microsoft® office 2007
A Professional Approach

OFFICE 2007

Deborah Hinkle
Kathleen Stewart
Pat R. Graves
Amie Mayhall
Jon Juarez
John Carter

**McGraw-Hill
Higher Education**

Boston   Burr Ridge, IL   Dubuque, IA   New York   San Francisco   St. Louis
Bangkok   Bogotá   Caracas   Kuala Lumpur   Lisbon   London   Madrid   Mexico City
Milan   Montreal   New Delhi   Santiago   Seoul   Singapore   Sydney   Taipei   Toronto

McGraw-Hill
Higher Education

MICROSOFT® OFFICE 2007: A PROFESSIONAL APPROACH
Published by McGraw-Hill, a business unit of The McGraw-Hill Companies, Inc., 1221 Avenue
of the Americas, New York, NY, 10020. Copyright © 2008 by The McGraw-Hill Companies, Inc.
All rights reserved. No part of this publication may be reproduced or distributed in any form
or by any means, or stored in a database or retrieval system, without the prior written consent of
The McGraw-Hill Companies, Inc., including, but not limited to, in any network or other
electronic storage or transmission, or broadcast for distance learning.

Some ancillaries, including electronic and print components, may not be available to customers
outside the United States.

This book is printed on acid-free paper.

3 4 5 6 7 8 0 BAN/BAN 0 9 8

ISBN   978-0-07-337351-5 (student edition)
MHID   0-07-337351-6 (student edition)
ISBN   978-0-07-721471-5 (annotated instructor's edition)
MHID   0-07-721471-4 (annotated instructor's edition)

Publisher: *Linda Schreiber*
Associate sponsoring editor: *Janna Martin*
Developmental editor: *Alaina Grayson*
Marketing manager: *Sarah Wood*
Media producer: *Marc Mattson*
Senior project manager: *Rick Hecker*
Production supervisor: *Janean A. Utley*
Designer: *Marianna Kinigakis*
Senior photo research coordinator: *Jeremy Cheshareck*
Media project manager: *Mark A. S. Dierker*
Cover design: *Asylum Studios*
Interior design: *JoAnne Schopler, Graphic Visions*
Typeface: *10.5/13 New Aster*
Compositor: *Aptara*
Printer: *R. R. Donnelley*

Library of Congress Cataloging-in-Publication Data

Microsoft Office 2007 : a professional approach / Deborah Hinkle ... [et al.].
      p. cm.
    Includes index.
    ISBN-13: 978-0-07-337351-5 (student edition : alk. paper)
    ISBN-10: 0-07-337351-6 (student edition : alk. paper)
    ISBN-13: 978-0-07-721471-5 (annotated instructor's edition : alk. paper)
    ISBN-10: 0-07-721471-4 (annotated instructor's edition : alk. paper)
    1. Microsoft Office. 2. Business—Computer programs. I. Hinkle, Deborah A.
HF5548.4.M525M524965 2008
005.5—dc22
                                                              2007024659

contents

Preface   *xxiv*

Installation Requirements   *xxvi*

Windows Tutorial   *xxviii*

WORD

Unit 1 *Basic Skills*

LESSON 1: CREATING A DOCUMENT   **WD-6**

Starting Word   **WD-6**
Exercise 1-1: Start Word   WD-7

Identifying Parts of the Word Screen   **WD-9**
Exercise 1-2: Identify the Microsoft Office
    Button and the Quick Access Toolbar   WD-9
Exercise 1-3: Identify Ribbon Commands   WD-10
Exercise 1-4: Identify Commands   WD-12

Keying Text   **WD-12**
Exercise 1-5: Key Text and Move the
    Insertion Point   WD-13
Exercise 1-6: Wrap Text and Correct
    Spelling   WD-13

Basic Text Editing   **WD-15**
Exercise 1-7: Delete Text   WD-16
Exercise 1-8: Insert Text   WD-16
Exercise 1-9: Combine and Split Paragraphs   WD-17

Naming and Saving a Document   **WD-18**
Exercise 1-10: Name and Save a Document   WD-18

Printing a Document   **WD-20**
Exercise 1-11: Print a Document   WD-20

Closing a Document and Exiting Word   **WD-21**
Exercise 1-12: Close a Document and
    Exit Word   WD-21

Lesson 1 Summary   **WD-23**

Concepts Review   **WD-25**

True/False Questions   **WD-25**

Short Answer Questions   **WD-25**

Critical Thinking   **WD-26**

Skills Review   **WD-26**
Exercise 1-13   WD-26
Exercise 1-14   WD-27
Exercise 1-15   WD-27
Exercise 1-16   WD-28

Lesson Applications   **WD-30**
Exercise 1-17   WD-30
Exercise 1-18   WD-31
Exercise 1-19   WD-31
Exercise 1-20   WD-32

On Your Own   **WD-33**
Exercise 1-21   WD-33
Exercise 1-22   WD-33
Exercise 1-23   WD-33

LESSON 2: SELECTING AND EDITING   **WD-34**

Opening an Existing Document   **WD-34**
Exercise 2-1: Open an Existing File   WD-35
Exercise 2-2: Create a New Folder   WD-37

Formatting Characters   **WD-38**
Exercise 2-3: Enter Formatting
    Characters   WD-39

Moving within a Document   **WD-40**
Exercise 2-4: Use the Keyboard to Move the
    Insertion Point   WD-40
Exercise 2-5: Scroll through a Document   WD-41

Undo and Redo Commands   **WD-43**
Exercise 2-6: Undo and Redo Actions   WD-44

Repeat Command   **WD-44**
Exercise 2-7: Repeat Actions   WD-45

Selecting Text   **WD-45**
Exercise 2-8: Select Text with the Mouse   WD-46
Exercise 2-9: Select Noncontiguous Text   WD-47
Exercise 2-10: Adjust a Selection Using
    the Mouse and the Keyboard   WD-48
Exercise 2-11: Edit Text by Replacing a
    Selection   WD-49

Saving a Revised Document   **WD-50**
Exercise 2-12: Save a Revised Document   WD-50
Exercise 2-13: Check Word's Auto
    Recover Settings   WD-50

Working with Document Properties   **WD-51**
Exercise 2-14: Review and Edit Document
    Properties   WD-51

Lesson 2 Summary   **WD-54**

Concepts Review   **WD-56**

True/False Questions   **WD-56**

Short Answer Questions   **WD-56**

Critical Thinking   **WD-57**

Skills Review   **WD-57**
Exercise 2-16   WD-57
Exercise 2-17   WD-58
Exercise 2-18   WD-58
Exercise 2-19   WD-59

Lesson Applications   **WD-61**
Exercise 2-20   WD-61
Exercise 2-21   WD-61
Exercise 2-22   WD-62
Exercise 2-23   WD-63

On Your Own   WD-64
    Exercise 2-24   WD-64
    Exercise 2-25   WD-64
    Exercise 2-26   WD-64

**LESSON 3: FORMATTING
CHARACTERS**   **WD-66**

Working with Fonts   **WD-66**
    Exercise 3-1: Change Fonts and Font
      Sizes Using the Ribbon   WD-67
    Exercise 3-2: Change Font Size Using
      Keyboard Shortcuts   WD-69

Basic Character Formatting   **WD-69**
    Exercise 3-3: Apply Basic Character
      Formatting Using the Ribbon   WD-70
    Exercise 3-4: Apply and Remove Basic
      Character Formatting Using Keyboard
      Shortcuts   WD-71
    Exercise 3-5: Apply and Remove Basic
      Character Formatting Using the Mini
      Toolbar   WD-72

Using the Font Dialog Box   **WD-72**
    Exercise 3-6: Choose Fonts and Font Styles
      Using the Font Dialog Box   WD-73
    Exercise 3-7: Apply Underline Options and
      Character Effects   WD-74
    Exercise 3-8: Use Keyboard Shortcuts for
      Underline Options and Font Effects WD-77
    Exercise 3-9: Change Character Spacing WD-77

Repeating and Copying Formatting   **WD-79**
    Exercise 3-10: Repeat Character
      Formatting   WD-79
    Exercise 3-11: Copy Character
      Formatting   WD-80

Changing Case and Highlighting Text   **WD-80**
    Exercise 3-12: Change Case   WD-81
    Exercise 3-13: Highlight Text   WD-81

Creating a Drop Cap   **WD-82**
    Exercise 3-14: Create a Drop Cap   WD-82

Word's AutoFormat Features   **WD-83**
    Exercise 3-15: Format Ordinal Numbers
      and Fractions Automatically   WD-84

Lesson 3 Summary   **WD-84**

Concepts Review   **WD-86**

True/False Questions   **WD-86**

Short Answer Questions   **WD-86**

Critical Thinking   **WD-87**

Skills Review   **WD-87**
    Exercise 3-16   WD-87
    Exercise 3-17   WD-88
    Exercise 3-18   WD-89
    Exercise 3-19   WD-90

Lesson Applications   **WD-91**
    Exercise 3-20   WD-91
    Exercise 3-21   WD-92
    Exercise 3-22   WD-93
    Exercise 3-23   WD-93

On Your Own   **WD-94**
    Exercise 3-24   WD-94
    Exercise 3-25   WD-94
    Exercise 3-26   WD-95

LESSON 4: WRITING TOOLS   **WD-96**

**Using AutoComplete, AutoCorrect,
and Smart Tags**   **WD-96**
    Exercise 4-1: Practice AutoComplete and
      AutoCorrect   WD-97
    Exercise 4-2: Create an AutoCorrect Entry WD-98
    Exercise 4-3: Control AutoCorrect Options WD-99
    Exercise 4-4: Create an AutoCorrect
      Exception   WD-100
    Exercise 4-5: Use Smart Tags   WD-101

**Working with AutoText and Building
Blocks**   **WD-103**
    Exercise 4-6: Create an AutoText Entry WD-103
    Exercise 4-7: Insert AutoText Entries WD-105
    Exercise 4-8: Edit and Delete AutoText
      Entries   WD-106

Inserting the Date and Time   **WD-107**
    Exercise 4-9: Insert the Date and Time WD-107

Checking Spelling and Grammar   **WD-108**
    Exercise 4-10: Spell- and Grammar-Check
      Errors Individually   WD-109
    Exercise 4-11: Spell- and Grammar-Check
      an Entire Document   WD-109

**Using the Thesaurus and Research
Task Pane**   **WD-112**
    Exercise 4-12: Use the Thesaurus   WD-112
    Exercise 4-13: Use References   WD-113

Lesson 4 Summary   **WD-114**

Concepts Review   **WD-116**

True/False Questions   **WD-116**

Short Answer Questions   **WD-116**

Critical Thinking   **WD-117**

Skills Review   **WD-117**
    Exercise 4-14   WD-117
    Exercise 4-15   WD-118
    Exercise 4-16   WD-120
    Exercise 4-17   WD-121

Lesson Applications   **WD-122**
    Exercise 4-18   WD-122
    Exercise 4-19   WD-123
    Exercise 4-20   WD-123
    Exercise 4-21   WD-124

On Your Own   **WD-125**
    Exercise 4-22   WD-125
    Exercise 4-23   WD-125
    Exercise 4-24   WD-125

UNIT 1 APPLICATIONS   **WD-127**

Unit Application 1-1   **WD-127**

Unit Application 1-2   **WD-127**

Unit Application 1-3   **WD-129**

Unit Application 1-4   **WD-130**

Unit 2 *Paragraph Formatting, Tabs, and Advanced Editing*

**LESSON 5: FORMATTING
PARAGRAPHS** **WD-132**

Paragraph Alignment **WD-132**
Exercise 5-1: Change Paragraph
Alignment WD-133
Exercise 5-2: Use Click and Type to
Insert Text WD-134
Line Spacing **WD-135**
Exercise 5-3: Change Line Spacing WD-135
Paragraph Spacing **WD-138**
Exercise 5-4: Change the Space Between
Paragraphs WD-138
Paragraph Indents **WD-139**
Exercise 5-5: Set Indents by Using Indent
Buttons and the Paragraph Dialog
Box WD-140
Exercise 5-6: Set Indents by Using
the Ruler WD-141
Borders and Shading **WD-143**
Exercise 5-7: Add Borders to Paragraphs WD-143
Exercise 5-8: Apply Borders to Selected
Text and a Page WD-145
Exercise 5-9: Add a Horizontal Line WD-147
Exercise 5-10: Apply Shading to a
Paragraph WD-148
Exercise 5-11: Apply Borders
Automatically WD-149
Repeating and Copying Formats **WD-149**
Exercise 5-12: Repeat, Copy, and Remove
Paragraph Formats WD-149
Bulleted and Numbered Lists **WD-150**
Exercise 5-13: Create a Bulleted List WD-150
Exercise 5-14: Create a Numbered List WD-152
Exercise 5-15: Change a Bulleted or
Numbered List WD-152
Exercise 5-16: Create Lists Automatically WD-153
Exercise 5-17: Create a Multilevel List WD-154
Symbols and Special Characters **WD-155**
Exercise 5-18: Insert Symbols WD-155
Exercise 5-19: Insert Special Characters WD-157
Exercise 5-20: Create Symbols
Automatically WD-157
Lesson 5 Summary **WD-158**
Concepts Review **WD-160**
True/False Questions **WD-160**
Short Answer Questions **WD-160**
Critical Thinking **WD-161**
Skills Review **WD-161**
Exercise 5-21 WD-161
Exercise 5-22 WD-162
Exercise 5-23 WD-163
Exercise 5-24 WD-164
Lesson Applications **WD-165**
Exercise 5-25 WD-165
Exercise 5-26 WD-165

Exercise 5-27 WD-166
Exercise 5-28 WD-166
On Your Own **WD-167**
Exercise 5-29 WD-167
Exercise 5-30 WD-167
Exercise 5-31 WD-167

**LESSON 6: TABS AND TABBED
COLUMNS** **WD-168**

Setting Tabs **WD-168**
Exercise 6-1: Set Tabs by Using the Tabs
Dialog Box WD-170
Exercise 6-2: Set Tabs by Using the
Ruler WD-171
Setting Leader Tabs **WD-173**
Exercise 6-3: Set Leader Tabs WD-173
Clearing Tabs **WD-173**
Exercise 6-4: Clear a Tab by Using the
Tabs Dialog Box and the Keyboard WD-174
Exercise 6-5: Clear a Tab by Using
the Ruler WD-174
Adjusting Tab Settings **WD-174**
Exercise 6-6: Adjust Tab Settings WD-175
Creating Tabbed Columns **WD-176**
Exercise 6-7: Set Tabbed Columns WD-176
Exercise 6-8: Select a Tabbed Column WD-178
Exercise 6-9: Insert Bar Tabs WD-179
**Sorting Paragraphs and Tabbed
Columns** **WD-180**
Exercise 6-10: Sort Tabbed Tables WD-181
Lesson 6 Summary **WD-182**
Concepts Review **WD-184**
True/False Questions **WD-184**
Short Answer Questions **WD-184**
Critical Thinking **WD-185**
Skills Review **WD-185**
Exercise 6-11 WD-185
Exercise 6-12 WD-186
Exercise 6-13 WD-187
Exercise 6-14 WD-187
Lesson Applications **WD-189**
Exercise 6-15 WD-189
Exercise 6-16 WD-190
Exercise 6-17 WD-190
Exercise 6-18 WD-191
On Your Own **WD-193**
Exercise 6-19 WD-193
Exercise 6-20 WD-193
Exercise 6-21 WD-193

LESSON 7: MOVE AND COPY **WD-194**

Using the Office Clipboard **WD-194**
Exercise 7-1: Display the Clipboard
Task Pane WD-195

Moving Text by Using Cut and Paste   **WD-196**

Exercise 7-2: Use the Ribbon to
Cut and Paste   WD-197

Exercise 7-3: Use the Shortcut Menu to
Cut and Paste   WD-197

Exercise 7-4: Use Keyboard Shortcuts to
Cut and Paste   WD-199

Exercise 7-5: Use the Office Clipboard to
Paste   WD-199

Moving Text by Dragging   **WD-200**

Exercise 7-6: Use Drag and Drop to
Move Text   WD-200

Copying Text by Using Copy and Paste   **WD-201**

Exercise 7-7: Use Copy and Paste   WD-201

Exercise 7-8: Use the Office Clipboard to
Paste Copied Text   WD-202

Copying Text by Dragging   **WD-202**

Exercise 7-9: Use Drag and Drop to
Copy Text   WD-203

**Working with Multiple Document
Windows**   **WD-204**

Exercise 7-10: Split a Document into
Panes   WD-204

Exercise 7-11: Move Between Panes to
Edit Text   WD-206

Exercise 7-12: Open Multiple Documents   WD-207

Exercise 7-13: Rearrange and Resize
Document Windows   WD-209

**Moving and Copying Text among
Windows**   **WD-209**

Exercise 7-14: Copy Text from One
Document to Another by Using Copy
and Paste   WD-210

Exercise 7-15: Move Text from One
Document to Another by Using Drag
and Drop   WD-210

Lesson 7 Summary   **WD-211**

Concepts Review   **WD-213**

True/False Questions   **WD-213**

Short Answer Questions   **WD-213**

Critical Thinking   **WD-214**

Skills Review   **WD-214**

Exercise 7-16   WD-214

Exercise 7-17   WD-215

Exercise 7-18   WD-216

Exercise 7-19   WD-217

Lesson Applications   **WD-219**

Exercise 7-20   WD-219

Exercise 7-21   WD-219

Exercise 7-22   WD-220

Exercise 7-23   WD-221

On Your Own   **WD-222**

Exercise 7-24   WD-222

Exercise 7-25   WD-222

Exercise 7-26   WD-222

LESSON 8: FIND AND REPLACE   **WD-224**

Finding Text   **WD-224**

Exercise 8-1: Find Text   WD-225

Exercise 8-2: Find Text by Using the
Match Case Option   WD-226

Exercise 8-3: Find Text by Using the
Find Whole Words Only Option   WD-228

Exercise 8-4: Find Text by Using the
Wildcard Option   WD-228

Exercise 8-5: Find Formatted Text   WD-230

Finding and Replacing Text   **WD-231**

Exercise 8-6: Replace Text by Using
Find Next   WD-231

Exercise 8-7: Replace Text by Using
Replace All   WD-232

Exercise 8-8: Delete Text with Replace   WD-232

**Finding and Replacing Special
Characters**   **WD-233**

Exercise 8-9: Find and Replace Special
Characters   WD-233

Finding and Replacing Formatting   **WD-235**

Exercise 8-10: Find and Replace
Character Formatting   WD-235

Exercise 8-11: Find and Replace
Paragraph Formatting   WD-236

Lesson 8 Summary   **WD-239**

Concepts Review   **WD-241**

True/False Questions   **WD-241**

Short Answer Questions   **WD-241**

Critical Thinking   **WD-242**

Skills Review   **WD-242**

Exercise 8-12   WD-242

Exercise 8-13   WD-243

Exercise 8-14   WD-245

Exercise 8-15   WD-246

Lesson Applications   **WD-248**

Exercise 8-16   WD-248

Exercise 8-17   WD-248

Exercise 8-18   WD-249

Exercise 8-19   WD-249

On Your Own   **WD-250**

Exercise 8-20   WD-250

Exercise 8-21   WD-250

Exercise 8-22   WD-250

UNIT 2 APPLICATIONS   **WD-251**

Unit Application 2-1   **WD-251**

Unit Application 2-2   **WD-252**

Unit Application 2-3   **WD-253**

Unit Application 2-4   **WD-254**

Unit 3 *Page Formatting*

LESSON 9: MARGINS AND PRINT OPTIONS **WD-256**

Changing Margins **WD-256**
Exercise 9-1: Change Margins for a Document Using the Page Setup Dialog Box **WD-258**
Exercise 9-2: Change Margins for Selected Text by Using the Page Setup Dialog Box **WD-260**
Exercise 9-3: Change Margins for a Section by Using the Page Setup Dialog Box **WD-262**
Exercise 9-4: Change Margins Using the Rulers **WD-262**
Exercise 9-5: Set Facing Pages with Gutter Margins **WD-265**

Using Print Preview **WD-267**
Exercise 9-6: View a Multiple-Page Document in Print Preview **WD-267**
Exercise 9-7: Change Margins in Print Preview **WD-269**
Exercise 9-8: Edit a Document in Print Preview **WD-269**

Paper Size and Orientation **WD-270**
Exercise 9-9: Change Paper Size and Page Orientation **WD-270**

Printing Envelopes and Labels **WD-271**
Exercise 9-10: Print an Envelope **WD-272**
Exercise 9-11: Choose Envelope Options **WD-273**
Exercise 9-12: Print Labels **WD-275**

Setting Print Options **WD-277**
Exercise 9-13: Choose Print Options from the Print Dialog Box **WD-277**

Lesson 9 Summary **WD-278**

Concepts Review **WD-280**

True/False Questions **WD-280**

Short Answer Questions **WD-280**

Critical Thinking **WD-281**

Skills Review **WD-281**
Exercise 9-14 **WD-281**
Exercise 9-15 **WD-282**
Exercise 9-16 **WD-283**
Exercise 9-17 **WD-283**

Lesson Applications **WD-285**
Exercise 9-18 **WD-285**
Exercise 9-19 **WD-286**
Exercise 9-20 **WD-286**
Exercise 9-21 **WD-287**

On Your Own **WD-288**
Exercise 9-22 **WD-288**
Exercise 9-23 **WD-288**
Exercise 9-24 **WD-289**

LESSON 10: PAGE AND SECTION BREAKS **WD-290**

Using Soft and Hard Page Breaks **WD-290**
Exercise 10-1: Adjust a Soft Page Break Automatically **WD-291**
Exercise 10-2: Insert a Hard Page Break **WD-292**
Exercise 10-3: Delete a Hard Page Break **WD-293**

Controlling Line and Page Breaks **WD-294**
Exercise 10-4: Apply Line and Page Break Options to Paragraphs **WD-294**

Controlling Section Breaks **WD-297**
Exercise 10-5: Insert Section Breaks by Using the Break Command **WD-297**

Formatting Sections **WD-298**
Exercise 10-6: Apply Formatting to Sections **WD-298**
Exercise 10-7: Change the Vertical Alignment of a Section **WD-299**
Exercise 10-8: Check Pagination in Print Preview and Page Layout View **WD-300**

Using the Go To Feature **WD-301**
Exercise 10-9: Go to a Specific Page or Section **WD-302**
Exercise 10-10: Go to a Relative Destination **WD-302**

Lesson 10 Summary **WD-303**

Concepts Review **WD-305**

True/False Questions **WD-305**

Short Answer Questions **WD-305**

Critical Thinking **WD-306**

Skills Review **WD-306**
Exercise 10-11 **WD-306**
Exercise 10-12 **WD-307**
Exercise 10-13 **WD-307**
Exercise 10-14 **WD-308**

Lesson Applications **WD-310**
Exercise 10-15 **WD-310**
Exercise 10-16 **WD-311**
Exercise 10-17 **WD-311**
Exercise 10-18 **WD-312**

On Your Own **WD-313**
Exercise 10-19 **WD-313**
Exercise 10-20 **WD-313**
Exercise 10-21 **WD-313**

LESSON 11: PAGE NUMBERS, HEADERS, AND FOOTERS **WD-314**

Adding Page Numbers **WD-314**
Exercise 11-1: Add and Preview Page Numbers **WD-315**
Exercise 11-2: Change the Position and Format of Page Numbers **WD-317**

Changing the Starting Page Number **WD-318**
Exercise 11-3: Add a Cover Page **WD-318**
Exercise 11-4: Remove Page Numbers **WD-319**

Adding Headers and Footers   **WD-320**
   Exercise 11-5: Add a Header to a
     Document   WD-320
   Exercise 11-6: Add a Footer to a
     Document   WD-323

**Adding Headers and Footers within
Sections**   **WD-324**
   Exercise 11-7: Add Sections to a
     Document with Headers and Footers   WD-324

Linking Section Headers and Footers   **WD-326**
   Exercise 11-8: Link and Unlink Section
     Headers and Footers   WD-326

Changing the Starting Page Number   **WD-327**
   Exercise 11-9: Change the Starting
     Page Number   WD-327

Creating Continuation Page Headers   **WD-328**
   Exercise 11-10: Add a Continuation Page
     Header to a Letter   WD-328

Creating Alternate Headers and Footers   **WD-330**
   Exercise 11-11: Create Alternate Footers
     in a Document   WD-331

Lesson 11 Summary   **WD-332**

Concepts Review   **WD-334**

True/False Questions   **WD-334**

Short Answer Questions   **WD-334**

Critical Thinking   **WD-335**

Skills Review   **WD-335**
   Exercise 11-12   WD-335
   Exercise 11-13   WD-336
   Exercise 11-14   WD-337
   Exercise 11-15   WD-338

Lesson Applications   **WD-339**
   Exercise 11-16   WD-339
   Exercise 11-17   WD-340
   Exercise 11-18   WD-340
   Exercise 11-19   WD-341

On Your Own   **WD-342**
   Exercise 11-20   WD-342
   Exercise 11-21   WD-343
   Exercise 11-22   WD-343

LESSON 12: STYLES AND THEMES   **WD-344**

Applying Styles   **WD-344**
   Exercise 12-1: Apply Styles   WD-345

Creating New Styles   **WD-347**
   Exercise 12-2: Create a Paragraph Style   WD-348
   Exercise 12-3: Create a Character Style   WD-350

Modifying and Renaming Styles   **WD-352**
   Exercise 12-4: Modify and Rename Styles   WD-352
   Exercise 12-5: Replace a Style   WD-353
   Exercise 12-6: Delete a Style   WD-354

Using Style Options   **WD-355**
   Exercise 12-7: Use the Style for
     Following Paragraph Option   WD-355
   Exercise 12-8: Use the Based on Option   WD-357
   Exercise 12-9: Display and Print Styles   WD-357
   Exercise 12-10: Change Style Set   WD-359

**Apply and Customize a Document
Theme**   **WD-359**
   Exercise 12-11: Apply a Theme   WD-359
   Exercise 12-12: Customize a Theme   WD-361

Lesson 12 Summary   **WD-364**

Concepts Review   **WD-366**

True/False Questions   **WD-366**

Short Answer Questions   **WD-366**

Critical Thinking   **WD-367**

Skills Review   **WD-367**
   Exercise 12-13   WD-367
   Exercise 12-14   WD-368
   Exercise 12-15   WD-369
   Exercise 12-16   WD-371

Lesson Applications   **WD-372**
   Exercise 12-17   WD-372
   Exercise 12-18   WD-372
   Exercise 12-19   WD-373
   Exercise 12-20   WD-374

On Your Own   **WD-375**
   Exercise 12-21   WD-375
   Exercise 12-22   WD-375
   Exercise 12-23   WD-375

LESSON 13: TEMPLATES   **WD-376**

Using Word's Templates   **WD-376**
   Exercise 13-1: Use a Word Template to
     Create a New Document   WD-377

Creating New Templates   **WD-380**
   Exercise 13-2: Create a New Template   WD-380
   Exercise 13-3: Create a New Template
     by Using an Existing Document   WD-383

Attaching Templates to Documents   **WD-383**
   Exercise 13-4: Attach a Template to a
     Document   WD-383

Modifying Templates   **WD-386**
   Exercise 13-5: Modify Template
     Formatting   WD-386

Using the Organizer   **WD-387**
   Exercise 13-6: Copy Styles to Another
     Template   WD-387

Lesson 13 Summary   **WD-389**

Concepts Review   **WD-390**

True/False Questions   **WD-390**

Short Answer Questions   **WD-390**

Critical Thinking   **WD-391**

Skills Review   **WD-391**
   Exercise 13-7   WD-391
   Exercise 13-8   WD-392
   Exercise 13-9   WD-394
   Exercise 13-10   WD-395

Lesson Applications   **WD-396**
   Exercise 13-11   WD-396
   Exercise 13-12   WD-396
   Exercise 13-13   WD-397
   Exercise 13-14   WD-398

On Your Own **WD-398**
  Exercise 13-15 .... WD-398
  Exercise 13-16 .... WD-399
  Exercise 13-17 .... WD-399

UNIT 3 APPLICATIONS **WD-400**

Unit Application 3-1 .... **WD-400**
Unit Application 3-2 .... **WD-401**
Unit Application 3-3 .... **WD-402**
Unit Application 3-4 .... **WD-404**

EXCEL

Unit 1 Introduction to Excel

LESSON 1: GETTING STARTED WITH EXCEL **EX-6**

Starting Excel **EX-6**
  Exercise 1-1: Work with the Excel Interface ... EX-8

Navigating in a Workbook **EX-10**
  Exercise 1-2: Move Between Worksheets ... EX-11
  Exercise 1-3: Go to a Specific Cell ... EX-11
  Exercise 1-4: Scroll Through a Worksheet ... EX-13
  Exercise 1-5: Change the Zoom Size ... EX-15
  Exercise 1-6: Close a Workbook ... EX-16

Opening an Existing Workbook ... **EX-16**
  Exercise 1-7: Open a Workbook ... EX-16

Editing a Worksheet **EX-17**
  Exercise 1-8: View Worksheets and Cell Contents ... EX-18
  Exercise 1-9: Replace Cell Contents ... EX-19
  Exercise 1-10: Edit Cell Contents ... EX-20
  Exercise 1-11: Clear Cell Contents ... EX-22
  Exercise 1-12: Use Undo and Redo ... EX-22

Managing Files **EX-24**
  Exercise 1-13: Create a New Folder and Use Save As ... EX-24

Printing Excel Files **EX-25**
  Exercise 1-14: Preview and Print a Worksheet ... EX-26
  Exercise 1-15: Print a Workbook ... EX-27
  Exercise 1-16: Save an XPS File ... EX-28
  Exercise 1-17: Exit Excel ... EX-29

Lesson 1 Summary **EX-30**
Concepts Review **EX-32**
True/False Questions **EX-32**
Short Answer Questions **EX-32**
Critical Thinking **EX-33**
Skills Review **EX-33**
  Exercise 1-18 .... EX-33
  Exercise 1-19 .... EX-34
  Exercise 1-20 .... EX-34
  Exercise 1-21 .... EX-35

Lesson Applications **EX-36**
  Exercise 1-22 .... EX-36
  Exercise 1-23 .... EX-36

  Exercise 1-24 .... EX-37
  Exercise 1-25 .... EX-37

On Your Own **EX-38**
  Exercise 1-26 .... EX-38
  Exercise 1-27 .... EX-38
  Exercise 1-28 .... EX-38

LESSON 2: CREATING A WORKBOOK ... **EX-40**

Entering Labels **EX-40**
  Exercise 2-1: Enter Labels in a Worksheet ... EX-41

Changing the Document Theme ... **EX-42**
  Exercise 2-2: Change the Theme ... EX-43
  Exercise 2-3: Change the Font, Font Size, and Style ... EX-45
  Exercise 2-4: Use the Format Painter ... EX-46

Selecting Cell Ranges **EX-47**
  Exercise 2-5: Select Ranges with the Mouse ... EX-47
  Exercise 2-6: Select Ranges with Keyboard Shortcuts ... EX-49

Modifying Column Width and Row Height ... **EX-51**
  Exercise 2-7: Modify Column Width ... EX-51
  Exercise 2-8: Modify Row Height ... EX-52

Entering Values and Dates **EX-53**
  Exercise 2-9: Enter Dates and Values ... EX-53
  Exercise 2-10: Apply Number Formats from the Ribbon ... EX-54
  Exercise 2-11: Apply Date Formats from the Dialog Box ... EX-55
  Exercise 2-12: Change the Font Color ... EX-56
  Exercise 2-13: Rename a Worksheet and Change the Tab Color ... EX-57

Saving a Workbook **EX-58**
  Exercise 2-14: Save a Workbook ... EX-59

Entering Basic Formulas **EX-59**
  Exercise 2-15: Key a Basic Formula ... EX-60
  Exercise 2-16: Enter a Formula by Pointing ... EX-62
  Exercise 2-17: Copy a Formula by Using the Copy and Paste Buttons ... EX-62
  Exercise 2-18: Use AutoSum, Average, and Max ... EX-63
  Exercise 2-19: Check Results with AutoCalculate ... EX-65

Lesson 2 Summary **EX-67**

Concepts Review **EX-69**

True/False Questions **EX-69**

Short Answer Questions **EX-69**

Critical Thinking **EX-70**

Skills Review **EX-70**
Exercise 2-20 .... EX-70
Exercise 2-21 .... EX-71
Exercise 2-22 .... EX-72
Exercise 2-23 .... EX-73

Lesson Applications **EX-75**
Exercise 2-24 .... EX-75
Exercise 2-25 .... EX-76
Exercise 2-26 .... EX-76
Exercise 2-27 .... EX-77

On Your Own **EX-77**
Exercise 2-28 .... EX-77
Exercise 2-29 .... EX-78
Exercise 2-30 .... EX-78

**LESSON 3: USING EDITING
AND STYLE TOOLS** **EX-80**

**Using AutoCorrect and
Error Checking** **EX-80**
Exercise 3-1: Use AutoCorrect to
    Correct Errors EX-81
Exercise 3-2: Set AutoCorrect Options EX-82
Exercise 3-3: Review Error Checking EX-83

Checking Spelling **EX-84**
Exercise 3-4: Spell-Check a Worksheet EX-84

Using Find and Replace **EX-86**
Exercise 3-5: Find Data EX-87
Exercise 3-6: Use Wildcards EX-89
Exercise 3-7: Replace Data EX-89
Exercise 3-8: Replace a Function in
    a Formula EX-90
Exercise 3-9: Correct Errors with
    Replace EX-90
Exercise 3-10: Find and Replace Formats EX-91
Exercise 3-11: Reset Find and Replace
    Formats EX-93

Using Series and AutoFill **EX-93**
Exercise 3-12: Create Month and Week
    Series EX-93
Exercise 3-13: Create a Number Series EX-94
Exercise 3-14: Copy Data with the Fill
    Handle EX-95
Exercise 3-15: Copy a Formula with the
    Fill Handle EX-95

Applying Table and Cell Styles **EX-96**
Exercise 3-16: Create a Table EX-96
Exercise 3-17: Change the Table Style EX-97
Exercise 3-18: Apply a Cell Style EX-98
Exercise 3-19: Print a Selection EX-99

Preparing Headers and Footers **EX-99**
Exercise 3-20: Set Headers and Footers EX-100
Exercise 3-21: Print Gridlines and Row
    and Column Headings EX-101

Exercise 3-22: Change Margins and
    Column Widths in Page Layout View EX-102

Lesson 3 Summary **EX-103**

Concepts Review **EX-105**

True/False Questions **EX-105**

Short Answer Questions **EX-105**

Critical Thinking **EX-106**

Skills Review **EX-106**
Exercise 3-23 .... EX-106
Exercise 3-24 .... EX-107
Exercise 3-25 .... EX-108
Exercise 3-26 .... EX-109

Lesson Applications **EX-111**
Exercise 3-27 .... EX-111
Exercise 3-28 .... EX-111
Exercise 3-29 .... EX-112
Exercise 3-30 .... EX-113

On Your Own **EX-114**
Exercise 3-31 .... EX-114
Exercise 3-32 .... EX-114
Exercise 3-33 .... EX-115

**LESSON 4: EXPLORING HOME TAB
COMMANDS** **EX-116**

Inserting and Deleting Sheets and Cells ... **EX-116**
Exercise 4-1: Insert Worksheets EX-117
Exercise 4-2: Move and Delete
    Worksheets EX-118
Exercise 4-3: Insert Cells EX-119
Exercise 4-4: Delete Cells EX-120

**Using AutoComplete and Pick From
Drop-Down List** **EX-120**
Exercise 4-5: Use AutoComplete EX-121
Exercise 4-6: Use Pick From Drop-Down
    List EX-122

**Copying, Cutting, and Pasting Cell
Contents** **EX-123**
Exercise 4-7: Cut and Paste Cell
    Contents EX-123
Exercise 4-8: Copy and Paste Cell
    Contents EX-124
Exercise 4-9: Use Drag and Drop EX-126
Exercise 4-10: Use the Office Clipboard EX-127

Working with Columns and Rows **EX-128**
Exercise 4-11: Insert Rows EX-129
Exercise 4-12: Delete Rows EX-131
Exercise 4-13: Insert and Delete Rows EX-131
Exercise 4-14: Hide and Unhide Columns
    and Rows EX-131
Exercise 4-15: Freeze and Split the
    Window EX-132

Working with Cell Alignment **EX-134**
Exercise 4-16: Change the Horizontal
    Alignment EX-135
Exercise 4-17: Use Center Across
    Selection EX-135
Exercise 4-18: Change the Vertical
    Alignment EX-137

Exercise 4-19: Wrap Text and Change
Indents   EX-137
Exercise 4-20: Use Merge and Center   EX-138
Exercise 4-21: Change Cell Orientation   EX-138

Applying Borders and Fill   **EX-139**
Exercise 4-22: Apply Borders Using the
Borders Button   EX-139
Exercise 4-23: Apply Borders Using the
Dialog Box   EX-141
Exercise 4-24: Add Solid Fill   EX-143
Exercise 4-25: Use Pattern Fill   EX-143
Exercise 4-26: Complete the Number
Formatting   EX-144

Using Data Bars   **EX-146**
Exercise 4-27: Use Data Bars   EX-146
Exercise 4-28: Edit the Data Bar Rule   EX-147

Lesson 4 Summary   **EX-149**

Concepts Review   **EX-151**

True/False Questions   **EX-151**

Short Answer Questions   **EX-151**

Critical Thinking   **EX-152**

Skills Review   **EX-152**
Exercise 4-29   EX-152
Exercise 4-30   EX-153
Exercise 4-31   EX-154
Exercise 4-32   EX-155

Lesson Applications   **EX-157**
Exercise 4-33   EX-157
Exercise 4-34   EX-158
Exercise 4-35   EX-158
Exercise 4-36   EX-159

On Your Own   **EX-160**
Exercise 4-37   EX-160
Exercise 4-38   EX-160
Exercise 4-39   EX-160

UNIT 1 APPLICATIONS   **EX-161**

Unit Application 1-1   **EX-161**

Unit Application 1-2   **EX-161**

Unit Application 1-3   **EX-163**

Unit Application 1-4   **EX-163**

Unit 2   *Working with Formulas and Functions*

**LESSON 5: EXPLORING
FORMULA BASICS**   **EX-166**

Using a Template to Create a Workbook   **EX-166**
Exercise 5-1: Create a Workbook from
a Template   EX-167

**Building Addition and Subtraction
Formulas**   **EX-168**
Exercise 5-2: Create and Copy Addition
Formulas   EX-168
Exercise 5-3: Create and Copy
Subtraction Formulas   EX-170

**Building Multiplication and
Division Formulas**   **EX-171**
Exercise 5-4: Create Multiplication
Formulas   EX-171
Exercise 5-5: Edit a Formula in the
Formula Bar   EX-172
Exercise 5-6: Create Division Formulas   EX-173
Exercise 5-7: Apply the Percent Style and
Increase Decimal Positions   EX-173

Using Order of Precedence in a Formula   **EX-174**
Exercise 5-8: Use Multiplication and
Addition in a Formula   EX-175
Exercise 5-9: Set Order of Precedence   EX-176

**Using Relative, Absolute, and
Mixed References**   **EX-177**
Exercise 5-10: Use a Line Break   EX-177
Exercise 5-11: Copy a Formula with a
Relative Reference   EX-178
Exercise 5-12: Create a Formula with
an Absolute Reference   EX-179
Exercise 5-13: Use a Color Scale   EX-179

Exercise 5-14: Use Mixed References   EX-181
Exercise 5-15: Add Borders and Fill
for Printing   EX-182

Working with the Page Layout Tab   **EX-183**
Exercise 5-16: Change Page Orientation   EX-183
Exercise 5-17: Change Scaling and Page
Margins   EX-183
Exercise 5-18: Copy a Worksheet and
Display Formulas   EX-185
Exercise 5-19: Add a Background   EX-186
Exercise 5-20: Save a Workbook as a
Web Page   EX-187

Lesson 5 Summary   **EX-189**

Concepts Review   **EX-191**

True/False Questions   **EX-191**

Short Answer Questions   **EX-191**

Critical Thinking   **EX-192**

Skills Review   **EX-192**
Exercise 5-21   EX-192
Exercise 5-22   EX-193
Exercise 5-23   EX-194
Exercise 5-24   EX-195

Lesson Applications   **EX-198**
Exercise 5-25   EX-198
Exercise 5-26   EX-198
Exercise 5-27   EX-199
Exercise 5-28   EX-200

On Your Own   **EX-200**
Exercise 5-29   EX-200
Exercise 5-30   EX-201
Exercise 5-31   EX-201

LESSON 6: WORKING WITH FUNCTIONS — EX-202

Using Math and Trig Functions — **EX-202**
Exercise 6-1: Use SUM and the Formula Bar — EX-203
Exercise 6-2: Use Insert Function — EX-205
Exercise 6-3: Use TRUNC — EX-207
Exercise 6-4: Use SUMIF — EX-208

Using Statistical Functions — **EX-209**
Exercise 6-5: Use the AVERAGE Function — EX-209
Exercise 6-6: Use AVERAGEIF — EX-210
Exercise 6-7: Use the MIN and MAX Functions — EX-210
Exercise 6-8: Use COUNT and COUNTBLANK — EX-212
Exercise 6-9: Use the COUNTA Function — EX-213

Using Icon Sets — **EX-214**
Exercise 6-10: Apply Icon Sets — EX-214
Exercise 6-11: Edit the Icon Formatting Rule — EX-215

Grouping Worksheets — **EX-216**
Exercise 6-12: Group and Delete Worksheets — EX-216
Exercise 6-13: Manage Worksheets — EX-217

Using Date and Time Functions — **EX-218**
Exercise 6-14: Use the TODAY() Function — EX-218
Exercise 6-15: Key and Format Dates — EX-219
Exercise 6-16: Use Fill Across Worksheets — EX-220
Exercise 6-17: Create a Custom Date Format — EX-221
Exercise 6-18: Key and Format Times — EX-222
Exercise 6-19: Use the NOW() Function — EX-223
Exercise 6-20: Create a Custom Time Format — EX-223
Exercise 6-21: Add a Header to Grouped Sheets — EX-224

Lesson 6 Summary — **EX-226**

Concepts Review — **EX-227**

True/False Questions — **EX-227**

Short Answer Questions — **EX-227**

Critical Thinking — **EX-228**

Skills Review — **EX-228**
Exercise 6-22 — EX-228
Exercise 6-23 — EX-229
Exercise 6-24 — EX-230
Exercise 6-25 — EX-231

Lesson Applications — **EX-233**
Exercise 6-26 — EX-233
Exercise 6-27 — EX-234
Exercise 6-28 — EX-234
Exercise 6-29 — EX-235

On Your Own — **EX-236**
Exercise 6-30 — EX-236
Exercise 6-31 — EX-236

Exercise 6-32 — EX-237

LESSON 7: USING LOGICAL AND FINANCIAL FUNCTIONS — EX-238

Using the IF Function — **EX-238**
Exercise 7-1: Use IF to Show Text — EX-239
Exercise 7-2: Use IF to Calculate a Value — EX-241

Using AND, OR, and NOT Functions — **EX-242**
Exercise 7-3: Use the AND Function — EX-242
Exercise 7-4: Use the OR Function — EX-244
Exercise 7-5: Use the NOT Function — EX-245

Working with Cell Styles — **EX-246**
Exercise 7-6: Use Cell Styles — EX-246
Exercise 7-7: Clear and Reapply Cell Styles — EX-247
Exercise 7-8: Create a Style — EX-247
Exercise 7-9: Edit a Style — EX-248

Working with Page Breaks — **EX-248**
Exercise 7-10: Preview and Change Page Breaks — EX-249
Exercise 7-11: Remove and Insert Page Breaks — EX-250
Exercise 7-12: Set Print Titles — EX-252
Exercise 7-13: Center a Page — EX-253
Exercise 7-14: Change the Footer Font and Print Page Numbers — EX-253
Exercise 7-15: Remove a Page Break — EX-254

Using the PMT and FV Functions — **EX-255**
Exercise 7-16: Use the PMT Function — EX-255
Exercise 7-17: Key a PMT Function — EX-256
Exercise 7-18: Use the FV Function — EX-258
Exercise 7-19: Format Negative Numbers — EX-259

Using Depreciation Functions — **EX-259**
Exercise 7-20: Use the DB Function — EX-260
Exercise 7-21: Copy and Edit the DB Function — EX-262

Lesson 7 Summary — **EX-263**

Concepts Review — **EX-265**

True/False Questions — **EX-265**

Short Answer Questions — **EX-265**

Critical Thinking — **EX-266**

Skills Review — **EX-266**
Exercise 7-22 — EX-266
Exercise 7-23 — EX-267
Exercise 7-24 — EX-268
Exercise 7-25 — EX-270

Lesson Applications — **EX-272**
Exercise 7-26 — EX-272
Exercise 7-27 — EX-272
Exercise 7-28 — EX-273
Exercise 7-29 — EX-273

On Your Own — **EX-274**
Exercise 7-30 — EX-274
Exercise 7-31 — EX-274
Exercise 7-32 — EX-275

LESSON 8: ROUNDING AND NESTING FUNCTIONS — **EX-276**

Using the INT Function — **EX-276**
Exercise 8-1: Use INT with a Cell Reference — EX-277
Exercise 8-2: Compare Values with INT — EX-277

Using the ROUND Function — **EX-278**
Exercise 8-3: Use ROUND — EX-278
Exercise 8-4: Compare Rounded Values — EX-279
Exercise 8-5: Change Colors and Borders — EX-280

Using Date and Time Arithmetic — **EX-281**
Exercise 8-6: Determine Ages and Dates — EX-281
Exercise 8-7: Determine Time Passed — EX-282
Exercise 8-8: Group Sheets to Add Footers — EX-283
Exercise 8-9: Hide and Unhide a Worksheet — EX-284

Creating Nested Functions — **EX-284**
Exercise 8-10: Nest SUM and ROUND — EX-284
Exercise 8-11: Create a Nested IF Function — EX-286
Exercise 8-12: Set Top/Bottom Conditional Formatting — EX-287

Creating a Hyperlink — **EX-288**
Exercise 8-13: Create a Hyperlink — EX-288
Exercise 8-14: Run the Compatibility Checker — EX-290

Lesson 8 Summary — **EX-291**
Concepts Review — **EX-293**
True/False Questions — **EX-293**
Short Answer Questions — **EX-293**
Critical Thinking — **EX-294**
Skills Review — **EX-294**
Exercise 8-15 — EX-294
Exercise 8-16 — EX-295
Exercise 8-17 — EX-296
Exercise 8-18 — EX-297

Lesson Applications — **EX-298**
Exercise 8-19 — EX-298
Exercise 8-20 — EX-298
Exercise 8-21 — EX-299
Exercise 8-22 — EX-300

On Your Own — **EX-301**
Exercise 8-23 — EX-301
Exercise 8-24 — EX-301
Exercise 8-25 — EX-301

UNIT 2 APPLICATIONS — **EX-302**

Unit Application 2-1 — **EX-302**
Unit Application 2-2 — **EX-302**
Unit Application 2-3 — **EX-303**
Unit Application 2-4 — **EX-304**

Unit 3 *Enhancing Worksheet Appearance*

LESSON 9: BUILDING CHARTS — **EX-306**

Viewing and Printing a Chart — **EX-307**
Exercise 9-1: View a Chart Object — EX-307
Exercise 9-2: Print a Chart Object — EX-308

Working with Chart Elements — **EX-308**
Exercise 9-3: Change the Chart Layout — EX-310
Exercise 9-4: Change the Chart Style — EX-311
Exercise 9-5: Edit and Format the Chart Title — EX-311
Exercise 9-6: Set Shape Fill and Effects — EX-313
Exercise 9-7: Set and Format Data Labels — EX-315
Exercise 9-8: Format the Axes — EX-315
Exercise 9-9: Format the Plot and Chart Areas — EX-316

Creating Charts — **EX-317**
Exercise 9-10: Create and Edit a Chart Sheet — EX-318
Exercise 9-11: Create a Chart Object — EX-319
Exercise 9-12: Move and Size a Chart Object — EX-319
Exercise 9-13: Change the Layout and Styles — EX-320
Exercise 9-14: Create a Bar Chart Sheet — EX-321
Exercise 9-15: Add Gridlines and a Data Table — EX-322

Editing Chart Data — **EX-323**
Exercise 9-16: Edit Chart Data — EX-323
Exercise 9-17: Add a Data Point — EX-323
Exercise 9-18: Add and Rename Data Series — EX-325
Exercise 9-19: Delete Data Points and a Data Series — EX-327

Using Images, Gradients, and Textures for a Data Series — **EX-327**
Exercise 9-20: Use an Image for a Data Series — EX-327
Exercise 9-21: Use a Gradient for a Data Series — EX-329
Exercise 9-22: Use a Texture for a Data Point — EX-330

Creating a Combination Chart — **EX-331**
Exercise 9-23: Create a Chart with Two Chart Types — EX-331
Exercise 9-24: Build a Chart with Two Series — EX-332
Exercise 9-25: Add a Secondary Axis — EX-333

Lesson 9 Summary — **EX-334**
Concepts Review — **EX-336**
True/False Questions — **EX-336**
Short Answer Questions — **EX-336**

Critical Thinking	**EX-337**
Skills Review	**EX-337**
Exercise 9-26	EX-337
Exercise 9-27	EX-338
Exercise 9-28	EX-339
Exercise 9-29	EX-340
Lesson Applications	**EX-342**
Exercise 9-30	EX-342
Exercise 9-31	EX-342
Exercise 9-32	EX-343
Exercise 9-33	EX-344
On Your Own	**EX-344**
Exercise 9-34	EX-344
Exercise 9-35	EX-345
Exercise 9-36	EX-345

LESSON 10: INSERTING SHAPES — EX-346

Adding and Formatting a Callout	**EX-347**
Exercise 10-1: Add a Callout to a Worksheet	EX-347
Exercise 10-2: Format and Move a Callout	EX-349
Exercise 10-3: Use the Format Shape Dialog Box	EX-350
Using Text Boxes	**EX-352**
Exercise 10-4: Add a Text Box	EX-352
Exercise 10-5: Format and Move a Text Box	EX-352
Exercise 10-6: Choose a Shape Style	EX-353
Inserting Basic Shapes and Arrows	**EX-354**
Exercise 10-7: Add a Shape and an Arrow	EX-354
Exercise 10-8: Resize the Name Box	EX-355
Exercise 10-9: Use the Selection and Visibility Pane	EX-356
Using the Drawing Tools Format Tab	**EX-357**
Exercise 10-10: Format Multiple Shapes	EX-357
Exercise 10-11: Copy and Move Objects	EX-357
Exercise 10-12: Size Shapes	EX-358
Exercise 10-13: Align and Nudge Shapes	EX-360
Exercise 10-14: Change a Shape	EX-360
Exercise 10-15: Use the Adjustment Handle	EX-361
Exercise 10-16: Rotate Shapes	EX-362
Exercise 10-17: Style Multiple Shapes	EX-363
Using Comments	**EX-363**
Exercise 10-18: Edit a Comment	EX-364
Exercise 10-19: Insert a Comment	EX-365
Exercise 10-20: Print Comments	EX-365
Exercise 10-21: Use Document Inspector	EX-365
Inserting WordArt	**EX-367**
Exercise 10-22: Insert WordArt	EX-367
Exercise 10-23: Edit WordArt	EX-368
Lesson 10 Summary	**EX-369**
Concepts Review	**EX-371**
True/False Questions	**EX-371**
Short Answer Questions	**EX-371**
Critical Thinking	**EX-372**

Skills Review	**EX-372**
Exercise 10-24	EX-372
Exercise 10-25	EX-373
Exercise 10-26	EX-375
Exercise 10-27	EX-376
Lesson Applications	**EX-377**
Exercise 10-28	EX-377
Exercise 10-29	EX-377
Exercise 10-30	EX-378
Exercise 10-31	EX-378
On Your Own	**EX-379**
Exercise 10-32	EX-379
Exercise 10-33	EX-379
Exercise 10-34	EX-379

LESSON 11: USING IMAGES AND SMARTART GRAPHICS — EX-380

Inserting a Picture	**EX-380**
Exercise 11-1: Insert a Picture from a File	EX-381
Exercise 11-2: Check Properties and Scale the Picture	EX-381
Exercise 11-3: Format and Copy an Image	EX-383
Exercise 11-4: Insert Clip Art	EX-383
Exercise 11-5: Crop, Size, and Style an Image	EX-384
Adding a Picture to a Header/Footer	**EX-385**
Exercise 11-6: Insert an Image in a Footer	EX-385
Exercise 11-7: Size an Image in a Footer	EX-386
Exercise 11-8: Create a Watermark	EX-387
Creating a Hierarchy SmartArt Shape	**EX-387**
Exercise 11-9: Create and Style an Organization Chart	EX-387
Exercise 11-10: Add a Shape to an Organization chart	EX-389
Exercise 11-11: Add Text to the Shapes	EX-390
Building a Cycle SmartArt Shape	**EX-391**
Exercise 11-12: Create a Cycle Diagram	EX-391
Exercise 11-13: Move Text in the Text Pane	EX-392
Exercise 11-14: Choose a New Layout	EX-393
Using the Research Tool	**EX-393**
Exercise 11-15: Find Synonyms	EX-394
Exercise 11-16: Translate Words	EX-396
Exercise 11-17: Use a Special Symbol	EX-397
Exercise 11-18: Set Document Properties	EX-398
Lesson 11 Summary	**EX-400**
Concepts Review	**EX-401**
True/False Questions	**EX-401**
Short Answer Questions	**EX-401**
Critical Thinking	**EX-402**
Skills Review	**EX-402**
Exercise 11-19	EX-402
Exercise 11-20	EX-403
Exercise 11-21	EX-404
Exercise 11-22	EX-405

Lesson Applications   **EX-407**
Exercise 11-23   EX-407
Exercise 11-24   EX-407
Exercise 11-25   EX-408
Exercise 11-26   EX-409
On Your Own   **EX-409**
Exercise 11-27   EX-409
Exercise 11-28   EX-410
Exercise 11-29   EX-410

UNIT 3 APPLICATIONS   **EX-411**
Unit Application 3-1   **EX-411**
Unit Application 3-2   **EX-411**
Unit Application 3-3   **EX-412**
Unit Application 3-4   **EX-412**

POWERPOINT

Unit 1 Basic Skills

LESSON 1: GETTING STARTED IN POWERPOINT   **PP-6**

Exploring PowerPoint   **PP-6**
Exercise 1-1: Identify Parts of the PowerPoint Window   PP-8
Exercise 1-2: Use the Quick Access Toolbar   PP-8
Exercise 1-3: Open an Existing Presentation   PP-9
Exercise 1-4: Work with Ribbons, Tabs, Groups, and Command Buttons   PP-10
Exercise 1-5: Use Microsoft Office PowerPoint Help   PP-10

Viewing a Presentation   **PP-11**
Exercise 1-6: Use Normal and Slide Sorter Views   PP-11
Exercise 1-7: Use the Slides and Outline Pane   PP-11
Exercise 1-8: Move from Slide to Slide   PP-12
Exercise 1-9: Use the Zoom and Fit to Window   PP-13
Exercise 1-10: Run a Slide Show   PP-14
Exercise 1-11: Observe Animation Effects   PP-14

Adding Text Using Placeholders   **PP-15**
Exercise 1-12: Key Placeholder Text   PP-15
Exercise 1-13: Change and Reset Placeholder Layout   PP-17

Naming and Saving a Presentation   **PP-17**
Exercise 1-14: Create a Folder for Saving Your Files   PP-18
Exercise 1-15: Name and Save a Presentation   PP-19

Preparing Presentation Supplements   **PP-19**
Exercise 1-16: Preview a Presentation   PP-19
Exercise 1-17: Print a Slide, Notes Page, Outline, and Handout   PP-20
Exercise 1-18: Choose Print Options   PP-22

Ending Your Work Session   **PP-23**
Exercise 1-19: Close a Presentation and Exit PowerPoint   PP-24

Lesson 1 Summary   **PP-24**
Concepts Review   **PP-26**
True/False Questions   **PP-26**
Short Answer Questions   **PP-26**
Critical Thinking   **PP-27**
Skills Review   **PP-27**
Exercise 1-20   PP-27
Exercise 1-21   PP-28
Exercise 1-22   PP-29
Exercise 1-23   PP-30

Lesson Applications   **PP-31**
Exercise 1-24   PP-31
Exercise 1-25   PP-32
Exercise 1-26   PP-32
Exercise 1-27   PP-33

On Your Own   **PP-34**
Exercise 1-28   PP-34
Exercise 1-29   PP-34
Exercise 1-30   PP-35

LESSON 2: DEVELOPING PRESENTATION TEXT   **PP-36**

Creating a New Blank Presentation   **PP-36**
Exercise 2-1: Start a New Blank Presentation   PP-37
Exercise 2-2: Add New Slides and Use Slide Layouts   PP-38

Using the Font Group Commands   **PP-41**
Exercise 2-3: Change the Font Face and Font Size   PP-42
Exercise 2-4: Apply Bold, Italic, Color, and Shadow   PP-43
Exercise 2-5: Change the Case of Selected Text   PP-44

Exercise 2-6: Change Line Spacing within
Paragraphs   PP-45
Exercise 2-7: Change Line Spacing between
Paragraphs   PP-46
Exercise 2-8: Use the Font Dialog Box to
Make Multiple Changes   PP-46

Adjusting Text Placeholders   **PP-48**
Exercise 2-9: Select a Text Placeholder   PP-48
Exercise 2-10: Change Text Horizontal
Alignment   PP-50
Exercise 2-11: Resize a Placeholder   PP-50
Exercise 2-12: Move a Placeholder   PP-52

Working with Bullets and Numbering   **PP-52**
Exercise 2-13: Remove Bullets   PP-53
Exercise 2-14: Promote and Demote
Bulleted Text   PP-53
Exercise 2-15: Change the Color and
Shape of a Bullet   PP-54
Exercise 2-16: Create a Bullet from
a Picture   PP-56
Exercise 2-17: Create Numbered
Paragraphs   PP-57
Exercise 2-18: Use the Ruler to Adjust
Paragraph Indents   PP-58

Working with Text Boxes   **PP-60**
Exercise 2-19: Create a Text Box   PP-60
Exercise 2-20: Change the Font and
Font Color   PP-61
Exercise 2-21: Rotate and Change Text
Direction   PP-61
Exercise 2-22: Wrap Text and Change
Alignment   PP-62

Lesson 2 Summary   **PP-63**

Concepts Review   **PP-66**

True/False Questions   **PP-66**

Short Answer Questions   **PP-66**

Critical Thinking   **PP-67**

Skills Review   **PP-67**
Exercise 2-23   PP-67
Exercise 2-24   PP-68
Exercise 2-25   PP-69
Exercise 2-26   PP-70

Lesson Applications   **PP-71**
Exercise 2-27   PP-71
Exercise 2-28   PP-72
Exercise 2-29   PP-73
Exercise 2-30   PP-74

On Your Own   **PP-75**
Exercise 2-31   PP-75
Exercise 2-32   PP-75
Exercise 2-33   PP-75

**LESSON 3: REVISING
PRESENTATION TEXT**   **PP-76**

**Selecting, Rearranging, and Deleting
Slides**   **PP-76**
Exercise 3-1: Select Multiple Slides   PP-77
Exercise 3-2: Rearrange Slide Order   PP-78
Exercise 3-3: Delete Slides   PP-79

Using the Clipboard   **PP-80**
Exercise 3-4: Use Cut, Copy, and
Paste to Rearrange Slides   PP-80
Exercise 3-5: Use Cut, Copy, and
Paste to Rearrange Text   PP-81
Exercise 3-6: Clear the Clipboard
Task Pane   PP-82
Exercise 3-7: Use Undo and Redo   PP-83
Exercise 3-8: Use Format Painter   PP-84

Checking Spelling and Word Usage   **PP-84**
Exercise 3-9: Check Spelling   PP-85
Exercise 3-10: Use Research   PP-86
Exercise 3-11: Use the Thesaurus   PP-86
Exercise 3-12: Use Find
and Replace   PP-87

Inserting Headers and Footers   **PP-88**
Exercise 3-13: Add Slide Date, Page
Number, and Footer   PP-89
Exercise 3-14: Add Handout Date,
Page Number, and Header   PP-90

**Applying a Consistent Background
and Color Theme**   **PP-91**
Exercise 3-15: Select a Design Theme   PP-91
Exercise 3-16: Change Theme Colors   PP-92
Exercise 3-17: Change Theme Fonts   PP-93
Exercise 3-18: Change Theme Effects   PP-93
Exercise 3-19: Create New
Theme Fonts   PP-94

Adding Movement Effects   **PP-95**
Exercise 3-20: Apply Slide
Transitions   PP-95
Exercise 3-21: Adjust Sounds
and Speeds   PP-95

Lesson 3 Summary   **PP-96**

Concepts Review   **PP-99**

True/False Questions   **PP-99**

Short Answer Questions   **PP-99**

Critical Thinking   **PP-100**

Skills Review   **PP-100**
Exercise 3-22   PP-100
Exercise 3-23   PP-101
Exercise 3-24   PP-102
Exercise 3-25   PP-103

Lesson Applications   **PP-105**
Exercise 3-26   PP-105
Exercise 3-27   PP-106
Exercise 3-28   PP-107
Exercise 3-29   PP-108

On Your Own   **PP-109**
Exercise 3-30   PP-109
Exercise 3-31   PP-109
Exercise 3-32   PP-109

UNIT 1 APPLICATIONS   **PP-110**

Unit Application 1-1   **PP-110**
Unit Application 1-2   **PP-111**
Unit Application 1-3   **PP-112**
Unit Application 1-4   **PP-113**

Unit 2 Presentation Illustration

LESSON 4: WORKING WITH GRAPHICS **PP-116**

Working with Shapes **PP-116**
Exercise 4-1: Draw Shapes—Rectangles, Ovals, and Lines PP-117
Exercise 4-2: Draw Horizontal Constrained Lines PP-119
Exercise 4-3: Add Connector Lines PP-121
Exercise 4-4: Create Squares and Circles PP-122
Exercise 4-5: Resize and Move Shapes PP-123
Exercise 4-6: Use Adjustment Handles to Modify Shapes PP-125
Exercise 4-7: Place Text in a Shape and Rotate PP-126

Inserting Clip Art Images **PP-127**
Exercise 4-8: Find Clip Art then Modify a Search PP-128
Exercise 4-9: Preview and Insert Clip Art Images PP-129
Exercise 4-10: Rearrange, Delete, Copy, Paste, and Duplicate Clip Art Images PP-130
Exercise 4-11: Group and Ungroup Images and Text PP-132

Inserting and Enhancing a Picture **PP-133**
Exercise 4-12: Insert Stock Photography PP-134
Exercise 4-13: Crop a Picture PP-135
Exercise 4-14: Recolor a Picture then Reset Colors PP-136
Exercise 4-15: Apply a Picture Style PP-136
Exercise 4-16: Insert a Picture from File PP-137
Exercise 4-17: Adjust Contrast and Brightness PP-138
Exercise 4-18: Change a Picture Shape PP-139
Exercise 4-19: Add a Border to a Picture PP-140
Exercise 4-20: Apply Picture Effects PP-140

Creating WordArt **PP-142**
Exercise 4-21: Create and Modify WordArt Text PP-142
Exercise 4-22: Apply WordArt Effects PP-143
Exercise 4-23: Edit WordArt Text Fill and Text Outline Colors PP-144

Creating a Photo Album **PP-145**
Exercise 4-24: Create Album Content by Inserting New Pictures PP-146
Exercise 4-25: Adjust Picture Order, Brightness, and Contrast PP-146
Exercise 4-26: Control Album Layout PP-147

Lesson 4 Summary **PP-148**
Concepts Review **PP-151**
True/False Questions **PP-151**
Short Answer Questions **PP-151**
Critical Thinking **PP-152**
Skills Review **PP-152**
Exercise 4-27 PP-152
Exercise 4-28 PP-154
Exercise 4-29 PP-155
Exercise 4-30 PP-156

Lesson Applications **PP-158**
Exercise 4-31 PP-158
Exercise 4-32 PP-159
Exercise 4-33 PP-161
Exercise 4-34 PP-163

On Your Own **PP-164**
Exercise 4-35 PP-164
Exercise 4-36 PP-164
Exercise 4-37 PP-165

LESSON 5: CREATING TABLES **PP-166**

Creating a Table **PP-166**
Exercise 5-1: Insert a Table PP-167
Exercise 5-2: Navigate in a Table PP-168
Exercise 5-3: Select Table Styles PP-169
Exercise 5-4: Apply Table Style Options PP-169

Drawing a Table **PP-170**
Exercise 5-5: Use Pencil Pointer to Draw a Table PP-170
Exercise 5-6: Change Table Text Direction PP-171
Exercise 5-7: Apply Shading and Borders PP-172
Exercise 5-8: Change Border and Shading Colors PP-174
Exercise 5-9: Erase Cell Borders PP-175

Modifying Table Structure **PP-175**
Exercise 5-10: Insert and Delete Rows and Columns PP-176
Exercise 5-11: Merge and Split Cells PP-177
Exercise 5-12: Apply a Diagonal Border PP-178
Exercise 5-13: Distribute Column Width and Row Height PP-179

Aligning Text and Numbers **PP-181**
Exercise 5-14: Align Text and Numbers Horizontally PP-181
Exercise 5-15: Change the Vertical Position of Text in a Cell PP-181
Exercise 5-16: Use Margin Settings to Adjust the Position of Text in a Cell PP-182
Exercise 5-17: Resize a Table PP-183

Enhancing the Table **PP-183**
Exercise 5-18: Apply and Modify a Cell Bevel Effect PP-184
Exercise 5-19: Apply and Modify a Shadow Effect PP-184
Exercise 5-20: Apply and Modify a Reflection Effect PP-185
Exercise 5-21: Insert a Picture and Apply Gradient Shading PP-186

Creating a Tabbed Table **PP-187**
Exercise 5-22: Set and Edit Tabs PP-187
Exercise 5-23: Create a Tabbed Table PP-189

Lesson 5 Summary **PP-190**
Concepts Review **PP-193**

True/False Questions   **PP-193**
Short Answer Questions   **PP-193**
Critical Thinking   **PP-194**
Skills Review   **PP-194**
Exercise 5-24   PP-194
Exercise 5-25   PP-195
Exercise 5-26   PP-197
Exercise 5-27   PP-199
Lesson Applications   **PP-201**
Exercise 5-28   PP-201
Exercise 5-29   PP-202
Exercise 5-30   PP-203
Exercise 5-31   PP-205
On Your Own   **PP-206**
Exercise 5-32   PP-206
Exercise 5-33   PP-207
Exercise 5-34   PP-207

LESSON 6: CREATING CHARTS   **PP-208**
Creating a Chart   **PP-208**
Exercise 6-1: Choose a Slide Layout
    for a Chart   PP-209
Exercise 6-2: Edit the Data Source   PP-210
Exercise 6-3: Switch Rows/Column Data   PP-212
Formatting a Column Chart   **PP-213**
Exercise 6-4: Explore Parts of a Chart   PP-213
Exercise 6-5: Change Chart Styles   PP-214
Exercise 6-6: Format the Vertical (Value)
    and Horizontal (Category) Axes   PP-215
Exercise 6-7: Apply Different Chart
    Layouts   PP-216
Exercise 6-8: Change or Remove the
    Legend   PP-216
Exercise 6-9: Apply or Remove Gridlines   PP-217
Using Different Chart Types   **PP-218**
Exercise 6-10: Switch to Other
    Chart Types   PP-218
Exercise 6-11: Add a Secondary
    Chart Axis   PP-219
Exercise 6-12: Combine Chart Types   PP-220
Exercise 6-13: Format a Primary
    and Secondary Axis   PP-221
Working with Pie Charts   **PP-223**
Exercise 6-14: Create a Pie Chart   PP-223
Exercise 6-15: Add Pie Slice Labels   PP-224
Exercise 6-16: Apply 3-D Rotation   PP-225
Enhancing Chart Elements   **PP-226**
Exercise 6-17: Adding Shapes for
    Emphasis   PP-226
Exercise 6-18: Change Colors in
    Chart Areas   PP-227
Exercise 6-19: Add a Picture Fill
    Behind Chart   PP-228
Lesson 6 Summary   **PP-230**
Concepts Review   **PP-232**
True/False Questions   **PP-232**
Short Answer Questions   **PP-232**
Critical Thinking   **PP-233**

Skills Review   **PP-233**
Exercise 6-20   PP-233
Exercise 6-21   PP-234
Exercise 6-22   PP-235
Exercise 6-23   PP-238
Lesson Applications   **PP-240**
Exercise 6-24   PP-240
Exercise 6-25   PP-241
Exercise 6-26   PP-242
Exercise 6-27   PP-244
On Your Own   **PP-247**
Exercise 6-28   PP-247
Exercise 6-29   PP-247
Exercise 6-30   PP-247

**LESSON 7: CREATING DIAGRAMS WITH
SMARTART GRAPHICS**   **PP-248**
Choosing SmartArt Graphics   **PP-248**
Exercise 7-1: Use Diagrams for
    Communication Purposes   PP-249
Exercise 7-2: Use Lists to Show Groups
    of Information   PP-250
Exercise 7-3: Use Process Diagrams to
    Show Sequential Workflow Steps   PP-252
Exercise 7-4: Use Cycle Diagrams to
    Show a Continuing Sequence   PP-254
Enhancing Diagrams   **PP-255**
Exercise 7-5: Apply Shape Quick Styles   PP-255
Exercise 7-6: Adjust 3-D Format and
    Rotation   PP-256
Exercise 7-7: Adjust the Overall Size
    and Layout of the Diagram   PP-256
Exercise 7-8: Add Shapes   PP-258
Exercise 7-9: Change Colors and Reset
    the Graphic   PP-259
Preparing an Organization Chart   **PP-261**
Exercise 7-10: Create an Organization
    Chart   PP-261
Exercise 7-11: Insert Subordinate Shapes   PP-262
Exercise 7-12: Add Assistant and
    Coworker Shapes   PP-264
Exercise 7-13: Change Layout, Delete, and
    Rearrange Shapes   PP-265
Exercise 7-14: Change Shape Sizing
    and Styles   PP-266
Creating Other Diagrams with SmartArt **PP-268**
Exercise 7-15: Create a Radial Diagram   PP-268
Exercise 7-16: Create a Gear Diagram   PP-269
Exercise 7-17: Insert a Continuous
    Picture List   PP-270
**Changing Diagram Types and
Orientation**   **PP-271**
Exercise 7-18: Change Diagram Types   PP-271
Exercise 7-19: Change the Orientation
    of Diagrams   PP-273
Lesson 7 Summary   **PP-274**
Concepts Review   **PP-276**
True/False Questions   **PP-276**
Short Answer Questions   **PP-276**

Critical Thinking	**PP-277**
Skills Review	**PP-277**
Exercise 7-20	PP-277
Exercise 7-21	PP-278
Exercise 7-22	PP-280
Exercise 7-23	PP-281
Lesson Applications	**PP-283**
Exercise 7-24	PP-283
Exercise 7-25	PP-284
Exercise 7-26	PP-285
Exercise 7-27	PP-286

On Your Own	**PP-287**
Exercise 7-28	PP-287
Exercise 7-29	PP-287
Exercise 7-30	PP-288
UNIT 2 APPLICATIONS	**PP-289**
Unit Application 2-1	**PP-289**
Unit Application 2-2	**PP-291**
Unit Application 2-3	**PP-293**
Unit Application 2-4	**PP-295**

ACCESS

Unit 1 Understanding Access Databases

LESSON 1 GETTING STARTED WITH A DATABASE — **AC-6**

Identifying Basic Database Structure	**AC-6**
Working with a Microsoft Access Database	**AC-8**
Exercise 1-1: Manage a Database	AC-8
Exercise 1-2: Start a Database	AC-9
Exercise 1-3: Open a Database	AC-10
Identifying Components of Access	**AC-11**
Exercise 1-4: Manipulate the Navigation Pane	AC-11
Exercise 1-5: Explore Tabs, Ribbons, and Groups	AC-12
Exercise 1-6: Open and Close Major Objects	AC-13
Exercise 1-7: Explore Datasheet and Design Views	AC-14
Navigating Access Recordsets	**AC-15**
Exercise 1-8: Use Navigation Buttons in a Table	AC-16
Exercise 1-9: Use Navigation Shortcut Keys in a Query	AC-16
Modifying Datasheet Appearance	**AC-17**
Exercise 1-10: Hide and Unhide Columns	AC-17
Exercise 1-11: Change Column Widths and Row Heights	AC-18
Exercise 1-12: Use the Font Command Group	AC-19
Printing and Saving a Recordset	**AC-20**
Exercise 1-13: Print a Query	AC-20
Exercise 1-14: Print a Table	AC-21
Exercise 1-15: Publish a Table	AC-22
Managing Access Files	**AC-23**
Exercise 1-16: Use Compact and Repair	AC-23
Exercise 1-17: Back Up a Database	AC-23
Exercise 1-18: Close a Database and Exit Access	AC-24

Lesson 1 Summary	**AC-24**
Concepts Review	**AC-27**
True/False Questions	**AC-27**
Short Answer Questions	**AC-27**
Critical Thinking	**AC-28**
Skills Review	**AC-28**
Exercise 1-19	AC-28
Exercise 1-20	AC-29
Exercise 1-21	AC-30
Exercise 1-22	AC-31
Lesson Applications	**AC-33**
Exercise 1-23	AC-33
Exercise 1-24	AC-33
Exercise 1-25	AC-33
Exercise 1-26	AC-34
On Your Own	**AC-34**
Exercise 1-27	AC-34
Exercise 1-28	AC-35
Exercise 1-29	AC-35
LESSON 2: VIEWING AND MODIFYING RECORDS	**AC-36**
Modifying Recordsets in a Table	**AC-36**
Exercise 2-1: Open a Database	AC-37
Exercise 2-2: Edit Fields in a Table	AC-37
Exercise 2-3: Add a Record in a Table	AC-38
Exercise 2-4: Delete a Record in a Table	AC-39
Modifying Recordsets through a Query	**AC-40**
Exercise 2-5: Edit Fields through a Query	AC-41
Exercise 2-6: Add a Record through a Query	AC-42
Exercise 2-7: Delete a Record through a Query	AC-42

Using Office Editing Tools   **AC-43**
  Exercise 2-8: Use AutoCorrect   AC-43
  Exercise 2-9: Use Copy, Paste, and the
    Office Clipboard   AC-45
  Exercise 2-10: Use Undo   AC-47

Viewing and Modifying Recordsets
through a Form   **AC-48**
  Exercise 2-11: Navigate through Forms   AC-48
  Exercise 2-12: Edit Fields through
    a Form   AC-50
  Exercise 2-13: Add Records through
    a Form   AC-51
  Exercise 2-14: Delete Records through
    a Form   AC-52

Managing Attachments   **AC-52**
  Exercise 2-15: Attach an Image   AC-53
  Exercise 2-16: Extract an Image from
    the Database   AC-54

Previewing, Printing, and Saving Data
Using a Report   **AC-55**
  Exercise 2-17: Preview a Report   AC-55
  Exercise 2-18: Print a Report   AC-56
  Exercise 2-19: Save a Report to a File   AC-57

Lesson 2 Summary   **AC-59**

Concepts Review   **AC-60**

True/False Questions   **AC-60**

Short Answer Questions   **AC-60**

Critical Thinking   **AC-61**

Skills Review   **AC-61**
  Exercise 2-20   AC-61
  Exercise 2-21   AC-62
  Exercise 2-22   AC-63
  Exercise 2-23   AC-64

Lesson Applications   **AC-66**
  Exercise 2-24   AC-66
  Exercise 2-25   AC-66
  Exercise 2-26   AC-67
  Exercise 2-27   AC-68

On Your Own   **AC-68**
  Exercise 2-28   AC-68
  Exercise 2-29   AC-68
  Exercise 2-30   AC-69

LESSON 3: FINDING, FILTERING,
SORTING, AND SUMMARIZING DATA   **AC-70**

Finding and Replacing Data   **AC-70**
  Exercise 3-1: Use the Search Tool   AC-71
  Exercise 3-2: Use the Find Command   AC-72
  Exercise 3-3: Use the Replace
    Command   AC-73

Using Wildcards   **AC-74**
  Exercise 3-4: Find Data Using an
    Asterisk "*"   AC-74
  Exercise 3-5: Find Data Using a Question
    Mark "?"   AC-75

Sorting Records   **AC-75**
  Exercise 3-6: Sort Records in
    Datasheet View   AC-75

  Exercise 3-7: Sort Records in a Form   AC-77
  Exercise 3-8: Sort Records in a Report   AC-77

Adding and Modifying the Totals Row
in Datasheets   **AC-78**
  Exercise 3-9: Add a Totals Row to
    a Query   AC-78
  Exercise 3-10: Modify a Totals Row in
    a Query   AC-79

Using Filters   **AC-80**
  Exercise 3-11 Create and Apply a Filter
    By Selection   AC-80
  Exercise 3-12: Filter for a Specific Value AC-83
  Exercise 3-13: Filter for a Range
    of Values   AC-83
  Exercise 3-14: Create and Apply a Filter
    By Form   AC-84
  Exercise 3-15: Use Filter By Form
    "Or" Option   AC-86

Using the Database Documenter   **AC-87**
  Exercise 3-16: Generate a Report for
    a Table   AC-87
  Exercise 3-17: Print/Save Reports for
    Multiple Objects   AC-88

Lesson 3 Summary   **AC-89**

Concepts Review   **AC-91**

True/False Questions   **AC-91**

Short Answer Questions   **AC-91**

Critical Thinking   **AC-92**

Skills Review   **AC-92**
  Exercise 3-18   AC-92
  Exercise 3-19   AC-93
  Exercise 3-20   AC-94
  Exercise 3-21   AC-94

Lesson Applications   **AC-96**
  Exercise 3-22   AC-96
  Exercise 3-23   AC-96
  Exercise 3-24   AC-96
  Exercise 3-25   AC-97

On Your Own   **AC-97**
  Exercise 3-26   AC-97
  Exercise 3-27   AC-97
  Exercise 3-28   AC-97

LESSON 4: CREATING NEW
DATABASES AND TABLES   **AC-98**

Creating Databases   **AC-98**
  Exercise 4-1: Create a Database Using a
    Template   AC-99
  Exercise 4-2: Set Database Properties   AC-100
  Exercise 4-3: Create a Blank
    Database   AC-101

Creating Tables   **AC-101**
  Exercise 4-4: Create a Table Using a
    Template   AC-102
  Exercise 4-5: Create a Table in
    Design View   AC-102
  Exercise 4-6: Copy a Table Structure   AC-105
  Exercise 4-7: Modify Table Properties   AC-105

Adding and Deleting Fields in a Table — AC-106

Exercise 4-8: Add and Delete Fields in Datasheet View — AC-106

Exercise 4-9: Add and Delete Fields in Design View — AC-107

Controlling Field Appearance — AC-108

Exercise 4-10: Change Field Property Caption — AC-109

Exercise 4-11: Change Field Property Default Value — AC-110

Exercise 4-12: Change Field Property Format — AC-110

Exercise 4-13: Change Field Property Input Mask — AC-111

Exercise 4-14: Change Field Property Date Picker — AC-113

Controlling Data Integrity — AC-113

Exercise 4-15: Set the Primary Key — AC-114

Exercise 4-16: Set the Field Property Field Size — AC-114

Exercise 4-17: Set the Field Property Validation Text and Rules — AC-115

Managing External Data — AC-116

Exercise 4-18: Export a Table to Access — AC-116

Exercise 4-19: Export Data to Word — AC-117

Exercise 4-20: Import Data from Excel — AC-118

Lesson 4 Summary — AC-119

Concepts Review — AC-121

True/False Questions — AC-121

Short Answer Questions — AC-121

Critical Thinking — AC-122

Skills Review — AC-122

Exercise 4-21 — AC-122

Exercise 4-22 — AC-123

Exercise 4-23 — AC-125

Exercise 4-24 — AC-125

Lesson Applications — AC-127

Exercise 4-25 — AC-127

Exercise 4-26 — AC-127

Exercise 4-27 — AC-128

Exercise 4-28 — AC-129

On Your Own — AC-130

Exercise 4-29 — AC-130

Exercise 4-30 — AC-130

Exercise 4-31 — AC-130

UNIT 1 APPLICATIONS — **AC-131**

Unit Application 1-1 — **AC-131**

Unit Application 1-2 — **AC-132**

Unit Application 1-3 — **AC-133**

Unit Application 1-4 — **AC-134**

Unit 2 Designing and Managing Database Objects

LESSON 5: MANAGING DATA INTEGRITY — AC-136

Creating Relationships Between Tables — AC-136

Exercise 5-1: Look at an Existing Relationship — AC-137

Exercise 5-2: Create a Relationship in the Relationships Window — AC-139

Exercise 5-3: Print/Save Relationships — AC-141

Working with Referential Integrity — AC-142

Exercise 5-4: Enforce Referential Integrity — AC-142

Exercise 5-5: Remove Referential Integrity — AC-144

Working with Subdatasheets — AC-145

Exercise 5-6: Insert a Subdatasheet — AC-145

Exercise 5-7: Remove a Subdatasheet — AC-147

Using the Lookup Wizard — AC-147

Exercise 5-8: Create a Lookup Field — AC-147

Exercise 5-9: Add Data with a Lookup Field — AC-148

Exercise 5-10: Modify a Lookup Field — AC-149

Exercise 5-11: Create a Multi-Valued Lookup Field — AC-150

Exercise 5-12: Add Data with a Multi-Valued Lookup Field — AC-151

Exercise 5-13: View Relationships Created by Lookup Fields — AC-152

Using Analyzing Tools — AC-153

Exercise 5-14: Analyze a Table — AC-153

Exercise 5-15: Analyze Performance — AC-155

Tracking Object Dependency — AC-155

Exercise 5-16: View Object Dependency — AC-155

Exercise 5-17: View a Missing Dependency — AC-156

Lesson 5 Summary — AC-157

Concepts Review — AC-159

True/False Questions — AC-159

Short Answer Questions — AC-159

Critical Thinking — AC-160

Skills Review — AC-160

Exercise 5-18 — AC-160

Exercise 5-19 — AC-161

Exercise 5-20 — AC-162

Exercise 5-21 — AC-164

Lesson Applications — AC-166

Exercise 5-22 — AC-166

Exercise 5-23 — AC-166

Exercise 5-24 — AC-166

Exercise 5-25 — AC-167

On Your Own — AC-168
Exercise 5-26 — AC-168
Exercise 5-27 — AC-168
Exercise 5-28 — AC-169

LESSON 6: DESIGNING QUERIES — **AC-170**

Creating and Modifying Select Queries — **AC-171**
Exercise 6-1: View a Select Query and Its Report — AC-171
Exercise 6-2: Create a Select Query Based on a Single Table — AC-172
Exercise 6-3: Add Fields to a Query — AC-173
Exercise 6-4: Create a Select Query based on Two Tables — AC-174

Adding Criteria and Operators to a Query — **AC-175**
Exercise 6-5: Use a Single Criterion — AC-176
Exercise 6-6: Use Comparison Operators — AC-177
Exercise 6-7: Use Wildcards In Criteria — AC-178
Exercise 6-8: Use Keywords in Criteria — AC-179

Applying Logical Operators — **AC-180**
Exercise 6-9: Use the and Criteria — AC-180
Exercise 6-10: Use the or Criteria — AC-181

Modifying Query Properties — **AC-182**
Exercise 6-11: Find the Top and Bottom Values — AC-182
Exercise 6-12: Create a Query with a Subdatasheet — AC-184

Adding Calculations to a Query — **AC-185**
Exercise 6-13: Use a Formula in a Calculated Field — AC-185
Exercise 6-14: Use a Function in a Calculated Field — AC-187

Creating Queries with Wizards — **AC-188**
Exercise 6-15: Use the Simple Query Wizard — AC-188
Exercise 6-16: Use the Crosstab Query Wizard — AC-190
Exercise 6-17: Use the Find Duplicates Query Wizard — AC-191
Exercise 6-18: Use the Find Unmatched Query Wizard — AC-192

Applying PivotChart/PivotTable Views — **AC-193**
Exercise 6-19: Use PivotTable View — AC-193
Exercise 6-20: Use PivotChart View — AC-194

Lesson 6 Summary — **AC-197**

Concepts Review — **AC-199**

True/False Questions — **AC-199**

Short Answer Questions — **AC-199**

Critical Thinking — **AC-200**

Skills Review — **AC-200**
Exercise 6-21 — AC-200
Exercise 6-22 — AC-202
Exercise 6-23 — AC-203
Exercise 6-24 — AC-204

Lesson Applications — **AC-206**
Exercise 6-25 — AC-206
Exercise 6-26 — AC-206

Exercise 6-27 — AC-207
Exercise 6-28 — AC-207

On Your Own — **AC-208**
Exercise 6-29 — AC-208
Exercise 6-30 — AC-208
Exercise 6-31 — AC-209

LESSON 7: ADDING AND MODIFYING FORMS — **AC-210**

Generating Forms Quickly — **AC-210**
Exercise 7-1: Create a Form with a Wizard — AC-211
Exercise 7-2: Generate a Form with One Click — AC-212

Modifying Controls in Layout View — **AC-213**
Exercise 7-3: Modify a Control Layout — AC-213
Exercise 7-4: Resize and Move Control Layouts — AC-214
Exercise 7-5: Align Control Layouts — AC-216
Exercise 7-6: Remove and Add Controls to a Control Layout — AC-217
Exercise 7-7: Set Tab Order — AC-219
Exercise 7-8: Format a Form in Layout View — AC-220

Working with Form Sections — **AC-221**
Exercise 7-9: Open and Size Form Sections — AC-221
Exercise 7-10: Add Labels and View Form Sections — AC-223

Modifying Controls in Design View — **AC-224**
Exercise 7-11: Format a Form in Design View — AC-224
Exercise 7-12: Resize and Move Controls — AC-226
Exercise 7-13: Modify Property Settings — AC-227
Exercise 7-14: Add a Label — AC-228

Adding Calculated Controls to a Form — **AC-228**
Exercise 7-15: Add Unbound Text Boxes — AC-229
Exercise 7-16: Add a Calculated Control — AC-229

Printing/Saving Forms — **AC-231**
Exercise 7-17: Print Specific Pages — AC-231
Exercise 7-18: Print One Record — AC-232
Exercise 7-19: Print Multiple Records — AC-233
Exercise 7-20: Save a Record — AC-233

Lesson 7 Summary — **AC-234**

Concepts Review — **AC-237**

True/False Questions — **AC-237**

Short Answer Questions — **AC-237**

Critical Thinking — **AC-238**

Skills Review — **AC-238**
Exercise 7-21 — AC-238
Exercise 7-22 — AC-239
Exercise 7-23 — AC-240
Exercise 7-24 — AC-242

Lesson Applications — **AC-244**
Exercise 7-25 — AC-244
Exercise 7-26 — AC-244
Exercise 7-27 — AC-245

On Your Own AC-246
   Exercise 7-28 AC-246
   Exercise 7-29 AC-246
   Exercise 7-30 AC-246
   Exercise 7-31 AC-247

**LESSON 8: ADDING AND
MODIFYING REPORTS** **AC-248**

Generating Reports Quickly **AC-248**
   Exercise 8-1: Create a Report with a
     Wizard AC-249
   Exercise 8-2: Generate a Report with
     One Click AC-250

Modifying Controls in Layout View **AC-251**
   Exercise 8-3: Format a Report in
     Layout View AC-251
   Exercise 8-4: Add and Rearrange
     Controls in a Report AC-252
   Exercise 8-5: Format a Report Using
     the Property Sheet AC-253

Working with Report Sections **AC-254**
   Exercise 8-6: Create a Grouped Report
     using a Wizard AC-255
   Exercise 8-7: Add a Group Section in
     Design View AC-256
   Exercise 8-8: Add a Group Section in
     Layout View AC-257
   Exercise 8-9: Modify Group Options AC-258
   Exercise 8-10: Add a Common Expression
     Control AC-259

Working with Controls in a Report **AC-260**
   Exercise 8-11: Move and Resize Controls AC-260
   Exercise 8-12: Align Controls AC-261
   Exercise 8-13: Add Lines to a Report AC-263
   Exercise 8-14: Edit Common Expression
     Controls AC-264

**Working with Format Painter and
Conditional Formatting** **AC-265**
   Exercise 8-15: Use the Format Painter AC-265
   Exercise 8-16: Use Conditional
     Formatting AC-266

**Creating a Multicolumn Report and
Labels** **AC-266**
   Exercise 8-17: Create a Multicolumn
     Report AC-267
   Exercise 8-18: Create Package Labels AC-267

Lesson 8 Summary **AC-269**
Concepts Review **AC-271**
True/False Questions **AC-271**
Short Answer Questions **AC-271**
Critical Thinking **AC-272**
Skills Review **AC-272**
   Exercise 8-19 AC-272
   Exercise 8-20 AC-273
   Exercise 8-21 AC-275
   Exercise 8-22 AC-276
Lesson Applications **AC-278**
   Exercise 8-23 AC-278
   Exercise 8-24 AC-278
   Exercise 8-25 AC-279
   Exercise 8-26 AC-280
On Your Own **AC-281**
   Exercise 8-27 AC-281
   Exercise 8-28 AC-281
   Exercise 8-29 AC-281

UNIT 2 APPLICATIONS **AC-282**

Unit Application 2-1 **AC-282**
Unit Application 2-2 **AC-283**
Unit Application 2-3 **AC-283**
Unit Application 2-4 **AC-284**

APPENDICES **A-1**
GLOSSARY **G-1**
INDEX **I-1**

preface

Microsoft Office 2007: A Professional Approach is written to help you master Microsoft Office. The text takes you step by step through the Office features that you are likely to use in both your personal and business life.

Case Studies

Learning the features of each application is one component of the text, and applying what you learn is another component. A case study was created for each application to offer the opportunity to learn in a realistic business context. Take the time to read the case studies. All the documents for this course relate to one of the case studies.

Organization of the Text

The text includes ten units, and each unit is divided into lessons. There are thirty-nine lessons, each self-contained but building on previously learned procedures. This building-block approach, together with the case studies and the following features, enables you to maximize the learning process.

Features of the Text

- Objectives are listed for each lesson.
- The estimated time required to complete each lesson up to the Lesson Applications section is stated.
- Within a lesson, each heading corresponds to an objective.
- Easy-to-follow exercises emphasize learning by doing.
- Key terms are italicized and defined as they are encountered.
- Extensive graphics display screen contents.
- Ribbon commands and keyboard keys are shown in the text when used.
- Large buttons in the margins provide easy-to-see references.
- Lessons contain important notes, useful tips, and helpful reviews.
- The Lesson Summary reviews the important concepts taught in the lesson.
- The Command Summary lists the commands taught in the lesson.
- Concepts Review includes true/false, short answer, and critical thinking questions that focus on lesson content.
- Skills Review provides skill reinforcement for each lesson.
- Lesson Applications apply your skills in a more challenging way.
- On Your Own exercises apply your skills creatively.
- Unit Applications give you the opportunity to practice the skills you learn throughout a unit.
- An Appendix includes Proofreaders' Marks, Standard Forms for Business Documents, a Glossary, and an Index.

Professional Approach Web Site

Visit the Professional Approach Web site at www.mhhe.com/pas07 to access a wealth of additional materials.

Conventions Used in the Text

This text uses a number of conventions to help you learn the program and save your work.

- Text to be keyed appears either in **red** or as a separate figure.
- Filenames appear in **boldface**.
- Options that you choose from tabs and dialog boxes, but that aren't buttons, appear in green; for example, "Choose **Print** from the Office menu."
- You're asked to save each document with your initials followed by the exercise name. For example, an exercise might end with this instruction: "Save the document as *[your initials]*5-12." Documents are saved in folders for each lesson.

If You Are Unfamiliar with Windows

If you are not familiar with Windows, review the "Windows Tutorial" available in the textbook or on the Professional Approach Web site at www.mhhe.com/pas07 before beginning Lesson 1. This tutorial provides a basic overview of Microsoft's operating system and shows you how to use the mouse. You might also want to review "File Management" on the Professional Approach Web site to get more comfortable with files and folders.

Screen Differences

As you practice each concept, illustrations of the screens help you follow the instructions. Don't worry if your screen is different from the illustration. These differences are due to variations in system and computer configurations.

installation requirements

You'll need Microsoft Office 2007 to work through this textbook. Office 2007 needs to be installed on the computer's hard drive or on a network. Use the following checklists to evaluate installation requirements.

Hardware

- Computer with 500MHz or higher processor and at least 256MB of RAM
- CD-ROM or DVD drive
- 1.5GB or more of hard disk space for a "Student" Office installation
- 1024 × 768 or higher-resolution video monitor
- Printer (laser or ink-jet recommended)
- Mouse
- Modem or other Internet connection

Software

- Word 2007, Excel 2007, PowerPoint 2007, and Access 2007 (from Microsoft Office 2007)
- Windows XP with Service Pack 2 or later, or Windows Vista, or later operating system
- Browser and Internet access

FEATURE	USE	HOW TO INSTALL/USE
Student template files	Build a new document based on template.	Copy template files to C:\Users\UserName\AppData\Roaming\Microsoft\Templates for files to appear on the My Templates tab of the New dialog box.
Clip art, additional	Use clip art related to the case.	Copy image files to any usable folder.
Templates	Build a new document based on template.	Part of typical installation; files are in C:\Program Files\Microsoft Office 11\Templates\1033.
Internet functionality	Use online help, use online Template Gallery, use additional research tools, view Web pages.	Specific to classroom.
Language tools	Use thesaurus and translation tools in the Research task pane.	Part of a typical installation for Office 2007 Professional. Install when prompted at first use. May require installation CD.

FEATURE	USE	HOW TO INSTALL/USE
Visual Basic Editor	View, edit, and save macros.	Part of a typical installation for Office 2007 Professional. Install when prompted. May require installation CD.
Digital Signature	Create a digital signature.	Part of a typical installation for Office 2007 Professional. Listed at Microsoft Office Button, Prepare.
XPS/PDF Add-in	Save files in XPS or PDF format.	
Compatibility Checker	Save files in XLS format.	Part of a typical installation for Office 2007 Professional.

If you are not familiar with Windows, review this "Windows Tutorial" carefully. You will learn how to

- Use a mouse.
- Start Windows.
- Use the taskbar, menus, Ribbon, dialog boxes, and other important aspects of Windows.

NOTE

All examples in this tutorial refer specifically to Windows Vista. If you are using any other version of Windows, your screen might differ slightly from the images shown in this tutorial. However, because most basic features are common to all versions of Windows, this tutorial should be helpful to you no matter which version of Windows you use.

If you are familiar with Windows but need help navigating Windows files and folders, refer to the section "File Management." There you will find information on how Windows stores information and how to use Windows Explorer, a tool for managing files and folders.

Computers differ in the ways they can be set up. In most cases, when you turn on your computer, Windows loads automatically and the Windows log-on screen appears. When you see the Windows log-on screen, you need to log on and key a password. In order to log on, you need to know how to use the mouse, a device attached to your computer.

Using the Mouse

A *mouse* is a pointing device that is typically attached to your computer. Optical versions, which are not attached, are also available. The mouse is your access to the computer screen, allowing you to accomplish specific tasks. It operates through a pointer, a screen object you use to point to objects on the computer screen. The normal shape for the mouse cursor is an arrow. To move the pointer arrow on the screen, you roll the mouse on any flat object, or on a mouse pad, which has a smooth surface designed for easy mouse rolling. Although you can use the keyboard with Windows, you will probably find yourself using the mouse most of the time.

To use the mouse to point to an object on the computer screen:

1. Turn on the computer (if it is not on already). Windows loads, and the log-on screen appears. The screen includes a log-on name and picture assigned to you by your instructor.

To log on, you need to move the mouse pointer to the log-on name that was assigned. The pointer on the computer screen mirrors the actions made by the mouse when you roll it. Place your hand over the mouse and roll it to the left. The pointer on the screen moves to the left.

2. Roll the mouse to the right, and watch the pointer on the screen move to the right.

3. Practice rolling the mouse in all directions.

4. Roll your mouse to the edge of the pad, and then lift it up and place it back in the middle of the pad. Try it now to see how it works. When you feel that you can control the mouse position on the screen, roll the mouse to the name you have been assigned.

To log on, you will need to click the name to select it. Mouse clicks are covered in the next section; instructions for logging onto Windows Vista are covered in succeeding sections.

Clicks and Double-Clicks

A mouse typically has two buttons at the front (the edge of the mouse where the cord attaches)—one on the left (primary) and one on the right (secondary). A mouse might also have a center button or a wheel.

Single-click actions with the mouse are used to position the pointer at a specific screen location. To perform a single click:

1. Roll the mouse around on the mouse pad until the pointer on the screen is over an object on the screen. Remember that the direction in which you move the mouse on the pad represents the pointer's movement on the screen.

2. Press and release the left mouse button once. Pressing and releasing the mouse button is referred to as a *click*. The computer tells you that the action has been performed when the object you click is *highlighted* (typically, the color of the selected object changes) to indicate to you that it has been *selected*. In Windows, you often need to select an object before you can perform an action. For example, you usually need to select an object before you can copy it.

Pressing and releasing the mouse button twice is referred to as a *double-click*. When you double-click an object on the screen, it is selected—the object is highlighted—and an action is performed. For example:

NOTE

Whenever you are told to "click" or "double-click" an object on the computer screen, use the left mouse button.

- When you double-click a folder, it is highlighted and opens to a window showing the items the folder contains.

- When you double-click a word in a text file, it is selected for a future action. In a text file, the pointer becomes an I-beam for selecting text in the document.

Selecting and Highlighting

You can also select a larger object such as a picture or a block of text by using the mouse.

1. Position the pointer on one side of the object, and hold down the left mouse button.
2. Roll the mouse until the pointer reaches the other side of the object.
3. Release the mouse button. The selected object is highlighted.

Drag and Drop—Moving an Object Using the Mouse

You can use the mouse to move an object on the screen to another screen location. In this operation, you select an object and drag the mouse to move the selected object, such as an icon. The operation is known as *drag and drop*.

1. Using the mouse, move the pointer over the object you want to drag.
2. Perform a single-click action by pressing the left mouse button but keep it pressed down. The selected object will be highlighted.
3. With the left mouse button still depressed, roll the mouse until the pointer and selected object are placed at the desired new location.
4. Release the mouse button to drop the object. The object is now positioned at the new location.

Using the Right Mouse Button

Pressing and quickly releasing the right mouse button is referred to as a *right-click*. Although the right mouse button is used less frequently, using it can be a real time-saver. When you right-click an icon, a *shortcut menu* appears with a list of commands. The list of commands displayed varies for each icon or object.

As you progress in this tutorial, you will become familiar with the terms in Table 1, describing the actions you can take with a mouse.

TABLE 1 Mouse Terms

TERM	DESCRIPTION
Point	Roll the mouse until the tip of the pointer is touching the desired object on the computer screen.
Click	Quickly press and release the left mouse button. Single-clicking selects objects.
Double-click	Quickly press and release the left mouse button twice. Double-clicking selects an object and performs an action such as opening a folder.
Drag	Point to an object on screen, hold down the left mouse button, and roll the mouse until the pointer is in position. Then release the mouse button (drag and drop).
Right-click	Quickly press and release the right mouse button. A shortcut menu appears.
Select	When working in Windows, you must first select an object in order to work with it. Many objects are selected with a single click. However, depending on the size and type of object to be selected, you may need to roll the mouse to include an entire area: Holding down the left mouse button, roll the mouse so that the pointer moves from one side of an object to another. Then release the mouse button.

Pointer Shapes

As you perform actions on screen using the mouse, the mouse pointer changes its shape, depending on where it is located and what operation you are performing. Table 2 shows the most common types of mouse pointers.

TABLE 2 Frequently Used Mouse Pointers

SHAPE	NAME	DESCRIPTION
⬉	Pointer	Used to point to objects.
I	I-Beam	Used in typing, inserting, and selecting text. When the I-beam is moved to a selected location, it turns into a blinking bar.
↔	Two-pointed arrow	Used to change the size of objects or windows.
✛	Four-pointed arrow	Used to move objects.
○	Busy	Indicates the computer is processing a command. While the busy or working in background pointer is displayed, it is best to wait rather than try to continue working. Note: Some of the working in background actions will not allow you to perform other procedures until processing is completed.
⬉○	Working in background	
🖑	Hand	Used to select a *link* in Windows' Help or other programs.

Starting Windows: The Log-on Screen

The Windows Vista log-on screen allows several people to use the same computer at different times. Each person is assigned a user account that determines which files and folders you can access and your personal preferences, such as your desktop background. Each person's files are hidden from the others using the computer. However, users may share selected files using the Public folder. The log-on screen lists each user allocated to the computer by name.

If the administrator has added your name to a given computer, the log-on screen will include your name. If the computers are not assigned to specific individuals, you may find a box for Guest or for a generic user. If your computer is on a network, your instructor might need to provide you with special start-up instructions.

After you have logged on to Windows Vista, the desktop is the first screen you will see. It is your on-screen work area. All the elements you need to start working with Windows appear on the desktop.

1. If you have not already turned on the computer, do so now to begin the Windows Vista loading process. The Windows log-on screen appears.

NOTE

On some computers, the log-on screen does not appear automatically. You might have to press the following keys, all at once, and then quickly release them: 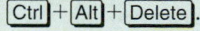 Ctrl + Alt + Delete .

2. Click your name to select it. The Password box appears with an I-beam in position ready for you to type your password.

3. Type your password.

4. Click the arrow icon to the right of the box. If you have entered the password correctly, the Windows desktop appears. If you made an error, the Password box returns for you to type the correct password.

The Windows Desktop

The Desktop includes the Start button, taskbar, and sidebar. You may also see icons on the desktop that represent folders, programs, or other objects. You can add and delete icons from the desktop as well as change the desktop background. The Start button is your entry into Vista functions.

Figure 1
Windows Vista
Desktop

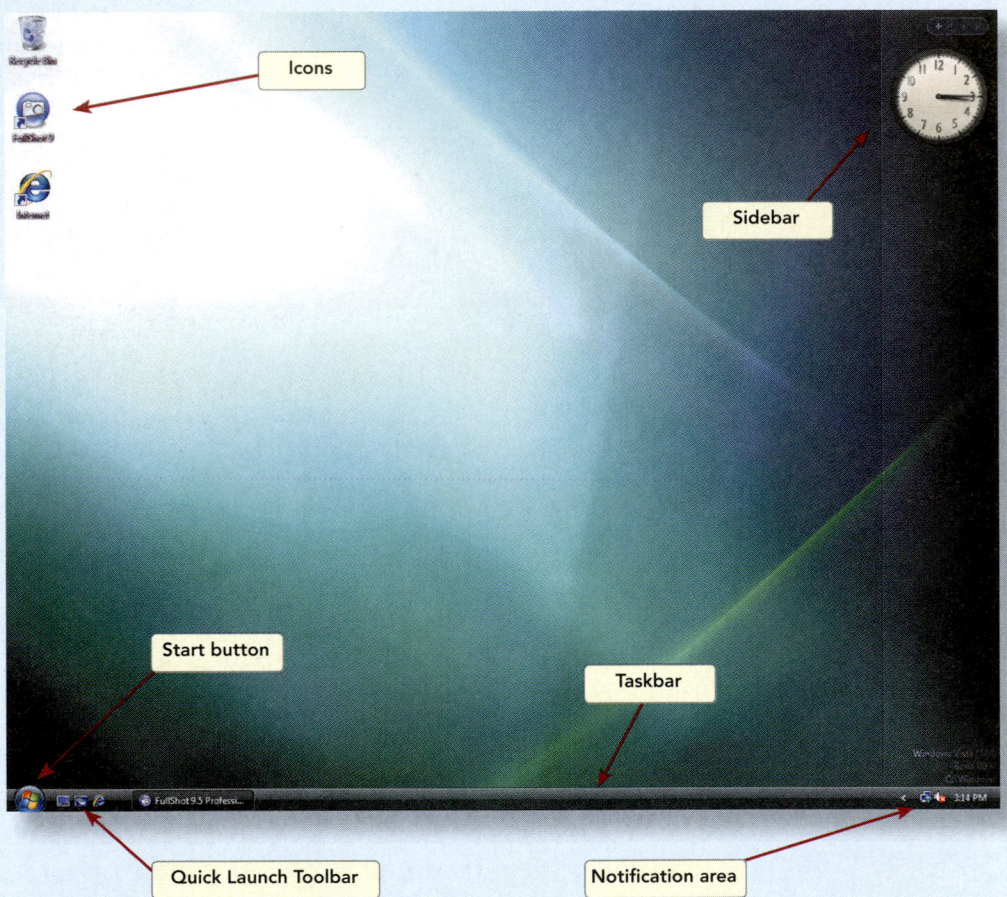

Using the Start Menu

Click the taskbar Start button to open the Start menu. You can also press the Windows logo key on the keyboard to open the Start menu. Use the Start menu to launch programs, adjust computer settings, search for files and folders, and turn off the computer. If this is a computer assigned to you for log-on, your Start menu may contain items that differ from those of another user assigned to the same computer. To open and learn about the Start menu, first click the Start button on the Windows taskbar. The Start menu appears.

Figure 2
Start menu

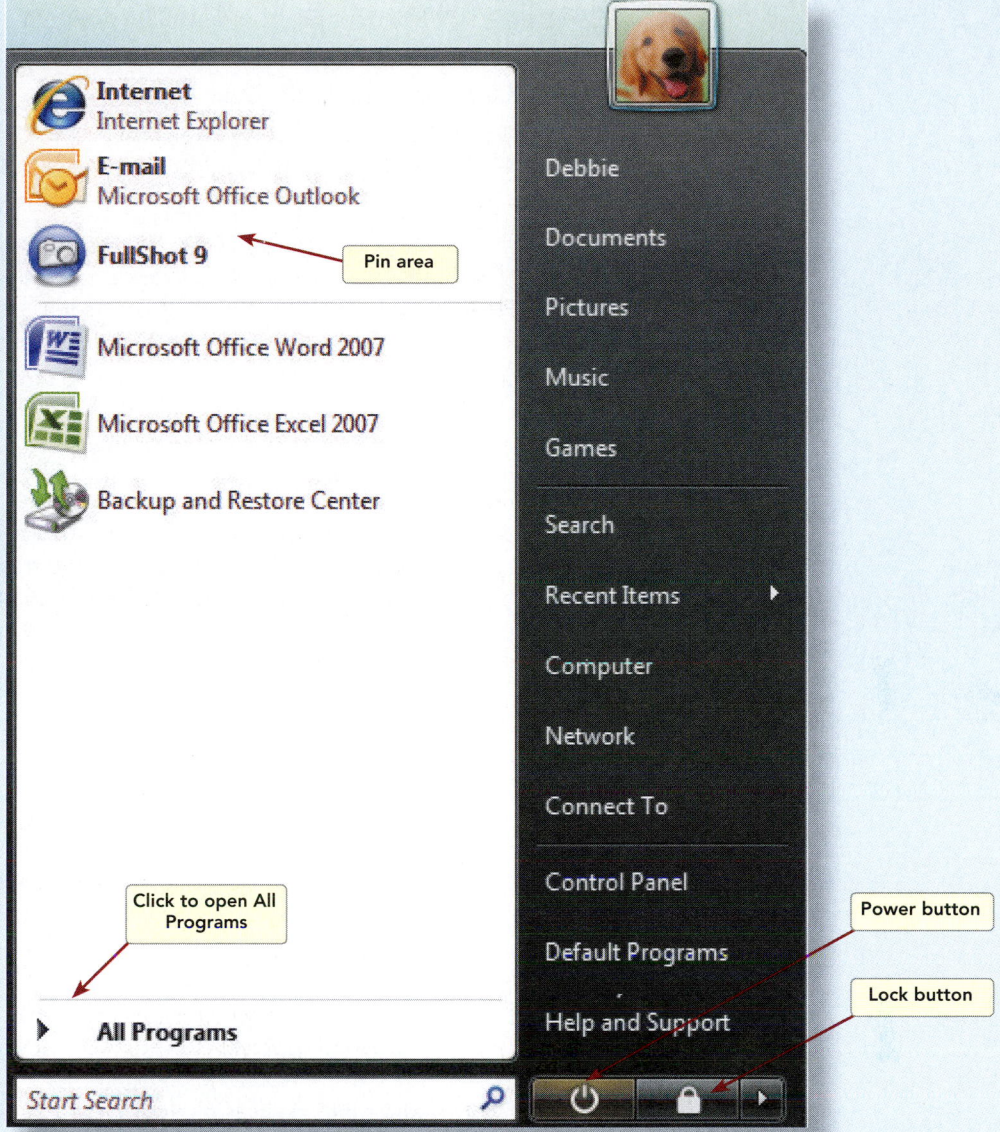

The left pane consists of three sections divided by separator lines. The top section, called the *pin area*, lists programs that are always available for you to click. These can include your Internet browser, e-mail program, your word processor, and so forth. You can remove programs you do not want listed, rearrange them, and add those you prefer.

Below the separator line are shortcuts to programs you use most often, placed there automatically by Windows. You can remove programs you do not want listed, rearrange them, but not add any manually.

All Programs displays a list of programs on your computer and is used to launch programs not listed on the Start menu.

Below the left pane is the *Search box* which is used to locate programs and files on your computer.

The right pane is also divided into three sections. It is used to select folders, files, and commands and to change settings. Use the icons at the bottom of the right pane to save your session, lock the computer, restart, switch users, and shut down.

Table 3 describes the typical components of the Start menu.

TABLE 3 Typical Components of the Start Menu

COMMAND	USE
Left Pane	
Pin area	Lists programs that are always available. You can add and delete items to the pin area.
Internet	Connects to the default browser.
E-mail	Connects to the chosen e-mail service.
Below the First Separator Line	
Programs	Lists programs that you use most often. You can add to and rearrange the programs listed.
Below the Second Separator Line	
All Programs	Click to display a list of programs in alphabetical order and a list of folders. Click to open a program.
Start Search	Use to search programs and folders. Key text and results appear.
Right Pane	
Personal folder	Opens the User folder.
Documents	Opens the Documents folder.
Pictures	Opens the Pictures folder.
Music	Opens the Music folder.
Games	Opens the Games folder.
Search	Opens the Search Results window. Advanced Search options are available.
Recent Items	Opens a list of the most recent documents you have opened and saved.
Computer	Opens a window where you can access disk drives and other hardware devices.
Network	Opens the Network window where you can access computers and other devices on your network.
Connect To	Opens a window where you can connect to a different network.
Control Panel	Opens the Control Panel.
Default Programs	Opens the Default Programs window where you can define default programs and settings.
Help and Support	Opens the Windows Help and Support window. Help offers instructions on how to perform tasks in the Windows environment.
Power button	Turns off the computer.
Lock button	Locks the computer, or click the arrow beside the Lock button to display a menu for switching users, logging off, restarting, or shutting down the computer.

Using the All Programs Command

Most programs on your computer can be started from the All Programs command on the Start menu. This is the easiest way to open a program not listed directly on the Start menu.

1. To open the All Programs menu, click the Start button. The Start menu appears.

2. Click **All Programs** or the triangle to the left near the bottom of the left pane. The All Programs menu appears, listing the programs installed on your computer. Every computer has a different list of programs. Notice that some menu entries have an icon to the left of the name and others display a folder. Click a folder, and a list of programs stored in that folder appears. Click a program to open it. Point to a program to see a short description of the program.

Figure 3
All Programs
window

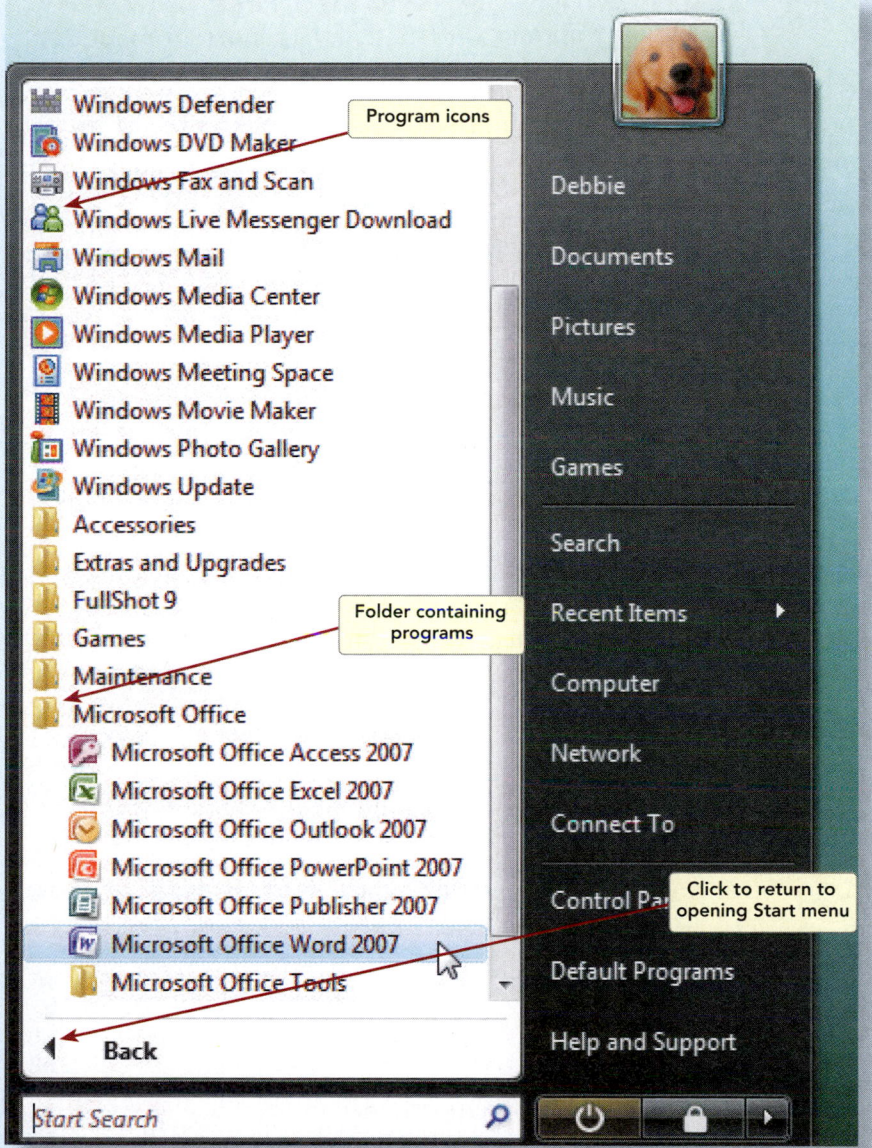

3. Click **Microsoft Office** to open a list of programs in the Microsoft Office folder. Click **Microsoft Office Word 2007**. (See Figure 3.) In a few seconds, the program you selected loads and the Word window appears. Notice that a button for the program appears on the taskbar. Leave Word open for the present.

Customizing the Start Menu

Both the Start menu and the desktop can be customized. You can add shortcuts to the desktop if you prefer, and you can add and delete items from the Start menu. However, if your computer is used by others, the administrator may limit some customization functions.

To add a program to the pin area of the Start menu:

1. Select the program you want to add to the pin list from the All Programs menu, and right-click it. A shortcut menu appears.
2. Click **Pin To Start Menu** on the shortcut menu. The program will be added to the pin list in the left pane above the first separator line.

To remove a program from the pin area of the Start menu:

1. Select the program you want to remove from the pin list, and right-click. A shortcut menu appears.
2. Click **Unpin From Start Menu**. The program will be removed from the pin list.

To change the order in which programs are listed in the pin area:

1. Point to the program icon.
2. Drag the icon to the desired position.

Using the Taskbar

The taskbar at the bottom of your screen is one of the most important features in Windows Vista. The taskbar is divided into several segments, each dedicated to a different use. It shows programs that are running, and you can use the taskbar to switch between open programs and between open documents within a program. If your computer has the Aero interface, a thumbnail preview appears when you move the mouse over a button on the taskbar.

Figure 4
The Desktop with the taskbar and the Word window

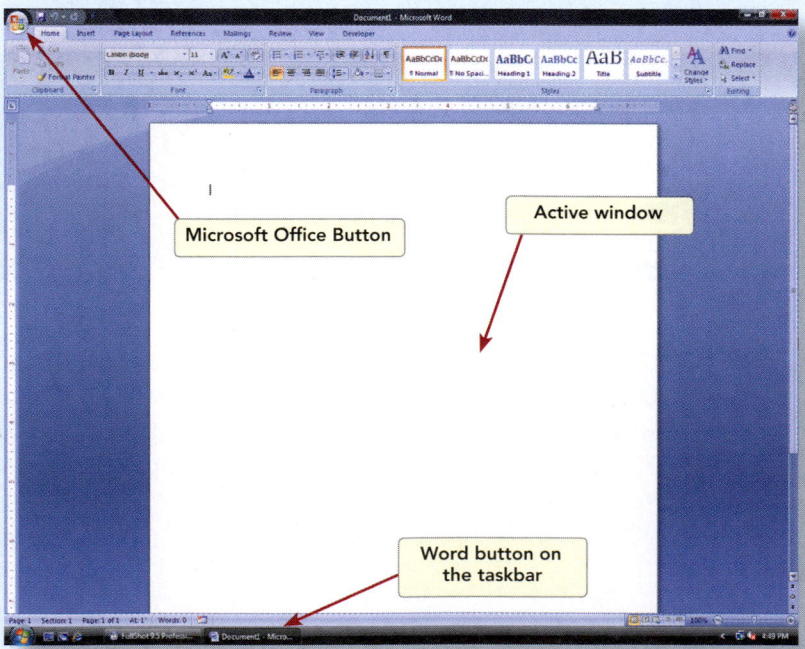

Microsoft Office Button

Active window

Word button on the taskbar

Windows displays a button on the taskbar for each opened program and document. Notice that there is a button for Word, showing the Word icon and the name of the program. Point to the Word button to view a thumbnail of the document window. Since the taskbar can become crowded, Windows combines access to documents or programs under single buttons. The button shows the name of the program (Microsoft Office Word) and the number of items in the group (9). The shape of the arrow varies, depending on what the button contains. Clicking the button opens the menu of available items.

Figure 5
Button contents for
Word documents

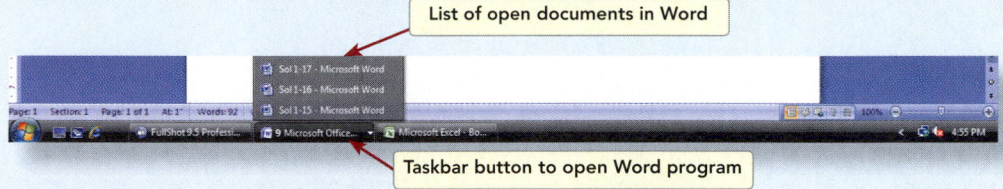

List of open documents in Word

Taskbar button to open Word program

Taskbar Notification Area

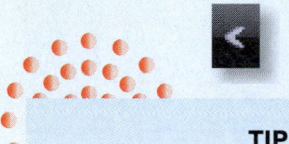

The *notification area* is on the right side of the taskbar, where the current time is usually displayed. Along with displaying the time, tiny icons notify you as to the status of your browser connection, virus protection, and so forth. It is also known as the *system tray*. In the interest of removing clutter, the notification area hides most of the icons. Clicking the Show Hidden Icons button ◄ "hides" or "unhides" the icons in the notification area. Click the left-pointing arrow next to the icons to expand the notification area. Click the right-pointing arrow to hide the notification area.

TIP

If you are not sure of what an item is or does, pointing to it without clicking displays a ScreenTip with a short description.

The Active Window

The window in which you are working is called the *active window*. The title bar for the active window is highlighted, and its taskbar button is also highlighted. The program window for Microsoft Word that you opened earlier should still be open. To examine additional features of the taskbar, open a second program, Microsoft Excel, a spreadsheet program in Microsoft Office.

1. If Word is not open, click the **Start** button and then click **All Programs**, **Microsoft Office**, **Microsoft Office Word 2007** from the Start menu. The Word window displays.

2. Click the **Start** button and then click **All Programs**, **Microsoft Office**, **Microsoft Office Excel 2007** from the Start menu. The Excel window displays. Notice how the Excel window covers the Word window, indicating that the window containing Excel is now active. Notice, too, that a new button for Excel has been added to the taskbar.

Figure 6
Excel (the active
window) covering
the Word window

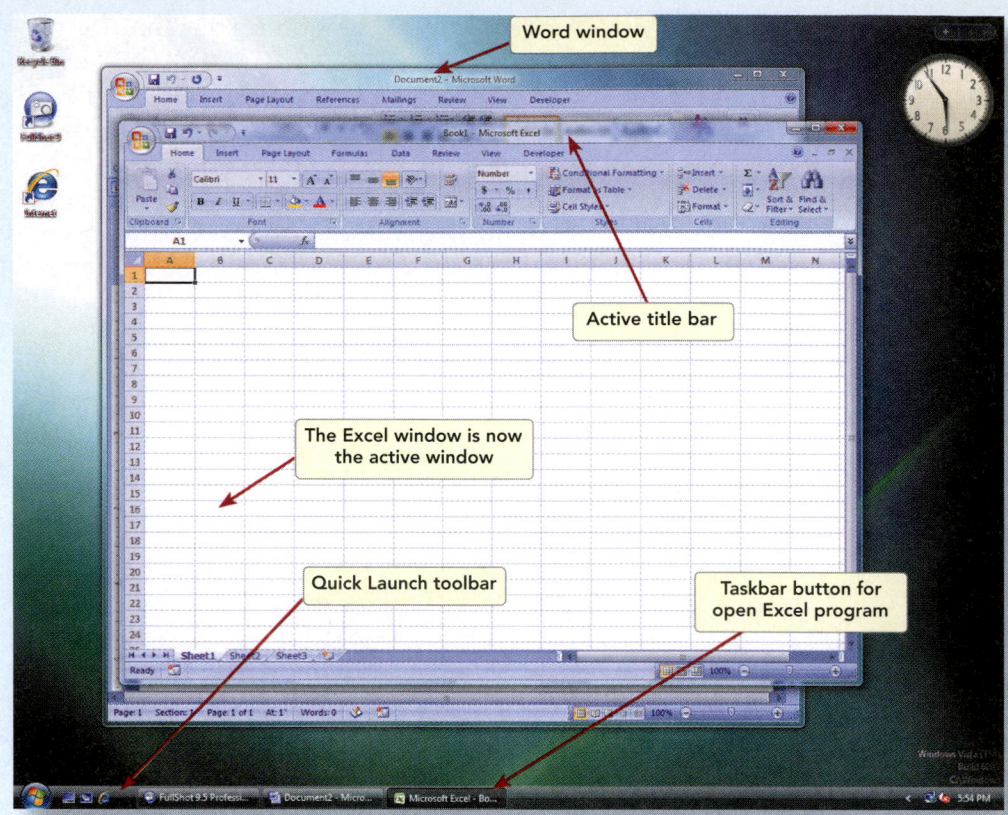

3. Click the button on the taskbar for Word, the first program you opened. Word reappears in front of Excel. Notice the change in the appearance of the title bar for each program.

4. Click the button on the taskbar for Excel. Notice that you switch back to Excel.

5. Click the button on the taskbar to return to Word.

6. Locate the Quick Launch toolbar to the right of the Start button, and point to the Switch between windows button ▣.

7. Click the Switch between windows button, and notice the desktop view.

8. Click the Excel window.

Changing the Size of the Taskbar

You can change the size of the taskbar using your mouse if your toolbar is crowded. It is usually not necessary, because of the multiple document style buttons and other hide/unhide arrows on the taskbar. Before you can change the size of the taskbar, it may be necessary for you to unlock it. To unlock the taskbar, right-click an open area of the taskbar and click **Lock the Taskbar** to remove the checkmark. A checkmark is a toggle command. Click to turn it off, and click a second time to turn it on.

1. Move the pointer to the top edge of the taskbar until it changes from a pointer to a two-pointed arrow ↕. Using the two-pointed arrow, you can change the size of the taskbar.

2. With the pointer displayed as a two-pointed arrow, hold down the left mouse button and move the arrow up until the taskbar enlarges upward.

3. Move the pointer to the top edge of the taskbar once again until the two-pointed arrow displays. Hold down the left mouse button, and move the arrow down to the bottom of the screen. The taskbar is restored to its original size.

Using Menus

Windows uses a system of menus that contain a choice of options for working with programs and documents. Most Windows programs use a similar menu structure. These operations are either mouse or keyboard driven. They are called commands because they "command" the computer to perform functions needed to complete the task you, the user, initiate at the menu level.

Executing a Command from a Menu

In Windows, a program may display a *menu bar*, a row of descriptive menu names at the top, just below the title bar. You open a menu by clicking the menu name listed in the menu bar. When a menu is opened, a list of command options appears. To execute a particular command from an open menu, press the left mouse button and then drag down and release the chosen option (click and drag). You can also click the command once the menu is open.

Keyboard Menu Commands

For people who prefer to use the keyboard to a mouse, Windows has provided keyboard commands for many menu items. You can use the keyboard to open menus and choose menu options.

Some menu items include not only the name of the command but a combination of keyboard keys. For example, under the File menu in WordPad, the Save command contains the notation Ctrl+S to its right. This means that you can also execute the command by pressing the Ctrl key together with the S key to save a document.

Figure 7
Title and menu bars
with the File menu
Open

Command name

Command with three
dots opens a dialog box.

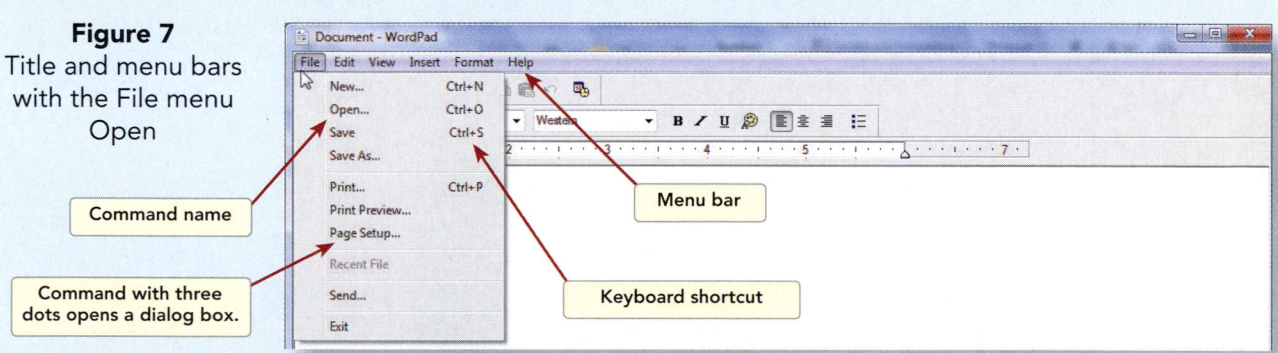

Other Menu Symbols

Three dots following a menu option indicate that a dialog box is displayed when that menu option is chosen. (Dialog boxes, discussed later, are small windows requesting and receiving input from a user.) Some commands also display a check box. Click an empty check box to select the option. A checkmark will appear in the square and indicates the option is selected. To turn off the option, click the check box to remove the checkmark. Commands that appear gray or dimmed are currently not available.

Perform the following steps for keyboard command practice:

1. Open the **Start menu**, click **All Programs**, and click the **Accessories** folder. Click **WordPad**. The WordPad program opens, and a button appears on the Windows taskbar.

2. Click **File** in the menu bar. The File menu displays. Click **File** to close the menu.

3. Press [Alt], and notice that the items in the menu bar display underlined letters (File, Edit). The underlined letters are a shortcut to open a menu. Press the letter "f" to open the File menu. Release [Alt], and click outside the menu in a blank area to close the menu.

4. Press [Alt]+[V], the keyboard shortcut for the View menu. The View menu displays.

5. Notice the four check boxes. All are selected. Click the **Options** command. The Options dialog box opens.

6. Click **Cancel** to close the dialog box.

7. Click **File** in the menu bar. Click **Exit**. Click **Don't Save** if prompted to save the document.

Displaying a Shortcut Menu

When the mouse pointer is on an object or an area of the Windows desktop and you right-click, a shortcut menu appears. A shortcut menu typically contains commands that are useful in working with the object or area of the desktop to which you are currently pointing.

1. Position the mouse pointer on a blank area of the desktop, and right-click. A shortcut menu appears with commands that relate to the desktop, including view and sort options.

2. Click outside the shortcut menu to close it.

3. Right-click the time in the bottom right corner of the taskbar. A shortcut menu appears.

4. Click Adjust Date/Time on the shortcut menu. The Date/Time Properties dialog box appears. You can use this dialog box to adjust your computer's date and time.

Figure 8
The Time shortcut menu

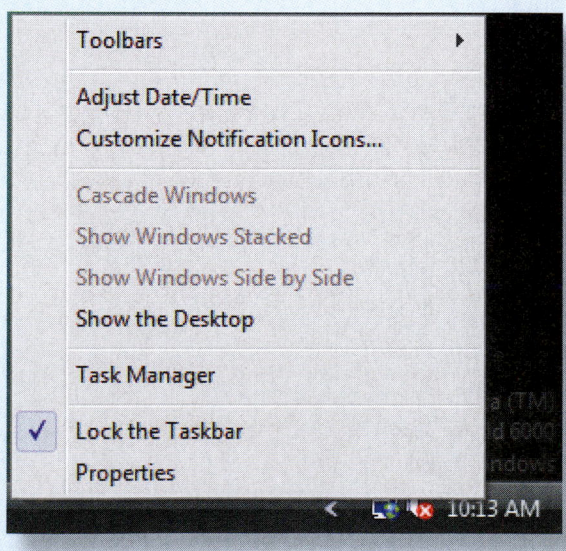

5. Click **Cancel**.

6. Right-click an icon on the desktop to display its shortcut menu, and then close the shortcut menu.

Using the Ribbon

Microsoft Office 2007 applications include a Microsoft Office Button, a Quick Access Toolbar, and a Ribbon. The *Microsoft Office Button* displays the Office menu which lists the commands to create, open, save, and print a document. The *Quick Access Toolbar* contains frequently used commands and is positioned to the right of the Microsoft Office Button. The *Ribbon* consists of seven tabs by default, and each tab contains a group of related commands. The number of commands for each tab varies. A command can be one of several formats. The most popular formats include buttons and drop-down lists.

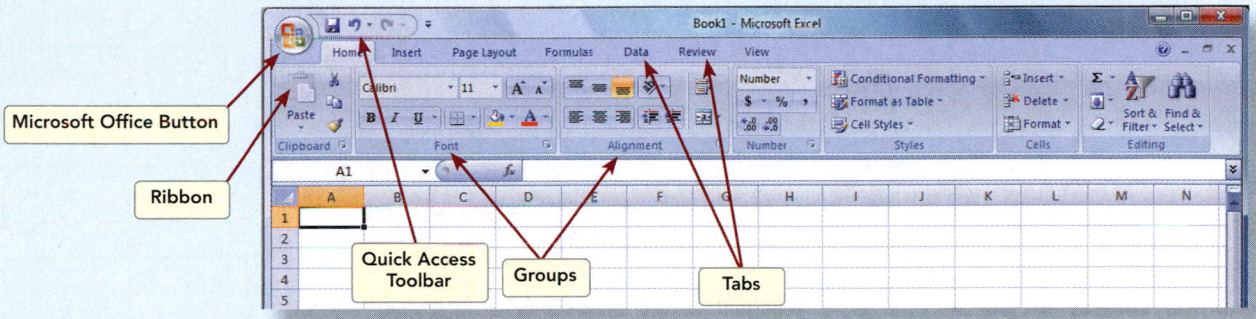

1. Activate the Excel program.

2. Point to and click the **Microsoft Office Button**. Notice the commands and icons in the menu.

3. Click a blank area of the window to close the menu.

4. Locate the Quick Access Toolbar beside the Microsoft Office Button. Point to each button in the Quick Access Toolbar to identify it. Notice that a keyboard shortcut displays beside each button.

5. Click the **Page Layout** tab. Notice the change in the groups and commands.

6. Click the **Home** tab.

Using Dialog Boxes

Windows programs make frequent use of dialog boxes. A *dialog box* is a window that requests input from you related to a command you have chosen. All Windows programs use a common dialog box structure.

1. Click the Excel program button on the taskbar to make Excel the active window if necessary.

2. Click the **Microsoft Office Button**. The File menu displays.

3. Click **Print** to display the Print dialog box.

4. The Print dialog box contains several types of dialog box options.

NOTE

A keyboard shortcut is available for the print dialog box: Press Ctrl + P to open the Print dialog box.

Figure 10
Print dialog box in Excel

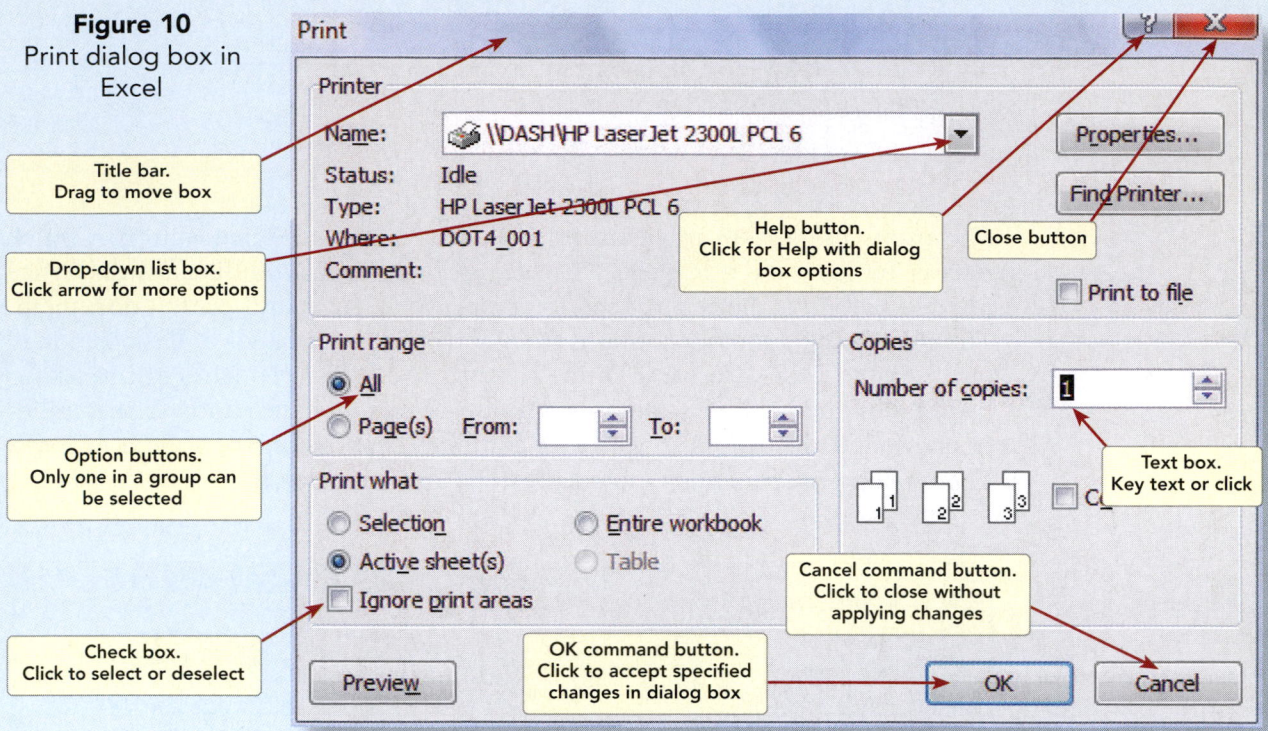

Title bar.
Drag to move box

Drop-down list box.
Click arrow for more options

Help button.
Click for Help with dialog box options

Close button

Option buttons.
Only one in a group can be selected

Cancel command button.
Click to close without applying changes

Check box.
Click to select or deselect

OK command button.
Click to accept specified changes in dialog box

Text box.
Key text or click

5. To close the Print dialog box, click **Cancel**, located in the lower right corner of the dialog box. The Print dialog box closes without applying any changes.

   Another type of dialog box uses tabs to display related options. Only one tab can display at a time. The Word Font dialog box offers many options for choosing character formatting.

1. Make Word the active window.

2. Click the **Home** tab, and click the small arrow that appears on the right of the Font group . The Font dialog box displays.

Figure 11
Font dialog box

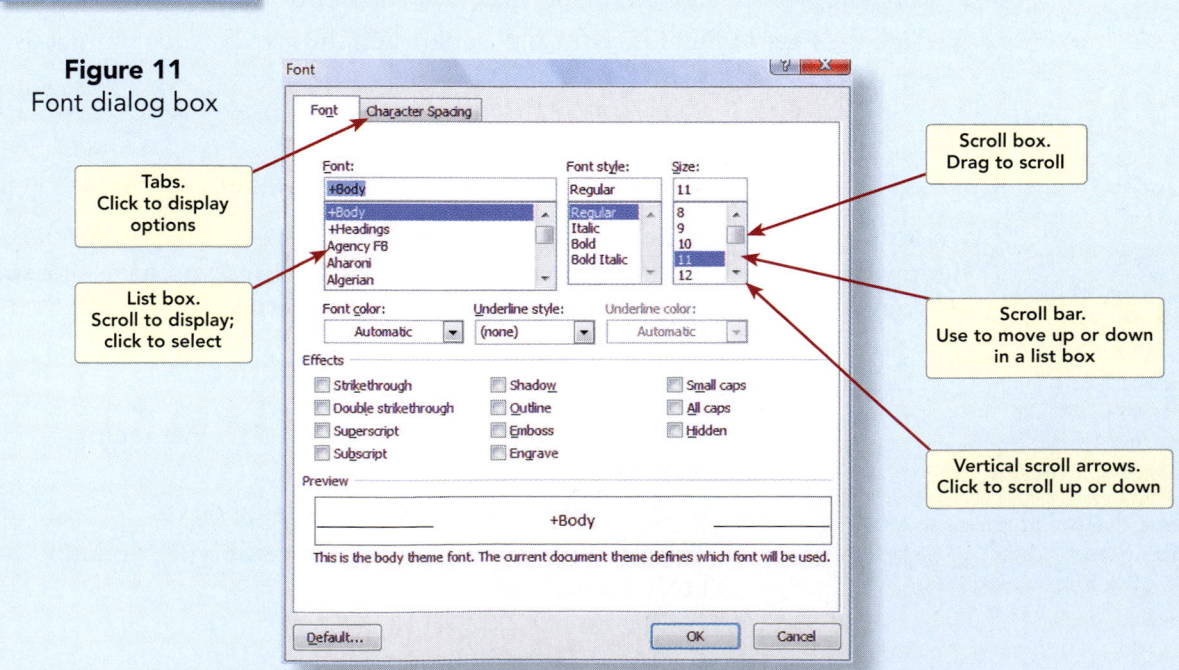

Tabs.
Click to display options

List box.
Scroll to display; click to select

Scroll box.
Drag to scroll

Scroll bar.
Use to move up or down in a list box

Vertical scroll arrows.
Click to scroll up or down

The scroll boxes are used to specify a font by name, its style, and its size. When you select a paragraph in a Word document, you can select its typographic features using this dialog box. The Font list box at the top left displays a list of all the typefaces installed on your computer. By clicking the name of the font, you select it for your paragraph.

The vertical scroll bar on the right side of a list box or a window indicates that there is more content to view. To view the hidden content, click the downward-pointing arrow or the upward-pointing vertical scroll arrow. You can also drag the scroll box on the scroll bar up or down to view all the content. The Character Spacing tab at the top of the Font dialog box displays additional character formatting options. Click the Character Spacing tab to view its contents, and then return to the Font tab.

Use the Font dialog box to style a paragraph as follows:

1. Type a very short paragraph in your Word document.
2. Position the I-beam at the beginning of the text, and hold down the left mouse button.
3. Drag the mouse to the end of the paragraph. The paragraph will change color, showing that it has been selected.
4. Open the Font dialog box by pressing Ctrl+D.
5. In the Font list box, click **Verdana**. You may need to scroll down to locate it.
6. In the Font style box, click **Bold**.
7. In the Size box, click **12**.
8. If you wish to change the color of your paragraph, move your pointer to the Font color drop-down list box and click the down-facing arrow. A color pallet appears. Point to the color you wish to use, and click.
9. When you have completed your selections, click **OK** at the bottom of the Font dialog box and look at the paragraph you have styled. If you wish, you can try other font formats, while your paragraph is selected.

Changing the Size of a Window

You can change the size of any window using either the mouse or the sizing buttons. Sizing buttons are the small buttons on the right side of the title bar that allow you to minimize or maximize the window (see Figure 12). This can be especially useful when you would like to display several open windows on your desktop and see them simultaneously.

1. Make Excel the active window, if it is not already. Click the Maximize button on the Excel title bar if the Excel window does not fill the entire desktop.

> **NOTE**
>
> Notice that the window occupies the entire desktop, and the Maximize button has changed to a Restore Down button. This type of function is known as a toggle: When a button representing one state (Maximize) is clicked, an action is performed, the button toggles to the alternate state, and the other button (Restore Down) appears. A number of actions in Windows operate this way.

Figure 12
Sizing buttons

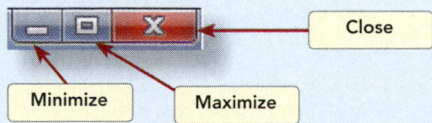

Close

Minimize   Maximize

Table 4 describes these buttons. To practice changing the size of a window, follow these steps:

TABLE 4 Sizing Buttons

BUTTON	USE
Minimize	Reduces the window to a button on the taskbar.
Maximize	Enlarges the window to fill the entire desktop (appears only when a window is reduced).
Restore Down	Returns the window to its previous size and desktop position (appears only when a window is maximized).

NOTE

You can double-click a window title bar to maximize or restore the window or right-click the program button on the taskbar and choose minimize, maximize, restore, or close.

2. Click the **Restore Down** button on the Excel title bar. The Excel window reduces in size, and the Word window appears behind it. The Restore Down button has now changed to a Maximize button. Notice that the highlighted title bar of the Excel window indicates it is the active window.

3. Click the **Minimize** button. The Excel window disappears, and its button appears on the taskbar.

How to Display Two Program Windows Simultaneously

1. Open the **Start** menu, and click **All Programs** to open Excel and Word if they are not already open from an earlier section of the tutorial.

TIP

Sometimes the borders of a window can move off the computer screen. If you are having trouble with one border of a window, try another border or drag the entire window onto the screen by using the title bar.

2. Click the **Excel** button on the taskbar to move its window to the front of the screen.

3. Click the **Restore Down** button if the Excel window is maximized.

4. Move the pointer to the right border of the Excel window. The pointer changes to a horizontal two-pointed arrow.

5. With the two-pointed arrow displayed , drag the border to the left to make the window narrower.

Figure 13
Sizing a window

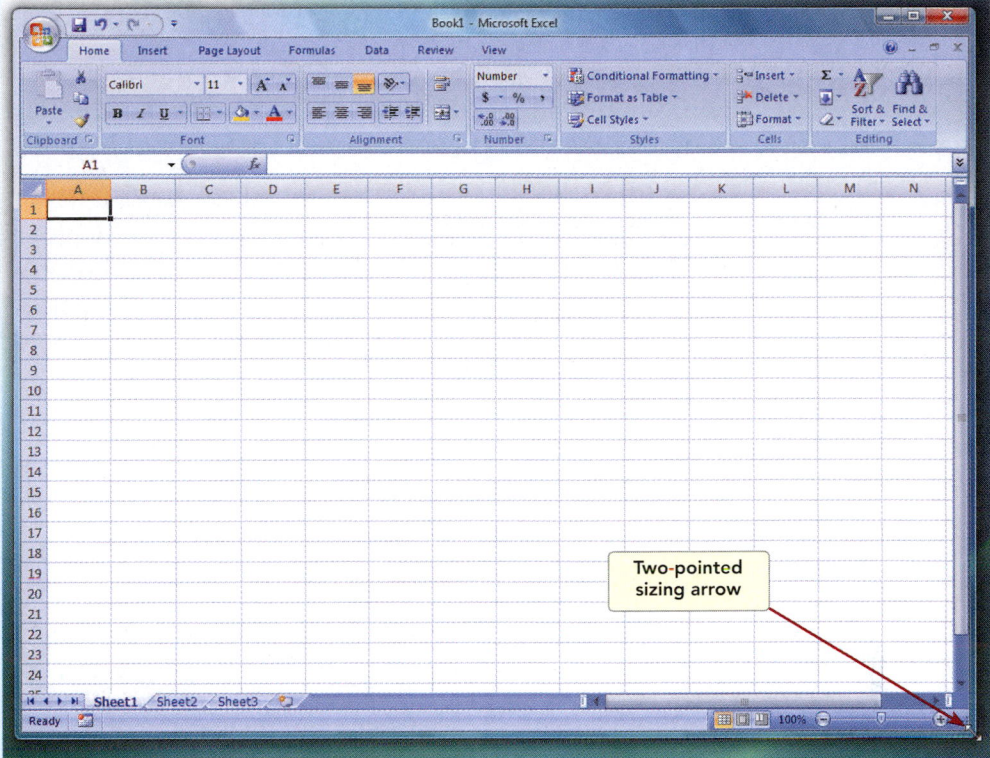

Two-pointed sizing arrow

NOTE

You can place the pointer on any part of the window border to change its size. To change both the height and width of the window, move the pointer to the bottom right corner of the window. The double-pointed arrow changes its orientation to a 45-degree angle (see Figure 13). Dragging this arrow resizes a window vertically and horizontally.

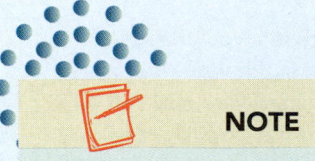

NOTE

The taskbar contains options to Show Windows Stacked, Cascade Windows, and Show the Desktop.

6. Click the title bar or any part of the Word window behind the Excel window. The Word window becomes the active window. The Excel window is still open, but it is now behind the Word window.

7. Click the **Maximize** button if the Word window does not fill the entire desktop.

8. Click the **Minimize** button on the title bar of the Word window. The Excel window becomes the active window.

9. Make the Word window the active window by clicking the **Word** button on the taskbar.

10. Click the **Restore Down** button on the Word window. The Word window reduces in size. The Excel window might be partially visible behind the Word window. You can drag the two reduced windows so that parts of both can be seen simultaneously.

11. Right-click the taskbar, and click **Show Windows Side by Side**. The windows display vertically.

12. Press the Alt key, and hold it down while pressing Tab. You can switch to the previous window by pressing this shortcut, or you can continue to press Tab to switch to an open window on the desktop.

13. Click the **Show Desktop** button located on the Quick Launch toolbar to see the desktop. The Word and Excel programs are minimized.

14. Click the **Show Desktop** button again to restore the programs.

15. Click the **Close** buttons on the title bars of each of the two program windows to close them and to show the desktop.

Using the Documents Command

Windows lets you open a recently used document by using the Recent Items command on the Start menu. This command allows you to open one of up to fifteen documents previously saved on your computer.

1. Click the **Start** button on the taskbar to display the Start menu.
2. Click **Recent Items**. The Recent Items submenu appears, showing you up to the last fifteen documents that were saved.
3. Click a document. The program in which the document was created opens, and the document displays. For example, if the document you chose is a Word document, Word opens and the document appears in a Word program window.
4. Click the program window's **Close** button. The program window closes, and the desktop is clear once again.

Changing the Desktop

The Control Panel lets you change the way Windows looks and works. Because your computer in school is used by other students, you should be very careful when changing settings. Others might expect Windows to look and work the standard way. Having Windows look or work in a nonstandard way could easily confuse other users. (Table 5 describes how to access other settings.)

To change the appearance of your computer, follow these steps. Talk to your instructor first, however, before changing any settings on your computer.

1. Click the **Start** button on the taskbar.
2. Click **Control Panel** on the right pane. The Control Panel window displays.
3. Click the **Appearance and Personalization** link. The Appearance and Personalization window displays.
4. Click **Personalization** and click **Window Color and Appearance**.
5. Click **Default** and click **OK**.
6. Close the Appearance and Personalization window.

TABLE 5 Setting Options

OPTION	USE
Control Panel	Displays the Control Panel window, which lets you change background color, add or remove programs, change the date and time, and change other settings for your hardware and software. The items listed below are accessed from the Control Panel.
Network and Internet	Includes options to view the network status, connect to a network, set up file sharing, change Internet options, and so on.
Hardware and Sound	Includes options to add a printer, change default settings for AutoPlay, sound, mouse settings, keyboard, and so on.
Appearance and Personalization	Includes options to change the desktop background, adjust screen resolution, customize the Start menu and icons on the taskbar, and change sidebar properties.

Using the Search Command

If you do not know where a file or folder is located, you can use the Search command on the Start menu to help you find and open it.

1. Click the **Start** button on the taskbar. Notice the blinking insertion point in the Start Search box. You can start typing the name of a program, folder, or file immediately.

2. Click **Search** in the right pane of the Start menu. The Search Results dialog box appears.

3. Click **Document** in the Show Only section.

Figure 14
Search Results
dialog box

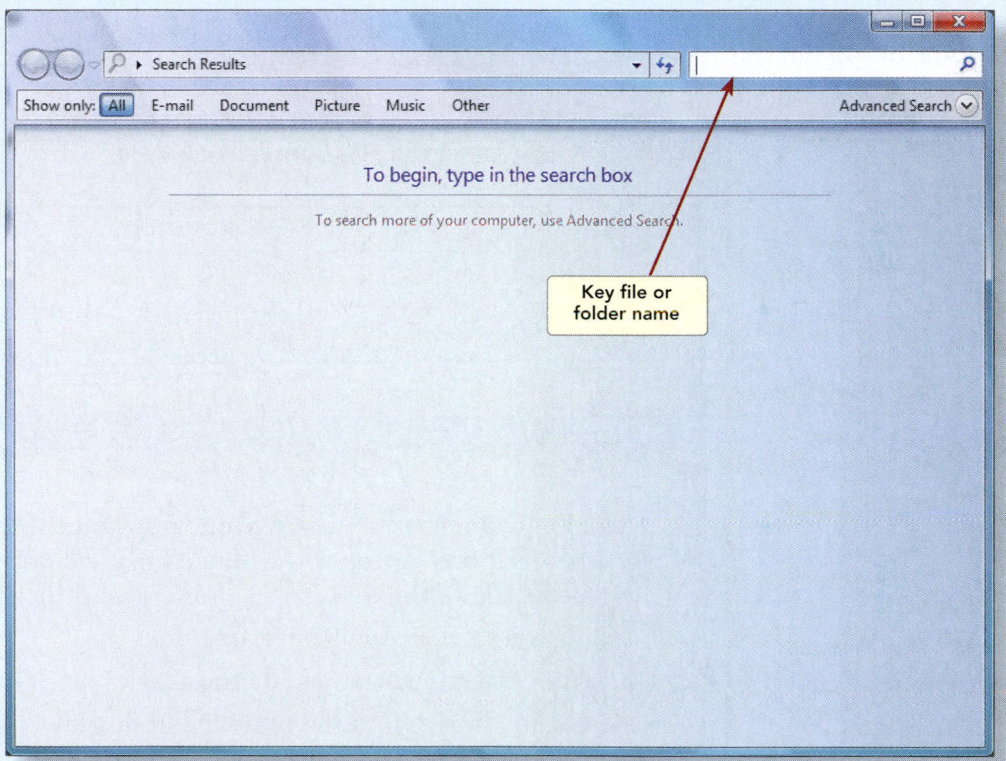

4. Type the name of the file or folder you want to find in the Search box. View the search results.

To search for files by date, size, type, or other attributes, click **Advanced Search**.

1. Click the arrow to the left of the Search Results text box to specify where you want Windows to search. The default location is the C drive.

2. Click **Search** to start the search. Any matches for the file are shown in the right pane of the dialog box.

3. Double-click any found item to open the program and view the file or folder Windows has located.

4. When you are finished with your search, close all open windows and clear your desktop.

Using the Run Command

Windows allows you to start a program by using the Run command and typing the program name. This command is often employed to run a "setup" or "install" program that installs a new program on your computer. It is best to use this command after you have become more familiar with Windows Vista.

1. Click the **Start** button on the taskbar.
2. Click All Programs, and click the Accessories folder.
3. Click **Run**.

Figure 15
Run dialog box

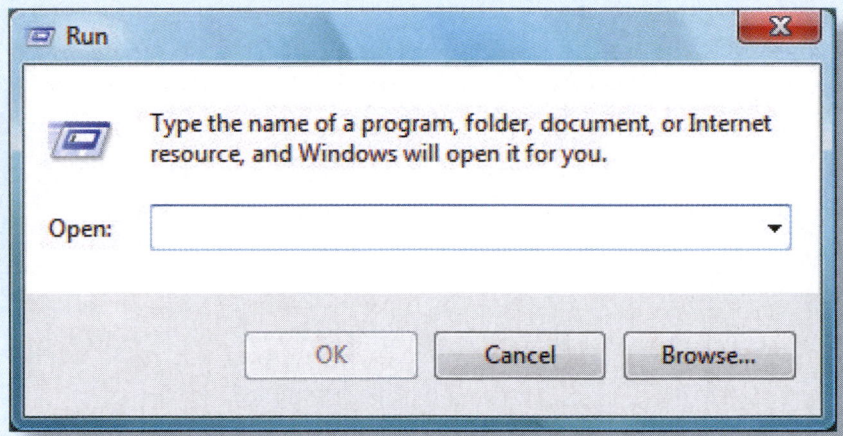

4. If you know the name of a program you want to run, type the name in the Open text box. Often you will need to click **Browse** to open a drop-down list of the disk drives, folders, and files available to you.
5. Click **Cancel** to close the Run dialog box.
6. Open the **Start** menu, and locate the Start Search box.
7. Key **run**, and notice that the Start menu displays the Run program.
8. Click the program name, and the Run dialog box displays.
9. Close the Run dialog box.

Deleting Files Using the Recycle Bin

The *Recycle Bin* is the trash can icon on your desktop. To delete a file:

NOTE

As a protection against deleting a file unintentionally, any file you have placed in the Recycle Bin can be undeleted and used again.

1. Click its icon, and drag it to the Recycle Bin.
2. Double-click the **Recycle Bin** icon. A window opens listing files you have deleted.
3. To undelete a file, merely drag it out of the Recycle Bin window and place it on the desktop or right-click the file and click Restore.
4. To empty the Recycle Bin and permanently delete files, click Empty Recycle Bin in the Recycle Bin dialog box, or right-click the Recycle Bin icon. The shortcut menu appears.
5. Click **Empty Recycle Bin**.

Exiting Windows

You should always exit any open programs and Windows before turning off the computer. This is the best way to be sure your work is saved. Windows also performs other "housekeeping" routines that ensure everything is ready for you when you next turn on your computer. Failure to shut down properly will often force Windows to perform time-consuming system checks the next time it is loaded. You can either log off the computer to make it available for another user, or shut it down entirely.

To Log Off

1. Click the **Start** button on the taskbar.
2. Click the arrow to the right of the Lock this computer button 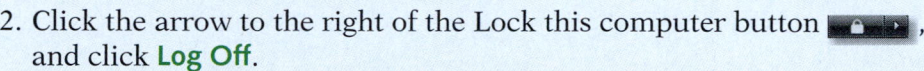, and click **Log Off**.

To Shut Down

To exit Windows, use the Lock this computer command on the Start menu. This command has several shut-down options.

- *Restart:* Restarts the computer without shutting off the power. This is sometimes necessary when you add new software.
- *Shut down:* Closes all open programs and makes it safe to turn off the computer. Some computers will turn off the power automatically.
- *Sleep:* Puts the computer in a low-activity state. It appears to be turned off but will restart when the mouse is moved. Press the computer power button to resume work.

1. Click the **Start** button on the taskbar.
2. Click the arrow beside the Lock this computer button.
3. Click the **Shut Down** option.
4. Windows prompts you to save changes in any open documents. It then prepares the computer to be shut down.

A Professional Approach

WORD 2007

Deborah Hinkle

There is more to learning a word processing program like Microsoft Word than simply pressing keys. You need to know how to use Word in a real-world situation. That is why all the lessons in this book relate to everyday business tasks.

As you work through the lessons, imagine yourself working as an intern for Campbell's Confections, a fictional candy store and chocolate factory located in Grove City, Pennsylvania.

Campbell's Confections

It was 1950. Harry Truman was president. Shopping malls and supermarkets were appearing in suburban areas. And Campbell's Confections began doing business.

Based in Grove City, Pennsylvania, Campbell's Confections started as a small family-owned business. Originally, Campbell's Confections was a candy store, with a few display cases in the front of the building and a kitchen in the back to create chocolates and to try new recipes. The store was an immediate success, and word traveled quickly about the rich, smooth, creamy chocolates made by Campbell's Confections. Today, the store includes several display cases for chocolates and hard candies and special displays for greeting cards and gifts. The factory is located in a separate building on Monroe Street and offers tours for visitors.

Within a few years of opening the first store, the company expanded, and Campbell's Confections opened candy stores in Mercer, New Castle, and

Meadville. Today there are 24 stores in three states—Pennsylvania, Ohio, and West Virginia.

The goal of Campbell's Confections is to offer "quality chocolate," and the company has grown from selling chocolate in retail stores exclusively to adding wholesale and fund-raising divisions. E-commerce has been the latest venture with Internet sales increasing monthly.

Currently, Thomas Campbell is the president-owner, and Lynn Tanguay is the vice president.

To understand the organization of Campbell's Confections, take a look at Figure CS-1. Notice each of the specialty areas and management divisions.

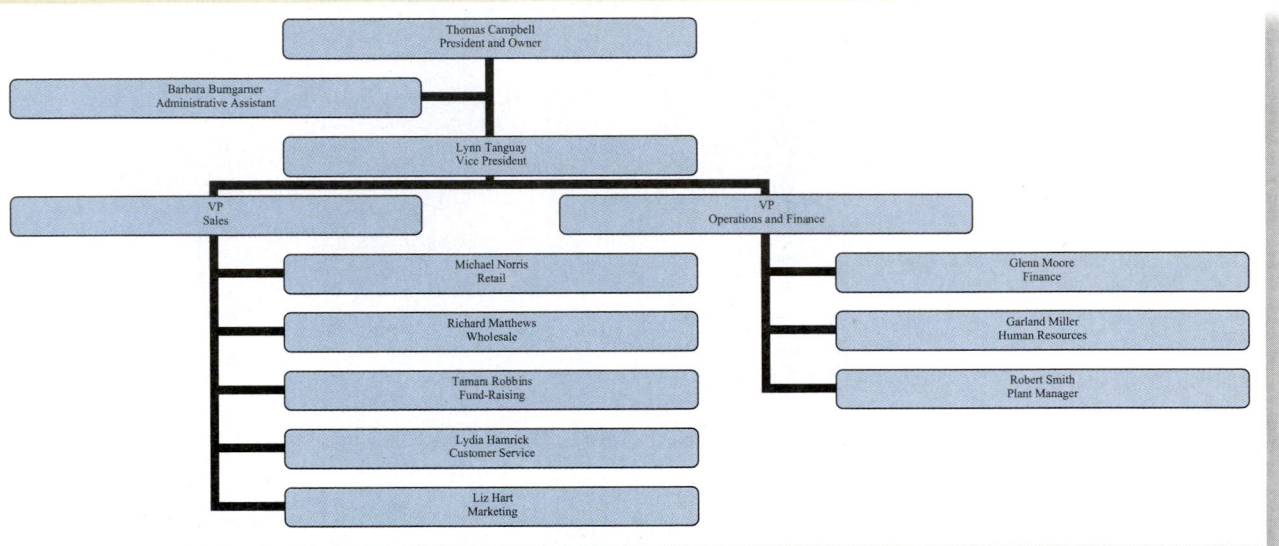

All the documents you will use in this text relate to Campbell's Confections. As you work through the documents in the text, take the time to notice the following:

- How the employees interact and how they respond to customers' queries.
- The format and tone of the business correspondence (if you are unfamiliar with the standard formats for business documents, refer to Appendix B).
- References to The Gregg Reference Manual, a standard reference manual for business writing and correspondence.
- The content of the correspondence (and its relation to Campbell's Confections).

As you use this text and become experienced with Microsoft Word, you will also gain experience in creating, editing, and formatting the type of documents that are generated in a real-life business environment.

unit 1

BASIC SKILLS

Lesson 1   Creating a Document   WD-6

Lesson 2   Selecting and Editing   WD-34

Lesson 3   Formatting Characters   WD-66

Lesson 4   Writing Tools   WD-96

UNIT 1   APPLICATIONS   WD-127

Creating a Document

OBJECTIVES

After completing this lesson, you will be able to:

1. Start Word.

2. Identify parts of the Word Screen.

3. Key text into a document.

4. Edit text.

5. Name and save a document.

6. Print a document.

7. Close a document and exit Word.

MCAS OBJECTIVES

In this lesson:
WW 07 6.1.1

Estimated Time: 1 hour

Microsoft Word is a versatile, easy-to-use word processing program that helps you create letters, memos, reports, and other types of documents. This lesson begins with an overview of the Word screen. Then you learn how to create, edit, name, save, print, and close a document.

Starting Word

There are several ways to start Word, depending on your system setup and personal preferences. For example, you can use the Start button on the Windows taskbar or double-click a Word shortcut icon that might be on your desktop.

NOTE

Windows provides many ways to start applications. If you have problems, ask your instructor for help.

Figure 1-1
Starting Word from
the Windows taskbar

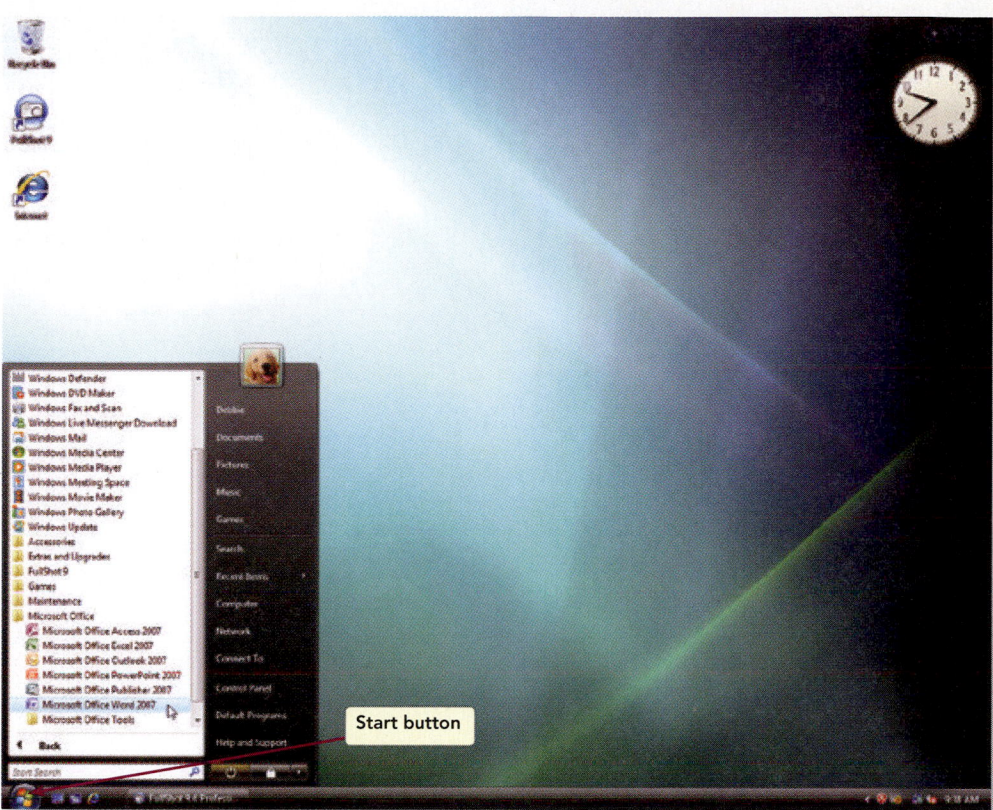

NOTE

Your screen will differ from the screen shown in Figure 1-1 depending on the programs installed on your computer.

Exercise 1-1   START WORD

1. Turn on your computer. Windows loads.

2. Click the Start button 🔵 on the Windows taskbar and point to **All Programs**.

3. On the All Programs menu, click **Microsoft Office**, and then click **Microsoft Office Word 2007**. In a few seconds, the program is loaded and the Word screen appears.

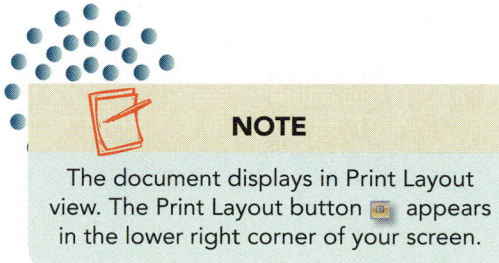

NOTE

The document displays in Print Layout view. The Print Layout button 🔳 appears in the lower right corner of your screen.

Figure 1-2
Word screen

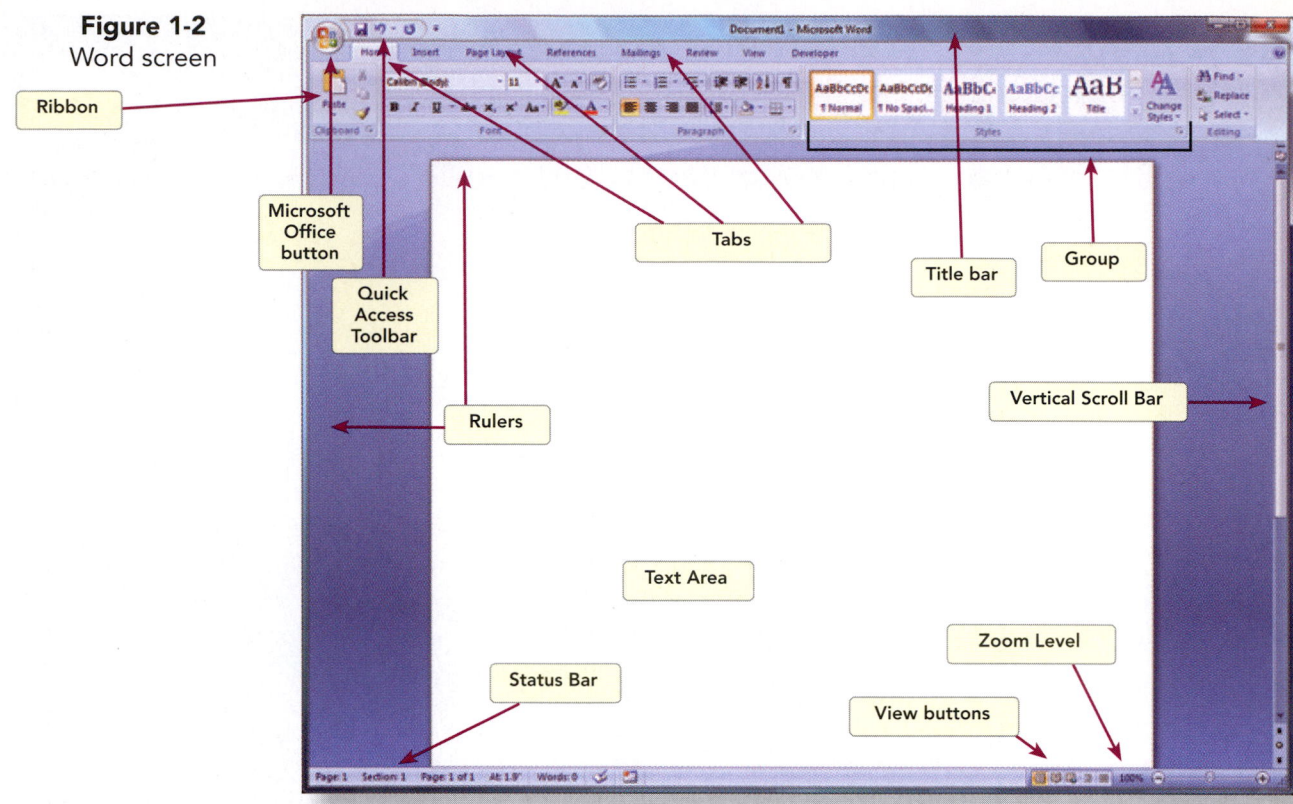

TABLE 1-1 Parts of the Word Screen

Part of Screen	Purpose
Microsoft Office Button	Displays the File menu, recently opened documents, and a command button to access Word Options.
Quick Access Toolbar	Displays icons for save, undo, and repeat. The Quick Access Toolbar can be customized, and the Quick Access Toolbar commands are available for all tabs on the Ribbon.
Title bar	Displays the name of the current document. The opening Word screen is always named "Document1."
Ribbon	Displays contextual tabs. Tabs contain groups of related commands. Commands can be buttons, menus, or drop-down list boxes.
Ruler	Shows placement of margins, indents, and tabs. The horizontal and vertical rulers display in Print Layout view.
Text area	Displays the text and graphics in the document.
Scroll bars	Used with the mouse to move right or left and up or down within a document.
Status bar	Displays the page number and page count of the document, the document view buttons, and the zoom control. It also displays the current mode of operation. The Status bar can be customized.

Identifying Parts of the Word Screen

To become familiar with Word, start by identifying the parts of the screen you will work with extensively, such as the Microsoft Office Button, the Quick Access Toolbar, and the Ribbon. As you practice using Word commands, you will see *ScreenTips* to help you identify screen elements such as buttons and commands.

Exercise 1-2 IDENTIFY THE MICROSOFT OFFICE BUTTON AND THE QUICK ACCESS TOOLBAR

The *Microsoft Office Button* displays the File menu which lists the commands to create, open, save, and print a document. Recently opened documents also appear when the File menu displays. The *Quick Access Toolbar* contains frequently used commands and is positioned to the right of the Microsoft Office Button and above the Ribbon by default. The commands on the Quick Access Toolbar are available for all tabs in the Ribbon.

1. Move the mouse pointer to the Microsoft Office Button . Notice a ScreenTip displays when you point to the button. Click the left mouse button to open the File menu. Word displays the File menu and a list of documents recently opened. The Word default setting is to show up to 17 documents in Recent Documents.

> **NOTE**
>
> You can also close the File menu by pressing [Esc] or click the Microsoft Office Button.

2. Click the text area to close the File menu.

3. Move the mouse pointer to the right of the Microsoft Office Button and point to the **Save** button . A ScreenTip and a keyboard shortcut to save a document display.

4. Point to the commands to the right of the Save command. Notice each command includes descriptive text and a keyboard shortcut. The Save, Undo, and Repeat commands are located in the Quick Access Toolbar by default. The Quick Access Toolbar contains commands you will use frequently and displays for each tab on the Ribbon.

>
>
> **TIP**
>
> Commands may appear in more than one location. For example, you can save a document by choosing **Save** from the File menu, by clicking the **Save** command on the Quick Access Toolbar, or by pressing [Ctrl]+[S].

Word 2007

Figure 1-3
Displaying Microsoft
Office button
commands

Exercise 1-3   IDENTIFY RIBBON COMMANDS

When you start Word, the Ribbon appears with the Home tab selected. The Ribbon consists of seven tabs by default. Each tab contains a group of related commands, and the number of commands for each tab varies. A command can be one of several formats. The most popular formats include buttons and drop-down lists. You can access Ribbon commands by using the mouse or Access Keys. Access Keys display badges or Key Tips. *Key Tips* are lettered or numbered squares that access or execute commands.

Figure 1-4
Ribbon

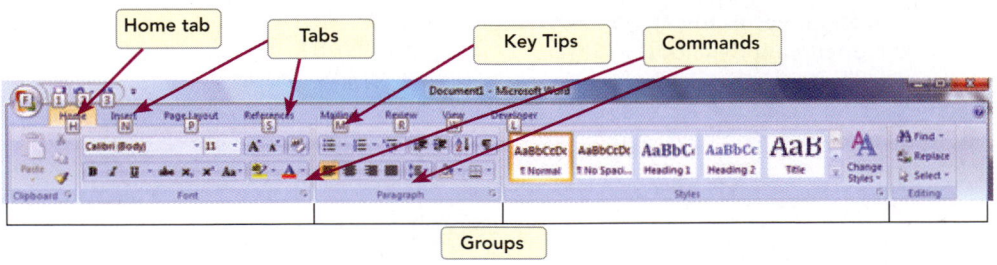

1. Move the mouse pointer to the **Insert** tab on the Ribbon and click **Insert**. Notice the change in the number and types of groups displayed. When you point to a Ribbon tab, the name of the tab is highlighted but not active. Click the Ribbon tab to display the commands.

2. Click the **Page Layout** tab. There are five groups of commands on the Page Layout tab.

Figure 1-5
Displaying the Page Layout tab

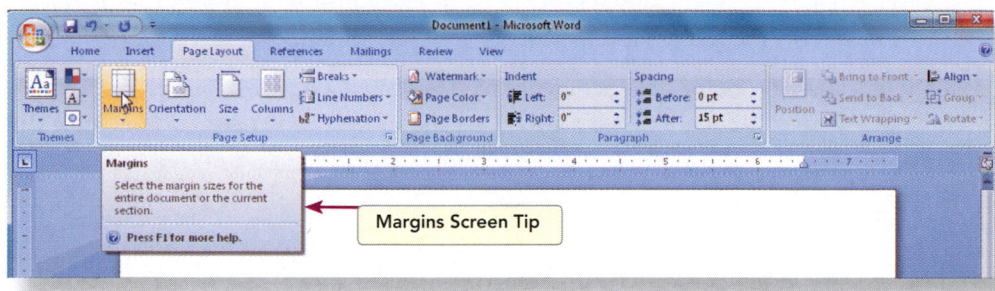

3. Click the **Page Layout** tab if necessary, and point to the **Margins** command. Read the ScreenTip.

4. Click the **Home** tab. Notice the groups and buttons available for formatting and editing.

5. Double-click the **Home** tab. The Ribbon is minimized.

6. Click the **Home** tab to restore the Ribbon.

7. Press the Alt key. Small lettered or numbered squares, called badges, appear on the Microsoft Office Button, Quick Access Toolbar, and Ribbon. The letters and numbers represent Key Tips and are used to execute a command.

8. Press the letter P on the keyboard to select the **Page Layout** tab.

9. Press the letter M on the keyboard to display the **Margins** gallery. Press Esc to close the gallery.

NOTE

Any Ribbon command with a light gray icon is currently not available. However, you can still identify the button by pointing to it with the mouse.

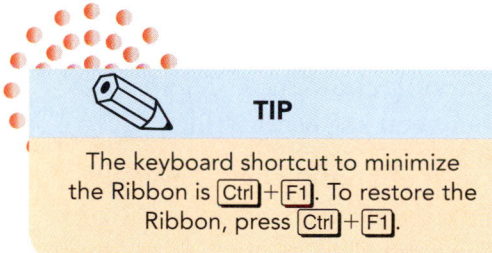

TIP

The keyboard shortcut to minimize the Ribbon is Ctrl + F1. To restore the Ribbon, press Ctrl + F1.

NOTE

The Quick Access Toolbar Key Tips are executed immediately.

TABLE 1-2 Ribbon Access Keys

Keystroke	Purpose
Alt	Select the active tab of the Ribbon and display badges for Key Tips. Press Alt a second time to cancel the access keys.
Alt, ← or →	Select the active tab of the Ribbon and move to the next or previous tab.
Alt, ↓ or ↑	Select the active tab of the Ribbon and move to the next or previous item on the Ribbon.
Alt, Tab	Select the active tab of the Ribbon and move to the first command of the first group. Each time you press Tab you move to the next command of the group. When you reach the last command of the group, press Tab to move to the next group of commands.
Alt, Shift + Tab	Rotate through Ribbon commands in the reverse direction.
Alt, Alt	Display Key Tips if they disappear.

Exercise 1-4   IDENTIFY COMMANDS

Use the Ribbon to locate and execute commands to format and edit your document. Commands also control the appearance of the Word screen.

1. Activate the **Home** tab.

2. Locate the Paragraph group and click the Show/Hide ¶ button ¶. This button is used to show or hide formatting marks on the screen. You can see special formatting for spaces, paragraph marks, and tab characters. The command toggles between show and hide.

> **NOTE**
>
> Drag the slider to the right to zoom in, and drag the slider to the left to zoom out. You can also use Ctrl + the wheel on your mouse to zoom in and zoom out. The View tab on the Ribbon contains Zoom commands.

3. Locate the vertical scroll bar and click the View Ruler button ⬜. Notice the rulers disappear from the Word screen. Click the View Ruler button again to display the rulers.

4. Locate the Zoom button on the status bar.

5. Click the Zoom button and click **200%**. Click **OK**. The text area is magnified, and you see a portion of the page.

6. Point to and drag the Zoom slider ⊖—▯——⊕ to 100%. The document returns to normal display.

Keying Text

When keying text, you will notice various shapes and symbols in the text area. For example:

- The *insertion point* is the vertical blinking line that marks the position of the next character to be entered.

- The mouse pointer takes the shape of an *I-beam* I when it is in the text area. It changes into an arrow $\searrow$ when you point to a command on the Quick Access Toolbar or the Ribbon.

¶

- The *paragraph mark* ¶ indicates the end of a paragraph. The paragraph mark displays when Show/Hide ¶ ¶ is selected.

Exercise 1-5   KEY TEXT AND MOVE THE INSERTION POINT

1. Before you begin, make sure the Show/Hide ¶ button ¶ on the Home tab Paragraph group is selected. When this feature is "turned on," you can see paragraph marks and spacing between words and sentences more easily.

2. Key the words **Campbell's Confections** (don't worry about keying mistakes now—you can correct them later). Notice how the insertion point and paragraph mark move as you key text. Notice also how a space between words is indicated by a dot.

Figure 1-6
The insertion point marks the place where you begin keying.

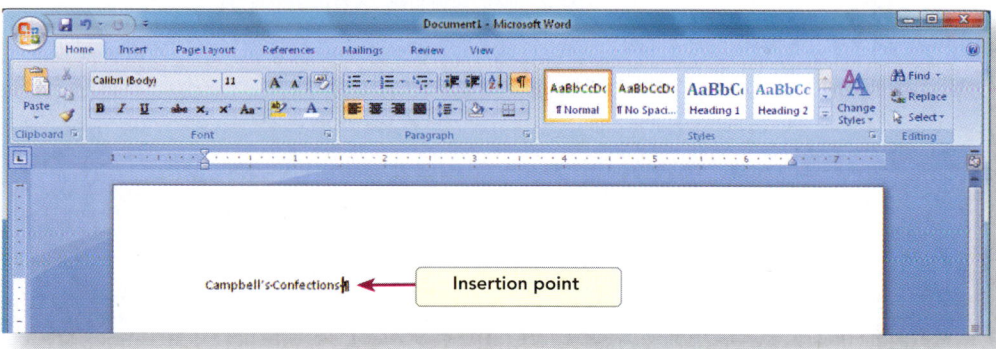

3. Move the insertion point to the left of the word "Campbell's" by positioning the I-beam and clicking the left mouse button.

4. Move the insertion point back to the right of "Confections" to continue keying.

Exercise 1-6   WRAP TEXT AND CORRECT SPELLING

As you key more text, you will notice Word performs several tasks automatically. For example, Word does the following by default:

- Wraps text from the end of one line to the beginning of the next line.

- Alerts you to spelling and grammatical errors.

- Corrects common misspellings, such as "teh" for "the" and "adn" for "and."

- Suggests the completed word when you key the current date, day, or month.

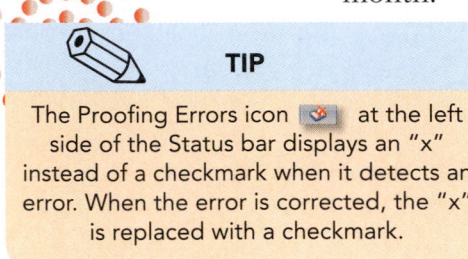

TIP

The Proofing Errors icon 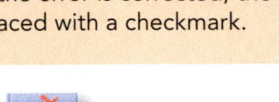 at the left side of the Status bar displays an "x" instead of a checkmark when it detects an error. When the error is corrected, the "x" is replaced with a checkmark.

1. Continue the sentence you started in Exercise 1-5, this time keying a misspelled word. Press [Spacebar], and then key **is western Pennsylvania's leeding candy maker** (don't key a period). Word recognizes that "leeding" is misspelled and applies a red, wavy underline to the word.

2. To correct the misspelling, use the mouse to position the I-beam anywhere in the underlined word and click the *right* mouse button. A shortcut menu appears with suggested spellings. Click "leading" with the *left* mouse button, and Word makes the correction. Notice the change in the Proofing Errors icon on the status bar.

Figure 1-7
Choose the correct spelling from the shortcut menu.

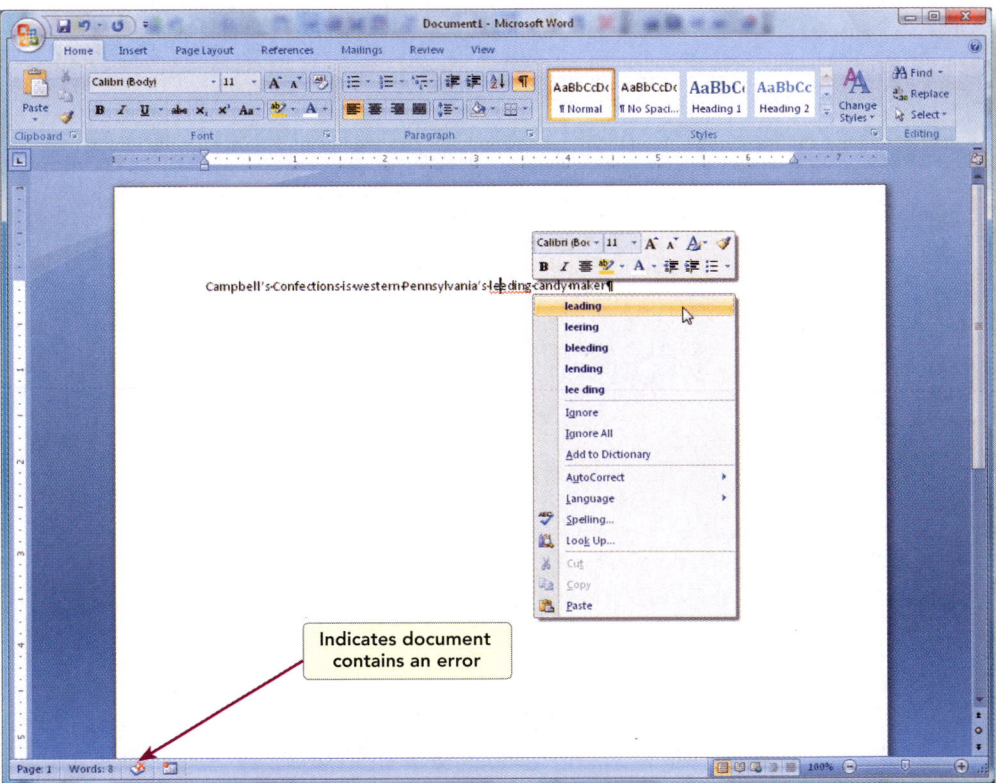

3. Move the insertion point to the right of "maker," and press [Spacebar]. Continue the sentence with another misspelled word by keying **adn**, and press [Spacebar]. Notice that "adn" is automatically corrected to "and" when you press [Spacebar].

4. Complete the sentence by keying **is located in Grove City on Main Street.**

5. Verify that the insertion point is to the immediate right of the period following Street, and then press the [Spacebar] once. Key the following text:

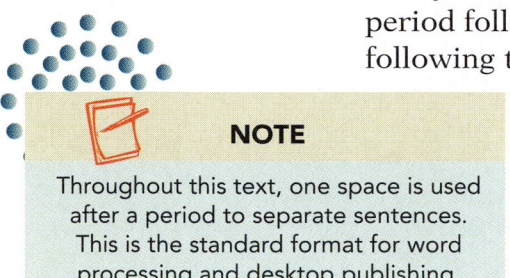

NOTE

Throughout this text, one space is used after a period to separate sentences. This is the standard format for word processing and desktop publishing.

It is a family-owned business with several stores located in western Pennsylvania, eastern Ohio, and northern West Virginia.

Notice how the text automatically wraps from the end of the line to the beginning of the next line.

6. Press [Enter] once to start a new paragraph.

NOTE

When Word suggests a completed word as you key text, you can ignore the suggested word and continue keying or insert it by pressing [Enter].

7. Key the second paragraph shown in Figure 1-8. When you key the first four letters of "Monday" in the first sentence, Word suggests the completed word in a small box. Press [Enter] to insert the suggested word, and then press [Spacebar] before you key the next word. Follow the same procedure for "Saturday."

Figure 1-8

For more information about Campbell's Confections, visit one of our stores Monday through Saturday, or visit our Web site anytime. Our sales associates will be happy to help you.

Basic Text Editing

The keyboard offers many options for basic text editing. For example, you can press [Backspace] to delete a single character or [Ctrl]+[Delete] to delete an entire word.

TABLE 1-3 Basic Text Editing

Key	Result
[Backspace]	Deletes the character to the left of the insertion point.
[Ctrl]+[Backspace]	Deletes the word to the left of the insertion point.
[Delete]	Deletes the character to the right of the insertion point.
[Ctrl]+[Delete]	Deletes the word to the right of the insertion point.

Exercise 1-7   DELETE TEXT

1. Move the insertion point to the right of the word "It" in the second sentence of the first paragraph. (Use the mouse to position the I-beam, and click the left mouse button.)

2. Press [Backspace] twice to delete both characters and key **Campbell's Confections**.

3. Move the insertion point to the left of "one" in the second paragraph.

4. Press [Delete] three times and key **any**.

> **NOTE**
>
> When keyboard combinations (such as [Ctrl]+[Backspace]) are shown in this text, hold down the first key as you press the second key. Release the second key, and then release the first key. An example of the entire sequence is this: Hold down [Ctrl], press [Backspace], release [Backspace], and release [Ctrl]. With practice, this sequence becomes easy.

5. Move the insertion point to the left of the word "information" in the second paragraph.

6. Hold down [Ctrl] and press [Backspace]. The word "more" is deleted.

7. Move the insertion point to the right of "Grove City" in the first sentence of the first paragraph.

8. Hold down [Ctrl] and press [Delete] to delete the word "on." Press [Ctrl]+[Delete] two more times to delete the words "Main Street."

Exercise 1-8   INSERT TEXT

When editing a document, you can insert text or key over existing text. When you insert text, Word is in regular *Insert mode*, and you simply click to position the insertion point and key the text to be inserted. To key over existing text, you switch to *Overtype mode*. The Overtype feature is turned off by default.

1. In the first sentence of the first paragraph, move the insertion point to the left of the "G" in "Grove City." Key **downtown**, and press [Spacebar] once to leave a space between the two words.

2. Move the insertion point to the beginning of the document, to the left of "Campbell's."

3. Click the **Microsoft Office Button**, and click the Word Options button 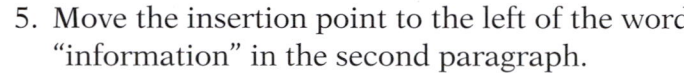 .

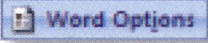

4. Click **Advanced**. Locate **Editing options**, and click to select **Use overtype mode**. Click **OK**.

5. Press [Caps Lock]. When you key text in Caps Lock mode, the keyed text appears in all uppercase letters.

TIP

Always remember to turn off Overtype mode as soon as you are done editing to avoid accidentally keying over text.

6. Key **campbell's confections** over the old text. Repeat the process for "Campbell's Confections" in the second sentence.

7. Press Caps Lock to turn off Caps Lock mode. Click the **Microsoft Office Button**, and click the Word Options button Word Options . Click **Advanced**, locate **Editing options**, and click to deselect **Use overtype mode**. Click **OK**.

Figure 1-9
Edited document

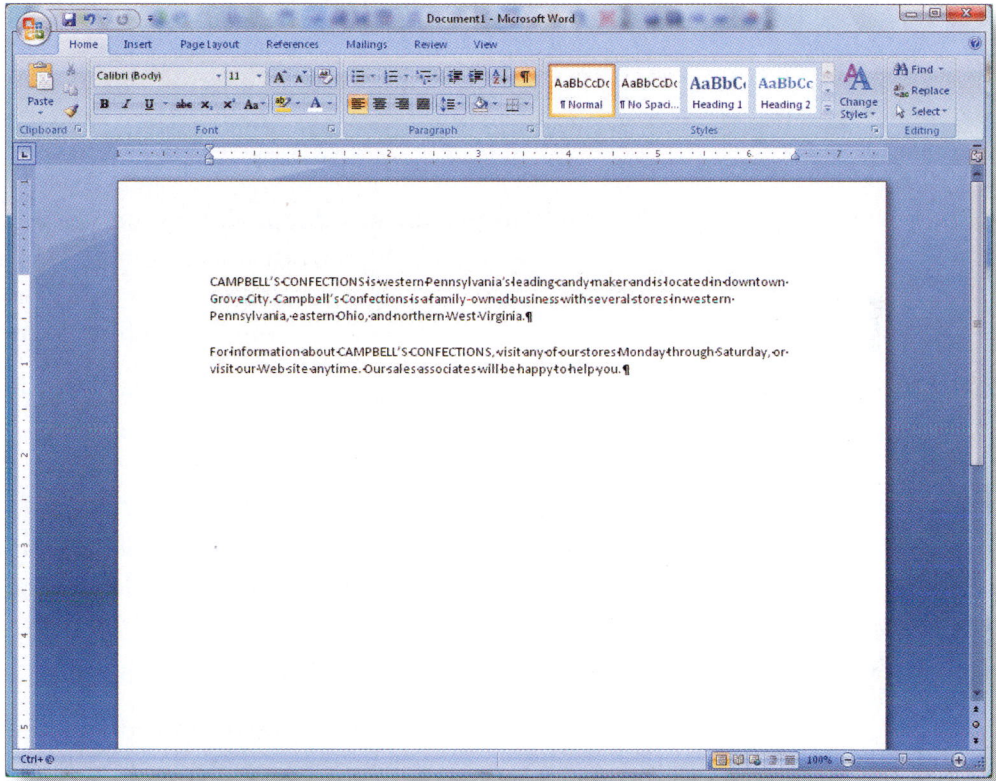

Exercise 1-9   COMBINE AND SPLIT PARAGRAPHS

1. At the end of the first paragraph, position the insertion point to the left of the paragraph mark (after the period following "West Virginia").

2. Press Delete. The two paragraphs are now combined, or merged, into one.

3. Press Spacebar once to insert a space between the sentences.

4. With the insertion point to the left of "For" in the combined paragraph, press Enter to split the paragraph.

Naming and Saving a Document

Your document, called "Document1," is stored in your computer's temporary memory. Until you name and save the document, the data can be lost if you have a power failure or a computer hardware problem. It is always good practice to save your work frequently.

The first step in saving a document for future use is to assign a *file name.* Study the following rules about naming documents:

- File names can be up to 255 characters long, including the drive letter and the folder name. The following characters cannot be used in a file name: **/ \ > < * ? ": |**

- File names can include uppercase letters, lowercase letters, or a combination of both. They can also include spaces. For example, a file can be named "Business Plan."

- Throughout this course, document file names will consist of *[your initials]* (which might be your initials or the identifier your instructor asks you to use, such as **rst**), followed by the number of the exercise, such as **4-1**. The file name would, therefore, be **rst4-1**.

You can use either the Save command or the Save As command to save a document. Here are some guidelines about saving documents:

- Use Save As when you name and save a document the first time.

- Use Save As when you save an existing document under a new name. Save As creates an entirely new file and leaves the original document unchanged.

- Use Save to update an existing document.

NOTE

Your instructor will advise you on the proper drive and folder to use for this course.

- Before you save a new document, decide where you want to save it. Word saves documents in the current drive and folder unless you specify otherwise. For example, to save a document to a floppy disk or a jump drive, you need to change the drive to A: or E:, whichever is appropriate for your computer.

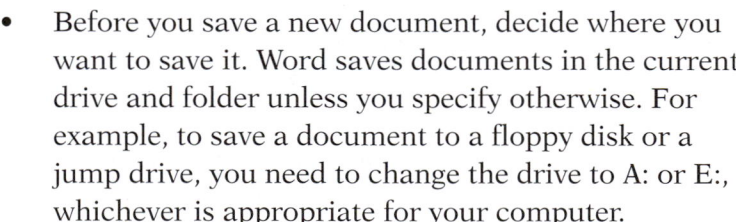

Exercise 1-10　NAME AND SAVE A DOCUMENT

1. Click the **Microsoft Office Button** to open the **File** menu and click **Save As**. The Save As dialog box appears.

2. In the File name text box, a suggested filename is highlighted. Replace this file name by keying *[your initials]***1-10**.

Word 2007

NOTE

The default document type is Word Document (.docx). You can specify other file types such as RTF (Rich Text Format, which is a format used to exchange text documents between applications and operating systems) and TXT (Plain Text, which contains no formatting). To change the file type, simply click the down arrow beside the Save as type text box.

3. Drag the scroll box in the navigation pane, and choose the appropriate drive for your data disk—Removable Disk (F:), for example. Make sure you have a formatted disk in the drive.

4. Click [Save]. Your document is named and saved for future use.

Figure 1-10
Save As dialog box

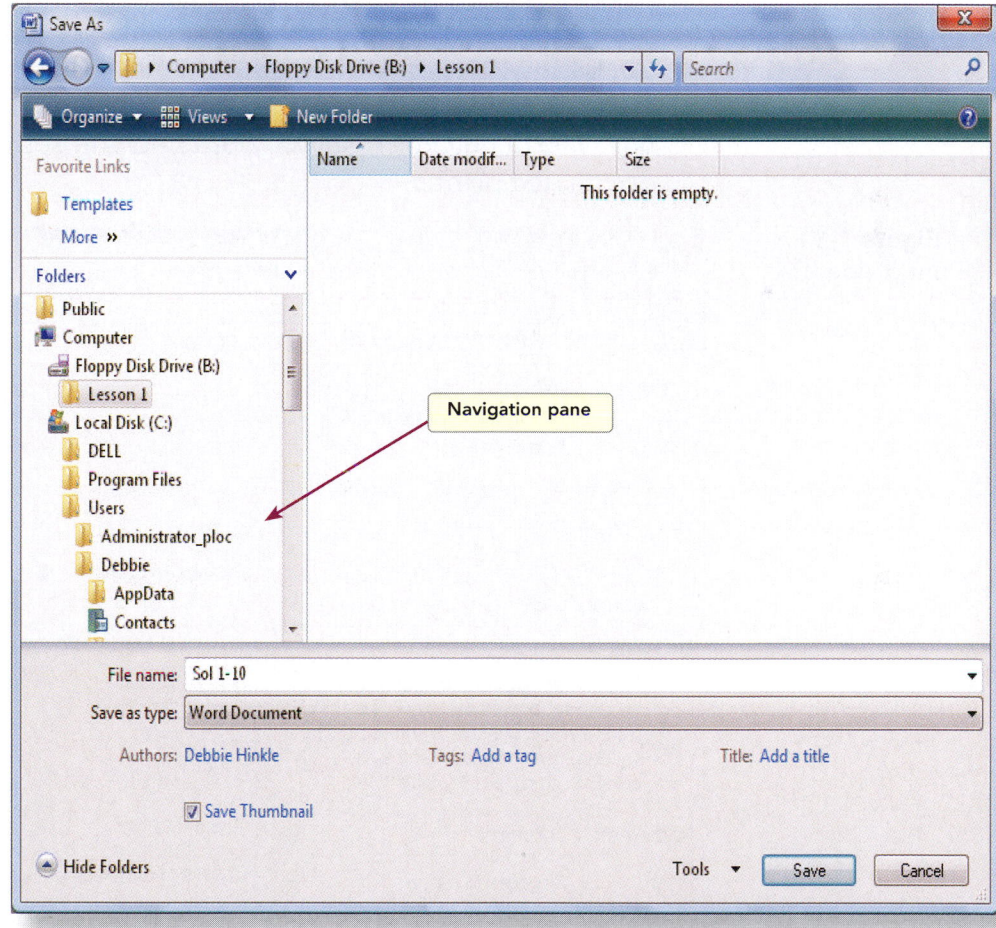

Printing a Document

After you create a document, printing it is easy. You can use any of the following methods:

- Choose Print from the File menu.

- Press Ctrl + P.

The Print option and the keyboard shortcut open the Print dialog box, where you can select printing options. Clicking Quick Print sends the document directly to the printer, using Word's default settings.

Exercise 1-11   PRINT A DOCUMENT

1. Click the Microsoft Office Button 🔘 to open the File menu. Click **Print**, then click **Print** from the submenu to open the Print dialog box. The dialog box displays Word's default settings and shows your designated printer.

Figure 1-11
Print dialog box

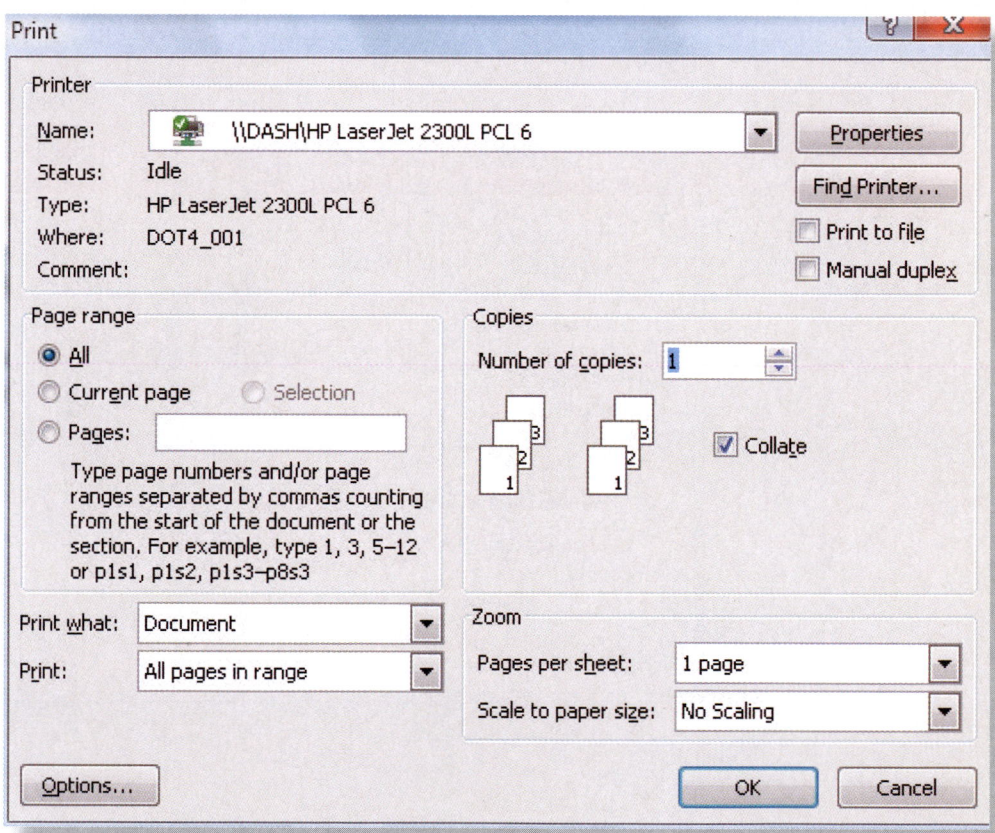

2. Click **OK** or press Enter to accept the settings.

Closing a Document and Exiting Word

When you finish working on a document and save it, you can close it and open another document or you can exit Word.

The easiest ways to close a document and exit Word include using the following:

- The Close button  in the upper right corner of the window.

- The Close command from the File menu.

- Keyboard shortcuts: Ctrl+W closes a document and Alt+F4 exits Word.

> **NOTE**
>
> When no document is open, the document window is blue. If you want to create a new document, choose New from the File menu, and click Blank Document. Click the Create button [Create]. The keyboard shortcut to create a new document is Ctrl+N.

Exercise 1-12   CLOSE A DOCUMENT AND EXIT WORD

1. Click the **Microsoft Office Button**, and choose **Close** from the File menu to close the document.

2. Click the Close button in the upper right corner of the screen to exit Word and display the Windows desktop.

Using Online Help

Online Help is available to you as you work in Word. Click the Help button or press F1 to open the Word Help window. You can click a Word Help link or key a word or phrase in the Search box.

FIND OUT MORE ABOUT USING HELP:

1. Start Word.

2. Locate the Help button in the upper right corner of the screen. Click the button to open the Word Help window.

Figure 1-12
Using the Word Help
window

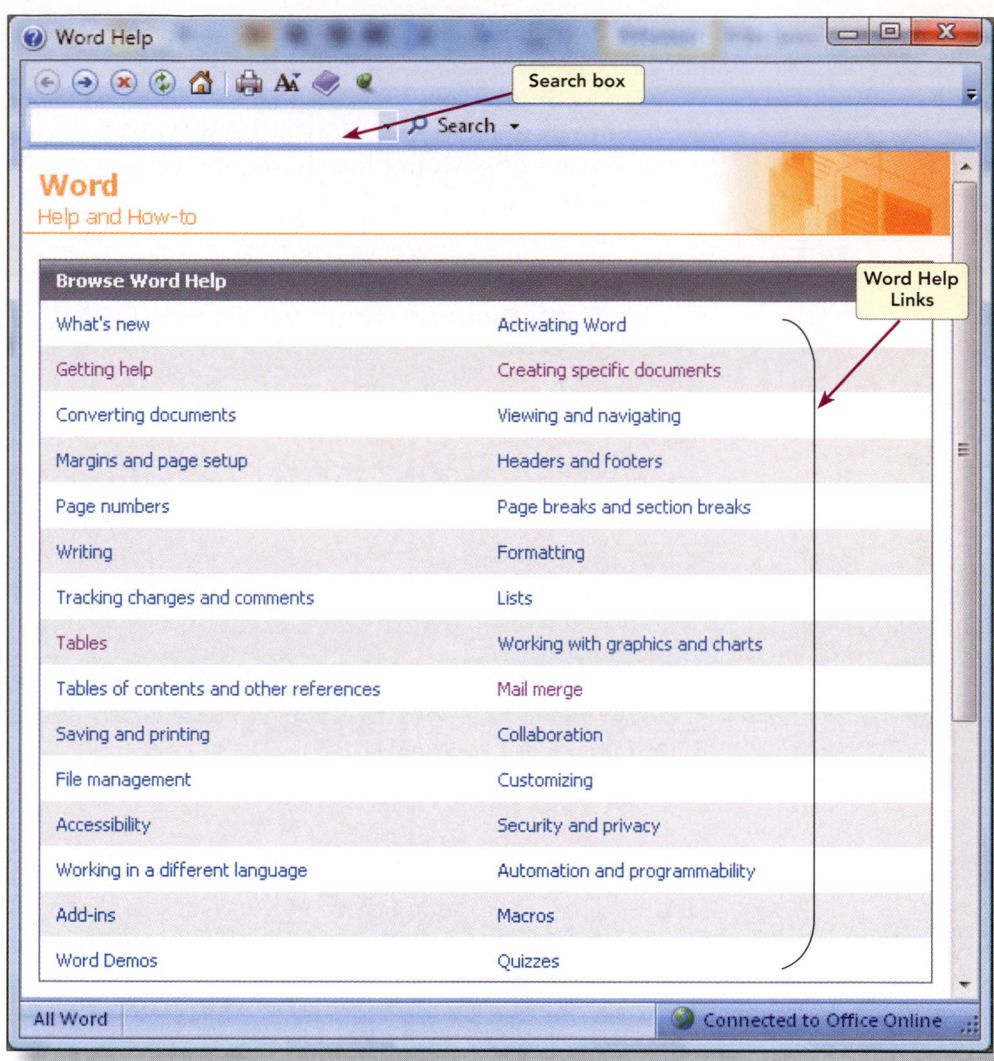

3. Locate and click the link **Getting help**.

4. Review the list of topics.

5. Click a topic and review the information.

6. Click the Back button ⊙ to return to the list of categories.

7. Close Help by clicking the Word Help window's Close button ▬ .

Lesson 1 Summary

- To start Microsoft Word, click the Start button on the Windows taskbar, point to All Programs, click Microsoft Office, and click Microsoft Office Word 2007.
- The Microsoft Office Button is located in the upper left corner of the Word screen. Click the button to open the File menu.
- The title bar is at the top of the Word screen and displays the current document name.
- The Quick Access Toolbar displays icons for Save, Undo, and Repeat.
- The Ribbon contains tabs which include groups of related commands. Commands can be buttons, menus, or drop-down list boxes.
- Click a tab name to display related groups of commands. The number of groups and commands varies for each tab.
- Identify a command by name by pointing to it with the mouse. Word displays a ScreenTip with the button name.
- The horizontal ruler appears below the Ribbon.
- Scroll bars appear as blue shaded bars to the right and bottom of the text area. They are used to view different portions of a document.
- The status bar is a blue shaded bar below the horizontal scroll bar. It displays the page number and page count of the document, the document view buttons, and the zoom control. It also displays the current mode of operation. Right-click the status bar to customize it.
- The blinking vertical line is called the insertion point. It marks the position of the next character to be keyed.
- The mouse pointer displays on the screen as an I-beam I when it is in the text area and as an arrow when you point to a command outside the text area.
- When the Show/Hide ¶ button is turned on, a paragraph mark symbol appears at the end of every paragraph. A dot between words represents a space.
- Word automatically wraps text to the next line as you key text. Press Enter to start a new paragraph or to insert a blank line.
- Word flags spelling errors as you key text by inserting a red, wavy line under the misspelled word. To correct the spelling, point to the underlined word, click the right mouse button, and choose the correct spelling.
- Word automatically corrects commonly misspelled words for you as you key text. Word can automatically complete a word for you, such as the name of a month or day. Word suggests the completed word, and you press Enter to insert it.
- Delete a single character by using Backspace or Delete. Ctrl+Backspace deletes the word to the left of the insertion point. Ctrl+Delete deletes the word to the right of the insertion point.

- To insert text, click to position the insertion point and key the text.
- To enter text over existing text, turn on Overtype mode by clicking the Microsoft Office Button. Click **Word Options**, and click **Advanced**. Click to select **Use overtype mode**. Click **OK**.
- Insert one space between words and between sentences.
- Document names, or file names, can contain 255 characters, including the drive letter and folder name, and can contain spaces. The following characters cannot be used in a file name: **/ \ > <* ? " : |**
- Save a new document by using the Save As command and giving the document a file name. Use the Save command to update an existing document.
- To start a new blank document, click the Microsoft Office Button. Click **New**, click **Blank document**, and click **Create**.
- To use Word Help, click the Microsoft Office Word Help button 🔵 or press F1.

LESSON 1		Command Summary	
Feature	**Button**	**Command**	**Keyboard**
Save As		**File** menu, **Save As**	F12
Print		**File** menu, **Print**	Ctrl + P
Close a document		**File** menu, **Close**	Ctrl + W or Ctrl + F14
Exit Word	X	**File** menu, **Exit Word**	Alt + F4

NOTE

Word provides many ways to accomplish a particular task. As you become more familiar with Word, you will find the methods you prefer.

Concepts Review

True/False Questions

Each of the following statements is either true or false. Indicate your choice by circling T or F.

T F   1. You can use the Ribbon to start or exit Word.

T F   2. Overtype mode appears on the Status bar by default.

T F   3. You can view more than one Ribbon tab at a time.

T F   4. The mouse pointer takes the shape of an arrow when it appears in the Ribbon.

T F   5. A red, wavy line appears under words that are misspelled in a document.

T F   6. Pressing [Delete] deletes characters to the left of the insertion point.

T F   7. [Ctrl]+[Delete] deletes the word to the right of the insertion point.

T F   8. You can save a document by choosing Save from the File menu.

Short Answer Questions

Write the correct answer in the space provided.

1. Which menu and menu option open the Print dialog box?

   _____

2. Which tab contains the Show/Hide ¶ button ¶ ?

   _____

3. If you begin keying a word such as "January" or "Thursday," how can you have Word complete the word for you automatically?

   _____

4. Which area of the Word screen shows the number of pages in the document and displays indicators that show the current mode of operation?

   _____

5. Which toolbar contains the Save button?

   _____

6. What shape is the mouse pointer when it appears in the text area of the screen?

_____

7. Which command is used to save a document under a different file name?

_____

8. What is the keyboard shortcut for Help?

_____

Critical Thinking

Answer these questions on a separate page. There are no right or wrong answers. Support your answers with examples from your own experience, if possible.

1. You can use the Show/Hide ¶ button to hide paragraph marks and space characters. When might it be useful to show these characters? When would you want to hide them?

2. Word allows great flexibility when naming files. Many businesses and individuals establish their own rules for naming files. What kinds of rules would you recommend for naming files in a business? For personal use?

Skills Review

Exercise 1-13

Identify parts of the Word screen.

1. Start Word, if necessary, by following these steps:
   a. Click the Start button 🌐 on the Windows taskbar.
   b. Point to **All Programs**, point to **Microsoft Office**, point to **Microsoft Office Word 2007**, and click.

2. Move the pointer to the Save button on the Quick Access Toolbar to identify it.

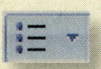

3. Click the **Page Layout** tab. Click the **Home** tab. Point to the Bullets button to identify it.

4. Point to, and then click the Microsoft Office Button 🌐. The File menu opens.

5. With the File menu still open, move the pointer up and down the menu list without clicking the mouse button. Notice the submenus for the Print and Save As commands.

6. Close the menu by clicking the Microsoft Office Button 🔵 or clicking in the blank text area.

7. Close the document by clicking the Close button ✕ in the upper right corner of the window located on the title bar.

Exercise 1-14

Key text, correct the spelling of a word, and save a document.

1. Start Word if necessary.

2. Open a new document window by clicking the Microsoft Office Button 🔵 . Click **New**, and click **Blank document**. Click **Create**.

3. Click the **Home** tab if necessary.

4. Locate the **Paragraph** group, and make sure the Show/Hide ¶ button ¶ is selected.

5. Key the text shown in Figure 1-13, including the intentional misspelling of "sponsored."

Figure 1-13

> Become a retail candy store owner and develop skills in business management! Come to the Small Business Fair and learn how to operate a business. The fair is sponsord by the Grove City Chamber of Commerce.

6. Correct the spelling of "sponsored" by following these steps:
   a. Move the I-beam anywhere within the word and click the right mouse button.
   b. Choose the correct spelling from the shortcut menu by clicking the word with left mouse button.

7. Save the document as *[your initials]***1-14** by following these steps:
   a. Open the **File** menu, and click **Save As** to open the Save As dialog box.
   b. Key the file name *[your initials]***1-14** in the **File name** text box.
   c. Choose the appropriate drive for your data disk—for example, Removable Drive (F:) or another drive specified by your instructor.
   d. Click **Save**.

8. Close the document by pressing Ctrl+W.

Exercise 1-15

Key, edit, and save a document.

1. Press Ctrl+N to create a new document.

2. Key the text shown in Figure 1-14. (Use default line spacing in all your documents, unless you are told otherwise.)

Figure 1-14

Campbell's Confections has just celebrated another anniversary in the candy business. The company has proudly created over 75,000 assorted chocolates including creams, nuts, and bark. Campbell's Confections has been at its current location for all of its 57 years.

3. Correct any spelling mistakes Word locates.
4. Delete the text "all of its" in the last sentence by following these steps:
   a. Move the insertion point to the right of the word "for" by positioning the I-beam and clicking the left mouse button.
   b. Hold down Ctrl and press Delete three times to delete the words "all of its."
5. Insert text after the word "creams" in the second sentence by following these steps:
   a. Move the insertion point to the immediate left of the the word "nuts."
   b. Key **melt-a-ways** followed by a comma and a space.
6. Split the paragraph by following these steps:
   a. Move the insertion point to the immediate left of the word "Campbell's" in the last sentence.
   b. Press Enter.
7. Save the document as *[your initials]***1-15** on your student data disk.
8. Close the document.

Exercise 1-16

Key, edit, save, and print a document.

1. Start a new blank document.
2. Key the text shown in Figure 1-15. Correct spelling mistakes as you key.

Figure 1-15

When you visit our inaugural store, take advantage of our factory tour where you can see each of the steps in candy making. All of our chocolates are hand decorated, and you will receive a free sample. You will follow the chocolate manufacturing line beginning with melting the chocolate, preparing the rich cream centers, and dipping.

3. Move the insertion point to the left of the word "inaugural" in the first line of the paragraph.

4. Press [Alt]+[F] to open the File menu. Click **Word Options**, and click **Advanced** in the left pane. Under Editing options, click **Use overtype mode** to turn on Overtype mode. Click **OK**.

5. Key **flagship** over the word "inaugural." Be sure to delete the extra character.

6. Turn off Overtype mode by clicking the **Microsoft Office Button**, and clicking **Word Options**. Click **Advanced** in the left pane, and click **Use overtype mode** to turn off Overtype mode. Click **OK**.

7. Use [Delete] to delete the word "manufacturing" and key **production** to replace it.

8. Check the spacing before and after the replacement text.

9. Save the document as *[your initials]*1-16 on your data disk.

10. Press [Ctrl]+[P] to open the Print dialog box. Click **OK** to print the document.

11. Close the document.

Lesson Applications

Exercise 1-17

Key, edit, and print a document.

1. Start a new document. Turn on Caps Lock mode and key **TO SALES ASSOCIATES:**

2. Turn off Caps Lock and press ⌷Enter⌷ to start a new paragraph.

3. Key the text shown in Figure 1-16, including the corrections. Refer to Appendix A, "Proofreaders' Marks," if necessary. *Proofreaders' marks* are handwritten corrections to text, often using specialized symbols.

Figure 1-16

Chocolate can be shipped between ~~June~~ **September** 1 and ~~August~~ **May** 15 only. Chocolate~~s~~ shipped to warm climates will be surrounded with ice packs. It is recommended that you select a personal or business address where someone will be available to handle the package as soon as it arrives. Remember: Fine chocolate~~s~~ **is** ~~are~~ perishable.

4. Key **anywhere** to the left of the word "between" in the first sentence." Delete the word "only."

5. Key the following sentence after the last sentence in the first paragraph. **During the hottest months of the year, shipments may be postponed.**

6. In the second paragraph, delete "Fine" after "Remember" and key **Quality** before "chocolate."

7. Save the document as *[your initials]***1-17** on your data disk.

8. Print the document, and then close it.

> **TIP**
>
> When Word suggests the completed word for "September," you can press ⌷Enter⌷ to insert the word. Remember to press ⌷Spacebar⌷ after the completed word.

Exercise 1-18

Key, edit, and print a document.

1. Start a new document and key the two paragraphs shown in Figure 1-17.

Figure 1-17

> Campbell's Confections has gained national recognition for its delectable chocolates. It is highly recognized for its unique, hand-molded chocolates in the mid-Atlantic area.
>
> The staff of all stores are considered experts in the history and manufacture of fine chocolate.

2. In the first paragraph, delete "area," and key **region** after "mid-Atlantic."

3. Switch to Overtype mode, and key **sales associates** over the text "staff of all stores." Delete the extra characters.

4. Turn off Overtype mode and move the insertion point to the beginning of the second sentence in the first paragraph.

5. Use Ctrl + Delete to delete "It" and key **Each of the 24 stores affiliated with Campbell's Confections in the mid-Atlantic region** in its place.

6. Delete "in the mid-Atlantic region" at the end of the first paragraph. Delete "its" before the word "unique."

7. Save the document as *[your initials]***1-18** on your data disk.

8. Print and then close the document.

Exercise 1-19

Key, edit, and print a document.

1. Start a new document. Key the text shown in Figure 1-18. Key each sentence on a new line.

Figure 1-18

> Reminder
>
> Will the first one to arrive at the store:
>
> Turn on the lights.
>
> Adjust the thermostat.
>
> Turn on the music.
>
> Turn on the computer.
>
> Thank you!

2. In the sixth line, change "computer" to **computer equipment**.

3. In the third line, change "the lights" to **all lighting fixtures**.

4. Click at the beginning of the third line, and insert another line by keying **Turn off the alarm and unlock the front door.**

5. Press [Caps Lock] and use Overtype mode to change "Reminder" and "Thank you!" to uppercase letters.

6. Insert an extra line after every line of text by pressing [Enter] once.

7. Save the document as *[your initials]*1-19 on your data disk.

8. Print and then close the document.

Exercise 1-20 ◆ Challenge Yourself

Key, edit, and print a document.

1. Start a new document and key the two paragraphs shown in Figure 1-19, including the corrections. Refer to Appendix A, "Proofreaders' Marks," if necessary.

Figure 1-19

Group tours are an imprtant part of campbell's. Tours include watching a video on the history of Campbell's Confections as well as the history of chocolate. After the video, a tour thru the factory is conducted by the plant manager.
Group tours arranged are for families visiting the area, school, or any group with an interest in learning about chocolate.

2. Correct the spelling of "thru" in the third sentence to **through**.

3. In the last sentence, key **type of** after "or any." Delete "families visiting the area" and key **tourists** in its place.

4. Add the following sentence to the end of the second paragraph. **Reservations are required two weeks in advance with a minimum of ten members in the tour.**

5. Save the document as *[your initials]*1-20 on your data disk.

6. Print, and then close the document

7. Exit Word.

On Your Own

In these exercises you work on your own, as you would in a real-life business environment. Use the skills you've learned to accomplish the task—and be creative.

Exercise 1-21

Write a short paragraph about yourself that includes your first and last name. Include information about your family, school, or employment. Switch to Overtype mode, turn on Caps Lock, and then key over your name in uppercase letters. Save the document as *[your initials]*1-21 and print it.

Exercise 1-22

Browse the various tabs on the Ribbon until you find a command that looks intriguing; then find out more about it by using the Help feature. In a new blank document, write a brief paragraph about your findings. Save the document as *[your initials]*1-22 and print it.

Exercise 1-23

Log onto the Internet and search for Web sites that relate to a particular interest of yours. Record a few Web addresses, and then key the addresses into a blank document, under an appropriate heading. Save the document as *[your initials]*1-23 and print it.

Lesson 2

Selecting and Editing

OBJECTIVES

After completing this lesson, you will be able to:

1. Open an existing document.
2. Enter formatting characters.
3. Move within a document.
4. Undo and Redo actions.
5. Repeat actions.
6. Select text.
7. Save a revised document.
8. Work with document properties.

Estimated Time: 1¼ hours

MCAS OBJECTIVES

In this lesson:
WW 07 1.3.3
WW 07 6.1.1
WW 07 6.1.2

To edit documents efficiently, you need to learn to select text and move quickly within a document. In this lesson you learn those skills, as well as how to open and save an existing document.

Opening an Existing Document

Instead of creating a new document, you start this lesson by opening an existing document. There are several ways to open a document:

- Choose **Open** from the File menu.
- Press Ctrl + O .
- Use the document links in the **Recent Documents** file listing.

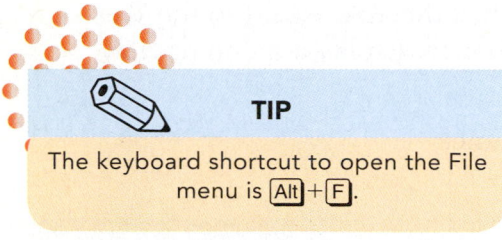

TIP

The keyboard shortcut to open the File menu is Alt + F.

NOTE

Click **Folders** to open and close the Folders list.

Exercise 2-1   OPEN AN EXISTING FILE

1. Click the **Microsoft Office Button** to open the File menu. The file names listed under **Recent Documents** are the files opened from this computer. If the file you want is listed, you can click its name to open it from this list. The Recent Documents section displays up to 17 documents.

2. Click **Open** to display the Open dialog box. You are going to open a student file named **Campbell-1**.

3. Locate the appropriate drive and folder according to your instructor's directions.

Figure 2-1
Files listed in the Open dialog box

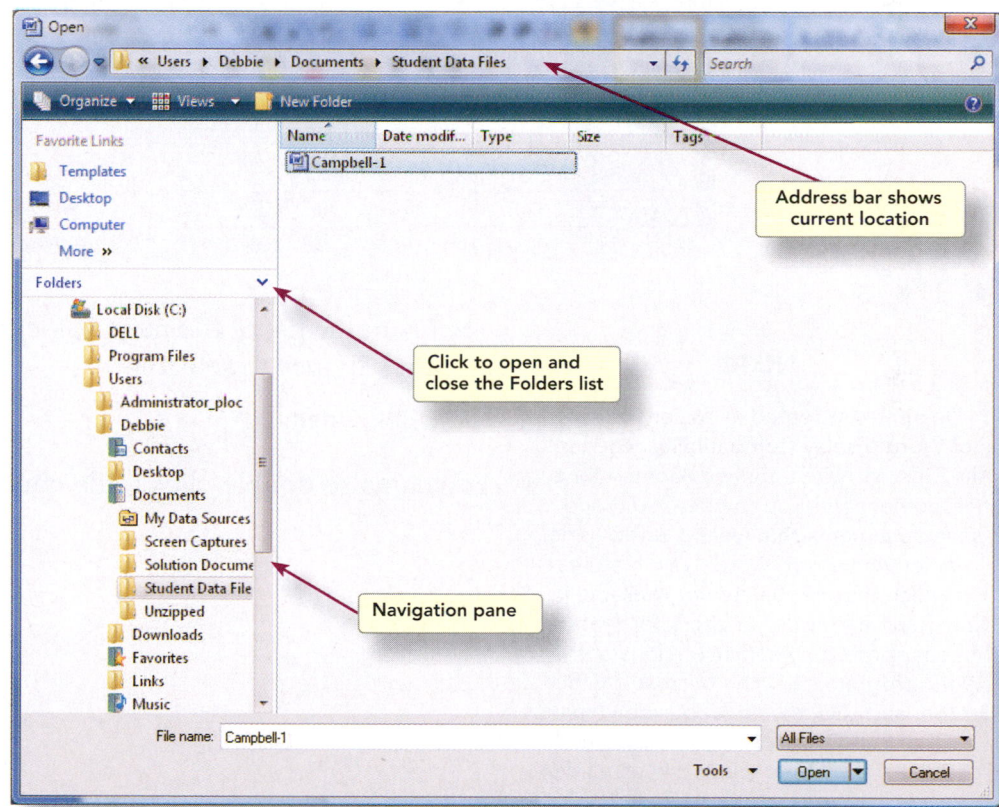

4. After you locate the student files, click the arrow next to the Views button  in the Open dialog box to display a menu of view options.

5. Choose **List** to list all files by file name.

Figure 2-2
Views menu in the Open dialog box

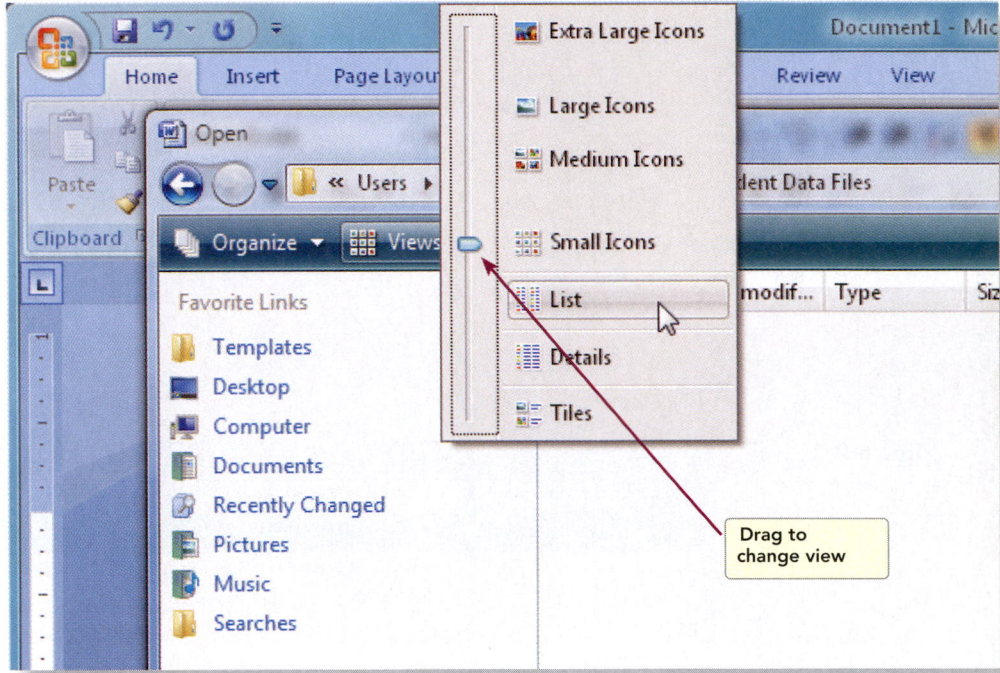

NOTE

Documents created in earlier versions of Word display Compatibility Mode in the Title bar when opened. Compatibility Mode enables you to open, edit, and save documents that were created using earlier versions of Word. New features in Office Word 2007 are not available in Compatibility Mode. To check for features not supported by earlier versions of the Word program, click the Microsoft Office Button, and click the arrow beside **Prepare**. Click **Run Compatibility Checker**. To convert a document created in an earlier version of Word to Office Word 2007, click the Microsoft Office Button, and click **Convert**. Click **OK**.

6. From the list of file names, locate **Campbell-1** and click it once to select it.

7. Click **Open**.

You can also double-click a file name to open a file.

TABLE 2-1 Open Dialog Box Buttons

Button	Name	Purpose
Debbie ▸ Documents ▸	Address bar	Navigates to a different folder.
(back arrow)	Back button	Works with the Address bar, and returns to most recent previous location.
(forward arrow)	Forward button	Works with the Address bar, and returns to location already opened.
Search	Search box	Looks for a file or subfolder.
Organize ▾	Organize	Opens a menu of file functions, such as cutting a file, copying a file, pasting a file, deleting a file, or renaming a file. Includes the Layout option to display the Navigation Pane, Details Pane, and the Preview Pane.
Views ▾	Views	Opens a menu of view options for displaying drives, folders, files, and their icons.
New Folder	New Folder	Creates a new folder to organize your files.

Exercise 2-2   CREATE A NEW FOLDER

Document files are typically stored in folders that are part of a hierarchal structure similar to a family tree. At the top of the tree is a disk drive letter (such as C: or A:) that represents your computer, network, floppy drive, jump drive, or CD-ROM drive. Under the disk drive letter, you can create folders to organize your files. These folders can also contain additional folders.

Here is a scenario: You store your files on the C: drive of your office computer. You create a folder on this drive named "Word Documents." Within this folder you create folders named "Letters," "Memos," and "Reports," each containing different types of documents.

For this course, you will create a new folder for each lesson and store your completed exercise documents in these folders.

1. Click the **Microsoft Office Button** and choose **Save As**. You are going to save **Campbell-1** under a new file name, in a new folder that will contain all the files you save in this lesson.

2. Choose the appropriate drive and folder location from the **Navigation pane**. (For example, to save your files to a jump drive, insert a jump

drive in the USB port, and make sure the **Address bar** indicates the appropriate drive).

3. Click the Create New Folder button . A New Folder icon appears in the File list section.

4. Key the folder name *[your initials]***Lesson2** and press Enter. The folder name appears in the Address bar and in the Navigation pane. Word is ready to save the file in the new folder.

5. Locate the **File name** box, and make sure the file's original name (**Campbell-1**) is selected. If not, double-click it.

6. Key the file name *[your initials]***2-2** and click **Save**.

> **NOTE**
>
> To rename a folder, locate the folder to rename and right-click the folder. Click Rename on the shortcut menu, key the new name, and press Enter.

Formatting Characters

The Show/Hide ¶ button ¶ on the Home tab shows or hides paragraph marks and other *formatting marks*. These characters appear on the screen, but not in the printed document. Formatting marks are included as part of words, sentences, and paragraphs in a document. Here are some examples:

• A word includes the space character that follows it.

• A sentence includes the end-of-sentence punctuation and at least one space.

• A paragraph is any amount of text followed by a paragraph mark.

The document you opened contains two additional formatting characters: *tab characters,* which you use to indent text, and *line-break characters,* which you use to start a new line within the same paragraph. Line-break characters are useful when you want to create a paragraph of short lines, such as an address, and keep the lines together as a single paragraph.

Another formatting character is a *nonbreaking space,* which you use to prevent two words from being divided between two lines. For example, you can insert a nonbreaking space between "Mr." and "Smith" to keep the name "Mr. Smith" undivided on one line.

TABLE 2-2 Formatting Characters

Character	To Insert, Press
Tab (→)	Tab
Space (·)	Spacebar
Nonbreaking space (°)	Ctrl + Shift + Spacebar
Paragraph mark (¶)	Enter
Line-break character (↵)	Shift + Enter

Exercise 2-3   ENTER FORMATTING CHARACTERS

1. Click the Show/Hide ¶ button ¶ if the formatting characters in the document are hidden.

2. Move the insertion point to the end of the document (after "family recipes.").

3. Press Enter to begin a new paragraph, and key **Campbell's Confections has been a member in good standing of the NCA for over 50** (do not press Spacebar).

4. Insert a nonbreaking space after "50" by pressing Ctrl + Shift + Spacebar. Then key **years.** (including the period). Word now treats "50 years" as a single unit.

Figure 2-3
Formatting characters

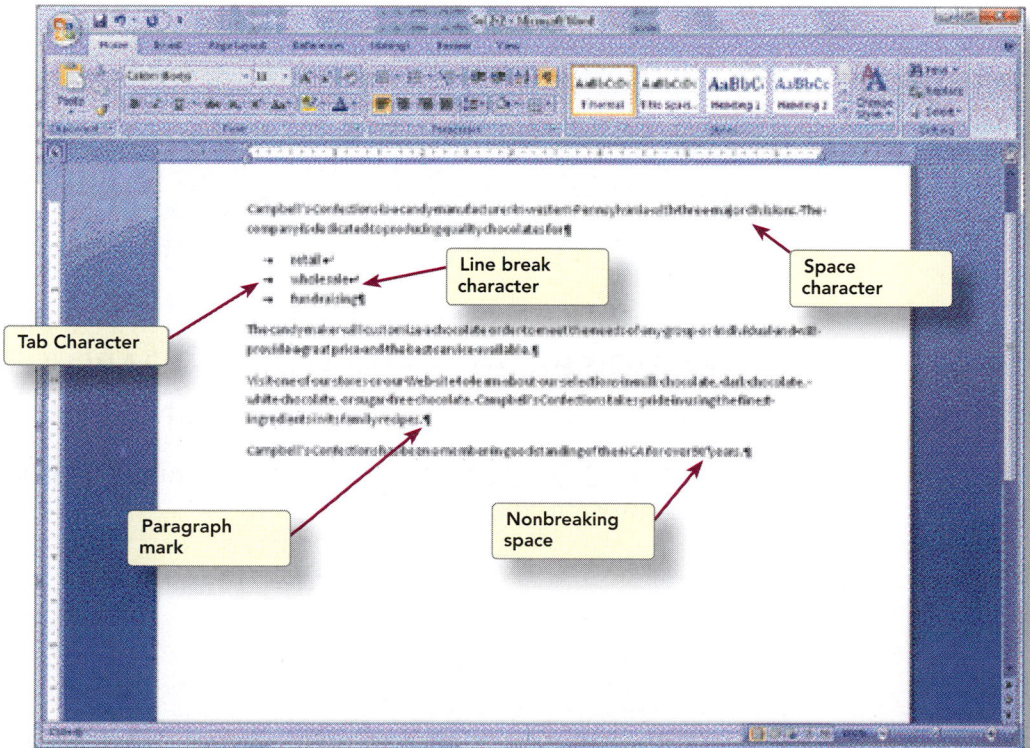

5. Press Enter and key the following text as one paragraph at the end of the document, pressing Shift + Enter at the end of the first and second lines instead of Enter.

Campbell's Confections
25 Main Street
Grove City, PA 16127

6. Click the Show/Hide ¶ button ¶ to hide the formatting characters, and click it again to redisplay them.

Moving within a Document

You already know how to move around a short document by positioning the I-beam pointer with the mouse and clicking. This is the easiest way to move around a document that displays in the document window. If a document is too long or wide to view in the window, you need to use different methods to navigate within a document.

Word offers two additional methods for moving within a document:

- *Using the keyboard:* You can press certain keys on the keyboard to move the insertion point. The arrow keys, for example, move the insertion point up or down one line or to the left or right one character. Key combinations quickly move the insertion point to specified locations in the document.

- *Using the scroll bars:* Use the vertical scroll bar at the right edge of the document window to move through a document. The position of the scroll box indicates your approximate location in the document, which is particularly helpful in long documents. To view and move through a document that is wider than the document window, use the horizontal scroll bar at the bottom of the document window.

Exercise 2-4   USE THE KEYBOARD TO MOVE THE INSERTION POINT

1. Press Ctrl + Home to move to the beginning of the document. Press End to move to the end of the first line.

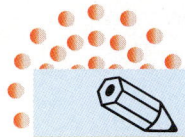

TIP

Word remembers the last three locations in the document where you edited or keyed text. You can press Shift+F5 to return the insertion point to these locations. For example, when you open a document you worked on earlier, press Shift+F5 to return to the place where you were last working before you saved and closed the document.

2. Press Ctrl+↓ several times to move the insertion point down one paragraph at a time. Notice how the text with the line-break characters is treated as a single paragraph.

3. When you reach the end of the document, press PageUp until you return to the beginning of the document.

TABLE 2-3 Keys to Move the Insertion Point

To Move	Press
One word to the left	Ctrl+←
One word to the right	Ctrl+→
Beginning of the line	Home
End of the line	End
One paragraph up	Ctrl+↑
One paragraph down	Ctrl+↓
Previous page	Ctrl+PageUp
Next page	Ctrl+PageDown
Up one window	PageUp
Down one window	PageDown
Top of the window	Alt+Ctrl+PageUp
Bottom of the window	Alt+Ctrl+PageDown
Beginning of the document	Ctrl+Home
End of the document	Ctrl+End

Exercise 2-5　SCROLL THROUGH A DOCUMENT

Using the mouse and the scroll bars, you can scroll up, down, left, and right. You can also set the Previous and Next buttons on the vertical scroll bar to scroll through a document by a specific object, such as tables or headings. For example, these buttons let you jump from one heading to the next, going forward or backward.

1. Locate the vertical scroll bar, and click below the scroll box to move down one window.

Figure 2-4
Using the Scroll bars

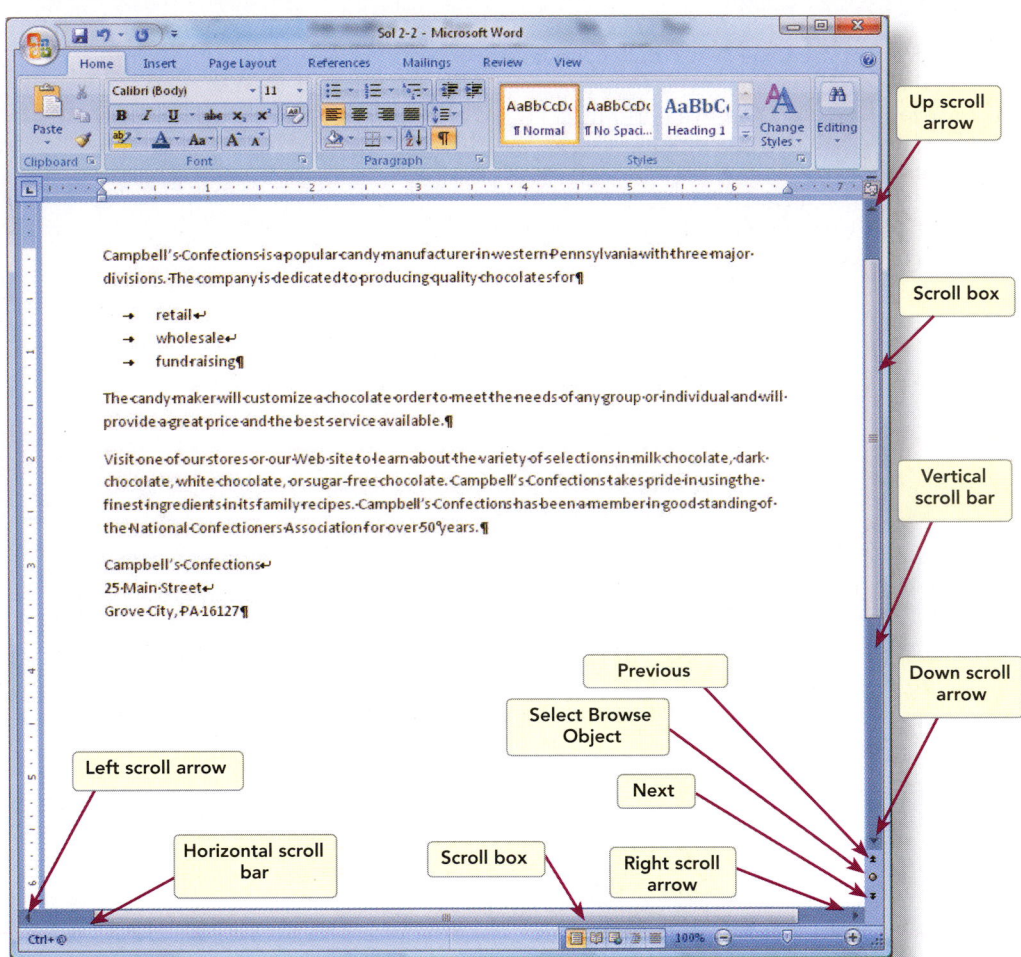

NOTE

The horizontal scroll bar does not display if the document window is wide enough to display the document text. To display the horizontal bar, size the window by dragging the resize handle (located in the lower right corner) to the left. When you resize the document window, the appearance of the Ribbon changes.

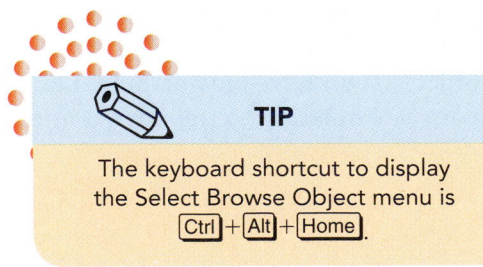

TIP

The keyboard shortcut to display the Select Browse Object menu is Ctrl + Alt + Home.

2. Drag the scroll box to the top of the scroll bar.

3. Click the down scroll arrow ▼ on the scroll bar three times. The document moves three lines.

4. Click the right scroll arrow ▶ on the horizontal scroll bar once, and then click the left scroll arrow ◀ once to return to the correct horizontal position.

5. Click the up scroll arrow ▲ on the vertical scroll bar three times to bring the document back into full view.
   Notice that as you scroll through the document, the insertion point remains at the top of the document.

6. Click the Select Browse Object button ⦿, located toward the bottom of the vertical scroll bar. A menu of icons appears.

7. Move the pointer over each icon to identify it. These browse options become significant as your documents become more complex. Click the Browse by Page icon 🗋.

TABLE 2-4 Scrolling through a Document

To Move	Do This
Up one line	Click the up scroll arrow ▲.
Down one line	Click the down scroll arrow ▼.
Up one window	Click the scroll bar above the scroll box.
Down one window	Click the scroll bar below the scroll box.
To any relative position	Drag the scroll box up or down.
To the right	Click the right scroll arrow ▶.
To the left	Click the left scroll arrow ◀.
Into the left margin	Hold down Shift and click the left scroll arrow ◀.
Up or down one page	Click Select Browse Object ●, click Browse by Page 🗋, and then click next ▼ or previous ▲.

TIP

If you are using a mouse with a wheel, additional navigating options are available. For example, you can roll the wheel forward or backward instead of using the vertical scroll bars, hold down the wheel and drag in any direction to pan the document, or hold down Ctrl as you roll the wheel to change the magnification.

Undo and Redo Commands

Word remembers the changes you make in a document and lets you undo or redo these changes. For example, if you accidentally delete text, you can use the Undo command to reverse the action and restore the text. If you change your mind and decide to keep the deletion, you can use the Redo command to reverse the canceled action.

There are two ways to undo or redo an action:

- Click the Undo button ↺ or the Redo button ↻ on the Quick Access Toolbar.

- Press Ctrl+Z to undo or Ctrl+Y to redo.

Exercise 2-6   UNDO AND REDO ACTIONS

1. Delete the first word in the document, "Campbell's," by moving the insertion point to the right of the space after the word and pressing Ctrl + Backspace. (Remember that a word includes the space that follows it.)

2. Click the Undo button to restore the word.

3. Move the insertion point to the left of the word "candy" in the first paragraph.

4. Key **mid-size** and press Spacebar once. The text now reads "mid-size candy manufacturer."

5. Press Ctrl + Z. The word "mid-size" is deleted.

6. Click the Redo button to restore the word "mid-size."

7. Click the down arrow to the right of the Undo button. Word displays a drop-down list of the last few actions, with the most recent action at the top. You can use this feature to choose several actions to undo rather than just the last action. Click the down arrow again to close the list.

8. Click the Undo button.

Figure 2-5
Undo Drop-Down list

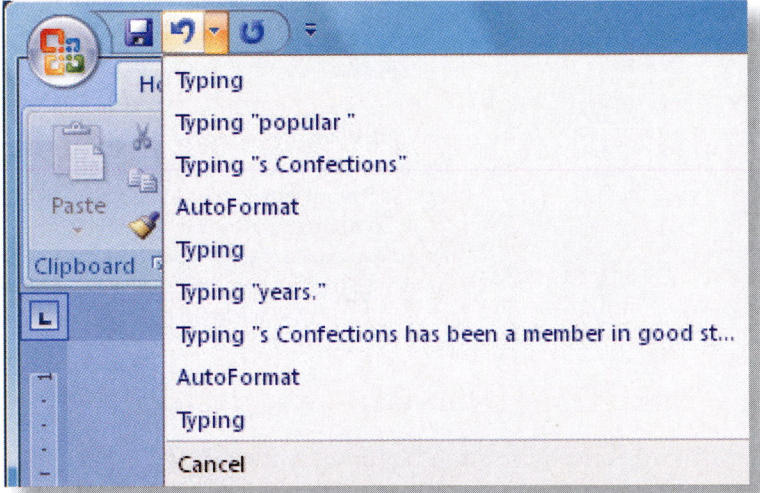

Repeat Command

Suppose you key text you want to add to other areas of a document. Instead of rekeying the same text, you can use the Repeat command to duplicate the text.
To use the Repeat command:

- Press Ctrl + Y or

- Press F4.

Exercise 2-7　　REPEAT ACTIONS

1. In the first paragraph position the insertion point to the left of the word "candy."

2. Key **popular** and press ⎡Spacebar⎤ once. The sentence now begins "Campbell's Confections is a popular candy."

3. Move the insertion point to the left of the word "selections" in the paragraph that begins "Visit one of our."

4. Press ⎡F4⎤ and the word "popular" is repeated.

NOTE

If you want to undo, redo, or repeat your last action, do so before you press another key.

Selecting Text

Selecting text is a basic technique that makes revising documents easy. When you select text, that area of the document is called the *selection*, and it appears as a highlighted block of text. A selection can be a character, group of characters, word, sentence, or paragraph or the whole document. In this lesson, you delete and replace selected text. Future lessons show you how to format, move, copy, delete, and print selected text.

You can select text several ways, depending on the size of the area you want to select.

TABLE 2-5　Mouse Selection

To	Use the Mouse to Select
A series of characters	Click and drag, or click one end of the text block, and then hold down ⎡Shift⎤ and click the other end.
A word	Double-click the word.
A sentence	Press ⎡Ctrl⎤ and click anywhere in the sentence.
A line of text	Move the pointer to the left of the line until it changes to a right-pointing arrow, and then click. To select multiple lines, drag up or down.
A paragraph	Move the pointer to the left of the paragraph and double-click. To select multiple paragraphs, drag up or down.
The entire document	Move the pointer to the left of any document text until it changes to a right-pointing arrow, and then triple-click (or hold down ⎡Ctrl⎤ and click).

Exercise 2-8 SELECT TEXT WITH THE MOUSE

1. Select the first word of the document by double-clicking it. Notice that the space following the word is also selected.

Figure 2-6
Selecting a word

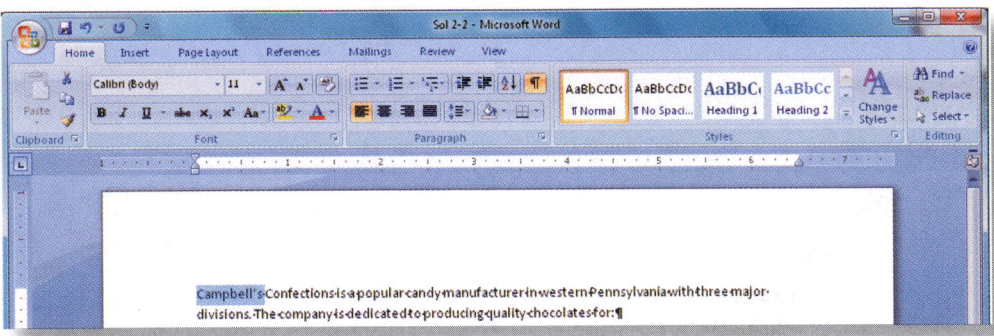

> **NOTE**
>
> When text is selected, a Mini toolbar appears with formatting options.

> **TIP**
>
> When selecting more than one word, you can click anywhere within the first word, and then drag to select additional text. Word will "smart-select" the entire first word.

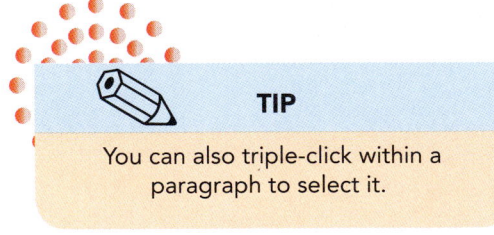

> **TIP**
>
> You can also triple-click within a paragraph to select it.

2. Cancel the selection by clicking anywhere in the document. Selected text remains highlighted until you cancel the selection.

3. Select the first sentence by holding down Ctrl and clicking anywhere within the sentence. Notice that the period and space following the sentence are part of the selection. Cancel the selection.

4. Locate the paragraph that begins "Visit one of our."

5. To select the text "milk chocolate," click to the left of "milk." Hold down the left mouse button and slowly drag through the text, including the comma and space after "chocolate." Release the mouse button. Cancel the selection.

6. To select the entire paragraph by dragging the mouse, click to position the insertion point to the left of "Visit." Hold down the mouse button, and then drag across and down until all the text and the paragraph mark are selected. Cancel the selection.

7. Select the same paragraph by moving the pointer into the blank area to the left of the text "Visit." (This is the margin area.) When the I-beam pointer changes to a right-pointing arrow ⍺, double-click. Notice that the first click selects the first line and the second click selects the paragraph, including the paragraph mark. Cancel the selection.

Figure 2-7
Selecting text

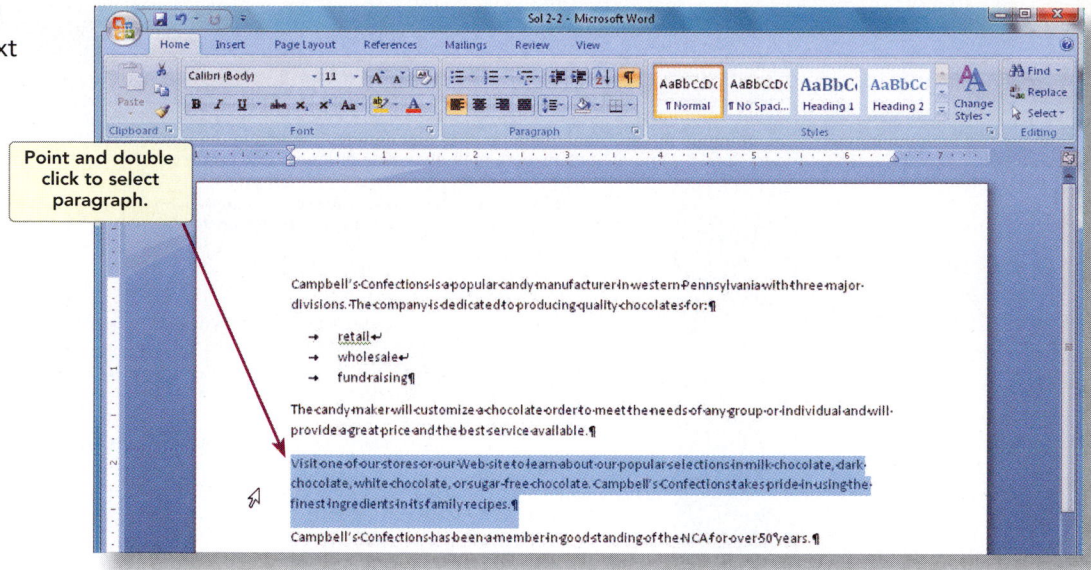

Exercise 2-9   SELECT NONCONTIGUOUS TEXT

In the previous exercise, you learned how to select *contiguous text*, where the selected characters, words, sentences, or paragraphs follow one another. But sometimes you would like to select *noncontiguous text*, such as the first and last items in a list or the third and fifth word in a paragraph. In Word, you can select noncontiguous text by using Ctrl and the mouse.

1. Select the first line of the list ("retail").

2. Press Ctrl and select the third line of the list ("fundraising"). With these two separate lines selected, you can delete, format, or move them without affecting the rest of the list.

3. Cancel the selection and go to the paragraph that begins "Visit one of our."

4. In the paragraph that begins "Visit one of our," double-click the word "our" before "Web site." With the word now selected, hold down Ctrl as you double-click the word "popular" in the same sentence and "finest" in the next sentence. (See Figure 2-8.) All three words are highlighted.

Figure 2-8
Selecting
noncontiguous
words

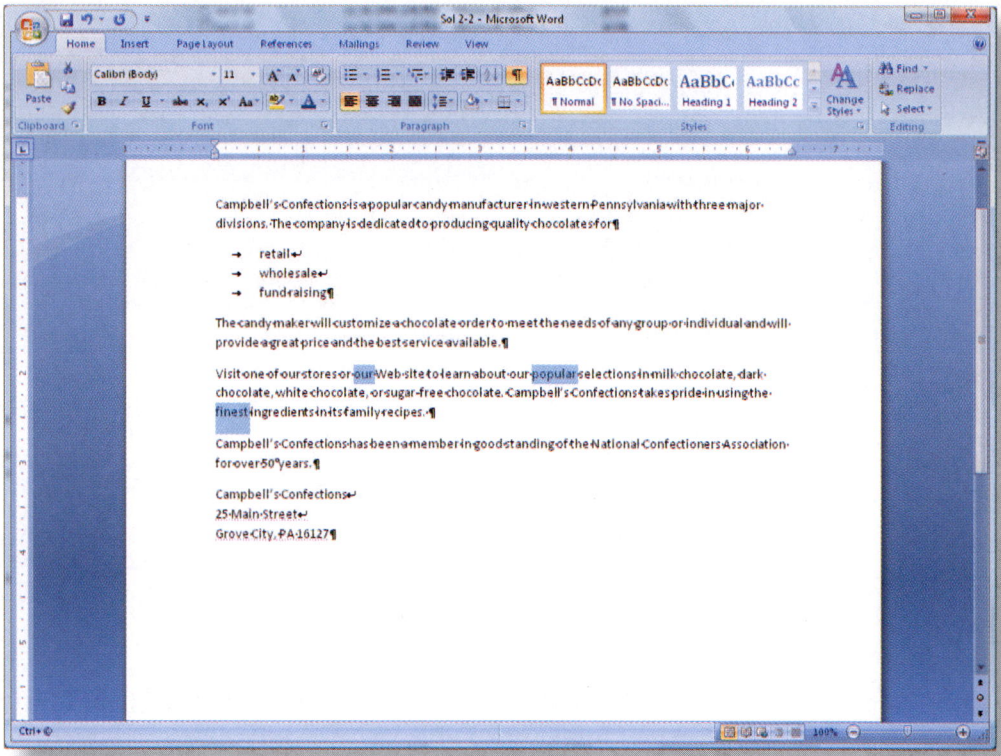

5. Cancel the selection.

Exercise 2-10   ADJUST A SELECTION USING THE MOUSE AND THE KEYBOARD

1. Select the paragraph beginning "Visit one of our."

2. Hold down `Shift` and press `←` until the last sentence is no longer highlighted. Release `Shift`.

3. Increase the selection to include the last sentence by holding down `Shift` and pressing `End` and then pressing `↓`. Release `Shift`.

4. Increase the selection to include all the text below it by holding down `Shift` and clicking at the end of the document (after the Zip Code).

5. Select the entire document by pressing `Ctrl`+`A`. Cancel the selection.

TABLE 2-6 Keyboard Selection

To Select	Press
One character to the right	Shift + →
One character to the left	Shift + ←
One word to the right	Ctrl + Shift + →
One word to the left	Ctrl + Shift + ←
To the end of a line	Shift + End
To the beginning of a line	Shift + Home
One line up	Shift + ↑
One line down	Shift + ↓
One window down	Shift + Page Down
One window up	Shift + Page Up
To the end of a document	Ctrl + Shift + End
To the beginning of a document	Ctrl + Shift + Home
An entire document	Ctrl + A

Exercise 2-11   EDIT TEXT BY REPLACING A SELECTION

You can edit a document by selecting text and deleting or replacing the selection.

NOTE

Although keying over selected text is an excellent editing feature, it sometimes leads to accidental deletions. Remember, when text is selected in a document (or even in a dialog box) and you begin keying text, Word deletes all the selected text with your first keystroke. If you key text without realizing a portion of the document is selected, use the Undo command to restore the text.

1. Locate the paragraph that begins "Visit one of our," select the words "our popular" using the Shift + click method: Click to the left of the word "our," hold down Shift, and click to the right of the word "popular."

2. Key **the variety of** to replace the selected text.

3. Locate the paragraph that begins "Campbell's Confections has been," select "NCA" and key **National Confectioners Association**. Notice that, unlike using Overtype mode, when you key over selected text, the new text can be longer or shorter than the selection.

Saving a Revised Document

You have already used the Save As command to rename the document you loaded at the beginning of this lesson. Now that you have made additional revisions, you can save a final version of the document by using the Save command. The document is saved with all the changes, replacing the old file with the revised file.

> **NOTE**
>
> If you wanted to save the current document with a different file name, you would use the **Save As** command.

Exercise 2-12 SAVE A REVISED DOCUMENT

1. Click the Save button  on the Quick Access Toolbar. This action does not open the Save As dialog box.

2. Open the **File** menu and point to the arrow beside **Print**. Click **Quick Print** to print the document.

Exercise 2-13 CHECK WORD'S AUTORECOVER SETTINGS

Word's *AutoRecover* feature can automatically save open documents at an interval you specify. However, this is not the same as saving a file yourself, as you did in the preceding exercise. AutoRecover's purpose is to save open documents "in the background," so a recently saved version is always on disk. Then if the power fails or your system crashes, the AutoRecover version of the document opens automatically the next time you launch Word. In other words, AutoRecover ensures you always have a recently saved version of your document.

Even with AutoRecover working, you need to manually save a document (by using the Save command) before closing it. AutoRecover documents are not always available; if you save and close your file normally, the AutoRecover version is deleted when you exit Word. Still, it is a good idea to make sure AutoRecover is working on your system and to set it to save recovery files frequently.

1. Open the **File** menu and click **Word Options** to open the Word Options dialog box.

2. Click **Save** in the left pane.

3. Make sure the **Save AutoRecover information every** box is checked. If it is not checked, click the box.

4. Click the up or down arrow buttons to set the **minutes** to 5. Click **OK**.

Figure 2-9
Setting AutoRecover options

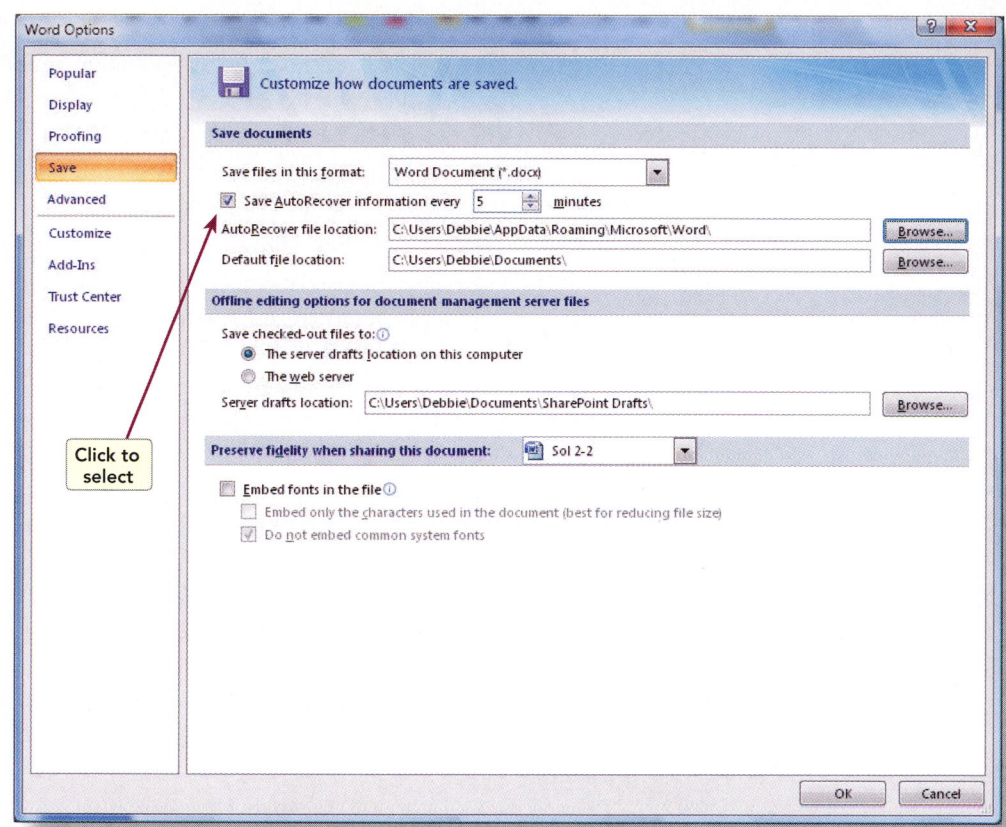

Working with Document Properties

Information that describes your document is called a *property*. Word automatically saves your document with certain properties, such as the file name, the date created, and the file size. You can add other properties to a document, such as the title, subject, author's name, and keywords. This information can help you organize and identify documents.

NOTE

You can also search for documents based on document properties by using the Search feature.

Exercise 2-14 **REVIEW AND EDIT DOCUMENT PROPERTIES**

1. With the file *[your initials]*2-2 still open, open the **File** menu and click **Prepare**. Click **Properties**. The Document Information Panel opens above your document.

Word 2007

Figure 2-10
Opening the
Properties dialog
box

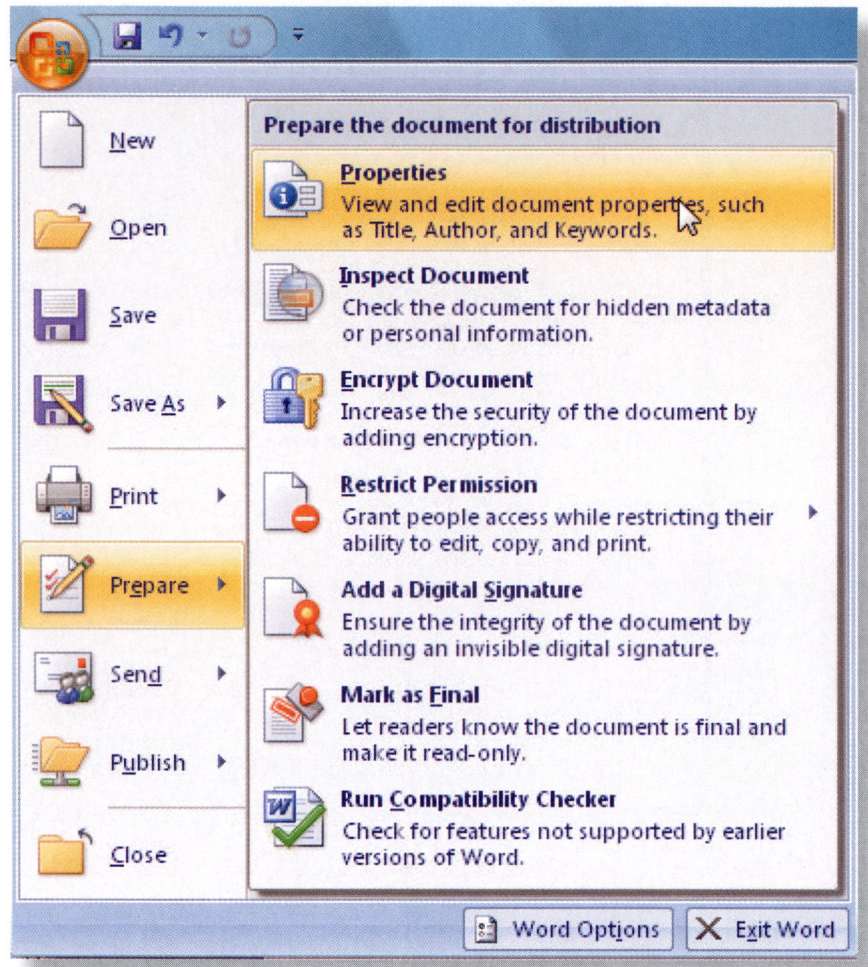

2. Notice the document properties displayed in the Document Information Panel.

Figure 2-11
Document
Information Panel

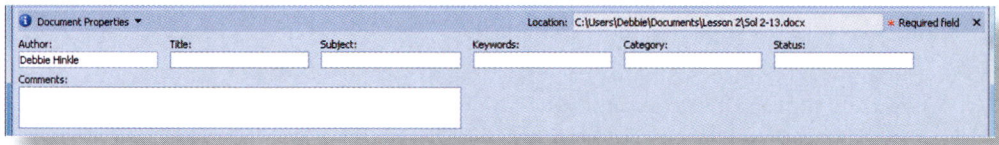

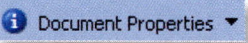

3. Click the Property Views and Options button . Click **Advanced Properties**. Click the **General** tab. This tab displays basic information about the file, such as file name, file type, location, size, and creation date.

4. Click the **Statistics** tab. This tab shows the exact breakdown of the document in number of paragraphs, lines, words, and characters.

5. Click the **Summary** tab. Here you can enter specific document property information or change existing information.

6. Edit the title to read **Campbell's Confections** and key *[your name]* as the author. Click **OK**.

 7. Click the Document Information Panel Close button to close the Document Information Panel.

Figure 2-12
Entering Summary
information

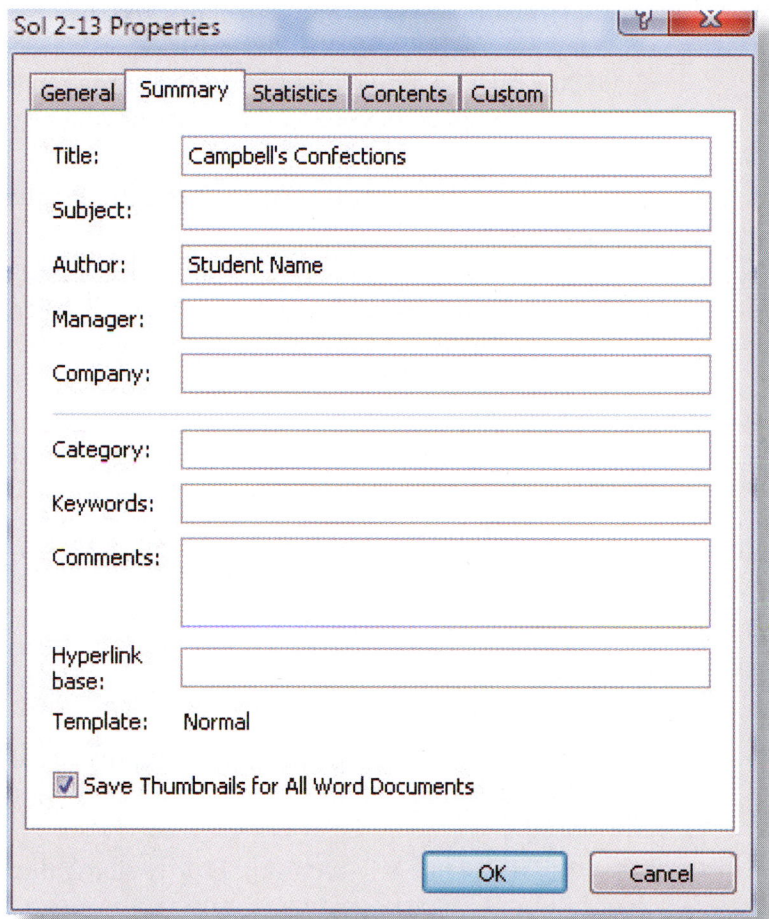

8. Save the document, and submit your work.

Lesson 2 Summary

- Use the Open dialog box to open an existing file. Use the Views button ▤ Views ▾ in the dialog box to change the way files are listed.

- Create folders to organize your files. You can do this in the Save As dialog box, using the New Folder button 📁 New Folder . Rename folders by locating and selecting the folder. Right-click the folder name and choose **Rename** from the shortcut menu.

- Formatting characters—such as blank spaces or paragraph marks— appear on-screen, but not in the printed document. Insert a line-break character to start a new line within the same paragraph. Insert a nonbreaking space between two words to make sure they appear on the same line.

- Use the Show/Hide ¶ button ¶ to turn the display of formatting characters on and off.

- When a document is larger than the document window, use the keyboard or the vertical scroll bar to view different parts of the document. Keyboard methods for moving within a document also move the insertion point.

- Keyboard techniques for moving within a document include single keys (such as PageUp and Home)and keyboard combinations (such as Ctrl + ↑). See Table 2-3.

- Scrolling techniques for moving within a document include clicking the up or down scroll arrows on the vertical scroll bar or dragging the scroll box. Scrolling does not move the insertion point. See Table 2-4.

- If you make a change in a document that you want to reverse, use the Undo command. Use the Redo command to reverse the results of an Undo command.

- If you perform an action, such as keying text in a document, and you want to repeat that action elsewhere in the document, use the Repeat command.

- Selecting text is a basic technique for revising documents. A selection is a highlighted block of text you can format, move, copy, delete, or print.

- There are many different techniques for selecting text, using the mouse, the keyboard, or a combination of both. Mouse techniques involve dragging or clicking. See Table 2-5. Keyboard techniques are listed in Table 2-6.

- You can select any amount of contiguous text (characters, words, sentences, or paragraphs that follow one another) or noncontiguous text (such as words that appear in different parts of a document). Use Ctrl along with the mouse to select noncontiguous blocks of text.

- When text is selected, Word replaces it with any new text you key, or it deletes the selection if you press Delete .

- Use the Save command to save any revisions you make to a document.

- Word's AutoRecover feature periodically saves open documents in the background so you can recover a file in the event of a power failure or system crash.

- Document properties are details about a file that help identify it. Properties include the file name, file size, and date created, which Word updates automatically. Other properties you can add or change include title, subject, author's name, and keywords. View or add properties for an open document by using the **Properties** command (File menu, Prepare).

LESSON 2		Command Summary	
Feature	**Button**	**Command**	**Keyboard**
Open		File menu, Open	Ctrl + O or Ctrl + F12
Undo		Quick Access Toolbar	Ctrl + Z or Alt + Backspace
Redo		Quick Access Toolbar	Ctrl + Y or Alt + Shift + Backspace
Repeat			Ctrl + Y or F4
Select entire document			Ctrl + A
Save		File menu, Save	Ctrl + S or Shift + F12

Concepts Review

True/False Questions

Each of the following statements is either true or false. Indicate your choice by circling T or F.

T F   1. You can view Document Properties in the Open dialog box.

T F   2. A line-break character is used to begin a new paragraph.

T F   3. A tab mark is a formatting character.

T F   4. The Save As dialog box can be used to create a new folder.

T F   5. Noncontiguous text is text that does not appear consecutively in a Word document.

T F   6. You can undo only the last change made to a document.

T F   7. To select a sentence, you can double-click anywhere within the sentence.

T F   8. You can increase a selection by using [Shift]+[End].

Short Answer Questions

Write the correct answer in the space provided.

1. How do you display a list of the files recently opened?

   _____

2. Which formatting character would you insert between two words to keep them together in a sentence?

   _____

3. What is the keyboard shortcut to move the insertion point to the beginning of a document?

   _____

4. Where does [Home] move the insertion point?

   _____

5. What portion of the vertical scroll bar can you drag up or down?

   _____

6. Which keyboard shortcut repeats the text you just keyed?

   _____

7. How do you open the Properties dialog box?

_____

8. Which feature automatically saves an open document at regular intervals?

_____

Critical Thinking

Answer these questions on a separate page. There are no right or wrong answers. Support your answers with examples from your own experience, if possible.

1. You can use a nonbreaking space to prevent a line break between two words. Give some examples of word combinations and word-and-number combinations in which you would use a nonbreaking space.

2. Word provides many ways to select text by using the mouse. For example, you can use just the mouse, the mouse in combination with the keyboard, or just the keyboard. When would each of these methods be preferable? Which method do you prefer, and why?

Skills Review

Exercise 2-16

Open a document and enter formatting characters.

1. Open the file **Pitt** by following these steps:
   a. Click the **Microsoft Office Button** and click **Open**.
   b. Click the arrow to the right of the Views button  and choose **List**.
   c. Click the appropriate drive and folder.
   d. Scroll to the file name **Pitt** and double-click.

2. Position the insertion point at the end of the document by pressing Ctrl + End.

3. Key the text shown in Figure 2-13 as one paragraph, using line-break characters, by following these steps:
   a. Press Enter at the end of the document.
   b. Key the first three lines of text, pressing Shift + Enter at the end of each line.
   c. Key the last line (the phone number) and press Enter.

Figure 2-13

```
Campbell's Confections
40 Station Square
Pittsburgh, PA 15219
412-555-2025
```

4. Add new text and a nonbreaking space by following these steps:
   a. Move the insertion point to the immediate left of the word "area" in the first paragraph.
   b. Key **Station** and then press Ctrl + Shift + Spacebar.
   c. Key **Square** after the nonbreaking space and press Spacebar.
5. Save the document as *[your initials]*2-16 in your Lesson 2 folder.
6. Submit and close the document.

Exercise 2-17

Move within a document.

1. Open the file **Order**.
2. Move the insertion point to the immediate left of "We will" in the second line, and press Enter to split the paragraph.
3. Move the insertion point to the immediate left of the third sentence in the new paragraph (beginning with "If you"), and press Enter to split the paragraph.
4. With the insertion point to the left of "If," press ← once to move the insertion point to the end of the previous paragraph and key **We are confident you will want to return to try all of our flavors!**
5. Press Ctrl + End to move to the end of the document. Press Spacebar and key **Our unique hand-molded chocolates are delightful.**
6. Press Ctrl + Home to move to the beginning of the document. Press Caps Lock and key **thinking of chocolate?** Press Enter to split the paragraph.
7. Save the document as *[your initials]*2-17 in your Lesson 2 folder.
8. Submit and close the document.

Exercise 2-18

Undo, redo, and repeat editing actions.

1. Open the file **Meeting Favors**.
2. Position the insertion point after the heading "Meeting Favors" and press Enter. Click the Undo button to undo the insertion.
3. Move the insertion point to the left of "flavors" in the first sentence of the second paragraph. Key **chocolate** to create the phrase "chocolate flavors."

4. In the same paragraph, move the insertion point to the left of "favor shapes." Press [F4] to create the phrase "chocolate favor shapes."

5. In the first sentence of the first paragraph, move the insertion point to the left of "for." Key **favors** and press [Spacebar].

6. Locate "premier chocolate" in the last paragraph, and use the **Repeat** command to insert "favors" to the left of "for your."

7. Click the Undo button ↻ to undo the text. Then click the Redo button ↺ to redo the text.

8. In the last sentence of the last paragraph, replace the sentence by following these steps:

   a. Select the last sentence by pressing [Ctrl] and clicking anywhere in the sentence.

   b. Key **Visit www.campbellsconfections.biz** for additional information.

9. Save the document as *[your initials]*2-18 in your Lesson 2 folder.

10. Submit your work.

Exercise 2-19

Select text, save a revised document, and enter summary information.

1. Start a new document. Key the text shown in Figure 2-14.

Figure 2-14

Campbell's Confections chocolate factory tour and candy store is one of Butler County's major attractions. The factory tour enables visitors to watch the entire cycle of candy making from melting the bulk chocolate to packing the individual pieces in air-tight containers. The information provided by the tour guide is informative and educational.

If you are planning a family trip to Mercer County, be sure to research the other attractions in the area. You are miles away from museums, antique stores, a forge that makes aluminum, bronze, and other metal gifts, and many outdoor activities. There are opportunities for camping, hiking, biking, boating, and fishing. Winter activities include sledding, ice fishing, ice skating, snowmobile trails, and cross-country skiing. Contact us for brochures and other information on area attractions.

2. Save the document as *[your initials]*2-19 in your Lesson 2 folder.

3. Select and replace a word by following these steps:

   a. Place the insertion point in the word "Butler" in the first sentence of the first paragraph.

   b. Double-click the word to select it and key **Mercer** to replace it.

4. Select and replace the text in the second paragraph by following these steps:

   a. Double click "us" in the last line of the second paragraph.

   b. Key **the Chamber of Commerce** in place of the selected text.

5. Select "miles" in the second paragraph and key **minutes** to replace the text.

6. Select a sentence by following these steps:

   a. Position the I-beam pointer over any sentence.

   b. Hold down `Ctrl` and click the mouse button. Release `Ctrl`.

   c. Deselect the sentence.

7. Select the first paragraph by following these steps:

   a. Move the pointer to the left of the paragraph until it changes to a right-pointing arrow `↗`.

   b. Double-click the mouse button.

8. Extend the current selection by following these steps:

   a. Hold down `Shift` and press `↓` twice to extend the selection two lines.

   b. Continue holding down `Shift` and press `End` to select the entire line.

   c. Continue holding down `Shift` and press `↓` to select the rest of the document. Release `Shift`.

9. Click anywhere to cancel the selection.

10. Select noncontiguous text by following these steps:

    a. Double-click the document's first word ("Campbell's").

    b. Move the pointer to the left of the paragraph's third line until the pointer changes to a right-pointing arrow. Hold down `Ctrl` and click to select the line.

    c. Hold down `Ctrl` and select the second paragraph by dragging the pointer from the beginning of the paragraph to the end.

11. Click anywhere to cancel the selection.

12. Review the document properties and enter summary information by following these steps:

    a. Open the **File** menu and click **Prepare**. Click **Properties**.

    b. Click the down arrow beside **Standard**, and click **Advanced.**

    b. Review the data on the **General** tab and the **Statistics** tab, and click the **Summary** tab.

    c. Click in the **Title** box and press `Home` to move the insertion point to the beginning of the title. Press `Shift`+`End` to select the current title. With the title selected, key **Mercer County** as the new title, replacing the existing text.

    d. Click **OK**.

13. Click the Save button to save the revised document.

14. Submit your work, and close the document.

Lesson Applications

Exercise 2-20

Select and edit text, and enter a nonbreaking space.

1. Open the file **Pitt**. Make the corrections shown in Figure 2-15 by selecting and then keying over the selected text.

Figure 2-15

Both tourists and local residents frequent the Pittsburgh candy store, ^of

Campbell's Confections. The store is in a bustling downtown location and

is well known for its chocolate-covered nuts, creams, and melt-a-ways. Be sure to

Drop in when you're visiting the area.

2. Press Ctrl + End to move to the end of the document. Press Enter to start a new paragraph. Then key:

   For information about monthly chocolate specials, or for directions to the store, call Rebecca Steigerwald at Campbell's Confections. You can also visit us on the Web at www.campbellsconfections.biz.

3. Insert a nonbreaking space between "Rebecca" and "Steigerwald" in the second paragraph. (Replace the regular space with a nonbreaking space.)

4. Save the document as *[your initials]*2-20 in your Lesson 2 folder.

5. Submit and close the document.

Exercise 2-21

Select and repeat text, and create a paragraph using line breaks.

1. Open the file **Video**.

2. In the first sentence, replace "our company" with **Campbell's Confections**.

3. Use the **Repeat** command to repeat the keyed text to the left of the word "Customers" in the last sentence. Enter a space after "Confections and change the "C" in "Customers" to lowercase.

4. In the second sentence, replace "the factory on Monroe Street" with **any of our 24 retail stores**.

5. Move to the end of the document and press Enter .

6. Key the text shown in Figure 2-16 as a single paragraph, using a line break for each new line.

Figure 2-16

```
Our newest stores are located in the following cities:
Fairmont, West Virginia
Edinboro, Pennsylvania
Massillon, Ohio
```

7. Save the document as *[your initials]*2-21 in your Lesson 2 folder.

8. Submit and close the document.

Exercise 2-22

Select and edit text, and insert a nonbreaking space.

1. Open the file **Factory - 2.**

2. Split the first paragraph at the sentence that begins "The chocolate factory."

3. Merge the second paragraph with the third paragraph. Be sure to insert a space between sentences.

4. Spell out "sq." and "ft." Replace "all of its" with **the**.

5. At the end of the last paragraph, key this sentence:

   Educational materials are available for elementary and middle school teachers.

6. Add a nonbreaking space between "June" and "30."

7. Insert the following sentence at the end of the first paragraph.

   The factory hosts special events throughout the year such as Candy Making 101 and Secrets of Dipping Strawberries. Each year it sponsors an expert chocolatier to demonstrate the art of making chocolate.

8. Save the document as *[your initials]*2-22 in your Lesson 2 folder.

9. Submit and close the document.

Exercise 2-23 ◆ Challenge Yourself

Select and edit text, use formatting characters, and enter summary information.

1. Open the file **Summer**.

2. Revise the document as shown in Figure 2-17.

Figure 2-17

Summer is a great time to visit Grove City. ~~In June,~~ the Grove City Area Chamber of Commerce hosts the annual Strawberry Days Art & Music Festival. *(in June)* *(Visitors can)* Enjoy free working exhibitions, live entertainment, and wonderful ethnic food. The July *(fourth of)* 4 patriotic celebration and fireworks are a special treat. Dozens of aerial *(fantastic)* ~~displays~~ and ~~fantastic~~ ground displays are all part of the Fireworks Spectacular at Memorial Park.

In August, the Chamber of Commerce hosts Art in the Park. This annual event features more than 100 artisans with a wide variety of fine art and handcrafted treasures.

3. Add the following sentence after "Music Festival in June" in the first paragraph. **The festival features more than 75 craftspeople and artists.**

4. In the last sentence of the first paragraph, replace "wonderful" with **a wide variety of**

5. Change the last paragraph so it becomes three lines of text, as follows (use line breaks to start new lines):
   Coming in August:
   Art in the Park
   Fine art and handcrafted treasures

6. Select the three-line paragraph you just created.

7. Press ⬛Delete⬛, and then undo the deletion.

8. At the end of the first paragraph, change "food" to **foods**

9. Save the document named *[your initials]***2-23** in your Lesson 2 folder.

10. Open the Properties dialog box. Key **Summer in Grove City** as the **Title**, key your name as the **Author**, and key **Summer tourist attractions** in the **Comments** box.

11. Save the document and submit your work.

On Your Own

In these exercises you work on your own, as you would in a real-life business environment. Use the skills you've learned to accomplish the task—and be creative.

Exercise 2-24

Write a short paragraph about a nearby town or city. Print the document. Edit the document, using the skills you learned in this lesson and changing the information to reflect the town or city where you live. Use nonbreaking spaces, if needed. Key your name as the author in the Document Property dialog box. Save the document as *[your initials]*2-24 and submit it.

Exercise 2-25

Open the file **Meeting Favors**. Use your editing skills to change each paragraph, making the document more concise and changing the subject to school favors. Save the document as *[your initials]*2-25. Submit your work.

Exercise 2-26

Key a short portion of a historical text or novel (written before the twentieth century)—approximately one-half page of document text. Edit the text to make the language more contemporary. On the Summary tab of the Document Properties dialog box, show the original author under Author. Under Comments, key **Modified by [your name]**. Save the document as *[your initials]*2-26. Submit your work.

Formatting Characters

MCAS OBJECTIVES

In this lesson:
WW 07 2.1.1
WW 07 2.1.3
WW 07 3.3.3

After completing this lesson, you will be able to:

1. Work with fonts.

2. Apply basic character formatting.

3. Work with the Font dialog box.

4. Repeat and copy character formats.

5. Change case and highlight text.

6. Create a drop cap.

7. Automatically format text and numbers.

Estimated Time: 1 hour

Every document is based on a theme. A *theme* is a set of formatting instructions for the entire document. Themes include fonts, colors, and effects.

Character formatting is used to emphasize text. You can change character formatting by making text bold or italic, for example, or by changing the style of the type. Word also provides special features to copy formats, highlight text, and automatically format text and numbers.

Working with Fonts

A *font* is a type design applied to an entire set of characters, including all letters of the alphabet, numerals, punctuation marks, and other keyboard symbols. Every theme defines two fonts—one for headings and one for body text.

Figure 3-1
Examples of fonts

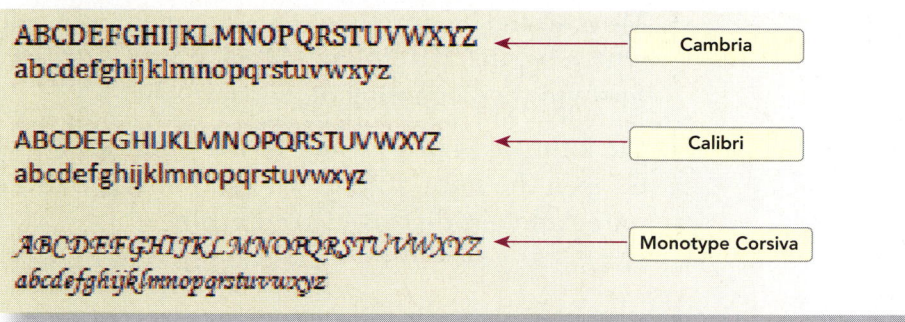

Cambria

Calibri

Monotype Corsiva

NOTE

The default theme fonts are Calibri, a sans serif font, and Cambria, a serif font. The default font size is 11.

Calibri is an example of a plain font; Cambria is more ornate; and Monotype Corsiva is an example of a more stylized font. Calibri is a *sans serif* font because it has no decorative lines, or serifs, projecting from its characters. Cambria is a *serif* font because it has decorative lines. Fonts are available in a variety of sizes, measured in *points*. There are 72 points to an inch. Like other character formatting, you can use different fonts and font sizes in the same document.

Figure 3-2
Examples of different point sizes

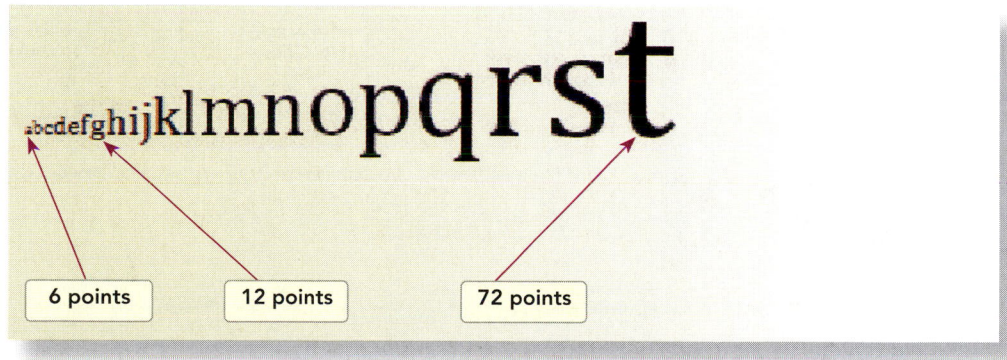

6 points   **12 points**   **72 points**

Exercise 3-1   CHANGE FONTS AND FONT SIZES USING THE RIBBON

The easiest way to choose fonts and font sizes is to use the Ribbon. The Home tab includes the Font group that contains frequently used formatting commands.

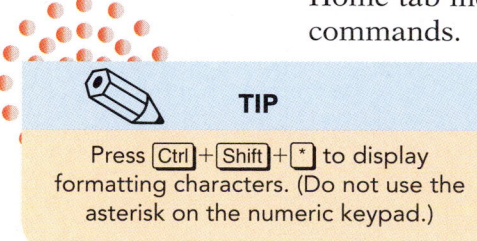

TIP

Press Ctrl + Shift + * to display formatting characters. (Do not use the asterisk on the numeric keypad.)

1. Open the file **Music**.

2. Click the Show/Hide ¶ button ¶ to display paragraph marks and space characters if they are not already showing.

3. Move to the beginning of the document and select the first line, which begins "Attention." (Remember, you can press Ctrl + Home to move to the beginning of a document.)

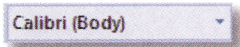

4. Click the down arrow next to the Font box Calibri (Body) on the Ribbon to open the Font drop-down list. Fonts are listed alphabetically by name and are displayed graphically.

Figure 3-3
Choosing a font

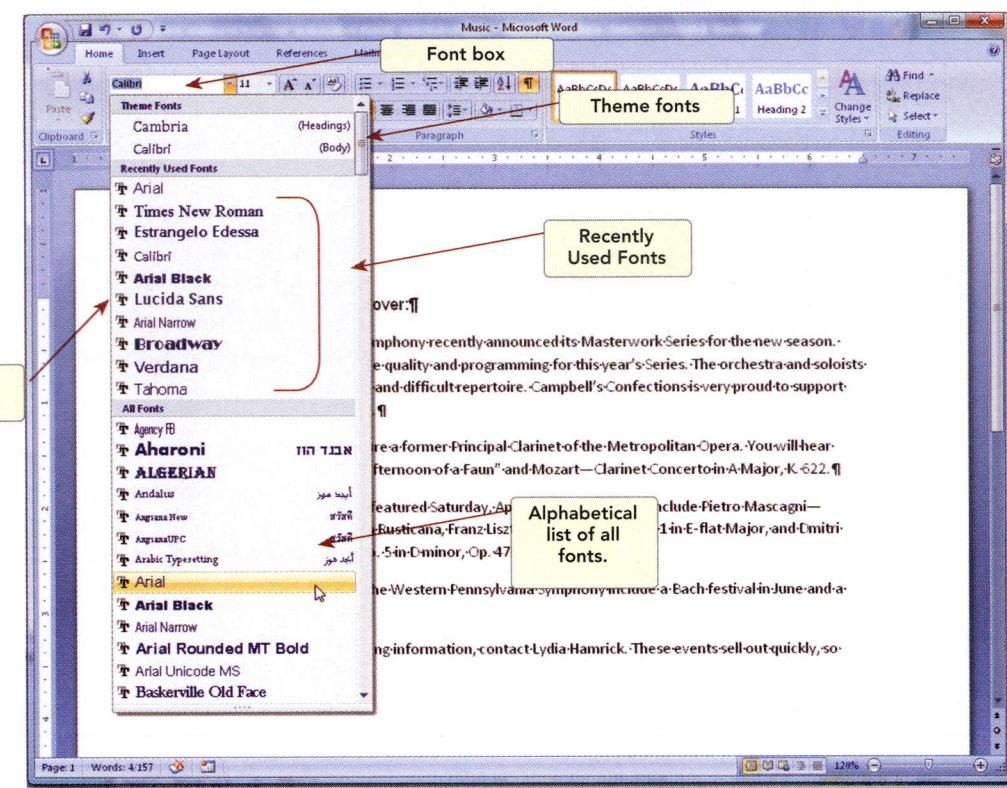

NOTE

The fonts you used most recently appear below the Theme Fonts. Shaded divider lines separate the Theme Fonts, Recently Used Fonts, and the list of All Fonts.

5. Using ↓ or the scroll box on the font list's scroll bar, choose Arial.

6. Click the down arrow to open the Font Size drop-down list ⒒ ▾ and choose 16 points. Now the first line stands out as a headline.

Figure 3-4
Choosing a font size

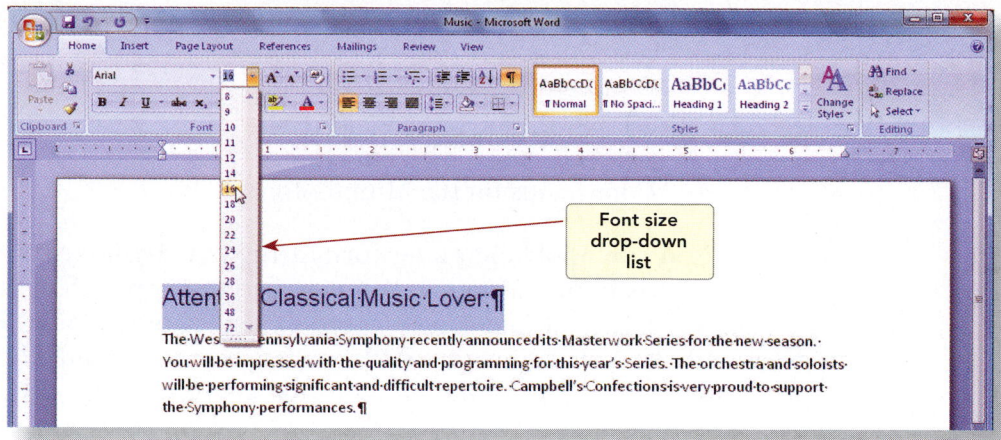

Font size
drop-down
list

Exercise 3-2   **CHANGE FONT SIZE USING KEYBOARD SHORTCUTS**

If you prefer keyboard shortcuts, you can press Ctrl+Shift+> to increase the font size or Ctrl+Shift+< to decrease the font size.

TIP

Sometimes text might appear bold on your screen when it is simply a larger font size.

1. Move the insertion point to the end of the paragraph that begins "For reservations," and press Enter to start a new paragraph.

2. Press Ctrl+Shift+> and key **Call Lydia at 555-2025**. The new sentence appears in 12-point type.

3. Press Enter to begin another paragraph. Press Ctrl+Shift+< to reduce the font size to 11 points and key **Credit card payments are accepted.**

Basic Character Formatting

The basic font styles or character formats are bold, italic, and underline. Text can have one or more character formats.

TABLE 3-1 Character Formatting

Attribute	Example
Normal	This is a sample.
Bold	**This is a sample.**
Italic	*This is a sample.*
Underline	<u>This is a sample.</u>
Bold and italic	***This is a sample.***

The simplest ways to apply basic character formatting are to use:

- Commands on the Ribbon
- Keyboard shortcuts
- Commands on the Mini toolbar

You can apply character formatting to existing text, including existing text that is noncontiguous. You can also turn on a character format before you key new text and turn it off after you enter the text. For example, you can click the Bold button **B**, key a few words in bold, click the button again to turn off the format, and continue keying regular text.

Exercise 3-3   APPLY BASIC CHARACTER FORMATTING USING THE RIBBON

1. Select "Mozart—Clarinet Concerto in A Major, K. 622" (not including the period).

2. Click the Bold button **B** on the Ribbon to format the text bold. (The Bold command is located in the Font group.)

3. With the text still selected, click the Italic button *I* on the Ribbon to format the text bold and italic.

4. Click the Bold button **B** again to turn off the bold format and to leave the text as italic only. Click the Bold button **B** again to restore the bold-italic formatting.

NOTE

The Home tab on the Ribbon displays by default. If the Home tab is not the active tab, click the Home tab to make it active and to display the Font group commands.

Figure 3-5
Using the Ribbon to apply character formatting

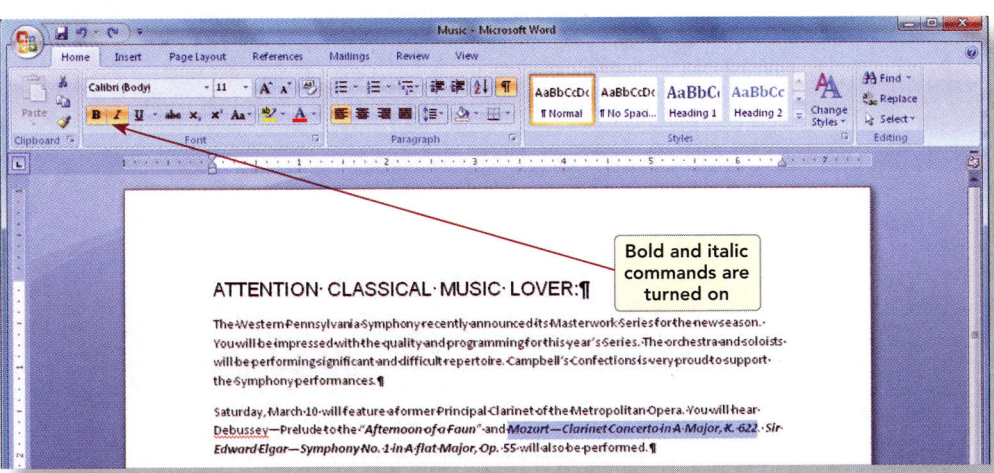

5. Move the insertion point to the end of the same paragraph and press Spacebar once.

6. Click the Bold button  and the Italic button , and key **Sir Edward Elgar—Symphony No. 1 in A-flat Major, Op. 55** in bold italic.

7. Click both buttons to turn off the formatting, press [Spacebar], and complete the sentence by keying **will also be performed.**

8. Select the bold italic text "Mozart—Clarinet Concerto in A Major, K. 622" again.

9. Press [Ctrl] and select the bold italic text **"Sir Edward Elgar—Symphony No. 1 in A-flat Major, Op. 55"** as well.

> **NOTE**
>
> When text is selected, a Mini toolbar appears with character and paragraph formatting commands.

10. Click the Underline button on the Ribbon to underline the noncontiguous selections.

11. Click the Undo button to remove the underlines.

12. Select the first line in the document.

13. Click the Change Case button and click **UPPERCASE**.

Exercise 3-4   APPLY AND REMOVE BASIC CHARACTER FORMATTING USING KEYBOARD SHORTCUTS

If you prefer to keep your hands on the keyboard instead of using the mouse, you can use keyboard shortcuts to turn basic character formatting on and off. You can press [Ctrl]+[B] for bold, [Ctrl]+[I] for italic, and [Ctrl]+[U] for underline. To remove character formatting from selected text, press [Ctrl]+[Spacebar].

1. Select the text "Afternoon of a Faun."

2. Press [Ctrl]+[B] to format the selected text bold and press [Ctrl]+[I] to add italic.

3. Move the insertion point to the end of the document, and press [Enter] to start a new paragraph.

4. Press [Caps Lock], press [Ctrl]+[B] to turn on the bold option, and key **jazz fans note:** in bold capital letters.

5. Press [Caps Lock] to turn it off, press [Spacebar], and continue keying in bold:

   The first annual Jazz Festival, featuring some of the world's greatest musicians, will be held next May.

6. Select the bold-italic text "Afternoon of a Faun" again and press [Ctrl]+[Spacebar] to remove the formatting.

7. Click the Undo button to restore the bold-italic formatting.

Exercise 3-5

APPLY AND REMOVE BASIC CHARACTER FORMATTING USING THE MINI TOOLBAR

The Mini toolbar appears when you select text in a document. You can click any of the buttons to apply or remove character formatting from the selected text.

1. Select the first line of text. Notice the Mini toolbar displays.

Figure 3-6
Mini toolbar

2. Click the drop-down arrow beside the Font Color button 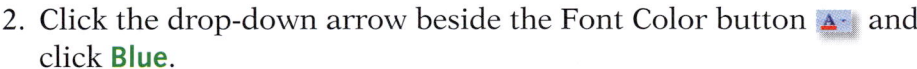 and click **Blue**.

3. Click the Grow Font button , and notice the change in the font size. Click the Shrink Font button .

Using the Font Dialog Box

The Font dialog box offers a wider variety of options than those available on the Ribbon. You can conveniently choose several options at one time.
There are several ways to open the Font dialog box:

- Click the Font Dialog Box Launcher.

- Right-click (use the right mouse button) selected text to display a *shortcut menu,* and then choose **Font**. A shortcut menu shows a list of commands relevant to a particular item you click.

- Keyboard shortcuts.

Figure 3-7
Shortcut menu

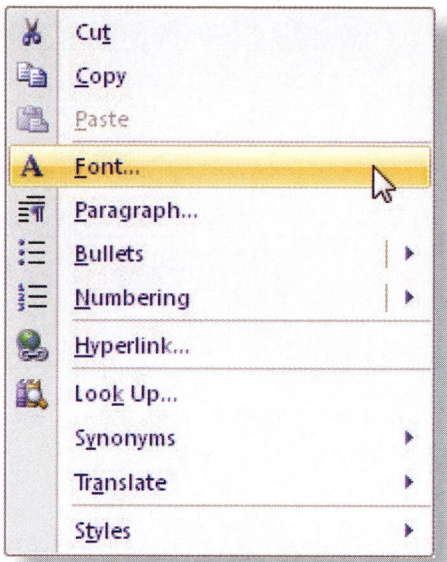

Exercise 3-6   **CHOOSE FONTS AND FONT STYLES USING THE FONT DIALOG BOX**

1. Select the first line of text, which is currently 16-point Arial and blue.

2. Click the arrow in the lower right corner of the Font group on the Ribbon. The Font dialog box displays.

Figure 3-8
Font Dialog Box
Launcher

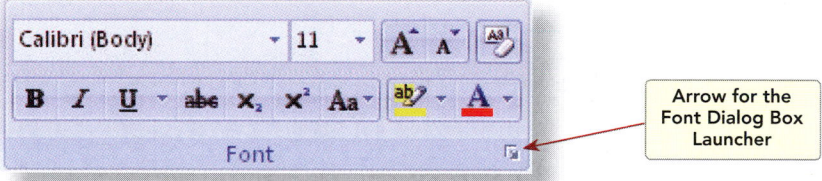

Arrow for the
Font Dialog Box
Launcher

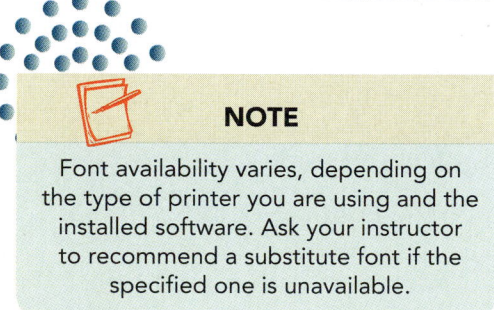

NOTE

Font availability varies, depending on the type of printer you are using and the installed software. Ask your instructor to recommend a substitute font if the specified one is unavailable.

3. Choose **Monotype Corsiva** from the **Font** list, **Bold Italic** from the **Font style** list, and **18** from the **Size** list. Look at your choices in the **Preview** box and click **OK**.

Figure 3-9
Using the Font
dialog box

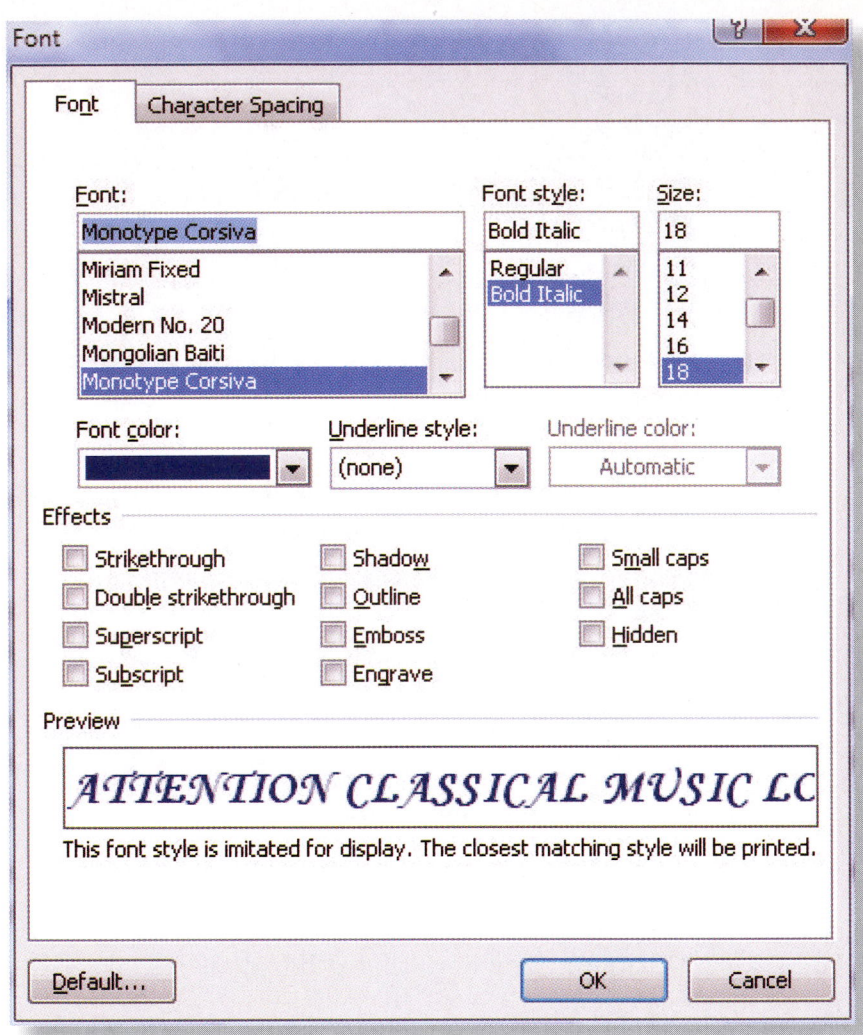

Exercise 3-7   APPLY UNDERLINE OPTIONS AND CHARACTER EFFECTS

In addition to choosing font, font size, and font style, you can choose font color, a variety of underlining options, and special character effects from the Font dialog box.

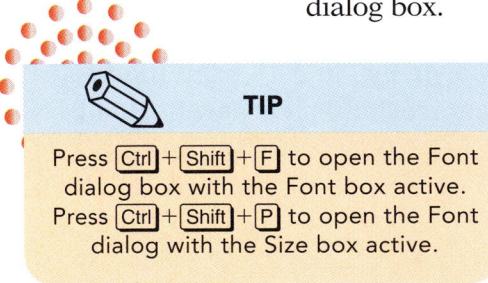

TIP

Press Ctrl + Shift + F to open the Font dialog box with the Font box active. Press Ctrl + Shift + P to open the Font dialog with the Size box active.

1. Select the text "JAZZ FANS NOTE" in the last paragraph (do not select the colon).

2. Press Ctrl + D to open the Font dialog box.

3. Click the down arrow to open the **Underline style** drop-down list. Drag the scroll box down to see all the available underline styles. Choose one of the dotted line styles.

4. Click the down arrow next to the Font color box and choose "Green". (Each color is identified by name when you point to it.) Both the text and the underline are now green in the **Preview** box.

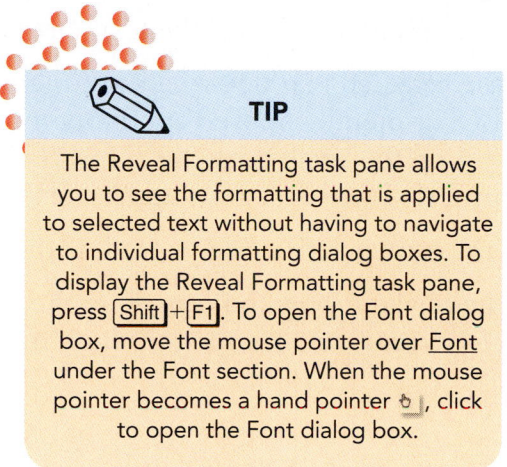

TIP

The Reveal Formatting task pane allows you to see the formatting that is applied to selected text without having to navigate to individual formatting dialog boxes. To display the Reveal Formatting task pane, press [Shift]+[F1]. To open the Font dialog box, move the mouse pointer over Font under the Font section. When the mouse pointer becomes a hand pointer 👆, click to open the Font dialog box.

Figure 3-10
Font color options in the Font dialog box

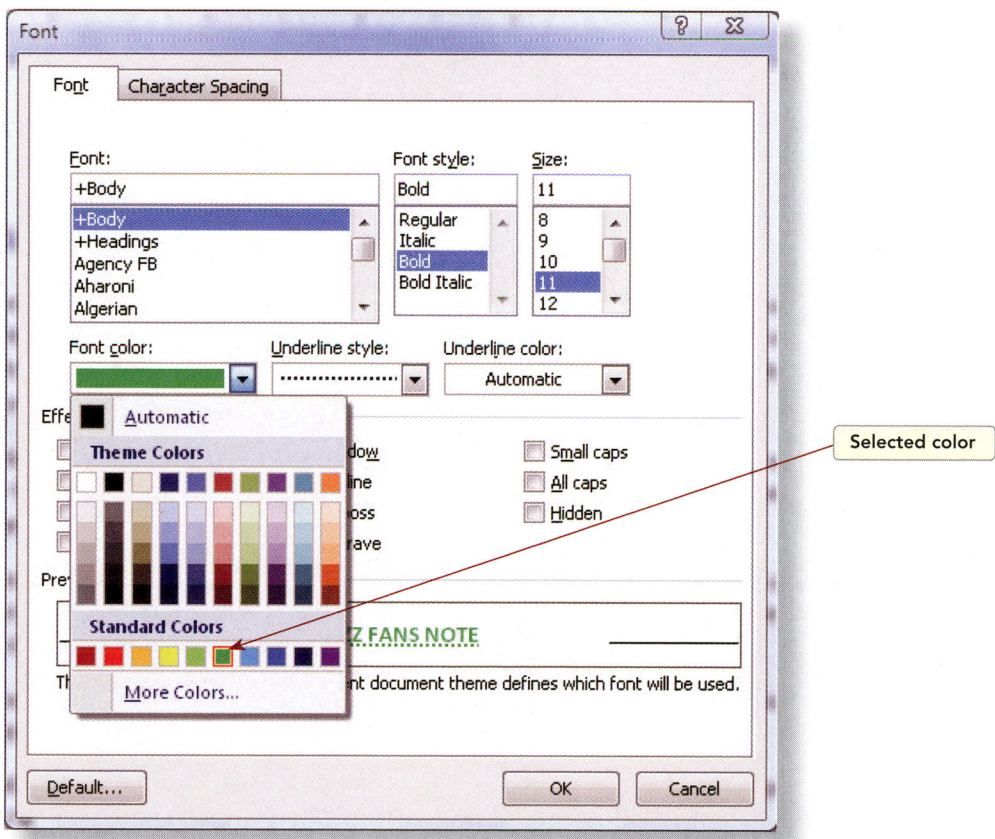

5. Click the down arrow next to the **Underline color** box and choose **Red**.

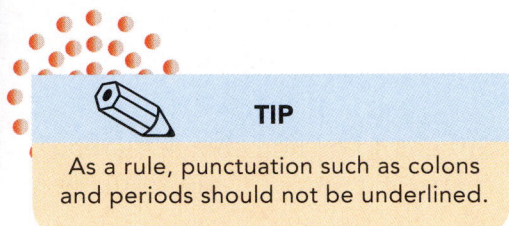

6. Click **OK**. The text is green with a red dotted underline.

7. Select the sentence after the green, dotted-underlined text "JAZZ FANS NOTE:"

8. Move the mouse pointer to the Ribbon and click the Clear Formatting button .

9. In the same sentence, select the text "Jazz Festival."

10. Click the selected text with the right mouse button, and from the shortcut menu, choose **Font** to open the Font dialog box. Under **Effects**, click the **Small caps** check box and click **OK**. The text that was formerly lowercase now appears in small capital letters.

11. Select the sentence that begins "Call Lydia."

12. Click the Strikethrough button on the Ribbon. The text appears with a horizontal line running through it.

TABLE 3-2 Font Effects in the Font Dialog Box

Effect	Description and Example
Strikethrough	Applies a ~~horizontal line~~.
Double strikethrough	Applies a ~~double horizontal line~~.
Superscript	Raises text ^{above} other characters on the same line.
Subscript	Places text $_{below}$ other characters on the same line.
Shadow	Applies a **shadow**.
Outline	Displays the inner and outer border of text.
Emboss	Makes text appear raised off the page.
Engrave	Makes text appear imprinted on the page.
Small Caps	Makes lowercase text SMALL CAPS.
All Caps	Makes all text UPPERCASE.
Hidden	Hidden text does not print and appears on-screen only if Word's Display options are set to display hidden text. See **File menu, Word Options.**

13. Click the Undo button to undo the strikethrough effect.

Exercise 3-8 — USE KEYBOARD SHORTCUTS FOR UNDERLINE OPTIONS AND FONT EFFECTS

Word provides keyboard shortcuts for some underlining options and font effects as an alternative to using the Ribbon or opening the Font dialog box.

REVIEW

Remember that Ctrl+U turns on and off standard underlining.

1. Start a new sentence at the end of the last paragraph by keying **To beat the heat, bring plenty of H2O.**

2. Select the "2" in H2O.

3. Press Ctrl+= to make it subscript.

4. Select the green, dotted-underlined text "JAZZ FANS NOTE." Press Ctrl+Shift+W to change the dotted underlining to words-only underlining.

TABLE 3-3 Keyboard Shortcuts for Underlining and Character Effects

Keyboard Shortcut	Action
Ctrl + Shift + W	Turn on or off words-only underlining.
Ctrl + Shift + D	Turn on or off double underlining.
Ctrl + Shift + =	Turn on or off superscript.
Ctrl + =	Turn on or off subscript.
Ctrl + Shift + K	Turn on or off small capitals.
Ctrl + Shift + A	Turn on or off all capitals.
Ctrl + Shift + H	Turn on or off hidden text.

Exercise 3-9 — CHANGE CHARACTER SPACING

The **Character Spacing** tab in the Font dialog box offers options for changing the space between characters or the position of text in relation to the baseline. Character spacing can be expanded or condensed horizontally, as well as raised or lowered vertically.

1. Select the first line of text, which begins "Attention."

2. Open the **Font** dialog box and click the **Character Spacing** tab.

3. Click the down arrow to open the **Scale** drop-down list. Click **150%** and notice the change in the **Preview** box. Change the scale back to **100%**.

Word 2007

Figure 3-11
Character Spacing
tab

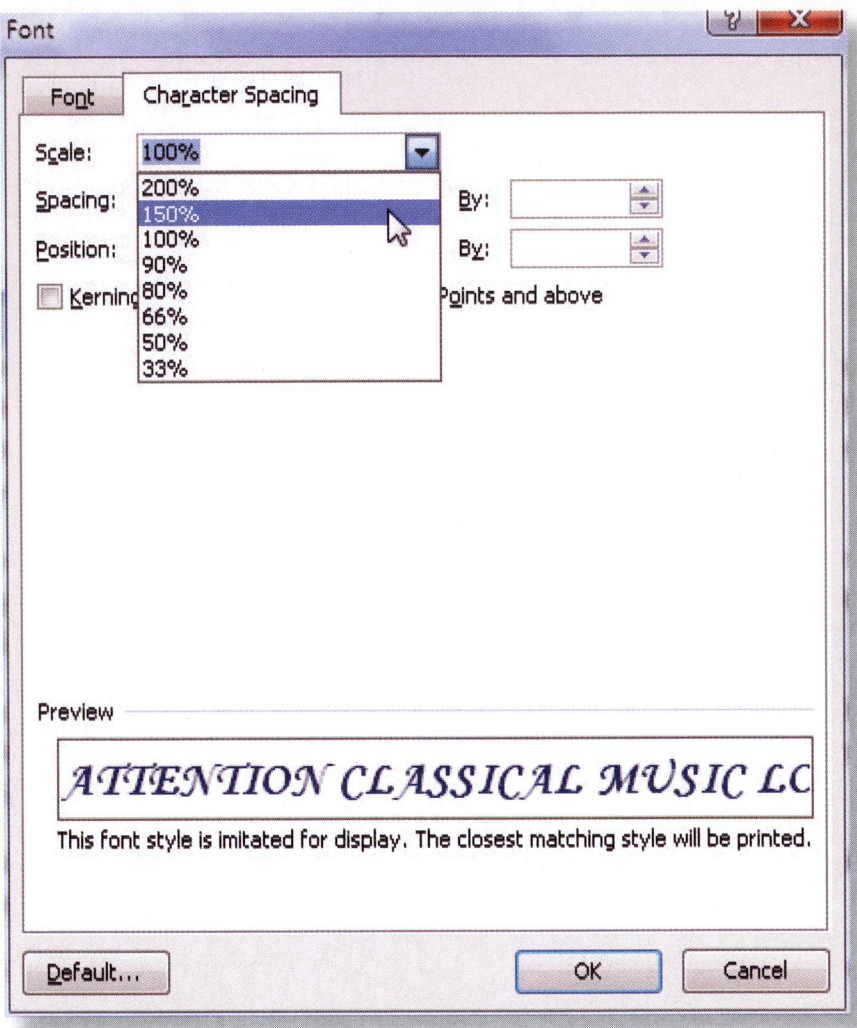

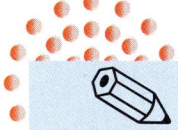
TIP

You can increase the space between characters even more by increasing the number in the **By** box (click the arrows or key a specific number). Experiment with the **Spacing** and **Scale** options on your own to see how they change the appearance of text.

4. Click the down arrow to display the **Spacing** options. Click **Expanded**, and then click **OK**. The text appears with more space between each character.

5. In the Save As dialog box, create a new folder for your Lesson 3 files and save the document as *[your initials]*3-9.

NOTE

Remember to use this folder for all the exercise documents you create in this lesson.

Repeating and Copying Formatting

You can use F4 or Ctrl+Y to repeat character formatting. You can also copy character formatting with a special tool on the Ribbon—the Format Painter button.

Exercise 3-10   REPEAT CHARACTER FORMATTING

Before trying to repeat character formatting, keep in mind that you must use the Repeat command immediately after applying the format. In addition, the Repeat command repeats only the last character format applied. (If you apply multiple character formats from the Font dialog box, the Repeat command applies all formatting.)

1. Select "Intermezzo" and click the Italic button to italicize the text.

2. Select "Piano Concerto No. 1 in E-flat Major" and press F4 to repeat your last action (turning on Italic format).

3. Select the sentence that begins "Call Lydia."

4. Open the **Font** dialog box. Click the **Font** tab, if it is not already displayed, and choose another font, such as Impact. Select the font size **12 points**, and change the font color to **red**. Click **OK**. The text appears with the new formatting.

5. Select the text "JAZZ FANS NOTE:" (including the colon) and press F4. Word repeats all the formatting you chose in the Font dialog box. If you apply each character format separately, using the Ribbon, the Repeat command applies only the last format you chose.

Figure 3-12
Repeating character formatting

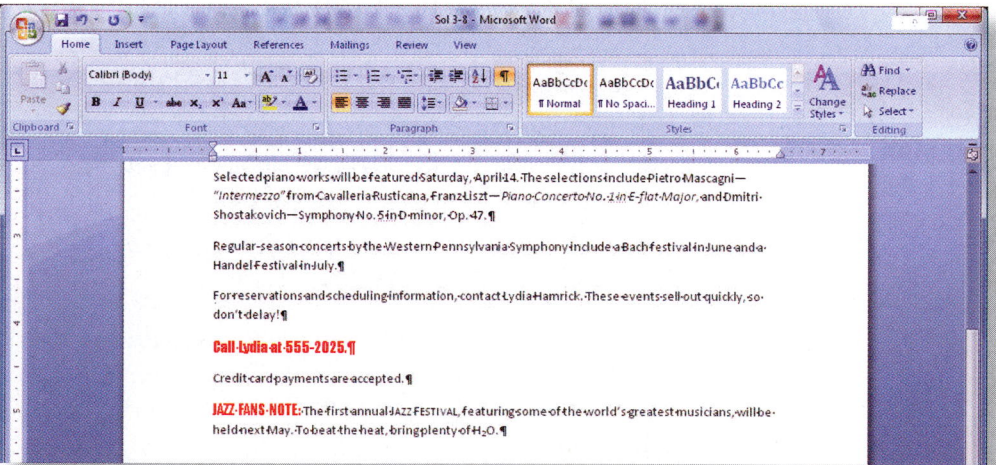

Exercise 3-11   COPY CHARACTER FORMATTING

The Format Painter button makes it easy to copy a character format. This is particularly helpful when you copy text with multiple formats, such as bold-italic small caps.

To use Format Painter to copy character formatting, first select the text with the formatting you want to copy, and then click the Format Painter button. The mouse pointer changes to a paintbrush with an I-beam pointer. Use this pointer to select the text to which you want to apply the copied formatting.

1. In the paragraph that begins "The Western," select "Masterwork Series" and click the Underline button.

2. With the text still selected, click the Format Painter button on the Ribbon. When you move the pointer back into the text area, notice the new shape of the pointer.

3. Use the paintbrush pointer to select "Series" in the next sentence. This copies the underlining to the selected text, and the pointer returns to its normal shape.

4. Select the small caps words "Jazz Festival" in the last paragraph.

5. Double-click the Format Painter button. Double-clicking lets you copy formatting repeatedly.

6. Scroll to the top of the document. Notice that the paintbrush pointer becomes an arrow when you move out of the text area to use the scroll bars.

7. Select the sentence that begins "The Western." The small caps formatting is applied to the sentence, and the pointer remains the paintbrush pointer.

8. Scroll down to the line that begins "Call Lydia" and select the sentence. The paintbrush pointer copies the new formatting over the old formatting.

9. Press Esc or click the Format Painter button to stop copying and to restore the normal pointer.

Changing Case and Highlighting Text

You have used Caps Lock to change case, and you have seen the Small Caps and All Caps options in the Font dialog box. You can also change the case of characters by using keyboard shortcuts and the Change Case command on the Ribbon.

Exercise 3-12   CHANGE CASE

1. Select the sentence that begins "Credit card payments." Press [Shift]+[F3]. This keyboard shortcut changes case. Now the text appears in all uppercase letters.

2. With the sentence still selected, press [Shift]+[F3] again. Now the sentence appears in all lowercase letters.

3. Press [Shift]+[F3] again and the original case (sentence case) is restored.

4. Select the first line of the document, and click the Change Case button on the Ribbon.

5. Click **Capitalize Each Word**. This option changes the first letter of each word to uppercase, the common format for titles.

6. Click anywhere in the document to deselect the text.

Exercise 3-13   HIGHLIGHT TEXT

To emphasize parts of a document, you can mark text with a color highlighter by using the Highlight button on the Ribbon, Font group. As with the Format Painter button, when you click the Highlight button, the pointer changes shape. You then use the highlight pointer to select the text you want to highlight. In addition, you can choose from several highlighting colors.

1. Make sure no text is selected. On the Ribbon, click the down arrow next to the Highlight button to display the color choices. Click **Yellow** to choose it as the highlight color. This turns on the Highlight button, and the color indicator box on the button is now yellow.

Figure 3-13
Choosing a highlight color

2. Move the highlight pointer into the text area.

3. Drag the pointer over the phone number in the paragraph that begins "CALL LYDIA."

4. Press ⎡Esc⎤ to turn off the highlighter and restore the normal pointer.

5. Select the first line of text, which begins "Attention."

6. Click the Highlight button  to highlight the selection. This is another way to use the highlighter—by selecting the text and then clicking the Highlight button.

7. Select the first line of text again. Remove the highlight by clicking the down arrow to display the highlight color choices and choosing **No Color**.

8. Select the remaining highlighted text and click the Highlight button. Because "None" was last chosen (as shown in the color indicator box on the button), this action removes the highlight from the selected text.

NOTE

You can use highlighting to mark text as you work on a document or to point out text for others opening the same document later. It might not work as well for printed documents because the colors might print too dark. You can use the shading feature to emphasize text in a printed document.

Creating a Drop Cap

One way to call attention to a paragraph is to use a dropped capital letter, or a *drop cap*. A drop cap is a large letter that appears below the text baseline. It is usually applied to the first letter in the first word of a paragraph.

Exercise 3-14   CREATE A DROP CAP

1. Place the insertion point at the beginning of the paragraph that begins "The Western."

2. Click the **Insert** tab on the Ribbon, and click the Drop Cap button . Click **Dropped**.

3. Undo the drop cap.

4. Click the Drop Cap down arrow and click **Drop Cap Options**. The Drop Cap dialog box opens.

Figure 3-14
Drop Cap dialog box

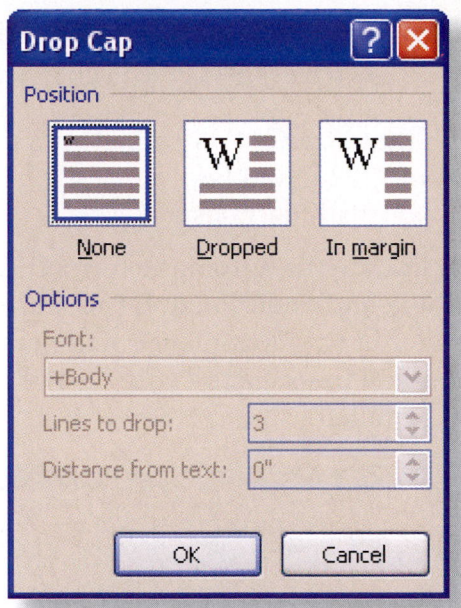

5. Under **Position**, click **Dropped**. This option is used to wrap the paragraph around the letter.

6. Click **OK**. Click within the document to deselect the "T" of "The," which is the height of three lines.

Word's AutoFormat Features

Word has several features that automatically change formatting as you key text or numbers. One of these *AutoFormat* features converts ordinal numbers and fractions into a more readable format, as shown in Table 3-4.

Another AutoFormat feature changes an Internet address into a hyperlink as you key the text. Clicking on the hyperlink takes you to another location, such as an HTML page on the Internet (assuming you are logged onto the Internet).

> **NOTE**
>
> Style manuals in general do not recommend superscript ordinals. To turn off the Ordinals and Fractions AutoFormat, open the Word Options dialog box, click Proofing, and click AutoCorrect Options to open the AutoCorrect dialog box. Click the AutoFormat tab, and click to deselect **Ordinals** and **Fractions** in the Replace section.

TABLE 3-4 Automatic Formatting of Ordinal Numbers and Fractions

Keyed Text	Format Change
1st	1st
2nd	2nd
1/2	$\frac{1}{2}$
1/4	$\frac{1}{4}$

Word 2007

Exercise 3-15   FORMAT ORDINAL NUMBERS AND FRACTIONS AUTOMATICALLY

1. In the paragraph that begins "Call Lydia," move the pointer to the immediate right of "2025" and key **or send an e-mail message to lydiahamrick@campbellsconfections.biz.**

2. Press Spacebar to initiate the automatic formatting. The e-mail address is now blue and underlined. If this were a real e-mail address, any reader of this document could press Ctrl and click the text to send an e-mail message to Lydia (providing the reader had an e-mail program installed).

Figure 3-15
Formatting Hyperlink text

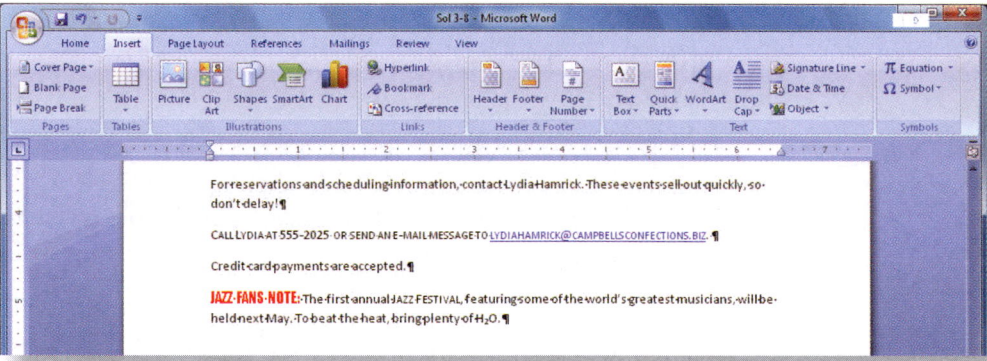

3. Move to the end of the paragraph that begins "Credit card payments." Add a new sentence by keying **Matinee performances are 1/2 price**. Notice that Word automatically converts the numbers and the slash into a fraction.

4. Save the document as *[your initials]*3-15 in your Lesson 3 folder.

5. Submit your work and close the document.

Lesson 3 Summary

- A font is a type design applied to an entire set of characters, including all the letters of the alphabet, numerals, punctuation marks, and other keyboard symbols.

- A font can be serif (with decorative lines) or sans serif (with no decorative lines).

- Fonts are available in a variety of sizes, which are measured in points. There are 72 points to an inch.

- You can use the Ribbon to change fonts and font sizes.

- Keyboard shortcuts can also be used to change font sizes: Ctrl+Shift+> increases the text size and Ctrl+Shift+< decreases the text size.

- Use the Ribbon, Home tab, Font group to apply basic character formatting (for example, bold, italic, and/or underline) to selected contiguous (text that is together) or noncontiguous text (text that is not together).

- Use keyboard shortcuts to apply and remove basic character formatting.

- Use the Mini toolbar to apply character formatting to selected text.

- The Font dialog box can be used to change fonts, font sizes, and font styles. The Font dialog box also has settings for underline styles, font and underline colors, effects such as small caps and shadow (see Table 3-2), and character spacing.

- A hyperlink often appears as blue underlined text you click to open a software feature (such as a dialog box or a Help topic) or to go to an e-mail or a Web address.

- Keyboard shortcuts are available for some underline styles and font effects (see Table 3-3).

- A shortcut menu shows a list of commands relevant to a particular item. To display a shortcut menu, point to the item and right-click the mouse.

- Use F4 or Ctrl+Y to repeat character formatting.

- Use the Format Painter command to copy character formatting. Double-click the button to apply formatting to more than one selection.

- To change the case of selected characters, use the keyboard shortcut Shift+F3 or the Change Case command on the Ribbon, Home tab.

- Use the Highlight command to apply a color highlight to selected text you want to emphasize on-screen.

- Use **Drop Cap** from the Insert tab to create a dropped cap. A drop cap is a large letter that appears below the text baseline. It is usually applied to the first letter in the first word of a paragraph.

- Take advantage of Word's automatic formatting of ordinal numbers and fractions as you key text. An ordinal number is a number that indicates an order (for example, 1st, 3rd, or 107th).

LESSON 3		Command Summary	
Feature	**Button**	**Command**	**Keyboard**
Bold	B	**Home** tab, **Font** group	Ctrl+B
Italic	I	**Home** tab, **Font** group	Ctrl+I
Underline	U	**Home** tab, **Font** group	Ctrl+U
Remove character formatting		**Home** tab, **Font** group	Ctrl+Spacebar
Increase font size	A	**Home** tab, **Font** group	Ctrl+Shift+>
Decrease font size	A	**Home** tab, **Font** group	Ctrl+Shift+<
Change case	Aa	**Home** tab, **Font** group	Shift+F3
Font color	A	**Home** tab, **Font** group	
Text Highlight Color		**Home** tab, **Font** group	

Concepts Review

True/False Questions

Each of the following statements is either true or false. Indicate your choice by circling T or F.

T F   1. You can apply single underlining from the Ribbon.

T F   2. To remove character formatting, press Ctrl + Delete .

T F   3. The Home tab on the Ribbon is used to insert a Drop Cap.

T F   4. Times New Roman is an example of a sans serif font.

T F   5. You can use F4 to repeat text or to repeat character formatting.

T F   6. After clicking the Format Painter button ✔ , you can press Esc to restore the normal pointer.

T F   7. You can use the Font dialog box to change character spacing.

T F   8. You must use the Font tab in the Font dialog box to apply the shadow effect.

Short Answer Questions

Write the correct answer in the space provided.

1. Which Ribbon tab contains a command to highlight text?

_____

2. Which dialog box do you use to choose bold-italic style?

_____

3. What unit of measurement is used to measure fonts?

_____

4. What keyboard shortcut increases the font size of selected text?

_____

5. What character effect places a horizontal line through text?

_____

6. Which command do you use to copy character formatting?

_____

7. What keyboard shortcut do you use to change the case of selected text?

_____

8. What character spacing setting inserts more space between characters?

_____

Critical Thinking

Answer these questions on a separate page. There are no right or wrong answers. Support your answers with examples from your own experience, if possible.

1. Select three examples of effective character formatting in magazine advertisements, articles, or other publications. Describe why you think the character formatting was particularly effective.

2. Using a large font size, key **Fonts & styles** 10 times on 10 separate lines (you can use the **Repeat Typing** command). Use a different font for each line. Describe the differences you see among the fonts.

Skills Review

Exercise 3-16

Apply basic character formatting. Change font and font size.

1. Open the file **Candy - 1**.
2. At the top of the document, press ⌷Enter⌷. Move to the paragraph mark and key **Fine Chocolates**.
3. Change the font for the entire document by following these steps:
   a. Select the entire document by pressing ⌷Ctrl⌷+⌷A⌷.
   b. Open the Font drop-down list on the Ribbon by clicking the down arrow.
   c. Locate and click **Arial**.
4. Change the first line you keyed to 16-point bold by following these steps:
   a. Select the text by moving the pointer to the left of the text. When the arrow points to the text, click the left mouse button.
   b. Choose **16** from the Font Size drop-down list on the Ribbon.

   c. Click the Bold button ⊞ on the Ribbon.
5. Apply italic formatting to noncontiguous text by following these steps:
   a. Move to the end of the document and press ⌷Enter⌷.
   b. Key **Call our toll-free number: 800-555-2025**.
   c. Select the sentence you just keyed.

d. Press and hold ⎡Ctrl⎤ and select the text "Campbell's Confections" in the previous paragraph.

    e. Click the Italic button ⎡*I*⎤.

6. Key new bold text by following these steps:

    a. Move to the end of the document and place the insertion point to the immediate left of the period.

    b. Click the Italic button ⎡*I*⎤ to turn off italic.

    c. Click the Bold button ⎡**B**⎤ to turn on bold. Press the ⎡Spacebar⎤ and key **or visit our Web site at www.campbellsconfections.biz.**

    d. Turn off bold.

7. Save the document as *[your initials]***3-16** in your Lesson 3 folder.

8. Submit and close the document.

Exercise 3-17

Apply formatting options using the Font dialog box and using repeat character formatting.

1. Open the file **Easter Eggs**.

2. Apply character formatting to the first line. Use the Font dialog box and follow these steps:

    a. Select the first line. Click the selected text with the right mouse button, and choose **Font** from the shortcut menu.

    b. Click the **Font** tab, if it is not already displayed. For font, font style, and size, choose **Arial, Bold**, and **14** points.

    c. Apply the effect **Small caps** by clicking the check box.

    d. View your options in the **Preview** box and click **OK**.

3. Apply and repeat character formatting by following these steps:

    a. Select the text "Fruit and Nut:" and press ⎡Ctrl⎤+⎡D⎤ to open the Font dialog box.

    b. Choose the font style **Bold Italic**.

    c. Open the **Font color** drop-down list and choose **Blue**. Click **OK**.

    d. Select the text "Chocolate Nut:" and press ⎡F4⎤. Repeat the formatting through "Chocolate Nut Fudge:"

4. Apply the **strikethrough** and **hidden** text effects from the Font dialog box by following these steps:

    a. Select the last line of text (beginning "Marshmallow:").

    b. Locate and click the Font Dialog Box Launcher icon on the Ribbon.

    c. Click the **Strikethrough** check box.

    d. Click **OK**. Notice the strikethrough effect.

    e. Open the Font dialog box by pressing Ctrl+D, and click the **Hidden** check box.

    f. Click **OK**. The text appears with a dotted underline.

    g. Click the Show/Hide button ¶ to hide the text and formatting characters.

5. Save the document as *[your initials]***3-17** in your Lesson 3 folder.

6. Submit your work.

Exercise 3-18

Copy character formatting and change case.

1. Open the file **WV Stores**.

2. Change the first line to read **Campbell's Confections—West Virginia Retail Stores**

3. At the end of the first line, press Enter and key **premiere chocolates and specialty items**

4. Select the first two lines of text and format them 14-point bold.

5. Use a keyboard shortcut to change the case of the first line to all uppercase by following these steps:

    a. Select the first line of text.

    b. Press Shift+F3.

6. Change the case of the second line using the Change Case dialog box by following these steps:

    a. Select the second line of text.

    b. Click the Change Case button Aa▾ on the Ribbon.

    c. Click **Capitalize Each Word**.

7. Use the Font dialog box to format the first store name, "Campbell's Confections," as bold-italic small caps.

8. Copy the character formatting to the other store names by following these steps:

    a. With the formatted text selected, double-click the Format Painter button.

    b. Drag the pointer over the next store name, "Campbell's Confections."

    c. Continue copying the formatting to the other store names. Use the scroll bar as needed. When you finish copying, click the Format Painter button to restore the normal pointer.

9. In the second line, change "and" to lowercase.

10. Save the document as *[your initials]***3-18** in your Lesson 3 folder.

11. Submit your work, and close the document.

Exercise 3-19

Highlight text, automatically format numbers, and create a dropped capital letter.

1. Start a new document by keying the text shown in Figure 3-16. Use 12-point Arial type.

Figure 3-16

> Bittersweet chocolate also known as semisweet chocolate is the darkest eating chocolate. It also has the highest percentage of chocolate liquor (unsweetened chocolate). Bittersweet chocolate usually consists of 50 percent chocolate liquor, and semi-sweet chocolate typically consists of 35 to 45 percent chocolate liquor. Both have a rich, smooth taste and are used for chocolate chips and baking.

2. Highlight part of the document by following these steps:
   a. Click the down arrow next to the Highlight button , and click the yellow highlight.
   b. Use the highlight pointer to select the text "50 percent."
   c. Press Esc to restore the normal pointer.

3. Create a dropped capital letter by following these steps:
   a. Position the insertion point at the beginning of the document.
   b. Click the **Insert** tab, and click **Drop Cap**.
   c. Click **Dropped**.

4. Remove the highlight by following these steps:
   a. Select the highlighted text "50 percent."
   b. Click the down arrow next to the Highlight button and choose **No Color**.

5. Format the first two words (beginning with "i") as 14-point bold.

6. Save the document as *[your initials]***3-19** in your Lesson 3 folder.

7. Submit and close the document.

Lesson Applications

Exercise 3-20

Apply and copy character formatting. Change font size.

1. Open the file **Milk Chocolate**.

2. Format the first line ("Milk Chocolate") to 14 points, and change the font to Impact. (If Impact is not available, choose another bold-looking font from the Font drop-down list.)

3. Select the text "10 percent" and format the text as italic. Change the font color to blue.

4. Use the Format Painter button 🖌 to apply the formatting of the text "10 percent" to "12 percent."

5. Apply the shadow and small caps effects to the first line.

6. Select "Milk chocolate" at the beginning of the descriptive paragraph under the heading. Use the Ribbon to bold the text and apply italic formatting.

7. Position the insertion point before the word "best." Press F4 to repeat the last selected character formatting (italic), key **very**, and press Spacebar.

8. Press Ctrl + End to go to the end of the document. Press Enter and key **Enjoy!**

9. Select the last line, and change the text to 12-point Times New Roman. Add red double underlining to the line, except the exclamation point.

10. Save the document as *[your initials]*3-20 in your Lesson 3 folder.

11. Submit your work, and close the document.

Exercise 3-21

Apply and copy basic character formatting. Change font size, case, and character spacing.

1. Start a new document by keying the text shown in Figure 3-17, including the corrections. Use 12-point Arial type.

Figure 3-17

> A chocolate glossary is helpful to understand the differences and similarities among chocolate ingredients. Chocolate liquor (unsweetened chocolate) is the ground up center (nibs) of the roasted cocoa bean. It is the basic ingredient of chocolate and cocoa products. Cocoa butter is the vegetable fat extracted during the refining process. ~~It is the base of white chocolate~~ (stet). Cocoa powder is made by removing most of the cocoa butter from the chocolate liquor. The remaining solids are ground to produce unsweetened cocoa powder. There are two types of cocoa powder: Dutch-processed and natural unsweetened cocoa powder.

2. In the first line, change the case of the text "chocolate glossary" to all capitals.

3. Copy or repeat the all-capitals formatting to the following words in the paragraph: "Chocolate liquor," "Cocoa butter," and "Cocoa powder."

4. Create a new paragraph for each term, beginning with "CHOCOLATE LIQUOR." (You should have four paragraphs in the document.)

5. At the beginning of the document, insert one blank line (press Enter once). Key the title **Guide to Chocolate Terminology** at the paragraph mark.

6. Change the text you just keyed to bold, dark blue, and small caps in 16-point type.

7. Format the text "nibs" as italic. Repeat the italic formatting to "Dutch-processed" and "natural unsweetened cocoa powder."

8. Select all the paragraphs below the heading, and change the font size to 11 points.

9. Use the Ctrl key to select noncontiguous text, and select "CHOCOLATE GLOSSARY," "CHOCOLATE LIQUOR," "COCOA BUTTER," AND "COCOA POWDER." Change the font color to light blue.

10. Save the document named *[your initials]*3-21 in your Lesson 3 folder.

11. Submit your work, and close the document.

Exercise 3-22

Apply and copy character formatting, highlight text, and create a dropped capital letter.

1. Open the file **Favors - 2**.

2. Key the text shown in Figure 3-18 at the end of the document. The text should be the last sentence of the last paragraph.

Figure 3-18

> For more information, call our toll-free number 800-555-2025 or visit our Web site www.campbellsconfections.biz.

3. Format the "C" of "Campbell's" in the first paragraph as a dropped capital letter.

4. Highlight the second paragraph (which begins "Our chocolate") in yellow.

5. Format the list of items from "wedding bells" through "other assorted shapes" as 11-point Arial italic small caps.

6. Repeat the formatting for the second list (from "solid milk chocolate" to "dark chocolate with mint filling").

7. Split the last paragraph so "For more information" starts a new paragraph.

8. Copy the formatting from one of the lists to the new last paragraph.

9. Format the phone number in the last paragraph as red, bold, and a dotted underline.

10. Remove the highlight from the second paragraph.

11. Select the first line of the document and format the text with bold, 14 points, and shadow effects.

12. Save the document as *[your initials]***3-22** in your Lesson 3 folder.

13. Submit your work, and close the document.

REVIEW

You need select only one, or a portion of, the formatted words, click the Format Painter button , and then select the new paragraph.

Exercise 3-23 ◆ Challenge Yourself

Apply character formatting, change case, and format numbers automatically.

1. Open the file **Club**.

2. Locate "CC" in the second paragraph. Select the text and apply the strikethrough format.

3. Repeat the strikethrough effect for "CC" in the next paragraph and in the last paragraph.

4. Select "Chocolate Club" in the second paragraph. Format the selected text as blue and small caps.

5. Move to the beginning of the document, and key **Chocolate Club**. Press Enter. Select the title and use the Ribbon to format the title as 14 points, bold, dark blue, and uppercase.

6. Select "$36." Use the Ribbon to format the text with a blue, dotted underline.

7. Copy the format applied to "$36" to "$400."

8. Select "Chocolate Club" in the second paragraph, and click the Clear Formatting button 🖫 on the Ribbon.

9. Save the document as *[your initials]*3-23 in your Lesson 3 folder.

10. Submit your work, and close the document.

On Your Own

In these exercises you work on your own, as you would in a real-life business environment. Use the skills you've learned to accomplish the task—and be creative.

Exercise 3-24

Create a list of 10 companies in which you are interested. (They could be potential employers, local companies, companies that make products in which you are interested—any companies you want.) Include the companies' addresses. Apply interesting font effects to the company name. Copy and repeat the formatting to the other companies in the list. Save the document as *[your initials]*3-24 and submit it.

Exercise 3-25

Create an itinerary for a trip to visit Hershey, Pennsylvania. (Be imaginative! This could be a real trip or a fantasy trip!) To make the itinerary interesting, use as many as possible of the character formatting features you learned in this lesson. Remember, though, the itinerary must be readable. Save the document as *[your initials]*3-25 and submit it.

Exercise 3-26

Log onto the Internet and find an interesting Web site about chocolate. Summarize the information from the site in a Word document at least a half page long. Add a title to the document. Format the first paragraph with a drop cap. Format the document using the character formats presented in the lesson. Save the document as *[your initials]*3-26 and submit it.

Writing Tools

OBJECTIVES

MCAS OBJECTIVES

In this lesson:
WW 07 1.4.1
WW 07 1.4.2
WW 07 4.1.1
WW 07 4.1.2

After completing this lesson, you will be able to:

1. Use AutoComplete, AutoCorrect, and Smart Tags.

2. Work with Building Blocks.

3. Insert the date and time as a field.

4. Check spelling and grammar.

5. Use the Thesaurus and Research task pane.

Estimated Time: 1 hour

Word provides several automated features that save you time when keying frequently used text and correcting common keying errors. Word also provides important writing and research tools: a spelling and grammar checker, a thesaurus, and access to research services. These tools help you create professional-looking documents.

Using AutoComplete, AutoCorrect, and Smart Tags

By now, you might be familiar with three of Word's automatic features, though you might not know their formal names:

*   *AutoComplete* suggests the completed word when you key the first four or more letters of a day, month, or date. If you key "Janu," for example, Word displays a ScreenTip suggesting the word "January," which you can insert by pressing Enter. Continue keying if you do not want the word inserted.

*   *AutoCorrect* corrects commonly misspelled words as you key text. If you key "teh" instead of "the," for example, Word automatically changes the spelling to "the." You can create AutoCorrect entries for text you frequently use, and you can control AutoCorrect options.

- *Smart tags* help you save time by performing actions in Word for which you would normally open other programs (such as Outlook). Word recognizes names, dates, addresses, and telephone numbers, as well as user-defined data types through the use of smart tags, which appear as purple dotted lines.

Exercise 4-1   PRACTICE AUTOCOMPLETE AND AUTOCORRECT

1. Open a new document. Open the **File** menu, and click **Word Options**. Click **Proofing**, and click **AutoCorrect Options** to open the AutoCorrect dialog box. Notice the available AutoCorrect options.

2. Scroll down the list of entries and notice the words that Word corrects automatically (assuming the **Replace text as you type** option is checked).

Figure 4-1
AutoCorrect dialog box

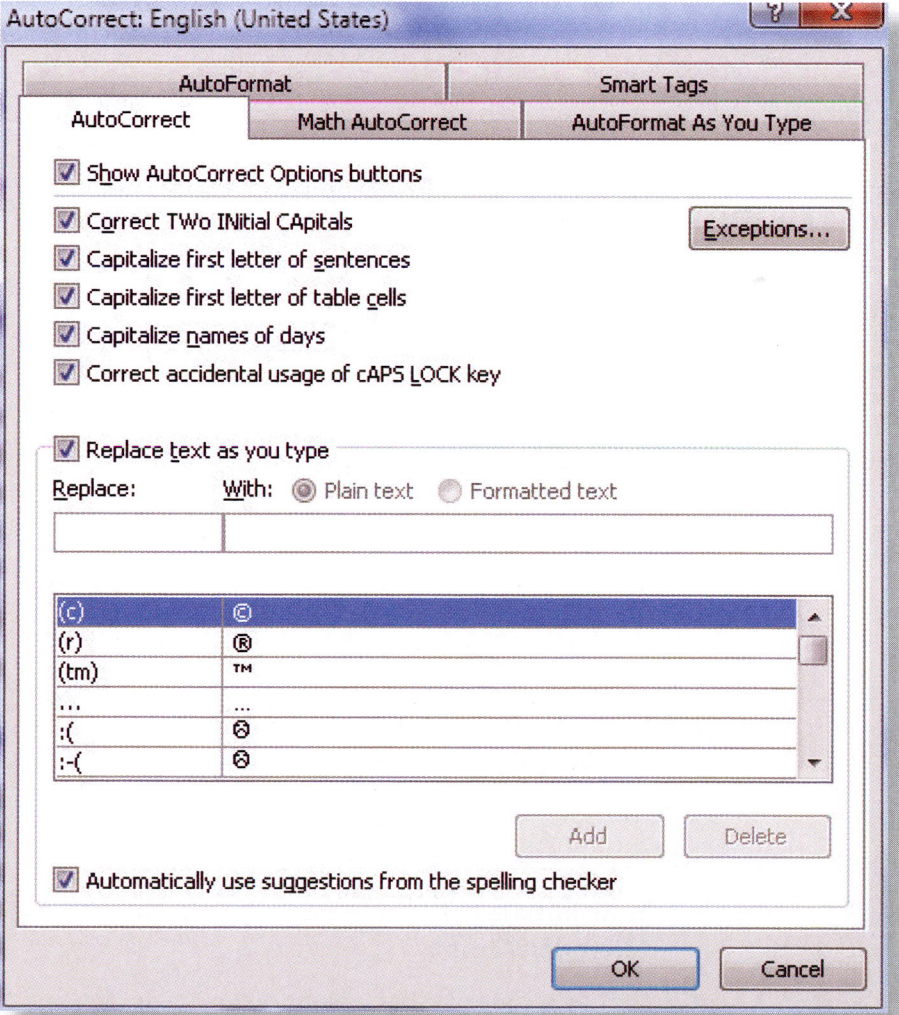

3. Click **Cancel** to close the dialog box. Click **Cancel** to close the Word Options dialog box.

4. Key **i am testing teh AutoCorrect feature.** Press Spacebar. Word corrects the "i" and "teh" automatically.

5. Try keying another incorrect sentence. Using the exact spelling and case as shown, key **TOdya is**. AutoCorrect corrects the spelling and capitalization of "Today."

6. Key today's date, beginning with the month, and then press Spacebar. When you see the AutoComplete ScreenTip that suggests the current date, press Enter.

7. Key a period at the end of the sentence.

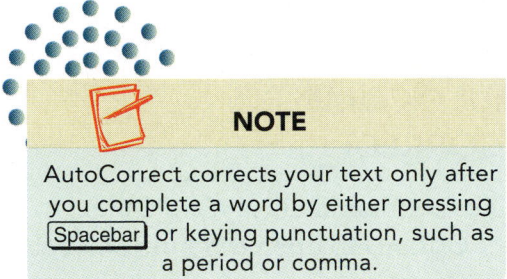

NOTE

AutoCorrect corrects your text only after you complete a word by either pressing Spacebar or keying punctuation, such as a period or comma.

TABLE 4-1 AutoCorrect Options

Options	Description
Correct TWo INitial Capitals	Corrects words keyed accidentally with two initial capital letters, such as "WOrd" or "THis."
Capitalize first letter of sentences	Corrects any word at the beginning of a sentence that is not keyed with a capital letter.
Capitalize first letter of table cells	Corrects any word at the beginning of a table cell that is not keyed with a capital letter.
Capitalize names of days	Corrects a day spelled without an initial capital letter.
Correct accidental usage of cAPS LOCK key	If you press Caps Lock accidentally and then key "tODAY," AutoCorrect changes the word to "Today" and turns off Caps Lock.
Replace text as you type	Makes all corrections automatically.

Exercise 4-2   CREATE AN AUTOCORRECT ENTRY

You can create AutoCorrect entries for words you often misspell. You can also use AutoCorrect to create shortcuts for text you use repeatedly, such as names or phrases. Here are some examples of these types of AutoCorrect entries:

- "asap" for "as soon as possible"

- Your initials to be replaced with your full name, such as **"jh"** for **"Janet Holcomb"**

- "cc" for "Campbell's Confections"

1. Click the Microsoft Office Button , and click **Word Options**. Click **Proofing**.

2. Open the AutoCorrect dialog box by clicking **AutoCorrect Options**. In the **Replace** box, key **fyi**.

3. In the **With** box, key **For your information**.

4. Click the **Add** button to move the entry into the alphabetized list. Click **OK** to close the AutoCorrect dialog box. Click **OK** to close the Word Options dialog box.

5. Start a new paragraph in the current document, and key **fyi, this really works**. Word spells out the entry, just as you specified in the AutoCorrect dialog box.

Exercise 4-3   CONTROL AUTOCORRECT OPTIONS

Sometimes you might not want text to be corrected. You can undo a correction or turn AutoCorrect options on or off by clicking the AutoCorrect Options button and making a selection.

1. Move the I-beam over the word "For" until a small blue box appears beneath it.

Figure 4-2
Controlling
AutoCorrect options

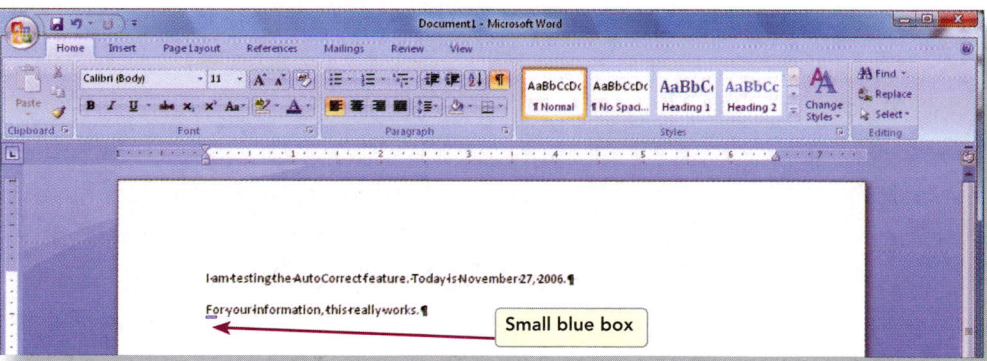

2. Drag the I-beam down over the small blue box until your mouse becomes a pointer and the box turns into the AutoCorrect Options button .

3. Click the button and choose **Change back to "fyi"** from the menu list.

Figure 4-3
Undoing automatic
corrections

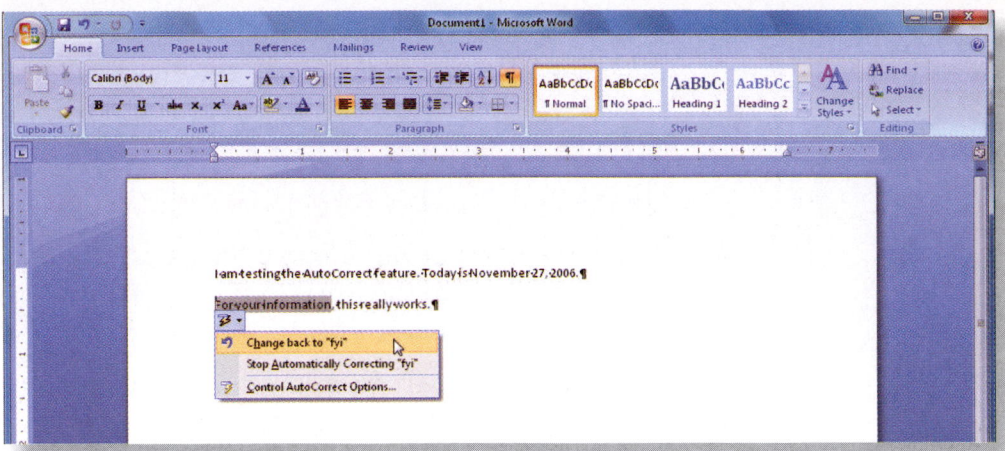

4. Click the AutoCorrect Options button again, and choose **Redo AutoCorrect** from the menu list. The words "For your information" are restored.

5. Click the button again and choose **Control AutoCorrect Options**. The AutoCorrect dialog box opens.

6. Position the insertion point in the Replace text box, and key **fyi**. The AutoCorrect entry displays and is highlighted. Click **Delete**, and then click **OK**.

Exercise 4-4   CREATE AN AUTOCORRECT EXCEPTION

Another way to keep Word from correcting text you do not want corrected is to create an AutoCorrect exception. For example, you might have a company name that uses nonstandard capitalization such as "tuesday's child." In such a case, you can use the AutoCorrect Exceptions dialog box to prevent Word from making automatic changes.

1. In a new paragraph, key the following on two separate lines:
   The ABCs of chocolate:
   ABsolute is a must.

   Notice that AutoCorrect automatically makes the "B" in "ABsolute" lowercase.

2. Open the AutoCorrect dialog box and click **Exceptions**. The AutoCorrect Exceptions dialog box displays.

3. Click the **INitial CAps** tab.

4. Key the exception **ABsolute** in the **Don't Correct** text box. Click **Add**. The entry is now in the list of exceptions.

Figure 4-4
AutoCorrect Exceptions dialog box

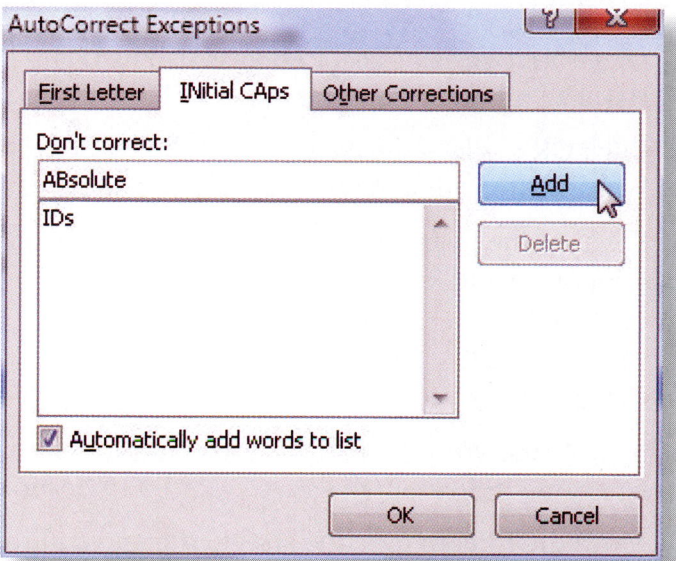

NOTE

Notice when you select "Absolute," the small blue box appears beneath the corrected word.

TIP

Another good example of an AutoCorrect exception is the use of lowercase initials, which are sometimes entered at the bottom of a business letter as reference initials (see Appendix B, "Standard Forms for Business Documents"). In this case, you would not want Word to capitalize the first letter.

5. Click **OK,** to close the AutoCorrect Exceptions dialog box, and then click **OK** again to close the AutoCorrect dialog box. Click **OK** to close the Word Options dialog box if necessary.

6. Select "Absolute" and then key **ABsolute Comfort**

7. Delete the exception: Open the AutoCorrect dialog box, click **Exceptions**, select "ABsolute" from the list, and click **Delete.** Click **OK** to close the AutoCorrect Exceptions dialog box, click **OK** to close the AutoCorrect dialog box, and then click **OK** again to close the Word Options dialog box if necessary.

Exercise 4-5   USE SMART TAGS

Just as Word recognizes an e-mail or Web address and automatically creates a hyperlink, it also recognizes names, dates, addresses, and telephone numbers, as well as user-defined data types through the use of smart tags. You can use this feature to perform actions in Word for which you would normally open other programs, such as Microsoft Outlook. Purple dotted lines beneath text in your document indicate smart tags.

1. Open the **File** menu, and click **Word Options**. Click **Proofing**, and click **AutoCorrect Options**.

2. Click the **Smart Tags** tab, and click the **Label text with smart tags** check box if it is not selected.

3. Under **Recognizers**, select **Address (English)** and **Date (Smart tag lists)**. Deselect all other **Recognizers**.

4. Click **OK** to close the AutoCorrect dialog box. Click **OK** to close the Word Options dialog box.

5. Position the insertion point at the end of the document, and press Enter twice and key:

   Campbells Confections
   25 Main Street
   Grove City, PA 16127

6. Notice that Word recognizes the text as an address and applies a smart tag indicator (the purple dotted underline).

7. Move the I-beam over the street address, and then move your pointer over the Smart Tag Actions button .

8. Click the button to see the list of actions.

Figure 4-5
Smart tag list of actions

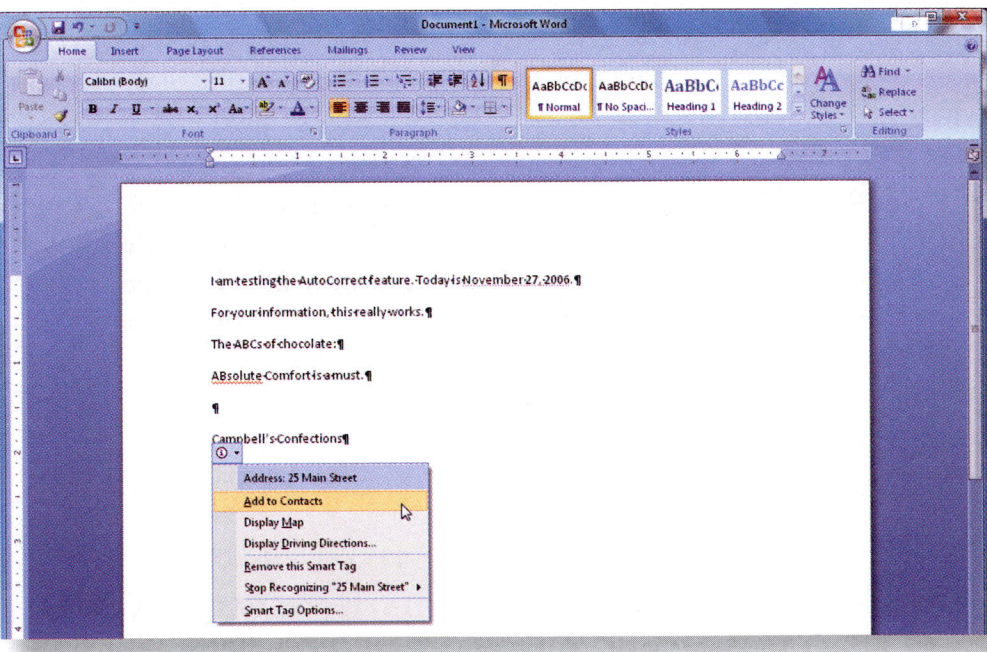

9. Choose **Add to Contacts**. Microsoft Outlook launches, and an Untitled-Contact dialog box opens. You can add the name and address as well as telephone numbers to the listing.

10. Look over the dialog box contents, and close the dialog box. Click **No** when you are asked if you want to save the changes.

11. Close the document without saving.

NOTE

Microsoft Outlook is a program included in the Microsoft Office suite. If it is not set up on your machine, just close the dialog box when it asks you to configure it, or ask your instructor for help. If Outlook does launch, the **Add to Contacts** option lets you record information about individuals and businesses. All this is done from within Word through the use of the smart tag.

Working with AutoText and Building Blocks

NOTE

You can also create AutoText entries for nontext items such as graphics and tables.

AutoText is another feature you can use to insert text automatically. This feature is extremely versatile. You can use it to create AutoText entries for text you use repeatedly (the AutoText entry can even include the text formatting). The text for which you create an AutoText entry can be a phrase, a sentence, paragraphs, logos, and so on.

After you create an entry, you can insert it with just a few keystrokes.

Exercise 4-6   CREATE AN AUTOTEXT ENTRY

To create an AutoText entry, you key the text that you want to save and select it, or you select text that already exists in a document. When you select the text to be used for an AutoText entry, be sure to include the appropriate spaces, blank lines, and paragraph marks.

1. Open the file **Letter - 1**.

2. Press Ctrl+A to select the document.

3. Click the **Insert tab** on the Ribbon.

4. Locate the **Text** group, and click **Quick Parts**. Click **Save Selection to Quick Part Gallery**. The Create New Building Block dialog box displays.

Figure 4-6
Quick Parts menu

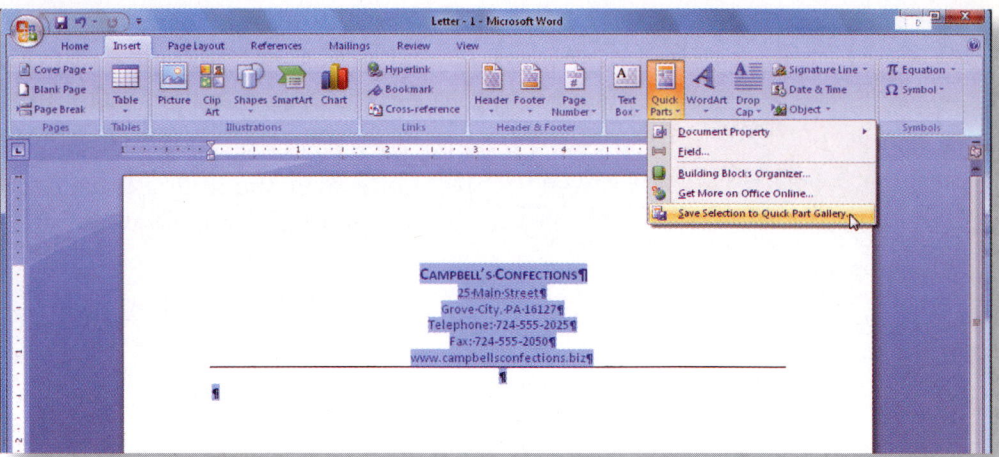

5. Key **[your initials]Letterhead** in the **Name** box. Each AutoText entry must have a unique name.

6. Select **AutoText** from the **Gallery** drop-down list box.

7. Select **General** from the **Category** drop-down list box.

8. Key **Grove City** in the **Description** text box.

NOTE

You can choose to insert AutoText entries as a separate paragraph by choosing **Insert content in its own paragraph**. Choose **Insert content in its own page** if you want the AutoText entry to appear on a new page.

9. Select **Building Blocks** from the **Save in** drop-down list.

10. Select **Insert content only** from the Options drop-down list. Click **OK**.

11. Press Ctrl+End to move to the end of the document. Key the text in Figure 4-7.

Figure 4-7

```
Sincerely,

Thomas Campbell

President

[your initials]
```

12. Select the text you just keyed, and press Alt+F3 to open the Create New Building Block dialog box.

13. Key or select the following information in the Create New Building Block dialog box.

Name:	**[your initials]Closing**
Gallery:	**AutoText**
Category:	**General**
Description:	**Closing**
Save in:	**Building Blocks**
Options:	**Insert content only**

14. Click **OK** to close the Create New Building Block dialog box.

15. Close the document, and do not save the changes.

Exercise 4-7 INSERT AUTOTEXT ENTRIES

To insert an AutoText entry, position the insertion point and open the Building Blocks Organizer. When the Building Blocks Organizer dialog box opens, click one of the column headings to sort the lists. Click the **Name** heading to sort the text alphabetically by name. Click the **Gallery** heading to display the lists by gallery type. AutoText entries will appear at the top of the Gallery listing. If you have an AutoText entry that is unique or short, you can key the first three letters of the entry name and press [F3] to insert the entry.

1. Create a new document.

2. Click the **Insert** tab and locate the **Text** group. Click **Quick Parts** and click **Building Blocks Organizer**. The Building Blocks Organizer dialog box displays.

Figure 4-8
Building Blocks
Organizer dialog box

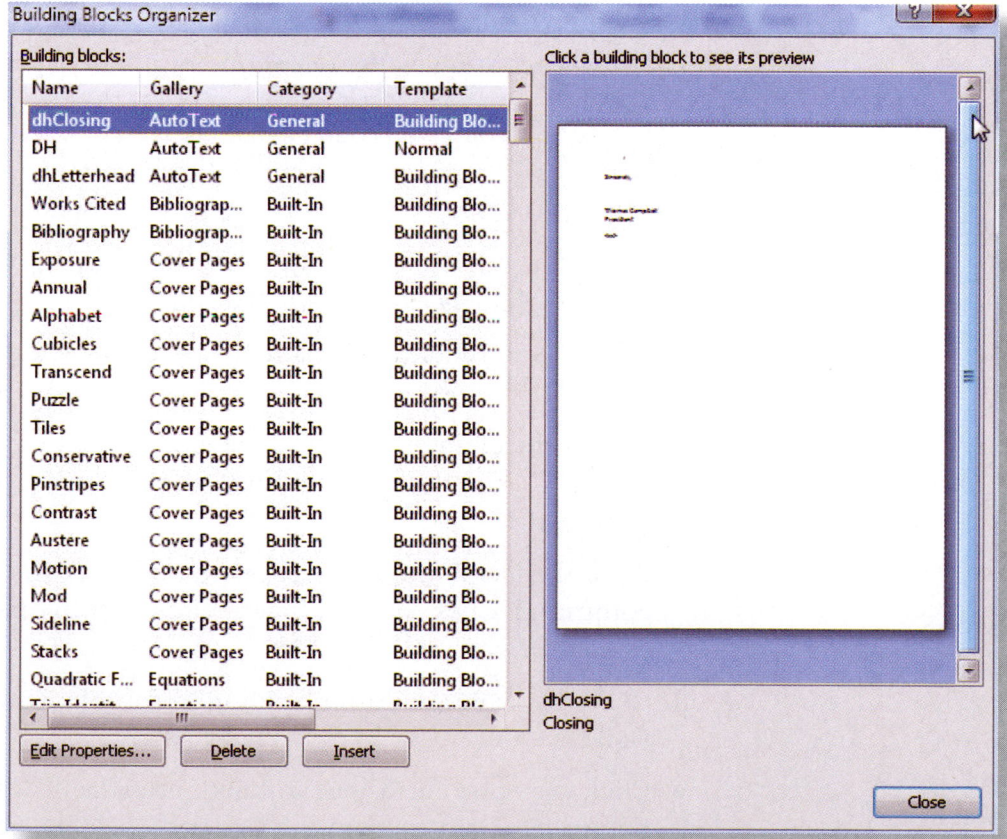

3. Click the **Gallery** heading, and the list sorts by gallery type.

4. Click the **Name** heading, and the list is sorted alphabetically by name.

5. Click the **Gallery** heading, and locate "[your initials]Letterhead" AutoText entry.

6. Click the ***[your initials]*Letterhead** entry, and click **Insert**. The letterhead information is automatically inserted.

7. Click 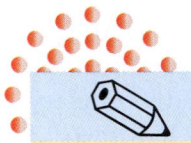 to remove the AutoText entry.

8. Key **[your initials]Letterhead** and press F3 to insert the Autotext entry using the keyboard shortcut.

9. Key **[your initials]Closing** and press F3 to insert the Closing AutoText entry.

> **TIP**
>
> Check Appendix B, "Standard Forms for Business Documents," to double-check that your letter has the correct number of blank lines between items.

Exercise 4-8   EDIT AND DELETE AUTOTEXT ENTRIES

After you create an AutoText entry, it may need to be edited. If you no longer use an entry, you can delete it.

1. Position the insertion point to the right of "Telephone:" in the letterhead, and key the telephone number **724-555-2025**.

2. Select the letterhead text beginning with "Campbell's Confections" and ending with the left aligned paragraph mark.

3. Press Alt + F3 to open the Create New Building Block dialog box.

4. Key **[your initials]Letterhead** in the **Name** box, and select **AutoText** from the **Gallery** drop-down list. Click **OK**.

5. Click **Yes** to redefine the AutoText entry. The entry now includes the telephone number.

6. To test the change, delete all the document text. Key **[your initials]Letterhead** and press F3 to insert the letterhead AutoText.

7. Click the **Insert** tab on the Ribbon, and click the **Quick Parts** command. Click **Building Blocks Organizer** to open the Building Blocks Organizer dialog box.

8. Click the **Gallery** column heading to sort the entries in the list by Gallery type.

9. Click the entry for "[your initials]Letterhead." Click **Delete** to remove the AutoText entry from the Gallery. Click **No**. Click **Close** to return to your document.

Inserting the Date and Time

You have seen that when you begin keying a month, AutoComplete displays the suggested date, and you press [Enter] to insert the date as regular text. You can also insert the date or time in a document as a field. A *field* is a hidden code that tells Word to insert specific text that might need to be updated automatically, such as a date or page number. If you insert the date or time in a document as a field, Word automatically updates it each time you print the document.

There are two ways to insert the date or time as a field:

- Click the **Insert** tab on the Ribbon, and click the **Date and Time** command. Select the desired format from the Date and Time dialog box.

- Press [Alt]+[Shift]+[D] to insert the date, and [Alt]+[Shift]+[T] to insert the time.

Exercise 4-9   INSERT THE DATE AND TIME

You can enter date and time fields that can be updated automatically. You can also choose not to update these fields automatically.

1. Move the insertion point to the end of the current document.

2. Press [Alt]+[Shift]+[D] to enter the default date field.

3. Click the Undo button 🔄.

4. Click the **Insert** tab on the Ribbon, and click the **Date and Time** command to open the Date and Time dialog box.

Figure 4-9
Date and Time
dialog box

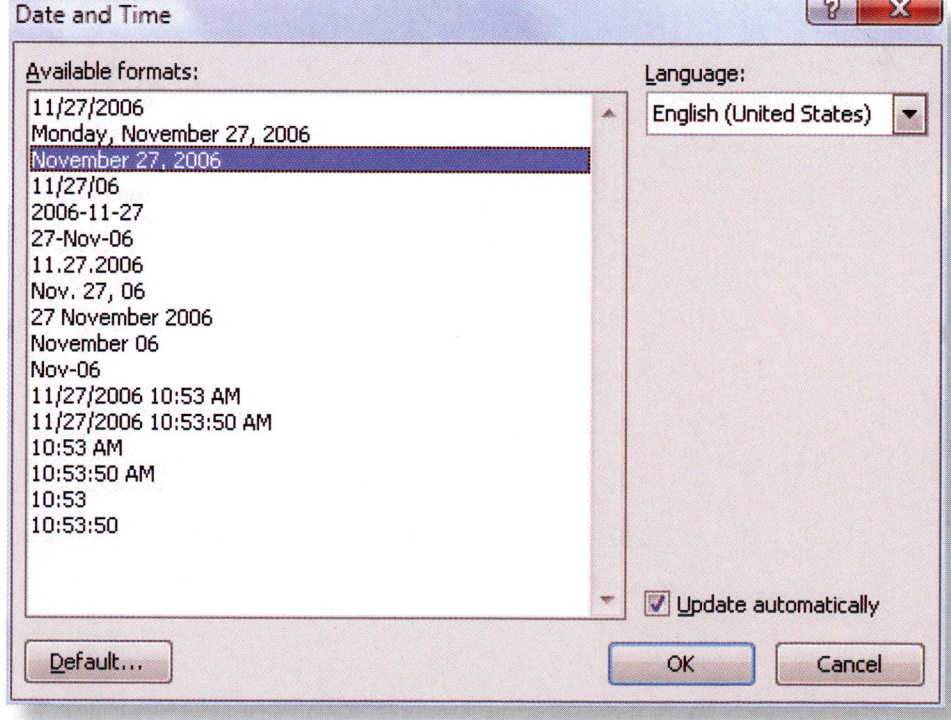

NOTE

You can also use this dialog box to insert the date and time in a particular text format without inserting it as an updatable field.

TIP

Although printing updates a field, you can also update a field on-screen by clicking the field and pressing F9.

5. Scroll the list of available time and date formats, and choose the third format in the list (the standard date format for business documents).

6. Check the **Update automatically** check box so the date is automatically updated each time you print the document. Click **OK**.

7. Move the insertion point after the date field, and press Spacebar twice.

8. Press Alt + Shift + T to insert the time as a field.

9. Save the document as *[your initials]*4-9 in your Lesson 4 folder.

10. Submit your work, and close the document.

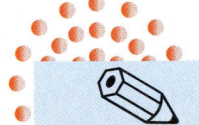

TIP

Remember that the **Update automatically** option will change the date in your document. If you are sending correspondence, do not choose this option because the date in the letter will then always reflect the current date, not the date on which you wrote the letter.

Checking Spelling and Grammar

Correct spelling and grammar are essential to good writing. As you have seen, Word checks your spelling and grammar as you key text and flags errors with these on-screen indicators:

- A red, wavy line appears under misspelled words.

- A green, wavy line appears under possible grammatical errors.

- A blue, wavy line appears under possible formatting inconsistencies.

- The Proofing Errors icon on the status bar contains an "X."

TABLE 4-2 Spelling and Grammar Status

Icon	Indicates
	Word is checking for errors as you key text.
	The document has errors.
	The document has no errors.

Exercise 4-10 SPELL- AND GRAMMAR-CHECK ERRORS INDIVIDUALLY

You can right-click text marked as either a spelling or a grammar error and choose a suggested correction from a shortcut menu.

> **NOTE**
>
> If no green, wavy lines appear in your document, open the **File** menu, and click **Word Options**. Click **Proofing** in the left pane. Click the **Check grammar with spelling** check box, and click **OK**.

> **TIP**
>
> Word's spelling and grammar tools are not foolproof. For example, it cannot correct a word that is correctly spelled but incorrectly keyed, such as "sue" instead of "use." It might also apply a green wavy line to a type of grammatical usage, such as the passive voice, which might not be preferred, but is not incorrect.

1. Open the file **Milk Chocolate - 2**. This document has several errors, indicated by the red and green wavy lines.

2. At the top of the document, press Enter and move the insertion point to the first paragraph mark. Notice that the Proofing Errors indicator 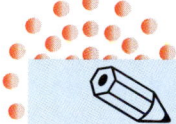 on the status bar now contains an "X."

3. Using 14-point bold type, key a misspelled word by keying the title **Mlk Chocolate**. When you finish, "Mlk" is marked as misspelled.

4. Right-click the misspelled word, and choose "Milk" from the spelling shortcut menu.

5. Right-click the grammatical error "It contain" in the second sentence. Choose "contains" from the shortcut menu.

Exercise 4-11 SPELL- AND GRAMMAR-CHECK AN ENTIRE DOCUMENT

Instead of checking words or sentences individually, you can check an entire document. This is the best way to correct spelling and grammar errors in a long document. Use one of these methods:

- Click the Spelling and Grammar button 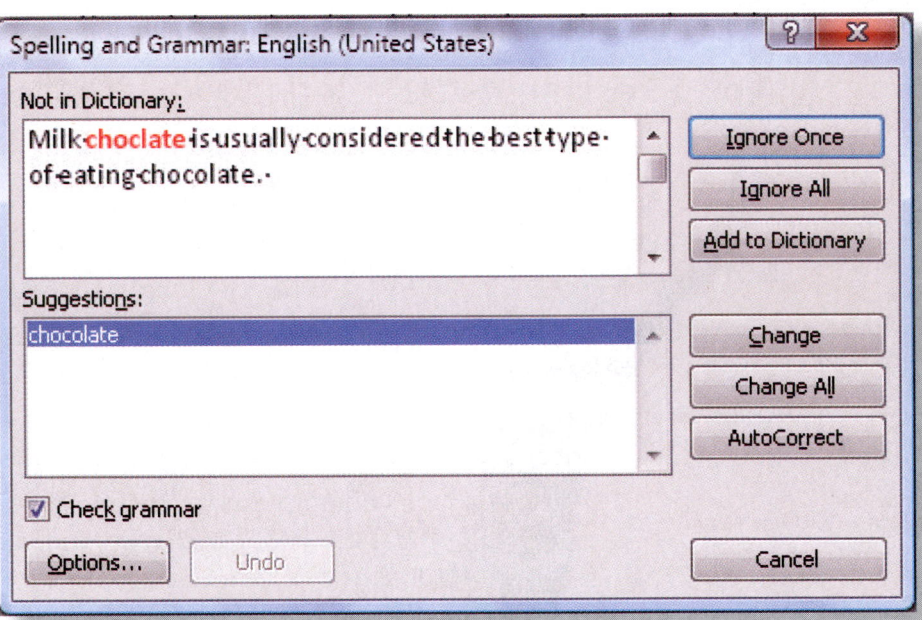 on the Review tab of the Ribbon.

- Press F7.

1. Position the insertion point at the beginning of the document and click the **Review** tab of the Ribbon. Click the Spelling and Grammar button . Word locates the first misspelling, "choclate."

Figure 4-10
Checking spelling

2. Click **Change** to correct the spelling to the first suggested spelling, "chocolate." Next, Word finds a word choice error, "hole."

3. Click **Change** to correct the word choice. Next, Word finds two words that should be separated by a space.

> **TIP**
>
> To check spelling without also checking grammar, click the **Check grammar** check box to clear it.

4. Click **Change** to correct the spacing. Next word finds a repeated word, "of."

5. Click **Delete** to delete the repeated word. Next Word finds a grammatical error—"it" is not capitalized.

6. Click **Change** to correct the capitalization in the document.

7. Click **OK** when the check is complete. Notice there are no more wavy lines in the document, and the Proofing Errors indicator shows a check mark.

8. Read the paragraph, and check for errors that were not found by the Spelling & Grammar checker.

9. Locate "10 per cent" in the second sentence. Delete the space between "per" and "cent."

10. Locate the sentence that begins "It is mild," and change "type" to "**types**."

11. Locate the sentence that begins "It used," and change it to read "**It is used**."

TABLE 4-3 Dialog Box Options When Checking Spelling and Grammar

Option	Description
Ignore Once	Skips the word.
Ignore All	Skips all occurrences of the word in the document.
Add to Dictionary	Adds the word to the default dictionary file in Word. You can also create your own dictionary and add words to it.
Change	Changes the word to the entry in the **Change To** box or to the word you chose from the **Suggestions** list.
Change All	Same as **Change**, but changes the word throughout the document.
AutoCorrect	Adds the word to the list of corrections Word makes automatically.
Options	Lets you change the Spelling and Grammar options in Word.
Undo	Changes back the most recent correction made.
Cancel	Discontinues the checking operation.

NOTE

You can create or add a custom dictionary for technical and specialized vocabulary. Open the **File** menu, click **Word Options**, and click **Proofing**. Click **Custom Dictionaries**, click **New**, and key a name for the custom dictionary. To add a custom dictionary that you purchased, follow the steps listed above, except choose Add instead of New. Locate the folder and double-click the dictionary file.

Using the Thesaurus and Research Task Pane

The *thesaurus* is a tool that can improve your writing. Use the thesaurus to look up a *synonym* (a word with a similar meaning) for a selected word to add variety or interest to a document. You can look up synonyms for any of these words to get additional word choices. The thesaurus sometimes displays *antonyms* (words with the opposite meaning) and related words.

After selecting a word to change, you can start the thesaurus in one of three ways:

- Click the **Review** tab, and click **Thesaurus**.

- Press [Shift]+[F7].

- Right-click the word and choose **Synonyms** from the shortcut menu.

Exercise 4-12   USE THE THESAURUS

1. Select the word "best" in the first paragraph, or place the insertion point in the word.

2. Press [Shift]+[F7]. The Research task pane appears with a list of synonyms for "best."

Figure 4-11
Using the Thesaurus

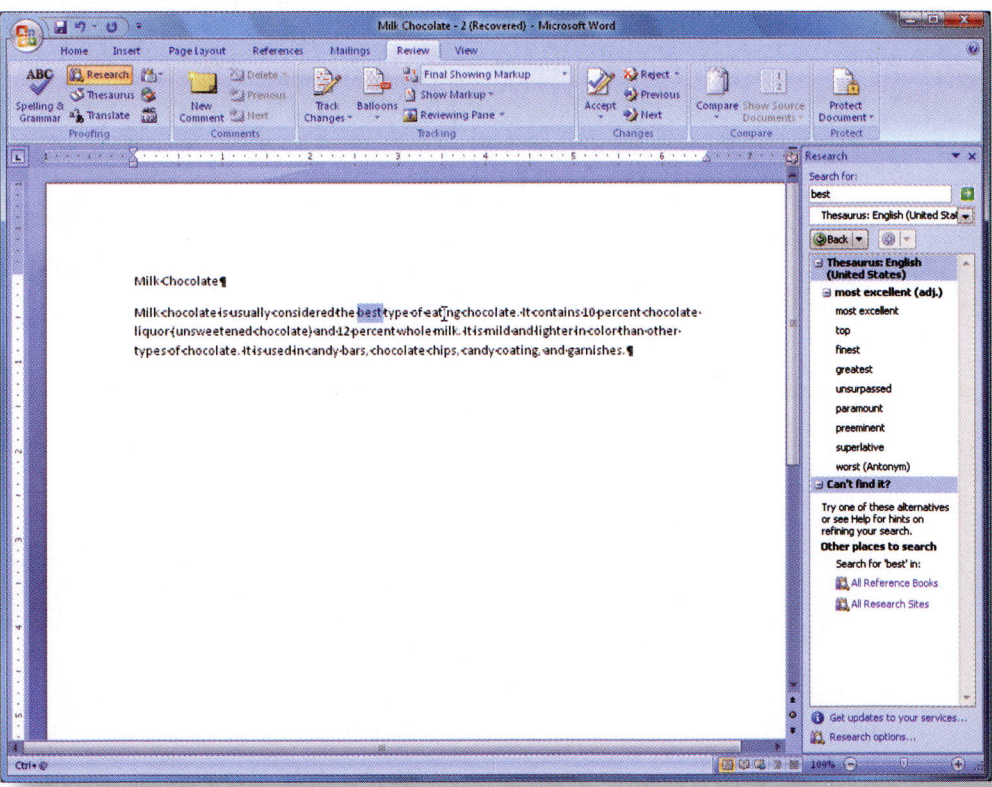

3. Point to the word "finest" and click the drop-down arrow. Click **Look Up**. A list of additional synonyms appears for "finest" in the task pane.

4. Go back to the word "finest" by clicking the Previous Search button 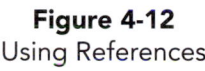 .

5. Point to "finest," click the down arrow, and choose **Insert**. Word replaces "best" with "finest" and returns to the document.

6. Save the document as *[your initials]***4-12** in your Lesson 4 folder.

7. Submit the document, but do not close it.

Exercise 4-13 USE REFERENCES

If you are connected to the Internet, you can access several research sources, such as a dictionary, an encyclopedia, and research sites such as MSN. From the Review tab on the Ribbon, you can click the Research button 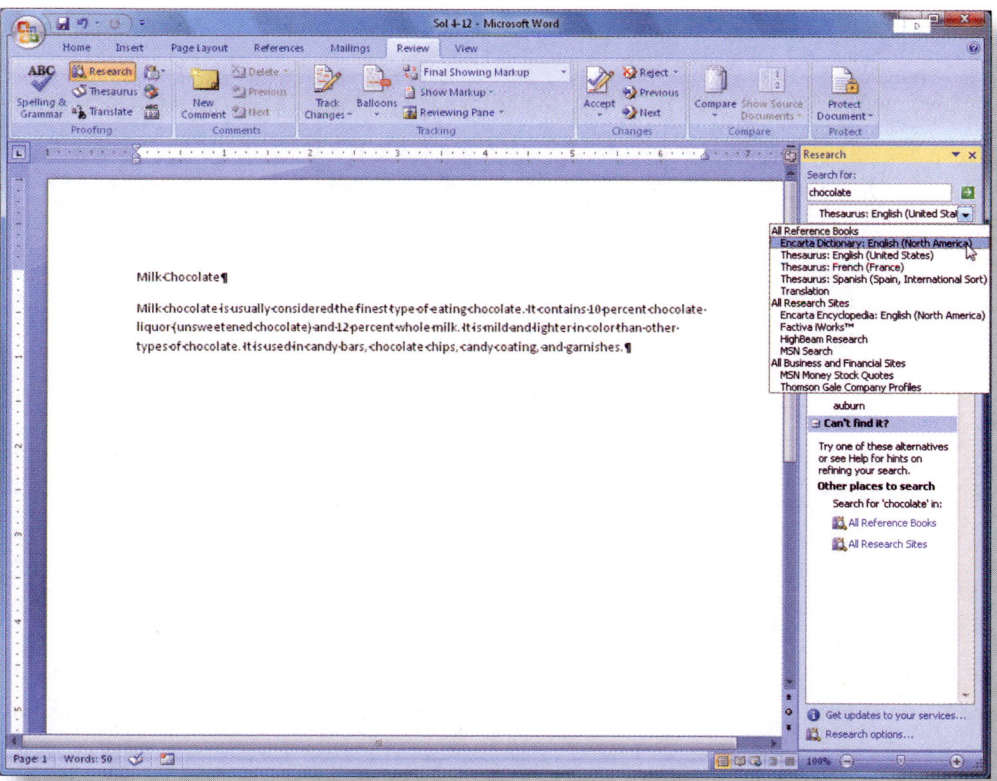 ; right-click a word and click **Look Up** in the shortcut menu; or press Alt and click a word to open the Research task pane.

1. Press Alt and click the word "chocolate" in the first sentence.

Figure 4-12
Using References

NOTE

Click Research options at the bottom of the Research task pane to open the Research Options dialog box.

TIP

Click the Translation Tool Tip button on the Ribbon to turn on or turn off a translation ScreenTip. Select a language to turn on the Translation ScreenTip. Click **Turn Off Translation ScreenTip** to turn off the ScreenTip.

2. Click the drop-down arrow beside the All Reference Books box and choose *Encarta Dictionary*. The task pane indicates the part of speech, syllabication, and several definitions for "chocolate."

3. Click the drop-down arrow beside the All Reference Books box, and choose Translation.

4. Choose **English** in the From box and **French (France)** in the To box. The bilingual dictionary displays the French word for chocolate—chocolat.

5. Close the document.

Lesson 4 Summary

- The AutoComplete feature suggests the completed word when you key the first four or more letters of a day, month, or date.

- The AutoCorrect feature corrects some misspelled words and capitalization errors for you automatically as you key text.

- Use the AutoCorrect dialog box to create entries for words you often misspell and the AutoCorrect Options button to control AutoCorrect options.

- Use the AutoCorrect Exceptions dialog box to create an AutoCorrect exception so Word will not correct it.

- Use smart tags to perform Microsoft Outlook functions, such as creating entries in Outlook's contact list.

- AutoText is another versatile feature you can use to insert text automatically. You create AutoText entries for text you use repeatedly, including text formatting.

- Use the Building Blocks Organizer to edit and delete AutoText entries.

- Insert the date and time in a document as an automatically updated field, which is a hidden code that tells Word to insert specific information—in this case, the date and/or time. Use the Date and Time dialog box to choose different date and time formats.

- Use the spelling and grammar checker to correct misspelled words in your document as well as poor grammar usage. Check errors individually or throughout your entire document.

- Use the thesaurus to look up synonyms (words with similar meaning) or sometimes antonyms (words with the opposite meaning) for a selected word to add variety and interest to your document.

- Use the Research task pane to look up words or phrases in a dictionary, to research topics in an encyclopedia, or to access bilingual dictionaries for translations. You can also access research sites such as MSN.

LESSON 4		Command Summary	
Feature	**Button**	**Command**	**Keyboard**
Create AutoText entry	Quick Parts ▾	**Insert** tab, **Text** group, **Quick Parts, Save Selection to Quick Part Gallery**	`Alt`+`F3`
Insert Date	Date & Time	**Insert** tab, **Text** group, **Date & Time**	`Alt`+`Shift`+`D`
Insert Time	Date & Time	**Insert** tab, **Text** group, **Date & Time**	`Alt`+`Shift`+`T`
Check spelling and grammar	ABC Spelling & Grammar	**Review** tab, **Proofing** group, **Spelling & Grammar**	`F7`
Thesaurus	Thesaurus	**Review** tab, **Proofing** group, **Thesaurus**	`Shift`+`F7`
Research	Research	**Review** tab, **Proofing** group, **Research**	`Alt`+Click

Concepts Review

True/False Questions

Each of the following statements is either true or false. Indicate your choice by circling T or F.

T F   1. AutoCorrect automatically changes "THis" to "This" and "monday" to "Monday."

T F   2. You can edit an AutoText entry by redefining an existing AutoText entry.

T F   3. You can start a grammar check from the Home tab.

T F   4. To start the thesaurus, press F7.

T F   5. The thesaurus finds synonyms for words.

T F   6. AutoComplete suggests a complete word or phrase for a date or an AutoText entry.

T F   7. You can choose to check only the spelling of a document, without checking the grammar.

T F   8. You can insert a date automatically by pressing Ctrl + D.

Short Answer Questions

Write the correct answer in the space provided.

1. Which function key starts a spell check?

_____

2. Which option in the Spelling and Grammar dialog box lets you skip over an incorrectly spelled word?

_____

3. Which dialog box is used to display and delete AutoText entries?

_____

4. When you click **Quick Parts** on the Ribbon, which option do you click to create an AutoText entry?

_____

5. Which tab on the Ribbon lists the Date and Time command?

_____

6. Which Word feature corrects accidental usage of [Caps Lock]?

_____

7. Which task pane is used to access references such as dictionaries and encyclopedias?

_____

8. What must you do to a word before using the thesaurus?

_____

Critical Thinking

Answer these questions on a separate page. There are no right or wrong answers. Support your answers with examples from your own experience, if possible.

1. Some educators believe the spell-checking feature in word processing programs will lead to decreased spelling skills in future generations. Do you think students' spelling skills will deteriorate? Explain your answer.

2. Key a sample of your writing that is at least one full page. Grammar-check the text. Did you find the analysis helpful? What are the advantages and disadvantages of using this tool?

Skills Review

Exercise 4-14

Use AutoCorrect and AutoComplete.

1. Start a new document.
2. Key the following sentence (including the errors in the first word):

   PEopel visiting western Pennsylvania enjoy its low humidity, blue skies, and rolling hills.

3. Press [Caps Lock] and key these sentences as shown. Be sure to press [Shift] to capitalize the first word in each sentence.

   The average high temperature is 60 degrees. The average low temperature is 35 degrees.

4. Continue the paragraph by keying the following sentence in all lowercase letters, letting AutoCorrect capitalize the first letter of each sentence. When you see the AutoComplete tip for the months, press [Enter] and continue keying.

   from january through december, you can find a wide variety of indoor and outdoor events and activities.

5. Start a new paragraph. Key the following sentence (including the errors in the first two words)

   thisyear, consider western Pennsylvania as a vacation destination.

6. Save the document as *[your initials]*4-14 in your Lesson 4 folder.

7. Submit your work, and close the document.

Exercise 4-15

Use AutoText and work with smart tags.

1. Open the file **Letter - 2**. Replace [Date] with the current date.

2. Select only the words "Campbell's Confections" in the letterhead of the document. (Do not select the space character or the paragraph mark.)

3. Using the text you just selected, create an AutoText entry by following these steps:

   a. Click the **Insert** tab on the Ribbon, and click **Quick Parts**.

   b. Click **Save Selection to Quick Part Gallery**.

   c. Key the AutoText entry name **[your initials]**.

   d. Select AutoText in the Gallery drop-down list.

   e. Click **OK**.

4. Change the formatting for the entire letterhead to small caps, dark blue, and regular text (no italic). Select the first line and change the font size to 14.

5. At the second blank paragraph mark below "Dear Mr. Matthews," key the following sentence, substituting your AutoText entry "**[your initials]**" where indicated in the paragraph. After you key "**[your initials]**," press F3 to insert the AutoText entry.

   Thank you for your interest in *[your initials]*, western Pennsylvania's most popular chocolate factory and candy store.

6. Press Enter twice to start a new paragraph.

7. Click the **Insert** tab on the Ribbon. Click **Quick Parts**, and click **Building Blocks Organizer**.

8. Click the **Gallery** column heading to sort the list. Locate and click **[your initials]** to select the AutoText entry. Click **Insert**.

9. Complete the sentence by keying the following text:

   is your full-service candy store, offering the greatest selections of milk, dark, white, and sugar-free chocolates. We also create specialty chocolates with logos, monograms, or custom artwork.

10. Start a new paragraph and key the following text. Use either of the previous two methods to insert your AutoText entry in place of "[your initials]."

    The enclosed brochures will provide more information about [your initials]. We look forward to helping you place your next order.

11. Press Enter twice and key **Sincerely yours,**.

12. Press Enter four times and key the following information:

    Lydia Hamrick

    Customer Service

13. Press Enter twice, key **[your initials]** in lowercase, and press Enter.

14. Control the AutoCorrect function with the AutoCorrect Options button ⁊⁻ by following these steps:

    a. Move the I-beam over your first initial until you see the small blue box.

    b. Move the pointer to the small blue box until the AutoCorrect Options button ⁊⁻ appears.

    c. Click the button icon and choose **Undo Automatic Capitalization**.

15. On the line below your initials, key **Enclosures (2)**

16. Delete the AutoText entry by following these steps:

    a. Click the **Insert** tab on the Ribbon, and click **Quick Parts**. Click **Building Blocks Organizer**.

    b. Select your AutoText entry, *[your initials],* from the list.

    c. Click **Delete** and click **Yes**. Click **Close**.

17. Work with smart tags by following these steps:

    a. Move the I-beam over the street address "Main Street," and then move your pointer over the Smart Tag Actions button ⓘ.

    b. Click the button to see the list of actions.

    c. Click **Add to Contacts**.

    d. Review the content of the Contact tab and close the window.

    e. Click **No** when you are asked if you want to save the changes.

18. Format all occurrences of Campbell's Confections in the body of the letter using italic, small caps, and dark blue font color.

19. Save the document as *[your initials]*4-15 in your Lesson 4 folder.

20. Submit and close the document.

Exercise 4-16

Spell-check and grammar-check a document.

1. Open the file **Favors - 3**.
2. Spell-check and grammar-check the document by following these steps:

   a. Click the **Review** tab on the Ribbon.
   b. Click the Spelling and Grammar button 🗹.
   c. When Word locates the first misspelled word, choose **Campbell's** from the **Suggestions** list and click **Change**. Next Word finds a misspelling, "ocasions." Click **Change**.
   d. When Word locates "sugarfree" as an error, click in the **Not in Dictionary** section of the Spelling & Grammar dialog box. Key a hyphen after the "r" and click **Change**.
   e. Correct the spelling of "wraped," "ribbon," and "minature." When Word locates "ment" as an error, click in the **Not in Dictionary** section, and press [Backspace] to delete the extra space and to form the word "assortment." Click **Change**.
   f. When Word locates "carmel" as an error, edit the text to read "caramel." Click **Change**.
   g. Continue checking the document, changing spelling, deleting words, or correcting grammar as appropriate.
3. Select the title, and change the font size to 14 and the font color to dark blue.
4. Save the document as *[your initials]*4-16 in your Lesson 4 folder.
5. Print and close the document.

Exercise 4-17

Use the thesaurus.

1. Open the file **Summer**.
2. Use the thesaurus to find another word for "wonderful" by following these steps:
   a. Select "wonderful" in the last sentence of the first paragraph.
   b. Press [Shift]+[F7].
   c. Point to a synonym, and click the drop-down arrow to the right of the word.
   d. Choose **Insert** from the drop-down list.
   e. Close the Research task pane by clicking the Research task pane Close button ⊠.

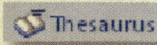

3. Start a new paragraph at the end of the document and key **Come and enjoy the fun!**

4. Select the word "fun."

5. Click the **Review** tab on the Ribbon. Click the Thesaurus button 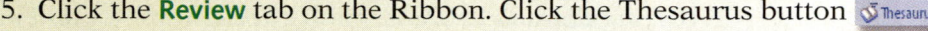.

6. Replace "fun" with a noun listed in the Research task pane. Remember to click the down arrow and choose **Insert**.

7. Save the document as *[your initials]*4-17 in your Lesson 4 folder.

8. Use the Research task pane to define a word by following these steps:

   a. Press Alt and click "ethnic" in the first paragraph.

   b. Choose the *Encarta Dictionary* from the All Reference Books drop-down list.

   c. Read the definition.

   d. Close the task pane.

9. Submit your work, and close the document.

Lesson Applications

Exercise 4-18

Create an AutoText entry and check grammar and spelling.

1. Create a new document, and key the text **Campbell's Confections** and press Enter.

2. Select the text and the paragraph marks and format them as 12-point Arial.

3. Select the text "Campbell's Confections" (excluding the paragraph marks), and create an AutoText entry named *[your initials]*.

4. Go to the end of the document, and key the text shown in Figure 4-13. Include the corrections. Wherever "[your initials]" appears, key the name of the AutoText entry you just created, pressing F3 to expand the entry.

Figure 4-13

The best hand made chocolate candy inWestern Pennsylvania is made by

<your initials>cc. The family owned business opened its first store in

1957. The ~~retail~~ store is located on Main ST grove city Pennsylvania, and
candy
chocolate   *east*
the factory is two blocks away on Monroe Street.

<your initials>cc specialize in assorted chocolate covered nuts, creams,
                                                                        candies
melt-a-ways, and truffles. You can also buy several varieties of hard and

soft candies. <your initials>cc takes pride inusing the finest ingredients in
family
its recipes.

<your initials>cc is open 6 days a week. In addition to buying your candy

at the store, you can call our toll free number at 800-555-2025, or visit our

Web site at www.campbellsconfections.biz.

5. Spell-check and grammar-check the document.

6. Format the title as 16-point bold, small caps with a text shadow.

REVIEW

Use the Repeat command F4 to format the name.

7. Format **Campbell's Confections** in small caps throughout the document.

8. Delete the AutoText entry you created.

9. Save the document as *[your initials]*4-18 in your Lesson 4 folder.

10. Submit your work, and close the document.

Exercise 4-19

Spell-check and grammar-check a document and use the Research task pane.

1. Open the file **Fountain - 2**.

2. Spell-check and grammar-check the document, making the appropriate corrections.

3. Proofread the document to ensure the document does not contain errors.

4. Use the thesaurus to look up the word "finest" in the second sentence of the paragraph that begins "Campbell's Confections."

5. Change the first line of the document to title case.

6. Format the title as 14-point bold, small caps with expanded character spacing.

7. Save the document as *[your initials]*4-19 in your Lesson 4 folder.

8. Submit and close the document.

Exercise 4-20

Format a document as a letter, check spelling and grammar, and use the thesaurus.

1. Open the document **Letter - 3**.

2. Position the insertion point on the second blank paragraph mark after the letterhead text.

3. Click the **Insert** tab, and click the **Date and Time** command. Click the third format in the Date and Time dialog box.

4. Press Enter four times, and key the text in Figure 4-14. Include one blank line after the address and the salutation. (Refer to Appendix B, "Standard Forms for Business Documents," for correct letter format.)

Figure 4-14

```
Mr. George Henderson

3850 Fifth Avenue

Altoona, PA 16602

Dear Mr. Henderson:
```

5. At the end of the document, press Enter twice. Key the closing **Sincerely**, and press Enter four times. Key **Lydia Hamrick**, and press Enter. On the next line, key **Customer Service**. Press Enter twice, and key your initials in lowercase. Press Enter and key **Enclosure**.

6. Use the AutoCorrect Options button 🖅 to undo the capitalization of your first initial.

7. Check the spelling and grammar of the document, making the appropriate corrections.

8. Use the thesaurus to find a synonym for "delighted" in the first sentence of the document.

9. Save the document as *[your initials]*4-20 in your Lesson 4 folder.

10. Submit and close the document.

Exercise 4-21 ◆ Challenge Yourself

Create an AutoText entry and check the grammar and spelling of a document.

1. Open the file **WV Stores**.

2. Select the complete address and contact information for the Clarksburg store, and create an AutoText entry named *[your initials]***clark**.

3. Close the document and open the file **Refer**.

4. Place the insertion point on the second paragraph mark after the letterhead text, and insert the date using the Ribbon. Use appropriate format for a business letter.

5. Press Enter four times and key the inside address listed in Figure 4-15.

Figure 4-15

```
Ms. Jill Gresh

360 Lincoln Street

Grafton, WV 26354
```

6. Press Enter twice, and key **Dear Ms. Gresh:**.

7. Verify that there is one blank line between the inside address and the salutation and one blank line between the salutation and the first paragraph.

8. Position the insertion point at the beginning of the paragraph that begins "Please let."

9. Key **[your initials]clark**, and press F3 to expand the Autotext entry. Press Enter if necessary to insert a blank line.

10. Spell- and grammar-check from the beginning of the document.

11. Delete the AutoText entry "*[your initials]***clark**."

12. Save the document as *[your initials]***4-21** in your Lesson 4 folder.

13. Submit your work, and close the document.

On Your Own

In these exercises you work on your own, as you would in a real-life business environment. Use the skills you've learned to accomplish the task—and be creative.

Exercise 4-22

Write a summary about a book you have recently read, but before you start the summary, create an AutoCorrect entry for a word you know you often misspell. Use this word in the summary as often as you can. Delete the entry when you have finished. Spell- and grammar-check your document. Format the document, save it as *[your initials]***4-22**, and submit it.

Exercise 4-23

Create a blank document, and create an AutoText to be used as a salutation in a letter. Create an AutoText entry to include a complimentary closing and signature line. Delete the text from the document, and write a letter to a friend. Insert the date using the Date and Time feature on the Insert tab of the Ribbon. Key your friend's inside address, and insert the AutoText entry you created for the salutation. Key the body of the letter, and insert the AutoText entry you created for the closing. Delete the AutoText entry when you have finished. Spell- and grammar-check your document. Format the document using correct business letter format. Save the document as *[your initials]***4-23**, and submit your work.

Exercise 4-24

Log onto the Internet, and find a Web site about one of your hobbies or interests. Summarize the information from the site in a Word document. Add a title to the document and apply basic character formatting. Use the thesaurus to insert synonyms. Spell- and grammar-check the document. Proofread and apply additional formatting to create an attractive document. Save the document as *[your initials]***4-24**, and submit your work.

Unit 1 Applications

Unit Application 1-1

Edit, spell-check, use the thesaurus, and apply formatting to a document.

1. Open the file **Chocolate**.

2. Format the entire document as 12-point Times New Roman.

3. Merge the first and second paragraphs.

4. Move to the top of the document, and key **Types of Chocolate**. Press Enter.

5. Format the title as 14-point bold, small caps, and brown font color.

6. Format the first paragraph with a dropped capital letter that drops three lines and is .1 inch from the text.

7. Spell-check and grammar-check the document. Ignore proper names.

8. In the first paragraph, use the thesaurus to choose a synonym for the word "type" in the last sentence.

9. Use noncontiguous text selection to format the names "Milk chocolate" in the second paragraph and "white chocolate" in the fifth paragraph as follows:

   - Small caps

   - Bold

   - Italic

   - Expanded character spacing

10. Copy the formatting to the remaining chocolate names: "Bittersweet chocolate" in the second paragraph, "semi-sweet chocolate" in the third paragraph, "Sweet or dark chocolate" in the fourth paragraph, and "Baking chocolate" in the last paragraph.

11. Save the document as *[your initials]***u1-1** in a new Unit 1 Applications folder.

12. Submit and close the document.

Unit Application 1-2

Create AutoText entries, use AutoComplete format, spell-check, and grammar-check a document.

1. Open the file **Form Letter Paragraphs**.

2. Select the letterhead information and one blank line below it, and create an AutoText entry named **[your initials]gcletterhead**.

3. Select the first paragraph, and create an AutoText entry named **[your initials]factorytour**. Remember to select the blank line following the paragraph.

4. Select each of the remaining paragraphs and create an AutoText entry using the naming pattern listed below.

Second paragraph beginning "Factory tours"	**[your initials]tourinfo**
Third paragraph beginning "We welcome"	**[your initials]size**
Fourth paragraph beginning "Call us"	**[your initials]call**
Fifth paragraph beginning "Enclosed"	**[your initials]brochure**
Sixth paragraph ending with "summer"	**[your initials]summer**
Seventh paragraph ending with "fall"	**[your initials]fall**
Eighth paragraph ending with "spring"	**[your initials]spring**
Ninth paragraph ending with "winter"	**[your initials]winter**
Remainder of document (closing)	**[your initials]closing**

5. Close the document without saving.

6. Start a new document. Insert the AutoText entry "**[your initials]gcletterhead.**"

7. Insert the date using the Date and Time dialog box and selecting the third format. Press ⌅Enter two times.

8. Address the letter as shown in Figure U1-1.

Figure U1-1

```
Ms. Margo Taylor

1660 North 13 Street

Reading, PA 19604

Dear Ms. Taylor:
```

9. For the body of the letter, insert the following AutoText entries. Insert in the order listed.

- *[your initials]***Factorytour**
- *[your initials]***Tourinfo**
- *[your initials]***Brochure**
- *[your initials]***Spring**
- *[your initials]***Closing**

10. Key your reference initials at the end of the document. Press ⌅Enter and key **Enclosure**. Control the capitalization of the first initial of your reference initials by using AutoCorrect Options.

11. Refer to Appendix B, "Standard Forms for Business Documents," to check your line spacing.

12. Insert nonbreaking spaces wherever a number appears at the end of a line.

13. Spell-check and grammar-check the document.

14. Delete the AutoText entries you created.

15. Save the document as *[your initials]***u1-2** in your Unit 1 Applications folder.

16. Submit and close the document.

Unit Application 1-3

Compose a document, apply formatting, and check grammar and spelling.

1. Start a new document.

2. Refer to Figure U1-2 to create a document describing the items listed in the table.

3. Format the title attractively using the Font dialog box.

4. Format the paragraph text attractively selecting an appropriate font, font size, and font effects.

Figure U1-2

Campbell's Confections—Product Listing			
Description	Choices	Weight	Price
Chocolate-covered nuts	Almond, Brazil, cashew, filbert, pecan	1 lb. Box 2 lb. Box	$12.95 $25.90
Chocolate-covered creams	Vanilla, chocolate, strawberry, butter, cherry, coconut, coffee, maple, orange, pineapple, raspberry, strawberry	1 lb. 2 lb.	$10.50 $21.00
Turtles	Pecan, cashew, peanut	1 lb. 2 lb.	$12.95 $25.90
Assortment—Chocolate-covered nuts and creams	See choices listed above.	1 lb. 2 lb.	$11.75 $23.50

5. Change the case of the title to all capitals.

6. Insert nonbreaking spaces in the document, if they are needed.

7. Spell-check and grammar-check the document.

8. Save the document as *[your initials]***u1-3** in your Unit 1 Applications folder.

9. Submit and close the document.

Unit Application 1-4 ◆ Using the Internet

Apply character formatting, use AutoFormat features, and check grammar and spelling.

1. Using the Internet, create a list of five organizations. Be creative. The organizations could be:

   • Companies where you would like to work

   • Schools you would be interested in attending

   • Associations related to your hobbies or interests

2. Include the organization's name and its Web site address.

3. Include any e-mail address, the physical address, and the telephone and fax numbers.

4. Allow AutoFormat to format the Web addresses and e-mail addresses as hyperlinks.

5. Create a title for the document, followed by a descriptive paragraph that describes the content of the list.

6. Apply appropriate formatting.

7. Check spelling and grammar, watching carefully as Word's spelling and grammar checker moves through the addresses.

8. Save the document named *[your initials]***u1-4** in your Unit 1 Applications folder.

9. Submit the document.

unit 2

PARAGRAPH FORMATTING, TABS, AND ADVANCED EDITING

Lesson 5   Format Paragraphs   WD-132

Lesson 6   Tabs and Tabbed Columns   WD-166

Lesson 7   Move and Copy   WD-194

Lesson 8   Find and Replace   WD-224

UNIT 2   APPLICATIONS   WD-251

Formatting Paragraphs

OBJECTIVES

After completing this lesson, you will be able to:

1. Align paragraphs.

2. Change line spacing.

3. Change paragraph spacing.

4. Set paragraph indents.

5. Apply borders and shading.

6. Repeat and copy paragraph formats.

7. Create bulleted and numbered lists.

8. Insert symbols and special characters.

MCAS OBJECTIVES

In this lesson:
WW 07 1.1.5
WW 07 2.1.4
WW 07 4.2.2
WW 07 4.2.3
WW 07 4.2.1

Estimated Time: 1½ hours

In Microsoft Word, a *paragraph* is a unique block of information. Paragraph formatting controls the appearance of individual paragraphs within a document. For example, you can change the space between paragraphs or change the space between lines. For emphasis, you can indent paragraphs, number them, or add borders and shading.

A paragraph is always followed by a *paragraph mark*. All the formatting for a paragraph is stored in the paragraph mark. Each time you press Enter, you copy the formatting instructions in the current paragraph to a new paragraph. You can copy paragraph formats to existing paragraphs and view formats in the Reveal Formatting task pane.

Paragraph Alignment

Paragraph alignment determines how the edges of a paragraph appear horizontally. There are four ways to align text in a paragraph, as shown in Figure 5-1.

Figure 5-1
Paragraph alignment
options

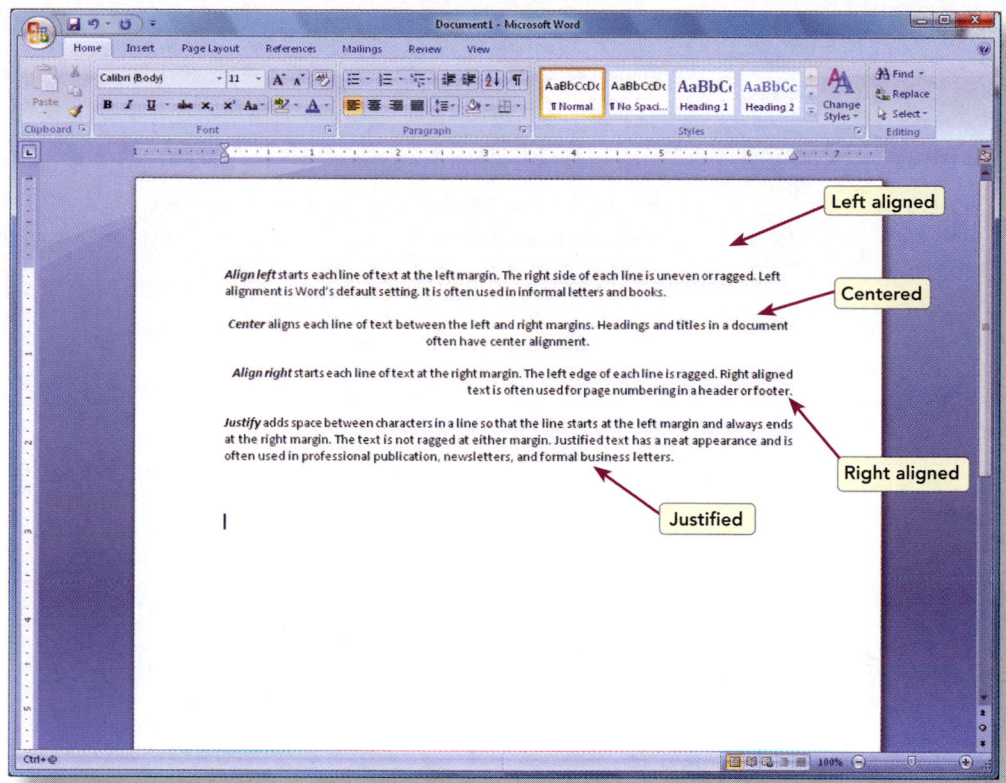

Exercise 5-1 — CHANGE PARAGRAPH ALIGNMENT

The easiest way to change paragraph alignment is to use the alignment buttons on the Ribbon, Home tab, Paragraph group. You can also use keyboard shortcuts: Ctrl+L left align; Ctrl+E center; Ctrl+R right align; Ctrl+J justify.

Figure 5-2
Alignment buttons
on the Ribbon

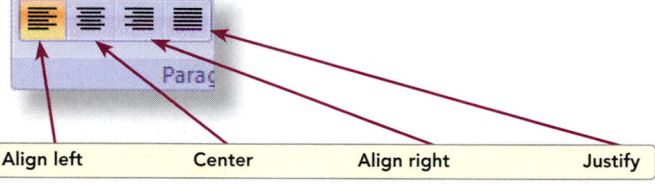

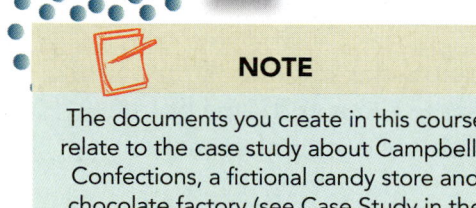

NOTE

The documents you create in this course relate to the case study about Campbell's Confections, a fictional candy store and chocolate factory (see Case Study in the frontmatter of the book).

1. Open the file **Corporate Gifts**. Click the Show/Hide ¶ button to display paragraph marks if they are turned off.

2. Position the insertion point anywhere in the first paragraph.

3. Click the Center button 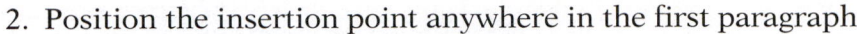 on the Ribbon (Home tab, Paragraph group) to center the paragraph.

4. Continue to change the paragraph's formatting by clicking the Align Right button ▤, the Justify button ▤, and the Align Left button ▤. Notice how the lines of text are repositioned with each change.

5. Position the insertion point in the second paragraph and press Ctrl+E to center the paragraph.

6. Use the keyboard shortcut Ctrl+R to right-align the third paragraph.

7. Press Ctrl+J to justify the fourth paragraph.

NOTE

When applying paragraph formatting, you do not have to select the paragraph—you just need to have the insertion point within the paragraph or just before the paragraph mark.

REVIEW

If you do not see one of the alignment buttons, check the Ribbon to verify that the Home tab is active.

TIP

To change the alignment of multiple paragraphs, select them, and then apply the alignment.

Exercise 5-2   USE CLICK AND TYPE TO INSERT TEXT

You can use *Click and Type* to insert text or graphics in any blank area of a document. This feature enables you to position the insertion point anywhere in the document without pressing Enter repeatedly. Word automatically inserts the paragraph marks before that point and also inserts a tab.

1. Open the file **Factory**, and leave the Corporate Gifts document open.

2. Click the **Microsoft Office Button** and click **Word Options.** Click **Advanced** in the left pane, and click **Enable click and type** if it is not already selected. Click **OK**.

3. Press Ctrl+End to move to the end of the document.

4. Position the I-beam about five lines below the last line of text, in the center of the page. The I-beam is now the Click and Type pointer ↧, which includes tiny lines that show right or center alignment.

Figure 5-3
Using Click and Type

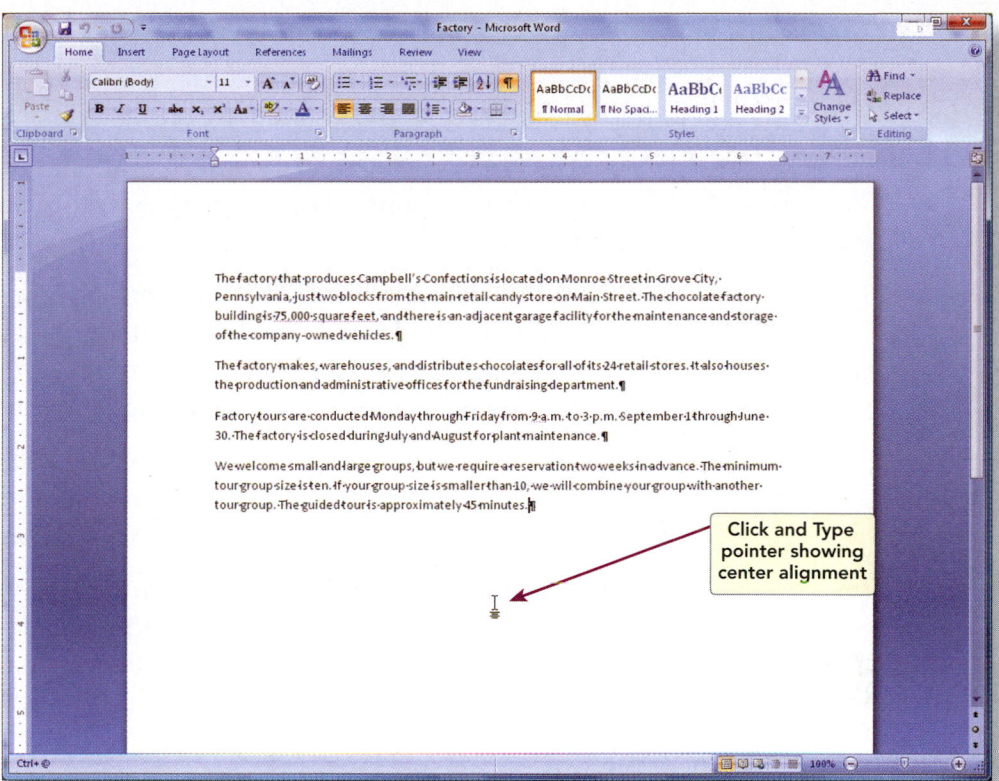

Figure 5-3
Using Click and Type

5. Move the I-beam back and forth until it shows center alignment. Double-click, and key **Visit us at www.campbellsconfections.biz**. The text is centered, and paragraph marks are inserted before it.

6. Save the document as *[your initials]*5-2 in your Lesson 5 folder.

7. Submit your work, and close the document.

Line Spacing

Line space is the amount of vertical space between lines of text in a paragraph. Line spacing is typically based on the height of the characters, but you can change it to a specific value. For example, some paragraphs might be single-spaced and some double-spaced. The default line spacing is Multiple 1.15.

Exercise 5-3 CHANGE LINE SPACING

You can apply the most common types of line spacing by using keyboard shortcuts: single space, Ctrl+1; 1.5-line space, Ctrl+5; double space, Ctrl+2. Additional spacing options, as well as other paragraph formatting options, are available in the Paragraph dialog box or from the Line Spacing button  .

Word 2007

1. Position the insertion point in the first paragraph of the Corporate Gifts document.

2. Press Ctrl+2 to double-space the paragraph.

3. With the insertion point in the same paragraph, press Ctrl+5 to change the spacing to 1.5 lines. Press Ctrl+1 to restore the paragraph to single spacing.

4. With the insertion point in the same paragraph, click the down arrow to the right of the Line Spacing button on the Ribbon, Home tab, Paragraph group, and choose **2.0** to change the line spacing to double. Choose **1.0** to restore the paragraph to single spacing.

5. Right-click the first paragraph and choose **Paragraph** from the shortcut menu. (You can also open the Paragraph dialog box by clicking the **Dialog Box Launcher** in the right corner of the Paragraph group.)

6. Click the down arrow to open the **Line spacing** drop-down list, and choose **Double**. The change is reflected in the **Preview** box.

Figure 5-4
Line-spacing options in the Paragraph dialog box

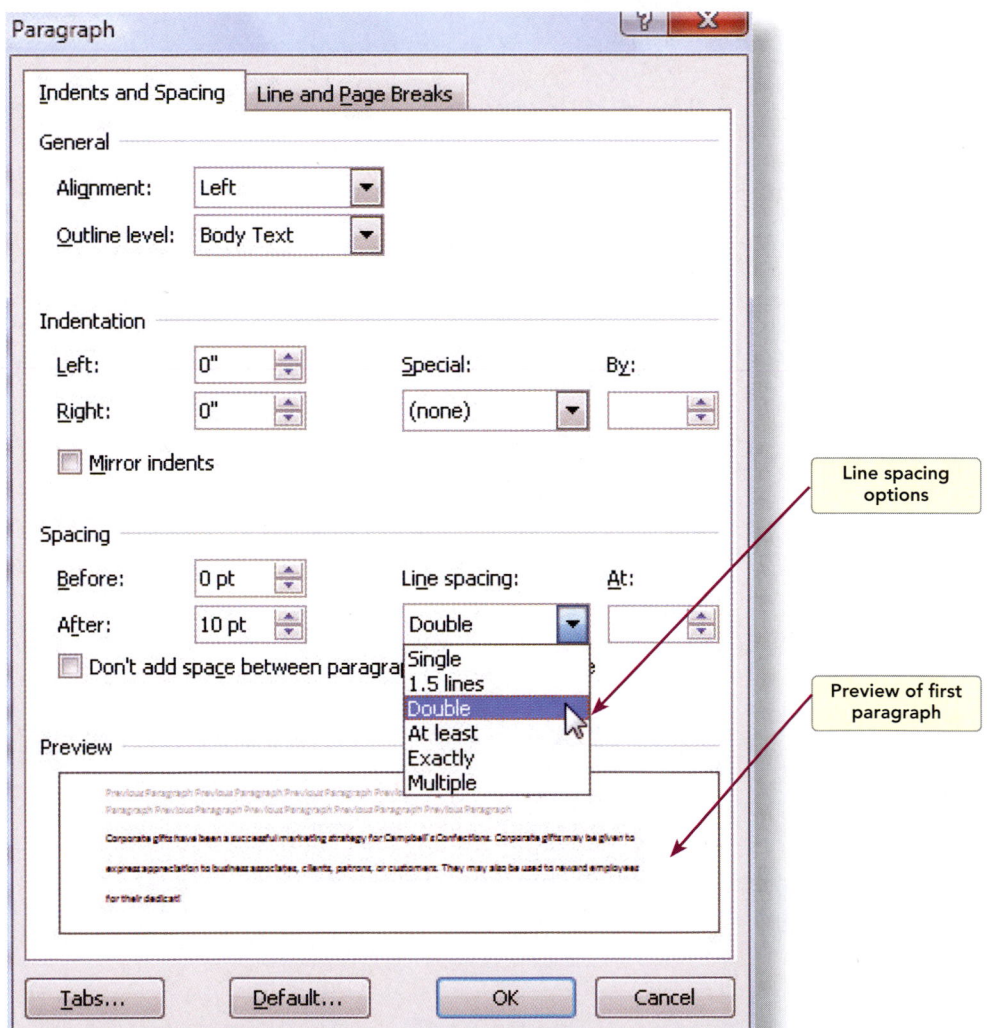

7. With the dialog box still open, choose **Single** from the **Line spacing** drop-down list. The **Preview** box shows the change.

8. Choose **Multiple** from the **Line spacing** drop-down list. In the **At** box, key **1.25**. (Select the text that appears in the box and key over it.) Press ⎆Tab to see the change displayed in the **Preview** box.

9. Click **OK**. Word adds an extra quarter-line space between lines in the paragraph.

Figure 5-5
Examples of line spacing

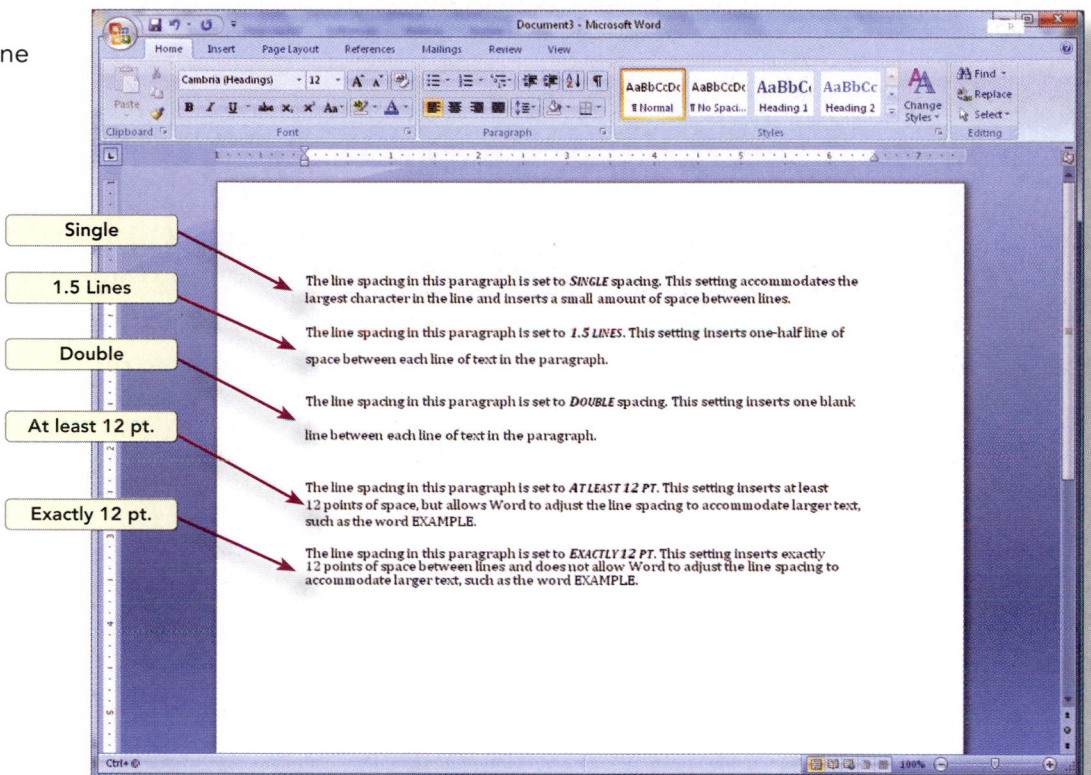

NOTE

The **At Least** option applies minimum line spacing that Word can adjust to accommodate larger font sizes. The **Exactly** option applies fixed line spacing that Word does not adjust. This option makes all lines evenly spaced. The **Multiple** option increases or decreases line spacing by the percentage you specify. For example, setting line spacing to a multiple of 1.25 increases the space by 25 percent, and setting line spacing to a multiple of 0.8 decreases the space by 20 percent.

Paragraph Spacing

In addition to changing spacing between lines of text, you can change *paragraph space*. Paragraph space is the amount of space above or below a paragraph. Instead of pressing Enter multiple times to increase space between paragraphs, you can use the Paragraph dialog box to set a specific amount of space before or after paragraphs.

Paragraph spacing is set in points. If a document has 12-point text, one line space equals 12 points. Likewise, one-half line space equals 6 points, and two line spaces equal 24 points. By default, **Paragraph Spacing** is **Before**: 0 points and **After**: 10 points.

Exercise 5-4   CHANGE THE SPACE BETWEEN PARAGRAPHS

1. Press Ctrl + Home to move the insertion point to the beginning of the document. Select the whole document by pressing Ctrl + A. Press Ctrl + L to left-align all paragraphs.

2. Use the keyboard shortcut Ctrl + 1 to change the entire document to single spacing.

3. Deselect the text and position the insertion point at the beginning of the document.

4. Click the Bold button to turn on bold, key **CORPORATE GIFTS** in all capitals, and press Enter.

5. Move the insertion point into the heading you just keyed. Although this heading includes only two words, it is also a paragraph. Any text followed by a paragraph mark is considered a paragraph.

NOTE

Most business documents start 2 inches from the top of the page. You can set this standard by using paragraph formatting, as done here, or by changing margin settings.

6. Open the Paragraph dialog box. You use the text boxes labeled **Before** and **After** to choose an amount of space for Word to insert before or after a paragraph.

7. Set the **Before** text box to 72 points (select the "0" and key **72**). Because 72 points equal 1 inch, this adds to the existing 1-inch top margin and places the title 2 inches from the top of the page.

TIP

Word provides these keyboard shortcuts for paragraph spacing: `Ctrl`+`0` adds 12 points of space before a paragraph; `Ctrl`+`Shift`+`0` removes space before a paragraph; `Ctrl`+`Shift`+`N` removes all paragraph and character formatting, restoring the text to default formatting.

8. Press `Tab`, set the **After** text box to **24** points, and click **OK**. The heading now starts at 2 inches and is followed by two line spaces.

9. Right-click the **Status bar** and click **Vertical Page Position**. Deselect the shortcut menu. The Status bar displays **At 2″** on the left side.

10. Click the Center button ≡ to center the heading.

Paragraph Indents

An *indent* increases the distance between the sides of a paragraph and the two side margins (left and right). Indented paragraphs appear to have different margin settings. Word provides a variety of indents to emphasize paragraphs in a document, as shown in Figure 5-6.

Figure 5-6
Types of paragraph indents

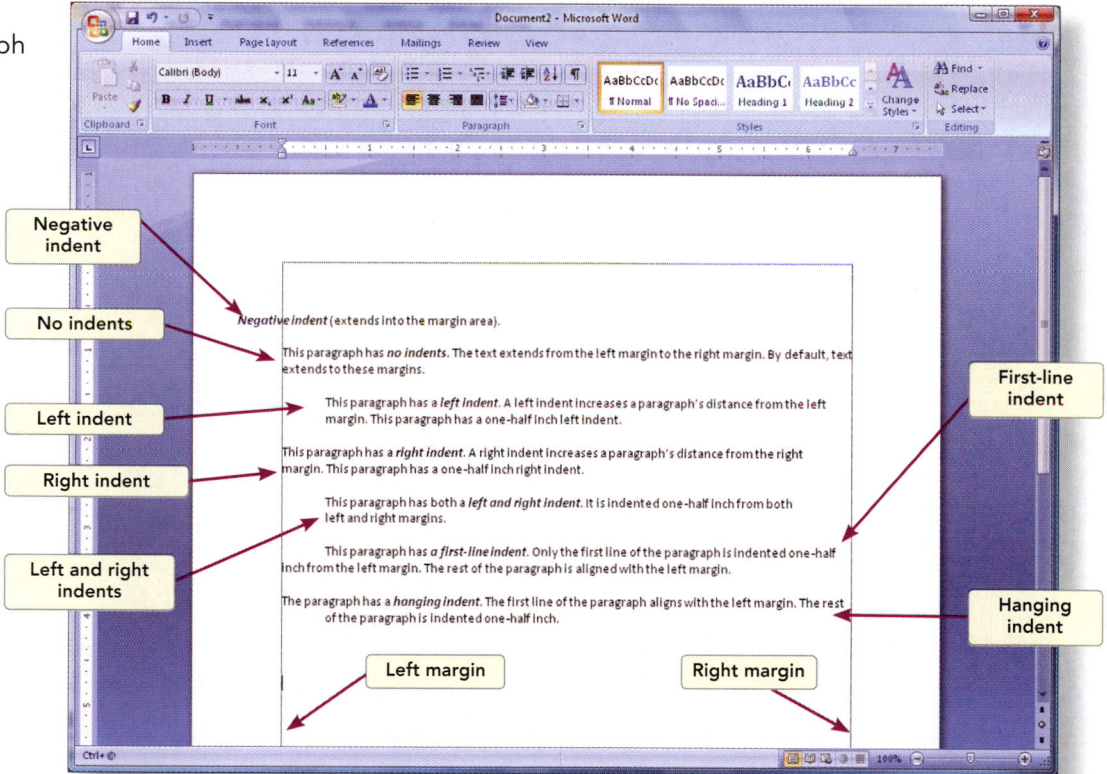

To set paragraph indents, you can use one of these methods:

- Indent buttons on the Ribbon, Home tab, Paragraph group
- Paragraph dialog box
- Keyboard
- Ruler

Word 2007

Exercise 5-5 SET INDENTS BY USING INDENT BUTTONS AND THE PARAGRAPH DIALOG BOX

1. Select the paragraph that begins "Our line" through the end of the document.

 2. Click the Increase Indent button on the Ribbon. The selected text is indented 0.5 inch from the left side.

3. Click the Increase Indent button again. Now the text is indented 1 inch.

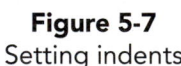 4. Click the Decrease Indent button twice to return the text to the left margin.

5. With the text still selected, open the Paragraph dialog box by clicking the Paragraph Dialog Box Launcher arrow.

6. Under **Indentation**, change the **Left** setting to **0.75** inch and the **Right** setting to **0.75** inch.

7. Click to open the **Special** drop-down list in the Paragraph dialog box and choose **First line**. Word sets the **By** box to 0.5″ by default. Notice the change in the Preview box.

NOTE

To set a *negative indent*, which extends a paragraph into the left or right margin areas, enter a negative number in the **Left** or **Right** text boxes. Any indent that occurs between the left and right margins is known as a *positive indent*.

Figure 5-7
Setting indents

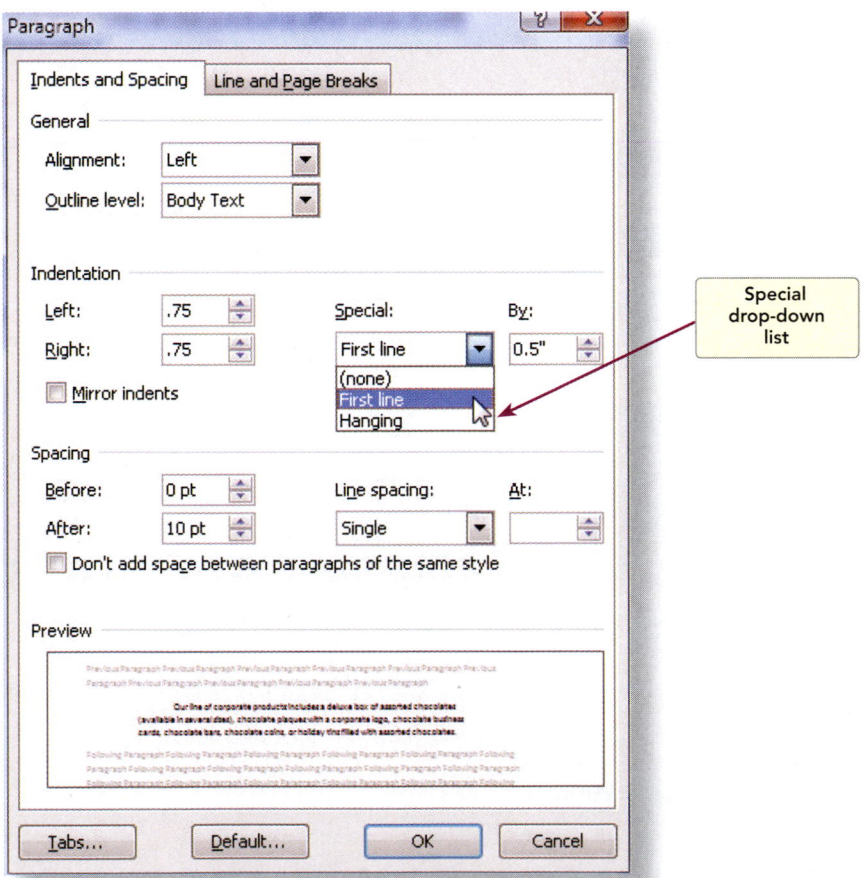

TIP

Word provides these keyboard shortcuts to set indents: Ctrl+M increases an indent; Ctrl+Shift+M decreases an indent; Ctrl+T creates a hanging indent; Ctrl+Shift+T removes a hanging indent.

8. Click **OK**. Now each paragraph is indented from the left and right margins by 0.75 inch, and the first line of each paragraph is indented another 0.5 inch.

Exercise 5-6 SET INDENTS BY USING THE RULER

You can set indents by dragging the *indent markers* that appear at the left and right of the horizontal ruler. There are four indent markers:

- The *first-line indent marker* is the top triangle on the left side of the ruler. Drag it to the right to indent the first line of a paragraph.

- The *hanging indent marker* is the bottom triangle. Drag it to the right to indent the remaining lines in a paragraph.

- The *left indent marker* is the small rectangle. Drag it to move the first-line indent marker and hanging indent marker at the same time.

- The *right indent marker* is the triangle at the right side of the ruler, at the right margin. Drag it to the left to create a right indent.

Figure 5-8
Indent markers on the ruler

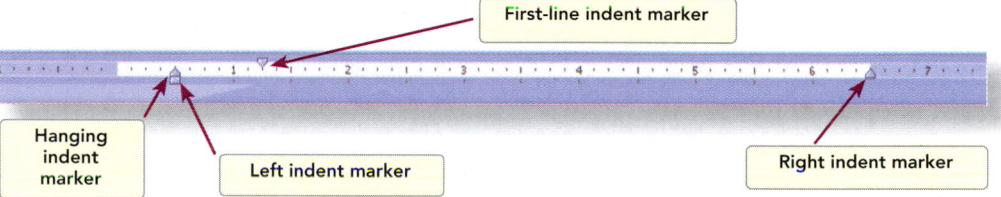

First-line indent marker

Hanging indent marker

Left indent marker

Right indent marker

1. Make sure the horizontal ruler is displayed. If it is not, click the **View Ruler button** or open the **Word Options** dialog box and click **Advanced** in the left pane and scroll to **Display**.

2. Position the insertion point in the first paragraph below the title.

3. Point to the first-line indent marker on the ruler. A ScreenTip appears when you are pointing to the correct marker.

4. Drag the first-line indent marker 0.5 inch to the right. The first line of the paragraph is indented by 0.5 inch.

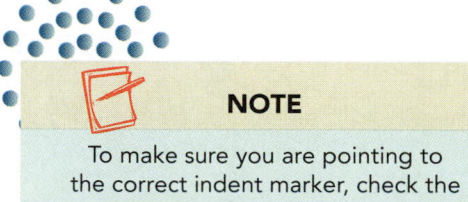

NOTE

To make sure you are pointing to the correct indent marker, check the ScreenTip identifier before you drag the marker.

5. Press Shift+F1 to display the **Reveal Formatting** task pane. Locate the Paragraph section, and notice the settings under **Indentation**.

6. Drag the first-line indent marker back to the zero position. Point to the hanging indent marker, and drag it 0.5 inch to the right. The lines below the first line are indented 0.5 inch, creating a hanging indent.

7. Drag the hanging indent marker back to the zero position. Drag the left indent marker (the small rectangle) 1 inch to the right. The entire paragraph is indented by 1 inch.

8. Select the first two paragraphs below the title, and press Ctrl + Shift + N to remove all formatting from the paragraphs. Notice that the line spacing and spacing after return to the default settings.

9. Position the insertion point in the second paragraph, which begins "Our line," and re-create the indents by using the ruler:

   • Drag the left indent marker 0.75 inch to the right to indent the entire paragraph.

   • Drag the first-line indent marker to the 1.25-inch mark on the ruler.

   • Drag the right indent marker 0.75 to the left (to the 5.75-inch mark on the ruler). Now the paragraph is indented like the paragraphs below it.

10. Select all the indented paragraphs, and drag the first-line indent marker to the 1-inch mark on the ruler. Now the opening line of each paragraph is indented only 0.25 inch.

Figure 5-9
Document with indented text

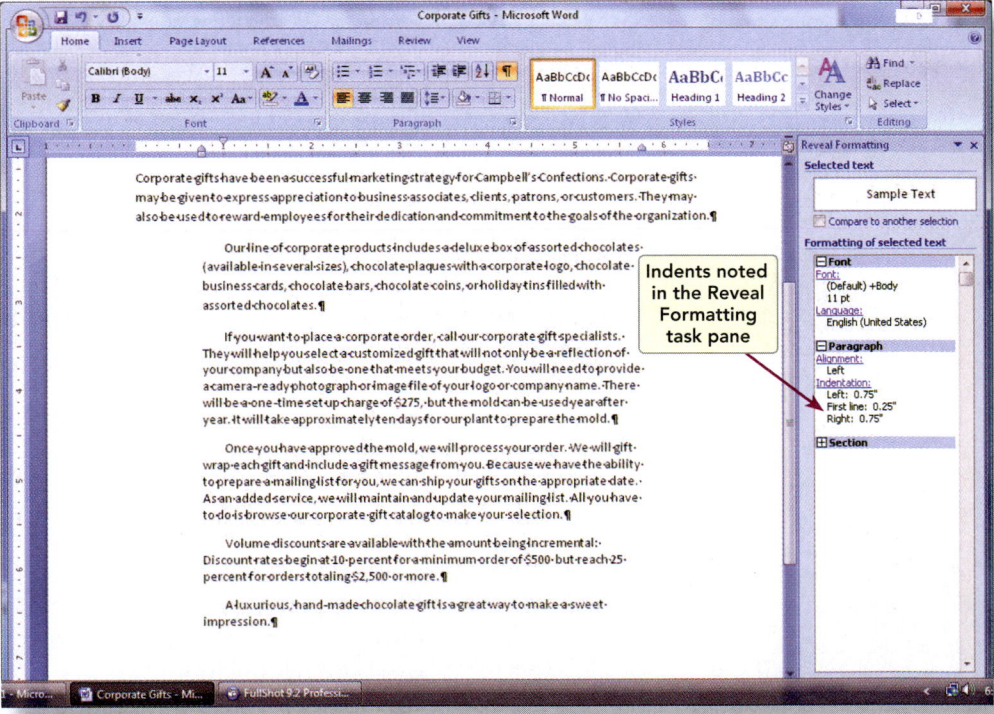

11. Save the document as *[your initials]5-6* in a new folder for Lesson 5.

12. Submit the document, but do not close it.

Borders and Shading

To add visual interest to paragraphs or to an entire page, you can add a *border*—a line, box, or pattern—around text, a graphic, or a page. In addition, you can use *shading* to fill in the background behind the text of a paragraph. Shading can appear as a shade of gray, as a pattern, or as a color. Borders can appear in a variety of line styles and colors.

This lesson explains how to use the Borders and Shading dialog box to set border and shading options, and how to use the Borders command on the Ribbon (which applies the most recently selected border style). The Borders button ScreenTip will change to display the most recently selected border style.

Exercise 5-7   ADD BORDERS TO PARAGRAPHS

1. With the file *[your initials]*5-6 open, go to the end of the document. Press ⬚Enter⬚ to start a new paragraph, and press ⬚Ctrl⬚+⬚Q⬚ to remove the paragraph formatting carried over from the previous paragraph.

2. Key the text shown in Figure 5-10.

Figure 5-10

> Let Campbell's Confections help you with your marketing strategy and your employees' recognition plan! We can provide you with a unique and personalized gift that will create a lasting impression. Call us today at 724-555-2025 for more information.

3. Make sure the insertion point is to the left of the current paragraph mark or within the paragraph.

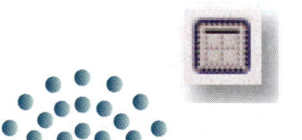

4. Click the down arrow beside the Borders button 🔲 and click **Borders and Shading** at the bottom of the drop-down list. The Borders and Shading dialog box appears. Click the **Borders** tab if it is not displayed.

NOTE

The appearance of the Borders button and the Screen Tip change according to the most recently selected border style.

5. Under Setting, click the **Box** option. The **Preview** box shows the Box setting. Each button around the **Preview** box indicates a selected border.

6. Scroll to view the options in the **Style** box. Choose the first border style (the solid line).

7. Open the **Color** drop-down list and choose Green. (ScreenTips identify colors by name.)

8. Open the **Width** drop-down list and choose **2¹/₄ pt**.

9. Click the top line of the box border in the **Preview** box. The top line is deleted, and the corresponding button is no longer selected. Click the Top Border button or the top border area in the diagram to restore the top line border.

Figure 5-11
Borders and Shading
dialog box

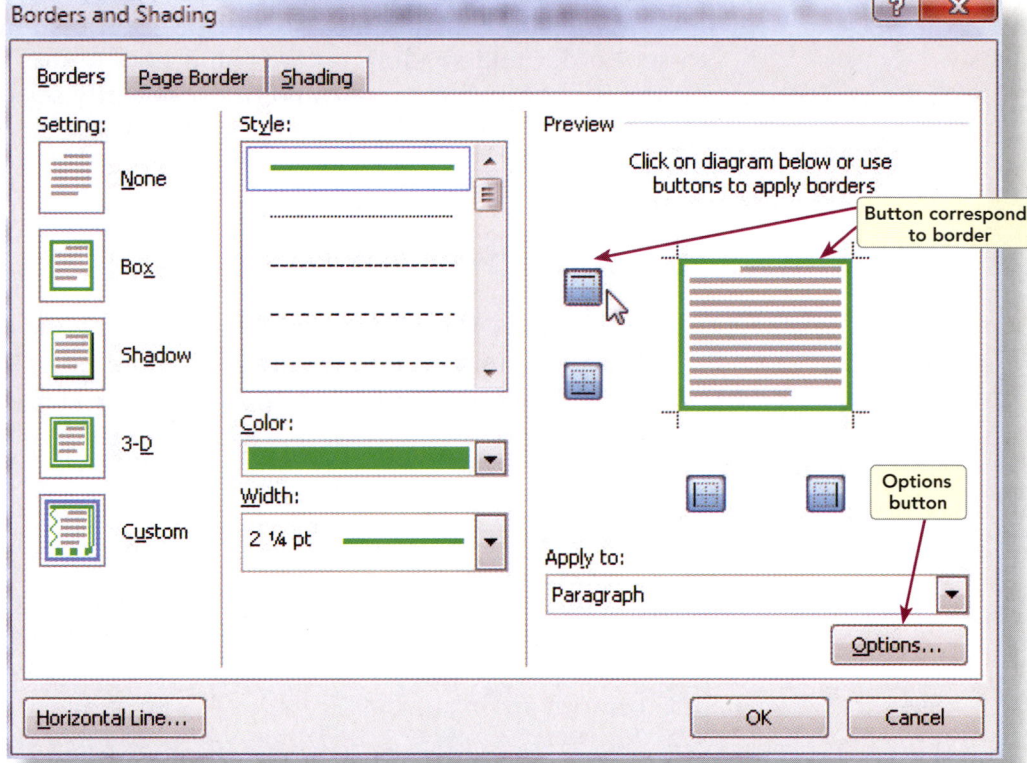

10. Click the **Options** button. In the Border and Shading Options dialog box, change the **Top**, **Bottom**, **Left**, and **Right** settings to **5 pt** to increase the space between the text and the border. Click **OK**.

11. Change the **Setting** from **Box** to **Shadow**. This setting applies a black shadow to the green border. Notice that the **Apply to** box is set to **Paragraph**. Click **OK**. The shadow border is applied to the paragraph.

12. Click anywhere within the title "CORPORATE GIFTS."

13. Click the down arrow next to the Borders button on the Ribbon. A drop-down menu of border options appears.

Figure 5-12
Border options on
the Ribbon

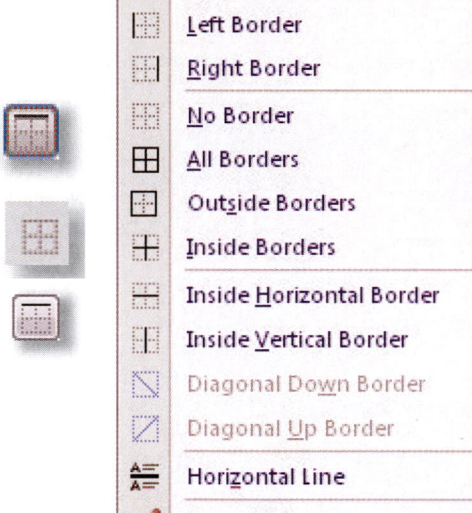

14. Click **Bottom Border**. A bottom border with the options previously set in the Borders and Shading dialog box is applied to the title.

15. Click the down arrow next to the Borders button . Click the **No Border** button to delete the border.

16. Reapply the bottom border, and click the Top Border button to add a top border as well.

17. Open the Paragraph dialog box, and change the left and right indents to *.5"*. Notice the border is indented from the left and right margins.

> **NOTE**
>
> Borders and shading, when applied to a paragraph, extend from the left margin to the right margin or if indents are set, from the left indent to the right indent.

Exercise 5-8   APPLY BORDERS TO SELECTED TEXT AND A PAGE

In addition to paragraphs, you can apply borders to selected text or to an entire page. When you apply a border to a page, you can choose whether to place the border on every page, the current page, the first page, or all but the first page in a document.

> **NOTE**
>
> When the **Apply to** box indicates **Text**, the borders are applied only to the selected text and not to the paragraph. If you include a paragraph mark in your selection, the borders are applied to all lines of the paragraph unless you change the **Apply to** setting to **Text**. It is important to notice the **Apply to** setting when applying borders and shading, or you might not get the results you intended.

1. In the third paragraph below the title (which begins "If you"), select the text "$275." Open the Borders and Shading dialog box.

2. From the **Style** box, scroll to the fifth line style from the bottom. Word automatically applies this style as the **Box** setting.

3. Change the **Color** to **Blue**. Notice that the **Apply to** box indicates **Text**.

Word 2007

Figure 5-13
Applying borders to
selected text

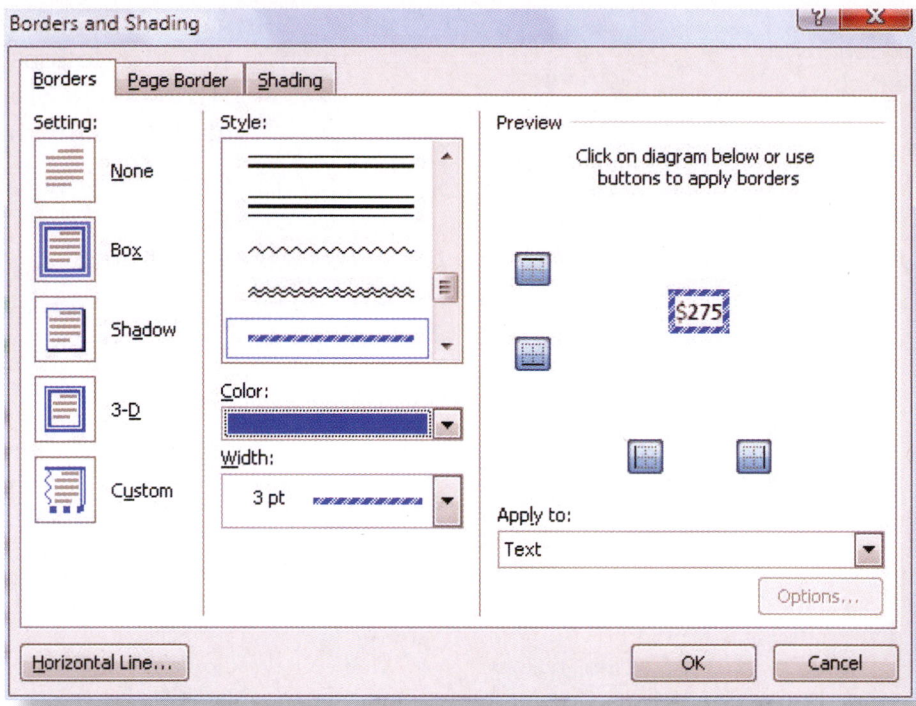

4. Click the **Page Border** tab. Choose the third-to-last line style (a band of three shades of gray), and click the **3-D** setting. The width should be **3 pt**.

5. Click **OK**. Notice the text border added to "$275" and the page border. Deselect the text so you can see the border color.

Figure 5-14
Document with
border formatting

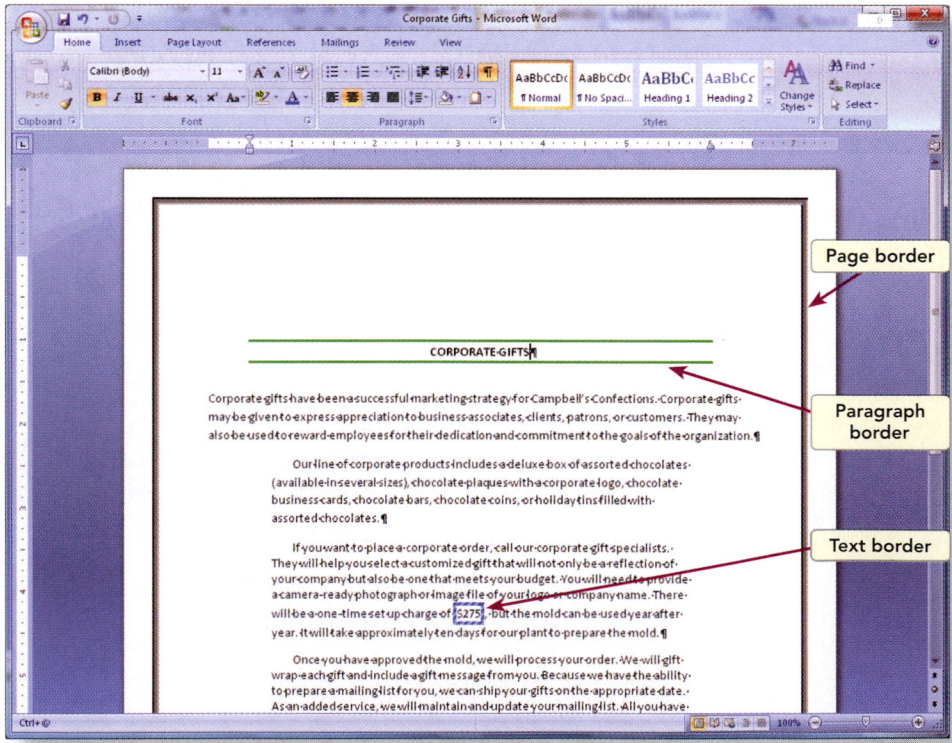

6. Save the document as *[your initials]*5-8 in your Lesson 5 folder. Print the document. Leave it open.

Exercise 5-9   ADD A HORIZONTAL LINE

Word provides special horizontal lines to divide or decorate a page. These lines are actually picture files (or "clips") in the shape of horizontal lines that are normally used when creating Web pages.

1. Position the insertion point anywhere in the last paragraph and open the Borders and Shading dialog box. Click the **Borders** tab.

2. Click **None** to remove the shadowed border. Click **OK**.

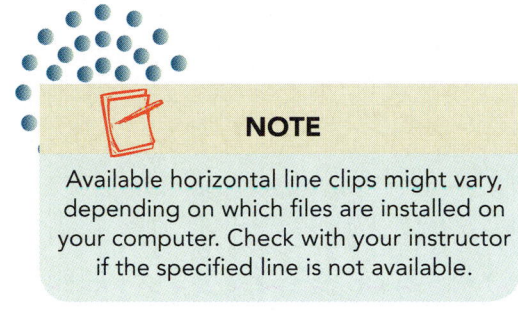

NOTE

Available horizontal line clips might vary, depending on which files are installed on your computer. Check with your instructor if the specified line is not available.

3. Position the insertion point at the beginning of the last paragraph.

4. Open the Borders and Shading dialog box. Click **Horizontal Line** at the bottom of the dialog box.

5. In the Horizontal Line dialog box, click the second box in the second row. Click **OK**. The line is inserted in the document.

Figure 5-15
Inserting a horizontal line

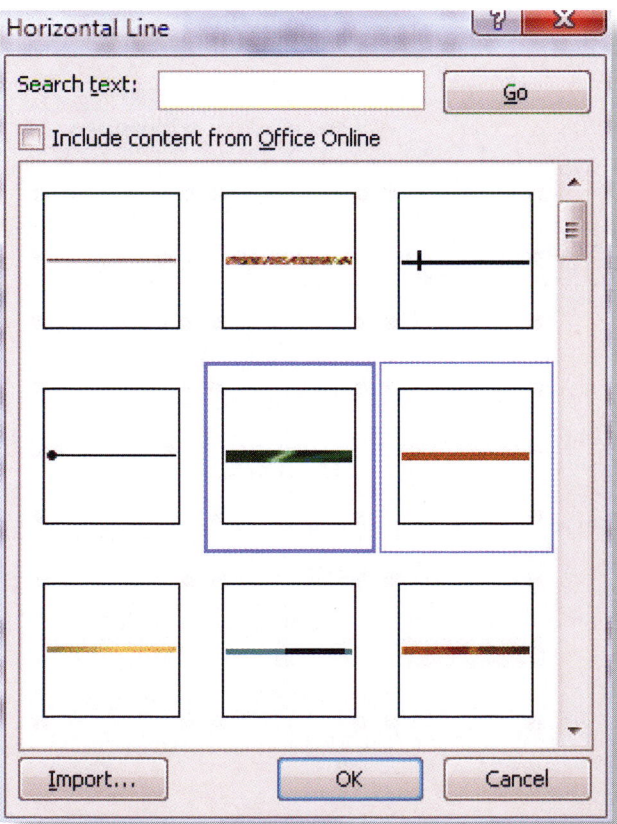

Exercise 5-10 APPLY SHADING TO A PARAGRAPH

1. Click anywhere in the last paragraph, and open the **Borders and Shading** dialog box.

2. Click the **Shading** tab.

3. Click the down arrow in the **Fill** box. Notice that you can apply Theme colors or Standard colors. Click the second gray color in the first column.

NOTE

You can click the Shading button  to apply a fill color.

Figure 5-16
Shading options in the Borders and Shading dialog box

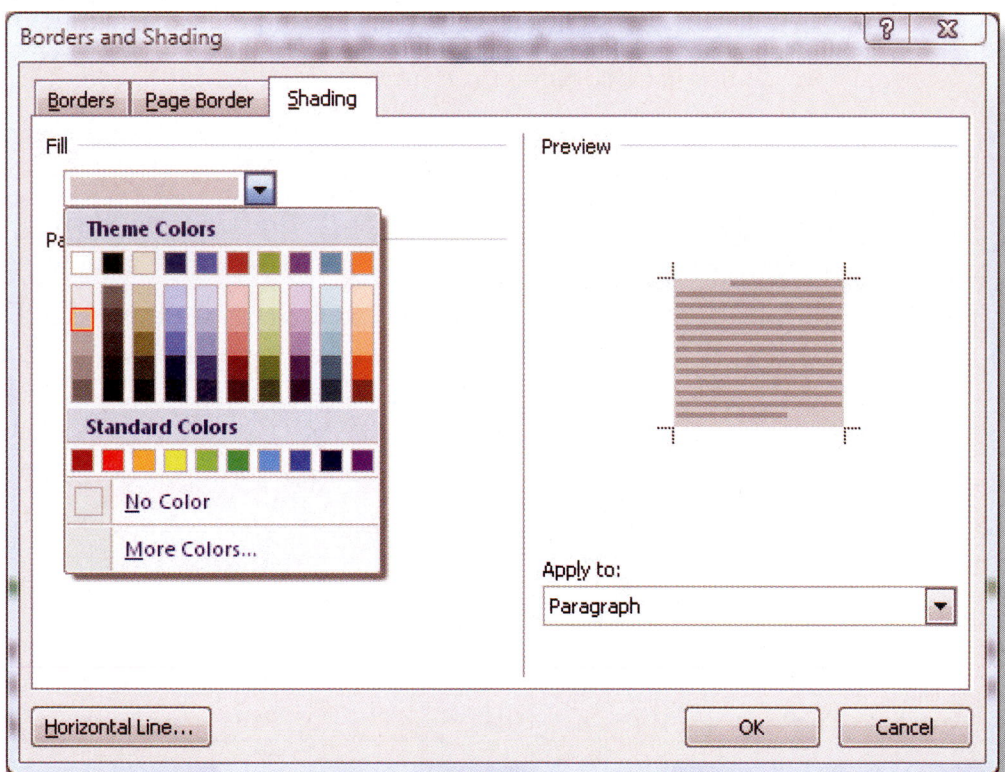

NOTE

Shading can affect the readability of text, especially when you use dark colors or patterns. It's a good idea to choose a larger type size and bold text when you use shading.

TIP

To remove all formatting from a paragraph (including borders, indents, and character formatting), click the Clear Formatting button in the Font group.

4. Open the **Style** drop-down list to view other shading options. Close the **Style** drop-down list without choosing a style.

5. Click **OK** to apply the gray shading to the paragraph.

6. With the insertion point still in the last paragraph, remove the gray shading by clicking the Shading button on the Ribbon. Click **No Color**.

7. Click the Undo button to restore the shading.

Exercise 5-11   APPLY BORDERS AUTOMATICALLY

Word provides an AutoFormat feature to apply bottom borders. Instead of using the Borders command or the Borders and Shading dialog box, you can key a series of characters and Word automatically applies a border.

1. Press Ctrl+N to create a new document and leave the current document open.

> **TIP**
>
> If you do not want to format borders automatically, click the AutoCorrect Options button ⓩ displayed after you key a series of characters and choose **Stop Automatically Creating Border Lines**.

2. Key **---** (three consecutive hyphens) and press Enter. Word applies a bottom border. Press Enter two times.

3. Key **===** (three consecutive equal signs) and press Enter. Word applies a double-line bottom border. Press Enter two times.

4. Key **——** (three consecutive underscores) and press Enter. Word applies a thick bottom border.

5. Close the document without saving.

TABLE 5-1 AutoFormatting Borders

You Key	Word Applies
Three or more hyphens (-) and press Enter	A thin bottom border
Three or more underscores (_) and press Enter	A thick bottom border
Three or more equal signs (=) and press Enter	A double-line bottom border

Repeating and Copying Formats

You can quickly repeat, copy, or remove paragraph formatting. For example, use F4 or Ctrl+Y to repeat paragraph formatting and the Format Painter button to copy paragraph formatting.

Exercise 5-12   REPEAT, COPY, AND REMOVE PARAGRAPH FORMATS

> **NOTE**
>
> You can click in a paragraph when repeating, copying, or removing formatting. You do not have to select the entire paragraph.

1. Click anywhere in the first paragraph under the title (which begins "Corporate Gifts"), and change the paragraph alignment to justified.

2. Select the rest of the indented paragraphs, starting with the paragraph that begins "Our line" through the paragraph that begins "A luxurious." Press F4 to repeat the formatting.

3. Click anywhere in the last paragraph (with the shading).

4. Click the Format Painter button 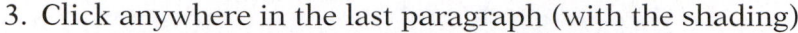; then click within the paragraph above the shaded paragraph to copy the formatting.

5. Click the Undo button 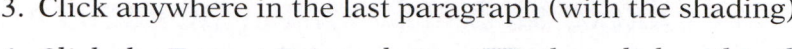 to undo the paragraph formatting.

6. Click anywhere in the shaded paragraph. Click the Clear Formatting button  on the Ribbon to remove the formatting.

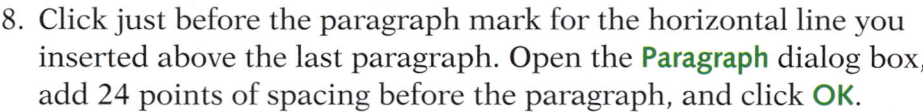

7. Click the Undo button 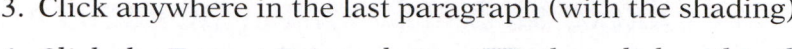 to restore the formatting.

8. Click just before the paragraph mark for the horizontal line you inserted above the last paragraph. Open the **Paragraph** dialog box, add 24 points of spacing before the paragraph, and click **OK**.

9. Save the document as *[your initials]***5-12** in your Lesson 5 folder.

10. Submit and close the document.

Bulleted and Numbered Lists

Bulleted lists and *numbered lists* are types of hanging indents you can use to organize important details in a document. In a bulleted list, a bullet (•) precedes each paragraph. In a numbered list, a sequential number or letter precedes each paragraph. When you add or delete an item in a numbered list, Word automatically renumbers the list.

To create bulleted lists or numbered lists, use the Bullets command or the Numbering command on the Ribbon (which apply the most recently selected bullet or numbering style).

Exercise 5-13   CREATE A BULLETED LIST

1. Open the file **Memo - 1**. This document is a one-page memo. Key the current date in the memo date line.

2. Locate and select the four lines of text beginning with "Monday" and ending with "Thursday."

3. Click the Bullets button  on the Ribbon, Home tab, Paragraph group. Word applies the bullet style that was most recently chosen in the Bullets list.

Figure 5-17
Bulleted list

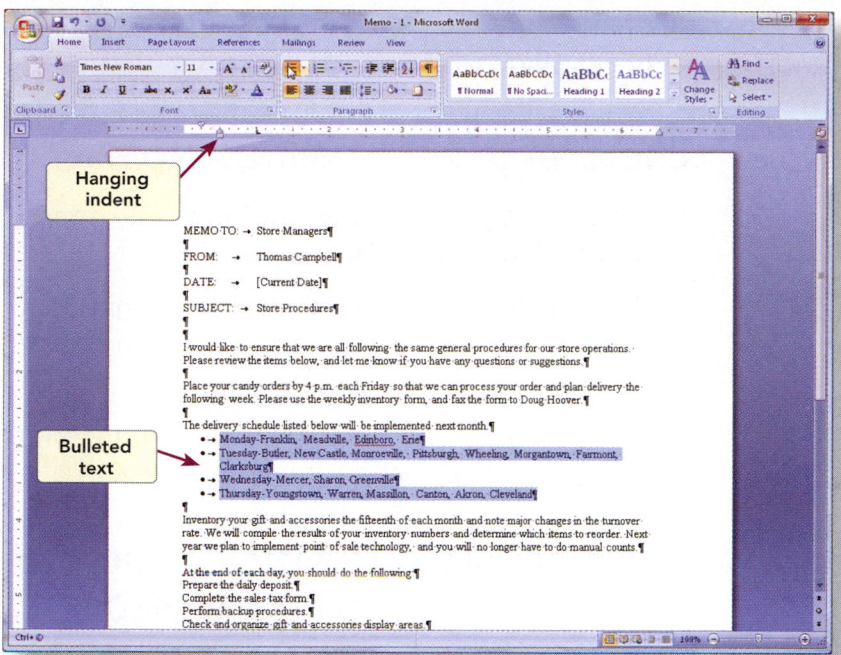

NOTE

When you create bulleted or numbered lists, Word automatically sets a 0.25-inch hanging indent.

4. With the list still selected, click the down arrow beside the **Bullets** button, and click one of the bullet shapes listed in the **Bullet Library**. The list is formatted with a different bullet shape. Deselect the list.

Figure 5-18
Bullet options

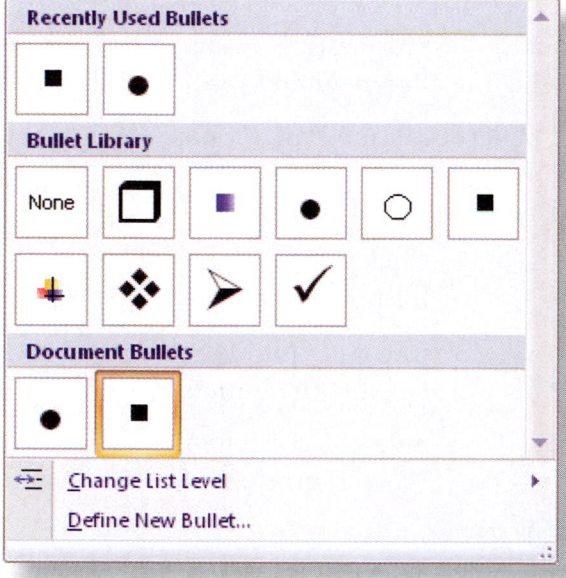

5. Click the first bullet in the bulleted list you just created to select all bullets.

6. Right-click the selected bullets, and click **Adjust List Indents** from the shortcut menu.

7. Change the **Bullet position** text box value to **.4**. Change the **Text indent** to **.65**. Click **OK**.

Exercise 5-14   CREATE A NUMBERED LIST

1. Select the last four paragraphs in the document, from "First Quarter" to "Fourth Quarter."

2. Click the Numbering button to format the list with the style that was most recently chosen from the Numbering list.

3. With the list still selected, click the down arrow beside the Numbering button. Click the roman numeral format. Word reformats the list with roman numerals.

Exercise 5-15   CHANGE A BULLETED OR NUMBERED LIST

Word's bulleting and numbering feature is very flexible. When a list is bulleted or numbered, you can change it in several ways. You can:

• Convert bullets to numbers or numbers to bullets in a list.

• Add or remove items in a bulleted or numbered list, and Word renumbers the list automatically.

• Interrupt a bulleted or numbered list to create several shorter lists.

• Customize the list formatting by changing the symbol used for bullets or changing the alignment and spacing of the bullets and numbers.

• Turn off bullets or numbering for part of a list or the entire list.

NOTE

When you select a bulleted or numbered list by dragging over the text, the list is highlighted but the bullets or numbers are not. You can select a list by clicking a bullet or number.

1. Select the bulleted list that starts with "Monday."

2. Click the down arrow beside the Numbering button.

3. Choose a numbered format that starts with "1" to convert the bullets to numbers.

4. Select and delete the line that begins "Wednesday." Word renumbers the list automatically.

5. Press Ctrl+Z to undo.

6. Place the insertion point at the end of the last item in the numbered list, after "Cleveland."

7. Press Enter and key **Friday-Emergency deliveries**. The formatting is carried to the new line.

8. Place the insertion point at the end of the fourth item (after "Cleveland.") and press Enter.

9. Key in italic ***When absolutely necessary:***

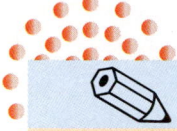

TIP

To change the shape, size, and color of a bullet, click the down arrow on the Bullets button and click **Define New Bullet**. Click the **Symbol** button to choose a new shape. Click the **Font** button to change size and color. Click the drop-down arrow of the **Alignment** box to change the bullet alignment. If you click the **Picture** button, you can insert a picture bullet—a decorative bullet often used in Web pages. You can format numbers or bullets of a list in a format different from the text of the list.

NOTE

After you format a list with bullets or numbering, each time you press [Enter] the format carries forward to the next paragraph. Pressing [Enter] twice turns off the format.

10. Click within the italic text, and click the Numbering button on the Ribbon to turn off numbering for this item. The list continues with the following paragraph.

11. Select and right-click the numbered text below the italic text (the numbered item that begins "Friday").

12. Click the **Set Numbering Value** option to open the Set Numbering Value dialog box. Select, if necessary, **Start new list** so the list does not continue the numbering. Change the **Set value to** box to **1**. Click **OK**. The new list starts with "1."

13. Insert a blank line above the italic text (click to the left of "*When*" and press [Enter]).

14. Select the list beginning with "At the" through "Check and organize."

15. Click the down arrow beside the Bullets button and click **Define New Bullet**.

16. Click **Symbol**, and change the **Font** to **Wingdings**. Scroll to locate and select the small, solid black square (▪). Click **OK** to close the Symbol dialog box, and click **OK** to close the Define New Bullet dialog box.

Exercise 5-16   CREATE LISTS AUTOMATICALLY

Word provides an AutoFormat feature to create bulleted and numbered lists as you type. When this feature is selected, you can enter a few keystrokes, key your list, and Word inserts the numbers and bullets automatically.

1. Press [Ctrl]+[End] to move to the end of the document.

2. Key the following: **Create a list of all equipment and fixtures in the store. Provide the following:**

3. Press [Enter]. Key ***** and press [Spacebar].

4. Key **Description/Model number** and press [Enter]. Word automatically formats your text as a bulleted list.

5. Key the following text to complete the list, pressing [Enter] at the end of each line except the last line:

   Serial number
   Date acquired
   Purchase price
   Location
   Inventory number

TABLE 5-2 AutoFormatting Numbered and Bulleted Lists

You Key	Word Creates
A number; a period, closing parenthesis, or hyphen; a space or tab; and text. Example, **1.**, **1**), or **1**-Press Enter.	A numbered list
An asterisk (*) or hyphen (-); a space or tab; and text. Press Enter.	A bulleted list

Exercise 5-17   CREATE A MULTILEVEL LIST

A *multilevel list* has indented subparagraphs. For example, your list can start with item number "1)," followed by another level of indented items numbered "a)," "b)," and "c)." An outline numbered list can have up to nine levels and is often used for technical or legal documents. The Multilevel List command is located on the Ribbon, Home tab, Paragraph group.

1. Go to the end of the document and press Enter four times.

2. Click the arrow beside the Multilevel List button 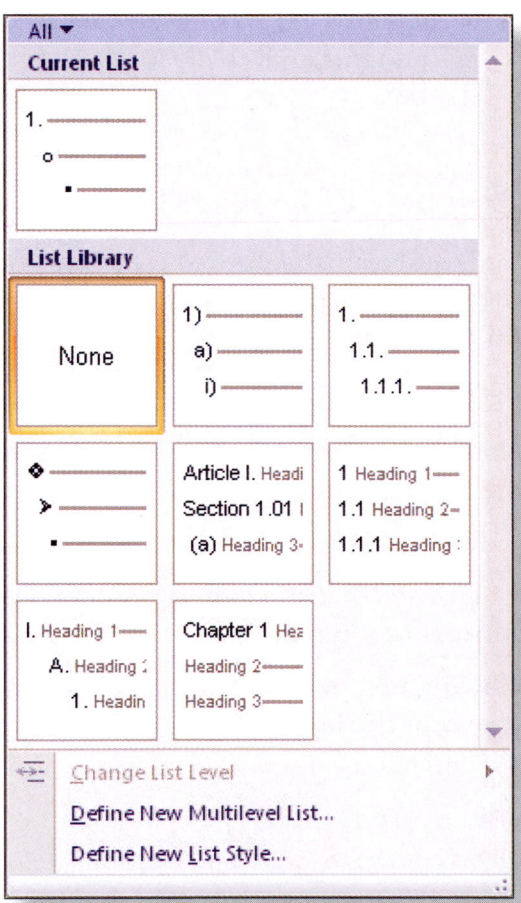. Notice the outline numbering styles available in the List Library.

Figure 5-19
Multilevel List Library

3. Click the outline numbering style that begins with **"I."** **Notice the uppercase roman numeral in the text.**

4. Key **January** and press Enter.

5. Click the Increase Indent button ▣ (or press Tab), and key **A.** Spacebar **Prepare memo to employees regarding changes to W-4 forms.**

6. Press Enter and key **B.** Spacebar **Prepare and mail W-2 forms to employees**. The numbered list now has two indented subparagraphs. Press Enter. Key **C.** Spacebar **Prepare and mail 1099 forms.** Press Enter.

7. With the insertion point at the beginning of a new line, click the Decrease Indent button ▣ (or press Shift + Tab) to position the insertion point at the left margin. You can now add a second first-level paragraph to your list.

8. Key **II. February**.

> **NOTE**
>
> You can create and define a multilevel list style and add it to the List Gallery. Click the arrow beside the Multilevel List button ▦ and click **Define New Multilevel List**. Enter the text and format for each level. Click **OK**.

Symbols and Special Characters

The fonts you use with Word include *special characters* that do not appear on your keyboard, such as those used in foreign languages (for example, ç, Ö, and Ω). There are additional fonts, such as *Wingdings* and *Symbol* that consist entirely of special characters.

To insert symbols and special characters in your documents, click the **Insert** tab on the Ribbon, locate the **Symbols** group, and click the **Symbol** command.

Exercise 5-18 INSERT SYMBOLS

1. Scroll toward the beginning of the document. Position the insertion point to the immediate left of the paragraph that begins *"When absolutely."*

2. Click the **Insert** tab. Locate the **Symbols** group, and click the arrow beside the Symbol button Ω. Click **More Symbols**. The Symbol dialog box appears.

3. Make sure the **Symbols** tab is displayed and choose **(normal text)** from the **Font** drop-down list box.

4. Scroll through the grid of available symbol characters for normal text, and notice that the grid contains diacritical marks that you can use for foreign languages. You will also see the symbol for cents (¢) and degrees (°).

5. Click the arrow to open the **Font** drop-down list box and choose **Symbol**. Review the available symbol characters.

6. Change the font to **Wingdings**. The characters included in the Wingdings font appear in the grid.

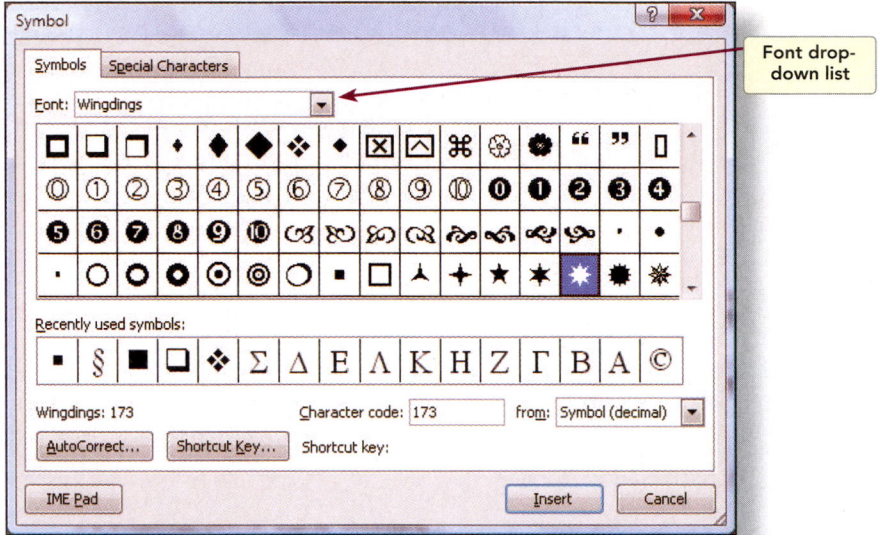

Figure 5-20
Symbol dialog box

7. Scroll down several rows until you see symbols similar to an asterisk (✳). Click one of the symbols.

8. Click **Insert,** and then click **Close**. The symbol appears in the document.

9. Select the list with roman numerals beginning with "I. First Quarter" through "IV. Fourth Quarter."

10. Click the Home tab and click the arrow beside the Bullets button 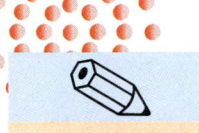.

11. Click **Define New Bullet** and click **Picture**. Click one of the picture bullets, and click **OK**, and then click **OK** again. The roman numerals are replaced with your chosen picture bullet.

TIP

Notice the recently used symbols shown at the bottom of the Symbol dialog box. Word displays the 16 most recently used symbols.

TIP

You can assign shortcut keys or AutoCorrect to a symbol by clicking **Shortcut Key** or **AutoCorrect** in the Symbol dialog box. You can also press Alt and key the numeric code (using the numeric keypad, if you have one) for a character. For example, if you change the font of the document to Wingdings and press Alt + 0 0 4 0 , you will insert the character for a Wingdings telephone. Remember to change the Wingdings font back to your normal font after inserting a special character.

Exercise 5-19 INSERT SPECIAL CHARACTERS

You can use the Symbol dialog box and shortcut keys to insert characters such as an en dash, an em dash, or SmartQuotes. An *en dash* is a dash slightly wider than a hyphen. An *em dash,* which is twice as wide as an en dash, is used in sentences where you would normally insert two hyphens. *Smart quotes* are quotation marks that open a quote curled in one direction (") and close a quote curled in the opposite direction (").

NOTE

By default, Word inserts smart quotes automatically.

1. Make sure nonprinting characters are displayed in the document. If they are not, click the Show/Hide ¶ button ¶.

2. On page 1, locate the paragraph that begins "1. Monday." Position the insertion point to the immediate right of "Monday." Press Delete to remove the hyphen.

3. Click the **Insert** tab, and click the arrow beside the Symbol button Ω. Click **More Symbols**, and click the **Special Characters** tab.

4. Choose **Em Dash** from the list of characters. (Notice the keyboard shortcut listed for the character.) Click **Insert**, and then click **Close**. The em dash replaces the hyphen.

5. Select the hyphen immediately following "Tuesday." Press Alt + Ctrl + – (the minus sign on the numeric keypad). An em dash is inserted. (If you don't have a numeric keypad, press F4 to repeat the character.)

6. Insert em dashes after "Wednesday," "Thursday," and "Friday."

Exercise 5-20 CREATE SYMBOLS AUTOMATICALLY

You can use Word's AutoCorrect feature to create symbols as you type. Just enter a few keystrokes, and Word converts them into a symbol.

NOTE

To review the symbols AutoCorrect can enter automatically, open the **Word Options** dialog box, and click **Proofing**. Click **AutoCorrect Options**, and click the AutoCorrect tab.

1. Scroll to the "SUBJECT" line, and click to the left of "Store."

2. Key **< = =** and notice that Word automatically creates an arrow (←).

3. Position the insertion point to the right of "Procedures." Key **= = >**. Word creates another pointing to the right.

4. Format the first line of the memo with 72 points of paragraph spacing before it. This starts the first line two inches from the top of the page. (See Appendix B, "Standard Forms for Business Documents.")

5. Save the document as *[your initials]***5-20** in your Lesson 5 folder.

6. Submit and close the document.

Lesson 5 Summary

- A paragraph is any amount of text followed by a paragraph mark.

- Paragraph alignment determines how the edges of a paragraph appear horizontally. Paragraphs can be left-aligned, centered, right-aligned, or justified.

- The Click and Type feature enables you to insert text in any blank area of a document by simply positioning the insertion point and double-clicking.

- Line space is the amount of vertical space between lines of text in a paragraph. Lines can be single-spaced, 1.5-line spaced, double-spaced, or set to a specific value.

- Paragraph space is the amount of space above or below a paragraph. Paragraph space is set in points—12 points of space equals one line space for 12-point text. Change the space between paragraphs by using the Before and After options in the Paragraph dialog box or by using the Ctrl+0, Ctrl+Shift+0 keyboard shortcuts to add or remove 12 points before a paragraph.

- A left indent or right indent increases a paragraph's distance from the left or right margin. A first-line indent indents only the first line of a paragraph. A hanging indent indents the second and subsequent lines of a paragraph.

- To set indents by using the horizontal ruler, drag the left indent marker (small rectangle), the first-line indent marker (top triangle), or the hanging indent marker (bottom triangle), which are all on the left end of the ruler, or drag the right indent marker (triangle) on the right end of the ruler.

- A border is a line or box added to selected text, a paragraph, or a page. Shading fills in the background of selected text or paragraphs. Borders and shading can appear in a variety of styles and colors.

- In addition to regular borders, Word provides special decorative horizontal lines that are available from the Borders and Shading dialog box.

- The AutoFormat feature enables you to create a border automatically. Key three or more hyphens –, underscores _, or equal signs =, and press Enter. See Table 5-1.

- Repeat paragraph formats by pressing F4 or Ctrl+Y. Copy paragraph formats by using the Format Painter command. Remove paragraph formats by pressing Ctrl+Q or choosing the **Clear Formatting** command from the Ribbon, Home tab, Font group.

- Format a list of items as a bulleted or numbered list. In a bulleted list, each item is indented and preceded by a bullet character or other symbol. In a numbered list, each item is indented and preceded by a sequential number or letter.

- Remove a bullet or number from an item in a list by clicking the Bullets command or the Numbering command on the Ribbon. Press Enter in the middle of the list to add another bulleted or numbered item automatically. Press Enter twice in a list to turn off bullets or numbering.

Change the bullet symbol or the numbering type by clicking the arrow beside the Bullets command to display the Bullet Library or the arrow beside the Numbering command to open the Numbering Library.

- The AutoFormat feature enables you to create a bulleted or numbered list automatically. See Table 5-2.

- Create a multilevel list by clicking the Multilevel List command. A multilevel list has indented subparagraphs, such as paragraph "1)" followed by indented paragraph "a)" followed by indented paragraph "i)." To increase the level of numbering for each line item, click the Increase Indent command or press Tab. To decrease the level of numbering, click the Decrease Indent command or press Shift+Tab.

- Insert symbols, such as foreign characters, by clicking the Insert tab and clicking the Symbol command. Wingdings is an example of a font that contains all symbols.

- Insert special characters, such as an em dash (—), by using the Special Characters tab in the Symbol dialog box.

- Create symbols automatically as you type by keying AutoCorrect shortcuts, such as keying (c) to produce the ©.

LESSON 5		Command Summary	
Feature	**Button**	**Command**	**Keyboard**
Left-align text		Home tab, Paragraph group	Ctrl+L
Center text		Home tab, Paragraph group	Ctrl+E
Right-align text		Home tab, Paragraph group	Ctrl+R
Justify text		Home tab, Paragraph group	Ctrl+J
Single space		Home tab, Paragraph group	Ctrl+1
Double space		Home tab, Paragraph group	Ctrl+2
1.5-line space		Home tab, Paragraph group	Ctrl+5
Borders and Shading		Home tab, Paragraph group	
Remove paragraph formatting		Home tab, Paragraph group	Ctrl+Q
Restore text to Normal formatting		Home tab, Font group	Ctrl+Shift+N
Increase indent		Home tab, Paragraph group	Ctrl+M
Decrease indent		Home tab, Paragraph group	Ctrl+Shift+M
Hanging indent		Home tab, Paragraph group	Ctrl+T
Bulleted list		Home tab, Paragraph group	
Numbered list		Home tab, Paragraph group	
Symbols and special characters		Insert tab, Symbols group	

Concepts Review

True/False Questions

Each of the following statements is either true or false. Indicate your choice by circling T or F.

T F   1. You can use the Ribbon, Home tab, Font group to right-align paragraphs.

T F   2. Text that is left-aligned has a ragged left edge.

T F   3. You can open the Paragraph dialog box from the shortcut menu.

T F   4. The keyboard shortcut Ctrl+5 changes line spacing to 1.5 lines.

T F   5. You can use Word's AutoCorrect feature to create symbols as you type by using certain keyboard combinations.

T F   6. To apply a page border to a document, click the Borders tab in the Borders and Shading dialog box.

T F   7. Ctrl+Q removes paragraph formatting.

T F   8. A hanging indent indents all lines in a paragraph except the first line.

Short Answer Questions

Write the correct answer in the space provided.

1. Which type of paragraph alignment adjusts spacing between words?

   _____

2. What is the keyboard shortcut for centering text?

   _____

3. Single, 1.5, and double are examples of what type of spacing?

   _____

4. If you click ⊞ once, what happens to selected text?

   _____

5. With an outline numbered list, instead of clicking ⊞, what key can you press to achieve the same result?

   _____

6. Which keystrokes apply a double-line border automatically?

_____

7. What is the procedure to display the Reveal Formatting task pane?

_____

8. Which indent marker is the top triangle on the left side of the ruler?

_____

Critical Thinking

Answer these questions on a separate page. There are no right or wrong answers. Support your answers with examples from your own experience, if possible.

1. You can use keyboard shortcuts to change paragraph alignment, or you can use the alignment buttons on the Ribbon. Which method do you prefer? Why? When might you use the other method?

2. Many people use bulleted lists and numbered lists interchangeably. Are there times when it would be more appropriate to use a bulleted list than a numbered list and vice versa? Explain your answer.

Skills Review

Exercise 5-21

Change paragraph alignment and line spacing.

1. Start a new document.
2. Change the character formatting and paragraph alignment for the first paragraph by following these steps:
   a. Select the paragraph mark and set the font to 14-point Cambria.
   b. Click the Center button ▣ on the Ribbon, Home tab, Paragraph group, to center the text you are about to key.
   c. Key the first two lines shown in Figure 5-21 in all capitals. Use a line break (press Shift + Enter) after the first line to make the two lines one paragraph.

Figure 5-21

```
CAMPBELL'S CONFECTIONS
OHIO STORE MANAGERS

Sarah Dunlap
Patrick Rhodes
Paul Kellogg
Scott Edwards
Nancy Epperson
Leigh Brittain
```

3. At the end of this paragraph, press [Enter] twice, turn off [Caps Lock], and key the six names shown in Figure 5-21. Again, use a line break after each name to make the names all one paragraph.

4. Change the alignment of each paragraph by following these steps:

a. Move the insertion point into the first paragraph and click the Align Right button ≡ on the Ribbon, Home tab, to right-align the first two lines.

b. Move the insertion point into the paragraph containing the six names and press [Ctrl]+[L] to left-align the names.

c. Select the entire document and click the Center button ≡ to center all the text.

5. Change line spacing by following these steps:

a. Click within the second paragraph.

b. Press [Ctrl]+[5] to change the line spacing to 1.5 lines.

6. Save the document as *[your initials]*5-21 in your Lesson 5 folder.

7. Submit and close the document.

Exercise 5-22

Change paragraph spacing and set indents.

1. Open the file **Club**. (Make sure the Show/Hide ¶ button ¶ is turned on.)

2. Change spacing between paragraphs by following these steps:

a. Select the entire document, click the right mouse button, and choose **Paragraph** from the shortcut menu.

b. Click the **Indents and Spacing** tab if it is not displayed.

c. Click the up arrow to the right of **After** to set the spacing after paragraphs to 12 points. Click **OK**.

3. Press [Ctrl]+[Home] to move to the top of the document. Key in bold uppercase letters **CAMPBELL'S CONFECTIONS' CHOCOLATE CLUB**.

4. Press [Enter] once. Click within the new title and open the **Paragraph** dialog box. Change **Spacing** to 72 points **Before** and 24 points **After**. Change the **Alignment** to **Centered** and click **OK**.

5. Apply a first-line indent to the paragraphs by following these steps:

a. Select all the paragraphs below the title.

b. Make sure the horizontal ruler is displayed. Point to the first-line indent marker on the ruler. When a ScreenTip identifies it, drag it 0.5 inch to the right.

6. Change the indentation of the last paragraph by following these steps:

a. Left-click to deselect the paragraphs.

b. Right-click the last paragraph and open the Paragraph dialog box.

c. Set the Left and Right indentation text boxes to 1 inch.

d. Remove the first-line indent by choosing **(none)** from the **Special** drop-down list. Click **OK**.

7. Key **Note:** at the beginning of the newly indented paragraph. Format "Note" in bold, small caps.

8. Justify the four paragraphs below the title.

9. Save the document as *[your initials]*5-22 in your Lesson 5 folder.

10. Submit and close the document.

Exercise 5-23

Apply borders and shading; repeat and copy formatting.

1. Open the file **Retail Stores**.

2. At the end of the document, key the following text as a separate paragraph. Use bold text and be sure to insert a blank line before the new paragraph.

   To learn more about our stores and products, call Campbell's Confections at 800-555-2025 or visit our web site at www.campbellsconfections.biz.

3. Apply borders and shading to the new paragraph by following these steps:

   a. Place the insertion point in the paragraph.

    b. Click the arrow beside the Borders button on the Ribbon, Paragraph group. Click **Borders and Shading**, and click the **Borders** tab if it is not displayed.

   c. Use the first line style, and change the line **Color** to **Blue**.

   d. Change the **Width** to **1¹/₂ pt**.

    e. In the **Preview** box, click the Top Border button and the Bottom Border button .

   f. Click the **Shading** tab. Click the down arrow beside the **Fill** box. From the **Theme Colors** palette, click the third box in the first column (**White, Background 1, Darker 15%**). Click **OK**.

4. Repeat the formatting by clicking within the first paragraph and pressing F4.

 5. Click the Undo button to undo the formatting in the first paragraph.

6. Apply a border to text automatically by following these steps:

   a. Key the following title at the top of the document: **Campbell's Confections**.

   b. Press Enter two times.

   c. Click in front of the blank paragraph mark. Key **= = =** and press Enter to automatically insert a double-line border under the first paragraph. Delete the blank paragraph mark.

7. Copy formatting from one paragraph to another by following these steps:

   a. Click in the last paragraph.

   b. Click the Format Painter button .

   c. Click in the title paragraph.

8. Change the title paragraph to bold and all capitals. Add 72 points of spacing before and 24 points after the paragraph and center the title.

9. Save the document as *[your initials]*5-23 in your Lesson 5 folder.

10. Submit and close the document.

Exercise 5-24

Align paragraphs, change paragraph spacing, create bulleted lists, and insert symbols and special characters.

1. Open the file **Designs**.

2. Format the title as bold, all caps, centered. Set the paragraph spacing to 72 points before and 24 points after.

3. Create a bulleted list by following these steps:

   a. Select the text beginning with "Milk chocolate" and ending with "White chocolate."

   b. Click the arrow beside the Bullets button .

   c. Choose a bullet option.

4. Insert symbols by following these steps:

   a. Position the insertion point to the right of "Computer."

   b. Click the **Insert** tab on the Ribbon. Click the Symbol button . Click **More Symbols**.

   c. Change the **Font** to **Wingdings**. Double-click the computer symbol in the second row.

   d. Click **Close**.

5. Click to the right of "Camera," and open the Symbol dialog box. Change the **Font** to **Webdings**, and scroll to the tenth row to locate the camera symbol. Click **Insert**. Click **Close**.

6. Click to the right of "Cell phone," and open the Symbol dialog box. Change the **Font** to **Webdings**, and scroll to the eleventh row to locate the cell phone symbol. Click **Insert**. Click **Close**.

7. Insert an em dash by following these steps:

   a. Position the insertion point in front of the computer symbol.

   b. Press [Alt]+[Ctrl]+[−] (the minus key on the numeric keypad). Or click the **Insert** tab on the Ribbon, click the arrow beside **Symbol**, click **More Symbols**, and click the **Special Characters** tab to select the em dash.

8. Insert an em dash before the camera symbol and the cell phone symbol. Select each symbol, and change the font size to 14.

9. Save the document as *[your initials]*5-24 in your Lesson 5 folder.

10. Submit and close the document.

Lesson Applications

Exercise 5-25

Change alignment, line spacing, and paragraph spacing and apply shading.

1. Start a new document.

2. Key the text shown in Figure 5-22, including the corrections. Use Times New Roman, single spacing, and 0 points spacing before and 0 points spacing after. Use line breaks (⎡Shift⎤+⎡Enter⎤) to format the text as two paragraphs.

Figure 5-22

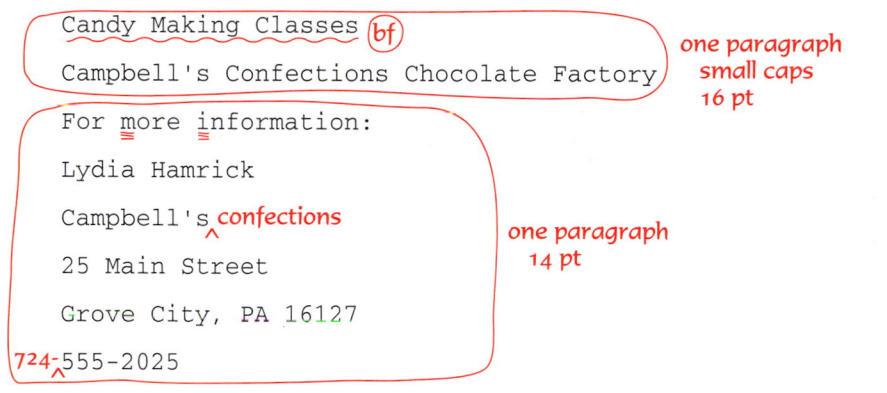

3. Center all text in the document.

4. Change the line spacing in only the second paragraph to 1.5 lines.

5. Change the paragraph spacing for only the first paragraph to 72 points before and 36 points after.

6. Add 10 percent gray shading to the first paragraph.

7. Add a page border, using the box setting and the double wavy line style.

8. Save the document as *[your initials]*5-25 in your Lesson 5 folder.

9. Submit and close the document.

Exercise 5-26

Change alignment, line spacing, and paragraph spacing; add a border; repeat formatting; and add symbols.

1. Open the file **WV Stores**.

2. Change the title to "Campbell's Confections—West Virginia Stores." There should be one blank line below the title and a blank line after each of the remaining office locations.

3. Format all lines of the first office location with 1.5-line spacing.

4. Repeat the formatting for the remaining locations.

5. Change the title to 20-point bold with paragraph spacing of 72 points before and 24 points after. Delete the blank paragraph mark after the title.

6. Add a 3/4-point double-line bottom border to the title.

7. Center the second and third office location text, and right-align the last office location text.

8. Replace the text "Telephone:" throughout the document with the telephone symbol from the Wingdings font (first row, eighth symbol). Leave the space between the symbol and the telephone number.

9. Replace the text "Fax:" throughout the document with a fax symbol from the Webdings font (eleventh row, tenth symbol).

10. Save the document as *[your initials]*5-26 in your Lesson 5 folder.

11. Submit and close the document.

Exercise 5-27

Indent paragraphs, create bulleted and numbered lists, and change paragraph spacing.

1. Open the file **Favors - 2**.

2. Select the title and apply bold, 14 point, and shadow formatting. Change the spacing before to 72 points and the spacing after to 24 points. Center the title.

3. Select the text from "wedding bells" to "other assorted shapes." Format the selected text as a bullet list using the standard round bullet.

4. Select the text from "solid milk chocolate" to "dark chocolate with mint filling." Format the selected text as a bullet list using a picture bullet.

5. Set 0.25-inch first-line indents for all paragraphs except the title, the bulleted lists, and the final paragraph.

6. Format the final paragraph with 0.75-inch left and right indents.

7. Add gray shading to the final paragraph.

8. Save the document as *[your initials]*5-27 in your Lesson 5 folder.

9. Submit and close the document.

Exercise 5-28 ◆ Challenge Yourself

Indent and align paragraphs, change paragraph spacing, apply a border, copy formatting, create bulleted lists, and insert a special character.

1. Open the file **Fundraising**.

2. Key the heading **Fundraising** at the top of the document. Format the heading in bold, uppercase letters with a negative left indent of –0.25 inch and 12 points of spacing before the paragraph and 24 points of spacing after the paragraph.

3. Format the paragraphs from "Solid milk chocolate" to "Milk chocolate with double chocolate filling" as a bulleted list, using the bullet of your choice, with 6 points of spacing after paragraphs.

4. Format the paragraphs from "Sales Department" to "555-2025" with a.75-inch left indent and with 6 points of spacing after paragraphs.

5. Add one blank paragraph mark above "Specialty fundraising." Position the insertion point at the blank paragraph mark. Open the Borders and Shading dialog box, and click **Horizontal Line**. Add a horizontal line of your choice.

6. Justify all paragraphs in the document except the title and bulleted lists.

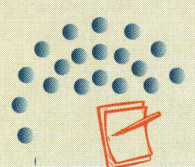

NOTE

If horizontal line clips are not available, use a border.

7. Add a page border to the document, using the third-to-last line style, 3-point width, and the 3-D setting.

8. Save the document as *[your initials]***5-28** in your Lesson 5 folder.

9. Submit and close the document.

On Your Own

In these exercises you work on your own, as you would in a real-life business environment. Use the skills you've learned to accomplish the task—and be creative.

Exercise 5-29

Create a flyer for an event, such as a meeting or concert. Use a variety of paragraph alignment settings, line spacing, and paragraph spacing. Add shading to one or more paragraphs and a page border. Include a bulleted list. Save the document as *[your initials]***5-29**. Submit the document.

Exercise 5-30

Create a set of instructions for how to make something. Use a bulleted list for the materials needed. Use a numbered list to describe the step-by-step instructions. Use borders or shading for emphasis or for paragraphs containing special notes or tips. Save the document as *[your initials]***5-30** and submit it.

Exercise 5-31

Review the foreign-language characters in the Symbols dialog box (normal text). Use a foreign-language dictionary (such as an online dictionary on the Internet) to find a few foreign words you can key in a document by inserting the appropriate foreign-language characters. Include the English translations. Display the Research task pane to help you define and translate vocabulary. Save the document as *[your initials]***5-31** and submit it.

Lesson 6

tabs and tabbed Columns

OBJECTIVES

After completing this lesson, you will be able to:

1. Set tabs.
2. Set leader tabs.
3. Clear tabs.
4. Adjust tab settings.
5. Create tabbed columns.
6. Sort paragraphs and tabbed columns.

MCAS OBJECTIVES

In this lesson:
WW 07 2.1.5
WW 07 4.2.2

Estimated Time: 1 hour

A *tab* is a paragraph-formatting feature used to align text. When you press Tab, Word inserts a tab character and moves the insertion point to the position of the tab setting, called the *tab stop*. You can set custom tabs or use Word's default tab settings.

As with other paragraph-formatting features, tab settings are stored in the paragraph mark at the end of a paragraph. Each time you press Enter, the tab settings are copied to the next paragraph. You can set tabs before you key text or for existing text.

Setting Tabs

Word's default tabs are left-aligned and set every half inch from the left margin. These tabs are indicated at the bottom of the horizontal ruler by tiny tick marks.

Figure 6-1
Default tabs

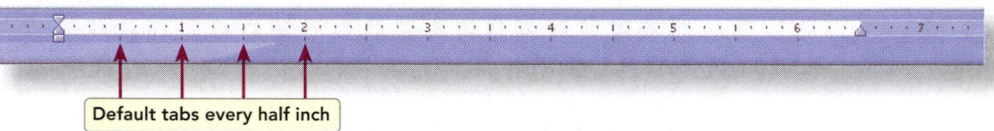

If you don't want to use the half-inch default tab settings, you have two choices:

- Change the distance between the default tab stops.

- Create custom tabs.

The four most common types of custom tabs are left-aligned, centered, right-aligned, and decimal-aligned. Custom tab settings are indicated by *tab markers* on the horizontal ruler. Additional custom tab options, such as leader tabs and bar tabs, are discussed in the section "Setting Leader Tabs" and in the exercise "Insert Bar Tabs."

Figure 6-2
Types of tabs

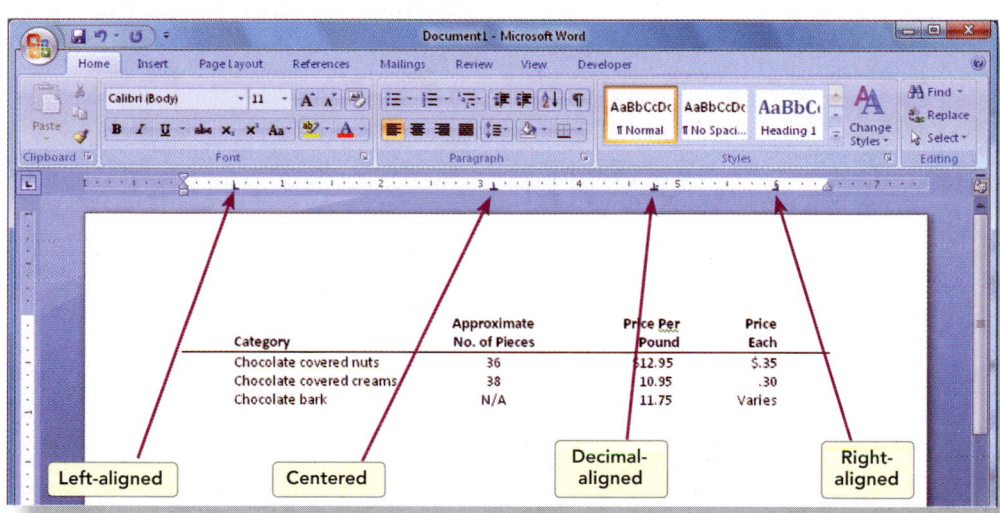

TABLE 6-1 Types of Tabs

Ruler Symbol	Type of Tab	Description
⌐	Left-aligned	The left edge of the text aligns with the tab stop.
⊥	Centered	The text is centered at the tab stop.
⌐	Right-aligned	The right edge of the text aligns with the tab stop.
⊥	Decimal-aligned	The decimal point aligns with the tab stop. Use this option for columns of numbers.
▯	Bar	Inserts a vertical line at the tab stop. Use to create a divider line between columns.

There are two ways to set tabs:

- Use the Tabs dialog box.
- Use the ruler.

Exercise 6-1   SET TABS BY USING THE TABS DIALOG BOX

1. Open the file **Memo - 2**.

2. Click the View Ruler button 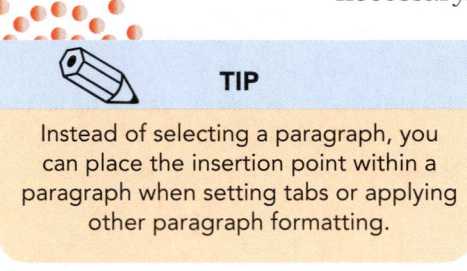 to display the horizontal ruler, if necessary.

3. Select the text near the end of the document that begins "Item New Price" through the end of the document.

> **TIP**
>
> Instead of selecting a paragraph, you can place the insertion point within a paragraph when setting tabs or applying other paragraph formatting.

4. Click the **Home** tab, and locate the **Paragraph** group. Click the **Paragraph Dialog Box Launcher** 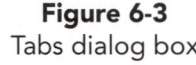. Click **Tabs**. The Tabs dialog box appears. Notice that the **Default tab stops** text box is set to 0.5 inch.

Figure 6-3
Tabs dialog box

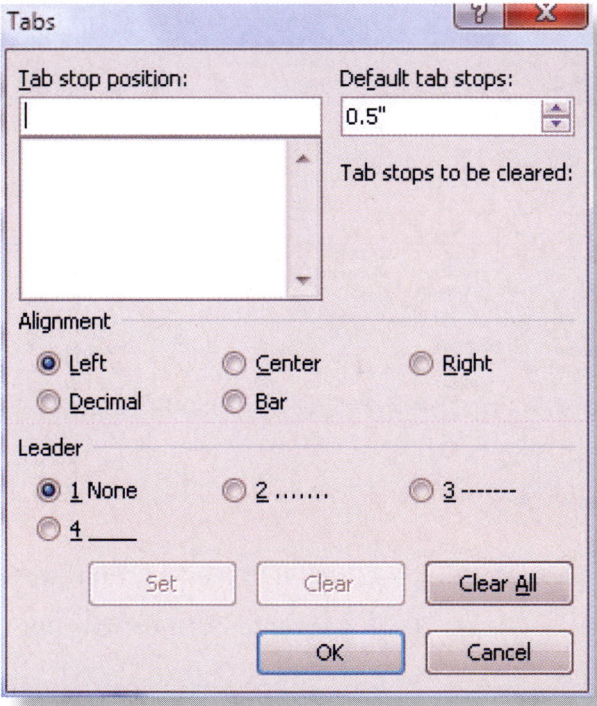

5. Key **.25** in the **Tab stop position** text box. The alignment is already set to **Left**, by default.

6. Click **OK**. The ruler displays a left tab marker ﹂, the symbol used to indicate the type and location of a tab stop on the ruler.

7. Move the insertion point to the left of the first word on the first line of the selected text, "Item".

8. Press [Tab]. The first line of the group is now indented 0.25 inch. This produces the same effect as creating a first-line indent.

REVIEW

Tabs are nonprinting characters that can be displayed or hidden. Remember, to display or hide nonprinting characters, click the Show/Hide ¶ button ¶.

NOTE

When you set a custom tab, Word clears all default tabs to the left of the new tab marker.

NOTE

The column heading "New Price" does not contain a decimal, but is aligned at the decimal point. You will adjust the tab for this heading later in this lesson.

9. Press ⎡Tab⎦ at the beginning of each of the lines that you formatted with the .25-inch left tab ("1.25 oz.," "1 lb.," "1 lb.," "4 oz.," and "4 oz.").

10. Select the same six lines of text ("Item" through "2.25") at the end of the document. Notice that there are tab characters between some of the words and that the text is crowded and difficult to read. The text is aligned at the default tab settings (every .5").

11. Open the Tabs dialog box by double clicking the tab marker at .25 on the ruler. Key **3.0** in the **Tab stop position** text box.

12. Under **Alignment**, choose **Decimal**. Click **Set**. Notice that the tab setting appears below the **Tab stop position** text box. The setting is automatically selected so that another tab setting can be keyed.

13. Click **OK**. The column headings "Item" and "New Price," along with the text below the headings, are now aligned at the tab stops.

Exercise 6-2   SET TABS BY USING THE RULER

Setting tabs by using the ruler is an easy two-step process: Click the Tab Alignment button on the left of the ruler to choose the type of tab alignment, and then click the position on the ruler to set the tab.

1. Go to the end of the document, and press ⎡Enter⎦ if necessary to begin a new paragraph.

2. Key **Category** at the left margin.

3. Click the **Tab Alignment** button on the horizontal ruler until it shows center alignment ⊥. Each time you click the button, the alignment changes.

Figure 6-4
Tab alignment button on the ruler

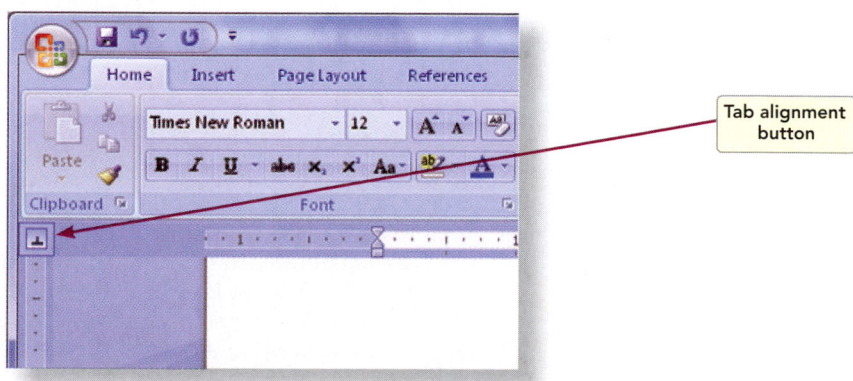

TIP

When choosing tab settings for information in a document, keep in mind that left-aligned text and right- or decimal-aligned numbers are easier to read.

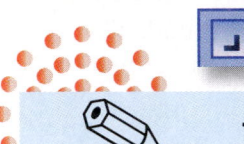

TIP

As you toggle through the Tab Alignment button symbols, notice the appearance of the first-line indent symbol and the hanging indent symbol. You can display one of these symbols, and then just click the ruler to the desired indent position instead of using the point and drag method.

4. Click the ruler at 3.25, and a center tab marker displays.

5. Press ⎯Tab⎯, and key **No. of Pieces**.

6. Click the **Tab Alignment** button on the horizontal ruler until it shows right alignment ⊞ , and then click the ruler at 5.5.

7. Press ⎯Tab⎯, and key **Price/Pound**.

8. Press ⎯Enter⎯ to start a new line. The tab settings will carry forward to the new line.

9. Key **Chocolate-covered nuts**, press ⎯Tab⎯, key **36**, press ⎯Tab⎯, and key **$12.95**.

10. Press ⎯Enter⎯ and key **Chocolate-covered creams**, press ⎯Tab⎯, key **38**, press ⎯Tab⎯, and key **10.95**. Press ⎯Enter⎯.

Figure 6-5
Document with tabbed text

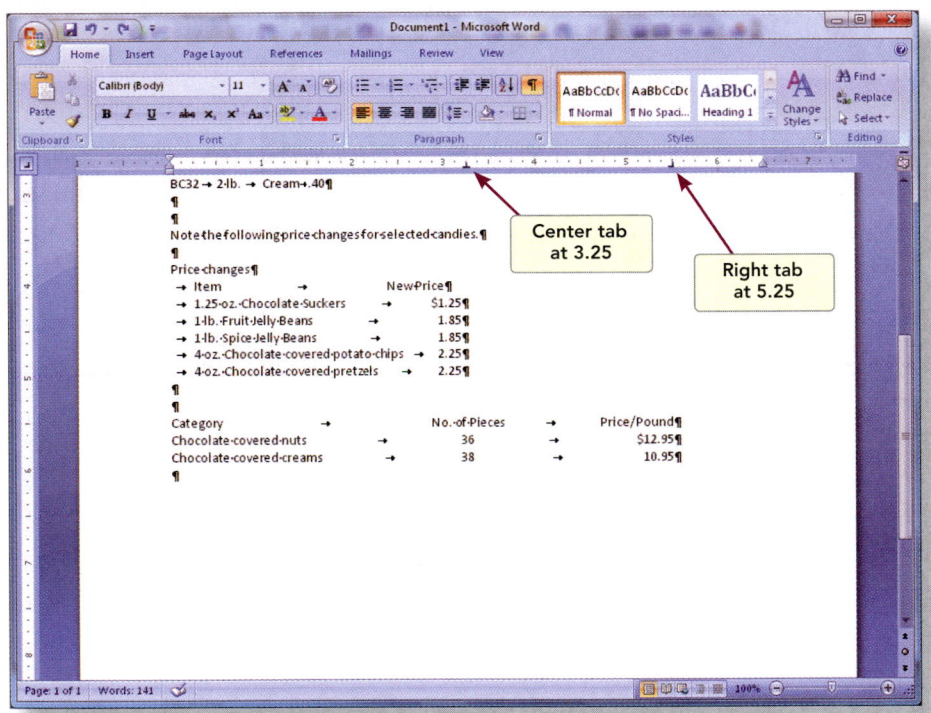

TIP

You can copy tab settings from one paragraph to another. Click in the paragraph whose tab settings you want to copy. Click the Format Painter button  . Click in the paragraph to which you are copying the tab settings.

Setting Leader Tabs

You can set tabs with *leader characters,* patterns of dots or dashes that lead the reader's eye from one tabbed column to the next. Leaders may be found in a table of contents, in which dotted lines fill the space between the headings on the left and the page numbers on the right.

Word offers three leader patterns: dotted line, dashed line, and solid line.

Figure 6-6
Leader patterns

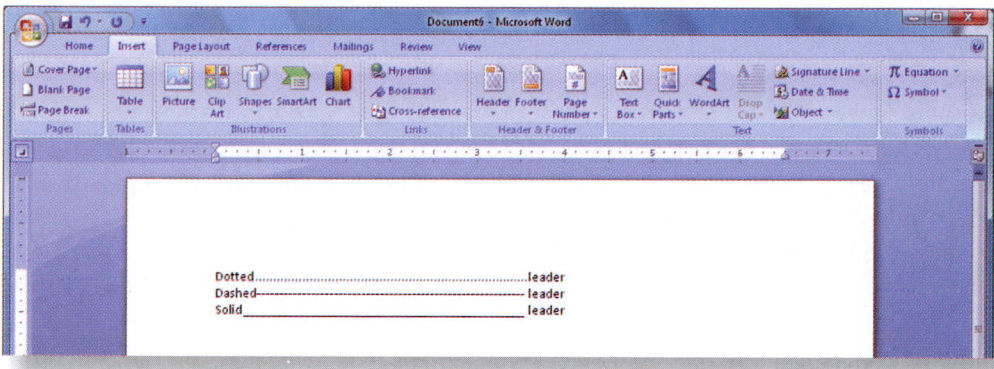

Exercise 6-3 SET LEADER TABS

1. Select the two columns of text under the headings "Item" and "New Price." The prices are aligned at a 3-inch decimal tab.

2. Open the **Tabs** dialog box. The tab settings for the selected text are displayed in the **Tab stop position** box with the **.25**-inch tab highlighted.

3. Click to select **3″** and under **Leader**, click the second leader pattern (the dotted line).

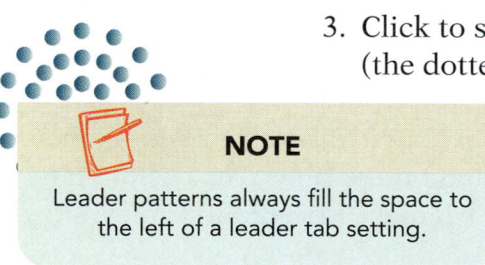

NOTE

Leader patterns always fill the space to the left of a leader tab setting.

4. Click **Set** and click **OK**. A dotted-line leader fills the space to the left of the 3-inch tab setting.

5. Select the heading "Price Changes" and apply bold, small caps formatting. Select the headings "Item" and "New Price" and apply bold and italic.

Clearing Tabs

You can clear custom tabs all at once or individually. When you clear custom tabs, Word restores the default tab stops to the left of the custom tab stop.

There are three ways to clear a tab:

- Use the Tabs dialog box.

- Use the ruler.

- Press Ctrl+Q.

Exercise 6-4   CLEAR A TAB BY USING THE TABS DIALOG BOX AND THE KEYBOARD

1. Select the six lines of text under the heading "Price Changes."

2. Open the Tabs dialog box. The 0.25-inch tab is highlighted in the **Tab stop position** box.

3. Click **Clear** and click **OK**. Word clears the 0.25-inch custom tab, and the text moves to the right to align at the tab at 3.0. (The text moves because each line is preceded by a tab character (→).

4. Delete the tab character (→) at the beginning of each line. The text in the first column moves to the left margin, and the second column is aligned at the tab setting.

5. Select the six lines of text under the heading "Price Changes" once again.

6. Press Ctrl+Q. The remaining tab setting is deleted, and the text is no longer aligned.

7. Click the Undo button to restore the 3-inch custom tab.

8. Save the document as *[your initials]*6-4 in your Lesson 6 folder.

NOTE

Remember, to remove tabs from text, you must delete the tab characters.

Exercise 6-5   CLEAR A TAB BY USING THE RULER

1. Position the insertion point at the beginning of the line of text with the heading "Category."

2. Position the pointer on the 5.5-inch right-aligned tab marker on the ruler.

3. When the ScreenTip "Right Tab" appears, drag the tab marker down and off the ruler. The custom tab is cleared, and the heading "Price/Pound" moves to a default tab stop.

4. Undo the last action to restore the tab setting.

5. Select the headings "Category," "No. of Pieces," and "Price/Pound," and apply bold, small caps formatting.

NOTE

When clearing or adjusting tabs by using the ruler, watch for the ScreenTip to correctly identify the item to which you are pointing. If no ScreenTip appears, you might inadvertently add another tab marker.

Adjusting Tab Settings

You can adjust tabs inserted in a document by using either the Tabs dialog box or the ruler. Tabs can be adjusted only after you select the text to which they have been applied.

Exercise 6-6   ADJUST TAB SETTINGS

1. Select the line with the headings "Item" and "New Price." The second heading is not aligned with the text below.

2. Point to the tab marker at 3 inches on the ruler.

3. Drag the tab marker to the right until the heading aligns with the text below.

4. Select the last three lines of text in the document ("Category" through "10.95").

5. Open the Tabs dialog box.

6. Click to select the tab setting **5.5** in the **Tab stop position** box.

7. Change the tab alignment setting by clicking **Left**. Click **OK**. Notice the change in the alignment of the heading and the text below.

8. Click the Undo button 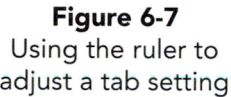.

Figure 6-7
Using the ruler to adjust a tab setting

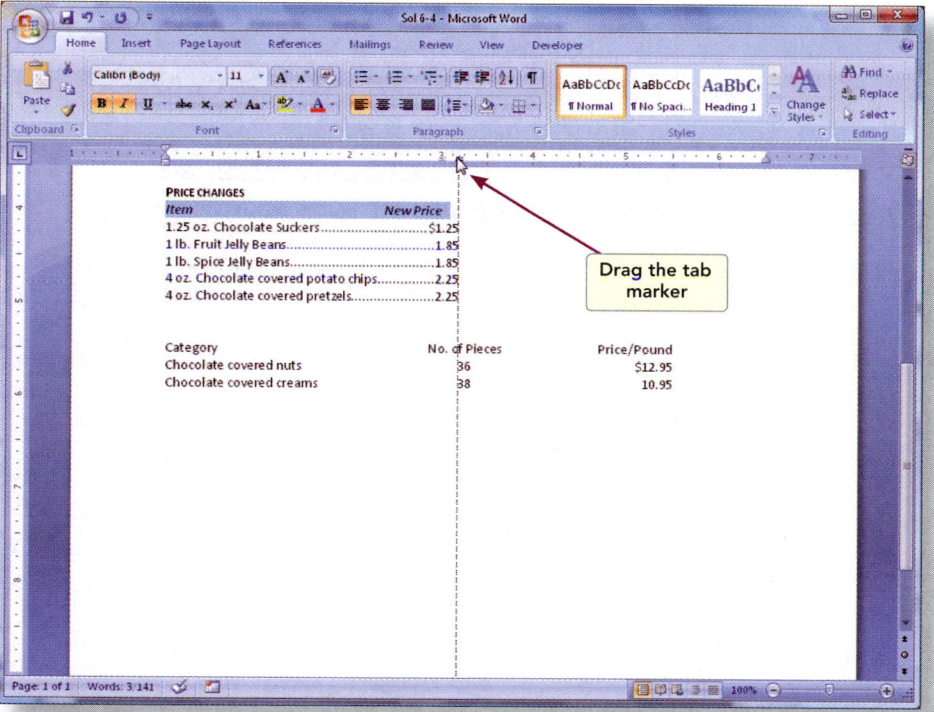

9. With the text still selected, drag the 5.5-inch tab marker to 6.5 inches on the ruler. The text is now aligned at the right margin.

NOTE

When you change tab settings with the ruler, be careful to drag the tab marker only to the right or to the left. If you drag the tab marker up or down, you might clear it from the ruler. If you inadvertently clear a tab marker, undo your action to restore the tab.

Creating Tabbed Columns

As you have seen in these practice documents, you can use tabs to present information in columns.

When you format a table using tabbed columns, follow these general rules based on *The Gregg Reference Manual*. Follow these rules for existing text or text to be keyed.

- The table should be centered horizontally within the margins.

- Columns within the table should be between six and ten spaces apart.

- The width of the table should not exceed the width of the document's body text.

- At least one blank line should separate the top and bottom of the table from the body text of the document.

Exercise 6-7   SET TABBED COLUMNS

1. Position the insertion point at the end of the document and press Enter twice.

2. Press Ctrl+Q to remove the tab settings from the paragraph mark; then key the text shown in Figure 6-8. Use single spacing.

Figure 6-8

```
The following stores offer a complete line of gifts and
accessories in addition to our fine chocolates. Other
stores offer a limited selection of gifts and accessories
due to space limitations.
```

3. Press Enter twice.

4. Study Figure 6-9 to determine the longest item in each column. (Pennsylvania is the longest item in the first column. Youngstown is the longest item in the second column, and West Virginia is the longest item in the third column.)

Figure 6-9

```
Pennsylvania        Ohio              West Virginia

Grove City          Akron             Clarksburg

Pittsburgh          Canton            Fairmont

Erie                Cleveland         Morgantown

Monroeville         Youngstown        Wheeling
```

5. Create a guide line that contains the longest item in each column by keying the following with 10 spaces between each group of words:

Pennsylvania   Youngstown   West Virginia

6. Click the Center button on the Ribbon to center the line.

7. Scroll down until the guide line is below the ruler.

8. Change the Tab Alignment button to left alignment . Using the I-beam as a guide, click the ruler to set a left-aligned tab at the beginning of each group of words.

Figure 6-10
Guide line for centering tabbed columns

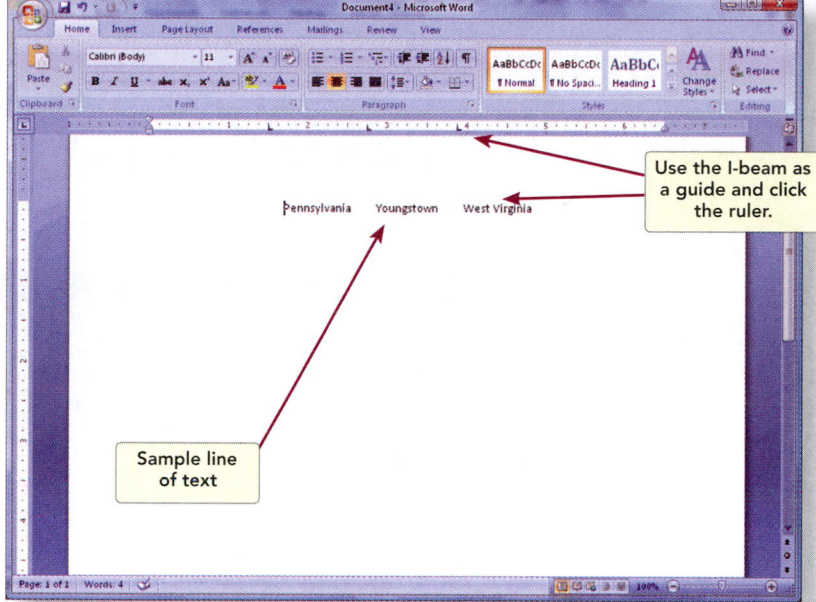

9. Delete the text in the guide line up to the paragraph mark. Do not delete the paragraph mark, which is now storing your left-aligned tab settings.

10. Click the Align Left button to left-align the insertion point.

11. Key the table text as shown in Figure 6-9, pressing `Tab` before each item and single-spacing each line. Underline each column heading.

12. Select the text near the top of the document beginning with "Item No." and ending with the line that begins "BC32."

13. Change the tab alignment button to left alignment and click the ruler at 2.5.

14. Change the tab alignment button to right alignment and click the ruler at 5.5.

15. Select the text if necessary, and click the Increase Indent button two times to move the text away from the left margin.

16. Drag the left tab marker (right or left) to position the middle column an equal distance from the first and third columns.

17. Bold and center the heading "Standard-Size Boxes." Format the title with all caps and 12 points spacing after. Apply bold and italic formatting to the column headings.

Exercise 6-8 SELECT A TABBED COLUMN

After text is formatted in tabbed columns, you can select columns individually by selecting a vertical block of text. Selecting tabbed text can be helpful for formatting or deleting text. You use [Alt] to select a vertical block of text.

> **NOTE**
>
> If you do not press [Alt] when trying to select text vertically, you will select the entire first line of text, rather than just the column header for the column you are selecting.

1. Hold down [Alt] and position the I-beam to the immediate left of "Ohio."

2. Drag across the heading, and then down until the heading and all four cities are selected. Do not select the tab characters to the right of the column.

Figure 6-11
Selecting text vertically

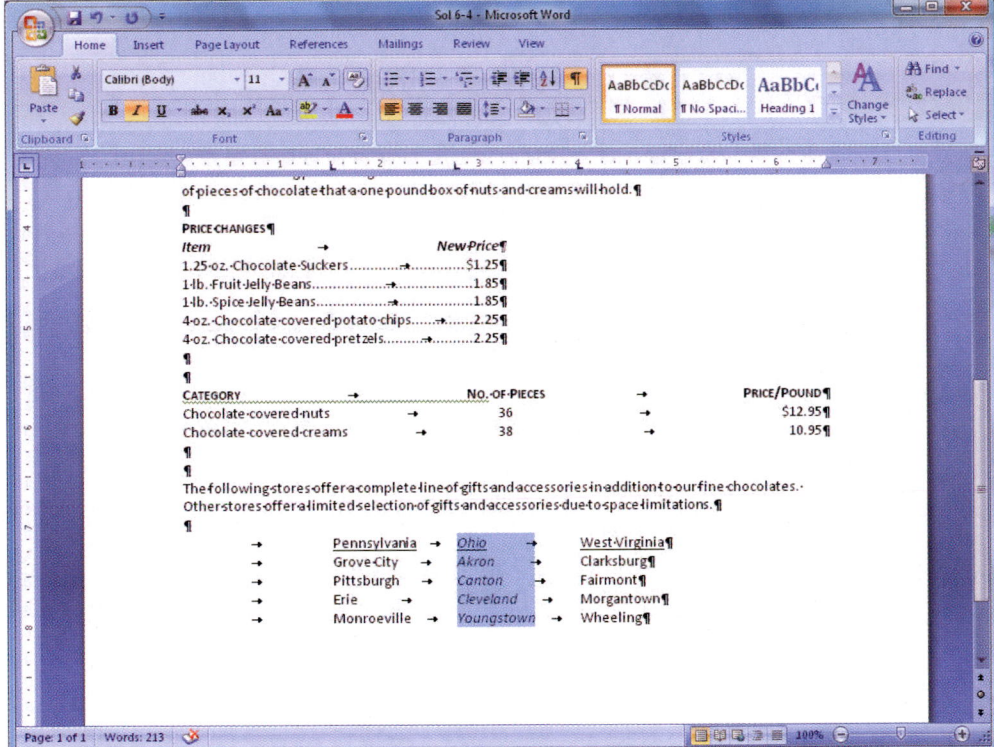

3. Press [Delete] to delete the column.

4. Undo the deletion.

5. Select the column again, this time selecting only the names under the column head "Ohio."

6. Click the Italic button 𝐼 to format the text.

Exercise 6-9   INSERT BAR TABS

Bar tabs are used to make tabbed columns look more like a table with gridlines. A bar tab inserts a vertical line at a fixed position, creating a border between columns. You can set bar tabs by using the ruler or the Tabs dialog box.

1. At the bottom of the document, select the four lines of tabbed text below the headings "Pennsylvania," "Ohio," and "West Virginia."

2. Open the **Tabs** dialog box. Key **2.5** in the text box, click **Bar**, and click **OK**. The vertical bar is placed between the first and second columns. Do not deselect the tabbed text.

3. To set bar tabs by using the ruler, click the Tab Alignment button until it changes to a bar tab ▯. Click the ruler at 3.75 inches. The bar tab markers appear as short vertical lines on the ruler.

4. Adjust the bar tab markers on the ruler to make them more evenly spaced, as needed.

5. Deselect the tabbed text. Click the Show/Hide ¶ button ¶ to view the document without nonprinting characters. The bar tabs act as dividing borders between the columns.

Figure 6-12
Tabbed text with bar tabs

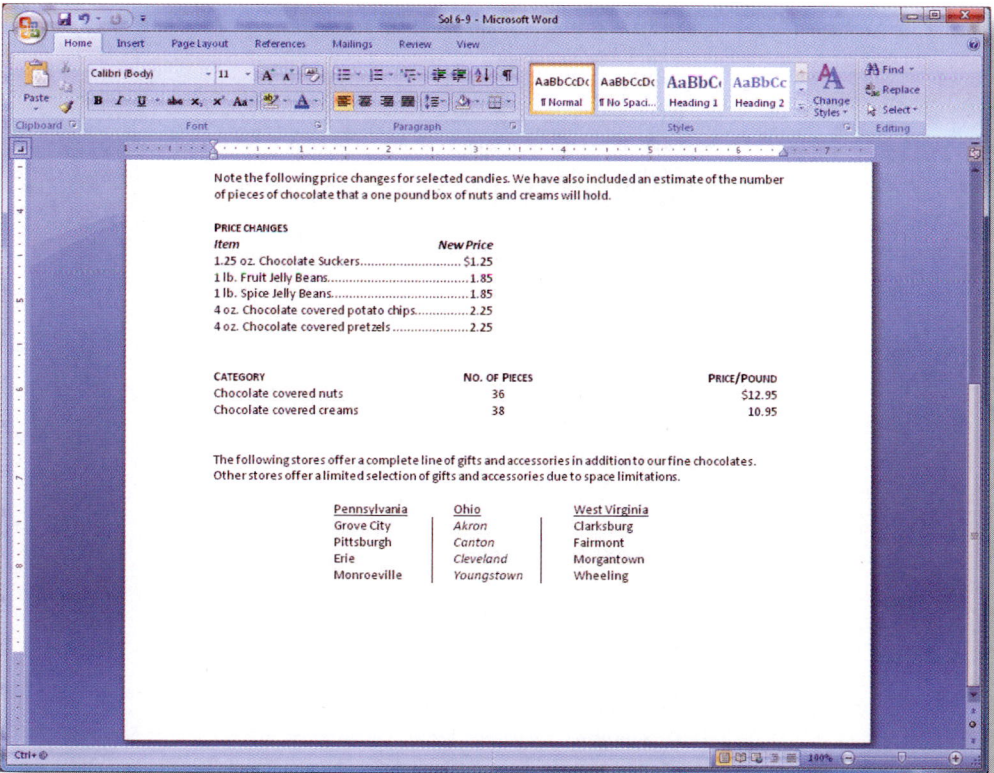

6. Position the insertion point in the line that contains "Grove City."

7. Point to the 3.75-inch bar tab on the ruler, and drag it off the ruler. The vertical line in the table disappears.

8. Undo the deletion to restore the bar tab.

9. Save the document as *[your initials]*6-9 in your Lesson 6 folder.

10. Submit the document.

Sorting Paragraphs and Tabbed Columns

Sorting is the process of reordering text alphabetically or numerically. You can sort to rearrange text in ascending order (from lowest to highest, such as 0–9 or A–Z) or descending order (from highest to lowest, such as 9–0 or Z–A).

You can sort any group of paragraphs, from a single-column list to a multiple-column table, such as one created by tabbed columns. When sorting a tabbed table, you can sort by any of the columns.

Figure 6-13
Sorting paragraphs and tables

PENNSYLVANIA STORES	NO. OF EMPLOYEES
Butler	14
Edinboro	15
Erie	18
Franklin	12
Greenville	10
Grove City	20
Meadville	12
Mercer	10
Monroeville	18
New Castle	14
Pittsburgh	20
Sharon	14

Alphabetical sort in ascending order

PENNSYLVANIA STORES	NO. OF EMPLOYEES
Grove City	20
Pittsburgh	20
Erie	18
Monroeville	18
Edinboro	15
Butler	14
New Castle	14
Sharon	14
Franklin	12
Meadville	12
Greenville	10
Mercer	10

Numerical sort in descending order

Exercise 6-10 SORT TABBED TABLES

1. Select the headings "Pennsylvania," "Ohio," and "West Virginia" and the four lines of text below the headings.

2. Click the Sort button on the Ribbon, Paragraph group.

3. Open the **Sort by** drop-down list to view the other sort options. Field numbers represent each of the columns. Open the **Type** drop-down list. Notice that the type options include **Text**, **Number**, and **Date**.

4. Click **Descending** to change the sort order and click the **Header row** option to select it. Click **OK**. The text in the first column is sorted alphabetically in descending order.

5. Press Ctrl+Z to undo the sort. Do not deselect the text.

6. Click the Sort button to open the Sort Text dialog box.

7. Click **Header row** at the bottom of the dialog box. This option indicates that the selection includes column headings, which should not be sorted with the text.

8. Open the **Sort by** drop-down list. Now you can sort by the table's column headings instead of by field numbers.

9. Choose **Ohio** from the drop-down list. Click **Descending** and click **OK**.

Figure 6-14
Sorting options in the Sort Text dialog box

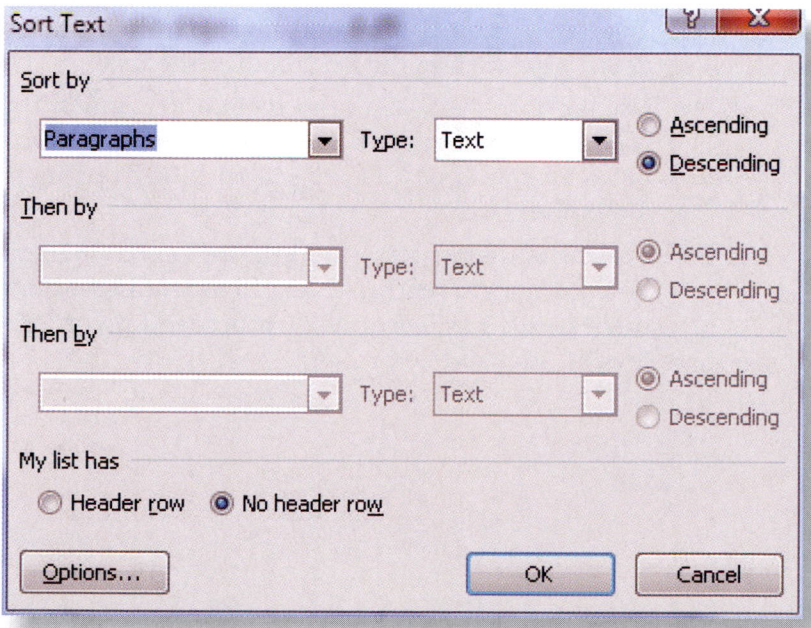

10. Save the document as *[your initials]*6-10 in your Lesson 6 folder.

11. Submit and close the document.

Lesson 6 Summary

- Tabs are a paragraph-formatting feature used to align text. When you press Tab, Word inserts a tab character and moves the insertion position to the tab setting, called the tab stop.

- Word's default tabs are left-aligned and set every half-inch from the left margin, as indicated at the bottom of the horizontal ruler.

- The four most common types of custom tabs are left-aligned, centered, right-aligned, and decimal-aligned. Custom tab settings are indicated on the horizontal ruler by tab markers.

- Set tabs by using the Tabs dialog box or the ruler. To use the ruler, click the Tab Alignment button on the left of the ruler to choose the type of tab alignment, and then click the position on the ruler to set the tab. See Table 6-1.

- A leader tab uses a series of dots, dashes, or solid underlines to fill the empty space to the left of a tab stop. Use the Tabs dialog box to set a leader tab.

- Clear custom tabs all at once or individually. To clear a tab, use the Tabs dialog box, or the ruler, or press Ctrl+Q.

- To adjust tab settings, position the insertion point in the tabbed text (or select the text), and then either open the Tabs dialog box or drag the tab markers on the ruler.

- Use tabs to present information in columns. Tabbed columns are a side-by-side vertical list of information.

- To select a tabbed column (for formatting or deleting the text), hold down Alt and drag the I-beam over the text.

- Use bar tabs to format tabbed columns similar to a table with gridlines. A bar tab inserts a vertical line at a fixed position, creating a border between columns. You can set bar tabs by using the ruler or the Tabs dialog box.

- Sorting is the process of reordering text alphabetically or numerically. You can sort to rearrange text in ascending order (from lowest to highest, such as 0–9 or A–Z) or descending order (from highest to lowest, such as 9–0 or Z–A).

LESSON 6		Command Summary	
Feature	Button	Command	Keyboard
Left tab	⌊	**Home** tab, **Paragraph** group	
Center tab	⊥	**Home** tab, **Paragraph** group	
Right tab	⌋	**Home** tab, **Paragraph** group	
Decimal tab	⊥	**Home** tab, **Paragraph** group	
Bar tab	⌶	**Home** tab, **Paragraph** group	
Leader tabs		**Home** tab, **Paragraph** group	
Clear tabs		**Home** tab, **Paragraph** group	Ctrl + Q
Sort text	A↓Z	**Home** tab, **Paragraph** group	

Concepts Review

True/False Questions

Each of the following statements is either true or false. Indicate your choice by circling T or F.

T   F   1. In Word, you can use [Spacebar] to precisely align text.

T   F   2. When you set a custom tab, Word clears all default tabs to the left of the tab stop.

T   F   3. You cannot set tabs for existing text.

T   F   4. You can either select a paragraph or place the insertion point within the paragraph when setting tabs for the paragraph.

T   F   5. When custom tabs are cleared, you must reestablish default tabs or you will have no tabs at all.

T   F   6. Tabs inserted in a document cannot be adjusted after they are set.

T   F   7. The symbol for a bar tab marker is a short vertical line.

T   F   8. You can use the ruler to set a leader tab.

Short Answer Questions

Write the correct answer in the space provided.

1. What are the two ways to set tabs?

_____

2. What are the five types of tabs you can set when using the Tab Alignment button?

_____

3. Which dialog box is used to set a leader tab?

_____

4. What type of tab do you use to create?

_____

5. What interval does Word use for default tabs?

_____

6. How do you clear a tab by using the ruler?

_____

7. Which key is used to select a tabbed column?

_____

8. Which Ribbon tab and group contains the Sort feature?

_____

Critical Thinking

Answer these questions on a separate page. There are no right or wrong answers. Support your answers with examples from your own experience, if possible.

1. Books and magazines may use leader tabs in the table of contents and index. Based on representative books and magazines, create a few general guidelines on when to use leader tabs. Support your view with examples.

2. Do you find it easier to read text that is centered in a column or text that is left-aligned? What about numbers that are centered or right-aligned? Create samples to support your position.

Skills Review

Exercise 6-11

Set tabs and create a business memo.

1. Start a new document, and set a 1-inch left-aligned tab by following these steps:
   a. Make sure the Tab Alignment button on the horizontal ruler shows left alignment ⊾.
   b. Click the ruler at the 1-inch mark.
2. Select the paragraph mark and open the Paragraph dialog box. Change the **Spacing After** to **0** and change the **Line spacing** to **Single**.
3. Key the text in Figure 6-15, using the spacing shown. Press Tab after each colon. Refer to Appendix B, "Standard Forms for Business Documents."

Figure 6-15

```
      MEMO TO:          Store Managers
one  ┌FROM:            Thomas Campbell
blank├
line └DATE:            <Current Date>
      SUBJECT:          Monroeville Store
two  →                                        tele                    412
blank The Monroeville store has added a second phone line. The number is 8⁄4-555-8228.
lines
      Please record the number and update the company directory.
```

4. In the date line, key today's date.

5. Select the first line of the memo heading and open the **Paragraph** dialog box. Change the **Spacing Before** to **72** points.

6. Add your reference initials at the end of the document.

7 Spell-check the document.

8. Save the document as *[your initials]***6-11** in your Lesson 6 folder.

9. Submit and close the document.

Exercise 6-12

Set leader tabs.

1. Start a new document. Format the paragraph mark as 14 points Arial Narrow. Change the **Spacing After** to **24 pt** and change the **Line spacing** to **Single**.

2. Key the first line in Figure 6-16.

3. Before keying the remaining text, set a solid leader tab that extends to the right margin by following these steps:

   a. Click the **Paragraph Dialog Box Launcher** to open the Paragraph dialog box. Click **Tabs**.

   b. In the **Tab stop position** box, key **6.5**. (The right margin setting.)

   c. Under **Alignment**, click **Right**.

   d. Choose the fourth leader option, click **Set**, and click **OK**.

Figure 6-16

```
Enter a drawing for a free pound of chocolate-covered nuts.
Complete the form below.

Name _____

Address _____

City/State/ZIP _____

Telephone _____
```

4. Key the remaining information, beginning with "**Name.**" Press Tab to move to the 6.5-inch right-aligned tab setting, and then press Enter. Continue keying the text in the figure.

5. Format the text with the solid-line leaders as small caps.

6. Save the document as *[your initials]***6-12** in your Lesson 6 folder.

7. Submit and close the document.

Exercise 6-13

Adjust and clear tab settings.

1. Open the file **Campbell - 1**.
2. Position the insertion point in the first line of the tabbed text that begins "retail." (The tabbed text is a single paragraph.)
3. Set a 1-inch left-aligned tab by using the ruler.
4. Use the ruler to adjust the tab setting by following these steps:
   a. Point to the 1-inch left tab marker.
   b. When you see the ScreenTip identifying the tab marker, drag the marker to 2.5 inches on the ruler.

5. Click the **Tab Alignment** button until it shows center alignment. Click the ruler at 2 inches to set a tab.
6. Use the Tabs dialog box to clear both tabs by following these steps:
   a. Open the Tabs dialog box.
   b. Click **Clear All** and click **OK**.

7. Click the Tab Alignment button until it shows right alignment. Click the ruler at 1.5 inches.
8. Drag the 1.5-inch tab marker on the ruler to adjust it to 2 inches.
9. Save the document as *[your initials]*6-13 in your Lesson 6 folder.
10. Submit and close the document.

Exercise 6-14

Create tabbed columns and sort text.

1. Start a new document. Key **MOST POPULAR HOLIDAY CHOCOLATES** in uppercase bold. Center the text and press [Enter].
2. Left-align the paragraph mark and turn off bold and uppercase. Change the **Spacing After** to 12 pt and change the **Line spacing** to Single.
3. Create a table with single-spaced, tabbed columns that are horizontally centered between the left and right margins by following these steps:
   a. Key a guide line containing the longest text from each column in Figure 6-17, with 10 spaces between columns. (Include the column headings when determining the longest item in each column.)
   b. Center the text.
   c. Scroll until the guide line is directly under the ruler.
   d. Using the I-beam for guidance, set a left-aligned tab for each of the columns.

e. Delete the guide line up to the paragraph mark. Left-align the paragraph mark.

f. Key the text shown in Figure 6-17, pressing [Tab] before each item in each column.

Figure 6-17

Holiday	Pennsylvania	Ohio	West Virginia
Valentine's Day	1 lb. chocolate nuts	1 lb. assorted	1 lb. turtles
Easter	1 lb. chocolate basket	8 oz. solid rabbit	8 oz. chocolate nut egg
Halloween	chocolate suckers	chocolate suckers	chocolate suckers

4. Bold the column headings. Format the first line of the document with 72 points spacing before.

5. Sort the table alphabetically by holiday by following these steps:

a. Select the entire table, including the column headings.

b. Click the Sort button 🔽 in the Paragraph group.

c. Click **Header row** to display the column headings in the Sort by drop-down list.

d. Choose **Holiday** from the **Sort by** drop-down list.

e. Choose **Text** from the **Type** list and choose **Ascending**. Click **OK**.

6. Save the document as *[your initials]*6-14 in your Lesson 6 folder.

7. Submit and close the document.

LESSON 6 Tabs and Tabbed Columns

WD-189

Lesson Applications

Exercise 6-15

Set tabs for a memo, and then adjust the tab settings.

1. Start a new document. Open the Paragraph dialog box, and change the line spacing to single, and change the spacing after to 0 points.

2. Set a 1-inch left tab and key the text for a memo heading.

3. The memo is to **Lydia Hamrick** from **Thomas Campbell**. The subject is **Renovation**. Remember to include today's date, and insert a blank line between lines in the memo heading.

4. Press Enter three times after the subject line, and key the text shown in Figure 6-18, including the corrections. Use single spacing and insert a blank line between paragraphs.

Figure 6-18

Renovation work is almost complete at Campbell's Confections in Erie *, Pennsylvania*. The Erie store is *our* the newest acquisition, and its modern up todate interior provides a spacious area for retail *-controlled* sales, *a* large temperature storage area, and a private office for the store manager.

The Erie store is close ~~enough~~ to the Peninsula to attract ~~visitors~~ *tourists is*, two-blocks from the hospital, *and is* conveniently located in a plaza with easy access to and *from* the parking lot for *local* residents.

The store renovation will be feature*d* in the Erie Times ① this weekend.

5. Change the font for the entire document to Arial.

6. Change the font for the memo-heading guidewords ("MEMO to:," "FROM:," "DATE:," and "SUBJECT:") to Arial Black.

7. Move to the beginning of the document, and change the spacing before to 72 points for the first line of the memo.

8. Spell-check the document.

9. Add your reference initials to the document.

10. Save the document as *[your initials]*6-15 in your Lesson 6 folder.

11. Submit and close the document.

Exercise 6-16

Set leader tabs and sort paragraphs.

1. Open the file **Chocolate Glossary**.

2. Select the title and change the spacing before to 72 points and the spacing after to 24 points.

3. Format the title size to 14 points, small caps, and center the text.

4. Position the insertion point at the beginning of the first line under the title, and key the paragraph shown in Figure 6-19. Use single spacing. Include one blank line below the paragraph.

Figure 6-19

```
The following list represents popular and commonly used
phrases in chocolate making. Refer to the list to help you
become familiar with the terms.
```

5. Select the list of terms and definitions. Drag the left tab marker off the ruler.

6. Set a dotted leader tab that right-aligns the glossary definitions at the right margin. (The right margin for this document is 6.5 inches as shown on the ruler.)

7. Sort each paragraph in the glossary alphabetically, from A to Z.

8. Change the spacing for each glossary definition to 6 points after paragraphs.

9. Apply a page border, using the box setting and the double wavy line style.

10. Spell-check the document.

11. Save the document as *[your initials]*6-16 in your Lesson 6 folder.

12. Submit and close the document.

Exercise 6-17

Set and adjust tab settings.

1. Start a new document.

2. Key the title in Figure 6-20. Format the title as 12-point Arial bold, uppercase, and centered.

3. Insert two blank lines below the title, and key the paragraph that begins "Even." Use left alignment, single spacing, 11 points, and Arial.

Figure 6-20

```
Chocolate Consumption

Even though Americans consume over 3 billion pounds of
chocolate a year, the United States is not ranked in the
top ten countries for worldwide consumption of chocolate.
Americans consume an average of 12 pounds of chocolate
per person per year. The following countries are listed
as the top five chocolate-consuming nations according to
the World Atlas of Chocolate.

             Country                Pounds/Year

             Switzerland               22.36

             Austria                   20.13

             Ireland                   19.47

             Germany                   18.04

             Norway                    17.93
```

4. Key the remaining text in the figure, beginning with "Country," using a 1.5-inch left indent and an appropriate right tab setting for the second column. The text should be evenly spaced between the left and right margins, as shown in the figure.

5. Format the paragraph that begins with "Even" with justified alignment and a dropped capital letter (use the default drop cap settings). There should be one blank line between this paragraph and the table below it.

6. Adjust the tab setting for the table, so it includes a dotted leader.

7. Change the line spacing for the table text to 1.5 lines.

8. Increase the font size of the title to 14 points and change the Spacing Before to 72 points. Apply bold and small caps to "Country" and "Pounds/Year."

9. Spell-check the document.

10. Save the document as *[your initials]*6-17 in your Lesson 6 folder.

11. Submit and close the document.

Exercise 6-18 ◆ Challenge Yourself

Create a memo with tabbed columns, sort the text, and add bar tabs.

1. Start a new document. Using the proper line spacing, margin settings, and a 1-inch left tab setting, create a memo to **Thomas Campbell** from **Lydia Hamrick**. The subject is **Weekend Hours for the Ohio Stores**.

2. For the body of the memo, key the text in Figure 6-21. Use single spacing. For the tabbed columns, create a guide line to set the tabs. Align the tabbed columns as indicated. Insert a blank line above and below the tabbed columns.

Figure 6-21

```
As you requested, the following is a list of the hours of
operation for the Ohio stores.

Store              Weekdays          Saturday          Sunday

Akron              9 to 5            9 to 3            Closed

Cleveland          10 to 6           9 to 4            1 to 6

Massillon          9 to 5            9 to 4            Closed

Warren             9 to 6            9 to 5            Closed

Youngstown         9 to 6            9 to 5            Closed

Canton             9 to 6            9 to 4            Closed

Let me know if you need additional information.
```

3. Apply a 3/4-point box border around the entire memo heading (excluding the blank lines below "SUBJECT:"). Add 10 percent gray shading to the memo heading. Click in the first line and apply 72 points spacing before.

4. Adjust the tab setting for the memo heading to 1.25 inches, and set a 1-inch bar tab to create a vertical dividing line.

5. Select the first column of the memo heading (which begins "MEMO TO:") and apply bold formatting.

6. Sort the tabbed table by store in ascending order.

7. Add your reference initials to the bottom of the memo.

8. Spell-check the document.

9. Save the document as *[your initials]*6-18 in your Lesson 6 folder.

10. Submit, and close the document.

On Your Own

In these exercises, you work on your own, as you would in a real-life business environment. Use the skills you've learned to accomplish the task—and be creative.

Exercise 6-19

Write a short business memo. The memo is from you, to a person you work with or a friend and about a subject related to work or a subject of your choosing. Use the correct spacing and tab settings for the memo heading. Save the document as *[your initials]*6-19 and submit it.

Exercise 6-20

Create a monthly budget in the form of a tabbed table. Set and adjust the tabs, using the ruler. Sort the table. Save the document as *[your initials]*6-20 and submit it.

Exercise 6-21

Log onto the Internet, and find a chocolate store you would like to visit. Create a tabbed table containing the names of your favorite chocolates, a brief description, and the price. Use leaders and sort the information. Save the document as *[your initials]*6-21 and submit it.

Lesson 7

Move and Copy

OBJECTIVES

After completing this lesson, you will be able to:

1. Use the Office Clipboard.

2. Move text by using cut and paste.

3. Move text by dragging.

4. Copy text by using copy and paste.

5. Copy text by dragging.

6. Work with multiple document windows.

7. Move and copy text among windows.

MCAS OBJECTIVES

In this lesson:
WW 07 2.2.1
WW 07 5.1.2

Estimated Time: 1 hour

One of the most useful features of word processing is the capability to move or copy a block of text from one part of a document to another or from one document window to another, without rekeying the text. In Word, you can move and copy text quickly by using the Cut, Copy, and Paste commands or the drag-and-drop editing feature.

Using the Office Clipboard

Perhaps the most important tool for moving and copying text is the *Clipboard,* which is a temporary storage area. Here's how it works: Cut or copy text from your document and store it on the Clipboard. Then move to a different location in your document and insert the Clipboard's contents using the Paste command.

There are two types of clipboards:

- The system Clipboard stores one item at a time. Each time you store a new item on this Clipboard, it replaces the previous item. This Clipboard is available to many software applications on your system.

- The Office Clipboard can store 24 items, which are displayed on the Clipboard task pane. The Office Clipboard lets you collect multiple items without erasing previous items. You can store items from all Office applications.

Exercise 7-1   DISPLAY THE CLIPBOARD TASK PANE

1. Click the **Home** tab. The **Clipboard** group contains a Dialog Box Launcher arrow to open the Clipboard task pane.

2. Click the **Clipboard Dialog Box Launcher** arrow. The Clipboard task pane opens. At the top of the task pane, notice the Paste All and Clear All buttons. At the bottom of the screen, at the right end of the Taskbar, notice the Clipboard icon, indicating that the Office Clipboard is in use.

Figure 7-1
Clipboard task pane

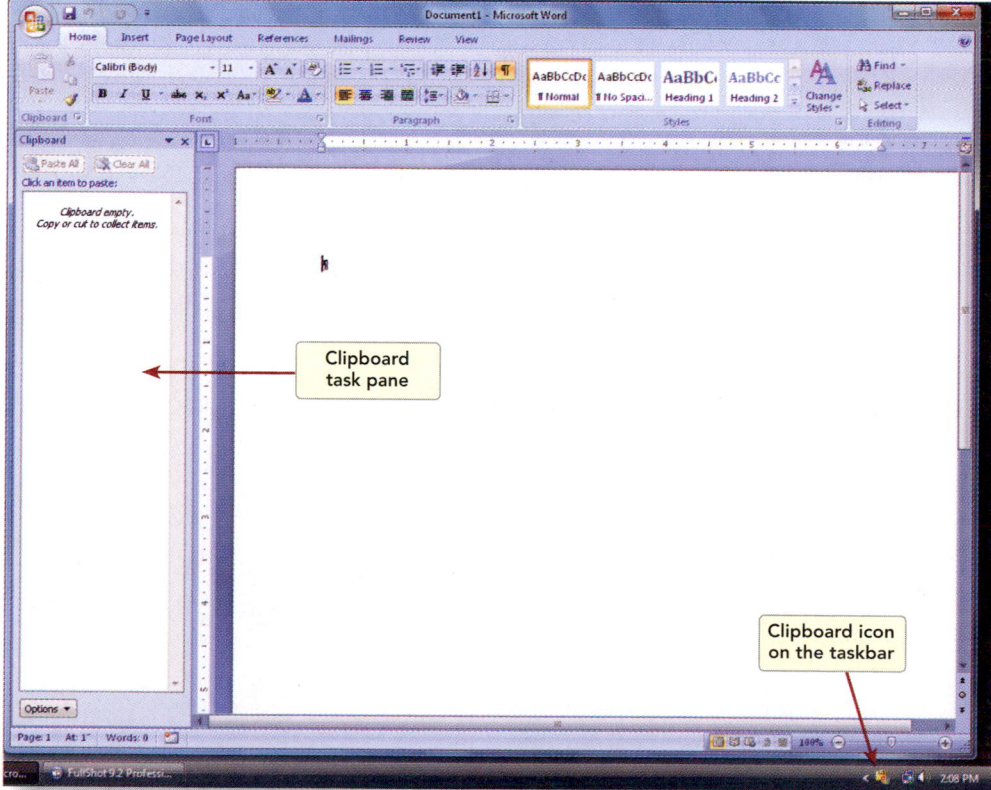

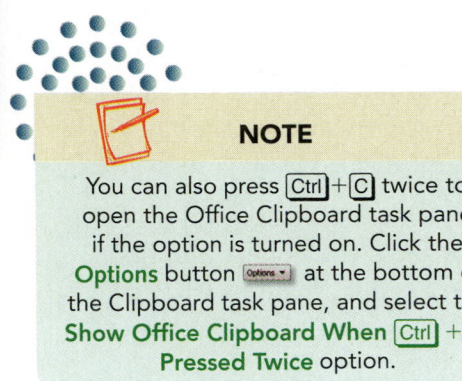

NOTE

You can also press Ctrl + C twice to open the Office Clipboard task pane if the option is turned on. Click the **Options** button Options ▾ at the bottom of the Clipboard task pane, and select the **Show Office Clipboard When** Ctrl + C **Pressed Twice** option.

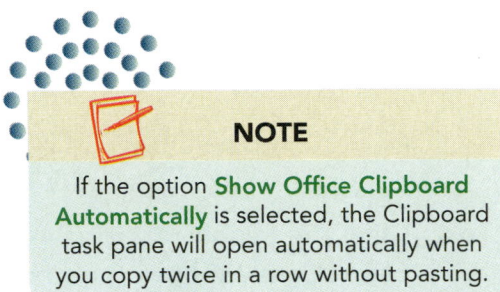

3. If the Office Clipboard contains items from previous use, click the Clear All button 🗙 Clear All to empty the Clipboard.

4. Click the **Options** button at the bottom of the task pane. Notice the options available for using the Office Clipboard.

5. Click outside the task pane, making sure not to choose any of the options in the list.

NOTE

If the option **Show Office Clipboard Automatically** is selected, the Clipboard task pane will open automatically when you copy twice in a row without pasting.

Moving Text by Using Cut and Paste

To move text by using the *cut-and-paste* method, start by highlighting the text you want to move and using the Cut command. Then move to the location where you want to place the text and use the Paste command. When you use cut and paste to move paragraphs, you can preserve the correct spacing between paragraphs by following these rules:

- Include the blank line below the paragraph you are moving as part of the selection.

- When you paste the selection, click to the left of the first line of text following the place where your paragraph will go—not on the blank line above it.

There are multiple ways to cut and paste text. The most commonly used methods are:

- Use the Cut ✂ Cut and Paste buttons 📋 on the Ribbon, Home tab.

- Use the shortcut menu.

- Use the keyboard shortcuts Ctrl + X to cut and Ctrl + V to paste.

- Use the Clipboard task pane.

Exercise 7-2   USE THE RIBBON TO CUT AND PASTE

1. Open the file **Festival Memo**. Display the Clipboard task pane if necessary.

2. Key the current year in the date line of the memo heading.

3. Select the text "Strawberry Days" in the subject line of the memo.

4. Click the **Home** tab, and click the Cut button 🔧 Cut to remove the text from the document and place it on the Clipboard. Notice the Clipboard item in the task pane.

5. Position the insertion point to the left of "Art" in the Subject line to indicate where you want to insert the text.

6. Click the Paste button 📋 to insert "Strawberry Days" in its new location. The Paste Options button 📋 appears below the pasted text, and the Clipboard item remains in the task pane.

7. Move the I-beam over the Paste Options button 📋. (The I-beam will change to an arrow when it passes over the Paste Options button.) When you see the button's drop-down arrow, click to view the list of options. Click in the document window to close the list of options.

8. Delete the em dash at the end of the subject line.

> **NOTE**
>
> When you point to the Paste button 📋, the button displays two colors and a divider line. Click the upper part of the button to paste text, or click the lower part of the button to display a list of options.

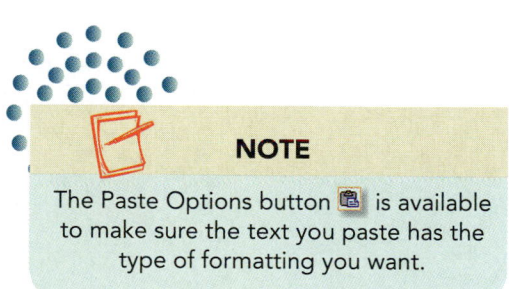

> **NOTE**
>
> The Paste Options button 📋 is available to make sure the text you paste has the type of formatting you want.

Exercise 7-3   USE THE SHORTCUT MENU TO CUT AND PASTE

1. Select the paragraph near the bottom of the document that begins "All hotels are." Include the paragraph mark on the blank line following the paragraph.

Figure 7-2
Using the shortcut
menu to cut

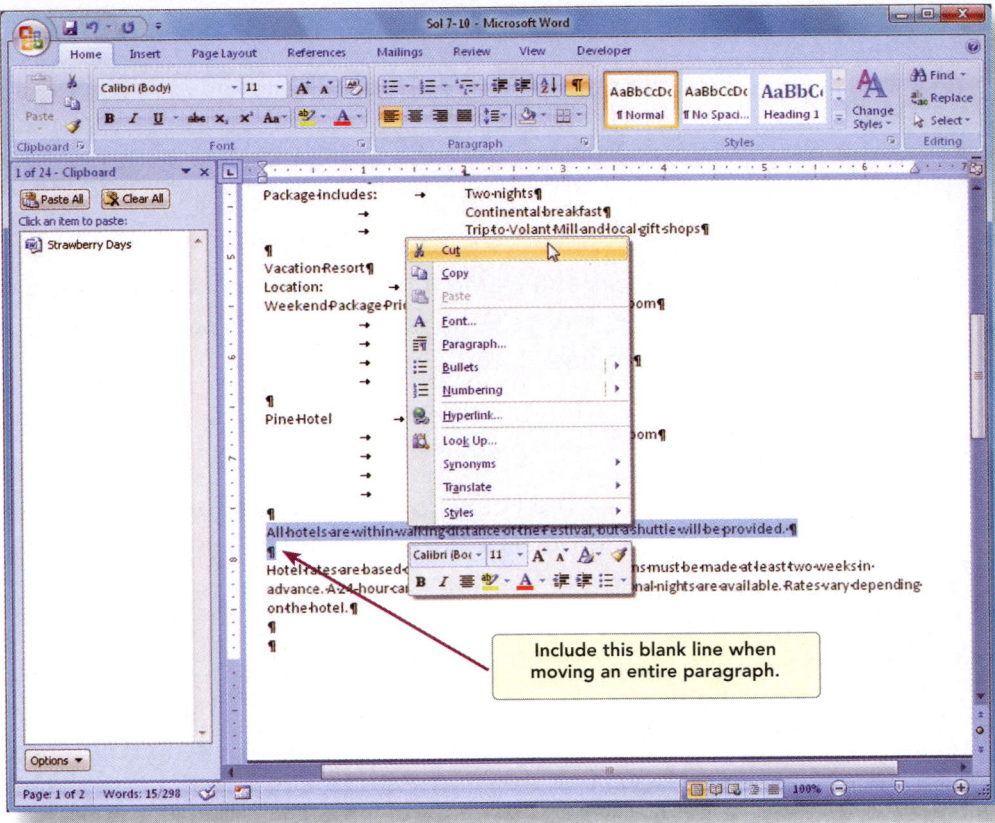

Include this blank line when
moving an entire paragraph.

2. Point to the selected text and right-click to display the shortcut
   menu.

3. Click **Cut**. The item is added to the Clipboard task pane.

NOTE

Each new item you cut (or copy) is added
to the top of the Clipboard task pane.

4. Position the I-beam to the left of the paragraph that begins "Several
   special." Right-click and choose **Paste** from the shortcut menu. The
   paragraph moves to its new location, and the Paste Options button
    appears below the pasted text.

Figure 7-3
Using the shortcut
menu to paste

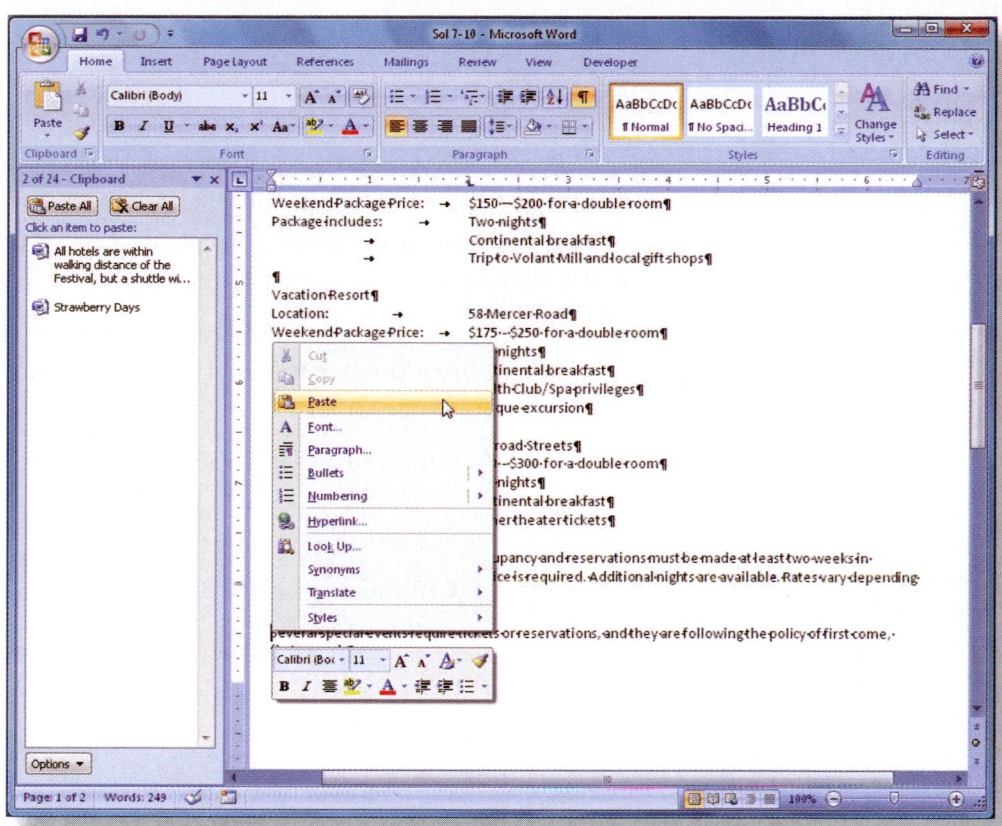

Exercise 7-4   USE KEYBOARD SHORTCUTS TO CUT AND PASTE

If you prefer using the keyboard, you can press `Ctrl`+`X` to cut text and `Ctrl`+`V` to paste text. You can also use `Ctrl`+`Z` to undo an action. The location of these shortcut keys is designed to make it easy for you to move your mouse with your right hand while you press command keys with your left hand.

1. Select the paragraph that begins "Several special." Press `Ctrl`+`X` to cut the text. A new item appears in the task pane.

2. Position the insertion point just before the paragraph that begins "Please refer." Press `Ctrl`+`V` to paste the text.

3. Press `Ctrl`+`Z` to undo the paste. Press `Ctrl`+`Y`. (Remember, you can also click the Undo button 🔄 to undo actions.) Notice that the Clipboard item remains in the task pane.

Exercise 7-5   USE THE OFFICE CLIPBOARD TO PASTE

Each time you cut text in the previous exercises, a new item was added to the Office Clipboard. You can paste that item directly from the task pane.

1. Select all the information that goes with the "Pine Hotel," including the title "Pine Hotel" and the blank line that follows the hotel information.

2. Cut this text, using the Cut button 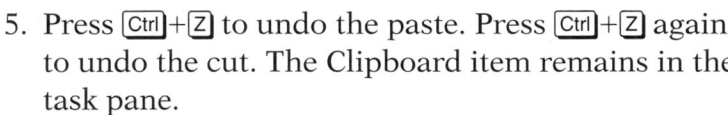 on the Ribbon. The text is stored as a new item at the top of the Clipboard task pane.

3. Position the insertion point to the left of the paragraph that begins "Wolf Creek Hotel."

4. Click the task pane item for the Pine Hotel text that you just cut. (Do not click the drop-down arrow.) This pastes the text at the location of the insertion point.

NOTE

Choosing the Paste option from the drop-down list pastes that item, just like clicking directly on the item. The Paste All button 🗒 Paste All on the Clipboard task pane is used to copy all Office Clipboard items to the location of the insertion point.

5. Press Ctrl+Z to undo the paste. Press Ctrl+Z again to undo the cut. The Clipboard item remains in the task pane.

6. Point to this Clipboard item in the task pane, and click the drop-down arrow that appears to its right.

7. Choose **Delete** from the list to delete the item from the Clipboard.

Moving Text by Dragging

You can also move selected text to a new location by using the *drag-and-drop* method. Text is not transferred to the Clipboard when you use drag and drop.

Exercise 7-6   USE DRAG AND DROP TO MOVE TEXT

1. Select all the information related to "Vacation Resort," including the title "Vacation Resort' and the blank line below the information.

2. Point to the selected text. Notice that the I-beam changes to a left-pointing arrow.

TIP

Use cut and paste to move text over long distances—for example, onto another page. Use drag and drop to move text short distances where you can see both the selected text and the destination on the screen at the same time.

3. Click and hold down the left mouse button. The pointer changes to the drag-and-drop pointer 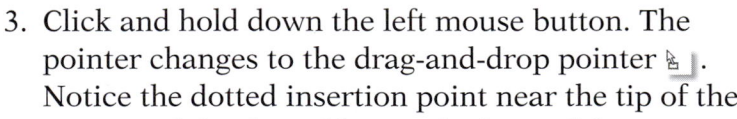. Notice the dotted insertion point near the tip of the arrow and the dotted box at the base of the arrow.

4. Drag the pointer until the dotted insertion point is positioned to the left of the line beginning "Wolf Creek Hotel." Release the mouse button. The paragraph moves to its new location and the Paste Options button 📋 appears.

Figure 7-4
Drag-and-drop
pointer

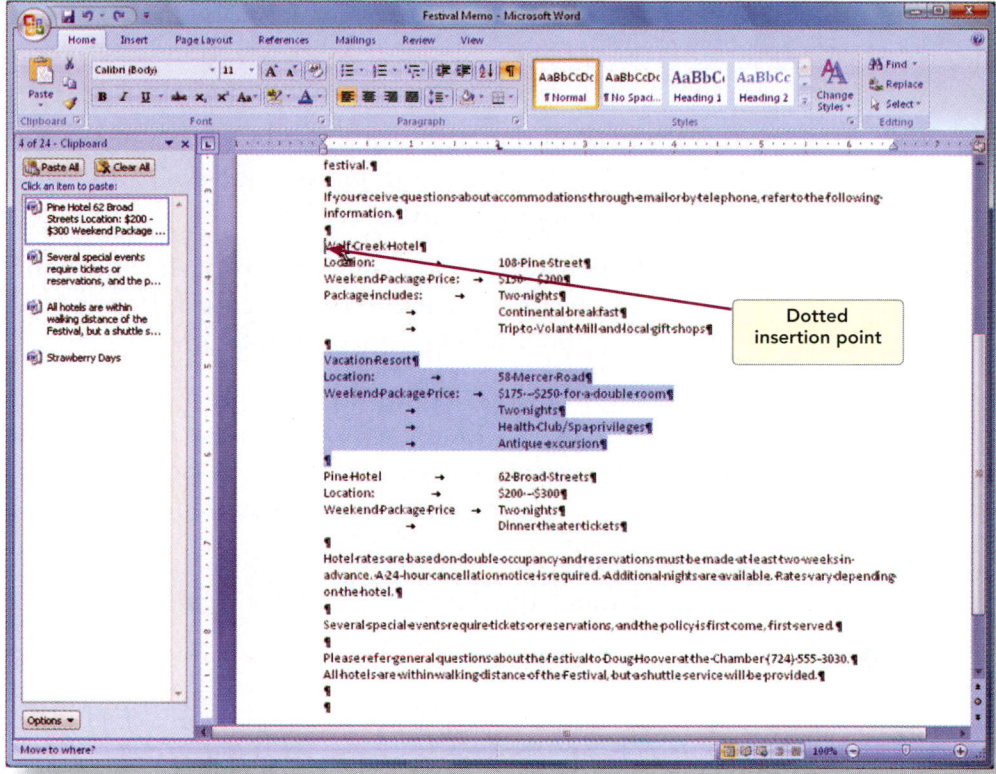

Dotted
insertion point

Copying Text by Using Copy and Paste

Copying and pasting text is similar to cutting and pasting text. Instead of removing the text from the document and storing it on the Clipboard, you place a copy of the text on the Clipboard.

There are several ways to copy and paste text. The most common methods are:

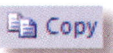

- Use the Copy 📋 Copy and Paste buttons 📋 on the Ribbon, Home tab.
- Use the shortcut menu.
- Use keyboard shortcuts Ctrl + C to copy and Ctrl + V to paste.
- Use the Clipboard task pane.

Exercise 7-7   USE COPY AND PASTE

1. Under "Wolf Creek Hotel," select the entire line that contains the text "Continental breakfast." Include the tab character to the left of the text and the paragraph mark to the right of the text. Click the Show/Hide button ¶ to display formatting characters. (The selected text should begin at the left margin and end with the paragraph mark.)

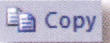

2. Click the Copy button on the Ribbon to transfer a copy of the text to the Clipboard. Notice that the selected text remains in its original position in the document.

3. Position the insertion point to the left of the paragraph that begins with a tab character and includes "Health Club/Spa privileges" in the text under "Vacation Resort."

4. Right-click and choose **Paste** from the shortcut menu. A copy of the paragraph is added to the "Vacation Resort" package description, and the Paste Options button 📋 appears.

5. Point to the Paste Options button 📋. When you see the down arrow, click the button. Notice that the same options are available when you copy and paste text. Click in the document window to close the list of options and keep the source formatting.

6. Position the insertion point to the left of the paragraph that begins "Dinner theater tickets." Press Ctrl+V to paste the text into the "Pine Hotel" package description.

Exercise 7-8   USE THE OFFICE CLIPBOARD TO PASTE COPIED TEXT

A new item is added to the Office Clipboard each time you copy text. You can click this item to paste the text into the document.

1. Under "Vacation Resort," select the text "for a double room." Include the space character to the left of the text and the paragraph mark to the right of the text.

NOTE

You can store up to 24 cut or copied items on the Office Clipboard. When the Clipboard is full and you cut or copy text, the bottom Clipboard item is deleted and the new item is added to the top of the task pane.

2. Press Ctrl+C to copy this text.

3. Position the insertion point to the right of the text that begins "$150–$200."

4. Click the Clipboard that contains the text "for a double room." The Clipboard content is pasted into the document at the location of the insertion point.

Copying Text by Dragging

To copy text by using the drag-and-drop method, press Ctrl while dragging the text. Remember, drag and drop does not store text on a Clipboard.

Exercise 7-9 USE DRAG AND DROP TO COPY TEXT

1. Scroll until you can see the text under "Wolf Creek Hotel" and "Pine Hotel."

2. Select the text under the Wolf Creek Hotel beginning with "for a double room." Include the paragraph mark.

3. While pressing ⌷Ctrl⌷, drag the selected text to the immediate right of the text "$200–$300" in the "Pine Hotel" section. The plus (⊞) sign attached to the drag-and-drop pointer indicates the text is being copied rather than moved.

4. The text is copied, and a space is automatically inserted between "$300" and "for."

> **NOTE**
>
> You may already have noticed that when you delete, cut, move, or paste text, Word automatically adjusts the spacing between words. For example, if you cut a word at the end of a sentence, Word automatically deletes the leftover space. If you paste a word between two other words, Word automatically adds the needed space as part of its Smart Cut-and-Paste feature. The Smart Cut-and-Paste feature is turned on by default.

Figure 7-5
Copying with the drag-and-drop pointer

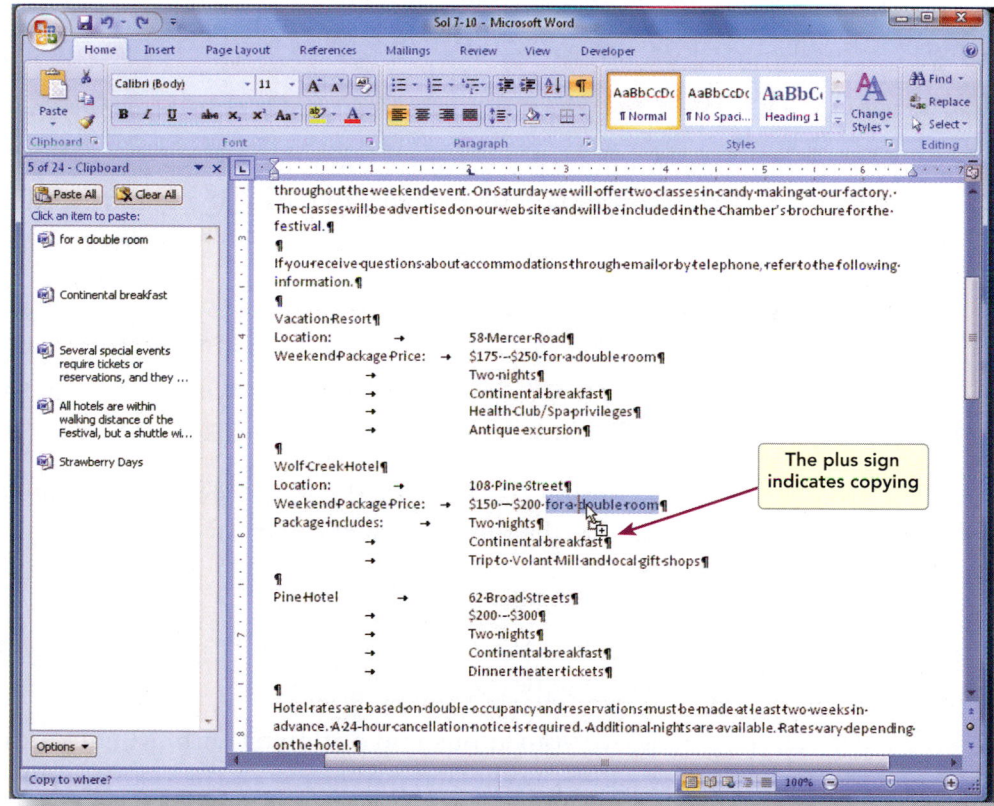

5. Move to the top of the document, and change the spacing before to 72 points, and insert your reference initials at the end of the document.

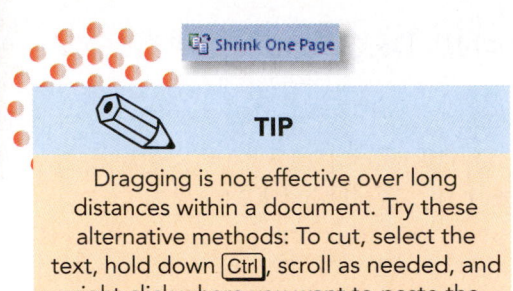

TIP

Dragging is not effective over long distances within a document. Try these alternative methods: To cut, select the text, hold down Ctrl, scroll as needed, and right-click where you want to paste the text. To copy, select the text, hold down Ctrl and Shift, scroll as needed, and right-click where you want to paste the text.

6. Open the **File** menu, and click the arrow beside **Print**. Click **Print Preview** to switch to Print Preview. Display both pages of the document by clicking **Two Pages**.

7. Locate and click the Shrink One Page button . The document is reduced to a one-page document.

8. Close Print Preview.

9. Save the document as *[your initials]*7-9 in a new folder for Lesson 7.

10. Click the Clear All button ⟨ Clear All ⟩ on the Office Clipboard to clear all items. Click the Close button ⟨ × ⟩ on the task pane to close the Office Clipboard.

11. Submit and close the document.

Working with Multiple Document Windows

In Word, you can work with several open document windows. Working with multiple windows makes it easy to compare different parts of the same document or to move or copy text from one document to another.

Exercise 7-10   SPLIT A DOCUMENT INTO PANES

Splitting a document divides it into two areas separated by a horizontal line called the *split bar*. Each of the resulting two areas, called *panes*, has its own scroll bar.

To split a screen, click the View tab and click the Split button or use the split box at the top of the vertical scroll bar.

1. Open the file **Fund2**.

2. Click the **View** tab and click the Split button ⟨ ⟩. A gray bar appears along with the split pointer ÷.

3. Move your mouse up or down (without clicking) until the gray bar is just below the last paragraph of the list of candy bars.

Figure 7-6
Splitting a document
into two panes

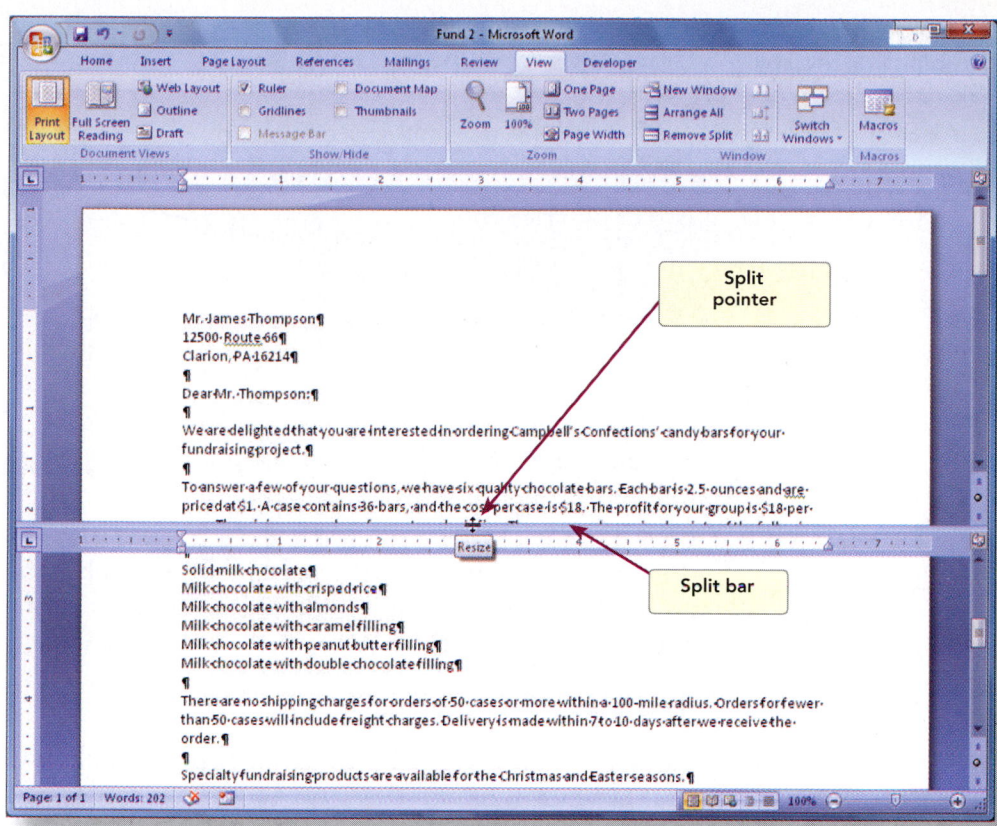

4. Click the left mouse button to set the split. The document divides into two panes, each with its own ruler and scroll bar.

5. To change the split position, move the mouse pointer over the split bar (between the top and bottom panes) until you see the split pointer ÷ and a ScreenTip that says "Resize." Then drag the bar above the list.

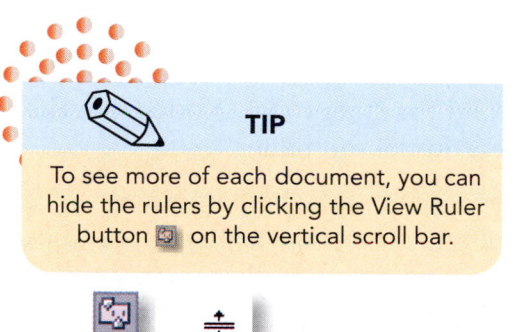

TIP

To see more of each document, you can hide the rulers by clicking the View Ruler button on the vertical scroll bar.

6. To remove the split bar, move the mouse pointer over it. When you see the split pointer, double-click. The split bar is removed.

7. Position the pointer over the *split box*—the thin gray rectangle at the top of the vertical scroll bar. (Refer to Figure 7–7 on the next page.)

8. When you see the split pointer ÷, double-click. Once again the document is split into two panes. (You can also remove the split bar by choosing Remove Split from the View tab.)

Word 2007

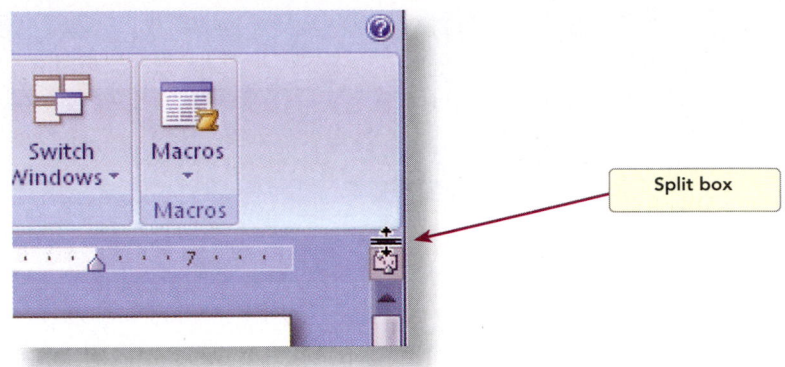

Split box

Exercise 7-11   MOVE BETWEEN PANES TO EDIT TEXT

After you split a document, you can scroll each pane separately and easily move from pane to pane to edit separate areas of the document. To switch panes, click the insertion point in the pane you want to edit.

1. Click in the top pane.

2. With the insertion point in the top pane, click the insertion point in the bottom pane.

3. Use the scroll bar in the bottom pane to scroll to the top of the document. Both panes should now show the inside address.

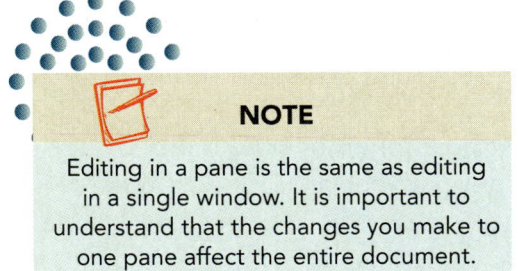

NOTE

Editing in a pane is the same as editing in a single window. It is important to understand that the changes you make to one pane affect the entire document.

4. In the bottom pane, change the street address to **12575 Route 66"** and the state to **PA**. Notice that the changes also appear in the top pane.

5. In the bottom pane, scroll until the paragraph beginning "Specialty fundraising" is displayed. Click within the top pane, and scroll until the paragraphs beginning "Specialty fundraising" and "There are no" are both displayed.

6. Go back to the bottom pane. Select the paragraph beginning "Specialty fundraising," and click the Cut button 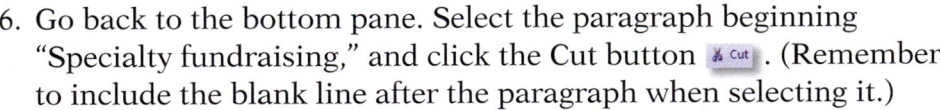. (Remember to include the blank line after the paragraph when selecting it.)

7. Move to the top pane, position the insertion point to the left of "There are no," and click the Paste button . The paragraph is moved from one part of the document to another.

8. Drag the split bar to the top of the screen. This is another way to remove the split bar. The document is again displayed in one pane.

TIP

See Appendix B, "Standard Forms for Business Documents," for standard business letter formatting.

9. Apply the correct letter formatting to the document by adding the date and your reference initials. Use the correct spacing between all letter elements, and place 72 points spacing before the date.

10. Save the document as *[your initials]*7-11 in your Lesson 7 folder.

11. Submit and close the document.

Exercise 7-12   OPEN MULTIPLE DOCUMENTS

In addition to working with window panes, you can work with more than one document file at the same time. This is useful if you keyed text in one document that you want to use in a second document.

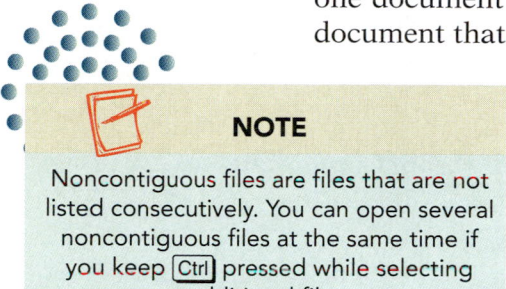

NOTE

Noncontiguous files are files that are not listed consecutively. You can open several noncontiguous files at the same time if you keep Ctrl pressed while selecting additional files.

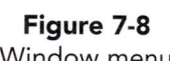

1. Display the Open dialog box. Simultaneously open the noncontiguous files **Bittersweet** and **Milk Chocolate**. To do this, click **Bittersweet** once, press Ctrl, and click **Milk Chocolate** once. With both files selected, click **Open**.

2. Click the **View** tab. Click the Switch Windows button, and notice that the two open files are listed at the bottom of this menu. The active file has a check next to it. Switch documents by clicking the file that is not active.

3. Press Ctrl+F6 to switch back.

4. Look at the taskbar at the bottom of your screen. Notice the two buttons that contain the names of your open documents. The highlighted button shows that it is the active document. Click the **Bittersweet** button to activate that document.

Figure 7-8
Window menu

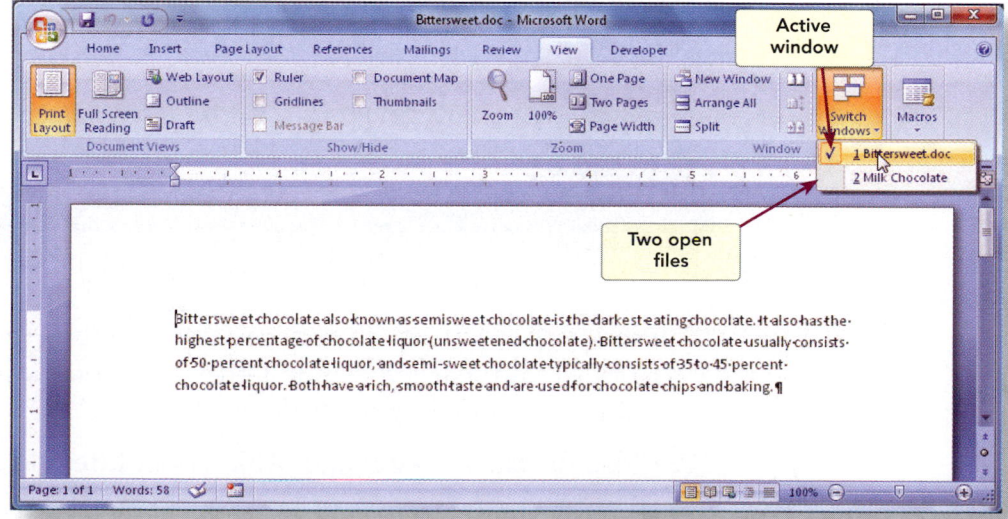

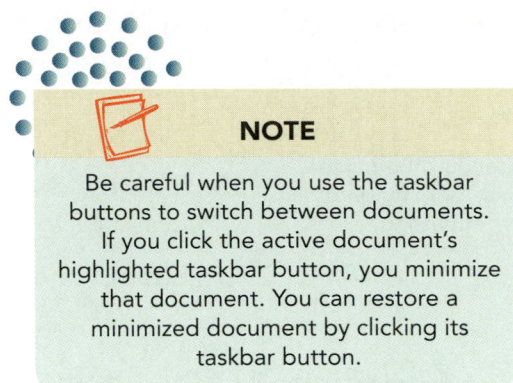

NOTE

Be careful when you use the taskbar buttons to switch between documents. If you click the active document's highlighted taskbar button, you minimize that document. You can restore a minimized document by clicking its taskbar button.

5. Click the **View** tab, if necessary. Click the Arrange All button to view both documents at the same time. The two documents appear one below the other.

Figure 7-9
Two documents displayed on one screen

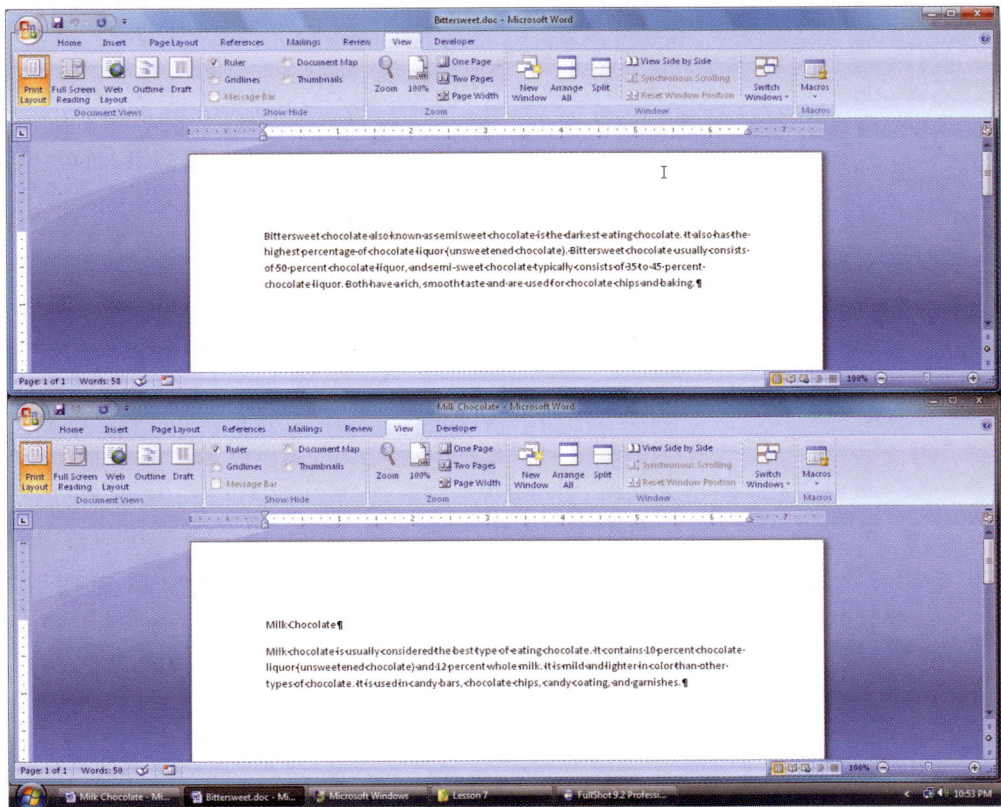

6. Press Ctrl+F6 to switch between documents. Press Ctrl+F6 again. Notice that the active window—the one containing the insertion point—has a highlighted title bar.

7. Close the **Bittersweet** and **Milk Chocolate** documents.

8. Click the Maximize button to maximize the Word window.

9. Simultaneously open three files, **Bittersweet**, **Chocolate - 2**, and **Milk Chocolate**, by accessing the Open dialog box. Select the first file, Bittersweet, and then press Ctrl and select the other two files. Click Open.

10. Choose Arrange All from the Window menu to display all three documents simultaneously.

Exercise 7-13 **REARRANGE AND RESIZE DOCUMENT WINDOWS**

You can rearrange the open documents in Word by using basic Windows techniques for minimizing, maximizing, restoring, and sizing windows.

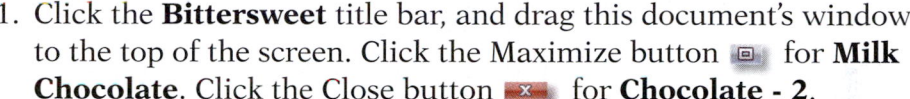

1. Click the **Bittersweet** title bar, and drag this document's window to the top of the screen. Click the Maximize button for **Milk Chocolate**. Click the Close button for **Chocolate - 2**.

2. Minimize the **Milk Chocolate** window by clicking its Minimize button . The document disappears from view. The **Milk Chocolate** button is on the taskbar, indicating that Word is still running.

3. Restore the **Milk Chocolate** document for viewing by clicking its taskbar button.

4. Drag a corner of the window's border diagonally down and to the right a few inches to make the window a different size.

5. Click the Maximize button in the **Milk Chocolate** window to return the window to full screen.

6. Click the Close button for **Milk Chocolate**.

Moving and Copying Text among Windows

When you want to copy or move text from one document to another, you can work with either multiple (smaller) document windows or full-size document windows. Either way, you can use cut and paste or copy and paste. If you work with multiple windows, you can also use drag and drop. To use this technique, you must display both documents at the same time.

Exercise 7-14   COPY TEXT FROM ONE DOCUMENT TO ANOTHER BY USING COPY AND PASTE

When moving or copying text from one document into another, the Paste command pastes text in the format of the document from which it was cut or copied. To control the formatting of pasted text, you can use the Paste Options button 📋 or the Paste Special function. In this exercise, you will use the Paste Special function to paste text without formatting.

1. Open the files **Bittersweet**, **Chocolate - 2**, and **Milk Chocolate**. Click the **Bittersweet** button on the taskbar to make it the active document.

2. In **Bittersweet**, select the entire document and change the font to 12-point Arial. Click the Copy button  .

3. Switch to the **Chocolate - 2** document.

4. Click the insertion point at the beginning of the paragraph that begins "Sweet or." Click the Paste button to insert the text copied from **Bittersweet**. Notice the format of the new text does not match the format of the current document.

5. Click the Undo button to remove the new text.

6. Click the **Home** tab, and click the lower part of the Paste button 📋. Click **Paste Special** and select **Unformatted Text**. Click **OK**. Now the format of the new text matches the format of the current document. Press Enter if necessary.

7. Click the **View** tab, and click the Switch Windows button 🗔 to activate **Bittersweet** again. Close this document without saving it.

> **TIP**
>
> You can insert an entire file into the current document by using the **Insert** tab. Move the insertion point to the place in the document where you want to insert the file. Then from the **Insert** tab, click the Object button 📋 Object ▾ . Click **Text from File** and double-click the filename. The text from the entire file is inserted at the insertion point.

Exercise 7-15   MOVE TEXT FROM ONE DOCUMENT TO ANOTHER BY USING DRAG AND DROP

1. Arrange the two open documents (**Milk Chocolate** and **Chocolate - 2**), so they are both displayed.

2. Switch to the **Milk Chocolate** document, and select the paragraph below the title.

3. Drag the selected paragraph to the **Chocolate - 2** document, and position the insertion point in front of the paragraph that begins "Sweet or."

Figure 7-10
Dragging a
paragraph between
document windows

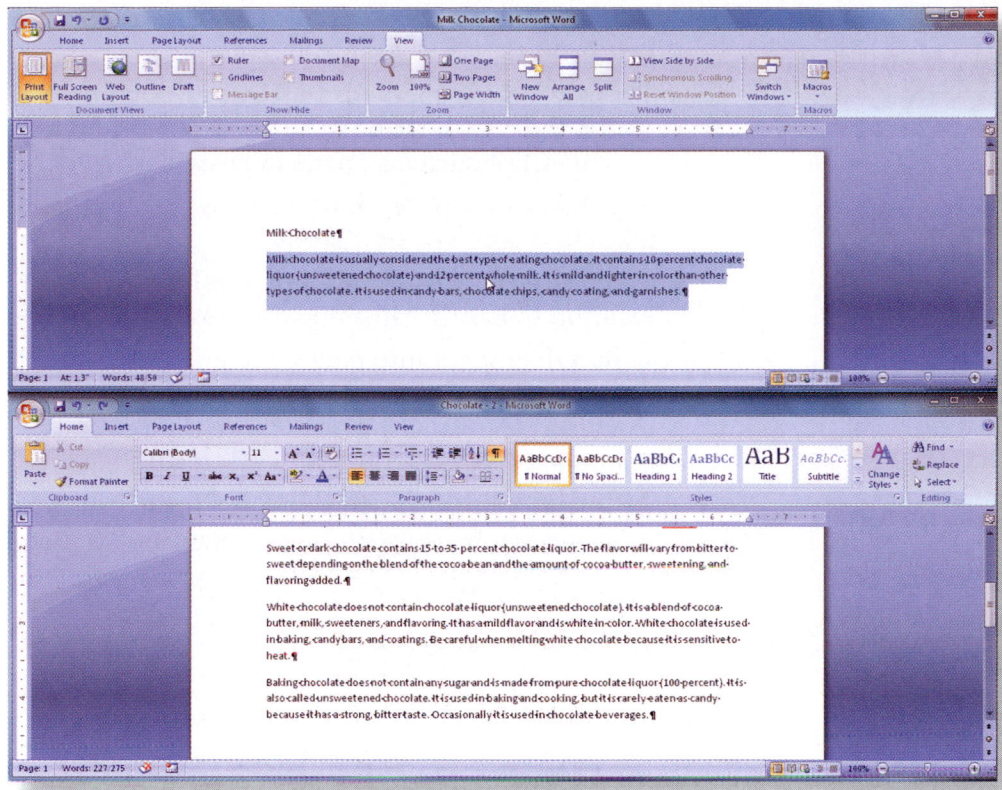

4. Close the **Milk Chocolate** document without saving.

5. Maximize the **Chocolate - 2** document. Correct the spacing between paragraphs (if you have extra paragraph marks, for example).

6. At the top of the document, add the title **TYPES OF CHOCOLATE**, formatted as 14-point bold and centered. Add 72 points spacing before and 24 points spacing after the title.

7. Save the document as *[your initials]***7-15** in your Lesson 7 folder; then print and close it.

Lesson 7 Summary

- The most important tool for moving and copying text is the Clipboard, which is a temporary storage space.

- When you display the Clipboard task pane, you are activating the Office Clipboard, which can store up to 24 cut or copied items. With the Clipboard task pane open, cut or copied text appears as a new item in the task pane.

- You move text by cutting and pasting—cut the text from one location and paste it to another.

- Copy and paste is similar to cut and paste, but instead of removing the text from the document, you place a copy of it on the Clipboard.
- There are many methods for cutting, copying, and pasting text. Use commands on the Ribbon, keyboard shortcuts, or the shortcut menu. Use the Clipboard task pane to paste stored text items.
- Use the Paste Options button 📋 to control the formatting of pasted text.
- You can use the drag-and-drop method to copy or move text from one location to another in a document or between documents.
- Split a document into panes to compare different parts of the document or to cut or copy text from one part of the document to another. Use the View tab or the split box above the vertical scroll bar to split a document.
- Open multiple documents and arrange them to fit on one screen to move or copy text from one document to another.

LESSON 7		Command Summary	
Feature	**Button**	**Command**	**Keyboard**
Open Office Clipboard	Clipboard	**Home** tab, **Clipboard** group	Ctrl + C twice
Cut	Cut	**Home** tab, **Clipboard** group	Ctrl + X
Copy	Copy	**Home** tab, **Clipboard** group	Ctrl + C
Paste	Paste	**Home** tab, **Clipboard** group	Ctrl + V
Split a document	Split	**View** tab, **Window** group	
Arrange multiple windows	Arrange All	**View** tab, **Window** group	
Next window		**View** tab, **Switch Windows**, *[filename]*	Ctrl + F6
Previous window		**View** tab, **Switch Windows**, *[filename]*	Ctrl + Shift + F6

Concepts Review

True/False Questions

Each of the following statements is either true or false. Indicate your choice by circling T or F.

T　F　1. Drag and drop stores text on the clipboard.

T　F　2. The content of the Office Clipboard is replaced each time you copy or cut text.

T　F　3. The keyboard shortcut for cut is ⌷Ctrl⌷+⌷C⌷.

T　F　4. You can drag text between two documents when they are maximized.

T　F　5. The Cut, Copy, and Paste commands are all available from the shortcut menu.

T　F　6. The only difference between cut and copy is that selected text remains in the document after copying.

T　F　7. When you move a paragraph, you should select the blank line following it to preserve proper line spacing.

T　F　8. When a document is split into panes, you can remove the split by double-clicking the split bar.

Short Answer Questions

Write the correct answer in the space provided.

1. How can you copy text without using the Clipboard?

_____

2. Which commands on the Ribbon, Home tab, do you use to move text?

_____

3. What is the keyboard shortcut for moving between two documents?

_____

4. For which command is ⌷Ctrl⌷+⌷V⌷ the keyboard shortcut?

_____

5. Which command displays all open documents at the same time?

_____

6. What is the keyboard shortcut to Undo?

_____

7. What is different about the drag-and-drop pointer when you are copying, as opposed to moving, text?

_____

8. Where is the split box located?

_____

Critical Thinking

Answer these questions on a separate page. There are no right or wrong answers. Support your answers with examples from your own experience, if possible.

1. Many people once wrote first-draft documents by hand or by using a typewriter. In either case, people would then literally cut and paste pieces of their document together and type a final draft. Some people say that word processing—specifically moving and copying text—has caused a basic change in the way people write. What do you think? Explain your answer.

2. You learned different methods for moving text by using cut and paste. You also learned the drag-and-drop method of moving text. Which method do you prefer? Why?

Skills Review

Exercise 7-16

Move text to a new location by using cut and paste and by dragging.

1. Open the file **Property**.
2. Display the Office Clipboard by following these steps:
   a. Click the **Home** tab, and click the **Clipboard Dialog Box Launcher**.
   b. Click Clear All [Clear All] if there are any items in the task pane.
3. Use keyboard shortcuts to move text by following these steps:
   a. Click the insertion point at the beginning of the line that starts "Equipment – Office." Press and hold [Shift]. Click at the end of the line beginning "Key employees."
   b. Press [Ctrl]+[X] to cut the text.
   c. Position the insertion point to the left of the line that begins "Types of coverage."
   d. Press [Ctrl]+[V] to paste the text. Press [Enter] to add a line space between the paragraphs.

4. Drag text by following these steps:

   a. Select the text "All employees" through "Customers."

   b. Point to the selected text. Press and hold down the left mouse button to display the drag-and-drop pointer and the dotted insertion point.

   c. Drag the dotted insertion point to the left of the word "Research" and release the mouse button.

   d. Press ⏎Enter after "Customers."

5. Use the Ribbon to cut and paste text by following these steps:

   a. Select the text "Fire" through "Loss of income."

   b. Click the Cut button .

   c. Position the insertion point at the beginning of the line that starts "Who to cover."

   d. Click the Paste button .

   e. Press ⏎Enter after "Loss of income."

6. Select "Types of insurance." Press ⏁Ctrl and select "Types of Coverage," "Who to cover," and "Research."

7. Apply bold, small caps, and 12 points format to the selected text. A blank line should precede each heading.

8. Clear and close the Office Clipboard by following these steps:

   a. Click Clear All  to remove all Clipboard items.

   b. Click the task pane's Close button .

9. Select the title of the document, and change it to bold, 14 points, uppercase, and apply 72 points spacing before and 24 points spacing after.

10. Save the document as *[your initials]*7-16 in your Lesson 7 folder.

11. Submit and close the document.

Exercise 7-17

Copy text by using copy and paste and by dragging.

1. Open the file **Stores - 2**.

2. Display the Office Clipboard, and clear the Office Clipboard if it contains any items.

3. Select all text in the document beginning with "Pennsylvania" through the end of the document.

4. Set a left tab at 2 inches on the ruler.

5. Position the insertion point to the right of "Grove City," and press ⏭Tab. Key **Carole Walters**.

6. Use the Office Clipboard to copy text by following these steps:

   a. Select the tab character (→) and "Carole Walters."

   b. Click the Copy button  to copy the text to a Clipboard.

   c. Position the insertion point to the right of "Meadville:"

   d. Paste the text by clicking the Clipboard.

7. Position the insertion point to the right of "Clarksburg" and press [Tab]. Key **Rebecca Surrena**.

8. Select the tab character and "Rebecca Surrena," and press [Ctrl]+[C] to place the selected text on a clipboard.

9. Position the insertion point to the right of "Fairmont," and press [Ctrl]+[V].

10. Use the drag-and-drop method to copy "Carole Walters" by following these steps:

    a. Select the tab character, the text "Carole Walters," and the paragraph mark.

    b. Point to the text. Press and hold down [Ctrl]; then click and hold down the left mouse button.

    c. Drag the dotted insertion point to the right of the word "Mercer:" and release both the mouse button and [Ctrl].

11. Click to the right of "Butler," press [Tab], and key **Cynthia Rhodes**. Select the tab character and the text you just keyed and copy it to the clipboard.

12. Click to the right of "Akron," press [Tab], and key **Jane Daniels**. Select the tab character and the text you just keyed and copy it to the clipboard. The clipboard should contain four names. Paste the text "Jane Daniels" to all cities listed under Ohio.

13. Use the Clipboard task pane to paste the text "Carole Walters" to the following cities: Edinboro, Erie, Sharon, Greenville, and Franklin.

14. Use the Clipboard task pane to paste the text "Rebecca Surrena" to Morgantown and Wheeling.

15. Use the Clipboard task pane to paste the text "Cynthia Rhodes" to New Castle, Pittsburgh, and Monroeville.

16. Bold and center the two lines at the top of the document. Format the first line in all caps and 16 points and 72 points spacing before. Format the second line in small caps and 14 points.

17. Format each of the state names as bold, italic, and small caps.

18. Select the text from "Pennsylvania" through the end of the document, and format the selected text with a 1-inch left indent. Drag the left tab marker on the ruler to 4 inches.

19. Clear and close the Office Clipboard.

20. Save the document as *[your initials]*7-17 in your Lesson 7 folder.

21. Submit and close the document.

Exercise 7-18

Split a document into panes.

1. Open the file **Favors - 2**.

2. Split the document into two panes by double-clicking the split box above the vertical scroll bar.

3. In the top pane, use the scroll bar to display the list beginning with "wedding bells" through "other assorted shapes." Format the selected text as a bulleted list.

4. In the bottom pane, scroll to the list that begins with "solid milk chocolate." Sort the list alphabetically.

5. In the bottom pane, format the list of chocolate squares as a bulleted list.

6. Remove the split by double-clicking the split bar.

7. Scroll through the document to view the changes.

8. Apply bold formatting to the title and change the spacing before to 72 points and the spacing after to 24 points.

9. Place the insertion point in the title line and apply a bottom border.

10. Save the document as *[your initials]***7-18** in your Lesson 7 folder.

11. Submit and close the document.

REVIEW

Click the Sort button in the Paragraph group.

Exercise 7-19

Arrange windows to move and copy text.

1. Start a new document. Key the text shown in Figure 7-11, and format it as a standard business memo. Use single spacing for the body of the memo and include today's date.

Figure 7-11

> Memo to Robert Smith from Pete Barnes
> Subject is Vehicle Reports
> Please review the following information, and let me know if the information provided is compatible with the new fleet management software.
> Mileage numbers will be provided the first of each month.

2. Save the document as *[your initials]***7-19** in your Lesson 7 folder.

3. Simultaneously open the files **Vehicle** and **Maintenance**.

4. Arrange the documents by following these steps:

   a. Switch to **Maintenance** if necessary, and minimize it by clicking the Minimize button 🗕 .

   b. Display the other two documents at the same time by clicking the **View** tab and clicking **Arrange All**.

5. Drag a paragraph between documents by following these steps:

   a. In the *[your initials]***7-19** window, scroll to display the sentence beginning "Mileage numbers."

   b. In the **Vehicle** window, select the entire document by pressing Ctrl + A .

   c. Holding down Ctrl to copy, drag the paragraph to the *[your initials]***7-19** window until it precedes the paragraph beginning "Mileage."

6. Close the **Vehicle** document and restore the **Maintenance** document by clicking its taskbar button.

7. Use **View tab**, **Arrange All** to display *[your initials]***7-19** and **Maintenance** at the same time, if necessary.

8. In **Maintenance**, select the text beginning "Scheduled Maintenance Guide" through the blank line preceding "10,000 miles." Copy and paste this text to the end of *[your initials]***7-19**.

9. Close the **Maintenance** document without saving it. Maximize *[your initials]***7-19**. Format the entire document in 12-point Times New Roman. Insert your reference initials at the bottom of the memo.

10. Select "Vehicle Listing" and "Scheduled Maintenance Guide," and format each heading with 14 point, bold and small caps. Format the column headings of the tabbed text to bold, small caps, and underlined.

11. Save the document again.

12. Submit and close the document.

13. If the Word window is not maximized, click the Maximize button ▣ .

Lesson Applications

Exercise 7-20

Move and copy text.

1. Open the file **OH Stores - 2**.

2. Move the address text for the Cleveland store to follow the address text for the Canton store.

3. Click on the blank line following the Akron address, and key the following text on two lines. Press Enter after each line.

   Telephone:
   Fax:

4. Select "Telephone:" and "Fax:" and copy the text to the Clipboard.

5. Paste the copied text at the end of each address.

6. Format the document heading as uppercase, bold, and 14 points with 72 points of spacing before and 24 points of spacing after. Delete the blank paragraph mark below the heading.

7. Apply bold, italic, and small caps formatting to each store name.

8. Save the document as *[your initials]*7-20 in your Lesson 7 folder.

9. Submit and close the document.

Exercise 7-21

Copy and move text in a memo.

1. Open the file **Walk**.

2. At the top of the document, insert a memo heading to the staff from you, using today's date.

3. Move the first line in the document (which begins "Getting ready") to the subject line and apply italic formatting. In the subject line, replace "walk" with a copy of the words "Chamber of Commerce Walk-a-Thon" found in the paragraph that begins "Here is." Match the destination formatting, and apply the appropriate capitalization to the subject line.

4. Delete the punctuation at the end of the subject line and extra blank lines below the subject line.

5. Use copy and paste to replace "walk-a-thon" in the last sentence of the document with the words "Chamber of Commerce Walk-a-Thon." Match destination formatting.

6. In the paragraph that begins "Once again," move the last two sentences (beginning with "We are") to the end of the document, combining them with the paragraph that begins "As I'm sure you all know."

7. At the top of the document, combine the paragraphs that begin "Once again" and "Here is."

8. In the paragraph that begins "We need," delete the words "We need a volunteer to" and capitalize the next word "check."

9. Format the three action paragraphs, beginning "Arrange," "Go through," and "Contact," as a numbered list.

10. Format the two uppercase and blue headings as uppercase, bold (no color), and with 6 points of spacing after them.

11. Save the document as *[your initials]*7-21 in your Lesson 7 folder.

12. Submit and close the document.

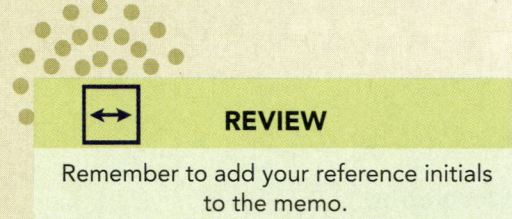

REVIEW

Remember to add your reference initials to the memo.

Exercise 7-22

Copy text from multiple documents into an existing document.

1. Open the file **Holtz**. Copy the inside address and salutation. Close the document without saving.

2. Create a new document, and insert the date using the Insert tab on the Ribbon. (Use appropriate format for a business letter.) Press Enter, and paste the copied text.

3. Format the date with 72 points spacing before and 36 points spacing after.

4. For the first paragraph of the new letter, key the text shown in Figure 7-12.

Figure 7-12

```
I am looking forward to your visit to Grove City in June.
You will be staying at the Wolf Creek Hotel as our guest.
```

5. From the file **Wolf Creek**, copy the second paragraph, beginning "The hotel has 200 rooms," and paste it at the end of the paragraph you keyed in step 4. Delete the last sentence in the paragraph.

6. Start a new paragraph by keying **When you arrive, the Strawberry Days Arts and Music Festival will be in full swing.**

7. From the file **Summer**, copy the last sentence of the first paragraph, and paste it at the end of the sentence you just keyed. Edit the beginning of the sentence to "You can enjoy."

8. Key the text shown in Figure 7-13 as a closing paragraph.

Figure 7-13

```
Jack, I am delighted that you are coming to Grove City! I
know you are going to have a great time at the Festival and
touring our facilities.
```

9. Add an appropriate closing. The letter is from Thomas Campbell, President.

10. Check for correct spacing, and spell-check the document.

11. Save the document as *[your initials]*7-22 in your Lesson 7 folder. Submit and close the document.

12. Close all other open documents without saving them. Maximize the Word window if needed.

Exercise 7-23 ◆ Challenge Yourself

Copy text from multiple documents to create a new document.

1. Start a new document. Key the title **west virginia contact information** in 12-point Arial small caps. Center the title and make it bold.

2. Insert two blank lines after the title.

3. Save the document as *[your initials]*7-23 in your Lesson 7 folder. Keep the document open.

4. Open the files **Stores - 3**, **WV Managers**, and **WV Stores**.

5. Refer to the three open documents to create a new document that includes the name and complete address for each store, the telephone and fax numbers for each store, the name of the store manager, and the name of the account executive.

6. Use tabs to arrange the text attractively.

7. Format document headings to include character and paragraph formatting.

8. Add 72 points of spacing before the first line in the document (the title). Increase the size of the title to 14 points.

9. Save the document again.

10. Submit and close the document.

On Your Own

In these exercises, you work on your own, as you would in a real-life business environment. Use the skills you've learned to accomplish the task—and be creative.

Exercise 7-24

Write a short proposal for changing something in your city, neighborhood, or school. Make the proposal at least three paragraphs long. At the end of the document, create a bulleted summary of the proposal, copying and pasting text from the proposal for the bulleted items. Save the document as *[your initials]*7-24 and submit it.

Exercise 7-25

Copy text from the Internet about a person (present day or historical) you admire. Use Paste Special to paste the text, without formatting, into a new document. Apply your own character and paragraph formatting. Save the document as *[your initials]*7-25 and submit it.

Exercise 7-26

Write a summary about a TV show you have recently seen. Save it as *[your initials]*7-26a. Keep this document open, and start a new document. Begin a letter to a friend, telling him or her about the TV show. Copy and paste or drag and drop text from the summary document into the letter. Save the document as *[your initials]*7-26b and submit both documents.

Lesson 8

Find and Replace

OBJECTIVES

After completing this lesson, you will be able to:

1. Find text.

2. Find and replace text.

3. Find and replace special characters.

4. Find and replace formatting.

MCAS OBJECTIVES

In this lesson:
WW 07 2.2.2
WW 07 5.1.1

Estimated Time: 1¼ hours

When you create documents, especially long documents, you often need to review or change text. In Word, you can do this quickly by using the Find and Replace commands.

The *Find* command locates specified text and formatting in a document. The *Replace* command finds the text and formatting and replaces it automatically with a specified alternative.

Finding Text

Instead of scrolling through a document, you can use the Find command to locate text or to move quickly to a specific document location.

Two ways to use Find are:

• Ribbon, Home tab, Editing group, Find command.

• Press Ctrl+F.

You can use the Find command to locate whole words, words that sound alike, font and paragraph formatting, and special characters. You can search an entire document or only selected text and specify the direction of the search. In the following exercise, you use Find to locate all occurrences of the word "Campbell."

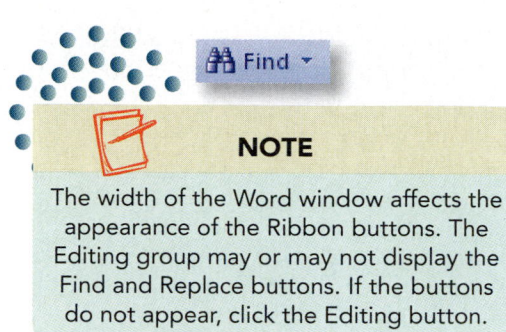

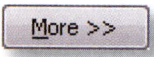

Exercise 8-1   FIND TEXT

1. Open the file **Stevenson - 1**.

2. Click the **Home** tab, and locate the **Editing** group. Click the Find button to open the Find and Replace dialog box. The **Find** tab is selected by default.

3. Delete any text in the **Find what** text box and key **Campbell**.

> **NOTE**
>
> The width of the Word window affects the appearance of the Ribbon buttons. The Editing group may or may not display the Find and Replace buttons. If the buttons do not appear, click the Editing button.

4. Click the **More** button [More >>], if it is displayed, to expand the dialog box.

Figure 8-1
Expanded Find and Replace dialog box

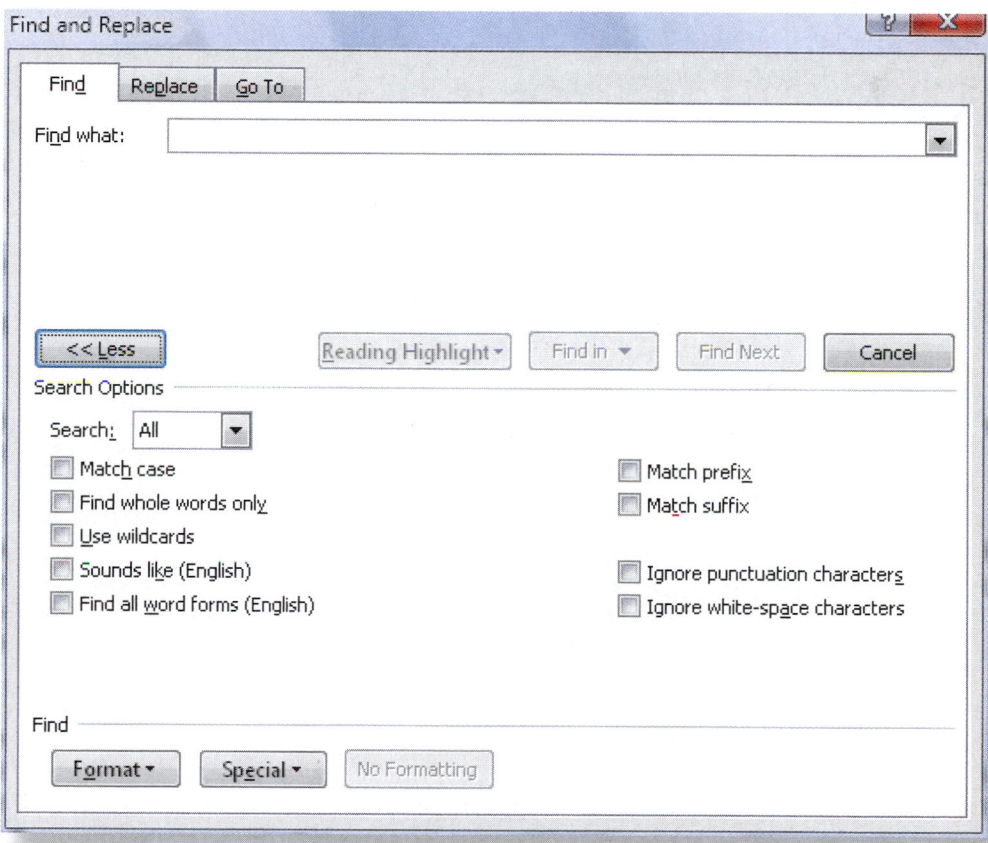

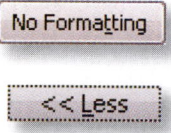

5. Click the **No Formatting** button [No Formatting] (if it is active) to remove any formatting from previous searches. Then click the **Less** button [<< Less] . The dialog box should look like the one in Figure 8-2.

Word 2007

Figure 8-2
Using the Find
feature

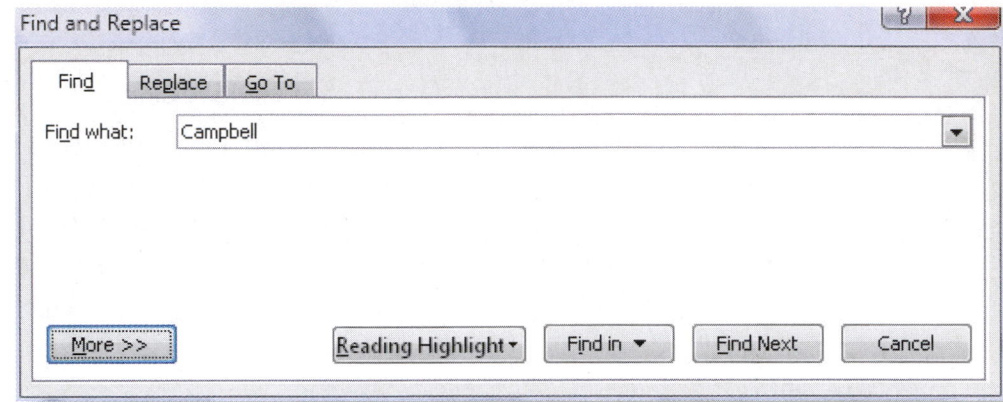

NOTE

To see more of the document text during
a search, drag the Find and Replace dialog
box by its title bar to the bottom right
corner of the screen.

6. Click the Find Next button [Find Next]. Notice that the first occurrence of "Campbell" found in the document is capitalized and italicized.

7. Continue clicking **Find Next** until you reach the end of the document. Notice that Word locates "Campbell" as a word and as text embedded in "Campbell's."

8. Click **OK** in the dialog box that says Word finished searching the document.

9. Click **Cancel** to close the Find and Replace dialog box.

10. Place the insertion point at the beginning of the paragraph that begins "Thank you." Press Ctrl+F to open the Find and Replace dialog box.

11. Key **Campbell's Confections** in the **Find what** text box. Click the Reading Highlight button [Reading Highlight ▾] and click **Highlight All**. The document highlights every occurrence of the text.

12. Click the Reading Highlight button [Reading Highlight ▾] and click **Clear Highlighting**. Close the dialog box.

Exercise 8-2   **FIND TEXT BY USING THE MATCH CASE OPTION**

The Find command includes options for locating words or phrases that meet certain criteria. One of these options is Match case, which locates text that matches the case of text keyed in the Find what text box. The next exercise demonstrates how the Match case option narrows the search when using the Find command.

1. Move to the end of the document by pressing Ctrl+End. Position the insertion point to the right of "Hamrick" in the closing.

2. Locate the **Editing** group, and click the Find button [🔍 Find ▾]. Click the More button [More >>] to display an expanded dialog box that contains search options.

3. Key **confections** in the **Find what** text box.

4. Click the **Match case** check box to select this option. Choose **Up** from the **Search:** drop-down list to reverse the search direction. Notice the **Options** that appear below the **Find what** text box.

Figure 8-3
Choosing search options

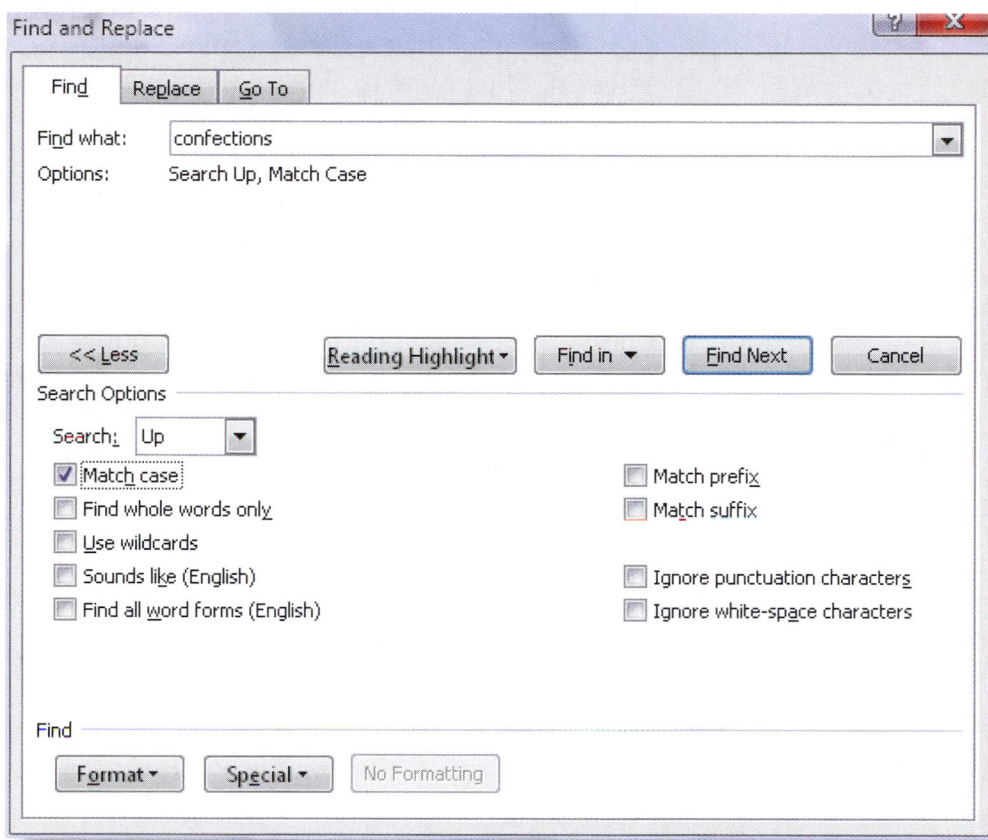

NOTE

The dialog box that appears when you end the search process is determined by the search direction and the position of the insertion point when you begin the search. When Word searches through the entire document, the dialog box tells you Word is finished searching, and the insertion point returns to its original position. When you search from a point other than the top or bottom of the document and choose Up or Down as your search direction, Word asks if you want to continue the search. If you choose not to continue, the insertion point remains at the last occurrence found.

5. Click the Less button  to collapse the dialog box. Click the Find Next button to begin the search. (If the dialog box is in your way, drag it to a preferred location.) Word ignores all occurrences of the word that do not match the search criteria ("confections").

6. Click **Find Next**. Word reaches the beginning of the document with no other matches found. Notice how the **Match case** option narrows the search.

7. Click **No** in the dialog box that asks if you want to continue searching.

8. Click **Cancel** to close the Find and Replace dialog box.

Exercise 8-3   FIND TEXT BY USING THE FIND WHOLE WORDS ONLY OPTION

The **Find whole words only** option is another way to narrow the search criteria. Word locates separate words, but not characters embedded in other words.

1. Move the insertion point to the beginning of the document. Press Ctrl+F to open the Find and Replace dialog box with the **Find** tab selected. Click **More** to expand the dialog box. Click **Match case** to clear the option.

2. Key **or** in the Find what text box. Click the down arrow next to the **Find what** text box, and notice that the previous entries are listed. The last seven entries of the **Find what** text box are displayed in this list. Click the arrow to close the list. Change the **Search:** drop-down list to **Down**.

3. Click the Find Next button � Find Next and notice that "for" is highlighted. Click the Find Next button ⎑ Find Next . "Factory" is highlighted because it contains the characters "or."

4. Click **Find whole words only** to select it. Click and choose **Down** from the **Search:** drop-down list.

5. Click **Less**, and then click **Find Next** to begin the search. Word locates the word "or," but not other word forms, such as "factory."

6. Click **Find Next** two times. Click **No** to end the search.

7. Click **Cancel** to close the Find and Replace dialog box.

Exercise 8-4   FIND TEXT BY USING THE WILDCARD OPTION

You can use the Use wildcards option to search for text strings using special search operators. A *wildcard* is a symbol that stands for missing or unknown text. For example, the Any Character wildcard "^?" finds any character. Using the "^?" wildcard, a search for "b^?te" would find both "bite" and "byte." The question mark is replaced by a character that follows "b" and precedes "te."

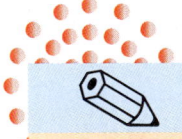

TIP

Press Esc to cancel a search. You can also interrupt a search by clicking outside the Find and Replace dialog box, editing the document text, and then clicking the dialog box to reactivate it.

1. Position the insertion point at the beginning of the document. Open the Find and Replace dialog box with the **Find** tab displayed.

2. Display the expanded dialog box and click **Use wildcards** to select this option.

3. Select the text in the **Find what** text box and key **ca**.

4. Click the **Special** button ⎓ Special ▾ and choose **Any Character** from the list. The "?" is inserted.

Figure 8-4
Choosing a Special search operator

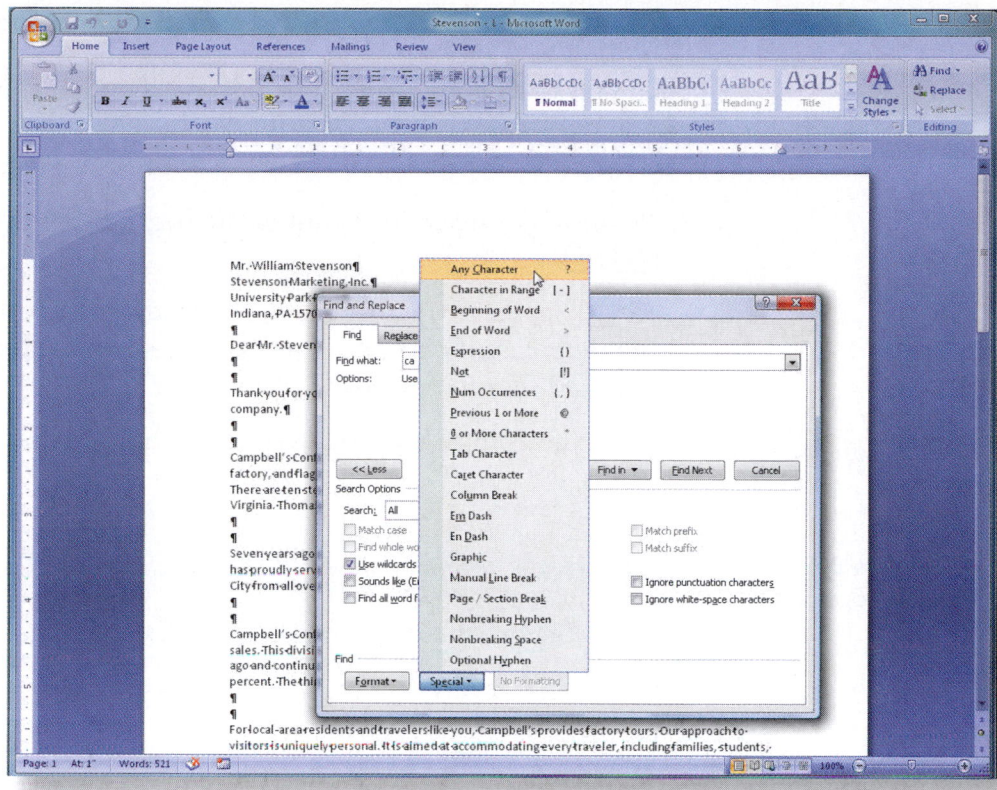

5. Choose **All** from the **Search:** drop-down list, if it is not already selected. Then click **Less**.

6. Click **Find Next**. The first occurrence appears in the word "candy."

7. Continue clicking **Find Next** and notice all the occurrences of "ca?" in the document.

8. Click **OK** in the dialog box that says Word finished searching the document.

9. Click **Cancel** to close the Find and Replace dialog box.

TIP

After you initiate a Find by using the Find and Replace dialog box, you can close the dialog box and use the Next Find/Go To button ⬇ and Previous Find/Go To button ⬆ located at the bottom of the vertical scroll bar to continue the search without having the dialog box in your way. (See Figure 8-5.)

Figure 8-5
Finding text without the Find and Replace dialog box

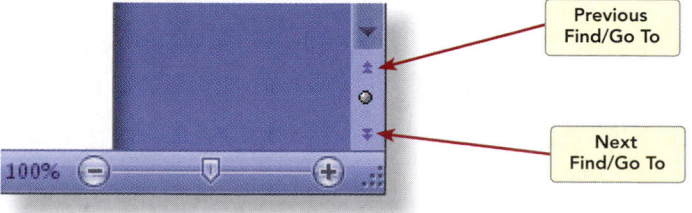

Previous Find/Go To

Next Find/Go To

Exercise 8-5   FIND FORMATTED TEXT

In addition to locating words and phrases, the Find command can search for text that is formatted. The formatting can include character formatting, such as bold and italic, and paragraph formatting, such as alignment and line spacing.

1. Position the insertion point at the beginning of the document. Press Ctrl + F.

2. Key **Campbell's Confections** in the **Find what** text box. Expand the dialog box and choose **All** from the **Search:** drop-down list. Click any checked search options to clear them.

3. Click the **Format** button [Format ▾] and choose **Font**.

Figure 8-6
Format options

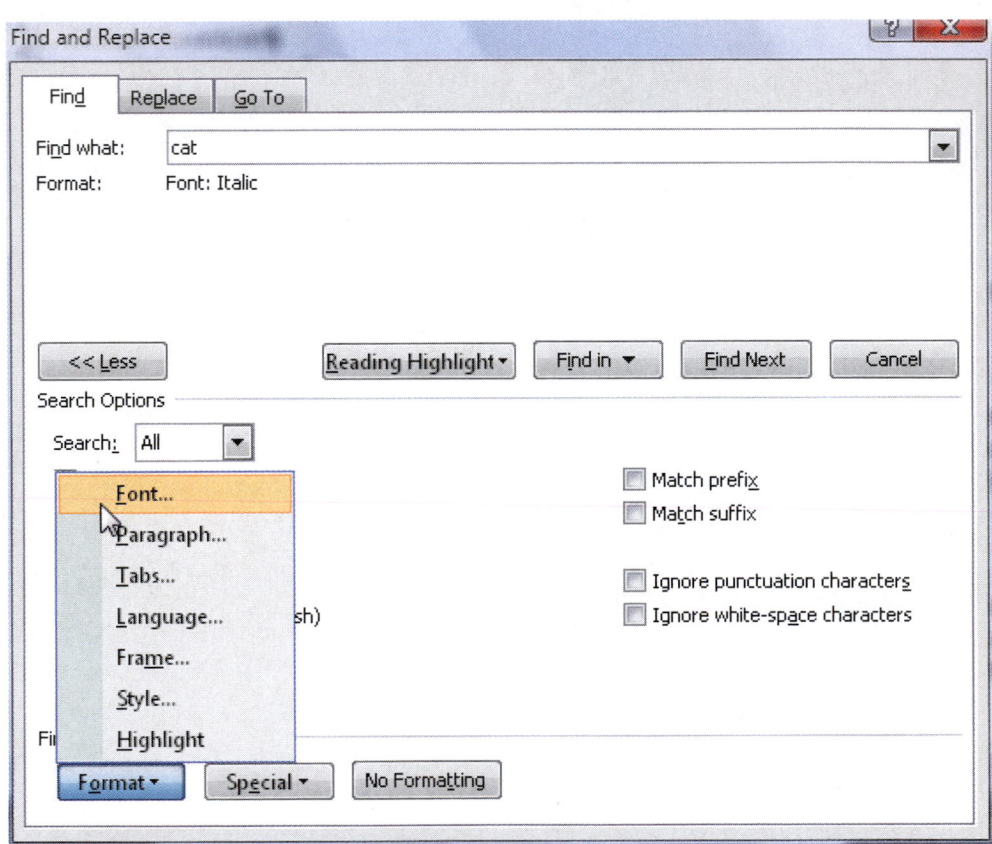

4. In the Find Font dialog box, choose **Italic** from the Font style list and click **OK**. Italic now appears below the Find what text box.

5. Click **Less**, and then click **Find Next**. Word locates "*Campbell's Confections.*"

6. Click **Cancel** to close the Find and Replace dialog box.

Finding and Replacing Text

The Replace command searches for specified text or formatting and replaces it with your specified alternative. You can replace all instances of text or formatting at once, or you can find and confirm each replacement.

Two ways to replace text are:

- Ribbon, Home tab, Editing group, Replace command.
- Press Ctrl + H.

Exercise 8-6   REPLACE TEXT BY USING FIND NEXT

1. Position the insertion point at the beginning of the document, locate the **Editing** group, and click the Replace button ![ab Replace]. The **Replace** tab is now selected in the dialog box.

2. Key **traveler** in the **Find what** text box. Expand the dialog box and click the **No Formatting** button to remove formatting from previous searches. Make sure no options under **Search:** are selected.

3. Press Tab to move to the **Replace with** text box, and key **visitor**. Click the **No Formatting** button if it is active.

Figure 8-7
Replacing text

Find and Replace

| Find | Replace | Go To |

Find what: traveler

Replace with: visitor

<< Less   Replace   Replace All   Find Next   Cancel

Search Options

Search: All

☐ Match case   ☐ Match prefix
☐ Find whole words only   ☐ Match suffix
☐ Use wildcards
☐ Sounds like (English)   ☐ Ignore punctuation characters
☐ Find all word forms (English) ☐ Ignore white-space characters

Replace

Format ▾   Special ▾   No Formatting

> **NOTE**
>
> Remember, pressing Tab in a dialog box moves the insertion point from one text box to another and highlights existing text. Pressing Enter executes the dialog box command.

4. Adjust the position and size (click **Less**) of the dialog box so you can see the document text. Click **Find Next**. Click **Replace** to replace the first occurrence of "traveler" with "visitor."

5. Continue to click **Replace** until Word reaches the end of the document.

6. Click **OK** when Word finishes searching the document.

7. Close the Find and Replace dialog box.

Exercise 8-7   REPLACE TEXT BY USING REPLACE ALL

The **Replace All** option replaces all occurrences of text or formatting in a document without confirmation.

1. Move the insertion point to the beginning of the document and press Ctrl+H to open the Find and Replace dialog box with the **Replace** tab selected.

> **NOTE**
>
> After replacing text or formatting, you can always undo the action. If you used **Replace All**, all changes are reversed at once. If you used **Replace**, only the last change is reversed, but you can undo the last several changes individually by selecting them from the Undo drop-down list.

2. Key **Campbell's Confections** in the **Find what** text box. Press Tab and key **CAMPBELL'S CONFECTIONS** in the **Replace with** text box.

3. Expand the dialog box, clear the **Match case** check box if necessary, and click **Replace All**. Word will indicate the number of replacements made.

4. Click **OK** and close the Find and Replace dialog box. "Campbell's Confections" now appears as "CAMPBELL'S CONFECTIONS" throughout the document.

5. Click the Undo button to undo the Replace All command.

Exercise 8-8   DELETE TEXT WITH REPLACE

You can also use the Replace command to delete text automatically. Key the text to be deleted in the **Find what** text box and leave the **Replace with** text box blank. You can find and delete text with confirmation by using the **Find Next** option or without confirmation by using the **Replace All** option.

1. Position the insertion point at the beginning of the document, and open the Find and Replace dialog box with the **Replace** tab selected.

2. Key **Campbell's** in the **Find what** text box and press Spacebar once. The space character is not visible in the text box.

3. Press ⌶Tab⌶ to move to the **Replace with** text box and press ⌶Delete⌶ to remove the previous entry.

4. Click the Replace All button  .

5. Click **OK** and close the dialog box. The word "Campbell's" followed by a space is deleted from the company name throughout the document. If the word "Campbell's" was followed by a punctuation mark, the word would not be deleted.

6. Click the Undo button 🔁 .

7. Save the document as *[your initials]*8-8 in a new folder for Lesson 8. Leave the document open for the next exercise.

TIP

The last option in the Find and Replace dialog box is **Find all word forms**. Use this option to find different forms of words and replace the various word forms with comparable forms. For example, if you key "walk" in the **Find what** text box and key "jump" in the **Replace with** text box, Word replaces "walk" with "jump" and "walked" with "jumped." Use **Replace**, rather than **Replace All**, when you choose this option to verify each replacement and ensure that correct word forms are used.

Finding and Replacing Special Characters

The Find and Replace features can search for characters other than ordinary text. Special characters include paragraph marks and tab characters. Special characters are represented by codes that you can key or choose from the Special drop-down list.

Exercise 8-9   **FIND AND REPLACE SPECIAL CHARACTERS**

1. Click the Show/Hide ¶ button to display special characters in the document if they are not showing.

2. Position the insertion point at the top of the document. Open the Find and Replace dialog box with the **Replace** tab selected. Expand the dialog box, if it is not already. Delete the text that appears in the **Find what** text box.

3. Click the **Special** button and choose **Paragraph Mark**. A code (^p) is inserted in the **Find what** text box. Add two additional paragraph mark codes in the **Find what** text box to search for three consecutive paragraph marks in the document. (Use the **Special** drop-down list or key **^p^p**.)

4. Move to the **Replace with** text box and insert two paragraph mark codes.

5. Clear any **Search Options** check boxes and click **Less**.

Word 2007

6. Click **Find Next**. Word locates the extra paragraph mark after the salutation of the letter.

Figure 8-8
Replacing special characters

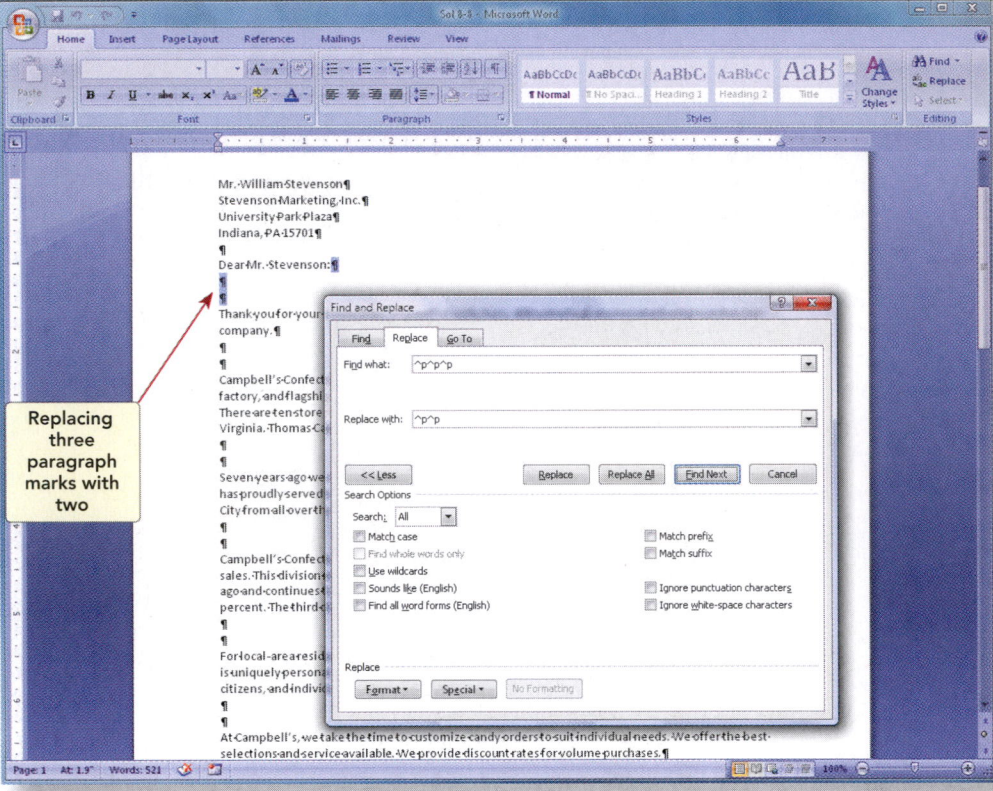

7. Click **Replace**. Notice the elimination of the extra paragraph mark. Continue to click **Replace** for each paragraph mark until you reach the paragraph marks just after "Sincerely."

8. Close the Find and Replace dialog box. The document paragraphs are now correctly spaced.

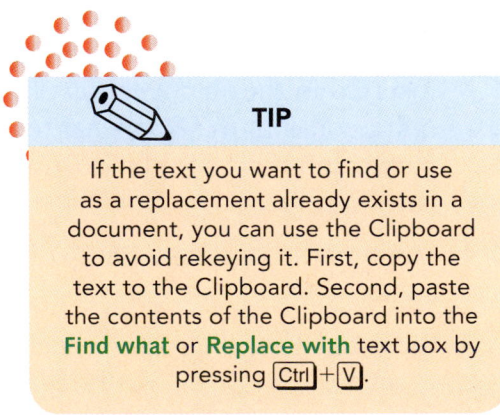

TIP

If the text you want to find or use as a replacement already exists in a document, you can use the Clipboard to avoid rekeying it. First, copy the text to the Clipboard. Second, paste the contents of the Clipboard into the **Find what** or **Replace with** text box by pressing Ctrl + V.

TABLE 8-1 Find and Replace Special Characters

Find or Replace	Special Character Code to Key
Paragraph mark (¶)	^p (must be lowercase)
Tab character →	^t (must be lowercase)
Any character (Find only)	^?
Any digit (Find only)	^#
Any letter (Find only)	^$
Column break	^n
Clipboard contents (Replace only)	^c
Em dash	^+
En dash	^=
Field (Find only)	^d
Footnote mark (Find only)	^f
Graphic (Find only)	^g
Manual line break	^l
Manual page break	^m
Nonbreaking hyphen	^~
Nonbreaking space	^s
Section break (Find only)	^b
White space (Find only)	^w

Finding and Replacing Formatting

Word can search for and replace both character and paragraph formatting. You can specify character or paragraph formatting by clicking the Format button [Format ▾] in the Find and Replace dialog box or using keyboard shortcuts.

Format ▾

Exercise 8-10   FIND AND REPLACE CHARACTER FORMATTING

1. Position the insertion point at the top of the document and open the Find and Replace dialog box with the **Replace** tab selected. Expand the dialog box.

2. Key **Campbell's Confections** in the **Find what** text box. Press ⎡Tab⎤ and delete the text in the **Replace with** text box.

3. Click the **Format** button and choose **Font**. Choose **Bold** for **Font style** and click **Small caps**. Click **OK**.

4. Click **Replace All**.

5. Click **OK** when Word finishes searching the document, and close the dialog box. "Campbell's Confections" appears bold and in small caps throughout the document.

6. Reopen the Find and Replace dialog box with the **Replace** tab selected.

7. Highlight the text in the **Find what** text box, if it is not already. Click the **Format** button and choose **Font**. Choose **Bold** and **Small caps** and click **OK**.

8. Press ⎡Tab⎤ to move the insertion point to the **Replace with** text box. Click the No Formatting button [No Formatting] to clear existing formatting.

9. Click the **Format** button [Format ▾] and choose **Font**. Choose the **Not Bold** style, deselect **Small caps**, and click **OK**.

10. Press ⎡Ctrl⎤+⎡I⎤ (the keyboard shortcut for italic text). Now the format for the **Replace with** text box is "**Not Bold, Not Small caps, Not All caps, Italic**."

11. Click **Replace All**.

12. Click **OK** and close the Find and Replace dialog box. "Campbell's Confections" is now italic, and not bold, throughout the document.

[No Formatting]

Exercise 8-11   FIND AND REPLACE PARAGRAPH FORMATTING

1. Position the insertion point at the end of the first paragraph that begins "Thank you." Open the Find and Replace dialog box with the **Replace** tab selected.

2. In the **Find what** text box, insert two paragraph mark special characters (use the **Special** list or key **^p^p**). Clear existing formatting.

3. Move to the **Replace with** text box, enter two paragraph mark special characters, and clear existing formatting.

4. Click the **Format** button and choose **Paragraph**. Click the **Indents and Spacing** tab if it is not active. Deselect **Mirror indents** if necessary.

5. Choose **First Line** from the **Special** drop-down list. If "0.5" is not the measurement displayed in the **By** text box, select the text in the **By** box and key **0.5**. Click **OK**.

6. Click **Find Next** and Word highlights the paragraph marks after "company." Click **Replace** to format that paragraph.

7. Click **Replace** seven more times (through the paragraph ending "enclosed brochure").

8. Close the Find and Replace dialog box. Scroll through the document to view the paragraph formatting changes. All these paragraphs should now have a 0.5-inch first-line indent.

9. Position the insertion point at the top of the document. Open the Find and Replace dialog box with the **Replace** tab selected.

10. Delete the text in the **Find what** text box, and set the text box to look for a 0.5-inch first-line indent. Deselect **Mirror indents** if necessary.

Figure 8-9
Defining paragraph
formatting

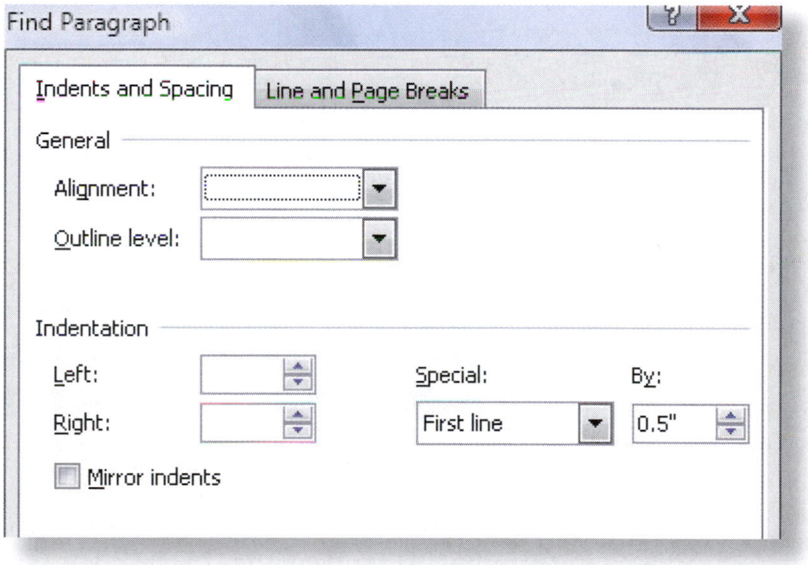

11. Delete the text in the **Replace with** text box, clear the formatting, and replace with 0.25-inch left and right indents and no first-line indent (choose **(none)** from the **Special** drop-down list in the Replace Paragraph dialog box).

Figure 8-10
Replacing paragraph
formatting

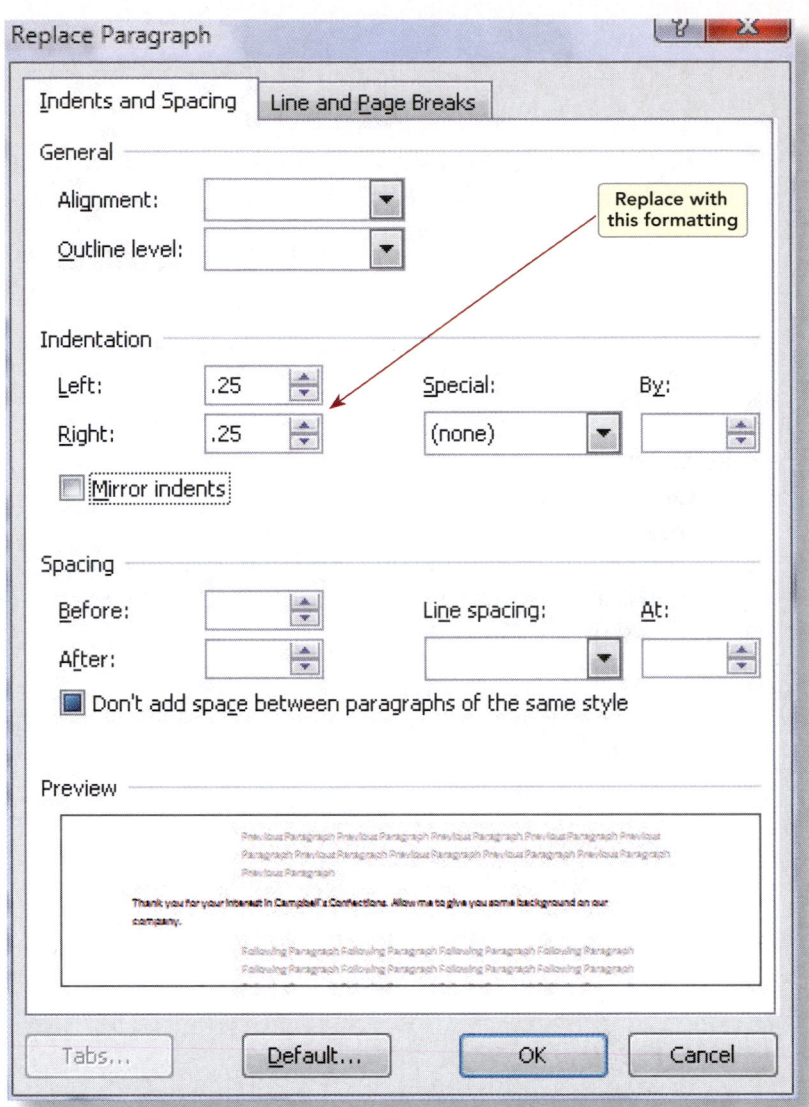

12. Click **Replace All** and click **OK**. Close the dialog box.

13. Scroll through the document to observe the replacement of first-line indented paragraphs with 0.25-inch left- and right-indented paragraphs.

14. Enter the date at the top of the document, with 72 points spacing before and three blank lines after it. Replace "xx" with your reference initials.

15. Save the document as *[your initials]*8-11 in your Lesson 8 folder.

16. Submit and close the document.

TABLE 8-2 Find and Replace Formatting Guidelines

Guideline	Procedure
Find specific text with specific formatting.	Key the text in the **Find what** text box and specify its formatting (choose **Font** or **Paragraph** from the **Format** drop-down list or use a keyboard shortcut).
Find specific formatting.	Delete text in the **Find what** text box, and specify formatting.
Replace specific text but not its formatting.	Key the text in the **Find what** text box. Click the **No Formatting** button to clear existing formatting. Key the replacement text in the **Replace with** text box, and clear existing formatting.
Replace specific text and its formatting.	Key the text in the **Find what** text box and specify its formatting. Delete any text in the **Replace with** text box, and specify the replacement formatting.
Replace only formatting for specific text.	Key the text in the **Find what** text box, and specify its formatting. Delete any text in the **Replace with** text box and specify the replacement formatting.
Replace only formatting.	Delete any text in the **Find what** text box, and specify formatting. Delete any text in the **Replace with** text box, and specify the replacement formatting.

Lesson 8 Summary

- The Find command locates specified text and formatting in a document. The Replace command finds text and formatting and replaces it automatically with specified alternatives.

- Use the Find command to locate whole words, words that sound alike, font and paragraph formatting, and special characters. Using the Find command, you can search an entire document or selected text. You can also specify the direction of the search.

- Use the Match case option to locate text that matches the case of document text. Example: When searching for "Confections," Word would not find "confections."

- When you want to locate whole words and not parts of a word, use the Find whole words only option. Example: When searching for the whole word "can," Word would find only "can," but not "candy" or "candidate."

- Use the Use wildcards option to search for text strings by using special search operators. A wildcard is a symbol that stands for missing or unknown text. Example: A search for "b^?yte" would find "bite" and "byte." See Table 8-1.

- Use the Sounds like option to find a word that sounds similar to the search text but is spelled differently or to find a word you do not know how to spell. When you find the word, you can stop the search process and edit your document.

- Use the Find command to search for formatted text. The formatting can include character formatting, such as bold and italic, and paragraph formatting, such as alignment and line spacing. Use the Replace command to replace the formatting. See Table 8-2.

- Use the Replace command to search for all instances of text or formatting at once or to find and confirm each replacement.

- Use the Replace command to delete text automatically. Key the text to be deleted in the Find what text box and leave the Replace with text box blank.

LESSON 8		Command Summary	
Feature	**Button**	**Command**	**Keyboard**
Find	🔍 Find ▾	**Home** tab, **Editing** group	Ctrl + F
Replace	Replace	**Home** tab, **Editing** group	Ctrl + H

Concepts Review

True/False Questions

Each of the following statements is either true or false. Indicate your choice by circling T or F.

T F   1. You can use keyboard shortcuts to specify formatting in the Find and Replace dialog box.

T F   2. To find text or formatting, you must have the insertion point at the beginning of the document.

T F   3. Line spacing and indents are two examples of paragraph formatting that you can specify in the Replace with text box.

T F   4. The question mark represents a special character code used to search for any character.

T F   5. You use the Match case option to specify only uppercase when finding or replacing text.

T F   6. The keyboard command to find text is Ctrl+H.

T F   7. The Undo command undoes all replacements made if you used the Replace All option.

T F   8. You can use the Find command to search either selected text or an entire document.

Short Answer Questions

Write the correct answer in the space provided.

1. What is the special character code for a paragraph mark?

2. Which button can you use to continue a Find operation when the Find and Replace dialog box is closed?

3. With the insertion point in the Find what text box, how do you move to, and automatically highlight the contents of, the Replace with text box?

4. Which Find option do you use to locate a specific word rather than all occurrences of the text?

5. If the insertion point is in the Find what text box, what is the shortcut to insert text for which you previously searched?

_____

6. How do you clear previous formatting when it appears below the text boxes in the Find and Replace dialog box?

_____

7. Which button expands the Find and Replace dialog box to show more options, and which button reduces the dialog box to make it smaller?

_____

8. Which option, Replace or Replace All, allows for selective replacement of text?

_____

Critical Thinking

Answer these questions on a separate page. There are no right or wrong answers. Support your answers with examples from your own experience, if possible.

1. Click the **Start** button, and click the link for Windows **Help and Support**. In the **Search Help** text box, key **find files** and press Enter. Read the information about finding files and folders. Create a document to summarize the facts. Be sure to include the instructions for finding a file that contains specific text as well as files created on a particular date.

2. The Replace All option can be very useful. It can also lead to occasional problems if you have not thought through a specific Replace All operation. After you experiment with the feature, describe some precautions you would suggest for the use of Replace All.

Skills Review

Exercise 8-12

Find and Replace text.

1. Open the file **Walk - 2**.
2. Use the Find command to locate the text "8 a.m." by following these steps:
   a. Position the insertion point at the beginning of the document and click the **Home** tab. Click the Find button 🔍 Find ▾ .
   b. Key 8 a.m. in the **Find what** text box. Click **More**, if the dialog box is not already expanded.

   c. Click **No Formatting** to clear previous formats. Make sure no search options are selected. Click **Find Next**.

   d. Click **Cancel** to close the dialog box, and edit the found text to **8:30 a.m.**

3. Change the text "walk-a-thon" to "Walk-a-Thon," using the Replace command, by following these steps:

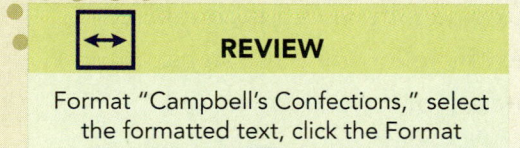

   a. Move the insertion point to the beginning of the document. Click the **Home** tab, and click the Replace button .

   b. Key **walk-a-thon** in the **Find what** text box, press Tab, and key **Walk-a-Thon** in the **Replace with** text box.

   c. Click **No Formatting** if any formatting remains.

   d. Click **Less** to reduce the size of the dialog box, and drag the dialog box to the bottom of the screen.

   e. Click **Find Next,** and then click **Replace**. Click **Replace** until Word reaches the end of the document. Click **OK**, and close the dialog box.

4. Change the date, using the Replace command, by following these steps:

   a. Position the insertion point at the beginning of the document and press Ctrl+H.

   b. Key **May 1** in the **Find what** text box.

   c. Press Tab and key **April 25** in the **Replace with** text box.

   d. Click **More** to expand the dialog box, and click any checked search options to deselect them.

   e. Click **Replace All**. Click **OK** and close the dialog box.

5. Replace the text "Education Fund" with "Outreach Program."

6. Move to the top of the document, and format the first line with 72 points spacing before. Edit the text to read "**Put on your walking shoes—Become a Friend of the Library Outreach Program**."

7. Format the first line of text as 14-point bold.

8. Move to the end of the document and format "Campbell's Confections" as bold italic. Copy the formatting to the text "Chamber of Commerce" located below the address.

REVIEW

Format "Campbell's Confections," select the formatted text, click the Format Painter button, and then select "Chamber of Commerce."

9. Spell-check the document.

10. Save the document as *[your initials]***8-12** in your Lesson 8 folder.

11. Submit, and close the document.

Exercise 8-13

Use Replace to replace special characters and delete text.

1. Start a new document.

2. Key the text shown in Figure 8-11, using single spacing. When keying the hyphens, do not insert space characters before or after the hyphen.

Figure 8-11

```
Campbell's Confections
Chocolate Factory Hours
September 1 through June 30
Monday-Saturday
9 a.m.-4 p.m.
Summer Schedule
July 1 through August 31
Monday-Friday
9 a.m.-5 p.m.
For more information, call 724-555-2025
```

3. Center the entire document horizontally, and change the font to Arial.

4. Change the first line to 16-point bold and the last line to bold italic. Apply bold and small caps format to the second line.

5. Replace special characters by following these steps:

   a. Position the insertion point at the end of the document and click the **Home** tab, and click the Replace button ![Replace]. Click **More** to expand the dialog box, if it is not already expanded.

   b. Key a hyphen in the **Find what** text box.

   c. Press Tab to move to the **Replace** with text box.

   d. Click the **Special** button and choose **En Dash**.

   e. Choose **Up** from the **Search:** drop-down list, and clear any search options that are selected.

   f. Click **Less**, and then click **Find Next**. Do not replace the hyphens in the telephone number.

   g. Click **Find Next** and click **Replace** to replace the hyphen in the time.

   h. Continue replacing hyphens until you reach the beginning of the document.

   i. Click **OK** and close the dialog box when the search is complete.

6. Use the Replace feature to delete text by following these steps:

   a. Position the insertion point at the top of the document and press Ctrl + H.

   b. Key **Summer Schedule** in the **Find what** dialog box.

   c. Expand the dialog box and clear any formatting.

   d. Delete any text or formatting in the **Replace with** text box.

   e. Select **All** for the **Search:** direction.

   f. Click **Replace All** to delete the text. Click **OK** and close the dialog box.

7. Undo the replacement by clicking the Undo button 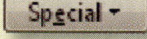 on the Quick Access Toolbar.

8. Change the spacing after to 12 points for the entire document. Change the spacing before for the first line to 72 points.

9 Spell-check the document.

10. Save the document as *[your initials]*8-13 in your Lesson 8 folder.

11. Submit and close the document.

Exercise 8-14

Use Replace to delete special characters, replace text, and replace formatting.

1. Open the file **OH Hours**.

2. Use the Replace command to delete all tabs by following these steps:

   a. Position the insertion point at the beginning of the document, and click the Replace button.

   b. Key **^t** (the code for a tab character) in the **Find what** text box, and clear existing formatting.

   c. Delete any text in the **Replace with** text box, and clear existing formatting and search options.

   d. Click **Replace All**, click **OK**, and click **Close**.

3. Undo the replacement.

4. Replace the em dash (—) with the word "to," by following these steps:

   a. Press Ctrl + H .

   b. Delete text or formatting that appears in the **Find what** text box. Click **More** to expand the dialog box. Click the Special button Special ▾ , and click **Em Dash**.

   c. In the **Replace with** text box, press Spacebar , key **to**, and press Spacebar .

   d. Click **Replace All**. Click **OK** and click **Close**.

5. Replace the underline format with bold small caps format by following these steps:

   a. Press Ctrl + H .

   b. Delete text or formatting that appears in the **Find what** text box. Click **More** to expand the dialog box. Press Ctrl + U . "**Underline**" should display under the Find what text box.

   c. In the **Replace with** text box, click the Format button Format ▾ , and click **Font**. Click the arrow in the **Underline Style** box, and click **(none)**. Select **Bold** and **Small caps** formatting. Click **OK**.

   d. Click **Replace All**. Click **OK** and click **Close**.

6. Change the heading of the document to 14 point with 72 points spacing before. Change the line spacing for all the tabbed text, including the tabbed heading, to double spacing.

7. Save the document as *[your initials]*8-14 in your Lesson 8 folder.

8. Submit and close the document.

Exercise 8-15

Replace character and paragraph formatting.

1. Open the file **Homecoming**.

2. Format the first page of the document as a memo. Key the memo heading information as shown in Figure 8-12. Add your reference initials and an enclosure notation (use the word "Attachment" instead of "Enclosure").

Figure 8-12

```
MEMO TO: Robert Smith

FROM: Thomas Campbell

DATE: May 30, 20—

SUBJECT: Homecoming Dates
```

3. Find and replace special characters by following these steps:

   a. Position the insertion point at the top of page 2, and open the Find and Replace dialog box with the **Replace** tab selected.

   b. Delete existing text in the **Find what** text box, and clear all search options and formatting. Click the Special button `Special▾` and click **Manual Line Break**.

   c. Tab to the **Replace with** text box, and delete all text. Click the **Special** button `Special▾` and click **Paragraph Mark**. (Notice that "^p" should appear in the Replace with text box.)

   d. Change the search direction to **Down** and click **Replace All**. When Word reaches the end of the document, click **No** to end the task and close the Find and Replace dialog box.

4. Find and replace character formatting by following these steps:

   a. Position the insertion point at the top of page 2, and open the Find and Replace dialog box with the **Replace** tab selected.

   b. Delete existing text in the **Find what** text box, and clear all search options and formatting. Press Ctrl+U to specify underline formatting.

   c. Tab to the **Replace with** text box, and delete all text. Click the **Format** button and choose **Font**.

   d. In the Replace Font dialog box, choose **Bold Italic** and set the **Underline style** to **(none)**. Click **OK**.

   e. Change the search direction to **Down** and click **Replace All**. When Word reaches the end of the document, click **No** to end the task and close the Find and Replace dialog box.

5. Find and replace paragraph formats by following these steps:

   a. Place the insertion point before the text *"Allegheny College"* on page 2, and open the Find and Replace dialog box with the **Replace** tab selected.

   b. In the **Find what** text box, enter two paragraph mark codes by keying **^p^p** or by using the **Special** button. Clear all search options and formatting.

   c. In the **Replace with** text box, clear any text, formatting, and search options. Enter one paragraph mark code.

   d. Click the **Format** button and choose **Paragraph**. Set **Spacing After** to 6 points (**6 pt**) and click **OK**.

   e. Click **Less**, and then click **Find Next**. Replace the formatting on page 2 only. Close the dialog box.

6. Format the title on page 2 ("Homecoming Events") as 14-point bold, uppercase, and centered. Format all the text below the title with a 2.25-inch left indent.

7. Spell-check the memo portion of the document.

8. Save the document as *[your initials]***8-15** in your Lesson 8 folder.

9. Submit and close the document.

Lesson Applications

Exercise 8-16

Replace text and character formatting.

1. Open the file **Chocolate - 3**.

2. Format the document as a memo to "Store Managers" from Thomas Campbell. Use today's date. The subject is "Chocolate Terms."

REVIEW

Remember to remove all formatting from previous search and replace actions.

TIP

The **Small caps** check box and all the other check boxes in the Find and Replace Font dialog boxes initially appear shaded. Click the **Small caps** check box once to select it.

3. Replace the text "cocoa bean" with **cacao bean** throughout the document.

4. Replace the italic formatting of the chocolate terms with bold, small caps formatting. Check the format options under the **Replace with** text box. (It should read "Bold, Not Italic, Small caps, Not All caps." Press Ctrl + I to turn off italic format if necessary.) Make sure no search options are checked before you begin replacing.

5. Add your reference initials to the document.

6. Save the document as **[your initials]8-16** in your Lesson 8 folder.

7. Submit and close the document.

Exercise 8-17

Find and replace text, special characters, and formatting.

1. Open the file **Holiday**. Format the document as a memo to "Store Managers" from Thomas Campbell. Use the current date, and the subject is holiday sales.

2. Revise the first paragraph as shown in Figure 8-13.

Figure 8-13

> The table below lists the most ^popular^ items sold f~~o~~r ^during^ our busiest holidays by state. We compiled the ~~numbers~~ results using sales from the ③-week period preceding each holiday. If you would like a breakdown by individual stores, let me know. We will use these figures to determine our production schedules. ^for next year^ If you have any comments regarding this information, please call me.

3. Replace the text "chocolate suckers" with **Halloween favors**.

4. Replace the 3 points spacing after paragraph formatting with double spacing.

5. Replace all bold formatting with blue underline, small caps, and blue font color formatting.

6. Format the first line of text in the document with 72 points of spacing before the paragraph.

7. Add your reference initials, and spell-check the document.

8. Save the document as *[your initials]*8-17 in your Lesson 8 folder.

9. Submit and close the document.

Exercise 8-18

Find and replace text and formatting.

1. Open the file **Club - 2**.

2. Alphabetize the list that begins "milk chocolate–covered nuts" through "three-tier."

3. Copy the text "CC Chocolate Club" and paste the text at the beginning of the document. Press Enter.

4. Replace the text "CC Chocolate Club" with "Campbell's Confections' Chocolate Club."

5. Replace the single-spaced paragraph format with 12 points spacing after (**12 pt**) and **.25** first-line indent.

6. Replace all hyphens with an en dash.

7. Format the list beginning with "caramel" through "truffles" as a bulleted list.

8. Format the first line as a title—uppercase, bold, 14 points, shadow, center alignment, and no indent. Apply 72 points spacing before and 24 points spacing after.

9. Add a page border to the document. (Open the Borders and Shading dialog box, and click the **Page Border** tab. Click **Box** under setting, and choose a geometric pattern located near the bottom of the Art drop-down list. Select an appropriate width and color.)

10. Spell-check the document.

11. Save the document as *[your initials]*8-18 in your Lesson 8 folder.

12. Submit and close the document.

Exercise 8-19 ◆ Challenge Yourself

Find and replace text, special characters, and formatting.

1. Open the file **Agenda**.

2. Replace each single paragraph mark with 12 points spacing after (**12 pt**).

3. Find the text "PM" and replace it with **p.m.** Include the **Match case** option.

4. Find the text "AM" and replace it with **a.m.**

5. Replace italic formatting with 12-point bold and small caps formatting.

6. Replace each hyphen (-) with an em dash.

7. Use the **Replace** command to format all session numbers (Session 1, Session 2, etc.) with italic format by using the wildcard "?".

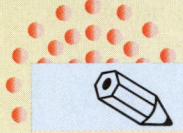

> **TIP**
>
> Click in the Find what text box. Key "Session" and press [Spacebar] then click Special and choose Any Character; that is, **Session ^?**.

8. Center the three-line title and apply 16-point bold and small caps formatting. Add 48 points of spacing before the first line and 24 points of spacing after the third line. Apply a bottom border to the third line of the title.

9. Format "Agenda" with center alignment, 14 points, bold, and small caps.

10. Save the document as *[your initials]*8-19 in your Lesson 8 folder.

11. Submit and close the document.

On Your Own

In these exercises, you work on your own, as you would in a real-life business environment. Use the skills you've learned to accomplish the task—and be creative.

Exercise 8-20

Key a song lyric you know, preferably one with a repetitive chorus. Copy the lyric, and paste it below the original. In the copy of the lyric, find an important word that is used repeatedly in the lyric and replace it with its opposite. Save the document as *[your initials]*8-20 and submit it.

Exercise 8-21

Write a summary about a book you recently read. Replace paragraph returns that begin new paragraphs with 6 points of spacing after paragraphs. Replace any occurrence of two spaces with one space. Save the document as *[your initials]*8-21. Submit the document.

Exercise 8-22

Log onto the Internet, and find a Web site about one of your favorite hobbies or interests. Copy-and-paste information from the Web site to a new document. Find and replace any formatting you do not want in the document. Give the document a title. Save the document as *[your initials]*8-22 and submit it.

Unit 2 Applications

Unit Application 2-1

Apply paragraph spacing, indent text, set tabs, add borders and shading, replace text.

1. Open the file **Customer Service**.

2. Format the document as a memo to "Customer Service Account Executives" from Thomas Campbell. Use today's date, and the subject is brochure information.

3. Select the first line of the memo heading ("MEMO TO") and apply 72 points spacing before.

4. Below the memo heading, key the text shown in Figure U2-1. Include the corrections. Use single spacing.

Figure U2-1

The ^marketing department ^is revising our brochre company and updating the information on our web site. Please review the following paragraphs, and let me know your suggestions or recommendations. If you would like to meet to discuss your proposed ^changes, let me know.

5. Format the paragraph heading ("Customer Service") as 14-point bold and small caps.

6. Format the "Customer Service" paragraph and the paragraph that follows the heading using a .5-inch left and right indent and Times New Roman.

7. Select the "SUBJECT" line, and apply a bottom border.

8. Apply a box border and light gray shading to the "Customer Service" paragraphs.

9. Replace each hyphen with an en dash.

10. Save the document as *[your initials]*u2-1 in a new folder for Unit 2 Applications.

11. Submit and close the document.

Unit Application 2-2

Apply paragraph spacing and change alignment; create a bulleted list; create tabbed text; find and replace text; copy and paste text.

1. Open the file **Ordering**. Change the font size of the document to 11 points.

2. Format the title in the first line of the document as 14-point uppercase, centered, with 72 points spacing before and 24 points spacing after.

3. Insert the following tabbed text near the end of the document so that it follows the paragraph that begins "Orders shipped." A blank line should precede and follow the tabbed text. Right-align the numbers in the second and third columns.

Figure U2-2

Amount	Standard	Rush
$0 to $20.00	$5.95	$18.95
20.01 to 40.00	8.95	21.95
40.01 to 60.00	11.95	24.95
60.01 to 80.00	14.95	27.95
80.01 to 100.00	17.95	30.95
100.01 to 125.00	20.95	33.95
125.01 to 150.00	23.95	36.95
150.01 to 200.00	26.95	39.95
Over $200.00	10% of Total	18% of Total

4. Key the text **Delivery Chart** as a heading above the tabbed text.

5. Format "Delivery Chart" as 14-point bold, centered, and small caps. Format the column headings for the tabbed text to be bold and underlined.

6. Select the paragraph headings ("Online," "Telephone," etc.), and format the headings as a bulleted list, using the small square-shaped bullet (▪).

7. Indent the text below the bulleted paragraphs so the paragraph text aligns with the text that follows the bullet.

8. Remove the bullet format from the paragraphs that begin "Note." Indent the "Note" paragraphs to match the other paragraphs (.5).

9. Use the Find and Replace commands to format the text "Note:" as bold, italic, and small caps.

10. Find the text "April through September" and key the following sentence after "September" but before the period: **or when temperatures reach 72**. Add the degree symbol to follow "72" (°).

11. Spell-check the document.

12. Save the document as *[your initials]*u2-2 in your Unit 2 Applications folder.

13. Submit and close the document.

Unit Application 2-3

Apply and change bulleted lists, create tabbed columns, apply indents, and sort text.

1. Start a new document and change the left and right indents to .5 inch.

2. Key the text shown in Figure U2-3, using 12-point Arial. Use leader tabs to create the lines under "Task completed." The leaders should extend to the right margin.

Figure U2-3

```
Before you go on vacation, use this handy checklist to make
sure you have not forgotten any details.

                                               Task completed

Change your voice mail recording            _____

Create an out-of-office message             _____

Meet with supervisor                        _____

Backup important files                      _____

Create a checklist for the temp             _____

Check calendar                              _____

File/archive papers and data files          _____
```

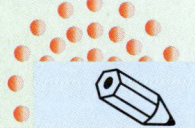

TIP

You need to set two tabs—one for the leader and one to begin the second column.

3. Center the text "Task completed" above the leader characters, and insert two blank lines above it. Apply bold and small caps format to "Task completed."

4. Format the list with 18-point spacing before paragraphs. Apply bullets to the list, using the checkmark bullet.

5. Format the opening paragraph as bold italic.

6. Select the list with the checkmark bullets, and customize the bullet as the 3-D box (❏) Wingding character.

7. Customize the 3-D box bullet format by increasing the bullet size to 14 points and changing the bullet color to blue.

8. Apply a 3-D page border, using the fourth-to-last line style.

9. Select the bulleted list, and sort the text in ascending order.

10. Save the document as *[your initials]*u2-3 in your Unit 2 Applications folder.

11. Submit and close the document.

Unit Application 2-4 ◆ Using the Internet

Work with a variety of paragraph formatting features, move and copy text, and find and replace text.

1. Locate three or more Web sites that contain information on your favorite hobby or on a topic that interests you.

2. Copy text from each site (make sure you select text only, no images, and press Ctrl+C to copy), and paste it into a new Word document.

3. Use the **Keep Text Only** option from the Paste Options button to remove Web formatting.

4. Create a formatted title for the document.

5. Use paragraph and character formatting features to format the document attractively.

6. Use the Find and Replace features to locate selected text, and apply formatting for emphasis.

7. Check spelling and grammar (Web sites may contain misspelled words or poor grammar).

8. Save the document as *[your initials]*u2-4 in your Unit 2 Applications folder.

9. Submit and close the document.

unit 3

PAGE FORMATTING

Lesson 9   Margins and Print Options   WD-256

Lesson 10   Page and Section Breaks   WD-290

Lesson 11   Page Numbers, Headers,
              and Footers   WD-314

Lesson 12   Styles and Themes   WD-344

Lesson 13   Templates   WD-376

UNIT 3   APPLICATIONS   WD-400

Margins and Print Options

MCAS OBJECTIVES

In this lesson:
WW 07 1.2.1
WW 07 4.5.3

OBJECTIVES

After completing this lesson, you will be able to:

1. Change margins.

2. Preview a document.

3. Change paper size and orientation.

4. Print envelopes and labels.

5. Choose print options.

Estimated Time: 1½ hours

In a Word document, text is keyed and printed within the boundaries of the document's margins. *Margins* are the spaces between the edges of the text and the edges of the paper. Adjusting the margins can significantly change the appearance of a document.

Word offers many useful printing features: changing the orientation (the direction, either horizontal or vertical, in which a document is printed), selecting paper size, and printing envelopes and labels.

Changing Margins

By default, a document's margin settings are:

- Top margin: 1 inch

- Bottom margin: 1 inch

- Left margin: 1 inch

- Right margin: 1 inch

Figure 9-1
Default margin
settings

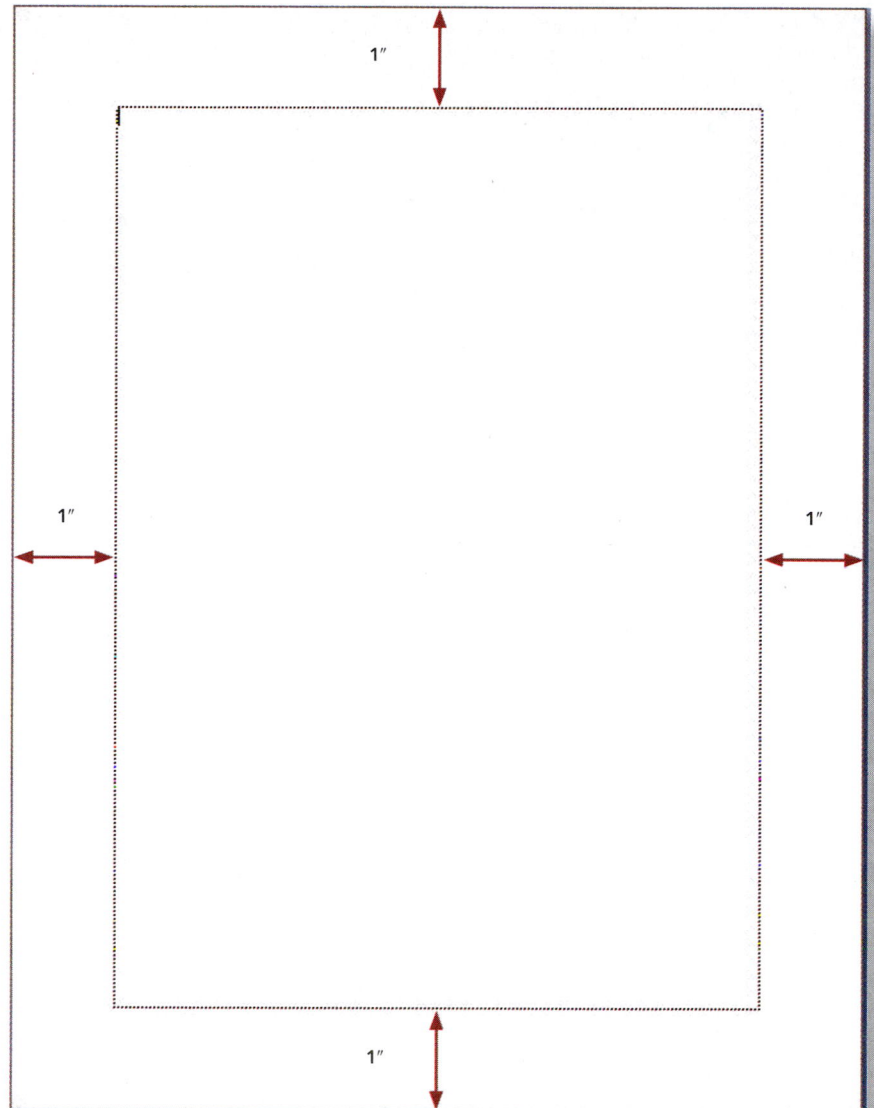

Using standard-size paper (8.5 by 11 inches) and Word's default margin settings, you have $6\frac{1}{2}$ by 9 inches on the page for your text. To increase or decrease this workspace, you can change margins by using the Page Setup dialog box or the rulers or Print Preview.

To set margins, you can use one of these methods:

- Change settings in the Page Setup dialog box.

- Drag margins using the horizontal and vertical rulers.

- Drag margins in Print Preview.

Figure 9-2
Actual workspace
using default
margin settings and
standard-size paper

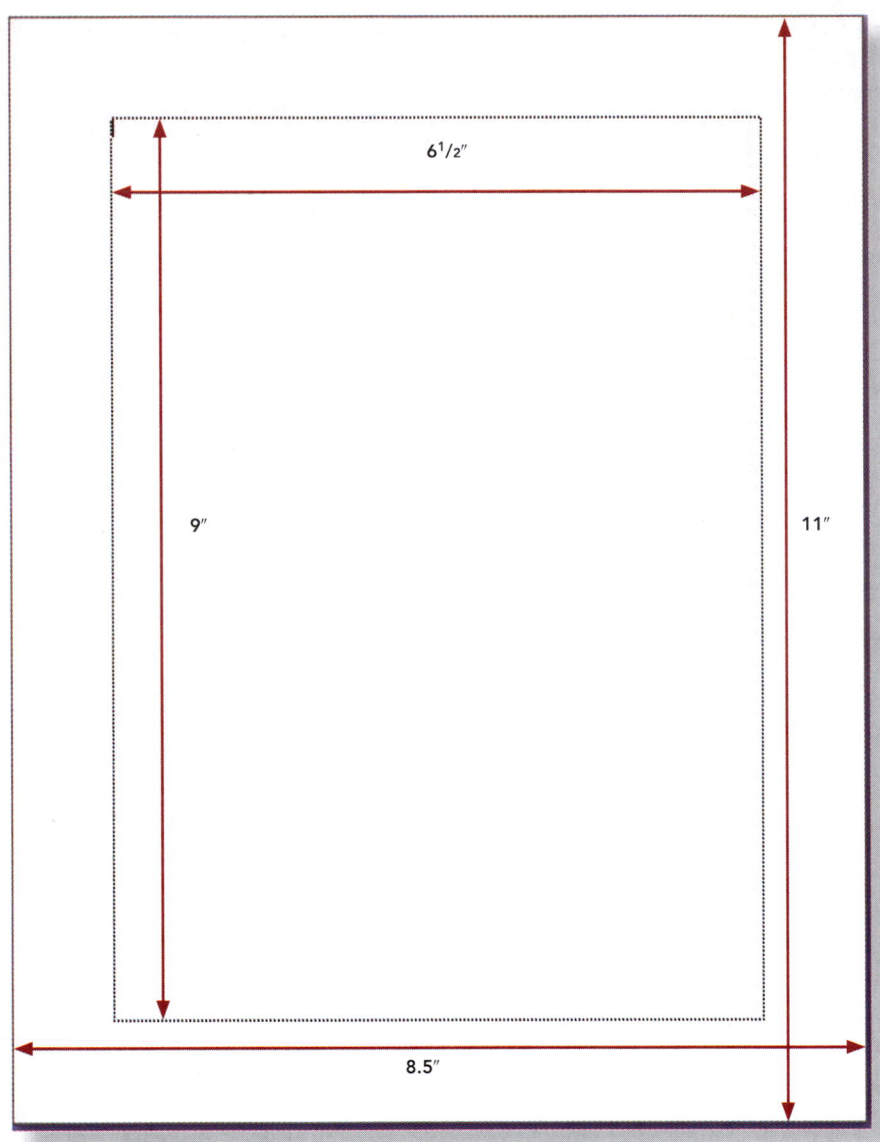

Exercise 9-1 CHANGE MARGINS FOR A DOCUMENT USING THE PAGE SETUP DIALOG BOX

One way to change margins for a document is to use the Page Setup dialog box. You can change margins for an entire document or selected text. You can open the Page Setup dialog by clicking the Margins command or clicking the Page Setup Dialog Box Launcher.

1. Open the file **Corporate Gifts**. (Make sure no text is selected.)

2. Click the **Page Layout** tab and click the Margins button ⬚. Notice that the first option is **Normal** which displays the default margin settings.

3. Click **Custom Margins** and click the **Margins** tab, if it is not active. The dialog box shows the default margin settings.

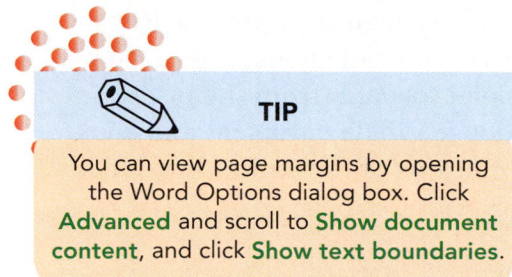

TIP

You can view page margins by opening the Word Options dialog box. Click **Advanced** and scroll to **Show document content**, and click **Show text boundaries**.

4. Edit the margin text box settings so they have the following values (or click the arrow boxes to change the settings). As you do so, notice the changes in the **Preview** box.

Top	**1.5**
Bottom	**1.5**
Left	**2**
Right	**2**

Figure 9-3
Changing margins in the Page Setup dialog box

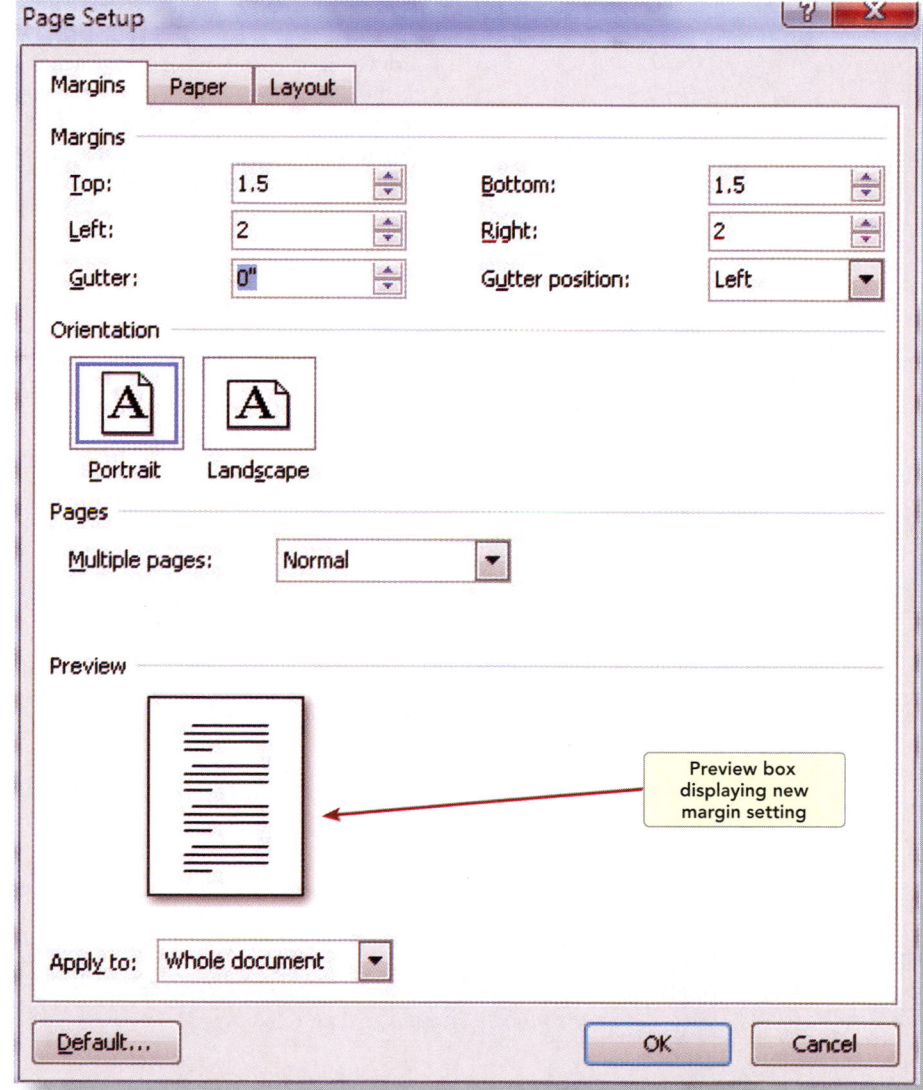

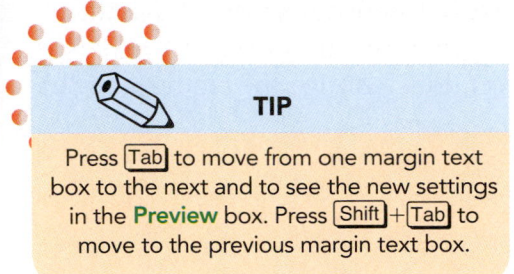

TIP

Press Tab to move from one margin text box to the next and to see the new settings in the **Preview** box. Press Shift + Tab to move to the previous margin text box.

5. Click the down arrow to open the **Apply to** drop-down list. Notice that you can choose either **Whole document** or **This point forward** (from the insertion point forward). Choose **Whole document** and click **OK** to change the margins of the entire document.

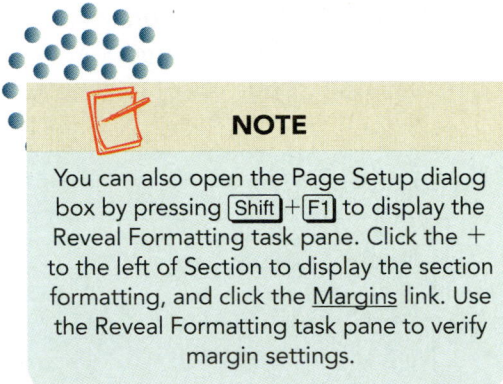

NOTE

You can also open the Page Setup dialog box by pressing Shift + F1 to display the Reveal Formatting task pane. Click the + to the left of Section to display the section formatting, and click the Margins link. Use the Reveal Formatting task pane to verify margin settings.

Exercise 9-2   **CHANGE MARGINS FOR SELECTED TEXT BY USING THE PAGE SETUP DIALOG BOX**

When you change margins for selected text, you create a new section. A *section* is a portion of a document that has its own formatting. When a document contains more than one section, *section breaks* indicate the beginning and end of a section. Section breaks in Draft view are represented by double-dotted lines.

1. Select the text from the second paragraph to the end of the document.

2. Click the **Page Layout** tab. Click the **Page Setup Dialog Box Launcher** to display the Page Setup dialog box.

Figure 9-4
Page Setup Dialog
Box Launcher

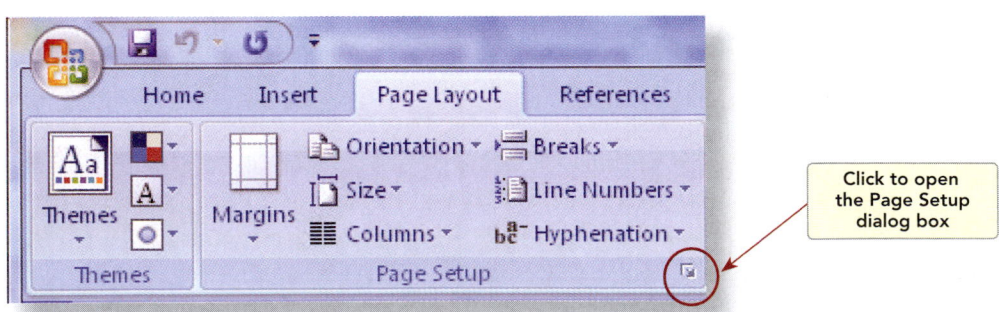

3. Change the margins to the following settings:

Top	2
Bottom	2
Left	1.5
Right	1.5

4. Choose **Selected text** from the **Apply to** box. Click **OK**.

5. Deselect the text, and scroll to the beginning of the selection. Word applied the margin changes to the selected text and created a new section. The section appears on a new page. The status bar displays section numbers and page numbers.

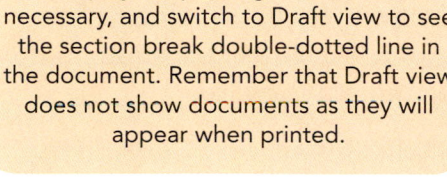

TIP

Display nonprinting characters if necessary, and switch to Draft view to see the section break double-dotted line in the document. Remember that Draft view does not show documents as they will appear when printed.

Figure 9-5
Changing margins for selected text creates a new section

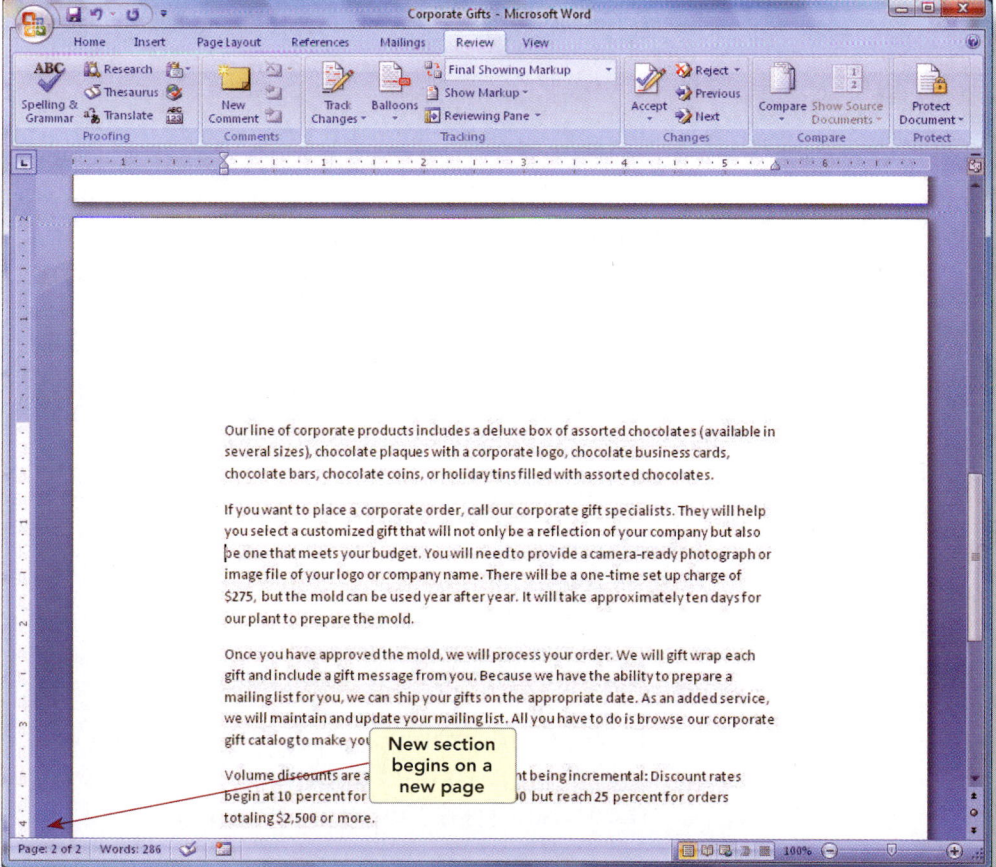

Exercise 9-3   CHANGE MARGINS FOR A SECTION BY USING THE PAGE SETUP DIALOG BOX

After a section is created, you can change the margins for just the section (not the entire document) by using the Page Setup dialog box. To help you know which section you are formatting, customize the status bar to display sections.

1. Move the insertion point anywhere in the new section (section 2), and right-click the status bar. Click **Section** and click in the document to close the shortcut menu. Open the **Page Setup** dialog box.

2. Change the left and right margin settings to **1.25** inches.

3. Open the **Apply to** drop-down list to view the options. Notice that you can apply the new margin settings to the current section, to the whole document, or from the insertion point forward.

4. Choose **This section** and click **OK** to apply the settings to the new section.

Exercise 9-4   CHANGE MARGINS USING THE RULERS

To change margins using the rulers, use Print Layout view. The status bar includes five buttons for changing document views: The default view for Word documents is Print Layout, which displays text as it will appear on the printed page. Print Layout view displays headers, footers, and other page elements.

There are two ways to switch document views:

• Click a view button on the right side of the status bar.

• Click the View tab, and click a view button.

Figure 9-6
View buttons

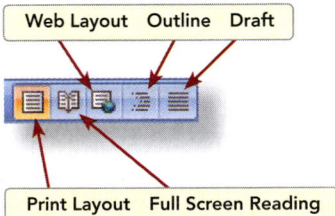

Web Layout   Outline   Draft

Print Layout   Full Screen Reading

1. Place the insertion point at the beginning of the document (⌈Ctrl⌉+⌈Home⌉). In bold uppercase letters, key **CORPORATE GIFTS** and then press ⌈Enter⌉. Center the title and add a blank line below it.

2. Click the **View Ruler** button at the top of the vertical scroll bar if the rulers are not displayed.

3. Click in the new section (page 2). The status bar shows that the document contains two pages and two sections. Notice the extra space at the top of the page. The new section has a larger top margin (2 inches).

4. To see more of the page, including the margin areas, click the Zoom button and then choose **Page width**. Click **OK**.

5. Move the insertion point to the top of the document (the first section). The blue area on the vertical ruler shows the 1.5-inch top margin. The blue areas on the horizontal ruler show the 2-inch left and right margins. The white area in the horizontal ruler shows the text area, which is a line length of 4.5 inches. (See Figure 9-7.)

Figure 9-7
Rulers in Print
Layout view

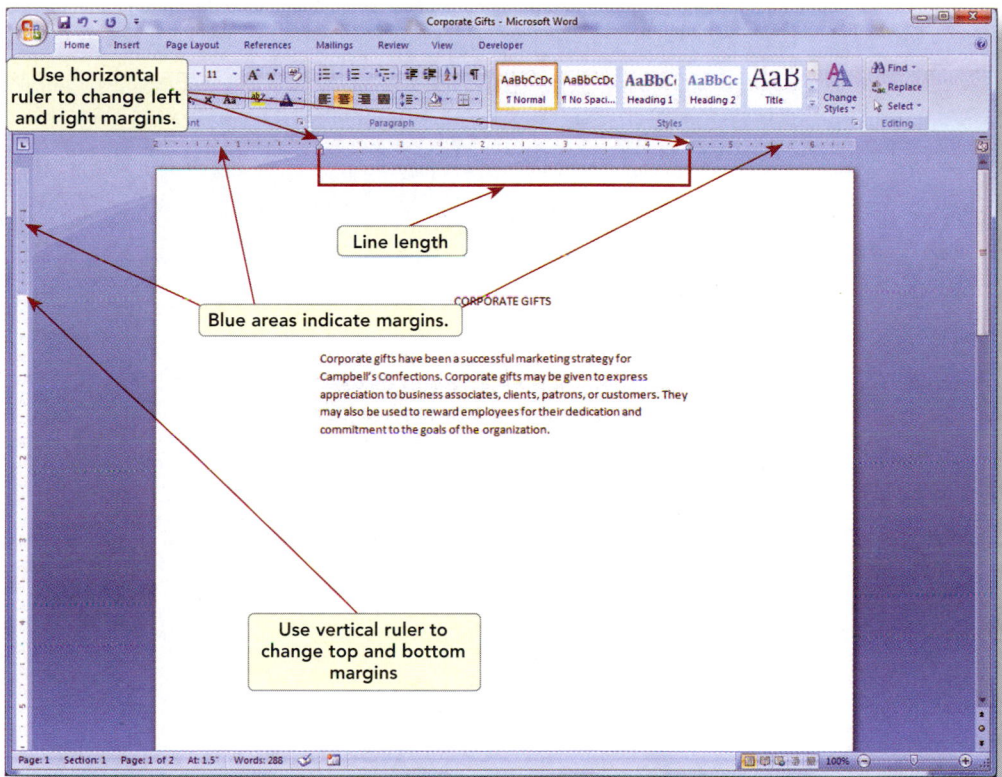

6. To change the top margin, position the pointer over the top margin boundary on the vertical ruler. The top margin boundary is between the blue area and the white area on the ruler. The pointer changes to a two-pointed vertical arrow ↕ and a ScreenTip displays the words "Top Margin."

7. Press and hold down the left mouse button. The margin boundary appears as a dotted horizontal line.

8. Drag the margin boundary slightly up, and release the mouse button. The text at the top of the document moves up to align with the new top margin.

9. Click the Undo button  to restore the 1.5-inch top margin.

10. Hold down the Alt key, and drag the top margin boundary down until it is at 2 inches on the ruler. Release Alt and the mouse button. Holding down the Alt key as you drag shows the exact margin and text area measurements.

11. To change the left margin, position the pointer over the left margin boundary on the horizontal ruler. The left margin boundary is between the blue area and the white area on the ruler. The pointer changes to a two-pointed horizontal arrow, and a ScreenTip displays the words "Left Margin."

Figure 9-8
Adjusting the left margin

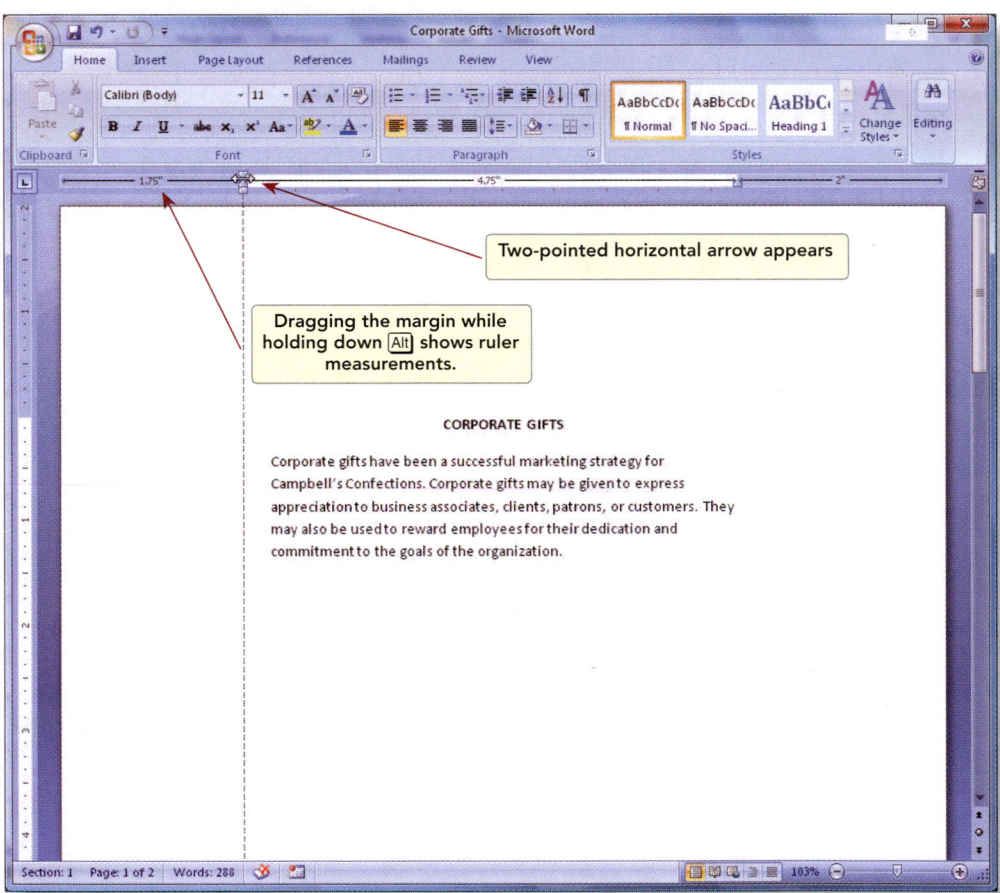

12. Hold down the Alt key, and drag the margin boundary to the left to create a 1.75-inch left margin. (See Figure 9-8.)

13. Using the same procedure, drag the right margin boundary until it is located 1.75 inches from the right. Be sure to watch for the two-pointed arrow

NOTE

You might have to fine-tune the pointer position to place it directly on the left margin boundary. Move the pointer slowly until you see the two-pointed arrow and the "Left Margin" ScreenTip.

before dragging. The first section now has 1.75-inch left and right margins and a 2-inch top margin.

14. Scroll to the next page (section 2). Click within the text to activate this section's ruler. Change the top margin to 1.75 inches.

15. Click the Microsoft Office Button 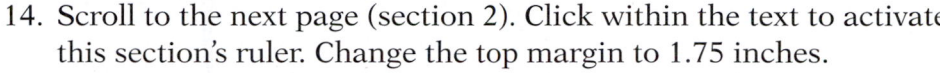, and click the Word Options button 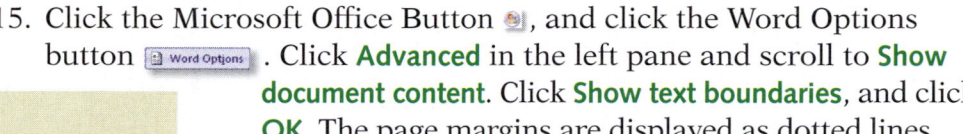. Click **Advanced** in the left pane and scroll to **Show document content**. Click **Show text boundaries**, and click **OK**. The page margins are displayed as dotted lines.

16. Remove the page margins from view by clicking the Microsoft Office Button, clicking the Word Options button, clicking **Advanced**, scrolling to **Show document content**, and deselecting **Show text boundaries**. Click **OK**.

17. Save the document as *[your initials]*9-4 in a new Lesson 9 folder, and leave the document open for the next exercise.

> **NOTE**
>
> If you move the pointer to the top of the page in Print Layout view, you will see the Hide White Space button. Double click the button to hide the white space (the margin area) at the top and bottom of each page and the gray space between pages so you can see more document text. Point to the top of the page, and double-click the Show White Space button to restore the space.

Exercise 9-5 SET FACING PAGES WITH GUTTER MARGINS

If your document is going to be bound—put together like a book, with printing on both sides of the paper—you will want to use mirror margins and gutter margins. *Mirror margins* are inside and outside margins on facing pages that mirror one another. *Gutter margins* add extra space to the left or top margins to allow for binding.

Figure 9-9
Mirror margins

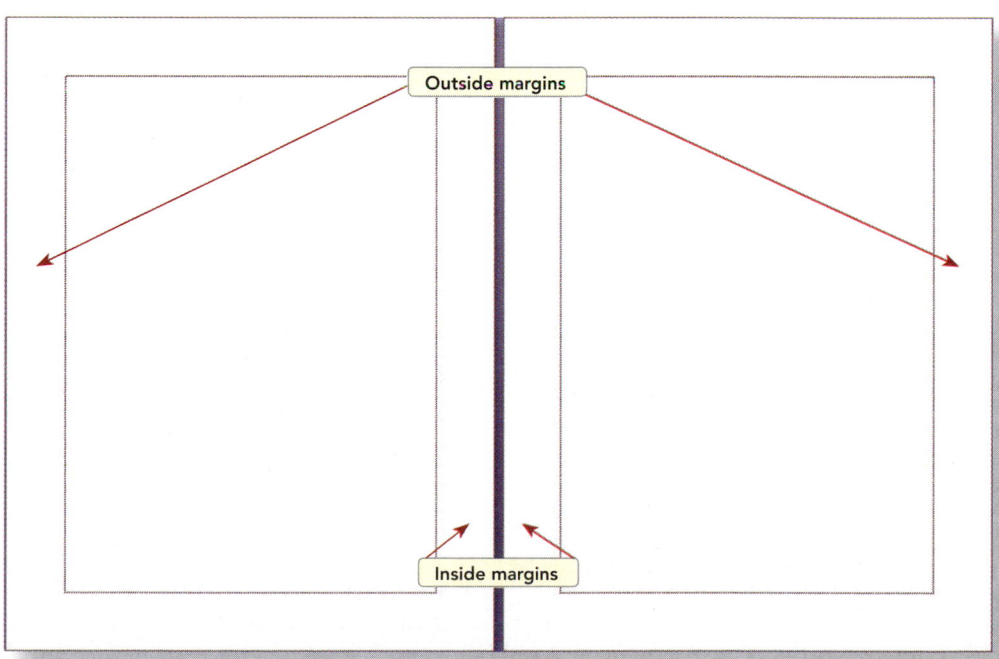

Figure 9-10
Gutter margins

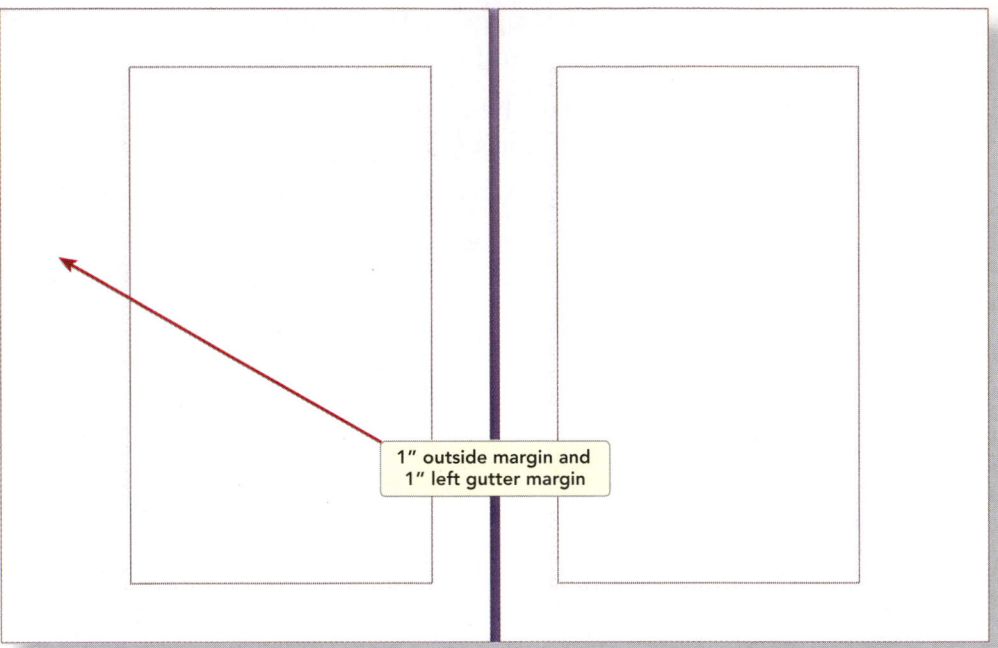

1" outside margin and
1" left gutter margin

1. Open the Page Setup dialog box, and open the **Multiple pages** drop-down list. Choose **Mirror margins**. Notice that the **Preview** box now displays two pages. The left and right margins are called the inside and outside margins.

2. Change the **Inside** margins to **1.25** inches and the **Outside** margins to **1** inch.

3. Set the **Gutter** margin to **1** inch, and press [Tab] to reflect the change in the Preview box. Click **OK**. A 1-inch gutter margin is added to the document. (Make sure you use at least 1-inch gutter margins to allow room for binding.)

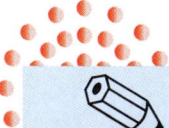

TIP

Visualize the document as double-sided, facing pages in a book by placing the back of page 2 against the back of page 1 and placing page 3 beside page 2. The gutter margin of page 1 is on the left. The gutter margin on the right of page 2 and on the left of page 3 allows space for the binding and represents facing pages. *Facing pages* appear as a two-page spread with odd-numbered right pages and even-numbered left pages.

4. Open the Page Setup dialog box, and open the **Multiple pages** drop-down list. Choose **Normal**. Change the **Gutter** setting to **.75** and change the **Gutter** position to **Top**. Click **OK**. The document is ready for top binding.

5. Open the Page Setup dialog box. Change the **Left** and **Right** margins to **1.5** inches, change the **Gutter** setting to **0"**, and change the **Gutter position** to **Left**. Click **OK**.

6. Save the document as *[your initials]***9-5** in your Lesson 9 folder.

7. Print the document, and keep it open for the next exercise.

Using Print Preview

Viewing a document in Print Preview is the best way to check how a document will look when you print it. You can view multiple pages at a time, adjust margins and tabs, and edit text.

To display a document in Print Preview, click the **Microsoft Office Button**, click the arrow beside **Print**, and click **Print Preview**. The keyboard shortcut for Print Preview is [Alt]+[Ctrl]+[I].

Exercise 9-6 VIEW A MULTIPLE-PAGE DOCUMENT IN PRINT PREVIEW

Print Preview displays entire pages of a document in reduced size. You can view one page at a time or two pages at a time.

1. Move the insertion point to the beginning of the document.

2. Click the **Microsoft Office Button**, click the arrow beside **Print**, and click **Print Preview**. Click the One Page button [One Page] on the Print Preview tab to display the first page of the document.

3. Click the Two Pages button [Two Pages] to see both pages.

Figure 9-11
Viewing multiple pages in Print Preview

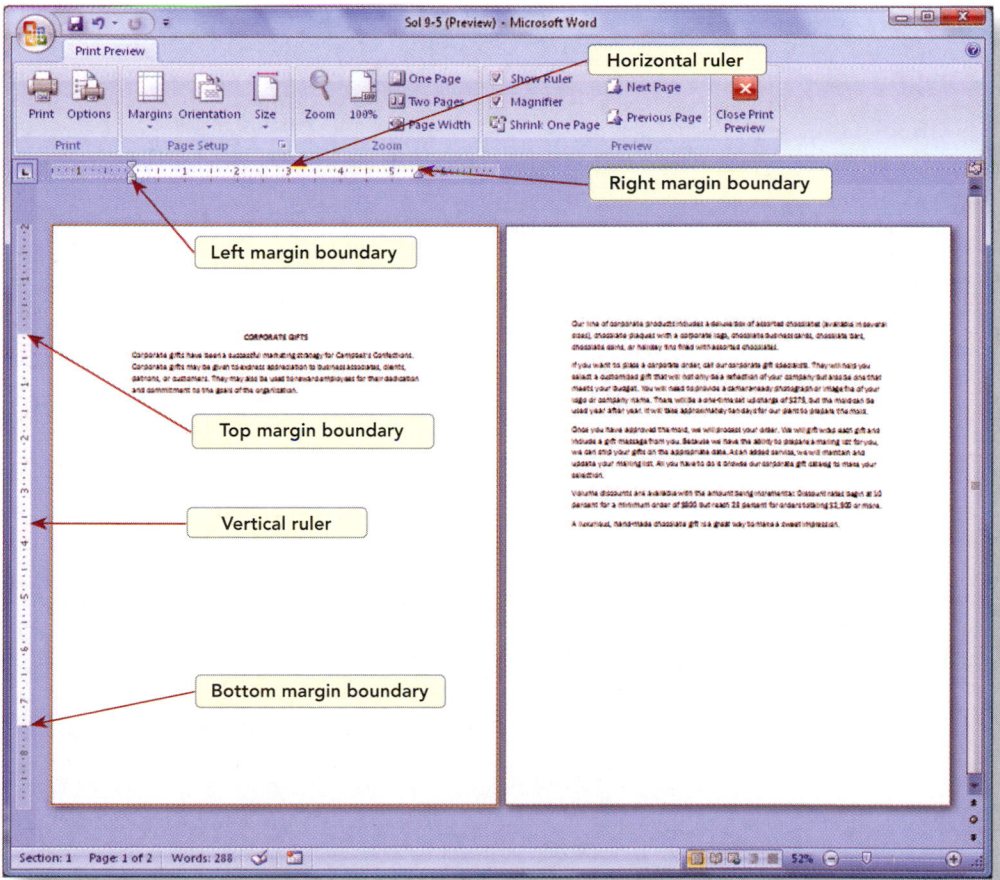

TIP

You use the Zoom box to view multiple pages of your document. Click the Zoom Level button on the status bar. Click Many Pages, and a grid appears to choose the number of pages you want to view and how they are configured in the window. If you drag the pointer as you move across the grid, you can expand the grid to display additional rows and pages, which is useful in a long document. Drag the Zoom Slider to 100% to return to a one-page view.

4. To zoom into page 2, click once on the page with the arrow pointer to make page 2 active and then click again with the magnifier pointer ⊕.

5. Click again to zoom out. Notice that the horizontal ruler shows the settings for page 2.

6. Click the Close Print Preview button 📄 to close the Print Preview window and to return to Print Layout view.

TABLE 9-1 Print Preview Toolbar

Button	Description	Function
	Print	Print the document in the Print Preview window.
	Options	List printing options.
	Margins	Change margin settings.
	Orientation	Switch between portrait and landscape orientation.
	Size	Select paper size.
	Zoom	Choose a magnification to reduce or enlarge the page or pages displayed.
	100%	Zoom document to 100 percent.
One Page	One Page	Display one page at a time.
Two Pages	Two Pages	Display two pages at a time.
Page Width	Page Width	Zoom the document to the width of the window.
Show Ruler	Show Ruler	Display or hide the Print Preview ruler, which you can use to change margins, tabs, and indents.
⊕	Magnifier	Change the I-beam pointer to a magnifying glass and vice versa. With the magnifying glass pointer, click in the document to zoom in and out. With the I-beam pointer, edit document text.
Shrink One Page	Shrink One Page	Shrink a document to fit on one less page when the last page contains only a few lines of text.
Next Page	Next Page	Move to the next page of the document.
Previous Page	Previous Page	Move to the previous page of the document.
Close Print Preview	Close Print Preview	Close the Print Preview window and return to the previous view

Exercise 9-7   CHANGE MARGINS IN PRINT PREVIEW

When you view a page in Print Preview, you can see all four margins and adjust margin settings using the horizontal and vertical rulers or by opening the Page Setup dialog box within the Print Preview window.

1. Move the insertion point to the beginning of the document (page 1, section 1).

2. Click the **Microsoft Office Button** and click the arrow beside **Print**. Click **Print Preview**.

3. Click the One Page button  on the Print Preview tab to display only page 1. Click the Show Ruler button  if it is not checked.

4. Move the pointer to the top margin boundary on the vertical ruler. The pointer changes to the two-pointed arrow, and the top margin is identified in a ScreenTip.

NOTE

Changing margins in Print Preview is similar to changing margins in Print Layout view. You use the vertical and horizontal rulers to drag the margins to the desired positions.

5. Hold down Alt as you drag the margin boundary to 1.5 inches on the blue area of the vertical ruler. Word adjusts the top margin to 1.5 inches.

6. Click the **Page Setup Dialog Box Launcher**.

7. Change the top margin to **2** inches and click **OK**.

8. Use the horizontal ruler to change the left and right margins to 1.25 inches.

TIP

You can check the exact measurement of a margin in Print Preview or Print Layout view by moving the pointer over the margin boundary, holding down the left mouse button without dragging it, and holding down Alt.

Exercise 9-8   EDIT A DOCUMENT IN PRINT PREVIEW

To edit text in Print Preview, you magnify a page to the desired size and then switch to edit mode. You would not, however, want to make extensive changes in Print Preview.

1. Click on page 1 to zoom in. The view of the document is enlarged to 100 percent.

2. Click the Magnifier button to deselect the option and change the pointer to the I-beam.

3. Select "Campbell's Confections" in the first paragraph, and press Ctrl+I to apply italic formatting.

4. Click the Magnifier button to cancel edit mode.

5. Click **Close Print Preview** to close the Print Preview window.

6. Save the document as *[your initials]***9-8**.

7. Submit the document, and leave it open for the next exercise.

Paper Size and Orientation

When you open a new document, the default paper size is 8.5 by 11 inches. Using the Page Setup dialog box, you can change the paper size to print a document on legal paper or define a custom-size paper.

The Page Setup dialog box also gives you a choice between two page orientation settings: portrait and landscape. A *portrait* page is taller than it is wide. This orientation is the default in new Word documents. A *landscape* page is wider than it is tall. You can apply page-orientation changes to sections of a document or to the entire document.

Exercise 9-9 **CHANGE PAPER SIZE AND PAGE ORIENTATION**

Figure 9-12
Changing page orientation

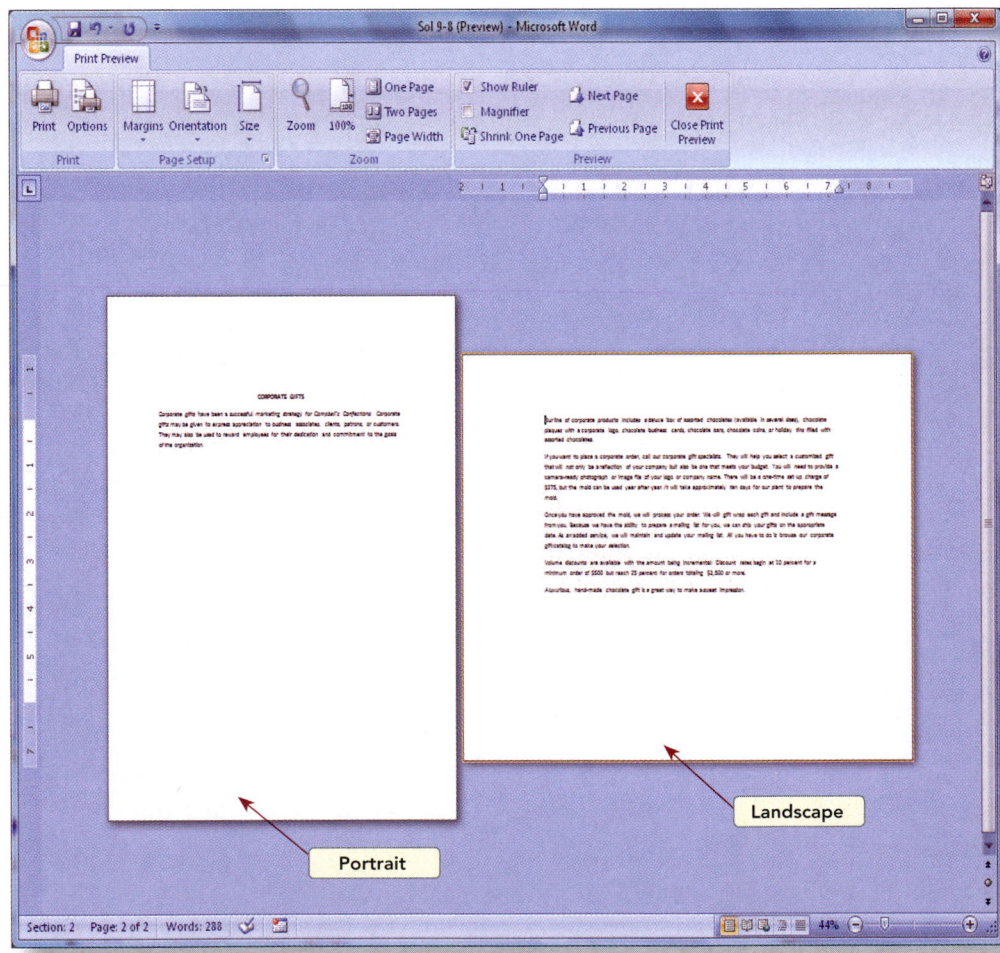

1. Open the **Page Setup** dialog box.

2. On the **Margins** tab, click **Landscape**.

3. Click the **Paper** tab. Notice the default paper size for letter paper.

4. Open the **Paper size** drop-down list and choose **Legal**. Click **OK**. Notice how the orientation and paper size changed.

5. Press Ctrl+Z to undo the changes to paper size and orientation.

6. Switch to Print Preview, and click the Two Pages button .

7. Click page 2, and click the Orientation button . Click **Landscape**. Section 2 on page 2 is formatted with landscape orientation and page 1 is formatted with portrait orientation. Click **Close Print Preview** to close the Print Preview window.

8. Save the document as *[your initials]*9-9.

9. Submit and close the document.

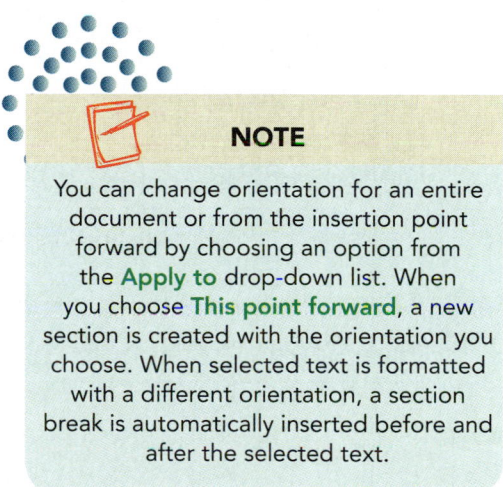

NOTE

You can change orientation for an entire document or from the insertion point forward by choosing an option from the **Apply to** drop-down list. When you choose **This point forward**, a new section is created with the orientation you choose. When selected text is formatted with a different orientation, a section break is automatically inserted before and after the selected text.

Printing Envelopes and Labels

Word provides a tool to print different-size envelopes and labels. Using the Envelopes and Labels command, you can:

- Print a single envelope without saving it or attach an envelope to a document for future printing. The attached envelope is added to the beginning of the document as a separate section.

- Print labels without saving them, or create a new document that contains the labels. You can print a single label or a full page of the same label.

Word 2007

Exercise 9-10   PRINT AN ENVELOPE

Printing envelopes often requires that you manually feed the envelope to your printer. If you print labels that are on other than 8½ by 11 inch sheets, you might need to feed the labels manually. Your printer will display a code and not print until you feed an envelope or label sheet manually.

1. Open the file **Matthews**. This document is a one-page letter.

2. Click the **Mailings** tab, and locate the **Create** group. Click the Envelopes button .

3. Click the **Envelopes** tab if it is not active. Notice that Word detected the address in the document and placed this text in the **Delivery address** text box. You can edit this text as needed.

Figure 9-13
Envelopes and
Labels dialog box

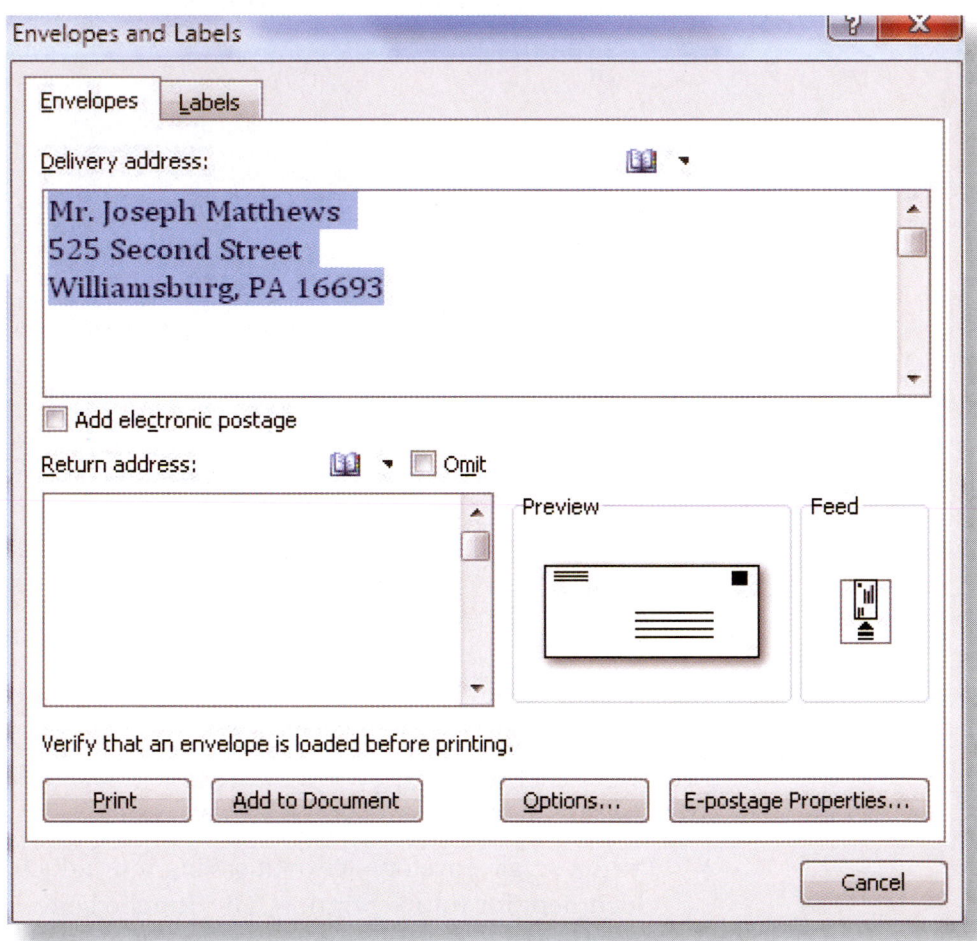

4. In the **Delivery address** text box, enter the full ZIP+4 Code by keying **-1129** after "16693."

5. Make sure the **Omit** box is not checked. Select and delete any text in the **Return address** text box, and then key the following return address, starting with your name:

[your name]
Campbell's Confections
25 Main Street
Grove City, PA 16127-0025

6. Place a standard business-size envelope in your printer. The **Feed** box illustrates the feeding method accepted by your printer.

7. Click **Print**. When Word asks if you want to save the return address as the default return address, click **No**. Word prints the envelope with the default font and text placement settings.

NOTE

If you don't have an envelope, you can use a blank sheet of paper to test the placement of the addresses. Ask your instructor how to proceed. You might have to feed the envelope or blank sheet manually.

NOTE

Check your printer to see what you need to do to complete a manual envelope feed. If the printer is flashing or displaying a message, you might have to press a button.

Exercise 9-11 CHOOSE ENVELOPE OPTIONS

Before printing an envelope, you can choose additional envelope options. For example, you can add the envelope content to the document for future use. You can also click the **Options** button in the Envelopes and Labels dialog box to:

- Change the envelope size. The default size is size 10, which is a standard business envelope.

- Change the font and other character formatting of the delivery address or return address.

- Verify printing options.

1. Open the **Envelopes and Labels** dialog box again.

2. Type your name and address in the **Return address** box.

3. Click the **Options** button in the Envelopes and Labels dialog box to open the Envelope Options dialog box. Click the **Envelope Options** tab if it is not active.

Word 2007

4. Under **Envelope size**, click the down arrow to look at the different-size options. Click the arrow again to close the list.

Figure 9-14
Envelope Options
dialog box

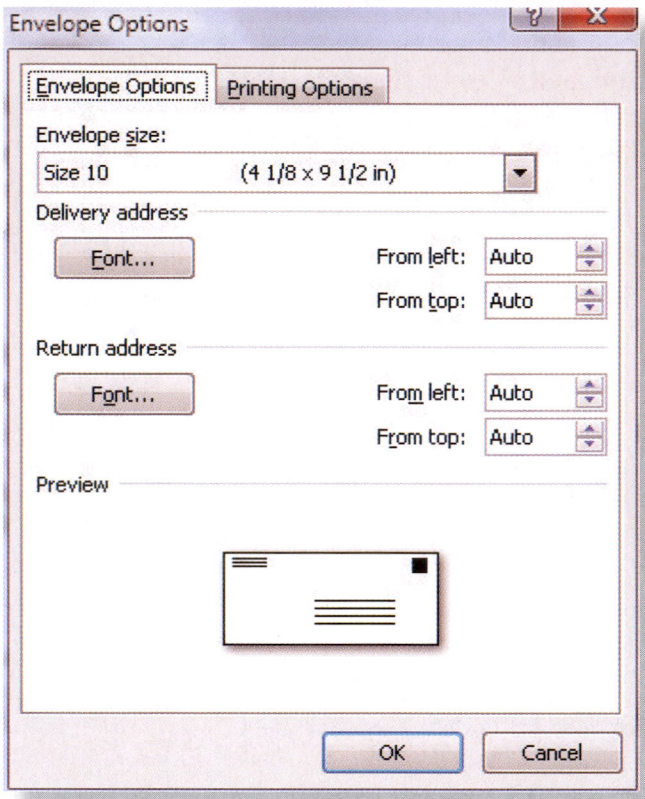

5. Click the **Font** button  for the **Delivery address**. The Envelope Address dialog box for the delivery address opens.

6. Format the text as bold and all caps and change the font size to **10**. Click **OK** to close the Envelope Address dialog box. Click **OK** to close the Envelope Options dialog box.

7. Delete the punctuation from the delivery address and add **-1129** to the ZIP Code.

> **NOTE**
>
> The delivery address format preferred by the U.S. Postal Service is all caps with no punctuation.

8. Click **Add to Document** to add the envelope information to the top of the document as a separate section. Don't save the return address as the default address.

> **NOTE**
>
> Once the envelope is added to the document, you can also format or edit the envelope text just as you would any document text. The default font for envelope addresses is Cambria.

9. Replace [Today's date] with the current date. Correct any spacing between the elements of the letter. Add your reference initials followed by **Enclosures (2)**. To make sure the letter follows the correct format, see Appendix B, "Standard Forms for Business Documents."

10. View the letter and envelope in Print Preview.

11. Close the Print Preview window, and save the document as *[your initials]***9-11** in your Lesson 9 folder.

12. Print the document.

13. Leave the document open for use in the next exercise.

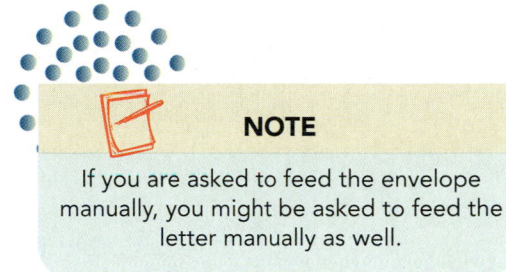

NOTE

If you are asked to feed the envelope manually, you might be asked to feed the letter manually as well.

Exercise 9-12   PRINT LABELS

The Labels tab in the Envelopes and Labels dialog box makes it easy to print different-size labels for either a return address or a delivery address.

1. Position the insertion point in the envelope section of the document. Click the **Mailings** tab. Click the Labels button .

2. Click the **Use return address** check box to create labels for the letter sender.

3. Select the address text, and press Ctrl+Shift+A to turn on all caps. Delete the comma after the city.

4. Click the option **Full page of the same label**, if it is not active, to create an entire page of return address labels.

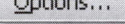

5. Click the Options button to choose a label size.

Figure 9-15
Label Options dialog
box

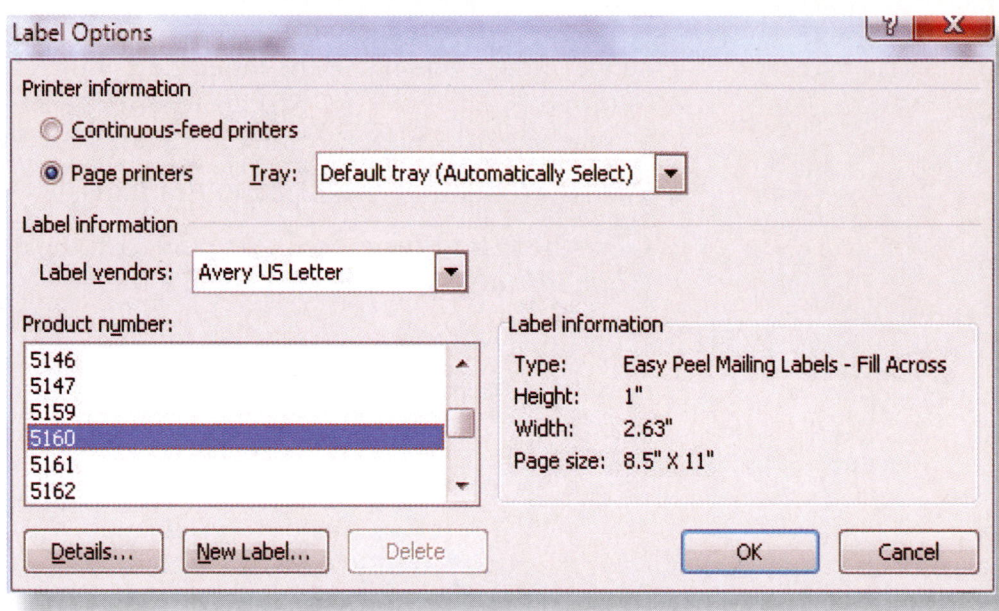

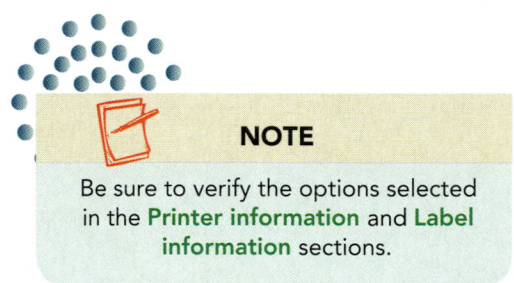

NOTE

Be sure to verify the options selected in the **Printer information** and **Label information** sections.

6. Verify that **Page printers** is selected under **Printer information** and that **Avery US Letter** is listed in the **Label vendors** box.

7. Scroll the **Product number** list to see the various label options, and choose **5160**, the product number for a standard Avery address label.

8. Click **OK**, and then click **New Document** to save the labels as a separate document. (If you click **Print**, you can print the labels without saving them.) Do not save the return address.

9. Select all text in the new document and reduce the font size to 11 points.

10. Save the document as *[your initials]***9-12** in your Lesson 9 folder.

11. Switch to Print Preview to view the labels on the page.

12. Prepare the printer for a sheet of 5160-size labels or feed a blank sheet of paper into the printer, and then print the labels.

13. Close the document containing the full sheet of labels.

Setting Print Options

When you click the Quick Print option, Word prints the entire document. If you open the Print dialog box, however, you can choose to print only part of a document. You can also select other print options from the dialog box, including collating copies of a multipage document, printing selected text, or printing multiple document pages on one sheet of paper.

Exercise 9-13   CHOOSE PRINT OPTIONS FROM THE PRINT DIALOG BOX

1. Position the insertion point to the left of the date in the letter to Mr. Joseph Matthews (*[your initials]*9-11). Click the **Microsoft Office Button**, and click the arrow beside **Print** to view the print options. Click **Print** to open the Print dialog box. (You can also click **Print** to open the Print dialog box.)

2. Click **Current Page** and click **OK**. Word prints page 1 of the document.

3. Open the Print dialog box again. Key **1-2** in the **Pages** text box. You can also enter specific page numbers or page ranges.

4. In the **Number of copies** text box, use the up arrow to change the number of copies to **2**.

5. If the **Collate** check box is not active, click it to select it. Notice the change in the preview of the number of copies. Click the **Collate** check box to uncheck it (make sure it is unchecked). With this box not checked, Word will print two copies of page 1 and then two copies of page 2.

6. Change the number of copies back to 1.

7. Click the down arrow to open the **Print what** drop-down list. It shows the various elements you can print in addition to the entire document. Click again to close the list.

8. Click the down arrow to open the **Print** drop-down list, which gives you the option to print even or odd pages. Click again to close the list.

9. Click the down arrow to open the **Pages per sheet** drop-down list, which gives you the option to print your selection over a specified number of sheets. Choose the **2 pages** setting. This option prints two pages on one sheet of 8$\frac{1}{2}$- by 11-inch paper, with each page reduced to fit on the sheet.

Word 2007

Figure 9-16
Print dialog box

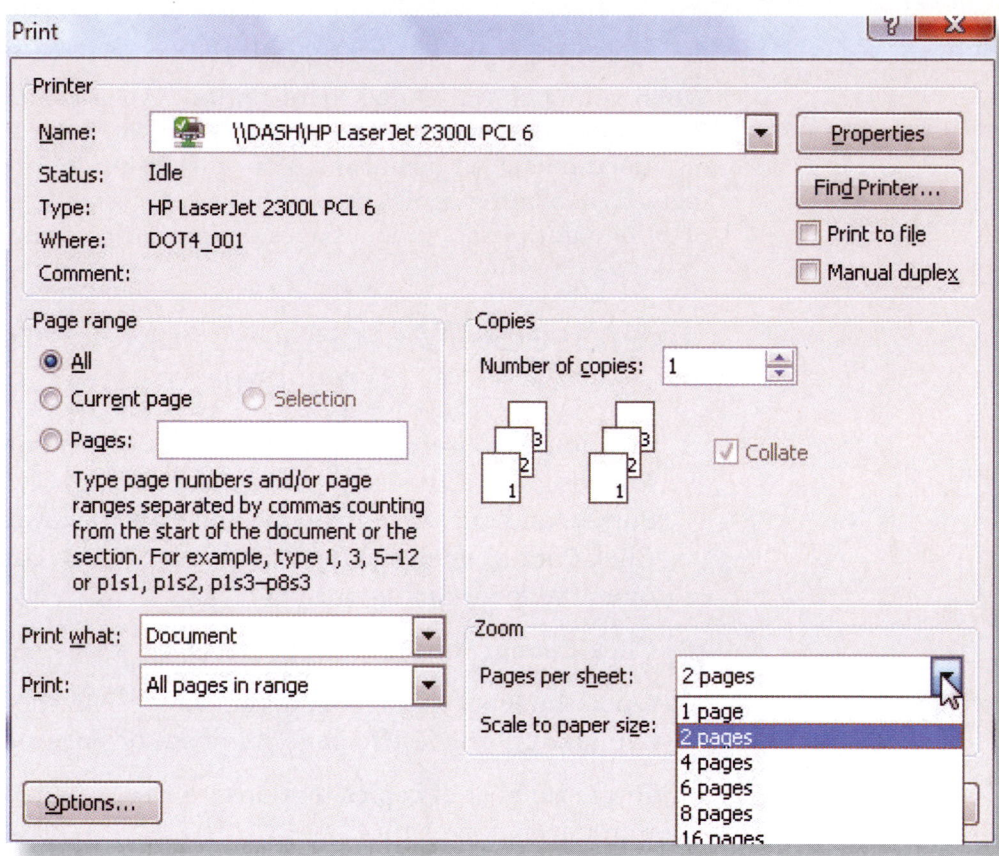

10. Open the **Scale to paper size** drop-down list, which gives you the option to print on a different paper or envelope size (Word adjusts the scaling of the fonts, tables, and other elements to fit the new size). Close the drop-down list.

11. Click **OK**. Word prints reduced versions of pages 1 and 2 on one sheet of paper.

12. Close the document without saving.

Lesson 9 Summary

- In a Word document, text is keyed and printed within the boundaries of the document's margins. Margins are the spaces between the edges of the text and the edges of the paper.

- Change the actual space for text on a page by changing margins (left, right, top, and bottom). You can key new margin settings in the Page Setup dialog box.

- Changing margins for selected text results in a new section for the selected text. A section is a portion of a document that has its own formatting. When a document contains more than one section, you see double-dotted lines, or section breaks, between sections to indicate the beginning and end of a section.

- Print Layout view shows how text is positioned on the printed page. Use the View buttons on the right of the status bar to switch between Print Layout view and Draft view.

- Print Preview shows how an entire document looks before printing. Use the One Page command, the Two Pages command, and the scroll bar to view all or part of the document. Change the Zoom as needed.

- Change margins in Print Layout view or in Print Preview by positioning the pointer over a margin boundary on a ruler and dragging. Press Alt to see the exact ruler measurement as you drag.

- Edit a document in Print Preview by clicking the Magnifier command to change the magnifier pointer to the I-beam pointer.

- For bound documents, use mirror margins and gutter margins. Mirror margins are inside and outside margins on facing pages that mirror one another. Gutter margins add extra space to the left and top margins to allow for binding

- A document can print in either portrait ($8\frac{1}{2}$- by 11-inch) or landscape (11- by $8\frac{1}{2}$-inch) orientation. Choose an orientation in the Page Setup dialog box, Margins tab.

- A document can be scaled to fit a particular paper size. Choose paper size options in the Page Setup dialog box, Paper tab.

- Use Word to print different-size envelopes. You can change address formatting and make the envelope part of the document for future printing. Use Word to print different-size address labels—either a single label or a sheet of the same label.

- Choose print options such as printing only the current page, specified pages, selected text, collated copies of pages, and reduced pages by opening the Print dialog box.

LESSON 9		Command Summary	
Feature	**Button**	**Command**	**Keyboard**
Print Preview		**Microsoft Office Button, Print, Print Preview**	Ctrl + F2 or Alt + Ctrl + I
Print Layout view		**View** tab, **Print Layout** command	Alt + Ctrl + P
Choose print options		**Microsoft Office Button, Print**	Ctrl + P
Print envelopes or lables		**Mailings** tab, **Envelopes** or **Mailings** tab, **Labels** command	

Concepts Review

True/False Questions

Each of the following statements is either true or false. Indicate your choice by circling T or F.

T F 1. Word has default settings for margins that are automatically set for each new document.

T F 2. You can change margins in Print Layout view by using the ruler.

T F 3. You can edit a document in Print Preview.

T F 4. Both Print Preview and the Page Setup dialog box use horizontal and vertical rulers to drag margins to desired positions.

T F 5. You can change margins for an entire document only by using the Page Setup dialog box.

T F 6. Gutter margins are outside margins on a bound document.

T F 7. The Shrink One Page feature reduces the size of the document by one page.

T F 8. Landscape is the default page orientation.

Short Answer Questions

Write the correct answer in the space provided.

1. What is the default document view?

2. What does the pointer look like when it is located over the margin boundary on the ruler in Print Layout view?

3. What is created when you change margins for selected text?

4. Which kind of document needs gutter margins?

5. Which tab, in which dialog box, do you use to change page orientation?

6. How do you switch to edit mode in Print Preview?

_____

7. Which key to you press to show the exact margin and text area measurements when using the ruler to change margins?

_____

8. What is the term for pages that appear as a two-page spread with odd-numbered right pages and even-numbered left pages?

_____

Critical Thinking

Answer these questions on a separate page. There are no right or wrong answers. Support your answers with examples from your own experience, if possible.

1. Collect samples of printed documents with interesting treatments of margins (such as books, advertisements, or reports). Pay particular attention to mirror margins and gutter margins. How does the margin treatment contribute to the overall feeling of the document?

2. Use Microsoft Office Word Help (F1) or practice on your own to explore the Book fold feature that is located in the Page Setup dialog box, Multiple Pages section. What type of document would you create to use this feature? Is the feature helpful?

Skills Review

Exercise 9-14

Set margins for an entire document and for selected text by using the Page Setup dialog box.

1. Open the file **Gresh**.

2. Change the margins for the entire document by following these steps:

   a. Click the **Page Layout** tab, and click the Margins button.

   b. Click **Custom Margins**, and set the **Top** margin to **2** inches, the **Bottom** margin to **.75** inch, and the **Left** and **Right** margins to **1.25** inches. Click **OK**.

3. Change the margins, and create a new section for selected text by following these steps:

   a. Select the text that begins "Campbell's Confections." through "Fax: 304-555-6660."

   b. Open the Page Setup dialog box.

   c. Set the left and right margins to **2** inches.

   d. Choose **Selected text** from the **Apply to** drop-down list, and click **OK**. The address appears by itself on a new page.

4. Click the Undo button to undo the new section.

5. Key the text **Matthew Garrett, Manager** as a separate line before "Campbell's Confections" in the body of the letter.

6. Save the document as *[your initials]***9-14** in your Lesson 9 folder.

7. Submit and close the document.

Exercise 9-15

Set margins in Print Layout view and Print Preview and change orientation.

1. Open the file **Chocolate**.

2. Change the left and right margins in Print Layout view by following these steps:

   a. Click the Print Layout View button located on the right of the status bar.

   b. If the rulers are not displayed, click the View Ruler button.

   c. Using the horizontal ruler, position the pointer on the left margin boundary until it becomes a two-pointed horizontal arrow (and the ScreenTip "Left Margin" appears).

   d. Hold down Alt and drag the margin boundary until the left margin measures 1.5 inches.

   e. Position the pointer on the right margin boundary and use the same method to drag it to 1.5 inches.

3. Change the top margin in Print Preview by following these steps:

   a. Click the **Microsoft Office Button**. Click the arrow beside **Print**, and click **Print Preview**.

   b. If the rulers are not displayed, click to select the Show Ruler command.

   c. Using the vertical ruler, position the pointer on the top margin boundary until it becomes a two-pointed arrow.

   d. Hold down Alt and drag the top margin boundary to 2 inches.

   e. Click the Close Print Preview button to return to Print Layout view. Drag the Zoom control to **100%** if necessary.

4. Add a bold, centered, and uppercase title **TYPES OF CHOCOLATE** to the top of the document, with 24 points spacing after.

5. Change the orientation to landscape by following these steps:

   a. Open the **Page Setup** dialog box.

   b. Click the **Margins** tab and choose **Landscape**.

   c. Change the top margin to **2** inches, change the bottom margin to **1** inch, and change the left and right margins to **1.25** inches.

   d. Click **OK** to close the Page Setup dialog box.

6. Save the document as *[your initials]***9-15** in your Lesson 9 folder.

7. Submit and close the document.

Exercise 9-16

Set mirror and gutter margins.

1. Open the file **Corporate Gifts - 2**.

2. Use the Page Setup dialog box to set mirror and gutter margins by following these steps:

   a. Open the **Page Setup** dialog box.

   b. Choose **Mirror margins** from the **Multiple pages** drop-down list.

   c. Change the inside and outside margins to **1.5** inches.

   d. Set the **Gutter** margin to **.5** inch.

   e. Click **OK**.

3. Scroll through the document in Print Layout view to see the new margin settings.

4. Switch to Print Preview.

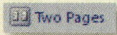

5. Click the Two Pages button , to see both pages display with the new margin settings. Click the Close Print Preview button.

6. Save the document as *[your initials]***9-16** in your Lesson 9 folder.

7. Print the document two pages per sheet, by following these steps:

   a. Click the **Microsoft Office Button**.

   b. Click **Print** to open the Print dialog box.

   c. Click the drop-down arrow beside the **Pages per sheet** option and choose **2 pages**.

   d. Click **OK**.

8. Submit and close the document.

Exercise 9-17

Set print options, print an envelope, and print labels.

1. Open the file **WV Stores**.

2. Print a portion of the document by following these steps:

   a. Select the text for the "Wheeling, WV" store—from "Campbell's Confections" through the fax number.

   b. Press Ctrl+P to open the Print dialog box.

   c. Choose **Selection** and click **OK**.

3. Insert the date by following these steps:

   a. Go to the end of the document, and press Enter four times. Key the text **Updated** and press Spacebar.

   b. Click the **Insert** tab, and click **Date and Time**.

   c. Choose the fourth date format, make sure **Update automatically** is not checked, and click **OK**.

   d. Insert a blank line after the date.

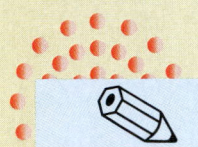

TIP

Because this document contains many addresses, you need to select the text you want to appear in the **Delivery address** box of the Envelopes and Labels dialog box.

4. Prepare an envelope addressed to the Morgantown store by following these steps:

   a. Select the name and address lines for the Morgantown store. Do not select the telephone and fax numbers.

   b. Click the **Mailings** tab. Click the **Envelopes** button. Click the **Envelopes** tab.

   c. In the **Delivery address** box, delete the comma in the address, and key **-3301** at the end of the ZIP Code.

   d. In the **Return address** box, key your name, followed by the office address:

      Campbell's Confections

      25 Main Street

      Grove City, PA 16127

5. Choose additional envelope options, and add the envelope to the document by following these steps:

   a. Click the **Options** button and choose the **Envelope Options** tab, if it is not already displayed.

   b. Make sure the envelope size is **10**.

   c. Click the **Font** button 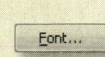 for the Delivery Address. Change the format to bold and all caps and click **OK**.

   d. Click **OK** in the Envelope Options dialog box. Click **Add to Document** in the Envelopes and Labels dialog box. Do not save the return address as the default.

6. Prepare the printer for a standard business envelope (or feed a blank sheet of paper into the printer). Print the document (envelope included).

7. Save the document as *[your initials]*9-17a in your Lesson 9 folder.

8. Create and print a page of return address labels by following these steps:

   a. With the insertion point in section 1 (the envelope), open the Envelopes and Labels dialog box and click the **Labels** tab.

   b. Examine the **Use return address** box. (Word recognizes the return address you previously entered for the envelope.)

   c. Choose the option **Full page of the same label**.

   d. Click **Options**. Set the **Product number** to **5160** and verify that **Page Printer** and **Avery US Letter** are selected. Click **OK**.

   e. Click **New Document** to save the labels as a separate document. Do not save the return address as the default.

   f. Save the labels as *[your initials]*9-17b in your Lesson 9 folder.

   g. Print the labels on a blank sheet of paper.

9. Close both documents.

Lesson Applications

Exercise 9-18

Set margins for a document and for selected text.

1. Open the file **PA Stores**.

2. At the beginning of the document, key the text shown in Figure 9-17, including the corrections. Use single spacing, and insert one blank line between paragraphs.

Figure 9-17

Than you for chosing Campbell's Confectoins to provide your company with our boxed chocolates. We began as small down town office over 50 *store* yeaars ago. Today we have offices in three states and we provide quality *stores* chocolates to all our customers.

All of our stores work together ot meet ~~all of your~~ group or individual needs. We offer our products in the following areas:

Retail
Wholesale *create as one paragraph using line breaks.*
Fundraising

For your convenience, Campbell's Confections offers complete service from any one of our Pennsylvania locations. Our storelocations and phone *# tele* numbers are listed on the following page. *s*

3. At the top of the document, key the title **Pennsylvania Stores** in 14-point bold small caps as a separate line. Center the title, and add 24 points spacing after. Copy the title, and paste it to the left of the first store.

4. Using the Page Setup dialog box, set the top margin to 2 inches and the left and right margins to 1.25 inches.

5. Select the text beginning with the second title "Pennsylvania Stores" through the end of the document. Use the Page Setup dialog box to change the left and right margins for *only* the selected text to 3 inches.

6. Change the top margin of the new section to 1.5 inches.

7. Use the Replace command to format all occurrences of "Campbell's Confections" in the second section as bold italic.

8. Save the document as *[your initials]*9-18 in your Lesson 9 folder.

9. Print the document using the 2 Pages per sheet option in the Print dialog box. Close the document.

Exercise 9-19

Set margins for a document and for selected text, change page orientation, and set print options.

1. Open the file **Memo - 3**.

2. Insert today's date in the date line.

3. In the opening paragraph of the memo, replace the text "items below" with **following information**.

4. Change the top margin to 2 inches and the left and right margins to 1.25 inches.

5. Select the text from "Beginning next quarter" through the end of the document. Change the orientation to landscape.

6. Format the new section as follows: change the top margin to 1.5 inches, change the bottom margin to 1 inch, and change the left and right margins to 1 inch.

7. Place a blank line above "Description/Model number." Delete the paragraph mark after "Model Number," and insert a tab character. Delete the paragraph mark after "Serial Number," and insert a tab character. Continue this procedure until the line includes all items. Adjust the tab settings to distribute the text evenly between the margins. Change the font of the headings to Arial Narrow, and apply bold and small caps formatting. Apply a bottom border to the headings.

8. Save the document as *[your initials]*9-19 in your Lesson 9 folder.

9. Print the document two pages per sheet. Close the document.

Exercise 9-20

Set margins, set mirror and gutter margins, and address an envelope.

1. Open the file **Orders**.

2. Change the left and right margins to 1.25 inches.

3. Set mirror margins and a .5-inch gutter margin.

4. Format the title as 14-point bold with a shadow effect. Add 72 points of paragraph spacing before the title.

5. Justify all text below the title except the tabbed information.

6. At the end of the document, format the address with 1.5-inch left and right indents (not margins), a 1-point box border, and gray shading. Key a colon after "at."

7. Add an envelope to the document, using the company address. Use your name and address as the return address. Do not save the return address.

8. Select the paragraph headings beginning with "Online" through "Customer Service," and change the font size to 12 points. Do not change the font size for the paragraphs beginning with "Note."

9. Save the document as *[your initials]*9-20 in your Lesson 9 folder.

10. Submit and close the document.

Exercise 9-21 ◆ Challenge Yourself

Create labels.

1. Open the file **Haas**.

2. Format the document as a standard business letter. (Refer to Appendix B, "Standard Forms for Business Documents," for margin and spacing requirements.) Enter the date as a field. The letter is from you with the title **Sales Associate** and to the following person:

   Mr. Mark Haas

   215 Lake Street

   Girard, PA 16417

3. Key the text shown in Figure 9-18 as the closing paragraphs.

Figure 9-18

```
Call our corporate gift specialists for assistance in
selecting your customized gifts, maintaining your mailing
list, and for information on volume discounts. The enclosed
brochure explains the procedure for ordering.

We look forward to doing business with you.
```

4. Add an enclosure notation to the letter.

5. Switch to Print Preview for a final view of the document.

6. Save the document as *[your initials]*9-21a in your Lesson 9 folder.

7. Create a sheet of labels (Avery Standard 5160) of Mr. Haas's address as a new document. Use all caps and no punctuation in the address.

8. Save the labels as *[your initials]*9-21b in your Lesson 9 folder.

9. Submit both documents and close them.

On Your Own

In these exercises you work on your own, as you would in a real-life business environment. Use the skills you've learned to accomplish the task—and be creative.

Exercise 9-22

Write a summary about a book you have recently read. Change the margins for the document, and change the margins of one of the sections of the summary that you want to highlight. Save the document as *[your initials]*9-22 and submit it.

Exercise 9-23

Create a document, and use the Page Layout tab to create a custom paper size. Change the width to 5 inches and the height to 3 inches. Change all margins to .4 inch, and change the orientation to landscape. Key a favorite recipe and format the text attractively. Save the document as *[your initials]*9-23 and submit it.

Exercise 9-24

Log onto the Internet, and find five Web sites about today's current political topic. Create a document summarizing the topic with a pro and con approach. Format the document using landscape orientation. Save the document as *[your initials]*9-24 and submit it.

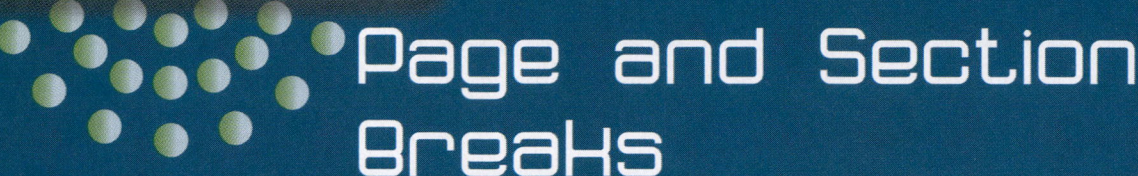

Lesson 10

Page and Section Breaks

OBJECTIVES

After completing this lesson, you will be able to:

1. Use soft and hard page breaks.

2. Control line and page breaks.

3. Control section breaks.

4. Format sections.

5. Use the Go To feature.

Estimated Time: 1 hour

MCAS OBJECTIVES

In this lesson:
WW 07 1.1.6
WW 07 1.2.1
WW 07 2.3.1
WW 07 2.3.2
WW 07 5.1.1

In Word, text flows automatically from the bottom of one page to the top of the next page. This is similar to how text wraps automatically from the end of one line to the beginning of the next line. You can control and customize how and when text flows from the bottom of one page to the top of the next. This process is called *pagination*.

Sections are a common feature of long documents and have a significant impact on pagination. This lesson describes how to use and manage sections.

Using Soft and Hard Page Breaks

As you work on a document, Word is constantly calculating the amount of space available on the page. Page length is determined by the size of the paper and the top and bottom margin settings. For example, using standard-size paper and default margins, page length is 9 inches. When a document exceeds this length, Word creates a *soft page break*. Word adjusts this automatic page break as you add or delete text. A soft page break appears as a horizontal dotted line on the screen in Draft view. In Print Layout view, you see the actual page break—the bottom of one page and the top of the next.

Draft view is frequently used to edit and format text. It does not show the page layout as it appears on a printed page, nor does it show special elements of a page such as columns, headers, or footers.

Exercise 10-1   ADJUST A SOFT PAGE BREAK AUTOMATICALLY

NOTE

When you format and edit a long documents, check the status bar settings to make sure Section and Page Numbers display. To verify the settings, right-click the status bar and click to select the options.

NOTE

The page breaks described in this lesson might appear in slightly different locations on your screen.

1. Open the file **History**. Switch to Draft view by clicking the Draft button 🗏 on the status bar. Change the zoom level to **100%** if necessary.

2. Scroll to the bottom of page 3. Notice the soft page break separating the heading "Gourmet Chocolate" from the paragraph below it.

3. Locate the paragraph just above the heading "Gourmet Chocolate" (it begins "In 2001"). Move the insertion point to the left of "The Web site has proven" in the middle of the paragraph, and press Enter to split the paragraph. Notice the adjustment of the soft page break. Undo 🔄 the paragraph split.

Figure 10-1
Adjusting the position of a soft page break

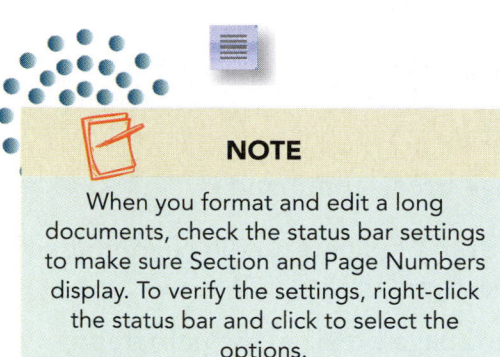

Exercise 10-2   INSERT A HARD PAGE BREAK

When you want a page break to occur at a specific point, you can insert a *hard page break*. In Draft view, a hard page break appears on the screen as a dotted line with the words "Page Break." In Print Layout view you see the actual page break.

There are two ways to insert a hard page break:

- Use the keyboard shortcut Ctrl + Enter.

- Click the **Insert** tab, and click the Page Break command.

1. Move the insertion point to the bottom of page 2, to the beginning of the paragraph that starts "The most popular."

2. Press Ctrl + Enter. Word inserts a hard page break so the paragraph and bulleted text are not divided between two pages.

3. Move to the middle of page 4, and place the insertion point to the left of the text that begins "Chronology."

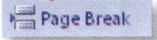

4. Click the **Insert** tab, and click the Page Break button 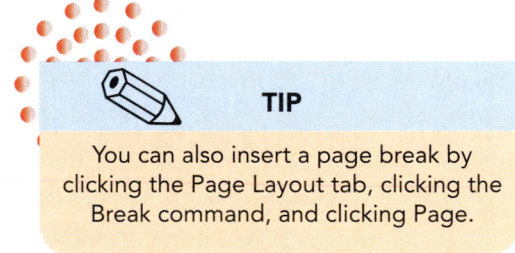 to insert a page break. Word inserts a hard page break and adjusts pagination in the document from this point forward.

Figure 10-2
Insert tab, Pages group

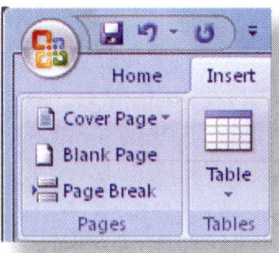

TIP

You can also insert a page break by clicking the Page Layout tab, clicking the Break command, and clicking Page.

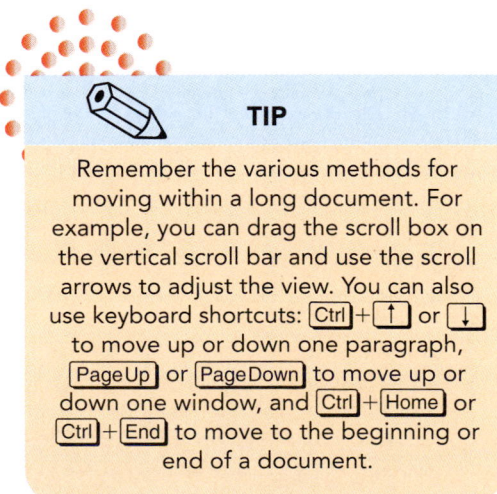

TIP

Remember the various methods for moving within a long document. For example, you can drag the scroll box on the vertical scroll bar and use the scroll arrows to adjust the view. You can also use keyboard shortcuts: Ctrl + ↑ or ↓ to move up or down one paragraph, PageUp or PageDown to move up or down one window, and Ctrl + Home or Ctrl + End to move to the beginning or end of a document.

Figure 10-3
Inserting a hard page break

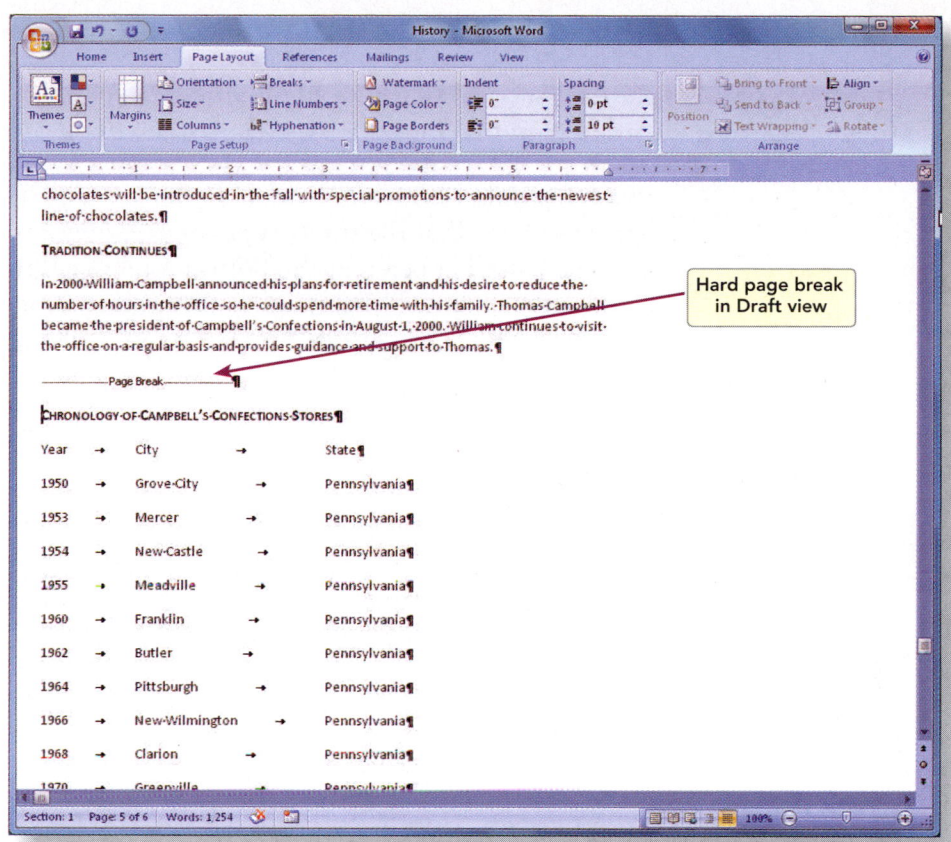

Exercise 10-3   DELETE A HARD PAGE BREAK

You cannot delete a soft page break, but you can delete a hard page break by clicking the page break and pressing Backspace or Delete.

1. Select the page break you just inserted by dragging the I-beam over the page break. Be sure to select the paragraph mark.

2. Press Delete to delete the page break.

3. Scroll back to the hard page break you inserted at the top of page 3. Position the insertion point to the left of "The most popular" and press Backspace two times (one time to delete the paragraph mark and one time to delete the page break). The page break is deleted, and Word adjusts the pagination.

Controlling Line and Page Breaks

To control the way Word breaks paragraphs, choose one of four line and page break options from the Paragraph dialog box:

- *Widow/Orphan control:* A *widow* is the last line of a paragraph and appears by itself at the top of a page. An *orphan* is the first line of a paragraph and appears at the bottom of a page. By default, this option is turned on to prevent widows and orphans. Word moves an orphan forward to the next page and moves a widow back to the previous page.

- *Keep lines together:* This option keeps all lines of a paragraph together on the same page rather than splitting the paragraphs between two pages.

- *Keep with next:* If two or more paragraphs need to appear on the same page no matter where page breaks occur, use this option. The option is most commonly applied to titles that should not be separated from the first paragraph following the title.

- *Page break before:* Use this option to place a paragraph at the top of a new page.

Exercise 10-4   APPLY LINE AND PAGE BREAK OPTIONS TO PARAGRAPHS

1. Close **History** without saving; then reopen the document. Switch to Draft view.

2. At the bottom of page 3, click within the heading "Gourmet Chocolate." You are going to format this heading so it will not be separated from its related paragraph.

3. Click the **Home** tab, and click the **Paragraph Dialog Box Launcher** to open the Paragraph dialog box. Click the **Line and Page Breaks** tab.

TIP

To reopen the file quickly, click the Microsoft Office Button and click the filename **History** under Recent Documents.

Figure 10-4
Line and Page
Breaks options in the
Paragraph dialog
box

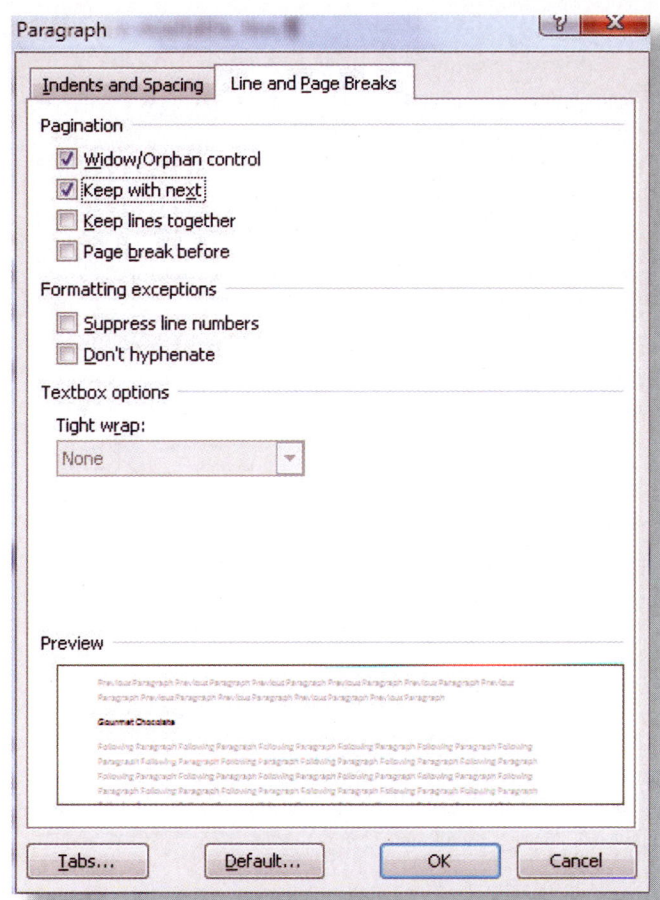

4. Click **Keep with next** to select it and click **OK**. Word moves the soft page break, keeping the two paragraphs together.

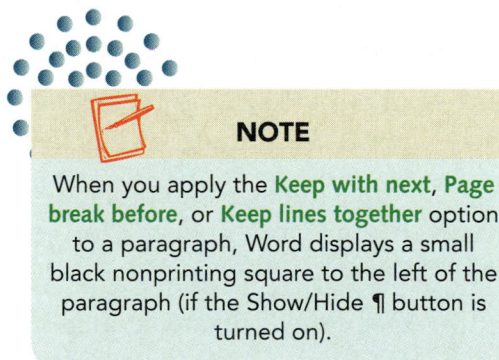

NOTE

When you apply the **Keep with next**, **Page break before**, or **Keep lines together** option to a paragraph, Word displays a small black nonprinting square to the left of the paragraph (if the Show/Hide ¶ button is turned on).

Figure 10-5
Applying the Keep
with next option

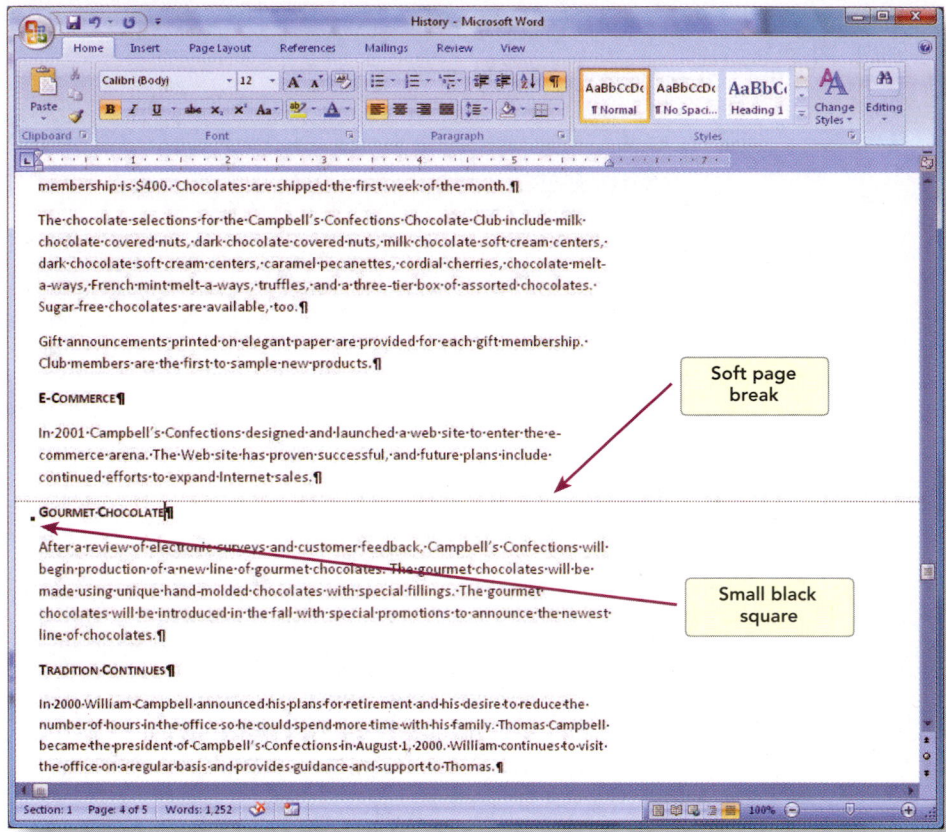

5. Press Ctrl + Home to go to the top of the document. Select the title, and apply 72 points spacing before.

6. Locate the text at the bottom of page 1 that begins "By 1980." The paragraph is divided by a soft page break.

7. Right-click the paragraph to open the shortcut menu. Click **Paragraph**. Click the **Line and Page Breaks** tab if necessary.

8. Choose **Keep lines together** and click **OK**. The soft page break moves above the paragraphs to keep the lines of text together.

9. Move to page 4, and place the insertion point in the paragraph that begins "Chronology." You will format this paragraph so it begins at the top of the page.

10. Open the **Paragraph** dialog box, click **Page break before**, and click **OK**. Word starts the paragraph at the top of page 5 with a soft page break.

11. Press Shift + F1 to open the **Reveal Formatting** task pane. Click the + to the left of Paragraph to display the paragraph formatting. Notice the link for **Line and Page Breaks**. Close the task pane.

12. Save the document as *[your initials]*10-4 in a new folder for Lesson 10. Leave it open for the next exercise.

Word 2007

Controlling Section Breaks

Section breaks separate parts of a document that have formatting different from the rest of the document. You may want to insert a section at the beginning of a document to include a title page with special formatting. A separate section is created when you change the left and right margins of selected text.

For better control in creating section breaks, you can insert a section break directly into a document at a specific location by using the Breaks command. You can also specify the type of section break you want to insert. Switch to Draft view to see the double-dotted section break lines.

TABLE 10-1 Types of Section Breaks

Type	Description
Next page	Section starts on a new page.
Continuous	Section follows the text before it without a page break.
Even page or Odd page	Section starts on the next even- or odd-numbered page. Useful for reports in which chapters must begin on either odd-numbered or even-numbered pages.

Exercise 10-5 INSERT SECTION BREAKS BY USING THE BREAKS COMMAND

1. Place the insertion point to the left of the paragraph at the top of page 5 that begins "Chronology."

2. Press Ctrl+Q. This clears the formatting for the paragraph, removing the soft page break you applied earlier.

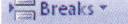

3. Click the **Page Layout** tab, and click the Breaks button . Under **Section Breaks**, click **Continuous**. Word begins a new section on the same page, from the position of the insertion point.

4. Click above and below the section mark. Notice that the section number changes on the status bar but the page number stays the same.

Word 2007

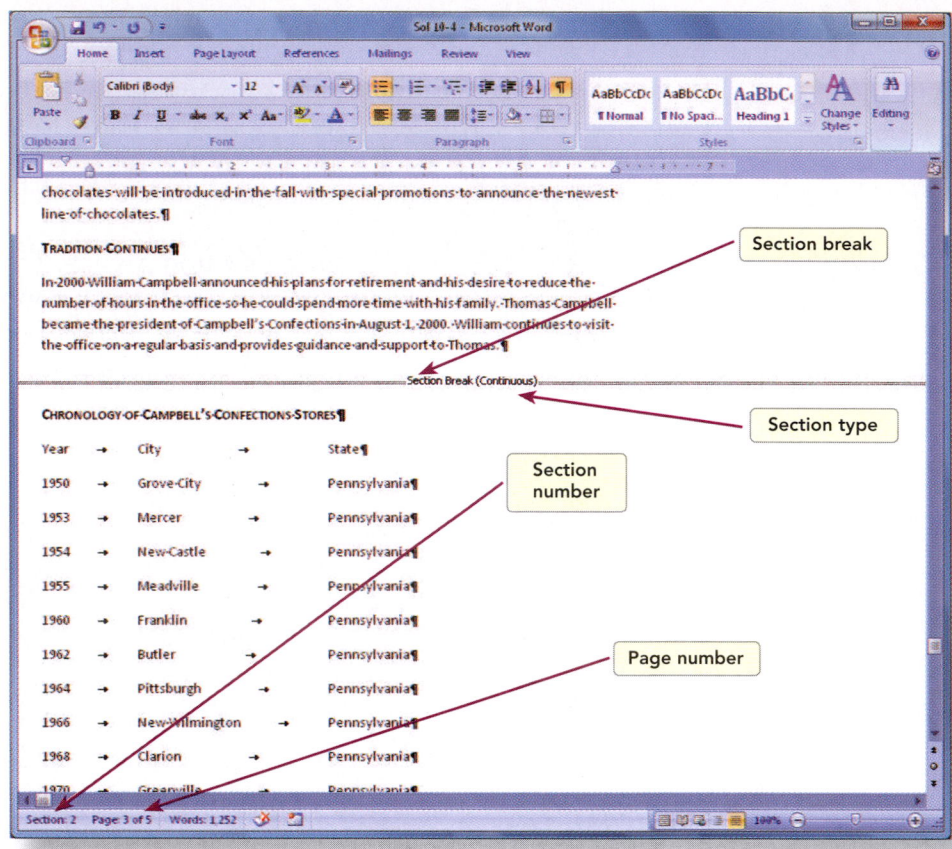

Formatting Sections

After you create a new section, you can change its formatting or specify a different type of section break. This is often useful for long documents, which sometimes contain many sections that require different page formatting, such as different margin settings or page orientation. For example, you can change a next page section break to a continuous section break, or you can change the page orientation of a section, without affecting the rest of the document.

> **NOTE**
>
> The formatting you apply to the section is stored in the section break. If you delete a section break, you also delete the formatting for the text above the section break. For example, if you have a two-section document and you delete the section break at the end of section 1, the document becomes one section with the formatting of section 2.

Exercise 10-6 APPLY FORMATTING TO SECTIONS

1. Position the insertion point before the text "Wholesale" on page 2. Use the **Page Layout** tab, Breaks button to insert a **Next page** section break.

2. With the insertion point in the new section (section 2), open the **Page Setup** dialog box by clicking the **Page Setup Dialog Box Launcher**.

3. Click the **Layout** tab, and click to open the **Section start** drop-down list. From this list you can change the section break from **Next page** to another type.

4. Choose **Continuous** so the section does not start on a new page.

Figure 10-7
Using the Page
Setup dialog box to
modify the section

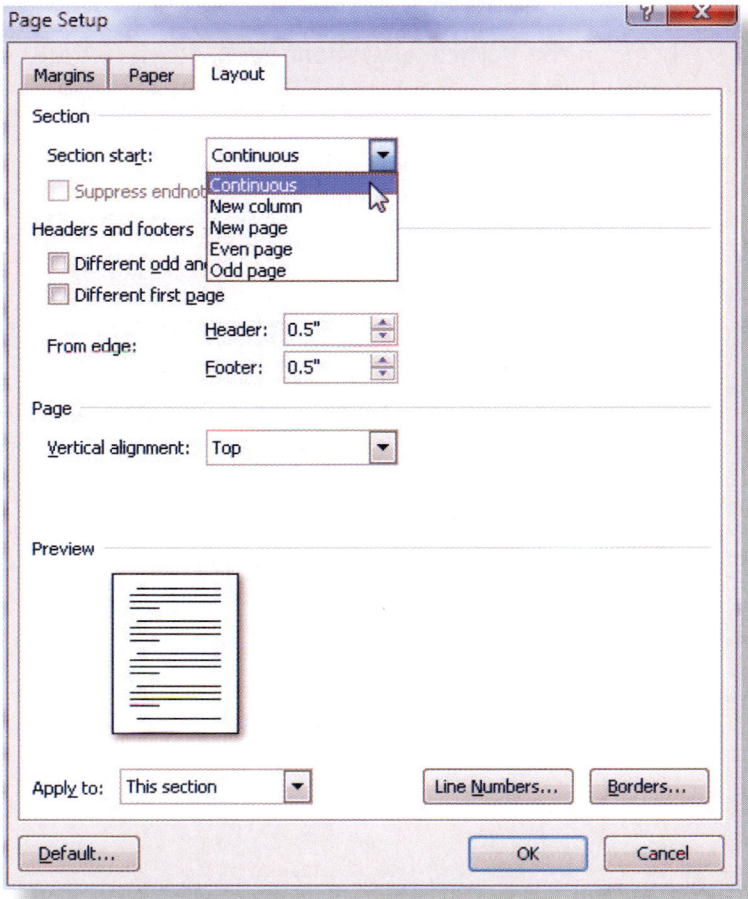

5. Click the **Margins** tab.

6. Set 1.5-inch left and right margins. Make sure **This section** appears in the **Apply to** box, and click **OK**. Section 2 of the document now has new margin settings.

Exercise 10-7   CHANGE THE VERTICAL ALIGNMENT OF A SECTION

Another way to format a section is to specify the vertical alignment of the section on the page. For example, you can align a title page so the text is centered between the top and bottom margins. Vertical alignment is a Layout option available in the Page Setup dialog box.

1. Move the insertion point to the last section of the document (which begins "Chronology"). Notice that, because this section does not start on a new page, a page break interrupts the list of stores.

2. Open the **Page Setup** dialog box and click the **Layout** tab.

3. Use the **Section start** drop-down list to change the section from **Continuous** to **New page**.

4. Open the **Vertical alignment** drop-down list and choose **Center**. Click **OK**.

TABLE 10-2 Vertical Alignment Options

Options	Description
Top	Aligns the top line of the page with the top margin (default setting).
Center	Centers the page between the top and bottom margins with equal space above and below the text.
Justified	Aligns the top line of the page with the top margin and the bottom line with the bottom margin, with equal spacing between the lines of text (similar in principle to the way Word justifies text between the left and right margins).
Bottom	Aligns the bottom line of a partial page along the bottom margin.

Figure 10-8
Vertical alignment options

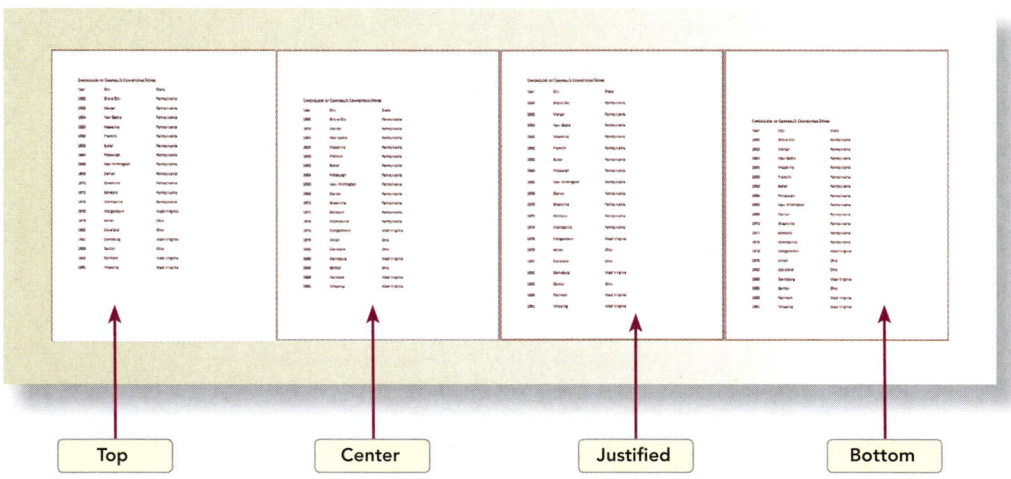

| Top | Center | Justified | Bottom |

Exercise 10-8   CHECK PAGINATION IN PRINT PREVIEW AND PAGE LAYOUT VIEW

After you apply page breaks, section breaks, or section formatting, use Print Preview or Print Layout view to check the document. Viewing the pages in relation to one another provides ideas for improvement before printing.

Remember, you can edit and change the formatting of a document in Print Layout view or Print Preview.

One Page

1. Click the **Microsoft Office Button** and click the arrow beside **Print**. Click **Print Preview** to preview the current section. Click the One Page button ⬛ One Page if necessary. Notice that the text is centered between the top and bottom margins. Notice also that Print Preview does not show the dotted lines of the section breaks, but it does show how the page will look when you print it.

2. While still in Print Preview, open the **Page Setup** dialog box, and change the vertical alignment to **Justified**. Click **OK**. Word justifies the last page of the document so the text extends from the top margin to the bottom margin.

Previous Page

3. Click the Previous Page button ⬛ Previous Page to scroll back, page by page, to page 2, section 1, of the document. (Check the status bar for location.)

100%

4. Click the Zoom Level button ⬛, choose **Page width** and click **OK**. You cannot see the continuous section break before "Wholesale. . ." but you can check the formatting and see how the document will look when printed.

5. Click the Print Layout View button to close Print Preview and to switch to Print Layout view.

6. Scroll to page 2, section 1. Notice that in Print Layout view, page breaks are indicated by the actual layout of each page as it will look when printed.

7. Click the Zoom Level button on the status bar to open the Zoom dialog box. Click **Many Pages** and click on the grid to display **1 × 2** (one row, two pages). Click **OK**. This reduces the document display so you can see two pages at the same time.

8. Scroll to the end of the document. Click the Draft View button ⬛ to switch to Draft view. Drag the **Zoom Slider** to **100%** if necessary.

Using the Go To Feature

You use Go To to move through a document quickly. For example, you can go to a specific section, page number, comment, or bookmark. Go To is a convenient feature for long documents—it is faster than scrolling, and it moves the insertion point to the specified location.

There are three ways to initiate the Go To command:

- Click the Home tab, and click the Find or Replace commands to open the Find and Replace dialog box. Click the Go To tab.

- Double-click on the status bar (anywhere to the left of "Words").

- Press Ctrl + G or F5.

Exercise 10-9   GO TO A SPECIFIC PAGE OR SECTION

1. With the document in Draft view, press F5. Word displays the **Go To** tab, located in the Find and Replace dialog box.

Figure 10-9
Using the Go To feature

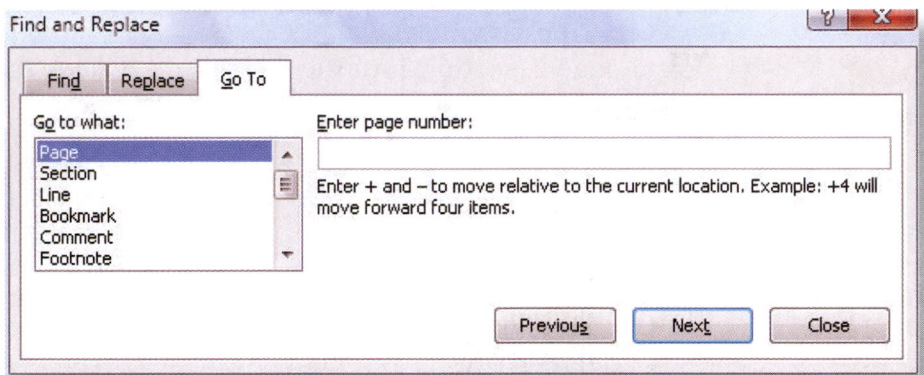

2. Scroll through the **Go to what** list to review the options. Choose **Section** from the list, and click **Previous** until you reach the beginning of the document.

3. Click **Next** until the insertion point is located at the beginning of the last section, which is section 3.

4. Choose **Page** from the **Go to what** list and click **Previous**. The insertion point moves to the top of the previous page.

5. Key **2** in the **Enter page number** text box and click **Go To**. The insertion point moves to the top of page 2.

6. **Close** the dialog box.

Exercise 10-10   GO TO A RELATIVE DESTINATION

You can use the Go To command to move to a location relative to the insertion point. For example, with **Page** selected in the **Go to what** list, you can enter "+2" in the text box to move forward two pages from the insertion point. You can move in increments of pages, lines, sections, and so on.

Another option is to move by a certain percentage within the document, such as 50 percent—the document's midpoint.

1. Double-click the word "Page" on the status bar to reopen the Find and Replace dialog box.

2. Choose **Line** from the **Go to what** list, and key **4** in the text box. Click **Go To**. The insertion point moves to the fourth line in the document.

NOTE

You must select Page in the Go to what list to use a percentage.

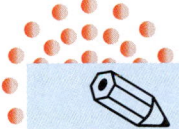

TIP

You can use the Go To feature to delete a single page of content. Position the insertion point, and open the Find and Replace dialog box. Click the Go To tab, and key **\page** in the text box. Click Go To. Click Close (the text will be highlighted), and press Delete.

3. Key **+35** in the text box, and click **Go To**. The insertion point moves forward 35 lines from the previous location.

4. Key **-35** in the text box, and click **Go To**. The insertion point moves back to the previous location.

5. Click **Page** in the **Go to what** list, key **50%** in the text box, and click **Go To**. The insertion point moves to the midpoint of the document.

6. Close the dialog box.

7. Save the document as *[your initials]***10-10** in a new Lesson 10 folder.

8. Open the Print dialog box, and choose **4 pages** in the **Pages per sheet** list box. Click **OK**.

9. Close the document.

Lesson 10 Summary

- Pagination is the Word process of flowing text from line to line and from page to page. Word creates a soft page break at the end of each page. When you edit text, you adjust line and page breaks. You can adjust the way a page breaks by manually inserting a hard page break (Ctrl + Enter).

- Delete a hard page break by clicking it and pressing Delete or Backspace.

- The Paragraph dialog box contains line and page break options to control pagination. To prevent lines of a paragraph from displaying on two pages, click in the paragraph and apply the **Keep lines together** option. To keep two paragraphs together on the same page, click in the first paragraph and apply the **Keep with next** option. To insert a page break before a paragraph, click in the paragraph and choose the **Page break before** option.

- Use section breaks to separate parts of a document that have different formatting. Apply a **Next page** section break to start a section on a new page or a **Continuous** section break to continue the new section on the same page. Apply an **Even page** or **Odd page** section break to start a section on the next even- or odd-numbered page.
- Change the vertical alignment of a section by clicking within the section and opening the Page Setup dialog box. On the **Layout** tab, under **Vertical alignment**, choose an alignment (Top, Center, Justified, or Bottom).
- Check pagination in Print Preview or Print Layout view. Scroll through the document or change the zoom level to display a different view.
- Use the Go To command to go to a specific page or section in a document. You can also go to a relative destination, such as the midpoint of the document or the 50th line.

LESSON 10		Command Summary	
Feature	**Button**	**Command**	**Keyboard**
Hard page break	Page Break	**Insert** tab, **Pages** group, **Page Break**	Ctrl + Enter
Line and page break options		**Home** tab, **Paragraph** group, **Paragraph** dialog box, **Line and Page Breaks** tab	
Section breaks	Breaks ▾	**Page Layout** tab, **Page Setup** group, **Breaks** command	
Formatting sections		**Page Layout** tab, **Page Setup** group, **Page Setup** dialog box	
Go To	Find ▾ Replace	**Home** tab, **Editing** group, **Find** or **Replace** command, **Go To** tab	Ctrl + G or F5

Concepts Review

True/False Questions

Each of the following statements is either true or false. Indicate your choice by circling T or F.

T F   1. You can delete a hard or soft page break by pressing Delete.

T F   2. To insert a section break, press Ctrl + Enter.

T F   3. One way to insert a page break is to choose Break from the Insert tab.

T F   4. Page break before is a paragraph formatting option that starts a paragraph at the top of a new page.

T F   5. A nonprinting character appears to the left of any paragraph to which you apply the Keep with next option.

T F   6. Section breaks appear in the Print Preview window as double-dotted lines.

T F   7. Page breaks appear in Print Layout view as single-dotted lines.

T F   8. You can use the Go To feature to move the insertion point from one section to another.

Short Answer Questions

Write the correct answer in the space provided.

1. Which type of page break is automatically adjusted as you key text?

   _____

2. Which type of section break does not start on a new page?

   _____

3. What is the term for the last line of a paragraph that appears alone at the top of a page?

   _____

4. Which option would you apply to a paragraph so it is not divided by a page break?

   _____

5. Which dialog box and tab would you display to change the vertical alignment of a section?

   _____

6. Which type of vertical alignment spaces text so the top line aligns with the top margin and the bottom line aligns with the bottom margin?

_____

7. In Print Layout view, which feature do you use to view two pages at the same time?

_____

8. Describe the appearance of the nonprinting character Word displays next to a paragraph when you apply certain line and page break options.

_____

Critical Thinking

Answer these questions on a separate page. There are no right or wrong answers. Support your answers with examples from your own experience, if possible.

1. In a long document that requires extensive editing, why would it be most efficient to perform all your edits before inserting hard page breaks?

2. Describe a situation where you would use a continuous section break.

Skills Review

Exercise 10-11

Adjust soft page breaks and insert hard page breaks.

1. Open the file **Terms**. Position the insertion point in the first line of the memo, and change the spacing before to 72 points.
2. Scroll to the bottom of page 1 to see where the soft page break occurs.
3. Change the font size for the entire document to 11 points. Notice how the change affects the soft page break.
4. Insert a page break before the text "Chocolate Terms" by following these steps:
   a. Place the insertion point to the left of the text.
   b. Press Ctrl+Enter.
5. Change the last line on page one to read: **is listed on the next page**. Change the font size of the title on page 2 to 14 points, and apply 24 points spacing after. Center the title.
6. Key today's date in the memo heading, and key your reference initials at the bottom of page 1.

7. View the document in Print Preview, one page at a time.

8. Click the Two Pages button 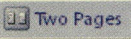 to view two pages at once. Return to a one-page view, and zoom to view the "SUBJECT:" line.

9. Click the Magnifier check box to deselect it. Select the text for the subject line ("Chocolate Terms"), and apply italic formating using the keyboard shortcut Ctrl+I.

10. Save the document as *[your initials]*10-11 in your Lesson 10 folder.

11. Submit and close the document.

Exercise 10-12

Apply line and page break options to paragraphs.

1. Open the file **Directory**.

2. Change the left and right margins to 1.25 inches.

3. Format the first line of the title as 14-point bold, centered, and uppercase. Add 36 points of spacing before. Format the second line as 12-point bold, small caps, and centered.

4. Key the current date.

5. Apply paragraph formatting to the heading "Ohio Stores" so it begins on a new page by following these steps:

   a. Move the insertion point within the heading.

   b. Click the Home tab, and click the Paragraph Dialog Box Launcher.

   c. Click the Line and Page Breaks tab.

   d. Choose Page break before and click OK.

6. Click within the heading "West Virginia Stores," and press F4 to repeat the format. Repeat the formatting to the heading "Pennsylvania Stores" if necessary.

7. Scroll through the document to verify that the stores are listed by state on a new page. The document should be four pages.

8. Save the document as *[your initials]*10-12 in your Lesson 10 folder.

9 Submit and close the document.

Exercise 10-13

Specify section breaks by type and change the margin settings in sections.

1. Open the file **Homecoming - 2**.

2. Insert a next page section break on page 1 before the heading "Homecoming Events" by following these steps:

   a. Place the insertion point to the left of the heading.

   b. Click the Page Layout tab, and click the Breaks button 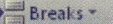. Click Next Page.

3. Move the insertion point to section 1. Change the top margin to 2 inches, and change the left and right margins to 1.25 inches. Be sure to apply the format to the section and not the whole document.

4. Use the **Page Setup** dialog box to format section 2 with 1.5-inch left and right margins. Make sure **This section** appears in the **Apply to** box.

5. Select the list of colleges, and change the left indent to 1.5 inches.

6. Change the vertical alignment for section 2 to centered by following these steps:

   a. Place the insertion point in the second section.

   b. Open the **Page Setup** dialog box, and click the **Layout** tab. Select **Centered** from the **Vertical alignment** drop-down list. Click **OK**.

7. Format page 2 (section 2) with a page border using the Box setting and a 3-point double line. Be sure to apply the border to "This Section."

8. Save the document as *[your initials]*10-13 in your Lesson 10 folder.

9. Submit and close the document.

Exercise 10-14

Vertically align a section and move around a document by using the Go To feature.

1. Open the file **Leadership**.

2. Insert **Next page** section breaks at "*Please join us for*" on page 1 and at "Possible Agenda Topics" at the bottom of the same page.

3. Vertically align the text in section 2 by following these steps:

   a. With the insertion point in section 2, click the **Page Layout** tab, and click the **Page Setup Dialog Box Launcher**. Click the **Layout** tab.

   b. Choose **Center** from the **Vertical alignment** drop-down list.

   c. Make sure **This section** appears in the **Apply to** box, and click **OK**.

4. Switch to Print Preview, and view only the second page (section 2).

5. From the Print Preview window, open the **Page Setup** dialog box again, and change the vertical alignment to **Justified**.

6. Close Print Preview.

7. Select all the text in section 2, and center the text horizontally.

8. Use the Go To feature to move within the document by following these steps:

   a. Press F5.

   b. Choose **Section** from the **Go to what** list, and enter **3** in the text box.

   c. Click **Go To** and close the dialog box.

9. Select the first line of section 3, and change the font to 14-point bold and small caps. Select the second line through the end of the document, and apply a bullet format.

10. Use the Zoom Level to view three pages at one time by following these steps:

    a. Click the Zoom Level button 100% on the status bar.

    b. Click the Many Pages button 🖳 and drag across the first row to highlight three pages.

    c. Click OK.

11. Drag the Zoom Slider to **100%**. Add 72 points of spacing before the first line on page 1. Add your reference initials to the bottom of page 1.

12. Save the document as *[your initials]***10-14** in your Lesson 10 folder.

13. Submit and close the document.

Lesson Applications

Exercise 10-15

Insert page breaks, apply line and page break options, and format text as a new section.

1. Open the file **Staff - 2**.

2. Key the text in Figure 10-10 at the beginning of the document.

Figure 10-10

> *format 14 points-bold-small caps*
>
> Corporate Staff—Brief Biographies
>
> Campbell's Confections has experienced growth and success since Wiliam [*significant* *financial*] Campbell started the company in 1905. One explanation for this success of [*the*] this company is the continued commitment to people—both customers [*t*] and employees. [*merge*]
>
> Campbell's Confections has been able to attract and hold employees and is proud of the fact that the average length of service for employees is 51 [*15*] years. William Campbell believed in the importance of demonstrating care for employee and Tom Campbell continues this philosophy. [*es*] [*Thomas*]

3. Use the Find feature or scroll to locate "Tamara Robbins." Use the Keep with next feature to place the heading "Tamara Robbins" with the descriptive paragraph.

4. Place the insertion point to the left of "Corporate Staff." And insert a next page section break.

5. Change the top margin for section 1 to 2 inches and the left and right margins to 1.5 inches.

6. Locate the text "Cynthia Parker," and insert a page break at the beginning of the line.

7. Increase the font size of the title in section 1 to 20 points, and apply the shadow text effect. Change the font size of the title in section 2 to 20 points, and apply bold, small caps, and the shadow text effect.

8. Add a 3-D page border to all pages of the document. Select a double-line style, dark blue color, and 3-point width.

9. In section 2, center the text vertically.

10. Preview the document.

11. Save the document as *[your initials]*10-15 in your Lesson 10 folder.

12. Print the document 4 sheets per page, and then close it.

Exercise 10-16

Add and format sections.

1. Open the file **Forman**.

2. Set a 2-inch top margin, and change the left and right margins to 1.25 inches. Key the current date at the top of the document, and include an enclosures notation.

3. Position the insertion point at the end of the document. Click the **Insert** tab, and click the arrow beside the **Object** button [Object ▾]. Click **Text from file**. Locate the file **Retail Stores - 2**, and click **Insert**.

4. Position the insertion point at the end of the document, and follow the same procedure to insert the file **Store Directory**.

5. Locate the text "There are 24" and insert a next page section break. In the new section, key the title **Campbell's Confections' Retail Stores** using bold uppercase text. Center the title, and increase the font size to 14 points. Add 24 points of spacing after.

6. Insert a next page section break before the text "Pennsylvania Stores."

7. Format section 2 so it is vertically centered and in landscape orientation. Set 1.5 inch left and right margins. Change the top and bottom margins to 1 inch. Select all paragraphs below the title and change the spacing after to 12 points.

8. Go to section 3, and insert a page break before "Ohio Stores" and "West Virginia Stores."

9. Change the top margin for section 3 to 1.5 inches.

10. Save the document as *[your initials]*10-16 in your Lesson 10 folder.

11. Submit and close the document.

Exercise 10-17

Apply line and page break options, add and format sections, and use the Go To feature.

1. Open the file **Price Change**.

2. Add a continuous section break before the line "Standard-size" and another at the bottom of the list (before the paragraph that begins "Price changes").

3. Format section 2 with a 1.5-inch left margin and double spacing. Adjust the tab settings to space the columns evenly between the margins. The third column should be formatted with a right tab at 5 inches. Bold and underline the column headings. Center, bold, and apply 14-point small caps to the title. Change the spacing before to 24 points.

4. Go to section 1, and key a memo heading to "Store Managers" from Thomas Campbell. Use the current date, and the subject is "Price changes." Align memo heading information with a left tab. Add your

reference initials at the end of section 1 with an attachment reference. Change the top margin to 2 inches and the bottom margin to 0.5 inch.

5. Go to section 3, and copy the formatting from the title in section 2 to the title in section 3.

6. Change the double-spaced text in section 2 to 1.5-line spacing.

7. Change the section layout for section 3 from a continuous section break to a section break that starts on a new page using the Page Setup dialog box.

8. Change the left and right margins for section 3 to 1 inch. Select the tabbed text in section 3, and change the left indent to 1 inch. Set a right dotted-leader tab at 5.5 inches. Bold and underline the column headings, and format the tabbed text with 1.5-line spacing. Remove the dotted leaders from the column heading. Format the title with 24 points spacing before and 12 points spacing after.

9. Change the alignment in section 3 so it is centered vertically.

10. Preview the document, and save it as *[your initials]*10-17 in your Lesson 10 folder.

11. Submit and close the document.

Exercise 10-18 ◆ Challenge Yourself

Add and delete page breaks, and add and format a new section.

1. Create a standard business memo from you to store managers. Key September 1 for the date. The subject is "Candy Bar Wrapper Contest." Key the body text shown in Figure 10-11.

Figure 10-11

```
Thank you for sending your comments regarding our first
candy bar wrapper contest. We want our first contest to be
a success, and we hope to use one of the winning designs for
one of our fundraising candy bar wrappers.

Please review the following list, and provide your comments
no later than Wednesday. We want to send the rules and
guidelines to the graphic artist for layout and printing. When
we receive the flyer, we will e-mail it to you for printing
and distribution to high schools in your service area.

Your comments regarding possible awards were enlightening.
Because Campbell's Confections' stores are located in a
tri-state area, we have taken great effort to work with
three state treasurers to establish our scholarship awards
program.
```

2. At the end of the memo, add an attachment reference. After the reference, create a new section that starts on a new page.

3. In the new section, insert the file **Wrapper**.

TIP

To insert a file, place the insertion point in the new section, click the **Insert** tab and click the arrow beside **Object**. Click **Text from File**. Locate the file and click **Insert**.

4. Format the two-line title as 14-point bold, all caps, and centered, with two blank lines below it.

5. Select all lines below the title and format with 12 points spacing after.

6. Select "Rules/Guidelines" and "Prizes" and apply bold, italic, and small caps formatting. Select the text below each side heading, and format it as a bulleted list.

7. Use the Replace feature to replace all occurrences of "contest" with **competition**.

8. Add a page border to section 2. Select a geometric-pattern border from the Art drop-down list. Select an appropriate width and color.

9. If you have not already done so, format section 1 with a 2-inch top margin. Make sure section 2 has the regular 1-inch top margin and is centered vertically.

10. Spell-check section 1 only.

11. Save the document as *[your initials]***10-18** in your Lesson 10 folder.

12. Submit and close the document.

On Your Own

In these exercises you work on your own, as you would in a real-life business environment. Use the skills you've learned to accomplish the task—and be creative.

Exercise 10-19

Write a short report about your 10 favorite television shows or movies. Include a document title. Each show or movie should be a separate paragraph with its own heading. Adjust page breaks as needed to keep headings with their related paragraphs. Save the document as *[your initials]***10-19** and submit it.

Exercise 10-20

Create a document that includes three poems by three different poets. Use headings to identify each poet and title. Use page breaks to start each poem on a separate page. Save the document as *[your initials]***10-20** and submit it.

Exercise 10-21

Create a document that lists three different categories of restaurants in your area. Include descriptions of two to three restaurants per category. Format each category as a separate section and apply a different, page, paragraph, and character format to each. Save the document as *[your initials]***10-21** and submit it.

Page Numbers, Headers, and Footers

OBJECTIVES

After completing this lesson, you will be able to:

1. Add page numbers.

2. Change the starting page number.

3. Add headers and footers.

4. Work with headers and footers within sections.

5. Link section headers and footers.

6. Change starting page numbers.

7. Create continuation page headers.

8. Create alternate headers and footers.

MCAS OBJECTIVES

In this lesson:
WW 07 1.2.1
WW 07 1.2.2
WW 07 4.1.1
WW 07 4.1.3
WW 07 4.1.4

Estimated Time: 1½ hours

Page numbers, headers, and footers are useful additions to multiple-page documents. Page numbers can appear in either the top or bottom margin of a page. The text in the top margin of a page is a *header;* text in the bottom margin of a page is a *footer.* Headers and footers can also contain descriptive information about a document, such as the date, title, and author's name.

Adding Page Numbers

Word automatically keeps track of page numbers and indicates on the left side of the status bar the current page and the total number of pages in a document. Each time you add, delete, or format text or sections, Word adjusts page breaks and page numbers. This process, called *background repagination,* occurs automatically when you pause while working on a document. Right-click the status bar to select **Formatted Page Numbers**, **Section**, and **Page Number** options when working with long documents.

Figure 11-1
How Word paginates
when you open a
document

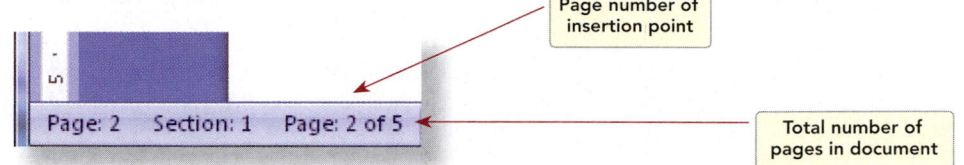

Page number of
insertion point

Total number of
pages in document

Exercise 11-1   ADD AND PREVIEW PAGE NUMBERS

Page numbers do not appear on a printed document unless you specify that they do. The simplest way to add page numbers is to click the Insert tab and click Page Number.

1. Open the file **History**.

2. With the insertion point at the top of the document, click the **Insert** tab and click the **Page Number** command. Word displays a list of options for placing your page number in the document. Notice that you can choose Top of Page, Bottom of Page, or Page Margins. Once you choose a position for the page number, you select a design from the gallery. A *gallery* is a list of design options for modifying elements of a page.

Figure 11-2
Page number
options

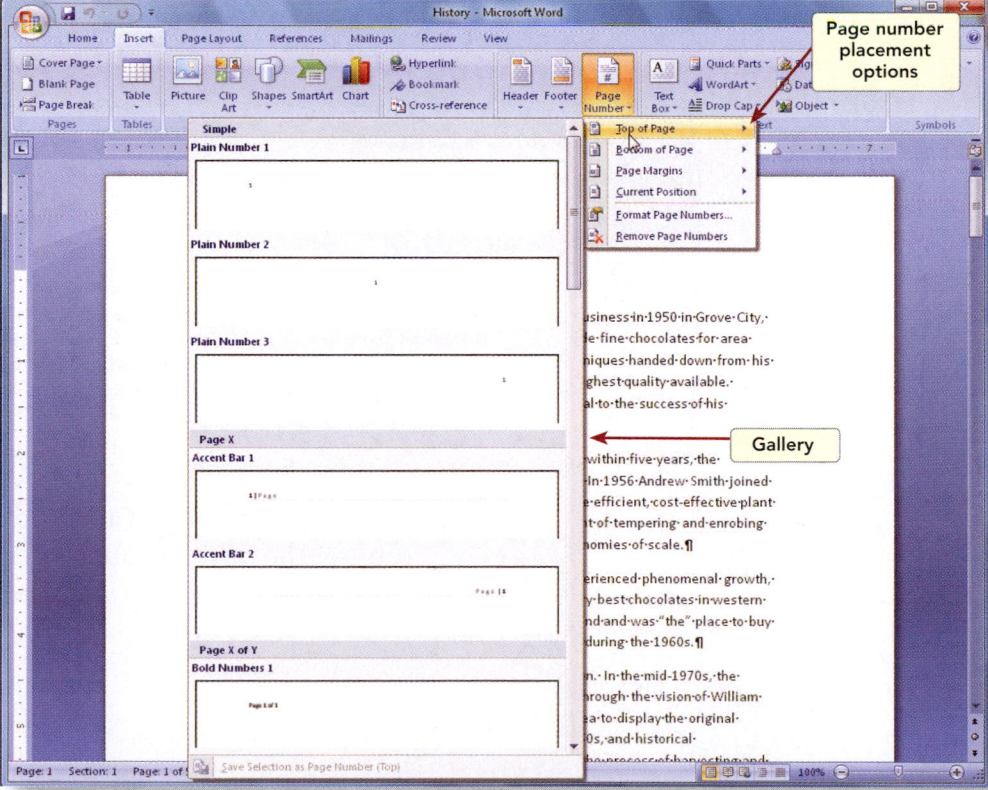

Word 2007

3. Click **Top of Page** to display the gallery for placing numbers at the top of the page. Click **Plain Number 3** to place a page number in the upper right corner of the document.

4. Scroll through the document to view the page numbers. By default Word places page numbers on every page.

5. Notice that the **Ribbon** adds a new tab when page numbers have been added to a document. The **Header and Footer Tools Design** tab includes additional options for formatting the document.

6. Click the Close Header and Footer button.

7. Click the **Insert** tab and click the Page Number button. Click **Bottom of Page** and scroll to the bottom of the gallery. Click **Triangle 2**. A page number appears at the bottom right corner of each page.

8. Switch to Print Preview, and notice that page numbers appear in the header and footer of the page.

9. Use the magnifier pointer to click the upper right corner of the first page. The page number appears within the 1-inch top margin. Specifically, the page number is positioned 0.5 inch from the top edge of the page at the right margin.

Figure 11-3
Viewing page numbers in Print Preview

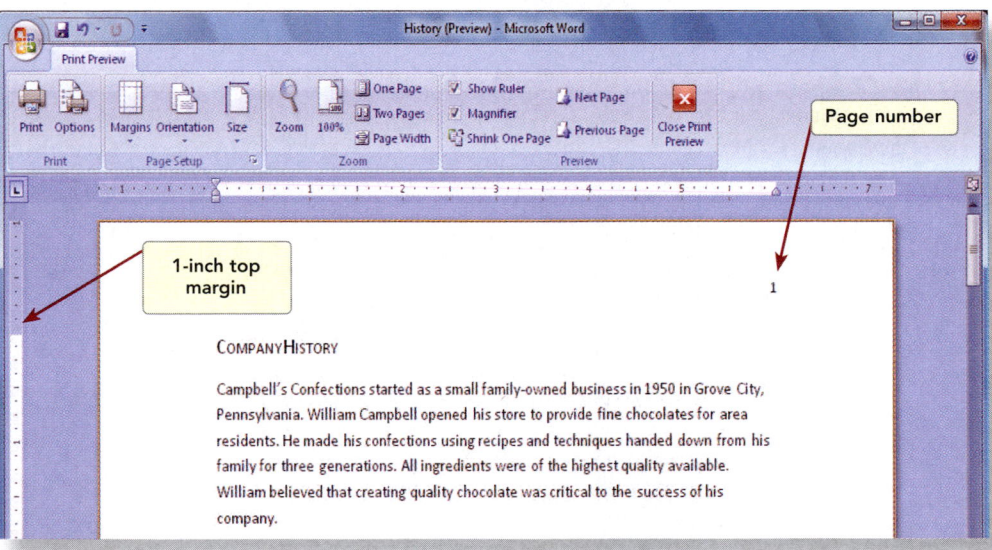

10. Close Print Preview. Click the Undo button to remove the page number in the footer.

Exercise 11-2   CHANGE THE POSITION AND FORMAT OF PAGE NUMBERS

Not only can you change the placement of page numbers and decide if you want to number the first page, but you can also change the format of page numbers. For example, instead of using traditional numerals such as 1, 2, and 3, you can use roman numerals (i, ii, iii) or letters (a, b, c). You can also start page numbering of a section with a different value. For instance, you could number the first page ii, B, or 2.

1. Double click the header of page 1. This activates the header pane (the area at the top of the page that contains the page number), displays the Headers and Footer Tools Design tab, and dims the document text.

2. Select the page number, and change the format of the number to italic using the Mini toolbar. Press Ctrl+E to center the number. Click the Undo button ↻ to undo the center alignment.

3. Locate the Header and Footer group on the Ribbon. Click the Page Number button 🔳 and click **Format Page Numbers**.

4. Open the **Number format** drop-down list, and choose uppercase roman numerals (I, II, III…). Click **OK**.

Figure 11-4
Page Number
Format dialog box

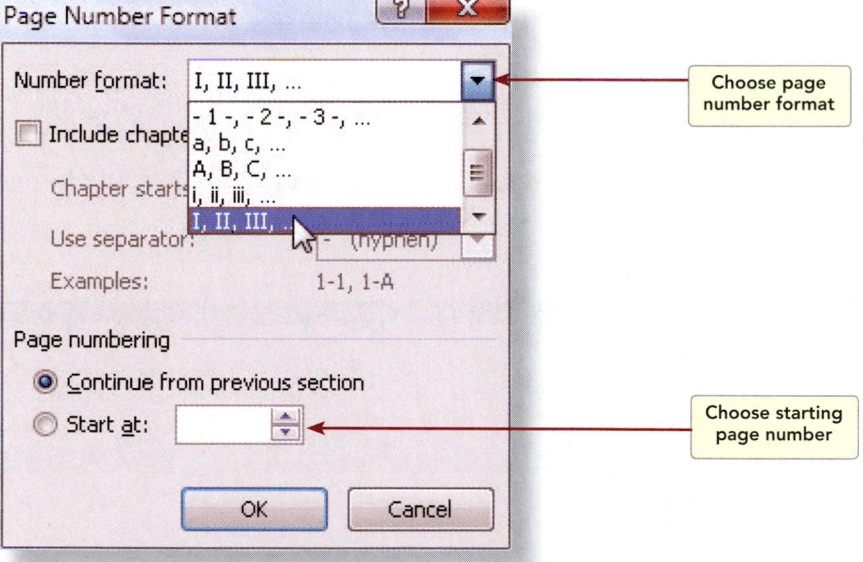

5. Locate the **Options** group on the Ribbon, and click **Different First Page**. Selecting the Different First Page option removes the page number from page 1 of the document. Click the Close Header and Footer button 🔳.

6. View the document in Print Preview, and note that page 1 does not display a page number. The header page numbering is now italic, starting with roman numeral II on page 2.

7. Close Print Preview.

Changing the Starting Page Number

In addition to formatting page numbers and changing the page number placement, you can change the starting page numbering. You can format a document with a cover page to display no page number on page 1 and define the actual page 2 of the document to display page number 1.

To add a cover page, click the Insert tab and click the Cover Page command. Select a design from the gallery, and the cover page automatically appears at the beginning of the document. You can also insert a blank page by clicking the Blank Page command on the Insert tab.

Exercise 11-3   ADD A COVER PAGE

1. Position the insertion point at the beginning of the document. Click the **Insert** tab, and click the Cover Page button . Click the **Sideline** design from the gallery. Click the text "[Type the document title]" and key **History**.

2. Notice that the cover page is not numbered. The second page of the document is numbered page 2.

3. Position the insertion point at the top of page 2. Click the **Insert** tab, and click the Page Number button . Click **Format Page Numbers**. Change the **Number format** to **1, 2, 3**, and change the **Start at** number to **0**. Click **OK**.

Figure 11-5
Preview Page Numbers

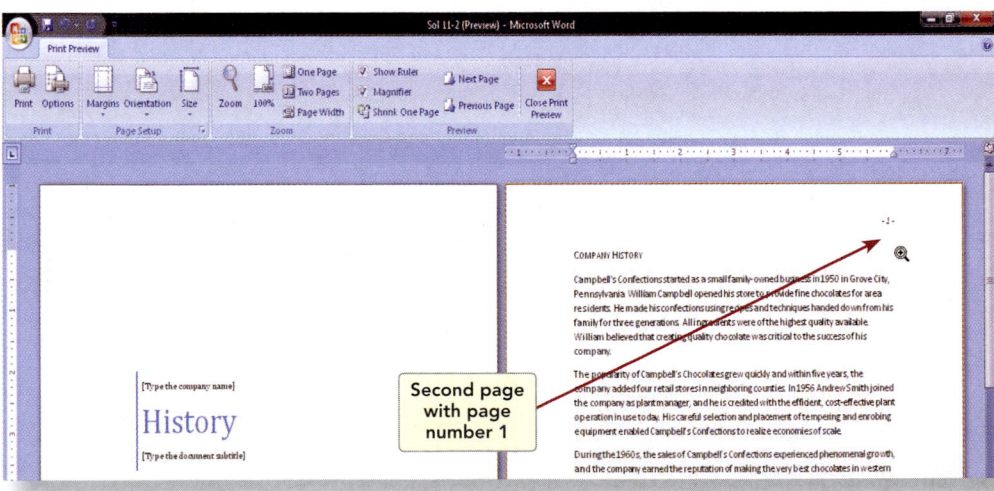

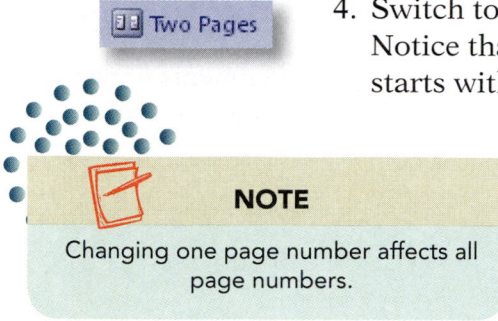

4. Switch to Print Preview, and click the Two Pages button 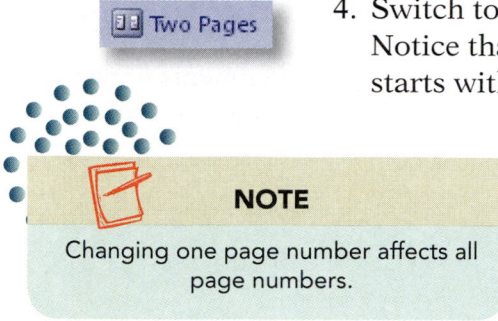. Notice that the cover page is not numbered and that page numbering starts with one on page 2. Close Print Preview.

5. Double-click the page number of page 2 of the document. Position the insertion point to the immediate left of the page number. Key **Page** and press Spacebar once.

NOTE

Changing one page number affects all page numbers.

6. Scroll to the header pane on page 3 to view the revised header text.

Figure 11-6
Formatted page number with "Page" added

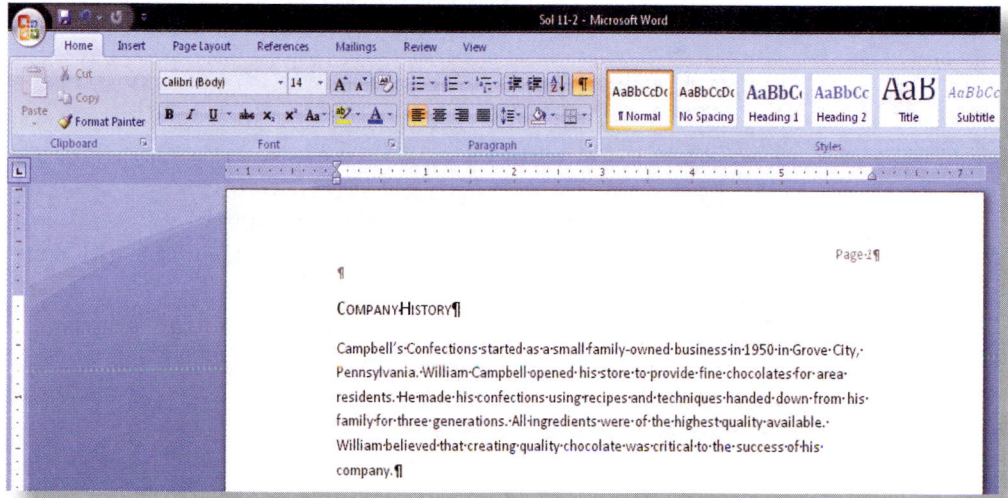

7. Save the document as *[your initials]*11-3 in your Lesson 11 folder.

Exercise 11-4   REMOVE PAGE NUMBERS

To remove page numbers, delete the text in the header or footer area or click the Remove Page Numbers command.

1. Click the **Insert** tab, and click the Page Number button . Click **Remove Page Numbers**.

2. Scroll the document and notice that the page numbers in the header and footer are deleted.

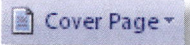

3. Click the Cover Page button , and click **Remove Current Cover Page**.

4. Close the document without saving it.

Adding Headers and Footers

Headers and footers are typically used in multiple-page documents to display descriptive information. In addition to page numbers, a header or footer can contain:

- The document name
- The date and/or the time you created or revised the document
- An author's name
- A graphic, such as a company logo
- A draft or revision number

This descriptive information can appear in many different combinations. For example, the second page of a business letter typically contains a header with the name of the addressee, the page number, and the date. A report can contain a footer with the report name and a header with the page number and chapter name. A newsletter might contain a header with a title and logo on the first page and a footer with the title and page number on the pages that follow.

Figure 11-7
Examples of headers and footers

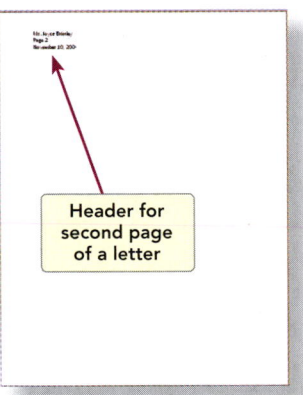

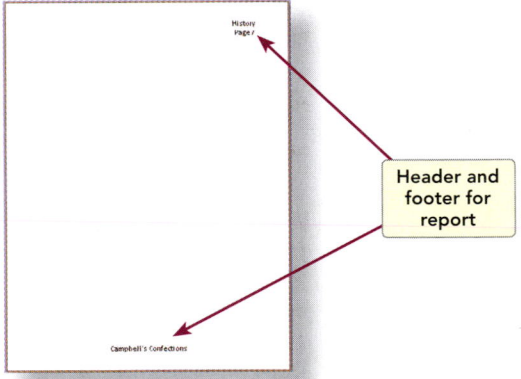

Exercise 11-5   ADD A HEADER TO A DOCUMENT

1. Open the file **History - 2**. This file is a six-page document with a title page. You will add a header and footer to pages 2 through 6.

2. Click the **Insert** tab, and click the Header button . Click the **Blank** design at the top of the Header gallery. Word displays the Header and Footer Tools Design tab, and the header pane is also visible.

3. Click the Different First Page check box [☑ Different First Page]. This enables you to give the document two different headers—a header for the title page, which you will leave blank, and a header for the rest of the document, which will contain identifying text. Notice that this header pane is labeled "**First Page Header**."

[⊞ Next Section]

4. Click the Next Section button [⊞ Next Section]. Notice that this header pane is labeled "**Header**." The Previous Section button [⊞ Previous Section] and the Next Section button [⊞ Next Section] are useful when you move between different headers and footers within sections of a document, as you will see later in the lesson.

> **NOTE**
>
> These preset tab settings are default settings for a document with the default 1-inch left and right margins. In such a document, the 3.25-inch tab centers text and the 6.5-inch tab right-aligns text. This document, however, has 1.25-inch left and right margins, so it is best to adjust the tabs.

5. Key **Campbell's Confections History** in the page 2 header pane. This text now appears on every page of the document except the first page.

6. Press [Tab] once. Notice that the ruler has two preset tab settings: 3.25-inch centered and 6.5-inch right-aligned. Drag the center tab marker to 3 inches on the ruler and the right-aligned tab marker to the right margin (6 inches). Press [Tab] again to move to the right-aligned tab setting.

[⊞ Quick Parts ▾]

7. Click the Quick Parts button [⊞ Quick Parts ▾], and click **Building Blocks Organizer**. Click the **Gallery** heading to alphabetize the Building Blocks by Gallery.

8. Scroll through the Building blocks to locate the **Page Numbers** Gallery. Click to select **Bold Numbers 3** and to preview the page number Building block.

9. Click **Insert**, and notice that the page number displays on the right margin, but the text on the left margin of the header disappeared. Click the Undo button [↶ ▾].

10. Click the Quick Parts button [⊞ Quick Parts ▾], and click **Field**. Scroll the list of **Field names** to locate the **Page** field and click it one time. Click the **1, 2, 3 Format**, and click **OK**. Word inserts the page number. Click to the immediate left of the page number, and key **Page**, and press [Spacebar].

[⊞ Previous Section]

11. Click the Previous Section button [⊞ Previous Section] and notice that the first-page header pane is still blank. Click the Next Section button [⊞ Next Section] to return to the header you created.

Word 2007

TABLE 11-1 Header and Footer Tools Design Tab

Button	Name	Purpose
Header	Header	Edit the document header.
Footer	Footer	Edit the document footer.
Page Number	Insert Page Number	Insert the page number.
Date & Time	Date and Time	Insert the current date or time.
Quick Parts ▾	Quick Parts	Insert common header or footer items, such as running total page numbers (for example, page 1 of 10).
Picture	Picture	Insert a picture from a file.
Clip Art	Clip Art	Insert clip art.
Go to Header	Go to Header	Activates header for editing.
Go to Footer	Go to Footer	Activates footer for editing.
Previous Section	Previous Section	Show the header or footer of the previous section.
Next Section	Next Section	Show the header or footer of the next section.
Link to Previous	Link to Previous	Link or unlink the header or footer in one section to or from the header or footer in the previous section.
☑ Different First Page	Different First Page	Create a header and footer for the first page of the document.
☐ Different Odd & Even Pages	Different Odd and Even Pages	Specify a header or footer for odd-numbered pages and a different header or footer for even-numbered pages.
☑ Show Document Text	Show Document Text	Display or hide the document text.
Header from Top: 0.5"	Header from Top	Specify height of header area.
Footer from Bottom: 0.5"	Footer from Bottom	Specify height of footer area.
Insert Alignment Tab	Insert Alignment Tab	Insert a tab stop.

Exercise 11-6   ADD A FOOTER TO A DOCUMENT

1. With the header on page 2 displayed, click the Go to Footer button to display the footer pane.

2. Key your name and press [Tab].

3. Save the document as *[your initials]*11-6 in your Lesson 11 folder.

4. With the insertion point at the center of the footer, click the Quick Parts button on the Header and Footer Tools Design tab. Click **Field**. The Field dialog box displays.

5. Click **CreateDate** from the **Field names** list. Click the third item in the **Date formats** list. Click **OK**. A field is inserted that displays the date the document was created.

6. Press [Tab] and click Quick Parts. Click **Field** and scroll the list of **Field names** to locate **FileName**. Click **FileName** and notice that a list of **Field properties** appears. Click **First capital**. Click **OK**.

Figure 11-8
Inserting fields

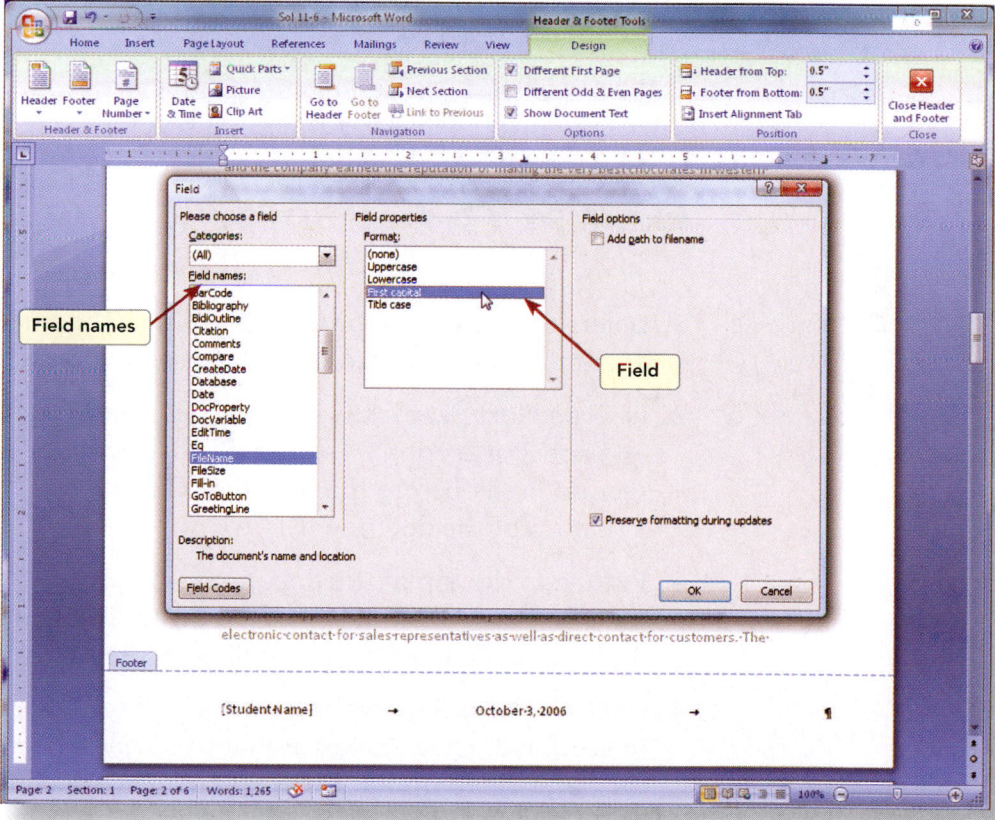

7. View the footer text. The document's filename is inserted. This footer information prints at the bottom of each page except the first.

8. Improve the tab positions by dragging the center tab marker to 3 inches and the right tab marker to 6 inches. (Remember, this document has 1.25-inch left and right margins, not the default 1-inch margins.)

9. Click the Close Header and Footer button to return to the document.

10. Switch to Print Preview. Check that no header or footer appears on the title page. Scroll through each page and view the header and footer.

11. Return to Page Layout view and save the document. Leave it open for the next exercise.

Adding Headers and Footers within Sections

Section breaks have an impact on page numbers, headers, and footers. For example, you can number each section differently or add different headers and footers.

When you add page numbers to a document, it is best to add the page numbers first and then add the section breaks.

Exercise 11-7   ADD SECTIONS TO A DOCUMENT WITH HEADERS AND FOOTERS

1. Delete the hard page break that follows the title page of the document, and insert a Next Page section break.

2. Insert a Next Page section break before the heading "Fundraising" on page 2 of section 2 (page 3 of the document) and a Next Page section break before the heading "Chronology" on page 2 of section 3 (page 5 of the document).

3. Return to the top of the document (by pressing Ctrl + Home), and click the **Insert** tab. Click the Header button . Click **Edit Header**. Notice that the blank header pane indicates the section number.

4. Click the Next Section button 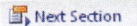 to move to the next header, in section 2, page 1. Notice that this header is also blank, because the Page Setup option **Different First Page** was selected for the entire document. This means the first page of each section can have a different header or footer than the rest of the pages in the section or it can have no header or footer.

5. Click the Next Section button 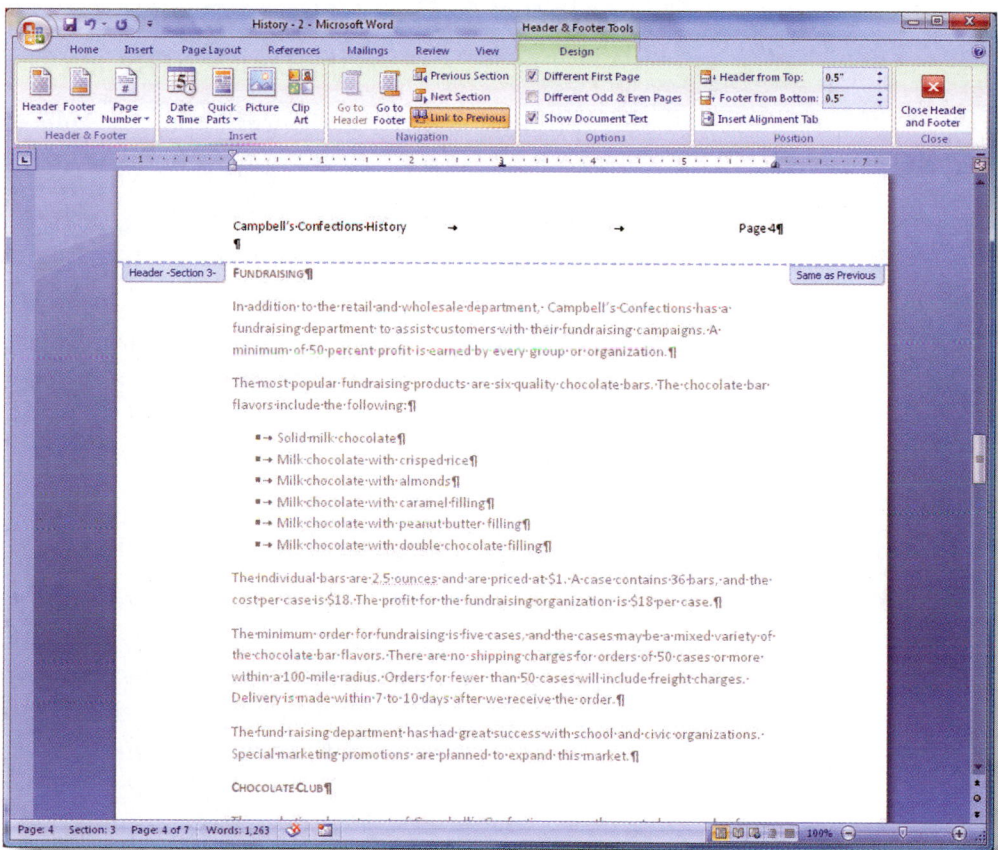 again to move to section 2, page 2. The header and footer begin on page 3.

6. Click the Next Section button to move to section 3, page 1. Because the **Different First Page** option applies to the document, the first page of this section also has no header or footer.

7. Turn off the **Different First Page** option for section 3 by clicking the Different First Page button on the Ribbon to clear the check box. Now page 1 of section 3 starts with the document header and footer. Turning off this option applies only to this section, as you will see in the next step.

Figure 11-9
The header on page 1, section 3, of the document

☑ Different First Page

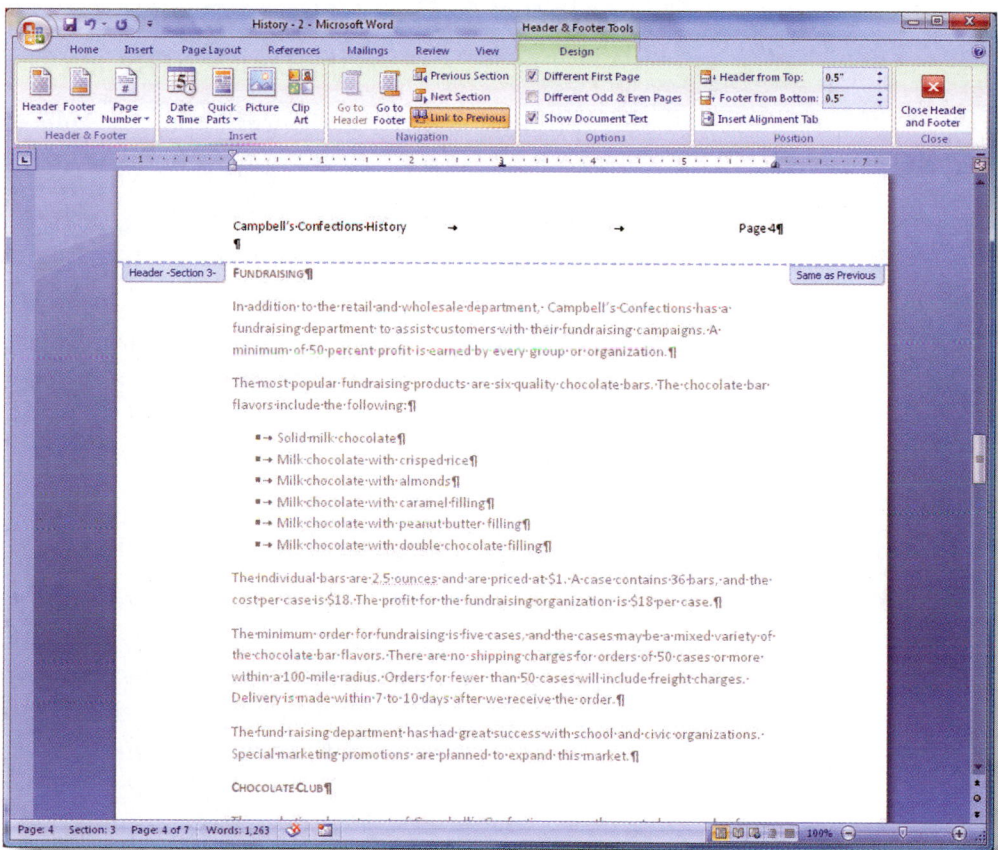

8. Click the Previous Section button twice to move to the header on page 1 of section 2. Notice that the header pane is still blank because the **Different First Page** option is still checked for this section.

9. Repeat step 7 to turn off the **Different First Page** option for this section. Now the header and footer start on page 1 of section 2. Repeat for section 4.

10. View each header in the document by dragging the scroll box (on the vertical scroll bar) down one page at a time. As you display each page's header, notice the page numbering. Also notice that the text "Same as Previous" appears on the header panes.

Linking Section Headers and Footers

By default, the Link to Previous command is "on" when you work in a header or footer pane. As a result, the text you originally enter in the header (and the footer) for the document is the same from section to section. Any change you make in one section header or footer is reflected in all other sections. You can use the Link to Previous command to break the link between header/footer text from one section to another section and enter different header or footer text for a section.

> **NOTE**
>
> Breaking the link for the header does not break the link for the footer. You must unlink them separately.

Exercise 11-8   LINK AND UNLINK SECTION HEADERS AND FOOTERS

1. Scroll to the header for section 3, page 1, select the text "Campbell's Confections History" and apply italic formatting.

2. Click the Previous Section button 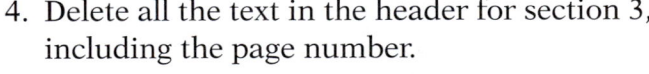 to move to the header in section 2. The header text is italic, demonstrating the link that exists between section headers and footers.

3. Click the Next Section button 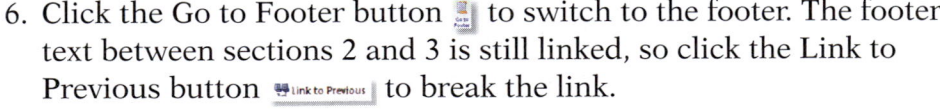 to return to section 3, page 1. Click the Link to Previous button to turn off this option. Now sections 2 and 3 are unlinked and you can create a different header or footer for section 3.

4. Delete all the text in the header for section 3, including the page number.

> **TIP**
>
> To select text in a header or footer, you can point and click from the area to the immediate left of the header or footer pane.

5. Press Tab to move to the center tab setting and key **Supplement**. Press Tab again and click the **Quick Parts** button. Click **Field**, and select **Page** in the **Field names** list box. Select the first number format, and click **OK**. Drag the center tab marker to 3 inches and the right tab marker to 6 inches, as needed.

6. Click the Go to Footer button to switch to the footer. The footer text between sections 2 and 3 is still linked, so click the Link to Previous button to break the link.

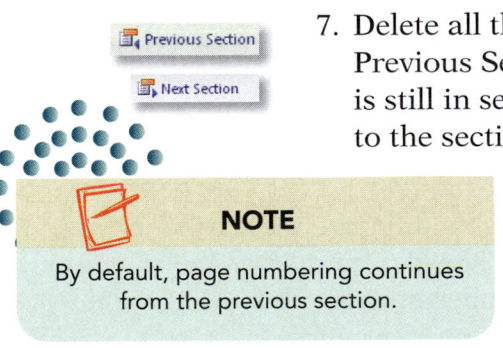

7. Delete all the footer text in section 3 except your name. Click the Previous Section button to see that the original footer text is still in section 2. Click the Next Section button to return to the section 3 footer.

8. Click the Link to Previous button to restore the link between section footers. When Word asks if you want to delete the current text and connect to the text from the previous section, click **Yes**.

> **NOTE**
>
> By default, page numbering continues from the previous section.

Figure 11-10
Restoring the link between section footers

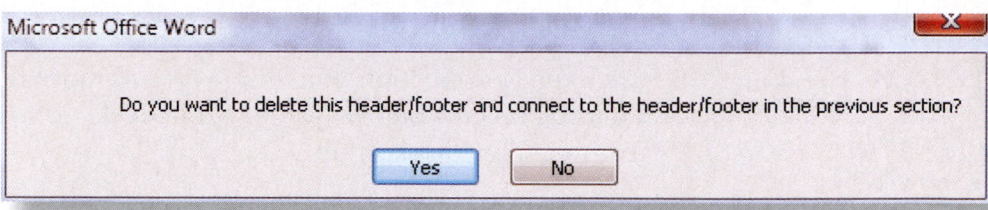

9. With the link and the original footer text restored, click the Close Header and Footer button .

10. Format the title page attractively. Adjust page breaks throughout the document as needed.

11. Save the document as *[your initials]***11-8**. Print the document six pages per sheet.

Changing the Starting Page Number

So far, you have seen page numbering start either with 1 on page 1 or 2 on page 2. When documents have multiple sections, you might need to change the starting page number. For example, in the current document, section 1 is the title page and the header on section 2 begins numbering with page 2. You can change this format so numbering starts in section 2, page 1, with page 1.

Exercise 11-9 CHANGE THE STARTING PAGE NUMBER

1. Double-click the page number on section 2, page 1 to display the header.

2. Click the Page Number button , and click **Format Page Numbers** to open the Page Number Format dialog box.

3. Change the **Start at** number to **1**.

Figure 11-11
Changing the starting page number for any part of a document

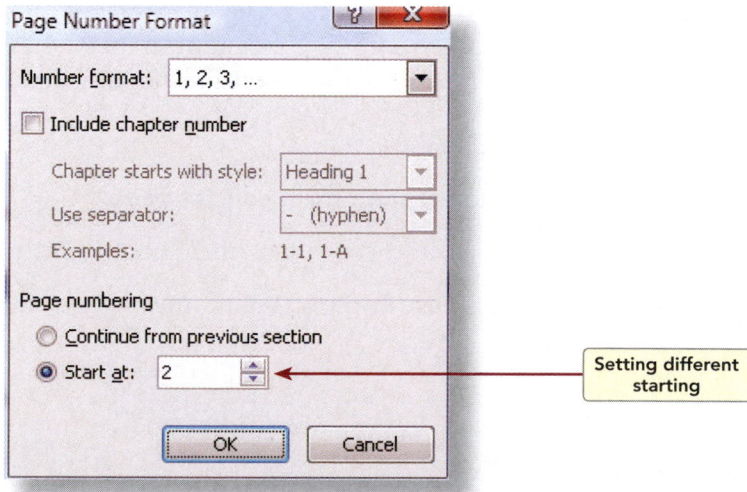

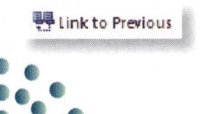

4. Click **OK**. Section 2 now starts with page 1.

5. Click the Next Section button 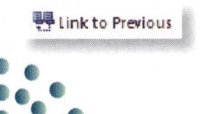 to move to section 3. Click the Link to Previous button and click **Yes** to restore the header from the previous section.

6. Open the **Page Number Format** dialog box. Choose the option **Continue from previous section** if necessary. Click **OK**. Notice that the section header begins with page 4.

7. Save the document as *[your initials]***11-9** in your Lesson 11 folder.

8. Submit and close the document.

Creating Continuation Page Headers

It is customary to use a header on the second page of a business letter or memo. A continuation page header for a letter or memo is typically a three-line block of text that includes the addressee's name, the page number, and the date.

There are three rules for letters and memos with continuation page headers:

- Page 1 must have a 2-inch top margin.

- Continuation pages must have a 1-inch top margin.

- Two blank lines must appear between the header and the continuation page text.

Exercise 11-10   ADD A CONTINUATION PAGE HEADER TO A LETTER

The easiest way to create a continuation page header using the proper business format is to apply these settings to your document:

- Top margin: 2 inches.

- Header position: 1 inch from edge of page.

- Page Setup Layout for Headers and Footers: Different First Page.

- Additional spacing: Add two blank lines to the end of the header.

By default, headers and footers are positioned 0.5 inch from the top or bottom edge of the page. When you change the position of a continuation page header to 1 inch, the continuation page appears to have a 1-inch top margin, beginning with the header text. The document text begins at the page's 2-inch margin, and the two additional blank lines in the continuation header ensure correct spacing between the header text and the document text.

1. Open the file **Mendez**.

2. Add the date to the top of the letter, followed by three blank lines.

3. Open the **Page Setup** dialog box, and display the **Layout** tab. Check **Different first page** under **Headers and Footers**. Set the **Header** to 1 inch **From edge**.

4. Click the **Margins** tab, and set a 2-inch top margin and 1.25-inch left and right margins. Click **OK**.

5. Click the **Insert** tab, and click the Header button 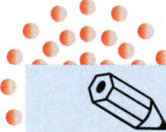. Click **Edit Header** to display the header pane.

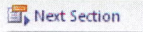

6. Click the Next Section button ![Next Section] to move to the header pane on page 2.

7. Create the header in Figure 11-12, inserting the information as shown. Press Enter twice after the last line.

Figure 11-12

```
Ms. Isabel Mendez

Page [Click Quick Parts, Field, Page for the page number.]

[Click Date and Time for the current date.]
```

TIP

Letters and memos should use the spelled-out date format (for example, December 25, 2007), and the date should not be a field that updates each time you open the document. To insert the date as text, with the correct format, click the Date and Time command and clear the Update automatically check box.

Word 2007

Figure 11-13
Continuation page header for a letter

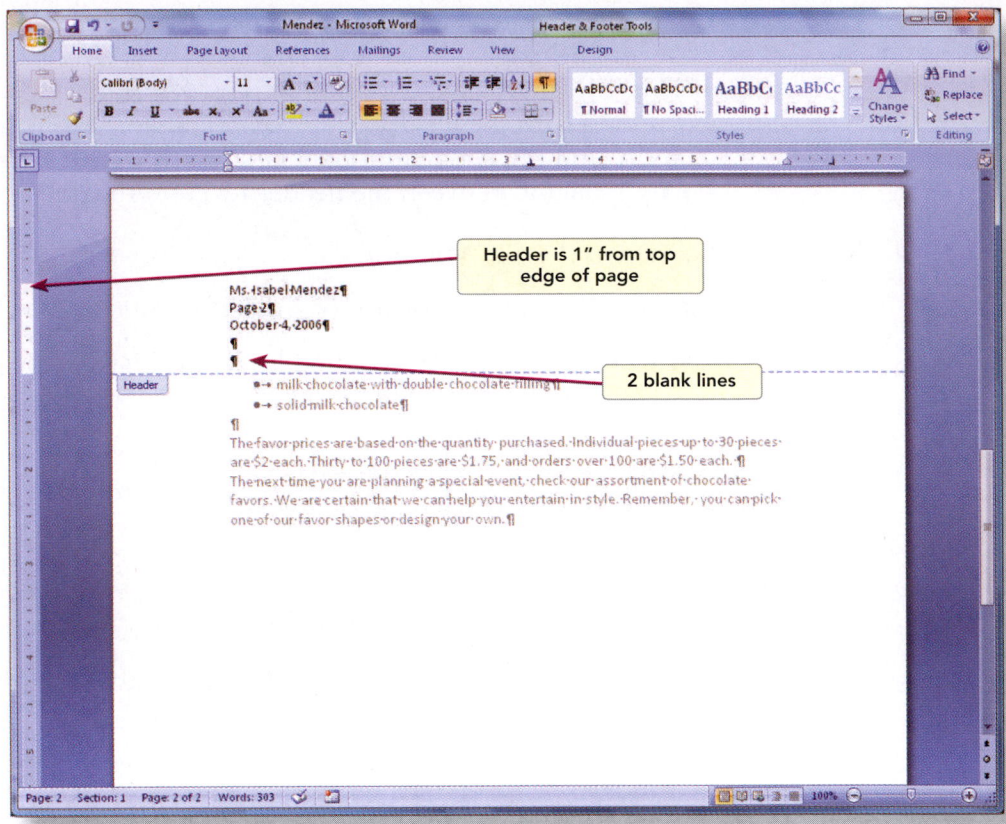

8. Close the header pane, and view both pages in Print Preview. Close Print Preview.

9. Add a complimentary closing, and key **Lydia Hamrick** and the title **Customer Service** at the end of the letter, followed by your reference initials.

10. Save the document as *[your initials]*11-10 in your Lesson 11 folder.

11. Submit, and close the document.

Creating Alternate Headers and Footers

In addition to customizing headers and footers for different sections of a document, you can also change them for odd and even pages throughout a section or document. For example, a textbook displays the unit name for even pages and displays the lesson name for odd pages.

Exercise 11-11   **CREATE ALTERNATE FOOTERS IN A DOCUMENT**

To create alternate headers or footers in a document, you use the **Different odd and even** check box and then create a header or footer for both even and odd pages.

1. Open the file **History - 2**. Delete the page break on page 1 and insert a next page section break.

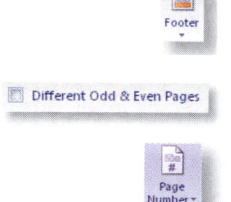

2. Position the insertion point in section 1, click the **Insert** tab, and click the Footer button .

3. Click **Edit Footer**, and click the Different Odd and Even Pages button 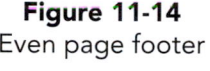 . Click the Different First Page button so the first page does not display a footer.

4. Click the Next Section button , and verify that the insertion point is in the Even Page Footer pane.

5. Click the Footer button , and scroll through the gallery. Select **Transcend (Even Page)**. The footer displays on page 2.

Figure 11-14
Even page footer

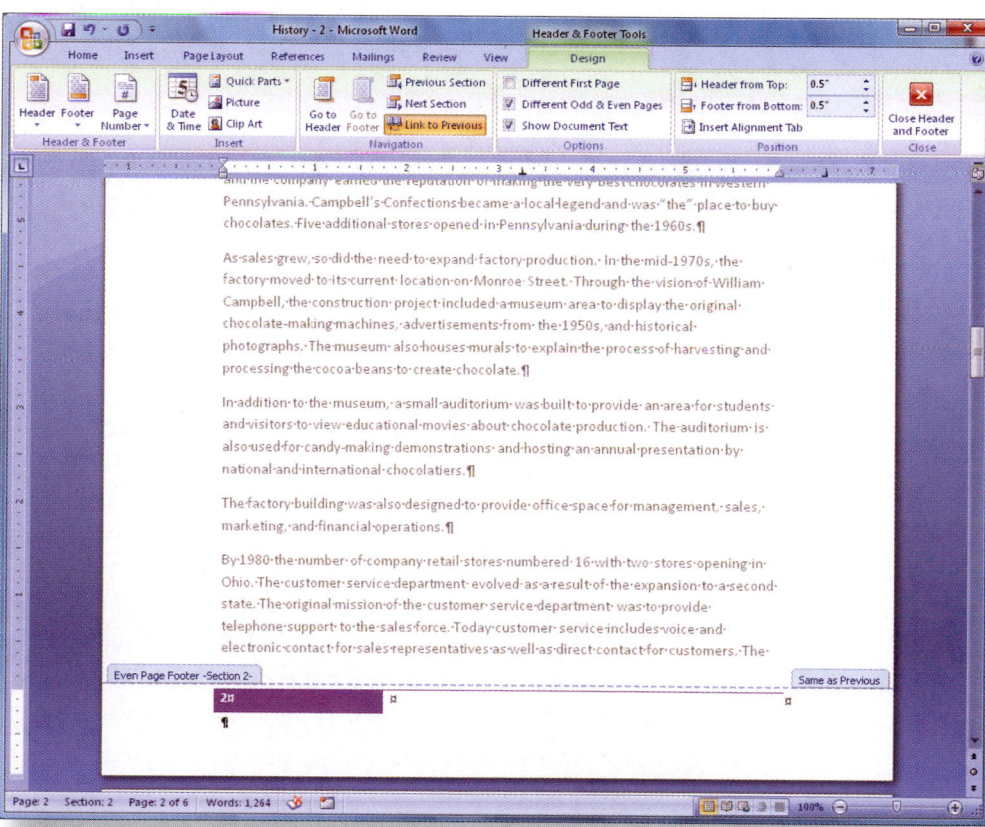

6. Click the Next Section button  to move to the footer on page 3. The footer pane is labeled "**Odd Page Footer**" and is blank.

7. Click the Footer button , and scroll through the gallery. Select **Transcend (Odd Page)**. The footer displays on page 3.

8. Click the Close Header and Footer button, and switch to Print Preview.

9. Click the Zoom Level button 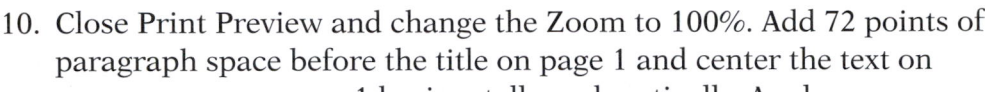, and click the Many Pages button. Drag over the grid to select six pages. Click **OK**. View each page of the document. Notice the position of the page number on the odd and even pages.

10. Close Print Preview and change the Zoom to 100%. Add 72 points of paragraph space before the title on page 1 and center the text on page 1 horizontally and vertically. Apply a page border to section 1. Adjust page breaks throughout the document as needed.

11. Save the document as *[your initials]***11-11** in your Lesson 11 folder.

12. Print the document four pages per sheet, or submit the document, and then close it.

NOTE

To create different odd and even headers or footers within a section, you must first break the link between that section's header or footer and the previous section's header or footer.

Lesson 11 Summary

- A header is text that appears in the top margin of the printed page; a footer is text that appears in the bottom margin. These text areas are used for page numbers, document titles, the date, and other information.

- Always add page numbers to long documents. You can choose the position of page numbers (examples: bottom centered or top right) and the format (examples: 1, 2, 3 or A, B, C). You can also choose to number the first page or begin numbering on the second page.

- Check page numbers in Print Preview or Print Layout view (they are not visible in Draft view). In Print Layout view, you can activate the header or footer pane that contains the page number by double-clicking the text and then modify the page number text (examples: apply bold format or add the word "Page" before the number).

- To remove page numbers, activate the header or footer pane that contains the numbering, select the text, and then delete it. You can also click the Page Number command and select Remove Page Numbers.

- To add header or footer text to a document, click the Insert tab, and click Header or Footer. Select a design from the gallery. Use the Header and Footer Tools Design tab buttons to insert the date and time or to insert Quick Parts for the filename, author, print date, or other information. See Table 11-1.

- Adjust the tab marker positions in the header or footer pane as needed to match the width of the text area.

- A document can have a header or footer on the first page different from the rest of the pages. Apply the Different first page option in the Page Setup dialog box (Layout tab), or use the Different First Page button on the Ribbon, Header & Footer Tools Design tab.

- Header and footer text is repeated from section to section because headers and footers are linked by default. To unlink section headers and footers, click the Link to Previous command. To relink the header or footer, click the button again.

- Sections can have different starting page numbers. Click the Page Number command to open the Page Number Format dialog box, and then set the starting page number.

- Memos or letters that are two pages or longer should have a continuation page header—a three-line block containing the addressee's name, page number, and date. Set the header to 1 inch from the edge, add two blank lines below the header, and use a 2-inch top margin. Apply the Different first page option, and leave the first-page header blank.

- Use the Ribbon, Header and Footer Tools Design Tab, or the Page Setup dialog box to change the position of the header or footer text from the edge of the page. The default position is 0.5 inch.

- A document can have different headers and footers on odd and even pages. Apply the Different odd and even option.

LESSON 11		Command Summary	
Feature	**Button**	**Command**	**Keyboard**
Add page numbers		**Insert** tab, **Page Number**	
Change page number format		**Insert** tab, **Page Number, Format Page Numbers**	
Add or edit header		**Insert** tab, **Header**	
Add or edit footer		**Insert** tab, **Footer**	
Change layout settings		**Page Layout** tab, **Page Setup** or **Header and Footer Tools Design** tab	

Concepts Review

True/False Questions

Each of the following statements is either true or false. Indicate your choice by circling T or F.

T F   1. The simplest way to add page numbers is to choose Page Numbers from the Page Layout tab.

T F   2. You can position a page number as a header or a footer.

T F   3. You can change the number format (for example, from numbers to roman numerals) by using the Page Number Format dialog box.

T F   4. You can apply character formatting to headers and footers in Draft view.

T F   5. A gallery displays designs for page numbers, headers, and footers.

T F   6. Deselect the Link to Previous command on the Header and Footer Tools Design tab to unlink a header in one section to the header in the previous section.

T F   7. Use Quick Parts to insert fields and document properties.

T F   8. The only way to create alternate page headers or footers is to use the Page Setup dialog box.

Short Answer Questions

Write the correct answer in the space provided.

1. What is the name of the process in which Word automatically adjusts page numbers and page breaks when you edit a document?

   _____

2. In addition to numbering such as 1, 2, 3 and roman numerals such as I, II, III, what other page number formatting can you use?

   _____

3. Which option do you use to leave the first page of a document blank and begin a header or footer on the second page?

   _____

4. Which Ribbon tab displays the Header and Footer buttons?

   _____

5. [Previous Section] is used for what purpose?

_____

6. What three items are included in a continuation page header for a letter?

_____

7. By default, how far from the edge of the page does Word print headers and footers?

_____

8. If you create different odd and even pages in a document, how is the header pane on page 1 labeled?

_____

Critical Thinking

Answer these questions on a separate page. There are no right or wrong answers. Support your answers with examples from your own experience, if possible.

1. What information do you think most businesses would include in the header or footer for a business report? Does the information included in a business report header or footer differ from the information found in a business letter header or footer?

2. Where do you prefer to place the page number in a business report? In a business letter? Explain your answer.

Skills Review

Exercise 11-12

Add and modify page numbers and add a header.

1. Open the file **Chronology - 2**.
2. Add page numbers to the bottom of each page by following these steps:

    a. Click the **Insert** tab, and click the Page Number button .
    b. Click **Bottom of Page**, scroll through the gallery, and click to select **Two Bars 1**. Close the **Header and Footer Tools Design** tab.
3. Modify the page numbers in Print Layout view by following these steps:
    a. Scroll to the bottom of page 1 to see the page number.
    b. Double-click the page number to activate the footer pane.

c. Drag the I-beam over the page number, and click the Bold button 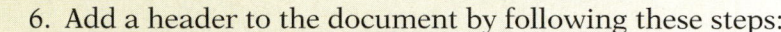 and the Italic button on the Mini toolbar. Change the **Font Size** to 14.

d. Close the Header and Footer Tools Design tab.

4. Add 72 points of spacing before the title on page 1.

5. View the document in Print Preview; then display it in Print Layout view.

6. Add a header to the document by following these steps:

a. Click the **Insert** tab, and click the Header button . Click the **Blank** design at the top of the gallery.

b. Press Tab twice to position the insertion point at the right-aligned tab setting.

c. Key your name, followed by a comma and space.

d. Click the Quick Parts button 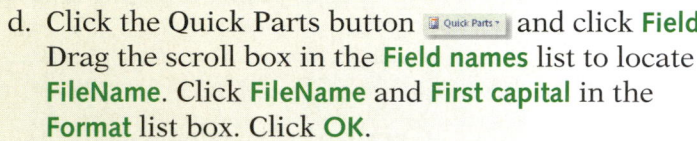 and click **Field**. Drag the scroll box in the **Field names** list to locate **FileName**. Click **FileName** and **First capital** in the **Format** list box. Click **OK**.

e. Close the Header and Footer Tools Design tab.

7. Save the document as *[your initials]*11-12 in your Lesson 11 folder.

8. Submit and close the document.

NOTE

The filename Chronology - 2 will change to the filename you assign the document after you close and reopen the document, print the document, or update the field.

Exercise 11-13

Add a footer to a document with sections, unlink the header, and change the starting page number.

1. Open the file **Wrapper - 2**.

2. Insert a **Next page** section break at "CAMPBELL'S CONFECTIONS."

3. On page 2, section 2, justify the text vertically on the page.

4. Create a footer for section 2 that is not linked to section 1 by following these steps:

a. Move the insertion point to section 2, and click the **Insert** tab. Click the Footer button and select the **Blank design**.

b. Click the Link to Previous button to unlink the section 2 footer from section 1 (to keep the section 1 footer blank) and key ***Instructions for the design of the wrapper are on the application form.**

c. Press Tab and key **Page**. Insert a space, click the Quick Parts button , click **Field**, click **Page** in the **Field names** list, and **1, 2, 3** in the **Format** list.

d. Click the Previous Section button to show the footer for section 1, which should be blank.

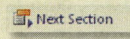

5. Change the starting page number of section 2 to page 1 by following these steps:

    a. Click the Next Section button to go back to section 2.

    b. Click the Page Number button 📄, and click **Format Page Numbers**.

    c. Click **Start at** and make sure the number 1 appears in the text box. Click **OK** and then close the Header and Footer Tools Design tab.

6. Change the top margin in section 1 to 2 inches.

7. Save the document as *[your initials]*11-13 in your Lesson 11 folder.

8. Print the document two pages per sheet, or submit the document, and then close it.

Exercise 11-14

Create a continuation page header for a memo.

1. Open the file **Bio Memo**. Delete the page break and insert a Next Page section break.

2. Key the current date in the memo heading.

3. Open the **Page Setup** dialog box, and change the top margin to 2 inches. Change the left and right margins to 1.25 inches. Click the Layout tab and click to select **Different first page**. Click **OK**.

4. Add a continuation page header to page 2 of the memo by following these steps:

    a. Click the **Insert** tab, and click the Header button 📄. Click **Blank.**

    b. Click the Next Section button to move to the header on page 2.

    c. Change the **Header from Top** setting to 1 inch. (**Header & Footer Tools Design** tab, **Position** group.)

    d. Key the text in Figure 11-15, inserting the information as shown.

Figure 11-15

```
Staff
Page [Click Quick Parts, Field, Page, and Format.]
[Key current date or insert as text.]
```

    e. To insert the current date in the correct format, click the Date and Time button 📅 and select the correct format. Be sure to clear the Update automatically box so the memo date does not change.

    f. Press [Enter] twice after the date and verify that there are two blank lines following the date.

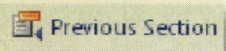

5. Click the Previous Section button to check that no header appears on page 1, and close the Header and Footer Tools Design tab.

6. Adjust line and page breaks if necessary.

7. Save the document as *[your initials]*11-14 in your Lesson 11 folder.

8. Submit and close the document.

Exercise 11-15

Add alternate footers to a document, and add a different first page footer.

1. Open the file **Guidelines - 2**.

2. Add a page break before the bold heading "Identification Numbers."

3. Move the insertion point to the top of the document (page 1).

4. Create a footer that appears only on even pages by following these steps:

   a. Click the **Insert** tab, and click the Footer button. Click Blank at the top of the gallery.

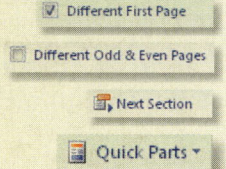

   b. Click the Different First Page button and the Different Odd and Even Pages button.

   c. Click the Next Section button to move to the Even Page Footer.

   d. Key **Guidelines—New Store Owners**. Press Tab twice.

   e. Key **Page** and press Spacebar. Click the Quick Parts button, click **Field**, click **Page**, and click the **1, 2, 3** format. Click **OK**.

   f. Select the footer text, and use the Mini toolbar to apply italic formatting.

5. Create and format a footer that appears only on odd pages by following these steps:

   a. Click the Next Section button to move to the odd page footer pane on page 3.

   b. Click the Date and Time button. Click the third format.

6. Close the Header and Footer Tools Design tab.

7. On page 1, format the two-line title in bold, 14 points, and all caps. Apply bold and small caps formatting to "Campbell's Confections." Apply italic formatting to "Preliminary Draft." Vertically center the text on the first page, and apply a page border to section 1.

8. View the document in Print Preview. Check the odd and even footers, and make sure the first page footer is blank.

9. Save the document as *[your initials]*11-15 in your Lesson 11 folder.

10. Submit and close the document.

Lesson Applications

Exercise 11-16

Add page numbers, change the page number font, and adjust the starting page number.

1. Open the file **Directory - 2**.

2. Position the insertion point at the beginning of the document, and click the Insert tab. Click Blank Page.

3. Format page 1 as a memo. The memo is to the staff from Barbara Bumgarner. Use today's date, and the subject is "Updated Directory." Key the text in Figure 11-16.

Figure 11-16

Attached is an updated directory for the corporate office and Campbell's *Confections'*
stores in (PA), (OH), and (WV). A few of *the* area codes have changed so you may
need to update your files.

Our goal is to have tollfree numbers for all stores by ~~the end of the year~~ *December*.
We will update the directory on an on going basis, and changes will be
emailed to you.

If information pertaining to your department changes, please notify me.
~~immediately~~.

4. Replace the page break after page 1 with a Next Page section break. Go to page 2, and insert a Next Page section break immediately preceding the bold heading "Pennsylvania." Insert a page break preceding the bold headings "Ohio" and "West Virginia."

5. Add page numbering to section 2 only. (Be sure to place the insertion point in section 2 first.) Position the page numbers at the bottom center of the section and select the Thick Line design from the gallery. Change the start number to 1.

6. In the footer of section 3, select the page number and change the format to 11-point Arial.

7. View the page numbers in Print Preview.

8. Format the memo on page 1 with a 2-inch top margin. Format the first three lines of section 2, and key today's date.

9. Spell-check the document.

10. Save the document as *[your initials]*11-16 in your Lesson 11 folder.

11. Print the document as four pages per sheet, or submit the document, and then close it.

Exercise 11-17

Create and unlink headers and footers within sections.

1. Open the file **Orders - 2**.

2. Insert a Next Page section break at the bold heading "How to Place an Order." Select the text on page 1, and format the text with a paragraph box border, using a double-line style, dark blue color, and width of 2¹/₄ points. On the title page, center the boxed title vertically and horizontally on the page, and reduce the width of the border by formatting the text in the box with 1-inch left and right indents.

3. Position the insertion point in section 1, and deselect any text that may be highlighted. Open the Borders and Shading dialog box, and click the Page Border tab. For the box setting, select the double-line style used in the previous step, with dark blue color and 1¹/₂ points wide. Apply the border to this section.

4. Format the tabbed text on page 2 (which starts with the text "Delivery Chart") as a separate section by placing a Next Page section break before it. Format this new section (section 3) with a 2-inch top margin.

5. Create a footer that starts on the first page of section 2 and is not linked to section 1. Key **Campbell's Confections** at the left margin. Move to the right margin, and key **Page** followed by a space and include the page number. Press Spacebar after the page number, and key **of** followed by a space. Open the Field dialog box, and click the NumPages field name and the 1, 2, 3 format. Click OK.

6. Italicize the footer text, and format the footer with a single-line, 1¹/₂-point top border.

7. Change the top margin for section to 2 to 1.5 inches.

8. View the document in Print Preview.

9. Save the document as *[your initials]*11-17 in your Lesson 11 folder.

10. Submit and close the document.

Exercise 11-18

Create a continuation page header for a business letter.

1. Open the file **Yang**.

2. Format the document as a business letter. Use the address shown in Figure 11-17. The letter will be from Tamara Robbins, Fundraising Coordinator.

Figure 11-17

```
Ms. Emiko Yang

7 South Diamond Street

Greenville, PA 16125
```

3. Adjust page setup options for a continuation page header by choosing the Different first page option, changing the header to 1 inch from the edge, and setting a 2-inch top margin and 1.25-inch left and right margins.

4. Insert a page break at the beginning of the paragraph that begins "Specialty."

5. Create a three-line continuation page header that prints on page 2. (Use the correct date format.)

6. Switch to Print Preview to view the document.

7. Add your reference initials, and spell-check the document.

8. Save the document as *[your initials]***11-18** in your Lesson 11 folder.

9. Submit and close the document.

Exercise 11-19 ◆ Challenge Yourself

Create alternate footers, unlink and format section footers, change starting page numbers, and change page formats.

1. Open the file **Company**.

2. Replace the page break after page 1 with a Next Page section break. On page 2, insert a Next Page section break at the bold heading "Pennsylvania." Insert Next Page Section breaks at the bold heading "Services" and one at the bold heading "Customer Service."

3. Insert page breaks at the bold headings "Ohio Stores," "West Virginia Stores," "Chocolate Club," "Corporate Gifts," "Favors," "Chocolate Fountains," "Fundraising," "Wholesale," and "Customer Service Account Executives."

4. Go to section 5 (Customer Service heading on page 13), and insert a blank footer. Deselect the Different First Page option and select the Different Odd and Even Pages options. Break the link for the even page footer for section 5 and the odd page footer for section 5. Key **Customer Service** in the odd page footer for section 5, and apply italic formatting. Center the footer text. Copy the text to the even page footer for section 5. Change the bottom margin for section 5 to 0.5 inch,

and change the font size for text beginning with "Pennsylvania" through the end of the document to 11 points. Verify that only section 5 has footer text.

5. Go to section 4 and unlink the first page footer from the previous section. Key **Campbell's Confections** at the left margin in the first page footer for section 4. Go to the odd page footer for section 4, and key **Page** followed by a space. Insert the Page field to add page numbering to the section. Change the start number to **1**. Go to the even page footer for section 4, and tab to the right margin. Key **Page** followed by a space. Insert the Page field to add numbering to the section.

6. Go to section 3, and unlink the first page footer from the previous section. Unlink the even page and odd page footers for section 3.

7. Key **Store Directory** at the left margin in the first page footer pane of section 3. Press Tab to move to the right margin, and key **Page** followed by a page number. Change the start the number for this section to **1**.

8. Go to section 2, and break the link from the previous section. Delete any text in the footer pane.

9. Go to section 1, and verify that the footer is blank. Add a page border to this section.

10. Go to section 5, and insert a blank header. Starting at section 5 and moving to the beginning of the document, break the link for all headers in the document. Go to the section 2 header, and click the header button to open the header gallery. Select the Annual design. Click the Company placeholder, and key **Campbell's Confections**. Key the current year.

10. Preview the document; then save it as *[your initials]*11-19 in your Lesson 11 folder.

11. Print the document four pages per sheet, or submit the document, and then close it.

On Your Own

In these exercises you work on your own, as you would in a real-life business environment. Use the skills you've learned to accomplish the task—and be creative.

Exercise 11-20

Write a two-page letter. Create your letterhead in the first-page header pane, and create a continuation header in the second-page header pane. Use correct business letter format. Save the document as *[your initials]*11-20 and submit it.

Exercise 11-21

Write a two-page report on a current event. Check pagination. Add appropriate headers and footers, and include page numbering. Create a title page as a separate section without a header or footer. Save the document as *[your initials]*11-21 and submit it.

Exercise 11-22

Write a short report about 10 places you would like to visit. Each place should be a separate paragraph with its own heading. Include a title page. Adjust page breaks as needed. Format the document for odd and even headers and footers, and then insert different identifying information in the headers or footers. Save the document as *[your initials]*11-22 and submit it.

Lesson 12

Styles and themes

OBJECTIVES

After completing this lesson, you will be able to:

1. Apply styles.

2. Create new styles.

3. Redefine, modify, and rename styles.

4. Use style options.

5. Apply and customize a theme.

MCAS OBJECTIVES

In this lesson:
WW 07 1.1.2
WW 07 1.1.3
WW 07 1.1.4
WW 07 2.1.1
WW 07 2.1.2

Estimated Time: 1¼ hours

A *style* is a set of formatting instructions you can apply to text. Styles make it easier to apply formatting and ensure consistency throughout a document.

In every document, Word maintains *style sets*—a list of style names and their formatting specifications. A style set, which is stored with a document, includes standard styles for body text and headings that appear in the Quick Style Gallery. You can apply styles, modify them, or create your own. A *theme* is a set of formatting instructions for the entire document. A theme includes style sets, theme colors, theme fonts, and theme effects. Themes can be customized and are shared across Office programs.

Applying Styles

The default style for text is called *Normal* style. Unless you change your system's default style, Normal is a paragraph style with the following formatting specifications: 11-point Calibri, English language, left-aligned, 1.15-line spacing, 10 points spacing after, and widow/orphan control.

To change the appearance of text in a document, you can apply five types of styles:

- A *character style* is formatting applied to selected text, such as font, font size, and font style.

- A *paragraph style* is formatting applied to an entire paragraph, such as alignment, line and paragraph spacing, indents, tab settings, borders and shading, and character formatting.

- A *linked style* formats a single paragraph with two styles. It is typically used to assign a heading style to the first few words of a paragraph.

- A *table style* is formatting applied to a table, such as borders, shading, alignment, and fonts.

- A *list style* is formatting applied to a list, such as numbers or bullet characters, alignment, and fonts.

Exercise 12-1   APPLY STYLES

There are two ways to apply styles:

- Open the Styles task pane and select a style to apply. To open the Styles task pane, click the Styles Dialog Box Launcher.

- Click the Home tab; click a Quick Style.

1. Open the file **Volume 1**.

2. Click the **Home** tab, and click the **Styles Dialog Box Launcher** to open the Styles task pane. The task pane lists formatting currently used in the document and includes some of Word's built-in heading styles.

3. Click the Change Styles button . Click **Style Set**, and click **Default**.

4. Click in the line "Choc Talk," and place the mouse pointer (without clicking) over the Heading 1 style in the task pane. A ScreenTip displays the style's attributes.

5. Click the **Heading 1** style in the Styles task pane. The text is formatted with 14-point bold Cambria, blue, 24 points spacing before, and 1.15-line spacing.

NOTE

The keyboard shortcut to open the Styles task pane is Ctrl + Alt + Shift + S.

NOTE

Define a style set before you apply formatting to ensure you are using the appropriate styles.

NOTE

To apply a style to a paragraph, you can simply click anywhere in the paragraph without selecting the text. Remember, this is also true for applying a paragraph format (such as line spacing or alignment) to a paragraph.

Figure 12-1
Using the Styles task
pane to apply a style

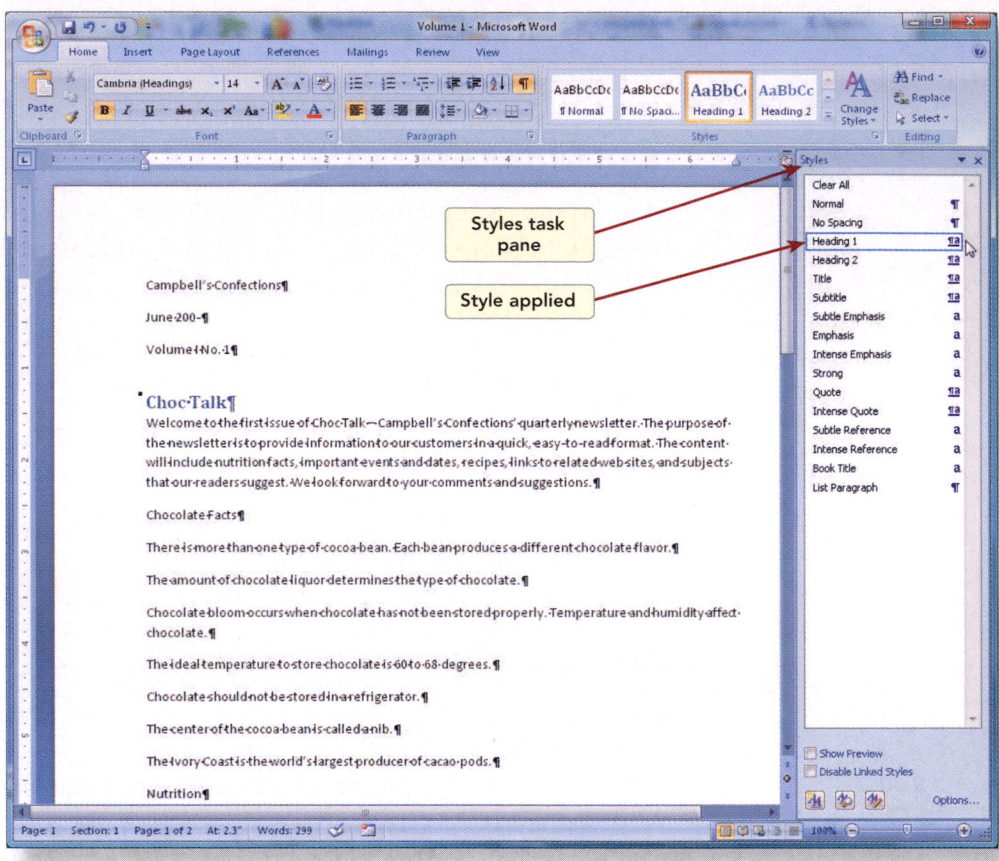

TIP

Style sets may only show those styles
already used in the document. To see all
styles available, click the Options link in the
Style task pane, and click the arrow beside
Select styles to Show. Select All styles.

6. Close the Styles task pane by clicking the Styles task pane Close button .

7. Position the insertion point in the text "Chocolate Facts."

8. Click the **Home** tab, and locate the **Styles** group. Click the More arrow 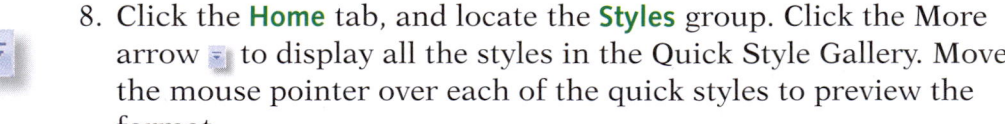 to display all the styles in the Quick Style Gallery. Move the mouse pointer over each of the quick styles to preview the format.

9. Choose **Heading 2**. Notice the applied formatting.

Figure 12-2
Using the Quick
Style Gallery

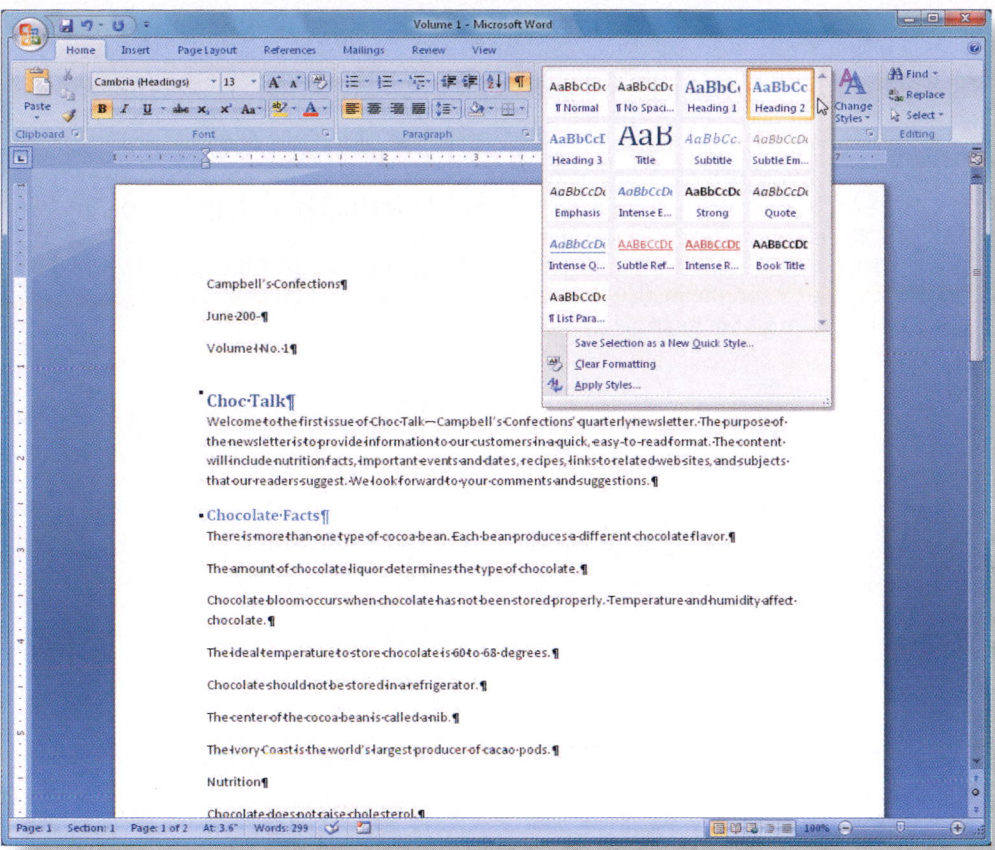

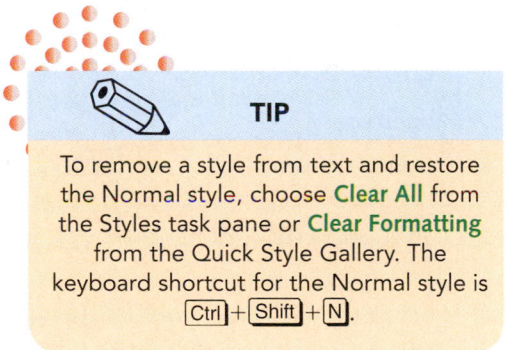

TIP

To remove a style from text and restore the Normal style, choose **Clear All** from the Styles task pane or **Clear Formatting** from the Quick Style Gallery. The keyboard shortcut for the Normal style is [Ctrl] + [Shift] + [N].

10. Position the insertion point in the heading "Nutrition." Press [F4] to repeat the Heading 2 style.

Creating New Styles

Creating styles is as easy as formatting text and then giving the set of formatting instructions a style name. Each new style name must be different from the other style names already in the document.

Word saves the styles you create for a document when you save the document.

Exercise 12-2   CREATE A PARAGRAPH STYLE

There are two ways to create a new paragraph style:

- Use the Quick Style Gallery.
- Click the **New Style** button in the Styles task pane.

1. Reopen the Styles task pane by clicking the **Styles Dialog Box Launcher**.

2. Select the heading "Chocolate Facts."

3. Increase the font size to 14 points, and press Ctrl + Shift + K to apply small caps.

4. Click the New Style button 🔲 at the bottom of the Styles task pane. The Create New Style from Formatting dialog box opens.

5. Key **Side Heading** in the **Name** box. Verify that **Paragraph** is the **Style type**.

Figure 12-3
Create New Style from Formatting dialog box

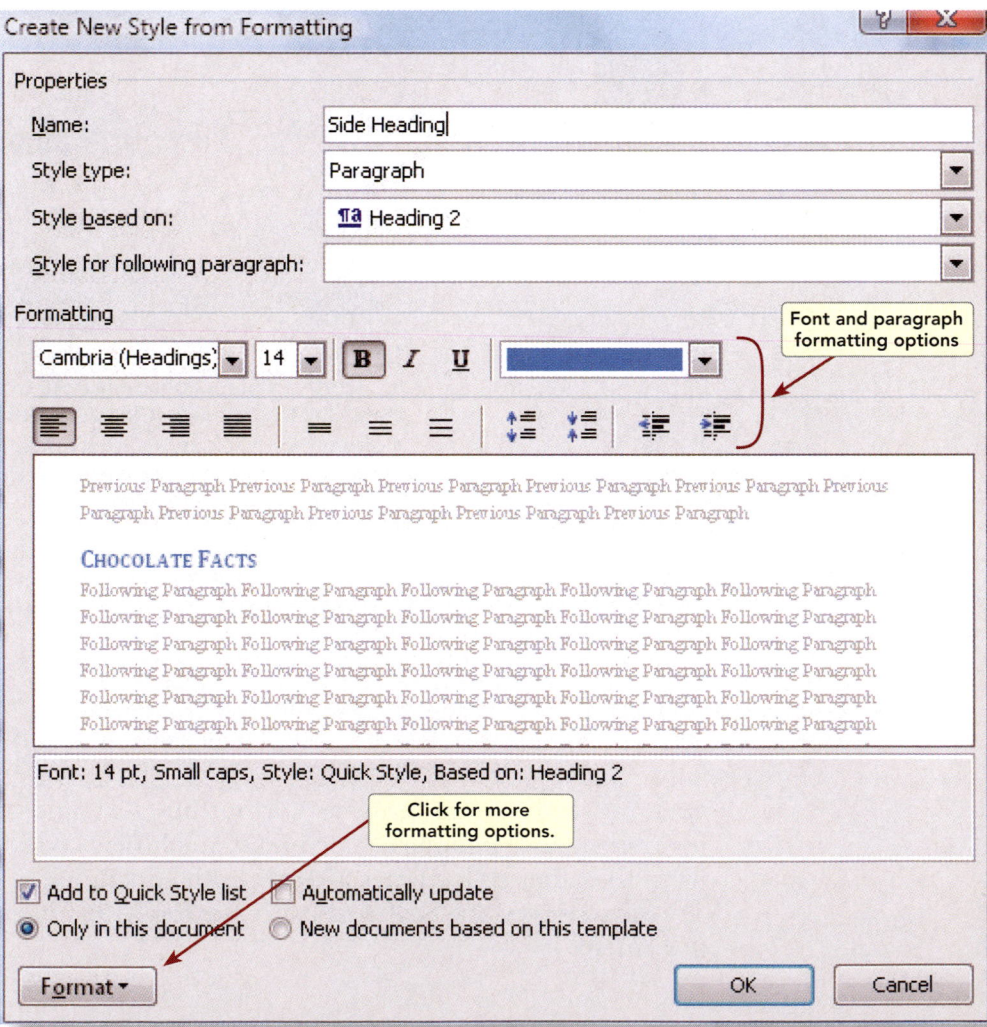

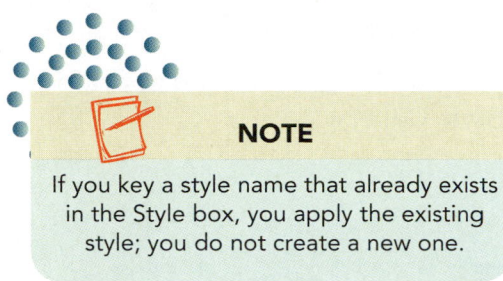

NOTE

If you key a style name that already exists in the Style box, you apply the existing style; you do not create a new one.

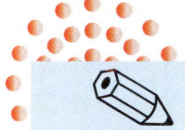

TIP

Use the Formatting buttons in the New Style dialog box to apply basic font and paragraph formatting. For more formatting options, click the Format button, and choose Font, Paragraph, Tabs, Border, or Numbering to open the corresponding dialog boxes.

6. Notice the two rows of buttons under **Formatting**. The first row is for font formatting, and the second row is for paragraph formatting. Point to the buttons, and notice a ScreenTip appears to identify each button.

7. Click **OK**.

8. Locate the heading "Nutrition." Click in the paragraph, and click the **Side Heading** style in the task pane. The new style is applied.

9. Repeat the formatting to the side headings "Pets and Chocolate" and "Important Chocolate Dates."

10. Select the text "June 200-" and change the font size to 12.

11. Right-click the selected text, and click **Styles** in the shortcut menu. Click **Save Selection as a New Quick Style**.

Figure 12-4
Creating a new style

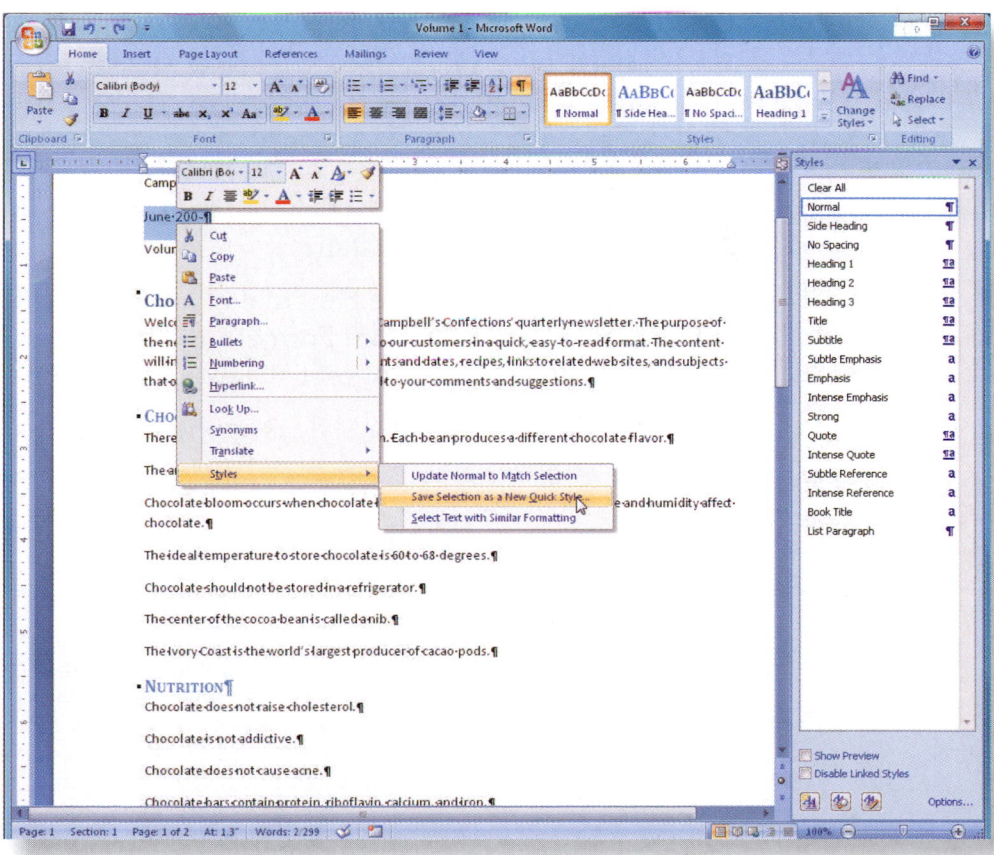

12. Key **Issue Date** in the **Name** box, and click **OK**.

13. Notice that the Side Heading style and the Issue Date style appear in the Style task pane and the Quick Style Gallery.

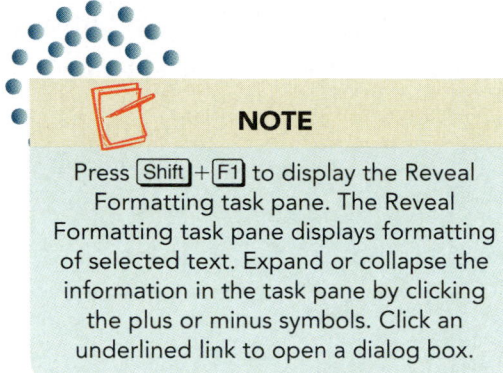

NOTE

Press Shift + F1 to display the Reveal Formatting task pane. The Reveal Formatting task pane displays formatting of selected text. Expand or collapse the information in the task pane by clicking the plus or minus symbols. Click an underlined link to open a dialog box.

Exercise 12-3   CREATE A CHARACTER STYLE

A character style is applied to selected text and only contains character formatting.

1. Select the text "Choc Talk" in the first paragraph under the heading "Choc Talk." Open the Create New Style from Formatting dialog box and key **Accent** in the **Name** box.

2. Choose **Character** from the **Style type** drop-down list box.

3. Click the **Format** button, choose **Font**, and set the formatting to 11-point Calibri and italic.

4. Click **OK** to close the Font dialog box. Click **OK** to close the Create New Style from Formatting dialog box. The selected text is formatted, and the Accent style appears in the task pane.

5. Note that a character style is applied to selected text, not the entire paragraph.

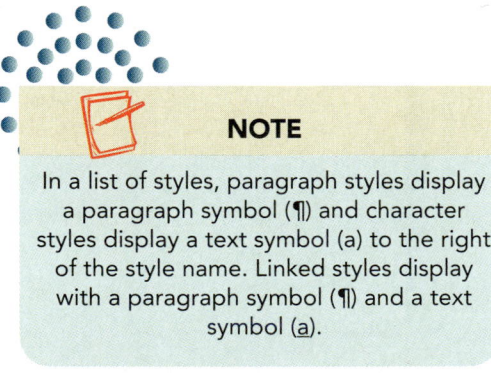

NOTE

In a list of styles, paragraph styles display a paragraph symbol (¶) and character styles display a text symbol (a) to the right of the style name. Linked styles display with a paragraph symbol (¶) and a text symbol (a).

Figure 12-5
Applying the
character style

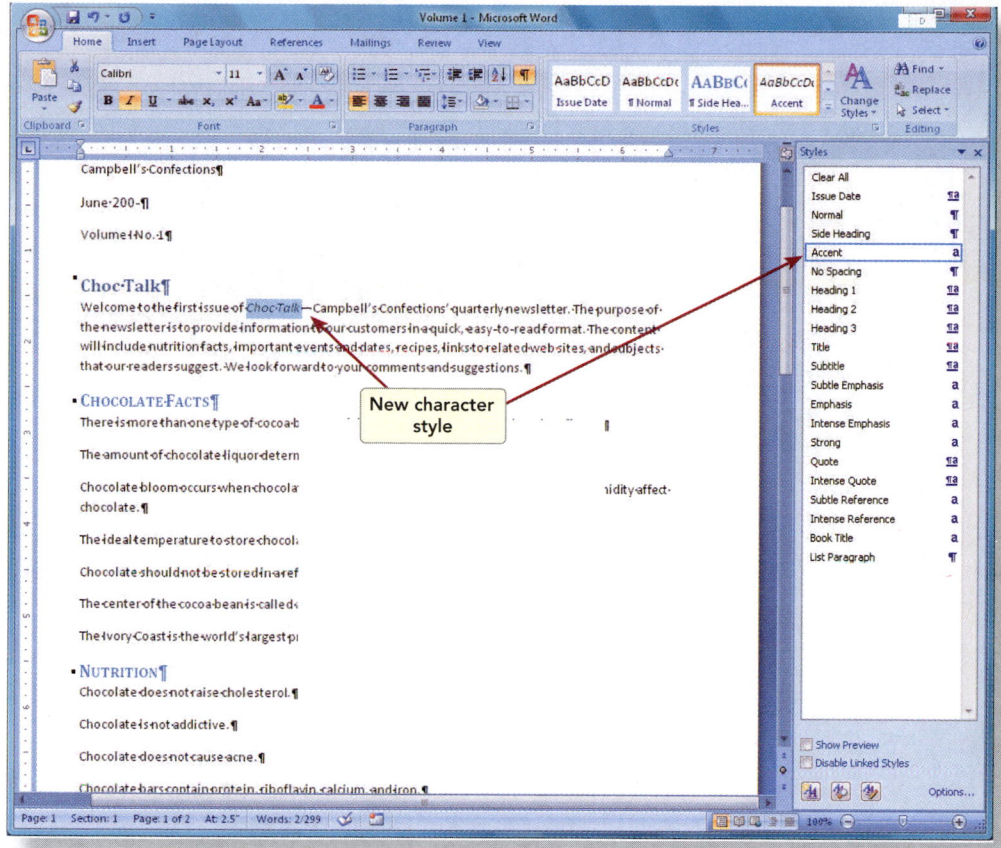

6. Save the document as ***[your initials]*12-3** in a new folder for Lesson 12. Do not print the document; leave it open for the next exercise.

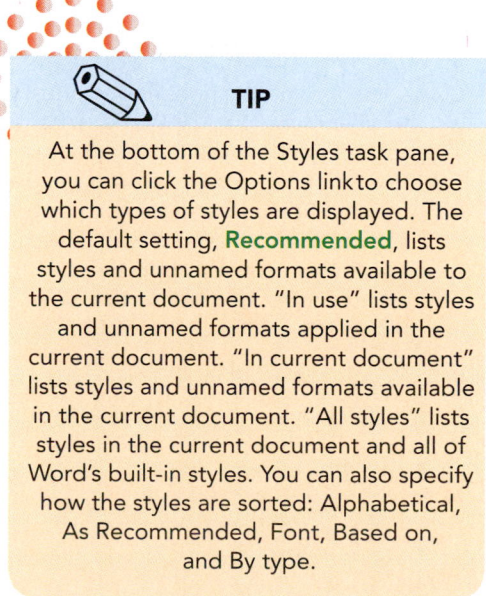

TIP

At the bottom of the Styles task pane, you can click the Options link to choose which types of styles are displayed. The default setting, **Recommended**, lists styles and unnamed formats available to the current document. "In use" lists styles and unnamed formats applied in the current document. "In current document" lists styles and unnamed formats available in the current document. "All styles" lists styles in the current document and all of Word's built-in styles. You can also specify how the styles are sorted: Alphabetical, As Recommended, Font, Based on, and By type.

Modifying and Renaming Styles

After creating a style, you can modify it by changing the formatting specifications or renaming the style. When you modify a style, the changes you make affect each instance of that style. You can quickly replace one style with another by using the Replace dialog box.

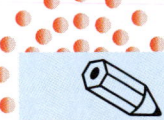

> **NOTE**
>
> You can modify any of Word's built-in styles as well as your own styles. However, you cannot rename Word's standard heading styles.

Exercise 12-4   MODIFY AND RENAME STYLES

To modify a style, right-click the style in the Styles task pane and then choose Modify. Or select the styled text, modify the formatting, right-click the style name in the Styles task pane, and choose Update to Match Selection.

1. In the Styles task pane, right-click the style name **Heading 1**. Choose **Modify** from the drop-down list.

2. In the **Modify Style** dialog box, change the point size to 18, and click **OK** to update the style.

3. Select the text "June 200-" and open the **Paragraph** dialog box. Change the spacing after to 0 points and click **OK**. Right-click the style name **Issue Date** in the task pane. Choose **Update Issue Date to Match Selection**. The style is updated to match the selected text formatting.

> **TIP**
>
> Instead of using the right mouse button to open the drop-down list of style options, you can use the left mouse button to click the down arrow next to a style name. Remember, if you click a style name (not its down arrow) with the left mouse button, you will apply the style to the text containing the insertion point.

> **TIP**
>
> You can also click the Select All button in the Styles task pane to select all instances of a style.

Figure 12-6
Modifying a style by updating it

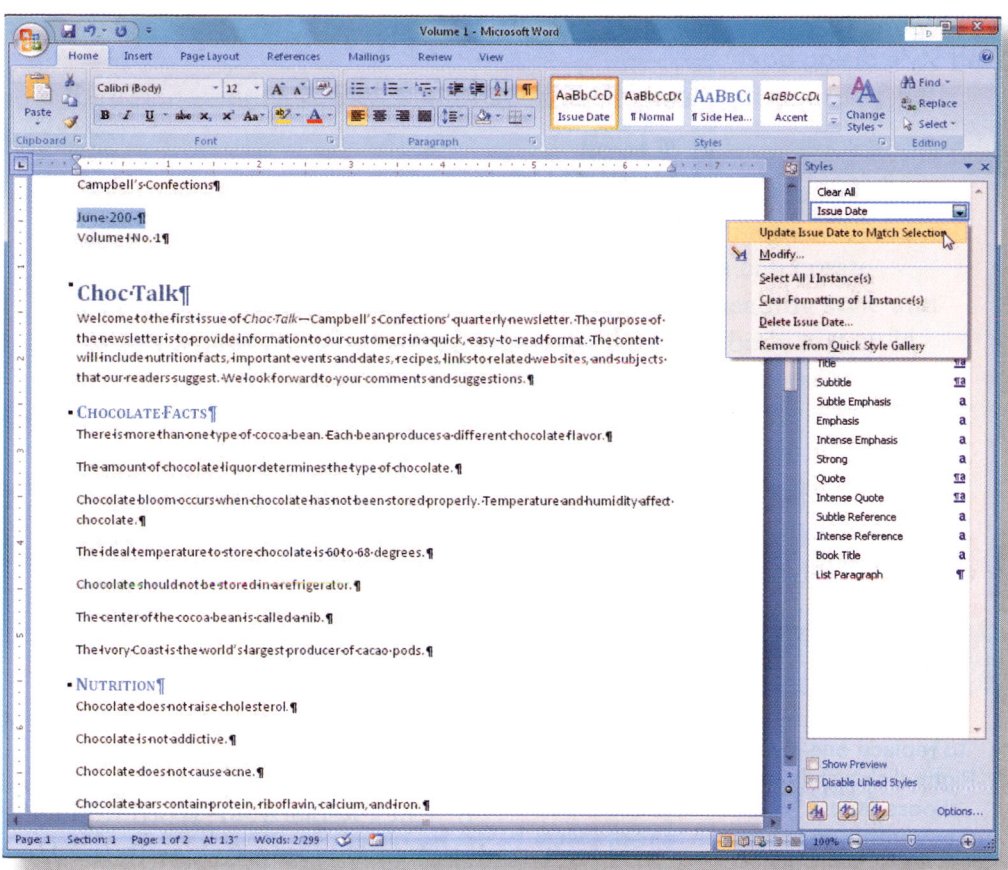

NOTE

After modifying or renaming a style, you can undo your action (for example, click Undo from the Quick Access toolbar).

4. Position the insertion point in the text "June 200-." Right-click the **Issue Date** style in the task pane and choose **Modify**.

5. Rename the Issue Date style by keying **Pub Date** in the **Name** text box. Click **OK**. The style Pub Date appears in the task pane, replacing the style name Issue Date.

Exercise 12-5   REPLACE A STYLE

1. Click the Home tab, and locate the **Editing** group. Click the Replace button ⬛Replace . Click the **More** button ⬛More >> , if needed, to expand the dialog box. Clear any text or formatting from a previous search.

2. Click the **Format** button and choose **Style**. The Find Style dialog box displays.

3. Click **Side Heading** from the **Find what style** list, and click **OK**.

Word 2007

Figure 12-13
Create New Theme
Colors dialog box

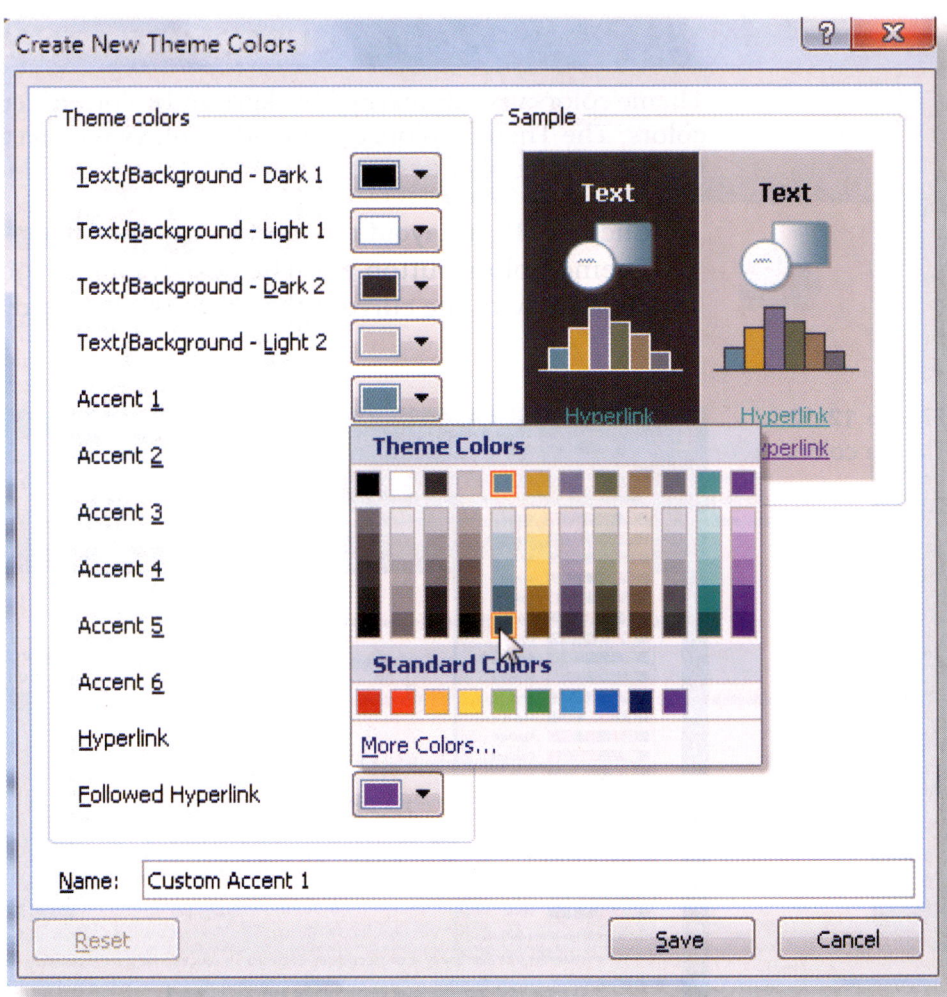

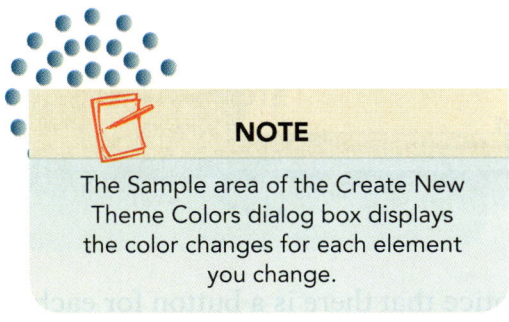

NOTE

The Sample area of the Create New Theme Colors dialog box displays the color changes for each element you change.

3. Click the Theme Colors button and notice that the Custom Accent 1 theme color appears at the top of the list. Right-click the Custom Accent 1 color, and click **Delete**. Click **No**.

4. Click the **Page Layout** tab, and click the Theme Fonts button . The heading and body text font for each theme displays.

5. Click the option to **Create New Theme Fonts**. The current Heading font and Body font are selected in the Create New Theme Fonts dialog box.

Figure 12-14
Create New Theme
Fonts

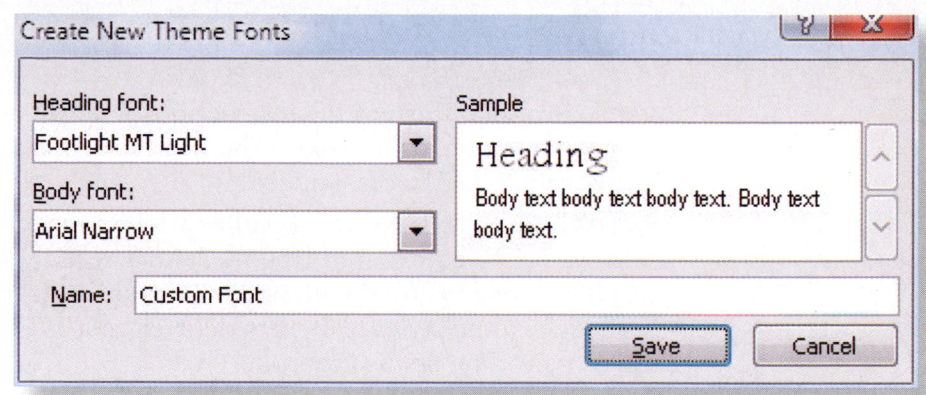

6. Change the **Heading font** to **Footlight MT Light**, and change the **Body font** to **Arial Narrow**. Key **Custom Font** in the **Name** box. Click **Save**.

7. Click the Theme Fonts button [A], and notice that "Custom Font" appears at the top of the list. Right-click **Custom Font**, and click **Edit**. Change the **Heading font** to **Eras Medium ITC**, and change the **Body font** to **Footlight MT Light**. Click **Save**.

8. Apply the Heading 5 style to the second line "June 200-." Apply the Heading 4 style to the line that begins "Volume."

9. Select the headings "Chocolate Facts," "Nutrition," "Pets and Chocolate," and "Important Chocolate Dates," and apply the Heading 3 style.

10. Select the lines of text under each of the headings formatted with the Heading 3 style, and format the lines as a bulleted list.

11. At the end of the document, delete the text that begins "Choc Talk" through the end of the document.

12. Click the **Page Layout** tab, and click the Themes button [ ]. Click **Save Current Theme**. Key **Custom Theme** in the **File name** box. Click **Save**.

13. Click the Themes button [ ], and notice that the design gallery displays Built In designs and Custom designs. Right-click the **Custom Theme** at the top of the gallery, and click **Delete**. Click **Yes** to delete the theme.

14. Save the document as *[your initials]***12-12** in your Lesson 12 folder.

15. Submit and close the document.

Lesson 12 Summary

- A style is a set of formatting instructions you can apply to text to give your document a unified look. The five types of styles are character, paragraph, linked, table, and list.

- Word's default style for text is called the Normal style. The default settings for body text are 11-point Calibri, left-aligned, 1.15-line spacing, 10 points spacing after, with widow-orphan control. Word provides built-in heading styles (for example, Heading 1, Heading 2). The default font for heading text is Cambria.

- To apply a style, select the text you want to style (or click in a paragraph to apply a paragraph style). Then choose the style from the Styles task pane or the Quick Styles gallery.

- View the attributes of a style by placing the mouse pointer over the style name in the Styles task pane and reading the text in the ScreenTip.

- Select all instances of a style by clicking the arrow for the style name in the Styles task pane or by right-clicking a style name in the task pane and choosing Select All Instance(s).

- To create a new paragraph style: Select text, modify the text, right-click the text, select Styles, select Save Selection as a New Quick Style, key a new style name, and click OK. Or click the New Style button in the Styles task pane, and set the style's attributes in the Create New Style from Formatting dialog box. You must use the Create New Style from Formatting dialog box to create a character style and specify Character as the style type.

- To modify or rename a style, right-click the style name in the Styles task pane (or point to the style name and click the down arrow), choose Modify, and then change the attributes. Or select text that uses the style, change the format, right-click the style name in the task pane, and choose Update to Match Selection.

- After applying a style throughout a document, you can replace it with another style. Click Replace on the Home tab (in the dialog box, click Format, choose Style, and select the style name in both the Find what and Replace with boxes).

- You can also replace styles by using the Styles task pane (select all instances of a style and then choose another style).

- To delete a style, click the Manage Styles button in the Styles task pane, select the style, and click Delete. Click Yes to delete the style, and click OK.

- When creating new styles, you can specify that they be based on an existing style. You can also specify that one style follows another style automatically. Both these options are offered in the Create New Style from Formatting dialog box.

- Display styles along the left margin of a document in Draft view by opening the Word Options dialog box, clicking Advanced, and scrolling to the Display group. Change the Style area width box to 0.5 inch. Do the reverse to stop displaying styles.

- Print a style sheet by choosing Print from the File menu and choosing Styles from the Print what drop-down list.
- The Theme feature formats an entire document using design elements. Themes include theme colors, theme fonts, and theme effects.

LESSON 12		Command Summary	
Feature	Button	Command	Keyboard
Styles task pane		**Home** tab, **Styles** group, **Styles Dialog Box Launcher**	Shift + Ctrl + Alt + S
Apply styles		**Home** tab, **Styles** group	
View style area		**Word Options, Advanced, Display**	
Themes		**Page Layout** tab, **Themes** group	

Concepts Review

True/False Questions

Each of the following statements is either true or false. Indicate your choice by circling T or F.

T F   1. Paragraph styles can include both paragraph- and character-formatting instructions.

T F   2. You can apply character styles to selected text within a paragraph.

T F   3. You can use either the Styles task pane or the Quick Styles Gallery to apply a paragraph style.

T F   4. If you select only part of a paragraph to change the paragraph style, only the selected portion is reformatted.

T F   5. You can create a character style by changing the formatting of selected text, right-click the selection, and select Styles.

T F   6. A style named and created for a specific document cannot be modified for that document.

T F   7. When you delete a style from the style sheet, any paragraph or text containing that style returns to the Normal style.

T F   8. You save the styles created for a document by saving the document.

Short Answer Questions

Write the correct answer in the space provided.

1. In the list of styles, what symbol designates a paragraph style?

_____

2. In the list of styles, what symbol designates a character style?

_____

3. How do you print a list of a document's styles?

_____

4. What is the purpose of a theme?

_____

5. How do you display style names in the left margin of a document?

_____

6. How do you open the New Style dialog box?

_____

7. What are the five types of styles?

_____

8. On what style are all standard styles based?

_____

Critical Thinking

Answer these questions on a separate page. There are no right or wrong answers. Support your answers with examples from your own experience, if possible.

1. The Based On option is often used to create a group of heading styles based on one style and a group of body text styles based on another style. Why aren't heading styles and body text styles typically based on the same style?

2. Create complementary styles for a heading and for body text, using two different fonts. Describe the formatting for each style, and provide a sample of the styles used together. Describe the type of document for which this combination would be suited.

Skills Review

Exercise 12-13

Apply styles and create new styles.

1. Open the file **Agenda - 1**.
2. Use the Quick Styles Gallery to apply a style to the document title by following these steps:
    a. Position the insertion point in the title (the first line).
    b. Click the More Arrow button to open the Quick Styles Gallery.
    c. Click **Title**.
3. Use the Styles task pane to apply a style by following these steps:
    a. Click the **Home** tab, and click the **Styles Dialog Box Launcher** to display the **Styles** task pane.
    b. Position the insertion point in the next heading, "Sponsored by."
    c. Click **Subtitle** in the task pane.
4. Apply the Heading 1 style to the heading "Agenda."

5. Create a new paragraph style for a heading by following these steps:

   a. Select the heading "Thursday, February 10."

   b. Click the New Style button 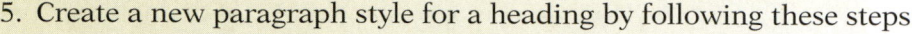, and key **Day** in the **Name** text box.

   c. Change the font formatting to 14-point bold and small caps.

   d. Change the paragraph formatting to 12 points spacing before and 6 points spacing after. Click **OK**.

   e. Apply the Day style to the line beginning "Friday."

6. Use the New Style dialog box to create a new style for the agenda text by following these steps:

   a. Position the insertion point at the beginning of the line that begins "12 Noon." Click **New Style** in the task pane.

   b. Key **Agenda Items** in the **Name** text box.

   c. Change the font size to 12.

   d. Click **Format** and choose **Paragraph**.

   e. Change the left indent to 0.25″ and change the spacing after to 3 points. Click **OK**.

   f. Click **OK** in the Create New Style from Formatting dialog box.

7. Select all the agenda text under the headings "Thursday" and "Friday." Choose the **Agenda Items** style from the Styles task pane.

8. Apply the Heading 2 style to the line that begins "Grove City College."

9. Change the document title to small caps and 72 points of spacing before paragraphs. Replace the hyphens following each session number with em dashes.

10. Save the document as *[your initials]*12-13 in your Lesson 12 folder.

11. Submit and close the document.

Exercise 12-14

Create, redefine, modify, and rename styles.

1. Open the file **OH Stores**. Display the Styles task pane.

2. For the document title, create and apply a paragraph style named **Office Heading** with the formatting 14-point Times New Roman, bold and italic.

3. For the text "Campbell's Confections," create and apply a paragraph style named **Subhead** with the formatting 12-point Arial, with bold and italic and with 12 points spacing before and 3 points spacing after paragraphs.

4. Position the insertion point in each line of text that contains a Campbell's Confections' store name, and apply the Subhead style (press F4 to repeat the style).

5. Redefine the Subhead style by following these steps:

   a. Select the first occurrence of "Campbell's Confections," and remove the italics by clicking the italic button .

   b. Right-click the **Subhead** style in the task pane. Choose **Update Subhead to Match Selection**.

6. Create a new character style for the word "Fax" by following these steps:

   a. Position the insertion point at the beginning of the second telephone number for the Akron Office. Click the **New Style** button in the Styles task pane.

   b. Key **Fax Num** in the **Name** text box.

   c. Choose **Character** from the **Style type** drop-down list.

   d. Click the Font Color button 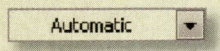 in the dialog box, and change the color to dark blue.

   e. Click **Format**, choose **Font**, and choose **Small caps**. Click **OK**. Click **OK** again.

7. Key the word **Fax:** followed by a space at the beginning of the second telephone number for the Akron office. Repeat for the other five offices.

8. Select the word "Fax" the first time it occurs, and apply the **Fax Num** style from the task pane. Apply the same style to each occurrence of "Fax" by selecting the word and pressing F4.

9. Rename the **Fax Num** style by following these steps:

   a. Right-click the Fax Num style in the task pane and choose **Modify**.

   b. In the Name text box, edit the text to "Fax" and click **OK**.

10. Delete the Office Heading style by following these steps:

    a. Right-click the **Office Heading** style in the task pane.

    b. Choose **Delete**. Click **Yes**.

11. Apply the Title style to the document title. Modify the style to include small caps. Delete the blank paragraph after the title.

12. Change the top margin to 1.5 inches and the bottom margin to 0.5.

13. Key **Telephone:** followed by a space to the left of each telephone number for all offices. (The telephone number is the first number listed.)

14. Save the document as *[your initials]*12-14 in your Lesson 12 folder.

15. Submit and close the document.

Exercise 12-15

Create styles, use style options, and display and print styles.

1. Open the file **Health Fair**. Display the Styles task pane. Change the date in the memo heading to today's date. Change the date in the third paragraph below the memo heading to a date two weeks from today's date. Delete the instruction text.

2. Select the text "Board Room No. 1," and create and apply a new paragraph style named **Room** with the formatting 12-point Arial, with bold and italic and with 3 points spacing after.

3. Apply the new style to "Board Room No. 2" and "Board Room No. 3."

4. Create a new paragraph style named "Session" that is based on the Room style by following these steps:

   a. Position the insertion point after "Board Room No. 1" and press Enter. Key **30-Minute Sessions**. Click the **New Style** button on the task pane.

   b. Key **Session** in the **Name** text box.

   c. Check that **Style based on** is set to the **Room** style.

   d. Using the Formatting buttons in the Create New Style from Formatting dialog box, change the font formatting to 11 points and turn off bold and italic.

   e. Click **OK**.

5. Click at the beginning of the paragraph that starts with the word "Topics." Create a new paragraph style named **Info** that is based on the Normal style. Use the formatting 11-point Arial, with 3 points of spacing after paragraphs.

6. Assign Session as the following paragraph style for Room and assign Info as the following paragraph style for Session by following these steps:

   a. Right-click the **Room** style in the task pane.

   b. Choose **Modify**.

   c. Choose **Session** from the **Style for following paragraph** drop-down list.

   d. Click **OK**. Repeat the procedure to assign Info as the following paragraph style for Session.

7. Position the insertion point at the end of the heading "Board Room No. 2," press Enter to apply the Session style, and key **45-Minute Sessions**.

8. Press Enter to apply the Info style and key **Topics:**.

9. At the end of "Board Room No. 3," press Enter, and key the following two lines of text:

   30-Minute Sessions
   Topics:

10. Select the text from "CPR" through "First Aid," and format the text as a bulleted list using a small square bullet (■). Right-click the selected text, and choose **Styles** from the shortcut menu. Click **Save Selection as a New Quick Style**. Name the style **Content**, and click **OK**.

11. Select the two lines of text that follow "Topics for Board Room No. 2," and apply the Content style. Repeat the style for the three lines of text under "Topics for Board Room No. 3."

12. Modify the Normal style to be Arial, with single spacing.

13. Display the style area for the document by following these steps:

    a. Open the **Word Options** dialog box, and click **Advanced**. Scroll to the **Display** group.

    b. Set the **Style area width** to 0.5 inch and click **OK**. Switch to Draft view.

14. Format the memo with the correct spacing at the top of the page, and remember to include your reference initials at the end of the document. Change the bottom margin to 0.5 inch.

15. Restore the style area width to zero. Switch to Print Layout view.

16. Print the document style sheet by following these steps:

    a. Open the **Print** dialog box.

    b. Choose **Styles** from the **Print what** drop-down list and click **OK**.

17. Spell-check the document, and save it as *[your initials]*12-15 in your Lesson 12 folder.

18. Submit and close the document.

Exercise 12-16

Apply and customize document themes.

1. Open the file **Health Fair - 2**. Display the Styles task pane.

2. Change the document theme by following these steps:

    a. Click the **Page Layout** tab, and click the Themes button .

    b. Click the **Median** design from the Themes gallery.

3. Change the theme font by following these steps:

    a. Click the Theme Fonts button .

    b. Click **Create New Theme Fonts**.

    c. Change the heading font to Tahoma, and change the body font to Tahoma.

    d. Key **Custom Font** in the **Name** text box. Click **Save**.

4. Modify the Normal style by changing the font size to 12.

5. Apply the style Heading 1 to the first line of the document. Apply the Heading 2 style to the text that begins "Saturday."

6. Apply the Heading 3 style to the headings "Employee's Full Name," "Store Location," and "Preferred Sessions." Modify the Heading 3 style to 24 points spacing before.

7. Format the document with a 1.5-inch top margin.

8. Spell-check the document.

9. Save the document as *[your initials]*12-16 in your Lesson 12 folder.

10. Submit and close the document.

Lesson Applications

Exercise 12-17

Create, apply, and modify styles; print styles.

1. Start a new document. Key the text shown in Figure 12-15. Create the styles as indicated for the first two lines.

Figure 12-15

```
Health Screening Day          New style: Headline 1
                              24-pt Arial bold, centered
For More Information:
                              New style: Headline 2
Garland Miller                18 pt Arial Italic, centered

Campbell's Confections

250 Monroe Street

Grove City, PA 16127

800-555-2025

Campbell's Confections-Makers of Fine Chocolate
```

2. Apply the Headline 2 style to the last line of text. Modify the style to include 18 points of paragraph spacing before and after.

3. Create a style called **Body 1** (based on the Normal style) for the remainder of the text; the style should be 12-point Arial, centered, with 1.5-line spacing.

4. Center the document vertically on the page.

5. Spell-check the document.

6. Save the document as *[your initials]*12-17 in your Lesson 12 folder.

7. Submit the document and the style sheet, and close the document.

Exercise 12-18

Create, modify, and rename styles; print styles.

1. Open the file **Screening**.

2. Create a character style named **Memo Heading** using Arial Black, 12 points.

3. Select "Memo To" and apply the Memo Heading style. Repeat the style formatting for "From," "Date," and "Subject."

4. Select the four lines in the memo heading, and adjust the tab setting to 1.25 inches.

5. Modify the Normal style to include 12-point Times New Roman and 12 points spacing after.

6. Select the text beginning "Height and weight" through "Asthma screening," and format the text using a picture bullet.

7. Rename the style Memo Heading with the name **Memo Head**.

8. Position the insertion point in the subject line of the memo heading, and change the spacing after to 24 points. Add a bottom border to the subject line.

9. Change the top margin to 2 inches and the bottom margin to 0.5 inch.

10. Add your reference initials to the document.

11. Save the document as *[your initials]***12-18** in your Lesson 12 folder.

12. Submit and close the document.

Exercise 12-19

Modify styles, use style options, and print styles.

1. Open the file **Property - 2**.

2. Format the document as a letter to the name and address shown below, from Lynn Tanguay, vice president. Remember to use the correct top margin and spacing and to include your reference initials. Change the bottom margin to 0.5 inch.

   Dr. James Wenner
   West College
   PO Box 1000
   New Wilmington, PA 16172

3. Edit the first line of the letter to read:

   Thank you for agreeing to present a seminar on property insurance for Campbell's Confections' store owners/managers. Please discuss the following topics.

4. Select the text "Types of insurance," and create a style named **Topic** with 12-point, bold, and small caps formatting.

5. Position the insertion point at the end of the document, and create a new style named **Subjects** with 12-point formatting.

6. Modify the Topic style by changing the style for following paragraph to Subjects.

7. Position the insertion point at the end of the line "Types of Insurance." Press Enter and key the text shown in Figure 12-16.

Figure 12-16

```
Equipment

Inventory

Buildings

Land

Liability

Business Interruption

Key Employees
```

8. Apply the Topic style to the text "Types of Coverage," press Enter, and key the following items. Place each on a separate line, and omit the commas.

   Fire, Theft, Catastrophes, Accidents, Loss of Income

9. Press Enter twice after keying "Loss of income," and apply the Normal style.

10. Key the following closing paragraph.

    If time permits, you may want to include comments on how to select an insurance agent. We look forward to your presentation next month.

11. Key the closing lines of the letter.

12. Modify the font size of the Normal style to 12 points.

13. Spell-check the document.

14. Save the document as *[your initials]*12-19 in your Lesson 12 folder.

15. Print the style sheet and the document, and close the document.

Exercise 12-20 ◆ Challenge Yourself

Create, apply, and modify styles; apply themes.

1. Open the file **Ordering**. Display the Styles task pane.

2. Apply the Opulent theme to the document.

3. Apply the Title style to the first line of the document.

4. Position the insertion point in the "Online" paragraph. Create a style called **Side Heading** using 14-point, bold, and small caps formatting.

5. Apply the Side Heading style to each of the document side headings. (There are seven side headings.)

6. Position the insertion point in the paragraph that begins "Note," and create a new style named **Special Note** using 11 points and 0.25-inch left indent.

7. Apply the Special Note style to each "Note" paragraph and the paragraph that follows "Note."

8. Modify the Normal style font to 11 points.

9. Modify the Title style to small caps.

10. Create a left-aligned header for page 2 to include the following text. Place two blank paragraphs after the second line of the header.

    Place an Order
    Page *[Number]*

11. Add a bottom border to the page number paragraph in the header.

12. Add your reference initials to the bottom of the document.

13. Save the document as *[your initials]***12-20** in your Lesson 12 folder.

14. Print the document and the style sheet, and close the document.

On Your Own

In these exercises you work on your own, as you would in a real-life business environment. Use the skills you've learned to accomplish the task—and be creative.

Exercise 12-21

Create your own one-page newsletter. Create and use styles for the different newsletter elements, such as the title, date line, body text, and publisher information. Save the document as *[your initials]***12-21**. Submit the document and the styles.

Exercise 12-22

Assume you have been on a job interview. Write a simple follow-up letter, and compare the document appearance by using three different themes. Apply the appropriate theme and styles to your letter. Save the document as *[your initials]***12-22**. Submit the document and the styles.

Exercise 12-23

Create a document that includes your five favorite songs. Each song should appear as a three-line description—song title, songwriter, and performer—with each line using a different style. The songwriter and performer styles should be based on the song title style. Specify the songwriter style as the style following the title style, and the performer style as the style following the songwriter style. Create the styles first; then key the text. Modify the styles as desired. Save the document as *[your initials]***12-23**. Submit the document and the styles.

templates

OBJECTIVES

After completing this lesson, you will be able to:

1. Use Word templates.

2. Create new templates.

3. Attach templates to documents.

4. Modify templates.

5. Use the Organizer.

MCAS OBJECTIVES

In this lesson:
WW 07 1.1.1
WW 07 1.1.5

Estimated Time: 1¹/₂ hours

If you often create the same types of documents, such as memos or letters, you can save time by using templates. Word provides a variety of templates that contain built-in styles to help you produce professional-looking documents. You can also create your own templates and reuse them as often as you like.

Using Word's Templates

A *template* is a file that contains formatting information, styles, and sometimes text for a particular type of document. It provides a reusable model for all documents of the same type. Every Word document is based on a template. You can modify templates to include formatting and text that you use frequently.

The following features can be included in templates:

- Formatting features, such as margins, columns, and page orientation.

- Standard text that is repeated in all documents of the same type, such as a company name and address in a letter template.

- Character and paragraph formatting that is saved within styles.

- Macros (automated procedures).

Templates also include *placeholder text* that is formatted and replaced with your own information when you create a new document.

The default template file in Word is called **Normal**. New documents that you create in Word are based on the Normal template and contain all the formatting features assigned to this template, such as the default font, type size, paragraph alignment, margins, and page orientation. The Normal template differs from other templates because it stores settings that are available globally. In other words, you can use these settings in every new document even if they are based on a different template. The file extension for template files is .dotx or .dotm. (A .dotm file is used to enable macros in the file.)

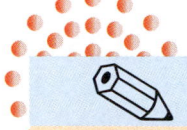

TIP

Pressing Ctrl+N or clicking the New button opens a new document but does not open the New Document dialog box. You can customize the Quick Access Toolbar to include a New button.

Exercise 13-1

USE A WORD TEMPLATE TO CREATE A NEW DOCUMENT

Starting Word opens a new blank document that is based on the Normal template.

1. Click the Microsoft Office Button 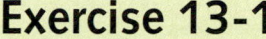, and click **New** to open the New Document dialog box.

Figure 13-1
New Document
dialog box

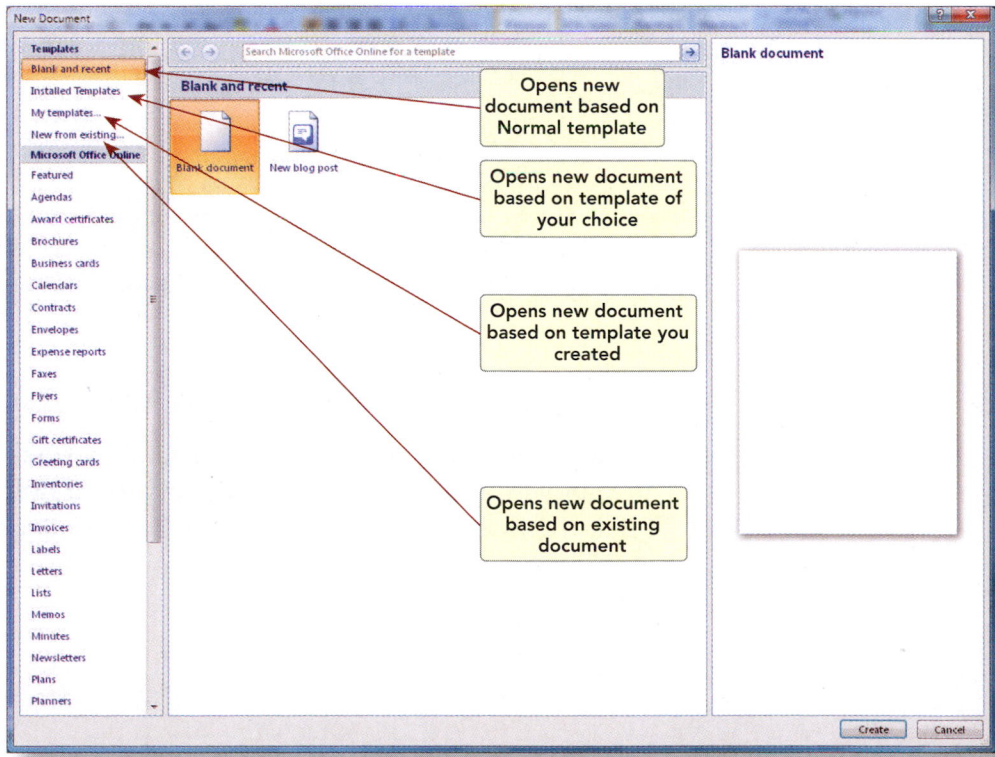

2. Under **Templates** in the New Document dialog box, click **Blank Document**, and click **Create**. Word opens a new document based on the default template Normal and closes the New Document dialog box. (You could also double-click **Blank Document**.)

3. Close the document without saving it.

4. Reopen the New Document dialog box, and click **Installed Templates**.

5. Click the **Equity Fax** icon. Notice the design of the template in the **Preview** box.

NOTE

Some templates might not be installed on your computer. Check with your instructor for instructions on locating the template.

Figure 13-2
Installed Templates

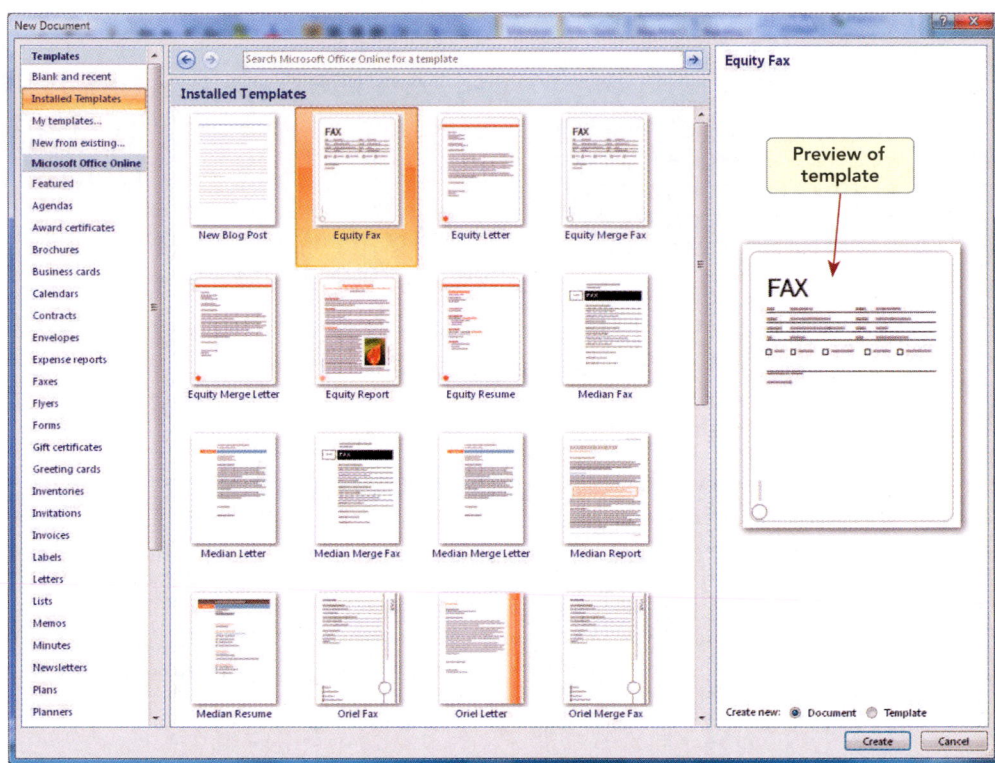

6. Use the **Preview** box to view other Word templates in the dialog box.

7. Click **Letters** under **Microsoft Office Online**. Click **Business**, and click **To Suppliers and vendors**. Click **Acceptance of bid** to preview the letter. Click the Download button [Download]. Click **Continue**. The document displays in a new window.

Figure 13-3
Creating a
document from
the downloaded
template

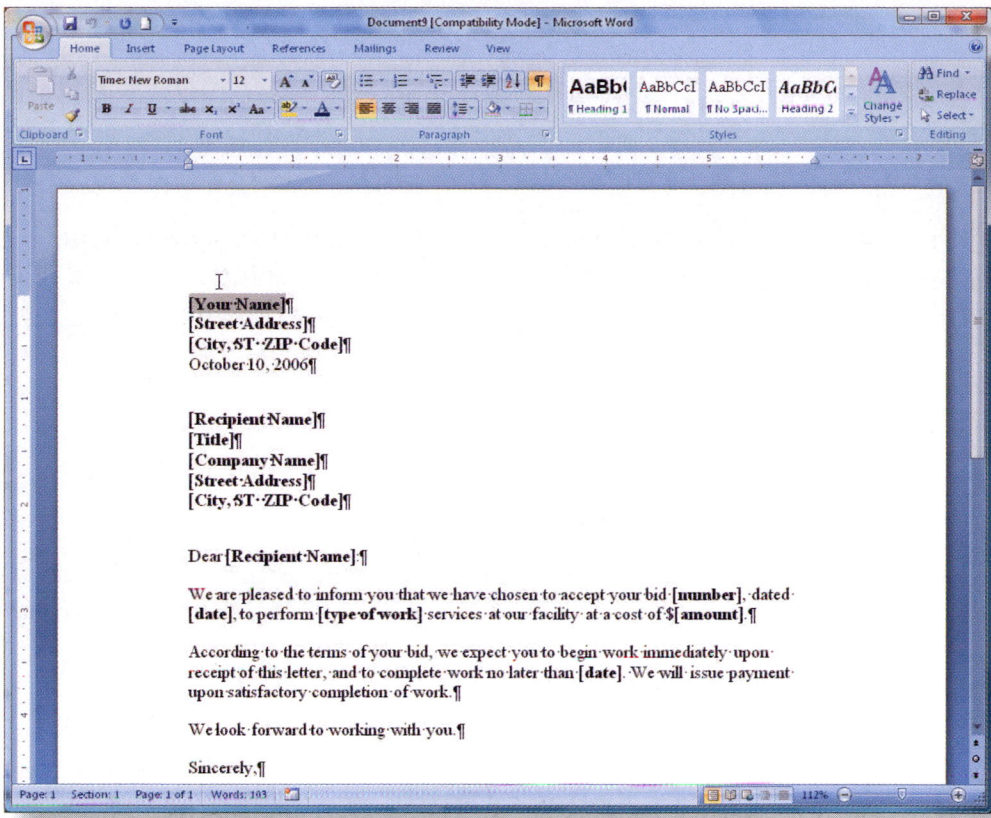

8. Select the first line of the return address, "[Your Name]," and key **Campbell's Confections**. Click to select the placeholder text that reads "[Street Address]." Key **25 Main Street**. Click to select the placeholder that reads "[City, ST ZIP Code]," and key **Grove City, PA 16127**.

9. Click each of the placeholders for the inside address, and key the following replacement text.

Mr. Paul Sakkal
President
Liberty Storage
1000 Millington Court
Cincinnati, OH 45242

10. Click the placeholder in the salutation, and key **Mr. Sakkal**.

11. Edit the first paragraph that begins "We are pleased" as shown in Figure 13-4.

Figure 13-4

We are pleased to inform you that we have chosen to accept your bid No. 876, dated February 1, to install chrome wire shelving at our Grove City factory at a cost of $1,500.

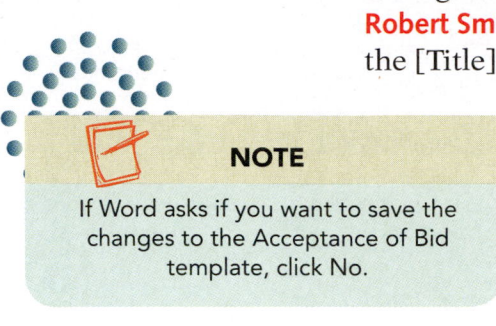

12. Change the date placeholder in the second paragraph to **April 15**. Key **Robert Smith** in the [Your Name] placeholder and **Plant Manager** in the [Title] placeholder. Key your initials at the end of the document.

> **NOTE**
>
> If Word asks if you want to save the changes to the Acceptance of Bid template, click No.

13. Format the first line of the return address (Campbell's Confections) using 14-point bold and small caps.

14. Save the document as *[your initials]***13-1** in a new Lesson 13 folder. Click **Yes**, if a message box appears.

15. Submit and close the document.

Creating New Templates

You can create your own templates for different types of documents by using one of three methods:

- Create a blank template file by using the default template and define the formatting information, styles, and text according to your specifications.

- Open an existing template, modify it, and save it with a new name.

- Open an existing document, modify it, and save it as a new template.

Exercise 13-2   CREATE A NEW TEMPLATE

1. Open the **New Document** dialog box (by clicking the **Microsoft Office Button** and **then New**), and click **My templates** under Templates. Click the **Blank Document** icon.

Figure 13-5
New dialog box showing My Templates

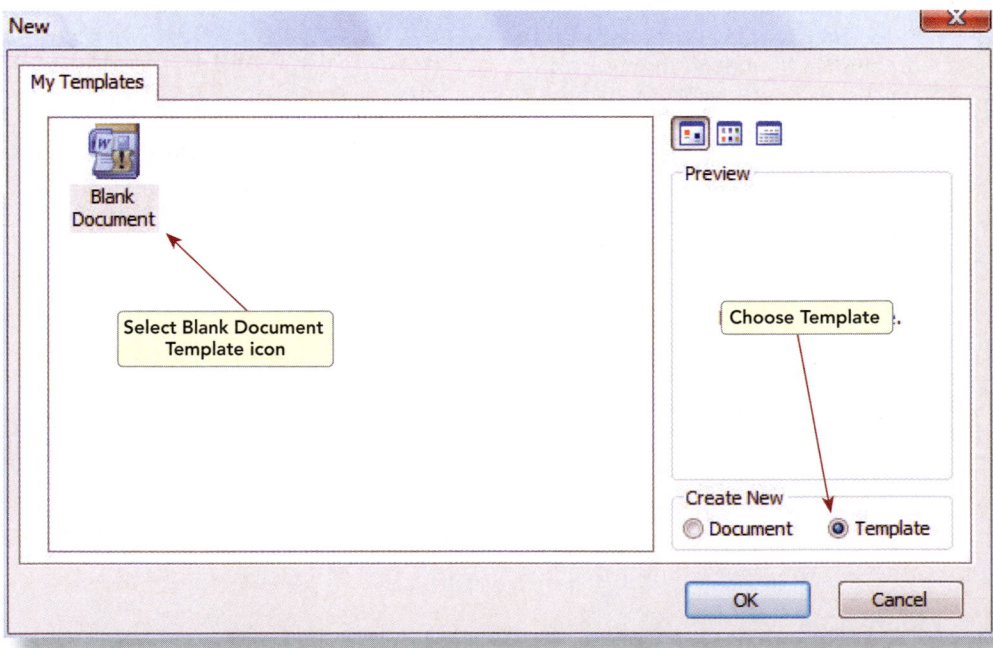

2. In the lower right corner of the dialog box, under **Create New**, click **Template** and then click **OK**. A new template file opens with the default name Template1.

3. Change the top margin to 0.5 inch.

4. Key the text shown in Figure 13-6.

Figure 13-6

```
Campbell's Confections

25 Main Street

Grove City, PA 16127

Telephone: 724-555-2025

Fax: 724-555-2050

www.campbellsconfections.biz
```

5. Select the letterhead information, and center the text horizontally. Select the first line, and apply 14-point bold and small caps formatting.

6. Modify the Normal style to 0 points spacing after and single spacing. Press Enter three times to insert blank lines after the Web address, and change the paragraph alignment to left.

7. Insert the date as a field at the third blank paragraph mark after the letterhead by clicking the **Insert** tab, and clicking **Date and Time**. Use the third date format in the **Available formats** list in the Date and Time dialog box. Check **Update automatically** so the date field is updated each time the document is printed. Click **OK**.

8. Press Enter four times.

9. Click the last line of the letterhead text, and apply a bottom border.

10. Click the **Microsoft Office Button**, click the arrow beside **Save As** and click **Word Template**. A folder named "Templates" should appear in the **Save As** dialog box, and **"Word Template"** should appear in the **Save as type** box.

Word 2007

Figure 13-7
Save As dialog box

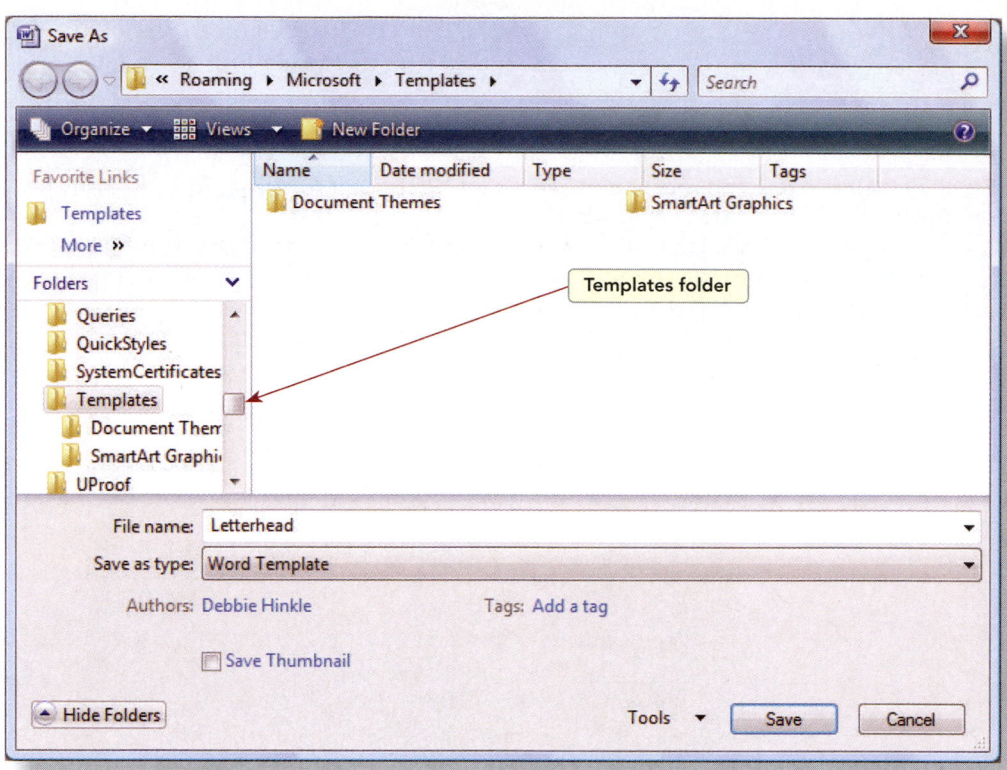

NOTE

By default, Word saves new templates in a User template folder on your hard disk. The specific location is C:\Users\ *Username*\Roaming\Microsoft\Templates (or a similar location in your computer). Before proceeding, ask your instructor where you should save your templates. If you use the default location, you can create new documents from your templates by using the New Document dialog box. If you use your Lesson 13 folder, you create new documents from your templates by using Windows Explorer or My Computer.

11. Save the template with the filename *[your initials]***Letterhead** in your Lesson 13 folder (unless your instructor advises you to save in the default Templates folder).

12. Close the template.

Exercise 13-3　CREATE A NEW TEMPLATE BY USING AN EXISTING DOCUMENT

1. Reopen the New Document dialog box by choosing New from the File menu. Under Templates, click New from existing.

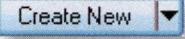

2. Locate and click to select the student data file **Memo - 1**. Click the Create New button ⬚. Word opens a copy of the document.

3. Change the top margin to 2 inches. Select the document, and change the font size to 12.

4. Delete all text to the right of each tab character in the memo heading.

5. Insert the date as a field; use the third date format. Check Update automatically so the date field is updated each time the document is printed.

6. Delete all the document paragraphs, but include the blank paragraph marks after the subject line.

7. Open the File menu, click the arrow beside Save As, and click Word Template. Verify that Word Template displays in the Save as type drop-down list box.

8. Save the file as *[your initials]*Memo in your Lesson 13 folder (unless your instructor advises you to save in the default Templates folder).

9. Close the template.

Attaching Templates to Documents

All existing documents have an assigned template—either Normal or another template that you assigned when you created the document. You can change the template assigned to an existing document by *attaching* a different template to the document. When you attach a template, that template's formatting and elements are applied to the document, and all the template styles become available in the document.

Exercise 13-4　ATTACH A TEMPLATE TO A DOCUMENT

1. Open the New Document dialog box. Click the Memos link for the Microsoft Office Online templates.

2. Click Memo (Professional design), and click the Download button ⬚. Click Continue.

3. Save the professional memo as a template file named *[your initials]*ProMemo in your Lesson 13 folder (unless your instructor advises you to save in the default Templates folder). Click OK if necessary, and close the template.

Word 2007

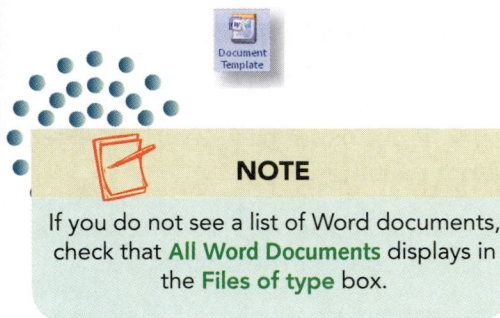

NOTE

If you do not see a list of Word documents, check that **All Word Documents** displays in the **Files of type** box.

4. Open the file **Memo - 4**.

5. Open the Word Options dialog box, and click **Popular** in the left pane. Click to select **Show Developer tab in the Ribbon**. Click **OK**.

6. Click the **Developer** tab in the Ribbon. Click the Document Template button 📄. The Templates and Add-ins dialog box shows that the document is currently based on the Normal template.

Figure 13-8
Templates and
Add-ins dialog box

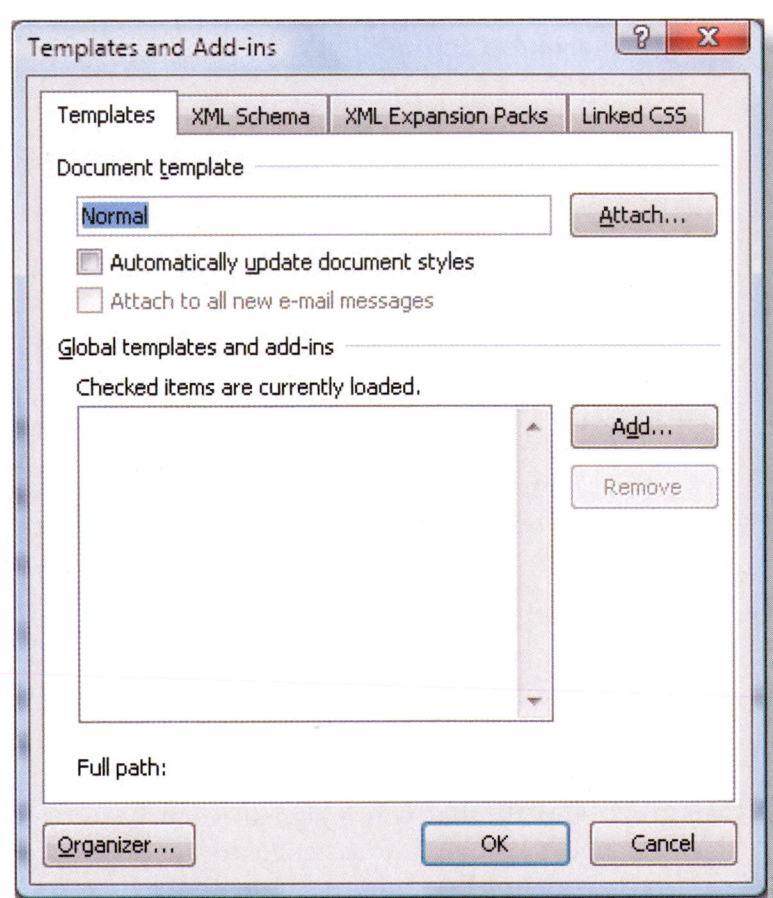

7. Click **Attach**. The Attach Template dialog box opens, displaying available templates and folders in the current folder.

8. Change to the folder that contains Word templates. The full default path of this folder is C:\Program Files\Microsoft Office\Templates\1033. (The folder may not be on the C: drive of your computer. Check with your instructor.)

9. Locate your Lesson 13 folder, and display **All Word Templates** in the **Files of type** box.

Figure 13-9
Attach Template
dialog box

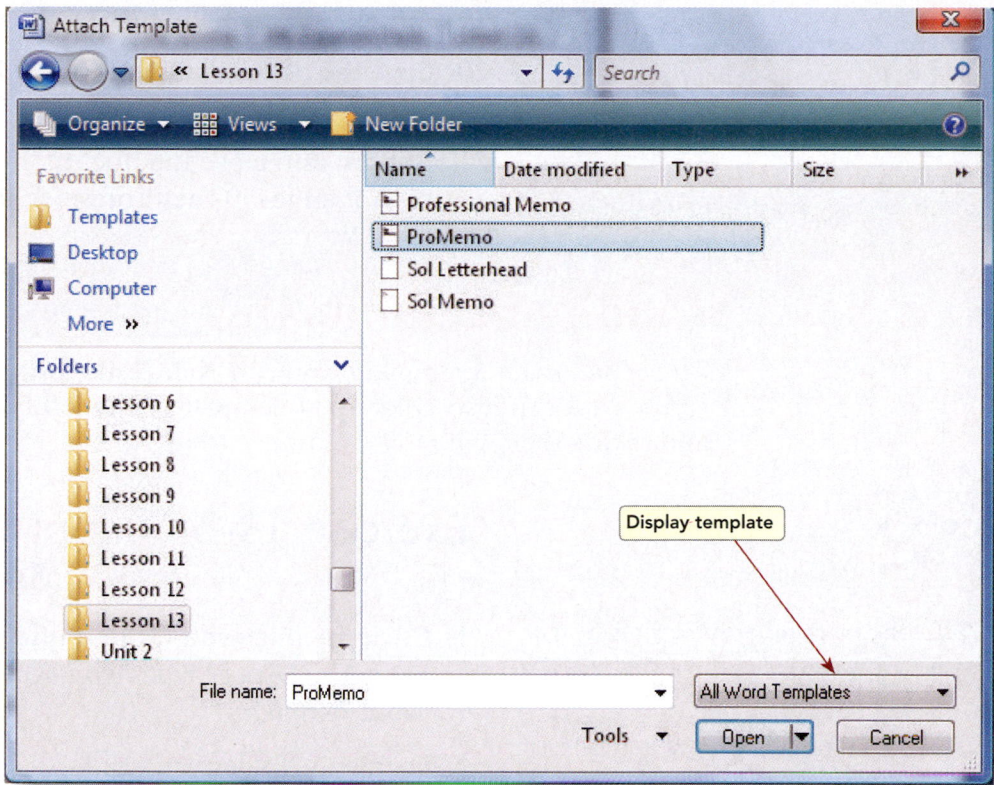

10. Double-click the template **ProMemo**.

11. Click the **Automatically update document styles** check box and click **OK**. Formatting from the Professional Memo template is applied to this document, and you can now apply any of the Professional Memo styles.

12. Display the Styles task pane.

13. Position the insertion point in the subject line of the memo heading, and apply the style **Message Header Last**.

14. Position the insertion point immediately to the left of "TO:" in the memo heading, and press [Enter]. Place the insertion point in the first line of text ("MEMO"), and apply the style **Document Label**.

↔ **REVIEW**

To modify a style before applying it, right-click the style name in the Styles task pane and choose **Modify**.

15. Apply the character style **Message Header Label** to the text "TO:," "FROM:," "DATE:," and "SUBJECT:" in the message header. (Remember, you must select text before applying a character style.) Select all four lines of the message header, and change the left tab setting to 1.5 inches to improve alignment.

16. Delete the text in the date line, and key today's date.

17. Set a 1-inch top margin and a 0.5 inch bottom margin.

18. Modify the Normal style to 12 points spacing after.

Word 2007

NOTE

Attaching a template replaces the template that is currently attached to the document.

19. Add your reference initials.

20. Save the document as *[your initials]***13-4** in your Lesson 13 folder.

21. Submit and close the document. If you are asked to save changes to the Professional Memo template, click **No**.

Modifying Templates

After you create a template, you can change its formatting and redefine its styles. You can also create new templates by modifying existing templates and saving them with a new name.

NOTE

Any changes you make to the formatting or text in a template affect future documents based on that template. The changes do not affect documents that were created from the template before you modified it.

Exercise 13-5   **MODIFY TEMPLATE FORMATTING**

1. Click the **Microsoft Office Button**, and click **Open**. From the **Files of type** drop-down list, choose **All Word Templates**.

2. Locate the folder you used to save your templates (for example, the Templates folder on your hard disk under either C:\Documents and Settings*<your name>*\ Application Data\Microsoft or your Lesson 13 folder).

3. Locate the file *[your initials]***Letterhead**.

4. Double-click the file *[your initials]***Letterhead** to open it. Display the Styles task pane.

5. Click the **Page Layout** tab, and click the Themes button . Change the document theme to **Flow**.

TIP

You can point to a file name to check its file type.

TIP

Opening a template through the Open dialog box opens the actual template. Double-clicking a template in Windows Explorer, My Computer, or the Templates dialog box opens a new document based on the template. Changes that you make to the new document do not affect the template.

6. Modify the Normal style font size to 12 points.

7. Click the Save button 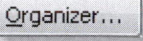 to save the changes. The earlier version of the template is overwritten by the new version.

8. Close the template.

Using the Organizer

Instead of modifying template styles, you can copy individual styles from another document or template into the current document or template by using the Organizer. The copied styles are added to the style sheet of the current document or template. When you copy styles, remember these rules:

- Copied styles replace styles with the same style names.

- Style names are case sensitive—if you copy a style named "HEAD" into a template or document that contains a style named "head," the copied style is added to the style sheet and does not replace the existing style.

You can also copy macros by using the Organizer. To open the Organizer, display and activate the Developer tab if necessary. Click the Document Template command. Click the Organizer button ⟨Organizer...⟩; then select the Styles tab.

Organizer...

Exercise 13-6 COPY STYLES TO ANOTHER TEMPLATE

1. Open the **New Document** dialog box, and click **Installed Templates**. Click to select the **Equity Lettter** icon, and click **Create**.

2. Save the document as a template named *[your initials]*EquityLetter in your Lesson 13 folder. Display the Styles task panel, and notice the list of styles. Close the document.

3. Open the template *[your initials]*Letterhead revised in Exercise 13-5.

4. Click the **Developer** tab, and click the Document Template button ⟨⟩. Click the **Organizer** button ⟨Organizer...⟩.

5. Click the **Styles** tab in the Organizer dialog box. On the left side of the dialog box, the Organizer lists the template and styles currently in use. You use the right side of the dialog box to copy styles to or from another template.

Close File

6. Click the **Close File** button  on the right side of the dialog box. The Normal template closes, and the **Close File** button changes to **Open File**.

Open File...

7. Click the **Open File** button ⟨Open File...⟩. In the Open dialog box, make sure **All Word Templates** appears in the **Files of type** box.

8. Locate the folder that contains the *[your initials]***EquityLetter** template.

9. Double-click the *[your initials]***EquityLetter** template. You can now choose styles from this template to copy into your letterhead template.

Figure 13-10
Organizer dialog box

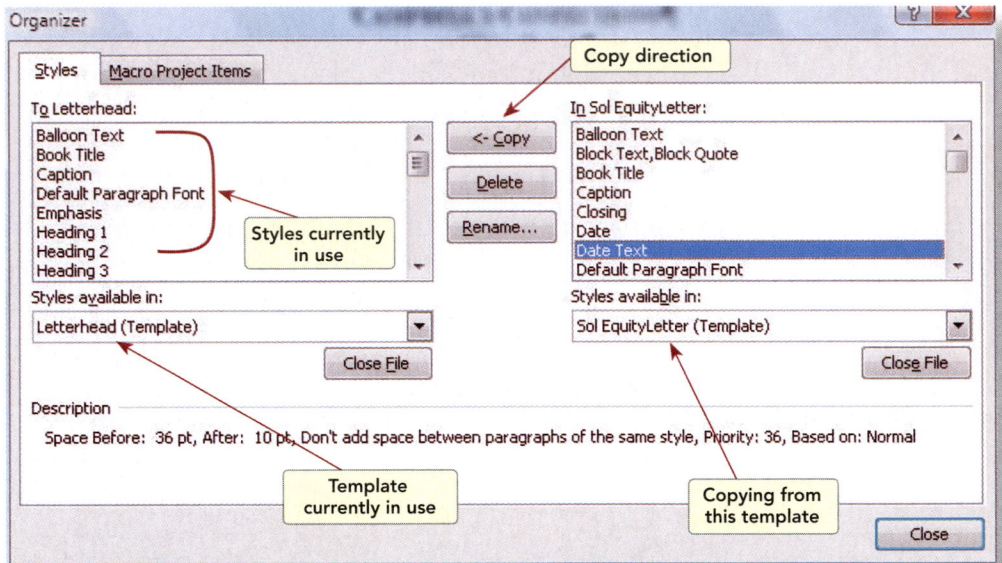

10. Scroll down the list of styles in the EquityLetter template. Click **Date Text** and click **Copy**.

11. Choose the **Normal** style from the EquityLetter style list. Notice the style description.

12. Click **Copy** and then click **Yes** to overwrite the existing style Normal.

13. Close the Organizer dialog box. The styles you chose from the EquityLetter template are copied to the current template. Notice that the Normal style from the EquityLetter template replaced the previous Normal style, so the text is formatted in Constantia 11 point with 8 points spacing after.

Options...

14. Click the Options link ⟨Options...⟩ at the bottom of the Styles task pane. Click the arrow for **Select styles to show** and select **All styles**. Click **OK**.

15. Apply the newly copied style Date Text to the date line.

16. Close the template without saving changes.

Lesson 13 Summary

- A template is a reusable model for a particular type of document. Templates can contain formatting, text, and other elements. By default, all new documents are based on the Normal template.

- Word provides a variety of templates upon which you can base a new document or a new template. You can modify any existing template and save it with a new name. You can also modify any existing document and save it as a new template.

- Every document is based on a template. You can change the template assigned to an existing document by attaching a different template to the document, thereby making the new template's styles available in the document.

- To modify a template you created, open it from the Open dialog box and choose All Word Templates from the Files of type drop-down list.

- Instead of modifying template styles, use the Organizer to copy individual styles from one document or template to another.

LESSON 13		Command Summary	
Feature	Button	Command	Keyboard
Use a template		Microsoft Office Button, New	
Attach template		Developer tab, Templates group, Document Template	
Copy styles		Developer tab, Templates group, Document Template, Organizer	

Concepts Review

True/False Questions

Each of the following statements is either true or false. Indicate your choice by circling T or F.

T   F   1. The file extension for a Word template is .tmp.

T   F   2. You can open the New Document dialog box by pressing Ctrl+N.

T   F   3. After a template is assigned to a document, it cannot be changed.

T   F   4. A Word template can contain placeholder text that you replace with your own information.

T   F   5. When styles are copied to a template, if the style names do not match the existing styles, they are added to the style sheet.

T   F   6. Existing templates cannot be modified.

T   F   7. If you do not specify a template when you create a new document, the document is created without one.

T   F   8. You can use the Organizer to copy styles between templates or documents.

Short Answer Questions

Write the correct answer in the space provided.

1. What is the file extension assigned to a template filename?

   _____

2. When you choose **New** from the Microsoft Office Button menu, what happens?

   _____

3. Which commands would you use to open the dialog box to attach a different template to a document?

   _____

4. How can you create a new template by using an existing document?

   _____

5. How can you change the styles in a template to match the styles in another template or document?

   _____

6. What is the procedure to download a template from Microsoft Office Online?

_____

7. What is the procedure to save a template?

_____

8. How do you change a template theme?

_____

Critical Thinking

Answer these questions on a separate page. There are no right or wrong answers. Support your answers with examples from your own experience, if possible.

1. Review Word's templates for letters, memos, and reports. How do they compare with the standard business format for these documents as described in *The Gregg Reference Manual* (or a similar handbook)?

2. Many businesses create templates that are used by all employees for internal and external correspondence. Why would a business take this approach? What advantages does it offer to a business?

Skills Review

Exercise 13-7

Use an existing Word template to create a letter.

1. Create a letter based on a template from Microsoft Office Online by following these steps:
   a. Click the **Microsoft Office Button** and click **New**.
   b. Click **Letters** under **Microsoft Office Online**, and click **Community**. Locate and click the **Congratulations on appointment to city council** icon. Click **Download**. Click **Continue**.
2. At the top of the document, click the placeholder text for [Your Name] and key **Campbell's Confections**. Key the following address in the appropriate placeholders.

   25 Main Street
   Grove City, PA 16127
3. Modify the Sender Address style to 14-point bold and small caps.

4. Replace or edit the placeholder text in the document with the text shown in Figure 13-11. Click or select each placeholder before entering the appropriate text. You might want to increase the zoom when keying the last two lines.

Figure 13-11

```
Ms. Ann Foster

Vice President

Foster Travel

600 Broad Street

Grove City, PA 16127

Dear Ms. Foster:

Thank you for your willingness to participate in our local
government. This recent appointment will enable you to
continue your longstanding commitment to the community and
our civic projects.

Thomas Campbell

President
```

5. At the blank paragraph marks below the closing, add your reference initials.
6. Modify the Normal style to the font Cambria. (This changes all the styles used below the company name, which are based on the Normal style.)
7. Change the paragraph spacing for the Date style to 24 points before and 36 points after.
8. Save the document as *[your initials]*13-7 in your Lesson 13 folder.
9. Submit and close the document.

Exercise 13-8

Create a new template, attach it to another document, and modify a template.

1. Create a new template by following these steps:
   a. Open the **File** menu, and click **New**.
   b. Click **My templates**, and click the icon for the **Blank Document** template.
   c. Under **Create New**, click **Template** and click **OK**.
2. Modify the Normal style to be 11-point Arial.

3. Modify the Heading 1 style so the paragraph formatting is center-aligned and the font size is 18 points.

4. Modify the Heading 2 style so the paragraph formatting is center-aligned with bold and italic formatting.

5. Modify the Heading 3 style to include small caps format. (If necessary click **Options** at the bottom of the Styles task pane and click the arrow for **Select styles to show** and select **All styles**.)

6. Save the template as *[your initials]*Agenda in your Lesson 13 folder or in the default Templates folder on the hard disk, whichever your instructor told you to use. Close the template.

7. Start a new document based on the Normal template by clicking the **Microsoft Office Button** and clicking **New**. Click the Blank Document icon and click **Create**.

8. Key the text shown in Figure 13-12. Use single spacing. Apply the heading styles to the paragraphs indicated.

Figure 13-12

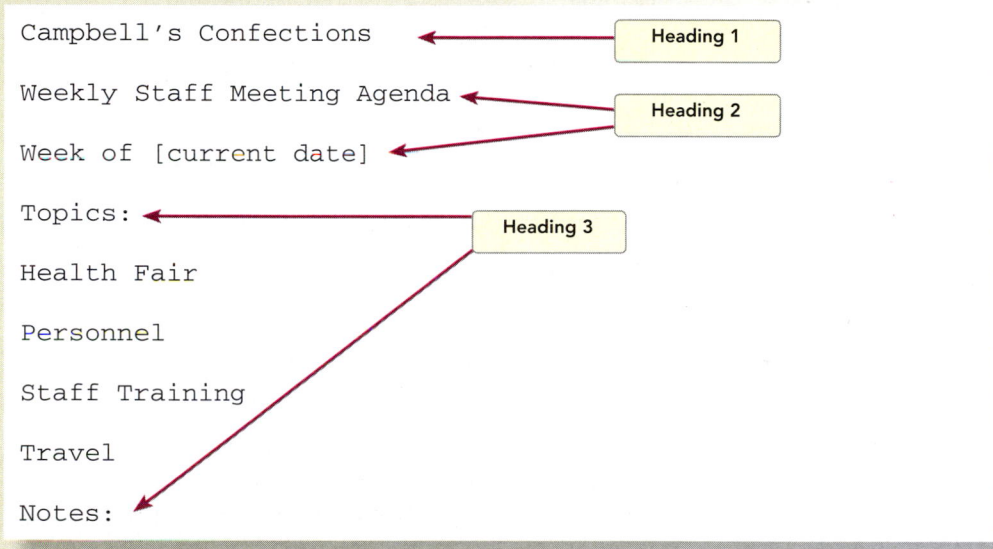

9. Attach the template you created, and automatically update the styles by following these steps:

a. Click the **Developer** tab, and click the Document Template button.

b. Click **Attach**.

c. Locate *[your initials]*Agenda and click **Open**.

d. Check the **Automatically update document styles** check box, and click **OK**.

10. Save the document as *[your initials]*13-8 in your Lesson 13 folder.

11. Submit and close the document.

Exercise 13-9

Use the Organizer to copy styles.

1. Open the **New Document** dialog box, and click **Installed Templates**. Locate and click the icon for **Equity Report**. Click **Create**.

2. Save the document template as *[your initials]***EquityReport** in your Lesson 13 folder. Close the template.

3. Open the file **Company - 2**.

4. Apply the Heading 1 style to the first line (the company name). Apply the Heading 2 style to the bold side headings.

5. Display all styles by following these steps:

   a. Click **Options** in the Styles task pane.

   b. Click the arrow to display the drop-down list for **Select styles to show**.

   c. Click **All styles**. Click **OK**.

6. Use the Organizer to copy styles from another template by following these steps:

   a. Click the **Developer** tab and click the Document Template button . Click **Organizer**.

   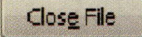

   b. Click the **Styles** tab. Click the Close File button on the right side of the dialog box (under **Normal.dot**).

   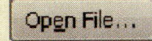

   c. Click the Open File button on the right side of the dialog box.

   d. Locate the folder that contains the *[your initials]***EquityReport** template, and click **Open**.

   e. Click **Normal** in the list on the right side of the dialog box (under **EquityReport**), and then click **Copy**. Click **Yes** to overwrite the existing style entry.

   f. Repeat the previous step to copy the Footer, Heading 1, Heading 2, and Heading 3 styles from the EquityReport template on the right to the **Company - 2** document on the left. To copy the styles simultaneously, hold down Ctrl while selecting each of the styles to copy. When prompted, overwrite the existing style entries in the **Company - 2** document.

   g. Click the **Close** button to close the Organizer dialog box.

7. Insert page numbers at the bottom right of the document, starting with 2 on page 2.

8. Modify the paragraph spacing for the Heading 1 style to 72 points before and 24 points after.

9. Save the document as *[your initials]***13-9** in your Lesson 13 folder.

10. Submit and close the document.

Exercise 13-10

Use an online template to create a new template.

1. Open the New Document dialog box, and click Gift certificates under Microsoft Office Online.

2. Click Employee gift certificate, and download the template. Save the template as *[your initials]*Gift in your Lesson 13 folder or in the default Templates folder on the hard disk, whichever your instructor told you to use.

3. Key Campbell's Confections in the [Company Name or Logo] placeholder for each gift certificate.

4. Key $25 Gift Certificate in the [Gift Name] placeholder for the first gift certificate. Key $50 Gift Certificate for the second certificate and $75 Gift Certificate for the third certificate.

5. Modify the Heading 1 style by changing the font color to black and applying bold and small caps formatting.

6. Modify the giftname style by changing the font color to black and applying small caps.

7. Use the replace command to modify the gift certificates. Change Group to Store. Change Department/Account to Certificate Number.

8. Save the template.

9. Submit and close the template.

Lesson Applications

Exercise 13-11

Use a template to create a document.

1. Create a document based on the template you created: *[your initials]*Letterhead.

2. Key the following information for the inside address:

   Ms. Barbara Scott
   National Fitness Center
   1237 West Main Street
   Grove City, PA 16127

3. Key Dear Ms. Scott for the salutation.

4. Open the file **Fitness**. Copy all the text and paste it into the letter.

5. Add as a closing paragraph.

   Thank you for your assistance. I will call for an appointment to discuss a formal agreement.

6. Key an appropriate complimentary closing and the following signature name and title:

   Garland Miller
   Human Resources

7. On the next line, key your reference initials followed by an enclosure notation.

8. Modify the Normal style by changing the font to Cambria.

9. Spell-check the document, and save it as *[your initials]*13-11 in your Lesson 13 folder.

10. Submit the document. Close both open documents.

Exercise 13-12

Use a template and copy styles by using the Organizer.

1. Start a new document based on the template you created: *[your initials]*Memo.

2. The memo is to "All Employees" from Garland Miller. The subject is "Fitness Center Membership."

3. Two blank lines below the subject line, key the text from Figure 13-13

Figure 13-13

> Campbell's Confections is contacting area fitness centers to negotiate a contract to provide lower membership fees for our employees.
>
> Please complete the attached survey so that we can determine which programs you prefer as well as your preferences for hours of operation, types of membership, and payment plans.
>
> Please return the completed survey by Friday.

4. Open the Organizer dialog box by displaying the Developer tab, and clicking Document Template. Click Organizer. On the right side of the dialog box, close the Normal template file and open *[your initials]*ProMemo template.

5. Copy the styles Company Name, Normal, Message Header First, Message Header Label, and Message Header Last to the current document, replacing the Normal style entry when prompted. Close the Organizer dialog box.

6. Insert a new paragraph mark above the "TO:" line. At the new paragraph mark, key Campbell's Confections and apply the Company Name style.

7. Modify the Company Name style by changing the font size to 24 points and adding 24 points spacing after. Change the line spacing to At least 12 pt. Change the top margin to 1 inch.

8. Key your reference initials at the end of the document.

9. Modify the Normal style by increasing the font size to 12 points.

10. Save the document as *[your initials]*13-12 in your Lesson 13 folder.

11. Submit and close the document.

Exercise 13-13

Modify a template and attach a template.

1. Open the template you created: *[your initials]*Letterhead. (Use the Open dialog box—do not create a document based on this template.)

2. Modify the Normal style to a 12-point font of your choice.

3. Save the template as *[your initials]*Letterhead2 in the folder where you saved the other templates. Close the template.

4. Open the file **Hernandez**.

5. Attach the template *[your initials]*letterhead2, updating document styles automatically.

6. Key the date at the top of the document followed by three blank lines.

7. Add your reference initials and an enclosure notation.

8. Set a 2-inch top margin. Add blank lines between paragraphs to format the document as a business letter.

9. Save the document as *[your initials]*13-13 in your Lesson 13 folder.

10. Submit and close the document.

Exercise 13-14 ◆ Challenge Yourself

Copy and apply styles.

1. Open the template file **Equity Fax** (Installed Templates).

2. Use the Organizer dialog box to copy all styles from the Origin Fax template (Installed Templates) to the Equity Fax template. (Remember: to select all styles, click the first file, scroll to the last file, press Shift and click.)

> **NOTE**
>
> To locate the Origin Fax template, change to the folder that contains the installed Word Templates (Program Files\Microsoft Office\Templates\1033\Fax).

3. Click Yes to overwrite the styles, and close the dialog box.

4. Open the Styles task pane.

5. Select "To:" in the heading, and apply the Message Header style.

6. Apply the Message Header style to all headings in the Equity Fax template.

7. Save the template as *[your initials]*13-14 in your Lesson 13 folder.

8. Submit and close the document.

On Your Own

In these exercises you work on your own, as you would in a real-life business environment. Use the skills you've learned to accomplish the task—and be creative.

Exercise 13-15

Use a résumé template to create your résumé. Include as much detail about yourself as possible. Modify the formatting as needed. Save the document as *[your initials]*13-15 and submit it.

Exercise 13-16

Create a cover letter for your résumé, using a matching template style. Address the cover letter to a prospective employer. Create an envelope for the letter. Save the document as *[your initials]*13-16 and submit it.

Exercise 13-17

Using the New Document dialog box, go to Microsoft Office Online and choose a template from any category. Preview and download the template, and then edit it in Word, using your own information. Save the document as *[your initials]*13-17 and submit it.

Unit 3 Applications

Unit Application 3-1

Create a cover letter for a document as a separate section; insert a page break and a continuation page header.

1. Open the file **Assortment**.

2. Add a blank page to the beginning of the document (use a section break to separate the cover letter from the **Assortment** document). To create the cover letter, key the text shown in Figure U3-1, including the corrections on page 1 of the document. Use the standard letter format. The letter should be from Richard Matthews, Wholesale Sales Division. Include your reference initials and an enclosure notation.

Figure U3-1

Mr. Patrick O'Reilly

Village Center

226 Pierce Avenue

Sharpsville, PA 16150

Dear Mr. O'Reilly:

As you requested, enclosed is the information about our wholesale division.

Campbell's Confections entered the wholesale market during the mid 1990s. A contract was negotiated with a large hotel chain to provide boxed chocolates for the gift stores. A second contract was approved ~~in 1997~~ with the Pittsburgh Airport.

Wholesale contracts are only negotiated with businesses that can provide multiple locations for our chocolates. Wholesale prices are based on a minimum order of $570. The wholesale agreements also stipulate the proper conditions for storing and displaying Campbell's Chocolates.

Initial chocolate offerings for the wholesale market include assorted chocolate-covered nuts (milk and dark chocolate), assorted chocolate-covered creams (milk and dark chocolate), and assorted melt-a-ways (milk and dark chocolate). Sugar-free chocolates and chocolate bars are also available.

Let me know if you have any questions. I look forward to speaking with you soon.

3. Change the top margin for section 1 to 2 inches.

4. Create a right-aligned footer for section 2. The text should include the text **Updated** followed by today's date inserted as a field that is automatically updated.

5. In section 2, delete blank paragraphs, and center the text vertically.

6. Select the bulleted list for each category on the page, and sort the text alphabetically.

7. Spell-check the letter only.

8. Change the first heading in section 2 to all caps, and center the heading.

9. Save the document as *[your initials]***u3-1** in a new folder for Unit 3 Applications.

10. Submit and close the document.

Unit Application 3-2

Create a memo; change page orientation; apply section formatting.

1. Open the file **Emboss**. Format the document as a memo to "Store Managers" from Robert Smith. Use the current date, and the subject is "New Products."

2. Add a Next Page section break at the end of the document, and key the text shown in Figure U3-2. Set a left-aligned tab for the text in each column under "Sample Letters." Use the Symbol dialog box (Symbol font) to insert the Greek letters.

Figure U3-2

```
Campbell's Confections

announces

Chocolate Embossing:

Greek Alphabet

Mascots

Sample Letters:

Alpha           A

Beta            B

Gamma           Γ

Delta           Δ

Epsilon         E
```

3. Change the top margin for section 1 to 2 inches. Key your reference initials and an attachment notation at the end of section 1.

4. Format section 2 with landscape orientation and centered vertically. Center the first six lines.

5. Open the Styles task pane, and modify the Heading 1 style for center alignment, 18 points, and small caps. Modify Heading 2 style for center alignment, 16 points spacing after, and 14-point small caps.

6. Select "Chocolate Embossing" through "Sample Letters," and apply 14-point bold and italic formatting.

7. Apply the Heading 1 style to the first line of section 2, and apply the Heading 2 style to the second line of section 2.

8. Format "Sample Letters" to have 24 points spacing before and small caps formatting.

9. Select the text from "Sample Letters" through "E," and apply 1-inch left and right indents, 18-point font size, and a $2^1/_4$ pt box border with 10 percent gray shading.

10. Add a double-line page border to section 2.

11. Preview the document, and then save it as *[your initials]*u3-2 in your Unit 3 Applications folder.

12. Submit and close the document.

Unit Application 3-3

Create a new template, create and apply paragraph and character styles, modify styles, and use style options.

1. Create a new document based on the default template. Change the left and right margins to 1.25 inches.

2. Key the title **Campbell's Confections**, and press Enter. Center the title, and change the font size to 20 points and apply small caps.

3. Key **Holiday Update** and press Enter two times.

4. Create a paragraph style named **Subhead** that is 14-point Arial, all caps, and centered, and apply it to the second line of text.

5. At the last paragraph mark, key **Chocolate Events**. Create and apply a paragraph style for this text based on the Normal style and named **UpdateHead**. Use 12-point Arial bold with all caps.

6. Save the document as a template named *[your initials]*update in your Unit 3 Applications folder or in the default Templates folder on the hard disk, whichever your instructor tells you to use. Close the template.

7. Start a new document based on the template *[your initials]*update.

8. Replace the words "CHOCOLATE EVENTS" with the current year.

9. One line below "200-," key **Akron, Ohio**, and apply the Normal style.

10. To the right of "Akron, OH," insert a tab character and key **January 3**.

11. To this line of text, create and apply a paragraph style named **CityName** using 12-point Arial bold with a 3-inch left tab setting.

12. Create a paragraph style named **IndentedPara** based on the CityName style, using 12-point Arial regular, with 12 points spacing after paragraphs and a 3-inch hanging indent.

13. Assign Indentedpara as the style for the paragraph following CityName.

14. Assign CityName as the style for the paragraph following Indentedpara.

15. Create a character style named **EventDate** using 11-point Arial bold italic, and apply it to the text "January 3."

16. Press Enter after "3," press Tab, and key **National Chocolate-Covered Cherry Day**.

17. Press Enter and key the text shown in Figure U3-3. Press Tab before each date and before each description. Apply the EventDate style to all the date text.

Figure U3-3

```
Clarksburg, WV        February 19
                      Chocolate Mint Day

Grove City, PA        March—Third Week
                      American Chocolate Week

Canton, OH            April 21
                      National Chocolate-Covered Cashews Day

Morgantown, WV        May 15
                      National Chocolate Chip Day

Monroeville, PA       June
                      National Candy Month

Youngstown, OH        July 7
                      Chocolate Day

Fairmont, WV          September 22
                      National White Chocolate Day

Butler, PA            October 28
                      National Chocolate Day
```

18. Modify the CityName style to 11 points.

19. Align the entire document vertically on the page.

20. Spell-check the document, and save it as *[your initials]*u3-3 in your folder for Unit 3 Applications.

21. Submit and close the document.

Unit Application 3-4 ◆ Using the Internet

Work with sections, page numbers, and headers and footers.

1. Using the Internet, research the history of chocolate.

2. Create a 3- to 5-page report, and organize the document into sections.

3. Include the following topics and create sections for each topic:

   • A timeline of the history of chocolate—include a brief description of major events for each century.

   • Mention Columbus, Aztecs, Mayas, and European influence.

   • Major producers of cacao pods.

   • Create a title page for the document as a separate section.

   • Title each subsequent section of the document.

   • Check pagination, and apply line and page break options where needed.

   • Include appropriate headers/footers and page numbering on all pages except the title page.

4. Save the document as *[your initials]*u3-4 in your Unit 3 Applications folder, and submit it.

microsoft® office excel®

A Professional Approach

EXCEL 2007

Kathleen Stewart

There's more to learning a spreadsheet program like Microsoft Office Excel than simply keying data. You need to know how to use Excel in real-world situations. That's why all the lessons in this book relate to everyday business tasks.

As you work through the lessons, imagine yourself working as an intern for Klassy Kow Ice Cream, Inc., a fictional San Francisco business that manufactures and sells ice cream.

Klassy Kow Ice Cream, Inc.

Klassy Kow Ice Cream, Inc., was formed in 1985 by Conrad Steele, shortly after the death of his father. Since 1967, Conrad's father and mother had been dairy farmers in Klamath Falls, Oregon. As an addition to their farm, Archibald and Henrietta Steele opened a small ice cream shop. They made their own ice cream from fresh cream, eggs, and butter—starting simply with vanilla, chocolate, and strawberry flavors. They also sold cones, sundaes, shakes, and malts.

As word spread about their delicious ice cream, Archie and Henrietta's business blossomed from a seasonal shop to a year-round store. Eventually, the Steeles expanded the number of flavors and started to offer hand-packed ice cream pies and cakes. They also started to sell to small supermarkets in southern Oregon under the "Klassy Kow" name, allowing their many local customers to buy half-gallons at their favorite supermarkets.

The business continued to expand and soon reached into supermarkets in the Pacific Northwest. Archibald and Henrietta opened new ice cream shops in Medford, Oregon, and Eureka and Red Bluff, California.

After Archibald Steele died, Conrad and his mother sold the dairy farm but kept the ice cream shops. They continue to buy ice cream from the new owners (the Klamath Farm) and have expanded the ice cream business to include 33 franchised ice cream shops in the western United States.

In 1998, with Klassy Kow continuing to grow steadily, Conrad decided to move the corporate headquarters to San Francisco, California. His mother, Henrietta, is retired and still lives in Klamath Falls, where she continues to help create and test new flavors for the Klamath Farm.

The company now has more than 200 employees, but the number of employees in the San Francisco office is surprisingly small. Most employees work in the ice cream shops scattered across Washington, Idaho, Oregon, Nevada, and northern California.

Conrad Steele, who is now president and chief executive officer of Klassy Kow, is responsible for the general operations of the company. He says, "I love to see a big smile on a customer's face after the first lick. It makes it all worth it."

Conrad visits many of the ice cream shops and likes to keep in touch with customers. He visits Klamath Farms at least four times a year to keep in contact with his major supplier.

All the worksheets, data, and graphics you will use in this course relate to Klassy Kow Ice Cream, Inc. As you work with the worksheets in the text, take the time to notice the following:

- The types of worksheets needed in a small business to carry on day-to-day business.
- The formatting of worksheets. Real businesses don't always pay attention to formatting internal worksheets. However, they do focus on formatting worksheets that customers will see.
- The types of business activities required by a company such as Klassy Kow. For example, it must deal with employees, internal accounting, and suppliers.

As you use this text and become more experienced with Microsoft Office Excel, you will also gain expertise in creating, editing, and formatting the sort of worksheets generated in a real-life business environment.

Klassy Kow Klassics

Sugar Cones	Waffle Cones
Ice Cream	Frozen Yogurt
Shakes	Malteds
Ice Cream Sodas	Ice Cream Sundaes
Ice Cream Cakes	Ice Cream Pies
Ice Cream Sandwiches	Soda
Coffee	

Kowabunga
(An ice cream beverage available in several flavors)

KowOwow
(A cow-shaped ice cream bar)

unit 1

INTRODUCTION TO EXCEL

Lesson 1   Getting Started with Excel   EX-6

Lesson 2   Creating a Workbook   EX-40

Lesson 3   Using Editing and Style Tools   EX-80

Lesson 4   Exploring Home Tab
            Commands   EX-116

UNIT 1   APPLICATIONS   EX-161

Lesson 1

Getting Started with Excel

OBJECTIVE

After completing this lesson, you will be able to:

1. Start Excel.

2. Navigate in a workbook.

3. Open an existing workbook.

4. Edit a worksheet.

5. Manage files.

6. Print Excel files.

MCAS OBJECTIVES

In this lesson:

XL07 1.3
XL07 1.4.1
XL07 1.4.3
XL07 5.4
XL07 5.4.2
XL07 5.5

Estimated Time: 1 hour

Microsoft Excel is *electronic spreadsheet software*. You can use Excel to create professional reports that perform business or personal calculations, display financial or scientific calculations, complete table management tasks, and show charts. Excel is powerful but easy to use. You'll become a productive Excel user as soon as you learn the basics.

Starting Excel

Excel opens showing a blank workbook, the Microsoft Office Button, the Quick Access toolbar, and the Ribbon (see Figure 1-1). New workbooks are named Book1, Book2, and so on during each work session.

The *Ribbon* is a set of command tabs. Each command tab has buttons, galleries, or other controls related to a specific task group or object. Some command tabs

NOTE

The command tabs in the Ribbon are similar to panes or tabs in a dialog box.

Figure 1-1
Excel screen

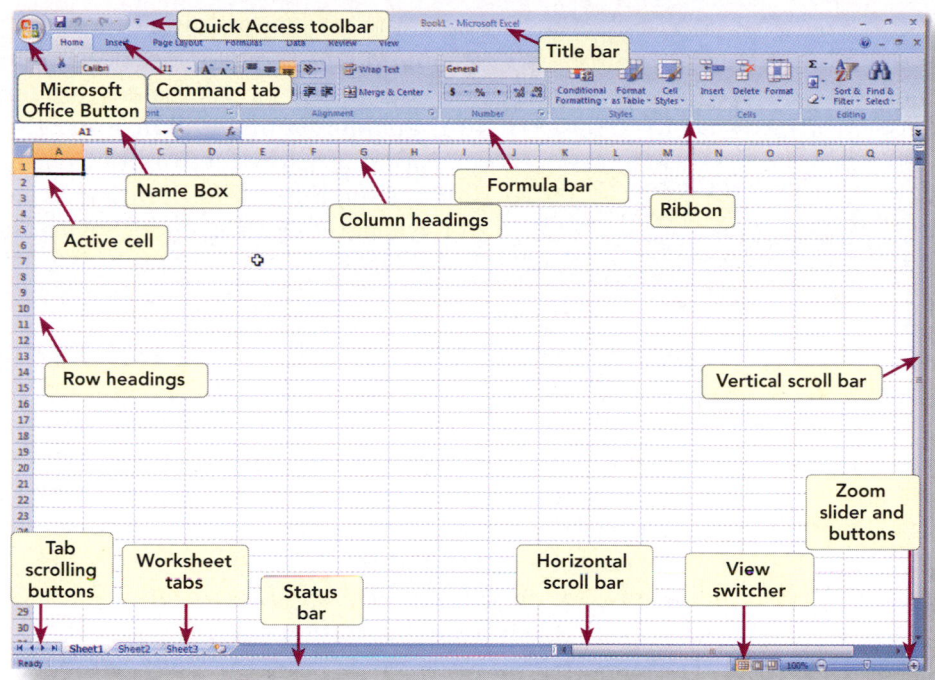

TABLE 1-1 Parts of the Excel Screen

Part of Screen	Purpose
Active cell	The cell outlined in a heavy black border. It is ready to accept new data, a formula, or your edits.
Column headings	Alphabetic characters across the top of the worksheet that identify columns.
Command tabs	A Ribbon tab control with command buttons, galleries, and other controls for creating, managing, editing, and formatting data.
Formula bar	Displays the contents of the active cell. You can also enter text, numbers, or formulas in the formula bar. It can be expanded and collapsed as needed.
Microsoft Office Button	Opens a menu with basic commands for working with the document.
Name Box	A drop-down combo box that shows the address of the active cell. You can also use it to move the pointer to a specific location.
Quick Access toolbar	Toolbar with shortcut command buttons for common tasks.
Ribbon	Organizes and displays command tabs.
Row headings	Numbers down the left side of the worksheet that identify rows.
Scroll bars	Used to move different parts of the screen into view.
Status bar	Displays information about the current task and mode of operation as well as View choices and the Zoom control.
Tab scrolling buttons	Navigation buttons to scroll through worksheet tabs.
Title bar	Contains the program name and the name of the workbook.
View switcher	Buttons to change the view of the current sheet among Normal, Page Layout, and Page Break Preview.
Worksheet tabs	Indicators at the bottom of the worksheet to identify sheets in the workbook.
Zoom controls	Buttons and slider to change the view magnification.

NOTE

Windows provides many ways to start applications. If you have problems, ask your instructor for help.

are context-sensitive and appear only when needed to accommodate what you are doing. The *Quick Access toolbar* provides one-click access to frequently used commands. You can add command buttons to this toolbar, and you can reposition it below the Ribbon. The *Microsoft Office Button* replaces the File menu in previous versions of Office, but it still lists commands such as Save and Print.

Exercise 1-1   WORK WITH THE EXCEL INTERFACE

There are several ways to start Excel, depending on how your software is installed. You can use the Start button on the Windows taskbar to choose Excel from the list of available programs. There may be an Excel icon on the desktop that you can double-click to start Excel.

Your screen size and resolution affects how the command buttons look and how much you see at once. Do not be concerned if your screen looks slightly different from illustrations in this text.

When the instructions tell you to "click" a tab, a command button, or a menu option, use the left mouse button. Use the left mouse button to carry out commands unless you are told explicitly to use the right mouse button.

1. Start Excel. A blank workbook opens.

2. Click the **Home** tab in the Ribbon. Commands on this tab are organized into seven groups: Clipboard, Font, Alignment, Number, Styles, Cells, and Editing.

NOTE

Super ScreenTips explain the purpose of the button, provide a keyboard shortcut, and when appropriate, describe when you might use the feature. They might also include a thumbnail image of a dialog box to be opened.

3. In the **Font** group, rest the mouse pointer on the Bold button ⓑ. A *Super ScreenTip* includes the button name, a brief description of the button's function, and its keyboard shortcut.

4. In the **Font** group, rest the mouse pointer on the Dialog Box Launcher. A Super ScreenTip describes and previews the dialog box that will be opened when you click this button. Many command groups have a Dialog Box Launcher.

Figure 1-2
Dialog Box Launcher
for the Font group

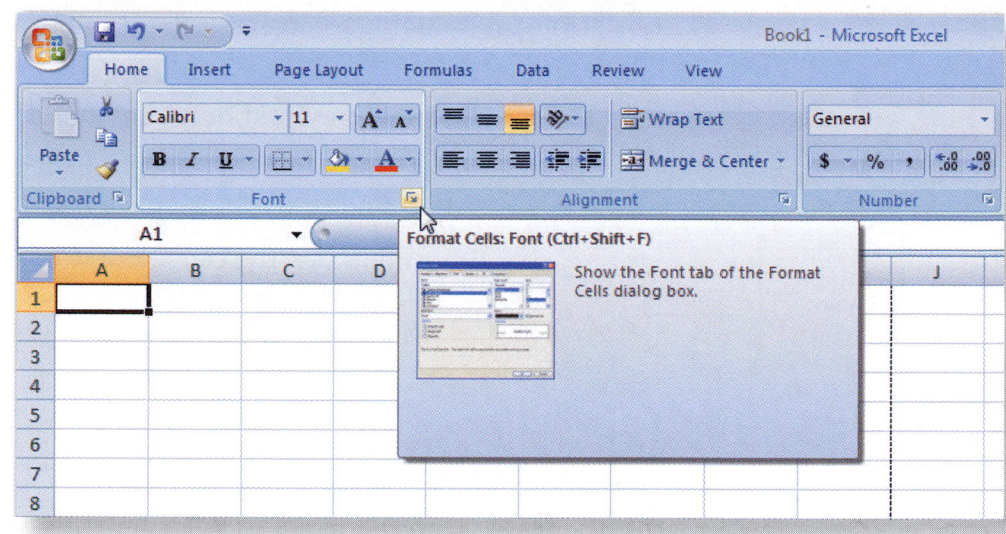

5. Click the Dialog Box Launcher for the **Font** group. The Format Cells dialog box opens with the **Font** tab visible.

6. Click **Cancel** to close the dialog box.

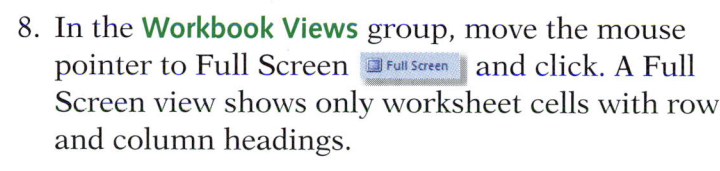

7. Click the **View** tab in the Ribbon. Commands on this tab are organized into five groups: Workbook Views, Show/Hide, Zoom, Window, and Macros.

8. In the **Workbook Views** group, move the mouse pointer to Full Screen and click. A Full Screen view shows only worksheet cells with row and column headings.

9. Press Esc on the keyboard to return to normal view.

10. Click the Page Layout View button . This view is an interactive preview of how the page will print and shows margins, the ruler, and header/footer areas. The grid does not print.

11. Click the Normal button .

12. Press and release the Alt key. *KeyTips* appear over a command name when you press the Alt key. They show keyboard shortcuts.

13. Key **h** to activate the **Home** tab.

14. Press Tab four times. The active task cycles through the commands in the Clipboard group, and the KeyTips are no longer visible. The Clipboard group is now active.

15. Press Esc.

16. Press F10 and key **h**. This is another keyboard shortcut to display KeyTips. Each task now shows a key.

NOTE

The Esc key is at the top left of most keyboards.

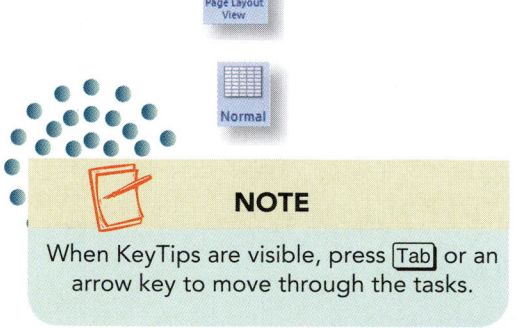

NOTE

When KeyTips are visible, press Tab or an arrow key to move through the tasks.

17. Key **1** to turn on bold. You can see that bold is applied by the button color.

18. Click the Bold button **B** . Bold is toggled off.

19. Double-click the **Home** tab. The ribbon collapses and more working space is available.

20. Right-click the **Home** tab. Click to deselect **Minimize the Ribbon**. You can right-click any tab to expand or collapse the ribbon.

TIP

The keyboard shortcut to collapse/expand the ribbon is Ctrl + F1.

Navigating in a Workbook

A *workbook* is the file Excel creates to store your data. When you look at the screen, you are viewing a worksheet. A *worksheet* is an individual page or sheet tab. A new workbook opens with three blank worksheets. You can insert or delete worksheets in the workbook. A workbook must have at least 1 worksheet and can have as many as your computer's memory allows.

TABLE 1-2 Navigation Commands in a Workbook

Press	To Do This
Ctrl + Home	Move to the beginning of the worksheet.
Ctrl + End	Move to the last used cell on the worksheet.
Home	Move to the beginning of the current row.
PageUp	Move up one screen.
PageDown	Move down one screen.
Alt + PageUp	Move one screen to the left.
Alt + PageDown	Move one screen to the right.
↑ , ↓ , ← , →	Move one cell up, down, left, or right.
Ctrl + arrow key	Move to the edge of a group of cells with data.
Ctrl + G or F5	Open the Go To dialog box.
Click	Move to the cell that is clicked.
Tab	Move to the next cell in a left-to-right sequence.
Shift + Tab	Move to the previous cell in a right-to-left sequence.
Ctrl + Backspace	Move to the active cell when it has scrolled out of view.
Ctrl + PageUp	Move to the previous worksheet.
Ctrl + PageDown	Move to the next worksheet.

A worksheet is divided into *rows* and *columns*. The rows are numbered and reach row 1,048,576. There are 16,384 columns, lettered from A to Z, then AA to AZ, BA to BZ, AAA to AAZ, ABA to ABZ, and so on, up to column XFD.

The intersection of a row and a column forms a rectangle known as a *cell*. You enter data (text, a number, or a formula) in a cell. Cells have *cell addresses* or *cell references*, which identify where the cell is located on the worksheet. Cell B2, for example, is the cell in column B, row 2.

The *active cell* is the cell that appears outlined with a thick border. It is ready to accept data or a formula, or if it already contains data or a formula, it is ready to be modified. It is the cell in which you are currently working. When you open a new workbook, the active cell is cell A1, the top-left cell in the worksheet. Cell A1 is referred to as "Home."

The mouse pointer displays as a thick white cross when you move it across cells in the worksheet. When you point at a Ribbon or worksheet tab, a command button, or a menu item, the pointer turns into a white arrow.

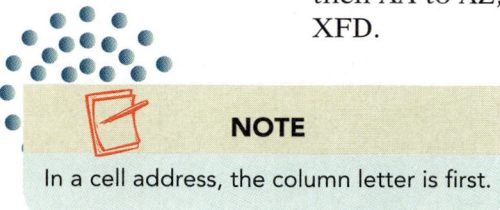

NOTE

In a cell address, the column letter is first.

NOTE

Pointing and resting the mouse pointer on a button is known as "hovering."

Exercise 1-2 MOVE BETWEEN WORKSHEETS

A new workbook has three worksheets named **Sheet1**, **Sheet2**, and **Sheet3**. **Sheet1** is displayed when a new workbook is opened.

1. Click the **Sheet2** worksheet tab. You can tell which sheet is active because its tab appears more white and the tab name is bold.

2. Click the **Sheet3** worksheet tab. All three sheets are empty.

3. Press Ctrl + PageUp. This shortcut moves to the previous worksheet, **Sheet2**, in this case.

4. Press Ctrl + PageDown. This command moves to the next worksheet, **Sheet3**.

5. Click the **Sheet1** tab to return to **Sheet1**.

NOTE

Cell A1 is the active cell on all three worksheets in a new workbook.

NOTE

When keyboard combinations (such as Ctrl + PageUp) are shown in this text, hold down the first key without releasing it and press the second key. Release the second key and then release the first key.

Exercise 1-3 GO TO A SPECIFIC CELL

When you move the mouse pointer to a cell and click, the cell you clicked becomes the active cell. It is outlined with a black border, and you can see the cell address in the *Name Box*. The Name Box is a drop-down combo box at the left edge of the formula bar. You can also determine the cell address by the orange-shaded column and row headings.

1. Move the mouse pointer to cell D4 and click. Cell D4 is the active cell, and its address appears in the Name Box. The column D and row 4 headings are shaded.

Figure 1-3
Active cell showing a thick border

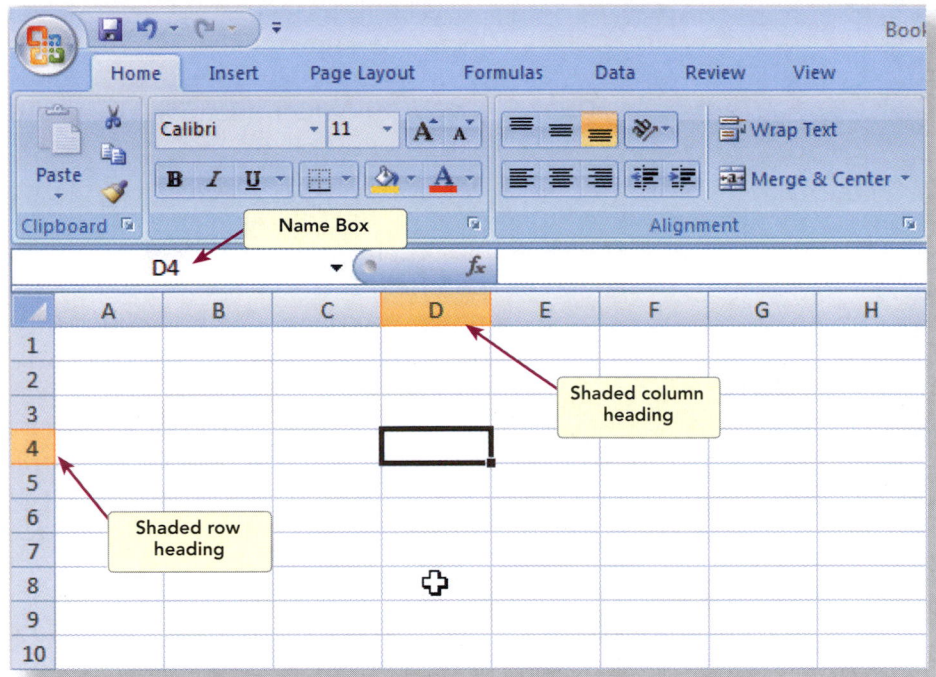

2. Press Ctrl+Home. This shortcut makes cell A1 the active cell.

3. Press Ctrl+G to open the Go To dialog box.

4. Key **b19** in the **Reference** box and press Enter. Cell B19 becomes the active cell, and its address is shown in the Name Box.

TIP

As an alternative, open the Go To dialog box by clicking the Find & Select button in the Editing group on the Home tab and choosing **Go To**.

Figure 1-4
Go To dialog box

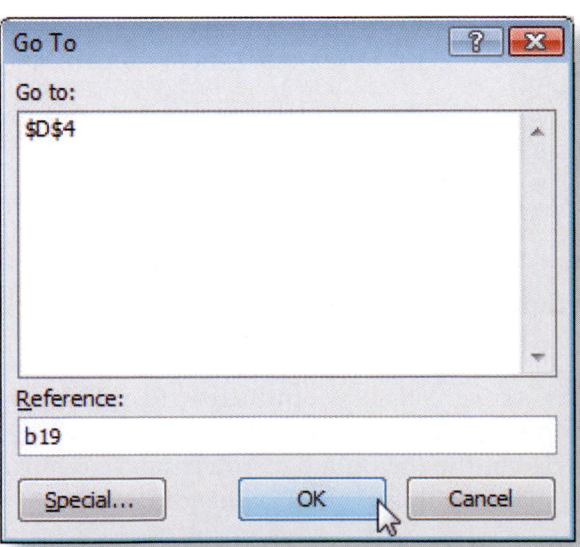

5. Press Ctrl+G. Recently used cell addresses are listed in the **Go to** list in the Go To dialog box.

6. Key **c2** and click **OK**.

7. Click in the **Name Box**. The current cell address is highlighted.

8. Key **a8** in the Name Box and press Enter.

Figure 1-5
Using the Name Box

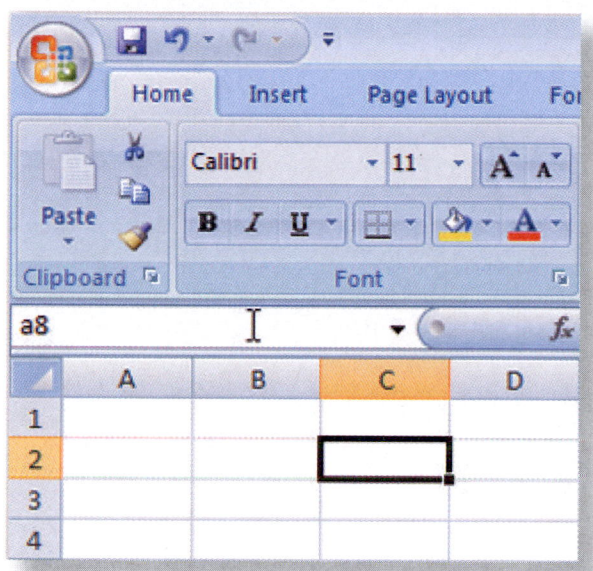

9. Press Ctrl + Home to return to cell A1.

Exercise 1-4   SCROLL THROUGH A WORKSHEET

When you scroll through a worksheet, the location of the active cell does not change. Instead, the worksheet moves on the screen so that you can see different columns or rows. The number of rows and columns you see at once depends on screen resolution and the Zoom size in Excel.

1. On the vertical scroll bar, click below the scroll box. The worksheet has been repositioned so that you see the next group of about 20 to 30 rows.

2. Click above the vertical scroll box. The worksheet has scrolled up to show the top rows.

3. Click the right scroll arrow on the horizontal scroll bar once. The worksheet scrolls one column to the right.

4. Click the left scroll arrow once to bring the column back into view.

5. Click the down scroll arrow on the vertical scroll bar twice.

6. Drag the vertical scroll box to the top of the vertical scroll bar. As you drag, a ScreenTip displays the row number at the top of the window. During all this scrolling, the active cell is still cell A1.

NOTE

You cannot see the active cell (cell A1) during your scrolling.

Figure 1-6
Using scroll bars

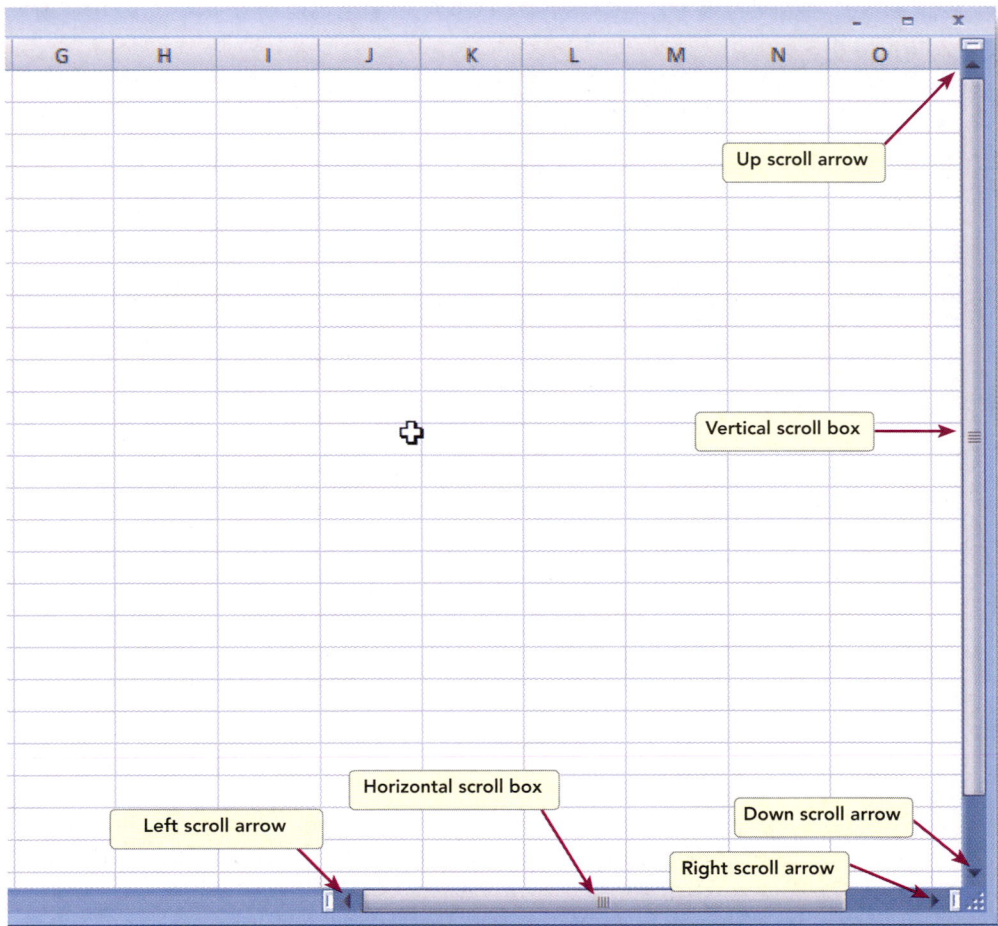

TABLE 1-3 Scrolling Through a Worksheet

To Move the View	Do This
One row up	Click the up scroll arrow.
One row down	Click the down scroll arrow.
Up one screen	Click the scroll bar above the scroll box.
Down one screen	Click the scroll bar below the scroll box.
To any relative position	Drag the scroll bar up or down.
One column to the right	Click the right scroll arrow.
One column to the left	Click the left scroll arrow.

Exercise 1-5   CHANGE THE ZOOM SIZE

The *Zoom size* controls how much of the worksheet you see on the screen. You can set the size to see more or less on screen and reduce the need to scroll. The **100%** size shows the data close to print size. A Zoom slider and two buttons are at the right edge of the status bar.

1. Click the Zoom In button on the status bar. The worksheet is resized to 110% and you see fewer columns and rows.

Figure 1-7
Changing the Zoom size

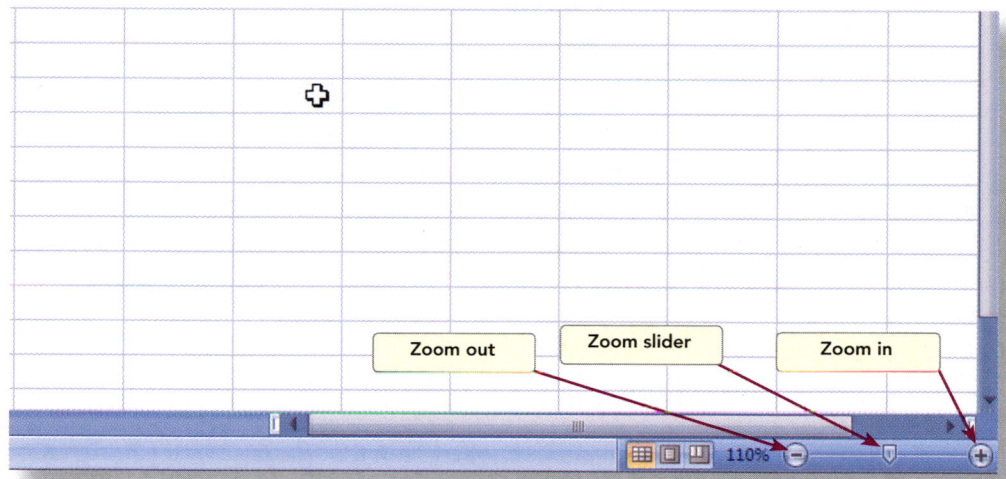

2. Click the Zoom Out button . The worksheet is reduced to 100% magnification.

3. Click the Zoom Out button again. Each click changes the magnification by 10%.

4. Point at the Zoom slider button , hold down the mouse button, and drag the slider slowly in either direction. You can set any magnification size.

5. Click the **View** tab in the Ribbon. There is a Zoom button on this tab.

6. Click the Zoom button . The Zoom dialog box opens.

7. Choose **200%**. Click **OK**.

8. Click **200%** in the status bar. The dialog box opens.

9. Choose **100%** and click **OK**.

TIP

It is usually quicker to change magnification by using the Zoom tools on the status bar.

Exercise 1-6 CLOSE A WORKBOOK

After you finish working with a workbook, you should save your work and close the workbook. You can close a workbook in several ways.

- Click the Microsoft Office Button and choose **Close**.
- Click the Close Window button [x] at the right end of the Ribbon tabs.
- Use keyboard shortcuts, Ctrl+W or Ctrl+F4.

1. Click the Microsoft Office Button.

2. Choose **Close**. (If you have made a change to the workbook, a dialog box asks if you want to save the changes. Click **No** if this message box opens.) The workbook closes, and a blank blue screen appears.

Opening an Existing Workbook

There are several ways to open an existing workbook.

- Click the Microsoft Office Button and choose **Open**.
- Use the keyboard shortcut Ctrl+O or Ctrl+F12.
- Navigate through folders in Windows Explorer or Computer to find and double-click the filename.

Exercise 1-7 OPEN A WORKBOOK

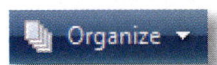

1. Click the Microsoft Office Button and choose **Open**. The navigation line shows the most recently used folder.

2. Choose the drive/folder according to your instructor's directions.

3. Click the arrow next to the Organize button and hover over **Layout**.

4. Click to select **Details Pane**. The Details pane is at the lower part of the dialog box. (Navigation Pane should also be selected. If it is not, repeat these steps to select it.)

NOTE

Your instructor will advise you on the drive/folder to use for this course.

5. Click the arrow next to the Views button and choose **Small Icons**.

Figure 1-8
Open dialog box

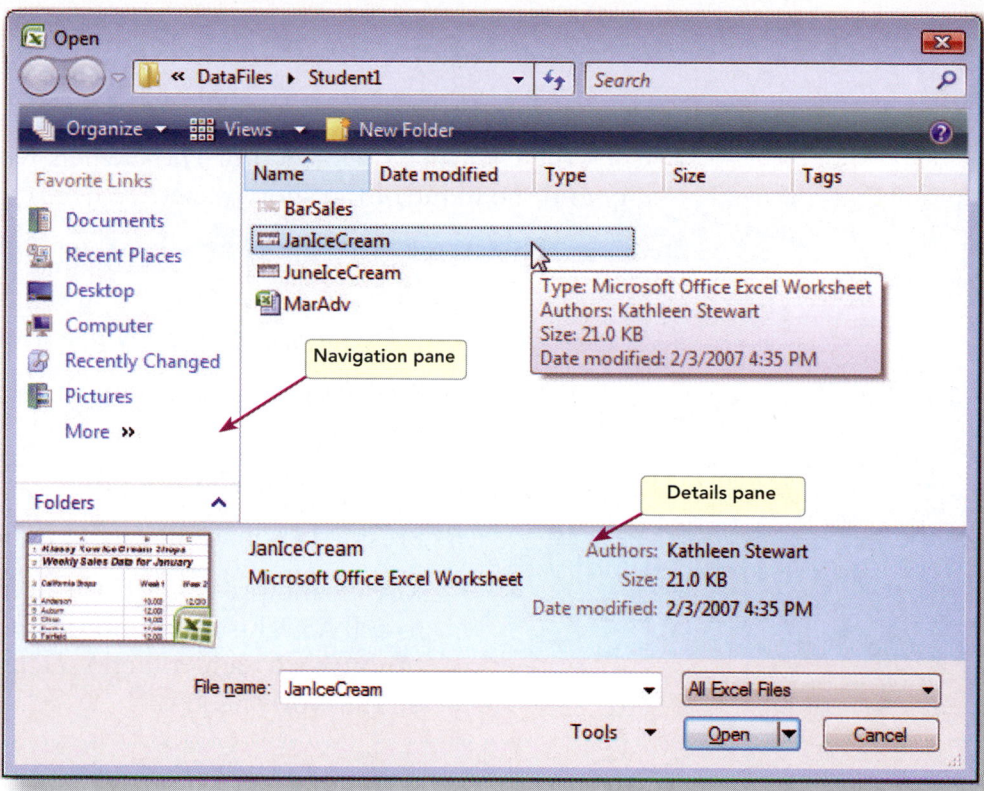

NOTE

The workbooks in this course relate to the Case Study about Klassy Kow Ice Cream, Inc., a fictional manufacturer of ice cream (see the Case Study in the frontmatter).

6. Find and click **JanIceCream**. The Details pane shows a thumbnail of the document.

7. Double-click **JanIceCream**. The workbook opens.

Editing a Worksheet

The **JanIceCream** workbook has three worksheets. The worksheets have been renamed **WeeklySales**, **Owners**, and **Chart** to better indicate what is on the sheet. For instance, the **WeeklySales** sheet shows sales for each city in each of the four weeks in January.

Worksheet cells contain text, numbers, or formulas. A formula calculates an arithmetic result. By simply viewing the worksheet, you might not know if the cell contains a number or a formula. However, you can determine a cell's contents by checking the formula bar. You can also use the formula bar to change the contents of cells.

Exercise 1-8   **VIEW WORKSHEETS AND CELL CONTENTS**

1. Click the **Owners** worksheet tab. The **Owners** worksheet shows the city and the name of the shop owner.

2. Click the **Chart** tab. This bar chart illustrates January sales for each city.

3. Press Ctrl + PageUp. This moves to the **Owners** worksheet.

4. Press Ctrl + PageDown. Now, the active tab is the **Chart** sheet.

5. Click the **WeeklySales** tab.

6. Press F5 to open the Go To dialog box.

7. Key **a5** and press Enter. The active cell is changed to cell A5. This cell contains the name of a city (Auburn), which you can see in the formula bar and on the worksheet.

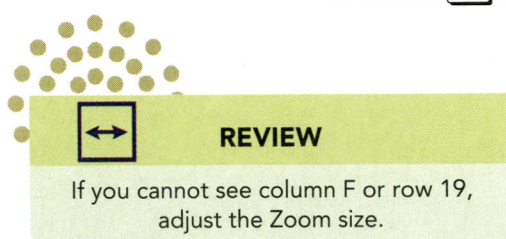

REVIEW

If you cannot see column F or row 19, adjust the Zoom size.

Figure 1-9
Cell contents and the formula bar
JanIceCream.xlsx
WeeklySales sheet

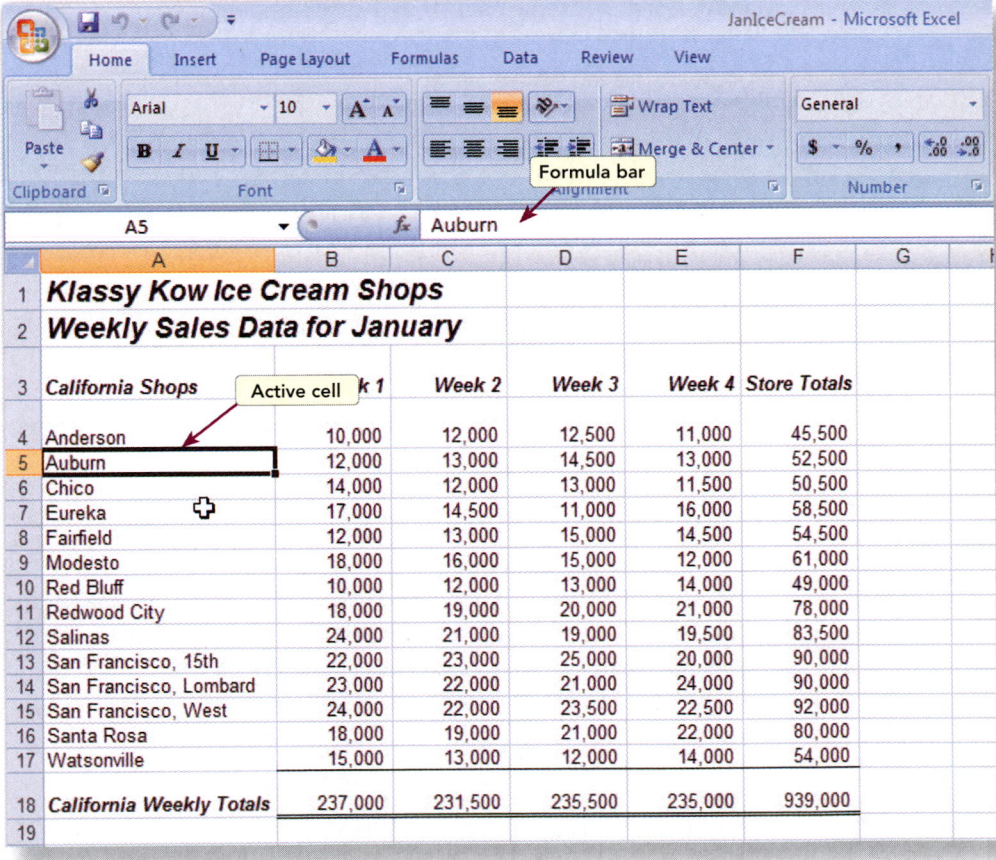

California Shops	Week 1	Week 2	Week 3	Week 4	Store Totals
Anderson	10,000	12,000	12,500	11,000	45,500
Auburn	12,000	13,000	14,500	13,000	52,500
Chico	14,000	12,000	13,000	11,500	50,500
Eureka	17,000	14,500	11,000	16,000	58,500
Fairfield	12,000	13,000	15,000	14,500	54,500
Modesto	18,000	16,000	15,000	12,000	61,000
Red Bluff	10,000	12,000	13,000	14,000	49,000
Redwood City	18,000	19,000	20,000	21,000	78,000
Salinas	24,000	21,000	19,000	19,500	83,500
San Francisco, 15th	22,000	23,000	25,000	20,000	90,000
San Francisco, Lombard	23,000	22,000	21,000	24,000	90,000
San Francisco, West	24,000	22,000	23,500	22,500	92,000
Santa Rosa	18,000	19,000	21,000	22,000	80,000
Watsonville	15,000	13,000	12,000	14,000	54,000
California Weekly Totals	237,000	231,500	235,500	235,000	939,000

8. Press F5, key **c10**, and press Enter. Cell C10 contains a number. In the formula bar, the number does not show the comma.

9. Press F5, key **f17**, and press Enter. Cell F17 contains a formula, which you can see in the formula bar. Formulas calculate a result.

Exercise 1-9 REPLACE CELL CONTENTS

When the workbook is in Ready mode, you can key, edit, or replace the contents of a cell. To replace a cell's contents, make it the active cell, key the new data, and press Enter. You can also click the Enter button ✓ in the formula bar or press any arrow key on the keyboard to complete the replacement.

If you replace a number used in a formula, the result of the formula automatically recalculates when you complete your change.

1. Click cell B5 to make it the active cell.

2. Key **20000** without a comma. As you key the number, it appears in the cell and in the formula bar. The status bar shows **Enter** to indicate that you are in Enter mode.

Figure 1-10
Replacing cell contents
JanIceCream.xlsx
WeeklySales sheet

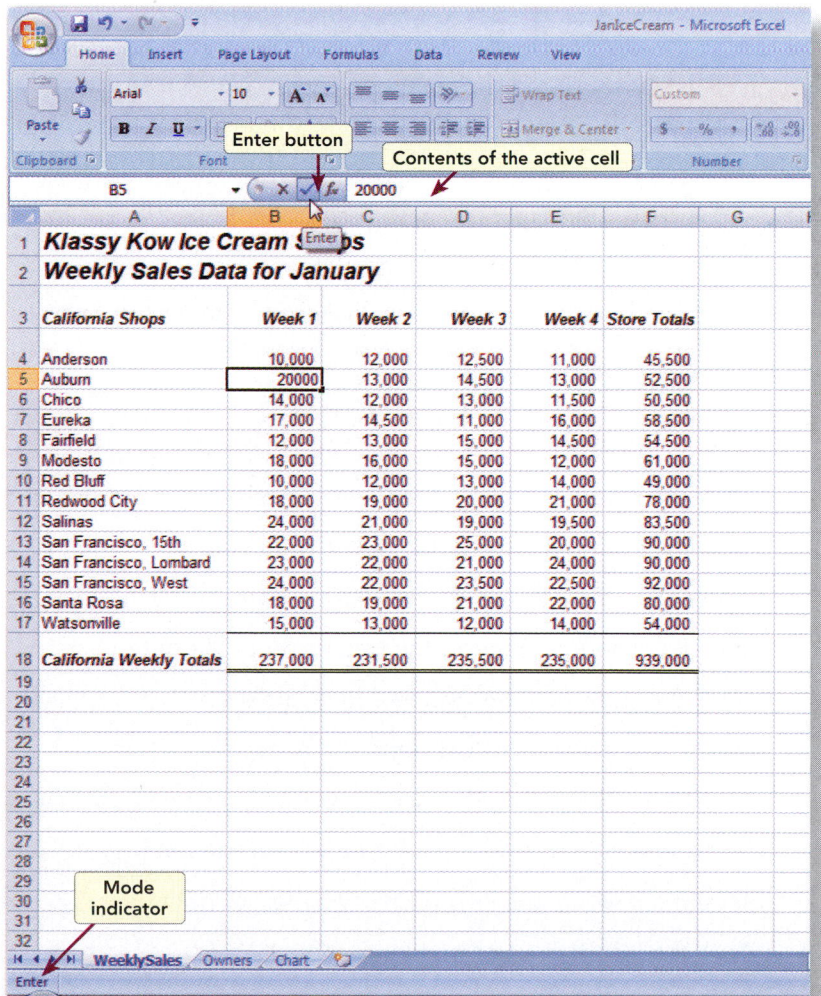

3. Press Enter. Excel inserts a comma, and the next cell in column B is active. The "Store Total" (cell F5, 60,500) and the "California Weekly Totals" amounts (in cells B18 and F18, 245,000 and 947,000) are recalculated. The worksheet returns to Ready mode.

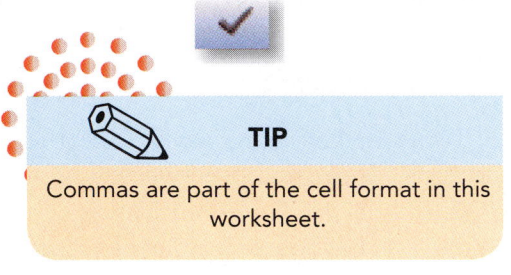

TIP

Commas are part of the cell format in this worksheet.

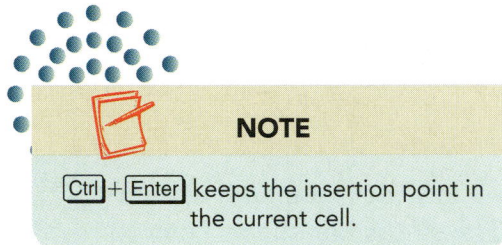

NOTE

Ctrl + Enter keeps the insertion point in the current cell.

4. Press ↑ to move to cell B5. Key **10000** without a comma. Click the Enter button ✓ in the formula bar. Notice that when you use the Enter button ✓, the pointer stays in cell B5.

5. Click the **Chart** tab. Notice the length of the Auburn bar, showing sales near $50,000.

6. Click the **WeeklySales** tab.

7. In cell B5, key **0**, and press Ctrl + Enter. A zero appears as a short dash in this worksheet.

8. Click the **Chart** tab. The chart on this worksheet is based on the data in the **WeeklySales** worksheet. Now that you have reduced sales, the Auburn bar is shorter.

9. Click the **WeeklySales** tab and key **10000** in cell B5. Press →.

Exercise 1-10   EDIT CELL CONTENTS

If a cell contains a long or complicated entry, you can edit it rather than rekeying the entire entry. Edit mode starts when you:

- Double-click the cell.
- Click the cell and press F2.
- Click the cell and then click anywhere in the formula bar.

TABLE 1-4 Keyboard Shortcuts in Edit Mode

Key	To Do This
Enter	Complete the edit, return to Ready mode, and move the insertion point to the next cell.
Alt + Enter	Move the insertion point to a new line within the cell, a line break.
Esc	Cancel the edit and restore the existing data.
Home	Move the insertion point to the beginning of the data.
End	Move the insertion point to the end of the data.
Delete	Delete one character to the right of the insertion point.
Ctrl + Delete	Delete everything from the insertion point to the end of the line.
Backspace	Delete one character to the left of the insertion point.
← or →	Move the insertion point one character left or right.
Ctrl + ←	Move the insertion point one word left.
Ctrl + →	Move the insertion point one word right.

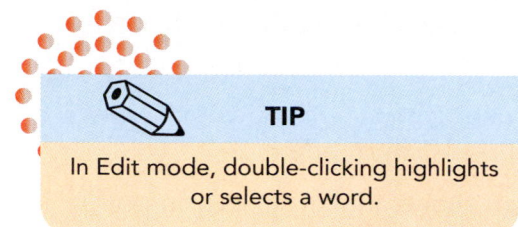

TIP

In Edit mode, double-clicking highlights or selects a word.

1. Click cell A2. The text in cell A2 is long, and its display overlaps into columns B and C.

2. Press F2. **Edit** mode is shown in the status bar. An insertion point appears in the cell at the end of the text.

3. Double-click "Data" in the cell. A Mini toolbar appears with buttons for font editing.

4. Point at the Mini toolbar. Its appearance brightens for easy viewing.

Figure 1-11
Using Edit mode
JanIceCream.xlsx
WeeklySales sheet

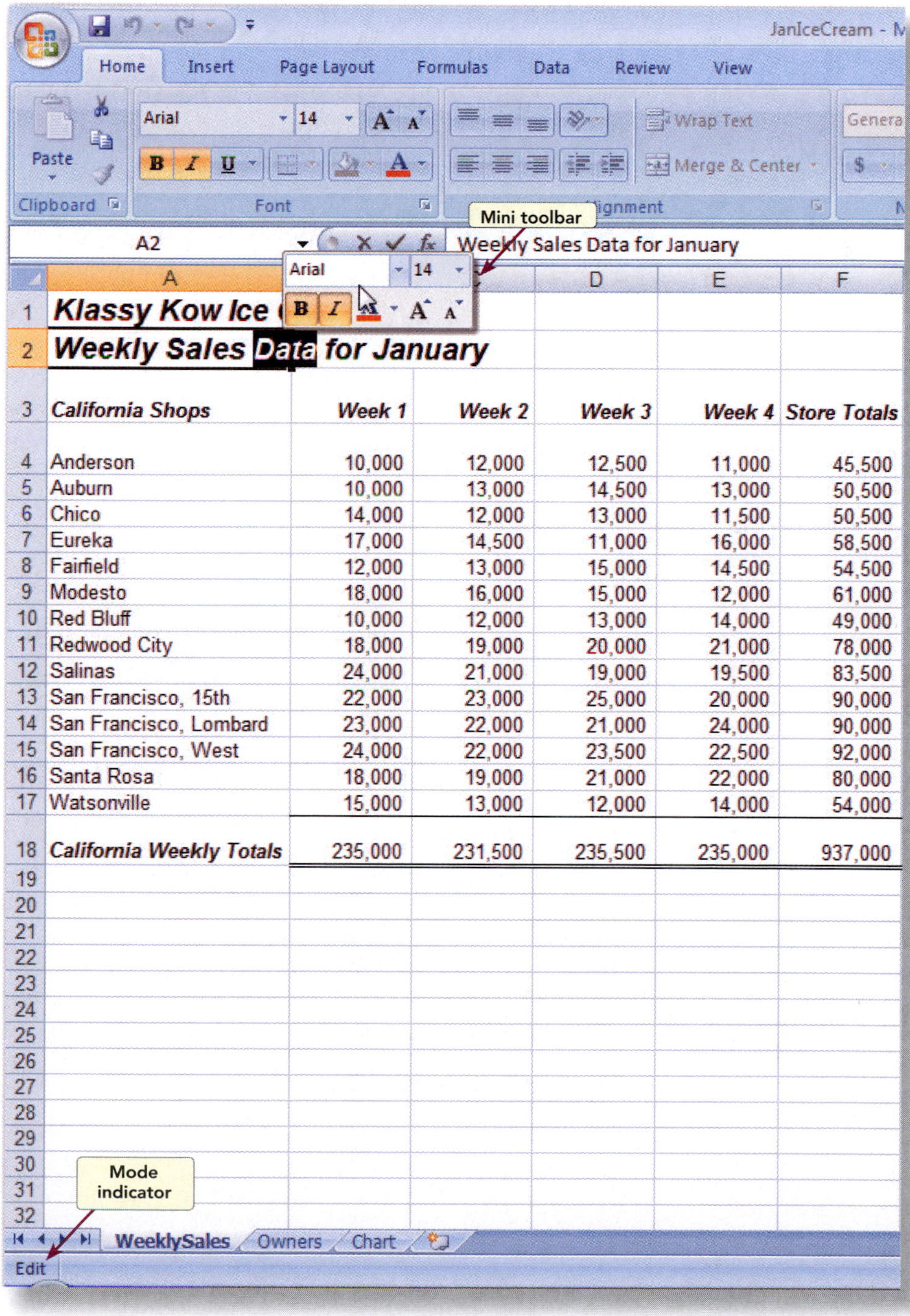

	A	B	C	D	E	F
1	*Klassy Kow Ice*					
2	*Weekly Sales Data for January*					
3	*California Shops*	*Week 1*	*Week 2*	*Week 3*	*Week 4*	*Store Totals*
4	Anderson	10,000	12,000	12,500	11,000	45,500
5	Auburn	10,000	13,000	14,500	13,000	50,500
6	Chico	14,000	12,000	13,000	11,500	50,500
7	Eureka	17,000	14,500	11,000	16,000	58,500
8	Fairfield	12,000	13,000	15,000	14,500	54,500
9	Modesto	18,000	16,000	15,000	12,000	61,000
10	Red Bluff	10,000	12,000	13,000	14,000	49,000
11	Redwood City	18,000	19,000	20,000	21,000	78,000
12	Salinas	24,000	21,000	19,000	19,500	83,500
13	San Francisco, 15th	22,000	23,000	25,000	20,000	90,000
14	San Francisco, Lombard	23,000	22,000	21,000	24,000	90,000
15	San Francisco, West	24,000	22,000	23,500	22,500	92,000
16	Santa Rosa	18,000	19,000	21,000	22,000	80,000
17	Watsonville	15,000	13,000	12,000	14,000	54,000
18	*California Weekly Totals*	235,000	231,500	235,500	235,000	937,000

Mini toolbar

A2 — Weekly Sales Data for January

Arial 14

Mode indicator

WeeklySales / Owners / Chart

Edit

5. Key **Information**. It replaces the word "Data." The Mini toolbar has disappeared.

6. Press ⎣Enter⎦ to complete the edit. Pressing ⎣Enter⎦ does not start a new line in the cell when the worksheet is in Edit mode.

7. Double-click cell A3. This starts Edit mode, and an insertion point appears in the cell.

8. In the cell, click to the left of the first "S" in "Shops."

9. Key **Retail** and press ⎣Spacebar⎦. Press ⎣Enter⎦.

10. Click cell F1. There is nothing in this cell.

11. Key your first name, a space, and your last name in the cell. Press ⎣Enter⎦. If your name is longer than column F, part of its display might overlap into column G and even into column H.

Exercise 1-11   CLEAR CELL CONTENTS

When you clear the contents of a cell, you delete the text, number, or formula in that cell.

NOTE

A green triangle may appear in the corners of cells F5 and B18 to indicate that a formula error has occurred. Ignore the triangles for now.

1. Click cell B5. Press ⎣Delete⎦ on the keyboard. The number is deleted, and Excel recalculates the formula results in cells F5, B18, and F18.

2. Press ⎣→⎦ to move the pointer to cell C5.

3. On the **Home** tab in the **Editing** group, click the Clear button ⌫⁻ .

4. Choose **Clear Contents**. The number is deleted, and formulas are recalculated.

Exercise 1-12   USE UNDO AND REDO

The Undo command reverses the last action you performed in the worksheet. For example, if you delete the contents of a cell, the Undo command restores what you deleted. The Redo command reverses the action of the Undo command. It "undoes" your Undo.

To use the Undo command, you can:

• Click the Undo button ↺⁻ on the Quick Access toolbar.

• Press ⎣Ctrl⎦+⎣Z⎦ or ⎣Alt⎦+⎣Backspace⎦.

To use the Redo command, you can:

- Click the Redo button on the Quick Access toolbar.

- Press Ctrl+Y or F4.

Excel keeps a history or list of your editing commands, and you can undo several at once.

> **NOTE**
>
> The ScreenTip for the Undo button includes the most recent task, such as Undo Clear.

1. Click the Undo button. The number in cell C5 is restored.

2. Click the Redo button. The number is cleared again.

3. Click cell A8 and key **Gotham**. Press Enter.

4. In cell A9 key **Los Angeles** and press Enter.

> **NOTE**
>
> Depending on the actions that have been undone and redone on your computer, your list might be different from the one shown in Figure 1-12.

5. Click the arrow next to the Undo button to display the history list.

6. Move the mouse to highlight the top two actions and click. The last two changes are undone, and the original city names are restored.

Figure 1-12
Undoing multiple edits
JanIceCream.xlsx
WeeklySales sheet

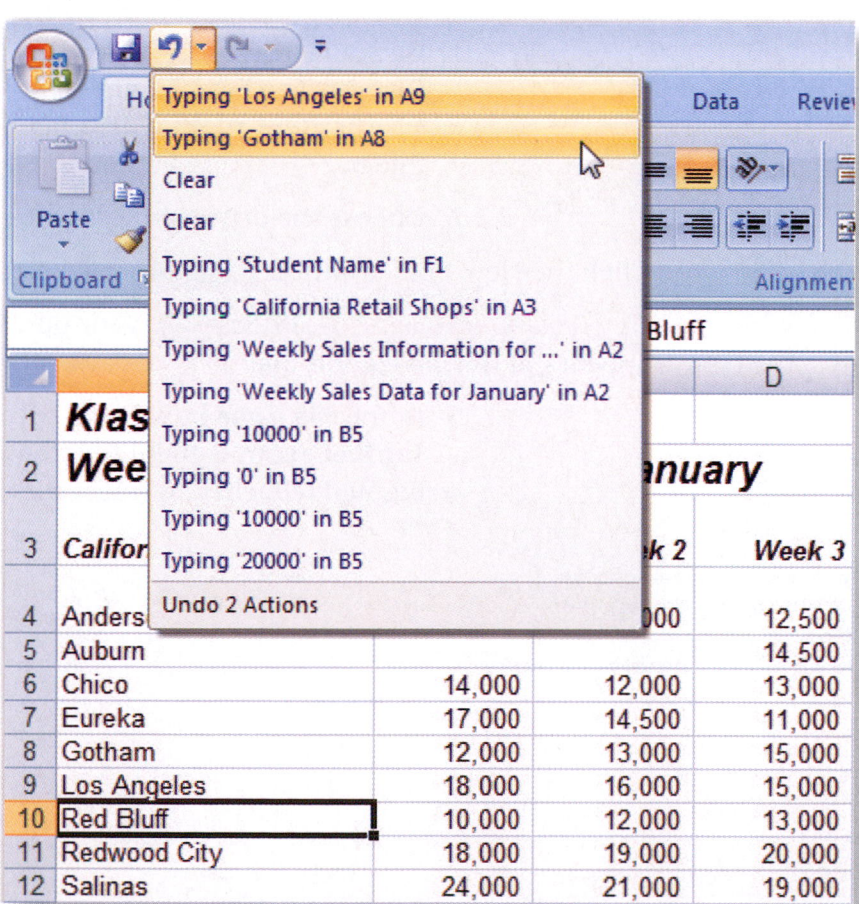

7. Click the Redo button. The first action is restored.

8. Click the Redo button again.

9. Press Ctrl+Home to place the pointer in cell A1.

Managing Files

Workbook files are usually stored in folders. A *folder* is a location on a disk, network, or other drive. Folders are organized in a structure like a family tree. The top level of the tree is a letter such as C, F, or G to represent the disk or other storage device. Under each letter, you can create folders to help you organize and manage your work.

For your work in this text, you will save your files in a folder you create for each lesson.

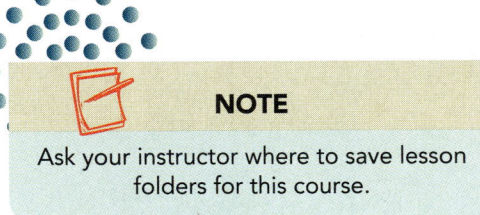

Exercise 1-13 CREATE A NEW FOLDER AND USE SAVE AS

1. Click the Microsoft Office Button and choose **Save As**. The Save As dialog box opens. You will save **JanIceCream** with a new filename in a lesson folder.

2. Choose the drive and folder location for your work.

 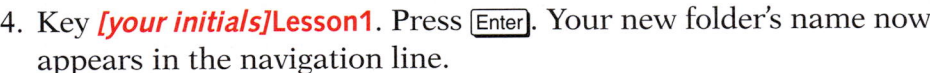

3. Click the New Folder button. A New Folder icon opens.

4. Key *[your initials]*Lesson1. Press Enter. Your new folder's name now appears in the navigation line.

5. In the **File name** box, make sure the filename **JanIceCream** is highlighted or selected. If it is not highlighted, click to select it.

6. Key ***[your initials]*1-13** and click **Save**. Your new filename now appears in the title bar.

Figure 1-13
Save As dialog box

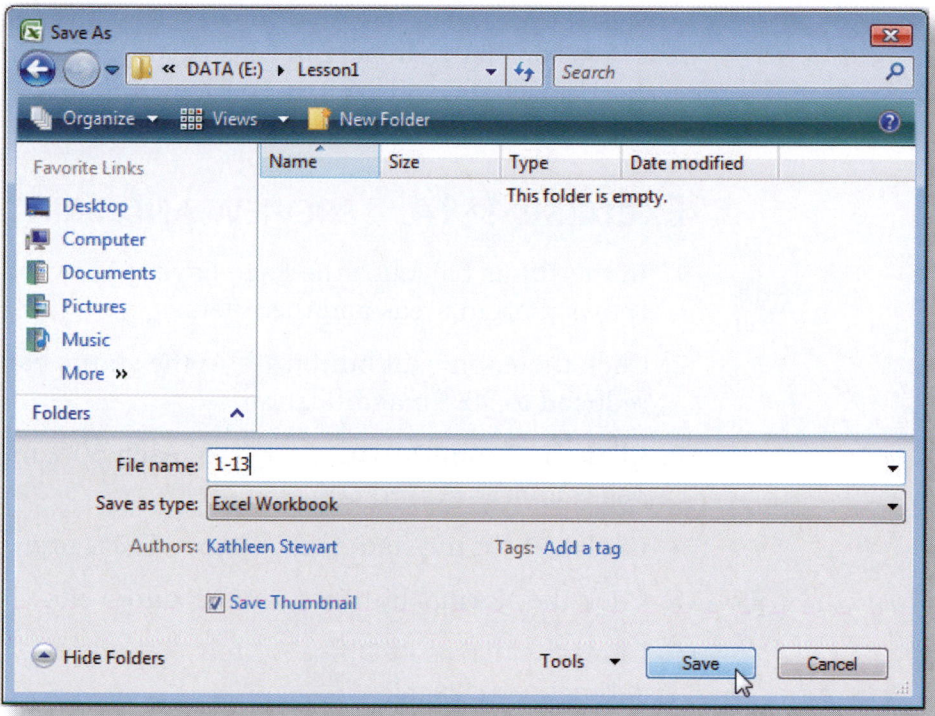

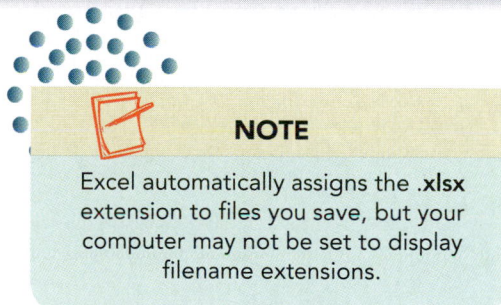

NOTE

Excel automatically assigns the **.xlsx** extension to files you save, but your computer may not be set to display filename extensions.

Printing Excel Files

You can use any of these methods to print a worksheet:

- Press ⌨Ctrl+⌨P.

- Click the Microsoft Office Button 🔘 and choose **Print** and then **Quick Print**.

- Click the Print button 🖨 while in Print Preview.

- Click the Quick Print button 🖨 on the Quick Access toolbar.

Some methods open the Print dialog box, in which you can change printing options. The Quick Print button, if it is on the Quick Access toolbar, and choosing Quick Print from the menu send the worksheet to the printer with default print settings.

Page Layout View displays your sheet with margin and header/footer areas. You can edit your work in Page Layout View. Print Preview also shows your worksheet as it will print in a normal or reduced view. You cannot make any changes in Print Preview.

Exercise 1-14   PREVIEW AND PRINT A WORKSHEET

1. In the status bar, click the Page Layout View button. The page shows margin areas and the rulers.

2. Click the Zoom Out button in the status bar. The worksheet is reduced to 90% magnification.

3. Click the Zoom Out button to reach 50% magnification. Unused pages appear grayed out.

4. Click **50%** in the status bar. Choose **100%** and click **OK**.

5. Click the Normal button in the status bar.

6. Click the Microsoft Office Button and hover over **Print**. A submenu opens.

7. Choose **Print Preview**. The worksheet is shown in a reduced size so that you can see the entire page.

Figure 1-14
Worksheet in Print Preview
1-13.xlsx
WeeklySales sheet

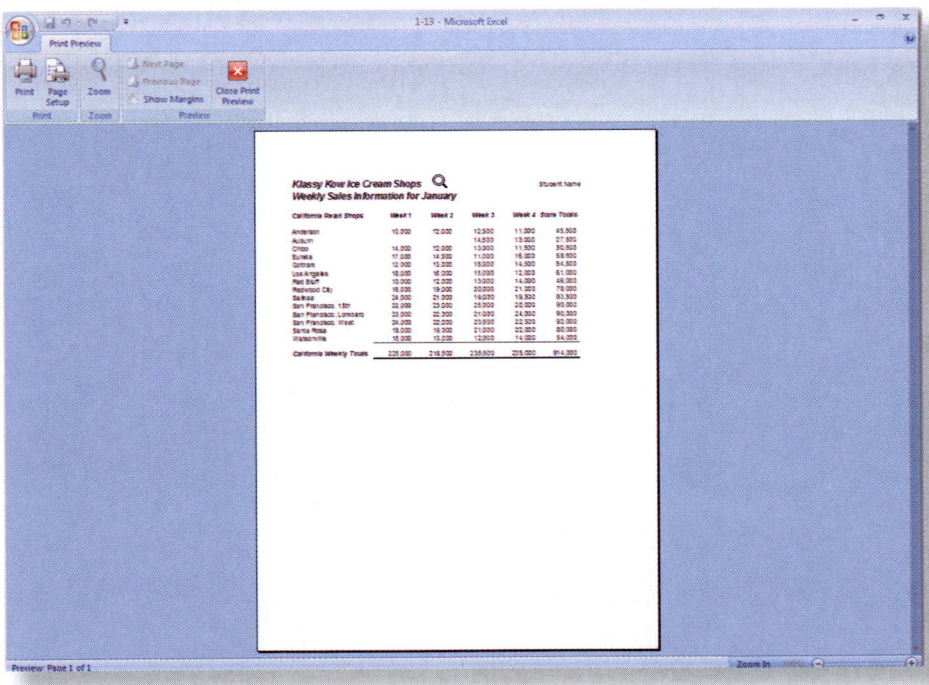

8. Move the mouse pointer near the main headings. The pointer appears as a small magnifying glass icon.

9. Click while pointing at the headings. The worksheet changes to a larger size, close to the actual print size.

10. Click anywhere to return to a reduced size. The mouse pointer appears as a white solid arrow when it will zoom out.

11. Zoom in on the "California Weekly Totals" row. Click anywhere to zoom out.

12. Click the Print button. The Print dialog box opens.

NOTE

Changing the size in the Print Preview window is called zooming in and out.

13. Press Enter. A printer icon appears on the taskbar as the worksheet is sent to the printer. Only the **WeeklySales** worksheet is printed.

Exercise 1-15   PRINT A WORKBOOK

You can print all sheets in a workbook with one command from the Print dialog box.

1. Press Ctrl+P. The Print dialog box opens with your default settings.

Figure 1-15
Print dialog box

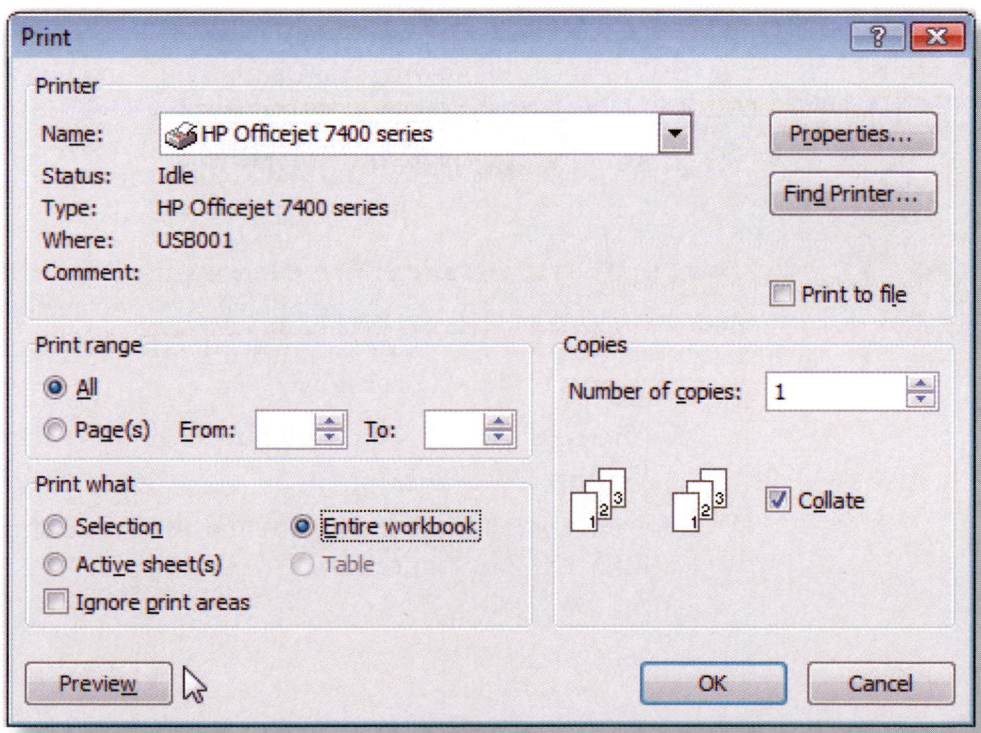

2. In the **Print what** section, choose **Entire workbook**.

3. Click **Preview**. The reduced size shows the first page, the **WeeklySales** sheet. The status bar shows that this is page 1 of 3.

4. Press PageDown. This is the second sheet, the **Owners** worksheet.

5. Press PageDown. This is the **Chart** sheet. It is set to print in landscape orientation.

6. Click **Previous Page** two times to return to the first sheet.

7. Click the Print button 🖨. All three sheets are sent to the printer and Print Preview closes.

Exercise 1-16   SAVE AN XPS FILE

XPS is *XML Paper Specification (XPS)*, a file type that maintains document formatting so that you or others can view or print the worksheet exactly as it was designed, with or without Excel. You need a viewer to open an XPS document, available in Windows Vista or free from Microsoft's Web site. To save a file as an XPS (or PDF) document, you must have installed this add-in at your computer.

1. Click the Microsoft Office Button 🔘 and choose **Save As**. The Save As dialog box opens. If you have opened the Publish as PDF or XPS dialog box, close it and try again.

2. Choose *[your initials]* **Lesson1** as the location.

3. In the **File name** box, make sure the file name *[your initials]***1-13** is highlighted or selected. If it is not highlighted, select it.

4. Key *[your initials]***1-16**.

TIP
You can also save a document as an Adobe PDF file so that others can view it without Excel.

5. Click the **Save as type** arrow. A list of file types opens.

6. Find and choose **XPS Document**. The same document name is assumed, but it will have a different extension.

7. Choose **Standard** as the **Optimize for** option. Click to deselect **Open file after publishing**.

8. Click **Options** and choose **Entire workbook** in the **Publish what** group. Click **OK** (see Figure 1-16).

9. Click **Save**. Your workbook is still open, and the XPS file is saved separately.

Figure 1-16
Saving an XPS
document

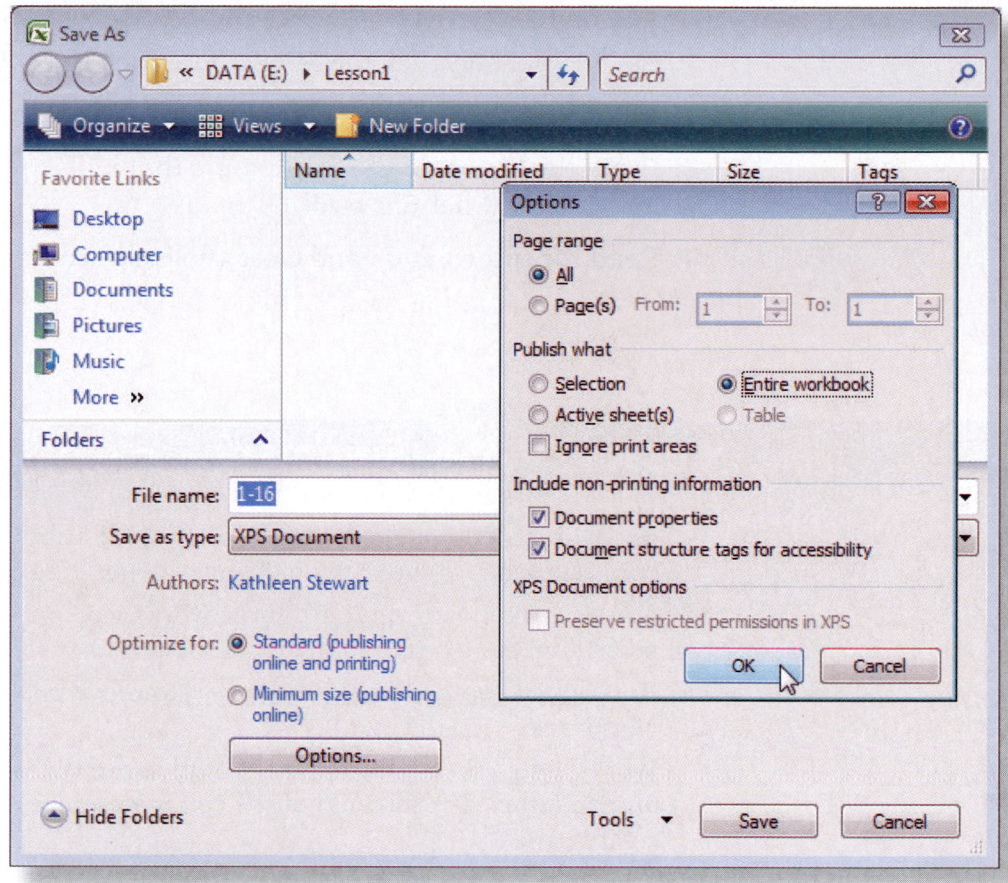

Exercise 1-17 EXIT EXCEL

You can exit Excel and close the workbook at the same time. If you give the command to exit Excel, you will see a reminder to save the workbook if you have not yet done so.

There are several ways to close a workbook and exit Excel:

- Click the Microsoft Office Button and choose **Exit Excel**.

- Use the Close button to first close the workbook and then to close Excel.

- Use the keyboard shortcut Alt+F4 to exit Excel.

1. Click the Microsoft Office Button.

2. Choose **Exit Excel**. Do not save changes if asked.

Using Online Help

Online Help is available at your computer and on the Microsoft Office Web site. An easy way to use Help is to key a short request in the search text box at the top of the opening screen.

GET ACQUAINTED WITH USING HELP

1. Start Excel and click the Microsoft Office Excel Help button ⓘ .

2. In the search box, key **get help** and press ⎡Enter⎤.

3. From the list of topics, find a topic that will explain how to use help and click it. Click **Show All**.

4. Read the information and close the Help window.

Lesson 1 Summary

- Excel opens with a blank workbook and the Ribbon. The active command tab on the Ribbon changes depending on what you are doing.

- A new workbook opens with three worksheets. A worksheet is an individual page or tab in the workbook.

- Press ⎡Ctrl⎤+⎡PageUp⎤ and ⎡Ctrl⎤+⎡PageDown⎤ to move between worksheets in a workbook.

- Worksheets are divided into cells, which are the intersections of rows and columns. The location of the cell is its address (also called its cell reference).

- Move the pointer to a specific cell with the Go To command or by clicking the cell.

- The active cell is outlined with a black border. It is ready to accept new data or a formula or to be edited.

- The Name Box shows the address of the active cell. You can also use it to change the active cell.

- If you use the scroll box or arrows to reposition the worksheet on the screen, the active cell does not change.

- The Zoom size controls how much of the worksheet you can see at once.

- Replace any entry in a cell by clicking the cell and keying new data. Edit long or complicated cell data rather than rekeying it.

- The Undo button ⎡↺⎤ and the Redo button ⎡↻⎤ both have history arrows so that you can undo or redo multiple commands at once.

- Preview your worksheet or the entire workbook before printing it. To preview and print all the worksheets in a workbook, click the Microsoft Office Button and choose Print. Then choose **Entire workbook**.

LESSON 1		Command Summary	
Feature	**Button**	**Task Path**	**Keyboard**
Collapse ribbon			Ctrl + F1
Clear cell contents		Home, Editing, Clear, Clear Contents	Delete
Close workbook		Microsoft Office, Close	Ctrl + W or Ctrl + F4
Exit Excel		Microsoft Office, Exit Excel	Ctrl + F4
Full Screen	Full Screen	View, Workbook Views, Full Screen	
Go To	Find & Select	Home, Editing, Find & Select, Go To	Ctrl + G or F5
KeyTips			Alt or F10
Normal View	Normal	View, Workbook Views, Normal	
Open workbook		Microsoft Office, Open	Ctrl + O
Page Layout View	Page Layout View	View, Workbook Views, Page Layout View	
Print		Microsoft Office, Print	Ctrl + P
Print Preview	Print	Microsoft Office, Print, Print Preview	
Redo			Ctrl + Y or F4
Save As		Microsoft Office, Save As	F12 or Alt + F2
Undo			Ctrl + Z or Alt + Backspace
Zoom In			
Zoom Out			
Zoom Size	Zoom	View, Zoom	

Concepts Review

True/False Questions

Each of the following statements is either true or false. Indicate your choice by circling T or F.

T F   1. A worksheet contains at least one workbook.

T F   2. The Name Box shows the address of the active cell.

T F   3. The Zoom size for a particular worksheet is permanent.

T F   4. You can use the scroll bars to move the pointer to a specific cell.

T F   5. You can replace a cell's contents by clicking the cell and keying new data.

T F   6. You must use Windows Explorer to create a new folder.

T F   7. Edit mode starts when you press [F2].

T F   8. If you click the Print button 🖨 while viewing a sheet in print preview, all worksheets in a workbook are printed.

Short Answer Questions

Write the correct answer in the space provided.

1. What is the name for the cell with a heavy black border that is ready to accept new data or a formula?

_____

2. Give an example of a cell address in the first column of a worksheet.

_____

3. What is the screen element that contains command tabs?

_____

4. What command enables you to use a different filename for a workbook as it is saved?

_____

5. What is the keyboard shortcut to move the pointer to cell A1?

_____

6. Which part of the Excel screen shows the contents of the active cell?

_____

7. How do you print all three sheets in a workbook with one command?

_____

8. What do you use to reposition the worksheet on the screen without changing the location of the active cell?

_____

Critical Thinking

Answer these questions on a separate page. There are no right or wrong answers. Support your answers with examples from your own experience, if possible.

1. You can replace or edit cell contents. Discuss when you might use each procedure.
2. Why should you use folders for organizing your files? Give examples of folder names that might be used in an auto dealership's office.

Skills Review

Exercise 1-18

Start Excel and navigate in a workbook.

1. Start Excel and navigate in a workbook by following these steps:
   a. Turn on the computer and start Excel.
   b. Press Ctrl + PageDown two times. Which sheet is active?
   c. Drag the scroll box on the vertical scroll bar to the bottom of the scroll bar. What is the last row shown on the worksheet?
   d. Press Ctrl + PageUp two times. Which sheet is active?
   e. Press Ctrl + G and key **a35**. Press Enter. What appears in the Name Box?
   f. Press Tab. What is the active cell?
   g. Press Shift + Tab. What is the active cell?

NOTE

Prepare your answers to questions in the Skills Review exercises as instructed for submission to your instructor. Include your name, the exercise number, and the question number.

NOTE

If Excel is already running, press Ctrl + N to start a new workbook.

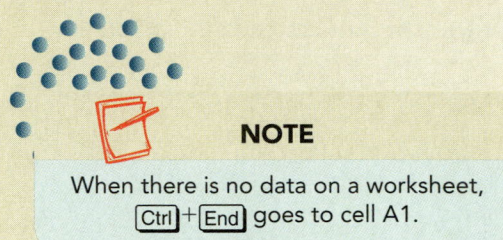

> **NOTE**
>
> When there is no data on a worksheet, Ctrl + End goes to cell A1.

h. Press Ctrl + Home. What is the active cell?

i. Press Ctrl + G, key **d15**, and press Enter. Press Ctrl + End. What is the active cell?

j. Press Alt. What is the KeyTip for the Formulas tab? Press Esc.

k. Press Ctrl + F1. What has happened?

l. Press Ctrl + F1 again.

m. Click the Close button ⊠. Do not save the workbook if a message box appears.

Exercise 1-19

Open a workbook. Edit a worksheet.

> **NOTE**
>
> This worksheet has an icon set, a conditional format. Values equal to or greater than 50 have a green circle; others have a yellow circle.

1. Open a workbook by following these steps:

   a. Click the Microsoft Office Button 🏢 and choose **Open**.

   b. Choose the drive and folder according to your instructor's directions.

   c. Find **MarAdv** and double-click it.

2. Edit a worksheet by following these steps:

   a. Press Ctrl + G, key **b5**, and press Enter.

   b. Key **2000** and press Enter. What is the new total for the Bremerton store?

   c. Click cell D10 and press Delete. What is the total for this week?

> **NOTE**
>
> Prepare your answers to questions in the Skills Review exercises as instructed for submission to your instructor. Include your name, the exercise number, and the question number.

   d. Click the arrow next to the Undo button ↺ ▾. What are the first two tasks listed?

   e. Press Esc.

   f. Click the Close Window button ⊠. Choose **No** to discard your changes.

Exercise 1-20

Edit a worksheet. Manage files.

1. Open **MarAdv**.

2. Edit a workbook by following these steps:

   a. Click cell A2 and press F2. What is the current mode for your worksheet?

REVIEW

The Mini toolbar will appear when you select text for editing.

b. Double-click "March" and key **April**. Press Enter. What is the active cell?

c. Double-click cell A11. How can you select or highlight the word "California"?

d. Delete "California." Delete the space before "W."

e. What key will finish your editing in cell A11?

3. Manage files by following these steps:

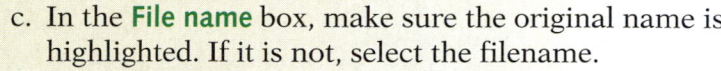

a. Click the Microsoft Office Button and choose **Save As**. What folder appears in the navigation line?

b. Set the folder to *[your initials]***Lesson1.** Where is this folder located?

TIP

Click or double-click to select a filename with no spaces.

c. In the **File name** box, make sure the original name is highlighted. If it is not, select the filename.

d. Key *[your initials]***1-20** and press Enter.

e. What filename appears in the title bar?

4. Click the Close Window button 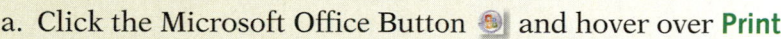.

Exercise 1-21

Edit cells. Print a worksheet.

1. Open **MarAdv.**

2. Press F12. Set the **Save in** folder to *[your initials]***Lesson1.**

TIP

F12 is the keyboard shortcut for File, Save As.

3. In the **File name** box, select the filename. Key *[your initials]***1-21** and press Enter.

4. Edit cells by following these steps:

a. Click cell A2 and press F2.

b. Double-click "March" and key **May**. Press Enter.

c. Double-click cell A11. Double-click "California."

d. Key **Washington** and press Enter.

e. Click cell F1. Key your first and your last name and press Enter.

5. Print a worksheet by following these steps:

a. Click the Microsoft Office Button  and hover over **Print**.

b. Choose **Print Preview**.

Print

c. Point near the main heading and click. Point anywhere and click again.

d. Click the Print button . Click **OK** in the dialog box.

6. Click the Close Window button .

7. Choose **Yes** to save changes.

Lesson Applications

REVIEW

Set the Zoom size so that you can see as much of the data as possible.

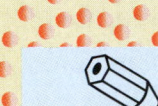

TIP

You do not need to key commas in this worksheet. They are part of the formatting.

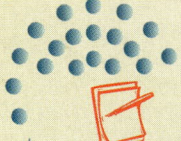

NOTE

Numbers align at the right edge of a cell; text aligns at the left edge. You may see green triangles in cells C11 and D11 to mark formula errors.

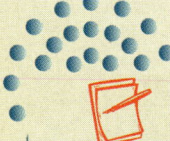

NOTE

This sheet uses separator rows and columns with borders.

Exercise 1-22

Open a workbook. Edit and print a worksheet.

1. Open **JanIceCream**.

2. Edit cell A2 to show the current month.

3. Change the first week total for Modesto to **15500**.

4. Key your first and your last name in cell A20. Press `Ctrl`+`Home`.

5. Save the workbook as *[your initials]*1-22 in your Lesson 1 folder.

6. Prepare and submit your work. Close the workbook.

Exercise 1-23

Open a workbook. Edit a worksheet. Print a worksheet.

1. Open **BarSales**.

2. Without changing the en dash (–), edit cell B4 to show **2006–2008**.

3. Change the fourth quarter amount for 2007 to **55000**.

4. Key your first and your last name in cell A14. Press `Ctrl`+`Home`.

5. Save the workbook as *[your initials]*1-23 in your Lesson 1 folder.

6. Prepare and submit your work. Close the workbook.

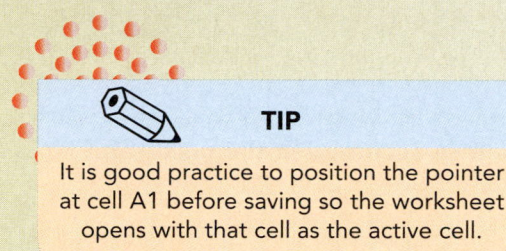

TIP

It is good practice to position the pointer at cell A1 before saving so the worksheet opens with that cell as the active cell.

NOTE

The chart shows shades of gray for the bars on a non-color printer.

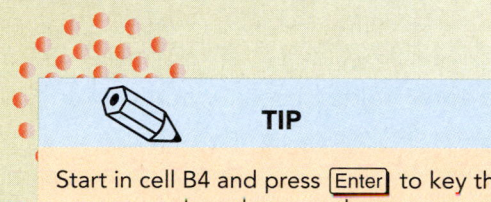

TIP

Start in cell B4 and press Enter to key the values down a column.

Exercise 1-24

Open and edit a workbook. Print a workbook.

1. Open **JuneIceCream**. This worksheet has data bars, another type of conditional format.

2. In cell F1 on the **WeeklySales** sheet, key your first and last name. Press Ctrl + Home.

3. In cell B18 on the **Owners** sheet, key your first and last name. Press Ctrl + Home.

4. Press Ctrl + P and select the option to print the entire workbook. Preview the workbook before printing it.

5. Save the workbook as *[your initials]*1-24 in your Lesson 1 folder.

6. Prepare and submit your work. Close the workbook.

Exercise 1-25 ◆ Challenge Yourself

Open a workbook. Edit worksheets. Print a workbook.

1. Open **JanIceCream**.

2. On the **WeeklySales** sheet, change the values for the first week as shown here.

3. In cell E1, key **Prepared by** *[your first and last name]*. Press Ctrl + Home. Preview and print the sheet.

4. On the **Owners** sheet, key your first and last name in cell C1. Press Ctrl + Home. Preview and print the sheet.

5. Save the workbook as *[your initials]*1-25 in your Lesson 1 folder.

6. Prepare and submit your work. Close the workbook.

Figure 1-17

	A	B
4	Anderson	12000
5	Auburn	14000
6	Chico	12000
7	Eureka	18000
8	Fairfield	15000
9	Modesto	16000
10	Red Bluff	11000
11	Redwood City	16000
12	Salinas	26000
13	San Francisco, 15th	24000
14	San Francisco, Lombard	24000
15	San Francisco, West	[Do not change]
16	Santa Rosa	19000
17	Watsonville	16000

On Your Own

In these exercises you work on your own, as you would in a real-life work environment. Use the skills you've learned to accomplish the task—and be creative.

Exercise 1-26

Open **JuneIceCream.** On the WeeklySales sheet, practice each of the navigation shortcuts shown in Table 1-2. On the Owners sheet, change each owner's name to someone you know. Include your own name as one of the owners. Print this worksheet. Save the workbook as *[your initials]*1-26 in your Lesson 1 folder. Prepare and submit your work. Close the workbook.

Exercise 1-27

Open **MarAdv.** Change the month to this month. Using the Internet or a map, change each city to a different city in your state. Change other labels to specify your state, too. Key your first and last name in cell A14. Save the workbook as *[your initials]*1-27 in your Lesson 1 folder. Prepare and submit your work.

Exercise 1-28

In the Open dialog box, experiment changing the views. Select and highlight the filename of each of the workbooks you used in this lesson (BarSales, JanIceCream, JuneIceCream, and MarAdv). Which of these files does not have a thumbnail preview? In the Excel Help system, look up document properties. Then open the Lesson 1 file(s) without a thumbnail and resave them with that property in your folder.

Creating a Workbook

OBJECTIVES

After completing this lesson, you will be able to:

1. Enter labels.
2. Change the document theme.
3. Select cell ranges.
4. Modify column width and row height.
5. Enter values and dates.
6. Save a workbook.
7. Enter basic formulas.

Estimated Time: 1¹/₂ hours

MCAS OBJECTIVES

In this lesson:
XL07 1.3
XL07 1.5.3
XL07 2.1.1
XL07 2.1.3
XL07 2.2.2
XL07 2.2.4
XL07 2.3.2
XL07 2.3.4
XL07 3.1.1
XL07 3.2.1
XL07 5.4

A new workbook opens with three blank worksheets. You can key text, numbers, or formulas in any cell in any of the worksheets. Excel uses a default document theme in a new workbook, but you can change the theme or any formatting elements used in the worksheet. You can also adjust the width and height of columns, edit colors, and more.

Entering Labels

When you key data that begins with a letter, Excel recognizes it as a *label*. Labels are aligned at the left edge of the cell and are not used in calculations.

As you key data, it appears in the active cell and in the formula bar. If you make an error, press Esc to start over. You can also press Backspace to edit the entry.

There are several ways you can complete an entry.

TABLE 2-1 Ways to Complete a Cell Entry

Key or Button	Result
Press [Enter]	Completes entry and moves the pointer to the cell below.
Press [Ctrl]+[Enter]	Completes entry and leaves the pointer in the current cell.
Press [Tab]	Completes entry and moves the pointer to the cell to the right.
Press [Shift]+[Tab]	Completes entry and moves the pointer to the cell to the left.
Press an arrow key	Completes entry and moves the pointer one cell in the direction of the arrow.
Click another cell	Completes entry and moves the pointer to the clicked cell.
Click the Enter button ✓	Completes entry and leaves the pointer in the current cell.

Exercise 2-1   ENTER LABELS IN A WORKSHEET

1. Start Excel with a blank workbook. Cell A1 on **Sheet1** is active.

2. In cell A1, key **Klassy Kow Sa** to start a label. The worksheet is in Enter mode, shown in the status bar. The label appears in the formula bar and in the cell.

3. Press [Backspace] to delete **Sa**.

4. Key **Promotions**. Notice that an Enter button ✓ and a Cancel button ✗ appear in the formula bar when you are in Enter mode.

NOTE

The first new workbook in a work session is named **Book1** until you save it with another name. The next new workbook is **Book2**, and so on.

Figure 2-1
Label appearing in the formula bar and the cell

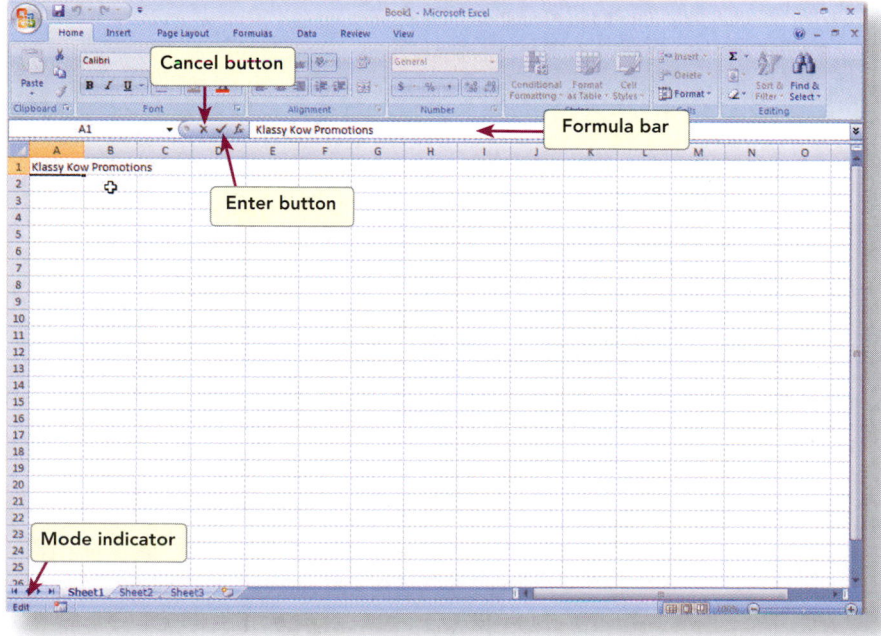

5. Press [Enter]. The label is completed in cell A1, and the pointer moves to cell A2. The label is longer than column A, so it appears to spill into columns B and C.

6. In cell A2, key **Market** to start a label. Press [Esc] to delete your entry. You can use [Esc] to delete an entry if you haven't yet pressed [Enter] or moved away from the cell.

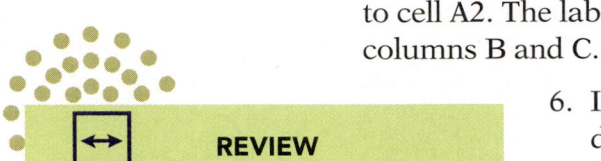

REVIEW

If you pressed [Enter] or moved away from the cell and need to edit it, click the cell. Key the new data and press [Enter].

7. Key **Company Plan** and click the Enter button ☑ in the formula bar. The label appears to spill into cell B2.

8. Click cell A3 to make it active.

9. Key **Name** and press [→]. The pointer is now in cell B3.

10. Key **Starting Date** and press [Tab]. The label is too long for column B and spills into column C.

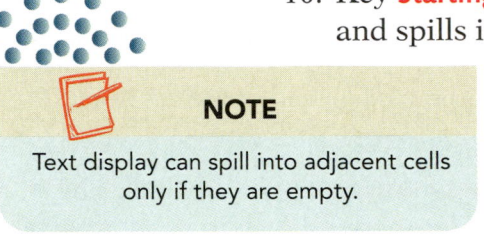

NOTE

Text display can spill into adjacent cells only if they are empty.

11. Key **Ending Date** in cell C3 and press [→]. This label cuts off the label from column B and spills into cell D3. You will fix these problems soon.

12. Key **Price** and press [Tab]. Key **Special Price** in cell E3 and press [Enter]. This label is not cut off, because there is nothing in the cell to the right.

13. Key the following labels in column A, starting in cell A4. Press [Enter] after each.

Berry Kowabunga
Easter Bunny Pie
Triple-Scoop Cone
24 oz. Shake

Changing the Document Theme

A *document theme* is a set of 2 fonts, 12 colors, and effects for shapes and charts. Each new workbook uses the Office document theme. The default body text font for this theme is 11-point Calibri. There is also a font for headings, Cambria.

NOTE

Although a theme includes 12 colors, 2 are for hyperlinks and do not appear in color palettes.

Document themes have been developed by designers to use fonts, colors, and effects that are coordinated and balanced. You can use any of the themes, or you can choose any available font, color, or effect.

Exercise 2-2 CHANGE THE THEME

If you have used theme fonts in your worksheet, you can change the document theme and immediately see font changes applied from the new theme. The *Live Preview* feature allows you to see the changes before they are applied.

NOTE

Your font list probably does not match the one in the text illustration.

1. Click cell A1. Click the **Home** tab. Hover over the **Font** box in the **Font** group to see the ScreenTip.

2. Click the arrow next to the **Font** box. The theme fonts are at the top of the list, Cambria for headings and Calibri for body data. Other fonts on your computer are listed below these two.

Figure 2-2
Choosing a theme font

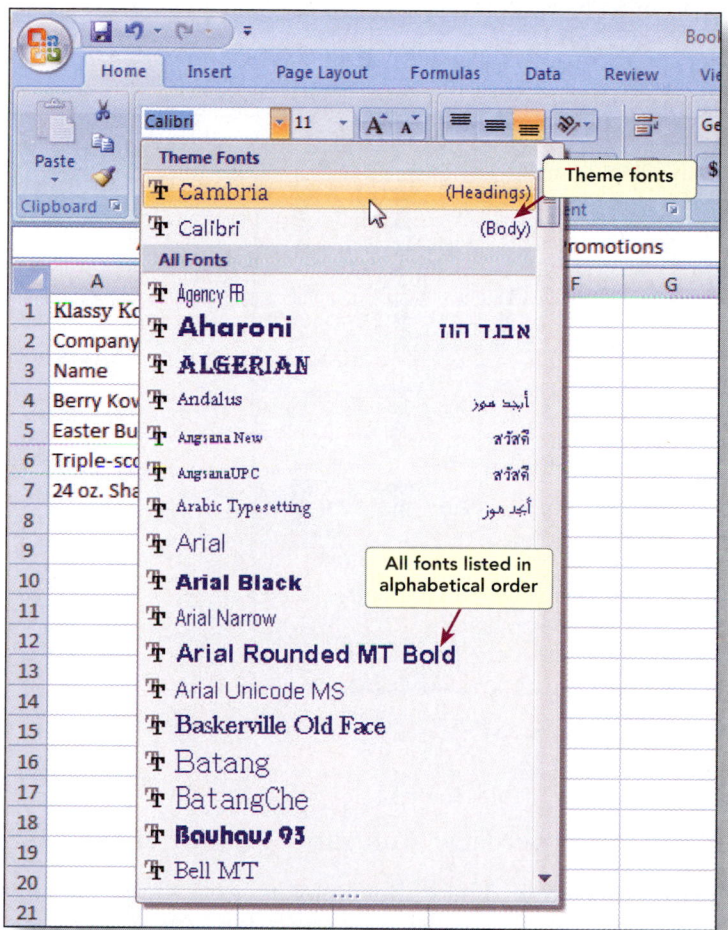

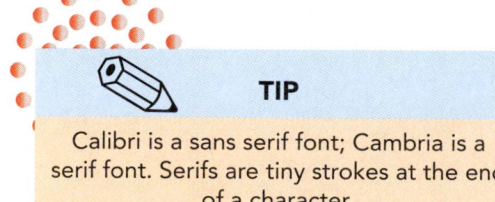

TIP

Calibri is a sans serif font; Cambria is a serif font. Serifs are tiny strokes at the end of a character.

3. Choose **Cambria**. The label in cell A1 is changed.

4. Choose the Cambria font for the label in cell A2. Your data now uses Cambria for these two labels and Calibri for the remaining data. These are both theme fonts.

5. Click the Zoom In button on the status bar four times. It will be easier to watch the changes in a larger view.

6. Click the **Page Layout** tab in the Ribbon. The first group is **Themes**.

7. Hover over the Themes button . The ScreenTip includes the current theme name.

8. Click the Themes button to open its gallery of built-in themes.

Figure 2-3
The Document
Theme gallery

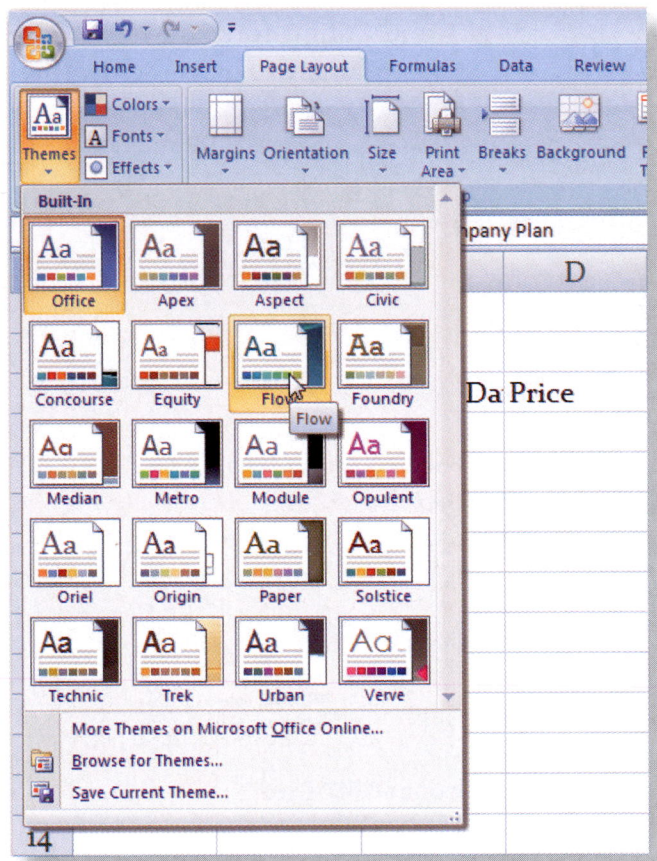

9. Hover over **Flow**. You can see a part of your data with the change.

10. Click **Flow**. The gallery closes, and the data uses new theme fonts.

11. Click the **Home** tab in the Ribbon.

12. Click the arrow next to the **Font** box. The theme fonts are Calibri for headings and Constantia for body text.

Exercise 2-3 CHANGE THE FONT, FONT SIZE, AND STYLE

You are not limited to the fonts in the document theme. You can use any font, font style, or size from the Font group on the Home tab or from the Format Cells dialog box. When you choose a larger font size, the height of the row is automatically made taller to fit the font. Font style includes bold, italic, and underline.

1. Click cell A1.

2. Click the arrow next to the **Font** box. A drop-down list box appears, showing font names for your computer.

3. Key **t** to move to the font names starting with "T." Live Preview shows the data in the new font as you scroll the list.

NOTE

You can also scroll in the Font list to a new font.

4. Find and choose **Times New Roman**.

5. Click the arrow next to the **Font Size** box. Choose **16**. Notice that row 1 is made taller to accommodate the larger font size.

Figure 2-4
Choosing a font size

TIP

You can key a font size that is not in the list.

6. Click the Italic button.

Exercise 2-4   USE THE FORMAT PAINTER

With the Format Painter, you can copy cell formats from one cell to another. This is often faster than applying formats individually.

To use the Format Painter, make the cell with formatting the active cell. Then click the Format Painter button ✔ in the Clipboard group on the Home tab. While the pointer is a white cross with a small paintbrush, click the cell to be formatted.

1. Make sure cell A1 is the active cell. Click the **Home** tab if necessary.

2. Hover over the Format Painter button ✔ and read the ScreenTip.

3. Click the Format Painter button ✔. Cell A1 shows a moving marquee, and the pointer is a thick white cross with a paintbrush.

Figure 2-5
Using the Format Painter

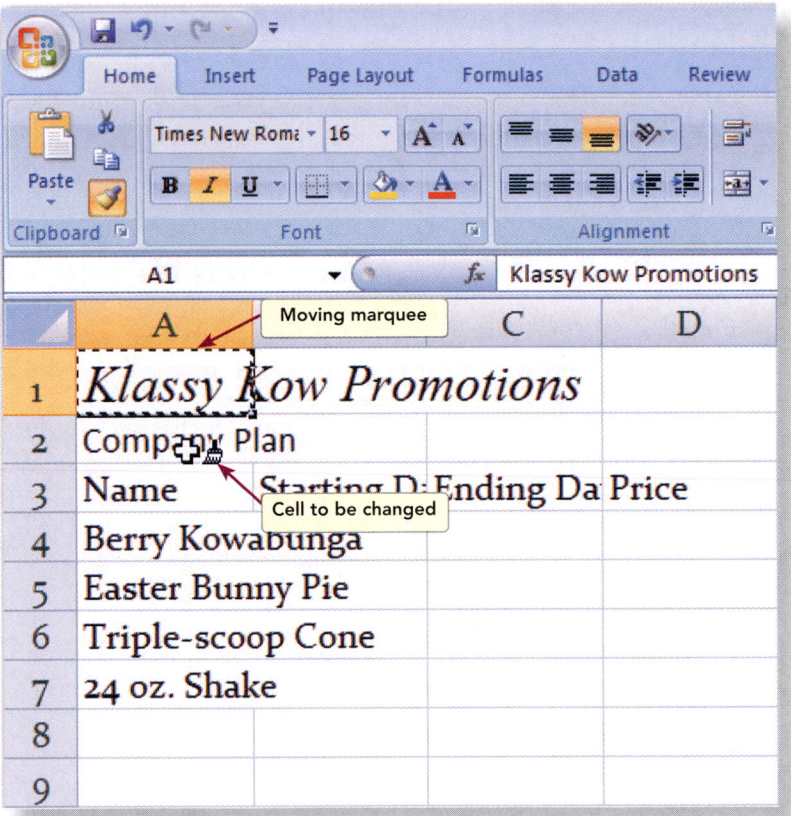

4. Click cell A2. The font, size, and style are copied, and row 2 is made taller. The Format Painter command is canceled.

5. Make sure cell A2 is now the active cell.

6. Double-click the Format Painter button ✔. This locks the painter on so that you can format more than one cell.

7. Click cell A3 to copy the format. Then click cell B3.

8. Click the Format Painter button ✓ to cancel the command.

9. Click the arrow next to the Undo button ↺▾. Excel shows Format Painter as **Paste Special** in the Undo history list.

10. Undo two **Paste Special** commands. The labels in row 3 return to the theme font (11-point Constantia).

11. Press Esc to cancel the marquee.

12. Click the Zoom Out button ⊖ to return to a 100% size.

Selecting Cell Ranges

A *range* is a group of cells that forms a rectangle on the screen. In many cases, you work with a range of cells. For example, you might need to format all the cells in rows 3 through 7 in the same style.

When a range is active, it is highlighted or shaded on the screen. Like an individual cell, a range has an address. A *range address* consists of the upper-left cell address and the lower-right cell address, separated by a colon.

TABLE 2-2 Examples of Range Addresses

Range Address	Cells in the Range
A1:B3	6 cells on 3 rows and in 2 columns
B1:B100	100 cells, all in column B
C3:C13	11 cells, starting at cell C3, all in column C
D4:F12	27 cells on 9 rows and in 3 columns
A1:XFD1	16,384 cells or the entire row 1

Exercise 2-5   **SELECT RANGES WITH THE MOUSE**

The *selection pointer* within the worksheet grid is a thick white cross shape. When you point at a row or column heading, the selection pointer appears as a solid black arrow. There are several ways to select a range of cells by using the mouse:

- Drag across adjacent cells to select the range.

- Click the first cell in the range. Hold down Shift and click the last cell in the range.

- Click a column heading letter to select a column or click a row heading number to select a row.

Excel 2007

- Drag across adjacent column heading letters or row heading numbers to select multiple columns or rows.

- Click the Select All button 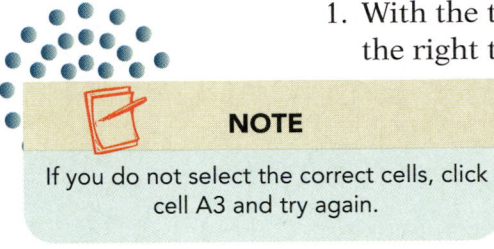 (see Figure 2-6) to select every cell on the worksheet.

1. With the thick white cross-shaped pointer, click cell A3 and drag to the right to cell E3.

2. Release the mouse button. Cells A3 through E3 are selected. The Name Box shows the first cell in the range, and the formula bar shows the first label. Cell A3 appears white, and the remaining cells are light blue-gray.

NOTE

If you do not select the correct cells, click cell A3 and try again.

Figure 2-6
Selecting a range of cells

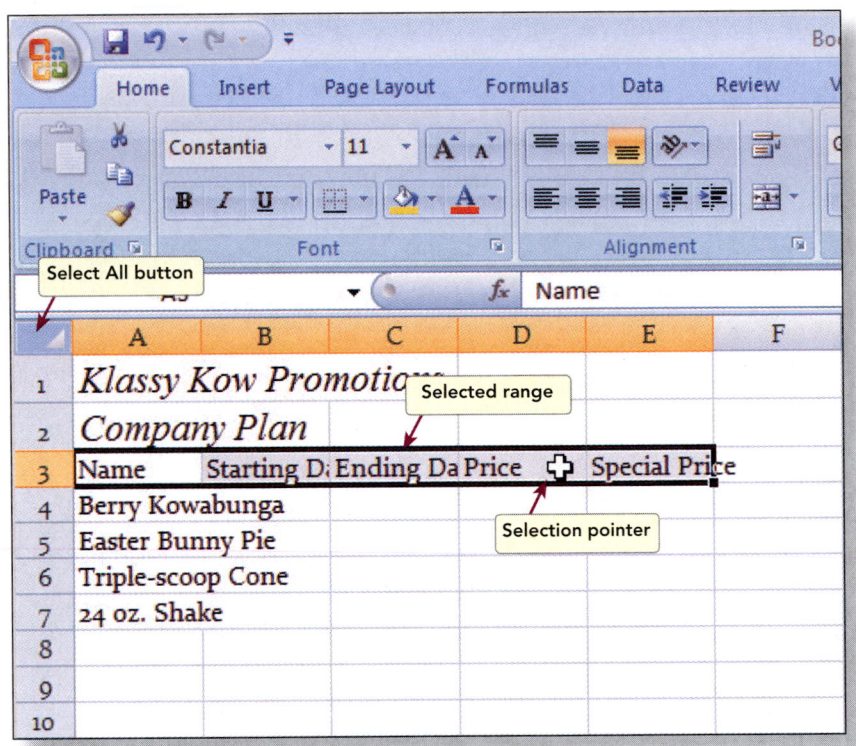

3. Click the Bold button ⓑ. The labels in the cells in the selected range are bold. Bold data is often slightly larger than data in the Regular style of the same font.

4. Click cell A1. This makes cell A1 active and deselects the range.

TIP

You can apply bold by using the keystroke combination [Ctrl]+[B]. You can apply italic by using [Ctrl]+[I].

5. Click cell A1 and drag to cell F1. Do not release the mouse button.

6. Drag down to cell F3 and then release the mouse button. The selected range is A1:F3.

7. Click cell A1 to deselect the range and make cell A1 active again.

8. Point to the row 1 heading. The pointer changes shape and is a solid black arrow.

9. Click the row 1 heading to select the row.

10. Click cell B2. You can click any cell to deselect a range.

11. Point to the row 1 heading. Click and drag down through the row headings from row 1 to row 5.

12. Release the mouse button. Five rows are selected.

13. Click any cell to deselect the rows.

14. Click the column A heading. This selects the column.

15. Click any cell to deselect the column.

16. Click the column B heading and drag to the column G heading. This selects a range that includes all the cells in columns B through G.

17. Click cell B5. Hold down Shift and click cell E18. This is another way to select a range. This range is B5:E18.

Exercise 2-6   SELECT RANGES WITH KEYBOARD SHORTCUTS

You can select a range of cells by using keyboard shortcuts. These shortcuts work for selecting data in many Windows programs.

TABLE 2-3 Keyboard Shortcuts to Select Cell Ranges

Keystroke	To Do This
Shift + arrow key	Select from the active cell, moving in the direction of the arrow.
Shift + Spacebar	Select the current row.
Shift + PageDown	Extend selection from active cell down one screen in the same column.
Shift + PageUp	Extend selection from active cell up one screen in the same column.
Ctrl + A	Select the entire range with data or the entire worksheet.
Ctrl + Spacebar	Select the current column.
Ctrl + Shift + Home	Extend selection from active cell to beginning of data.
Ctrl + Shift + End	Extend selection from active cell to end of data.
F8	Start Extend Selection mode.
F8 + arrow key	Extend selection from active cell in the direction of the arrow.
Esc	End Extend Selection mode.

1. Click cell A3. Hold down Shift and press → four times. The range is A3:E3.

Excel 2007

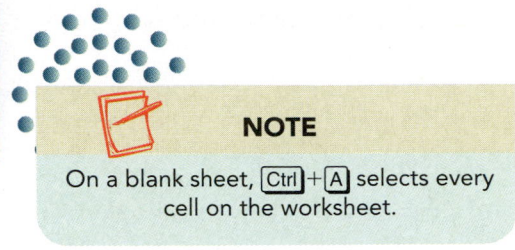

NOTE

On a blank sheet, Ctrl+A selects every cell on the worksheet.

2. Click the arrow next to the Font box. Key **c** and choose **Calibri** (or scroll to the font).

3. Click the arrow next to the Font Size box. Choose **14**.

4. Click the Bold button **B** to remove bold.

5. Click cell A1. Hold down Shift and press ↓ once. Choose **Calibri** for the font.

6. Click cell A3 and press F8. This starts Extend Selection mode. Notice that **Extend Selection** appears in the status bar.

7. Press → four times. Press ↓ to reach row 15. The range A3:E15 is selected.

TIP

If you go too far, press ↑ to reach row 15.

8. Press Esc to cancel Extend Selection mode.

9. Click cell A3. Hold down Shift and click cell E15. This is another way to select the range.

10. Hold down Ctrl. Click cell A17 and drag across to cell E17.

11. Release the Ctrl key. Two different-sized ranges that are not next to each other are selected at the same time.

Figure 2-7
Selecting two ranges

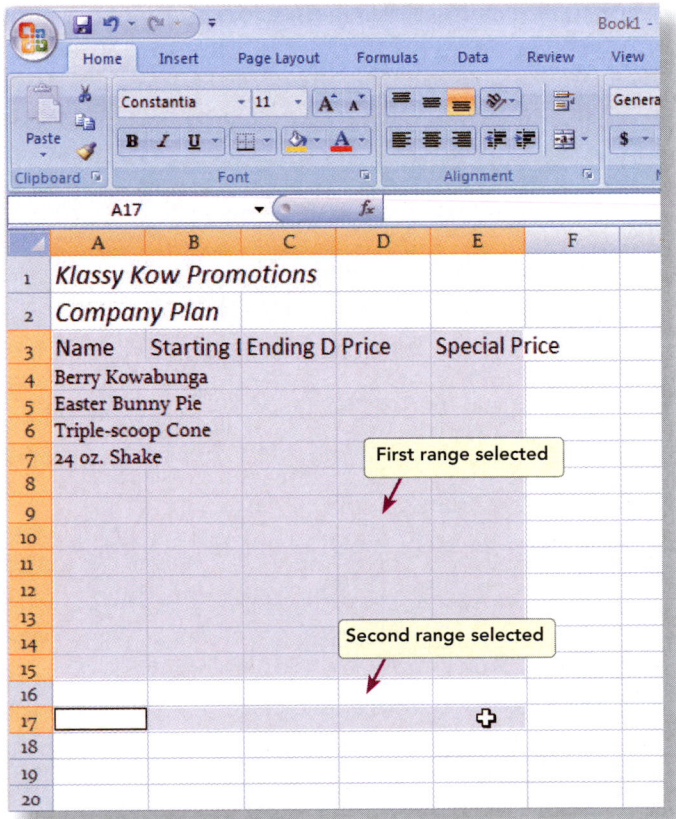

12. Press Ctrl+Home.

Modifying Column Width and Row Height

In a new workbook with the Office document theme, columns are 8.43 spaces (64 pixels) wide. If the column on the right is empty, a label larger than 8.43 spaces spills into it so that you can see the entire label on screen.

If the column on the right is not empty, you can widen the column so that the label is not cut off.

Rows in a new workbook are 15.00 points (20 pixels) high to fit the default 11-point Calibri font. A *point* is 1/72 inch. Generally Excel resizes the row height as needed, but you can size it manually, too.

Here are the ways you can resize column widths and row heights:

> **NOTE**
>
> If you change the document theme before keying any data, column width and row heights are set for the new theme.

- Drag a column or row border to a different size.

- Double-click a column's right border to AutoFit the column. *AutoFit* means the column is widened to fit the longest entry in the column.

- Double-click a row's bottom border to AutoFit the row height. A row is AutoFitted to fit the largest font size currently used in the row.

- On the Home tab in the Cells group, click the Format button [Format ▾] and then choose Row Height or Column Width.

When you use the mouse to change the row height or column width, you will see the size in a ScreenTip. For rows, the height is shown in points (as it is for fonts) as well as in pixels. For columns, the width is shown in character spaces and in pixels. A *pixel* is a screen dot, a single point of color on the screen. A *character space* is the average width of a numeric character in the standard font used in the worksheet.

If you use Ribbon commands to change the column width or row height, you must key the entry by using points for row height or character spaces for column width.

Exercise 2-7   MODIFY COLUMN WIDTH

1. Place the pointer on the vertical border between the column headings for columns A and B. The pointer changes to a two-pointed arrow with a wide vertical bar.

2. Drag the sizing pointer to the right until the ScreenTip shows **15.63 (130 pixels)** and release the mouse button. At this width, the column should be wide enough for the longest promotion item.

Excel 2007

Figure 2-8
Resizing columns

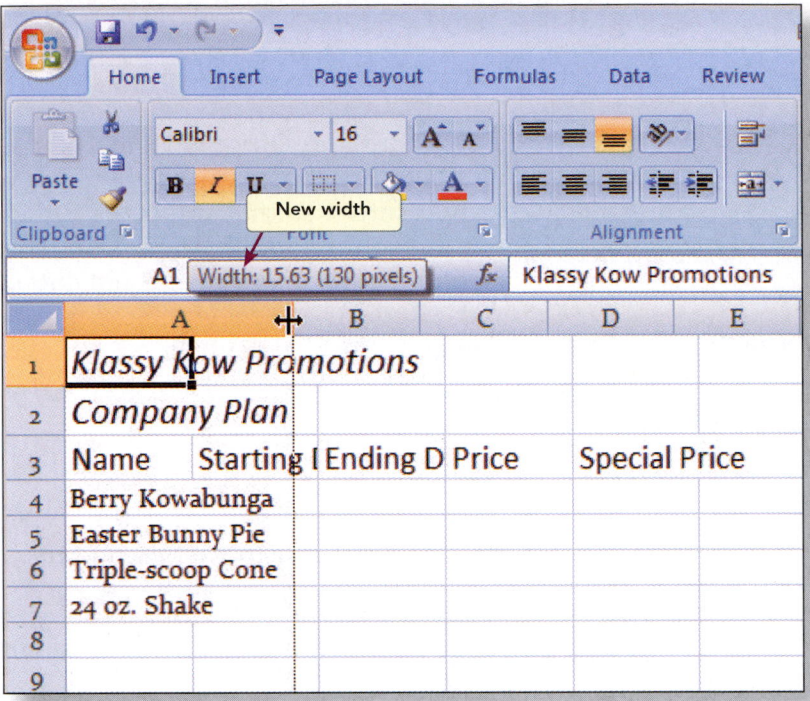

TIP

Be careful about AutoFitting columns that include titles in rows 1 or 2. Excel will AutoFit a column to accommodate long labels.

Format ▾

NOTE

If you change data in a column that you've AutoFitted, the column does not automatically AutoFit for the new entry.

3. Place the pointer between the column headings for columns B and C. Double-click. Excel AutoFits column B to fit the label.

4. Double-click the border between the column headings for columns C and D. Excel AutoFits column C.

5. Click anywhere in column D.

6. In the **Cells** group, click the Format button and then choose **Column Width**. The Column Width dialog box opens.

7. Key **10** and press Enter. The column width is changed to 10 spaces.

8. Double-click the border between the column headings for columns E and F to AutoFit column E.

Exercise 2-8 MODIFY ROW HEIGHT

1. Place the pointer on the horizontal border between the headings for rows 3 and 4. The pointer turns into a two-pointed arrow.

2. Drag down until the ScreenTip shows **22.50 (30 pixels)** and release the mouse button.

Figure 2-9
Resizing rows

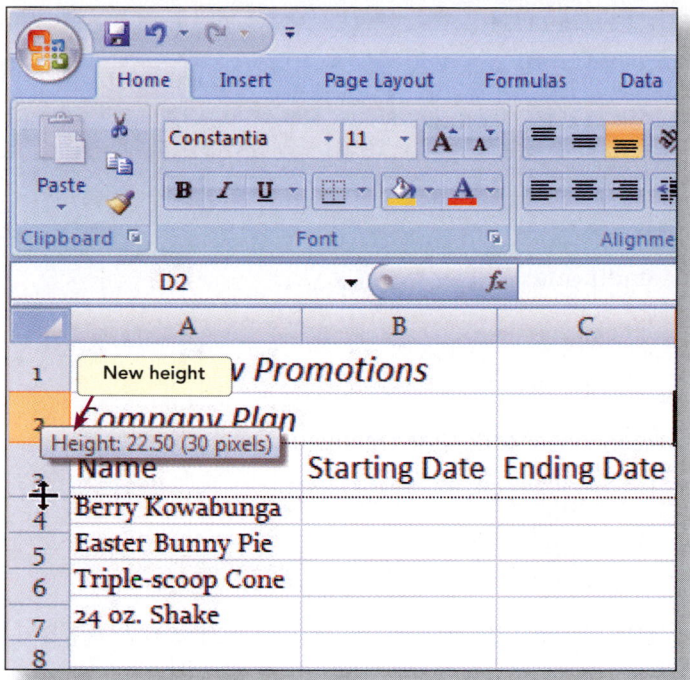

3. Click anywhere in row 4.

4. In the **Cells** group, click the Format button 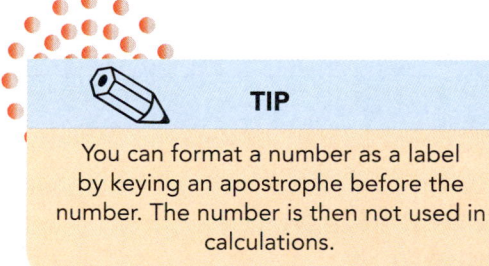 and then **Row Height**. The Row Height dialog box opens.

5. Key **22.5** and press [Enter]. The row is 22.5 points (30 pixels) high.

Entering Values and Dates

When you key an entry that starts with a number or an arithmetic symbol, Excel assumes it is a *value*. A value is right-aligned in the cell and is included in calculations. Arithmetic symbols include =, −, and +.

TIP

You can format a number as a label by keying an apostrophe before the number. The number is then not used in calculations.

Exercise 2-9 **ENTER DATES AND VALUES**

Excel recognizes dates if you key them in a typical date style. For example, if you key "1/1/08," Excel formats it as a date. Dates have special formats and can be used in date arithmetic.

1. Click cell B4.

2. Key **12/1/08** and press Enter. Excel recognizes the numbers as a date and shows four digits for the year. If SmartTags are enabled, you will see an indicator in the lower-right corner of the cell. Ignore the indicator for now.

3. Continue keying the following dates in column B. Press Enter after each one:
   3/15/08
   8/1/08
   10/15/08

4. Key these dates in cells C4:C7:
   12/31/08
   4/15/08
   8/31/08
   11/15/08

5. Click cell D4. Drag to select cells D4:E7. With the range selected, you can press Enter to move from cell to cell, going top to bottom and then left to right.

6. Key the prices shown in the "Price" and "Special Price" columns in Figure 2-10.

Figure 2-10
Worksheet data entry completed

	A	B	C	D	E	F
1	*Klassy Kow Promotions*					
2	*Company Plan*					
3	Name	Starting Date	Ending Date	Price	Special Price	
4	Berry Kowabunga	12/1/2008	12/31/2008	3.19	2.99	
5	Easter Bunny Pie	3/15/2008	4/15/2008	24.99	20.99	
6	Triple-scoop Cone	8/1/2008	8/31/2008	3.29	2.99	
7	24 oz. Shake	10/15/2008	11/15/2008	3.29	2.99	
8						

Exercise 2-10   **APPLY NUMBER FORMATS FROM THE RIBBON**

If you key only a value, it is formatted in a General style. This style shows only digits, no commas. If the value has a decimal point, it is shown with as many places after the decimal point as you key.

To increase the readability of your worksheet, you can apply common formats from the Ribbon. You first select the range of cells to be formatted and then click a task button in the Ribbon.

1. Click cell D4. Drag to select cells D4:E7.

2. In the **Number** group, click the Accounting Number Format button [$ ▾]. The cells in the range are formatted to show a dollar sign and two decimal places. The dollar signs are aligned at the left edge of the cell.

Exercise 2-11   APPLY DATE FORMATS FROM THE DIALOG BOX

Excel includes many date formats in the Format Cells dialog box. You can open the Format Cells dialog box for the active cell or range by:

- Pressing [Ctrl]+[1].

- Right-clicking the cell or range and choosing Format Cells from the shortcut menu.

- On the Home tab in the Cells group, clicking the Format button [Format ▾] and then choosing Format Cells.

1. Click cell B4. Click and drag to select cells B4:C7.

2. Point at any of the selected cells and right-click. A shortcut menu opens with the Mini toolbar.

3. Choose **Format Cells**. The Format Cells dialog box opens; it should show the appropriate tab and category.

4. Click the **Number** tab if necessary.

5. Click **Date** in the **Category** list on the left if necessary. Many preset date formats are displayed in the **Type** box on the right.

6. Click a type in the list that shows the date first, a hyphen, an abbreviation for the month, another hyphen, and a two-digit year (example "14-Mar-01") and click **OK**. (See Figure 2-11 on the next page.) All of the dates are reformatted.

Figure 2-11
Choosing a date
format

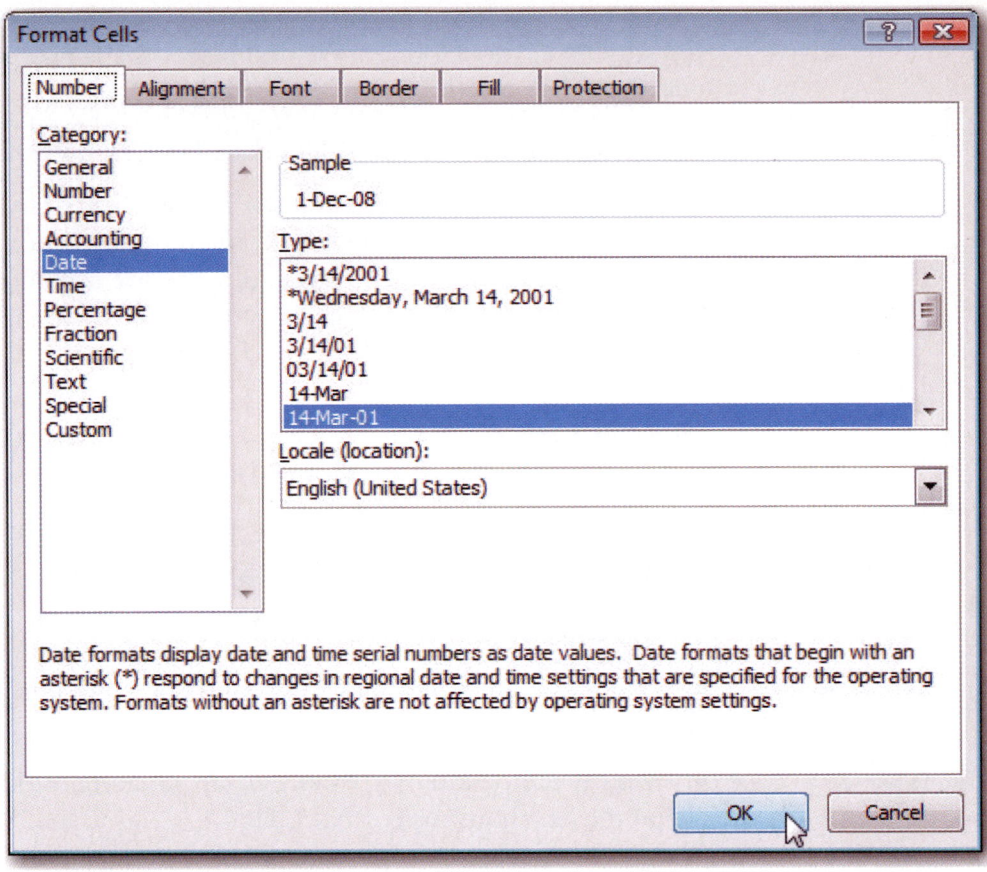

NOTE

Two-digit years between 00 and 29 are assumed to be the twenty-first century (2000, 2001, 2015). Two-digit years between 30 and 99 are assumed to be the twentieth century (1930, 1950, and 1999).

NOTE

Two theme colors are for hyperlinks. These colors do not appear in the palettes. The color swatches in the palette have ScreenTips indicating the color's purpose, intensity, or name.

Exercise 2-12   CHANGE THE FONT COLOR

In addition to changing the font, size, and style, you can set a new font color. The document theme includes 12 colors and various intensities (or saturations) of that color. You can also choose from standard colors, too. You can change the font color for a selected cell or range by:

- On the Home tab in the Font group, clicking the Font Color button.

- Opening the Format Cells dialog box and choosing the Font tab.

1. Select cells E4:E7 (the special prices).

2. Click the Font Color button. The color shown on the button is applied to the selected range, probably red.

3. Click the arrow next to the Font Color button. A color palette opens with 10 theme colors in the top row. The first 4 are text/background colors; the remaining 6 are accent colors. Standard colors are near the bottom of the palette.

4. Hover over several colors anywhere in the palette and watch the live preview in the worksheet.

5. Click **Dark Teal, Text 2** in the fourth column, first row. This is one of the theme colors. The palette closes, and the color is applied to the selected range.

6. Select cells A1:A2.

7. Press [Ctrl]+[1] and click the **Font** tab.

8. Click the arrow for **Color**. The same theme colors are listed as well as the standard colors.

9. Choose **Dark Teal, Text 2** and click **OK**.

> **TIP**
>
> Deselecting the range enables you to see the color more clearly.

Figure 2-12
Changing the color from the Format Cells dialog box

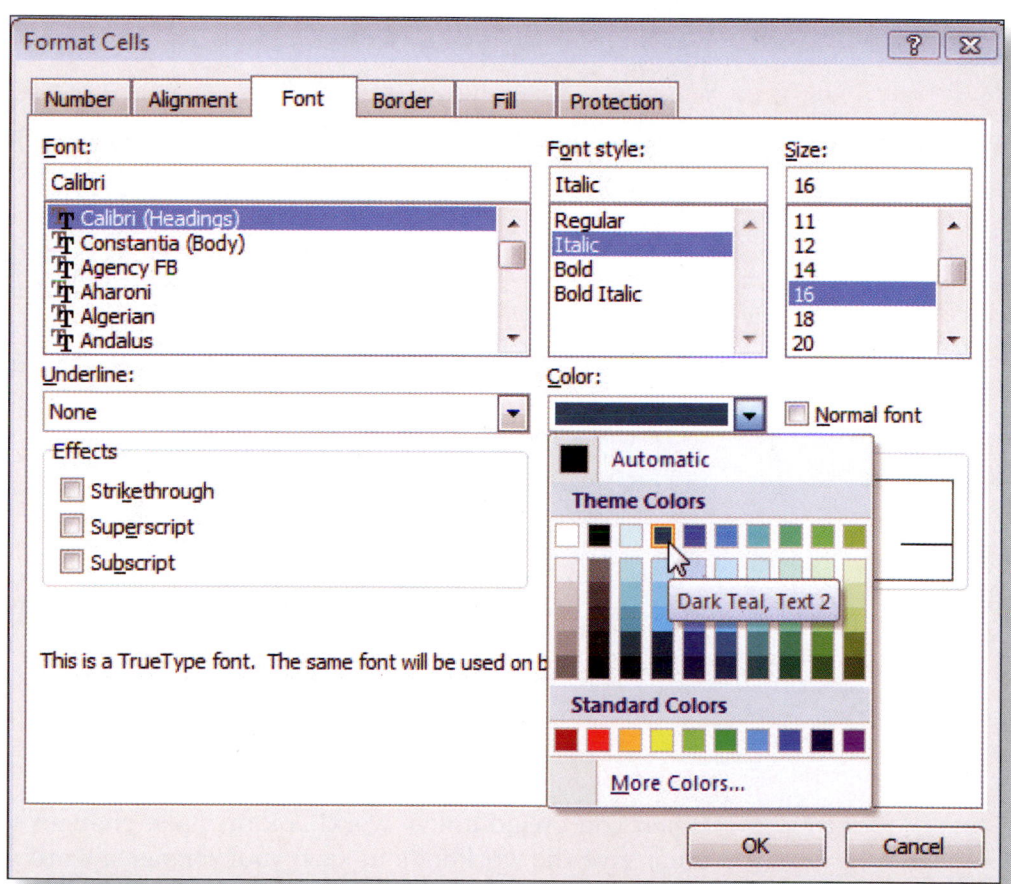

Exercise 2-13   **RENAME A WORKSHEET AND CHANGE THE TAB COLOR**

You can rename a worksheet tab with a more descriptive name to help you and others remember the worksheet's purpose. Worksheet names can be up to 31 characters. You can use spaces in the name of a worksheet tab.

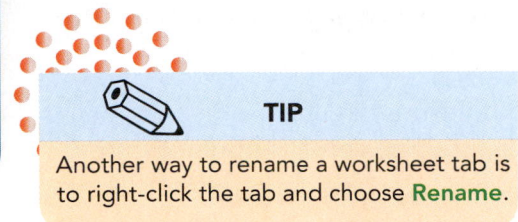

TIP

Another way to rename a worksheet tab is to right-click the tab and choose **Rename**.

1. Double-click the worksheet tab for **Sheet1**. The tab name is selected.

2. Key **Promos** and press ⌐Enter⌐.

3. Double-click **Sheet2** and name it **Plans**. The **Plans** sheet is empty.

4. Right-click the **Promos** tab and choose **Tab Color**. The Theme Colors dialog box opens with the palette of colors.

5. Choose **Dark Teal, Text 2** as the tab color.

Figure 2-13
Changing the tab color

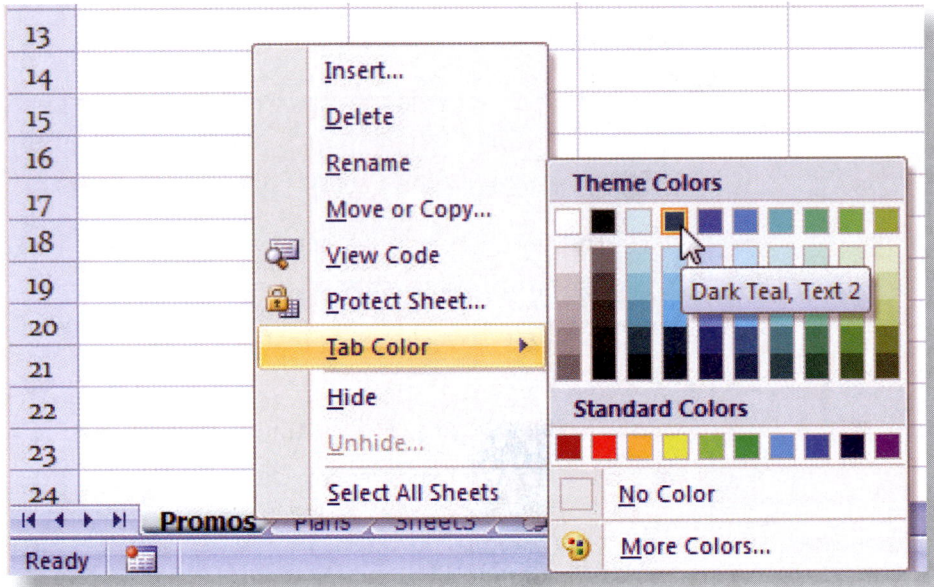

6. Click the **Plans** tab. Now you can see the color of the **Promos** tab better.

7. Click the **Promos** tab to make it the active sheet.

Saving a Workbook

When you create a new workbook or make changes to an existing one, you must save the workbook to keep your changes. Until you save your changes, your work can be lost if there is a power failure or computer problem.

To save a workbook, you must first give it a filename. A *filename* is the file identifier you see in the Open dialog box, Computer, or Windows Explorer. When you name a file in Windows, you can use up to 255 characters. Included in those 255 characters are the drive and folder names, so the actual filename is really limited to fewer than 255 characters. Generally, it is a good idea to keep filenames as short as possible.

You can use uppercase or lowercase letters, or a combination of both, for filenames. Windows is case-aware, which means it does recognize uppercase and lowercase that you key. However, it is not case-sensitive, so it does not distinguish between "BOOK1" and "book1." You can use spaces in a filename, but you cannot use the following characters: \ ?: * " <> |

Filenames are followed by a period and a three- or four-letter extension, supplied automatically by the software. Excel 2007 workbooks have the extension ".xlsx." Extensions identify the type of file.

For a new workbook, you can use either the Save or the Save As command to save and name the workbook. When you make changes to an existing workbook and want to save it with the same filename, use Save. If you want to save a workbook with a different filename, use Save As.

Excel saves workbooks in the current drive or folder unless you specify a different location. You can easily navigate to the appropriate location in the Save dialog box.

Throughout the exercises in this book, filenames consist of two parts:

- *[your initials]*, which might be your initials or an identifier your instructor asks you to use, such as **kms**

- The number of the exercise, such as **2-14**

NOTE

You may not see filename extensions if your Folder Options (Organize button in the Explorer dialog box) are set to hide them.

TIP

Wherever the pointer is when you save a workbook is where it appears the next time you open the workbook.

Exercise 2-14   SAVE A WORKBOOK

Depending on how difficult it would be to redo the work, you should save your file every 15 to 30 minutes.

1. Click cell A1.

2. Click the Save button on the Quick Access toolbar.

3. Choose the appropriate drive and folder location.

4. Click the New Folder button .

5. Key *[your initials]*Lesson2 and press Enter. The location is updated to your folder.

6. In the **File name** box, double-click **Book1** and key *[your initials]*2-14.

7. Click **Save**. The title bar shows the new filename.

NOTE

Your instructor will tell you what drive/folder to use to save your workbooks.

Entering Basic Formulas

A *formula* is an equation that performs a calculation on values in your worksheet and displays an answer. You key a formula in a cell. After you press a completion key, the formula results appear in the cell. The formula itself is visible in the formula bar.

Formulas are one of the main reasons for using Excel, because a formula performs calculations for you. If you later change any of the numbers used for the calculations, Excel quickly recalculates the formula to show a revised answer.

Formulas begin with an = sign as an identifier. After the = sign, you enter the address of the cells you want to add, subtract, multiply, or divide.

NOTE

Arithmetic operations are calculated in a specific order: first, exponentiation; second, multiplication and division; and finally, addition and subtraction.

Then you use *arithmetic operators* in the 10-key pad or at the top of the keyboard to complete the calculation. You probably recognize all of the arithmetic operators shown in Table 2-4, with the possible exception of exponentiation. The *exponentiation* operator raises a number to a power. For example, 2^3 represents 2 to the third power, or 2^3, which means $2 \times 2 \times 2$ or 8.

TABLE 2-4 Arithmetic Operators

Key or Symbol	Operation
^	Exponentiation
*	Multiplication
/	Division
+	Addition
−	Subtraction

Exercise 2-15   KEY A BASIC FORMULA

In your workbook, you can calculate the difference between the regular price and the promotion price. This is a simple subtraction formula. You will be working in column F. If you cannot see column F, set your Zoom size to a smaller size so you can see it.

1. Click cell F3. Key **Difference** and press Enter. The label is formatted with the same style as other labels in the row.

NOTE

Excel applies the same format to a cell in which you are entering data as the three or more cells to the immediate left or top of the cell.

2. Double-click the border between the column headings for columns F and G to AutoFit column F.

3. Key **=d** in cell F4 to start the formula. *Formula AutoComplete* shows a list of built-in formulas that begin with the letter "d." You can continue keying your own formula for now.

Figure 2-14
Formula
AutoComplete list
2-14.xlsx
Promos sheet

	A	B	C	D	E	F	G
	Klassy Kow Promotions						
	Company Plan						
	Name	Starting Date	Ending Date	Price		Special Price	Difference
	Berry Kowabunga	1-Dec-08	31-Dec-08	$	3.19	$	2.99	=d
	Easter Bunn	*Returns the number that represents the date in Microsoft Office Excel date-time code*					
	Triple-scoop Cone	1-Aug-08	31-Aug-08	$	3.29	$	2.99	
	24 oz. Shake	15-Oct-08	15-Nov-08	$	3.29	$	2.99	

AutoComplete dropdown: _fx_ DATE, _fx_ DATEVALUE, _fx_ DAVERAGE, _fx_ DAY, _fx_ DAYS360, _fx_ DB, _fx_ DCOUNT, _fx_ DCOUNTA, _fx_ DDB, _fx_ DEC2BIN, _fx_ DEC2HEX, _fx_ DEC2OCT

4. Key **4-e4** in cell F4. You'll see another Formula AutoComplete list when you key **e**. Your formula should be **=d4-e4** and it appears in the cell and in the formula bar. The cells used in the formula are outlined in colors that match the colors of the formula in the cell.

Figure 2-15
Keying a formula
2-14.xlsx
Promos sheet

Formula bar: ✕ ✓ _fx_ | =d4-e4

B	C	D		E		F
motions						
Starting Date	Ending Date	Price		Special Price		Difference
1-Dec-08	31-Dec-08	$	3.19	$	2.99	=d4-e4
15-Mar-08	15-Apr-08	$	24.99	$	20.99	
1-Aug-08	31-Aug-08	$	3.29	$	2.99	
15-Oct-08	15-Nov-08	$	3.29	$	2.99	

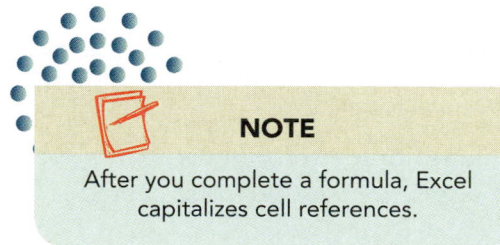

NOTE

After you complete a formula, Excel capitalizes cell references.

5. Press ⎆Enter⎵. The difference in price is 20 cents. It is shown in the same number format as the cells used in the formula.

6. Press ⬆ to return to cell F4. Notice that the formula bar shows the formula, but the cell displays the result of the formula.

Exercise 2-16   ENTER A FORMULA BY POINTING

You can use the mouse to point to cells used in a formula. This increases accuracy, because you don't have to worry about keying the wrong cell address.

1. Click cell F5. Key = to start the formula.

2. Click cell D5. The address appears in cell F5 and in the formula bar. Cell D5 has a moving marquee.

3. Key – to subtract the next cell.

4. Click cell E5. It is placed in the formula after the minus sign and now has the moving marquee.

Figure 2-16
Entering a formula
by pointing
2-14.xlsx
Promos sheet

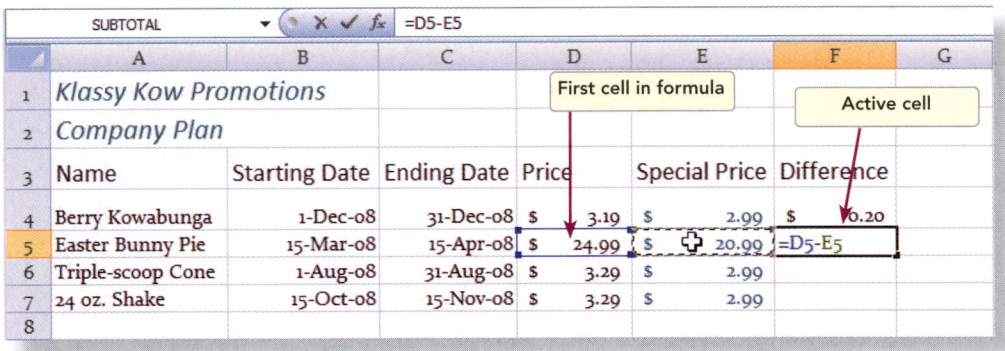

5. Click the Enter button ✓ in the formula bar. The difference of $4 is calculated.

Exercise 2-17   COPY A FORMULA BY USING THE COPY AND PASTE BUTTONS

The formula in cell F5 is the same as the one in cell F4 except for the row references. The formula is relative to its location on the worksheet. When you copy a formula with row or cell references, Excel makes this adjustment automatically.

1. Click cell F5. Click the Copy button 📋 . The cell now has a moving marquee. The status bar tells you to select the destination for the copy.

2. Click cell F6 and drag to select the range F6:F7.

3. Click the Paste button 📋 . The formula is copied to both cells in the range. The Paste Options button 📋 appears just below the pasted data.

4. Hover over the Paste Options button 📋. A down arrow appears next to the button. Click the down arrow; options for copying the data are listed. You need not change the option.

Figure 2-17
Copying a formula
2-14.xlsx
Promos sheet

	A	B	C	D	E	F	G	H	I	J
1	*Klassy Kow Promotions*									
2	*Company Plan*									
3	Name	Starting Date	Ending Date	Price	Special Price	Diffe	Paste Options button			
4	Berry Kowabunga	1-Dec-08	31-Dec-08	$ 3.19	$ 2.99	$ 0.20				
5	Easter Bunny Pie	15-Mar-08	15-Apr-08	$ 24.99	$ 20.99	$ 4.00				
6	Triple-scoop Cone	1-Aug-08	31-Aug-08	$ 3.29	$ 2.99	$ 0.30				
7	24 oz. Shake	15-Oct-08	15-Nov-08	$ 3.29	$ 2.99	$ 0.30				

Keep Source Formatting
Use Destination Theme
Match Destination Formatting
Values Only
Values and Number Formatting
Values and Source Formatting
Keep Source Column Widths
Formatting Only
Link Cells

Status bar message

Promos Plans Sheet3

Select destination and press ENTER or choose Paste   Average: $0.30   Count: 2   Sum: $0.60   100%

NOTE

You can press Enter to complete a Copy or Paste command. This automatically cancels the moving marquee.

5. Press Esc twice to cancel the moving marquee and finish the Paste command.

6. Click cell F6 and review the formula. Notice that Excel has adjusted the formula to take into account the relative position of the cell.

7. Click cell F7. Review the formula. Excel has adjusted it as well.

Exercise 2-18   USE AUTOSUM, AVERAGE, AND MAX

NOTE

The screen resolution at your computer affects how a button looks. It may include an icon and text, and the text may be below or next to the button. Check the ScreenTip when in doubt.

Some calculations are so common in business and personal use that Excel includes them as functions. A *function* is a built-in formula in Excel. An example of a function is "SUM," in which Excel automatically totals a column or row. A function starts with =, just like a formula. Excel has several "auto" functions available on the Formulas tab and the Home tab.

Excel 2007

TABLE 2-5 Function Library Group

Button	Action
Insert Function	Opens the Insert Function dialog box
AutoSum	Displays the sum, average, count, maximum, or minimum of selected cells
Recently Used	Lists the most recently used functions
Financial	Displays a list of financial functions
Logical	Displays a list of logical functions
Text	Displays a list of text functions
Date & Time	Displays a list of date and time functions
Lookup & Reference	Displays a list of lookup and reference functions
Math & Trig	Displays a list of mathematical and trigonometry functions
More Functions	Displays a list of statistical, engineering, cube, and information functions

TIP

Click the AutoSum button, not its arrow.

1. Click the **Formulas** tab in the Ribbon. The Function Library group includes buttons for each major function category.

2. Click cell F8. Click the AutoSum button in the Function Library group. A formula is placed in the cell followed by the range that will be summed. A moving marquee surrounds cells that will be summed. A ScreenTip for the function appears.

Figure 2-18
Using AutoSum
2-14.xlsx
Promos sheet

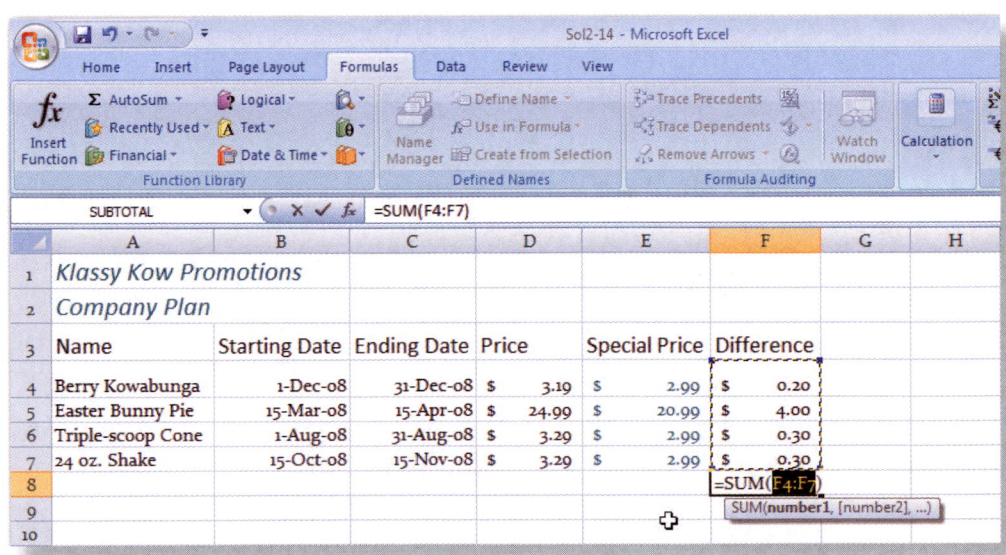

3. Press [Enter]. The formula is completed.

4. Click cell F8. Notice that the formula includes the function name SUM and an assumed range in parentheses.

5. Click cell D8.

6. Click the arrow with the AutoSum button Σ AutoSum ▾.

7. Choose **Average**. The AVERAGE function appears in the formula bar and in the active cell. A moving marquee surrounds the cells in the assumed range.

8. Press [Ctrl]+[Enter] to complete the function. Notice that now the formula includes the function name AVERAGE and the range of cells that is averaged.

9. Click cell D9. Click the arrow with the AutoSum button Σ AutoSum ▾.

10. Choose **Max**. A moving marquee surrounds the cells that will be used by the MAX function. The MAX function is used to determine the largest value in a range.

11. Click cell D4 and drag to select the range D4:D7. Don't include cell D8 in this function, because it is the average you just calculated.

12. Press [Ctrl]+[Enter]. The result of the formula shows the highest price in the column.

TIP

There is a Sum button in the Editing group on the Home tab. Both buttons are called AutoSum in this text.

NOTE

The SUM function adds the values in the cells. The AVERAGE function adds the values in the range and then divides by the number of cells in the range.

NOTE

Functions ignore titles in a column/row because they are not values; they are labels, which are not used in calculations.

Exercise 2-19   CHECK RESULTS WITH AUTOCALCULATE

The *AutoCalculate* feature displays formula results for a selected range in the status bar. AutoCalculate can display sums, averages, counts, maximums, or minimums. You set AutoCalculate choices by right-clicking the status bar.

1. Right-click the status bar. Verify that there are check marks for **Average**, **Count**, and **Sum**. Press [Esc].

2. Select the range F4:F7. AutoCalculate shows the average, a count, and the sum for the selected range in the status bar.

Excel 2007

Figure 2-19
Using AutoCalculate
2-14.xlsx
Promos sheet

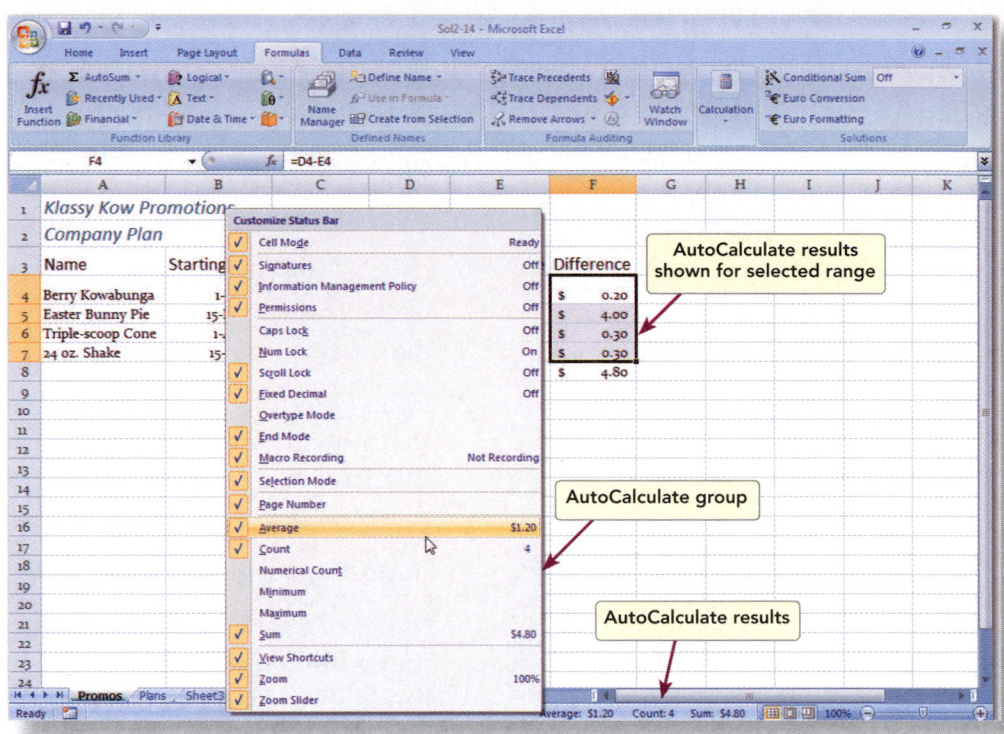

3. Right-click the status bar and click to select **Minimum** and **Maximum**. Press Esc.

4. Select the range D4:D7. AutoCalculate shows more information about these cells.

5. Select cells A4:A7. These are labels, so AutoCalculate only shows a count.

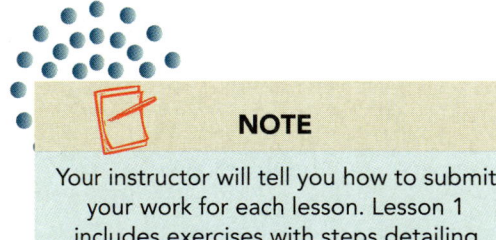

NOTE

Your instructor will tell you how to submit your work for each lesson. Lesson 1 includes exercises with steps detailing how to print your work or save it as an XPS file.

6. Right-click the status bar and click to deselect **Minimum** and **Maximum**. Press Esc.

7. Key your first and last name in cell A10.

8. Press F12 and save the workbook as *[your initials]2-19* in your Lesson 2 folder.

9. Prepare and submit your workbook.

10. Close the workbook.

Using Online Help

Building basic formulas is an important skill. You will use it as the basis for becoming a proficient Excel user.

LOOK UP FORMULAS

1. Start Excel and click the Microsoft Office Excel Help button [icon].

2. Click in the Search box, key **create formula**, and press [Enter].

3. In the list of topics, find and click a topic related to creating a formula.

4. Click **Show All** at the top of a Help window to expand all explanations.

5. When you finish investigating formulas, close the Help window.

Lesson 2 Summary

- In a blank workbook, you can key values, labels, dates, or formulas. Excel recognizes data by the first character you key in the cell.

- Labels are aligned at the left edge of a cell. If they are longer than the column width, they spill into the next column if it is empty. Otherwise, they appear cut off on the screen.

- To complete a cell entry, press [Enter], [Tab], or any arrow key or click another cell. You can also click the Enter button [icon] in the formula bar.

- New workbooks use the Office document theme. The default font for data is 11-point Calibri. You can change the font, the font size, the color, and the style.

- Use the Format Painter to copy formats from one cell to other cells.

- Many commands require that you first select a range of cells. You select a range of cells by using the mouse or keyboard shortcuts.

- The default row height matches the default font size in the document theme. The row height adjusts if you choose a larger font.

- Common formats, such as Accounting, can be applied to cells from the Number group on the Home tab. Many other formats are available in the Format Cells dialog box.

- It's usually a good idea to change the default worksheet tab name to a more descriptive name. You can also change the worksheet tab color for visual cues.

- You must save a new workbook to keep your work. For a new workbook, you can use the Save or the Save As command.

- To create a formula in a cell, you can key it or you can construct it by pointing to the cells used in the formula. All formulas begin with the = symbol.

- When you copy a formula, Excel adjusts it to match the row or column where the copy is located.
- Excel has functions for common calculations such as Sum, Average, Maximum, Minimum, and Count.
- You can see results for common functions without keying a formula if you use AutoCalculate.

LESSON 2   Command Summary

Feature	Button	Task Path	Keyboard
Accounting Number	$ ▾	Home, Number	
AutoSum	Σ AutoSum ▾	Formulas, Function Library	
Column Width	Format ▾	Home, Cells, Format, Column Width	
Copy		Home, Clipboard	Ctrl + C
Font		Home, Font	Ctrl + 1
Font Color	A ▾	Home, Font	Ctrl + 1
Font Size		Home, Font	Ctrl + 1
Format Painter		Home, Clipboard	
Paste	Paste ▾	Home, Clipboard	Ctrl + V
Rename sheet	Format ▾	Home, Cells, Format, Rename Sheet	
Row Height	Format ▾	Home, Cells, Format, Row Height	
Save		Microsoft Office, Save	
Tab color	Format ▾	Home, Cells, Format, Tab Color	
Themes	Themes ▾	Page Layout, Themes	

Concepts Review

True/False Questions

Each of the following statements is either true or false. Indicate your choice by circling T or F.

T F 1. If you key **ABC Company** in a cell, Excel will recognize it as a label.

T F 2. When text is too long for a row, it spills to the next row.

T F 3. A range is a rectangular group of cells.

T F 4. Formulas must be keyed in the formula bar.

T F 5. Common number formats are shown as buttons on the Page Layout tab.

T F 6. The AutoSum button includes options for other common functions.

T F 7. AutoCalculate and AutoSum both display results in a cell.

T F 8. If you copy a formula from one cell to another, Excel changes it to match the new row and column.

Short Answer Questions

Write the correct answer in the space provided.

1. What symbol is used to start a formula?

   _____

2. Describe how to rename a worksheet tab.

   _____

3. What is included in a document theme?

   _____

4. If the pointer is in cell B3 as you key a label and you want to key a label in cell C3, what key can you press to go directly to cell C3?

   _____

5. Give an example of a range address.

   _____

6. What function key starts Extend Selection mode?

   _____

7. How can you AutoFit a column to the longest text in it?

_____

8. List three arithmetic operators that might be used in a formula.

_____

Critical Thinking

Answer these questions on a separate page. There are no right or wrong answers. Support your answers with examples from your own experience, if possible.

1. A new workbook opens with three worksheets. Give examples of how you might use different sheets in the same workbook if you worked in the office for a movie theater.

2. Why does Excel have different data types such as values, labels, and dates? What are some of the differences among these types?

Skills Review

Exercise 2-20

Enter labels. Change the font and the document theme.

REVIEW

Press Backspace to correct errors in a cell, or press Esc to start over. Remember that labels in some cells might spill over to other cells.

1. Create a workbook and enter labels by following these steps:

    a. Press Ctrl + N. This opens a new workbook.
    b. Double-click the **Home** tab to collapse the Ribbon.
    c. Key the labels shown in Figure 2-20.

Figure 2-20

	A	B	C	D	E
1	Klassy Kow Ice Cream				
2	Ice Cream Pie Sales for September				
3		1st Qtr	2nd Qtr	3rd Qtr	4th Qtr
4	Chocolate				
5	Vanilla				
6	Strawberry				
7	Turtle				

2. Change the font by following these steps.

   a. Click cell A1. Click the **Home** tab.

   b. Click the down arrow next to the Font box. Key **c** and choose **Cambria**.

   c. Click the down arrow next to the Font Size box. Choose **18**.

   d. Click cell A2 and change it to 14-point Cambria.

3. Key your first and last name in cell A9. Press Ctrl + Home.

4. Save the workbook as *[your initials]***2-20a** in your Lesson 2 folder.

5. Change the document theme by following these steps.

   a. Click the **Page Layout** tab in the Ribbon.

   b. Click the Themes button.

     c. Choose **Concourse**.

     d. Click the Microsoft Office Button. Point at the **Print** arrow and choose **Print Preview**. Close the preview.

6. Save the workbook as *[your initials]***2-20b** in your Lesson 2 folder.

7. Prepare and submit your work. Close the workbook.

Exercise 2-21

Select cell ranges. Change the font and the document theme.

1. Open **CakeSales** and click the **CakeSales** worksheet tab.

2. Press F12 and save the workbook as *[your initials]***2-21** in your Lesson 2 folder.

3. Select cell ranges and change the font by following these steps:

   a. Click cell A1 and drag to select cells A1:A2. Change the size to 16.

   b. Click cell B3 and press F8 to start Extend Selection mode.

   c. Press End.

   d. Click the Bold button. Change the font size to 12 points.

   e. Click cell A4 and press F8. Press Ctrl + ↓. Then press Ctrl + →.

   f. Change the font size to 10 points.

4. Key your first and last name in cell A9. Press Ctrl + Home.

5. Click the Microsoft Office Button. Choose **Print** and then **Quick Print**. This worksheet prints with row and column headings.

6. Change the document theme by following these steps.

   a. Click the **Page Layout** tab. Click the Themes button. Choose the **Urban** theme.

   b. Click cell B3 and press F8 and then End.

   c. Change the font to the headings font for this document theme.

d. Click cell A4 and press F8. Press Ctrl+→. Then press Ctrl+↓. Change the font size to 11 points.

   e. Click the Microsoft Office Button. Point at the **Print** arrow and choose **Print Preview**. Close the preview.

   f. Click the Save button. This resaves the workbook with the same name.

7. Prepare and submit your work. Close the workbook.

Exercise 2-22

Set column width and row height. Enter and format values and dates.

1. Open **PromoPlans**. Press F12 and save the workbook as *[your initials]*2-22 in your Lesson 2 folder.

2. Set column width and row height by following these steps:

   a. Place the pointer on the border between the column headings for columns A and B.

   b. Drag the pointer to the right to **17.86 (130 pixels)**.

   c. Click the column B heading and drag to select columns B through F.

   d. Double-click the border between the column headings for columns F and G to AutoFit the selected columns.

   e. Click the row heading for row 3. Drag to select rows 3 through 7.

   f. Drag the bottom border for row 7 to **22.50 (30 pixels)**.

3. Enter the values and dates shown in Figure 2-21. Ignore SmartTag Options buttons that may appear.

Figure 2-21

	B	C	D	E	F
4	3/3/08	4/15/08	3.29	2500	2500
5	9/1/08	9/30/08	20.99	950	1800
6	1/15/09	1/31/09	3.19	4000	4700
7	5/1/08	5/31/08	2.99	3500	3900

4. Format values and set font colors by following these steps:

   a. Select the range E4:F7. Press Ctrl+1.

   b. Click the **Number** tab. Choose **Number** in the **Category** list.

   c. Click the down spinner arrow for **Decimal places** to reach **0**.

   d. Click to select the **Use 1000 Separator** (,) box and click **OK**.

e. Select the range D4:D7.

f. Click the Accounting Number Format button  on the Home tab.

g. Select the range B4:C7. In the **Number** group, click the Dialog Box Launcher. Click the **Number** tab. Choose **Date** in the **Category** list.

h. Choose the format in the **Type** list that spells out the month, shows a comma after the date, and four digits for the year. Click **OK**.

NOTE

Currency format from the Format Cells dialog box uses a floating currency symbol; the symbols are to the immediate left of the first digit.

5. Key your first and last name in cell A9 and press `Ctrl`+`Home`.

6. Double-click the **Sheet1** tab and key **PricePromos**. Press `Enter`.

7. Click the Save button .

8. Prepare and submit your work. Close the workbook.

Exercise 2-23

Save a workbook. Enter labels and values. Enter and copy formulas.

NOTE

You can click the Microsoft Office Button , choose New, and then choose Blank Workbook to create a new workbook. New workbooks use the Office theme.

1. Save a workbook by following these steps:

a. Press `Ctrl`+`N` to create a new workbook.

b. Double-click the **Sheet1** tab. Key **MediaPlans** and press `Enter`.

c. Right-click the **MediaPlans** tab and choose **Tab Color**. Choose **Accent 2** from the top row.

d. Click the Save button . Find and choose your Lesson 2 folder.

e. Key *[your initials]*2-23 in the **File name** box. Click **Save**.

2. Enter labels and values by following these steps:

a. In cell A1, set the font for 16-point Cambria.

b. Key **Klassy Kow Media Schedule** and press `Enter`.

TIP

You can set the font for selected cells before keying data.

c. Select the range A2:D2 and set the font to 12-point Calibri bold italic.

d. In cell A2, key **Media** and press `Enter`.

e. In cell B2, key **Frequency**. In cell C2, key **Cost per Ad**. In cell D2, key **Total** and press `Enter`.

f. Click the column B heading and drag to select columns B through D.

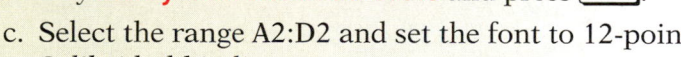

REVIEW

If you AutoFit column A, the column will be sized to accommodate the label in cell A1.

g. Double-click the border between the column headings for columns D and E to AutoFit the selected columns.

h. Place the pointer on the border between the column headings for columns A and B. Drag the pointer to the right to **15.00 (110 pixels)**.

i. Key the labels and values shown in Figure 2-22.

Figure 2-22

	A	B	C
3	WOW Radio	15	150
4	Channel 3 Cable	10	125
5	Star Newspaper	4	105
6	Clipper Mailer	1	200

   j. Click the row heading for row 1. Drag to select rows 1 through 6. Drag the bottom border for row 6 to **22.50 (30 pixels)**.

3. Enter and copy a formula by following these steps:

   a. Click cell D3. Key **=** to start the formula.

   b. Click cell B3.

   c. Key ⁕ to multiply the next cell.

   d. Click cell C3. Press Enter.

   e. Click cell D3 and click the Copy button  in the Clipboard group.

      f. Click cell D4 and drag to select cells D4:D6. Press Enter to complete the copy.

4. Select cells C3:D6. Click the Accounting Number Format button $ ▾.

5. Key your first and last name in cell A9. Press Ctrl + Home.

6. Click the Save button .

7. Prepare and submit your work. Close the workbook.

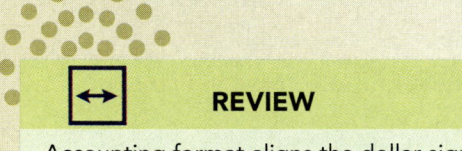

REVIEW

Accounting format aligns the dollar signs at the left edge of the cell and adds two decimal places.

Lesson Applications

Exercise 2-24

Enter and format labels and values. Enter and copy a formula.

1. Open **WeeklySales**. Save it as *[your initials]*2-24 in your Lesson 2 folder.

2. Key these labels in the specified cells:
A1	**Klassy Kow Ice Cream**
A2	**Specialty Pie Sales**
A3	**March 31, *<and the current year>***

3. Select all three cells and make them 16-point Cambria.

4. Format the date to show the month spelled out, the date, a comma, and four digits for the year.

5. Make column A **20.71 (150 pixels)** wide.

> **↔ REVIEW**
>
> Press ⟨Ctrl⟩+⟨1⟩ to format the date.

6. Select cells B5:E8. Key the values shown in Figure 2-23, pressing ⟨Enter⟩ to move in a top-down, left-right direction.

Figure 2-23

4		Week 1	Week 2	Week 3	Week 4	Total
5	Turtle Candy	10	30	50	80	
6	Rainbow	20	40	60	20	
7	Neapolitan	20	10	30	10	
8	Cookie Crunch	30	50	20	30	

7. Make the labels in row 4 bold. Change the height of rows 4 through 8 to **22.50 (30 pixels)**.

8. Click cell F5 and use AutoSum. Copy the formula in cell F5 to cells F6:F8.

9. Key your first and last name in cell A10. Return the pointer to cell A1.

10. Change the tab name to **SpecialtyPies** and choose a tab color.

11. Prepare and submit your work. Save and close the workbook.

Exercise 2-25

Enter labels and format data. Use a formula. Save a workbook.

1. Open **PieSales**.

2. Select cells B9:E9 and click the AutoSum 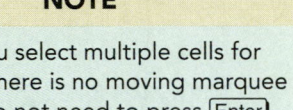 button.

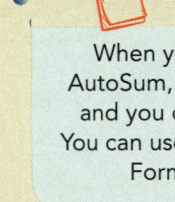

3. Key an appropriate label in cell A9 and make it bold.

4. Set the font size for this row to match the other data rows.

> **NOTE**
>
> When you select multiple cells for AutoSum, there is no moving marquee and you do not need to press Enter. You can use the AutoSum button on the Formulas or the Home tab.

5. In cell F4, key **Year Totals**. Copy the format from another label and widen the column.

6. Select cells F5:F9 and use AutoSum. Set the font size to match.

7. Select all the values and use the Format Cells dialog box to set **Number** format with no decimals and the thousands separator.

8. Make the totals in row 9 and in column F bold.

9. Rename the worksheet **Pies**. Choose a color for the tab.

10. Change to the **Metro** theme.

11. Key your first and last name in cell A12. Preview the worksheet.

12. Make cell A1 the active cell, and save the workbook as *[your initials]*2-25 in your Lesson 2 folder.

13. Prepare and submit your work. Close the workbook.

Exercise 2-26

Enter and copy a formula. Save a workbook.

1. Open **MediaPlans**. Save it in your Lesson 2 folder as *[your initials]*2-26.

2. In cell E4, use a formula to multiply "# of Times Run" by "Individual Cost." Copy the formula to appropriate cells.

3. Use AutoSum in cell E10. Set the values in column E to match the color used in the main label and borders.

4. Match the row height for rows 5 through 10 to that of row 3. Check for other problems that you should fix.

> **NOTE**
>
> This sheet uses narrow columns and short rows as separators for adding borders.

5. Rename the sheet **MediaPlans**. Choose the tab color to match the font and borders.

6. Key your first and last name in cell A13.

7. Preview the worksheet. Return the pointer to cell A1.

8. Prepare and submit your work. Save and close the workbook.

Exercise 2-27 ◆ Challenge Yourself

Create a workbook. Enter and format labels and values. Enter formulas.

1. In a new workbook, name **Sheet1** as **DailySales**.

2. Choose a document theme and then choose a tab color. Save the workbook as *[your initials]*2-27 in your Lesson 2 folder.

3. Key the following labels in the specified cells with the Headings font for your theme:

A1	**Klassy Kow Ice Cream Shops**
A2	**Daily Double Scoop Sales in** *<your home city>*
B3	**Friday**
C3	**Saturday**
D3	**Sunday**

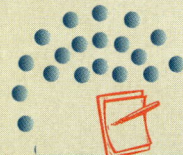

NOTE

If you type a flavor name that begins with a *k*, *d*, or the same letter as one of your other flavors, you might see an AutoComplete ScreenTip. Ignore it and continue typing.

4. In cells A4 through A8, key the names of five flavors of ice cream, one in each cell.

5. Decide how to format these labels.

6. Key values to show how many double-scoop cones were sold on each day. Format the values with no decimals and with a thousands separator.

7. Key **Number of Flavors** in cell A9 and then use **Count Numbers** from the AutoSum options in cell B9.

8. Key your first and last name in cell A12. Return the pointer to cell A1. Preview the worksheet. Prepare and submit your work.

9. Save the workbook and close it.

On Your Own

In these exercises you work on your own, as you would in a real-life work environment. Use the skills you've learned to accomplish the task—and be creative.

Exercise 2-28

Open **MediaPlans**. Change the names in column A to the names of radio stations, TV stations, newspapers, or magazines in your city. Key a new cost for a weekday ad for each medium. Change to the Verve theme. Add your name and the exercise number to the worksheet. Make sure all data is visible and save the workbook as *[your initials]*2-28 in your Lesson 2 folder. Prepare and submit your work and close the workbook.

Exercise 2-29

Sketch on paper a worksheet with the names of five people in your class or with whom you work. List each person's city, phone number (with area code in parentheses), and birthday. Determine a main title and titles for the columns.

Create a workbook based on your sketch. Format it attractively. Add your name and the exercise number to the worksheet. Save it as *[your initials]*2-29 in your Lesson 2 folder. Prepare and submit your work and close the workbook.

Exercise 2-30

Look through a print or Internet catalog and list five products to purchase. In a new workbook, list the product name, the store or Web site, and the price for each product. Add a quantity column to show how many of each item you would purchase. Create a formula to show what it would cost to buy your items (do not include sales tax or shipping charges). Decide how to format your sheet. Add your name and the exercise number to the worksheet. Save it as *[your initials]*2-30 in your Lesson 2 folder. Prepare and submit your work.

Lesson 3

Using Editing and Style tools

OBJECTIVES

After completing this lesson, you will be able to:

1. Use AutoCorrect and Error Checking.

2. Check spelling.

3. Use Find and Replace.

4. Use series and AutoFill.

5. Apply table and cell styles.

6. Prepare headers and footers.

Estimated Time: 1¹/₂ hours

MCAS OBJECTIVES

In this lesson:
XL07 1.1.1
XL07 1.1.2
XL07 1.3
XL07 2.1.2
XL07 2.3
XL07 2.4.1
XL07 5.5.1
XL07 5.5.3
XL07 5.5.4

Excel has many tools to increase your accuracy. Excel finds and flags common types of formula errors. It has electronic dictionaries that correct spelling errors as you type. Other tools enable you to quickly find and replace data or formats and to fill in data automatically.

Using AutoCorrect and Error Checking

AutoCorrect makes spelling corrections as you type. It recognizes common errors such as "teh," and changes it to "the." It capitalizes the days of the week and the months and corrects capitalization errors, such as THis. You can also set it to enter routine data automatically.

AutoCorrect makes its change when you press the spacebar, the Enter key, or a punctuation mark.

Exercise 3-1   USE AUTOCORRECT TO CORRECT ERRORS

The **KowaSales** workbook measures sales of the Kowabunga ice cream novelty over a three-year period. For the years 2008 and 2009, a percentage increase is estimated.

NOTE

As you key the labels for this exercise, be sure to key the errors that are shown.

1. Open **KowaSales**. The Kowabunga worksheet has a two-color scale applied to columns F and G.

2. Double-click the Home tab to collapse the ribbon. This provides more working space.

Figure 3-1
Keying a deliberate error
KowaSales.xlsx
Kowabunga sheet

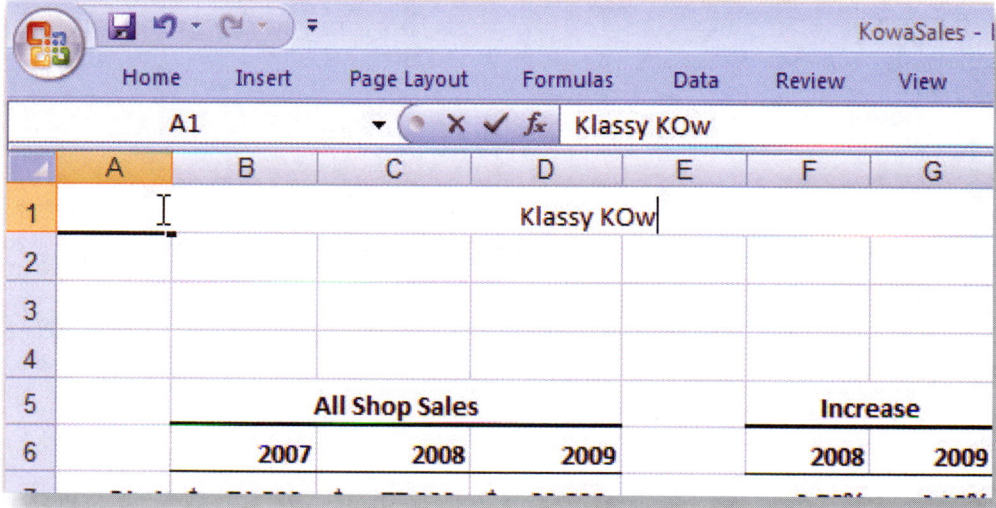

3. In cell A1, key **KLassy KOw** and press ⎁Spacebar⎁. The two incorrect uppercase letters are corrected. Notice that horizontal centering is preset for cell A1.

4. Key **Ice Cream Shops** to complete the label. Press ⎁Enter⎁.

5. Key **saturday and sunday Sales** and press ⎁Enter⎁. As you can see, AutoCorrect capitalizes the days of the week.

6. Double-click the Home tab. Select cells A1:A2 and set them to Cambria 18 point.

NOTE

This workbook uses the Office document theme. Cambria is the headings font; Calibri is for body text.

7. In cell A3, change the font to 9-point Calibri.

8. Key **these aer sales fro all Kowagunga flavors**. Press ⎁Enter⎁. Not all errors are found by AutoCorrect. "Aer" and "fro" have not been corrected, and neither has "Kowagunga." Leave these errors for now.

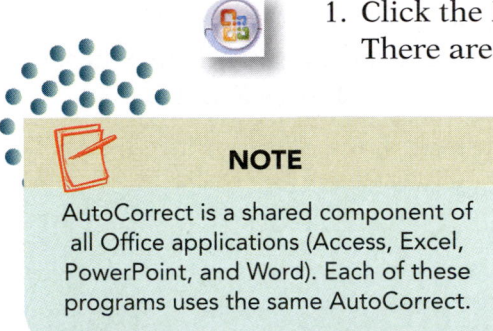

Exercise 3-2   SET AUTOCORRECT OPTIONS

If you key "acn," AutoCorrect changes your typing to "can." If "ACN" were the initials of an employee or a company, you would want to delete this correction from AutoCorrect. You can also add new corrections to AutoCorrect.

1. Click the Microsoft Office Button 🔵 and choose **Excel Options**. There are nine panes with features that can be customized.

2. Choose **Proofing**. Click **AutoCorrect Options**. The errors and corrections in AutoCorrect are listed in alphabetical order.

3. In the **Replace** box, key **kk**. Press ⌑Tab⌑.

4. In the **With** box, key **Klassy Kow**. Click **Add** to add this entry to the AutoCorrect list. Click **OK**.

NOTE

AutoCorrect is a shared component of all Office applications (Access, Excel, PowerPoint, and Word). Each of these programs uses the same AutoCorrect.

Figure 3-2
AutoCorrect dialog box

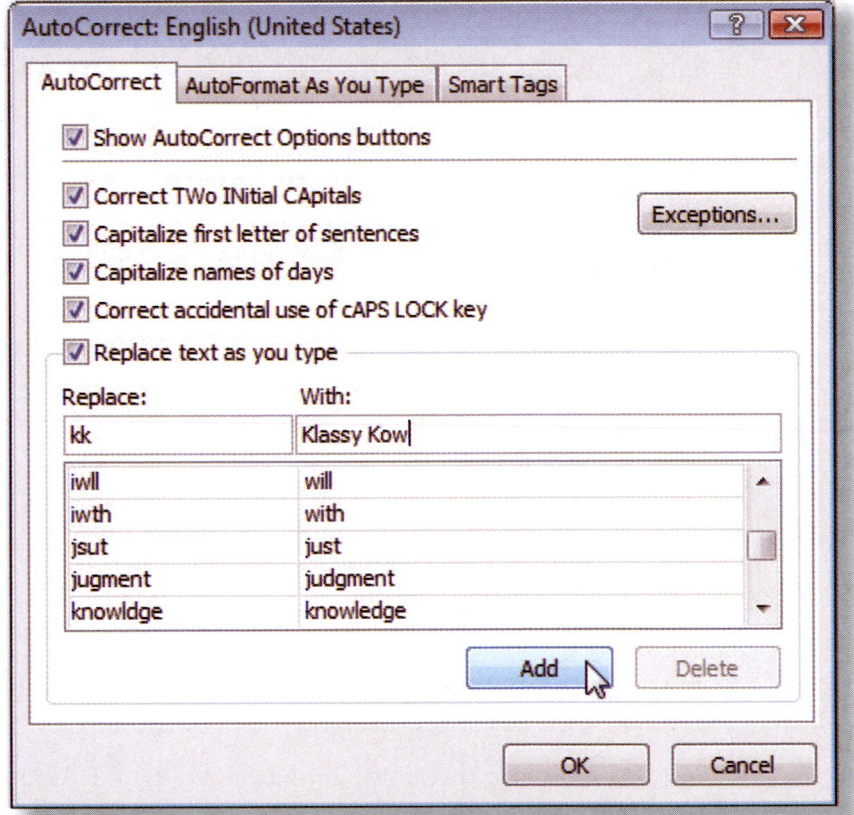

5. Click **OK** to close the Excel Options dialog box.

6. Click cell B25, key **kk**, and press ⌑Spacebar⌑. The initials are changed to "Klassy Kow."

7. Key **Marketing Department** to finish the label. Press ⌑Enter⌑.

8. Click the Microsoft Office Button 🔵 and choose **Excel Options**. Choose **Proofing**. Click **AutoCorrect Options**.

9. In the **Replace** box, key **kk** to move to the "Klassy Kow" entry.

10. Click **Delete** to remove the entry. Click **OK**.

> **NOTE**
>
> You have been instructed to delete the "Klassy Kow" AutoCorrect entry so that students in other classes can use the computer without having this entry listed among the AutoCorrect entries.

11. Click **OK** to close the Excel Options dialog box.

12. Click cell G25, key **kk**, and press Enter. The initials are not changed, because the entry has been deleted from AutoCorrect.

13. Delete the contents of cells B25 and G25.

14. Press Ctrl + Home.

Exercise 3-3   REVIEW ERROR CHECKING

Excel automatically alerts you to problems with formulas by showing an error indicator and an Error Checking Options button. The error indicator is a small green triangle in the top-left corner of the cell. The Error Checking

> **NOTE**
>
> If you do not see error indicators, click the Microsoft Office Button and choose Excel Options. In the Formulas pane, select Enable background error checking.

Options button is a small exclamation point within a diamond. It appears when you click the cell with the error indicator. When an error indicator warns of a potential error, you can review the type of error, fix it, or ignore the error.

1. Click cell B11. The Error Checking Options button appears to the left of the cell.

2. Position the mouse pointer on the Error Checking Options button to see a ScreenTip.

3. Click the arrow next to the button. Its shortcut menu opens. The first menu item explains the error, that the formula omits adjacent cells. Excel assumes that a SUM formula in cell B11 would sum the cells directly above, cells B6:B10. However, the formula is correct because the year in cell B6 should not be included in the formula.

Figure 3-3
Error Checking options
KowaSales.xlsx
Kowabunga sheet

	A	B	C	D	E	F	G
1		Klassy Kow Ice Cream Shops					
2		Saturday and Sunday Sales					
3		these aer sales fro all Kowagunga flavors.					
4							
5		All Shop Sales				Increase	
6		2007	2008	2009		2008	2009
7	Qtr 1	$ 74,500	$ 77,300	$ 80,530		3.76%	4.18%
8	Qtr 2	70,130	80,100	87,000		14.22%	8.61%
9	Qtr 3	72,300	78,150	80,100		8.09%	2.50%
10	Qtr 4	77,500	82,350	84,560		6.26%	2.68%
11		$ 294,430	$ 317,900	$ 332,190			
12		Formula Omits Adjacent Cells					
13		Update Formula to Include Cells					
14		Help on this error					
15		Ignore Error			actual and extimated		
16					artr for 2007, 2008, and		
17		Edit in Formula Bar			ase is is computd by		
18		Error Checking Options...			s year from the current		
19					the current year.		

Excel 2007

4. Choose **Ignore Error**. The small triangle is removed.

5. Click the **Formulas** command tab. There are four command groups on this tab.

6. In the Formula Auditing group, click the Error Checking button. The Error Checking dialog box opens with the next error noted, cell C11. This formula is correct.

Figure 3-4
Error Checking
dialog box
KowaSales.xlsx
Kowabunga sheet

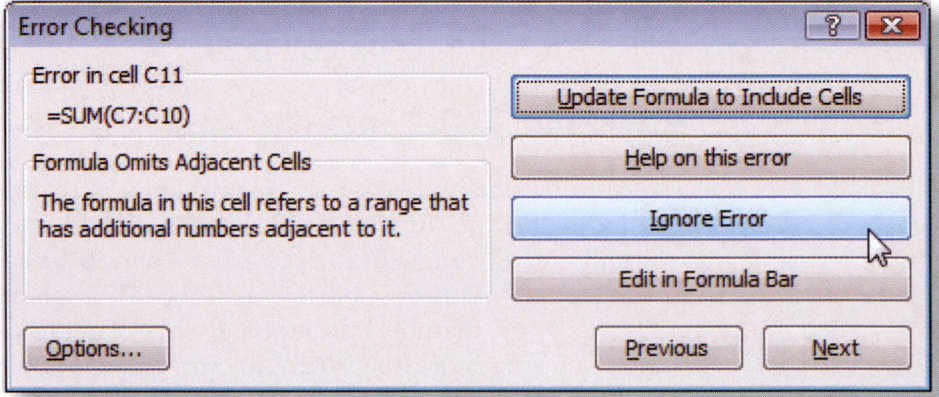

7. Click **Ignore Error** in the dialog box. The error triangle in cell C11 is removed. Cell D11 is flagged.

8. Click **Ignore Error**. A message box notes that error checking is complete.

9. Click **OK**. Press Ctrl+Home.

Checking Spelling

Excel's Spelling feature scans the worksheet and finds words that do not match entries in its dictionaries. It also finds repeated words. The Spelling dialog box provides options for handling errors. These options are described in Table 3-1.

Exercise 3-4   **SPELL-CHECK A WORKSHEET**

Excel starts spell-checking at the active cell and checks to the end of the worksheet. When the spell-checker reaches the end of the worksheet, a dialog box opens, asking if you want to continue spell-checking from the beginning of the worksheet.

The **Kowabunga** worksheet has a text box below the data with several spelling errors. A text box is used for special text displays and notations. If you accidentally click the text box in this lesson, click any cell away from the box to continue working.

TABLE 3-1 Spelling Dialog Box Options

Command	Action
Ignore Once	Do not change the spelling of this occurrence of the word. If it is a repeated word, do not delete one of the words.
Ignore All	Do not change the spelling of any occurrences of the word. If it is a repeated word, do not delete the double word.
Add to Dictionary	Add this word to the dictionary so that Excel will not regard it as misspelled.
Change	Replace the current spelling with the highlighted alternative in the **Suggestions** box.
Delete	Appears only for repeated words. Click to delete one occurrence of the word.
Change All	Replace the current spelling with the highlighted alternative every time this mis-spelling occurs.
AutoCorrect	Add the misspelled word with its correction to the AutoCorrect list.
Undo Last	Reverse/undo the last spelling correction.
Options	Offers choices for changing the dictionary language, ignoring uppercase and words with numbers, and ignoring Internet addresses.

TIP

You can select a range of cells and then click the Spelling button to spell-check only that range.

1. Click the **Review** command tab. Three command groups on this tab are used to examine and annotate your worksheet.

2. Click the Spelling button. Excel finds "worksheet" in the text box. It offers a suggestion for the correct spelling.

Figure 3-5
Spelling dialog box
KowaSales.xlsx
Kowabunga sheet

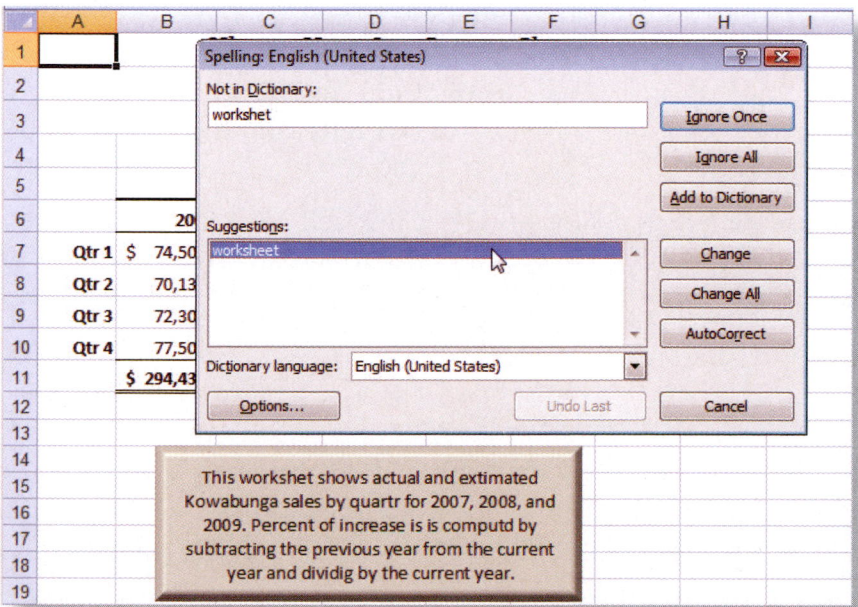

TIP

Move the dialog box so that you can see the text box. You can move a dialog box by dragging its title bar.

3. Double-click **worksheet** in the **Suggestions** list. A double-click is the same as clicking the word and then clicking **Change**. The correction is made, but you will not see it until you close the Spelling dialog box.

4. The next error is "extimated." Double-click **estimated** in the **Suggestions** list. "Kowabunga" in the text box is next. This word is correct.

5. Click **Ignore Once**. The word "quartr" appears next in the text box.

6. Double-click **quarter** in the **Suggestions** list. The next error is a **Repeated Word**, two occurrences of the word "is."

7. Click **Delete** to remove one occurrence of the word.

8. Correct "computd" and "dividng."

9. Excel shows "Klassy" in the **Not in Dictionary** box and offers one suggestion for the correct spelling. Since this is how the company spells its name, you can ignore all occurrences of this spelling.

10. Click **Ignore All**. Excel will ignore any more occurrences of "Klassy" in this worksheet. The word "Kow" is the next error. This is the same issue.

11. Click **Ignore All**. The word "aer" appears next with a list of possible corrections.

12. Click **are** in the **Suggestions** list and click **Change**. The next error is "Kowagunga."

13. Click in the **Not in Dictionary** box. There are no suggestions, but you can key the correction.

14. Edit the spelling to **Kowabunga** in the **Not in Dictionary** box.

15. Click **Change**. A message box notes that this word is not in the dictionary.

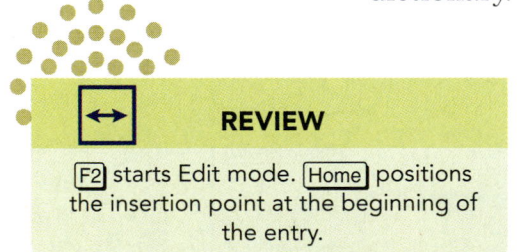

REVIEW

F2 starts Edit mode. Home positions the insertion point at the beginning of the entry.

16. Click **Yes**. When Spelling is complete, a message box tells you that the spell check is complete. Click **OK**.

17. Click cell A3. Press F2 and press Home. Spelling has not found all errors in this sheet.

18. Capitalize **These** and change "fro" to **for**. Press Enter.

Using Find and Replace

You use the Find command to locate a *character string,* a sequence of letters, numbers, or symbols. You can also use the Find command to locate formats, such as everything in the worksheet that is bold.

You can use wildcards in a Find command when you are not sure about spelling or want to find a group of data. A *wildcard* is a character that represents one or more numbers or letters. Excel recognizes two common wildcard characters:

- * Represents any number of characters

- ? Represents any single character

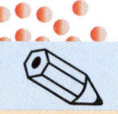

TIP

If you want to find a word or value that includes an asterisk or a question mark, precede the wildcard with a tilde (~). For example, "25~*" would find **25***.

The character string "ce*" would find everything in the worksheet that includes the characters "ce" followed by any number of letters or values. This might include "central," "nice," and "ocean." The character string "s?t" would locate entries that have an "s" followed by any character and a "t." Examples are "sit," "reset," and "S4T."

There are two ways to start the Find command:

- Click the Find & Select button in the Editing group on the Home tab and choose **Find**.

- Press Ctrl+F or Shift+F5.

The Replace command locates occurrences of a character string and substitutes a replacement string. A *replacement string* is a sequence of characters that is exchanged for existing data. The Replace command can also search for a format, replacing it with another format.

There are two ways to start the Replace command:

- Click the Find & Select button in the Editing group on the Home tab and choose **Replace**.

- Press Ctrl+H or Shift+F5.

Find and Replace share a dialog box, so you can actually use any of these four methods to start either command.

Exercise 3-5   FIND DATA

In the Find and Replace dialog box, you can choose whether to search the worksheet or the workbook. You can search by column or row. If you know that the name you are looking for is in column A or B, it is faster to search by column. You can also choose to search formulas or the value results. Other options let you match capitalization or the entire cell contents. The Find command searches cells. It does not search *objects* in a worksheet such as the text box in **KowaSales**.

NOTE

An object is a separate, clickable element or part of a worksheet.

In Find and Replace character strings, do not key format symbols such as the dollar sign or a comma.

1. Press Ctrl+Home.

2. Press Ctrl+F. The Find and Replace dialog box opens. Notice that each command has a separate tab.

3. Key **2008** in the **Find what** box.

4. Click **Find All**. The dialog box expands to list information about two cells that include this string of numbers. The first occurrence is outlined in the worksheet and highlighted in the list.

Figure 3-6
Find and Replace
dialog box, Find tab

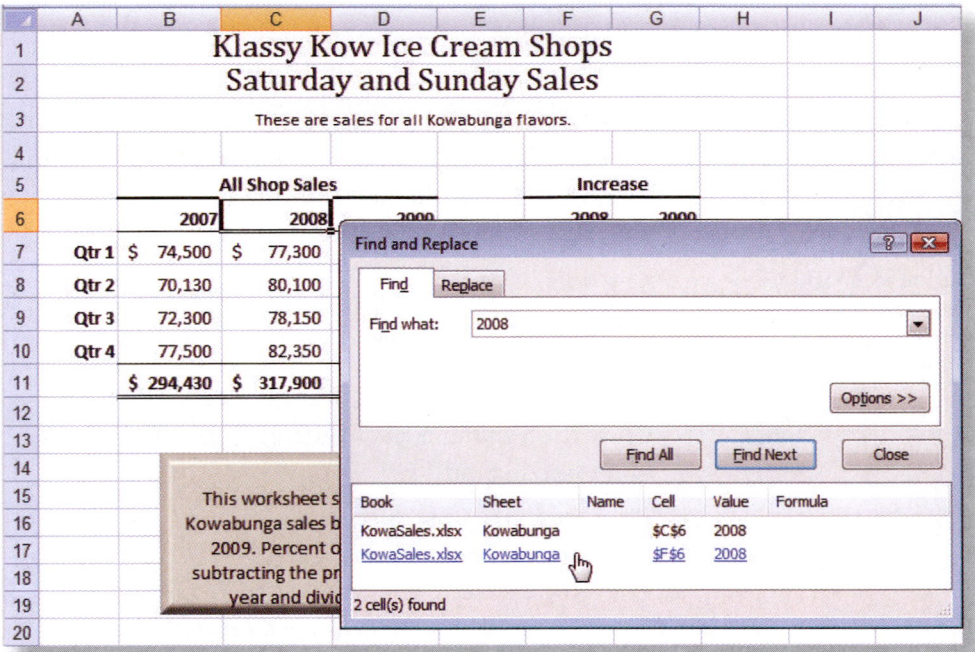

5. Click the second cell identifier in the dialog box. The pointer moves to that cell in the worksheet.

6. Double-click **2008** in the **Find what** box and key **qtr**. Character strings you key in the **Find what** box are not case-sensitive unless you turn on the **Match case** option.

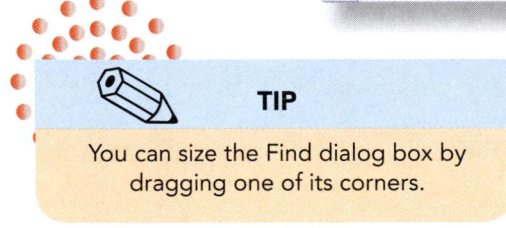

TIP

You can size the Find dialog box by dragging one of its corners.

7. Click **Options >>**. The dialog box expands with additional settings.

8. Click the arrow next to the **Within** box. You can find data within the active sheet or the entire workbook.

9. Choose **Sheet**.

NOTE

If the dialog box shows Options <<, it is expanded.

10. Click the arrow next to the **Search** box. For many worksheets, you might not see much difference in speed if you search by columns or by rows.

11. Choose **By Rows**.

12. Click the arrow next to the **Look in** box. Excel searches the underlying formula or the values. A *comment* is a text message attached to a cell.

13. Choose **Formulas**.

14. Click **Find All**. Four cells include the "qtr" character string.

15. Drag the sizing handle at the lower-right corner of the dialog box to see the list.

Exercise 3-6   USE WILDCARDS

1. Double-click **qtr** in the **Find what** box and key ***500**. This character string is used to find all cells with an entry that ends in "500."

2. Click **Find All**. Two values in the worksheet match this character string.

3. Double-click ***500** in the **Find what** box and key **u*** (lowercase letter "U" and an asterisk). This character string is used to find all cells with an entry that includes the letter "u" followed by any number of other characters.

4. Click **Find All**. There are several cells with such entries. Some appear to be values.

> **NOTE**
>
> Cell addresses in the Find and Replace dialog box are shown with dollar signs ($) to indicate an absolute reference. Absolute references are covered in another lesson.

5. Click the cell identifier for cell B11 in the dialog box. The value of **$294,430** is calculated from a SUM formula. That's the "u."

6. Click the arrow next to the **Look in** box. Choose **Values**.

7. Click **Find All**. The Values option checks the actual contents of the cells.

8. Double-click **u*** and key **t?e** in the **Find what** box.

9. Click **Find All**. There is one cell that includes this three-letter string.

10. Select **Match entire cell contents**. Click **Find All**. There are no cells that contain only this string. The message box says that Excel cannot find data to match.

11. Click **OK** to close the message box. Click **Close** to close the Find and Replace dialog box.

Exercise 3-7   REPLACE DATA

You can replace a character string one occurrence at a time or all at once. Sometimes replacing them all at once can be a problem, because you might locate some character strings you didn't anticipate.

1. Press Ctrl+Home to make cell A1 active.

2. Press Ctrl+H. The same Find and Replace dialog box opens, this time with the **Replace** tab active. Excel remembers your most recent Find character string.

3. Double-click **t?e** in the **Find what** box and key **2009**.

4. Click in the **Replace with** box and key **2010**. This will change occurrences of "2009" to "2010."

5. Click to deselect **Match entire cell contents**.

6. Click **Find Next** to locate the first occurrence of "2009."

Figure 3-7
Find and Replace
dialog box,
Replace tab

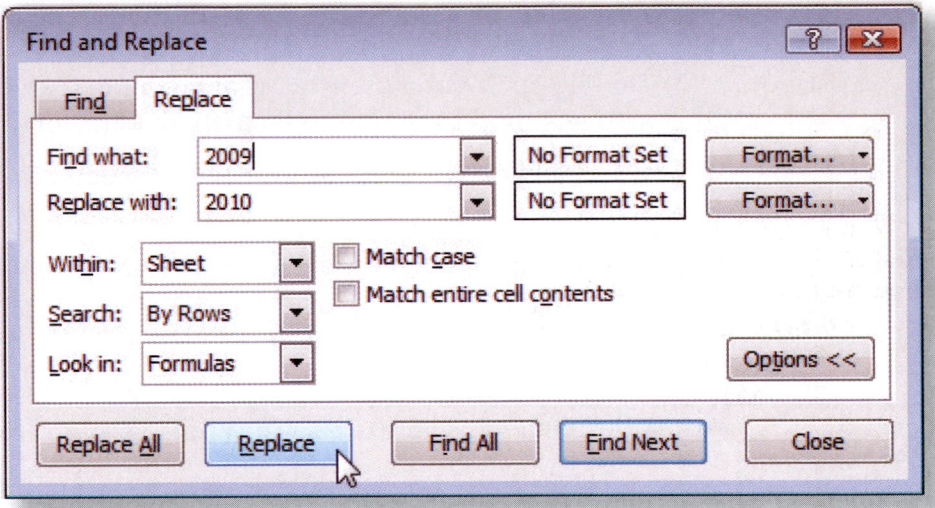

7. Click **Replace** to change "2009" to "2010." Excel locates the next occurrence.

8. Click **Replace**. The replacement is made.

9. Click **Replace**. There are no more occurrences of "2009."

10. Click **OK** in the message box.

Exercise 3-8   REPLACE A FUNCTION IN A FORMULA

1. Double-click **2009** in the **Find what** box and key **sum**.

2. Click **Find All**. Excel locates three cells with the SUM function.

3. Double-click **2010** in the **Replace with** box and key **avg**. This is not the correct spelling for the AVERAGE function.

4. Click **Replace**. The first occurrence is replaced. The cell shows **#NAME?**, a type of error.

5. Click **Replace All**. Two more replacements are made.

6. Click **OK**. You have replaced all instances of "sum" with a misspelled function name.

7. Click **Close** to close the Find and Replace dialog box. You will correct the errors in the next exercise.

Exercise 3-9   CORRECT ERRORS WITH REPLACE

1. Click cell B11. Position the pointer on the Error Checking Options button ![icon].

2. Click the arrow next to the button. This is an **Invalid Name Error**. The name of the function is "average," not "avg."

Figure 3-8
Error messages
KowaSales.xlsx
Kowabunga sheet

		All Shop Sales			Increase	
6		2007	2008	2010	2008	2010
7	Qtr 1	$ 74,500	$ 77,300	$ 80,530	3.76%	4.18%
8	Qtr 2	70,130	80,100	87,000	14.22%	8.61%
9	Qtr 3	72,300	78,150	80,100	8.09%	2.50%
10	Qtr 4	77,500	82,350	84,560	6.26%	2.68%
11		#NAME?	#NAME?	#NAME?		

Invalid Name Error

Help on this error

Show Calculation Steps...

Ignore Error

Edit in Formula Bar

Error Checking Options...

shows actual and estimated
by quarter for 2007, 2008, and
of increase is computed by
revious year from the current
ding by the current year.

3. Click cell B11 to close the shortcut menu.

4. Press Ctrl+H. Double-click in the **Find what** box and key **avg**.

5. Press Tab. In the **Replace with** box, key **average**, the correct spelling.

6. Click **Find All**. All the cells with the misspelled function are listed.

7. Click **Replace All**. The replacements are made, and the function is now correct.

8. Click **OK** and then click **Close**. Another Error Checking Options button has appeared.

9. Click cell B11 and display the Error Checking Options menu. The AVERAGE function assumes that all cells immediately above the cell with the function should be included in the range, cells B6:B10. Cell B6 is the year and should not be included.

10. Drag to select the range B11:D11. Position the mouse pointer on the Error Checking Options button. Click the arrow and choose **Ignore Error**.

Exercise 3-10   FIND AND REPLACE FORMATS

In addition to finding or replacing characters, you can find and replace formats. For example, you can find labels and values that are 11-point bold Calibri and change them to bold italic. When you replace formats, you should not show any text or numbers in the Find what or Replace with boxes.

1. Press Ctrl+Home. Press Ctrl+H.

2. Double-click in the **Find what** box and press Delete. The box is empty.

3. Double-click in the **Replace with** box and press Delete.

4. Click the arrow next to **Format** to the right of the **Find what** box.

5. Click **Choose Format From Cell**. The dialog box closes, and the pointer shows the selection pointer with an eyedropper. This pointer will copy the format of the cell to the dialog box.

6. Click cell A7. The dialog box expands. The format from cell A7 (11-point bold Calibri) is shown in the **Preview** area for **Find what**. These cells are also right-aligned.

7. Click the arrow next to **Format** to the right of the **Replace with** box.

8. Choose **Format**. The Replace Format dialog box opens. You can set a new format here.

9. Click the **Font** tab. In the **Font** list, choose **Cambria (Headings)**.

10. In the **Font style** list, choose **Bold Italic**. In the **Size** list, choose **11**.

11. Click **OK**. The previews show what format will be found and how it will be replaced.

12. Click **Find All**. Four cells are listed.

Figure 3-9
Replacing formats

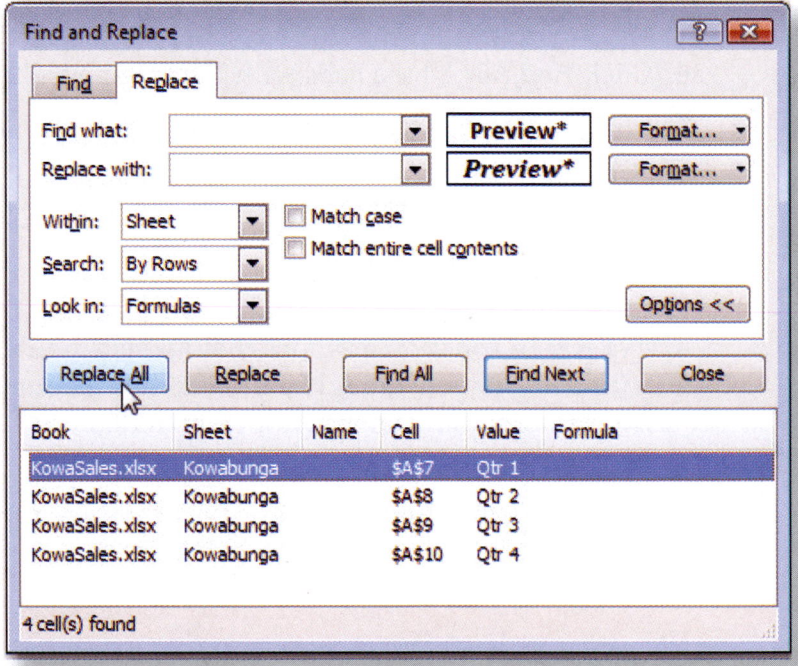

13. Click **Replace All**. The replacements are made.

14. Click **OK** and then click **Close**. The labels in row 5 include a centering command, so they were not matched. Values in row 6 include top and bottom borders, and the other values include some type of number formatting.

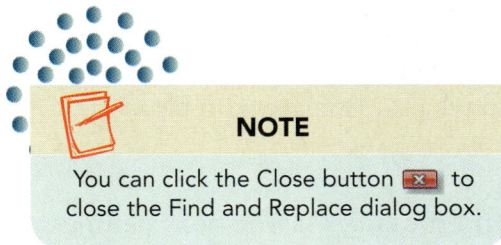

NOTE

You can click the Close button ⊠ to close the Find and Replace dialog box.

Exercise 3-11 RESET FIND AND REPLACE FORMATS

After replacing formats, you should reset the dialog box. If you don't, the formats will be in effect the next time you use Find and Replace and could affect your results.

1. Press Ctrl+H.

2. Click the arrow next to **Format** for the **Find what** box.

3. Click **Clear Find Format**. The area shows **No Format Set**.

4. Click the arrow next to **Format** for the **Replace with** box.

5. Click **Clear Replace Format**. Click **Close**.

Using Series and AutoFill

A *series* is a list of labels, numbers, dates, or times that follows a pattern. The days of the week are a series that repeats every seven days. Months repeat their pattern every 12 months. These are common series that Excel recognizes if you key a label in the series.

You can create your own series by keying two values or labels to set an interval or pattern. The *interval* is the number of steps between numbers or labels. For example, the series "1, 3, 5, 7" uses an interval of two because each number is increased by 2 to determine the next number. The series "Qtr 1, Qtr 2, Qtr 3" uses an interval of one.

Exercise 3-12 CREATE MONTH AND WEEK SERIES

The easiest way to create a series is by using the *AutoFill command,* which copies and extends data from a cell or range of cells to adjacent cells. The AutoFill command uses the *Fill handle,* a small rectangle at the lower-right corner of a cell or range.

TIP

AutoFill works only if you spell the first entry correctly.

1. Press Ctrl+G. The Go To dialog box opens.

2. Key **a26** and press Enter. The insertion point is in cell A26.

3. Key **January** and press Enter.

4. Click cell A26. Scroll the worksheet until you can see rows 26 through 37.

5. Place the pointer on the Fill handle for cell A26. The pointer changes to a solid black cross.

6. Drag down to cell A37. As you drag, a ScreenTip shows each month as it is filled in.

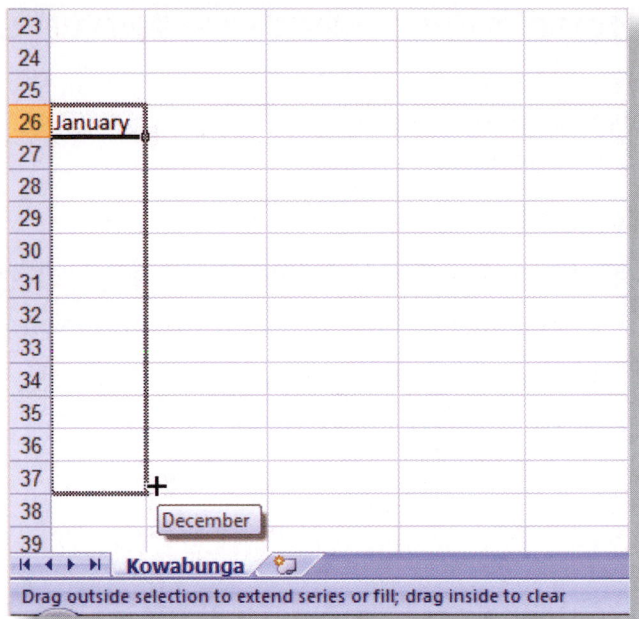

7. Release the mouse button. The series is filled. The AutoFill Options button appears below your filled selection. It includes options for filling data.

8. Hover over the AutoFill Options button 📑 and click its arrow.

9. Choose **Fill Series** for a regular AutoFill task.

10. In cell B25, key **Week 1** and press Ctrl+Enter.

11. Place the mouse pointer on the Fill handle for cell B25.

12. Drag right to cell E25. Release the mouse button. The series is filled.

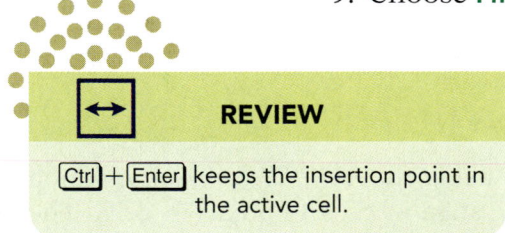

REVIEW

Ctrl+Enter keeps the insertion point in the active cell.

Exercise 3-13   CREATE A NUMBER SERIES

To establish a value series, first key two values in the series. Then select both cells and drag the Fill handle. If you drag the Fill handle too far, just drag it back to where you wanted to finish.

1. Click cell B26. Key **5** and press Enter.

2. Key **10** in cell B27. This sets a pattern with an interval of 5, increasing each value by 5.

3. Click cell B26 and drag to select cell B27. There is one Fill handle for the range.

4. Place the pointer on the Fill handle for cell B27.

5. Drag down to cell B37 and release the mouse button. The series is filled in, and the range is selected.

6. Hover over the AutoFill Options button 🔢 and click its arrow.

7. Choose **Copy Cells**. The series is adjusted to be a copy.

8. Click the arrow with the AutoFill Options button 🔢. Choose **Fill Series**.

Exercise 3-14 COPY DATA WITH THE FILL HANDLE

When there is no apparent pattern in the range, the Fill handle copies data rather than creating a series.

1. The series you just filled in should still be selected. The Fill handle for the range is located in cell B37. Place the mouse pointer on the Fill handle.

2. Drag right to column E and release the mouse button. The range is copied, because no pattern was set for going from one column to the next.

Figure 3-11
Using the Fill pointer to copy
KowaSales.xlsx
Kowabunga sheet

		Weel 1	Weel 2	Weel 3	Weel 4	
23						
24						
25		Weel 1	Weel 2	Weel 3	Weel 4	
26	January	5				
27	February	10				
28	March	15				
29	April	20				
30	May	25				
31	June	30				
32	July	35				
33	August	40				
34	Septemb	45				
35	October	50				
36	Novemb	55				
37	Decembe	60				
38				5		
39						

3. Make column A **10.00 (75 pixels)** wide.

Exercise 3-15 COPY A FORMULA WITH THE FILL HANDLE

1. Click cell F26. Click the **Home** tab.

Σ ▾

2. In the **Editing** group, click the AutoSum button Σ ▾. The SUM function shows the range to be summed as B26:E26.

3. Press Ctrl + Enter. The formula is completed.

4. Look at the formula bar. You can copy this formula to the rest of the rows by using the Fill handle.

5. Place the pointer on the Fill handle for cell F26.

6. Drag down to cell F37 and release the mouse. Excel copies the formula, and the AutoFill Options button  appears.

7. Display the AutoFill Options menu. You do not need to make a change.

8. Click cell F27. The copied formula is relative to where it is on the worksheet, just as when you use Copy and Paste.

Applying Table and Cell Styles

A *table* is an arrangement of data in which each row represents one item or element. In your worksheet, each item is a month. Tables usually have a *header row* for each column to define the column's data. In this lesson, you will learn how to create a table from your data using built-in table styles.

Excel also has many cell styles for formatting labels and values based on the current document theme. These styles can include font and border settings, number formats, alignment settings, background colors, and more.

Exercise 3-16   CREATE A TABLE

1. In cell F25, key **Total** and press ⎄Enter⎄. In cell A25, key **Month** and press ⎄Enter⎄. Each column now has a header.

2. On the **Home** tab in the **Styles** group, click the Format as Table button. The Table Styles gallery opens with previews of many table styles. The styles are categorized as Light, Medium, or Dark based on the color scheme.

Figure 3-12
Table Styles gallery

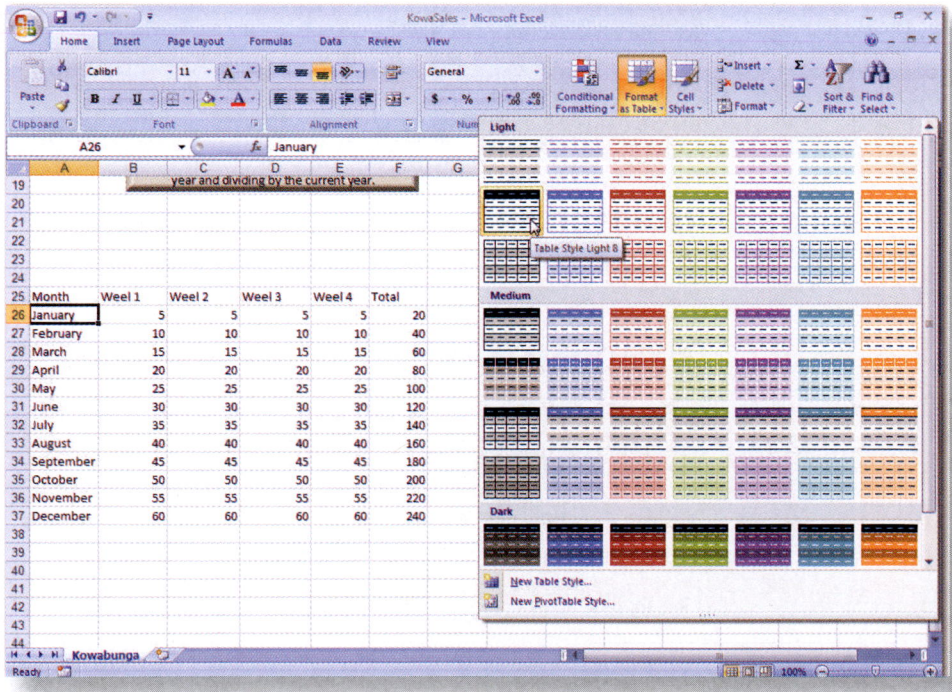

3. Hover the mouse pointer over several thumbnails to find **Table Style Light 8** and click the icon. The gallery closes, your data is marqueed, and the Format As Table dialog box opens with a suggested range for your table.

Figure 3-13
Format As Table
dialog box
KowaSales.xlsx
Kowabunga sheet

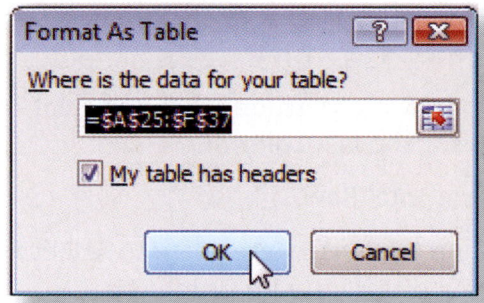

4. Make sure there is a check mark for **My table has headers**. Click **OK**. Excel applies the style, adds Filter buttons to the header labels, and displays the **Table Tools Design** command tab.

> **NOTE**
>
> Filter buttons are used to sort and filter the rows. The buttons do not print.

5. Click cell G23. **Table Tools Design** is a context-sensitive tab that only appears when the insertion point is within a table.

6. Click cell D27. The **Table Tools Design** tab appears.

Figure 3-14
New Table
KowaSales.xlsx
Kowabunga sheet

	Month	Weel 1	Weel 2	Weel 3	Weel 4	Total	
24							
25	Month	Weel 1	Weel 2	Weel 3	Weel 4	Total	
26	January	5	5	5	5	20	
27	February	10	10	10	10	40	
28	March	15	15	15	15	60	
29	April	20	20	20	20	80	
30	May	25	25	25	25	100	
31	June	30	30	30	30	120	
32	July	35	35	35	35	140	
33	August	40	40	40	40	160	
34	September	45	45	45	45	180	
35	October	50	50	50	50	200	
36	November	55	55	55	55	220	
37	December	60	60	60	60	240	
38							

Exercise 3-17   CHANGE THE TABLE STYLE

You can easily change the style of a table and adjust several other design elements.

1. Click the **Table Tools Design** tab.

2. Click the More button ⊟ in the **Table Styles** group to open the gallery.

3. Hover over several different styles. Live Preview shows the table as it would appear with each style as you hover.

4. Find **Table Style Medium 8** and click the icon. The gallery closes, and the table is restyled.

5. In the **Table Style Options** group, click to deselect **Header Row**. The header row is no longer visible.

6. In the **Table Style Options** group, click to select **Total Row**. A grand total is shown for the last column.

7. Click to deselect **Total Row**.

8. In the **Table Style Options** group, click to select **First Column**. The first column is styled differently for emphasis.

9. Click to deselect **First Column**.

10. Click to select **Header Row** to show the header row again.

Exercise 3-18   APPLY A CELL STYLE

1. In cell A23, key **Monthly Estimates** and press Enter.

2. Click cell A23. In the **Styles** group on the Home tab, click the Cell Styles button 🖳. The Cell Styles gallery opens. The styles are divided into five groups. You can use any style for any worksheet cell; the categories are just guidelines.

Figure 3-15
Cell Styles gallery
KowaSales.xlsx
Kowabunga sheet

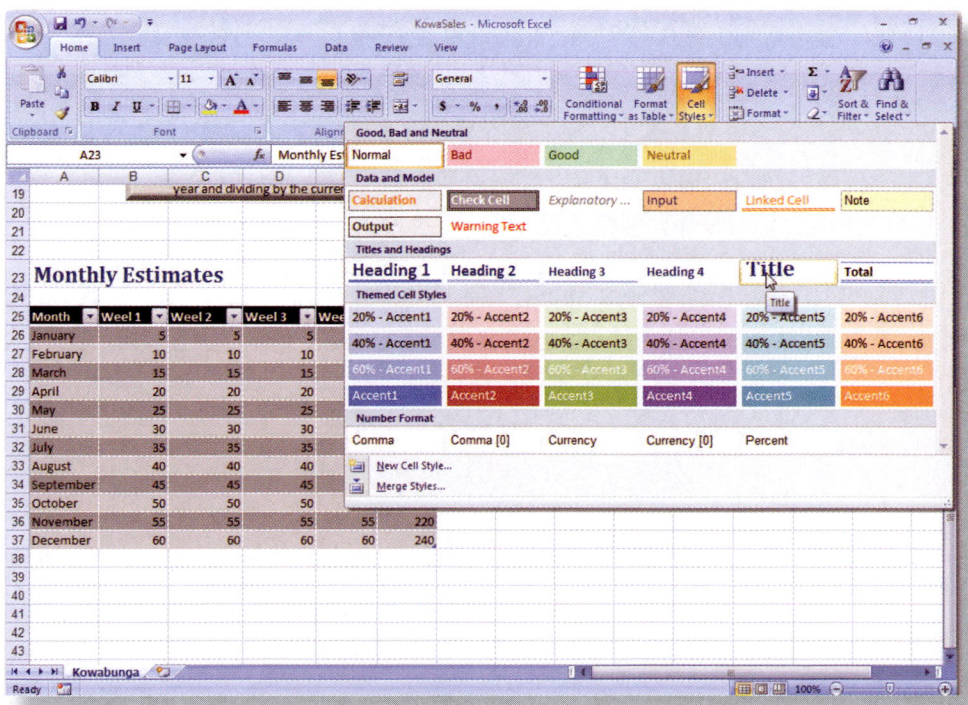

3. Hover the mouse pointer over different thumbnails and watch cell A23. Live Preview shows how the label will appear with the style.

4. Find and click the **Title** style (under Titles and Headings). The label is reformatted as Cambria 18 point in a theme color.

5. In the **Font** group, click the Font Color button . The color on the button is applied (probably red). You can apply your own formatting after choosing a cell style.

Exercise 3-19   PRINT A SELECTION

In the current worksheet, you might want to print only the table. To print a portion of a worksheet, select the range of cells you want to print. Open the Print dialog box and choose **Selection**.

1. Go to cell A38 and key your first and last name. Excel assumes your name is another row in the table and formats it to match.

> **NOTE**
>
> A table has a sizing handle at the bottom right corner.

2. Rest the mouse pointer on the table-sizing handle in cell F38. The pointer changes to a two-pointed arrow.

3. Drag the handle up to row 37. Your name is no longer part of the table.

4. Click cell F38 and press Delete. The formula was copied, too.

5. Click cell A23 and press F8. Extend Selection mode starts.

6. Press → five times to reach column F.

7. Press Ctrl+↓ three times. Each press of this key combination highlights up to the current range of your data.

8. Press Ctrl+P. The Print dialog box opens.

9. Choose **Selection** in the **Print what** area.

10. Click **Preview**. The Print Preview shows the range that will be printed.

11. Click the Print button. Only the range that you specified is printed.

12. Save the workbook as *[your initials]*3-19 in a folder for Lesson 3.

Preparing Headers and Footers

Headers and footers can be used to display a company name, a department, the date, or a company logo. A *header* prints at the top of each page in a worksheet. A *footer* prints at the bottom of each page. Excel has preset headers and footers, and you can create your own.

A header or footer can have up to three sections. The left section prints at the left margin. The center section prints at the horizontal center of the page. The right section aligns at the right margin.

You can create headers and footers by:

- Clicking the Header & Footer button 📄 in the Text group on the Insert tab.

- Clicking the Page Layout View button 🔳 on the status bar.

- Clicking the Page Layout View button 📄 in the Workbook View group on the View tab.

- Clicking the Dialog Box Launcher in the Page Setup group on the Page Layout tab.

- Clicking the Page Setup button 📄 in Print Preview.

Exercise 3-20   SET HEADERS AND FOOTERS

1. With *[your initials]*3-19 open, press Ctrl + Home.

2. Click the **Insert** tab in the Ribbon.

3. In the **Text** group, click the Header & Footer button 📄. The Header/ Footer Tools Design tab is a context-sensitive tab that opens when the insertion point is within a header or footer section. The worksheet is in Page Layout View.

4. Click the Header button 📄 to display a gallery of header arrangements. Header sections are separated by commas. If you choose a single item, it prints in the center section. Two items print in the center and at the right margin. Three items print at the left margin, in the center, and at the right margin.

NOTE

The same preset layouts are available for footers and headers.

Figure 3-16
Choosing a preset header
3-19.xlsx
Kowabunga sheet

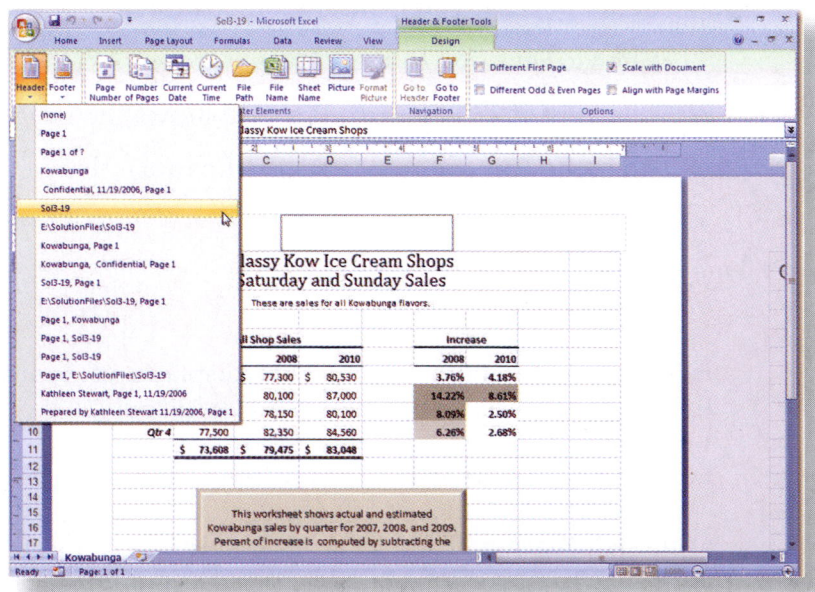

5. Find and click the first occurrence of your filename. You can see the header in the center section.

6. Point at the filename in the header and click. The code for displaying the filename is **&[File]**.

Go to Footer

7. In the **Navigation** group, click the Go to Footer button. The insertion point is in the center section.

8. Point at the left section and click. The insertion point moves there.

Page Number

9. Key your first and last name in the left section and press Tab. The insertion point moves to the center section.

10. In the **Header and Footer Elements** group, click the Page Number button.

Number of Pages

11. Press Spacebar, key **of**, and press Spacebar again.

12. In the **Header and Footer Elements** group, click the Number of Pages button.

13. Press Tab. The insertion point moves to the right section.

Current Date

14. Click the Current Date button. The code for displaying the current date is **&[Date]**.

Figure 3-17
Creating a custom footer
3-19.xlsx
Kowabunga sheet

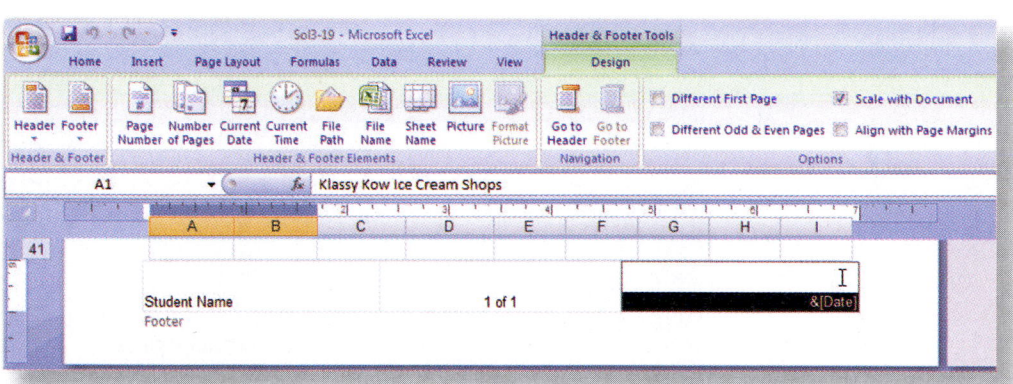

15. Click a cell above the footer area. This completes the footer and returns the focus to your worksheet.

16. Press Ctrl+Home. The worksheet is in Page Layout View while you work with headers and footers.

Exercise 3-21 **PRINT GRIDLINES AND ROW AND COLUMN HEADINGS**

Gridlines and row and column headings are visible while you work on a worksheet. They do not print as a default, but you can set them to print. Printing a worksheet with the gridlines and row and column headings makes it easy to locate data or to re-create a worksheet, if needed.

1. With *[your initials]*3-19 in Page Layout view, click the **Page Layout** tab in the Ribbon.

2. In the **Sheet Options** group, click to select the **Print** box below **Gridlines**.

3. Click to select **Print** below **Headings**.

Exercise 3-22 CHANGE MARGINS AND COLUMN WIDTHS IN PAGE LAYOUT VIEW

Excel sets 0.75 inch for left and right margins in a new workbook. The top and bottom margins are both set at 0.7 inch. The header and footer are preset to print 0.3 inch from the top and bottom of the page, within the top and bottom margin areas.

You can change the margins and the column widths in Page Layout View by dragging a margin marker or a column heading border. As you drag, the margin setting or column width is shown in inches or character spaces.

1. Hover over the left margin marker. The pointer changes to a two-pointed arrow.

2. Click and drag right to set a left margin of about **1.00**. Watch the ScreenTip for the setting as you drag. Your margin setting does not need to be exact.

Figure 3-18
Changing page margins in Page Layout View
3-19.xlsx
Kowabunga sheet

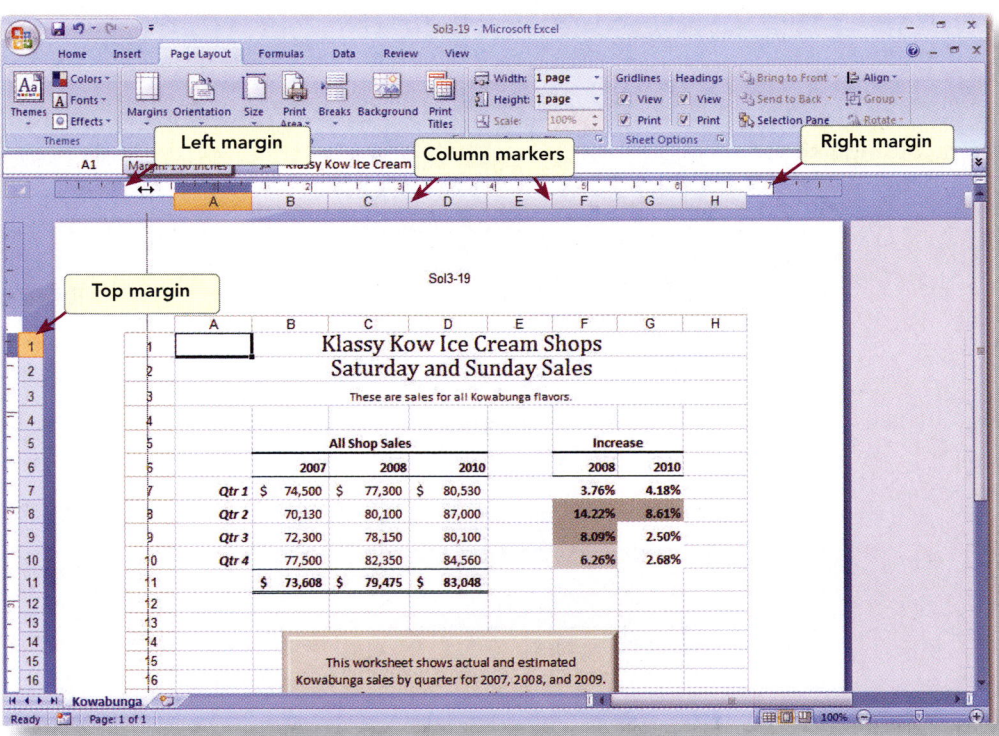

3. Hover the pointer over the right margin marker. Click and drag left to reach about **1.00**.

NOTE

The column headings for adjusting the width are just below the ruler.

4. Place the pointer on the column marker between columns A and B. The pointer changes to a two-pointed arrow. Drag right to make column A wider at **1.00 inches (101 pixels)**.

5. Make column E slightly less wide.

6. Press F12 and save the workbook as *[your initials]3-22* in your Lesson 3 folder.

7. Prepare and submit your work. Close the workbook.

Using Online Help

Series and AutoFill are time-saving features of Excel. They enable you to work more quickly and more accurately. Read more about series and the AutoFill command.

LOOK UP AUTOFILL AND SERIES

1. In a new workbook, press F1.

2. In the Search text box, key **autofill** and press Enter.

3. Find topics about filling in data in cells. Read the help information.

4. Close the Help window.

Lesson 3 Summary

- AutoCorrect corrects common typing errors as you work. You can add your own entries or delete existing ones.

- The Spelling command spell-checks a worksheet by comparing labels to dictionary entries. Options let you decide if and how to make the correction.

- The Find command locates and lists all occurrences of data that match your Find what character string. You can use wildcards in the character string.

- The Replace command locates and substitutes new data for existing data. You can complete the changes one at a time or all at once.

- Excel displays options buttons for some commands and formula errors. You can look at the message for the button, make a change, or ignore it.

- All cells have a Fill handle that can be used for filling in a series or for copying data.

- Excel recognizes common series for the days of the week, the months, and patterns such as "Week 1," "Week 2," and so on.

- You can create your own series with any interval by keying at least two cells that define the pattern.
- A table is a consistent pattern of data rows with a header row. Tables can be formatted with a style from the gallery.
- Cell styles apply colors, fonts, and other formatting options to a cell or range.
- Headers and footers print at the top or bottom of every page. There are preset headers and footers, or you can create your own.
- You can view and print a worksheet with or without the gridlines and row and column headings.
- You can change margins and column widths in Page Layout View and immediately see the results.

LESSON 3		Command Summary	
Feature	**Button**	**Task Path**	**Keyboard**
Error checking		Formulas, Formula Auditing	
Error checking options		Formulas, Formula Auditing	
Fill series		Home, Editing	
Find		Home, Editing, Find	Ctrl + F
Gridlines, print/view		Page Layout, Sheet Options	
Header/Footer		Insert, Text	
Header, preset		Header & Footer Tools Design, Header & Footer	
Headings, print/view		Page Layout, Sheet Options	
Print selection		Microsoft Office, Print	Ctrl + P
Replace		Home, Editing	Ctrl + H
Spelling		Review, Proofing	F7
Style, cell		Home, Styles	
Table, create		Home, Styles	
Table, style		Table Tools Design, Table Styles	

Concepts Review

True/False Questions

Each of the following statements is either true or false. Indicate your choice by circling T or F.

T F   1. If you key **THe** as part of a label, AutoCorrect will automatically fix the error.

T F   2. Options buttons are screen messages that tell you what command to choose next.

T F   3. The Replace command can be used to locate and change the font size.

T F   4. The Spelling command completes columns of month or day names.

T F   5. You can format data as a table if it has a header row followed by data rows.

T F   6. The Fill handle displays a small hollow circle.

T F   7. A series is a list with a recognizable pattern.

T F   8. The option to print a selected range is in the Page Layout dialog box.

Short Answer Questions

Write the correct answer in the space provided.

1. How can you collapse the Ribbon?

_____

2. Name the feature that enables you to automatically complete a list of 12 months after you key one month.

_____

3. What keyboard shortcut opens the Replace dialog box?

_____

4. How are table styles categorized or grouped in the gallery?

_____

5. Name two context-sensitive command tabs.

_____

6. How can you print row and column headings?

_____

7. How can you change the margins in Page Layout View?

_____

8. What does Excel display when you release the mouse button after using the Fill handle?

_____

Critical Thinking

Answer these questions on a separate page. There are no right or wrong answers. Support your answers with examples from your own experience, if possible.

1. Find and Replace are powerful time-saving commands. Think of times/ situations when they might create problems in your work.

2. You can copy a formula with the Copy and Paste buttons (as you did in Lesson 2) or with the Fill handle. Which do you prefer and why? When wouldn't it be a good idea to use the Fill handle to copy a formula?

Skills Review

Exercise 3-23

Use AutoCorrect. Use Error Checking. Check spelling.

1. Open **ExpWA**. Press F12 and save the workbook as *[your initials]*3-23 in your Lesson 3 folder. This worksheet has a two-color scale to differentiate high and low values.

2. Use AutoCorrect by following these steps:

   a. Click cell A2.

   b. Key (with the error) **Expenses Already Sceduled** and press Spacebar.

   c. Click cell A14.

   d. Key (with errors) **Thsi workshet was prepared by STudent [your last name] on monday.** Press Enter.

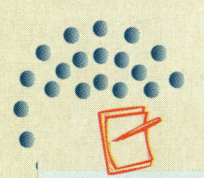

NOTE

Row 4 is a separator row with a bottom border as part of the worksheet design.

3. Change the height of rows 5 and 12 to **22.50 (30 pixels)**. Select rows 6:11 and make them **16.50 (22 pixels)** tall. Make row 4 **6.00 (8 pixels)** tall.

4. Select cells A1:A2 and change to the Headings font for the theme.

5. Click the Save button 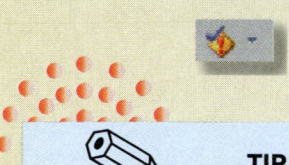.

6. Use Error Checking by following these steps:

   a. Click the **Formulas** tab.

   b. In the **Formula Auditing** group, click the Error Checking button 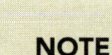.

   c. Look at the formula for cell F7. It is not the same as others in the column; it does not include cell E7.

   d. Click **Copy Formula from Above**.

   e. Look at the formula for cell B12. This formula is missing cell B11.

   f. Choose **Update Formula to Include Cells**.

   g. Click **OK** in the message box.

7. Check spelling by following these steps.

   a. Press Ctrl + Home.

   b. Click the **Review** tab. Click the Spelling button .

   c. What is the first misspelled word? What will you do about it?

   d. Take the action you described in the previous step.

   e. List each error and how you correct it.

   f. There is one more error on this sheet. Find it and correct it.

8. Press Ctrl + Home.

9. Click the Microsoft Office Button  and hover over the arrow next to **Print**. Choose **Print Preview**. Preview your worksheet in a reduced and in a normal size.

10. Prepare and submit your work. Save and close the workbook.

Exercise 3-24

Use Find. Use Replace.

1. Open **MayPromo**. Save it as *[your initials]*3-24 in your Lesson 3 folder.

2. Use Find by following these steps:

   a. Press Ctrl + F.

   b. Key **ee** in the **Find what** box.

NOTE

This workbook uses the Zenith document theme.

TIP

Drag the dialog box so that you can see the cells with formulas.

NOTE

Prepare your answers to questions in the Skills Review exercises as instructed for submission to your instructor. Include your name, the date, the exercise number, and the question number.

NOTE

Follow your usual class procedures for submitting work.

   c. Click **Find All**. How many cells include this character string?

   d. Double-click **ee** in the **Find what** box and key **a?** in its place.

   e. Click **Find All**. How many cells include an **a** followed by any character?

   f. Double-click **a?** and key **r*** and click **Find All**. How many cells include an "r" followed by any character?

   g. Double-click **r*** and key **P** in the **Find what** box.

   h. Click **Options** to expand the dialog box and click to select **Match case**. Click **Find All**. How many cells include an uppercase "P"?

   i. Turn off **Match case** and hide the options.

3. Use Replace by following these steps:

   a. Click the **Replace** tab.

   b. Double-click **P** and key **20** in the **Find what** box.

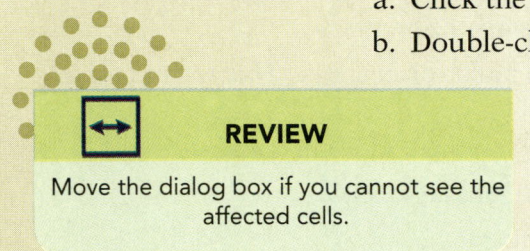

REVIEW

Move the dialog box if you cannot see the affected cells.

   c. In the **Replace with** box, key **50**. Click **Find All**. There are four cells with this value.

   d. Click **Replace** to change the first occurrence.

   e. Click **Replace** to change the second occurrence.

   f. Click **Find Next** to skip the next occurrence.

   g. Double-click **20** and key **25** in the **Find what** box.

   h. Press `Tab` to reach the **Replace with** box and press `Delete`. Click **Find All**. There are five cells with a value of 25.

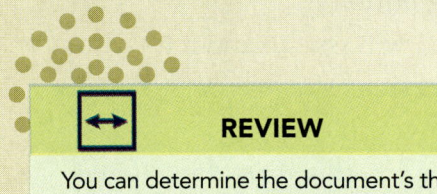

REVIEW

You can determine the document's theme from the Page Layout Tab. Just hover over the Themes button.

   i. Click **Replace All** to make these cells blank. Click **OK** in the message box.

   j. Close the dialog box.

4. Key your first and last name in cell A13. Change the tab name to **MayExp** and choose a tab color from the theme colors.

5. Press `Ctrl`+`Home`. Prepare and submit your work.

6. Save and close the workbook.

Exercise 3-25

Create series. Use AutoFill to copy values.

1. Create a new workbook. Save it as *[your initials]*3-25 in your Lesson 3 folder.

2. Change the document theme to **Flow**.

3. Key **Klassy Kow Ice Cream Shops** in cell A1. Format it as 18-point Calibri.

4. Use 12-point Calibri in cell A2 and key **Summary prepared by** *[your first and last name]*.

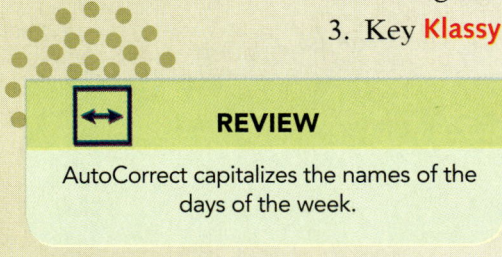

REVIEW

AutoCorrect capitalizes the names of the days of the week.

5. Create a series by following these steps:

   a. Click cell B3 and key **monday**. Press `→`.

   b. Key **wednesday** in cell C3 and press `←`.

TIP

Make the first label bold and then use AutoFill.

REVIEW

If you use the Home tab, Cells group, Format, and Row Height, use points (not pixels) to change the row height.

c. Select cells B3:C3. Make these labels bold.

d. Place the pointer on the Fill handle.

e. Drag right far enough to build a series ending with Sunday.

f. Key **Week 1** in cell A4 and make it bold.

g. Place the pointer on the Fill handle for cell A4 and drag down to build a series ending with Week 4.

6. Set the height of rows 2, 3, and 8 to **22.50 (30 pixels)**. Then choose a height slightly less than that for the other rows.

7. Use AutoFill to copy values by following these steps:

   a. Click cell B4 and key **10**. Press .

   b. In cells C4:E4, key **20**, **40**, and **30**.

   c. Select cells B4:E4. Place the mouse pointer on the Fill handle for the range. Drag down to reach row 7.

8. Select cells B8:E8. Click the AutoSum button on the **Home** tab. Make these values bold.

9. Adjust column widths using your judgment.

10. Press Ctrl + Home. Click the Save button .

11. Prepare and submit your work. Then close the workbook.

Exercise 3-26

Create a table. Use cell styles. Prepare headers/footers.

1. Open **MayCakes**.

2. Save the workbook as *[your initials]*3-26 in your Lesson 3 folder.

3. Create a table by following these steps:

   a. Click cell B3.

   b. In the **Styles** group on the **Home** tab, click the Format as Table button .

   c. Scroll to find **Table Style Medium 10** and click the icon.

   d. In the Format As Table dialog box, change the range to **=$A$3:$E$7**.

   e. Click to select **My table has headers**. Click OK.

4. Use cell styles by following these steps:

   a. Select cells A1:A2.

   b. In the **Styles** group on the **Home** tab, click the Cell Styles button.

   c. Click **Accent2** in the gallery.

   d. Set 14-point Cambria as the font for cells A1:A2. Make both cells bold.

  e. Autofit column A. Make rows 3:7 each **30.00 (40 pixels)** tall.

  f. Click cell A3 and key **Flavor**. Press Ctrl + Home.

5. Prepare a footer by following these steps:

  a. Click the **Insert** tab.

  b. In the **Text** group, click the Header & Footer button .

  c. Click the Go to Footer button in the **Navigation** group.

  d. Click in the left section and key your first and last name.

  e. Press Tab to move to the center section.

  f. Click the File Name button in the **Header & Footer Elements** group. Press Tab.

  g. Click the Current Date button .

  h. Click a cell in the worksheet and press Ctrl + Home.

  i. Click the **Page Layout** tab.

  j. In the **Sheet Options** group, click to deselect both **Print** boxes.

  k. Hover over the left margin marker. Drag left to set a left margin of about **.50** inches.

  l. Hover the pointer over the right margin marker. Click and drag right to reach about **.50**.

  m. Click the Normal button in the status bar.

6. Prepare and submit your work. Save and close the workbook.

Lesson Applications

Exercise 3-27

Use Find and Replace. Create a footer. Change the left margin.

1. Open **MayPromo**. Save it as *[your initials]*3-27 in your Lesson 3 folder.

NOTE

You do not need to key uppercase characters in a Find character string, but you should key them in the Replace character string.

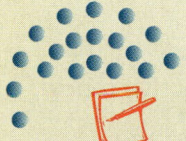

NOTE

A zero (0) in this worksheet will display as a hyphen. Zero is treated differently from empty/blank in calculations.

2. Replace all occurrences of **california** with **Washington**.

3. Replace all occurrences of **75** with **0** (zero).

4. Find and correct formula errors.

5. Change the tab name to **MayExpense** and choose a tab theme color.

6. Create a footer that shows your name in the left section. In the center section, click the Sheet Name button. Add the date to the right section.

7. Change the left margin to about 1.25 inches.

8. Preview the worksheet and prepare and submit your work. Save and close the workbook.

Exercise 3-28

Create a series. Create a table and use cell styles. Prepare a header.

1. Create a new workbook and choose the **Paper** document theme. Save the workbook as *[your initials]*3-28 in your Lesson 3 folder.

2. Using the Headings font, key **Klassy Kow Specials** in cell A1. In cell A2, key **Price Promotions** with the same font.

REVIEW

Press Ctrl + 1 to format the date.

3. In cell B3, key **Regular Price**. In cell C3, key **Special Price**. In cell D3, key **Savings**. AutoFit each column to show the label.

4. In cell A5, key **Ice Cream Cakes**.

5. In cell A6, key **January 1, 200x** (using next year in place of the "x"**).** Key **February 1, 200x** in cell A7, with the same year. Select both cells and format the date to spell out the month and show the date, a comma, and a four-digit year.

NOTE

Ignore Smart Tag Actions buttons.

6. Select cells A6:A7 and use the Fill handle to extend the dates to May 1.

7. Format cells B6:D10 as Accounting format.

8. Key **24.5** in cell B6. Copy this value to cells B7:B10.

9. Key the following special prices:

January	20.5
February	21.5
March	20.5
April	19.99
May	22.5

10. Use a formula in cell D6 to compute the difference between the regular price and the special price. Copy the formula to cells D7:D10.

11. Press Ctrl + Home. Rename the tab as **Cakes** and choose a tab theme color.

12. Select cells A5:D10 and format them using a medium style table. Your table does not have a header row. In the Table Style Options group on the Table Tools Design tab, deselect **Header Row**.

13. Make row 4 very small. Then choose font sizes, styles, and colors for the labels and set row heights and column widths to build an attractive report.

14. Add a header to show your name at the left, the sheet name in the center, and the filename at the right. Change the left margin to make the sheet appear centered on the page.

15. Prepare and submit your work. Save and close the workbook.

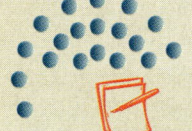

NOTE

Blank cells in the Quantity column are formatted to appear red. This is a conditional format. The color changes when you enter a value.

Exercise 3-29

Spell-check a worksheet.

1. Open **OrderSheet**. Find and correct misspelled words.

2. In cell C5, key today's date in this format: mm/dd/yy.

3. In cell C6, key *[your last name]*'s Supermarket.

4. Key the following quantities for the ice cream flavors shown. No quantity appears for flavors that are not being ordered.

Vanilla	25
Chocolate	25
Strawberry	20
Butter Pecan	10
French Vanilla	10
Chocolate Chip	10
Chocolate Mint Melody	10
Peppermint Candy	10
Raspberry Swirl	15
Purple Kow	12

   The flavors in Rows 17-24 are not being ordered.

Apple Pie	5
Rum Raisin	5
Blueberry	5
New York Cherry	5

5. Select the cells with dollar values and use the Format Cells dialog box to change to the Currency format (floating dollar sign). Paint this format to cell F34.

6. Press ⌈Ctrl⌉+⌈Home⌉. Save the workbook as *[your initials]3-29* in your Lesson 3 folder.

7. Prepare and submit your work. Close the workbook.

Exercise 3-30 ◆ Challenge Yourself

Create a series. Create a table and use cell styles. Prepare a footer.

1. Create a new workbook. Rename **Sheet1** as **ShakeSales**. Save the workbook as *[your initials]3-30* in your Lesson 3 folder.

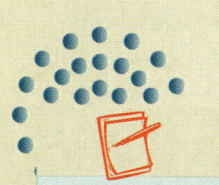

NOTE

New workbooks use the Office document theme.

2. Key **Klassy Kow Ice Cream Shops** in cell A1. Key **Daily Shake Sales in** *[your home city]* in cell A2.

3. In cell B3, key **Chocolate**. In cell C3, key **Vanilla**.

4. In cell A4, key **monday**. Fill in the days of the week up to and including Sunday in column A. Key **Day** in cell A3.

5. In cell B4, key **4**. In cell B5, key **8**. Extend this series down column B to fill in values up to Sunday. Copy the entire range of values to the Vanilla column.

6. Create a table for rows 3:11 using any style. Set your own row heights.

7. Use the cell style gallery to format the labels in cells A1:A2 to coordinate with your table, or apply your own formatting.

8. Select the **Total Row** from the Table Tools Design tab. Show totals for both columns.

9. Add a footer with your name at the left, the filename in the center, and the sheet name at the right.

10. Prepare and submit your work. Close the workbook.

On Your Own

In these exercises you work on your own, as you would in a real-life work environment. Use the skills you've learned to accomplish the task—and be creative.

Exercise 3-31

Open **SepPies**. Change the labels to the Headings font and the values to the Body font. Change the date to today's date. Use AutoFill to complete the labels in row 3. Key the names of four ice cream pies in cells A5:A8. Create a table for the data rows and use cell styles for the main labels. Make your own changes, too, for an attractive layout. Add a footer with your name, the filename, and the date. Save the worksheet as *[your initials]*3-31. Prepare and submit your work. Save and close the workbook.

Exercise 3-32

Create a new workbook and save it as *[your initials]*3-32. In cell A1, key **Using AutoFill and Series**. Create a 15-month series in column A, using a 3-month interval (January, April; fill 15 rows; start with any month). Build a 15-day series in column B, using an every-other-day interval (Monday, Wednesday; 15 rows; start with any day). In row 20, build a 10-year series, using a 4-year interval (2000, 2004; start with any year). In row 22, build a 10-value series starting at 2 and using an interval of 2 (2, 4). In cell A24, key today's date. In cell A25, key the date one week from today. Build a 12-date series in column A from these two dates. Apply a different cell style to each series and the main label, too.

Add a header with appropriate information. On the Page Layout tab, find and use the command to print the worksheet in landscape orientation. Prepare and submit your work. Save and close the workbook.

Exercise 3-33

Use the Internet or printed maps to determine the mileage between your city and five major cities in your part of the country. Calculate a driving time to each city from your city. Create a workbook that shows this information in an easy-to-read layout. Include a main label and column titles. Spell-check it and use a table or cell styles. Add an appropriate header. Save the workbook as *[your initials]*3-33. Prepare and submit your work. Close the workbook.

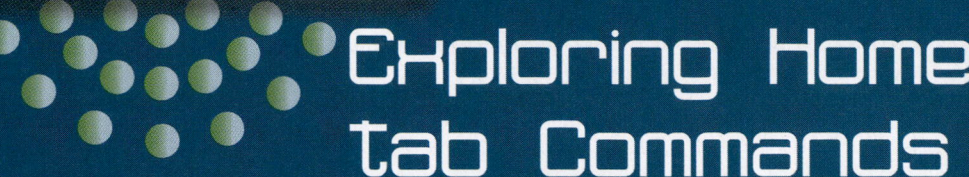

Exploring Home tab Commands

OBJECTIVES

After completing this lesson, you will be able to:

1. Insert and delete sheets and cells.

2. Use AutoComplete and Pick From Drop-Down List.

3. Copy, cut, and paste cell contents.

4. Work with columns and rows.

5. Work with alignment.

6. Apply borders and fill.

7. Use data bars.

Estimated Time: 1¼ hours

MCAS OBJECTIVES

In this lesson:
XL07 1.2
XL07 1.3.1
XL07 1.4.2
XL07 1.5.1
XL07 1.5.5
XL07 2.2.1
XL07 2.2.3
XL07 2.3.2
XL07 2.3.3
XL07 2.3.4
XL07 2.3.6
XL07 2.3.7
XL07 4.3.1
XL07 4.3.3

The Home tab includes commonly used tasks and commands. The groups on this tab are Clipboard, Font, Alignment, Number, Styles, Cells, and Editing. The Home tab is the active tab when you open a new workbook.

Inserting and Deleting Sheets and Cells

A new workbook opens with three blank sheets. You can insert and delete sheets as needed. You insert a new worksheet when you:

- Click the **Insert Worksheet** tab.

- Press Shift + F11.

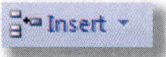
- In the Cells group, click the arrow with the Insert Cells button 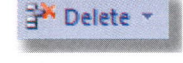 and choose **Insert Sheet**.

- Right-click a worksheet tab and choose **Insert**. Then choose **Worksheet** in the dialog box.

You delete a worksheet when you:

- Right-click the worksheet tab and choose **Delete**.

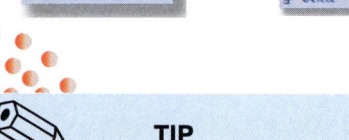
- In the Cells group, click the arrow next to the Delete Cells button  and choose **Delete Sheet**.

TIP

You can change the default number of sheets in a new workbook in the Popular pane in the Excel Options dialog box.

Exercise 4-1   INSERT WORKSHEETS

Excel names new sheets starting with the next number in sequence. For example, if the workbook already has **Sheet1**, **Sheet2**, and **Sheet3**, a new sheet would be named **Sheet4**.

1. Open **AcctRec**. This workbook has one worksheet named **AR2007** for Accounts Receivable in 2007. Notice that there is no **Sheet1**.

2. Click the **Insert Worksheet** tab.

3. Double-click the **Sheet1** worksheet tab.

4. Key **SalesReps** and press Enter. The worksheet tab is renamed.

5. Right-click the **SalesReps** tab. Choose a color different from the color of the **AR2007** sheet.

6. Press Shift+F11. A new worksheet named **Sheet2** is placed in front of the **SalesReps** sheet.

NOTE

Your sheet numbers might be different.

7. Right-click the **AR2007** tab and choose **Insert**. The Insert dialog box opens.

8. Click the **General** tab. This tab shows the types of objects you can insert in your workbook. You likely have objects different from the text figure.

Figure 4-1
Insert Worksheet
dialog box

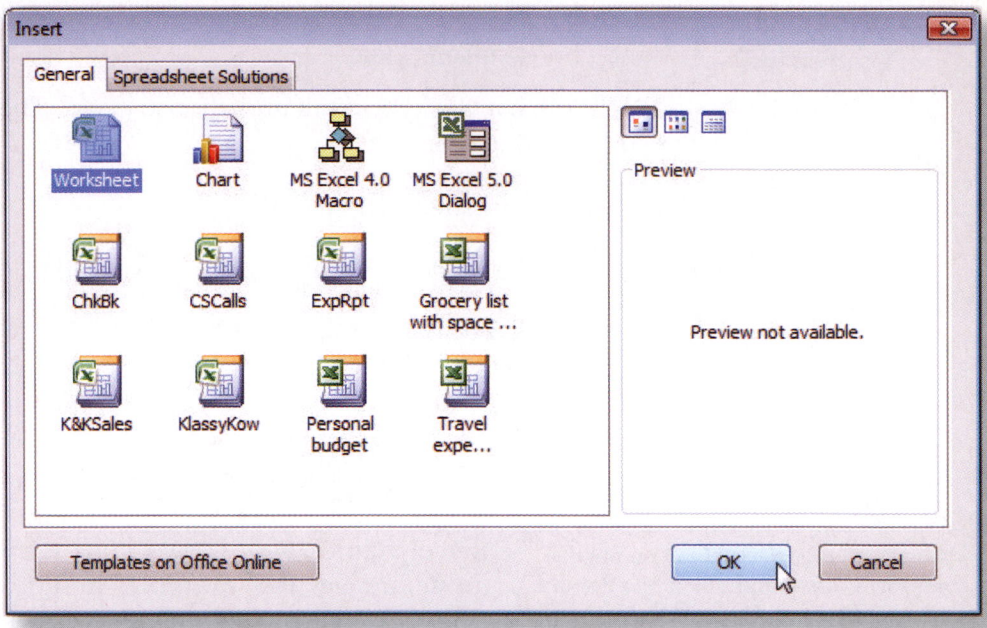

9. Click **Worksheet** and click **OK**. **Sheet3** is placed before the **AR2007** worksheet.

Exercise 4-2   MOVE AND DELETE WORKSHEETS

You can rearrange worksheet tabs in any order. Additionally, if you don't need all the sheets in a workbook, you can delete blank ones to conserve file space. You cannot delete the only sheet in a workbook.

1. Click the **AR2007** tab to make it active.

2. Point at the tab to display a white arrow pointer.

3. Click and drag the tab to the left of **Sheet3**. As you drag, you see a small sheet icon and a triangle that marks the new position of the sheet.

4. Release the mouse button. The **AR2007** sheet is now the leftmost tab.

5. Right-click the **Sheet3** tab. The sheet becomes the active sheet and a shortcut menu opens.

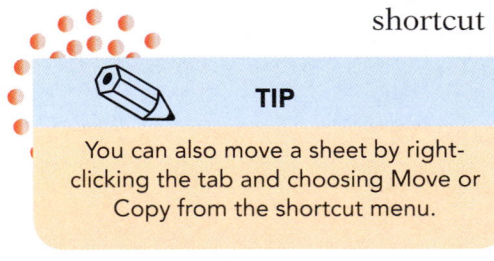

TIP

You can also move a sheet by right-clicking the tab and choosing Move or Copy from the shortcut menu.

6. Choose **Delete**. The sheet is deleted, and **Sheet2** is active.

7. In the **Cells** group, click the arrow with the Delete Cells button [Delete]. Choose **Delete Sheet**. The sheet is deleted, and the **SalesReps** worksheet is active.

Exercise 4-3 INSERT CELLS

When you insert or delete cells, you affect the entire worksheet, not just the column or row where you are working. You can accidentally rearrange data if you don't watch the entire sheet. When you insert or delete cells, you decide if existing cells should move up, down, left, or right.

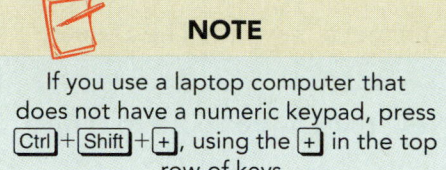

NOTE

If you use a laptop computer that does not have a numeric keypad, press Ctrl+Shift++, using the + in the top row of keys.

1. Click the **AR2007** tab. Set the Zoom size so that you can see columns A through H.

2. Click cell B8.

3. Press Ctrl++ in the numeric keypad. (The *numeric keypad* is the set of number and symbol keys at the right side of the keyboard.) An Insert dialog box opens with choices about what happens after the cell is inserted.

Figure 4-2
Insert dialog box
AcctRec.xlsx
AR2007 sheet

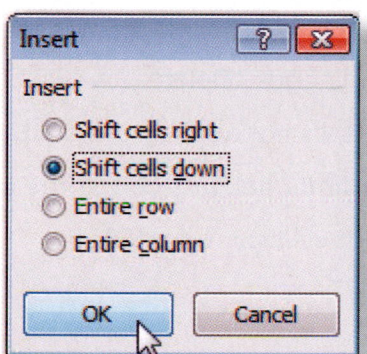

4. Choose **Shift cells down** if it's not already selected and click **OK**. A blank cell is inserted. The cells originally in cells B8:B15 have moved down to cells B9:B16. The data in the other columns did not shift.

5. Click cell C12. The reference number and related paid date are in the wrong columns.

6. Right-click cell C12 and choose **Insert**.

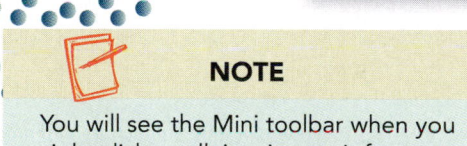

NOTE

You will see the Mini toolbar when you right-click a cell; just ignore it for now.

7. Choose **Shift cells right** and click **OK**. All the cells in the worksheet shift to the right, including those in column H and beyond.

Figure 4-3
One cell inserted, with other cells shifted right
AcctRec.xlsx
AR2007 sheet

	A	B	C	D	E	F	G	H	I	J	K
1	Date	Account Name	Amount Due	Reference No.	Date Paid			Account Name	Sales Representative	YTD Sales	Count
2	1/1/2007	Regan Superma	4501.26	20101	2/1/2007			Regan Supermarkets	José Garcia	11321	
3	1/7/2007	Southwest Offi	345	20107	3/1/2007			Southwest Office	Gary Johnson	9875	
4	2/5/2007	Stop and Shop	1000.55	20205	2/26/2007			Stop and Shop	Kathleen D'Alvia	4533	
5	2/15/2007	Corner Store	541.32	20215	3/15/2007			Corner Store	Lisa Watson	7566	
6	4/2/2007	SafeTop Stores	15245.78	20402	4/30/2007			SafeTop Stores		14500	
7	4/15/2007		12567	20415	5/15/2007					12375	
8	5/8/2007	Internatio	*Inserted cell* 7	20508	6/8/2007			International Groceries		8655	
9	5/24/2007	Internatio	0	20524	6/24/2007					7544	
10	6/18/2007	Tom's Foods	25125.24	20601	7/18/2007					11900	
11	6/23/2007	Regan Superma	15200.35	20612	7/30/2007					10555	
12	7/6/2007				20618	8/2/2007		*Cell shifted right*	Tom's Foods		560
13	8/14/2007		11245.56	20623	9/14/2007			Dominic's Foods		9877	
14	8/24/2007		8750	20706	9/30/2007			Diamond Food Stores		13000	
15	9/7/2007	South Island Foods		20814	9/30/2007			Bryce Groceries			
16	9/23/2007	Fresh Foods		20824	10/23/2007			South Island Foods			
17								Fresh Foods			
18											

Exercise 4-4 DELETE CELLS

When you delete cells, watch the entire worksheet for changes.

> **NOTE**
>
> On a laptop, press Ctrl + Shift + - in the top row of keys.

1. Scroll the worksheet so that you can see columns D through I.

2. Click cell H7.

3. Press Ctrl + - in the numeric keypad. The Delete dialog box opens.

4. Choose **Shift cells up** and click **OK**. Now there is no room to return "Tom's Foods" to column H.

5. Click the Undo button in the Quick Access toolbar.

6. Click cell H12. Press Ctrl + - on the numeric keypad.

7. Choose **Shift cells left** and click **OK**. Only the cells in columns H and beyond are shifted to the left.

8. Right-click cell H7 and choose **Delete**.

9. Choose **Shift cells up,** if it's not already selected, and click **OK**.

10. Select cells H8:H10. Right-click any cell in the range.

11. Choose **Delete** and **Shift cells up**. Click OK.

12. Press Ctrl + Home.

Using AutoComplete and Pick from Drop-Down List

Excel has two features that make it easy to enter labels in a column. Both features use text already in the column.

- *AutoComplete* displays a suggested label after you key the first character(s) in a cell. AutoComplete works for text and labels that are a combination of text and numbers.

- *Pick From Drop-Down List* displays a list of labels already in the column for your selection. This method is helpful when it is important that you use exactly the same data as already entered. It's a way to validate data as it is entered.

Exercise 4-5   USE AUTOCOMPLETE

When you key the first few characters of a label, Excel scans the column for the same characters. If it finds a match, it displays a proposed entry. If the suggestion is correct, press Enter. If the suggested label is not what you want, ignore it and continue to key the new label. You may need to key more than one character before Excel proposes a label.

> **TIP**
>
> You can key lower- or uppercase letters to see a proposed label.

1. Click cell B7.

2. Key **r** to see an AutoComplete suggestion. In this case, Excel's suggestion is accurate.

Figure 4-4
An AutoComplete suggestion
AcctRec.xlsx
AR2007 sheet

	A	B	C	D
1	**Date**	**Account Name**	**Amount Due**	**Reference No.**
2	1/1/2007	Regan Superma	4501.26	20101
3	1/7/2007	Southwest Offi	345	20107
4	2/5/2007	Stop and Shop	1000.55	20205
5	2/15/2007	Corner Store	541.32	20215
6	4/2/2007	SafeTop Stores	15245.78	20402
7	4/15/2007	regan Supermarkets		20415
8	5/8/2007		3677.87	20508
9	5/24/2007	International G	5590	20524
10	6/18/2007	Tom's Foods	25125.24	20601

3. Press Enter. The label is entered with the same capitalization as the existing label in the column.

4. Key **s** in cell B8. No suggestion is made, because several labels in the column start with "s." Excel needs more information.

5. Key **t** to see a suggestion for "Stop and Shop."

6. Press Enter.

7. Click cell B12 and key **south**. Excel has not found a match.

8. Press Spacebar. Excel suggests "South Island Foods," because the space distinguishes it from "Southwest."

9. Press Enter.

10. Key **PDQ Shop** in cell B13 and press Enter. No suggestion was made, because no existing label starts with "p."

11. Click cell C15 and key **87**. Excel does not make AutoComplete suggestions for values.

12. Press Esc.

Exercise 4-6   USE PICK FROM DROP-DOWN LIST

The Pick From Drop-Down List option appears on the shortcut menu when you right-click a cell.

1. Right-click cell I6.

2. Choose **Pick From Drop-Down List.** Excel displays a list of labels already in column I.

3. Click **José Garcia**.

Figure 4-5
Using Pick From Drop-Down List
**AcctRec.xlsx
AR2007 sheet**

H	I
Account Name	**Sales Representative**
Regan Supermarkets	José Garcia
Southwest Office	Gary Johnson
Stop and Shop	Kathleen D'Alvia
Corner Store	Lisa Watson
SafeTop Stores	
International Grocerie	Gary Johnson
Tom's Foods	José Garcia
Dominic's Foods	Kathleen D'Alvia
Diamond Food Stores	Lisa Watson
Bryce Groceries	
South Island Foods	
Fresh Foods	

4. Right-click cell I7. Choose **Pick From Drop-Down List**.

5. Click **Lisa Watson**.

6. Right-click cell B14. Choose **Pick From Drop-Down List**. The list is longer and includes a scroll bar.

7. Find and click **Tom's Foods**.

8. Right-click cell C12. Choose **Pick From Drop-Down List**. Excel does not display a list for values.

9. Press Esc.

Copying, Cutting, and Pasting Cell Contents

You can copy, cut (move), and paste cell contents in a worksheet. When you copy or cut a cell or range of cells, a duplicate of the data is placed on the *Windows Clipboard*. This is a temporary memory area used to keep data you have copied or cut.

Data that is cut can be pasted once. Data that is copied can be pasted many times and in many locations. Copied data stays on the Windows Clipboard until you copy or cut another cell or range. Then that data replaces the data on the Clipboard.

The Cut and Paste commands are used to move labels and values from one cell to another. To use Cut and Paste, first select the cells you want to cut, and then you can:

- Click the Cut button ✄ in the Clipboard group. Position the pointer at the new location and click the Paste button 📋 or press ⌈Enter⌋.

- Press ⌈Ctrl⌋+⌈X⌋. Position the pointer at the new location and press ⌈Ctrl⌋+⌈V⌋ or press ⌈Enter⌋.

- Right-click the selected cells. Choose **Cut** from the shortcut menu. Right-click the new cell location and choose **Paste** from the shortcut menu.

- Select the cell or range. Drag it to a new location.

The Copy and Paste commands make a duplicate of the data in another location. To use copy and paste, select the cells you want to copy, and then you can:

- Click the Copy button 📑 in the Clipboard group. Position the pointer at the new location and click the Paste button 📋 or press ⌈Enter⌋.

- Press ⌈Ctrl⌋+⌈C⌋. Position the pointer at the new location and press ⌈Ctrl⌋+⌈V⌋ or press ⌈Enter⌋.

- Right-click the selected cells. Choose **Copy** from the shortcut menu. Right-click the new cell location and choose **Paste**.

- Select the cell or range. While holding down the ⌈Ctrl⌋ key, drag it to a new location.

Exercise 4-7   CUT AND PASTE CELL CONTENTS

When you paste cells that have been cut, the cut data replaces existing data unless you tell Excel to insert the cut data.

1. Click cell C14. Click the Cut button ✄. A moving marquee surrounds the cell.

2. Click cell C12 and then click the Paste button 📋. The data is removed from cell C14 and pasted in C12. The marquee is canceled.

3. Select cells B15:B16. Press ⌈Ctrl⌋+⌈X⌋. The range displays the moving marquee.

4. Click cell B17 and press ⎡Enter⎤. The pasted range is selected.

Figure 4-6
Cutting cell contents
AcctRec.xlsx
AR2007 sheet

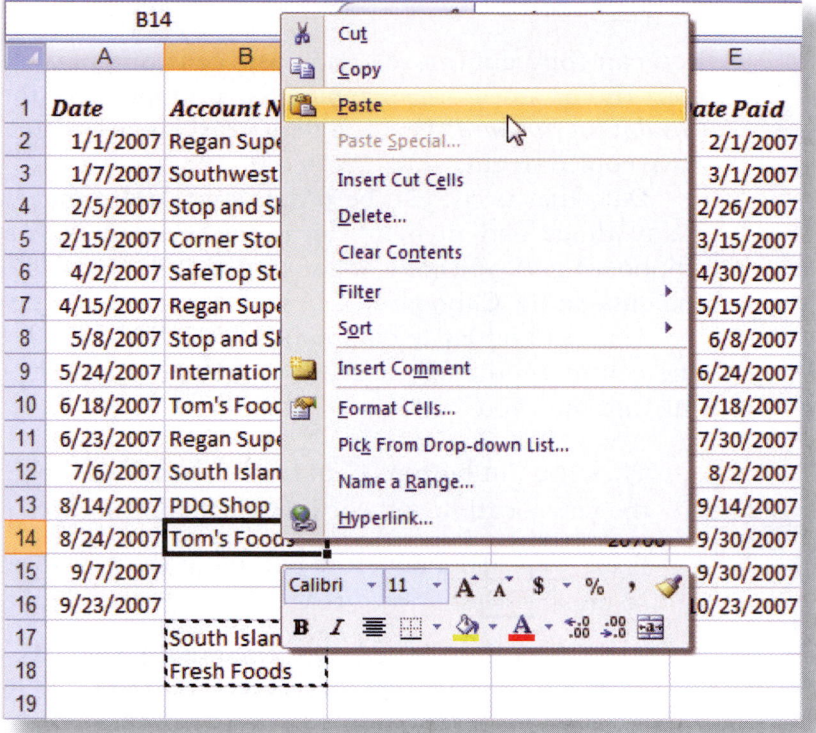

5. Click the Cut button ✂. The range displays the moving marquee.

6. Right-click cell B14. Choose **Paste**. A regular Paste command replaces existing data. "Tom's Foods" is gone from cell B14.

7. Select cells B5:B6. Press ⎡Ctrl⎤+⎡X⎤.

8. Right-click cell B4 and choose **Insert Cut Cells**. The data from cells B5:B6 is inserted before Stop and Shop, which has shifted down.

Exercise 4-8   COPY AND PASTE CELL CONTENTS

The Paste Options button 📋 appears below a pasted selection. When you click it, you see a list of options that establish how the selection can be pasted.

1. Click cell B1 and click the Copy button 📋. The cell is surrounded by the moving marquee.

2. Click cell B13 and click the Paste button 📋. The label is pasted, the original data is removed, and the Paste Options button 📋 appears.

NOTE

Close the Clipboard pane if it opens.

3. Rest the mouse pointer on the Paste Options button 📋. Click its arrow.

4. Choose **Formatting Only**. This option copies only the formatting; it does not copy the actual label.

Figure 4-7
Using Paste Options
AcctRec.xlsx
AR2007 sheet

	A	B	C	D	E
1	*Date*	*Account Name*	*Amount Due*	*Reference No.*	*Date Paid*
2	1/1/2007	Regan Superma	4501.26	20101	2/1/2007
3	1/7/2007	Southwest Offi	345	20107	3/1/2007
4	2/5/2007	Corner Store	1000.55	20205	2/26/2007
5	2/15/2007	SafeTop Stores	541.32	20215	3/15/2007
6	4/2/2007	Stop and Shop	15245.78	20402	4/30/2007
7	4/15/2007	Regan Superma	12567	20415	5/15/2007
8	5/8/2007	Stop and Shop	3677.87	20508	6/8/2007
9	5/24/2007	International Gr	5590	20524	6/24/2007
10	6/18/2007	Tom's Foods	25125.24	20601	7/18/2007
11	6/23/2007	Regan Superma	15200.35	20612	7/30/2007
12	7/6/2007	South Island Fo	8750	20618	8/2/2007
13	8/14/2007	*Account Name*	11245.56	20623	9/14/2007
14	8/24/2007	South Island Foo		20706	9/30/2007
15	9/7/2007	Fresh Foods			9/30/2007
16	9/23/2007				9/23/2007

Paste Options menu:
- ○ Keep Source Formatting
- ◉ Use Destination Theme
- ○ Match Destination Formatting
- ○ Values and Number Formatting
- ○ Keep Source Column Widths
- ○ Formatting Only
- ○ Link Cells

TIP

The marquee is not automatically canceled after you click the Paste button. This enables you to paste the data again in a different location.

REVIEW

Copied cells replace existing data unless you choose the option to insert them.

5. Click the Undo button. Press **Esc**.

6. Click cell I2 and drag to select the range I2:I7.

7. Press **Ctrl**+**C**. Excel displays a marquee around the range.

8. Click cell I8. You only need to click in the first cell for the copy as long as the destination range is empty.

9. Press **Ctrl**+**V**. The range of names is duplicated. The marquee is shown as well as the Paste Options button.

10. Click cell I14. Press **Ctrl**+**V** to paste the data again.

11. Press **Esc** to cancel the marquee.

12. Select the range C8:C10 and press **Ctrl**+**C** to copy the range.

13. Right-click cell C11.

14. Choose **Insert Copied Cells**. The Insert Paste dialog box opens.

15. Choose **Shift cells down**. Click **OK**. The copied cells are inserted, and the existing cells are shifted down in the column.

16. Press Esc to cancel the marquee.

Exercise 4-9   USE DRAG AND DROP

Use the drag-and-drop method to cut or copy data when you can see the original and the destination cell on screen. The *drag-and-drop pointer* is a four-pointed arrow.

1. Select cell C16. Place the pointer at the top or bottom edge/border of the cell. The drag-and-drop pointer appears.

2. Hold down the mouse button and drag to cell C17. A ScreenTip identifies the destination cell. You can also see a ghost highlight that shows where the data will be placed.

Figure 4-8
Using drag and drop to cut and paste
AcctRec.xlsx
AR2007 sheet

10	6/18/2007	Tom's Foods	25125.24	20601
11	6/23/2007	Regan Superma	3677.87	20612
12	7/6/2007	South Island Fo	5590	20618
13	8/14/2007	PDQ Shop	25125.24	20623
14	8/24/2007	South Island Fo	15200.35	20706
15	9/7/2007	Fresh Foods	8750	20814
16	9/23/2007		11245.56	20824
17				
18			C17	
19				

3. Release the mouse button. You have used the drag-and-drop method to perform a cut and paste.

4. Place the pointer at the top or bottom edge/border of cell C17 to display the drag-and-drop pointer.

5. Hold down Ctrl. You will see a tiny plus sign (+) with a solid white arrow to signify this will be a copy and paste. Do not release Ctrl.

6. Click and drag to cell C16. Release the mouse button first and then release Ctrl. This is drag and drop to perform a copy and paste.

7. Select cells B6:B7. Place the pointer at the top or bottom edge of the range to display the drag-and-drop pointer.

NOTE

Drag and drop works in most Windows applications.

8. Hold down the Ctrl key to display the plus sign (+) and the white arrow pointer. Do not release the Ctrl key.

9. Click and drag down to cells B16:B17. Release the mouse button and then Ctrl. Both labels are copied.

Exercise 4-10   USE THE OFFICE CLIPBOARD

The *Office Clipboard* is a temporary memory area that can hold up to 24 copied items. It is separate from the Windows Clipboard. The Office Clipboard is available when any Office application (Excel, Access, Word, or PowerPoint) is running. It is shared among these programs, so something you copy in Excel can be pasted in Word. The options for the Office Clipboard allow you to set it to open automatically when you first copy an object and to show a screen message after copying.

1. Click the Dialog Box Launcher in the Clipboard group. The Clipboard task pane opens. You may see values and labels from your last copy task.

> **NOTE**
>
> If the Clear All button ☒ Clear All is grayed or dimmed, you have nothing on the Clipboard and can continue.

2. Click the Clear All button ☒ Clear All in the task pane.

3. Select the range A4:E4 and click the Copy button. An Excel icon and the data appear in the task pane. There is an icon in the lower-right corner of the Windows taskbar.

4. Select the range A6:A7 and click the Copy button. Another icon and data appear in the pane, above the first set.

5. Select the range A8:E8 and click the Copy button. Three items have been copied and are on the Office Clipboard.

6. Press Esc. The marquee is removed.

7. Click cell A17. Click the date object in the task pane to paste two dates (see Figure 4-9 on the next page).

5. Use cell alignment by following these steps:

   a. Select the range A1:D2.

   b. In the **Alignment** group, click the Dialog Box Launcher.

   c. Click the **Horizontal** arrow and choose **Center Across Selection**. Click **OK**.

   d. Select the labels in row 3 and click the Center button .

   e. Select cells D6:D10 and click the Dialog Box Launcher in the **Alignment** group.

   f. Click the **Horizontal** arrow and choose **Right (Indent)**. In the **Indent** box, choose or key **2**. Click **OK**.

6. Apply borders by following these steps:

   a. Click the row 4 heading and drag to select row 5. Right-click and choose **Insert**.

   b. Select the range A3:D3.

   c. In the **Font** group, click the arrow next to the Borders button . Choose **Top and Bottom Border.**

   d. Select the range A4:D4. Click the Dialog Box Launcher in the **Font** group. Click the **Border** tab.

   e. In the **Style** list, choose the dot-dot-dash line (first line, second column). Click the bottom border area in the preview box. Close the dialog box.

   f. Set row 4 to a height of **4.50 (6 pixels)**. Set the height of row 5 to **15.00 (20 pixels).**

   g. Select the range A12:D12. Click the down arrow next to the Borders button . Choose **Bottom Border**.

   h. Select the range A11:D11. Press Ctrl+1. Click the **Border** tab.

   i. In the **Style** list, choose the dot-dot-dash line. Click the bottom border area in the preview box. Close the dialog box.

   j. Set the height of row 11 to **15.00 (20 pixels)** and row 12 to **4.50 (6 pixels)**. Make row 3 the same height as row 2.

7. Use data bars by following these steps:

   a. Select cells D6:D10. Click the Conditional Formatting button in the **Styles** group.

   b. Choose **Data Bars** and then **Green Data Bar**.

   c. Click the Conditional Formatting button . Choose **Manage Rules**.

   d. Choose **Edit Rule**. Set the **Bar Color** to a shade of gray. Click **OK** to return to the worksheet.

8. Press Ctrl+Home. Delete **Sheet2** and **Sheet3**. Rename **Sheet1** as **Interviews** and choose a tab color to coordinate with the data bar.

9. In Page Layout View, change the left and right margin to **2.25** inches.

10. Create a header with your first and last name at the left, the sheet name in the center, and the date at the right.

11. Prepare and submit your work. Save and close the workbook.

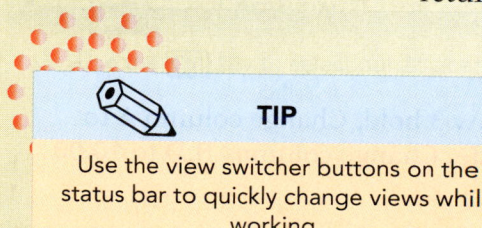

TIP

Use the view switcher buttons on the status bar to quickly change views while working.

Lesson Applications

Exercise 4-33

Cut, copy, and paste data. Use borders and cell alignment. Add data bars.

1. Open **KowOwow** and save it as *[your initials]*4-33 in your folder.

2. On the **Oregon** sheet, cut the "Ashland" row and insert it before the "Eugene" row. Cut the "Medford" row and insert it before the "Roseburg" row.

3. Copy the range A7:A11 to cells A15:A20.

4. Key the following values for 2007:

Figure 2-24

	Chocolate	Vanilla
2007		
Ashland	22000	21000
Eugene	27000	28000
Klamath Falls	20000	18000
Medford	18000	16000
Roseburg	17000	15000

5. Shows sums in the range D7:D11 and in the range B12:D12. Apply the Comma style with no decimals to cells B7:D12.

6. Center the labels in rows 1:2 over the data. Align the labels in row 3 to balance the data in each column.

7. Set the row height for rows 14:19 to match the 2007 data. Create borders in rows 20:21 to mirror those in rows 4:5.

8. Use orange data bars for cells D7:D11.

9. Add a footer. Set the left margin so that the sheet appears centered on the page.

NOTE

Use the Borders dialog box to design special borders.

10. On the **California** sheet, copy cells A5:A19 to cells A22:A36. Show totals for 2007.

11. Format values to show commas and no decimals. Center the labels in rows 1:2 over the data. Adjust the alignment of the labels in row 3 for better balance.

12. Select cells A5:D18. Apply dotted-line middle and bottom horizontal borders. Do the same for the lower half of the sheet.

13. Add a custom header to the sheet. Set the left margin so that the sheet appears centered.

14. Prepare and submit your work. Save and close the workbook.

Exercise 4-34

Insert and move worksheets. Align labels; use borders and fill. Copy data and formats.

1. Open **EstKowO** and save it as *[your initials]*4-34 in your folder.

2. Insert two new worksheets and name them **Nevada** and **Washington**.

3. Arrange the worksheets so that they are in alphabetical order, left to right. Use a different accent color for each tab.

4. On the **Oregon** sheet, center the labels in rows 1:2 over the data and apply a lighter shade of the tab color as fill. Right-align the labels in row 3.

5. Use the tab color for a double top border for row 1. Apply a double bottom border to row 2 using the same color. Make each of these rows slightly taller. Then set the vertical alignment of cell A2 to **Center** so that the amount of space above the labels appears to be equal to the space below.

6. Select cells A3:D18. Use the **Border** tab to apply single inside borders and single left, right, and bottom borders (same color as the tab). Apply single side borders to rows 1:2 to complete the design.

NOTE

Do not press [Enter] to complete a paste command if you want to use the Paste Options.

7. Copy and paste cells A1:D4 on the **Oregon** sheet to the same range on the **Nevada** sheet. Click the Paste Options button 📋 and choose **Keep Source Column Widths**. Paste with the same options to the **Washington** sheet.

8. Copy cells B5:D11 from the **Oregon** sheet to the **Nevada** sheet. From the Paste Options, choose **Formatting Only**. Paste with the same options to the **Washington** sheet.

9. Change the fill and border colors on the **Nevada** sheet to match its tab color. Add a footer. Do the same for the **Washington** sheet.

10. Add a header to the **Oregon** sheet. Prepare and submit your work.

11. Save and close the workbook.

Exercise 4-35

Insert columns. Cut cells. Use cell alignment and borders. Add data bars.

1. Open **EstKowO** and save it as *[your initials]*4-35 in your folder.

2. On the **California** sheet, insert a column at column C. Move the label in cell A4 to cell B4. Move the label in cell A21 to cell C4.

TIP

If you prefer to use drag and drop, reduce the Zoom size to see more on screen.

TIP

A column filled with # symbols means the column is not wide enough.

3. Move cells B22:B36 to cells C5:C19.

4. Insert a column at column E. Copy the labels in cells B4:C4 to cells D4:E4. Move cells D22:D36 to cells E5:E19.

5. Fix the formula in cell F5 and copy it to the appropriate cells.

6. Center-align the labels in row 4 and cell F3. Merge and center cells B3:C3; do the same for **Vanilla**. Center the labels in rows 1:2 over the data. Delete all data below row 21.

7. Apply **Accounting Number Format** for rows 5 and 19 but remove the decimal places.

8. Insert a column at column D and make it **2.14 (20 pixels)** wide. Then set single left and right borders for cells D3:D19. Apply a single-line top border to cells A3:G3.

9. Set gray data bars for cells G5:G18.

10. Add a header and prepare and submit your work.

11. Save and close the workbook.

Exercise 4-36 ◆ Challenge Yourself

Cut and paste rows. Change cell alignment and data bars.

1. Open **JulyCakes** and save it as *[your initials]***4-36**.

2. Arrange the flavors in alphabetical order. Show quarterly sums.

3. Change the labels in rows 1:3 to the headings font. Then choose a larger size for the labels in rows 1:2 and center them across the data.

4. Format the values with **Comma** style but no decimals.

5. Change to the **Concourse** document theme. Make other adjustments and/or format enhancements that you think are necessary.

6. Delete the data bars.

7. Add a header. Turn off printing and viewing for gridlines and row and column headings.

8. Prepare and submit your work. Save and close the workbook.

On Your Own

In these exercises you work on your own, as you would in a real-life work environment. Use the skills you've learned to accomplish the task—and be creative.

Exercise 4-37

Create a new workbook and save it as *[your initials]*4-37 in your Lesson 4 folder. Key the names of eight people in your class, relatives, or coworkers. List each person's city, state, favorite color, and preferred season, using AutoComplete or Pick From Drop-Down List when possible. Include a main label and labels for the columns. Apply fill and borders to enhance the readability. Add a header and save the workbook. Prepare and submit your work.

Exercise 4-38

Create a new workbook and save it as *[your initials]*4-38 in your folder. In cell A1, key **Restaurants and Fast Food Shops**. Enter column labels for the names of restaurants, phone numbers, cuisine ("Italian," "Seafood,"), and average price. Key data for 15 establishments. Set data bars for the price cells. Format your work attractively. Add a footer and save the workbook. Prepare and submit your work.

Exercise 4-39

Create a new workbook that lists the day of the week and the actual date for every day last month in two columns. In a third column, key the outdoor temperature. Experiment with alignment and borders. Add data bars to the temperature data. Add a header and save the workbook as *[your initials]*4-39. Prepare and submit your work.

Unit 1 Applications

Unit Application 1-1

Rename and delete sheets. Use Find and Replace and Spelling. Key formulas. Format data.

Klassy Kow Ice Cream maintains a statement of assets that includes cash, equipment, and supplies. You will be editing the worksheet.

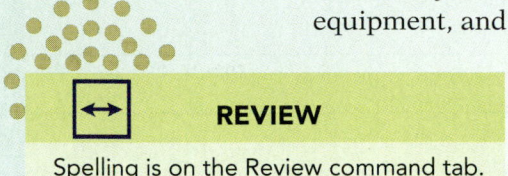

REVIEW

Spelling is on the Review command tab.

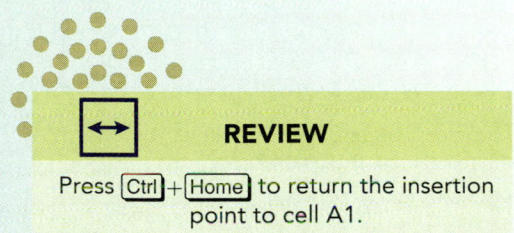

REVIEW

Formulas begin with =. Point and click to enter a cell address in a formula.

REVIEW

Press Ctrl + Home to return the insertion point to cell A1.

1. Open **Assets**. Rename **Sheet1** as **Assets** and choose a tab color from the theme colors. Delete the other sheets. Save the workbook as *[your initials]***u1-1** in a folder for Unit 1.

2. Format the headings in rows 1:2 with the Headings font for the document theme. Adjust column widths as needed. Use Comma style with no decimals for cells C4:C13.

3. Replace all occurrences of **valuables** with **assets**. Check spelling and look for inconsistent capitalization.

4. Sum the value of current assets in cell C8. In cell C12, subtract depreciation from the property, plant, and equipment amount. Add the current and fixed assets in cell C13. Add a dollar sign to the first value in each section and to the total.

5. Use borders, fill, or other methods to better design the worksheet.

6. Add a header and place the insertion point in cell A1.

7. Prepare and submit your work. Save and close the workbook.

Unit Application 1-2

Enter and format values and labels. Key formulas. Insert rows. Format data.

An income statement shows revenues (money from sales), expenses, and net income (sales minus expenses). You are to prepare and format this month's statement.

1. Create a new workbook with one sheet named **IncStatement** and save the workbook as *[your initials]***u1-2** in your Unit 1 folder.

2. Key the data as shown in Figure Unit 1-1.

Figure Unit 1-1

	A	B
1	Revenue	1500000
2	Cost of goods sold	975000
3	Sales expenses	57000
4	Administrative expense	50000
5	Depreciation	8000
6	Other expenses	2500
7	Total operating expenses	
8	Earnings before interest and taxes	
9	Interest expense	10000
10	Income taxes	150000
11	Net income	

3. Move the contents of cell B1 to cell C1.

4. In cell B7, sum the values in column B up to and including row 6. In cell C8, subtract total operating expenses from revenues. For net income (C11), subtract both interest expense and income taxes from earnings. Apply **Top and Double Bottom Borders** to the earnings and net income cells.

5. Insert two rows at the top of the data. As the first label, key **Klassy Kow Ice Cream, Inc.** In cell A2, key *[This Month]* **Income Statement**.

6. Format all values to show a comma with no decimals and the values in column C to include a dollar sign.

7. Use cell alignment, borders, fill, font styles and colors, and other tools to format the sheet.

8. Add a footer and use margins that place the data attractively on the page.

9. Prepare and submit your work. Save and close the workbook.

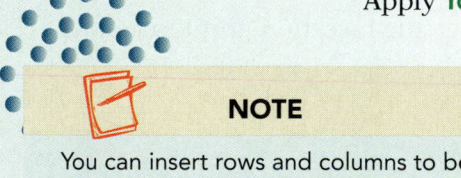

NOTE

You can insert rows and columns to be used as separators in designing borders and shading effects.

TIP

Position the pointer in cell A1 before you save a workbook.

Unit Application 1-3

Use AutoComplete or Pick From Drop-Down List. Find and correct errors. Use AutoCalculate.

The corporate office offers training for employees on various topics in various locations. You are to edit the worksheet that tracks this data.

1. Open **HRClasses** and choose a more descriptive name for the sheet. Save the workbook as *[your initials]***u1-3** in your Unit 1 folder.

2. Key the missing e-mail addresses using the same pattern as the other e-mail addresses.

3. Use AutoComplete or Pick From Drop-Down List to choose a department, location, and class for the missing entries. You may make your own selections.

REVIEW

Right-click the status bar to change AutoCalculate options.

NOTE

This worksheet is set for landscape printing.

4. Check the data carefully for errors and correct them.

5. In cell B27, key the value that results from AutoCalculate **Numerical Count** for the last names. Show the appropriate result in cell E27. Format these two values to use the same font and size as the related label.

6. Adjust the height of rows 2 and 3 so that there is a bit more fill below the labels.

7. Add a header and use margins that make the sheet appear centered on the landscape page.

8. Prepare and submit your work. Save and close the workbook.

Unit Application 1-4 ◆ Using the Internet

Search online booksellers for book and video titles about Excel. Make a list of 10 titles, including author(s), publisher(s), number of pages, price, and type of media.

Prepare a worksheet for your data with additional columns for shipping charges and a total cost. Format the data as a table or develop your own design. Use a header or a footer with appropriate information. Save your workbook as *[your initials]***u1-4** in your Unit 1 folder. Prepare and submit your work. Close the workbook.

unit 2

WORKING WITH FORMULAS AND FUNCTIONS

Lesson 5   Exploring Formula Basics   EX-166

Lesson 6   Working with Functions   EX-202

Lesson 7   Using Logical and Financial
Functions   EX-238

Lesson 8   Rounding and Nesting
Functions   EX-276

UNIT 2   APPLICATIONS   EX-302

Exploring Formula Basics

OBJECTIVES

MCAS OBJECTIVES

In this lesson:
XL07 1.2
XL07 1.5.1
XL07 2.1.4
XL07 2.3.1
XL07 2.3.4
XL07 2.3.7
XL07 3.1
XL07 3.1.1
XL07 3.8
XL07 4.3.3
XL07 5.4.2
XL07 5.5.5
XL07 5.5.6

After completing this lesson, you will be able to:

1. Use a template to create a workbook.

2. Build addition and subtraction formulas.

3. Build multiplication and division formulas.

4. Use order of precedence in a formula.

5. Use relative, absolute, and mixed references.

6. Work with the Page Layout tab.

Estimated Time: 1½ hours

NOTE

The workbooks you create and use in this course relate to the Case Study (see the Case Study in the frontmatter of the book) about Klassy Kow Ice Cream, Inc., a fictional ice cream company.

Formulas use common arithmetic operations (addition, subtraction, multiplication, and division). When building formulas, you should keep in mind mathematical order of precedence, which determines how Excel completes a series of calculations.

Excel usually updates a reference in a formula relative to its position when the formula is copied. It also has other types of references for copying formulas.

Using a Template to Create a Workbook

A *template* is a model workbook that can include labels, values, formulas, themes, styles, alignment settings, borders, and more. A template is used as the starting point for routine workbooks.

You can use a template as the model for a workbook by:

- Choosing My Templates in the Templates group of the New Workbook dialog box.

- Choosing Installed Templates in the Templates group of the New Workbook dialog box.

- Choosing the template name from the Blank and Recent pane in the New Workbook dialog box.

NOTE

Copy the templates to the folder Users\
UserName\AppData\Roaming\Microsoft\
Templates. Check with your instructor
if you need help locating the templates
used in this lesson.

Templates are saved with an **.xltx** filename extension in a Templates folder for your computer. Templates must be in this Templates folder to be listed in the New Workbook dialog box.

Exercise 5-1 CREATE A WORKBOOK FROM A TEMPLATE

When you create a new workbook from a template, a copy of the template opens as the new workbook. It has the same name as the template, followed by a number.

1. Click the Microsoft Office Button 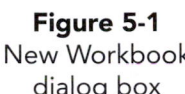 and choose **New**. The New Workbook dialog box opens.

Figure 5-1
New Workbook
dialog box

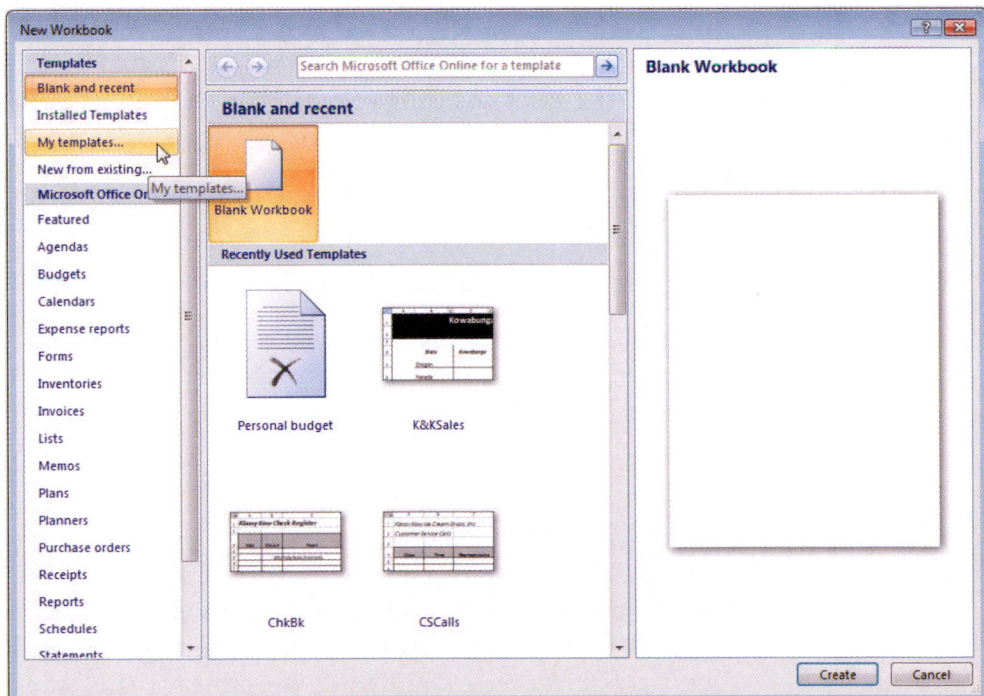

Excel 2007

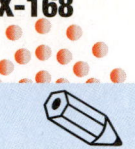

TIP

Excel includes several professionally designed templates, and you can download more from the Microsoft Office Web site.

2. Click **My templates**. The New dialog box opens.

3. Find the template **KlassyKow**.

4. Click **KlassyKow** and click **OK**. A new workbook opens with labels, values, and images. The title bar shows the template name with a number, probably 1.

Building Addition and Subtraction Formulas

Addition formulas total or sum cell values using the plus sign (+). Subtraction formulas compute the difference between cell values using the minus sign (−).

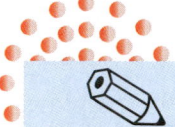

TIP

When cells are next to each other in a row or a column, it is usually faster to use AutoSum than to key a formula for addition.

Exercise 5-2   CREATE AND COPY ADDITION FORMULAS

This worksheet tracks monthly expenses of sales representatives. The budgeted amounts are part of the template, but expenses are keyed.

1. Click the Microsoft Office Button and choose **Excel Options**. Open the **Formulas** pane.

2. In the **Error checking rules**, verify that all rules show a check mark. Click **OK**.

3. Set the Zoom size so that you can see rows 1 through 30. Then click cell B27.

4. Press **=** to start a formula.

5. Click cell B8, the budget amount for the first week for Kim Tomasaki. A marquee appears around the cell, and it is outlined in a color.

TIP

You can use + on the numeric keypad or at the top of the keyboard to key the plus symbol in a formula.

6. Key **+** and click cell B13, the second week budget amount.

7. Key **+** and click cell B18, the third week.

8. Key **+** and click cell B23, the fourth week. This addition formula determines the monthly total budgeted amount for this salesperson.

Figure 5-2
Entering an addition
formula
KlassyKow.xltx
Expenses sheet

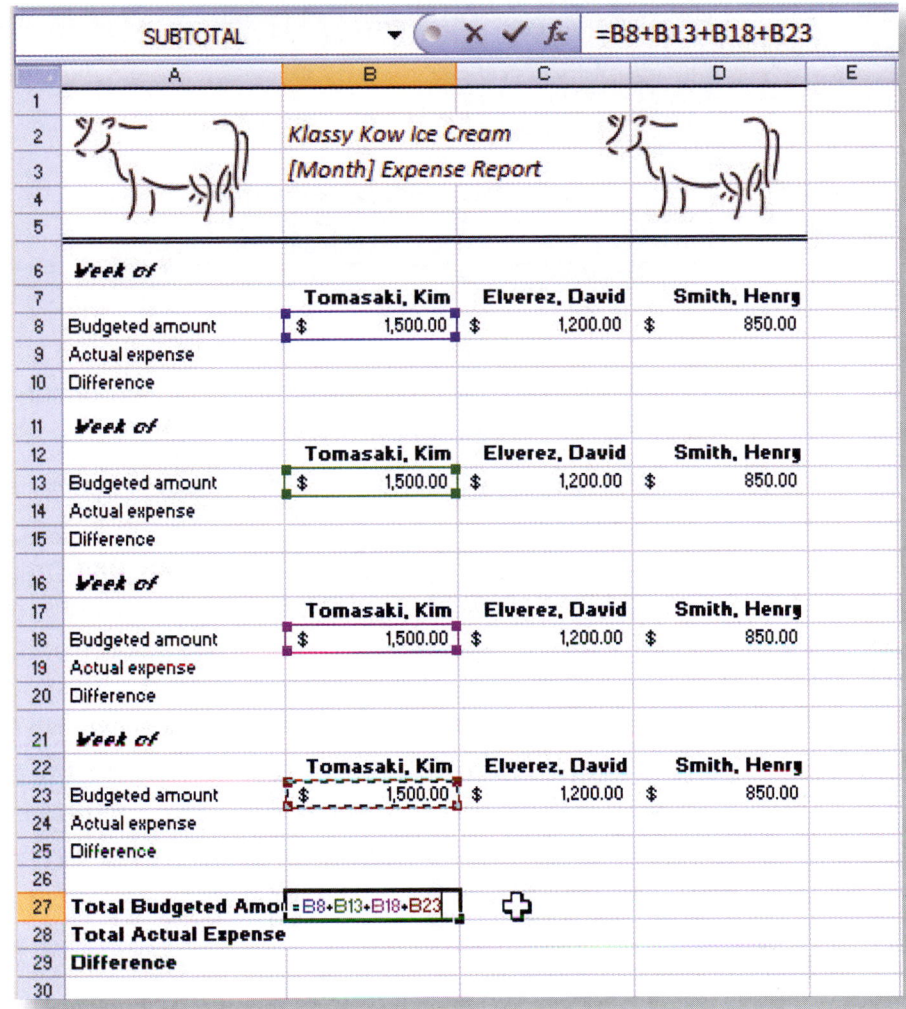

9. Press ⌈Enter⌉. The result is $6,000.

10. In cell B28, key = to start the formula.

11. Click cell B9, the cell where the first week's actual amount will be keyed.

REVIEW

You can click the Enter button ☑ in the formula bar to complete a formula.

12. Key + and click cell B14, the second week.

13. Key + and click cell B19, and then key + and click cell B24.

14. Key + again to make a deliberate error.

15. Press ⌈Enter⌉. A message box opens. The last plus sign is not necessary, and Excel proposes a correction, eliminating it.

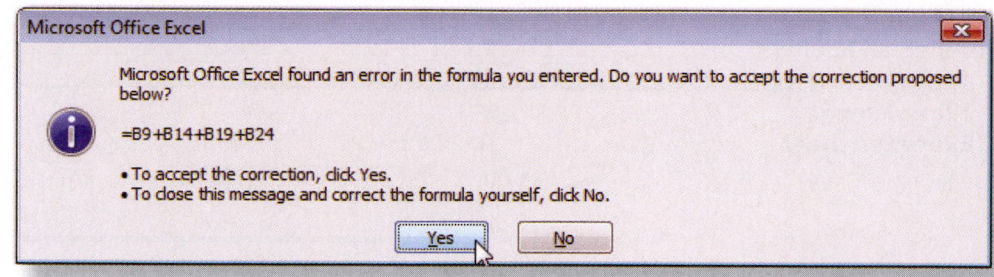

16. Choose **Yes**. This worksheet displays a single dash to indicate zero, and the cell shows a small green triangle indicating an error.

17. Click cell B28 and position the mouse pointer on the Error Checking Options button .

18. Click the arrow next to the button to see that the formula refers to empty cells.

19. Choose **Ignore Error**.

20. Select cells B27:B28. Position the mouse pointer on the Fill handle.

21. Drag the Fill handle to cell D28 to copy the formulas. The AutoFill Options button appears below the filled range. Results appear in row 27, and green triangles mark errors in cells C28:D28.

22. Select cells C28:D28 and ignore the errors.

Exercise 5-3 CREATE AND COPY SUBTRACTION FORMULAS

The difference between budgeted and actual expenditures is computed by subtracting the actual amount from the budgeted amount. You can use − on the numeric keypad or at the top of the keyboard.

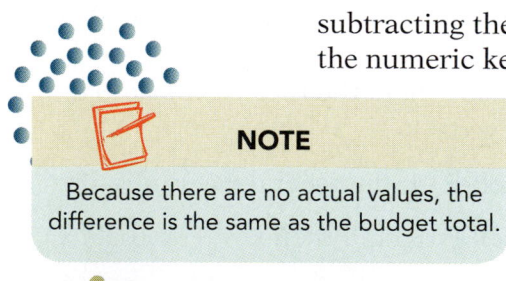

NOTE

Because there are no actual values, the difference is the same as the budget total.

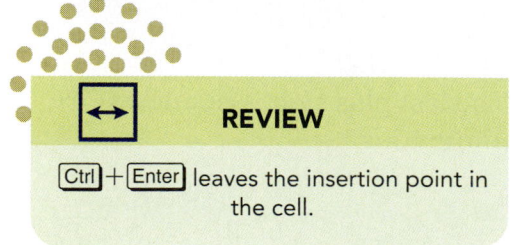

REVIEW

Ctrl + Enter leaves the insertion point in the cell.

1. Click cell B29 and key = to start a formula.

2. Click cell B27, the budget total.

3. Key − and click cell B28, the actual total. Press Enter.

4. Copy the formula in cell B29 to cells C29:D29.

5. Click cell B10. Key = and click cell B8, the budgeted amount for the week.

6. Key − and click cell B9, the actual amount. Press Ctrl + Enter.

7. Copy cell B10 to cells C10:D10. The AutoFill Options button 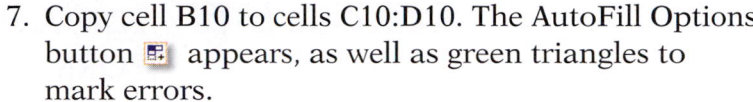 appears, as well as green triangles to mark errors.

8. While cells B10:D10 are selected, click the Copy button.

9. Click cell B15 and click the Paste button.

10. Click cell B20 and click the Paste button. Paste again in cell B25.

11. Press [Esc] to cancel the marquee. The differences are the same as the budget amounts, because no actual expenses are shown yet.

 NOTE

Error triangles do not print and have no effect on your worksheet, so you can ignore them when you know that nothing is wrong.

Building Multiplication and Division Formulas

A multiplication formula can calculate an employee's weekly wages by multiplying hours worked by the rate of pay. Multiplication formulas use an asterisk (*).

Division formulas can be used to determine percentages, averages, individual prices, and more. A division formula uses a forward slash (/).

The result of a multiplication or division formula is formatted with decimals if the result is not a whole number. A *whole number* is a value without a fraction or decimal.

 **TIP**

You can use [*] and [/] on the numeric keypad or [*] at the top of the keyboard and [/] at the bottom.

Exercise 5-4 · CREATE MULTIPLICATION FORMULAS

You can multiply the current total amounts by 10 percent to determine next year's amounts, assuming a 10 percent increase. When you multiply by a percent, you can key the value with the percent sign (%) in the formula. If you do not key the percent sign, you must key the decimal equivalent of the value.

1. Select cell A27. Display the drag-and-drop pointer, hold down [Ctrl], and drag a copy of the cell to cell A31.

2. Click cell A31 and press [F2]. Press [Home] and key **Increased**.

3. Delete **Total** and press [Enter].

4. Widen column A to fit the label.

5. Click cell B31 and key **=**.

6. Click cell B27, key *****, and then key **10%**. Press [Ctrl]+[Enter]. This amount is the increase in dollars, but not the new total.

 **TIP**

Convert a percent to its decimal equivalent by dividing the percent amount by 100. For example, 89% is 89/100 or 0.89.

 **REVIEW**

Display the drag-and-drop pointer by pointing at the top or bottom edge of a selection.

Exercise 5-5 EDIT A FORMULA IN THE FORMULA BAR

To determine the new total amount, multiply by 110%, because 110% is the current amount (100%) plus the increase (10%).

1. With cell B31 active, click in the formula bar. A text insertion point appears, and the cell in the worksheet is outlined in the same color as the cell address in the formula bar.
2. Click between the **1** and the **0** in the formula bar.
3. Key **1** to change the percent to **110%**.

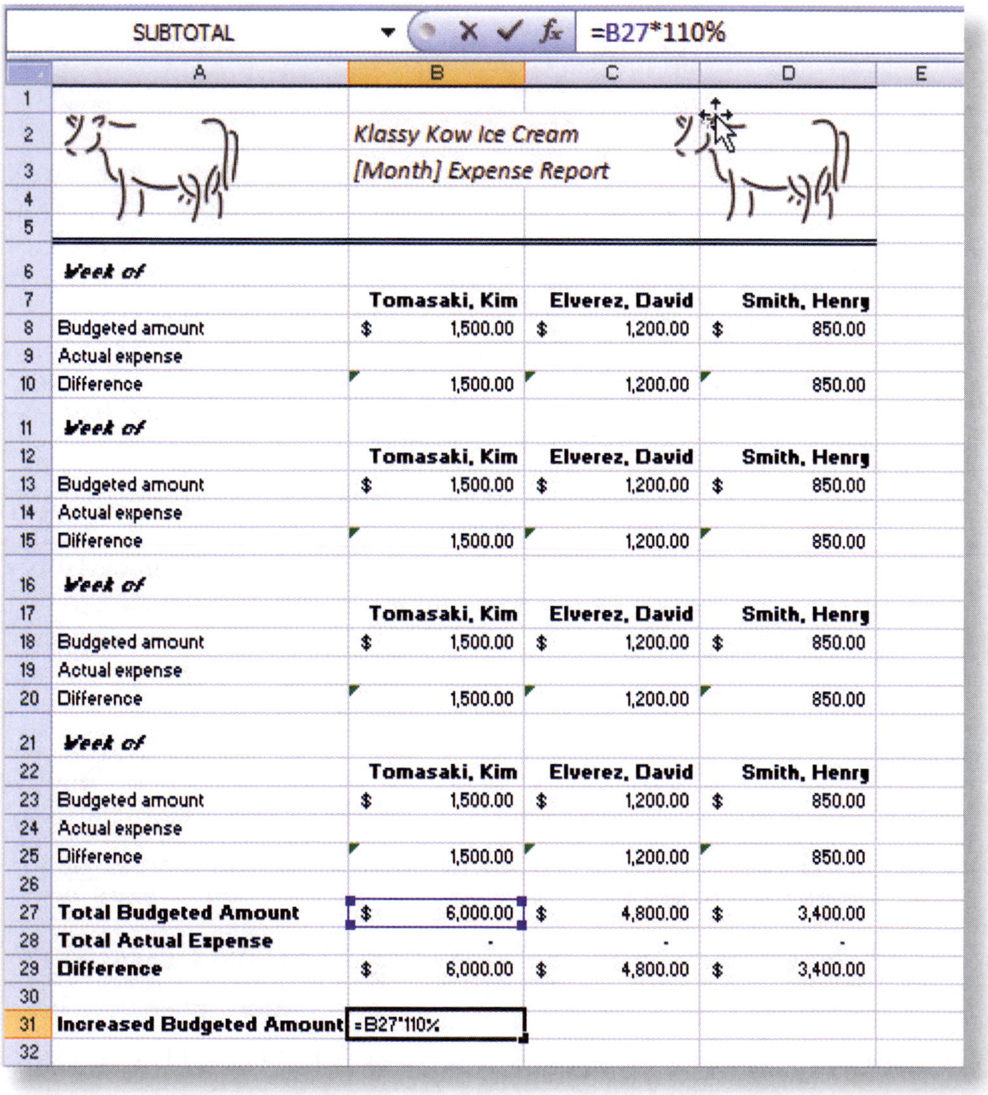

	A	B	C	D	E
1					
2		Klassy Kow Ice Cream			
3		[Month] Expense Report			
4					
5					
6	Week of				
7		Tomasaki, Kim	Elverez, David	Smith, Henry	
8	Budgeted amount	$ 1,500.00	$ 1,200.00	$ 850.00	
9	Actual expense				
10	Difference	1,500.00	1,200.00	850.00	
11	Week of				
12		Tomasaki, Kim	Elverez, David	Smith, Henry	
13	Budgeted amount	$ 1,500.00	$ 1,200.00	$ 850.00	
14	Actual expense				
15	Difference	1,500.00	1,200.00	850.00	
16	Week of				
17		Tomasaki, Kim	Elverez, David	Smith, Henry	
18	Budgeted amount	$ 1,500.00	$ 1,200.00	$ 850.00	
19	Actual expense				
20	Difference	1,500.00	1,200.00	850.00	
21	Week of				
22		Tomasaki, Kim	Elverez, David	Smith, Henry	
23	Budgeted amount	$ 1,500.00	$ 1,200.00	$ 850.00	
24	Actual expense				
25	Difference	1,500.00	1,200.00	850.00	
26					
27	Total Budgeted Amount	$ 6,000.00	$ 4,800.00	$ 3,400.00	
28	Total Actual Expense	-	-	-	
29	Difference	$ 6,000.00	$ 4,800.00	$ 3,400.00	
30					
31	Increased Budgeted Amount	=B27*110%			
32					

Figure 5-4
Editing a formula in the formula bar
KlassyKow.xltx
Expenses sheet

4. Press Ctrl+Enter. The new total ($6,600) is calculated.
5. Copy cell B31 to cells C31:D31.

Exercise 5-6   CREATE DIVISION FORMULAS

If you select a range before keying data, you can press Enter to move from one cell to the next in top-to-bottom, left-to-right order.

1. Select cells B9:D9.

2. Key **1000** and press Enter.

3. Key **950** and press Enter.

4. Key **725** and press Enter. As you fill in the amounts, the difference is calculated.

5. Select cells B14:D14 and key these values:

   1300   **1250**   **925**

6. Key these values in cells B19:D19 and cells B24:C24. The totals are calculated in rows 28 and 29 as you key the values:

   900   **850**   **625**
   1000   **750**   **575**

7. Click cell B30 and key **=** to start a formula.

8. Click cell B28 and key **/** for division. Dividing the actual amount (cell B28) by the budget amount (cell B27) determines the percent actual expenses are of the budget amount.

9. Click cell B27 and press Enter. The result is formatted as a decimal.

Exercise 5-7   APPLY THE PERCENT STYLE AND INCREASE DECIMAL POSITIONS

Excel converts a decimal to a percent when you apply the Percent Style. It multiplies the decimal value by 100. For example, 0.7 is 0.7*100 or 70%.

1. Click cell B30. In the **Number** group on the **Home** tab, click the Percent Style button %. The percent symbol is added, and the value is converted.

2. Click the Increase Decimal button two times. A decimal position is added with each click.

3. Copy the formula in cell B30 to cells C30:D30.

4. In cell A30, key **Actual as % of Budget** and press Enter. Because three rows precede this row, the format of those rows is applied.

5. Press Ctrl+Home. Press F12 and save the workbook as *[your initials]5-7* in a new folder for Lesson 5.

6. Close the workbook.

Using Order of Precedence in a Formula

Excel follows mathematical rules as it calculates a formula. These rules include an *order of precedence,* sometimes called *order of operation* or *math hierarchy.* The order of precedence determines what part of a formula is calculated first. Generally, a formula is calculated from left to right, but some arithmetic operators take priority over others. For example, if you key a formula with both a multiplication symbol (*) and an addition symbol (+), Excel calculates the multiplication first even if it is the second symbol as you move from left to right. You can override the order of precedence by enclosing parts of the formula within parentheses.

When two operators have the same order of precedence—for example, multiplication and division—the operations are performed from left to right (see Table 5-1).

Figure 5-5 shows three formulas with the same values and the same operators. The results differ depending on the placement of the parentheses.

Figure 5-5

Parentheses change the order of operations

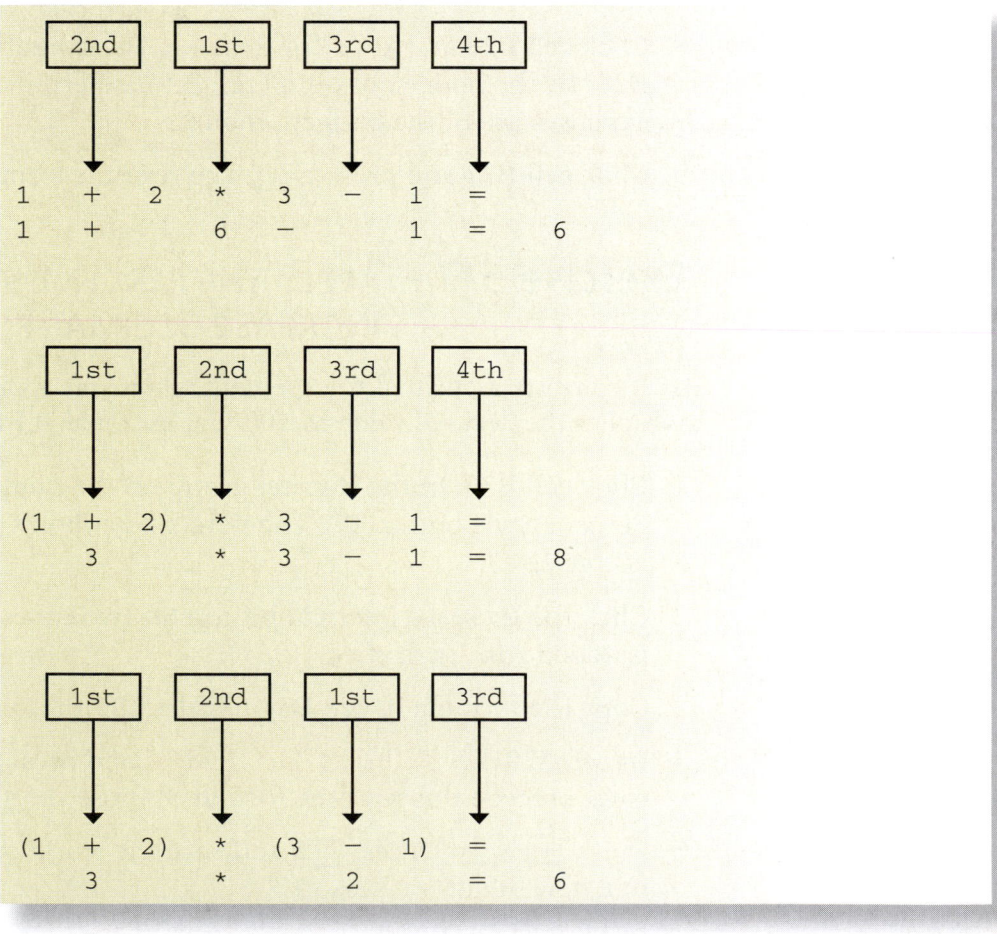

TABLE 5-1 Operator Precedence in Excel

Operator		Precedence Description
^	1st	Exponentiation
*	2nd	Multiplication
/	2nd	Division
+	3rd	Addition
−	3rd	Subtraction
&	4th	Concatenation (symbol used to join text strings)
=	5th	Equal to
<	5th	Less than
>	5th	Greater than

Exercise 5-8   USE MULTIPLICATION AND ADDITION IN A FORMULA

TIP

You can memorize the order of precedence for parentheses and the first five operators: "<u>P</u>lease <u>e</u>xcuse <u>m</u>y <u>d</u>ear <u>A</u>unt <u>S</u>ally" (parentheses, exponentiation, multiplication, division, addition, subtraction).

In this exercise, you use a formula that seems logical to determine a dollar amount of sales. You will see, however, that it results in an incorrect total.

1. Open **DrinkSize**. Click cell E15. You need to total the items for each state and multiply by the price.

2. Key **=** and click cell C6, the price for a 16-ounce soda.

3. Key ***** to multiply the price by the number sold.

4. Select cell D6 and key **+**.

5. Click cell E6, key **+**, click cell F6, key **+**, and click cell G6. This part of the formula adds state unit totals.

6. Press Enter. The result looks reasonable, but it is wrong.

7. Click cell E15. The formula includes a multiplication symbol, so cell C6 is first multiplied by cell D6. Then the other cells are added to the result of C6*D6.

REVIEW

AutoCalculate results are visible in the status bar.

8. Right-click the AutoCalculate area and verify that **Sum** is selected.

9. Select cells D6:G6. Check AutoCalculate for the sum of 30,000.

10. Click cell J6 and key **=** to start a formula. You are temporarily using this empty cell to calculate the correct amount.

11. Click cell C6, key ***30000**, and press ⌷Enter⌷. This is the correct amount—the total number sold (30,000) multiplied by the price.

12. Delete the contents of cell J6.

Exercise 5-9   SET ORDER OF PRECEDENCE

1. Double-click cell E15 to start Edit mode. The formula is in the cell and in the formula bar. The referenced cells are outlined in color.

2. In the worksheet cell, click in front or to the left of **D6**.

3. Key a left parenthesis **(** in front of **D6**.

4. Press ⌷End⌷. The insertion point moves to the end of the formula.

5. Key a right parenthesis **)**.

6. Press ⌷Enter⌷. These parentheses force the additions to be calculated first. That result is multiplied by the value in cell C6.

Figure 5-6
Changing the order of precedence
DrinkSize.xlsx
DrinkSales sheet

	A	B	C	D	E	F	G	H
1								
2			*Klassy Kow Ice Cream Shops*					
3			*Comparison of Drink Sizes Sold*					
4			*Count of Items for June*					
5			**Price**	**California**	**Washington**	**Oregon**	**Nevada**	
6		16 oz. Soda	$0.89	8,000	6,000	5,000	11,000	
7		32 oz. Soda	$1.59	12,000	7,500	4,000	15,000	
8		12 oz. Coffee	$1.29	7,500	8,000	5,000	11,500	
9		20 oz. Coffee	$1.59	5,400	8,500	5,500	16,000	
10		Tea	$1.29	2,500	2,000	2,300	4,000	
11								
12								
13								
14				**Total Dollar Values Sold**				
15				16 oz. Soda	=C6*(D6+E6+F6+G6)			
16				32 oz. Soda				
17				12 oz. Coffee				
18				20 oz. Coffee				
19				Tea				
20								
21								

7. Apply Accounting format to cell E15 but show no decimals.

8. Copy the formula in cell E15 to cells E16:E19.

9. Click cell E16. Notice that the formula multiplies the price in cell C7 by the values in row 7 for a 32-ounce soda. This is correct.

10. Widen columns as needed. Press Ctrl + Home.

11. Save the workbook as *[your initials]5-9* in your Lesson 5 folder.

12. Close the workbook.

Using Relative, Absolute, and Mixed References

When you copy a formula, Excel adjusts the formula relative to the row or column where the copy is located. This is known as a *relative reference*.

There are situations, however, when you want Excel to copy the formula exactly. A formula with an *absolute reference* does not change when it is copied into another cell. An absolute reference uses two dollar signs ($) in its address, one in front of the column reference and one in front of the row reference. $B$5 is an absolute reference to cell B5.

Excel can also use a *mixed reference,* in which a dollar sign is placed in front of the reference for either the row or the column. In a mixed reference, part of the cell reference is adjusted when a formula is copied; the other is not. $B5 is a mixed reference with an absolute reference to column B but a relative reference to row 5.

Dollar signs used in a cell address do not signify currency. They are a reserved symbol used to mark the type of cell reference.

TABLE 5-2 Cell References

Address	Type of Reference	
B1	Relative	
$B$1	Absolute	
$B1	Mixed	Column letter is absolute; row number is relative.
B$1	Mixed	Row number is absolute; column letter is relative.

Exercise 5-10   USE A LINE BREAK

You can place labels on two lines in a cell by pressing Alt + Enter at the point where you want the second line to start. This is known as a *line break* in a cell. You often need to adjust the row height or the column width if you use line breaks.

1. Open **ShopDownTime**.

2. In cell G5, key **Cost per** and press Alt + Enter.

3. Key **Down Hour** and press Enter.

4. Adjust the column width so that the label splits only between "per" and "Down."

5. Click cell G5 and look at the formula bar. It is not tall enough to show the complete label.

6. Rest the mouse pointer on the splitter bar above the column headings.

Figure 5-7
Sizing the formula bar
ShopDownTime.xlsx
AllStates sheet

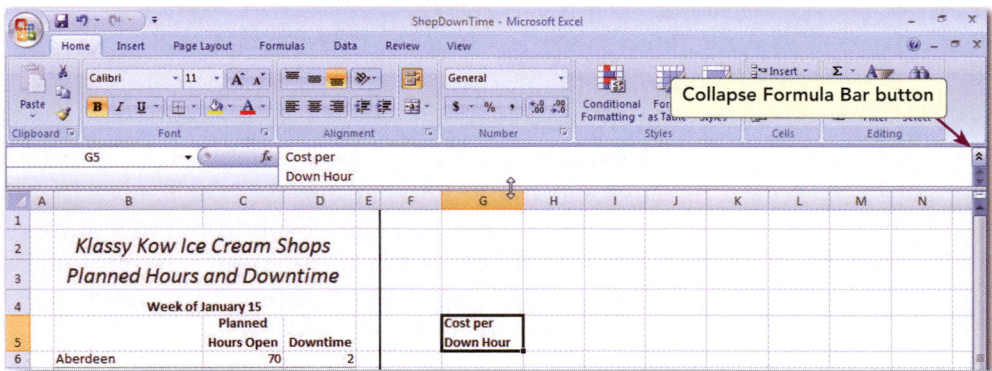

7. Drag down until you see the label in the formula bar. The formula bar occupies more space and your data rows occupy less.

8. In cell G6, key **25** and format it as Accounting with two decimals.

Exercise 5-11   COPY A FORMULA WITH A RELATIVE REFERENCE

1. Insert a column at column E. In cell E5, key **Cost**. Its formatting matches the preceding columns.

2. Click cell E6. Key **=** to start the formula.

3. Click cell D6, key *****, and then click cell H6. This formula uses relative references.

4. Press Enter. The result is $50.

5. Drag the Fill handle for cell E6 to copy the formula to cell E25. The copied formulas show a dash for zero and an error triangle. The cells that should show a total cost do not.

6. Click each copied cell in column E and look in the formula bar. Each time the formula went down a row, the row reference adjusted. That works for column D, but not for column H.

7. Click the Undo button.

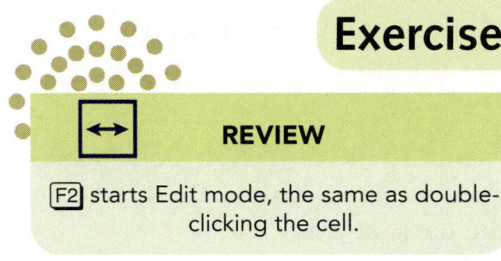

Exercise 5-12 CREATE A FORMULA WITH AN ABSOLUTE REFERENCE

REVIEW

F2 starts Edit mode, the same as double-clicking the cell.

Because absolute references are common to many calculations, Excel has a quick way of adding dollar signs to a cell reference. It's the F4 key.

1. Click cell E6 and press F2.

2. Click between **H** and **6** in the worksheet cell.

3. Press F4. Two dollar signs are inserted, one before **H** and one before **6**.

Figure 5-8
Making a cell reference absolute
ShopDownTime.xlsx
AllStates sheet

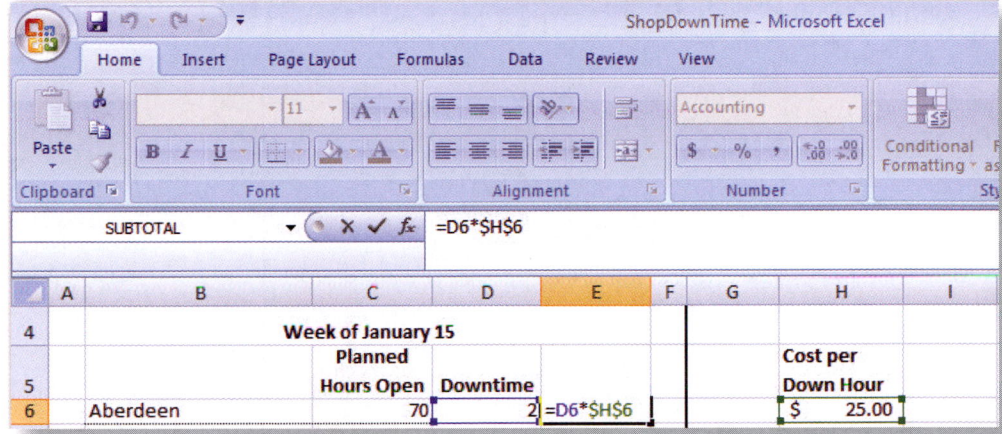

4. Press F. The dollar sign appears only with **6**.

5. Press F again. The dollar sign appears only with **H**.

6. Press F again. The dollar signs are removed.

7. Press F once more. The absolute reference appears again.

8. Press Ctrl+Enter. Look in the formula bar.

9. Use the Fill handle for cell E6 to copy the formula into cells E7:E37.

10. Click each copied cell and look in the formula bar. Cell H6 did not change in any of the copies.

11. Select cells E6:E37 and apply a dashed middle and bottom horizontal border.

Exercise 5-13 USE A COLOR SCALE

In addition to data bars, the Conditional Formatting command includes color scales. This command applies fill to the range based on the values. You can use two- or three-color arrangements.

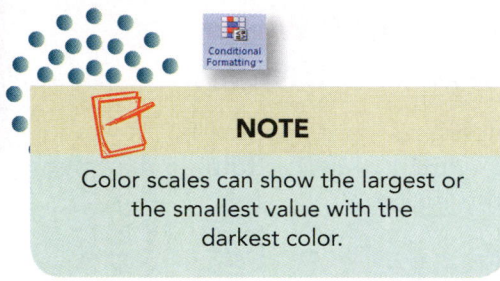

NOTE

Color scales can show the largest or the smallest value with the darkest color.

1. Select cells E6:E37. In the **Styles** group on the **Home** tab, click the Conditional Formatting button.

2. Choose **Color Scales** and the **Red – Yellow Color Scale** in the second row, second icon. This scale shows the highest values in the darkest color.

Figure 5-9
Choosing a color scale
ShopDownTime.xlsx
AllStates sheet

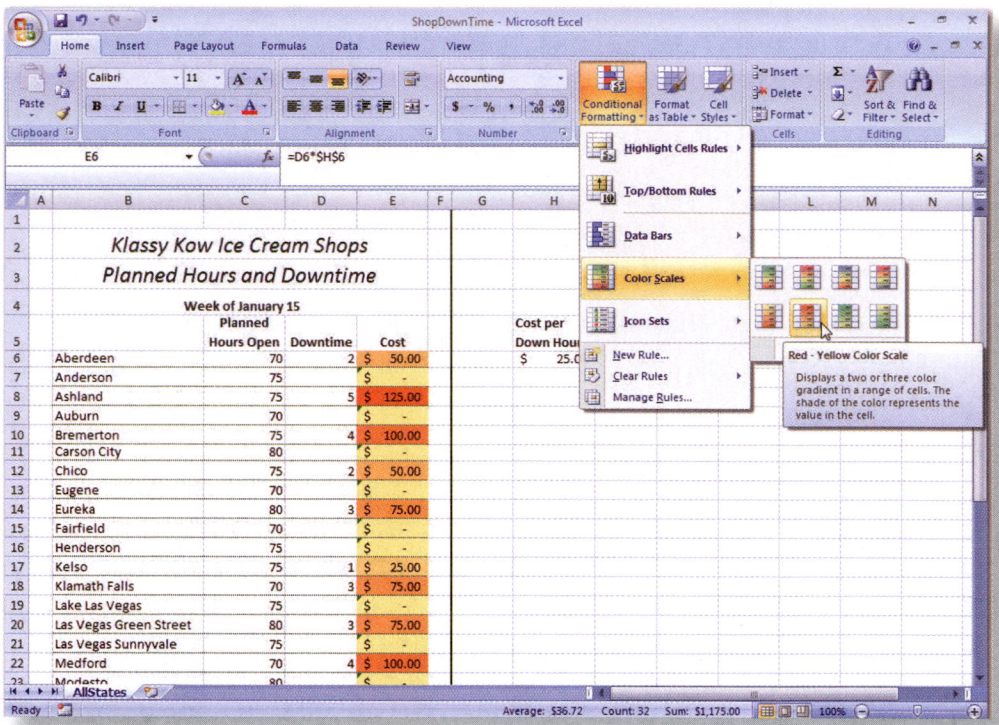

3. Click in column H to better see the color scale.

4. Select cells E6:E37 and click the Conditional Formatting button.

5. Choose **Manage Rules**. The Conditional Formatting Rules Manager dialog box opens.

6. Click **Edit rule**. The Edit Formatting Rule dialog box is the same as the one for data bars.

7. Choose a different light and dark color from the same hue.

8. Click **OK** twice to see your changes.

9. Press Ctrl + Home. Save the workbook as ***[your initials]*5-13** in your folder.

10. Close the workbook.

11. At the right end of the formula bar, click the Collapse Formula Bar button. The formula bar collapses to its default height.

Exercise 5-14   USE MIXED REFERENCES

A multiplication table will be printed as a promotional item and posted on the company's Web site. This multiplication table uses mixed references.

1. Open **MultTable**.

2. Set the Zoom percent to a size that lets you see the entire worksheet.

3. Click cell B3. You want to show the result of multiplying 1 by 1 in cell B3.

4. Key **=** and click cell A3. This will be a mixed reference.

5. Press F4 three times to show **$A3**. This part of the formula will always use column A, but the row will change.

6. Press ***** and click cell B2.

7. Press F4 two times to show **B$2**. This part of the formula will always use row 2, but the column will change.

Figure 5-10
Mixed reference
formula
MultTable.xlsx
Sheet1 sheet

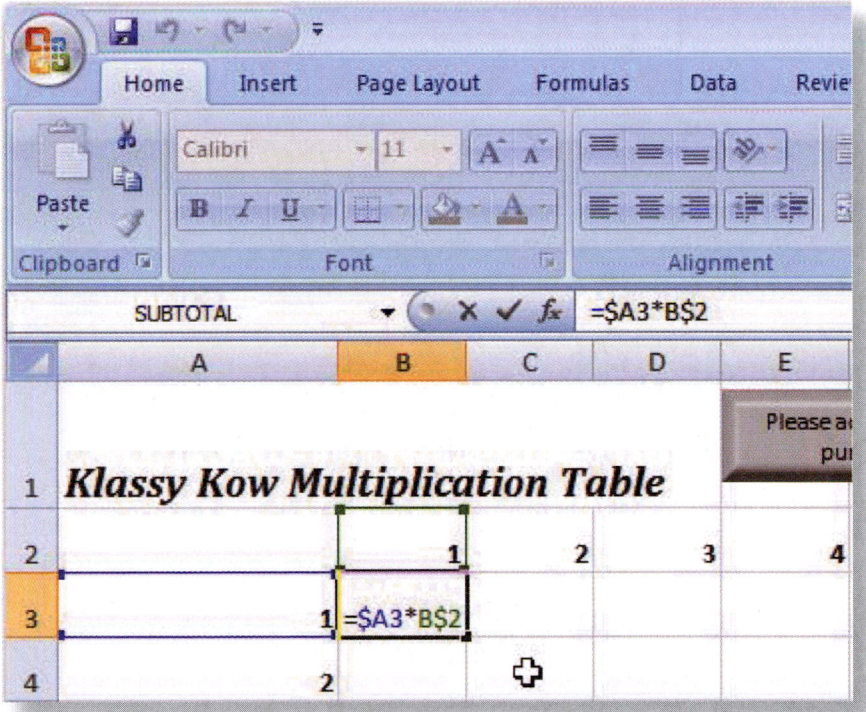

8. Press Ctrl + Enter.

9. Use the Fill handle to copy cell B3 to cell K3.

10. Use the Fill handle to copy cells B3:K3 down to row 12.

Excel 2007

Exercise 5-15   ADD BORDERS AND FILL FOR PRINTING

Borders and fill will make it easier to follow numbers across a wide layout.

1. Select cells A2:K12 and press Ctrl + 1.
2. Click the **Border** tab.
3. In the **Border** preset group, click the Top Border button.
4. Click the Middle Horizontal Border and then the Bottom Border buttons. Click the Left Border and the Right Border buttons. Click **OK**.

Figure 5-11
Setting top, middle, bottom, left, and right borders

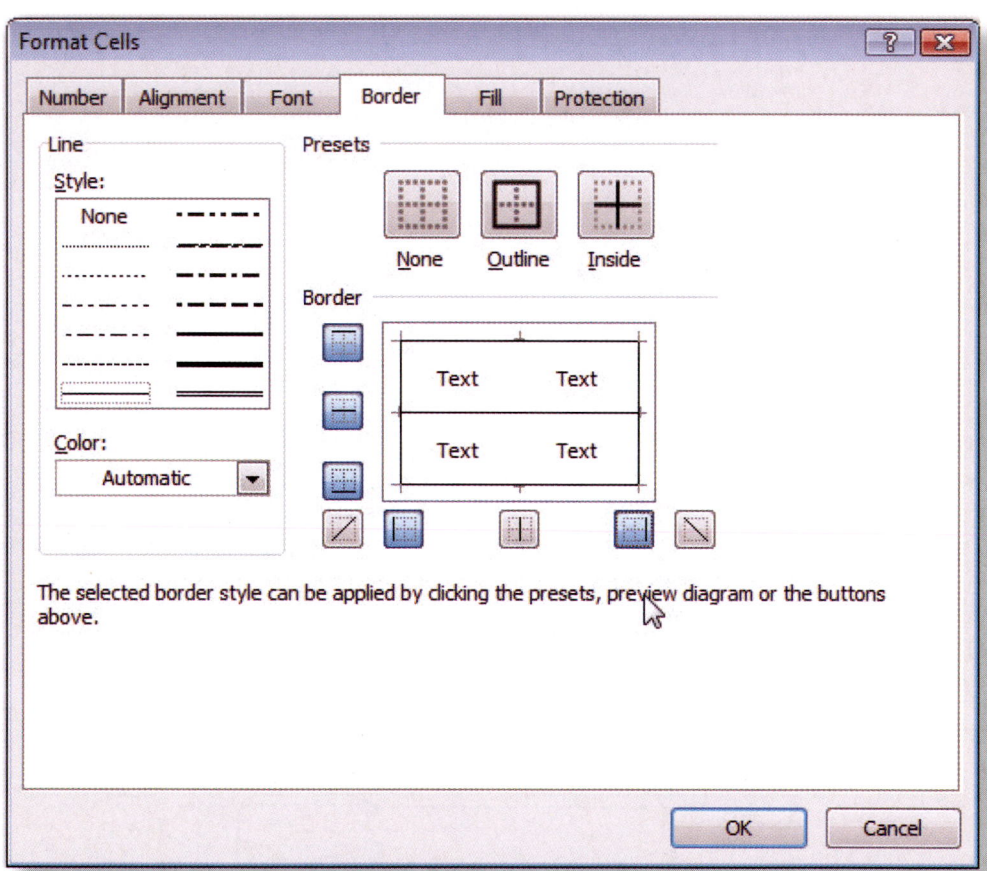

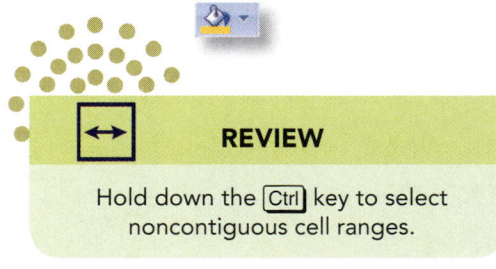

REVIEW

Hold down the Ctrl key to select noncontiguous cell ranges.

5. Select cells A2:K2 and cells A3:A12.
6. Click the arrow next to the Fill Color button.
7. Choose **White, Background 1, Darker 25%** in the first column.
8. Press Ctrl + Home.

Working with the Page Layout Tab

There are many options for how to print a worksheet as well as several ways to change these options. From the Page Layout tab, you can:

- Change margins.

- Change the page orientation.

- Choose a paper size.

- Set a print area or print titles.

- Scale the worksheet to fit the page or print larger than the page.

- Change page breaks.

- Add a background image.

Page orientation determines if the worksheet prints landscape or portrait. The default is *portrait* orientation, one that is taller than it is wide.

Scaling commands enable you to set a size percentage for the printed page. This size can be smaller or larger.

Exercise 5-16   CHANGE PAGE ORIENTATION

Many worksheets are too wide to fit portrait orientation on 8½ by 11 inch paper. A *landscape* orientation is horizontal—the page is wider than it is tall.

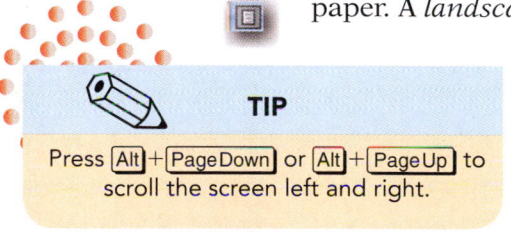

TIP

Press Alt + PageDown or Alt + PageUp to scroll the screen left and right.

1. Click the Page Layout View button in the status bar. The worksheet does not fit on a single page in portrait orientation. You can see in the status bar (at the left) that the worksheet requires more than one page.

2. Click the Zoom Out button to reach **80%**. Excel splits the worksheet between columns.

3. Click the **Page Layout** command tab.

4. In the **Page Setup** group, click the Page Orientation button . Choose **Landscape**. The worksheet fits on a single page in landscape orientation.

Exercise 5-17   CHANGE SCALING AND PAGE MARGINS

You can set a worksheet to print at 50 percent of its size or 150 percent of its size. You might need to do this if you want to print the worksheet on a 5- by 7-inch card or if you want to enlarge it for a special display. When you enlarge a worksheet, the output device will split the pages between columns so that you can tape the parts together.

You change margins by dragging the margin markers in Page Layout View. If you need to set a precise margin, you can use the Margins tab in the Page Setup dialog box to key a specific setting.

1. In the **Scale to Fit** group, double-click **100** and key **75**. Click any cell or press Enter. The worksheet is reduced to 75 percent of its normal size. This is only an output adjustment and does not change any format settings.

Figure 5-12
Scaling the worksheet
MultTable.xlsx
Sheet1 sheet

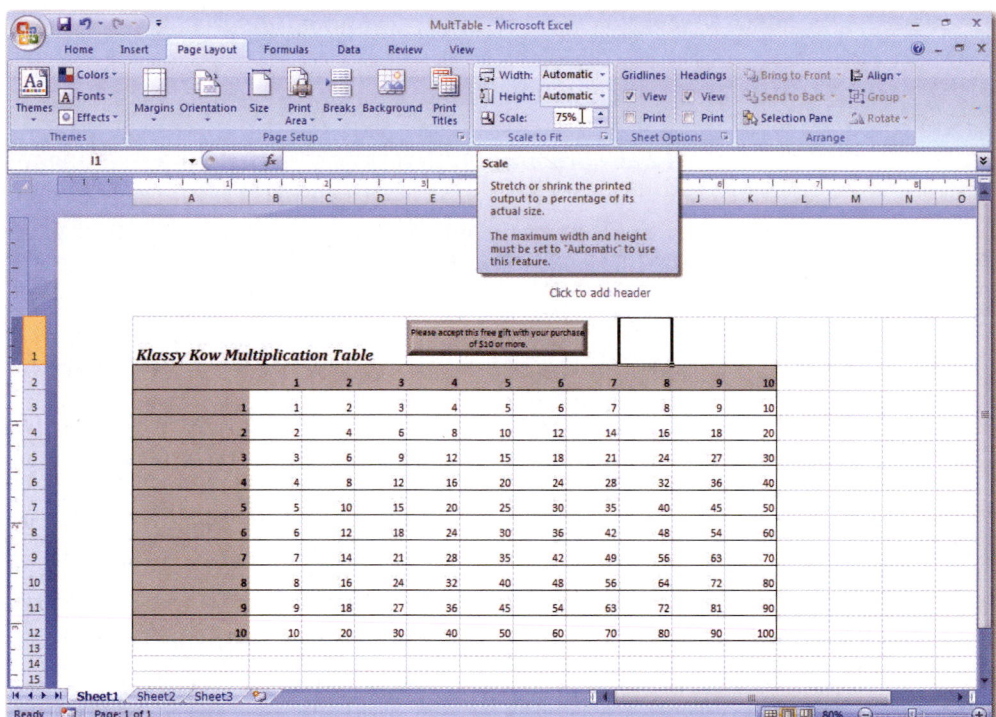

2. In the **Page Setup** group, click the Margins button . Choose **Custom Margins**. The Page Setup dialog box opens with the **Margins** tab active.

3. Double-click in the **Left** box and key **2.25**.

4. Double-click in the **Right** box and key **1**. Click **OK**.

5. Zoom out to **70%**.

6. In the **Sheet Options** group, click to deselect **Gridlines: View** and **Headings: View**. This represents how the worksheet will print.

7. Save the workbook as *[your initials]5-17* in your folder.

Exercise 5-18   COPY A WORKSHEET AND DISPLAY FORMULAS

You can easily review and troubleshoot formulas by displaying them all at once on screen. A copy of the worksheet with formulas visible also provides clear documentation for your work.

In order to keep the original version of your worksheet, you'll make a copy and show formulas on the copy.

1. Rename **Sheet1** as **PrintTable**.

2. Right-click the **PrintTable** tab and choose **Move or Copy**.

3. In the Move or Copy dialog box, click to select **Create a copy**. Click **OK**. The copy is named **PrintTable (2)** and is inserted in front of the original.

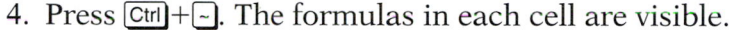

4. Press $\boxed{\text{Ctrl}}$+$\boxed{\sim}$. The formulas in each cell are visible.

5. In the **Sheet Options** group on the **Page Layout** tab, click to select **Gridlines: View**, **Gridlines: Print**, **Headings: View**, and **Headings: Print**.

6. Click the column A heading. Scroll right and hold down $\boxed{\text{Shift}}$ while clicking the column K heading. All the columns are selected.

7. Double-click the border between columns K and L. Excel AutoFits each column to its longest entry.

8. In the **Scale to Fit** group, double-click **75**, key **100**, and click any cell. The worksheet occupies two pages, because formulas require more space than values.

9. Click the Margins button. Choose **Custom Margins**. Double-click in the **Left** box and key **.5**. Press $\boxed{\text{Tab}}$ and key **.5** in the **Right** box.

10. Click the **Page** tab. In the **Scaling** section, click to select **Fit to**.

11. Choose **1 page(s) wide** by **1 tall**.

12. Click **OK**. Excel fits the worksheet to a single landscape page with 0.5-inch left and right margins (see Figure 5-13 on the next page).

NOTE

The tilde (~) is located at the top left of the keyboard. You can display formulas by clicking the Microsoft Office Button and choosing **Excel Options, Advanced** pane (Display Options for this Worksheet).

NOTE

Column headings are above the header area.

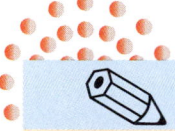

TIP

You can set your own scaling percentage or choose the **Fit to** option.

Figure 5-13
Formulas visible
5-17.xlsx
PrintTable (2) sheet

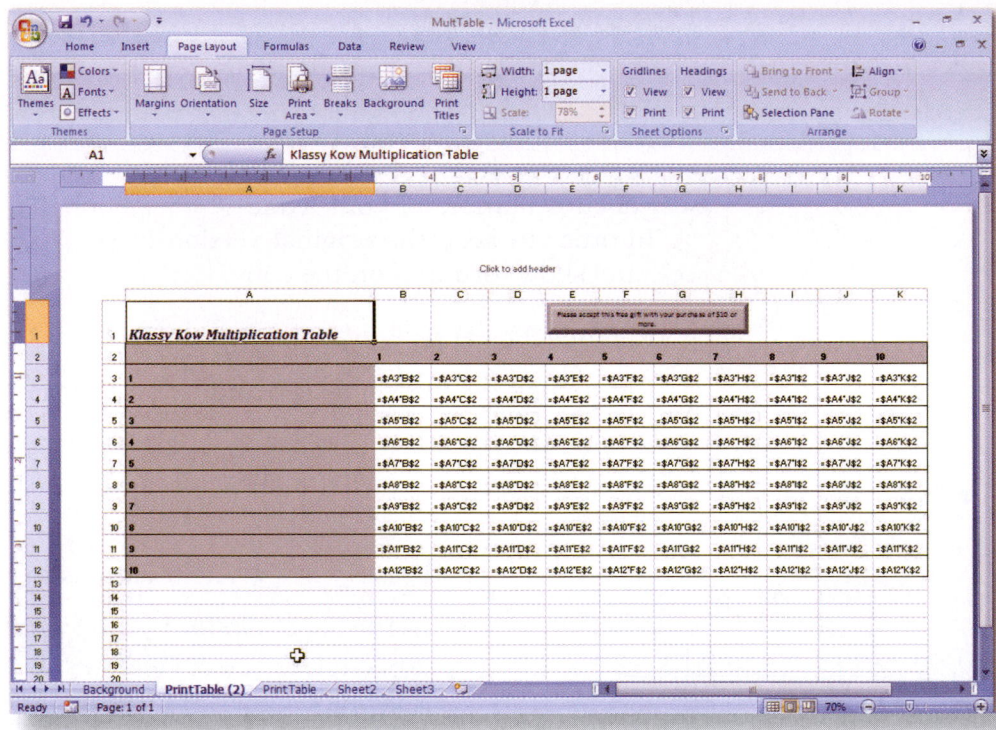

13. Press Ctrl+Home. Save the workbook as *[your initials]***5-18** in your folder.

Exercise 5-19   ADD A BACKGROUND

A *background* is an image that appears on screen and on the Web. It fills or spans the entire worksheet. It does not print.

1. Right-click the **PrintTable** tab and choose **Move or Copy**.

2. In the Move or Copy dialog box, click to select **Create a copy**. Click **OK**. The copy is named **PrintTable (3)**.

3. Rename **PrintTable (3)** as **Background**.

4. Click the Normal button on the status bar.

5. On the **Page Layout** tab, click to select **Gridlines: View** and **Headings: View**.

6. Click the Background button in the **Page Setup** group. The Sheet Background dialog box opens.

7. Navigate to the folder with the **KKBack** file. Click to select the file.

Figure 5-14
Using a sheet
background
5-18.xlsx
Background sheet

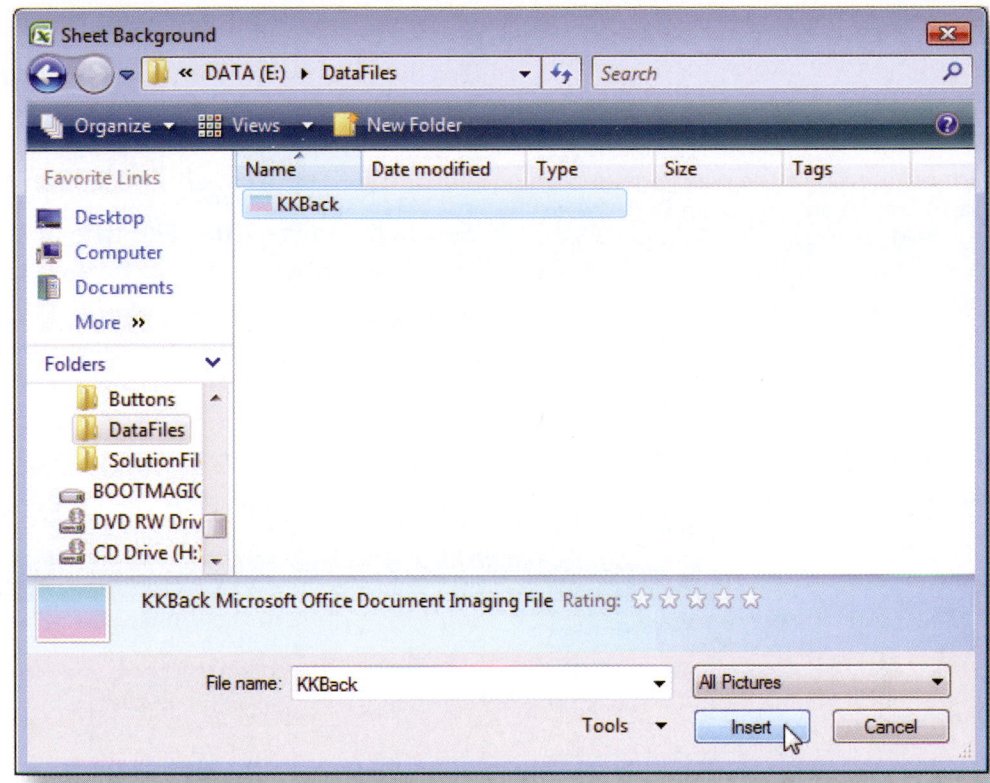

8. Click **Insert**. The background is a blend of colors and fills the worksheet.

9. Select cells A2:K2 and cells A3:A12.

10. Click the **Home** tab. Click the arrow with the Fill Color button and choose **No Fill**. You don't need a fill color with the background.

11. Press Ctrl + Home.

12. Press Ctrl + P. The Print dialog box opens.

13. Press Alt + W to open Print Preview. Backgrounds do not print; they are visible on screen and on a Web site.

14. Close Print Preview.

Exercise 5-20   SAVE A WORKBOOK AS A WEB PAGE

You can save an Excel workbook as an HTML file so that it can be viewed on the World Wide Web. An *HTML* file uses *Hypertext Markup Language,* a widely used and recognized format for Web pages. Web pages are saved with an **.htm** extension. You can save the entire workbook or an individual worksheet as a Web page. When you save the entire workbook, the Web page shows the worksheet tabs.

Excel 2007

NOTE

Do not use Single File Web Page to save a Web page unless you are familiar with HTML and can edit it on your own.

1. Press F12. The Save As dialog box opens.

2. Click the arrow for **Save as type** and choose **Web Page**.

3. Set the **Save in** folder to your Lesson 5 folder.

4. In the **Save** area, choose **Entire Workbook**.

5. Click **Change Title**. The title appears in the title bar of the browser.

6. Key **Klassy Kow Multiplication Table** and click **OK**.

Figure 5-15
Saving a Web page

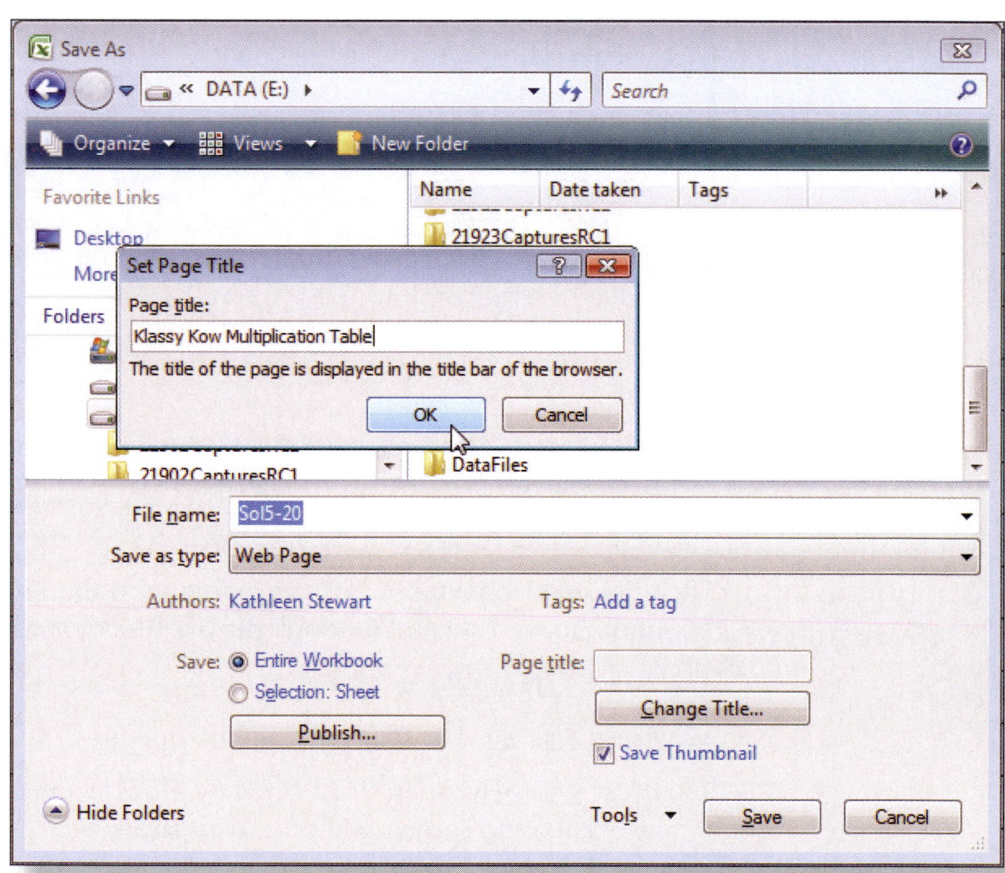

7. Name the file *[your initials]5-20*. Click **Save**. If a message box opens about incompatible features, choose **Yes**.

8. Close the workbook.

9. Start your Web browser and maximize the window.

10. Press Ctrl+O. Click **Browse** and navigate to your folder. Find and click *[your initials]5-20* and click **Open**. Click **OK**.

11. Look for the title and at each of the tabs in the browser.

 12. Click the Close button to close the browser.

Using Online Help

USE HELP TO VIEW ADDITIONAL INFORMATION ABOUT FORMULAS

1. In a new workbook, press F1.

2. In the Search box, key **create formula** and press Enter.

3. Find and review topics to learn more about building formulas. Read the help information.

4. Close the Help window.

Lesson 5 Summary

- Use a template to create workbooks that use the same labels and other basic information on a routine basis.

- Templates can include labels, values, formatting, formulas, and pictures.

- You can edit a formula in the formula bar and within the cell in Edit mode.

- The Percent Style converts a decimal value to its percent equivalent.

- In calculating formulas, Excel follows mathematical order of precedence.

- You can establish a different order of precedence in a formula by keying parentheses around the calculations that you want performed first.

- Excel has relative, absolute, and mixed references. These references determine what happens when a formula is copied.

- A color scale is a conditional formatting rule that fills a range of cells with various intensities of a color based on the values.

- A portrait orientation prints a vertical page. A landscape page prints a horizontal page.

- The Scale to Fit group on the Page Layout tab enables you to print the worksheet in a reduced or enlarged size. You can also choose to have Excel fit the worksheet on a page.

- To set a precise margin, use the Margins tab in the Page Setup dialog box.
- You can print a worksheet with formulas displayed for documentation or help in locating problems.
- You can add an image as a sheet background for display on a Web page.
- You can save a workbook as a Web page for viewing in most browsers.

LESSON 5		Command Summary	
Feature	**Button**	**Task Path**	**Keyboard**
Absolute reference			F4
Background	Background	Page Layout, Page Setup	
Collapse formula bar	⌃		Ctrl + Shift + U
Color scale	Conditional Formatting	Home, Styles, Conditional Formatting	
Copy sheet		Home, Cells, Format, Move or Copy Sheet	
Show/hide formulas	Show Formulas	Formulas, Formula Auditing	Ctrl + ~
Edit mode			F2
Fit to page	Height: Automatic / Width: Automatic	Page Layout, Scale to Fit	
Increase Decimal	⬅.0 .00	Home, Number	Ctrl + 1
Margins	Margins	Page Layout, Page Setup	
New, from template		Microsoft Office, New	
Page Orientation	Orientation	Page Layout, Page Setup	
Percent Style	%	Home, Number	Ctrl + 1
Scaling		Page Layout, Scale to Fit	
Web page		Microsoft Office, Save As	F12

Concepts Review

True/False Questions

Each of the following statements is either true or false. Indicate your choice by circling T or F.

T F   1. A template opens as a new workbook with the template name and a letter.

T F   2. You can apply one-, two-, and three-color scales to a range.

T F   3. The multiplication symbol in a formula is /.

T F   4. To multiply by a percent, you must key the decimal equivalent of the percent.

T F   5. You can control the order of precedence in a formula with parentheses.

T F   6. Division is calculated before addition in a formula without parentheses.

T F   7. Column widths adjust automatically when you display formulas.

T F   8. An absolute reference does not adjust when the formula is copied to another cell.

Short Answer Questions

Write the correct answer in the space provided.

1. What is the keyboard shortcut to display or hide formulas?

_____

2. Which page orientation is taller than it is wide?

_____

3. How would the cell reference **$F$3** be described?

_____

4. What are the four arithmetic symbols that can be used in a formula?

_____

5. What type of operation is being performed in the formula = A4*B4?

_____

6. What command option allows you to print a worksheet on a smaller piece of paper?

_____

7. What term describes a model workbook used as the basis for other workbooks?

_____

8. How can you start Edit mode to edit a formula?

_____

Critical Thinking

Answer these questions on a separate page. There are no right or wrong answers. Support your answers with examples from your own experience, if possible.

1. Why is it helpful to adjust the Zoom percentage while working? How is this different from scaling the worksheet?

2. Why is it necessary to have an absolute cell reference in some formulas? Why can't all formulas use relative references?

Skills Review

Exercise 5-21

Use a template to create a new workbook. Build addition and subtraction formulas.

1. Create a workbook from a template by following these steps:
   a. Click the Microsoft Office Button 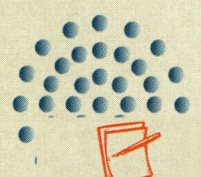 and choose **New**.
   b. Click **My templates**.
   c. Choose **ChkBk** and click **OK**.

> **NOTE**
>
> Copy the **ChkBk** template file into the appropriate folder for your computer before starting this exercise.

2. In cell A4, key today's date in mm/dd/yy format. Key tomorrow's date in cell A5 in the same format. Adjust the column width if necessary.

3. Press F12 and save the workbook as *[your initials]*5-21 in your Lesson 5 folder.

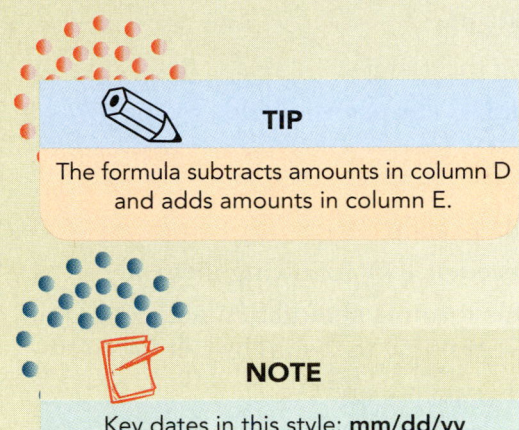

TIP

The formula subtracts amounts in column D and adds amounts in column E.

NOTE

Key dates in this style: **mm/dd/yy**

4. Build addition and subtraction formulas by following these steps:

   a. Click cell F5. Key **=** to start a formula.

   b. Click cell F4 and key **–** for subtraction.

   c. Click cell D5 and key **+** for addition.

   d. Click cell E5. Press Enter and ignore any error triangles.

5. Copy the formula in cell F5 to cells F6:F15. The results are all the same at this point.

6. Key the following information, starting in cell A6.

Figure 5-16

		Date	Check #	Payee	Credit Amount	Deposit
6		[2 days from today]	1002	Helpful Hand Computers	1250	
7		[3 days from today]				2500
8		[4 days from today]	1003	Greenberg and Whitefield	575	
9		[5 days from today]	1004	[your school name]	435	
10		[6 days from today]				1200

7. Hide rows 11 through 15.

8. Add a footer with your name at the left and the filename at the right.

9. In Page Layout View, adjust the margins if necessary to fit the worksheet on a single portrait page.

10. Press Ctrl + Home. Prepare and submit your work. Save and close the workbook.

Exercise 5-22

Build multiplication and division formulas. Set the order of precedence.

1. Open **TasteTest**. Save the workbook as *[your initials]*5-22 in your Lesson 5 folder.

2. Build a multiplication formula by following these steps:

   a. Click cell F4 and key **=**. Click cell D4. This is a taste-tester's regular hourly pay rate.

   b. Key **+**. Click cell E4. The tester receives a holiday rate increase, added to the regular pay rate.

   c. Key *****. Click cell C4. The hourly rate is multiplied by the number of hours worked to determine pay.

   d. Press Enter.

NOTE

This pay formula is not correct. You will correct it later.

3. Copy the formula in cell F4 to cells F5:F8.

4. Build a division formula by following these steps:

   a. Click cell H4 and key **=**. Click cell F4. The pay is divided by the number of items tested.

   b. Key **/**. Click cell G4. Press [Enter].

   c. Copy the formula to cells H5:H8.

5. Set the order of precedence by following these steps:

   a. Click cell F4. This formula should first add cells D4 and E4 and then multiply that sum by cell C4.

   b. Press [F2]. Click between **=** and **D**.

   c. Key **(** and click before *****. Key **)** and press [Enter].

   d. Recopy the formula in cell F4 to cells F5:F8. Column H is recalculated.

6. Apply the Accounting format to cells D4:F8 and cells H4:H8.

7. Apply bold to cells A3:H3 and use Wrap Text. Center-align these labels. Make row 3 **45.00 (60 pixels)** tall.

8. Make column A **13.57 (100 pixels)** wide. AutoFit the other columns.

9. Center the labels in rows 1:2 over the worksheet data. Apply a medium tint of one of the accent colors to these cells and **Outside Borders**.

10. Select cells A9:H9 and apply a **Bottom Border**. Make this row **7.50 (10 pixels)** tall. Apply a **Bottom Border** to the labels in row 3 and set row 4 to a height of **20.25 (27 pixels)**.

11. Add a header with your name at the left, the filename in the center, and the date at the right. Use a left margin that allows the sheet to fit on one portrait page and makes the data appear to be horizontally centered.

12. Press [Ctrl]+[Home]. Prepare and submit your work. Save and close the workbook.

REVIEW

Multiplication is calculated before addition.

REVIEW

Use Center Across Selection to center multiple rows over data.

Exercise 5-23

Build formulas. Use an absolute reference.

1. Open **InsClaims**. Save it as *[your initials]*5-23 in your Lesson 5 folder.

2. Right-click the row 21 heading and choose **Insert**. Click the Insert Options button and choose **Format Same as Below**. A row without fill is inserted.

3. Insert two more rows without fill so that there are four empty rows above the row with solid black fill.

4. In cell B22, key **Total Number of Claims** and make it bold. If Excel copies the fill used in the rows, set the cell to use **No Fill**.

5. Build formulas by following these steps:

   a. Click cell C22. Key **=** to start the formula.

   b. Click cell C7 and click **+** to build an addition formula.

   c. Click C10 and click **+** to continue.

   d. Continue by adding each cell in column C with a value. When all cells are listed, press Enter.

6. Create similar formulas in cells D22 and E22. Center-align the results.

7. In cell B23, key **Total Processing Cost**. In cell B24, key **Single Claim Processing**. Make these labels bold.

8. In cell C24, key **15.45** and format it as Accounting.

9. Use an absolute reference in a formula by following these steps:

   a. Click cell C23. Key **=** to start the formula.

   b. Click C24 and press F4 to make it absolute.

   c. Key ***** and click cell C22. Press Ctrl+Enter.

10. Copy this formula to cells D23:E23.

11. Select all cells with currency values and apply **Currency** format from the Format Cells dialog box to show the dollar sign ($) next to the first digit.

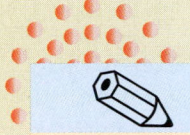

TIP

A dollar sign that is next to the first digit is known as a "floating" symbol.

12. Add a footer with your name at the left, the sheet name and the filename in the center, and the date at the right. Adjust the margins to fit the sheet to a single page.

13. Press Ctrl+Home. Prepare and submit your work. Save and close the workbook.

Exercise 5-24

Use relative, absolute, and mixed references. Change page orientation and margins. Display formulas. Save a Web page.

1. Open **Henderson** and save it as *[your initials]*5-24 in your Lesson 5 folder. Change to the **Opulent** document theme.

2. Click cell G3 and click after the **m** in **Cream** in the formula. Press Alt+Enter and then press Enter. Adjust the column width to show **Ice Cream** on one line and **Cost** on the second.

3. Center the labels in row 3.

4. Key the values shown below.

		Friday	Saturday	Sunday
4	One scoop	100	150	125
5	Two scoops	155	175	135
6	Three scoops	70	85	55

5. Use relative references by following these steps:

   a. Click cell B7 and click the AutoSum button Σ▾.

   b. Copy the formula to cells B7:G7.

   c. Click cell E4 and click the AutoSum button Σ▾.

   d. Copy the formula to cell E5:E6.

6. Use absolute references by following these steps:

   a. Click cell F4 and key **=** to start a formula.

      b. Click cell E4 and key ***** to multiply.

      c. Click cell B10 and press ⌨F4. Press ⌨Ctrl+⌨Enter.

      d. Copy this formula to cells F5:F6.

7. Use mixed references by following these steps:

   a. Click cell G4 and key **=** to start.

   b. Click cell E4 and key ***** to multiply.

   c. Click cell B11 and press ⌨F4 three times to show **$B11**. Press ⌨Ctrl+⌨Enter.

   d. Copy this formula to cells G5:G6.

8. In cell E9, key **Grand Total** and make it bold. In cell G9, create a formula to add the total cone and ice cream costs. Copy formatting as needed.

9. Change the page orientation and margins by following these steps:

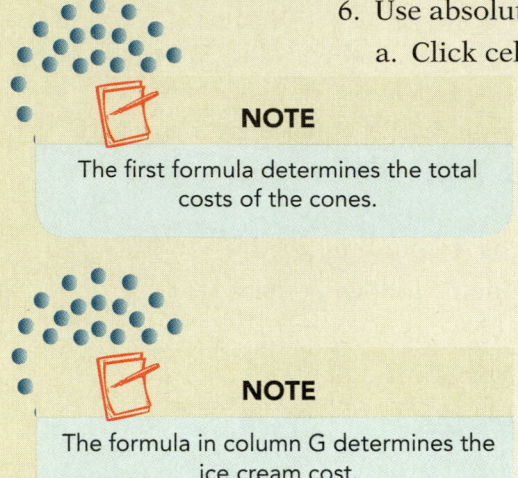

   a. Click the **Page Layout** tab.

   b. In the **Page Setup** group, click the Page Orientation button. Choose **Landscape**.

   c. In the **Page Setup** group, click the Margins button. Choose **Custom Margins**.

   d. Double-click in the **Left** box and key **2.5**. Double-click in the **Top** box and key **2**. Click **Print Preview**.

   e. Close Print Preview.

10. Add a footer.

11. Display formulas by following these steps:

   a. Right-click the **Sheet1** tab and choose **Move or Copy**.

   b. Click to select **Create a copy**. Click **OK**.

   c. Rename the copied sheet **Formulas**. Press ⌨Ctrl+⌨~.

   d. Click the column A heading. Scroll the worksheet, hold down ⌨Shift, and click the column G heading. Double-click the border between the column headings for columns G and H.

   e. Click the **Page Layout** tab.

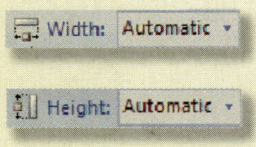

   f. In the **Scale to Fit** group, click the arrow for the Width button. Choose **1 page**.

   g. In the **Scale to Fit** group, click the arrow for the Height button. Choose **1 page**.

12. Add a background by following these steps:

   a. Right-click the **Sheet1** tab and choose **Move or Copy**. In the **Before sheet** list, choose **Formulas**. Click to select **Create a copy**. Click **OK**.

   b. Rename the copied sheet **Background**.

   c. Click the **Page Layout** tab. In the **Page Setup** group, click the Background button.

   d. Navigate to the folder with the **KKBack** file. Click to select the file and click **Insert**.

e. Press Ctrl + Home . Delete **Sheet2** and **Sheet3**.

　　f. Click the Save button  to resave your workbook.

13. Save the workbook as a Web page by following these steps:

　　a. Press F12 . Click the arrow for **Save as type** and choose **Web Page**.

　　b. Set the **Save in** folder to your Lesson 5 folder.

　　c. In the **Save** area, choose **Entire Workbook**.

　　d. Click **Change Title**. Key **Henderson Costs** and click **OK**.

TIP

You can use the same filename for the workbook and the Web page because they use different extensions.

　　e. Name the file *[your initials]*5-24. Click **Save**. Choose **Yes** in the message box about incompatible formats.

　　f. Close the workbook.

　　g. Start your Web browser and maximize the window.

　　h. Press Ctrl + O . Click **Browse** and navigate to your folder. Find and click *[your initials]*5-24 and click **Open**. Click **OK**.

　　i. Look for the title and at each of the sheets in the browser.

　　j. Click the Close button to close the browser.

14. Prepare and submit your work.

Lesson Applications

Exercise 5-25

Create a workbook from a template. Build addition and subtraction formulas.

TIP

Check the Recently Used Templates list in the New Workbook dialog box. Double-click the filename if it is listed.

REVIEW

Select cells in a row, key data, and press Enter to move left to right from cell to cell.

NOTE

Negative numbers are shown in parentheses in this workbook. A negative number means the sales rep spent more money than budgeted.

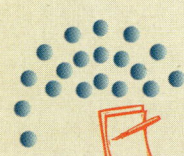

NOTE

Unless your instructor tells you otherwise, include your name, the sheet name, the filename, and the date in a header/footer.

1. Use the **KlassyKow** template as the basis for a workbook. Save the new workbook as *[your initials]*5-25.

2. Edit the label in cell B3 to show the current month.

3. Edit cells A6, A11, A16, and A21 to show the date of each Friday in the current month. If the month has a fifth Friday, do not include it.

4. In cells B9:D9, key the following expenses:

1300	1000	895

5. Key actual expenses for the weeks as follows:

Second week	1600	900	750
Third week	1000	1300	850
Fourth week	1200	2000	500

6. In cell B10, subtract the actual expense from the budgeted amount. Copy the formula to cells C10:D10 and then to the appropriate cells in rows 15, 20, and 25.

7. In cell B27, add the budget amounts for Kim Tomasaki. Copy the formula for the other salespeople.

8. In row 28, copy or create formulas to add the actual expense amounts for the salespeople. In row 29, calculate the differences.

9. Select cells E27:E29 and click the AutoSum button. Widen the column to show the data.

10. Add a footer. Prepare and submit your work. Save and close the workbook.

Exercise 5-26

Use a mixed reference. Change page orientation and scaling.

1. Open **DrinkSize** and save it as *[your initials]*5-26 in your folder.

2. Copy/paste cells A1:H11 to cells A23:H33. Compare and fix row heights. Delete the unit values for the states in rows 28:32.

3. In cell D28, multiply the item count for California by the price of a 16-ounce soda, using a mixed reference so that you can copy this formula for the other states and then for the other rows.

4. Format these results as Currency with two decimals and a dollar sign (from the Format Cells dialog box). Adjust column widths. Change the label to **Dollar Sales for June**.

5. In cells E15:E19, use a formula to calculate the total dollar sales for each beverage. Use the same currency format as other values on the sheet.

6. Use a two-color scale for cells E15:E20 that shows a darker shade for the largest values. Edit the rule to show a color that coordinates with the existing sheet.

7. Change the page orientation to landscape. Set the scaling to print the worksheet at **90%** of normal size.

8. Add a header.

9. Make a copy of the worksheet and name the tab **Formulas**. Choose a blue color for the tab to match the font.

10. Display the formulas and fit the columns. Scale the worksheet to **75%**.

11. Prepare and submit your work. Save and close the workbook.

Exercise 5-27

Use order of precedence. Change page layout options. Print formulas.

1. Open **ICOrder** and save it as *[your initials]*5-27 in your folder.

2. Center the two main labels across columns A:C.

3. Insert a row at row 1 and make it **7.50 (10 pixels)** tall. Apply a dash-dot-dash-dot top border to this row up to column C.

4. Apply the same border to the bottom of row 3. Apply a solid vertical border to the right edge of cells A5:A12 and cells B5:B12.

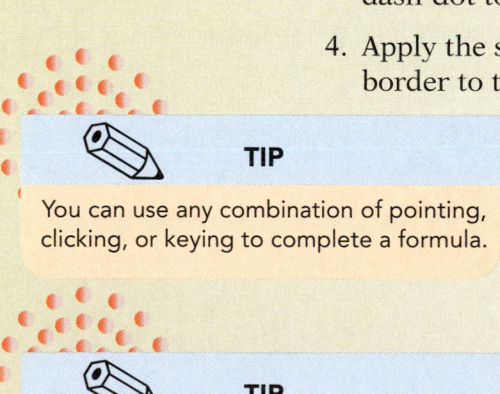

TIP

You can use any combination of pointing, clicking, or keying to complete a formula.

TIP

Key sample data to test your formulas.

5. Apply **White, Background 1, Darker 25%** fill to cell C16 with a single top and double bottom solid border.

6. In cell C14, create a formula to calculate a subtotal by multiplying the quantity by the price for each item. In cell C15, create a formula to calculate the sales tax. Finally, in cell C16, create the formula to calculate the total amount due.

7. Select cells A1:C16 and press Ctrl+C to copy. Click cell E1 and press Ctrl+V to paste. Right-click the Paste Options button and choose **Keep Source Column Widths**.

NOTE

The Footer margin is on the Margins tab of the Page Setup dialog box.

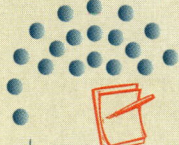

NOTE

Choose a print range in the Print dialog box.

8. Copy and paste cells A1:G16 to start in cell A18 so that there are four copies of the order form on your worksheet. Check for discrepancies in row height and make adjustments.

9. Change the page orientation to landscape. Scale the worksheet to 95% and set the top and bottom margins at .5 inches and the left margin at 1 inch. Change the footer margin to .35 inches.

10. Add a footer.

11. Make a copy of the worksheet and name it **Formulas**. Display the formulas. Size the columns to show the complete formulas. Set 75% scaling and print only the first page.

12. Prepare and submit your work. Save and close the workbook.

Exercise 5-28 ◆ Challenge Yourself

Use order of precedence. Print formulas.

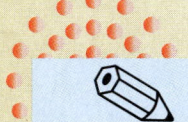

TIP

A 4.5% tax rate makes the final cost 104.5% of the pre-tax total. Correct the first occurrence of the formula and copy it to the other locations.

1. Open **OrderForm**. Save it as *[your initials]*5-28 in your folder.

2. The **Amount Due** formula calculates the total amount due by multiplying quantity by price, summing these results, and multiplying by 104.5%, the tax rate. Review and correct the formula.

3. Add a header.

4. Make a copy of the worksheet and name it **Formulas**. Hide all columns except those with formulas.

5. Prepare and submit your work. Save and close the workbook.

On Your Own

In these exercises you work on your own, as you would in a real-life work environment. Use the skills you've learned to accomplish the task—and be creative.

Exercise 5-29

Open **MultTable** and edit it to build a division table. Apply borders and/or fill to make the worksheet easy to read. Add a header or footer. Save the workbook as *[your initials]*5-29 in your Lesson 5 folder. Set the page for landscape orientation on one page. Make a copy of the sheet with formulas. Prepare and submit your work. Save and close the workbook.

Exercise 5-30

Create a new workbook and save it as *[your initials]*5-30 in your folder. In cell A1, key **Tip Calculator**. In cell B2, key **10%**; in cell C2, **15%**; in cell D2, **18%**; and in cell E2, **20%**. Starting in cell A3, create a series with a $5 interval that goes from $10 to $100. Using mixed references, create and copy formulas to determine the tip based on the sales amount and a tip percentage. Show two decimal places for the results. Apply formatting, borders, and fill for an attractive appearance. Prepare a formulas sheet. Prepare and submit your work. Save the workbook and close it.

Exercise 5-31

Develop a worksheet that tracks the number of e-mail and instant messages you receive per day. Build a date series in column A for a four-week period. In column B, key a value to show the number of messages with some variety of numbers. Make all data bold. Apply a three-color scale that uses a dark color for the smallest value. Add a header or footer. Save your workbook as *[your initials]*5-31. Prepare and submit your work. Save and close the workbook.

Lesson 6

Working with Functions

OBJECTIVES

After completing this lesson, you will be able to:

1. Use math and trig functions.

2. Use statistical functions.

3. Use icon sets.

4. Group worksheets.

5. Use date and time functions.

Estimated Time: 1½ hours

MCAS OBJECTIVES

In this lesson:
XL07 1.3.1
XL07 1.5.1
XL07 1.5.2
XL07 1.5.5
XL07 2.3.1
XL07 2.3.2
XL07 3.2
XL07 3.2.1
XL07 3.4.1
XL07 4.3.1
XL07 4.3.3
XL07 5.5

Excel has several categories of functions that perform common mathematical, statistical, financial, and other calculations. A *function* is a built-in formula.

Many functions do things automatically that would be difficult or time-consuming for you to do manually. For example, in a list of accounts with each customer's amount due, Excel can quickly calculate a total, find the largest amount due, or calculate an average amount due.

Using Math and Trig Functions

All functions have a *syntax*, which defines the necessary parts of the formula and the order of those parts. The syntax consists of an equal sign and the name of the function, followed by parentheses. Inside the parentheses, you place arguments.

An *argument* is the information the function needs to complete its calculation, usually one or more values or cell ranges. A few functions do not have arguments, but most have at least one argument. If a function has more than one argument, the arguments are separated by commas. A function's arguments can consist of:

- Cell references (individual cells or ranges)
- Constants (a number keyed in the formula)
- Another function (known as a nested function)
- Range names

Figure 6-1
Syntax for the SUM function

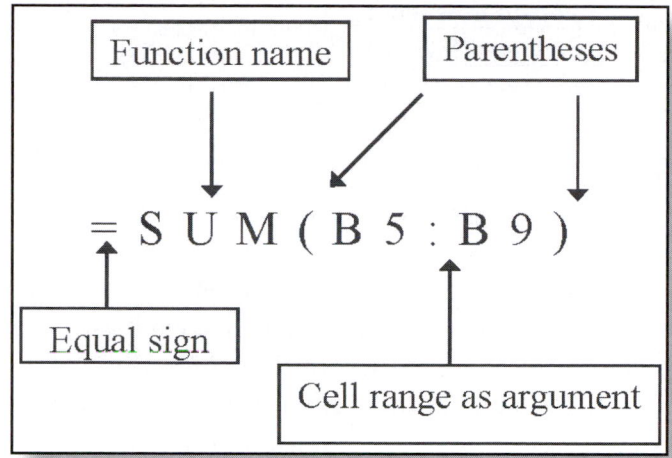

Exercise 6-1   **USE SUM AND THE FORMULA BAR**

The SUM function in the Math & Trig category adds columns or rows of values. The SUM function ignores cells with:

NOTE

Excel inserts the SUM function when you use the AutoSum button Σ AutoSum ▾ .

- Text
- Error values such as #NAME?

TABLE 6-1 Examples of the SUM Function

Function(argument/s)	Cell Data	Result
=SUM(A1:A3)	A1=10, A2=20, A3=30	60
=SUM(50,60)	None	110
=SUM(A1,250)	A1=25	275
=SUM(A1,B2,C1:C2)	A1=10, B2=20, C1=10, C2=30	70
=SUM(A1,B2)	A1=25, B2="Ice Cream"	25
=SUM(A1,B2)	A1=25, B2=#NAME?	25

1. Open **DownTime**.

2. Click cell E17.

3. Key **=su**. *Formula AutoComplete* displays a list of functions that match what you have keyed so far. There is also a descriptive ScreenTip for the highlighted function.

Figure 6-2
Formula
AutoComplete
**DownTime.xlsx
Jan15Plan sheet**

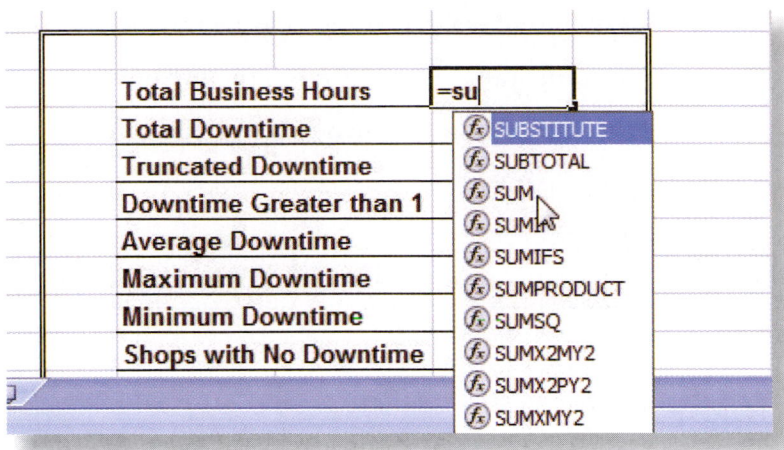

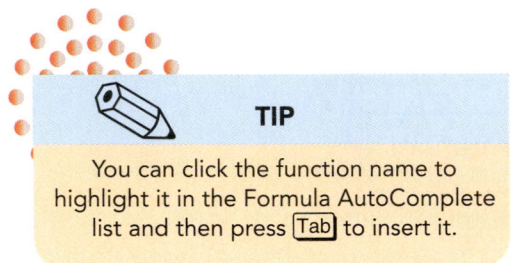

TIP

You can click the function name to highlight it in the Formula AutoComplete list and then press [Tab] to insert it.

4. Double-click **SUM** in the list. The opening parenthesis is inserted with the function name. An Argument ScreenTip illustrates the syntax for the function with the first argument shown in bold.

5. Click cell C7 and drag to select cells C7:C14. As you drag, the ScreenTip shows the number of rows and columns. The function will sum the range C7:C14.

Figure 6-3
SUM function with its Argument ScreenTip
**DownTime.xlsx
Jan15Plan sheet**

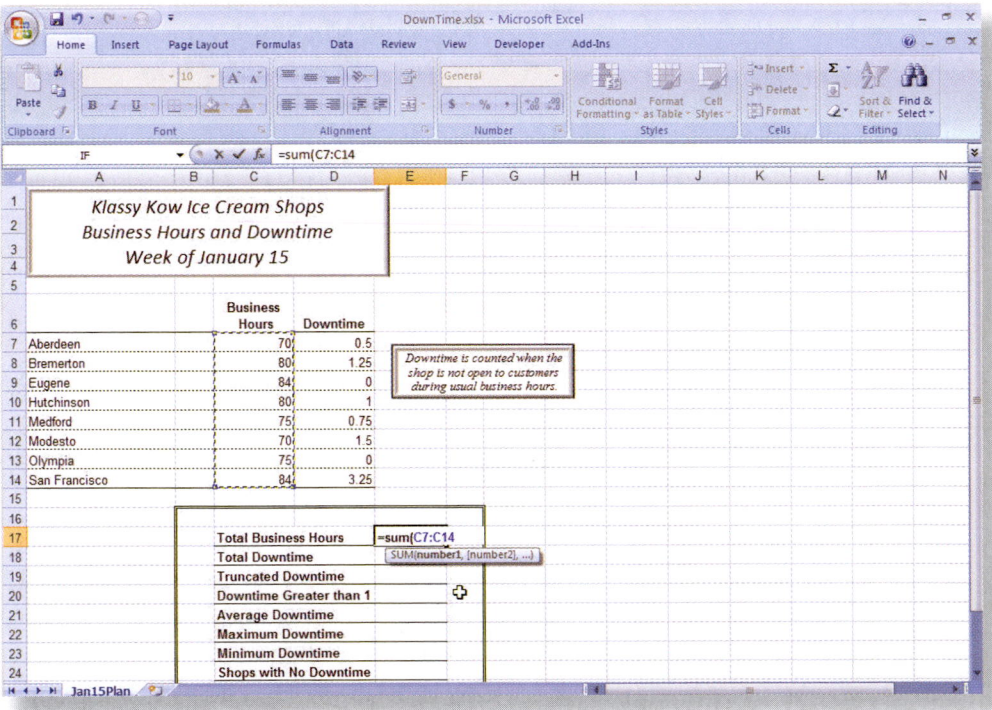

6. Press [Ctrl]+[Enter]. The result is 618.

7. Look in the formula bar. For the SUM function, Excel adds a closing parenthesis for you. This formula is the same as keying **=c7+c8+ c9+c10+c11+c12+c13+c14**.

Exercise 6-2 USE INSERT FUNCTION

The Insert Function dialog box enables you to choose a function from all available. After you choose a function, the Function Arguments dialog box opens and guides you in building the formula. An Insert Function button appears at the left of the formula bar. There is also an Insert Function button on the Formulas tab.

1. Click cell E18. This will be a sum of the values from column D.

2. Click the Insert Function button in the formula bar. The Insert Function dialog box opens.

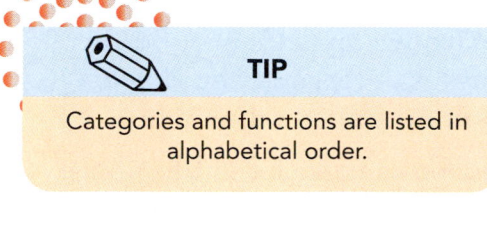

TIP

Categories and functions are listed in alphabetical order.

3. Click the arrow next to the **Or select a category** list. Choose **Math & Trig**.

4. In the **Select a function** list, scroll to find **SUM**.

5. Click **SUM** to see its syntax and a description in the dialog box.

Figure 6-4
Insert Function dialog box

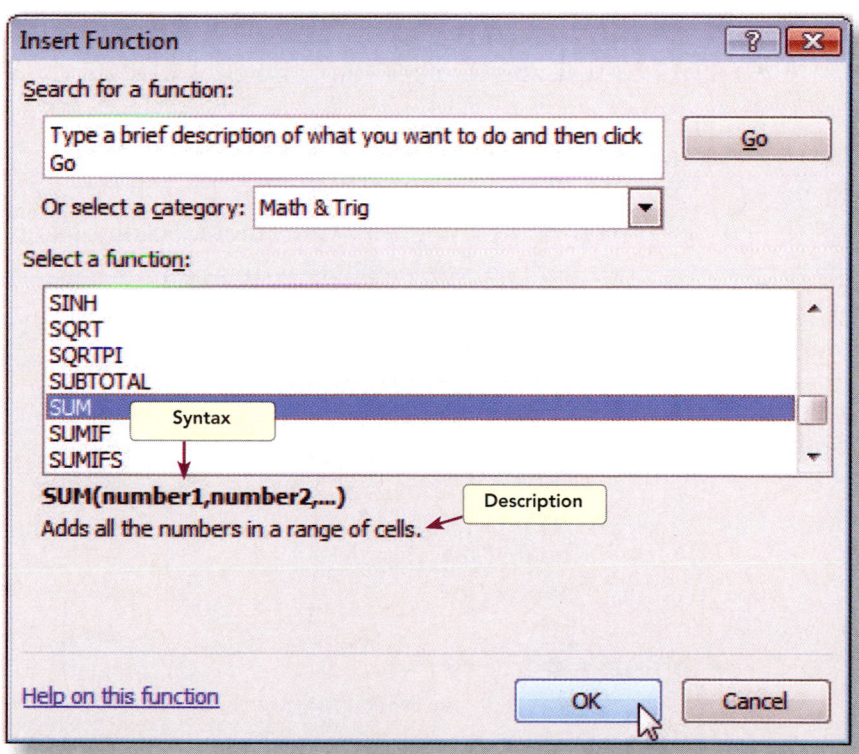

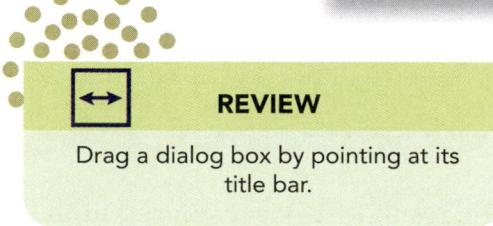

REVIEW

Drag a dialog box by pointing at its title bar.

6. Click **OK**. The Function Arguments dialog box opens. In the **Number1** box, Excel assumes that you want to sum the range above cell E18.

7. Move the dialog box so that you see columns C and D (see Figure 6-5).

Figure 6-5
Function Arguments
dialog box
DownTime.xlsx
Jan15Plan sheet

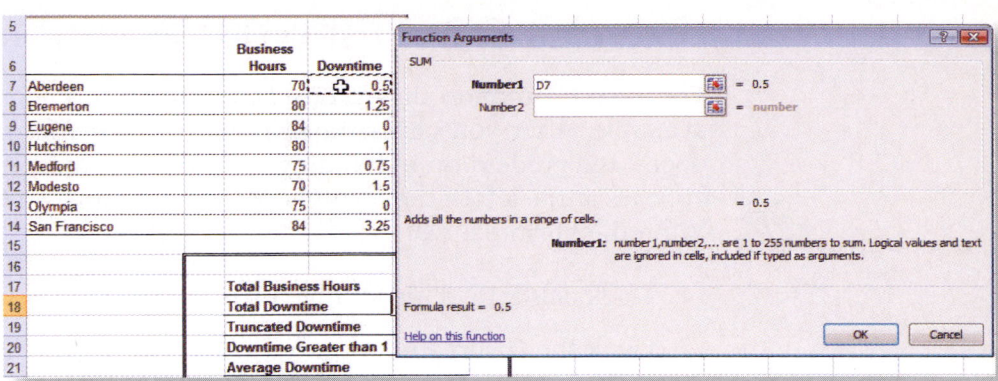

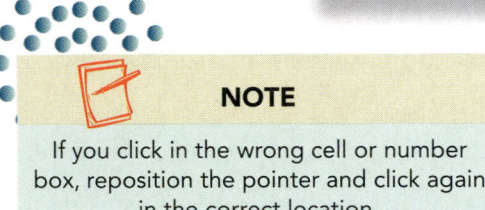

NOTE

If you click in the wrong cell or number box, reposition the pointer and click again in the correct location.

8. Click cell D7. A marquee appears around the cell, and its address is entered in the **Number1** box in the Function Arguments dialog box.

9. Click in the **Number2** box and click cell D8. Notice that the formula appears in both the formula bar and the cell. When cells are listed one by one, they are separated by commas in the function.

10. Click in the **Number3** box and click cell D9.

11. Click in the **Number4** box and click cell D10.

12. Click in the **Number5** box and click cell D11.

13. Scroll in the Function Arguments dialog box and complete the arguments up to **Number8** with cell D14.

Figure 6-6
Function Arguments
dialog box with cells
entered separately

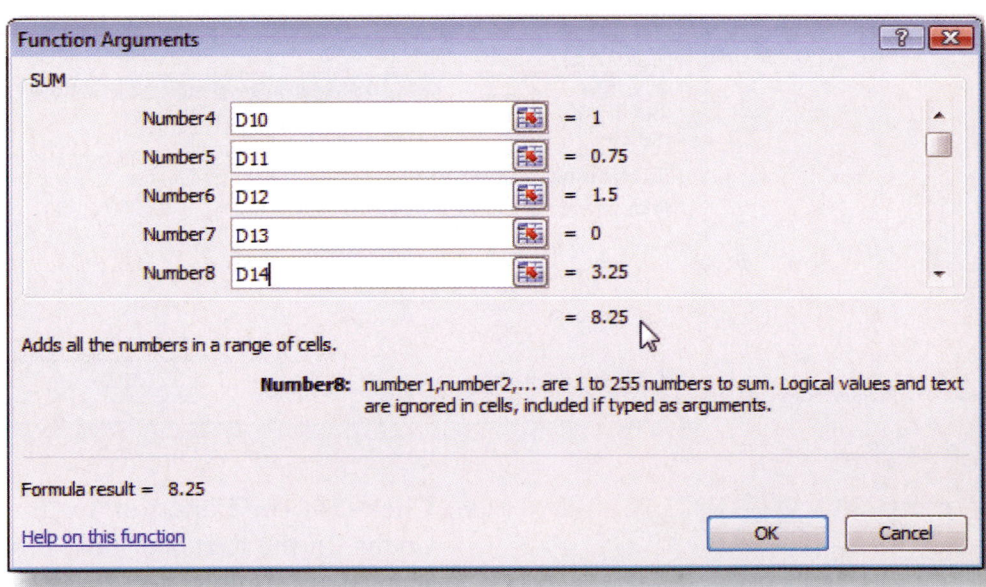

14. Press Enter. The dialog box closes; the result (8.25) is displayed in the cell.

Exercise 6-3   USE TRUNC

The TRUNC function removes the decimal part of a number or shows a certain number of decimal positions without adjusting the value.

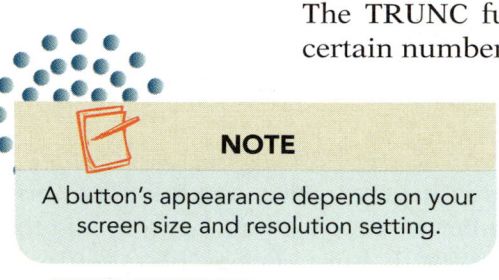

NOTE

A button's appearance depends on your screen size and resolution setting.

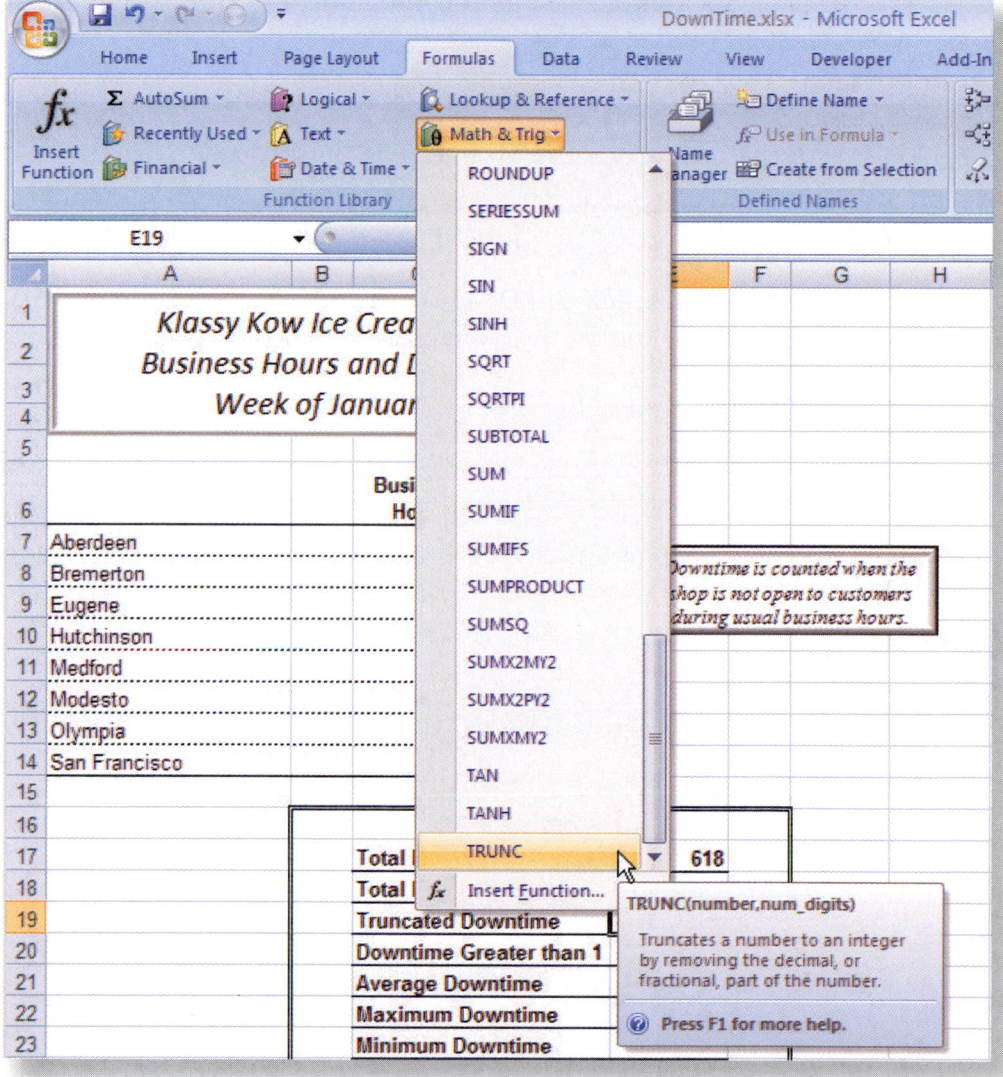

Figure 6-7
Choosing TRUNC

1. Click cell E19. You are going to truncate the results in cell E18 to show no decimals.

2. Click the **Formulas** tab in the Ribbon.

3. In the **Function Library** group, click the Math & Trig button . The list of functions opens.

4. Scroll to find **TRUNC** and click. The TRUNC Function Arguments dialog box opens. The insertion point is in the **Number** box.

5. Click cell E18. Its address appears in the **Number** box.

6. Click in the **Num_digits** box. Key **0** to truncate the value to show no decimal positions.

7. Click **OK**. The truncated value of cell E18 is 8.

Exercise 6-4   USE SUMIF

The SUMIF function adds cell values only if they meet a condition. In this case, you will determine the total number of down hours for shops with downtime greater than one hour. The SUMIF function has two required arguments, Range and Criteria. The range is the group of cells to be added. The criteria is a condition that must be met for the cell to be included in the addition. The optional argument is Sum_range, which allows for additional limits on which cells to add.

1. Click cell E20. Click the **Formulas** tab.

2. Click the Math & Trig button ⟨🔢 Math & Trig ⟩.

3. Scroll to find **SUMIF** and click. The Function Arguments dialog box opens with the insertion point in the **Range** entry box.

4. Click cell D7 and drag to select the range D7:D14. As you drag, the dialog box collapses so that you can see your work better.

5. Release the mouse button. The dialog box expands, and the range you selected is entered in the **Range** box.

6. Click in the **Criteria** box. Key **>1** to set a rule that the value in the range D7:D14 be greater than 1 to be included in the sum.

NOTE

A value of 1 is not greater than 1.

Figure 6-8
SUMIF function in the Function Arguments dialog box

Function Arguments					? ✕
SUMIF					
Range	D7:D14	🔢	=	{0.5;1.25;0;1;0.75;1.5;0;3.25}	
Criteria	>1	🔢	=		
Sum_range		🔢	=	reference	
			=		

Adds the cells specified by a given condition or criteria.

Criteria   is the condition or criteria in the form of a number, expression, or text that defines which cells will be added.

Formula result =

Help on this function   OK   Cancel

7. Click **OK**. The result is 6 because only the values in cells D8, D12, and D14 are totaled. You can verify this result with AutoCalculate.

8. Click cell D8. Hold down Ctrl and click cells D12 and then D14. These are values greater than 1. The sum appears in the status bar.

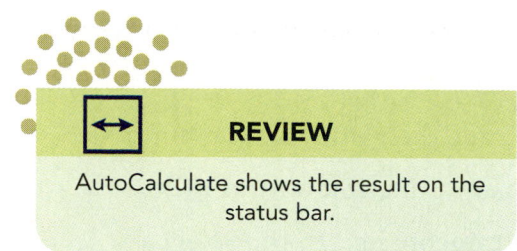

REVIEW

AutoCalculate shows the result on the status bar.

9. Click cell E20 and view the formula in the formula bar. The criteria has been inserted with quotation marks. Note that the values in cells E19 and E20 are not aligned.

10. Copy the format from cell E19 to cell E20 to adjust the alignment.

Using Statistical Functions

Another category of Excel functions is the Statistical group. Some of these functions are useful even if you are not a statistician.

Exercise 6-5   USE THE AVERAGE FUNCTION

The AVERAGE function calculates the arithmetic mean of a range of cells. The *arithmetic mean* adds the values in the cells and then divides by the number of values. The AVERAGE function ignores:

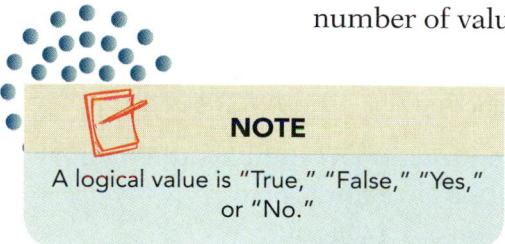

NOTE

A logical value is "True," "False," "Yes," or "No."

- Text

- Blank or empty cells (but not zeros)

- Error values such as #NAME?

- Logical values

TABLE 6-2 Examples of the AVERAGE Function

Function(argument/s)	Cell Data	Result
=AVERAGE(A1:A3)	A1=10, A2=20, A3=30	20
=AVERAGE(50,60)	None	55
=AVERAGE(A1,250)	A1=25	137.5
=AVERAGE(A1,B2,C1:C2)	A1=10, B2=20, C1=10, C2=30	17.5
=AVERAGE(A1, B2)	A1=25, B2="Ice Cream"	25
=AVERAGE(A1, B2)	A1=25, B2=#NAME?	25
=AVERAGE(A1:A3)	A1=20, A2=0, A3=TRUE	10
=AVERAGE(A1:A3)	A1=20, A2=Empty, A3=40	30

1. Right-click the row 21 row heading and choose **Insert**. A row is inserted.

2. Key **Average Business Hours** in cell C21.

3. Click cell E21. This cell should average the values from column C.

4. Click the **Formulas** tab. Click the Insert Function button .

5. Choose **Statistical** in the **Or select a category** list. In the **Select a function** list, locate **AVERAGE**.

6. Click **AVERAGE** to see its syntax and description. Click **OK**.

7. Move the dialog box until you can see column C. The **Number1** box shows the range directly above cell E21.

8. Click cell C7 and drag to select cells C7:C14 to reset the range.

9. Release the mouse button. The dialog box expands, and the range you selected is entered in the **Number1** box.

10. Click **OK**. The result is 77.25.

Exercise 6-6   USE AVERAGEIF

The AVERAGEIF function averages cell values only if they meet a condition. Like SUMIF, AVERAGEIF has two required arguments, Range and Criteria.

1. Click cell E22. Click the Insert Function button .

2. Choose **Statistical**. In the **Select a function** list, find **AVERAGEIF**.

3. Click **AVERAGEIF** and click **OK**. The Function Arguments dialog box opens with the insertion point in the **Range** entry box.

4. Click cell D7 and drag to select the range D7:D14.

5. Click in the **Criteria** box. Key **>0** to set a rule that the value in the range D7:D14 must be greater than 0 to be included in the average.

6. Click **OK**. The result is 1, formatted without any decimals.

7. Click the **Home** tab. Click the Increase Decimal button three times. The values are not properly aligned.

8. Press Ctrl+1 and click the **Number** tab. Click **General** and click **OK**.

Exercise 6-7   USE THE MIN AND MAX FUNCTIONS

MIN and MAX are statistical functions that show the minimum (smallest) value or the maximum (largest) value in a range. The MIN and MAX functions ignore:

- Text

- Blank or empty cells (but not zeros)

- Error values such as #NAME?

- Logical values

TABLE 6-3 Examples of the MIN and MAX Functions

Function(argument/s)	Cell Data	Result
=MAX(A1:A3)	A1=10, A2=20, A3=30	30
=MAX(50,60)	None	60
=MIN(A1,250)	A1=25	25
=MIN(A1,B2,C1:C2)	A1=10, B2=20, C1=10, C2=30	10
=MAX(A1, B2)	A1=25, B2="Ice Cream"	25
=MAX(A1, B2)	A1=25, B2=#NAME?	25
=MIN(A1:A3)	A1=20, A2=10, A3=FALSE	10
=MIN(A1:A3)	A1=20, A2=Empty, A3=40	20

1. Click cell E23.

2. Press [Shift]+[F3]. This shortcut opens the Insert Function dialog box.

3. Choose **Statistical** and **MAX**. In the Function Arguments dialog box, the **Number1** box shows the range directly above cell E23.

4. Select cells D7:D14 to determine the largest value from column D. The range is shown as **Number1**. Click **OK**. The maximum value is 3.25.

5. Click cell E24 and key **=min** to start the MIN function. Formula AutoComplete shows the function and its ScreenTip.

Figure 6-9
Formula
AutoComplete
and descriptive
ScreenTip
DownTime.xlsx
Jan15Plan sheet

6. Press [Tab]. The opening parenthesis is inserted.

7. Select cells D7:D14 and press [Enter]. The function does not ignore zeros, so the minimum value is zero.

NOTE

An empty cell is not the same as a cell with a value of 0.

8. Delete the contents of cells D9 and D13. The results in cell E24 are recalculated and some cells show error triangles because the formulas now refer to empty cells.

Exercise 6-8   USE COUNT AND COUNTBLANK

The COUNTBLANK function counts empty cells in a range. The COUNT function tallies the number of values in a range. The COUNT function ignores:

- Text

- Blank or empty cells (but not zeros)

- Error values such as #NAME?

- Logical values

TABLE 6-4 Examples of the COUNT Function

Function(argument/s)	Cell Data	Result
=COUNT(A1:A3)	A1=Empty, A2=20, A3=30	2
=COUNT(A1:A3)	A1=30, A2=Empty, A3=#NAME?	1
=COUNT(A1:A3)	A1=25, A2="Ice Cream," A3=3	2
=COUNT(13, 21, 111)	None	3
=COUNT(A1, B2, C1:C2)	A1=25, B2=0, C1="Hello," C2=4	3

1. Key **0** (zero) in cells D9 and D13. The results in cell E24 change.

2. Click cell E25 and click the **Home** tab. Click the Insert Function button 𝑓ₓ in the formula bar.

3. Choose **Statistical** and **COUNT**. Click **OK**.

4. Select cells D7:D14. The range appears in the **Value1** box.

5. Click **OK**. The cells with zero (0) are included in the count.

6. Delete the contents of cells D9 and D13. The count tallies the cells with downtime. Blank cells are not included.

7. Edit the label in cell C25 to delete **No**.

8. Right-click the row heading for row 25 and insert a row.

9. Click cell E25 and click the Insert Function button 𝑓ₓ.

10. Choose **Statistical** and **COUNTBLANK**. Click **OK**. Select cells D7:D14. Click **OK**.

11. Key **Shops with No Downtime** in cell C25.

12. Insert a row at row 27. Key **Number of Shops** in cell C27.

13. Click cell E27, key **=count**, and press ⎄Tab.

14. Drag to select cells A7:A14. The range is **value1** in the ScreenTip.

Figure 6-10
Keying the COUNT
function
DownTime.xlsx
Jan15Plan sheet

	A	B	C	D	E	F	G	H
6			Business Hours	Downtime				
7	Aberdeen		70	0.5				
8	Bremerton		80	1.25				
9	Eugene		84					
10	Hutchinson		80	1				
11	Medford		75	0.75				
12	Modesto		70	1.5				
13	Olympia		75					
14	San Francisco		84	3.25				
15								
16								
17			Total Business Hours	618				
18			Total Downtime	8.25				
19			Truncated Downtime	8				
20			Downtime Greater than 1	6				
21			Average Business Hours	77.25				
22			Average Downtime	1.375				
23			Maximum Downtime	3.25				
24			Minimum Downtime	0.5				
25			Shops with No Downtime	2				
26			Shops with Downtime	6				
27			Number of Shops	=COUNT(A7:A14				
28				COUNT(**value1**, [value2], ...)				
29								

Downtime is counted when the shop is not open to customers during usual business hours.

15. Press [Enter]. The result is 0, because the COUNT function ignores text.

Exercise 6-9   USE THE COUNTA FUNCTION

The COUNTA function tallies values and labels. The COUNTA function ignores:

- Blank or empty cells (but not zeros)
- Error values such as #NAME?
- Logical values

TABLE 6-5 Examples of the COUNTA Function

Function(argument/s)	Cell Data	Result
=COUNTA(A1:A3)	A1=Empty, A2=20, A3=30	2
=COUNTA(A1:A3)	A1=30, A2=Empty, A3=#NAME?	1
=COUNTA(A1:A3)	A1=25, A2="Ice Cream," A3=3	3
=COUNTA(13, 21, 111)	None	3
=COUNTA(A1, B2, C1:C2)	A1=25, B2=0, C1="Hello," C2=TRUE	3

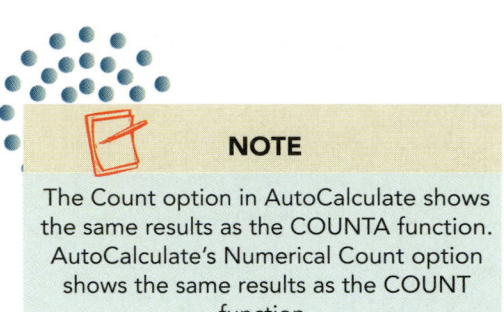

NOTE

The Count option in AutoCalculate shows the same results as the COUNTA function. AutoCalculate's Numerical Count option shows the same results as the COUNT function.

1. Double-click cell E27.

2. Position the insertion point and key **a** after **COUNT**.

3. Press Enter. The new function COUNTA includes labels; there are eight shops in the list.

4. Add a bottom border to the data in row 27.

5. Save the workbook as *[your initials]*6-9 in a folder for Lesson 6.

Using Icon Sets

Data visualizations are simple conditional formatting rules. They use data bars, color scales, and icon sets. An icon set consists of three to five icons that appear in a range of cells based on the value in the cell.

Exercise 6-10   APPLY ICON SETS

1. With *[your initials]*6-9 open, click the **Home** tab.

2. Select cells D7:D14. In the **Styles** group, click the Conditional Formatting button.

3. Hover at **Icon Sets**. A gallery opens with the available styles.

4. Hover at several sets to see the results. Live Preview displays the icon sets before you apply them.

Figure 6-11
Choosing an icon set
6-9.xlsx
Jan15Plan sheet

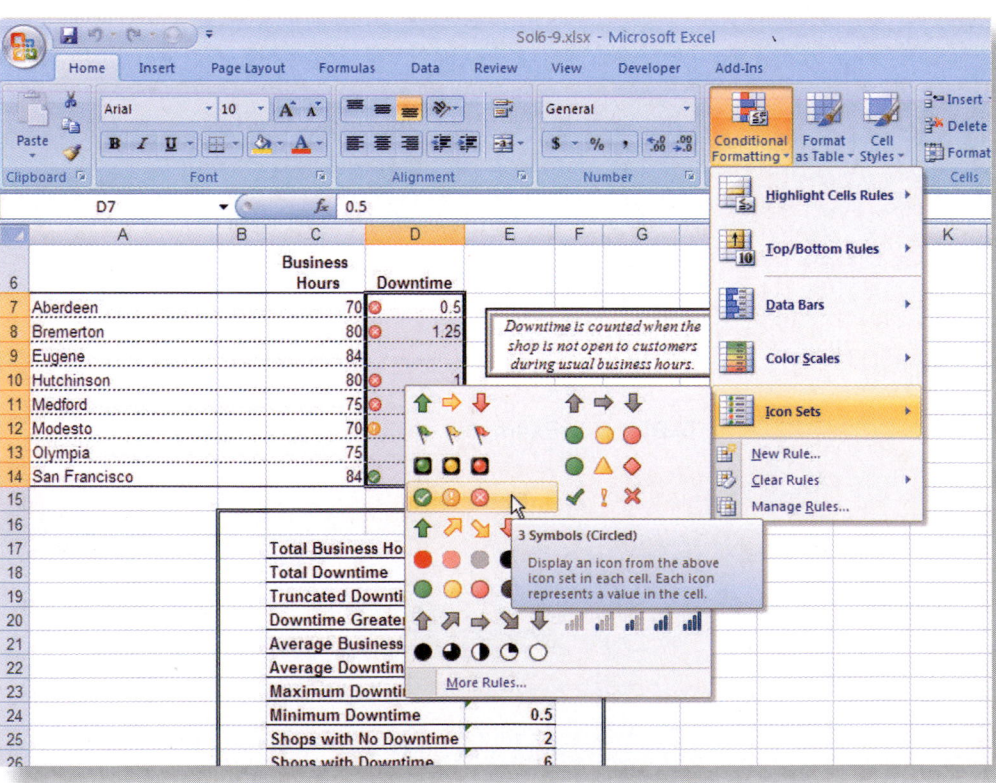

5. Choose **3 Symbols (Circled)** in the first column. The icons appear at the left edge of the cell. The highest value has the green check mark.

Exercise 6-11   EDIT THE ICON FORMATTING RULE

1. Select cells D7:D14 and click the Conditional Formatting button 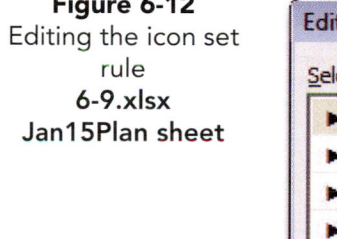.

2. Choose **Manage Rules**. The icon set is listed in the Conditional Formatting Rules Manager dialog box.

3. Click **Edit Rule**. The Edit Formatting Rule dialog box includes options that you can edit for this rule.

4. Click the arrow with **Percent** for the first icon. Choose **Number**. This will set the rule to use a specific value rather than a percent.

5. Change the **Type** for the second icon to **Number**.

6. Click to select **Reverse Icon Order**. This will set the rule to show the green check mark for the lowest value.

7. Key **10** in the **Value** box for the first icon (red X). There are no values greater than or equal to 10 in your list, so this icon won't be shown at all.

8. Key **1** in the **Value** box for the second icon (yellow exclamation point).

Figure 6-12
Editing the icon set rule
6-9.xlsx
Jan15Plan sheet

Edit Formatting Rule	? ✕

Select a Rule Type:

▶ Format all cells based on their values
▶ Format only cells that contain
▶ Format only top or bottom ranked values
▶ Format only values that are above or below average
▶ Format only unique or duplicate values
▶ Use a formula to determine which cells to format

Edit the Rule Description:

Format all cells based on their values:

Format Style: Icon Sets ▼

Display each icon according to these rules:

Icon		Value		Type
❌	when value is	>= ▼	10	Number ▼
⚠️	when < 10 and	>= ▼	1	Number ▼
✅	when < 0			

Icon Style: 3 Symbols (Circled) ▼   ☑ Reverse Icon Order   ☐ Show Icon Only

[OK]   [Cancel]

9. Click **OK**. Click **OK** again. Empty cells are not formatted; they have no value.

10. Key **0** in cells D9 and D13. The icons are inserted.

11. Press ⌈Ctrl⌉+⌈Home⌉. Save the workbook as *[your initials]6-11* in your folder. Close the workbook.

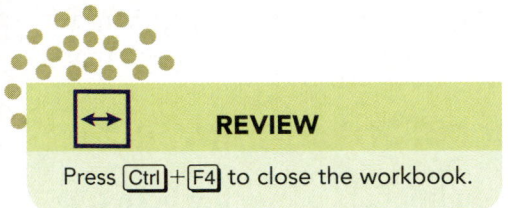

REVIEW

Press ⌈Ctrl⌉+⌈F4⌉ to close the workbook.

Grouping Worksheets

An Excel workbook can have as many worksheets as your machine's memory allows. Multiple sheets enable you to separate related data when necessary but have it available for managing information. When you work with multiple sheets, you can group the sheets to edit or format them as a group.

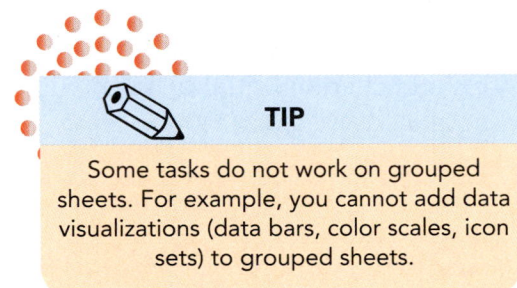

TIP

Some tasks do not work on grouped sheets. For example, you cannot add data visualizations (data bars, color scales, icon sets) to grouped sheets.

Exercise 6-12   GROUP AND DELETE WORKSHEETS

When worksheets are grouped, editing and formatting commands affect all sheets in the group. This is an efficient way to make changes to several worksheets at once, as long as the sheets are identical.

1. Choose the Microsoft Office Button 🔘 and choose **New**. Choose **My templates** in the New Workbook dialog box.

2. Choose **CSCalls** and click **OK**.

3. Click the **Sheet2** tab, hold down ⌈Ctrl⌉, and click the **Sheet3** tab. Both worksheets are selected or active. The word **[Group]** appears in the title bar. The tabs appear more white.

NOTE

The **CSCalls** template file should be copied to the appropriate Templates folder on your computer.

Figure 6-13
Grouped worksheets
CSCalls.xltx

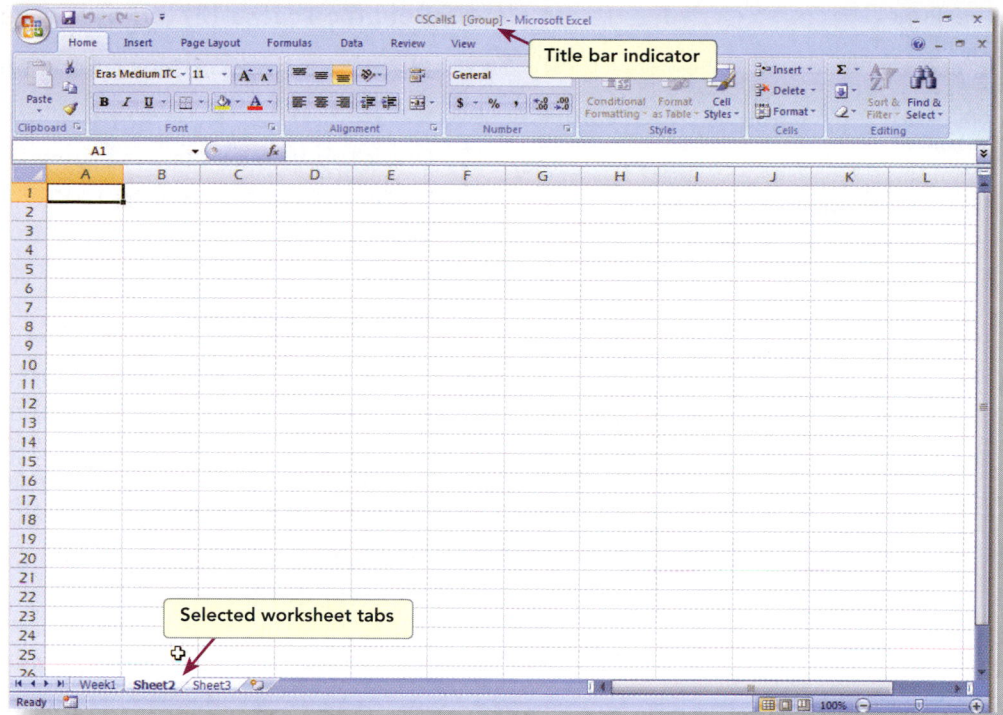

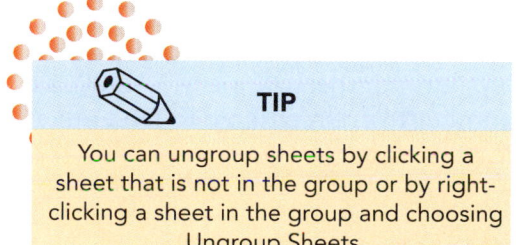

TIP

You can ungroup sheets by clicking a sheet that is not in the group or by right-clicking a sheet in the group and choosing Ungroup Sheets.

4. Click the **Week1** tab. Selecting a tab outside the group ungroups the sheets.

5. Click **Sheet2**, hold down Ctrl, and click **Sheet3** again.

6. Right-click either tab in the group and choose **Delete**. Both sheets are deleted.

Exercise 6-13   MANAGE WORKSHEETS

When you copy a worksheet with the Move or Copy dialog box, formatting and data are included.

1. Right-click the **Week1** tab. Choose **Move or Copy**. The **To book** list includes the names of open workbooks as well as a new book. The **Before sheet** list allows you to move or copy the sheet to a specific location in the tabs.

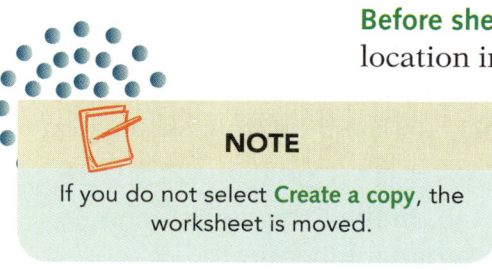

NOTE

If you do not select Create a copy, the worksheet is moved.

2. Select **(move to end)** in the **Before sheet** list.

3. Click to select **Create a copy**.

4. Click **OK**. The new worksheet named **Week1 (2)** is an exact duplicate of the **Week1** sheet.

REVIEW

You can double-click or right-click a sheet tab to rename it.

REVIEW

You can insert a sheet by right-clicking a worksheet tab and choosing Insert or by clicking the Insert Worksheet tab.

5. Rename **Week1 (2)** tab as **Week2**.

6. Make two more copies of the **Week1** sheet and name them **Week3** and **Week4**.

7. Click the **Week1** tab and press Shift+F11. A blank worksheet is inserted in front of (to the left of) the **Week1** sheet. New sheet numbers start at the next available number in the workbook.

8. Rename the new sheet as **FirstQuarter**.

9. Right-click the **FirstQuarter** tab and choose **Move or Copy**. Choose **(move to end)** and click **OK**. This moves the sheet without making a copy.

10. Choose a different accent color for each tab.

11. Save the workbook as *[your initials]*6-13 in your Lesson 6 folder.

Using Date and Time Functions

Date and time functions can be used to display the current date and time, determine ages, and calculate hours worked, days passed, and future dates.

With dates and times, Excel uses a *serial number* system. A serial number is a date shown as a value. Excel's date system numbers January 1, 1900, as 1 and January 2, 1900, as 2; it assigns a number to every date up to December 31, 9999.

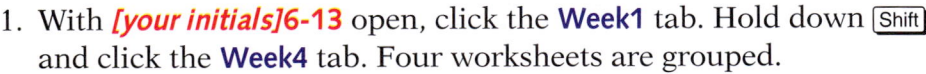

Exercise 6-14   **USE THE TODAY() FUNCTION**

The TODAY() function displays the current date, using the computer's clock. This function has no arguments, and Excel formats the results in a standard date style. The TODAY() function is *volatile,* which means that the formula results depend on the computer on which the workbook is opened.

1. With *[your initials]*6-13 open, click the **Week1** tab. Hold down Shift and click the **Week4** tab. Four worksheets are grouped.

NOTE

Ignore Formula AutoComplete.

2. Click cell A3. Key **=today()** and press Enter. The current date is inserted. The ##### symbols indicate that the column is not wide enough to show the date in the current font size.

3. Click cell A3 and look in the formula bar. Excel capitalizes function names after you complete the cell.

4. Press Ctrl+1 and click the **Number** tab. In the **Category** list, choose **General**. The sample box shows the serial number for today.

5. Click **OK**. The serial number that represents today's date is shown.

6. Click the Undo button  . The format change is reversed.

7. Press Ctrl+1 and click the **Alignment** tab.

8. In the **Text control** group, click to select **Shrink to fit**.

9. Click **OK**. The display date is sized to fit the column width, but the font size still shows the original size.

Exercise 6-15   KEY AND FORMAT DATES

When you key a date, Excel assigns the closest matching date format to the date you key. The resulting format may not match what you key. You can, however, use one of many built-in date formats or create your own format.

TABLE 6-6 Sample Keyed Dates and Initial Screen Display

Keyed Characters	Screen Display
1-1-08	1/1/2008
1/1/08	1/1/2008
1-jan-08	1-Jan-08
january 1, 2008	1-Jan-08
jan 1, 2008	1-Jan-08

NOTE

Remember that four worksheets are grouped.

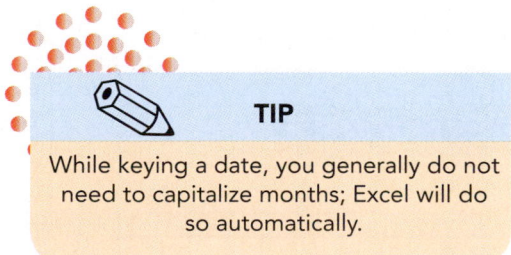

TIP

While keying a date, you generally do not need to capitalize months; Excel will do so automatically.

1. In cell A5, key **01/01/08** and press Enter. The date is formatted without leading zeros and shows the year with four digits.

2. In cell A6, key **1-jan-08** and press Enter. The format matches what you keyed.

3. In cell A7, key **january 1, 2008** and press Enter.

4. In cell A8, key **1-1-08** and press Enter.

5. Select cells A5:A8. Press Ctrl+1.

6. Click the **Number** tab and choose **Date** in the **Category** list.

7. Choose **March 14, 2001** in the **Type** list.

8. Click **OK**. Widen column A. All the dates are formatted in the same style.

9. Click cell A3.

10. Right-click the **Week4** tab. The **Week4** sheet becomes the active sheet.

11. Choose **Ungroup Sheets**. The **Week4** worksheet shows the dates.

12. Click the **Week1** tab, then the **Week2** tab, then the **Week3** tab. All sheets have the same formatting and data.

Exercise 6-16   USE FILL ACROSS WORKSHEETS

Another way to copy selected data from one worksheet to another is the Fill Across Worksheets command. To use this command, you first select the worksheet with the data and the one(s) where the data should be copied.

1. Click the **FirstQuarter** tab. This is the blank sheet you inserted.

2. Click the **Week4** tab.

3. Hold down the Ctrl key and click the **FirstQuarter** worksheet tab. The title bar shows **[Group]**.

4. On the **Week4** sheet, select cells A1:D8. These are the cells that will be copied to the **FirstQuarter** sheet.

5. On the **Home** tab, click the Fill button in the **Editing** group. Its submenu opens.

6. Choose **Across Worksheets**. The Fill Across Worksheets dialog box has options to copy everything, only the data, or only the formatting.

Figure 6-14
Using Fill Across
Worksheets
6-13.xlsx
Week4 sheet

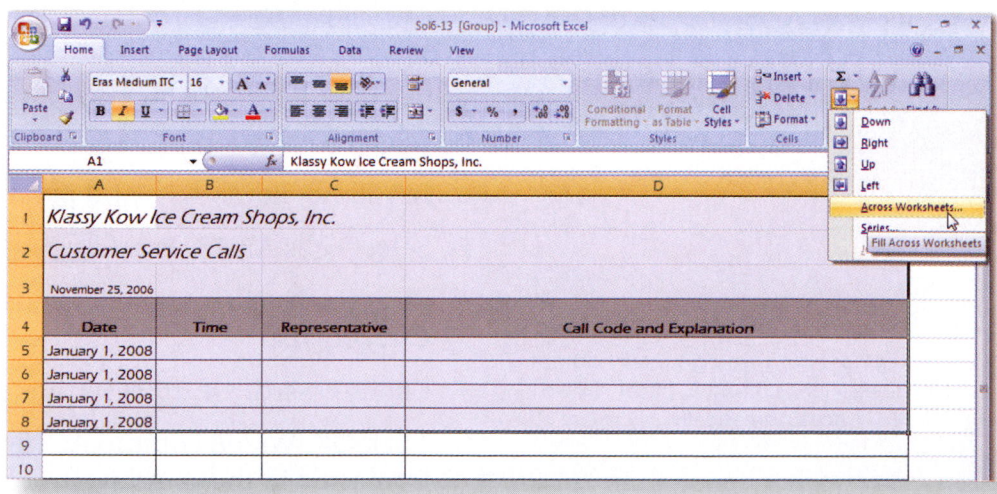

7. Choose **All** and click **OK**.

8. Right-click the **Week4** worksheet tab. Choose **Ungroup Sheets**.

9. Click the **FirstQuarter** worksheet tab. The data and some formatting have been copied. Column widths and row heights are not copied.

10. Make columns A:C **12.56 (120 pixels)** wide. Make column D **57.56 (525 pixels)** wide.

11. Make row 4 **30.00 (30 pixels)** tall. Make rows 5:8 **18.75 (25 pixels)** tall.

Exercise 6-17   CREATE A CUSTOM DATE FORMAT

To create your own date format, you key formatting codes in the Custom category. You can see formatting codes and samples in the Format Cells dialog box.

1. Select cells A5:A8 and press Ctrl + 1.

2. Click the **Number** tab and choose **Date** in the **Category** list.

3. Scroll through the **Type** list. There is no preset format to show the date, the month spelled out, and a two-digit year (14 March 01).

4. Click **Custom** in the **Category** list. The **Type** list shows the codes for a variety of formats, not just dates. You can choose one as a starting point to build your own format.

5. Scroll the **Type** list to find **d-mmm**.

6. Click the code to select it. The **Sample** box shows the date with that format.

7. Click in the **Type** box above the **Type** list.

8. Delete the hyphen and press Spacebar.

9. Edit the code to show **dd mmmm y**. Two **dd**'s show the date with a leading zero. Four **mmmm**'s spell out the month. A single **y** shows a two-digit year.

10. Look at the **Sample** box.

Figure 6-15
Creating a custom
date format

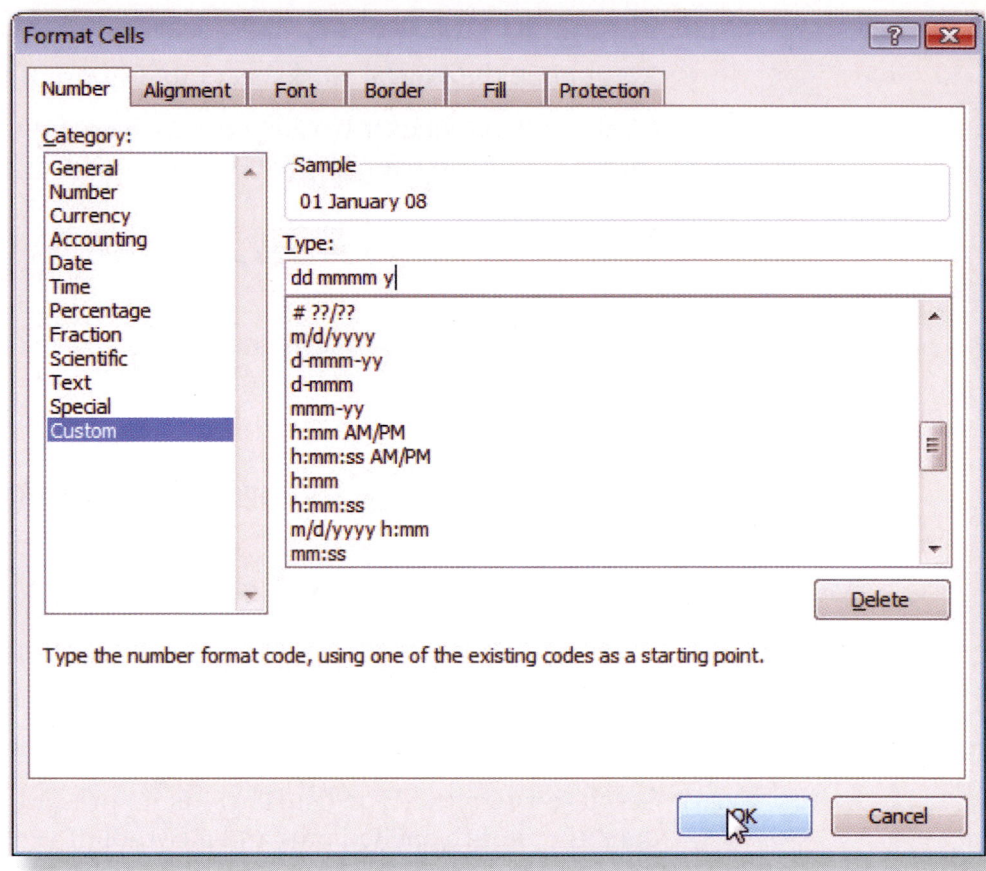

11. Click **OK**. The dates are reformatted. Widen the column if necessary.

Exercise 6-18   KEY AND FORMAT TIMES

> **TIP**
>
> It does not matter which worksheet is on top when you edit data in grouped worksheets.

1. Click the **Week1** tab. Hold down ⎙Shift⎙ and click the **Week4** tab. Four worksheets are grouped.

2. Click cell B5 and key **11 am**.

3. Press ⎙Ctrl⎙+⎙Enter⎙. The time is shown and AM is capitalized.

4. Look in the formula bar to see minutes and seconds.

5. Click cell B6 and key **4:30** and press ⎙Ctrl⎙+⎙Enter⎙.

6. Look at the time in the formula bar. If you do not key **am** or **pm**, Excel assumes morning.

7. In cell B7 key **4:30 pm** and press ⎙Enter⎙.

8. In cell B8 key **13:30** and press ⎙Enter⎙. Excel shows the time using the 24-hour clock.

9. In cell B9 key **2:45 pm**, and in cell B10 key **14:30**.

10. Select cells B5:B10.

11. Press ⌷Ctrl⌷+⌷1⌷. Click the **Number** tab and choose **Time** in the **Category** list.

12. Scroll the **Type** list. Then choose **1:30 PM** and click **OK**.

Exercise 6-19   USE THE NOW() FUNCTION

The NOW() function is similar to the TODAY() function. It uses the computer's clock to show the current date and time.

1. Click cell A11. Key **=now(** and press ⌷Enter⌷. Excel supplies the closing parenthesis.

2. Widen the column as needed. The default format may not include the time.

3. Click cell A11 and press ⌷Ctrl⌷+⌷1⌷.

4. Click the **Number** tab and choose **Time** in the **Category** list.

5. Scroll through the **Type** list. Then choose **3/14/01 1:30 PM** and click **OK**. The function shows the current date and time.

Exercise 6-20   CREATE A CUSTOM TIME FORMAT

1. Click cell A11 and press ⌷Ctrl⌷+⌷1⌷.

2. Click **Custom** in the **Category** list.

3. Scroll the **Type** list to find **m/d/yyyy h:mm**.

4. Click the code to select it. The **Sample** box shows the date and time with that format.

5. Click in the **Type** box before the first **m**.

6. Edit the code to show **mmm d, yyyy- -h:mm AM/PM**. Be sure to insert the spaces, the comma, and the hyphens. Check the **Sample** box to verify your format as you build it.

Figure 6-16
Creating a custom
time format

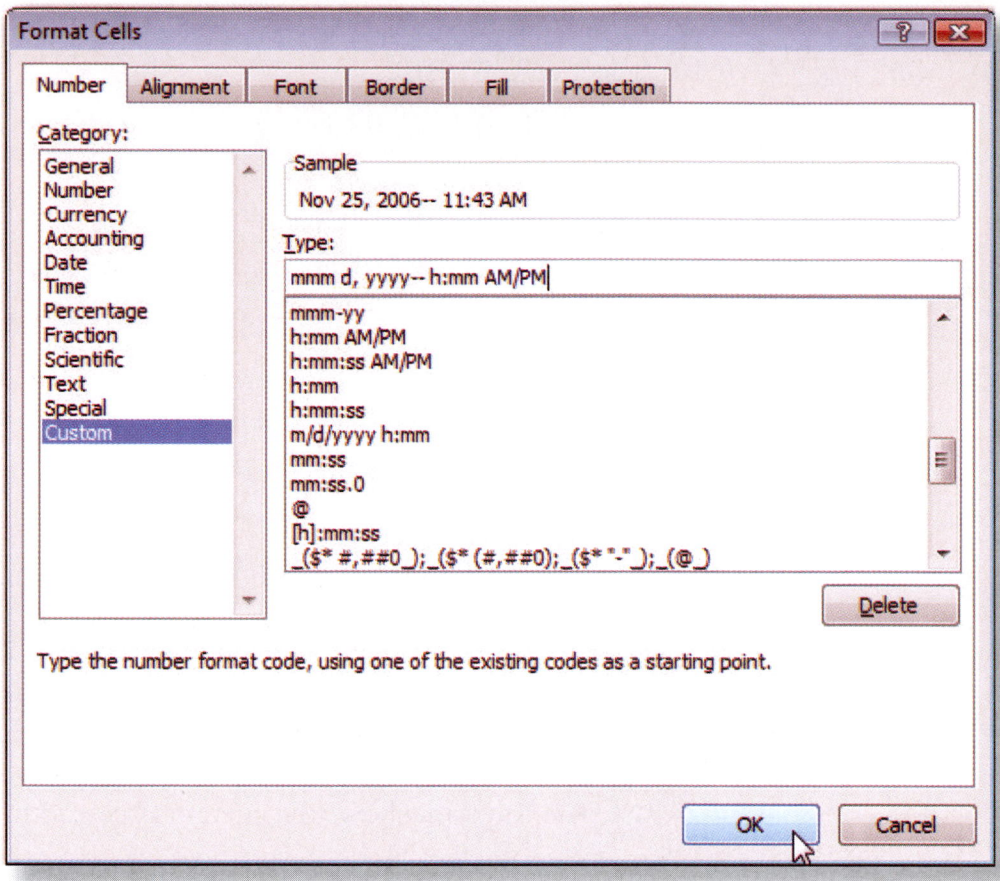

7. Click the **Alignment** tab. In the **Text control** group, click to select **Shrink to fit**.

8. Click **OK**. The time is reformatted and shrunk.

9. Right-click any sheet and choose **Ungroup Sheets**.

Exercise 6-21   ADD A HEADER TO GROUPED SHEETS

You can add the same header or footer to all sheets in a group through the Page Setup dialog box. You can also center the sheets at the same time.

1. Click the **Week1** tab. Hold down ⇧Shift and click the **FirstQuarter** tab.

2. Click the **Page Layout** tab. Click the Dialog Box Launcher for the **Page Setup** group. The Page Setup dialog box opens.

3. Click the **Header/Footer** tab. Click **Custom Header**. The Header dialog box includes the usual three sections.

4. Key your name in the left section.

5. Click in the center and click the Insert Sheet Name button . Click in the right section and click the Insert Date button.

Figure 6-17
Adding a header in the Header dialog box

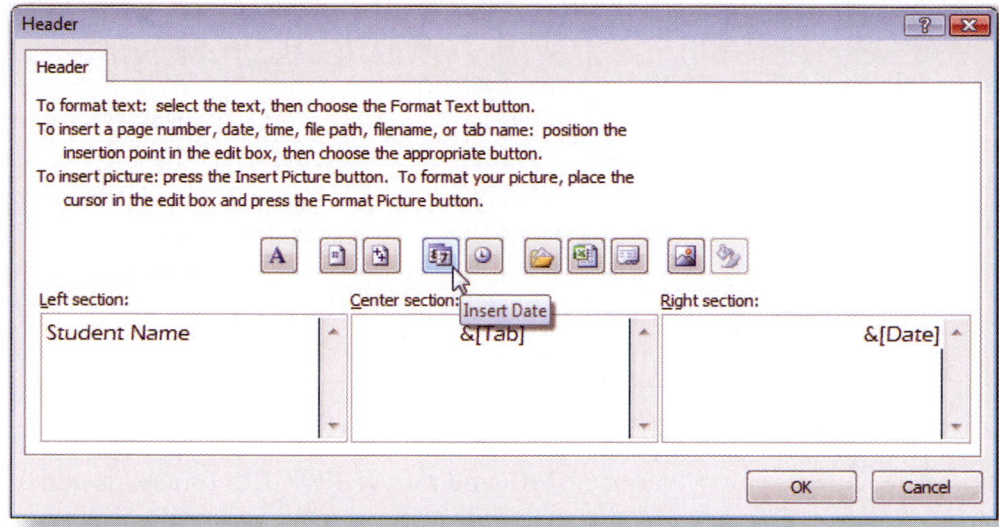

6. Click **OK**. The Page Setup dialog box includes a preview of your header.

7. Click the **Margins** tab. In the **Center on page** group, click to select **Horizontally**.

8. Click **Print Preview** in the **Page Setup** dialog box. This is the first page of five.

9. Press PageDown to see the next sheet. Press PageUp to return to previous pages.

TIP

A workbook is saved with the sheets grouped.

10. Click **Close Print Preview**.

11. Save the workbook as *[your initials]*6-21 in your folder.

12. Click the Microsoft Office Button . Choose **Print** and then **Quick Print** while the worksheets are grouped. All five sheets print with the same header.

13. Close the workbook.

Using Online Help

USE HELP TO VIEW ADDITIONAL INFORMATION ABOUT FORMAT CODES

1. In a new workbook, press F1.

2. In the Search box, key **format codes** and press Enter.

3. Find and review topics to learn more about format codes. Read the help information.

4. Close the Help window.

Lesson 6 Summary

- Excel has several categories of date, time, mathematical, and statistical functions. You can key them or use the Insert Function dialog box.

- When you key a function name, Formula AutoComplete displays a list of functions that match your keystrokes.

- Functions have a syntax that must be followed. The syntax includes an equal sign, the name of the function, and arguments inside parentheses.

- The SUM function adds the values of the cells indicated in its argument.

- The TRUNC function removes the decimal part of a number.

- The AVERAGE function calculates the arithmetic mean.

- The SUMIF and the AVERAGEIF functions add and average values only if they meet the criteria specified in the argument.

- The MIN function displays the smallest value in a range. The MAX function displays the largest value in a range.

- The COUNT function counts the number of values in a range. The COUNTA function does the same and includes labels. COUNTBLANK counts empty cells in a range.

- The TODAY and NOW functions show the current date and time. Both functions can be formatted using preset or custom formats.

- An icon set is a data visualization that displays an icon at the left edge of the cell based on the value.

- Icon sets can use three, four, or five icons to represent the values.

- Copy selected data from one worksheet to another using the Fill Across Worksheets command.

- You can group multiple worksheets to edit, format, or print several sheets at once.

- Use the Page Setup dialog box to add a footer or header to grouped sheets.

LESSON 6		Command Summary	
Feature	**Button**	**Task Path**	**Keyboard**
Custom format	Format	Home, Cells, Format, Format Cells	Ctrl + 1
Custom header/footer		Page Layout, Page Setup, Dialog Box Launcher	
Fill across worksheets		Home, Editing, Fill	
Icon set		Home, Styles, Conditional Formatting	
Insert Function	fx		Shift + F3
Insert Function	fx Insert Function	Formulas, Function Library	Shift + F3

Concepts Review

True/False Questions

Each of the following statements is either true or false. Indicate your choice by circling T or F.

T F 1. To complete a function, you must include its arguments.

T F 2. Icon sets display an image in the range based on the value.

T F 3. The SUM function calculates a text value as 1.

T F 4. The first character for all functions is a left parenthesis.

T F 5. The TODAY function does not have arguments.

T F 6. Custom formats include **?** and ***** to show days and months.

T F 7. Most statistical functions ignore text in their calculations.

T F 8. You can copy data from one worksheet to another with the Fill handle.

Short Answer Questions

Write the correct answer in the space provided.

1. Name the three types of data visualizations.

   _____

2. How can you select more than one worksheet tab?

   _____

3. Name the function that adds cell values only if they meet your criteria.

   _____

4. What function displays the arithmetic mean of a range of cells?

   _____

5. What does Excel do if a function is volatile?

   _____

6. What term is used to describe the information between parentheses in a function?

   _____

7. What feature helps you complete a function after you key = and its first character in the cell?

_____

8. What function would display the highest sales amount in a column?

_____

Critical Thinking

Answer these questions on a separate page. There are no right or wrong answers. Support your answers with examples from your own experience, if possible.

1. What are some math and trig functions that you did not use in this lesson? How might they be helpful in school work or on the job?

2. What type of businesses might use calculations that would use the date and time functions? Give examples of how they would use the functions.

Skills Review

Exercise 6-22

Use Math & Trig functions. Use Statistical functions.

1. Open **HolidayPay**. Save it as *[your initials]6-22* in your Lesson 6 folder.
2. Click the Select All button . Then click the Bold button **B** . All cells are set for bold.
3. Move the data in cells C13:H16 to start in cell C9.
4. In cell C15, key **Number of Employees**.
5. Use math and trig functions by following these steps:
   a. Click cell H13.
   b. Key **=sum(** to start the function.
   c. Click cell H6 and drag to select cells H6:H12. Press Enter.
   d. In cell E15, key **=counta(** to start the function.
   e. Click cell C6 and drag to select cells C6:C12. Press Enter.
6. In cell I6, key a formula to multiply the hours worked by the holiday rate. Widen the column slightly and copy the formula through row 12.
7. Use math and trig and statistical functions by following these steps:
   a. Click cell I13. Click the **Formulas** tab.
   b. Click the Math & Trig button 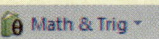 .

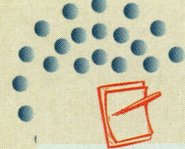

NOTE

If the assumed range is not correct, click and drag to select the correct range.

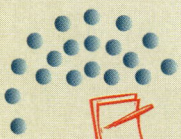

NOTE

The COUNTIF function is similar to the SUMIF function, but it is in the Statistical category.

c. Scroll and click **SUM**.

d. Check that the range to be summed is I6:I12. Click **OK**.

e. Widen column I as needed.

f. Click cell E16. Click the Insert Function button 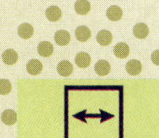.

g. In the **Or select a category** list, choose **All**. Quickly key **coun** and find **COUNTIF**. Select it and click **OK**.

h. For the **Range** box, select cells I6:I12.

i. In the **Criteria** box, key **>250** to count employees who earned more than $250. Click **OK**.

8. Key **Over $250** in cell C16.

9. Add **Top and Double Bottom** borders to cells H13:I13.

10. Press Ctrl + Home. Add a footer and adjust the left and/or right margin to fit the sheet to a portrait page.

11. Make a copy of the worksheet and name it **Formulas**.

12. Press Ctrl + ~. AutoFit the columns.

13. Click the **Page Layout** tab. Click the Page Orientation button  and choose **Landscape**.

14. In the **Scale to Fit** group, click the arrow with the Width button 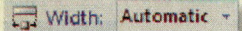. Choose **1 page**. Use the same choice for **Height**.

15. Prepare and submit your work. Save and close the workbook.

Exercise 6-23

Use Math & Trig and Statistical functions. Use an icon set.

1. Open **Insurance**. Save it as *[your initials]*6-23 in your Lesson 6 folder.

2. Key math and trig and statistical functions by following these steps:

   a. Click cell D17. Key **=coun** and press Tab.

   b. Click cell C4 and drag to select cells C4:C14. Press Enter.

   c. In cell D18, key **=sum** and press Tab. Select cells C4:C14 and press Enter.

REVIEW

For many functions, you need not key the entire name for AutoComplete to find it.

NOTE

The **Most Recently Used** list shows the functions you have used during the work session.

3. Use Insert Function by following these steps:

   a. Click the **Formulas** tab.

   b. Click cell D19. Click the Insert Function button . Choose **Statistical** and **COUNTA**. Click **OK**.

   c. Select cells D4:D14. Click **OK**.

   d. Click cell D20 and press Shift + F3.

   e. In the **Or select a category** list, choose **Most Recently Used** and **COUNTA**. Click **OK**.

   f. Select cells A4:A14. Click **OK**.

4. Remove the decimals from the values in column D. Center the labels in rows 1:2 across the data. Change the document theme to **Paper**.

5. Use icon sets by following these steps:

   a. Select cells E4:E14 and click the Conditional Formatting button .

   b. Choose **Icon Sets** and **Red to Black** in the first column.

   c. Select cells E4:E14 and click the Conditional Formatting button.

   d. Choose **Manage Rules**. Click **Edit Rule**.

   e. Click the arrow with **Percent** for the first icon. Choose **Number**.

   f. Change the **Type** for the second and third icons to **Number**.

   g. Click to select **Reverse Icon Order**.

   h. Key **2000** in the **Value** box for the first icon (black).

   i. Key **1000** in the **Value** box for the second icon (gray).

   j. Key **500** in the **Value** box for the third icon (light red).

   k. Click **OK**. Click **OK** again.

6. Press `Ctrl`+`Home`. Add a header and change the left margin to 1.50 inches.

7. Prepare and submit your work. Save and close the workbook.

Exercise 6-24

Group worksheets. Use Date & Time functions. Use Math & Trig and Statistical functions.

REVIEW

Copy the template to the appropriate folder for your computer. Then choose **My Templates** in the **New Workbook** dialog box.

1. Use the **ChkBk** template to create a new workbook. Save it as *[your initials]*6-24 in your Lesson 6 folder.

2. Group worksheets by following these steps:

   a. Right-click the **Sheet1** tab. Choose **Move or Copy**. Select **Sheet2** in the **Before sheet** list. Click to select **Create a copy**. Click **OK**.

   b. Make another copy and place it before **Sheet2**.

   c. Click the **Sheet2** tab. Hold down `Ctrl` and click the **Sheet3** tab.

   d. Right-click either tab and choose **Delete**.

   e. Rename the sheets as **Week1**, **Week2**, and **Week3**. Assign an accent color to each tab.

   f. Click the **Week1** tab. Hold down `Shift` and click the **Week3** tab.

3. Use a date function by following these steps:

   a. Click cell A4, key **=to**, and press `Tab`. Press `Ctrl`+`Enter`.

   b. Click cell A5 and key **=** to start a formula.

   c. Click cell A4 and key **+5** to add five days to today's date.

   d. Press `Ctrl`+`Enter`.

TIP

You can use the Fill handle for the check numbers.

e. Copy the formula in cell A5 to cells A6:A15.

f. Key your name in cell A20 while the sheets are grouped.

4. Ungroup worksheets by following these steps:

   a. Right-click any sheet tab in the group. Choose **Ungroup Sheets**.

   b. Click the **Week1** tab.

5. Key the data for columns B:D as shown here.

Figure 6-18

	Check #	Payee	Credit Amount	Deposit
6	1002	[your first and last name]	1250	
7	1003	Sutter, Howe, & Jones	2500	
8	1004	Holberg Markets	575	
9	1005	[your school name]	435	
10	1006	Hacienda Martinez	575	
11	1007	Smithfield Stores	435	
12	1008	Grocerytown Enterprises	1200	

6. Use math and trig and statistical functions by following these steps:

   a. Click cell D16.

   b. Key **=sum** and press Tab.

   c. Click cell D5 and drag to select cells D5:D12. Press Enter.

   d. In cell B16, key **=count(** and ignore Formula AutoComplete.

   e. Click cell B5 and drag to select cells B5:B12. Press Enter.

   f. Press Ctrl + Home.

7. Group the worksheets and click the **Page Layout** tab. In the **Scale to Fit** group, click the arrow with the Height button . Choose **1 page**. Use the same choice for the **Width**.

8. Prepare and submit your work. Save and close the workbook.

Exercise 6-25

Use Date & Time functions. Format times and dates.

1. Create a new workbook and save it as *[your initials]*6-25 in your Lesson 6 folder.

2. Click the Select All button . Set the font to Calibri 12 point bold.

3. In cell A1, key **Klassy Kow Ice Cream Shops**. In cell A2, key **Olympia Shop**. Choose a larger font size for these labels.

4. Key **Date** in cell A3, **Open Time** in cell B3, and **Close Time** in cell C3. Center-align these labels. Make all three columns **12.14 (90 pixels)** wide.

5. Use date functions by following these steps:
    a. In cell A4, key **=today(** and press ⌷Enter⌷.
    b. Click cell A5 and key **=** to start the formula.
    c. Click cell A4 and key **+1** to add one day. Press ⌷Enter⌷.
    d. Copy the formula in cell A5 to cells A6:A10.

6. Format dates by following these steps:
    a. Select cells A4:A10. Press ⌷Ctrl⌷+⌷1⌷.
    b. Click the **Number** tab and choose **Date** in the **Category** list.
    c. Choose **March 14, 2001** in the **Type** list. Click **OK**.
    d. Widen column A to show the dates if necessary.

7. Key the times as shown in the figure below.

Figure 6-19

	Open Time	Close Time
4	9 am	10 pm
5	10 am	11 pm
6	10 am	12 am
7	11 am	12 am
8	11 am	9 pm
9	11 am	11 pm
10	11 am	11 pm

8. Format times by following these steps:
    a. Select cells B4:C10. Press ⌷Ctrl⌷+⌷1⌷.
    b. Click the **Number** tab and choose **Custom** in the **Category** list.
    c. Choose **h:mm** in the **Type** list.
    d. Edit the code in the **Type** box to show **h AM/PM**. Click **OK**.

9. Center the labels in rows 1:2 across the data. Make all rows **26.25 (35 pixels)** tall.

10. Insert a row at row 1. Insert a column at column A. Select cells A1:E12. Press ⌷Ctrl⌷+⌷1⌷ and choose a double border as an outline.

11. Select cells A1:E3 and change the font color to white. Then apply black fill.

12. Add a header and change the left margin to about 1.75 inches.

13. Make a copy of the worksheet and change the tab name to **Formulas**. Display the formulas and adjust the column widths; columns A and E can be very narrow. Change the left margin to .75 inches. Fit the sheet to a portrait page.

14. Prepare and submit your work. Save and close the workbook.

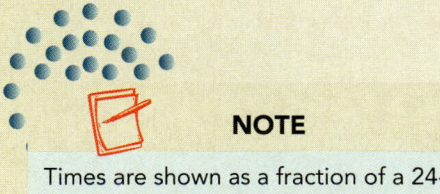

NOTE

Times are shown as a fraction of a 24-hour day in formula view.

Lesson Applications

Exercise 6-26

Use Date functions. Group worksheets.

1. Create a new workbook using the **CSCalls** template. Save the workbook as *[your initials]*6-26.

2. Use the TODAY function in cell A3 and format the cell as white so that it is not visible. Key a formula in cell A5 that adds one day to cell A3. Shrink the data to fit if needed.

3. Key a formula in cell A6 that adds one day to the date in cell A5. Copy the formula in cell A6 down to row 25.

4. Format cells B5:B25 to show the time using the **1:30 PM** preset format.

5. Key the times and representative names as shown. Use AutoComplete where appropriate.

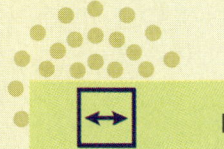

REVIEW

Set the Zoom size if you prefer to see the entire worksheet at once.

Figure 6-20

5	9:30 am	Anderson
6	10:25 am	Olmstead
7	12:30 pm	Rogers
8	1:30 pm	Devantes
9	10:45 am	LaPluie
10	2:30 pm	Anderson
11	11:30 am	Anderson
12	8:45 am	Olmstead
13	4:30 pm	LaPluie
14	10 am	Devantes
15	8 am	Devantes
16	3:30 pm	Rogers
17	9:45 am	LaPluie
18	10:15 am	Olmstead
19	12 pm	Devantes
20	12:15 pm	Olmstead
21	11:15 am	LaPluie
22	11:45 am	Olmstead
23	2:25 pm	Devantes
24	9 am	Anderson
25	10:25 am	Olmstead

6. Select cells A1:D25. Then hold down ⌃Ctrl and click the **Sheet2** tab. Fill all across the worksheets.

7. Name **Sheet2** as **Week2**. Make the column widths and row heights the same as the **Week1** sheet.

8. On the **Week2** sheet, edit the formula in cell A5 to add seven days to the function.

NOTE

Use the Page Setup dialog box to apply settings to grouped sheets.

9. Group the two sheets and open the Page Setup dialog box. From this dialog box, add a footer. Then set landscape orientation and change the top and bottom margins to .5 inch. Delete **Sheet3**.

10. Prepare and submit your work. Save and close the workbook.

Exercise 6-27

Group worksheets. Use Statistical functions.

1. Open **ShopPart** and save it as *[your initials]*6-27 in your folder.

2. Group all four sheets.

3. In cell A22, key **Number of Shops**. Make it 11-point Calibri bold italic.

NOTE

The worksheets should remain grouped throughout this exercise.

4. In cell B22, use **COUNTIF** to count the shops that participated in the Tip Calculator promotion. Copy the formula to cells C22:D22.

5. Center-align the contents in cells B22:D22. Use 11-point Calibri bold italic.

6. Insert a column at column A and make it **3.57 (30 pixels)** wide. Apply a double outline border around cells A5:E23.

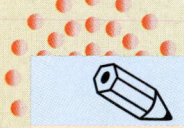

TIP

Use the Insert Function dialog box to build the COUNTIF function.

7. From the Page Setup dialog box, add a footer and change the page orientation to landscape.

8. Prepare and submit your work. Save and close the workbook.

Exercise 6-28

Use Math & Trig functions.

1. Open **ORSundaes** and save it as *[your initials]*6-28 in your folder.

2. In cell H3, use **AVERAGE** with cells C4:C8 as **Number1**. Ignore the error.

3. Compute the average sales for medium and large sundaes in cells H4 and H5. Adjust column F to show the labels, and make column G very narrow.

4. In cell H6, calculate the revenue by summing the appropriate sales and multiplying by the related price. Use a similar formula to determine revenue for medium and large sundaes.

5. In cell H13, add the three revenues to find a total.

6. Delete row 14. Add a double top border to the data cells to match the other price listings.

7. Format all non-money values as Comma style with no decimal places.

8. Apply a double outline border around cells E1:I10. Move this entire range so that it starts in row 5.

9. Add a header.

10. Make a copy of the worksheet and change the tab name to **SundaesFormulas**. Display the formulas. Delete columns with no data and AutoFit the other columns. Fit the formula sheet to one landscape page.

11. Prepare and submit your work. Save and close the workbook.

Exercise 6-29 ◆ Challenge Yourself

Use date arithmetic.

1. Open **CoPay**. Save it as *[your initials]6-29* in your folder.

2. Insert a column before column D. Key **Date Eligible** on two lines as the label for this column.

3. In cell D5, key a formula to determine the date eligible for a reduced copay. The formula should add the appropriate number of days to the enrollment date to determine when the employee is eligible.

4. Copy the formula for the other employees. Make adjustments as needed.

5. Increase the indent once for the department names to create space between the dates in column D and the labels in column E. Then widen column E to show more space between its labels and those in column F.

6. Add a footer and fit the worksheet to one portrait page.

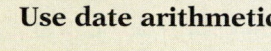

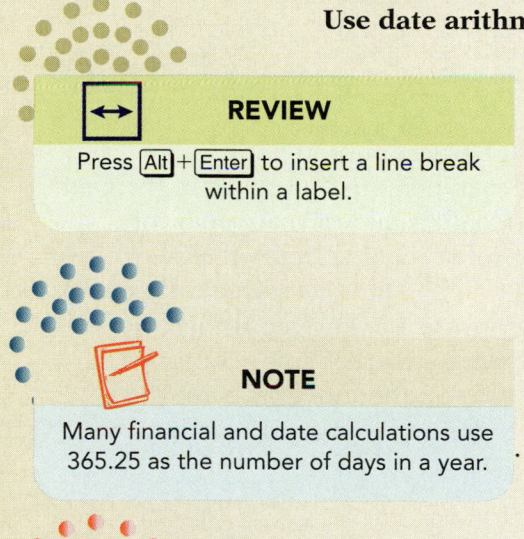

REVIEW

Press [Alt]+[Enter] to insert a line break within a label.

NOTE

Many financial and date calculations use 365.25 as the number of days in a year.

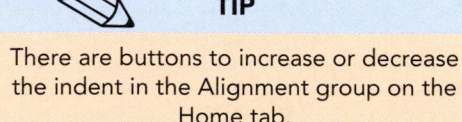

TIP

There are buttons to increase or decrease the indent in the Alignment group on the Home tab.

REVIEW

Horizontal centering for the page is on the Margins tab in the Page Setup dialog box.

7. Create a formula sheet. Turn off horizontal centering and fit the formulas to one landscape page.

8. Prepare and submit your work. Save and close the workbook.

On Your Own

In these exercises you work on your own, as you would in a real-life work environment. Use the skills you've learned to accomplish the task—and be creative.

Exercise 6-30

Create a new workbook and save it as *[your initials]*6-30. Key **My Age in Days and Years** as a label. In column A, key the TODAY() function. In the cell below the date, key a formula to add 365.25 days to today. Copy this formula to reach 10 years from now. Key your birthdate in column F. In column B, use the **DAYS360** function to calculate your age in days for each date in column A. In column C, divide the number of days by 360. Format your work attractively. Add a footer. Prepare and submit your work.

Exercise 6-31

In a new workbook, key the first names of 10 people you know in a column. In the column to the right, key each person's eye color. In the next column, key each person's hair color. Add labels and format your work with borders and/or fill so that it looks professional. In a row below your data, key **Number of Persons with Blonde Hair and Blue Eyes**. In a cell next to or below this label, use **COUNTIFS** to determine the answer. If there are no such persons in your list, change your label to another color combination or change some of the colors in your list to test the function. Save the workbook as *[your initials]*6-31. Add a header and prepare and submit your work.

Exercise 6-32

Open **HolidayPay**. Delete column G and then column H. Move rows so that there is no blank space in the middle of the data. Key new labels below row 12 so that you can show these calculations: average regular rate, average rate increase, and average hours worked. Save the worksheet as *[your initials]*6-32. Add a header or footer. Create a formula sheet. Prepare and submit your work.

Lesson 7

Using Logical and Financial Functions

OBJECTIVES

After completing this lesson, you will be able to:

1. Use the IF function.

2. Use the AND, OR, and NOT functions.

3. Work with cell styles.

4. Work with page breaks.

5. Use the PMT and FV functions.

6. Use the Depreciation functions.

MCAS OBJECTIVES

In this lesson:
XL07 2.3.1
XL07 2.3.3
XL07 3.1
XL07 3.6.1
XL07 5.5
XL07 5.5.2
XL07 5.5.4

Estimated Time: 1¹/₂ hours

A *logical function* is a formula that calculates if an expression is true. There are seven logical functions: AND, FALSE, IF, IFERROR, NOT, OR, and TRUE. Except for the IF and IFERROR functions, a logical function shows the word "TRUE" or "FALSE" as a result.

A *financial function* performs a business calculation that involves money. These include how to figure loan payments and how to determine depreciation.

Using the IF Function

The IF function is a simple analysis and decision-making tool. When working with accounts receivable, for example, you can determine if a late fee should be assessed.

The IF function has three arguments. It follows the form "If X, then Y; otherwise Z." X, Y, and Z represent the arguments.

The syntax for the IF function is:

=IF(logical_test, value_if_true, value_if_false)
Example: =IF(C5>50,C5*2, "None")

- Logical_test is the first argument, the condition. It's a statement or expression that is either true or false. In the example, the expression C5>50 is either true or false, depending on the value in cell C5.

- Value_if_true, the second argument, is what the formula shows if the logical_test is true. In the example, if C5 is greater than 50, the value in cell C5 is multiplied by 2. The value_if_true can be a formula, a value, text, or a cell reference.

- Value_if_false, the third argument, is what the formula shows if the logical_test is not true. The value_if_false can be a formula, a value, text, or a cell reference. In the example, if the value in cell C5 is 50 or less, the result is the word "None."

Exercise 7-1   USE IF TO SHOW TEXT

You can create an IF function to display text. When you use the Function Arguments dialog box, Excel inserts quotation marks around text in an IF function. When you key an IF function, you must key quotation marks.

IF functions can use relational or comparison operators as well as the arithmetic operators.

TABLE 7-1 Relational (Comparison) Operators

Operator	Description
=	Equal to
<>	Not equal to
>	Greater than
<	Less than
>=	Greater than or equal to
<=	Less than or equal to

1. Open **BonusPay** and click cell C4. If a salesperson sells more than $60,000 in goods, this cell should display "Yes."

2. Click the **Formulas** tab.

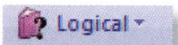

3. Click the Logical button 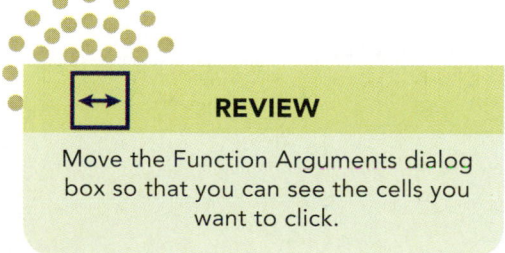.

4. Choose **IF** in the list. The insertion point is in the **Logical_test** box.

5. Click cell B4. The address appears in the **Logical_test** box.

6. Key **>60000** in the **Logical_test** box after **B4**. This logical test will determine if the value in cell B4 is greater than 60000.

7. Click in the **Value_if_true** box.

REVIEW

Move the Function Arguments dialog box so that you can see the cells you want to click.

8. Key **Yes**. If the value in cell B4 is greater than 60000, cell C4 will display the word "Yes."

9. Click in the **Value_if_false** box. Note the quotation marks for "Yes."

10. Key **No**. If the value in cell B4 is not greater than 60000, cell C4 will display the word "No."

Figure 7-1
Function Arguments dialog box for IF
BonusPay.xlsx
Bonus sheet

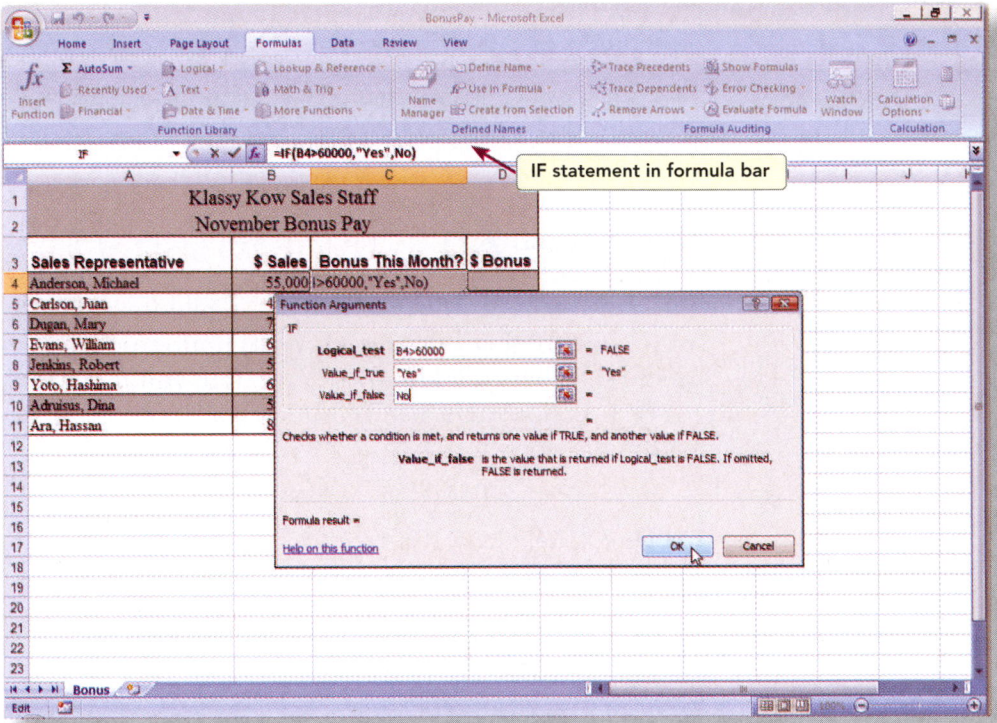

11. Click **OK**. The result of this IF formula for cell C4 is **No**.

12. Look at the formula in the formula bar. You can see the quotation marks for **No** now.

13. Click the **Home** tab and then the Center button. Copy the formula to cells C5:C11. Formatting is copied with the formula.

14. Click the Undo button. Press [Esc] if you see a marquee.

15. Click cell C4 and press [Ctrl]+[C].

16. Select cells C5:C11 and right-click one of the selected cells.

17. Choose **Paste Special**. Choose **Formulas** and click **OK**.

18. Click the Center button for the selected range.

Exercise 7-2   USE IF TO CALCULATE A VALUE

Excel can calculate the bonus if a salesperson is eligible. In this case, the bonus will be 2.5% of the sales value.

1. Click cell D4. Key **=if** to see the Formula AutoComplete list.

2. Press Tab. The ScreenTip displays the syntax for the function, and the argument to be keyed next is bold.

3. Click cell C4. A marquee appears around the cell, and the address appears after the left parenthesis. This starts the **Logical_test**.

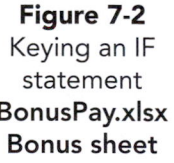

NOTE

When you key text as part of the Logical_test, you must include quotation marks.

4. Key **="yes"** after **C4**. This logical test will determine if cell C4 shows "Yes." Text in a logical test is not case-sensitive.

5. Key a comma after **"yes"** to separate the logical test from the value_if_true. **Value_if_true** in the ScreenTip is bold.

6. Click cell B4. A marquee appears around the cell, and the address appears after the comma.

7. Key ***2.5%** after **B4**. The formula multiplies the value in cell B4 by 2.5% if cell C4 shows "Yes." This is what the function will do if the test is true (C4 does show "yes").

8. Key a comma after **2.5%** to separate the value_if_true from the value_if_false. Value_if_false in the ScreenTip is bold.

9. Key **""** (two quotation marks with nothing between them). This represents no text, or nothing. If cell C4 does not show "Yes," cell D4 will show nothing. It will be blank.

Figure 7-2
Keying an IF statement
BonusPay.xlsx
Bonus sheet

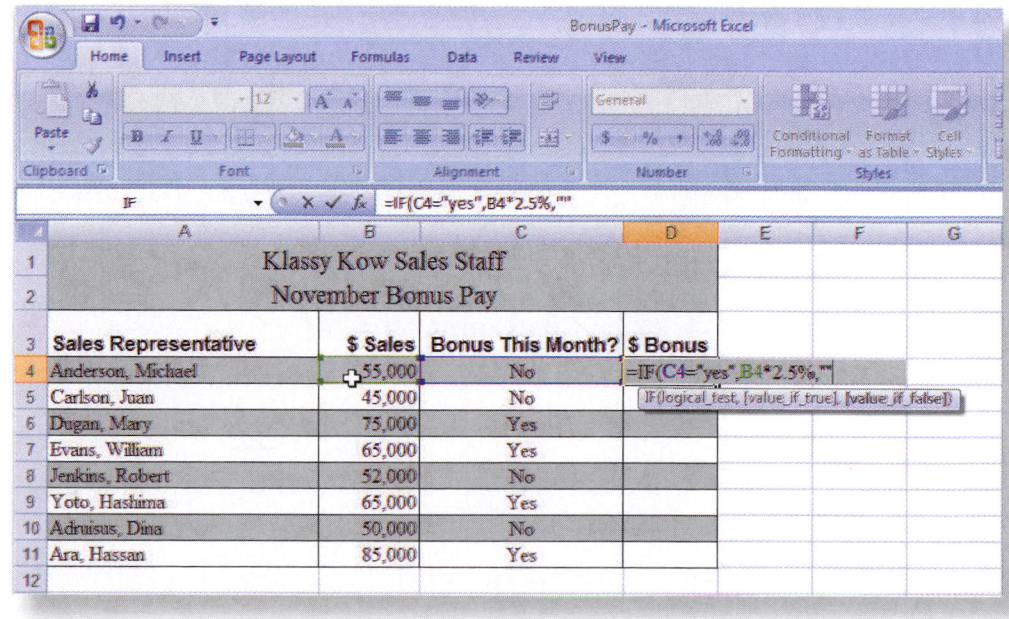

10. Press [Enter]. Excel added the closing right parenthesis for you. Cell D4 shows nothing, because this sales rep does not receive a bonus.

11. Click cell D4 and press [Ctrl]+[C].

12. Select cells D5:D11 and right-click. Choose **Paste Special**. Choose **Formulas** and click **OK**. Press [Esc] to remove the marquee.

13. Select cells D4:D11 and click the Comma Style button .

14. Click the Decrease Decimal button two times.

15. Add a footer and save the workbook *[your initials]*7-2 in a folder for Lesson 7. Close the workbook.

Using AND, OR, and NOT Functions

AND, OR, and NOT are logical functions that show either "TRUE" or "FALSE" as a result. These functions ignore labels and empty cells, so you use them only with values (numbers).

Exercise 7-3   USE THE AND FUNCTION

In an AND function, you can use multiple logical tests. All tests or expressions must be true for the result cell to show TRUE. Otherwise, it shows FALSE.

TABLE 7-2 Examples of the AND Function

Expression	Result
AND(C4>10, D4>10)	TRUE if both C4 and D4 are greater than 10; FALSE if either C4 or D4 is 10 or less.
AND(C4>10, C4<100)	TRUE if C4 is greater than 10 but less than 100; FALSE if C4 is 10 or less than 10 or 100 or greater than 100.
AND(C4>10, D4<10)	TRUE if C4 is greater than 10 and D4 is less than 10; FALSE if C4 is equal to or less than 10 or if D4 is equal to or greater than 10.
AND(C4=10, D4<100)	TRUE if C4 is equal to 10 and D4 is less than 100; FALSE if C4 is equal to any value except 10.

1. Open **CustCount**.

2. In cell J3, key **All Over 150 on** and hold down [Alt] and press [Enter].

3. Key **on Weekend?** and press [Enter].

4. Make the label bold. Make row 3 **30.00 (40 pixels)** tall. AutoFit the column.

5. Click cell J4. Click the **Formulas** tab.

6. Click the Logical button 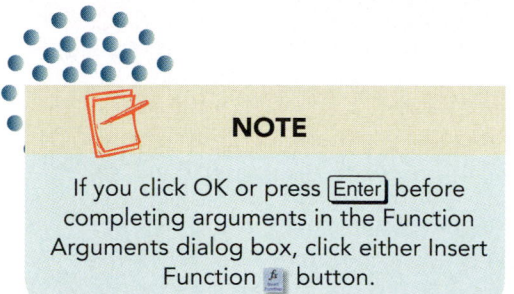. Choose **AND** in the list. The insertion point is in the **Logical1** box.

7. Click cell G4. The address appears in the **Logical1** box.

8. Key **>** in the **Logical1** box after **G4**.

9. Key **150** but don't press Enter. This test will determine if the value in cell G4 is greater than 150.

10. Click in the **Logical2** box. Click cell H4 and key **>150**. The second condition is that the value in cell H4 be greater than 150.

11. Click in the **Logical3** box. Click cell I4 and key **>150**. The third condition is that the value in cell I4 be greater than 150.

NOTE

If you click OK or press Enter before completing arguments in the Function Arguments dialog box, click either Insert Function f_x button.

Figure 7-3
Function Arguments dialog box for AND
CustCount.xlsx
CustCount sheet

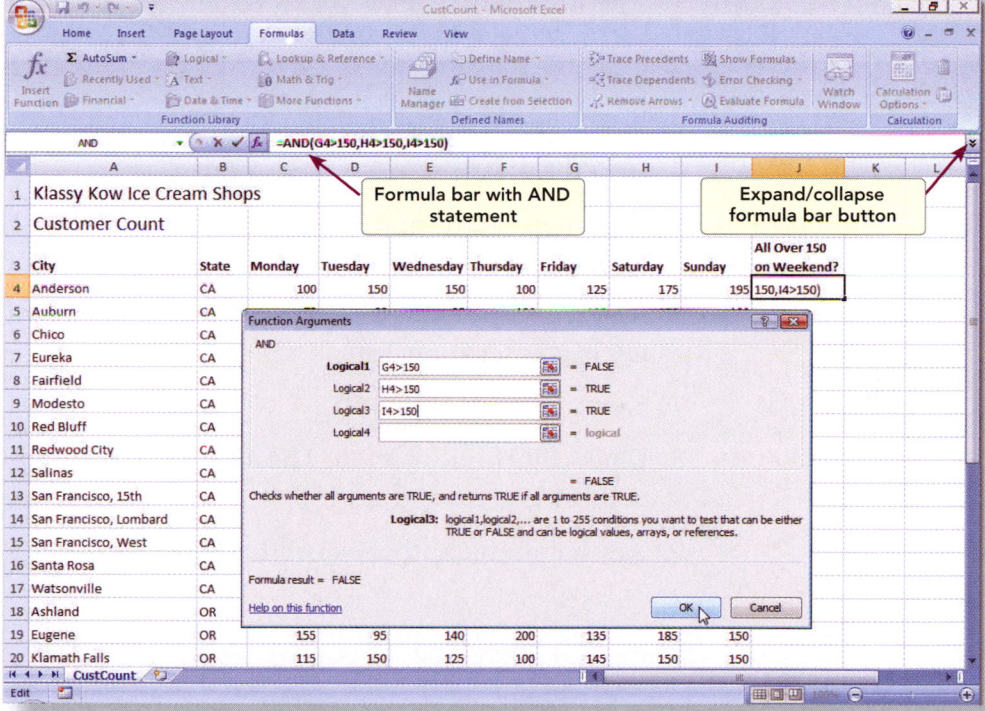

12. Click **OK**. The customer count must be greater than 150 each weekend day to show TRUE; it's not. Look at the formula in the formula bar.

13. Copy the formula to cells J5:J35. Only weekends in which all three days had greater than 150 customers show TRUE (Las Vegas Green Street, Reno, and Olympia). A day's count equal to 150 is not greater than 150.

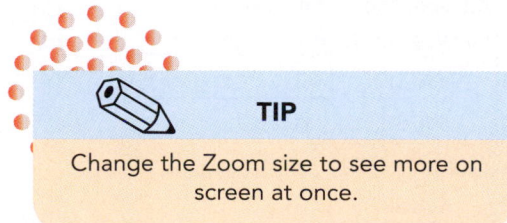

TIP

Change the Zoom size to see more on screen at once.

Exercise 7-4 USE THE OR FUNCTION

In an OR function, any one of your logical tests can be true for the result cell to show TRUE. If they are all false, the result is FALSE.

TABLE 7-3 Examples of the OR Function

Expression	Result
OR(C4>10, D4>10)	TRUE if either C4 or D4 is greater than 10; FALSE only if both C4 and D4 are less than or equal to 10.
OR(C4>10, D4<100)	TRUE if C4 is greater than 10 or if D4 is less than 100; FALSE only if C4 is equal to or less than 10 and if D4 is equal to or greater than 100.
OR(C4>10, D4=10)	TRUE if C4 is greater than 10 or if D4 is equal to 10; FALSE if C4 is equal to or less than 10 and if D4 is any value other than 10.

1. Copy the label in cell J3 to cell K3.

2. Click the Expand Formula Bar button. Click in the formula bar and edit the label to **Any Over 150 on Weekend?**

3. Press Enter and AutoFit the column.

4. In cell K4, key **=or** and press Tab.

5. Click cell G4. A marquee appears around the cell, and the address appears in the formula.

6. Key **>150** after **G4**. This logical test will determine if the value in cell G4 is greater than 150.

7. Key a comma after **150**.

8. Click cell H4. Key **>150**. The second condition will test if the value in cell H4 is greater than 150.

9. Key a comma and click cell I4. Key **>150** as the third logical test.

Figure 7-4
Keying an OR function
CustCount.xlsx
CustCount sheet

	Thursday	Friday	Saturday	Sunday	All Over 150 on Weekend?	Any Over 150 on Weekend?	
	100	125	175	195	FALSE	=or(G4>150,H4>150,	
	100	135	150	100	FALSE	I4>150	
	225	135	175	1		OR(logical1, [logical2], [logical3], [logical4], …)	
	100	125	135	150	FALSE		
	100	135	150	100	FALSE		

10. Press Enter. If the customer count is greater than 150 people on any one of the weekend days, the result is TRUE.

11. Copy the formula into cells K5:K35.

12. Click the Collapse Formula Bar button.

REVIEW

You can click the Enter button ✔ in the formula bar to complete a formula.

Exercise 7-5 **USE THE NOT FUNCTION**

In a NOT function, the reverse or opposite of your logical_test must be true for the result cell to show TRUE. The NOT function has one argument.

TABLE 7-4 Examples of the NOT Function

Expression	Result
NOT(C4>10)	TRUE if C4 is 10 or less than 10; FALSE if C4 is 11 or greater.
NOT(C4=10)	TRUE if C4 contains any value other than 10; FALSE if C4 is 10.

1. Click cell L3. Key **Sunday>150?**

2. Click cell L4. Key **=not(** and click cell I4.

3. Key **<150**. The formula tests if the value in cell I4 is less than 150. If the value is 150 or a value greater than 150, cell L4 will show TRUE.

Figure 7-5
Keying a NOT function
CustCount.xlsx
CustCount sheet

H	I	J	K	L	M
		All Over 150 on Weekend?	Any Over 150 on Weekend?	Sunday>150?	
Saturday	Sunday				
175	195	FALSE	TRUE	=NOT(I4<150	
150	100	FALSE	FALSE	NOT(logical)	
175	150	FALSE	TRUE		
135	150	FALSE	FALSE		
150	100	FALSE	FALSE		

4. Press Enter.

5. Copy the formula to cells L5:L35. Look at the results for counts of 150 or more on Sunday.

Working with Cell Styles

A *cell style* is a set of formatting specifications for labels or values. A cell style can contain number format, font, border, alignment, fill, and cell protection. You used cell styles when you clicked the Accounting Number Format button $ ▾ , the Comma Style button ▸ , or the Percent Style button % . The default cell style for all new data keyed in a workbook is Normal.

Exercise 7-6   USE CELL STYLES

1. Click the **Home** tab.

2. Select cells C36:I36 and click the AutoSum button Σ ▾ .

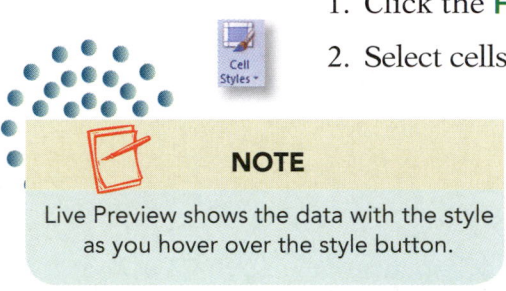

3. While the cells are selected, click the Cell Styles button in the **Styles** group. The Cell Styles gallery opens.

4. Hover over several cell styles to see the change in row 36.

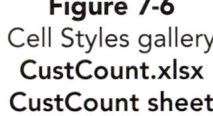

NOTE

Live Preview shows the data with the style as you hover over the style button.

Figure 7-6
Cell Styles gallery
CustCount.xlsx
CustCount sheet

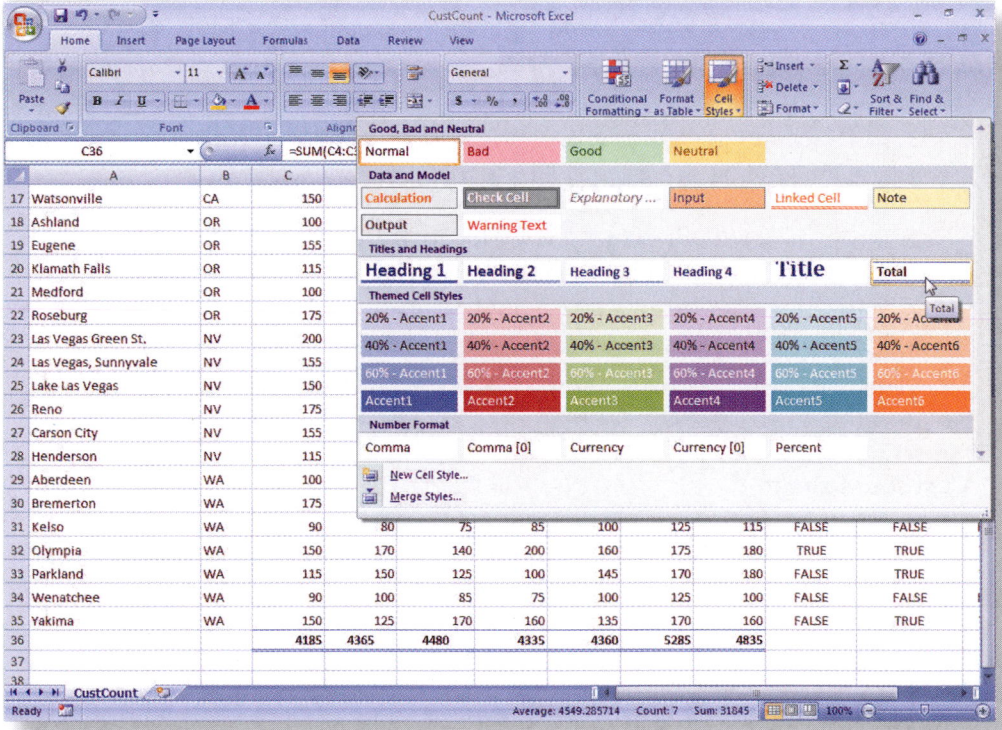

5. Find **Total** in the **Titles and Headings** category. Click to select it. The gallery closes and the style is applied.

6. Click a cell away from the range to see the style. The values are bold and have a top and double bottom blue border.

7. Select cells C36:I36 again. Click the Cell Styles button 🔲 again. Number styles are near the bottom of the gallery.

8. Choose **Comma [0]**. This is the comma style with no decimal places. It overwrites the previous style. Notice that these cells are not right-aligned with other values in the columns. Other values use a different style.

Exercise 7-7 CLEAR AND REAPPLY CELL STYLES

You can remove a cell style or your own formatting from a cell or a range of cells. The cells then return to the default Normal style.

1. While cells C36:I36 are selected, click the Clear button 🔲 in the **Editing** group. Choose **Clear Formats**. The cells are returned to the Normal style.

2. Click cell C4 and press F8 to start Extend Selection mode.

3. Press → six times to select up to column I.

4. Hold down Ctrl and press ↓. This shortcut selects to the last row of data.

5. Click the Cell Styles button 🔲.

6. Choose **Comma [0]**. The style is applied, and all values are aligned.

7. Select cells C36:I36 and apply the **Total** cell style.

8. Select cells A1:A2 and apply the **Title** cell style.

9. Press Ctrl+Home.

Exercise 7-8 CREATE A STYLE

You can create your own styles. Styles that you create are listed in the **Custom** category and saved with the workbook.

1. Click the Cell Styles button 🔲. Click **New Cell Style**.

2. In the **Style name** box, key **Mine** and click **Format**. The Format Cells dialog box opens.

3. Click the **Font** tab. Choose 11-point regular Calibri. Do not click **OK** yet.

4. Click the **Border** tab. Set a single bottom black border. Do not click **OK** yet.

5. Click the **Fill** tab. Choose a light shaded accent color to match the blue in cells A1:A2. Click **OK**. This style will apply fill and a bottom border.

6. Click **OK** again.

7. Select cells A4:L4. Hold down Ctrl and select cells A6:L6. Repeat these steps to cells A8:L8 to the selection.

NOTE

Cell styles use the document theme colors.

8. Click the Cell Styles button . Choose **Mine** at the top of the gallery. Notice that the alignment of values is not correct. The number format in your style does not match the **Comma [0]** style. You'll fix this in the next exercise.

9. Select cells A10:L10. Press Ctrl+Y. This is the keyboard shortcut to repeat the most recent command.

10. Repeat these steps to apply the style to every other row in the sheet, up to and including row 34.

11. Make row 36 the same height as the other rows.

TIP

Press F8 and Ctrl+→ to select a row.

Exercise 7-9   EDIT A STYLE

If you edit a style, all cells with the style are reformatted.

1. Click cell C5 and press Ctrl+1. Click the **Number** tab. The **Number** format (from **Comma [0]**) uses the Accounting option with no decimals and no symbol. Close the dialog box.

2. Click cell C4. This is your style.

3. Click the Cell Styles button . Right-click **Mine** and choose **Modify**.

4. Click **Format**. The Format Cells dialog box opens.

5. Click the **Number** tab. Choose **Accounting**, **0** decimals. In the **Symbol** box, choose **None**. Do not click **OK**.

6. Click the **Fill** tab. Choose a different color if your first choice was too dark. Click **OK**.

7. Click **OK** again. All the cells with the Mine style are restyled. The values are properly aligned, but the number alignment is affecting the labels in columns A:B (cities and states).

8. Select cells A4:B35 and press Ctrl+1. On the **Number** tab, choose **General** and click **OK**. You can override an individual setting of any style.

9. Click the **Page Layout** tab. Click the Margins button. Choose **Custom Margins**.

10. Set the left and right margins at 1 inch; set the top and bottom margins at 1.25 inches. Click **OK**.

Working with Page Breaks

A *page break* is a code that tells the printer to start a new page. When a worksheet is too wide or too tall to fit on the paper, Excel inserts an automatic page break. This page break appears as a dashed line on the screen. You can accept Excel's location for page breaks, you can move the break to a new location, or you can insert your own.

Exercise 7-10 PREVIEW AND CHANGE PAGE BREAKS

1. Click the Microsoft Office Button . Hover over the **Print** arrow and choose **Print Preview**.

> **NOTE**
>
> In Print Preview, ⌈PageDown⌉ moves to the next page if your screen is showing a reduced view.

2. Point at the page and click anywhere to zoom in/out. The worksheet is too large to print on a single page in portrait orientation.

3. Click to set a reduced view and press ⌈PageDown⌉. Rows(s) that do not fit on the first page are on page 2.

4. Press ⌈PageDown⌉ again. Columns that do not fit on the first two pages are on page 3. Look at page 4, too.

5. Close Print Preview.

> **NOTE**
>
> The background page number does not print.

6. Click the Page Break Preview button  in the status bar. A message box explains how you can adjust page breaks.

7. Click **OK**. Pages are arranged in top-to-bottom, left-to-right order with a background page number. Page breaks are blue dashed lines.

Figure 7-7
Page Break Preview
CustCount.xlsx
CustCount sheet

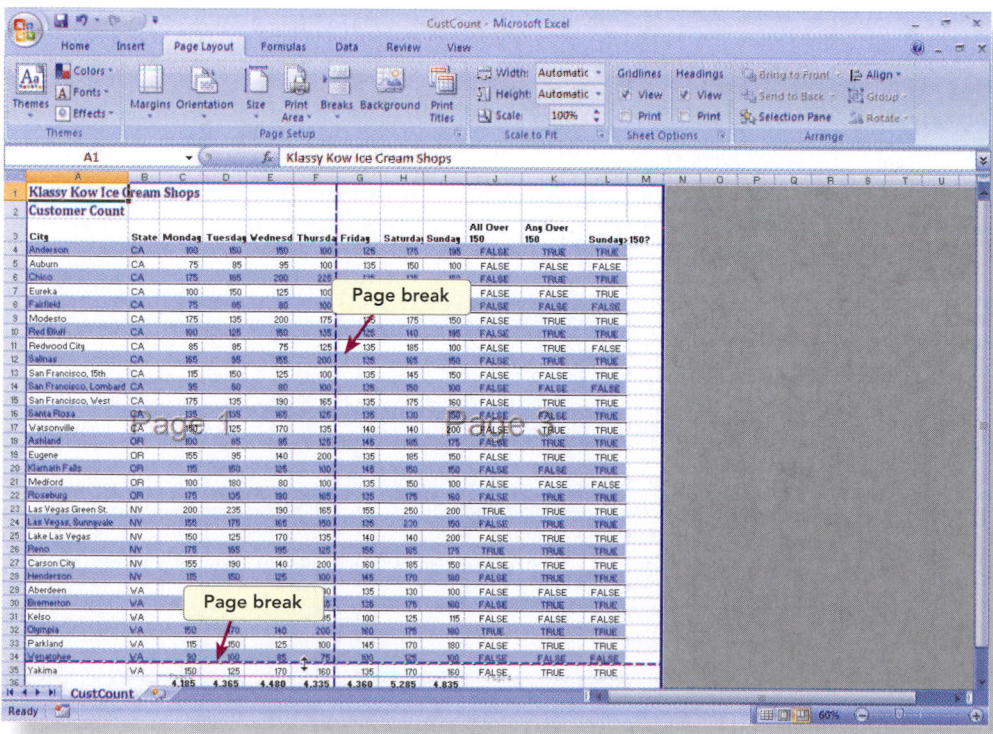

Excel 2007

8. Place the pointer on the horizontal blue dashed line below row 35 to display a two-pointed arrow. Your dashed line might be anywhere between rows 33 and 36.

9. Click and drag the dashed blue line up so that it is between rows 22 and 23. The line becomes solid blue if you manually set or adjust it.

10. Click and drag the vertical blue dashed line between columns F and G to the left so that it is between columns E and F.

11. Widen any column in which the label in row 3 is not visible.

12. Click the Normal button 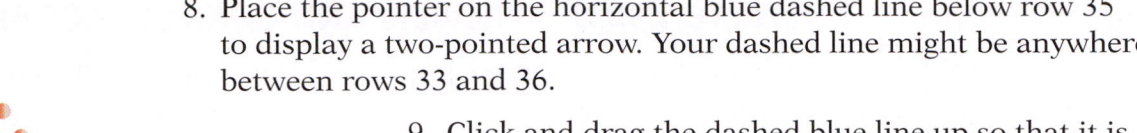 in the status bar. You can see dashed lines for page breaks in Normal view.

TIP

You can AutoFit columns and rows while in Page Break Preview.

Exercise 7-11   REMOVE AND INSERT PAGE BREAKS

You can delete page breaks if necessary, or you can insert your own breaks where you want. When you insert a page break, it is placed to the left of the active cell or column. The placement of page breaks is affected by the currently installed printer, so your worksheet may have different breaks than those shown in this lesson.

1. Click the Page Break Preview button. Click **OK** in the message box.

2. Click and drag the page break below row 22 down and below row 36. You should now have only two pages.

3. Click cell J1. If you insert a page break here, it will be between columns I and J.

4. Click the **Page Layout** tab. In the **Page Setup** group, click the Breaks button.

Figure 7-8
Inserting a page break
CustCount.xlsx
CustCount sheet

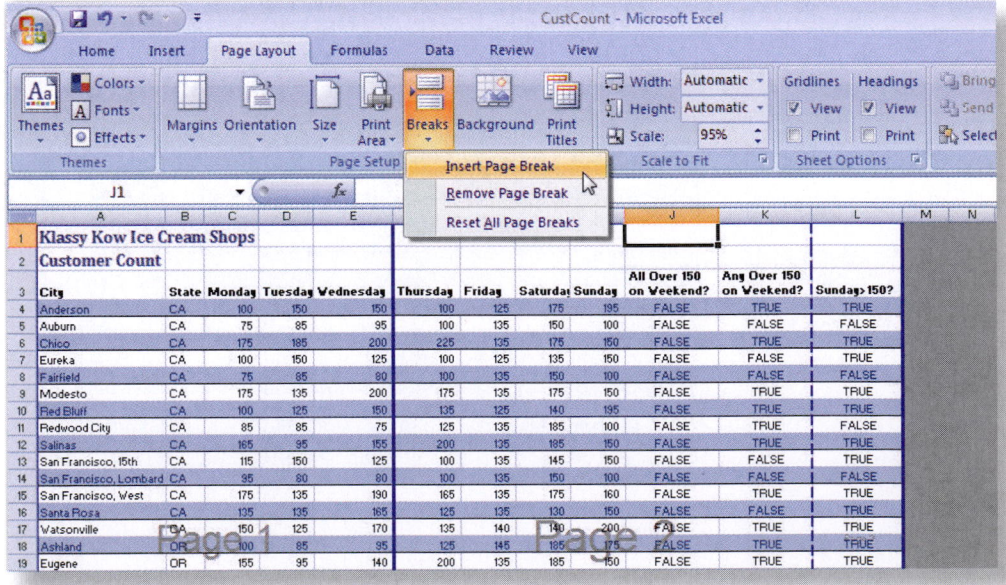

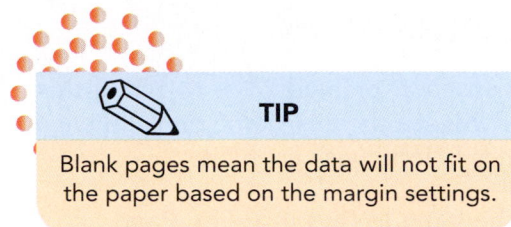

TIP

Blank pages mean the data will not fit on the paper based on the margin settings.

5. Choose **Insert Page Break**. The page break is solid blue because you inserted it manually. Your worksheet should now occupy three pages. If your worksheet is longer, you probably have some blank pages.

6. Click the Microsoft Office Button. Hover over the **Print** arrow and choose **Print Preview**. Press `PageDown` to view the pages.

7. In Print Preview, click to select **Show Margins**. The page shows markers for all margins, including the header and footer. The top margin is the lower of the two horizontal lines; the marker is the tiny rectangle at either edge.

8. Click the top margin marker and drag it up to reach about **.75**. The setting is shown in the status bar as you drag.

Figure 7-9
Changing margins in
Print Preview
CustCount.xlsx
CustCount sheet

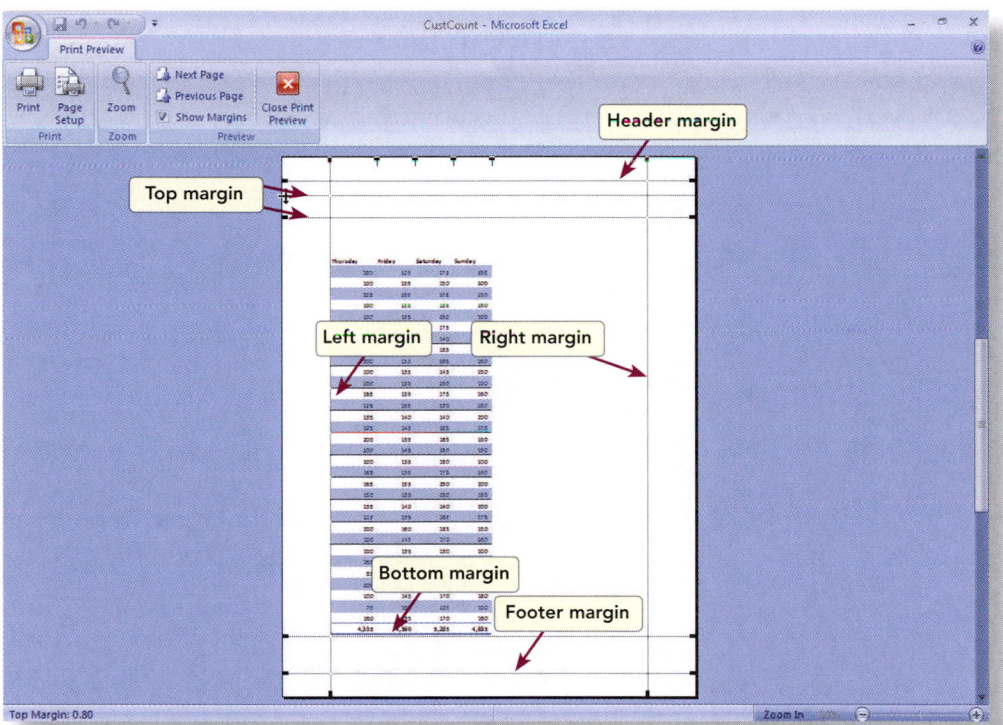

9. Do the same for the bottom margin. Less margin space eliminates any blank pages. Now the worksheet fits on three pages.

10. Close Print Preview.

Exercise 7-12   SET PRINT TITLES

You can repeat the labels in column A on each printed page to make this three-page worksheet easier to read. You will see the city name on each page so that it is easy to determine which values belong with each city.

1. Click the Print Titles button on the **Page Layout** tab. The Page Setup dialog box opens with the **Sheet** tab active.

2. Click in the **Columns to repeat at left** text box.

3. Click anywhere in column A. The dialog box shows **$A:$A** as the range for print titles.

Figure 7-10
Setting print titles
CustCount.xlsx
CustCount sheet

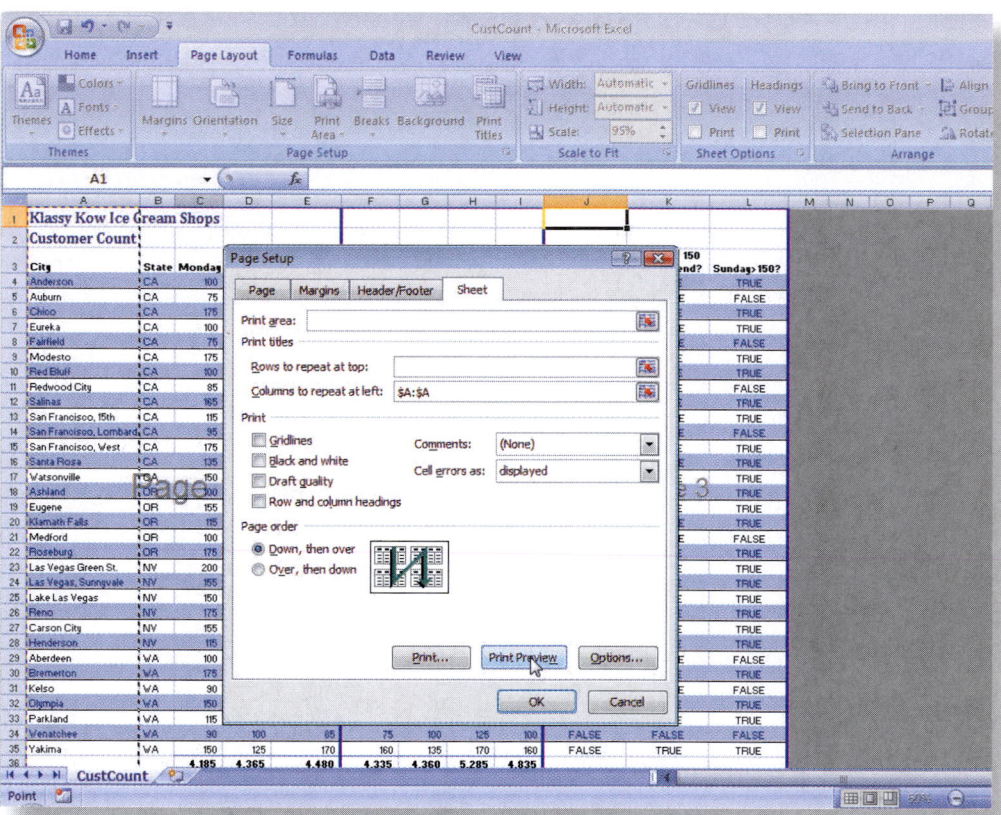

4. Click **Print Preview** in the dialog box.

5. Press [PageDown] and [PageUp] to view the pages. Notice that the label in cell A1 is cut off on pages 2 and 3.

6. Close Print Preview. AutoFit column A. Hide column B. Excel probably inserted a new automatic page break, because column A is wider now.

Exercise 7-13 CENTER A PAGE

Although you can change the left and right margins to make a page appear centered, Excel can center a worksheet horizontally or vertically on the printed page. Centering occurs between the margins.

1. On the **Page Layout** tab, click the Margins button. Choose **Custom Margins**.

2. In the **Center on page** section, click to select **Horizontally**.

3. Click to select **Vertically**.

4. Change the left and right margins to **.50**. Change the top and bottom margins to **.75**.

5. Click **Print Preview** in the dialog box. All pages are horizontally centered, and the smaller margins better fit the first page.

6. Close Print Preview.

7. Click the Normal button in the status bar.

Exercise 7-14 CHANGE THE FOOTER FONT AND PRINT PAGE NUMBERS

The default font for data in headers and footers is 11-point Calibri for the default Office theme. You can change the formatting for any section in the footer to any font and size available on your computer.

1. Click the **Insert** tab and then click the Header & Footer button.

2. Click the Go To Footer button in the **Navigation** group. Click in the left section.

3. Click the **Home** tab. Click the Font Size arrow and choose **8**.

4. Key *[your first and last name]*. The font size is applied as you type.

5. Click in the center section. Click the **Header & Footer Tools Design** tab.

6. Click the Page Number button. The code is **&[Page]**, and it is 11-point Calibri.

7. Press [Spacebar] to insert a space after **&[Page]**.

8. Key **of** and press [Spacebar].

9. Click the Number of Pages button. The code is **&[Pages]**. This footer will display **Page 1 of 3** on the first page.

10. Drag across **&[Page] of &[Pages]** to select all of it. The Mini toolbar appears.

11. Click the Decrease Font Size button three times. Each click reduces the size by 1 point.

Figure 7-11
Printing page
numbers
CustCount.xlsx
CustCount sheet

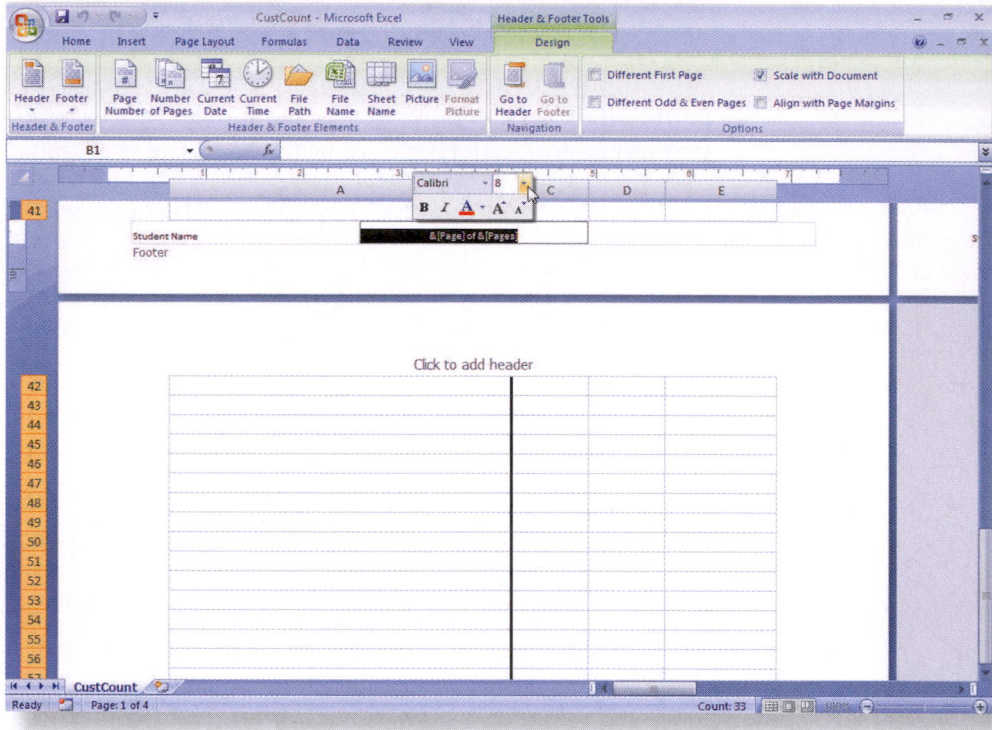

12. Insert the filename in the right section with the same font. Click a worksheet cell.

13. Click the Normal button ⊞ in the status bar.

14. Save the workbook as *[your initials]7-14* in your Lesson 7 folder.

Exercise 7-15   REMOVE A PAGE BREAK

You can remove a manual page break and let Excel resume automatic page breaks.

1. Click the Page Break Preview button 🔲. Click **OK** in the message box.

2. Click cell J1. The page break is to the left of this column.

3. Click the **Page Layout** tab. Click the Breaks button 🔳 and choose **Remove Page Break**. An automatic page break is inserted, probably after column J.

4. Click the Normal button ⊞ in the status bar.

5. Save and close the workbook.

Using the PMT and FV Functions

Financial functions analyze money transactions such as loans and savings or investment plans. Many financial functions, including PMT and FV, use the concept of an annuity. An *annuity* is a series of equal payments made at regular intervals for a specified period of time.

Many of Excel's financial functions use these arguments:

- *Rate* is the interest for the period. If you make monthly payments, you must divide the rate by 12 to find the monthly interest rate.

- *Nper* is the total number of periods during which a payment is made. It represents the total number of payments. A five-year loan with monthly payments would have an Nper of 60 (12 months a year * 5 years).

- *PV* is present value or the amount of the loan. It is the current cash value of the money transaction.

- *FV* is future value or the cash balance at the end of the time period. For an investment, FV is how much you will have at the end of your savings or investment time. For a loan, the FV is 0 because you must pay back every penny.

- *Type* specifies whether payments are made at the beginning or the end of the period.

Exercise 7-16   USE THE PMT FUNCTION

The PMT (Payment) function can be used to determine monthly payments if you borrow money to buy a computer, a car, or a house.

1. Open **CU**.

2. In cell C7, key **4** to plan a four-year loan.

3. In cell C8, key **=** to use a formula to compute the number of payments.

4. Click cell C7 and key ***12**. Press [Enter]. You will make a total of 48 payments (4 years * 12 months in a year).

5. In cell C9, key **20000**, the amount of money borrowed.

6. In cell C10, key **4.9%** as the interest rate.

7. Click cell C12. Click the **Formulas** tab.

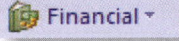

8. Click the Financial button . Scroll and click **PMT**. The PMT Function Arguments dialog box opens with the insertion point in the **Rate** box, the first argument.

> **TIP**
>
> By using a formula in cell C8 to determine the number of payments, you only need to change the number of years to test different loan lengths.

9. Click cell C10, the interest rate. The cell address appears in the **Rate** box.

10. Key **/12** in the **Rate** box after **C10**. An annual interest rate must be divided by 12 to figure a monthly payment.

11. Click in the **Nper** box. This argument is the total number of payments.

12. Click cell C8 for the number of payments.

13. Click in the **Pv** box and click cell C9. The present value is cash you receive now.

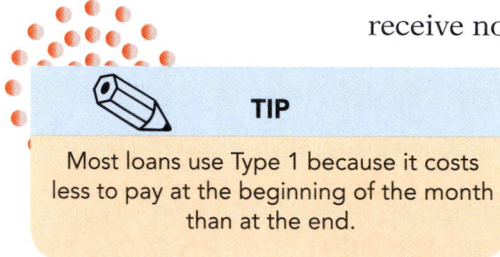

TIP

Most loans use Type 1 because it costs less to pay at the beginning of the month than at the end.

14. Click in the **Fv** box. Future value for a loan is what you will owe at the end of the loan, 0. You do not need to enter anything in this box.

15. Click in the **Type** box and key **1** for a payment at the beginning of the month.

Figure 7-12
Function Arguments
dialog box for PMT
CU.xlsx
CreditUnion sheet

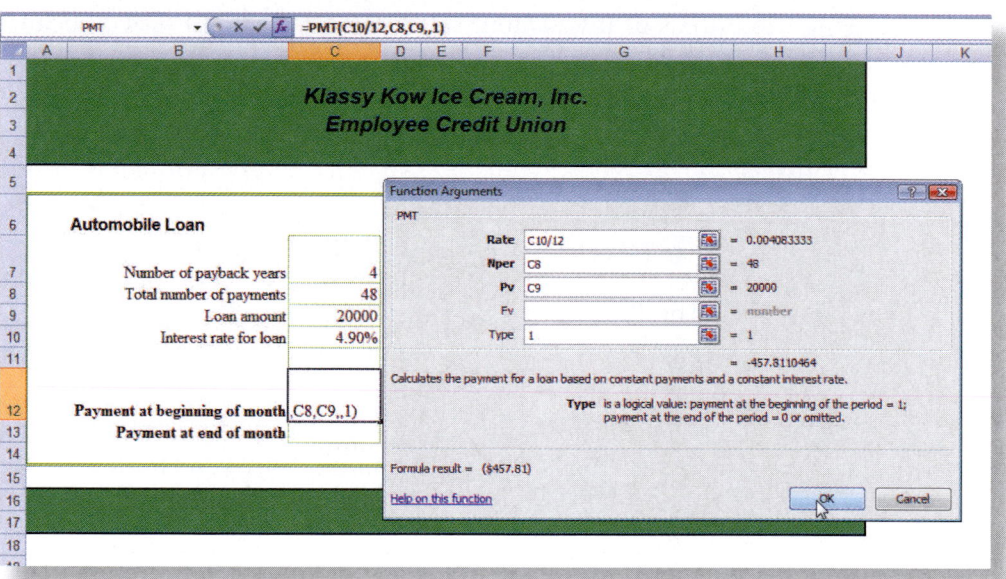

16. Click **OK**. The result ($457.81) is a negative number, because it is money that you have to pay. It is money out of your pocket. Negative formula results are shown in red with parentheses in this worksheet.

Exercise 7-17   KEY A PMT FUNCTION

Key a PMT function from scratch in this exercise to determine the payment if made at the end of the month.

1. Click cell C13.

2. Key **=pm** to display the Formula AutoComplete list and press Tab. The ScreenTip reminds you that the first argument is the **Rate**.

3. Click cell C10 for the rate.

4. Key **/12** to divide the rate by 12.

5. Key a comma to separate the arguments. The second argument, **Nper**, is bold in the ScreenTip.

6. Click cell C8 for the number of payments.

7. Key a comma. The ScreenTip shows the next argument as bold, which is the present value or the amount of the loan.

8. Click cell C9. The square brackets with **[fv]** and **[type]** in the ScreenTip mean that these two arguments are optional. If you do not key a future value, Excel assumes the FV is 0. If you do not key a type, it is assumed to be a 0 type.

9. Press Enter. Notice that payment at the end of the month is slightly more than at the beginning of the month.

Figure 7-13
Keying a PMT function
CU.xlsx
CreditUnion sheet

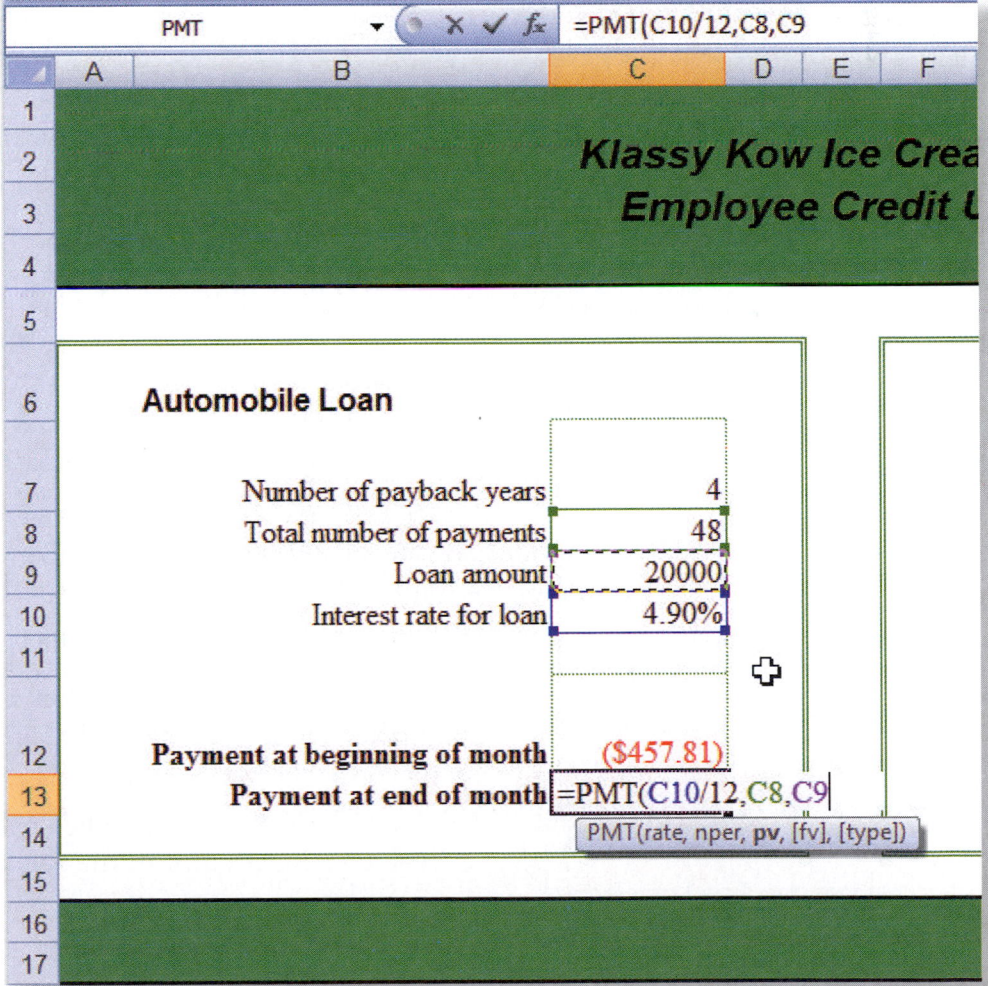

10. Click cell C7. Key **5** and press Enter for a five-year loan. Both functions are recalculated as well as the total number of payments.

11. In cell C10, key **3.9%** and press Enter. Payments with a lower interest rate are lower.

12. Click cell C9 and press F2 to edit the value.

13. Press Home to position the insertion point and key **−** to make this a negative number.

14. Press Enter. The payments now are positive numbers.

Exercise 7-18   USE THE FV FUNCTION

The FV (Future Value) function can be used to determine such things as how much you will have in your savings account at some point in the future if you make regular deposits. You can include money already in the account when you start your savings program.

1. Click cell H7 and key **5** to plan a five-year savings plan.

2. In cell H8, key **=** and click cell H7. Key ***12** and press Enter. You would make 60 total deposits if you save monthly for five years.

REVIEW

If you do not key the % sign, you must key the decimal equivalent of the value.

3. In cell H9, key **50** as the amount saved each month.

4. In cell H10, key **1000** as the amount of money already in the account.

5. In cell H11, key **5.25%** as the interest rate.

6. In cell H12, click the Financial button . Scroll and click **FV**. The insertion point is in the **Rate** box for the first argument.

NOTE

The Function Arguments dialog box shows the syntax and a description of each argument when you click its box.

7. Click cell H11 for the **Rate**. Key **/12** in the **Rate** box after **H11** to divide the rate by 12.

8. Click in the **Nper** box and then click cell H8.

9. Click in the **Pmt** box and click cell H9. The payment is the amount you plan to deposit into your savings account each month.

TIP

In a savings plan, Type 1 pays more interest.

10. Click in the **Pv** box and click cell H10. The present value is the amount in the account to start.

11. Click in the **Type** box and key **1** for a deposit at the beginning of the month.

Figure 7-14
Function Arguments
dialog box for FV
CU.xlsx
CreditUnion sheet

Function Arguments

FV

Rate	H11/12		= 0.004375
Nper	H8		= 60
Pmt	H9		= 50
Pv	H10		= 1000
Type	1		= 1

= -4736.486919

Returns the future value of an investment based on periodic, constant payments and a constant interest rate.

Type is a value representing the timing of payment: payment at the beginning of
the period = 1; payment at the end of the period = 0 or omitted.

Formula result = -4736.486919

Help on this function   OK   Cancel

12. Click **OK**. The result is shown as a negative number, because the FV
    function assumes the bank's or lender's point of view. This is money
    that they would have to pay to you.

Exercise 7-19   FORMAT NEGATIVE NUMBERS

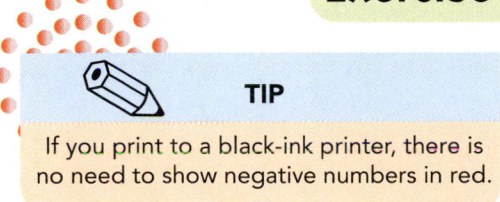

TIP

If you print to a black-ink printer, there is
no need to show negative numbers in red.

Many business reports show negative numbers in red.
Excel's number formats can show negative numbers in red
or black, with or without parentheses, or with a leading
minus sign.

1. Select cells C9, C12:C13, H9:H10, and H12.

2. Press Ctrl+1. Click the **Number** tab and choose **Currency**. Verify that
   there will be two decimals and a dollar sign.

3. In the **Negative numbers** list, choose the non-red **($1,234.10)**. Click **OK**.

4. Make cells C12 and H12 bold.

5. Press Ctrl+Home. Add a header.

6. Save the workbook as ***[your initials]7-19*** in your Lesson 7 folder.
   Close the workbook.

Using Depreciation Functions

Depreciation is the decline in value of an asset. Your car depreciates. You
pay an amount for the car, but it is not worth that amount in three years
because it has been used. In a business, depreciation is an expense that can

reduce income taxes. There are widely accepted methods of determining depreciation, and Excel has several functions to calculate the amounts.
Excel's depreciation functions use these basic arguments:

- *Cost* is the original price of the item.

- *Salvage* is the value of the item after it has been depreciated. It is what the item is worth at the end of its life.

- *Life* is the number of periods over which the item will be depreciated. This is usually expressed in years for expensive assets.

- *Period* is the time for which depreciation is calculated. It uses the same units as Life. If an asset has a 10-year life, you would usually figure depreciation for a single year (the period).

Exercise 7-20   USE THE DB FUNCTION

The DB (Declining Balance) function calculates depreciation at a fixed rate and assumes that the value declines each year. You calculate depreciation for each year separately.

1. Open **Depreciation**.

2. Select cells B11:B12. Use the Fill handle to extend the labels down column A to "10th Year." Extend the values in column C to match.

3. Click the **Formulas** tab.

4. In cell D11, click the Financial button .

5. Hover over **DB** and read the ScreenTip.

6. Click **DB**. The insertion point is in the **Cost** box for the first argument.

7. Click cell D7 for the **Cost**.

8. Click in the **Salvage** box and then click cell D8. This is the value of the tanks after 10 years.

9. Click in the **Life** box and click cell D9. The life is how long the tanks are expected to last.

10. Click in the **Period** box and click cell C11 to calculate depreciation for the first year.

11. Click in the **Month** box. This allows you to start depreciating an asset in the middle of a year. The label "Month" is not bold, which means this argument is optional. Leave it empty.

Figure 7-15
Function Arguments
dialog box for DB
Depreciation.xlsx
Sheet1 sheet

Function Arguments

DB

Cost	D7		=	250000
Salvage	D8		=	10000
Life	D9		=	10
Period	C11		=	1
Month			=	number

                                    = 68750

Returns the depreciation of an asset for a specified period using the fixed-declining balance
method.

              Month is the number of months in the first year. If month is
                      omitted, it is assumed to be 12.

Formula result = $68,750.00

Help on this function   OK   Cancel

12. Click **OK**. The depreciation for the first year is $68,750.

13. Click cell D12 and key **=db(** to start the function. The ScreenTip
    shows that the first argument is the **cost**.

14. Click cell D7.

15. Key a comma to separate the arguments. The second argument,
    salvage, is bold in the ScreenTip.

16. Click cell D8 for the salvage value.

17. Key another comma. The ScreenTip reminds you that the next
    argument is the **life** of the asset.

18. Click cell D9 and key a comma. The **period** argument is next.

19. Click cell C12 for the second year. The next argument in square
    brackets is **[month]** in the ScreenTip. Do not enter anything here.

Excel 2007

Figure 7-16
Keying a DB function
Depreciation.xlsx
Sheet1 sheet

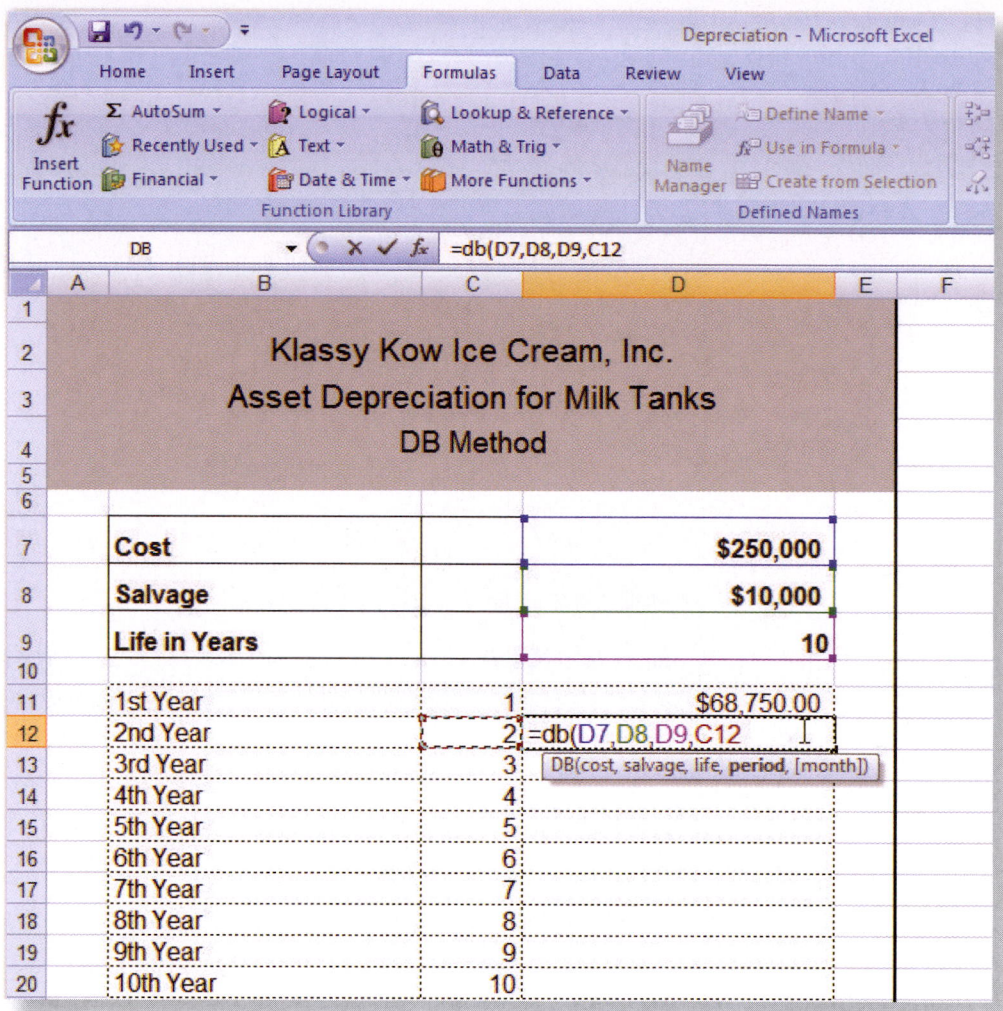

20. Press Enter. The depreciation for the second year is less because the asset was worth less at the beginning of the second year.

Exercise 7-21   EDIT AND COPY THE DB FUNCTION

With absolute references to the first three cells, you can copy the formula.

1. Click cell D12.

2. Press F2. The references to cells D7, D8, and D9 should be absolute.

3. Click between the **D** and the **7** and press F4. The reference is absolute.

4. Do the same for D8 and D9 in the formula and press Enter.

5. Hide coloumn C.

6. Press Ctrl + Home. Edit the footer to show your name and save the workbook as *[your initials]7-21* in your folder.

7. Close the workbook.

Using Online Help

Excel has many financial functions that calculate common business arithmetic, including several methods for determining depreciation.

USE HELP TO VIEW ADDITIONAL INFORMATION ABOUT DEPRECIATION

1. In a new workbook, click the Microsoft Office Excel Help button ⊚.

2. In the Search box, key **depreciation** and press Enter.

3. Find and review topics about the SLN, SYD, and VDB functions.

4. Close the Help window.

Lesson 7 Summary

- The IF function enables you to create formulas that test whether a condition is true. If it is true, you specify what should be shown or done. You also set what appears or is done if the condition is false.

- The **IF** function can show text in its result, it can calculate a value, or it can show a cell reference.

- AND, OR, and NOT are logical functions that show either TRUE or FALSE as a result.

- Logical functions use relational or comparison operators.

- A style is a set of formatting attributes for labels and values.

- Cell styles appear in a gallery with Live Preview. They are coordinated with the document theme.

- You can remove all formatting from a cell and return to the default Normal style.

- You can create your own style and save it with the worksheet.

- Page breaks determine where a new page starts. Excel inserts page breaks based on the paper size and the margins.

- You can insert and delete your own page breaks.

- Page Break Preview shows the page breaks as solid or dashed blue lines.

- If a worksheet requires more than one page, you can repeat column or row headings from page to page to make it easier to read the worksheet.

- The Margins tab in the Page Setup dialog box includes options to center a page horizontally or vertically.

- You can print each page number as well as the total number of pages in a worksheet as a header or a footer.

- Financial functions include PMT and FV and other common business calculations such as depreciation.

- The **PMT** function calculates a regular payment for a loan, using an interest rate.
- The **FV** function calculates how much an amount will be worth in the future at a given interest rate.
- The **DB** function calculates how much of its value an asset loses each year during its life.
- Negative numbers can be shown in red, within parentheses, or with a leading minus ($-$) sign.

LESSON 7		Command Summary	
Feature	**Button**	**Task Path**	**Keyboard**
Apply cell style		Home, Styles, Cell Styles	
Center page		Page Layout, Page Setup, Margins, Custom Margins	Ctrl + 1
Collapse formula bar			
Create cell style		Home, Styles, Cell Styles, New Cell Style	
Delete page break		Page Layout, Page Setup, Breaks, Remove Page Break	
Edit cell style		Home, Styles, Cell Styles	
Expand formula bar			
Insert page break		Page Layout, Page Setup, Breaks, Insert Page Break	
Page break preview			
Print titles		Page Layout, Page Setup	
Repeat command			Ctrl + Y

Concepts Review

True/False Questions

Each of the following statements is either true or false. Indicate your choice by circling T or F.

T F   1. You can repeat the most recent command by pressing Ctrl + R.

T F   2. You must key quotation marks around text that you key in a Function Arguments dialog box.

T F   3. The AND and OR functions usually show the same results.

T F   4. All financial functions include a rate argument.

T F   5. Arguments in a function are separated by commas.

T F   6. The Cell Styles gallery includes styles for values as well as labels.

T F   7. The PMT function determines how much your money will grow over a period of time.

T F   8. The Print Titles option can repeat rows or columns on each page of a worksheet.

Short Answer Questions

Write the correct answer in the space provided.

1. What dialog box helps you complete built-in functions with entry boxes for each argument?

_____

2. Which argument in a financial function refers to the total number of periods (also the total number of payments or deposits)?

_____

3. Which logical function shows the opposite of the condition?

_____

4. What Excel feature lets you see the results of a cell style before applying it?

_____

5. Which command tab includes choices for page breaks and print titles?

_____

6. How can you distinguish between an automatic page break and one that you placed?

_____

7. Which financial function would help you determine how much money will be in your account at the end of a year if you make regular deposits?

8. What is the purpose of the Type argument in financial functions?

Critical Thinking

Answer these questions on a separate page. There are no right or wrong answers. Support your answers with examples from your own experience, if possible.

1. Why are there separate logical operators for greater than (>) and greater than or equal to (>=)?

2. Which financial functions do you recognize or can you figure out from the Financial category? Explain how two financial functions that you did not use in this lesson might work in a business setting.

Skills Review

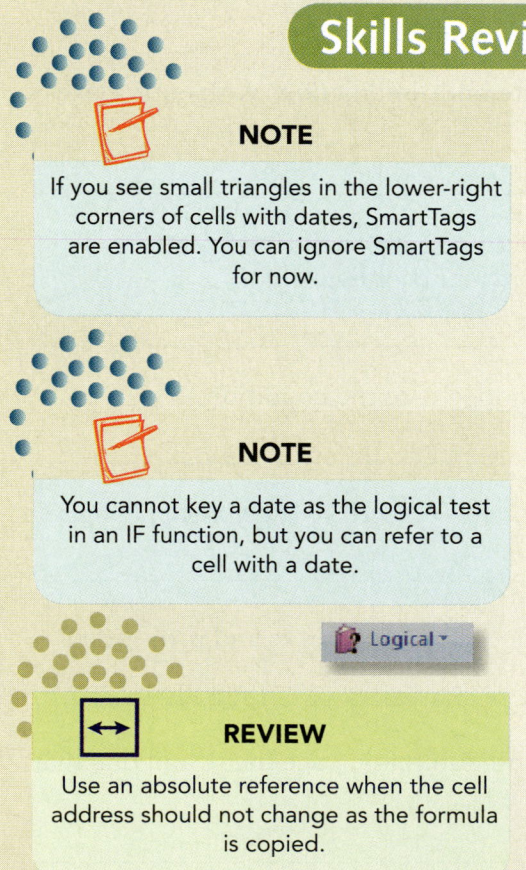

NOTE

If you see small triangles in the lower-right corners of cells with dates, SmartTags are enabled. You can ignore SmartTags for now.

NOTE

You cannot key a date as the logical test in an IF function, but you can refer to a cell with a date.

REVIEW

Use an absolute reference when the cell address should not change as the formula is copied.

Exercise 7-22

Use the IF function.

1. Open **CustBirth** and save it as *[your initials]*7-22 in your Lesson 7 folder.

2. Right-click the column D heading and insert a column. In cell D3, key **Born after 2000?**

3. In cell A21, key **12/31/00**. This is the last date in 2000, and you will refer to this cell in the IF function.

4. Use the IF function by following these steps:

   a. Click cell D4 and click the **Formulas** tab.

   b. Click the Logical button [Logical] and choose **IF**.

   c. Click cell C4 and key >.

   d. Click cell A21 and press [F4] to make the reference absolute. The logical test determines if the date in cell C4 is greater than the date in cell A21 (that is, it is after that date).

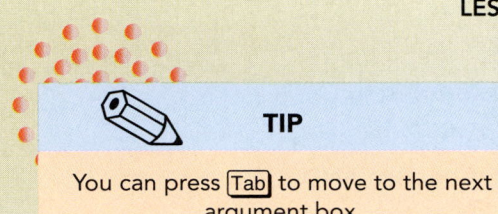

TIP

You can press Tab to move to the next argument box.

TIP

Set the alignment before copying the formula. The copied format does not include a bottom border.

REVIEW

Hidden rows/columns are used in formulas.

NOTE

Ask your instructor for help if you cannot find the template.

    e. Click in the **Value_if_true** box. Key **Yes**.

    f. Click in the **Value_if_false** box. Key **No** and click **OK**.

5. Center the results. Copy the formula to cells D5:D20.

6. Right-click the row 21 heading and hide the row. Add the missing border. Press Ctrl + Home.

7. Add a header. On the Page Layout tab in the Scale to Fit group, set both the Width and Height commands to **1 page**.

8. Make a copy of the worksheet and name it **CustBirthdaysFormulas**. Display the formulas, fit the columns, and fit the sheet to one landscape page.

9. Prepare and submit your work. Save and close the workbook.

Exercise 7-23

Use AND, OR, and NOT functions.

1. Open the New Workbook dialog box. Click **My templates** and double-click **KlassyBirth**.

2. Save the workbook as *[your initials]*7-23 in your folder.

3. Key the following information, starting in cell A8.

Figure 7-17

Name	Shop	Age	Male/Female
[your first and last name]	Wenatchee	[your age]	[your gender]
Carole Greenfield	Olympia	10	F
Michael Westberg	Yakima	5	M
Hashima Yeng	Kelso	6	M
Krystal Chavez	Bremerton	8	F
Pedro Juarez	Yakima	7	M
David Hutchinson	Wenatchee	5	M
Melinda Brown	Kelso	4	F

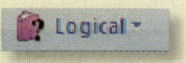

4. Use an AND function by following these steps:

   a. Click cell E8 and click the **Formulas** tab.

   b. Click the Logical button and choose **AND**.

   c. Click cell C8 and key **>=6** in the **Logical1** box.

   d. Click in the **Logical2** box. Click cell C8 and key **>=8**. Click **OK**.

   e. Copy the formula in cell E8 to cells E9:E15.

5. Key an OR function by following these steps:

   a. Click cell F8 and key **=or(** to start the formula.

   b. Click cell C8 and key **<=5**.

   c. Key a comma to separate the arguments.

   d. Click cell D8, key **="f"** and press [Enter].

   e. Copy the formula in cell F8 to cells F9:F15.

6. Use a NOT function by following these steps:

   a. In cell G8, key **=not** and press [Tab].

   b. Click cell D8 and key **="f"** and press [Enter].

   c. Copy the formula.

7. Add your footer. Fit the sheet to one landscape page.

8. Make a copy of the sheet and name it **CustBirthdaysFormulas**. Display the formulas and fit this sheet to one landscape page.

9. Prepare and submit your work. Save and close the workbook.

NOTE

Text in an AND/OR function must be enclosed in quotation marks.

Exercise 7-24

Work with styles. Work with page breaks. Set print titles.

1. Open **PerfRating**. Save the workbook as *[your initials]*7-24.

2. Apply styles by following these steps:

   a. Press [F8] and then press [Ctrl]+[End].

   b. On the **Home** tab, click the Clear button in the **Editing** group. Choose **Clear Formats**.

   c. Select cells A1:A2. Click the Cell Styles button and choose **Title**.

   d. Select cells A3:F3 and apply the **Heading 2** style.

   e. Make columns A:C each **15.00 (110 pixels)** wide.

3. Create and apply styles by following these steps:

   a. Click the Cell Styles button and choose **New Cell Style**.

   b. Key **Amounts** in the **Style name** box and click **Format**.

   c. Click the **Number** tab. Set **Currency** with 0 decimal places and a dollar sign, and click **OK**. Click **OK** again.

NOTE

Column E uses a nested IF formula.

NOTE

Your style starts as a copy of the Normal style.

     d. Click the Cell Styles button and choose **New Cell Style**. Key **Increase** in the **Style name** box and click **Format**.

     e. Click the **Number** tab. Set **Currency** with 0 decimal places and a dollar sign.

     f. Click the **Font** tab. Set 11-point Calibri bold. Choose a dark blue theme color from the **Color** list. Click **OK**. Click **OK** again.

     g. Create a style named **Ratings**. Click the **Font** tab. Set 11-point Calibri bold. On the **Alignment** tab, choose **Center** for the **Horizontal** setting. Click **OK**. Click **OK** again.

     h. Select cells C4:C16 and F4:F16. Apply the **Amounts** style.

     i. Apply the **Increase** style to cells E4:E16 and the **Ratings** style to cell D4:D16 and to cells D18:D20.

     j. Apply the **Percent** style to cells E18:E20.

4. Click cell D3 and press ⌗F2⌗. Click after the final "e" in "Performance" and press ⌗Alt⌗+⌗Enter⌗. Then press ⌗Enter⌗.

5. Make columns D:E each **15.00 (110 pixels)** wide. Center the label in cell D3.

6. Work with page breaks by following these steps:

     a. Click the Page Break Preview button . Click **OK** in the message box.

     b. Rest the mouse pointer on the blue dashed line to display a two-pointed arrow.

     c. Drag the dashed-line page break so that it is between columns C and D.

7. Set print titles by following these steps:

     a. Click the **Page Layout** tab. Click the Print Titles button .

     b. In the **Print titles** section, click in the **Rows to repeat at top** box.

     c. Select cells A1:A2. Excel inserts an absolute reference for rows 1:2.

     d. Click in the **Columns to repeat at left** box. Click anywhere in column A.

     e. Click **Print Preview**. Check the labels in column A on both pages.

     f. Close Print Preview.

     g. Click the Normal button . AutoFit column A.

8. Add a header, but change the font to 8 points for each section.

9. Prepare and submit your work. Save and close the workbook.

REVIEW

Page breaks that you place appear as solid lines.

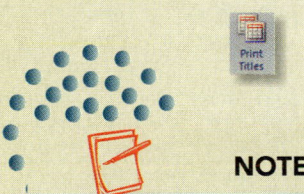

NOTE

Your worksheet will expand to three printed pages when you AutoFit column A.

TIP

Enter the header data, select it, and use the Mini toolbar to change the font size.

Exercise 7-25

Use PMT and FV functions. Use a depreciation function.

1. Open **Comparison** and save it as *[your initials]7-25*.

2. In cells B3:B5, key data for a $15,000 loan at 5.9% for three years. In cell B6, key **=** and click cell B5. Key ***12** and press Enter.

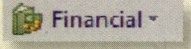

3. In cells E3:E5, key data for a $15,000 loan at 6.5% for four years. Use the formula in cell E6 to determine the number of payments.

4. Use the PMT function by following these steps:

   a. Click the **Formulas** tab.

   b. In cell B7, click the Financial button . Choose **PMT**.

   c. Click cell B4 and key **/12** in the **Rate** box.

   d. Click in the **Nper** box and then click cell B6.

   e. Click in the **Pv** box and then click cell B3.

   f. Click in the **Type** box and key **1**. Click **OK**.

   g. Copy the formula in cell B7 to cell E7.

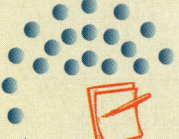

5. Copy cells A1:A2 to **Sheet2**. Edit the label in cell A2 to say **Savings Comparison**. In cells A3:A6, key the following labels:
   Savings Amount
   Rate
   Years for Savings
   Total # of Deposits

6. Widen column A for the longest label and format row 3 as **27.00 (36 pixels)** high. Copy cells A3:A6 to cells D3:D6. Make column D the same width as column A.

7. In column B, key data for saving $50 a month at 6.25% for three years. Use a formula to determine the number of deposits.

8. In column E, key data for saving $100 a month at 6.5% for four years.

9. Use the FV function by following these steps:

   a. In cell B7, click the **Formulas** tab and the Financial button . Choose FV.

   b. Click cell B4 and key **/12** in the **Rate** box.

   c. Click in the **Nper** box and then click cell B6. Click in the **Pmt** box and then click cell B3.

d. Click in the **Type** box and key **1**. Click **OK**.

e. Copy the formula in cell B7 to cell E7. Widen columns as needed.

10. Rename **Sheet2** as **Savings**. Group these two sheets and insert a column at column A and a row at row 1.

11. Apply a double outline border to cells A1:G9. Apply dotted middle horizontal and bottom borders to cells B4:C7 and cells E4:E7. Center the two main labels across the data. Ungroup the sheets.

12. Rename **Sheet3** **Depreciation**. Set cells A1:A2 for 16-point Calibri. In cell A1, key **Klassy Kow Ice Cream, Inc.** In cell A2, key **Asset Depreciation for Storage Tanks**.

13. Use 14-point Calibri for cell A3 and key **DDB Method**. Make columns A and C each **27.86 (200 pixels)** wide.

14. Set Calibri bold for cells A4:C15. Key the following labels and values:

	A	B	C
4	Cost		$300,000
5	Salvage		$15,000
6	Life in Years		8

15. In cell A8, key **1st Year** and in cell A9, key **2nd Year**. Select these two cells and use the Fill handle to fill down column A to **8th Year**. In cell B8, key **1** and in cell B9, key **2**. Fill this series down to **8**.

16. Use a depreciation function by following these steps:

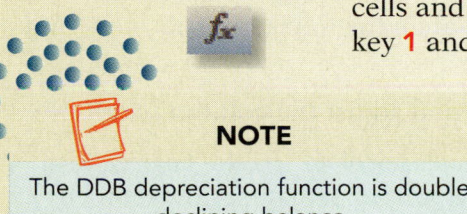

a. In cell C8, click the Insert Function button .

b. Choose **Financial** and **DDB**. Click **OK**.

NOTE

The DDB depreciation function is double-declining balance.

c. Click cell C4 for the **Cost** and press F4 to make the reference absolute.

d. Click in the **Salvage** box, click cell C5, and press F4.

e. Click in the **Life** box, click cell C6, and make it absolute.

NOTE

By showing the years as simple values, you can copy the formula.

f. Click in the **Period** box, click cell B8, and leave it a relative reference.

g. Leave the **Factor** box empty. Click **OK**.

h. Copy the formula down to row 15.

17. Hide column B. Center the labels in rows 1:3 across the data.

18. Group all three worksheets and click the **Page Layout** tab. Click the Dialog Box Launcher for the **Page Setup** group. Horizontally center the sheets. Add a footer to the grouped sheets from this dialog box.

19. Prepare and submit your work. Save and close the workbook.

Lesson Applications

Exercise 7-26

Use the IF function.

1. Use the **KlassyBirth** template to create a workbook. Save it as *[your initials]7-26*.

2. Click the Expand Formula Bar button and edit the label in cell B3 to show **Favorite Flavor** on the second line. Change **Age** in cell C7 to **Flavor**. Collapse the formula bar.

3. In cells A8:D13, key the following information:

TIP

Look for recently used templates in the New Workbook dialog box.

Figure 7-18

	Name	Shop	Favorite Flavor	M/F
4	Marian Most	Las Vegas, Green	Chocolate	F
5	Tommy Dunne	Lake Las Vegas	Bubble Gum Goo	M
6	Luella Orr	Carson City	Chocolate	F
7	Patrick Adams	Reno	Vanilla	M
8	Asata Akai	Henderson	Strawberry	F
9	Efren Aldo	Las Vegas, Sunnyvale	Chocolate	M

4. Widen columns B and C slightly. Left-align the flavors in column C and increase the indent once.

5. Key **Chocolate?** as the label in cell E7 and adjust the column width.

6. Use the IF function in cell E8 with **C8="chocolate"** as the **Logical_test**. Show **Yes** if the customer's favorite flavor is chocolate. Show **Other** if chocolate is not the favorite. Copy the formula for the rest of the names and center the results.

7. Delete columns F and G. One of the images may be deleted with the columns. Center the sheet horizontally. Add a header.

8. Make a copy of the worksheet and name it **CustBirthdaysFormulas**. Display the formulas and adjust column widths. Don't size the picture. Fit the sheet to one landscape page.

9. Prepare and submit your work. Save and close the workbook.

Exercise 7-27

Work with page breaks.

The financial staff keeps track of retirement accounts for Klassy Kow employees. The worksheet should be printed with each year on a separate page. Each year details five funds.

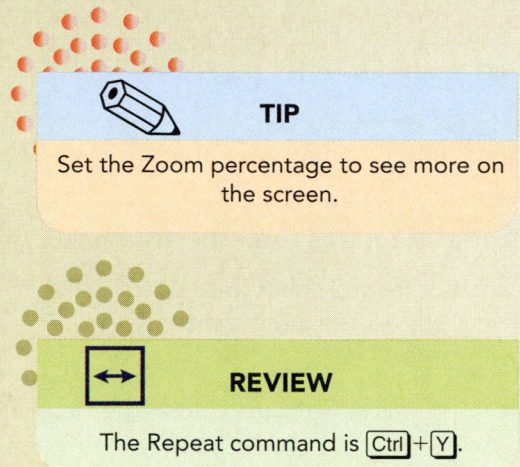

TIP

Set the Zoom percentage to see more on the screen.

REVIEW

The Repeat command is Ctrl + Y.

1. Open **RetireAcct** and save it as *[your initials]*7-27.

2. Increase the left indent 2 spaces for cell A10. Change the page orientation to landscape.

3. Center cell B3 across cells B3:G3. Repeat these steps for all years.

4. Set page breaks so that each year's data is on a separate page. Set rows 1:2 and column A as print titles. Use the Scale to Fit group to fit the sheet to three pages wide, one page tall.

5. Add a header with your name at the left. In the center section, show the filename and the sheet name on one line. Press Enter and on the second line in the center, show **&Page of &Pages**. Include the date in the right section.

6. Prepare and submit your work. Save and close the workbook.

Exercise 7-28

Use AND and OR functions.

1. Open **SerAwards**. Save it as *[your initials]*7-28 in your folder.

2. In cell E4, use an AND function to show TRUE if the employee has greater than two years of service and a performance rating equal to 4. Copy the formula to cells E5:E16.

3. In cell F4, use an OR function to show TRUE if the employee has greater than four years of service or a performance rating equal to 4. Copy the formula.

4. Add an icon set using **3 Symbols (Circled)** for column D. Edit the rule to show a green check mark for any rating equal to or greater than 3. Show an exclamation point for any other number. The red X should not appear at all.

5. Set the page to be horizontally centered. Add a footer using a 9-point font for all sections.

6. Make a formula sheet and fit it to one landscape page.

7. Prepare and submit your work. Save and close the workbook.

Exercise 7-29 ◆ Challenge Yourself

Use the PMT function to calculate mortgage payments at different interest rates.

Klassy Kow Ice Cream, Inc., must choose a construction loan to finance expansion at the headquarters building. This worksheet analyzes information from four lenders. The loan will be for $500,000, 10 years, payments made at the beginning of each month.

1. Open **LoanComp** and save it as *[your initials]*7-29.

2. Review the formulas. There are two errors in formulas that result in incorrect values on this worksheet.

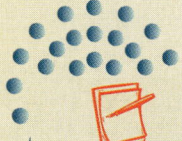

NOTE

A total cost is calculated by multiplying the monthly payment by the total number of payments.

3. Correct the errors and make format adjustments as needed.

4. Add a header and fit the sheet to a single portrait page.

5. Prepare a formula sheet. On this sheet, add different fill to the cells that you edited. Fit the formula sheet to a portrait page.

6. Prepare and submit your work. Save and close the workbook.

On Your Own

In these exercises you work on your own, as you would in a real-life work environment. Use the skills you've learned to accomplish the task—and be creative.

Exercise 7-30

Assume you are a bank professional who expects a 6% return on money you lend. Create a new workbook to determine how much you can lend to a customer who can afford to pay $200 a month for five years. Use Help to learn about the PV function and use it in your workbook. Assume payments will be made at the beginning of the month. Decide how to format your data, and add a header or footer. Save the workbook as *[your initials]*7-30. Prepare and submit your work.

Exercise 7-31

Open **CustCount**. Select the rows for a state and apply a cell style from the Themed Cell Styles group. Use a different style for each state. Set landscape orientation and insert page breaks so that each state is on its own page. Add a footer that includes page numbers. Save the workbook as *[your initials]*7-31. Prepare and submit your work.

Exercise 7-32

Open **AR** and save it as *[your initials]*7-32. Copy cells A2:E16 to cell A17 and again to cells A32 and A47. Add your usual footer and include the page number in the center. Look at the worksheet in Print Preview and in Page Break Preview. Excel prints the pages down and then over. On the **Sheet** tab of the Page Setup dialog box, change this setting to print over and then down. Prepare and submit your work.

Lesson 8

Rounding and Nesting Functions

OBJECTIVES

After completing this lesson, you will be able to:

1. Use the INT function.

2. Use the ROUND function.

3. Use date and time arithmetic.

4. Create nested functions.

5. Create a hyperlink.

Estimated Time: 1½ hours

MCAS OBJECTIVES

In this lesson:
XL07 1.5.4
XL07 2.3.7
XL07 2.3.8
XL07 3.1.1
XL07 4.3.3
XL07 5.4.1
XL07 5.5.4

The INT and ROUND functions can be used with formulas or functions to convert a value with decimals. You will learn about these two functions as well as how to nest one function inside another to solve complex problems.

Using the INT Function

Excel stores the full number of decimals that are keyed or calculated in a cell, even if the cell is formatted to show fewer decimal places. For example, if you key 1.2345 and format the cell for two decimal places, Excel displays 1.23 in the cell. In a calculation, however, Excel uses the full value, 1.2345, which you see in the formula bar.

If you want Excel to use the value shown in the cell (not the one in the formula bar), you can use the INT or ROUND functions.

INT stands for "Integer." An *integer* is a whole number, a number with no decimal or fractional parts. The INT function (in the Math & Trig category) shows only the nondecimal portion of a number. To do this, it truncates or cuts off all digits after the decimal point. The INT function has one argument, the value or cell to be adjusted.

TABLE 8-1 Examples of the INT Function

Expression	Cell Data	Result
INT(C4)	C4=9.7	9
INT(9.792)	None	9
INT(A1)	A1=−9.7	−9

Exercise 8-1   USE INT WITH A CELL REFERENCE

1. Open **Recipes.**

2. On the **Recipes** sheet in cell C7, key **=int** to see the Formula AutoComplete list and the ScreenTip.

3. Press Tab to select the INT function. The argument is the value.

4. Click cell B7.

Figure 8-1
Keying an INT function
Recipes.xlsx
Recipes sheet

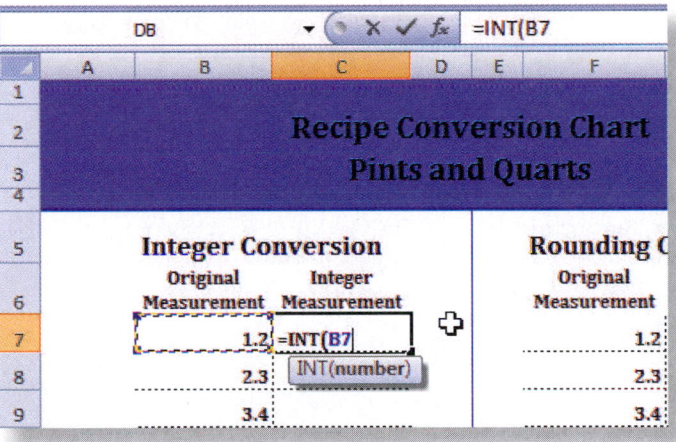

5. Press Enter. The integer value of 1.2 is 1.

6. Copy the formula in cell C7 to cells C8:C12.

Exercise 8-2   COMPARE VALUES WITH INT

1. Key **=** in cell B14 and click cell B7.

2. Key ***2** and press Enter. This is a multiplication formula, doubling the value in cell B7.

3. Use the Fill handle to copy the formula to cells B15:B19.

4. Key **=** in cell C14 and click cell C7.

5. Key ***2** and press Enter. This doubles the integer value in cell C7.

6. Copy the formula to cells C15:C19. Compare the values in columns A and B. There are some noticeable differences between doubling the original value and doubling the integer value.

7. Delete the contents of cells C14:C19.

8. In cell C14, key **=int(** and click cell B14. Press Enter. This is the integer value of 2.4.

9. Copy the formula to cells C15:C19.

Using the ROUND Function

The ROUND function "rounds" a value to a specified digit to the left or right of the decimal point. *Rounding* a number means that it is made larger or smaller, a greater or lesser value. The ROUND function uses two arguments: the value to be rounded and the number of digits used for rounding. If the second argument is zero or a negative number, the rounding occurs to the left of the decimal point.

TABLE 8-2 Examples of the ROUND Function

Expression	Cell Data	Result
ROUND(C4, 1)	C4=9.736	9.7
ROUND(C4, 2)	C4=9.736	9.74
ROUND(C4, 0)	C4=9.736	10
ROUND(C4, −1)	C4=9.736	10

> **TIP**
>
> Rounding can be used in financial calculations to round to the nearest dollar.

Exercise 8-3 USE ROUND

1. Click the **Formulas** tab and click cell G7.

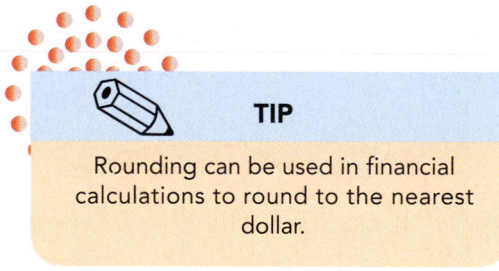

2. Click the Math & Trig button . Hover over **ROUND** to read the ScreenTip.

3. Choose **ROUND**.

4. In the **Number** box, click cell F7.

5. In the **Num_digits** box, key **0**. The value in cell F7 will be rounded to show no decimal positions.

Figure 8-2
Using ROUND in the dialog box
Recipes.xlsx
Recipes sheet

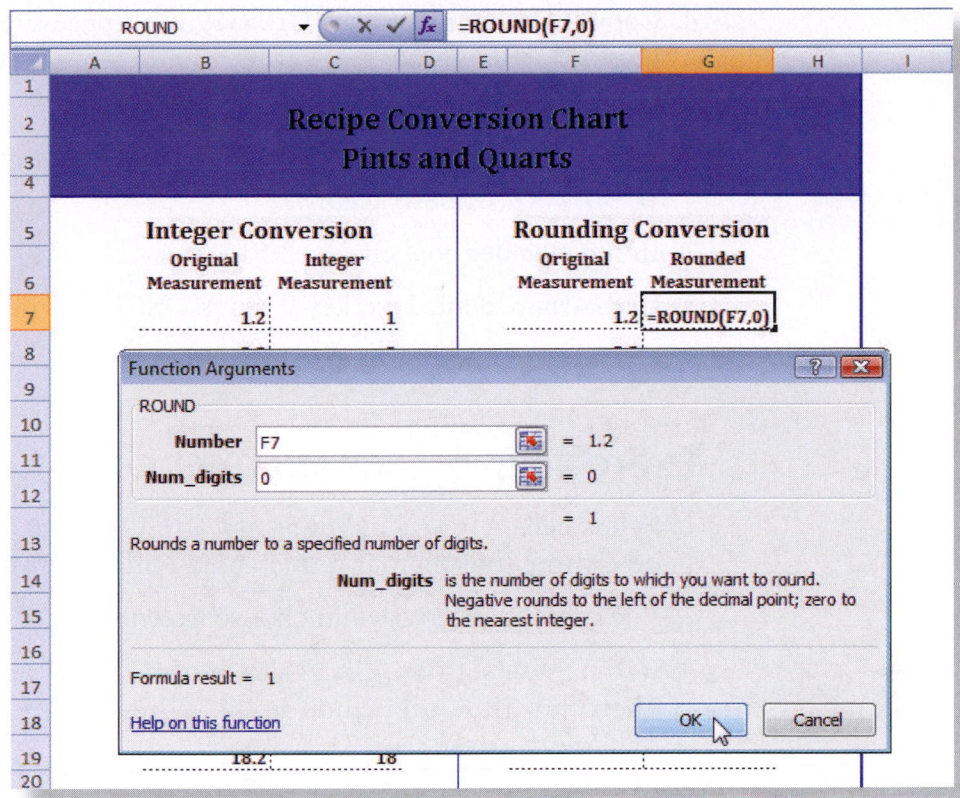

6. Click **OK**. The value 1.2 is rounded to 1. It rounds down because the value after the decimal point is less than 5.

7. Copy the formula down to cell G12.

8. Edit cells F8:F11 to show the following values. As you do, notice how the values in column G are rounded up or down.
    1.6
    3.2
    5.5
    7.2

9. Click the arrow next to the Undo button <img> and undo the last four edits.

Exercise 8-4   COMPARE ROUNDED VALUES

Note the difference between doubling the rounded values and rounding the doubled values in this exercise.

1. Key **=** in cell F14 and click cell F7. Key ***2** and press Enter.

2. Copy the formula to cells F15:F19.

3. Key **=** in cell G14 and click cell G7. Key ***2** and press Enter. This doubles the rounded value in cell G7.

4. Copy the formula to cells G15:G19. Compare the values in columns C and D.

5. Delete the contents of cells G14:G19.

6. Click the **Formulas** tab. In cell G14, click the Math & Trig button  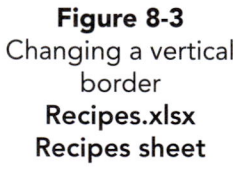 . Choose **ROUND**.

7. In the **Number** box, click cell F14.

8. In the **Num_digits** box, key **0**. Click **OK**. The value **2.4** is rounded to **2**.

9. Copy the formula to cells G15:G19.

Exercise 8-5 CHANGE COLORS AND BORDERS

1. Select cells A1:H21 and press [Ctrl]+[1]. Click the **Border** tab. You can determine that there is a thick blue outline border.

2. Click the **Color** arrow and choose **Accent 1** for a softer blue.

3. In the **Presets** group, click None button to remove all borders. Then click the Outline button . Click **OK**. The same border thickness is used.

4. Click the **Home** tab. Select cells A1:H4 and click the arrow next to the Fill Color button .

5. Choose **Blue, Accent 1**.

6. Select cells D5:D21. There should be a vertical border for these cells. Since columns D and E share borders, you can edit this border from either column.

Figure 8-3
Changing a vertical border
Recipes.xlsx
Recipes sheet

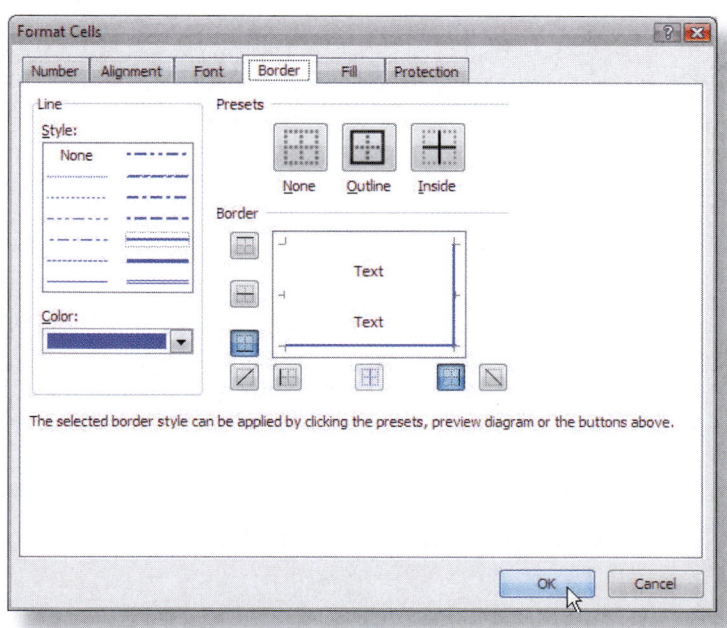

7. Press Ctrl + 1. Click the **Border** tab.

8. Click the right vertical border preview area or the Right Vertical button to remove the border.

9. Click the **Color** arrow and choose **Blue, Accent 1**. Then click the right vertical border area or its button. Click **OK**.

10. Change the sheet tab color to **Blue, Accent 1**.

11. Save the workbook as *[your initials]*8-5 in a new folder for Lesson 8.

Using Date and Time Arithmetic

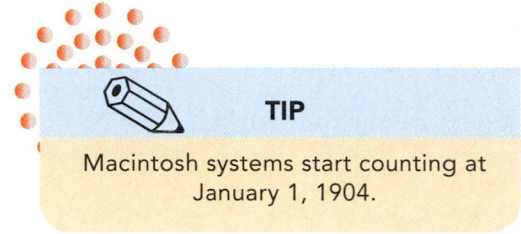

TIP

Macintosh systems start counting at January 1, 1904.

Because of its serial number system, Excel's Date & Time functions can calculate ages, hours worked, or days passed. The serial number system treats dates as values. January 1, 1900, is 1; January 2, 1900, is 2; and so on.

Exercise 8-6   DETERMINE AGES AND DATES

To determine a product's age, subtract the manufacture date from today. The result is a serial number that can be converted to an age in years.

1. In *[your initials]*8-5, click the **ExpireDate** tab. Replace all occurrences of the year in column A with last year.

2. In cell C4, key **=today()-** to start the formula.

3. Click cell A4. The formula subtracts the manufacture date from today.

REVIEW

A series of #### symbols in a cell means that the value is too wide to be displayed in the currently selected font size.

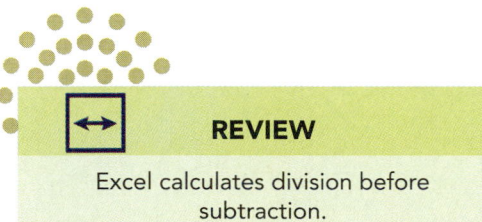

REVIEW

Excel calculates division before subtraction.

4. Press Enter. The age is formatted as a date and is probably too wide to display.

5. Click cell C4 and press Ctrl + 1. On the **Number** tab, choose **Number** with two decimal places and click **OK**. This is the age in days.

6. Press F2. Press Home and → to position the insertion point after the equal sign.

7. Key a left parenthesis **(** after the equal sign.

8. Press End and key a right parenthesis **)** after **A4** in the formula.

Figure 8-4
Converting the age
formula to years
8-5.xlsx
ExpireDate sheet

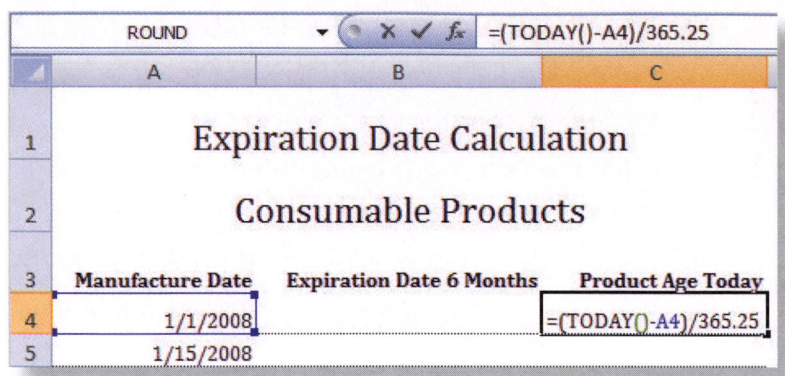

9. Key **/365.25** to divide by the number of days in a year. Press Enter.

10. Copy the formula in cell C4 to row 19.

11. Click cell B4 and key **=** to start a formula.

12. Click cell A4 and key **+** to add days to the manufacture date.

NOTE

Dividing by 365.25 includes a leap year once every four years.

13. Key **6** and press Enter. This adds six days to the date.

14. Click cell B4, press F2, and edit the formula to add 180 days.

15. Copy the formula to row 19.

Exercise 8-7   DETERMINE TIME PASSED

Calculating time passed is similar to determining an age. You subtract the beginning time from the ending time. Excel usually shows time results as a fraction of a 24-hour day. To convert to hours, multiply the results by 24.

1. Click the **FreezerTime** tab.

2. In cell C6, key **8:30 am** and press →. Excel capitalizes the AM/PM reference.

3. In cell D6, key **4:30 pm**. Excel shows times as you key them, using a 12-hour AM/PM clock.

4. Key the following times in columns C and D.

	C	D
7	9 am	5 pm
8	10:30 am	6:15 pm
9	12 pm	8:30 pm
10	6 am	4 pm
11	1 pm	11 pm

5. In cell E6, key **=** and click cell D6, the ending time.

6. Key a minus sign (**–**) and click cell C6, the starting time. Press Enter.

7. Click cell E6 and press Ctrl+1. Click the **Number** tab.

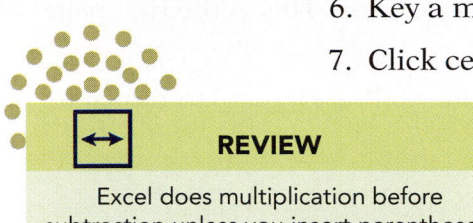

REVIEW

Excel does multiplication before subtraction unless you insert parentheses.

8. Choose **Number** with **3** decimal places. Click **OK**. The result is **.333**, representing one-third of a day.

9. Press F2 and press Home.

10. Press → and key a left parenthesis **(** after the equal sign.

11. Press End and key a right parenthesis **)**.

Figure 8-5
Converting time
to hours
8-5.xlsx
FreezerTime sheet

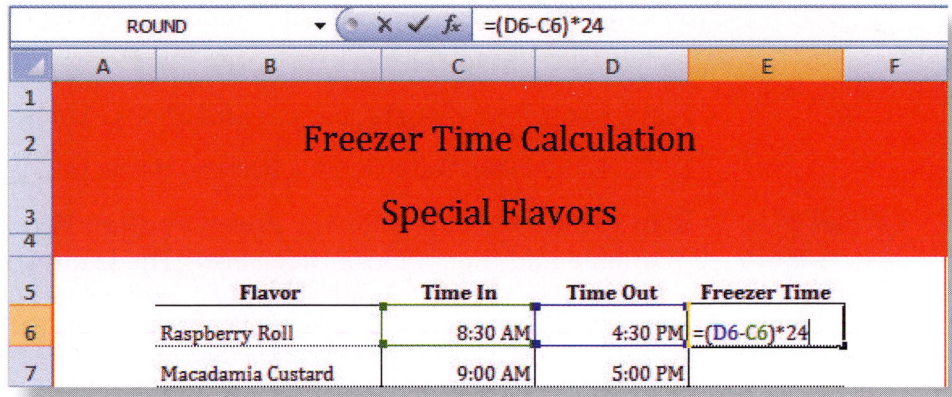

12. Key ***24** to multiply by the number of hours in a day. Press Enter.

13. Copy the formula to row 11.

Exercise 8-8   GROUP SHEETS TO ADD FOOTERS

1. Save the workbook as **[your initials]8-8** in your Lesson 8 folder.

2. While the **FreezerTime** sheet is active, hold down Shift and click the **Recipes** tab.

3. Click the **Page Layout** tab. Click the Dialog Box Launcher for the **Page Setup** group.

4. Click the **Header/Footer** tab. Click **Custom Footer**.

5. Click the Format Text button A and choose 9-point regular Calibri. Key your name in the left section.

6. In the center section, click the Format Text button A and choose 9-point regular Calibri. Click the Insert Sheet Name button.

7. Insert the date using the same font in the right section. Click **OK**.

8. In the **Page Setup** dialog box, click the **Margins** tab. In the **Center on page** section, click to select **Horizontally**.

9. Click **Print Preview** in the **Page Setup** dialog box. This is the first page of three.

10. Press ⌈PageDown⌋ to see the other worksheets. Press ⌈PageUp⌋ to return to previous pages.

11. Click **Close Print Preview**.

12. Print while the worksheets are grouped. All three sheets print with the same footer.

Exercise 8-9   HIDE AND UNHIDE A WORKSHEET

You can hide a worksheet so that you do not see its tab while the workbook is open. This allows you to hide sheets that include sensitive information.

1. Right-click any worksheet tab and choose **Ungroup Sheets**.

2. Click the **ExpireDate** sheet. Click the **Home** tab.

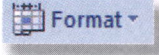

3. In the **Cells** group, click the Format button . Choose **Hide & Unhide** and then choose **Hide Sheet**. The **ExpireDate** sheet no longer appears in the workbook.

4. Save and close the workbook. If you save and close a workbook with hidden sheets, the workbook will reopen just like that.

5. Open *[your initials]*8-8. There is no **ExpireDate** sheet visible.

6. In the **Cells** group, click the Format button. Choose **Hide & Unhide** and then choose **Unhide Sheet**. The Unhide dialog box lists the names of hidden sheets.

7. Choose **ExpireDate** in the list and click **OK**. The sheet is visible.

8. Save and close the workbook.

Creating Nested Functions

A *nested* function is a function inside another function. The argument for the main function is another function. The IF function is a function that is often used in nested functions as well as the ROUND function.

Exercise 8-10   NEST SUM AND ROUND

1. Open **CookieCrunch**.

2. Click cell C6 and notice the formula. Click cell D6 and check its formula. This worksheet uses a formula to compute a 5 percent sales increase from one month to the next and results in decimal values for most of the months.

> **NOTE**
>
> A 5 percent increase multiplies the previous month's sales by 105 percent.

3. Click cell H11. Click the Insert Function button 𝑓ₓ in the formula bar.

4. In the **Select a category** box, choose **Math & Trig**. Key **r** to move to the functions that begin with "r." Scroll and choose **Round**. Click **OK**.

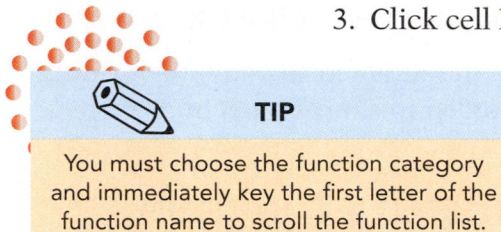

TIP

You must choose the function category and immediately key the first letter of the function name to scroll the function list.

5. Move the Function Arguments dialog box to see column headings and column H.

6. In the **Number** argument box, you will nest the SUM function. With the insertion point in the **Number** box, click the arrow for the **Name Box**.

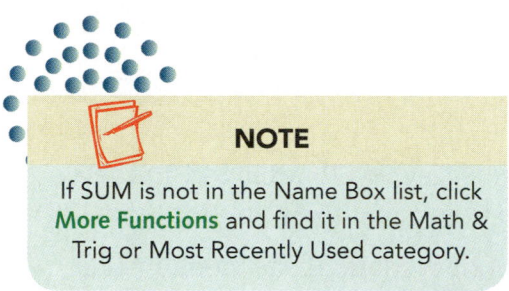

NOTE

If SUM is not in the Name Box list, click **More Functions** and find it in the Math & Trig or Most Recently Used category.

7. Choose **SUM**. The Function Arguments dialog box now shows the SUM function, but it is nested in the ROUND function in the formula bar. The SUM function is bold in the formula bar, and the suggested range for the argument is highlighted and is correct (H6:H10).

Figure 8-6
Nesting SUM in a ROUND function
CookieCrunch.xlsx PieSales sheet

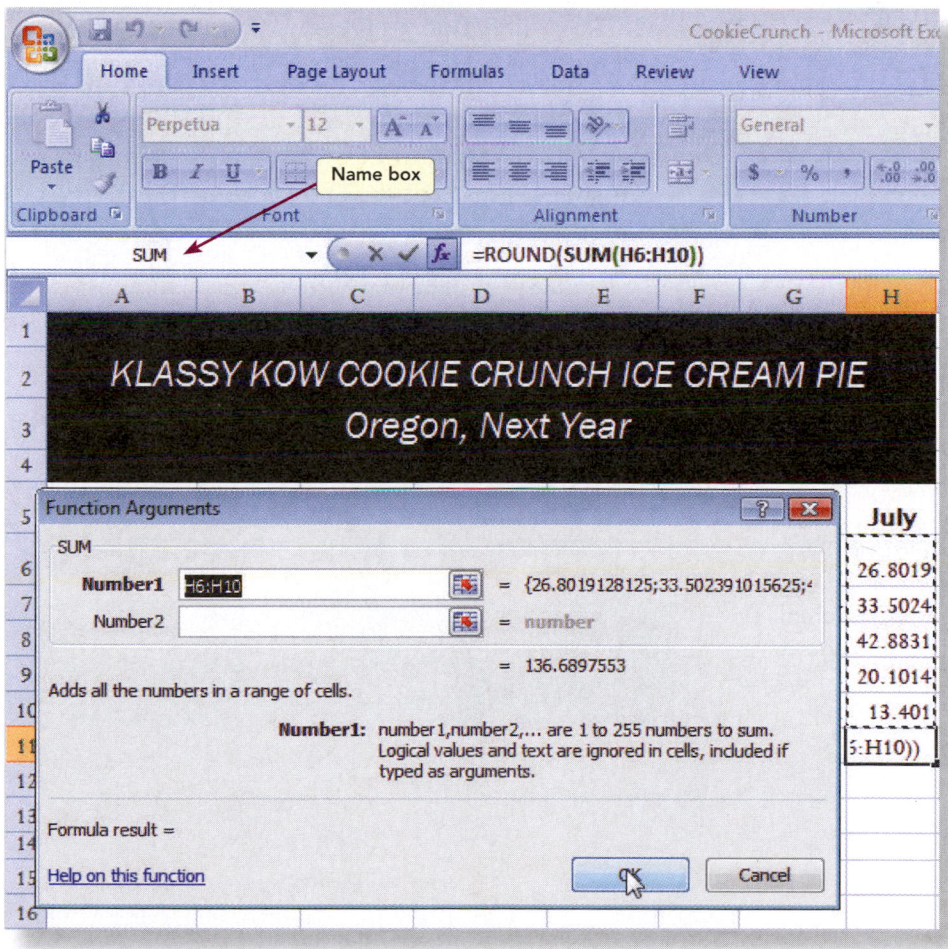

8. Click anywhere in the word **ROUND** in the formula bar. The Function Arguments dialog box returns to the ROUND function and displays **SUM(H6:H10)** as the **Number** argument.

9. Click in the **Num_digits** argument box and key **0**. Click **OK**.

10. Display the Fill handle for cell H11 and drag left to copy the formula to cells G11:B11. All results are rounded to show no decimal places.

Exercise 8-11　CREATE A NESTED IF FUNCTION

A nested IF function tests for more than one logical test. In your worksheet, you will first check to see if the monthly total is greater than 110, and then you'll test if it is greater than 120.

1. Click cell B12 and click the **Formulas** tab. Click the Logical 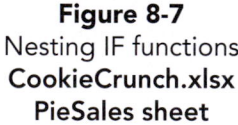. Choose **IF**.

2. In the **Logical_test** box, click cell B11. Key **>=120** after **B11** in the box. This tests if the value in cell B11 is equal to or greater than 120.

3. Click in the **Value_if_true** box. Key **120 or More**. If the value in cell B11 is greater than 120, the text "120 or More" will be shown.

4. Click in the **Value_if_false** box. If the value is not over 120, you will check if it is equal to or over 110. This is another IF function.

5. While the insertion point is in the **Value_if_false** box, click **IF** in the Name Box. The Function Arguments dialog box updates to show another IF statement. The second IF function is bold in the formula bar to show that it is the one you are now building.

6. In the **Logical_test** box, click cell B11. Key **>=110** after **B11**. Now you are determining if the value in cell B11 is equal to or greater than 110.

7. Click in the **Value_if_true** box. Key **110 or More** as the result text.

8. Click in the **Value_if_false** box. Key **Less than 110** and click **OK**.

Figure 8-7
Nesting IF functions
CookieCrunch.xlsx
PieSales sheet

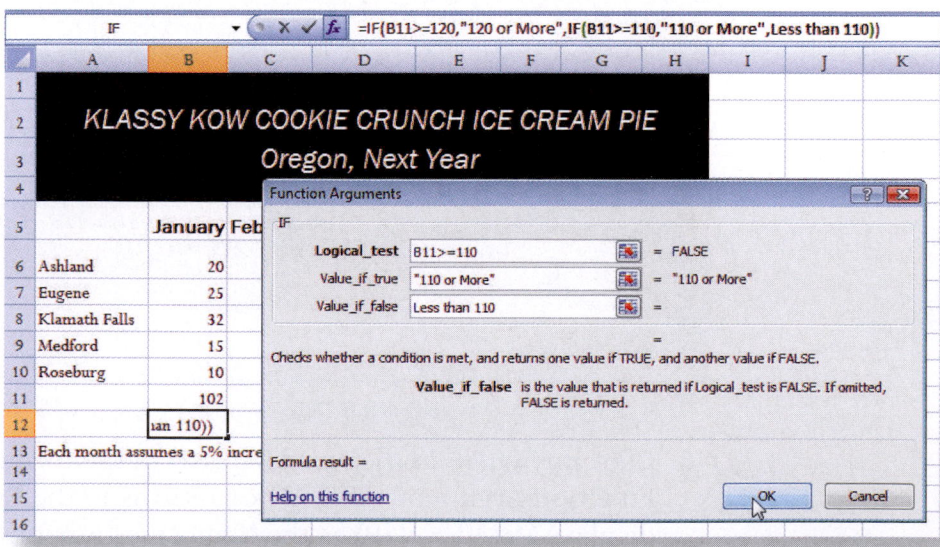

9. Copy the formula to cells C12:H12 and AutoFit columns B:H.

10. Set the height of row 13 to **67.50 (90 pixels)**.

11. Click the **Home** tab. Select cells A13:H13. In the **Alignment** group, click the Merge & Center button ⊞ . Click the Middle Align button ≡ .

12. Right-align the data in row 12.

13. Set the page to landscape orientation and use horizontal centering.

Exercise 8-12 SET TOP/BOTTOM CONDITIONAL FORMATTING

In addition to data visualizations, you can use conditional formatting to display cells with a particular format based on common numerical rankings. The Top/Bottom Rules command has options to format the top or bottom number of items or a percentage. It can also distinguish values above or below average.

1. Select cells B6:H10. On the Home tab in the Styles group, click the Conditional Formatting button.

2. Choose **Top/Bottom Rules** and then **Top 10 Items**. The Top 10 Items dialog box allows you to set how many and which format.

Figure 8-8
Setting top/bottom conditional formatting
CookieCrunch.xlsx
PieSales sheet

3. Click the arrow next to the **With** box and choose **Custom Format**. The Format Cells dialog box opens. You cannot change the font, but you can change the style, color, fill, and borders.

4. Choose **Bold Italic** on the **Font** tab.

5. Click the **Fill** tab. Choose a medium gray color and click **OK**.

6. Click **OK**. Click a cell away from the values to better see the formatting.

7. Select cells B6:H10. Click the Conditional Formatting button 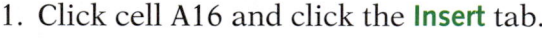 and choose **Manage Rules**.

8. Click **Edit Rule**. The Edit Formatting Rule dialog box opens.

9. Click **Format**. Set the font to be bold, but not italic. Click **OK** to return to your worksheet.

10. Save the workbook as *[your initials]*8-12 in your Lesson 8 folder.

Creating a Hyperlink

A *hyperlink* is a clickable object or text that, when clicked, displays another file, opens another program, shows a Web page, or displays an e-mail address. A hyperlink is a shortcut to files on your computer, your network, or the World Wide Web. As you insert hyperlinks in your work, Excel keeps a list of the addresses in the Insert Hyperlink dialog box. You can key a new entry or choose an existing link from the list.

A text hyperlink is shown in color and is underlined. There are several ways to add a hyperlink to your worksheet:

- Click the Hyperlink button 🌐 on the **Insert** tab.

- Right-click the cell and choose **Hyperlink** from the shortcut menu.

- Press Ctrl+K.

Exercise 8-13   CREATE A HYPERLINK

1. Click cell A16 and click the **Insert** tab.

2. Click the Hyperlink button 🌐. The Insert Hyperlink dialog box opens.

3. Click the **E-mail Address** button in the **Link to** bar. Key **YourE-MailAddress** in the **E-mail address** text box. Excel adds **mailto:** for e-mail addresses and shadows your address in the **Text to display** box.

4. Drag to select the address in the **Text to display** box.

5. Key **Click here to contact our office.**

6. Click the **ScreenTip** button. Key **Oregon Shops Only**. Click **OK**.

Figure 8-9
Insert Hyperlink
dialog box
8-12.xlsx
PieSales sheet

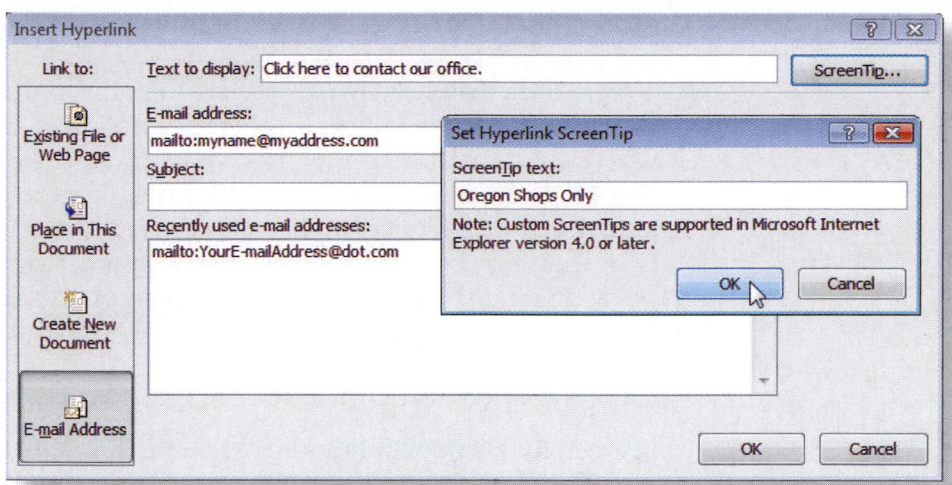

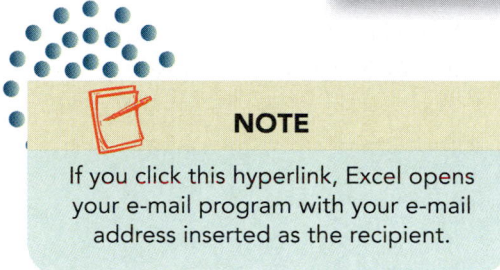

NOTE

If you click this hyperlink, Excel opens your e-mail program with your e-mail address inserted as the recipient.

7. Click **OK** again. Hyperlink text appears in color and is underlined. Hyperlink text is styled by the document theme, but its font and color are not shown in any galleries.

8. Position the mouse pointer on cell A16 to see the ScreenTip.

Figure 8-10
Hyperlink and
ScreenTip
8-12.xlsx
PieSales sheet

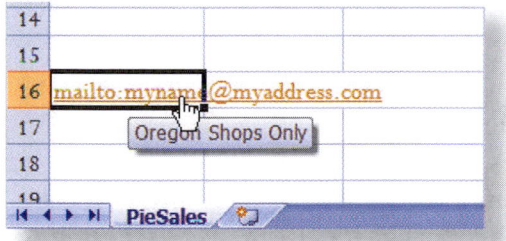

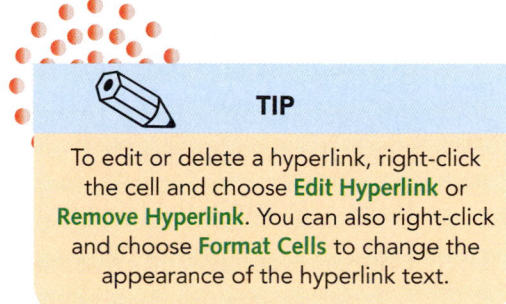

TIP

To edit or delete a hyperlink, right-click the cell and choose **Edit Hyperlink** or **Remove Hyperlink**. You can also right-click and choose **Format Cells** to change the appearance of the hyperlink text.

9. Press Ctrl+Home. Save the workbook as *[your initials]*8-13 in your folder.

Excel 2007

Exercise 8-14   RUN THE COMPATIBILITY CHECKER

If you work with people who use previous versions of Excel, you can save your work in an appropriate format for them. Two formats that are fairly common are *XLS* (earlier Excel version) and *CSV* (comma-separated values).

Before saving a workbook as an XLS file, you can determine if any of its elements won't be effective or visible in the previous version.

CSV files are simple text files with commas to separate the columns. CSV files generally do not include any type of formatting. Many software applications, including Word, can open a CSV file.

1. Click the Microsoft Office Button 🔵 and hover over **Prepare**.

2. Choose **Run Compatibility Checker**. The dialog box opens and shows which features will not be functional in the earlier Excel file. Although earlier versions of Excel do have conditional formatting, they do not include all the subtleties of this version.

Figure 8-11
Compatibility
Checker dialog box
8-13.xlsx
PieSales sheet

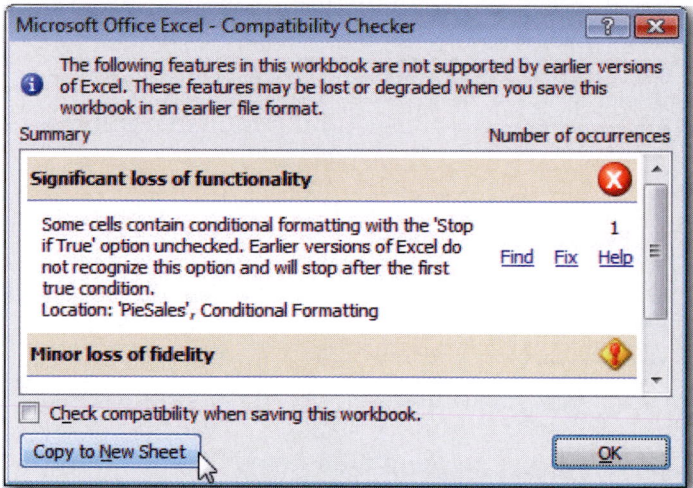

3. Click **Copy to New Sheet**. This creates a documentation sheet that explains the compatibility issues. These issues are more related to formatting than to the actual data.

4. Click the **PieSales** tab.

5. Press F12. Click the **Save as type** arrow.

6. Choose **Excel 97-2003 Workbook**. This workbook will have the **xls** extension, so you can use the same name.

7. Click **Save**. The Compatibility Checker runs automatically when you choose this file type.

8. Click **Continue**. The file has been saved. To really see the difference, you need to open the **.xls** file in an earlier version of Excel.

9. Press F12. Click the **Save as type** arrow.

10. Choose **CSV(Comma delimited)** for a different format. The filename is the same, but the workbook will have the **csv** filename extension.

11. Click **Save**. A message box alerts you that the second sheet will not be included.

12. Click **OK**. There are more problems in converting the file to this format.

Figure 8-12
Message box about converting file
8-13.xlsx
PieSales sheet

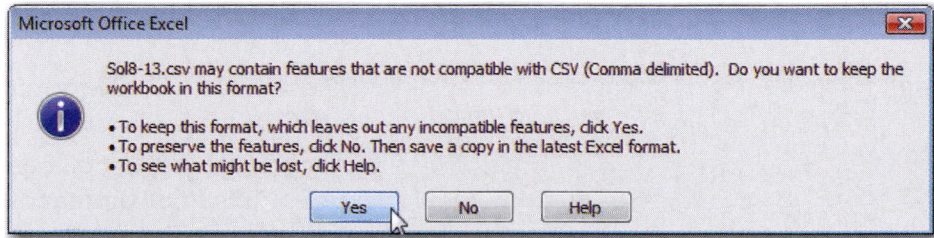

13. Click **Yes**. The file is saved.

14. Close the workbook without saving.

Using Online Help

Excel is a *mail-enabled* program, which means you can e-mail a workbook to a coworker from within Excel.

USE HELP TO LEARN ABOUT EXCEL'S E-MAIL CAPABILITIES

1. In a new workbook, click the Microsoft Office Excel Help button [icon].

2. In the Search box, key **e-mail** and press Enter. Find and review topics about sending a workbook in e-mail.

3. Close the Help window when you are finished reading about e-mail.

Lesson 8 Summary

- Use the INT function to display a value with no decimal positions.
- The ROUND function adjusts a value up or down, depending on how many digits you use for rounding. It can round to the left or right of the decimal point.
- Excel uses a serial number system for dates and times. This allows it to make date and time calculations.

- In most date and time calculations, you need to convert the results to the proper format. This may require additional arithmetic to change days to years or fractional days to hours.

- You can hide a worksheet so that its tab is not visible.

- A nested function is a function used as an argument for another function.

- The Conditional Formatting command includes a Top/Bottom Rules setting that formats the highest or lowest values or percentages in a range.

- Hyperlinks enable you to jump to other files, e-mail addresses, or Web sites.

- Workbooks can be saved in a variety of file formats for exchanging data with others. These include CSV text files and earlier versions of Excel.

- The Compatibility Checker scans a workbook before it is saved as an earlier Excel file. It notes features and commands that will not work in the earlier version.

LESSON 8		Command Summary	
Feature	**Button**	**Task Path**	**Keyboard**
Compatibility Checker		Microsoft Office, Prepare	
CSV file		Microsoft Office, Save As	F12
Hide sheet	Format ▾	Home, Cells, Format, Hide & Unhide	
Insert hyperlink	Hyperlink	Insert, Links	Ctrl + K
Top/Bottom Rule	Conditional Formatting	Home, Cells, Conditional Formatting	
Unhide sheet	Format ▾	Home, Cells, Format, Hide & Unhide	
XLS file		Microsoft Office, Save As	F12

Concepts Review

True/False Questions

Each of the following statements is either true or false. Indicate your choice by circling T or F.

T   F   1. The INT and ROUND functions use the same arguments.

T   F   2. An integer is a whole number, a nondecimal number.

T   F   3. Excel uses a serial number system for dates.

T   F   4. A nested function is placed in the cell below the first formula.

T   F   5. You can hide a worksheet in a workbook.

T   F   6. A hyperlink is a blinking cell with a formula.

T   F   7. An XLS file has all the same features and functions as an XLSX file.

T   F   8. To convert a fraction of a day to hours, multiply by 365.25.

Short Answer Questions

Write the correct answer in the space provided.

1. What is the term used to describe a function inside a function?

_____

2. What would this function display in the cell =INT(3.5643)?

_____

3. What button, when clicked, reveals the Top/Bottom Rules command?

_____

4. What does a hyperlink do?

_____

5. Which function inserts the current date?

_____

6. How can you convert days into years?

_____

7. How would Excel display this value =ROUND(1.567,2) in the cell?

_____

8. Name two functions that are often used in nested formulas.

_____

Critical Thinking

Answer these questions on a separate page. There are no right or wrong answers. Support your answers with examples from your own experience, if possible.

1. How would you determine the number of days until Christmas?

2. Which function do you think has more value in business use: INT or ROUND? Why?

Skills Review

Exercise 8-15

Use the INT and ROUND functions.

1. Open **Miles&Bulk** and save it in your Lesson 8 folder as *[your initials]*8-15.

2. On the **DeliveryMiles** sheet, format cell A1 as 18-point Calibri. Make the labels in row 3 bold. Then make all three columns **27.86 (200 pixels)** wide.

REVIEW

Drag across three column headings to select them and then set the width.

3. Use the INT function by following these steps:

   a. Key **=int** in cell C4 and press Tab.

   b. Click cell B4 and press Enter.

   c. Copy the formula in cell C4 to cells C5:C8.

4. Format rows 3:8 each **22.50 (30 pixels)** high.

5. Insert a column at column A. Apply a double-line **Outline** border to cells A2:E9. Right-align cells B3 and C3. Apply a dotted middle horizontal and bottom border to cells B3:D8.

6. Move the label in cell B1 to cell A1 and center it across the appropriate selection of cells. Set landscape orientation and horizontal centering. Add a footer.

7. On the **BulkCosts** sheet, click cell C6. Key **=** and click cell B6. Press F4 three times to make the column reference absolute. Key ***** and click cell C5. Press F4 two times to make the row reference absolute. Press Enter.

8. Copy the formula in cell C6 to cells C7:E14.

9. Use the ROUND function by following these steps:

   a. Copy cells A6:B14 to cells A19:A27. Copy cells C5:E5 to cells C18:E18.

   b. Click cell C19 and click the **Formulas** tab.

   c. Click the Math & Trig button 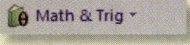 and choose **ROUND**.

   d. Click cell C6 for the **Number** box. Click in the **Num_digits** box and key **0**. Click **OK**.

   e. Copy the formula in cell C19 to cells C20:E27.

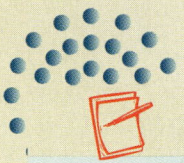

NOTE

The formula multiplies the cost per unit by a quantity of 10500 units.

10. Format cells C6:E14 and cells C19:E27 as **Accounting**. Apply **Tan, Background 2** fill to every other row, starting at rows 6 and 19.

11. Center the main labels across the data and center the page horizontally.

12. Add a header using a 9-point font for each section.

13. Prepare and submit your work. Save and close the workbook.

Exercise 8-16

Use date and time arithmetic.

1. Open **PTWorkers** and save it as *[your initials]*8-16 in your Lesson 8 folder.

2. On the **Status** sheet, key **=today()** in cell A20. Edit cell A5 to show your first and last name.

3. Use date arithmetic by following these steps:

   a. Click cell C4 and key **=** to start the formula.

   b. Click cell A20 and press [F4].

   c. Key **–** and click cell B4. Press [Enter].

   d. Click cell C4 and press [Ctrl]+[1]. Choose **Number** as the **Category** and use 2 decimal places. Click **OK**.

   e. Copy the formula in cell C4 to cells C5:C8.

   f. Click cell D4, key **=(**, and click cell A20. Press [F4].

   g. Key **–** and click cell B4. Key **)/365.25** and press [Enter].

   h. Format cell D4 as **Number** with 2 decimal places.

   i. Copy the formula in cell D4 to cells D5:D8.

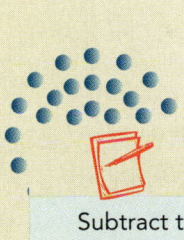

NOTE

Subtract the hire date from today to determine how long an employee has worked at the shop.

REVIEW

The subtraction is enclosed in parentheses, so it is calculated first.

4. Format cells D4:D8 as 12-point Calibri.

5. Insert a column at column A and a row at row 1. Set an **Outline** border for cells A1:F10. Set dashed middle horizontal and bottom borders for cells B5:E9.

6. Select cells B2:E3 and use **Center Across Selection**. Right-align the labels in row 4.

7. Click the Microsoft Office Button 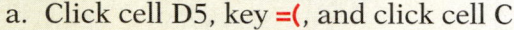 and hover at **Print**. Choose **Print Preview**. Click to select **Show Margins**. Drag the left margin marker to set a 1-inch margin.

8. On the **PartTimeHours** sheet, replace Tom Santana's name (C6 and C12) with your first and last name.

9. Use time arithmetic by following these steps:

    a. Click cell D5, key **=(**, and click cell C5.

    b. Key **–** and click cell B5.

    c. Key **)*24** and press Enter.

    d. Copy the formula in cell D5 to cells D6:D15.

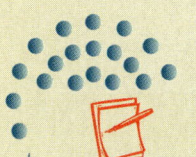

NOTE

Subtract the start time from the finish time to determine hours worked.

10. Center the labels in cells A1:A2 across the data.

11. Click the Microsoft Office Button 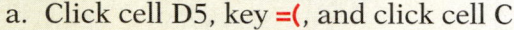 and choose **Excel Options**. On the Advanced pane, click to deselect **Show a zero in cells that have zero value** in the **Display options for this worksheet** group. Click **OK**.

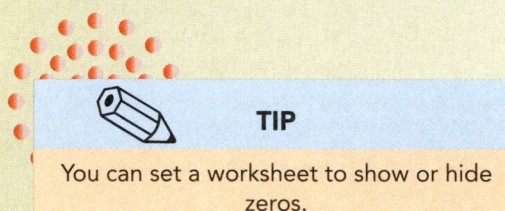

TIP

You can set a worksheet to show or hide zeros.

12. Press Ctrl+P and then press Alt+W. Click to select **Show Margins**. Drag the left margin marker to set a 1.50-inch margin.

13. Prepare and submit your work. Save and close the workbook.

Exercise 8-17

Use ROUND. Create nested functions.

1. Open **CASupplies**. Save it in your Lesson 8 folder as *[your initials]*8-17. Change to the **Flow** document theme.

2. Use ROUND and create a nested function by following these steps:

    a. Click cell B18. Click the **Formulas** tab. Click the Math & Trig button [🔢 Math & Trig ▾] and choose **ROUND**.

    b. In the **Number** argument box, click the arrow with the **Name Box** and choose **AVERAGE** again. The suggested range is B4:B17 for **Number1**.

    c. Click cell B4 and drag to select cells B4:D17 as the **Number1**.

    d. In the formula bar, click anywhere in **ROUND**.

    e. Click in the **Num_digits** box and key **0**. Click **OK**.

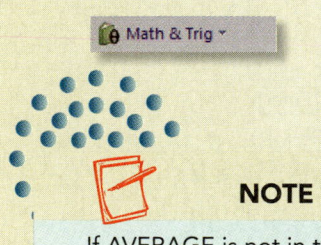

NOTE

If AVERAGE is not in the Name Box list, click **More Functions** and find it in the Statistical or Most Recently Used category.

3. Use ROUND and key a nested function by following these steps:

    a. Click cell B19. Key **=rou** and press Tab.

    b. Key **aver** and press Tab to start the nested function.

    c. Select cells E4:E17 and key a comma to separate the arguments.

    d. Select cells F4:F17 and key **)** to close the **AVERAGE** function.

    e. Key **,** to start the **Num_digits** argument.

    f. Key **0)** to complete the **ROUND** function. Press Enter.

4. Use either method to determine the average number of sundae cups ordered (columns G:I).

5. Format cells A1:A2 as 18-point Calibri. Format the labels in row 3 as Constantia 10-point. Apply **Comma Style** with 0 decimal places to all values.

6. Select the cells for cones ordered and apply conditional formatting that shows the top five values in bold text with gray fill.

7. Click the **Page Layout** tab and the Dialog Box Launcher in the **Page Setup** group. On the **Page** tab, choose **Landscape** and **Fit to** 1 page wide by 1 page tall. On the **Header/Footer** tab, click **Custom Footer**. Prepare a footer.

8. Prepare and submit your work. Save and close the workbook.

Exercise 8-18

Insert a hyperlink.

1. Open **CACount** and save it as *[your initials]***8-18** in your Lesson 8 folder.

2. Insert a hyperlink by following these steps:

    a. Right-click cell G1 and choose **Hyperlink**.

    b. Click in the **Text to display** box and key **Show Supplies Sheet**.

    c. Click the **Existing File or Web Page** in the **Link to** list.

    d. Find **CASupplies**, click the filename, and click **OK**.

3. On the Home tab, click the Format button 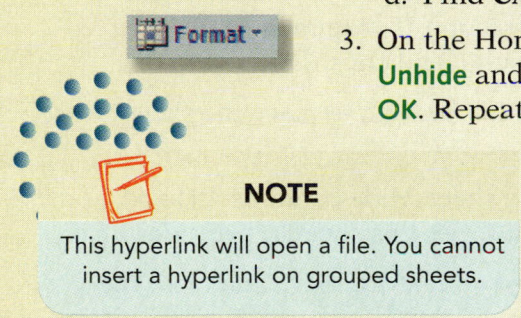. Choose **Hide & Unhide** and then **Unhide Sheet**. Click **CustCount (2)** in the list and click **OK**. Repeat these steps to unhide **CustCount (3)**.

4. Add the same hyperlink to each of these sheets.

5. Group the sheets, right-click the column B heading, and hide it.

NOTE

This hyperlink will open a file. You cannot insert a hyperlink on grouped sheets.

6. Click the **Page Layout** tab and open the **Page Setup** dialog box. Set landscape orientation. Add a header from this dialog box.

7. Prepare and submit your work. Save and close the workbook.

Lesson Applications

Exercise 8-19

Use date arithmetic. Create a nested function.

1. Open **PastDue** and save it as *[your initials]8-19*.

2. Select cells C4:C15. Replace all occurrences of "2005" with the current year. If, after replacing, some dates are in the future, change those cells to the same date but last year.

> **TIP**
>
> You can limit a Find and Replace task to selected cells.

> **NOTE**
>
> Some customers might be very late, and some might show a negative number of days, meaning bills are not yet due.

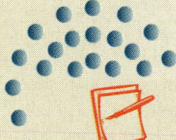

> **NOTE**
>
> Headings and Gridlines are options on the Page Layout tab as well as on the Sheet tab in the Page Setup dialog box.

3. In cell D4, key a formula to compute the due date 30 days after the invoice date. Copy the formula.

4. In cell E4, use a formula to subtract cell D4 from today. Format the result with no decimal places and negative numbers in red with no parentheses and no minus sign. You may not have negative numbers at this point. Copy the formula.

5. In cell F4, create an IF formula. The first logical test is that cell E4 be greater than 120 days. If this is so, the Value_if_true is **Over 120**. As the Value_if_false, nest another IF function. The logical test for the second IF function is that cell E4 be greater than 60. The Value_if_true for this IF statement is **Over 60**. The Value_if_false entry for the second IF statement is **Acceptable**. Right-align the results, and copy the formula.

6. Add a footer. Set a left margin to place the sheet more centered on the page.

7. Make a copy of the sheet. Hide columns A:C and display the formulas. Set this sheet to print **Headings**.

8. Prepare and submit your work. Save and close the workbook.

Exercise 8-20

Use time arithmetic.

1. Create a new workbook and save it as *[your initials]8-20*.

2. Choose the **Urban** document theme. In cell A1, key **Klassy Kow Parkland Shop**. Key **Part-Time Hours** in cell A2.

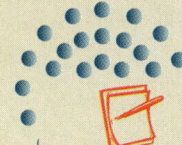

NOTE

When the time is on the hour, you do not need to key the colon or the zeros. Excel inserts them and capitalizes AM and PM.

3. In cell B3:D3, key the following labels.

   Starting Time   Ending Time   Hours Worked

4. In cell A4, key **Monday**.

5. Key the data shown in the figure below.

Figure 8-13

	A	B	C
5	Keiko Yang	11 am	8:30 pm
6	Eugene Sanchez	12 pm	10 pm
7	Millie Hanes	9:30 am	4 pm
8	Michael Bianciotto	10 am	5:30 pm
9	Aneta Monroe	2 pm	10 pm

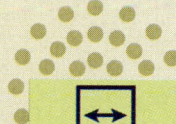

REVIEW

Convert a fraction of a day to hours by multiplying by 24.

6. In cell D5, key a formula to determine hours worked. Format the result as a **Number** with two decimal places. Copy the formula.

7. Format the sheet in an attractive, easy-to-read style. Add a header.

8. Prepare and submit your work. Save and close the workbook.

Exercise 8-21

Use date arithmetic. Use the INT function.

1. Create a new workbook and save it as *[your initials]*8-21. Set the **Metro** document theme.

2. Key **Klassy Kow New Employees** in cell A1. Key **Birthday and Age** in cell A2.

3. Key these labels in cells A3:C3.

   Name   Birthday   Age

4. In cells A4:A10, key the first and last names of six persons. Use classmates' or family members' names, or create new names.

5. Key birth dates in column B for each of your employees. Format the birthdays in a date format of your choice.

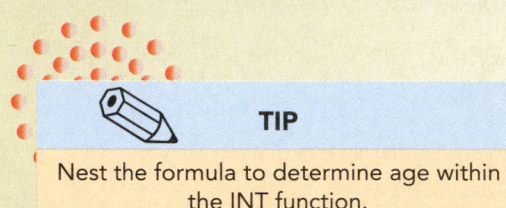

TIP

Nest the formula to determine age within the INT function.

6. Key a formula that determines the person's age as an integer.

7. Format your worksheet in a professional manner. Add a header or footer.

8. Copy the worksheet to prepare a formula sheet.

9. Prepare and submit your work. Save and close the workbook.

Exercise 8-22 ◆ Challenge Yourself

Create a nested function.

A nested IF statement in this worksheet determines the state with the maximum value for each product.

1. Open **JulyDrinks**. Save it as *[your initials]*8-22.

NOTE

Do not include the Totals column as you check for the highest sales.

2. In cell G5, start an IF function. Click cell B5 for the **Logical_test**, key **=** after **B5**, and nest the **MAX** function after the equal sign. Select cells B5:E5 as **Number1** for the MAX function.

3. Click anywhere in the word **IF** in the formula bar. Key **California** in the **Value_if_true** box. Your function states that "California" will be displayed in cell G5 if the value in cell B5 is the maximum value in the range B5:E5.

4. In the **Value_if_false** box, nest a second **IF** function. For the **Logical_test**, click cell C5, key **=** after **C5**, and nest the **MAX** function with cells B5:E5 as **Number1**. If California is not the maximum value, the function will test if cell C5 (Washington) is the maximum.

5. Click in the second occurrence of **IF** in the formula bar. In the **Value_if_true** box, key **Washington**. "Washington" will be shown in cell G5 if the value in cell C5 is the maximum value in the range B5:E5.

NOTE

The structure of the nested IF function does not require a logical test for the Nevada value.

6. In the **Value_if_false** box, nest a third **IF** function. The **Logical_test** is **D5 =MAX(B5:E5)**. Click in the third occurrence of **IF**, and key **Oregon** in the **Value_if_true** box.

7. In the **Value_if_false** box, key **Nevada**. If the value in cell B5, C5, or D5 is not the maximum value, then Nevada is. Click **OK**.

8. Center the results and copy the formula to row 9. Add a **Top and Double Bottom** border to cells B10:F10.

9. Select cells B5:E5 and set a conditional formatting top/bottom rule to show the largest value in bold. Repeat this for each item.

10. Set the page to be horizontally centered. Add a footer.

11. Copy the worksheet and display the formulas. Hide rows 1:3 and fit the columns to the visible data. Remove the horizontal centering, and fit this sheet to one landscape page.

12. Prepare and submit your work. Save and close the workbook.

TIP

Use the Page Setup dialog box to remove horizontal setting and fit the page.

On Your Own

In these exercises you work on your own, as you would in a real-life work environment. Use the skills you've learned to accomplish the task—and be creative.

Exercise 8-23

In a new workbook, key your name and the names of three family members in a column. In the next column, key birth dates for this year for each person. In the third column, calculate the number of days until the person's next birthday. Select a document theme and use your own format choices to make the worksheet attractive. Add a footer. Save the workbook as *[your initials]*8-23. Prepare and submit your work.

Exercise 8-24

Open **PerfRating** and review the nested IF function in column E to determine how an increase is calculated. Make a copy of the sheet and delete the contents of column E and re-create the nested IF function. Format the sheet in a professional way. Add a footer and save the workbook as *[your initials]*8-24. Prepare and submit your work.

Exercise 8-25

Create a new workbook with a list of 10 persons' first names in column A. In column B, key each person's height in inches, showing heights in inches. In column C, use an IF formula to show "Tall" if the person is 72 inches or more, "Average" if the person is between 63 and 71 inches, and "Short" if the person is less than 62 inches tall. Add labels and format the sheet with your own design. Add a header. Save the workbook as *[your initials]*8-25. Prepare and submit your work.

Unit 2 Applications

Unit Application 2-1

Use an absolute reference. Use the ABS and MIN functions. Apply a border.

Klassy Kow Ice Cream has a contest in which customers guess how many gumballs are in a large jar. You keep track of customers and their guesses to determine who has won. The correct count is shown in cell B4.

1. Open **Gumballs**. Save the workbook as *[your initials]*u2-1 in a folder for Unit 2.

> **NOTE**
>
> The ABS function calculates the absolute value of a negative number. The formula should use an absolute reference for cell B4.

2. In cell C5, key **Difference**. In cell D5, key **Lowest Difference**. Copy the format from cell D5 to the other labels in row 5.

3. In cell C6, key **=abs** to start the ABS function from the Math & Trig category. As the **Number** argument, subtract the value of cell B6 from the absolute value of cell B4. Copy the formula.

4. In cell D6, use the MIN function to determine which difference in column C is the smallest.

5. Format all values as 11-point regular Calibri with commas and no decimals.

6. Apply a double top and double bottom border to highlight the winner's name and numbers.

7. Add a footer.

8. Prepare and submit your work. Save and close the workbook.

Unit Application 2-2

Use order of precedence. Determine ages. Nest AND and IF functions.

On the customer birthday list, you need to indicate whether a customer is between 1 and 4 years old, between 5 and 10 years old, or over 10. The formula uses AND functions nested in IF functions.

1. Open **CustAge** and save the workbook as *[your initials]*u2-2.

> **REVIEW**
>
> The IF function is in the **Logical** category.

2. In cell E3, key **Category** and copy the format from one of the other labels in this row.

3. Determine the customer's age in column D. Format the results as **Number** with two decimals.

4. In cell E4, start an IF function. For the **Logical_test**, nest **AND**. In the **Logical1** box, click cell D4 and key **>=5**. For the **Logical2** entry, set **D4<=10**. This AND function tests if a customer is between 5 and 10 years old.

5. Return to the **IF** function. For **Value_if_true**, key **Between 5 and 10**. If the results of the AND function are true, this statement will be shown.

6. For **Value_if_false**, nest another **IF** function. For the **Logical_test**, nest **AND**. For **Logical1**, use **D4>=1**. For **Logical2**, use **D4<5**. This tests if the customer is between 1 and 4 years old.

7. Return to the second **IF** function and key **Between 1 and 4** as the **Value_if_true**. For the **Value_if_false**, key **Over 10**. Click **OK**.

8. Format the results to match other labels in the row, and copy the formula. Set a horizontal left indent of 1 for the results.

TIP

Use the Mini toolbar to change the header font.

9. Center the labels in rows 1:2 across the data. Use borders, fill, row height, and column width to enhance the readability of your worksheet.

10. Change the birthday for Maureen Weinberg to one that will make her over 10 years old.

11. Add a header using a 9-point font in all sections. Make sure the sheet will fit on a portrait page.

12. Make a copy of the worksheet and name it **CustBirthdaysFormulas**. Hide column C and display the formulas. Fit this sheet to one landscape page.

13. Prepare and submit your work. Save and close the workbook.

Unit Application 2-3

Use mixed references.

TIP

Group sheets and delete them at once.

Each ice cream shop buys supplies from the San Francisco headquarters. A shop receives a discount based on the quantity ordered. You need to determine the total cost based on the quantity and the discount.

1. Open **SupplyDisc**. Rename **Sheet1** as **Discounts**. Delete **Sheet2** and **Sheet3**. Save the workbook as *[your initials]*u2-3.

2. In cell C6, multiply the quantity by the price using mixed references. Then multiply that result by 1 minus the discount (another mixed reference). You should be able to copy the formula to the rows in column C and then to the other columns.

3. Center cells C4:F4 across the data.

4. Choose a different document theme. Format all values in rows 6:14 with a floating dollar sign and two decimals. Show commas, no decimals, for the values in row 3.

5. Add a header or footer.

6. Make a formula sheet named **DiscountsFormulas**. Fit all the columns to the data and to one landscape page.

7. Prepare and submit your work. Save and close the workbook.

Unit Application 2-4 ◆ Using the Internet

Search online travel sites to determine travel times for trips from cities in the United States to cities in Canada, Mexico, China, France, and Italy (5 rows of data). For each trip, choose a departure city and a destination city (Chicago to Vancouver, Omaha to Paris). Develop your data so that at least one trip is by train and one is by car.

Prepare a worksheet that lists the departure and arrival cities and travel time. Include type of transportation. Show the current date somewhere on the sheet as well as an average travel time for your trips. Choose a document theme and use cell styles to design your work.

Add appropriate labels and a footer. Save your workbook as *[your initials]*u2-4. Prepare and submit your work.

unit 3

ENHANCING WORKSHEET APPEARANCE

Lesson 9   Building Charts   EX-306

Lesson 10   Inserting Shapes   EX-346

Lesson 11   Using Images and SmartArt
             Graphics   EX-380

UNIT 3   APPLICATIONS   EX-411

Lesson 9

Building Charts

OBJECTIVES

MCAS OBJECTIVES

In this lesson:
XL07 4.1
XL07 4.1.1
XL07 4.1.2
XL07 4.1.3
XL07 4.2
XL07 4.2.1
XL07 4.2.2
XL07 4.2.3

After completing this lesson, you will be able to:

1. View and print charts.

2. Work with chart elements.

3. Create charts.

4. Edit chart data.

5. Use images, gradients, and textures for a data series.

6. Create a combination chart.

Estimated Time: 2 hours

A *chart* is a visual representation of information in a worksheet. Charts can help you make comparisons, identify patterns, and recognize trends.

You can create a chart on the same sheet as its data or on its own sheet in the workbook. In either case, a chart is linked to the data used to create it and is updated when you edit the data.

NOTE

The workbooks you create and use in this course relate to the Case Study (see the frontmatter of the book) about Klassy Kow Ice Cream, Inc., a fictional ice cream company.

Viewing and Printing a Chart

A chart that appears on the same sheet as the data is a graphic object and can be selected, sized, moved, and edited. An object is a separate, clickable element or part of a worksheet or chart. When a workbook has objects, you can use the Selection pane to select, view, and rearrange them.

Exercise 9-1   VIEW A CHART OBJECT

When you select a chart, the Chart Tools are activated. These tools include three command tabs: the Design tab, the Layout tab, and the Format tab.

1. Open **SeptChart**. The Zoom size is set to 75% so that you can see more of the worksheet and the chart without scrolling.

2. Click in the white chart background area to select the chart. The Chart Tools command tabs are now visible. The chart is surrounded by a light frame.

3. Press Alt to see the KeyTips. Key **jo** to select the Chart Tools Format tab. The Current Selection group shows that the chart area is the active chart element.

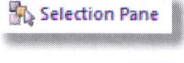

4. In the **Arrange** group, click the Selection Pane button 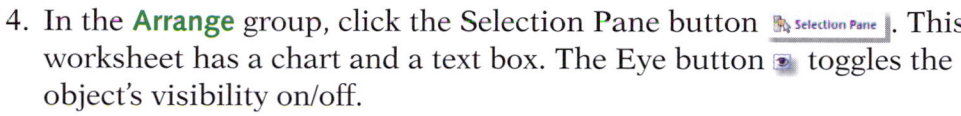. This worksheet has a chart and a text box. The Eye button 👁 toggles the object's visibility on/off.

Figure 9-1
Chart selected in the worksheet
SeptChart.xlsx
WeeklySales sheet

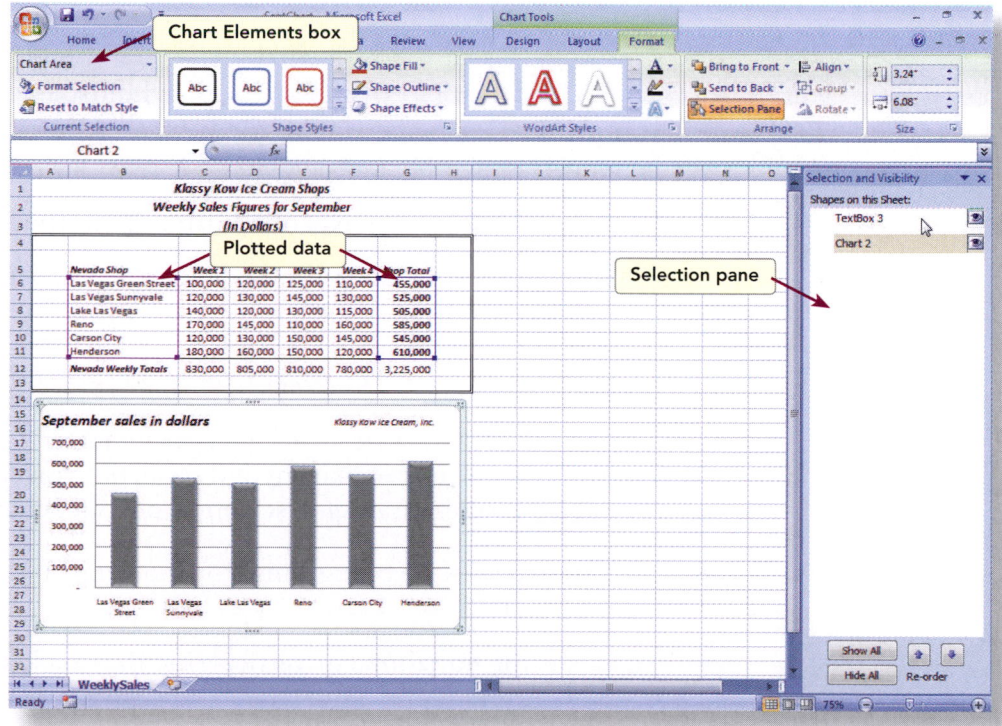

5. Click the Eye button 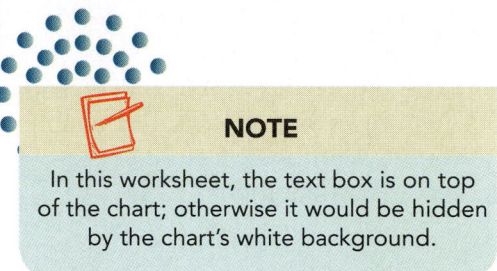 for **TextBox 3**. The text box is the company name in the top-right corner of the chart. It's hidden now.

6. Click the Eye button for **TextBox 3** again to display it.

7. Toggle the visibility of **Chart 2** on/off.

NOTE

In this worksheet, the text box is on top of the chart; otherwise it would be hidden by the chart's white background.

Exercise 9-2   PRINT A CHART OBJECT

1. Click cell A1 to deselect the chart. The background frame is removed from the chart.

2. Press [Alt] and key **n**. The Insert tab is active.

3. Key **h** to choose **Header & Footer**.

4. Click the Header button. A list of header arrangements opens.

5. Choose the second option from the bottom of the list—the user name, the page number, and the date.

6. Click the user name and change it to your name.

NOTE

The user name in a classroom setting is set by the class or network administrator.

7. Click cell A1 and print the sheet. The worksheet and the chart print on a single page.

8. Click in the white background chart area to select the chart.

9. Press [Ctrl]+[P]. In the **Print what** group, **Selected Chart** is chosen. Click **OK**. The chart prints by itself in landscape orientation. When you print a selected element, the header is not included, because a header is a page setting.

10. Click cell A1. Click the Normal button in the status bar.

11. Click the Close button in the **Selection & Visibility** pane.

Working with Chart Elements

A chart is composed of many clickable elements or objects. These elements are formatted by the current layout and style, but you can change each object on its own, too. Here is a brief description of Excel chart elements:

- The *chart area* is the background for the chart. It can be filled with a color or pattern.

- An *axis* is the horizontal or vertical line that encloses the data.

- The *horizontal (category) axis* is created from row or column headings in the data. A category describes what is shown in the chart.

- The *vertical (value) axis* shows the numbers on the chart. Excel creates a range of values (the *scale*) based on the data.

- An *axis title* is an optional title for the categories or values.

- The *plot area* is the rectangular area bounded by the horizontal and vertical axes.

- The *chart title* is an optional title or name for the chart.

- A *data series* is a collection of related values from the worksheet. These values are in the same column or row and translate into the columns, lines, pie slices, and so on.

- A *data point* is a single value or piece of data from the data series.

- A *data marker* is the object that represents individual values. The marker can be a bar, a column, a point on a line, or an image.

- A *legend* is an element that explains the symbols, textures, or colors used to differentiate series in the chart.

- A *gridline* is a horizontal or vertical line that extends across the plot area to make it easier to read and follow the values.

- A *tick mark* is a small line or marker on the horizontal (category) and vertical (value) axes to help in reading the values.

Figure 9-2
Excel chart elements

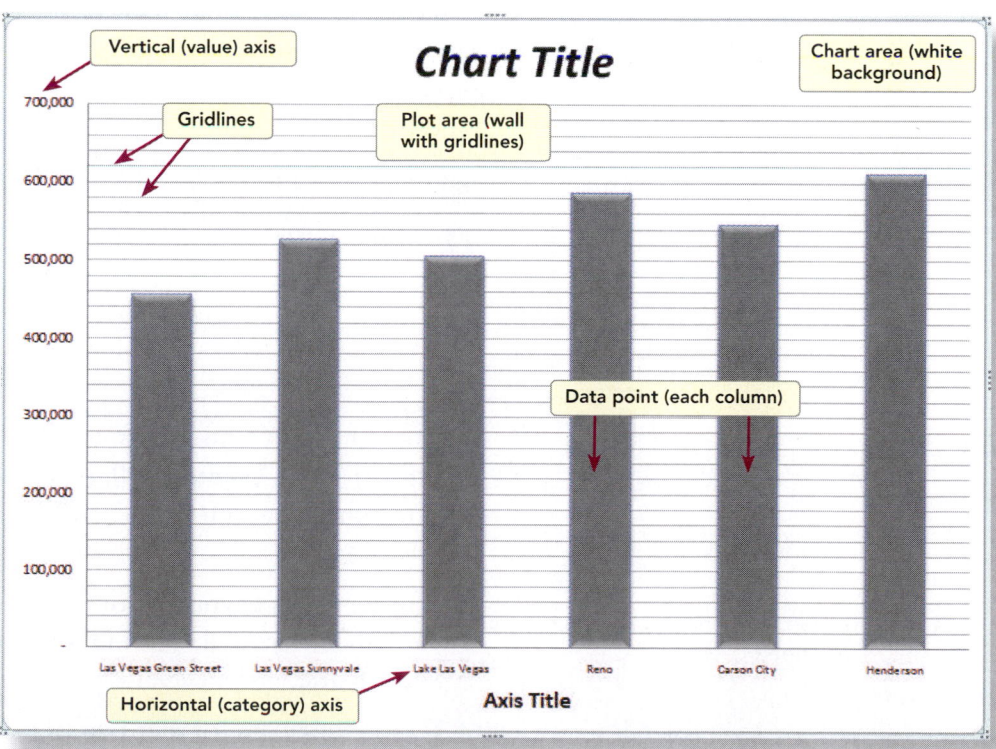

Exercise 9-3   CHANGE THE CHART LAYOUT

The Chart Tools command tabs include layout and style choices to help you build a professional-looking chart. The Chart Layouts gallery offers various arrangements of chart elements for each chart type.

1. Click the chart background. Click the **Chart Tools Design** tab.

 2. In the **Chart Layouts** group, click the More button. The Chart Layout gallery opens.

3. Click **Layout 2**. The chart is redesigned to show values above the columns with no values along the vertical axis.

Figure 9-3
The Chart Layouts gallery
SeptChart.xlsx
WeeklySales sheet

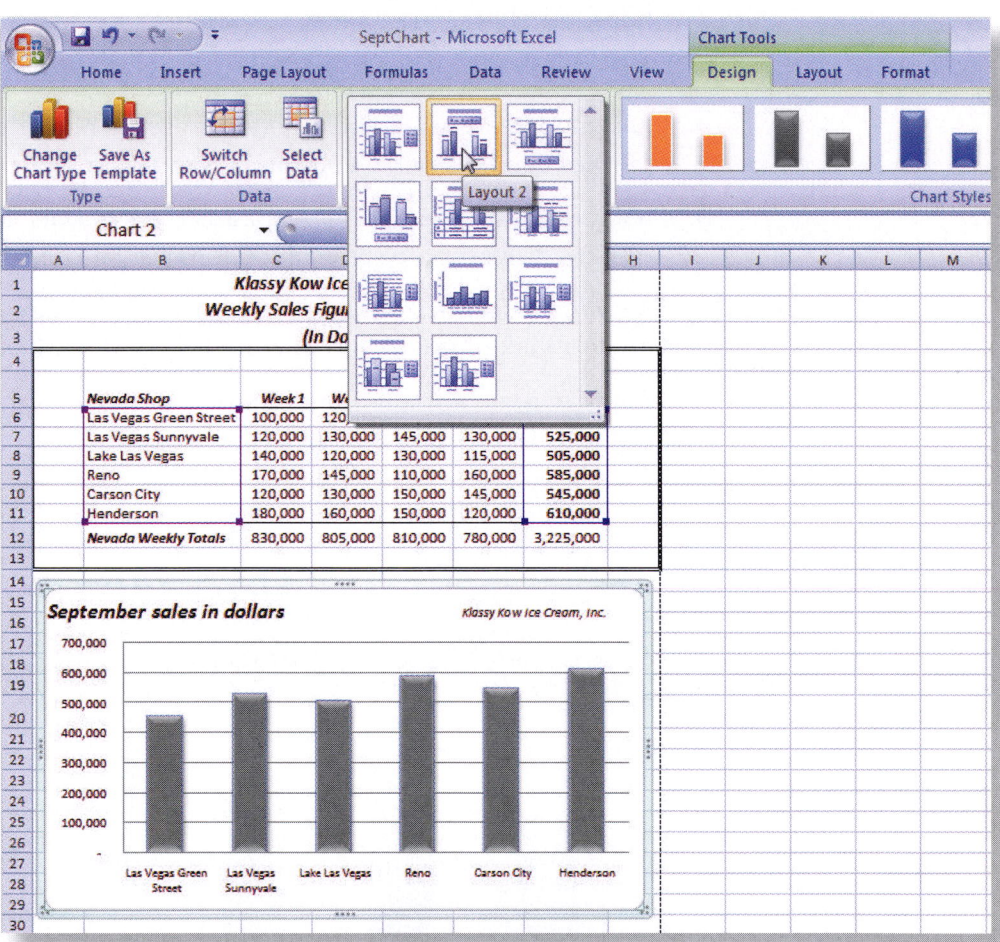

4. In the **Chart Layouts** gallery, click **Layout 3**. This is similar to Layout 1 but with a legend at the bottom (**Series 1**).

5. In the **Chart Layouts** group, click the More button. Click **Layout 4**. This layout does not include a chart title.

6. Choose **Layout 3**. The chart title object is a placeholder and will need to be rekeyed (later in the lesson). There is a legend at the bottom.

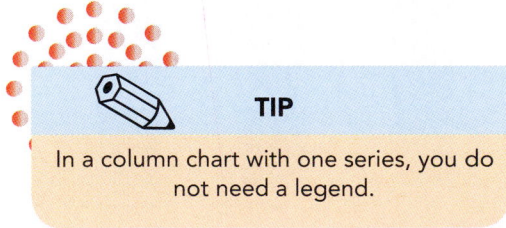

TIP

In a column chart with one series, you do not need a legend.

Exercise 9-4 CHANGE THE CHART STYLE

The Chart Styles gallery provides variations in colors and effects for chart elements using the document theme. There are many predefined styles that combine theme colors and effects.

1. In the **Chart Styles** group, click the More button ⬇. The Chart Styles gallery opens. Your chart uses Style 19, but the column colors were modified.

2. Click **Style 34**. The columns show a flat effect in a new color.

Figure 9-4
The Chart Styles gallery
SeptChart.xlsx
WeeklySales sheet

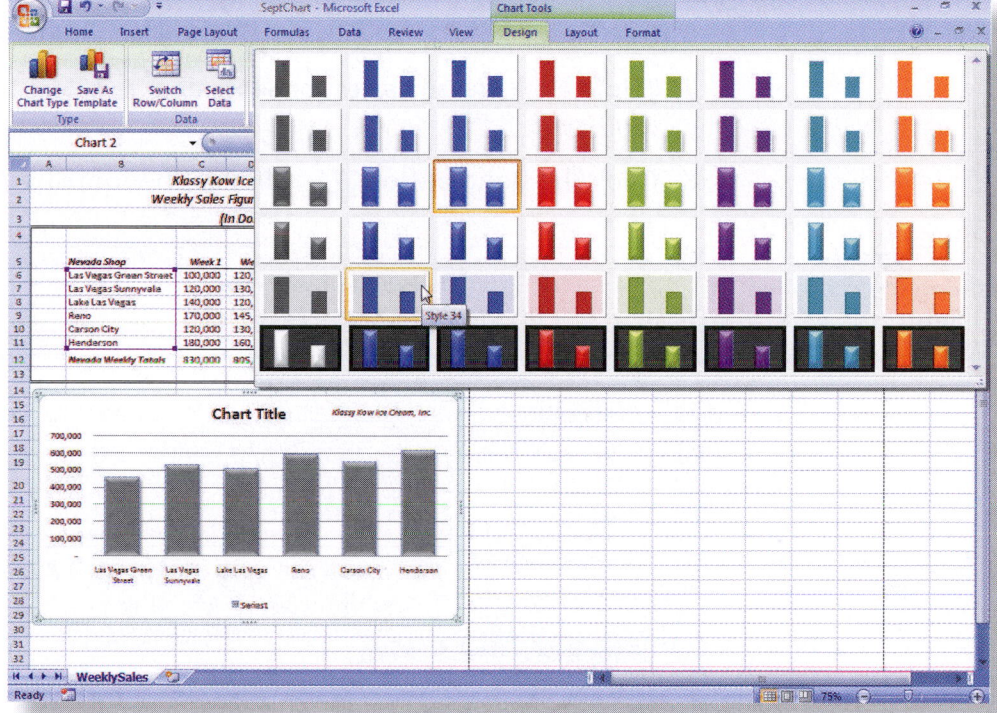

3. In the **Chart Styles** group, click the More button ⬇. Click **Style 44**. This style changes the background color, too.

4. Choose **Style 20**. The columns again have a beveled effect.

Exercise 9-5 EDIT AND FORMAT THE CHART TITLE

Chart elements show a ScreenTip when you hover over them. To edit an element, select it by pointing and clicking. When an element is selected, it shows a bounding frame and selection handles, and its name appears in the Chart Elements box on the Chart Tools Format tab. *Selection handles* are small circles, rectangles, or dots at the corners and along each border of the bounding frame. They can be used to size the element.

Excel 2007

1. Click the **Chart Tools Format** tab.

2. Point at the placeholder text **Chart Title** on the chart and click. The object is selected and shows a bounding border with four selection handles. Its name appears in the Chart Elements box in the Current Selection group.

3. Point at an edge of the object to display a four-pointed arrow. This is the move pointer.

4. Drag the object left to align with the values on the vertical axis.

5. Triple-click **Chart Title**. This is placeholder text.

6. Key **Nevada sales for September**. The placeholder text is replaced.

7. Triple-click **Nevada sales for September** to select it. Point at the Mini toolbar.

8. Click the Italic button _I_. Change the font size to 16.

Figure 9-5
Editing the chart title
SeptChart.xlsx
WeeklySales sheet

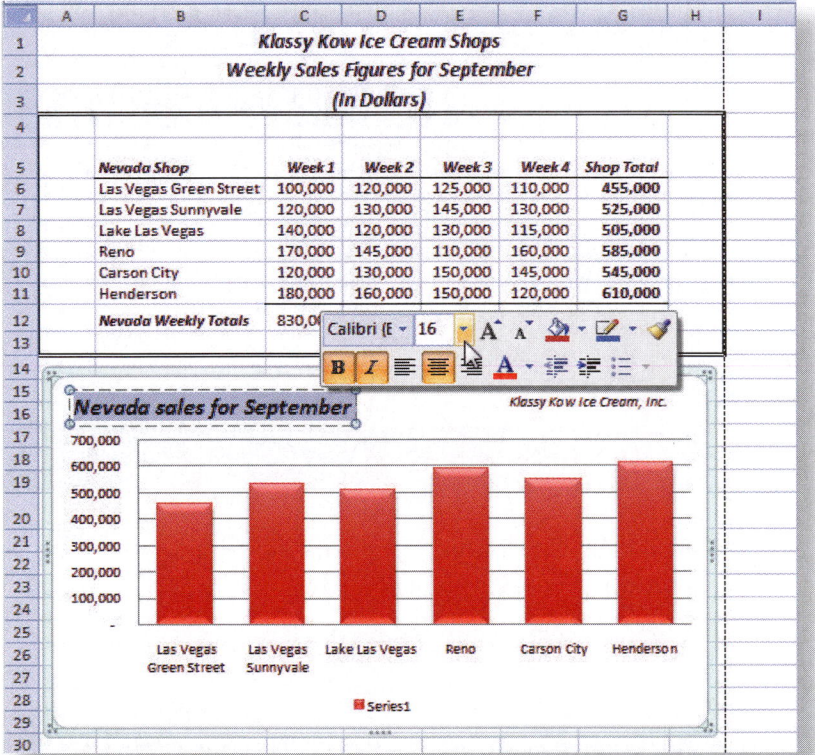

9. Click the white background area of the chart to deselect the title.

Exercise 9-6   SET SHAPE FILL AND EFFECTS

> **TIP**
>
> Many chart experts refer to the value axis as the y-axis and the category (horizontal) axis as the x-axis.

The data series in this chart are the values from column G. Each value is represented by the height of its column. The values are plotted against the value (vertical) axis, the column of numbers at the left. The category for this chart is the city name, shown along the horizontal axis.

1. Make sure the chart is selected.

2. Rest the mouse pointer on the Reno column to see its ScreenTip. It is one data point from the series.

3. Click the Reno column. The entire data series is selected, and the Chart Elements box shows **Series 1**. This is the first (and only) series in this chart.

4. In the **Shape Styles** group on the **Chart Tools Format** tab, click the More button for the **Shape Styles**. The styles include some with an outline and no fill, some with both outline and fill, and beveled and shadow styles.

Figure 9-6
Changing the shape's style
SeptChart.xlsx
WeeklySales sheet

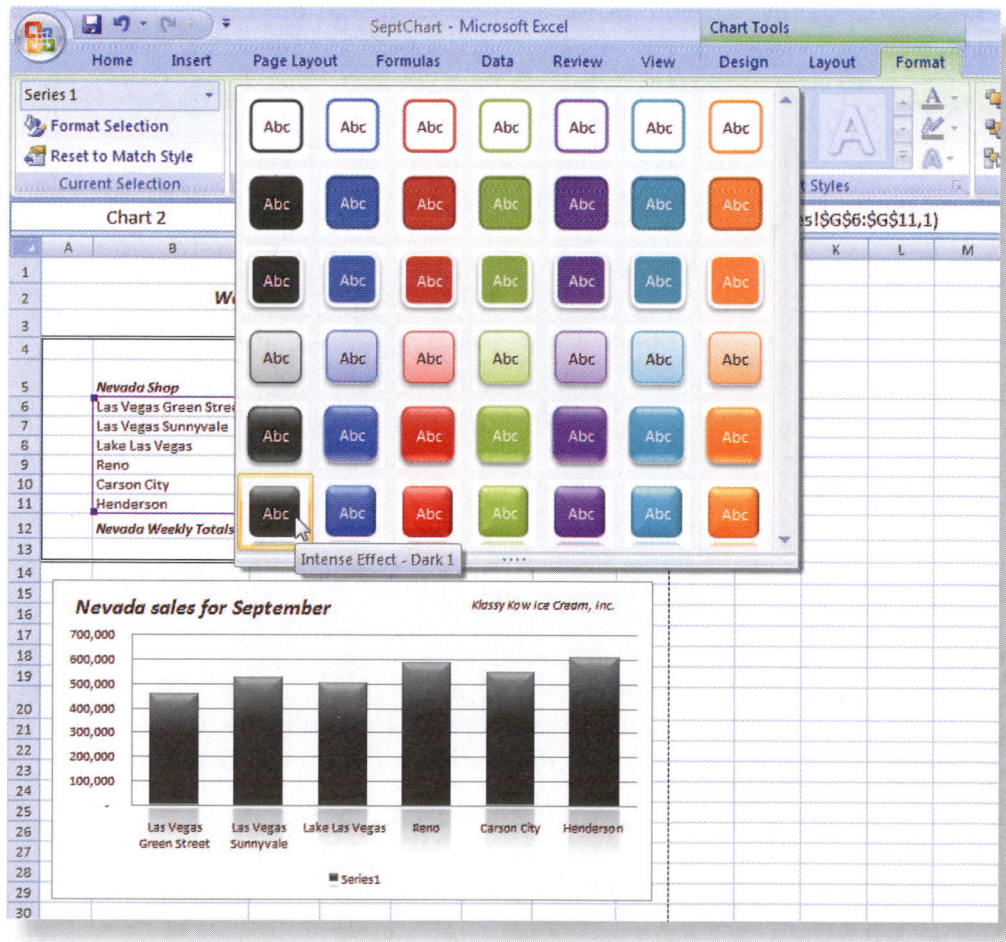

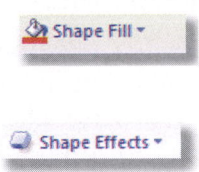

5. Choose **Intense Effect, Dark 1**. Each column now has a reflection, too.

6. In the **Shape Styles** group, click the Shape Fill button .

7. Choose **White, Background 1, Darker 35%** in the first column.

8. In the **Shape Styles** group, click the Shape Effects button. Most effects are available for this shape.

Figure 9-7
Changing the shape's effect
SeptChart.xlsx
WeeklySales sheet

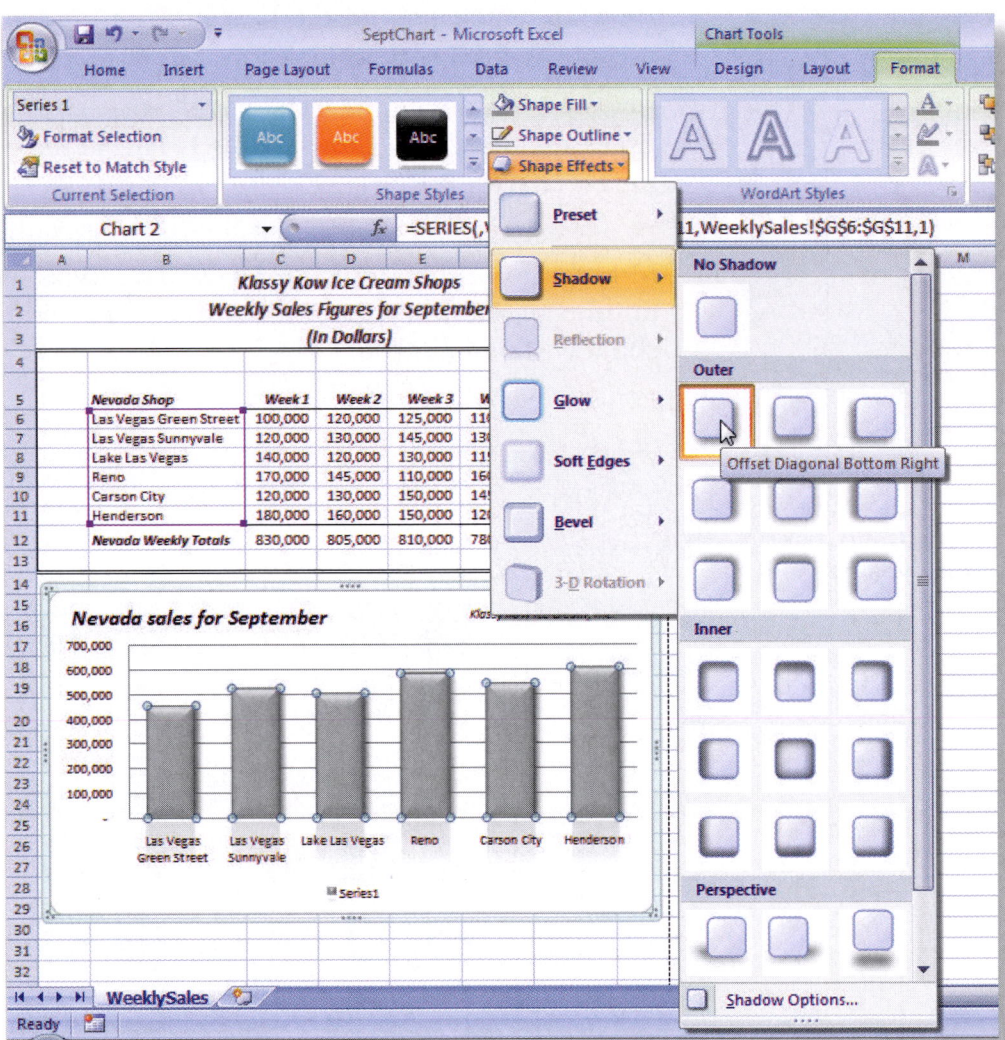

9. Hover over **Shadow** to display its gallery. Then choose **Offset Diagonal Bottom Right** (first effect in the Outer group).

10. Click the white chart background.

Exercise 9-7 SET AND FORMAT DATA LABELS

A *data label* is an optional title shown for each value. It is the value from column G in this case. The Chart Tools Layout tab provides options for setting and positioning individual chart elements.

1. Click the **Chart Tools Layout** tab.

2. Hover over the Data Labels button  and read its ScreenTip. Click one of the labels.

3. Click the Data Labels button and choose **Outside End**. The value of each data point appears above its column.

4. Rest the mouse pointer on one of the data labels to see the ScreenTip.

> **NOTE**
>
> The Chart Elements box is in the Current Selection group on both the Layout and Format command tabs.

5. Click the **Chart Tools Format** tab. Click the arrow next to the **Chart Elements** box and choose **Series 1 Data Labels**. The data labels are selected and show bounding boxes and selection handles.

6. Click the **Home** tab and change the font size to 9 points.

Exercise 9-8 FORMAT THE AXES

The Horizontal (Category) Axis is the x-axis in this chart, the city names.

1. Position the mouse pointer on a city name to see its ScreenTip.

2. Click the **Chart Tools Format** tab. Click the **Chart Elements** arrow and choose **Horizontal (Category) Axis**. The city names are selected and show a bounding box and selection handles.

3. On the **Home** tab, change the font size to 8 points.

4. Click one of the values along the Vertical (Value) Axis, the y-axis, the sales in dollars.

5. Click the **Chart Tools Layout** tab. Click the Axes button. Choose **Primary Vertical Axis** and **None**. With the data labels displayed, you don't need the axis values.

6. Right-click one of the data labels (above the columns). Choose **Format Data Labels**.

7. Click **Number**. Choose **Currency** with **0** decimals and **$** as the **Symbol**. Click **Close**.

Excel 2007

Figure 9-8
Formatted data
labels
SeptChart.xlsx
WeeklySales sheet

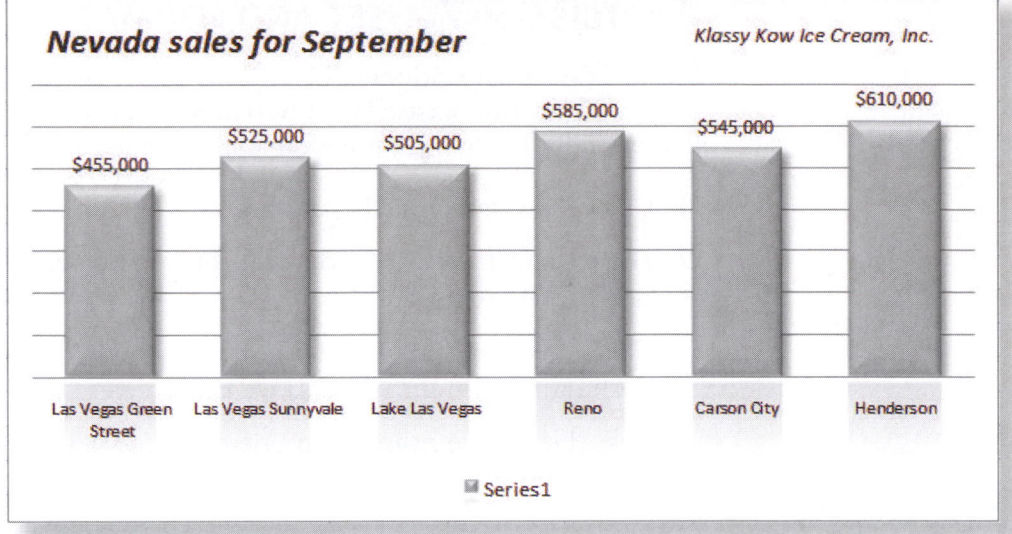

8. Click a cell in column I to better see the chart.

Exercise 9-9   FORMAT THE PLOT
AND CHART AREAS

1. Click **Series 1** at the bottom of the chart. This is the legend. There is one series in this chart, the amount shown by each column.

2. Press Delete.

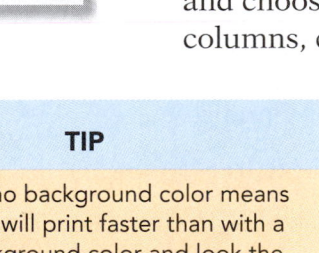

3. Click the **Chart Tools Format** tab. Click the **Chart Elements** arrow and choose **Plot Area**. The plot area is the background grid for the columns, currently white. It is selected.

4. In the **Current Selection** group, click the Format Selection button Format Selection.

5. On the **Fill** pane, choose **No fill**. Click **Close**. The color (white) is removed but is not noticeable yet.

6. Click the **Chart Elements** arrow and choose **Chart Area**. The chart's background is selected; it is white, too.

TIP

Choosing no background color means your chart will print faster than with a white background color and look the same on white paper.

7. Click the Format Selection button Format Selection.

8. On the **Fill** pane, choose **No fill**. Click **Close**. You can now see that there is no fill color.

9. Click cell A1.

10. Save the workbook as *[your initials]*9-9 in a folder for Lesson 9.

11. Close the workbook.

Creating Charts

Before you build your own chart, you must consider two questions. First, what data should you use for the chart? And, second, what type of chart is best for that data? With practice and experience, you can develop a good sense of how to identify data and choose chart types.

You can create basic chart types such as column charts, bar charts, pie charts, and line charts. You can also create specialized charts such as doughnut and radar charts. Table 9-1 describes the chart types available.

NOTE

The appearance of a button in the Ribbon is affected by the screen size and resolution setting. All buttons have ScreenTips for clarification.

TABLE 9-1 Chart Types in Excel

Type		Definition
	Column	A column chart is the most popular chart type. Column charts show how values change over a period of time or make comparisons among items. They can be prepared with 3-D effects or stacked columns. Categories are on the horizontal axis (x), and values are on the vertical axis (y). The shape can also be a cone, a cylinder, or a pyramid.
	Line	Line charts show trends in data over a period of time. They emphasize the rate of change. 3-D effects are available. Lines can be stacked and can show markers, a symbol that indicates a single value.
	Pie	Pie charts show one data series and compare the sizes of each part of a whole. Pie charts should have fewer than six data points to be easy to interpret. A pie chart can use 3-D effects and can show exploded slices.
	Bar	Bar charts illustrate comparisons among items or show individual figures at a specific time. Bar charts can use 3-D effects and stacked bars. Categories are on the vertical axis (y). Values are on the horizontal axis (x). The shape can also be a cone, a cylinder, or a pyramid.
	Area	Area charts look like colored-in line charts. They show the rate of change and emphasize the magnitude of the change. 3-D effects are available.
	Scatter	Scatter charts are used to show relationships between two values, such as comparing additional advertising to increased sales. Scatter charts do not have a category; both axes show numbers/values.
	Stock	Stock charts are often called "high-low-close charts." They use three series of data in high, low, close order. They can also use volume as a fourth series.
	Surface	Surface charts illustrate optimum combinations of two sets of data. They show two or more series on a surface. Surface charts can use 3-D effects.
	Doughnut	Doughnut charts compare the sizes of parts. A doughnut chart has a hole in the middle. A doughnut chart shows the relative proportion of the whole. A doughnut chart can show more than one data series, with each concentric ring representing a series.
	Bubble	Bubble charts compare sets of three values. They are like scatter charts with the third value displayed as the size of the bubble. Bubble charts can be 3-D.
	Radar	Radar charts show the frequency of data relative to a center point and to other data points. There is a separate axis for each category, and each axis extends from the center. Lines connect the values in a series.

Exercise 9-10   CREATE AND EDIT A CHART SHEET

After you select values and labels, press F11 to create a chart sheet with the default chart type. It is inserted on a new sheet, and you can edit it like any chart.

1. Open **MayChart**. There is no chart yet.

2. Select cells B6:C11. This range includes the province/country category and the values.

3. Press F11. A column chart is inserted on its own sheet.

4. On the **Chart Tools Design** tab in the **Chart Layouts** group, click the More button ▾.

5. Choose **Layout 3**. This layout includes a chart title and a legend (at the bottom).

6. Click the chart title object. Its bounding box and selection handles are visible.

7. Triple-click the placeholder text. Key **Number of Kowabungas Sold**.

8. Click any column and notice that the entire series is selected.

9. While all columns are selected, click the "British Columbia" column. It is selected alone.

10. Click the **Chart Tools Format** tab. In the **Shape Styles** group, click the Shape Fill button .

11. Choose **Red, Accent 2** in the sixth column. Only the selected column is changed.

Figure 9-9
Changing an individual column
MayChart.xlsx
Chart1 sheet

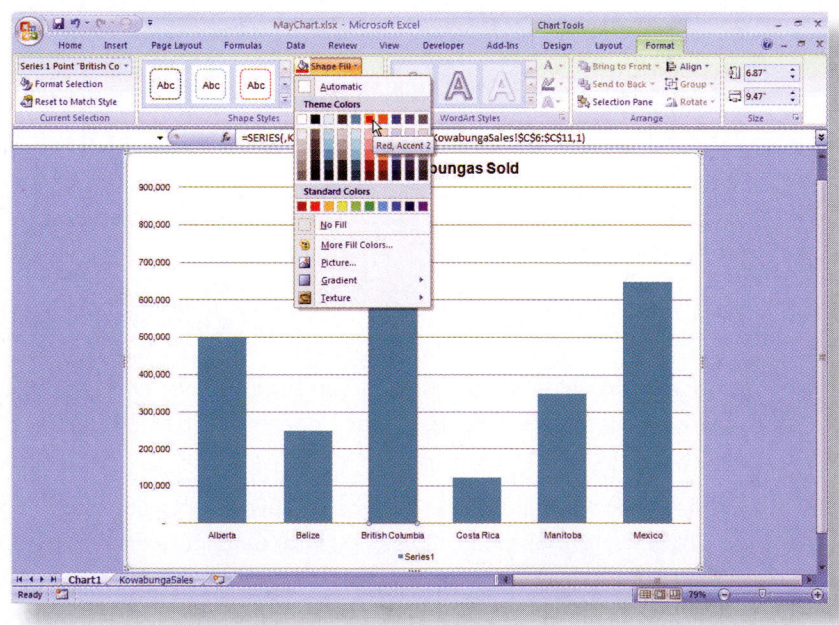

12. Click the legend at the bottom of the sheet and press Delete.

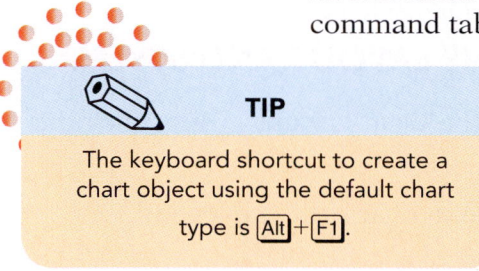

Exercise 9-11   CREATE A CHART OBJECT

A *chart object* appears on the same sheet as the data; it may also be called an *embedded chart*. You create it by choosing the chart type from the Insert command tab.

> **TIP**
>
> The keyboard shortcut to create a chart object using the default chart type is Alt + F1.

1. Click the **KowabungaSales** tab. Cells B6:C11 are still selected.

2. Click the **Insert** tab. The Charts group includes buttons for the most commonly used chart types.

3. Click the Pie button 🥧. You can create two- or three-dimensional charts. A ScreenTip describes each type when you hover over the icon.

Figure 9-10
Creating a pie chart
MayChart.xlsx
KowabungaSales
sheet

4. In the **2-D** list, choose **Pie**. The chart is on the worksheet with its data.

Exercise 9-12   MOVE AND SIZE A CHART OBJECT

The selection handles for the chart object are three dots arranged in a triangle shape on the corners. The handles are four dots arranged in a row in the middle of each edge. The move pointer is a four-pointed arrow; the sizing pointer is two-pointed.

1. Point at the top edge of the chart object to display a four-pointed arrow. Drag the chart so that its top-left corner aligns at cell A14.

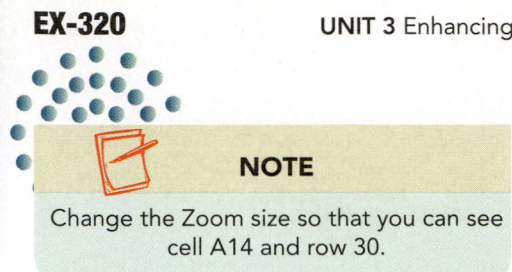

NOTE

Change the Zoom size so that you can see cell A14 and row 30.

2. Point at the bottom-right selection handle. A two-pointed sizing pointer appears.

3. Click and drag the bottom-right selection handle to cover cell E32. As you drag, the chart is made larger.

Exercise 9-13   CHANGE THE LAYOUT AND STYLES

1. Click the **Chart Tools Design** tab. In the **Chart Layouts** group, click the More button .

2. Choose **Layout 5**. This layout includes a chart title, no legend, and data labels inside the pie slices.

3. In the **Chart Styles** group, click the More button .

4. Choose **Style 17**. The slices are shown in shades of gray.

5. Click the **Chart Tools Format** tab. Make sure that the chart area is the current selection.

6. For **Shape Styles**, click the More button .

7. Hover over several different styles. Since the chart area is selected, the entire object is affected.

8. Press Esc to close the gallery without making a change.

9. Point at any pie slice, but away from the label and click.

10. For **Shape Styles**, click the More button .

11. Hover over several styles. Now the slices would be affected, not the background.

12. Press Esc to close the gallery without making a change.

13. While the slices are selected, click only the Alberta slice. You should see selection handles for just this slice.

Figure 9-11
Pie chart with a single slice selected
MayChart.xlsx
KowabungaSales
sheet

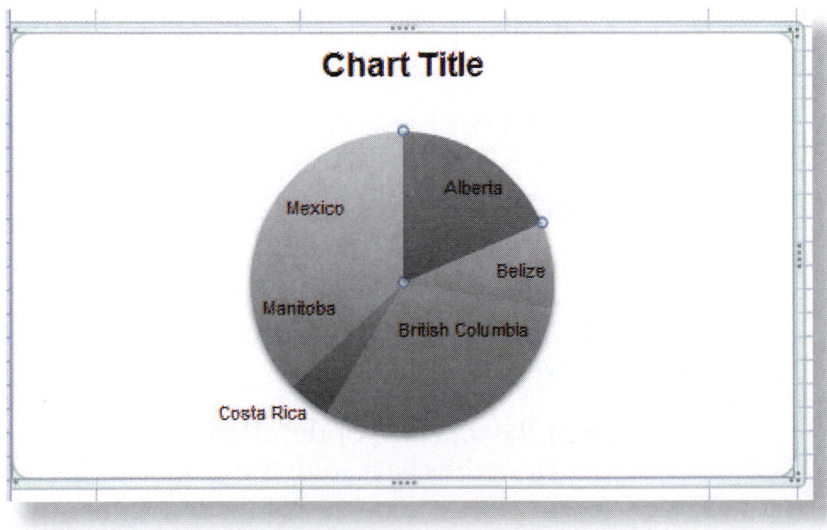

14. Click the More button  for **Shape Styles**.

15. Hover over several styles. Now just one slice would be affected.

16. Press Esc.

17. Click the chart title object.

18. Triple-click the placeholder text and key **Kowabunga Sales**.

19. Right-click the pie and choose **Format Data Labels**.

20. On the **Label Options** pane, click to select **Percentage**.

21. Click **Close**. The slices now show the name and the percentage.

Exercise 9-14   CREATE A BAR CHART SHEET

You can create a chart object and later move it to its own sheet. It is still linked to the data in the worksheet.

1. Select cells B6:C11 and click the **Insert** tab.

2. In the **Charts** group, click the Bar button.

3. In the **3-D** group, choose **Clustered Bar in 3-D**, the first icon. The chart object appears on your worksheet.

4. In the **Location** group, click the Move Chart button. The Move Chart dialog box allows you to move the chart to its own sheet or to another worksheet in the workbook.

Figure 9-12
Move Chart dialog box
MayChart.xlsx
KowabungaSales sheet

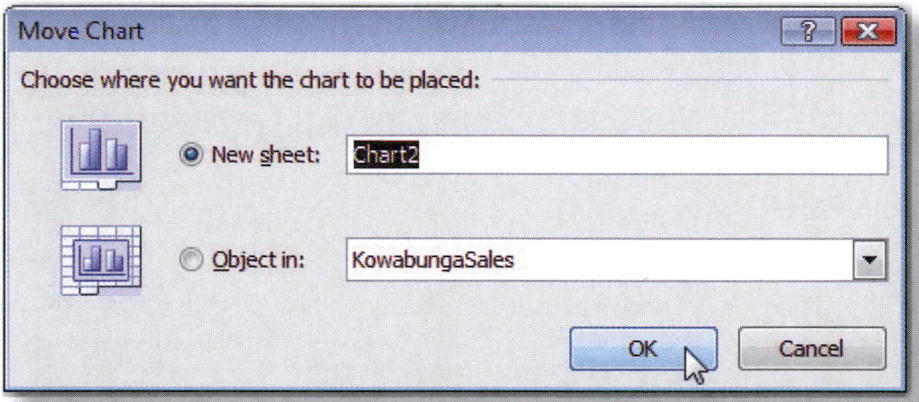

5. Choose **New sheet** and click **OK**. The chart is placed on a new sheet.

6. Click **Series 1** and press Delete. That was the legend.

7. Click the **Chart Tools Layout** tab. In the **Labels** group, click the Chart Title button.

8. Choose **Above Chart**. A placeholder object is inserted.

9. Triple-click **Chart Title** and key **Comparison of Weekly Sales**.

10. Click anywhere in the side panel to deselect the chart.

Exercise 9-15   ADD GRIDLINES AND A DATA TABLE

A data table lists the values and names displayed in the chart. It is separate from the chart and appears below the horizontal axis. Gridlines appear on the plot area to make it easy to relate values to the bars or columns. Only major vertical gridlines are shown in this chart.

1. Click the white chart background to select the chart.

2. On the **Chart Tools Layout** tab, click the Gridlines button .

3. Choose **Primary Vertical Gridlines** and then choose **Major and Minor Gridlines**.

4. Click the Data Table button.

5. Choose **Show Data Table**. It appears below the chart and shows "Series 1" as the name.

6. Right-click anywhere in the data table and choose **Select Data**. The source worksheet data is active and the Select Data Source dialog box opens.

7. Click **Series 1** in the Legend Entries list and then click **Edit**. There is no series name at this point.

8. Key **$ Sales** and click **OK**. Click **OK** again. The data table shows the new series name.

Figure 9-13
Editing the series name
MayChart.xlsx
KowabungaSales
sheet

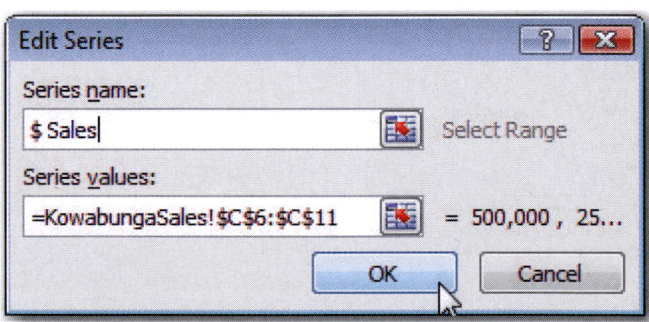

REVIEW

You can right-click a tab to rename it.

9. Name the sheet **BarChart**.

10. Save the workbook as **[your initials]9-15** in your folder.

Editing Chart Data

Because a chart is linked to its data, changes that you make in the worksheet are reflected in the chart. You can add categories or value series to your data and then to its chart.

Exercise 9-16   EDIT CHART DATA

1. Click the **KowabungaSales** tab in *[your initials]*9-15. Notice the pie-slice size for Manitoba and its corresponding value in the worksheet.

2. Click the **BarChart** tab. Note the length of the bar for Manitoba.

3. Click the **Chart1** tab. Note the height of the Manitoba column.

4. Click the **KowabungaSales** tab.

5. Click cell C10, key **900000**, and press Enter. Notice the larger pie slice for Manitoba.

6. Click the **Chart1** tab. The height of the Manitoba column is increased.

7. Click the **BarChart** tab. Note the length of the Manitoba bar.

Exercise 9-17   ADD A DATA POINT

If you add another country and its total to the worksheet, you add a data point to the data series. If you insert the new data within the chart's current data range, it appears automatically in all charts linked to the data. If you add data below or above the chart's original source data range, you need to reset the data range for each chart.

1. On the **KowabungaSales** sheet, insert a row at row 12.

2. Key **Ontario** in cell B12. Key **1000000** in cell C12. This data is not within the existing data range for the charts.

3. Right-click the white background area for the pie chart. Choose **Select Data**. The Select Data Source dialog box opens, and a moving marquee encloses the current data range.

4. Click **Cancel**. The data range shows sizing handles at each corner.

5. Position the pointer on the bottom-right handle for cell C11. A two-pointed sizing arrow appears.

6. Drag the sizing arrow to include the Ontario information. The chart is updated when you release the mouse button.

Excel 2007

Figure 9-14
Adding a data point
9-15.xlsx
KowabungaSales
sheet

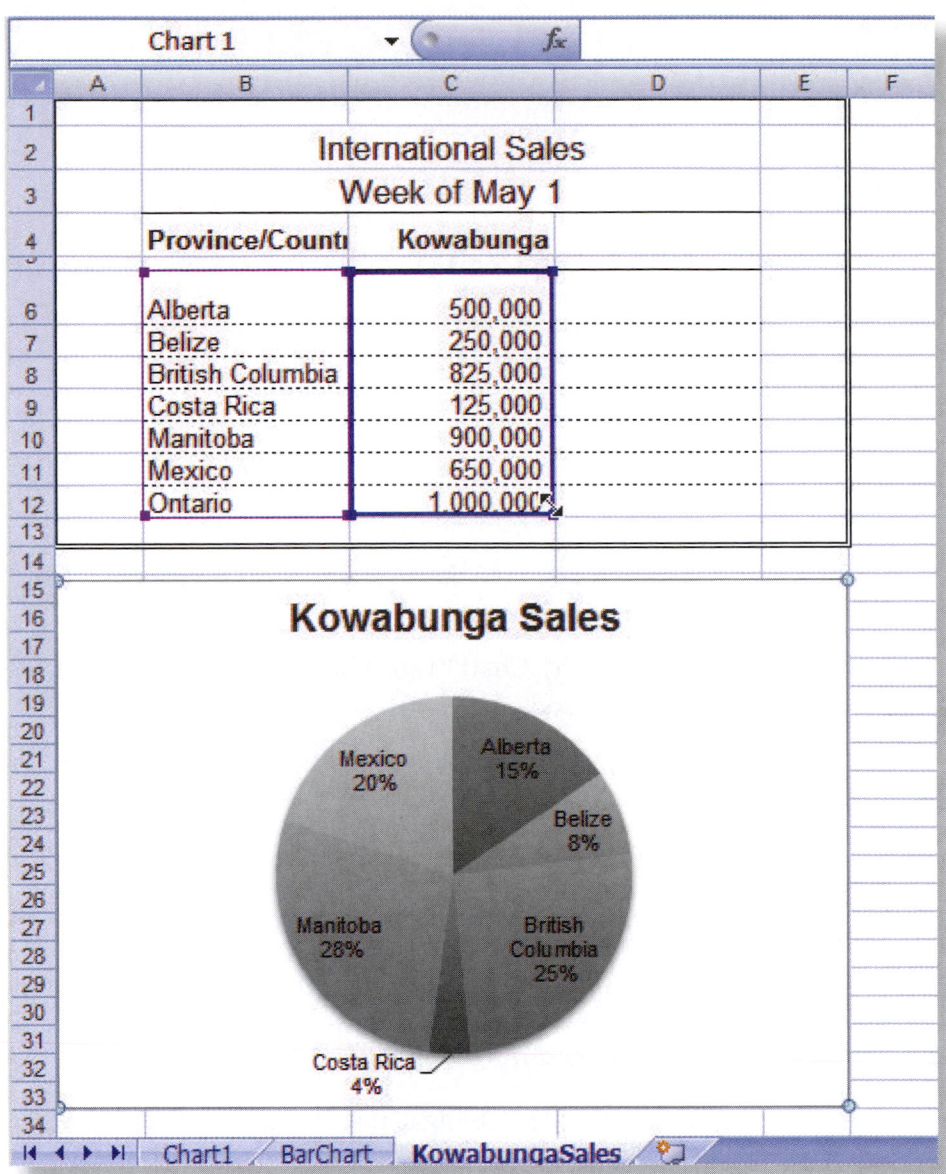

7. Click the **Chart1** tab.

8. Right-click the white chart background. Choose **Select Data**. The Select Data Source dialog box opens on top of the **KowabungaSales** tab with the current data range selected.

9. In the **Chart data range** entry box, edit the address to show **$C$12** instead of $C$11. Click **OK**. The column chart is updated to include Ontario.

Figure 9-15
Edit Data Source
dialog box
9-15.xlsx
**KowabungaSales
sheet**

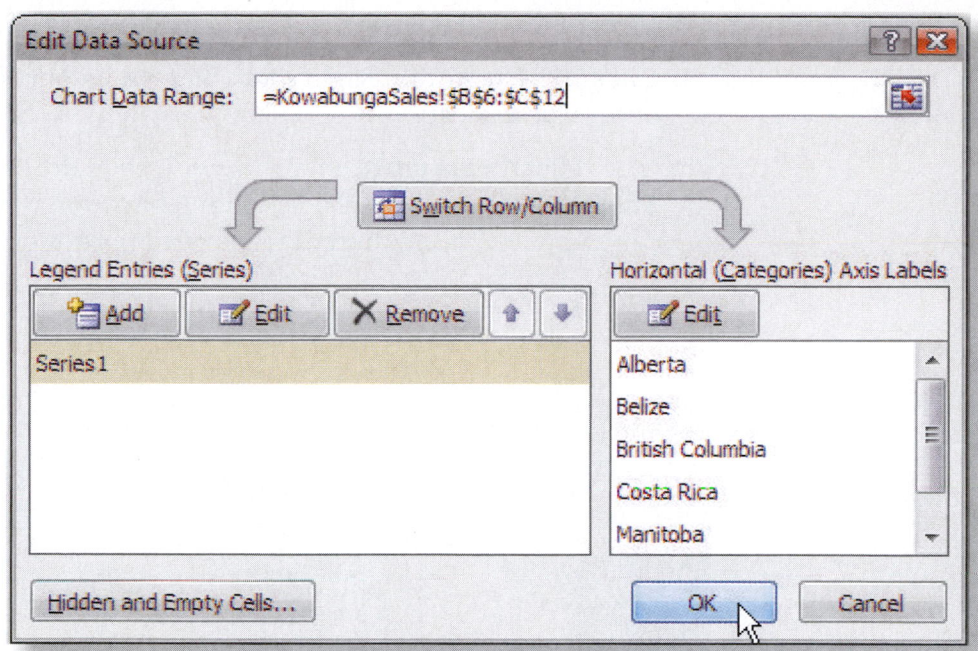

REVIEW

The dialog box collapses as you drag.
It expands when you release the mouse
button.

10. Click the **BarChart** tab. Right-click the white chart
background.

11. Choose **Select Data**. Move the dialog box so that you
can see the range.

12. Click cell B6 and drag to select cells B6:C12. Click
OK. There is now an Ontario bar.

13. Insert a row at row 10 on the **KowabungaSales** sheet.

14. Key **Great Britain** in cell B10 and **250000** in cell C10. This data point
is within the existing data range for the charts.

15. Click each sheet tab to see the Great Britain data.

Exercise 9-18 ADD AND RENAME
DATA SERIES

NOTE

A pie chart has only one series.

If you add a second product to the data, you can then create
a second series for the column and bar charts.

1. On the **KowabungaSales** sheet, key **KowOwow** in cell D4.

2. Key the following values in cells D6:D13:

D6	60000
D7	120000
D8	45000
D9	150000
D10	300000
D11	250000
D12	100000
D13	750000

3. Format the label and values to match the rest of the worksheet.

4. Click the **Chart1** tab. Right-click the white chart background and choose **Select Data**.

5. In the **Chart data range** entry box, edit the address to show **$B$6:d13**. Click **OK**. The column chart now shows two columns for each province/country, one for each product. The British Columbia data has a different color scheme due to your earlier change. Your colors may be different from the text figures.

Figure 9-16
Adding a data series
9-15.xlsx
KowabungaSales
sheet

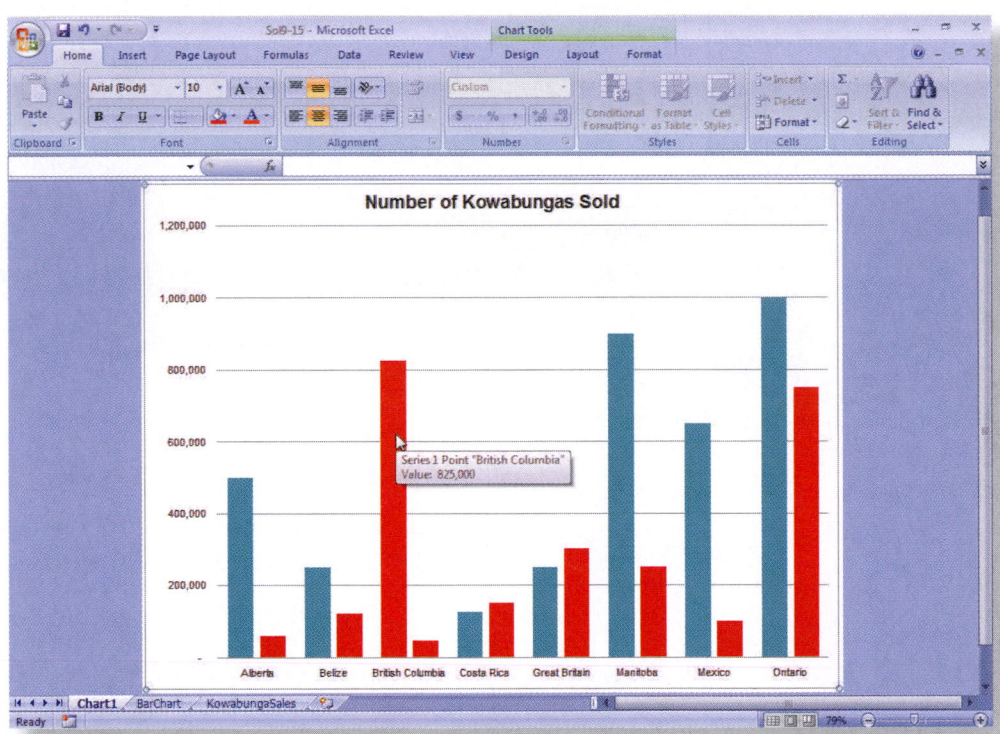

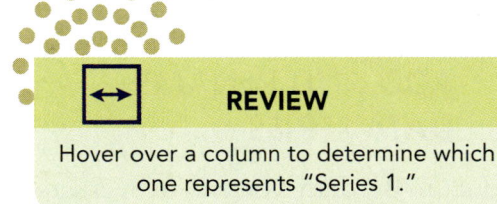

REVIEW

Hover over a column to determine which one represents "Series 1."

6. Right-click any column for **Series 1** (Kowabunga). Choose **Select Data**.

7. Click **Series 1** in the Legend Entries list and click **Edit**.

8. Key **Kowabunga** and click **OK**.

9. Click **Series 2** in the list and click **Edit**. Key **KowOwow** and click **OK**.

10. Click **OK** again. Hover over several columns to view the series' names.

11. Right-click the **Kowabunga** column for British Columbia. Choose **Reset to Match Style**.

12. Click the white background.

13. On the **Chart Tools Design** tab, choose **Style 6**.

Exercise 9-19   DELETE DATA POINTS AND A DATA SERIES

1. Click the **KowabungaSales** tab.

2. Delete rows 8 and 9. The pie chart is updated.

3. Click the **BarChart** tab. Click the **Chart1** tab. The British Columbia and Costa Rica data is removed from all charts.

4. Click the **KowabungaSales** tab.

5. Delete cells D6:D11. This is an entire data series.

6. Click the **Chart1** tab. The second column (KowOwows) is gone, but the category labels appear out of alignment with the columns.

7. Right-click any column and choose **Select Data**. KowOwow is still listed as a series.

8. Click **KowOwow** in the Legend Entries list and click **Remove**.

9. Click **OK**.

> **NOTE**
>
> You can delete any chart object or the entire chart by selecting it and pressing [Delete].

Using Images, Gradients, and Textures for a Data Series

You can change from a solid color to a gradient or an image for columns, bars, pie slices, and other chart objects. Gradients and textures can be used to better distinguish bars, columns, or slices on a black-and-white printer. Images allow you to show a picture to represent the data.

You can insert an image, a gradient, or a texture by selecting the chart object and:

• Clicking the Shape Fill button [Shape Fill ▾] on the Chart Tools Format tab.

• Clicking the Format Selection button [Selection Pane] on the Chart Tools Format tab or the Chart Tools Layout tab.

• Right-clicking the object and choosing Format Data Series or Format Data Point.

Exercise 9-20   USE AN IMAGE FOR A DATA SERIES

If you want to use an image in a bar or column chart, it looks best if you use a two-dimensional chart rather than 3-D.

1. Click the **BarChart** tab. Select the chart and then click the **Chart Tools Design** tab.

2. Click the Change Chart Type button ⬛. The Change Chart Type dialog box lists all the available types.

3. In the **Bar** group, choose **Clustered Bar** (first icon, first row) to change the chart to a two-dimensional chart. Click **OK**.

4. Click any bar in the chart. All the bars show selection handles.

5. Click the **Chart Tools Format** tab. Click the Format Selection button ⬛ Format Selection . The Format Data Series dialog box opens.

6. On the **Fill** pane, choose **Picture or texture fill**.

7. In the **Insert from** group, click **File**.

8. Navigate to the folder with **Kowabunga** to find the image.

9. Choose **Kowabunga** and click **Insert**. The picture is inserted in the bars and stretched to fit the length of the bar. Move the dialog box to see.

10. In the dialog box, click to select **Stack**. The image is scaled to fit and repeat across the bars.

Figure 9-17
Inserting a picture
9-15.xlsx
BarChart sheet

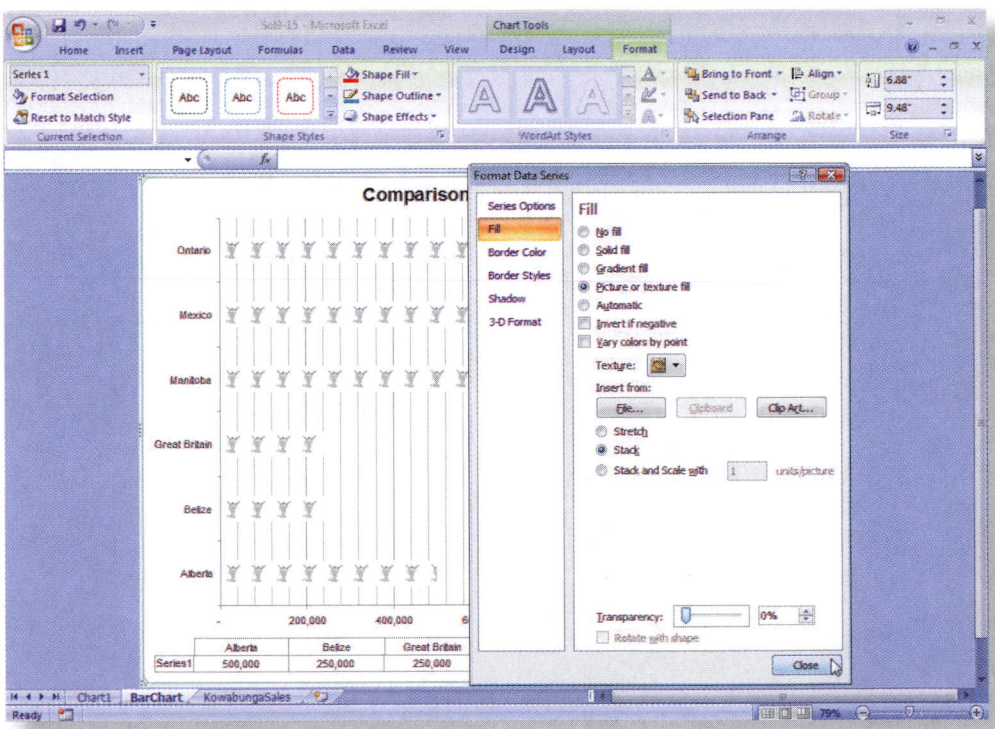

11. Click **Close**.

Exercise 9-21   USE A GRADIENT FOR A DATA SERIES

A *gradient* is a blend of colors. A gradient can give a special effect to bars, columns, or pie slices in a chart. In Excel, you can build blends that use one, two, or more colors, or you can choose from preset gradients.

1. Click the **Chart1** tab.

2. Right-click any column and choose **Format Data Series**.

3. On the **Fill** pane, choose **Gradient fill**. The dialog box updates to show the related options.

4. Click the arrow for **Preset colors**. A gallery of preset color blends opens.

5. Find and click **Moss** (first tile, third row). Click **Close**.

6. Right-click any column again and choose **Format Data Series**. Click **Fill**.

7. In the **Gradient stops** group, verify that **Stop 1** is current. A *stop* is a color in a gradient and refers to a position on a color scale.

8. Click the arrow for **Color** and choose **White, Background 1**.

9. Click the arrow next to **Stop 1** and choose **Stop 2**. This will be your second color.

10. Click the arrow for **Color** and choose **Black, Text 1**.

11. Click the arrow next to **Stop 2** and choose **Stop 3**. This is a third color from the **Moss** gradient.

Figure 9-18
Building a gradient fill
9-15.xlsx
BarChart sheet

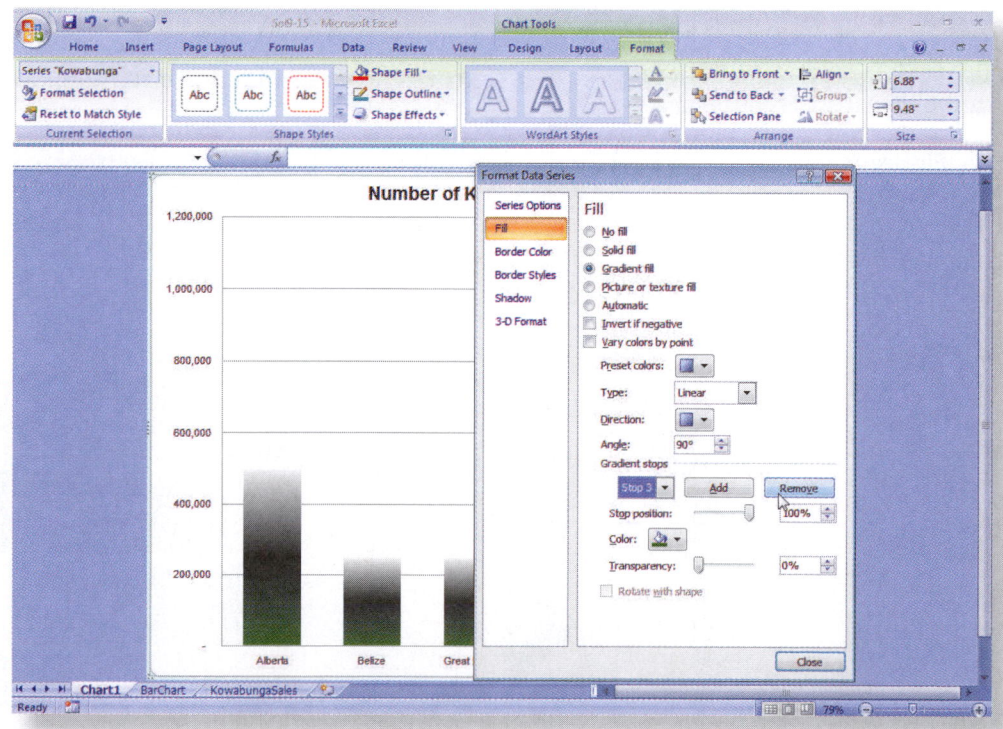

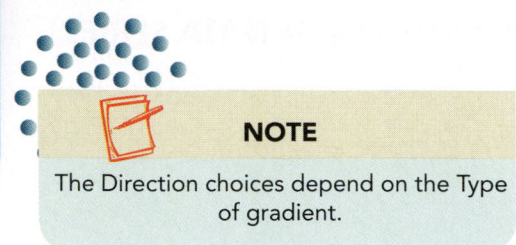

NOTE

The Direction choices depend on the Type of gradient.

12. Click **Remove** to use only two colors (two stops).

13. Click the arrow for **Direction**. Several variations of the way in which the colors blend are shown in a gallery.

14. Find and choose **Linear Up**.

15. Click **Close**.

NOTE

If you're using a black-and-white printer, colorful gradients print as shades of gray.

Exercise 9-22   USE A TEXTURE FOR A DATA POINT

A *texture* is a background that appears as a grainy, nonsmooth surface.

TIP

Point at the slice, not the data label within the slice.

1. Click the **KowabungaSales** tab.

2. Click the pie to select it. Click the Manitoba slice to select that slice only.

3. Right-click the slice and choose **Format Data Point**.

4. On the **Fill** pane, choose **Picture or texture fill**.

5. Click the arrow with **Texture**. A gallery of available textures opens. Notice that textures look similar to marble, wood, or canvas.

Figure 9-19
Using a texture as fill
9-15.xlsx
KowabungaSales
sheet

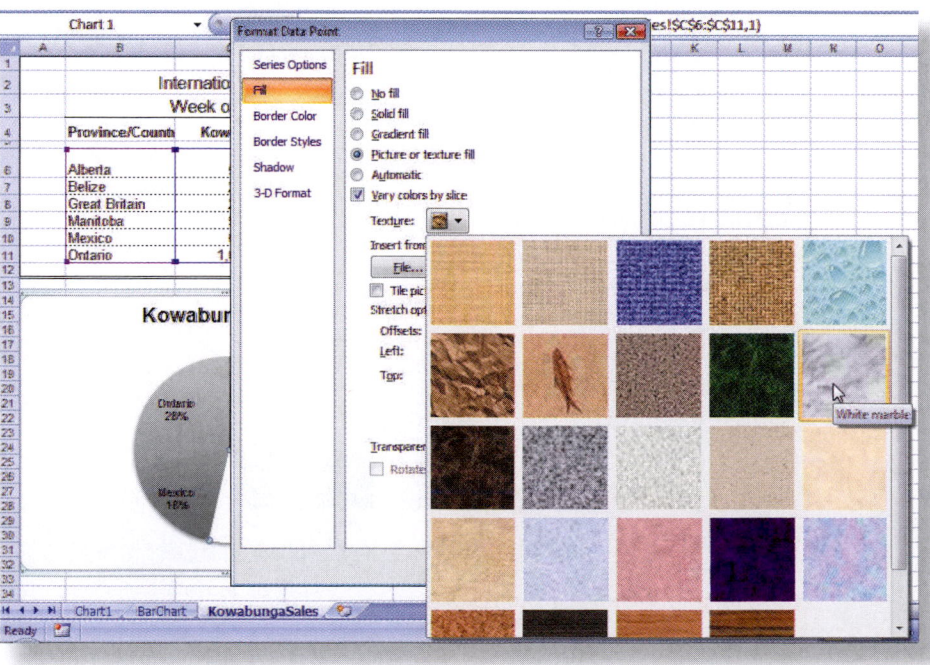

6. Hover over several texture tiles. A description appears with the name.

7. Choose **White marble**. Click **Close**.

8. Select only the Ontario slice. Click the **Chart Tools Format** tab and then click the Format Selection button .

9. On the **Fill** pane, choose **Picture or texture fill**.

10. Click the arrow with **Texture** and choose a different texture. Click **Close**.

11. Click a cell in the worksheet. Save your workbook as *[your initials]9-22* in your folder.

12. Close the workbook.

Creating a Combination Chart

A *combination chart* is a single chart that uses more than one chart type or different number scales. A combination chart has at least two series or sets of values. Some combination charts use the same chart type for each series, but a secondary number scale. A *secondary axis* is a set of axis values that is different from the first (primary) set.

Exercise 9-23 **CREATE A CHART WITH TWO CHART TYPES**

1. Open **ComboChart**.

2. Select cells A4:C9 and press F11. A new chart sheet is inserted and plots two products.

3. On the **Chart Tools Design** tab, click the Select Data button.

NOTE

The formulas in columns D and E multiply the price by the number sold.

4. Choose **Series 1** in the Legend Entries list and click **Edit**.

5. Key **Kowabunga** and click **OK**.

6. Edit **Series 2** to display **KowOwow** and click **OK**.

7. Click **OK** again. The legend is updated.

8. Right-click any Kowabunga bar and choose **Change Series Chart Type**.

9. In the **Line** category, choose **Line with Markers**. Click **OK**. The Kowabunga series is now a line chart.

Excel 2007

Figure 9-20
Changing the chart type for a data series
ComboChart.xlsx
Chart1 sheet

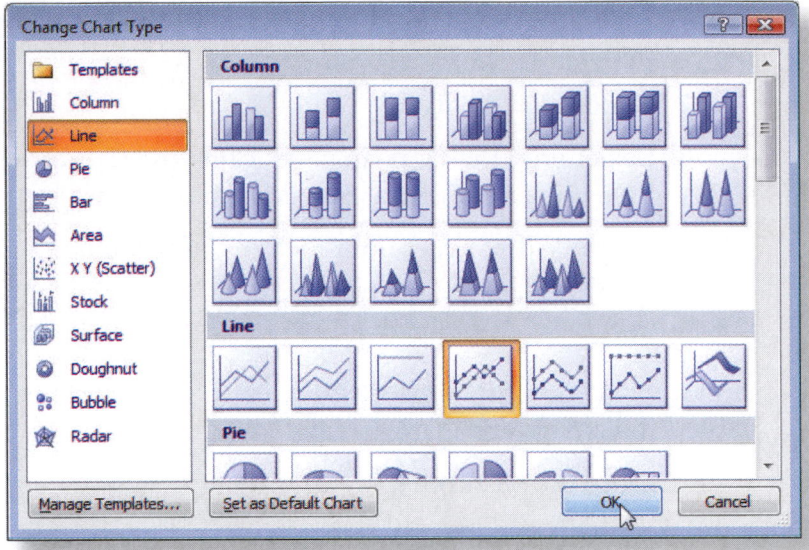

10. Right-click the line and choose **Format Data Series**.

11. On the **Line Style** pane, set the **Width** to **2 pt**.

12. On the **Line Color** pane, choose **Black Text 1** as the **Color**.

13. On the **Marker Options** pane, choose **Built-in**. Set the **Size** to **10**. Click **Close**.

14. Click the white chart background. The markers should be the same color as the line.

15. Right-click the line and choose **Format Data Series**. On the **Marker Fill** pane, choose **Solid fill**. Then set the color to match the line color.

16. On the **Marker Line Color** pane, choose **Solid fill** and the same color. Click **Close**.

17. Save the workbook as *[your initials]9-23*.

Exercise 9-24   BUILD A CHART WITH TWO SERIES

You can show the dollar sales and the number of items sold on the same chart. These values will be two different series on the chart.

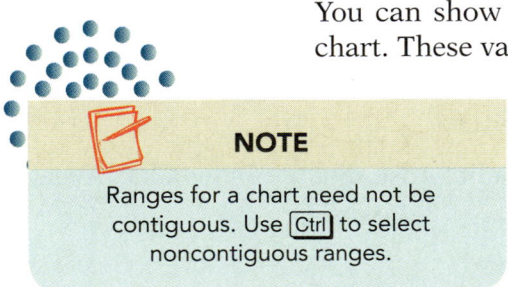

NOTE

Ranges for a chart need not be contiguous. Use Ctrl to select noncontiguous ranges.

1. Click the **KowabungaSales** tab.

2. Select cells A4:A9, C4:C9, and E4:E9. This represents the number of KowOwows sold and the sales dollars.

3. Click the **Insert** tab. Choose a **Clustered Column** 2-D chart.

4. Click the Move Chart button and place the chart on its own sheet. There are two series, one for the product and one for the dollars. Both series use the same value axis, so the dollar column is disproportionately taller.

5. Right-click the legend and choose **Select Data**.

6. Change **Series 1** to display **Number Sold**.

7. Change **Series 2** to **Dollar Sales** and click **OK**. Click **OK** again.

8. On the **Chart Tools Layout** tab, click the Chart Title button . Choose **Above Chart**.

9. Edit the placeholder to show **Units and Dollars**.

Exercise 9-25   ADD A SECONDARY AXIS

Because the values are very different, you should use two axes on the chart, one for the number of items and one for the dollar amounts. To use a secondary axis, use different chart types for each data series.

1. Right-click any Dollar Sales column and choose **Change Series Chart Type**.

NOTE

Some chart types cannot be combined. Excel displays a message if you choose charts that cannot be combined.

2. In the **Area** category, choose **Area**. Click **OK**.

3. Right-click somewhere in the area and choose **Format Data Series**.

4. On the **Fill** pane, choose **Gradient fill**. Click the arrow with **Preset colors** and choose **Moss**. Click **Close**.

5. Right-click a Number Sold column and choose **Format Data Series**.

6. On the **Series Options** pane, choose **Secondary axis**. The selected series will be plotted on a separate value axis. Click **Close**.

Figure 9-21
Using a secondary axis in a chart
9-23.xlsx
Chart2 sheet

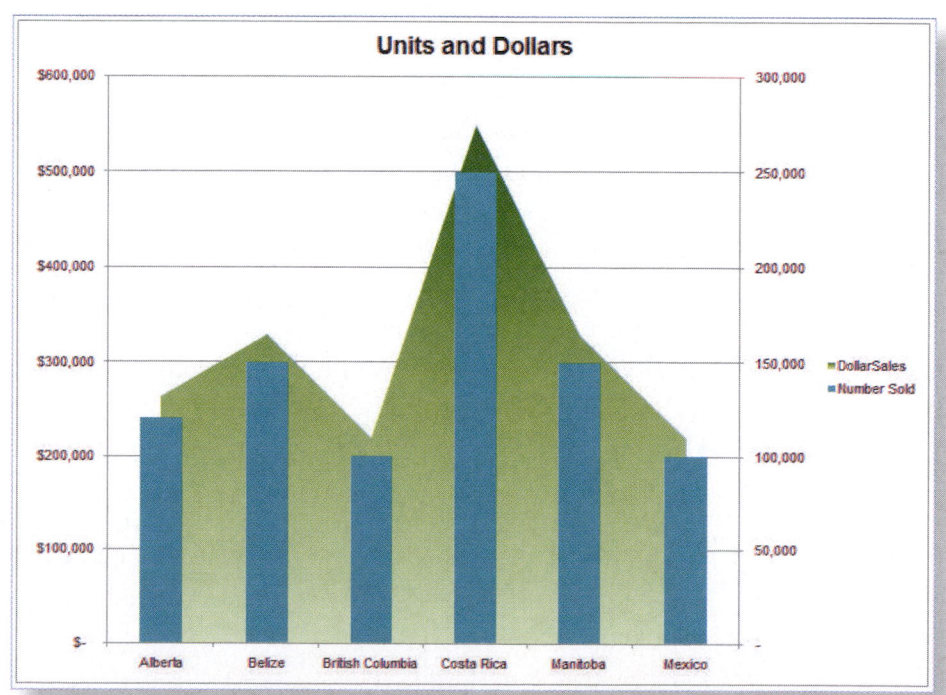

7. Right-click the legend and choose **Format Legend**.

8. On the **Legend Options** pane, choose **Bottom** and click **Close**.

9. Save the workbook as *[your initials]9-25*. Close the workbook.

Using Online Help

In addition to charts, you can use many types of images and graphics in a worksheet. Unlike charts, SmartArt graphics and shapes are usually not based on worksheet data.

USE HELP TO LEARN ABOUT GRAPHICS

1. In a new workbook, press F1.

2. Find and review topics about using SmartArt Graphics in a worksheet. Then find topics about shapes.

3. Close the Help window when you are finished reading about graphics and shapes.

Lesson 9 Summary

- Charts can be objects in a worksheet, or they can be separate chart sheets.
- A chart is linked to the data that it is plotting. If the data is edited, the chart reflects the changes.
- A chart includes many individual elements that can be formatted and edited.
- Right-click a chart element to see its shortcut menu.
- Charts show data series, which are the chart's values. A pie chart can have only one series, but other types of charts can show multiple data series.
- You can make many chart changes directly on the chart.
- If you select data and press F11, Excel creates an automatic column chart sheet.
- Excel's standard types of business charts include bar, column, line, and pie charts.
- Move a chart by selecting it and dragging it. Size a chart by dragging one of its selection handles.
- After a chart is created, you can add a data point or an entire series to it.
- Although charts typically use solid color for columns, slices, and bars, you can use images, textures, or gradients to add visual appeal to your charts.

- You can apply effects to the shapes used in a chart to include shadows, glows, bevels, and more.
- A combination chart has at least two series and uses different chart types for each series.
- Some combination charts use a single chart type but a secondary axis because the series values are disproportionate.

LESSON 9		Command Summary	
Feature	**Button**	**Task Path**	**Keyboard**
Axis, add	Axes	Chart Tools Layout, Axes	
Axis, format	Format Selection	Chart Tools Format, Current Selection	Ctrl + 1
Axis titles, add	Axis Titles	Chart Tools Format, Labels	
Chart object, create		Insert, Charts	Alt + F1
Chart sheet, create		Insert, Charts	F11
Chart title, add	Chart Title	Chart Tools Layout, Labels	
Chart type	Change Chart Type	Chart Tools Design, Type	
Data labels, add	Data Labels	Chart Tools Layout, Labels	
Data labels, format	Format Selection	Chart Tools Format, Current Selection	Ctrl + 1
Data series, edit	Select Data	Chart Tools Design, Data	
Data series, format	Format Selection	Chart Tools Format, Current Selection	Ctrl + 1
Data table, add	Data Table	Chart Tools Layout, Labels	
Legend, add	Legend	Chart Tools Layout, Labels	
Legend, format	Format Selection	Chart Tools Format, Current Selection	Ctrl + 1
Move chart	Move Chart	Chart Tools Design, Location	
Selection pane	Selection Pane	Chart Tools Format, Arrange	

Concepts Review

True/False Questions

Each of the following statements is either true or false. Indicate your choice by circling T or F.

T   F   1. A chart sheet includes the related worksheet data.

T   F   2. A selected chart element displays selection handles and a bounding frame.

T   F   3. The markers for a line chart can be formatted separately from the line.

T   F   4. Excel determines the best type of chart for your data after you select it.

T   F   5. Some chart layouts do not include a chart title.

T   F   6. If you insert a new item in the range used in a chart, you add a data point.

T   F   7. Each slice in a pie chart represents a data series.

T   F   8. The chart style includes colors for the plot area as well as other chart elements.

Short Answer Questions

Write the correct answer in the space provided.

1. What name describes a chart that appears on the worksheet with the data?

_____

2. What command tab includes the chart layout and style choices?

_____

3. What is the keyboard shortcut to create a chart sheet?

_____

4. If you have one data series with five data points, what type of chart might be best?

_____

5. What term describes a blend of colors for filling a bar or column?

_____

6. What can you use when two data series have drastically different values?

_____

7. What happens if you delete a data series used in a column chart from the worksheet?

_____

8. What is a data table?

_____

Critical Thinking

Answer these questions on a separate page. There are no right or wrong answers. Support your answers with examples from your own experience, if possible.

1. Discuss and determine what data and related charts might be developed for your school.

2. What are some advantages of using charts over tabular data? What are some pitfalls of charts?

Skills Review

Exercise 9-26

View and print a chart.

1. Open **DecChart** and save it as *[your initials]*9-26.

2. View a chart by following these steps:

   a. Click the **Page Layout** tab.

   b. Click the Selection Pane button 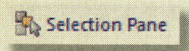. There are two objects on this sheet, a chart and a text box.

   c. Click **Chart 4** in the **Selection & Visibility** pane.

      d. Click **Text Box 2**. The bounding box and selection handles are visible; the box is beneath the chart.

      e. At the bottom of the **Selection & Visibility** pane, click the Bring Forward button. The text box must be on top of the chart to be visible over the white background.

      f. Click cell A1. The chart is deselected.

REVIEW

The chart and text box numbers are not important.

3. Print a chart object by following these steps:

    a. Close the **Selection & Visibility** pane.

    b. Insert a header that includes the user name, but change it to your name.

    c. Press `Ctrl`+`P` and click **OK**. The worksheet and chart print on the same page.

4. Prepare and submit your work. Save and close the workbook.

Exercise 9-27

Change the chart layout and style. Edit the chart title. Format axes. Add data labels.

1. Open **NovReceipts** and save it as *[your initials]*9-27. Change the Zoom size to **80%** and adjust column widths if necessary.

2. Change the chart layout and style by following these steps:

    a. Click the chart background to select the chart.

    b. Click the **Chart Tools Design** tab and change to **Layout 1**.

    c. Change to **Style 45**.

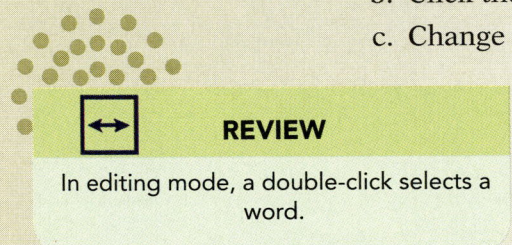

REVIEW

In editing mode, a double-click selects a word.

3. Edit the chart title by following these steps:

    a. Click the chart title to select it.

    b. Double-click **November** and key **December** in its place.

    c. Point at the chart title to display a four-pointed arrow. Drag the title left to align with the state names.

    d. Triple-click the title and point at the Mini toolbar. Click the Italic button *I*.

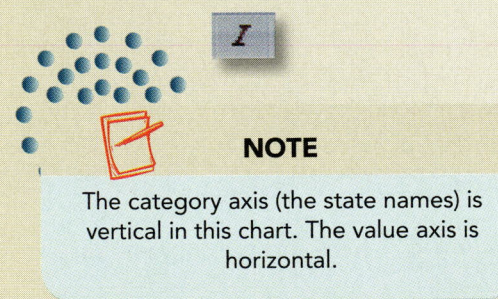

NOTE

The category axis (the state names) is vertical in this chart. The value axis is horizontal.

4. Format an axis and delete the legend by following these steps:

    a. Right-click any value on the horizontal axis. Choose **Format Axis**.

    b. On the **Axis Options** pane, click the arrow for **Display units**. Choose **Thousands** and click **Close**. Excel automatically scales the values.

    c. Click **Series 1** (the legend). Press `Delete`.

5. Add data labels by following these steps:

    a. Right-click any bar and choose **Add data labels**.

    b. Right-click one of the data labels. Choose **Format Data Labels**.

    c. Click **Number**. Choose **Currency** with **0** decimals and **$ English (United States)** as the **Symbol**. Click **Close**.

6. Prepare and submit your worksheet. Save and close the workbook.

Exercise 9-28

Create a chart object. Edit chart data and objects. Edit the data source.

1. Create a new workbook and save it as *[your initials]*9-28.

2. In cell A1, key **Sales of Waffle Cones**. Make it 18-point Cambria.

3. In cell A2, key **May 1**. Fill dates to reach **May 15** in cell A16.

> **NOTE**
>
> Excel will assume the current year in the date.

4. Key the following values in column B:

Figure 9-22

01-May	1000
02-May	1200
03-May	1000
04-May	1500
05-May	1400
06-May	1000
07-May	1200
08-May	1000
09-May	1500
10-May	1400
11-May	1400
12-May	1500
13-May	1200
14-May	1000
15-May	800

5. Create a chart object by following these steps:

   a. Select cells A2:B16 and click the **Insert** tab. Click the Line button .

   b. Choose **Line with markers** in the second row.

   c. On the **Chart Tools Design** tab, choose **Layout 3** from the Chart Layouts gallery.

   d. Point at the top edge of the chart to display a four-pointed arrow. Drag the chart so that its top-left corner aligns at cell A18.

   e. Point at the bottom-right selection handle to display a two-pointed arrow. Drag the bottom-right selection handle to cell L32.

   f. Click the **Page Layout** tab. Set landscape orientation.

6. Edit data and objects by following these steps:

   a. Edit cell B5 to show **600** and cell B12 to show **800**.

   b. Right-click the line and choose **Format Data Series**.

   c. On the **Line Style** pane in the **Width** box, set **3 pt**.

d. Click **Marker Options**. In the **Marker type** group, choose **Built-in**. Set the marker **Size** to **10**.

e. On the **Marker Fill** pane, choose **Solid fill**. Set the color to match the line.

f. On the **Marker Line Color** pane, use the same color as the line.

g. Click **Shadow**. Click the arrow for **Presets** and choose **Offset Bottom** in the **Outer** group. Click **Close**.

h. Triple-click **Chart Title** and key **Waffle Cone Sales**.

i. Click the "Series1" legend and press Delete.

TIP

Click away from the chart to see your changes.

7. Format the axes by following these steps:

a. Click the **Chart Tools Layout** tab. Click the Axis Titles button. Choose **Primary Horizontal Axis Title** and then **Title Below Axis**.

b. Triple-click **Axis Title** and key **May 1 through May 15**.

c. Click the Axes button. Choose **Primary Horizontal Axis** and then **Show Left to Right Axis**.

d. Click the Gridlines button. Choose **Primary Vertical Gridlines** and then **Major Gridlines**.

e. Click the chart background.

f. Click the **Chart Tools Format** tab. Verify that the chart area is the selected element.

g. In the **Shape Styles** group, click the More button.

h. Choose **Subtle Effect – Dark 1**.

8. Edit the data source by following these steps:

a. Select the chart and press Ctrl+C. Click the **Sheet2** tab and press Ctrl+V.

b. On **Sheet1**, insert a row at row 17. Key **May 16** in cell A17 and **2000** in cell B17.

c. Right-click the chart on **Sheet2** and choose **Select Data**.

d. Click cell A2 and drag to select cells A2:B17. Click **OK**.

e. Triple-click the horizontal axis title and change it to **...through May 16**.

f. Click one of the dates to select them. On the **Home** tab, change the font to 9 point.

9. Prepare and submit your work. Save and close the workbook.

Exercise 9-29

Create a combination chart. Use a gradient for a data series. Format a data series. Size a chart.

1. Open **ConeSales** and save it as *[your initials]*9-29.

2. Create a combination chart by following these steps:

   a. Click the **Insert** tab.

   b. Select cells A3:C18 and click the Line button 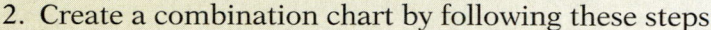.

   c. Choose **Stacked line with markers** (second icon, second row).

   d. Click the Move Chart button. Choose **New sheet** and click **OK**.

   e. Right-click the waffle cone line and choose **Change Series Chart Type**. Choose **Area** in the **Area** group and click **OK**.

   f. Click the **Chart Tools Layout** tab. Click the Chart Title button. Choose **Centered Overlay Title**.

   g. Triple-click **Chart Title** and key **Waffle and Sugar Cone Sales**.

   h. Click the Gridlines button. Choose **Primary Horizontal Gridlines** and then **Major and Minor Gridlines**.

3. Use a gradient for a series by following these steps:

   a. Right-click in the area for the waffle cone series. Choose **Format Data Series**.

   b. Click **Fill** and then **Gradient fill**. Click the arrow for **Preset colors** and choose **Wheat**.

   c. Click the arrow for **Direction** and choose **Linear Up**.

   d. Click **Close**.

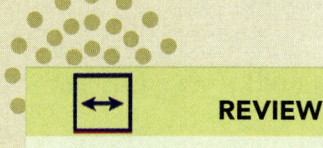
4. Format a data series by following these steps:

   a. Right-click the sugar cone line and choose **Format Data Series**.

   b. Choose **Line Color** and **Solid line**. For the color, choose **Black, Text 1**.

   c. Choose **Line Style**. Set the **Width** to **3 pt**.

   d. Choose **Marker Options**. Choose **Built-in** and set the size to **10**.

   e. Choose **Marker Fill** and use the same color as the line.

   f. Choose **Marker Line Color** and set the same color. Click **Close**.

5. Size a chart by following these steps:

   a. Click the white chart background and click the **Chart Tools Format** tab.

   b. In the **Size** group, click in the **Shape Height** box and key **5.75**.

   c. Set the shape width to **8.5**.

   d. Point at an edge of the chart to display a four-pointed arrow. Drag the chart so that it appears centered on the page.

6. Right-click **Sheet1** and choose **Hide**. The data is hidden but is still used for the chart.

7. Prepare and submit your work. Save and close the workbook.

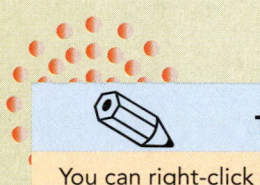

Lesson Applications

Exercise 9-30

Create a scatter chart. Edit chart objects.

A scatter chart (a "scattergram") does not have a category axis. Both axes show values. In the chart for this exercise, you show the relationship between a price decrease and increased sales.

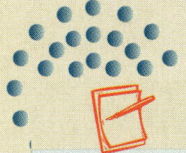

> **NOTE**
>
> The worksheet uses the Aspect document theme.

1. Open **Scatter** and save it as *[your initials]*9-30.

2. Select cells B6:C11 and create a scatter chart with straight lines and markers. Move the chart to its own sheet.

3. Apply **Chart Layout 5** and **Chart Style 38**.

4. Choose a thickness for the line and a size/style for the markers. The line and markers should use **Red Accent 2** as the color.

5. Format the data labels so that there is no Y value included. Delete the legend.

6. Edit the chart title placeholder to **Percentage Price Decrease and Increased Sales**.

7. Edit the vertical axis title to **Additional Sundaes Sold** and make it 9-point Verdana. Edit the horizontal axis title to **Promotional Price Decrease** and make it 9-point.

8. Use 9-point for the numbers along each axis.

9. Prepare and submit your work.

Exercise 9-31

Create an exploded pie chart. Edit chart objects.

An exploded pie chart shows one or more of the slices detached from the rest of the pie to emphasize the slice(s). The Excel chart types show all the slices detached, but you can create your own chart with a single exploded slice.

1. Open **ExPie** and save it as *[your initials]9-31*.

2. Create a 2-D pie chart below the data. Make the chart area as wide as the worksheet data borders. Align the top-left corner near cell A12 and the lower-right corner at about cell D35.

3. Use **Chart Layout 5** and **Chart Style 1**. Key **Shake Flavor Comparison** as the chart title.

4. Format the data labels to use 9-point Calibri and place the labels in the center.

5. Format the data series to set the angle of the first slice to **90**.

6. Select the pie and then the **Butterscotch** slice. Drag the **Butterscotch** slice away from the pie, but not too far.

7. Select the pie and format the data series with a solid black border.

8. Format the **Vanilla** slice as solid white. Format each of the other slices with a color, gradient, or texture that represents the flavor.

9. Prepare and submit your work.

Exercise 9-32

Create and format a bubble chart.

The Klassy Kow Credit Union provides savings account records for employees who contribute regularly. You are to prepare a bubble chart to demonstrate why it is best to start saving as soon as possible. A bubble chart is similar to a scatter chart with an additional series.

1. Open **BubbleChart** and save it as *[your initials]9-32*.

2. In column E, use the FV function to determine the value of an account with the interest rate shown. The original amount is the PV, the amount in the account when the savings program starts. Assume that payments are made at the beginning of the month.

3. Create a 3-D bubble chart using cells C6:E10. Place the chart below the data. Choose **Layout 1** and **Style 21**.

4. As the chart title, key **Growth of Your Deposits**. Delete the legend.

5. Edit the horizontal axis title to **Years in Program**. Edit the vertical axis title to **Monthly Savings**.

6. Format the values for both axes appropriately.

7. Size the chart as needed. On the **Chart Tools Format** tab, choose a shape style.

8. Prepare and submit your work.

Exercise 9-33 ◆ Challenge Yourself

Edit chart data. Create and format a stock chart.

A stock chart plots daily stock price information. In the worksheet, the prices must be in this order from left to right: high price, low price, closing price. There are several variations for this chart type with some that include the open price and volume.

1. Open **HighLow** and unhide the **Apr** worksheet. Save the workbook as *[your initials]*9-33.

NOTE

When preparing a stock chart, you should eliminate weekend and other nontrading days.

2. Review the April data and its chart. The close prices are correct. There are, however, other errors in the data. Review the data and edit it as needed.

3. There are errors in the May data. Find and correct them.

4. Create a stock chart for the May data using cells A4:D13. Move the chart to its own sheet. Use **Chart Style 29**. Delete the legend.

5. Format the vertical axis on the chart with a maximum value of 30 and a minimum value of 23.

6. Add a chart title and position it at the left. (Check the April chart.)

7. There are data points at the top and bottom tips of the vertical lines. Select each and format the markers so that they are visible.

8. Prepare and submit your work.

On Your Own

In these exercises you work on your own, as you would in a real-life work environment. Use the skills you've learned to accomplish the task—and be creative.

Exercise 9-34

In a new workbook, key your city, state, and ZIP code in cell A1. In cells A3:A12, enter the dates for the past ten days. Use a local newspaper or an Internet site to determine the high temperature for each of those days and key the values in column B. Create a line chart that plots the daily temperatures with a layout and style of your choice. Place the chart as a separate sheet. Save the workbook as *[your initials]*9-34. Prepare and submit your work.

Exercise 9-35

Build a worksheet with a doughnut chart object to show your weekly expenses. Use at least six expense categories (food, gas, entertainment, books, etc.). Add a chart title and decide whether to show labels or percentages on the segments. Save the workbook as *[your initials]*9-35. Prepare and submit your work.

Exercise 9-36

Create a worksheet that lists first names of six friends in one column and their heights in inches in a second column. Create a column chart sheet with the names on the horizontal axis and heights on the vertical axis. Use a gradient or texture fill for the columns. Make other formatting choices so that your chart is easy to interpret. Hide the worksheet. Save the workbook as *[your initials]*9-36. Prepare and submit your work.

Lesson 10

Inserting Shapes

OBJECTIVES

After completing this lesson, you will be able to:

1. Add and format a callout shape.

2. Create and format text boxes.

3. Insert basic shapes and arrows.

4. Use the Drawing Tools Format tab.

5. Use comments.

6. Insert WordArt.

MCAS OBJECTIVES

In this lesson:
XL07 4.4.3
XL07 5.1.2
XL07 5.3.1

Estimated Time: 1¾ hours

Excel has many design elements that can add visual appeal to your worksheets. A *shape* is a common, recognizable figure, form, or outline. Shapes include rectangles, flowchart symbols, stars, banners, text boxes, lines (with or without arrows), and callouts that can be sized, moved, and styled.

Shapes are placed on a draw layer. The *draw layer* is an invisible, transparent working area that is separate from and on top of worksheet data.

REVIEW

An object is a separate, clickable element in a worksheet. Shapes and charts are objects on the draw layer.

Adding and Formatting a Callout

Shapes, as well as other drawing elements, are available on the Insert tab. A *callout* is descriptive text enclosed in a shape. Callouts typically include a line or arrow that points to data or another object on the worksheet.

Exercise 10-1   ADD A CALLOUT TO A WORKSHEET

Callouts and most other shapes have the following features:

- A *bounding box*, a rectangular outline around the object.

- *Selection handles*, small circles and/or rectangles surrounding the shape's bounding box.

- An *adjustment handle*, a yellow diamond used to change the appearance and design of the shape. Each shape has its own type of adjustments; a few shapes do not have an adjustment handle.

- A *rotation handle*, a green circle that acts like a wand to rotate a shape.

1. Create a new workbook from the **K&KSales** template. The worksheet includes a comment with instructions about keying the date.

> **↔ REVIEW**
>
> Copy the template file to the appropriate folder on your computer. Then click the Microsoft Office Button 🔘 and choose **New**. Click **My Templates**.

2. Right-click the **K&KSales** tab and choose **Unhide**. Choose **ComboChart** and click **OK**. The chart is incomplete because there is no data yet.

3. Unhide the **Unit&Dollars** sheet.

4. Add the following data to columns D and F on the **K&KSales** sheet. Columns H and J have formulas that will calculate as you key values.

Figure 10-1

State	Kowabunga	KowOwow
Oregon	2575	2000
Nevada	3550	3000
Washington	5600	4500
California	6500	6700

> **📝 NOTE**
>
> This template has very narrow columns used as separators.

5. Click the **Insert** tab. Notice that the command buttons in the **Illustrations** group are dimmed. This template has sheet protection so that you can edit only certain cells.

Excel 2007

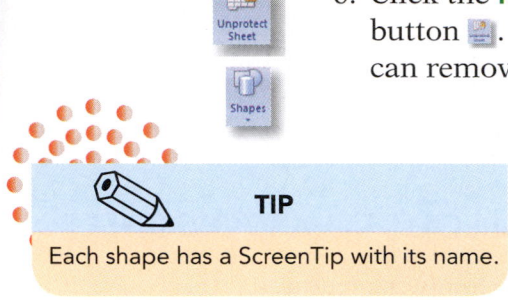

6. Click the **Review** tab. In the **Changes** group, click the Unprotect Sheet button ☐. As long as sheet protection does not use a password, you can remove it.

7. Click the **Insert** tab. In the **Illustrations** group, click the Shapes button ☐. Several categories of shapes are shown in the gallery.

8. In the **Callouts** group, choose **Oval Callout**, first row, third shape. The pointer changes to a thin cross.

TIP

Each shape has a ScreenTip with its name.

Figure 10-2
Choosing a callout

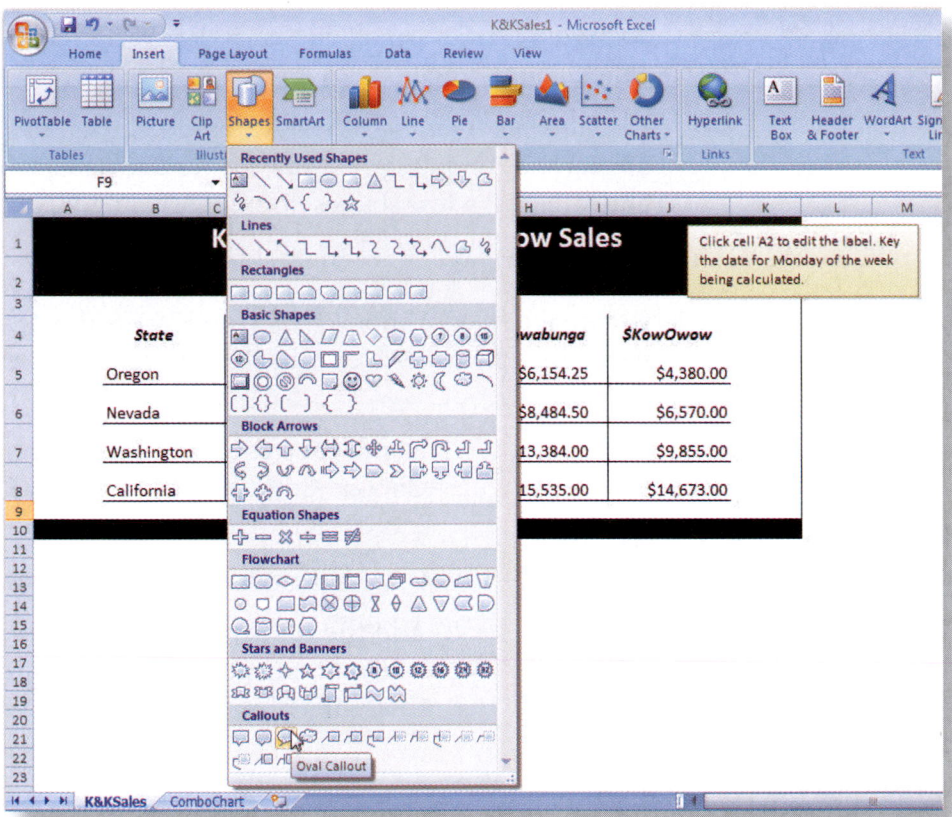

9. Click and drag to draw a rectangular shape starting near cell C12 and extending down to about cell G16. The shape appears with round and square selection handles, one adjustment handle, and a rotation handle. There is a rectangular bounding box, too. The Drawing Tools Format tab is available.

10. Key **Rolling blackouts in Nevada contributed to poor sales.** Since the shape is active, you can simply start keying your text. As you key text, the bounding frame changes to a dashed line.

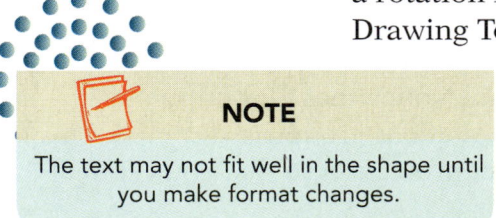

NOTE

The text may not fit well in the shape until you make format changes.

Figure 10-3
New callout on the
sheet
K&KSales.xltx
K&KSales sheet

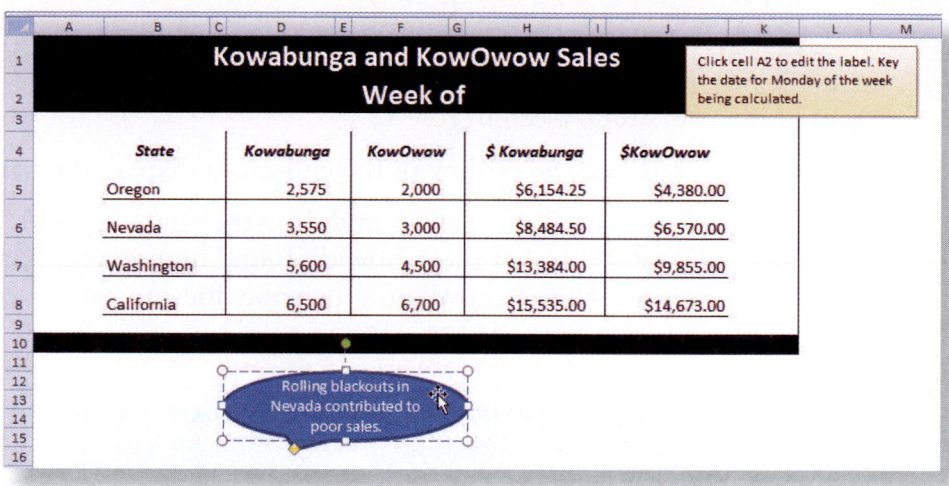

11. Click a cell in row 12. The shape is deselected.

12. Using the four-pointed arrow, click the outline of the callout. It is selected and shows a solid line as its bounding box. The solid line means the entire callout is active and can be edited.

13. Click inside the callout. The text insertion point appears, and the solid line becomes a dashed line. The dashed line boundary means you can work with the text inside the box.

14. Click a cell in row 12. The shape is deselected.

Exercise 10-2   FORMAT AND MOVE A CALLOUT

1. With the four-pointed arrow, click the outline of the callout. The shape displays the solid line boundary. This means edits will affect all text in the shape or the shape itself.

2. Click the **Home** tab. Choose **Cambria** as the font and **10** as the size. All the text in the callout changes.

3. Click inside the callout to display a text insertion point. The boundary displays a dashed line, meaning that your edits will affect only selected text.

4. Double-click **Nevada** to select the word.

Figure 10-4
Changing font of
selected text in a
callout
K&KSales.xltx
K&KSales sheet

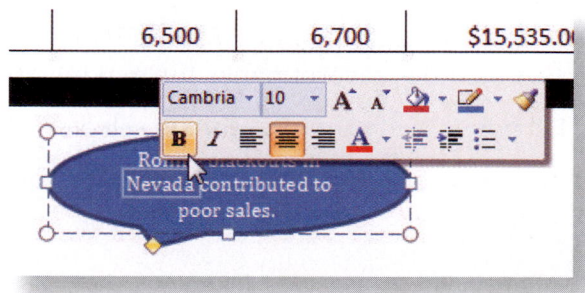

5. Click the Bold button **B** in the Mini toolbar. Only the selected text is changed.

6. Click a cell in row 12.

7. Click the outline of the callout to display the solid line outline.

8. Point at the outline and drag the shape up and toward columns K:M so that the yellow diamond adjustment handle is aligned with the Nevada row and the shape does not obscure any data.

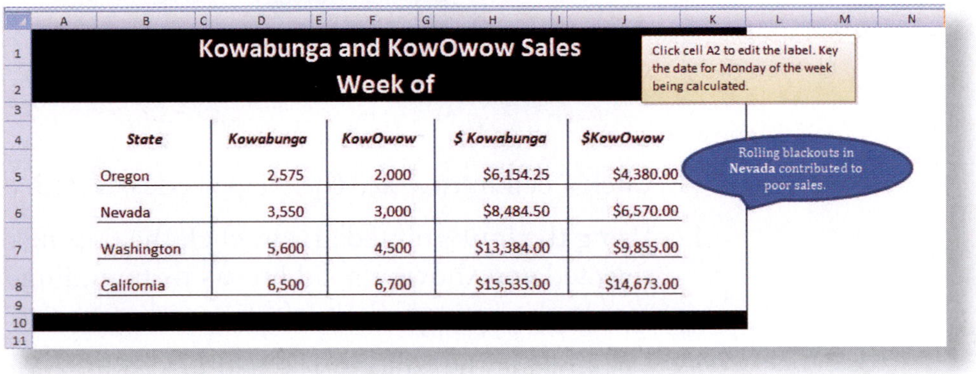

Figure 10-5
Repositioned shape
K&KSales.xltx
K&KSales sheet

9. Click a cell in the worksheet.

Exercise 10-3   USE THE FORMAT SHAPE DIALOG BOX

Although you can make many changes to objects using the command tabs and galleries, you can also use the Format Shape dialog box.

You can open the Format Shape dialog box by:

- Right-clicking the shape and choosing Format Shape from the shortcut menu.

- Selecting the shape so that it displays the solid line boundary and pressing Ctrl+1.

- Selecting the shape so that it displays the solid line boundary and clicking the Dialog Box Launcher in the Shape Styles group on the Drawing Tools Format tab.

1. Right-click the oval and choose **Format Shape**. The Format Shape dialog box includes several panes for making changes to the shape.

2. In the **Fill** pane, verify that **Solid fill** is selected.

3. Click the arrow for **Color**. Choose **White, Background 1, Darker 35%**.

4. Click **Line Color** and choose **No line**.

5. Choose **3-D Format** to open the pane. A *3-D format* applies a three-dimensional look to an object so that it appears to have a depth as well as a height and width.

6. Click the arrow for **Top** to display the gallery of bevels. A *bevel* is a 3-D effect that resembles the edge of a tabletop.

Figure 10-6
Setting a bevel in
the Format Shape
dialog box
K&KSales.xltx
K&KSales sheet

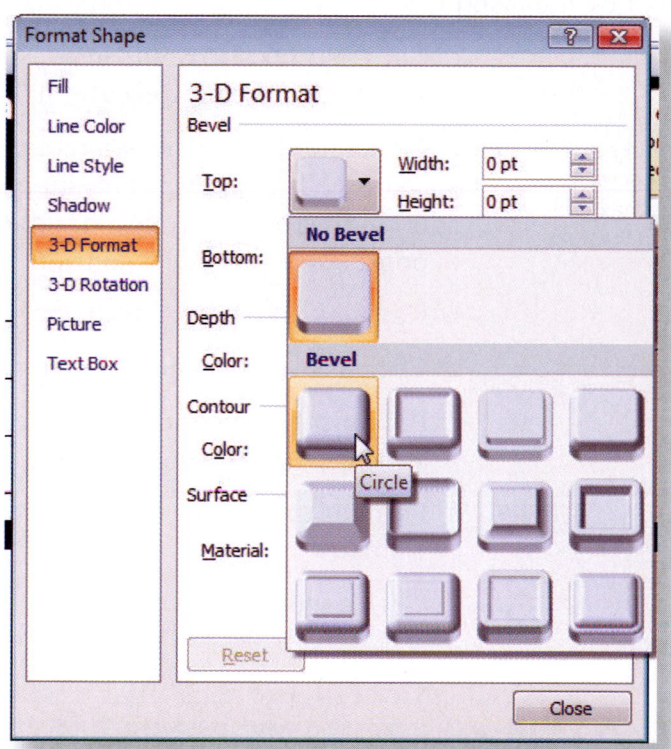

NOTE

A bevel can be displayed as the top part of the object or the bottom. Experiment to see which looks more natural.

7. Choose **Circle**. This is a preset bevel. The other settings in the dialog box enable you to create your own bevel or edit this one.

8. Click **Close**. Click a worksheet cell.

9. Save the workbook as *[your initials]*10-3 in a folder for Lesson 10.

TIP

Be careful when designing special effects on your own so that you do not use too many settings in any one format.

Using Text Boxes

A *text box* is similar to a callout but does not have connector lines or arrows. You can use a text box to display titles, comments, or notes. It can be formatted with or without borders, fill colors, shadows, or 3-D effects.

Exercise 10-4   ADD A TEXT BOX

1. Click the **Insert** tab.

2. Click the Text Box button . The pointer changes to an upside-down lowercase "T."

3. Click and drag to draw a rectangular shape that spans cells H12:K13. The shape appears with the bounding box, selection handles, a text insertion point, and a dashed-line frame.

4. Key **Klassy Kow Ice Cream, Inc.**

5. Click a worksheet cell. The text box is deselected.

6. Point at the text and click. The dashed-line border appears with the insertion point.

7. Point at the border and click to display a solid line frame.

8. Click a worksheet cell.

> **NOTE**
>
> Whether a Ribbon button includes an icon and text is determined by your screen size and resolution. Your buttons may look slightly different from those in the text.

> **NOTE**
>
> If you draw a shape that you do not like, click to select it (it will show the solid bounding line), and press Delete. Then try again.

Figure 10-7
Text box on a worksheet
10-3.xltx
K&KSales sheet

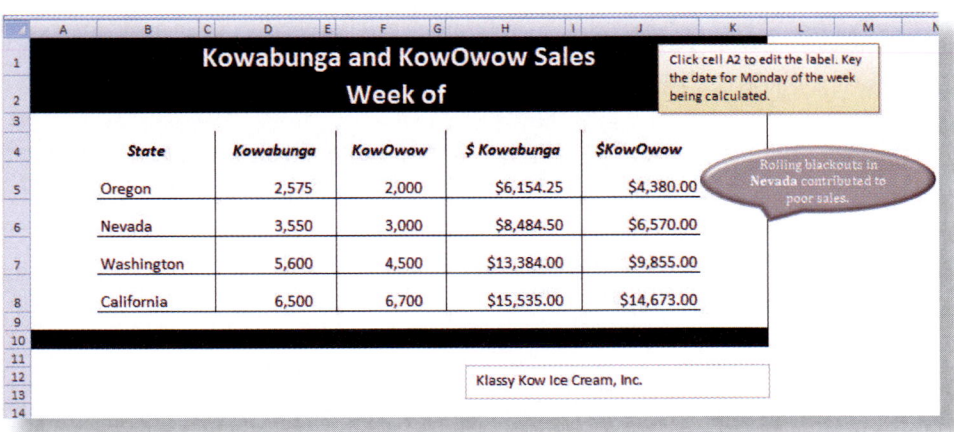

Exercise 10-5   FORMAT AND MOVE A TEXT BOX

1. Point at the text box and click to display a text insertion point.

2. Point at the text and triple-click. This selects all the text.

3. Choose **8-point Cambria** from the Mini toolbar.

4. Click the Italic button. Click the Align Text Right button.

5. Point at the bottom-left selection handle. Click and drag left until the frame fits closely to the text with the text on a single line.

6. Right-click the text box and choose **Format Shape**.

7. In the **Fill** pane, choose **No fill**.

8. Click **Line Color** and choose **No line**. Click **Close**.

9. Drag the text box with the four-pointed arrow so that it rests within row 10 at cells J10:K10. The black text is not visible on the black border.

10. Triple-click inside the text box to select all the text.

11. In the Mini toolbar, click the arrow with the Font Color button. Choose **White, Background 1**.

12. Click the text box to display the solid line border.

TIP

You can nudge a selected shape with any arrow key.

Figure 10-8
Completed text box
10-3.xltx
K&KSales sheet

$ Kowabunga	$KowOwow
$6,154.25	$4,380.00
$8,484.50	$6,570.00
$13,384.00	$9,855.00
$15,535.00	$14,673.00

Rolling blackouts in Nevada contributed to poor sales.

Klassy Kow Ice Cream, Inc.

13. Press ↑ or ↓ to nudge the text box so that it appears in the middle of row 10.

Exercise 10-6   CHOOSE A SHAPE STYLE

1. Click a worksheet cell.

2. Click the **Insert** tab. Click the Text Box button.

3. Click and drag to draw a text box from cell C20:I22.

4. Key the following paragraph:

   There are two charts for this data. One shows units and one shows units and sales dollars.

5. Point at the text box border and click. Click the **Drawing Tools Format** tab.

6. In the **Shape Styles** group, click the More button 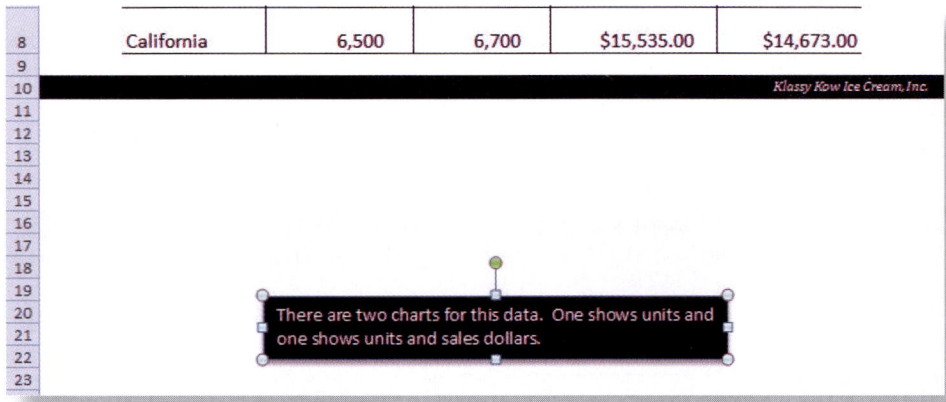. Choose **Moderate Effect, Dark 1**.

7. Rest the mouse pointer on any selection handle to size the box if the text does not fit. Fit the text box as needed.

8. Click a worksheet cell.

Figure 10-9
Text box with a
shape style
10-3.xltx
K&KSales sheet

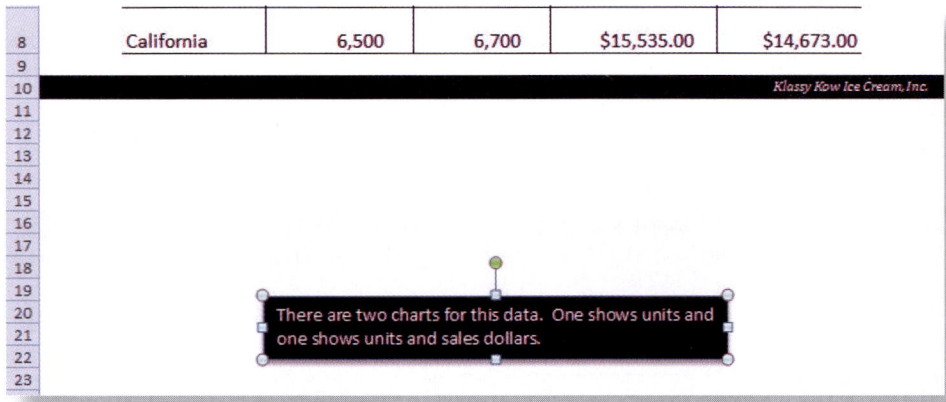

| 8 | California | 6,500 | 6,700 | $15,535.00 | $14,673.00 |

Klassy Kow Ice Cream, Inc.

There are two charts for this data. One shows units and one shows units and sales dollars.

Inserting Basic Shapes and Arrows

The Shapes gallery includes several categories of common shapes. The Basic Shapes group includes a variety of geometric shapes, a sun, a moon, a smiley face, and more. The Lines group has straight, zig-zag, and wavy lines with and without arrows. There is a separate group for block-style arrows, too. Shapes with an enclosed interior can include text and display effects, fills, and outlines. Adjustment handles depend on the shape and its editability.

Exercise 10-7   ADD A SHAPE AND AN ARROW

1. On the **K&KSales** sheet, click the **Insert** tab.

2. In the **Illustrations** group, click the Shapes button.

3. In the **Basic Shapes** group, choose **Double Bracket** in the last row, first shape. The pointer changes to a thin cross.

4. Draw a rectangular shape that starts near cell B12 and extends to cell E14. The shape shows a frame, selection handles, an adjustment handle, and a rotation handle.

5. Key **The most recently opened shops are in Oregon.**

6. Triple-click the text and then click the Bold button **B** in the Mini toolbar.

7. Click the shape's outline to display the solid boundary. Then click a cell to better see the shape.

8. Click the **Insert** tab. In the **Illustrations** group, click the Shapes button. In the **Lines** group, choose **Arrow** (the second shape).

9. Point near cell C5.

TIP

Holding down the [Shift] key while drawing a line keeps it straight.

10. Hold down [Shift] and drag down to draw a straight line that points to the double-bracketed shape, just below the row 10 border. Release the mouse button first, then the [Shift] key. The line with the arrow has two selection handles, no adjustment handle, and no rotation handle.

11. Click an empty cell. The line is deselected.

Exercise 10-8   RESIZE THE NAME BOX

You can resize the Name Box and the formula bar so that you can see longer object names in full. The sizing button resembles a recessed button, between the Insert Function button f_x in the formula bar and the Name Box.

1. Using the four-pointed arrow, select the line with an arrow. The Name Box shows the name of the active shape, but the name may not be completely visible.

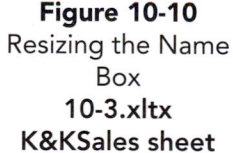

NOTE

Shapes are named according to their design and numbered in consecutive order. The number is not important.

2. Point at the sizing button. A two-pointed horizontal arrow appears.

3. Click and drag to the right until you can see the complete shape name.

Figure 10-10
Resizing the Name Box
10-3.xltx
K&KSales sheet

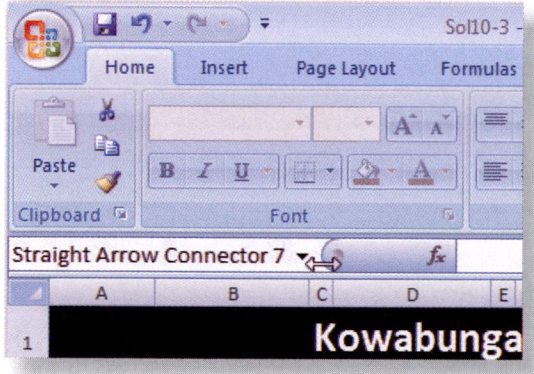

4. Using the four-pointed arrow, select the double-bracketed shape. Look at the Name Box.

5. Click an empty cell.

Exercise 10-9   USE THE SELECTION AND VISIBILITY PANE

The Selection and Visibility pane lists objects (shapes, images, graphics, and charts) on a worksheet. You can use the Selection and Visibility pane to select an object, hide or show it, and reset its order. Shapes, objects, and charts are on the invisible drawing layer in a stacking order. This can result in one shape covering another that is beneath it.

NOTE

The numbers for your shapes may be different from the text illustration.

1. Select the line. Click the **Drawing Tools Format** tab.

2. In the **Arrange** group, click the Selection Pane button 🔲 Selection Pane . The pane opens on the right side of the screen. The most recently added shape is at the top of the list and is on the top of the drawing layer. The first shape inserted is at the bottom of the list and at the bottom in the stacking order.

3. In the Selection and Visibility pane, click **Oval Callout *n***. It is selected in the worksheet.

4. In the pane, click **Double Bracket *n***. It is active and selected, and the oval shape is deselected.

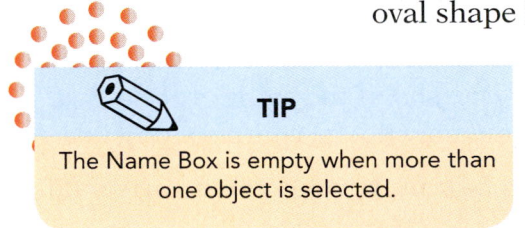

TIP

The Name Box is empty when more than one object is selected.

5. Hold down the Ctrl key and click **Straight Arrow Connector *n*** in the Selection and Visibility pane. Two shapes are selected.

6. Hold down Ctrl and click **Oval Callout *n***. All three shapes are selected.

Figure 10-11
Selecting multiple shapes in the Selection and Visibility pane
10-3.xltx K&KSales sheet

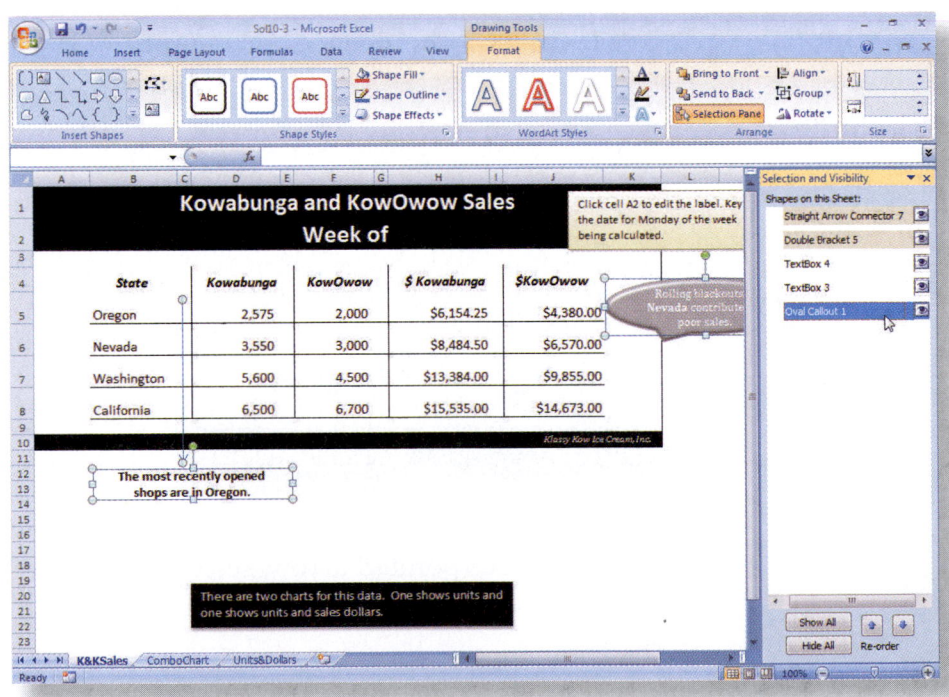

7. Click the Eye button 👁 for **Oval Callout *n***. It is hidden.

8. Hide and then display each of the shapes.

Using the Drawing Tools Format Tab

The Drawing Tools Format tab includes commands that allow you to customize a shape in several ways. You can change it to another shape, rotate it, change colors, and more. The Drawing Tools Format tab is a contextual drawing tool that appears only when a shape is selected.

Exercise 10-10   FORMAT MULTIPLE SHAPES

1. Click a worksheet cell.

2. In the Selection and Visibility pane, click **Straight Arrow Connector *n***.

3. Hold down ⌈Ctrl⌉ and click **Double Bracket *n*** in the pane. Both shapes are selected.

4. Click the **Drawing Tools Format** tab.

5. Click the Shape Outline button 🖊 Shape Outline ▾ in the **Shape Styles** group.

6. Choose **Black, Text 1**.

7. Click the Shape Outline button 🖊 Shape Outline ▾ and hover over **Weight**. A list of line thicknesses is displayed.

8. Choose **1½ pt**.

NOTE

You can format multiple shapes from the Ribbon or from the Format Shape dialog box.

Exercise 10-11   COPY AND MOVE OBJECTS

1. Click the **Home** tab. Both shapes should still be selected.

2. Click the Copy button 🗐 and then click the Paste button 📋. A copy of the grouped shapes is made, on top of the original. You can see the names in the Selection and Visibility pane.

3. Point at the copied shapes to display a four-pointed arrow. Drag the copy to the left of the dollar amount in cell H5 (see Figure 10-12 on the next page).

4. Triple-click the text in the copied bracket shape.

5. Key **Kowabunga flavors have been enhanced.**

Figure 10-12
Copied shapes
10-3.xltx
K&KSales sheet

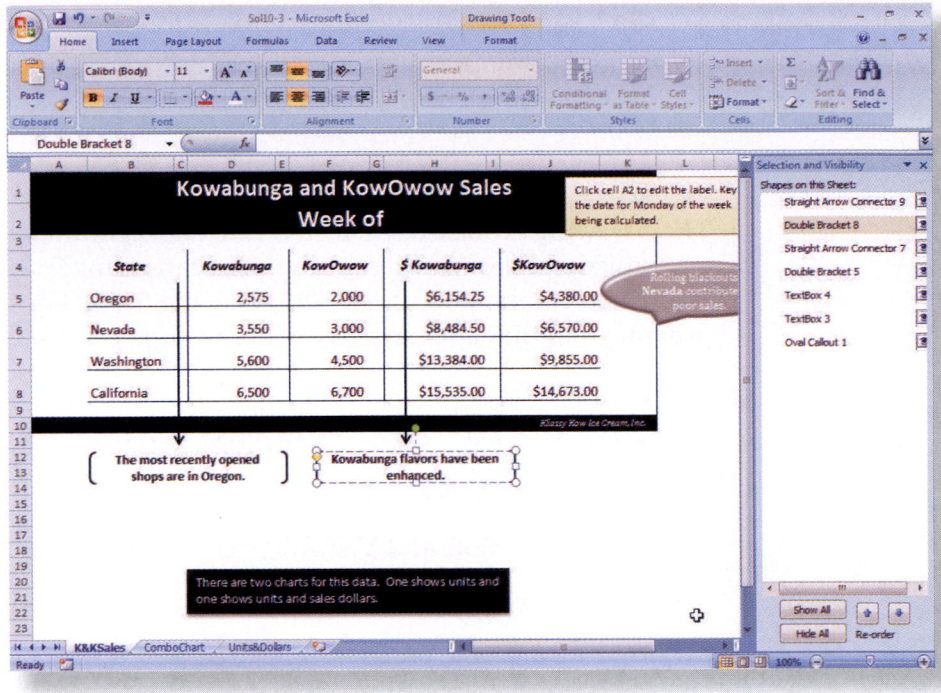

6. Click an empty cell.

Exercise 10-12   SIZE SHAPES

You can size a shape by dragging any of its selection handles. Use a corner handle to size the shape on all sides at once. Use a side handle to change only the width or height. Specific sizes can be set using the Size group on the Drawing Tools Format tab or the Size and Properties dialog box.

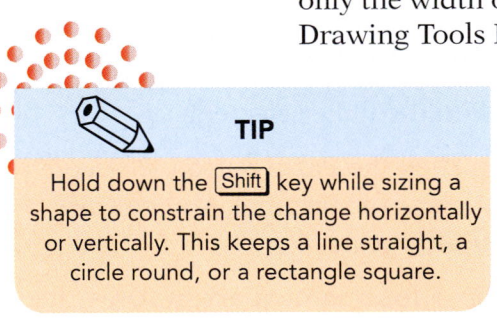

TIP

Hold down the Shift key while sizing a shape to constrain the change horizontally or vertically. This keeps a line straight, a circle round, or a rectangle square.

1. Click the connector line for the first bracket shape. It has two selection handles, one at each end. Its name is shaded in the Selection and Visibility pane.

2. Position the pointer on the bottom handle to display a two-pointed arrow.

3. Hold down the Shift key and drag the selection handle down to make the line slightly longer, until you see faint red handles around the bracket shape.

4. Release the mouse and then the Shift key. Red handles indicate that the objects overlap.

5. Press Ctrl+Z to undo.

6. Click the first bracket shape to show the solid boundary and eight selection handles. The corner handles are round.

7. Position the pointer on the bottom-right handle to display a two-pointed arrow.

8. Drag the selection handle down and to the right to about cell E15.

9. Click the **Drawing Tools Format** tab. In the **Size** group, note the Shape Height and Shape Width settings for the shape.

10. Click the second bracket shape to show the solid boundary.

11. In the **Size** group, click the **Shape Height** box and key the same height as the first bracket shape. Press Enter.

12. Click the **Shape Width** box and key the same width as the first bracket shape. Press Enter.

13. Click the first line, hold down Shift, and click the second line. Both lines should be selected.

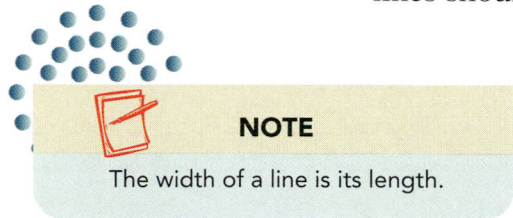

NOTE

The width of a line is its length.

14. Click the **Drawing Tools Format** tab. In the **Size** group, click the Dialog Box Launcher. The Size and Properties dialog box opens.

15. Click in the **Width** box and key **1.85**. Click **Close**. Both lines are the same length.

Figure 10-13
Size and Properties
dialog box
10-3.xltx
K&KSales sheet

Size and Properties

Size | Properties | Alt Text

Size and rotate

Height: 0"   Width: 1.85"

Rotation: 90°

Scale

Height: Width:

☐ Lock aspect ratio

☐ Relative to original picture size

Crop from

Left: Top:

Right: Bottom:

Original size

Height: Width:

Reset

Close

Exercise 10-13   ALIGN AND NUDGE SHAPES

When you use more than one drawing element, you can arrange the shapes so that they align at their top, left, right, or bottom edges. To align objects, you must select more than one object. With only one object selected, the Align commands are not available. Alignment of shapes uses each object's bounding box and selection handles.

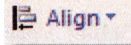

1. Make sure both lines are selected.

2. In the **Arrange** group on the **Drawing Tools Format** tab, click the Align button . Choose **Align Top**. The top selection handles are aligned horizontally.

3. Click one bracket shape. Add the second bracket shape to the selection. Align the bracket shapes at the top.

4. Click an empty cell and then select the first line.

5. Press ⬅ or ➡ to nudge the line as needed away from or closer to the text. Do the same for the second line.

6. Select and nudge each of the bracket shapes as needed.

7. Click an empty cell.

Exercise 10-14   CHANGE A SHAPE

Many shapes, but not all, can be changed to another shape. The connector lines, for example, cannot be changed but the bracket shape can be.

1. Select the second bracket shape so that the solid boundary is visible.

2. Click the **Drawing Tools Format** tab. In the **Insert Shapes** group, click the Edit Shape button.

3. Choose **Change Shape**. A list of shape categories opens.

4. In the **Basic Shapes** group, find and click **Folded Corner**. The folded corner is the bottom-right one. This shape has one adjustment handle.

5. Click an empty cell.

Figure 10-14
Changing the shape
10-3.xltx
K&KSales sheet

6. Change the first bracket shape to the same folded corner shape, and click an empty cell.

7. Close the Selection and Visibility pane.

Exercise 10-15   USE THE ADJUSTMENT HANDLE

Most shapes have one or more adjustment handles, shown as a yellow diamond. What an adjustment handle does depends on the shape. Some shapes do not have adjustment handles. If they don't, they can only be sized.

1. Click the **ComboChart** tab. Click the chart to select it.

2. Click the **Chart Tools Layout** tab. The **Insert** group has commands for inserting pictures, shapes, and text boxes.

3. In the **Insert** group, click the Shapes button.

4. In the **Block Arrows** group, choose **Left Arrow** in the first row, second shape.

5. Draw a shape that starts left of and above the Nevada column between the 5,000 and 6,000 gridlines, reaching to about the Washington column/point (see Figure 10-15). The shape shows a frame, selection handles, two adjustment handles, and a rotation handle.

6. Point at the adjustment handle near the arrowhead and click. The pointer changes to a solid white arrowhead.

7. Drag the adjustment handle left and right to see how it changes the shape. You cannot move this handle up or down.

8. Experiment with the second adjustment handle. It can only be moved up or down.

9. Adjust the shape to resemble the original arrow.

Exercise 10-16   ROTATE SHAPES

Many shapes have a rotation handle. This allows you to move the shape so that it angles differently from the original. The rotation handle is a small green circle. You can also specify a precise degree of rotation from the Arrange group on the Drawing Tools Format tab.

1. While the arrow is selected, place the mouse pointer over the green rotation handle and click. A circulating arrow surrounds the handle.

Figure 10-15
Ready to rotate
10-3.xltx
ComboChart sheet

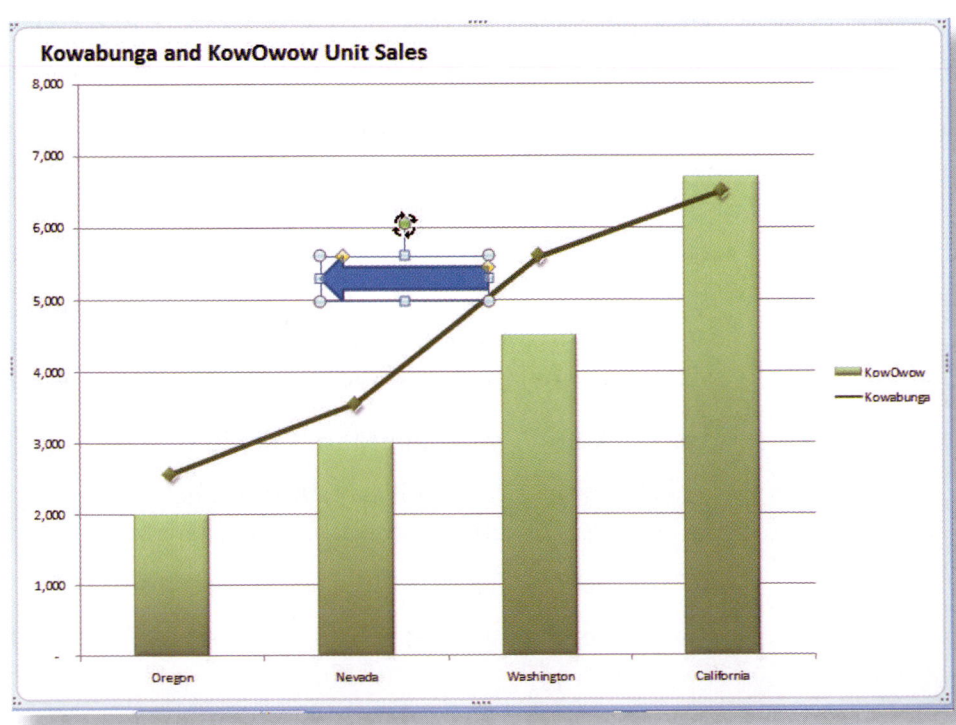

2. While holding down the mouse button, drag the mouse in any direction in a small arc. The shape rotates.

3. Click the Undo button 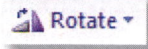.

4. Repeat Steps 2 and 3 several times so that you get a feel for how the rotation handle moves the shape.

5. With the shape selected and in its original position, click the **Drawing Tools Format** tab. Click the Rotate button .

6. Hover at each option and watch the shape. Live Preview shows the results before you click.

7. Click **Flip Horizontal**. The arrow now points at the Washington data.

Exercise 10-17   STYLE MULTIPLE SHAPES

1. Hold down Ctrl and point at the shape.

2. While holding down Ctrl, drag a copy of the arrow to point at the Nevada point on the line. Release the mouse button first and then Ctrl.

NOTE

If you release the Ctrl key first, you will move the shape.

3. Select both arrow shapes.

4. Click the **Drawing Tools Format** tab. In the **Shapes Styles** group, click the More button and choose **Moderate Effect, Accent 3**.

5. Click away from the chart.

6. Click the **ComboChart** tab. Hold down Ctrl and click the **Units&Dollars** tab. The sheets are grouped.

7. Right-click either tab and choose **Hide**.

8. Save the workbook as *[your initials]*10-17.

Using Comments

A *comment* is pop-up explanatory text attached to a cell. In a comment you can inform others what you did or what they should do in the sheet. Comments can be set to display only when you hover over the cell, or they can be displayed at all times.

Cells with comments show a small red triangle in the upper-right corner. The comment appears in a text box when you hover over the cell with the comment.

Excel 2007

Exercise 10-18 EDIT A COMMENT

A comment attached to cell J2 is set to show at all times and was repositioned. It hides the red triangle and does not get in the way of any work you might do on the sheet. This is a common practice for templates as a way to include directions to the user.

1. Click the **Review** command tab. There is a **Comments** group on this tab.

2. In *[your initials]*10-17, click cell A2 and press F2. Key **September 1** and press Enter.

3. Point at the comment box to display a four-pointed arrow and click. The comment box has selection handles and the dotted line boundary.

4. Drag the comment box to the right until you see the red triangle indicator in cell J2.

5. Click inside the comment box. The boundary changes to diagonal lines. This means you can edit the text inside the box.

6. Delete **to edit the label** from the comment.

Figure 10-16
Editing a comment
10-17.xltx
K&KSales sheet

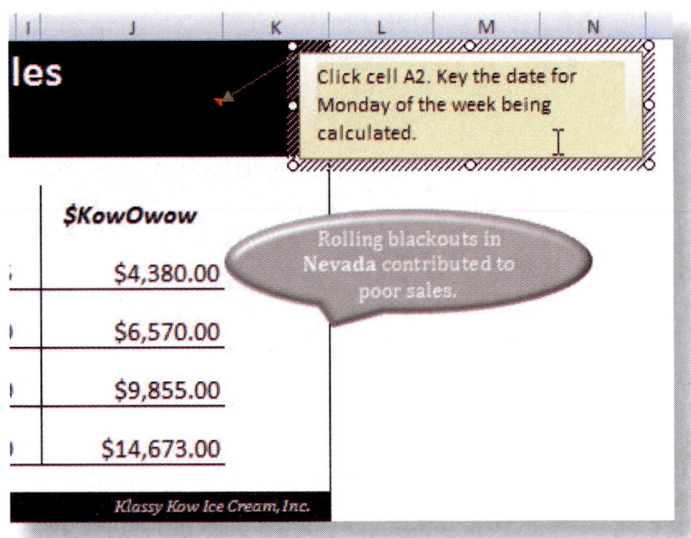

7. Click any cell.

8. Click cell J2. Click the Show All Comments button [Show All Comments]. The comment is no longer displayed.

9. Hover over cell J2 to display its comment.

10. Click cell J9.

Exercise 10-19 INSERT A COMMENT

1. Right-click cell J9 and choose **Insert Comment**. The comment text box opens and displays the user name for your computer, followed by a colon.

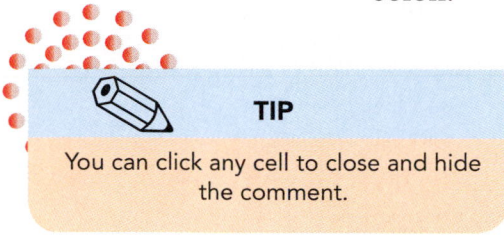

TIP

You can click any cell to close and hide the comment.

2. Key **Units sold are multiplied by average price for the previous month.**

3. Click cell J11 to close the comment text box.

4. Move the mouse pointer over cell J9 to display the comment.

Exercise 10-20 PRINT COMMENTS

1. Right-click cell J2 and choose **Show/Hide Comments**. The comment stays visible.

2. Show the comment for cell J9.

3. Click the Microsoft Office Button. Hover at **Print** and choose **Print Preview**. Comments do not print as a default.

NOTE

You can print comments as they appear on the sheet or at the end of the data on a separate sheet.

4. Close the preview.

5. Click the **Page Layout** tab. In the **Sheet Options** group, click the Dialog Box Launcher. The Page Setup dialog box opens to the **Sheet** tab.

6. In the **Print** group, click the **Comments** arrow. You must use this setting to print comments.

7. Choose **As displayed on sheet**. Click **Print Preview** in the dialog box.

8. Click the Print button in Print Preview and click **OK**. The comments print as they appear on the worksheet.

9. Click cell J2 and click the Show/Hide Comment button [Show/Hide Comment] on the **Review** tab.

10. Hide the comment for cell J9.

11. Save the workbook as *[your initials]*10-20.

Exercise 10-21 USE DOCUMENT INSPECTOR

The *Document Inspector* is a feature that checks a document for metadata and personal information. *Metadata* is information that is saved with a document such as your computer name, your user name, the name of the folder, hidden rows/columns/cells, document properties, and more. In some cases, you may want to remove such information from your work before you make it available to others.

1. With *[your initials]*10-20 open, click the Microsoft Office Button and hover at **Prepare**.

2. Choose **Inspect Document**. You may see a message box that asks if you want to save the file; choose **Yes**. The Document Inspector dialog box lists the information that can be found and removed from a workbook.

Figure 10-17
Document Inspector
dialog box
10-20.xltx
K&KSales sheet

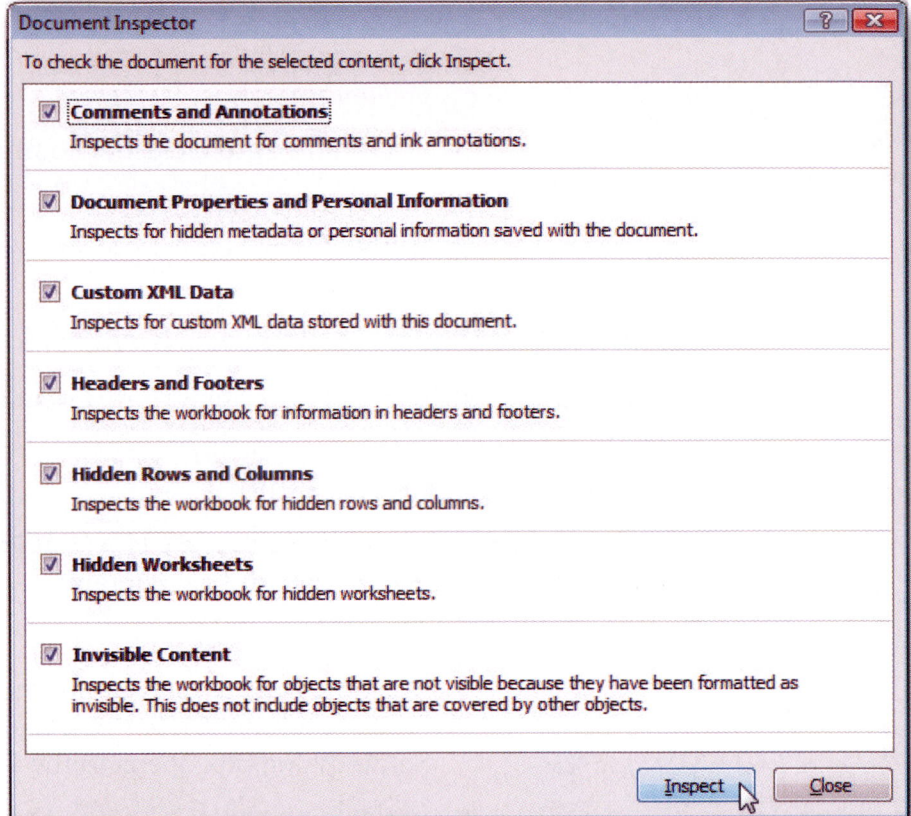

3. Click **Inspect**. This workbook includes comments, document properties, and hidden worksheets. Before removing the data, check the properties.

4. Click **Close**.

5. Click the Microsoft Office Button and hover at **Prepare**.

6. Choose **Properties**. The Document Information Panel opens above the worksheet. There is an author name and a general comment. These settings were part of the template.

Figure 10-18
Document
Information Panel
10-20.xltx
K&KSales sheet

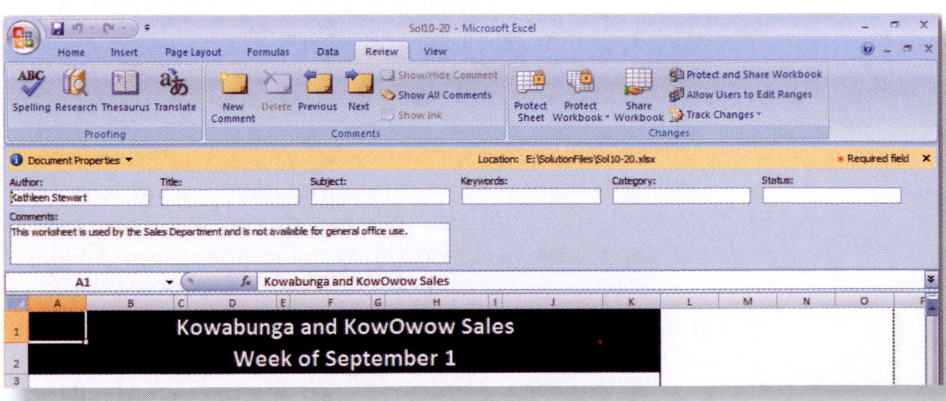

7. Click the Close the Document Information Panel button 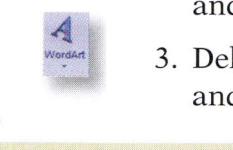.

8. Click the Microsoft Office Button ⊙ and hover at **Prepare**. Choose **Inspect Document**. Click **Yes** if prompted to save the document.

9. Click **Inspect**. For **Comments and Annotations**, click **Remove All**.

10. Remove the document properties but not the hidden sheets.

11. Click **Close**.

Inserting WordArt

A *WordArt* image is shaped text that may be filled and outlined. A WordArt shape is an object with selection handles, an adjustment handle, and a rotation handle. WordArt is available in all the Office applications.

Exercise 10-22   INSERT WORDART

1. Make a copy of the **K&KSales** sheet.

2. On the copied sheet, click to select one of the folded corner shapes and press ⌈Delete⌉.

3. Delete the second text box, each of the two lines, the oval callout, and the text box near row 20.

> **NOTE**
>
> The shape must show the solid line boundary to be deleted. You can delete multiple shapes.

4. Delete the labels in cells A1 and A2.

5. Click the **Insert** tab. Click the WordArt button ⒜. The WordArt Gallery displays several variations.

6. Find and click **Fill-White, Drop Shadow**. The shape appears on the sheet with placeholder text.

Figure 10-19
WordArt Gallery

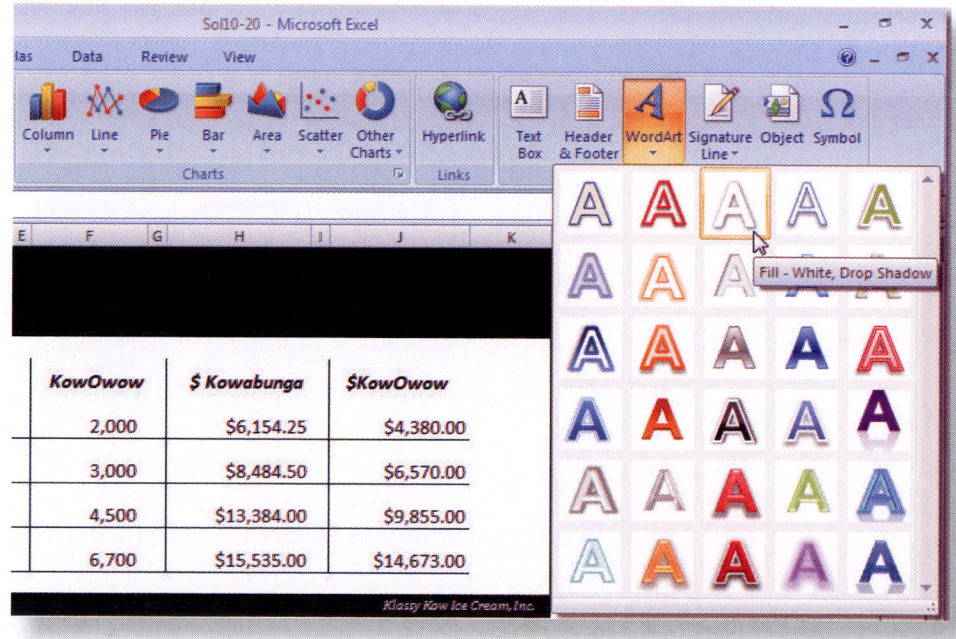

7. With the four-pointed arrow, drag the shape so that it starts near cell A12.

8. Click an empty cell. Then click the WordArt shape. The shape has a dashed line boundary for editing the text and a solid line boundary for changes to the shape itself.

9. Click the WordArt shape several times to see the difference between the boundary appearances.

NOTE

You can place WordArt on a chart sheet, too.

10. Display the dashed line boundary and triple-click the placeholder text. Use the Mini toolbar to set 28 points as the font size.

11. Key **Kowabunga and KowOwow Sales**. The text you key replaces the sample text.

Exercise 10-23   EDIT WORDART

1. Select the WordArt shape so that it shows the solid line boundary.

2. Click the **Drawing Tools Format** tab.

3. Click the More button ⬇ for **WordArt Styles**. A gallery of WordArt styles opens.

4. Hover over a few styles. Live Preview shows the reformatted shape. Some styles use uppercase and some use upper- and lowercase letters.

5. Find and select **Fill-Text 1, Inner Shadow** in the second row.

Figure 10-20
Edited WordArt shape

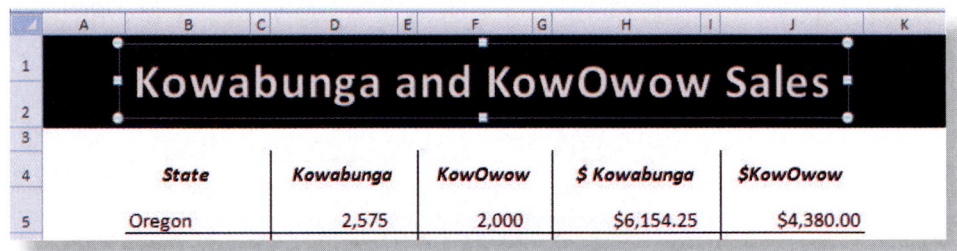

6. With the four-pointed arrow, drag the WordArt shape so that it fits in rows 1:2.

7. Click cell A3.

8. Save your workbook as *[your initials]*10-23. Close the workbook.

Using Online Help

The 3-D Format pane enables you to create shapes that have a professional appearance. As you learn more about the options, you can experiment creating your own bevels and other effects.

USE HELP TO LEARN ABOUT 3-D FORMATS

1. In a new workbook, click the Microsoft Office Excel Help button ⓘ.

2. Find and review topics about using 3-D format.

3. Close the Help windows.

Lesson 10 Summary

- A shape is a common figure or form. A callout is used to attach an explanation to a cell or other object.

- Shapes are placed on an invisible draw layer, a transparent work area separate from the worksheet data.

- You can change the font within a shape or change its size, shape, rotation angle, and colors.

- Shapes that have a closed interior can have a fill color, as well as an outline or border color. Text within a shape has a color, too. A line shape cannot have fill or text.

- The Format Shape dialog box includes most of the same commands that are on the Drawing Tools Format tab.

- Shape effects include bevels (3-D appearance), shadows, reflections, and more. Not all shapes can use all effects.

- A text box is a rectangle shape for displaying text on the sheet. It can have a fill, a line (border), and special effects.

- Lines, with or without arrows, are shapes.

- The Selection and Visibility pane lists all objects on a worksheet and provides a way to select and reorder the shapes.

- Shapes can be aligned and distributed for a balanced appearance on the sheet. They can also be rotated.

- Most shapes have at least one adjustment handle to redesign the shape into a variation of itself.

- Comments can be used as annotations, notes, or explanations for data on a worksheet.

- Comments are attached to cells and display when the mouse pointer touches a cell with the comment.

- The Document Inspector looks for personal and other information that might not be easily visible in a document.

- You can remove all information found by the Document Inspector before sharing a workbook with other workers.
- Use WordArt to create a design object that is shaped text.
- WordArt is a shape and can be edited and formatted like most shapes.

LESSON 10		Command Summary	
Feature	**Button**	**Task Path**	**Keyboard**
Bevel, add	Shape Effects ▾	Drawing Tools Format, Shape Styles	
Comment, delete	Delete	Review, Comments	
Comment, edit	Edit Comment		Shift + F2
Comment, new	Edit Comment	Review, Comments	Shift + F2
Document Inspector		Microsoft Office, Prepare, Inspect Document	
Shape, change		Drawing Tools Format, Insert Shapes	
Shape, format		Drawing Tools Format, Shape Styles	Ctrl + 1
Shape, insert	Shapes	Insert, Illustrations	
Shape, rotate	Rotate ▾	Drawing Tools Format, Arrange	
Shape, size		Drawing Tools Format, Size, Height/Width	
Shapes, align	Align ▾	Drawing Tools Format, Arrange	
Text box, insert	Text Box	Insert, Text	
WordArt, insert	WordArt	Insert, Text	
WordArt, edit		Drawing Tools Format, WordArt Styles	

Concepts Review

True/False Questions

Each of the following statements is either true or false. Indicate your choice by circling T or F.

T F   1. Any selection handle can be used to size a shape.

T F   2. Callouts can use various shapes to display text.

T F   3. You can change the fill color of a shape from the Ribbon.

T F   4. Metadata and personal information is removed when you save a workbook.

T F   5. The boundary box for a shape displays a dotted line at all times.

T F   6. The adjustment handle is a small green circle.

T F   7. Shadows and bevels are available as special effects for many shapes.

T F   8. A cell with a comment displays a small red triangle.

Short Answer Questions

Write the correct answer in the space provided.

1. What is the small green circle that appears when a shape is selected?

_____

2. What should the pointer look like when you move a shape?

_____

3. What if you cannot see an object's name in the Name Box?

_____

4. What name describes an annotation that appears only when the mouse pointer passes over the cell?

_____

5. What command arranges objects so that the tops are even?

_____

6. Name two categories of Shapes.

_____

7. How can you determine if a cell has a comment without moving the pointer around the sheet?

_____

8. How can you see a list of all shapes and objects on a worksheet?

_____

Critical Thinking

Answer these questions on a separate page. There are no right or wrong answers. Support your answers with examples from your own experience, if possible.

1. What are the differences between comments and callouts? Why and when would you use each?

2. Discuss why and when you should remove metadata and personal information from your work.

Skills Review

Exercise 10-24

Add and format a callout. Create and format a text box.

1. Create a new workbook from the **K&KSales** template. Save the workbook as *[your initials]*10-24.

2. Key the values shown in Figure 10-21.

Figure 10-21

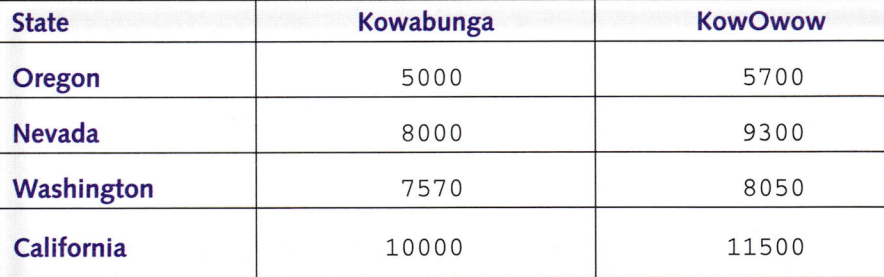

State	Kowabunga	KowOwow
Oregon	5000	5700
Nevada	8000	9300
Washington	7570	8050
California	10000	11500

NOTE

The worksheet protection is set so that you can enter values; you cannot insert shapes until it is removed.

3. Add a callout to a worksheet by following these steps:

a. Click the **Review** tab. Click the Unprotect Sheet button ⬚.

b. Click the **Insert** tab. In the **Illustrations** group, click the Shapes button ⬚.

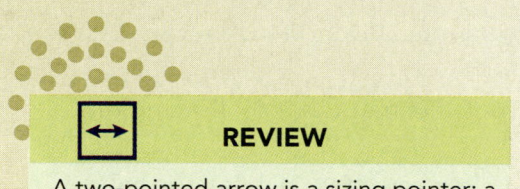

REVIEW

A two-pointed arrow is a sizing pointer; a four-pointed arrow is the move pointer.

   c. In the **Block Arrows** group, choose **Left Arrow**.

   d. Draw a shape starting at cell K8 and extending to about cell N9.

   e. Key California benefited from a price promotion.

   f. Triple-click the text in the callout. In the Mini toolbar, choose 9-point bold.

   g. Click an empty cell.

4. Format a callout by following these steps:

   a. Click the shape to display the solid line boundary.

   b. Place the pointer on the right-middle handle to display a sizing pointer. Drag the pointer right to fit the text on a single line.

   c. Place the pointer on the boundary line to display a four-pointed arrow. Drag the shape so that it points at the vertical middle of row 8.

   d. Right-click the shape and choose **Format Shape**.

   e. On the **Fill** pane, use **Solid fill**. Click the arrow for **Color**. Choose **Black, Text 1**.

   f. Click **Line Color** and choose **No line**.

   g. On the **Shadow** pane, click the arrow for **Presets**. From the Outer group, choose **Offset Diagonal Top Right** (first icon, third row).

   h. Close the dialog box and click an empty cell.

5. Create a text box by following these steps:

   a. Click the **Insert** tab. Click the Text Box button.

   b. Draw a box that starts at cell C12 and extends to cell I15.

   c. Key Weekly sales are calculated each Saturday evening for the previous week.

   d. Triple-click the text and make it bold and centered.

6. Format a text box by following these steps:

   a. Click the text box to display the solid line boundary.

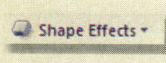

   b. Click the **Drawing Tools Format** tab. Click the Shape Effects button.

   c. In the **Preset** gallery, choose **Preset 2**.

   d. Drag a side handle to size the box so that the text displays evenly on two lines. Then drag the shape so that it appears centered below the data.

   e. Click an empty cell.

7. Edit cell A2 to show the date for Sunday of this week.

8. Prepare and submit your work.

Exercise 10-25

Use the Drawing Tool Format tab. Insert basic shapes.

1. Open **Contest** and save it as *[your initials]*10-25.

2. In cell C6, use a formula to subtract the guess in column B from the correct amount. Copy the formula through row 19.

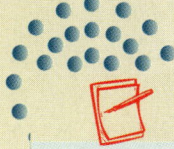

NOTE

The wave shape is linked to cell D6 and displays the results of the formula.

 Shape Fill ▾

 Shape Outline ▾

Shape Effects ▾

3. Use the MIN function in cell D6 to find the smallest value in column C.

4. Use the Drawing Tools Format tab by following these steps:

   a. Click the wave below row 20 to display the solid boundary.

   b. Click the **Drawing Tools Format** tab.

   c. Click the Shape Fill  button. Choose **White/Background 1, Darker 25%**.

   d. Click the Shape Outline [Shape Outline ▾] button. Choose **No Outline**.

   e. Click the Shape Effects [Shape Effects ▾] button. In the **Shadow** gallery, in the **Inner** group, choose **Inside Diagonal Bottom Left** (first icon, third row).

   f. Click the **Home** tab.

   g. Click the Center button ▤. Click the Middle Align button ▤.

   h. Change the font size to 24 points.

   i. Click an empty cell.

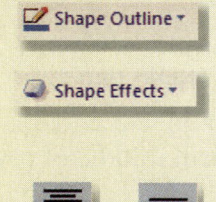 Shapes

5. Insert basic shapes by following these steps:

   a. Click the **Insert** tab. In the **Illustrations** group, click the Shapes button ▤.

   b. In the **Basic Shapes** group, choose **Smiley Face**.

   c. Hold down the [Shift] key. Click and drag to draw a shape starting at cell D21 and extending the bottom edge of the face to row 26.

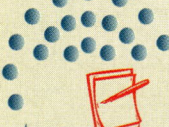

NOTE

Holding down the [Shift] key while drawing an elliptical object makes it a circle. Release the mouse button first when finished.

   d. Drag the shape so that it appears in the horizontal center of column D.

   e. Select the **Smiley Face** shape to display the solid boundary.

   f. Point at the boundary and hold down the [Ctrl] key. Drag a copy of the shape to the horizontal center of column A. Release the mouse first and then the [Ctrl] key.

6. Use the Drawing Tools Format tab by following these steps:

REVIEW

Holding down the [Ctrl] key when you drag and drop creates a copy of the object.

   a. Click the first **Smiley Face**.

   b. Hold down the [Ctrl] key and click the second face. Hold down the [Ctrl] key and click the wave. Three shapes are selected.

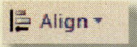 Align ▾

   c. On the **Drawing Tools Format** tab, click the Align button [Align ▾]. Choose **Align Middle**.

   d. Click the Align button [Align ▾] again. Choose **Distribute Horizontally**. The objects are evenly spaced between the left face and the right face.

7. Center the sheet horizontally.

8. Prepare and submit your work.

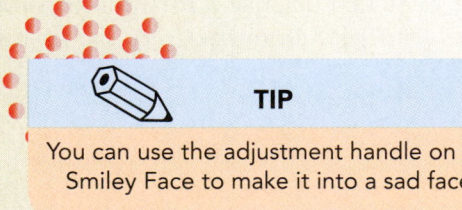

TIP

You can use the adjustment handle on the Smiley Face to make it into a sad face.

Exercise 10-26

Edit and insert comments. Print comments. Use the Document Inspector.

1. Create a new workbook from the **ExpRpt** template and save the workbook as *[your initials]*10-26.

2. Edit a comment by following these steps:

   a. Click cell E1. Click the **Review** tab.

   b. Click the Edit Comment button .

   c. Edit the text to show **Spacebar** instead of **End**.

   d. Click any cell to complete the edit.

NOTE

The comments are set to display at all times.

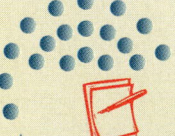

NOTE

When the dotted line boundary is active, changes affect the shape and all text.

3. Insert and format comments by following these steps:

   a. Right-click cell E8 and choose **New Comment**.

   b. Key **Edit cells B3, B8, B13, and B18 to show the date for Monday in the specified week**.

   c. Click the border of the comment box to display a dotted line boundary.

   d. Click the **Home** tab and click the Italic button .

   e. Right-click cell E1 and choose **Edit Comment**.

   f. Click the border of the comment box to display a dotted line boundary. Click the Italic button .

   g. Insert a comment in cell C30 that shows your first and last name.

4. Print comments on the worksheet by following these steps:

   a. On the **Review** tab, click the Show All Comments button 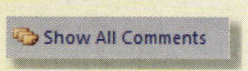.

   b. Click the **Page Layout** tab. In the **Sheet Options** group, click the Dialog Box Launcher.

   c. In the **Print** group, click the arrow for **Comments**. Choose **As displayed on sheet**.

   d. Click **Print** in the dialog box and then click **OK**.

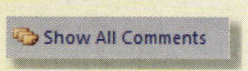

5. Print comments on a separate sheet by following these steps:

   a. On the **Review** tab, click the Show All Comments button 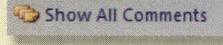. The button is a toggle (on/off).

   b. Click the **Page Layout** tab. In the **Sheet Options** group, click the Dialog Box Launcher.

NOTE

Comments need not be visible on screen when you choose to print them on a separate page.

   c. In the **Print** group, click the arrow for **Comments**. Choose **At end of sheet**. Click **Print** and then click **OK**.

6. Use the Document Inspector by following these steps:

   a. Click the Microsoft Office Button and hover at **Prepare**. Choose **Inspect Document**.

   b. Click **Inspect**. For **Comments and Annotations**, click **Remove All**.

   c. Remove the document properties.

   d. Click **Close**.

7. Prepare and submit your work.

Exercise 10-27

Insert WordArt. Format WordArt.

1. Open **CASales** and save it as *[your initials]*10-27.

2. Delete the contents of cells A1:A2. Insert a row at row 3.

3. Insert WordArt by following these steps:

   a. Click the **Insert** tab. Click the WordArt button .

   b. Find and click **Fill-White, Drop Shadow**.

   c. Triple-click the placeholder text and key **Klassy Kow Ice Cream**. Press Enter to start a new line.

   d. Key **Weekly Sales Data**.

4. Format WordArt by following these steps:

   a. Triple-click the first line in the shape and use the Mini toolbar to set 24 points.

   b. Do the same for the second line.

   c. Select the shape to display a solid line boundary and drag it to appear centered in rows 1:4.

   d. In the **WordArt Styles** group, click the arrow next to the Text Fill button. Choose **Black, Text 1**.

   e. In the **WordArt Styles** group, click the arrow next to the Text Outline button. Choose **No Outline**.

5. Prepare and submit your work.

Lesson Applications

Exercise 10-28

Create and format a shape. Inspect a document.

A text box is a rectangle, but you can use many shapes to display text.

1. Create a new workbook, using the **K&KSales** template. Save the workbook as *[your initials]*10-28. Unprotect the sheet (Review tab).

2. Key the values shown in Figure 10-22.

Figure 10-22

State	Kowabunga	KowOwow
Oregon	15000	16500
Nevada	18000	19200
Washington	17570	18050
California	19000	19500

3. Draw a rounded rectangle shape below the worksheet data that spans from column B to column J. Key **This report is filed each week during the peak selling season for novelty products.**

4. Format the shape box to show the text as bold italic. Use black fill, no outline, and a shadow. Size the shape so that the text is on two lines with equal amounts of text on each. Position the shape to look centered below the data.

5. Remove all comments and properties from the workbook.

6. Prepare and submit your work.

Exercise 10-29

Add and format shapes.

The Stars and Banners category has shapes that can highlight a cell in eye-catching ways.

1. Open **CASales** and save it as *[your initials]*10-29.

2. Select rows 6 through 18 and make them **25.50 (34 pixels)** high.

3. Insert an **Explosion 1** shape from **Stars and Banners** to encircle cell F16. Use no fill and a 1-point black outline.

NOTE

No fill means you can see the cell contents through the shape. The Line Style pane is in the Format Shape dialog box.

4. From the **Basic Shapes** category, draw a lightning bolt in cells D1 through F3. Flip the shape so that it points toward the data. Use a gradient fill, no outline, and a shadow.

5. Prepare and submit your work.

Exercise 10-30

Display cell contents in a shape.

You can link a shape to a cell to display the cell's contents in the shape.

1. Open **Contest**. Save the workbook as *[your initials]*10-30.

2. Delete the wave shape below the data.

3. From the Stars and Banners category, insert a **16-Point Star** that spans cells B20 to C28.

4. While the shape is selected, click in the formula bar. Key **=d4** and press Enter. The value from cell D4 appears in the shape.

5. Center the contents horizontally and vertically and use 24 point as the font size. Set the page for horizontal centering, too.

6. Format cell D4 to use white as the font color.

7. Edit the text box at the top of the sheet so that it reads . . . **number in the star wins** . . . instead of "in cell D4."

8. Prepare and submit your work.

REVIEW

Use the Home tab to apply centering and font choices.

Exercise 10-31 ◆ Challenge Yourself

Use WordArt. Display cell contents in a shape.

You can link a cell on one worksheet to a shape on another sheet in the same workbook to create a separate display about your data.

1. Open **CASales** and save it as *[your initials]*10-31.

2. Insert a new sheet and name it **BestWeek**.

3. On the new sheet, insert WordArt that says **Best California Sales!** Choose any style, and position the shape so that its bottom edge rests on row 5 and so that it starts in column A.

4. Draw a 16-point star that covers approximately cells B8:F22.

5. On the WeeklySales sheet, key **Best Week** in cell A20. Match its format to cell A19. In cell B20, use the MAX function with the range B19:E19.

6. On the BestWeek sheet, select the star. In the formula bar, key **=** to start a formula. Click the WeeklySales tab and click cell B20. Press Enter.

7. Format the shapes so that they form a cohesive design.

8. Center the sheet horizontally and vertically.

9. Prepare and submit your work.

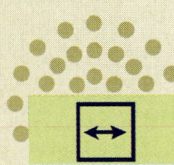

REVIEW

Click the Insert Worksheet tab or press Shift + F11 to insert a new worksheet.

On Your Own

In these exercises you work on your own, as you would in a real-life work environment. Use the skills you've learned to accomplish the task—and be creative.

Exercise 10-32

Create a workbook using the **K&KSales** template. Fill in values for the two products, and unhide both chart sheets. Delete the title object on each chart and insert WordArt as a title. Save the workbook as *[your initials]*10-32. Prepare and submit your work.

Exercise 10-33

In a new workbook, insert and format seven different shapes. Format each one differently and attractively. Position the shapes so that they overlap in several places. Use the Selection pane to experiment reordering the shapes on the sheet. Save the workbook as *[your initials]*10-33. Prepare and submit your work.

Exercise 10-34

In a new workbook, insert a text box and key your name. Format the shape to have a solid black outline and no fill. Copy the box four times. Next change each text box to a different shape. Use different fills, outlines, and effects for each shape. Experiment with the adjustment handle(s). Save your workbook as *[your initials]*10-34. Prepare and submit your work.

Using Images and SmartArt Graphics

OBJECTIVES

After completing this lesson, you will be able to:

1. Insert a picture.
2. Add a picture to a header or footer.
3. Create a hierarchy SmartArt shape.
4. Build a cycle SmartArt shape.
5. Use the Research tool.

Estimated Time: 1 1/2 hours

MCAS OBJECTIVES

In this lesson:
XL07 1.2
XL07 2.1.4
XL07 2.3.4
XL07 4.4.1
XL07 4.4.2
XL07 5.3.3
XL07 5.5.4

In a worksheet, you can insert images from a disk, from the Clip Organizer, or from Web galleries. SmartArt Graphics include lists, hierarchy charts (organization charts), matrixes, and other common business diagrams.

The Research tool enables you to insert information from various sources into your worksheet. You can use reference information from your own computer, from a network, or from the Web.

Inserting a Picture

Images can add visual appeal as well as help to explain your work. When you insert an image, Excel treats it as an object, like a shape. You can edit the size, position, and other properties, depending on the type of image.

TIP

For best effect, don't use too many images on a sheet. One or two related images or shapes should work.

Exercise 11-1 INSERT A PICTURE FROM A FILE

To insert a picture from a file, the picture must be in a graphics format that Excel can use. The **KowOwowTrans** file used in this exercise is a *GIF* file (Graphics Interchange Format), a popular graphics format for images on the Web.

1. Open **KowSales**.

2. Click the **Insert** tab. In the **Illustrations** group, click the Insert Picture from File button. The Insert Picture dialog box opens.

3. Navigate to the folder with the **KowOwowTrans** file and click the thumbnail or filename to select it.

4. Click the arrow next to the Views button and choose **Medium Icons**. You can verify that you have chosen the correct image.

Figure 11-1
Inserting a picture from a file
KowSales.xlsx
K&KSales sheet

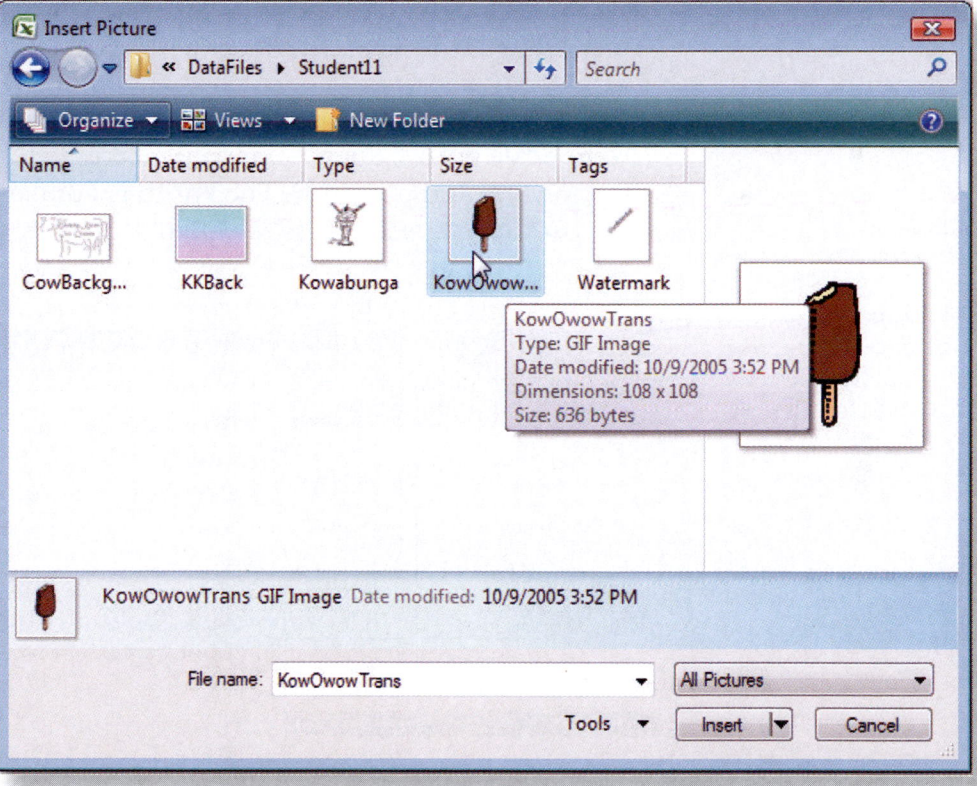

REVIEW

Contextual tools appear at the right side of the Ribbon.

5. Double-click **KowOwowTrans**. The image is inserted at a default size in a default position on the worksheet's drawing layer. Contextual Picture Tools are now available.

6. Point to the bounding box to display a four-pointed arrow. Drag the image below the worksheet data.

Exercise 11-2   CHECK PROPERTIES AND SCALE THE PICTURE

Depending on the type of picture, the Picture Tools Format tab provides various commands. An important command is the one to scale the image. *Scaling* means that you can size the picture by a percentage, larger or smaller.

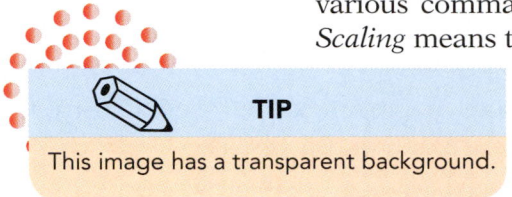

TIP

This image has a transparent background.

1. Click the **Picture Tools Format** tab. In the **Size** group, click the Dialog Box Launcher. The Size and Properties dialog box opens.

2. Click the **Properties** tab. The settings on this tab depend on whether the image is used on a worksheet or a chart sheet.

3. If it's not already selected, click to select **Move but don't size with cells**. This will allow you to size the picture independent of the data.

4. If it's not already selected, click to select **Print object**. You can turn this setting off to print the sheet without the picture.

5. Click the **Size** tab.

6. In the **Scale** group, double-click the percentage value in the **Height** box, key **40**, and press Tab. The **Width** is adjusted automatically because **Lock aspect ratio** is selected.

Figure 11-2
Size and Properties
dialog box
KowSales.xlsx
K&KSales sheet

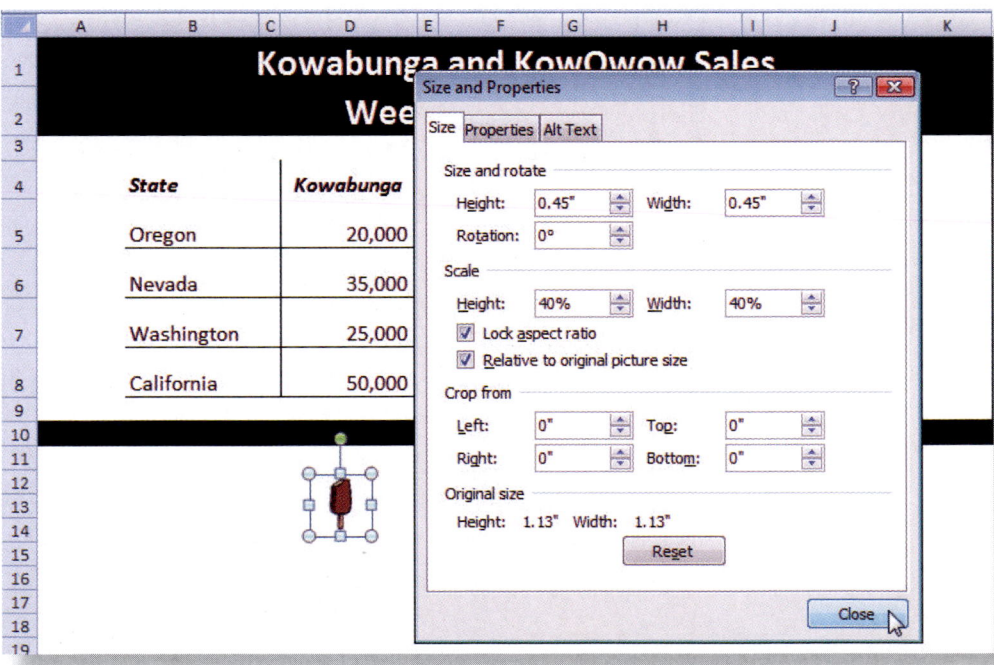

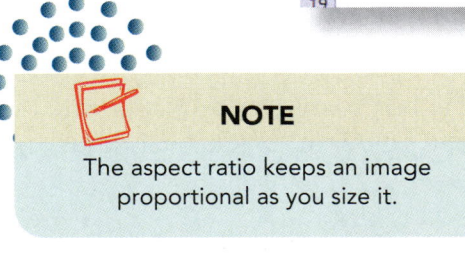

NOTE

The aspect ratio keeps an image proportional as you size it.

7. Click **Close**. The image is 40 percent of its original size.

Exercise 11-3   FORMAT AND COPY AN IMAGE

A picture has many of the same style elements as a shape. You can add 3-D effects, shadows, and more. You may also be able to change the colors for some pictures, based on their original format.

You can copy a picture with regular Copy and Paste commands. And, like shapes, a picture can be dragged using the four-pointed arrow.

1. Make sure the picture is selected.

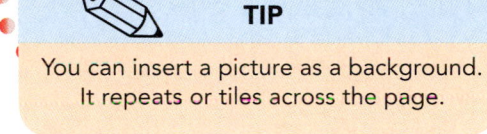 2. In the **Picture Styles** group, click the Picture Effects button 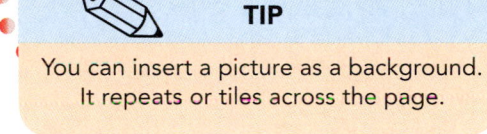.

3. Hover over **Shadow**. In the **Outer** group, choose **Offset Right**.

4. Point at the image to display a four-pointed arrow. Drag the picture to cells A3:A4.

5. Press Ctrl+C and then Ctrl+V. The pasted copy is located in a default location.

6. Drag the copy near cell C6.

7. Press Ctrl+V to paste again. Drag this copy near cell G5.

8. Paste one more copy near cell K8.

9. Click an empty cell to deselect the image.

> **TIP**
>
> You can insert a picture as a background. It repeats or tiles across the page.

Exercise 11-4   INSERT CLIP ART

The Clip Organizer sorts and arranges images from Microsoft and other sources that are on your hard disk. The images are cataloged so that they appear in the Clip Art task pane.

 1. Click the **Insert** tab. Click the Clip Art button. The Clip Art task pane opens.

2. In the **Search for** box, key **money**. This searches for images on your computer that have the word "money" in the title or the description.

3. Click **Go**. (If a message box asks if you want to search online, choose **No**.) Clip art images that illustrate money are shown in the task pane. Your images may not be the same as those shown in this text.

4. Double-click the first image (or any available picture). It is inserted on the worksheet.

Figure 11-3
Searching for an image in the Clip Art task pane
KowSales.xlsx
K&KSales sheet

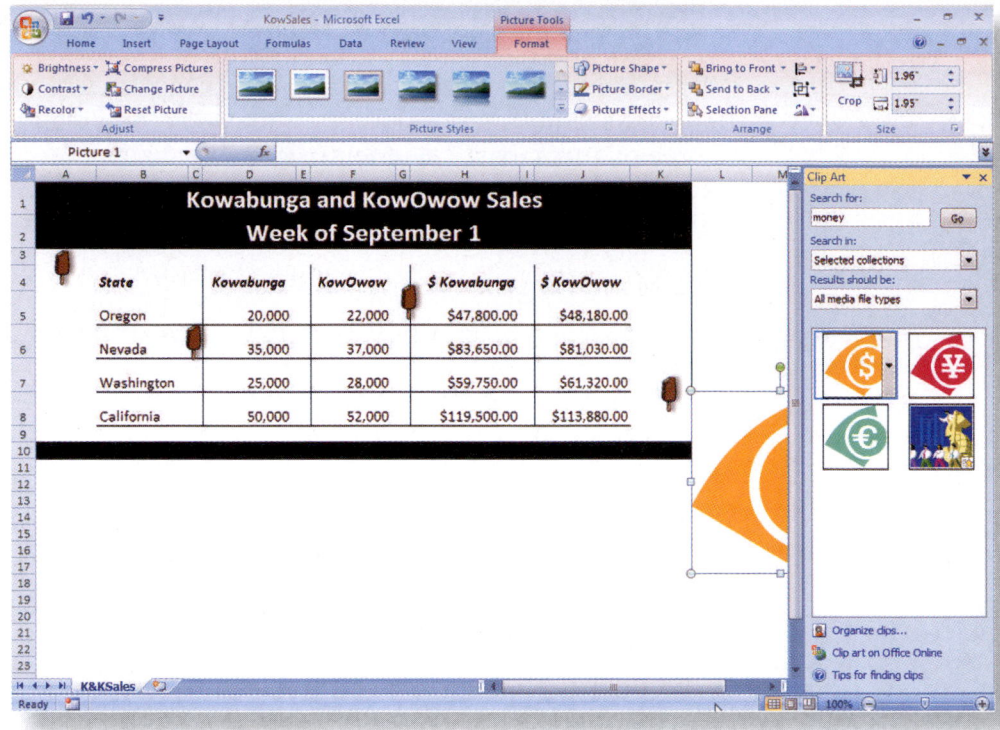

5. Close the Clip Art task pane.

Exercise 11-5   CROP, SIZE, AND STYLE AN IMAGE

Cropping an image allows you to remove part of the picture, working from any of the edges. It takes some guesswork and practice to learn how to crop an image so that it shows what you want to see.

1. Click the **Picture Tools Format** tab.

Crop

2. In the **Size** group, click the Crop button. The insertion point resembles a rectangle with extended edges and includes an arrow.

3. Align the top-left corner of the insertion point shape on the top-left corner handle of the image. The pointer mimics the handle.

4. Drag down and right so that the bounding line just touches the top of the circle design.

NOTE

If you click away from the image and see regular selection handles, click the Crop button again.

5. Align the bottom-left corner of the insertion point on the bottom-left handle of the shape. Drag left so that the bounding line just touches the left of the circle design.

6. Use either corner now to display the original image.

Figure 11-4
Cropped image
KowSales.xlsx
K&KSales sheet

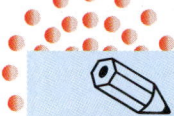

7. Crop the image so that it appears as a dollar sign on a rectangle as shown in Figure 11-4. Click an empty cell to finish cropping.

8. Select the clip art image. Click the **Picture Tools Format** tab.

9. In the **Picture Styles** group, click the More button. A gallery of preset styles opens.

10. Choose **Bevel Rectangle** in the fourth row for a beveled 3-D effect.

11. Point at the image and drag it to rows 1:2 between columns J:K.

12. Point at the bottom-right handle to display a two-pointed arrow. Drag up to size the shape so that it fits in rows 1:2.

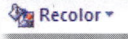

13. In the **Picture Tools** group, click the Recolor button . A gallery of preset color variations opens.

14. In the **Light Variations** group, choose **Background color 2 Light**, the first icon.

15. Click an empty cell.

Adding a Picture to a Header/Footer

Exercise 11-6   INSERT AN IMAGE IN A FOOTER

You can insert an image from disk into a header or a footer. A company logo is an example of an image that might be used as such.

1. Click the **Insert** tab. Click the Header & Footer button.

2. Click the Go to Footer button. The insertion point is in the center section.

3. Click in the left section. In the **Header and Footer Elements** group, click the Picture button. The Insert Picture dialog box opens.

4. Navigate to the folder with **KowOwowTrans** and click to highlight the filename or icon.

5. Click **Insert**. The code is **&[Picture]**.

6. Click in the center section for the footer. Now you can see the image.

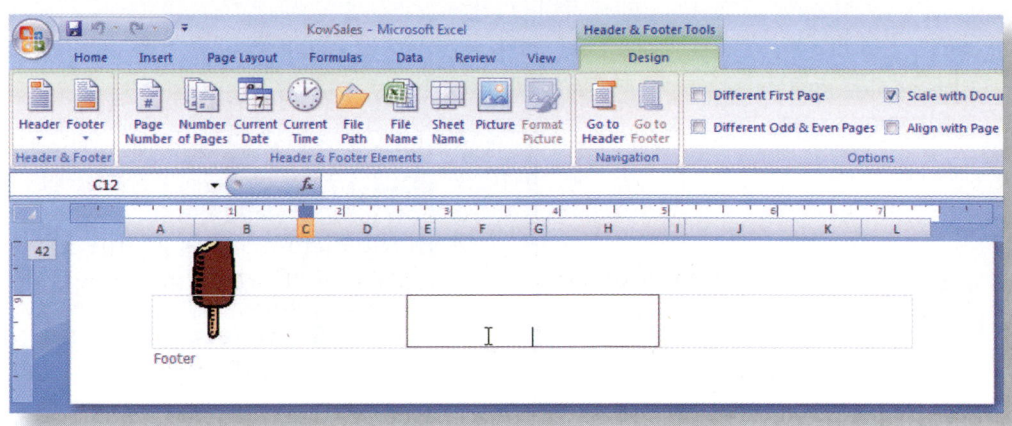

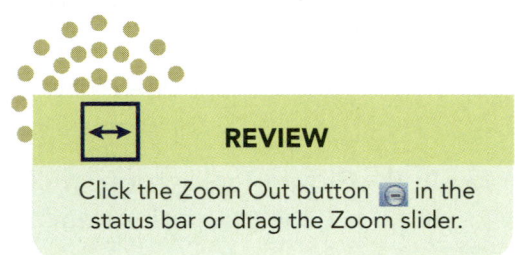

REVIEW

Click the Zoom Out button [−] in the
status bar or drag the Zoom slider.

7. Click a cell above the footer area. Set a Zoom size of **40%** and scroll
   to see the page.

Exercise 11-7   SIZE AN IMAGE IN A FOOTER

1. Return to **100%** Zoom size.

2. Scroll to the footer area and click in the left section.

3. In the **Header and Footer Elements** group, click the Format Picture
   button 🖼. The Format Picture dialog box has two tabs for a footer
   image.

4. Click the **Size** tab. In the **Scale** group, double-click the value in the
   Height box, key **65**, and press [Tab]. Click **OK**.

5. Click after the right square bracket with **&[Picture]**. Press [Enter] and
   key your first and last name.

6. Click a cell in the worksheet. Press [Ctrl]+[Home].

7. Press [Ctrl]+[P] and then [Alt]+[W] to open Print Preview. Close Print
   Preview.

Exercise 11-8 CREATE A WATERMARK

A *watermark* is text or an image that appears on top of or behind the data. A watermark is similar to a background image, but it is intended for printed documents. You can simulate a watermark in Excel by inserting the appropriate image in a header or footer.

1. Click the **Insert** tab. Click the Header & Footer button 🔲. The insertion point is in the header center section.

2. In the **Header and Footer Elements** group, click the Picture button 🔲.

3. Navigate to the folder with **Watermark** and click to highlight the filename or icon

4. Click **Insert**. The **&[Picture]** code is the same.

5. Click a worksheet cell and set the Zoom size to **60%**. This image is text that has been sized and rotated.

6. Click in the center header section.

7. In the **Header and Footer Elements** group, click the Format Picture button 🔲.

8. Click the **Picture** tab. In the **Image control** group, set the **Brightness** to **90%**. Click **OK**.

9. Click a cell in the worksheet. Press Ctrl + Home.

10. Return to normal view and 100% Zoom size.

11. Save the workbook as *[your initials]*11-8 in a Lesson 11 folder.

12. Close the workbook.

Creating a Hierarchy SmartArt Shape

SmartArt is a graphics feature that enables you to quickly display data as a high-quality illustration. These illustrations include bulleted lists, organization charts, cycles, matrixes, pyramids, and more. These graphics include a text pane for ease in keying text. They resize automatically based on how much text you enter. The layouts can be converted to another graphic with little or no extra work. SmartArt graphics are not linked to worksheet data but can be used to clarify and enhance data.

Exercise 11-9 CREATE AND STYLE AN ORGANIZATION CHART

An *organization chart* is an object that displays relationships, usually among workers in a company. Organization charts show hierarchical associations between people. This means there is someone at the top (the superior) with assistants, subordinates, or coworkers.

1. Create a new workbook. Set landscape orientation.

2. Click the **Insert** tab. Click the SmartArt button. The Choose a SmartArt Graphic dialog box shows seven categories of diagrams that can be built as well as an All group. When you click a thumbnail in any category, the pane on the right describes its use.

3. Click **Hierarchy** to open its pane. Click **Organization Chart** (first icon). Read the information at the right and click **OK**. An organization chart with five shapes opens with its Text pane. The SmartArt Tools include a Design and a Format tab.

Figure 11-6
New organization chart

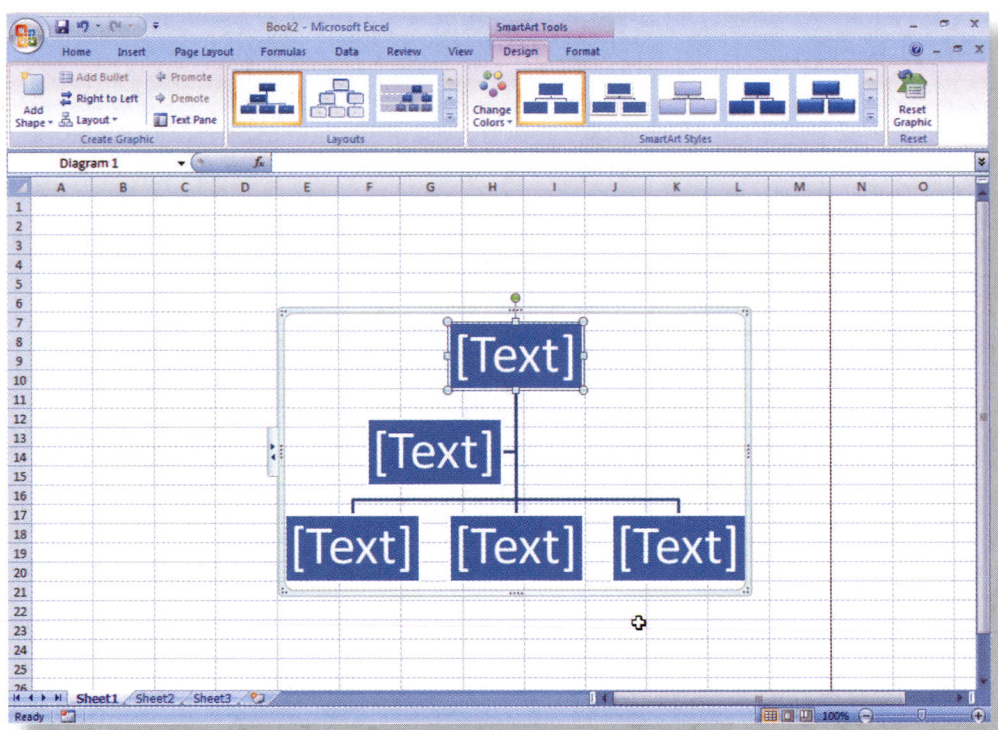

4. Click the **SmartArt Tools Design** tab. In the **SmartArt Styles** group, click the More button. Find and choose **Polished** in the 3-D category.

5. In the **SmartArt Styles** group, click the Change Colors button. In the **Primary Theme Colors** group, choose **Dark 1 Outline**.

6. In the **Create Graphic** group, click the Text Pane button. The Text pane opens or closes. Display the Text pane.

7. Click the **SmartArt Tools Format** tab. Click the Size button.

8. Double-click the value in the **Height** box, key **4**, and press Enter.

9. Set the **Width** to **6**.

10. Point at the border of the graphic's frame to display the four-pointed arrow. Drag the shape so that its top-left selection handle is in cell A1. The Text pane moves to the other side.

> **NOTE**
>
> The Text Pane button [Text Pane] toggles the pane on/off. Remember that your screen resolution and size has an effect on how buttons appear.

Exercise 11-10   ADD A SHAPE TO AN ORGANIZATION CHART

Each box in the organization chart is a shape. The top shape is the highest in the hierarchy, and generally there is one top shape. An *assistant shape* represents a helper and is attached to the line that connects the top shape to the rest of the chart. The other three shapes are below the top shape and represent *subordinate* employees.

1. Click the border of the top shape. It shows a solid line boundary, selection handles, and a rotation handle.

2. Click inside the top shape. The text insertion point is visible with a dashed line boundary.

3. Click the shape to display a solid line boundary.

4. Click the **SmartArt Tools Design** tab.

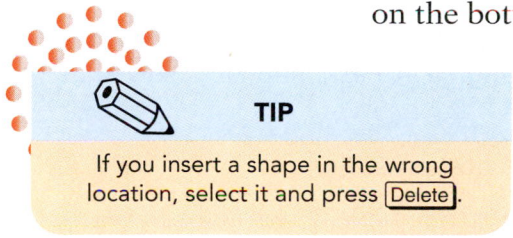

5. In the **Create Graphic** group, click the arrow on the Add Shape button . The menu lists where a shape can be placed.

6. Choose **Add Shape Below**. A fourth shape is added as a subordinate on the bottom row, and the entire graphic is resized.

7. Click the border of the leftmost subordinate shape (bottom row) to display a solid line boundary.

TIP

If you insert a shape in the wrong location, select it and press Delete.

8. Click the arrow on the Add Shape button . Choose **Add Shape Below**. A shape is added as a new subordinate to the subordinate.

Figure 11-7
Adding shapes

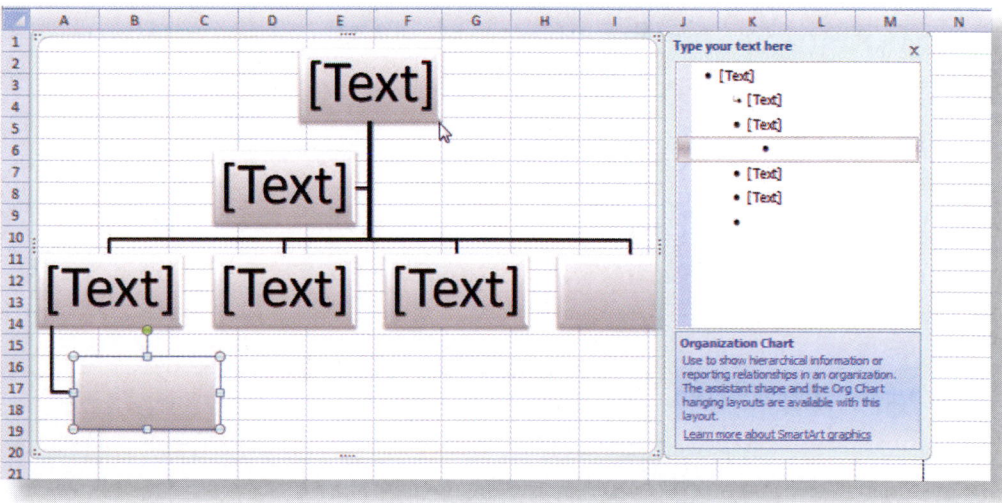

9. Select the top shape to display a solid line boundary.

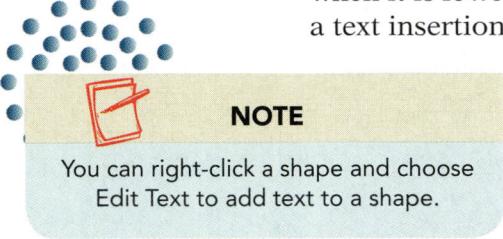

Exercise 11-11   ADD TEXT TO THE SHAPES

The *Text pane* is a dialog box that is attached to a SmartArt shape. It works like a bulleted or numbered list in Word or PowerPoint. When you're working in the Text pane, pressing Enter inserts a new shape at the current level. Pressing Tab or Shift+Tab demotes or promotes a shape in the graphic. A shape is promoted when it is moved up a level in the hierarchy; it is demoted when it is lowered in the hierarchy. You can also click inside a shape to place a text insertion point for keying data.

> **NOTE**
>
> You can right-click a shape and choose Edit Text to add text to a shape.

1. Click the **SmartArt Tools Design** tab. If necessary, click the Text Pane button [Text Pane] to display it.

2. Click inside the top shape. The text insertion point appears, and the shape's border displays dashed lines.

3. Key **Conrad Steele** and press Enter. A new line within the shape is available.

4. Key **President and CEO**. Do not press Enter.

5. In the Text pane, click the line below **President and CEO**. This is the entry line for the assistant shape; it is selected with a solid line boundary.

6. Key *[your first and last name]*. Press Enter. A new shape is inserted at the same level.

7. Click the new shape in the graphic and press Delete.

8. In the Text pane, click immediately after the last character in your name and press Shift+Enter. This is a second line in the shape.

9. Key **Executive Assistant** on the second line.

10. In the Text pane, click the next line. This represents the leftmost subordinate shape.

Figure 11-8
Keying text in a shape

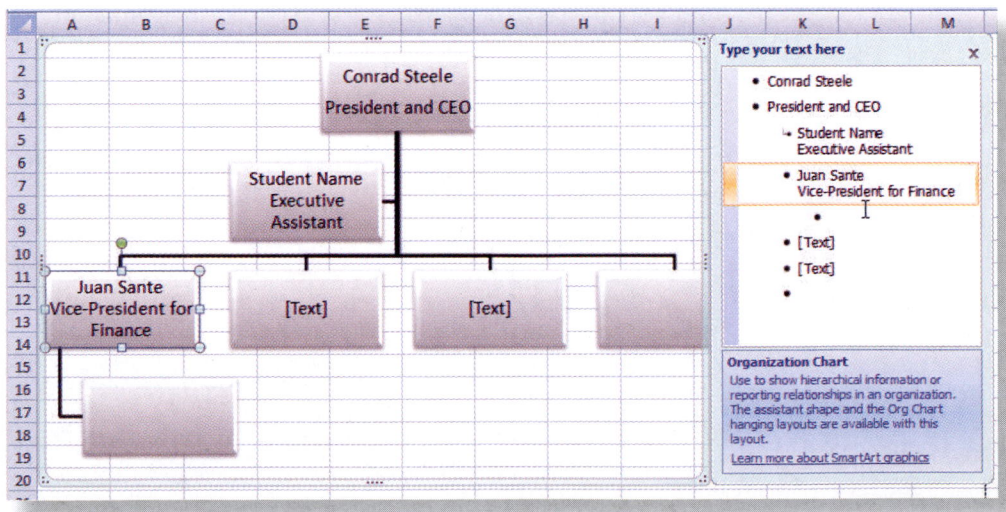

11. Key **Juan Sante** and press [Shift]+[Enter]. Key **Vice-President for Finance** as his title.

12. Click inside the second subordinate shape to display a dashed line boundary. Key **Keiko Sumara** and press [Shift]+[Enter].

13. Key **Sales and Marketing** as her second line.

14. For the third subordinate shape, key **Robin McDonald**, and press [Shift]+[Enter]. Key **Human Resources**.

NOTE

If you have extra shapes in your layout, delete them.

15. In the fourth subordinate shape, key **Unknown** on the first line and **Communications** on the second line.

16. Click inside the shape below **Juan Sante** and key **[your instructor's first and last name]**.

17. Click outside the shapes but within the graphic's border. All text boxes are deselected, and you can see the position of the text in the Text pane.

NOTE

The selection handles for the graphic frame are dots arranged in a triangle or in a row.

18. Close the Text pane.

19. Place the pointer on the right middle selection handle for the graphic's frame. With a two-pointed sizing arrow, drag the right edge to reach column L.

20. Drag the bottom middle handle to reach row 25.

21. Save the workbook as **[your initials]11-11**.

Building a Cycle SmartArt Shape

As part of SmartArt graphics, Excel can build several styles of business diagrams, including List, Cycle, Process, and Relationship diagrams. A *diagram* is an object that illustrates a concept. Diagrams are not linked to worksheet data.

Cycle diagrams illustrate a series of tasks, events, or stages that continue and repeat in a circular manner. Some graphics are called cycles and others are called radials.

Exercise 11-12   CREATE A CYCLE DIAGRAM

1. Click the **Sheet2** worksheet tab.

2. Click the **Insert** tab. Click the SmartArt button 📊.

3. Click **Cycle** in the Choose a SmartArt Graphic dialog box. There are several cycle and radial shapes in this category.

4. Find and click **Block Cycle** in the first row. Read its description and click **OK**. A cycle diagram with five shapes is inserted.

5. In the **Create Graphic** group, click the Text Pane button 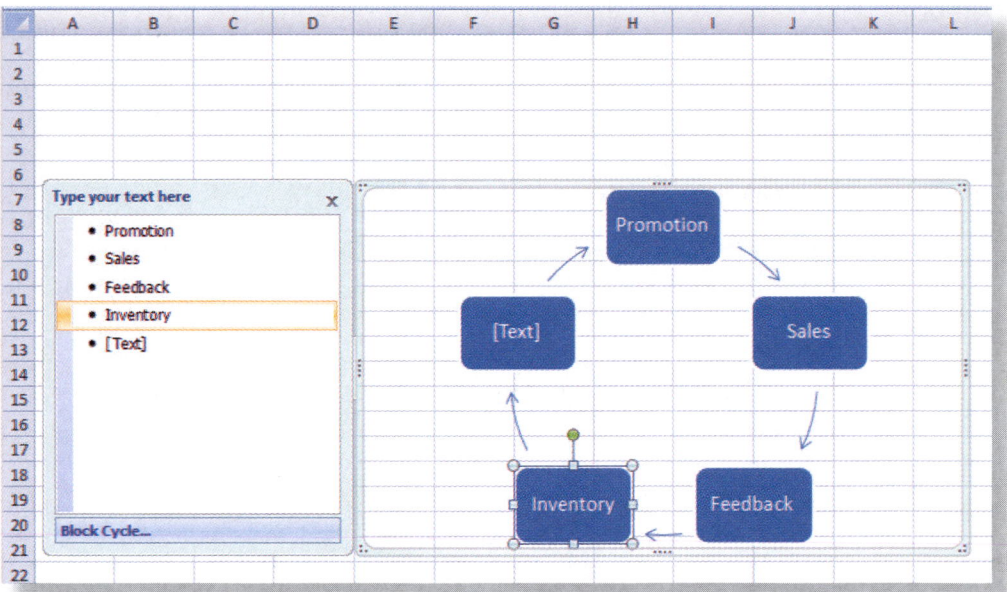 to display the pane.

6. Key **Promotion**. It appears in the top shape and as the first line in the Text pane.

7. Press ↓ to move to the second line in the Text pane and key **Sales**.

8. Press Enter. Another shape is inserted.

9. Press Backspace. The shape is deleted.

10. In the Text pane, click the third line. Key **Feedback**.

11. In the Text pane on the fourth line, key **Inventory**.

Figure 11-9
Cycle diagram
11-11.xlsx
Sheet2 sheet

12. Click a worksheet cell away from the graphic. Only the shape appears.

13. Click a cell near the graphic. The frame and the Text pane open when the graphic is selected.

Exercise 11-13   MOVE TEXT IN THE TEXT PANE

You can make edits in the Text pane as if it were a bulleted Word list. For example, in your cycle shape, "Inventory" should be the top of the cycle. This can be accomplished as a cut-and-paste task.

1. Triple-click **Inventory** in the Text pane. It is selected, and the Mini toolbar opens.

2. Press Ctrl+X. The text and the shape are cut.

3. Click to the left of **Promotion** in the Text pane.

4. Press Enter. A blank line is inserted in the Text pane as well as the new shape.

5. Click the blank line and press Ctrl+V. The cut text is pasted in its new location in the shape and in the Text pane.

6. Click the **SmartArt Tools Design** tab.

7. In the **SmartArt Styles** group, click the More button ⬚. Choose **Polished**.

8. Click the Change Colors button ⬚. Choose **Dark 1 Outline**.

9. Click the empty shape in the graphic and press Delete.

10. Point at the border of the graphic to display the four-pointed arrow. Drag the shape so that its top-left selection handle is in cell A1. The Text pane moves to the other side of the frame.

11. Drag the bottom-right selection handle to reach cell H22.

12. Close the Text pane and click a worksheet cell.

13. Rename the sheet tab as **Cycle**. Save the workbook as *[your initials]*11-13.

Exercise 11-14   CHOOSE A NEW LAYOUT

Most SmartArt graphics can be changed to another layout. When you choose another layout, the text is remapped to the new shape. In some cases, not all layouts are well-suited to your text.

1. In *[your initials]*11-13, select the main cycle shape, not an individual box.

2. On the **SmartArt Tools Design** tab in the **Layouts** group, click the More button ⬚.

3. Hover over several thumbnails to see the new layout. Live Preview shows how the graphic will appear.

4. Find and choose **Segmented Cycle**. Close the workbook without saving.

Using the Research Tool

The Research task pane helps you find and insert data from an outside source. Excel has a Research Library that includes a multilanguage thesaurus and dictionary, a translation utility, and an encyclopedia. A *thesaurus* is a reference that lists words that mean the same thing as the word you select.

You can open the Research task pane by:

- Clicking the Research button on the Review tab.

- Clicking a word while holding down the Alt key.

Exercise 11-15   FIND SYNONYMS

A *synonym* is a word that means the same thing as another word. The Research tool can look up labels in cells; it cannot research text that is inside a graphic or shape.

> **NOTE**
>
> If you have different reference books and resources on your computer, expand/collapse each one and check its findings.

> **NOTE**
>
> Click the − sign to collapse a list and the + sign to expand it.

1. Open **Research**. This is a matrix graphic.

2. Hold down Alt and click cell L1. The Research task pane opens with preliminary results for the word "sales." It has searched All Reference Books on your computer. Each resource has an expand or collapse button (+ or −) to indicate whether its list is hidden or shown.

3. Collapse each of the resource items to start.

4. Click the Expand button ⊞ for **Thesaurus: English (United States)**. There is only one related word, **sale**, so you will not change that label in the diagram.

Figure 11-10
Using the Research task pane
Research.xlsx
Matrix sheet

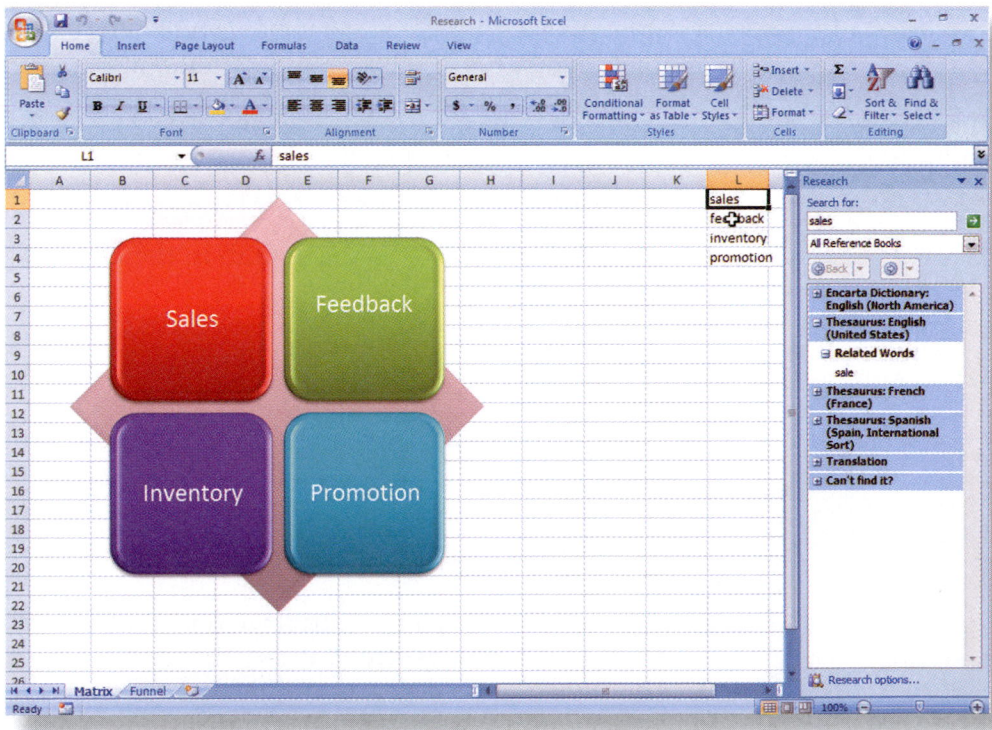

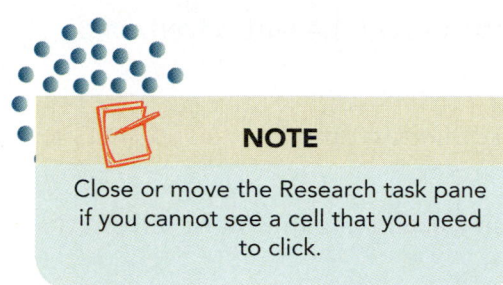

NOTE

Close or move the Research task pane if you cannot see a cell that you need to click.

5. Hold down Alt and click cell L2. The task pane updates to show related words for "feedback."

6. Expand/scroll the **Thesaurus: English (United States)** list. You will replace the word "feedback" in cell L2 with "reaction."

7. Place the mouse pointer on **reaction** in the **criticism (n.)** category.

8. Click the arrow and choose **Insert**. The replacement is made in cell L2, not in the graphic.

Figure 11-11
Choosing a word from the thesaurus
Research.xlsx
Matrix sheet

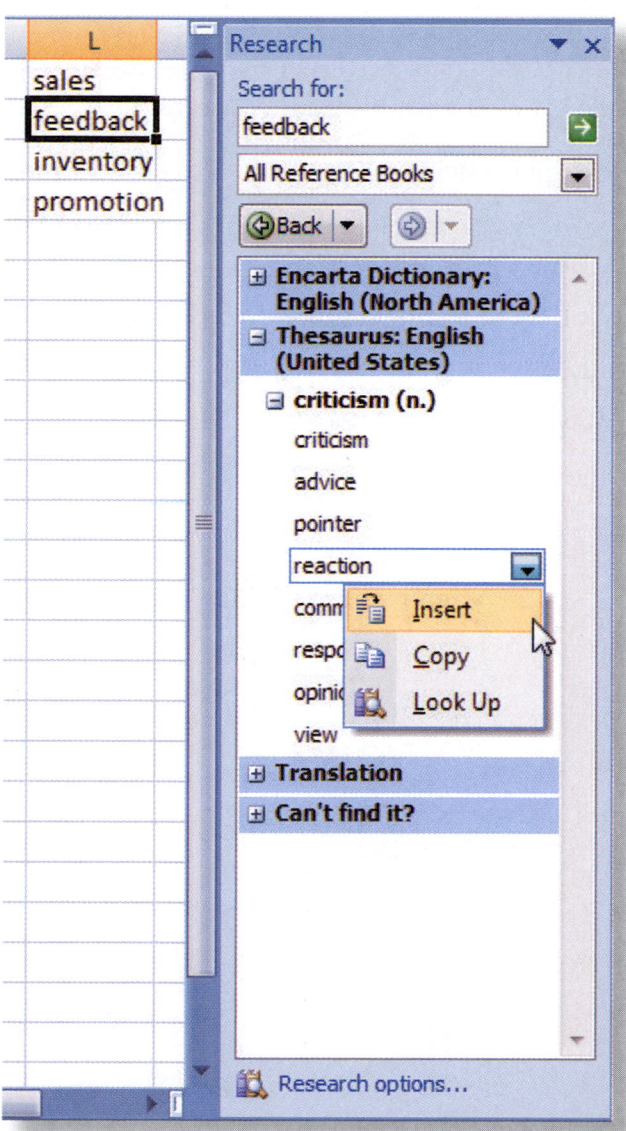

9. Hold down Alt and click cell L3. If necessary, scroll to see the results.

10. Place the mouse pointer on **stock** in the **supply (n.)** category. Click the down arrow and choose **Insert**.

11. Use the Thesaurus to replace **promotion** in cell L4 with **advertising**.

12. Close the Research task pane.

13. Double-click **Promotion** in the matrix diagram and key **Advertising** as its replacement.

14. Replace **Feedback** in the diagram with **Reaction** and **Inventory** with **Stock**.

15. Click a worksheet cell.

Exercise 11-16   TRANSLATE WORDS

As part of the Research tool, Excel can translate words into another language. Although this is a handy feature, you will find that you must be familiar with the language you choose so that you can use the correct grammar, such as the gender of nouns and the tense of verbs.

1. Click the **Funnel** worksheet tab. This is a funnel graphic.

2. Click near the shape to select it. The frame includes a tab at the left with two arrows.

3. Click the tab at the left of the frame. The Text pane opens.

4. Hold down Alt and click cell J1.

5. Click the Expand button ⊞ for **Translation** in the Research task pane.

6. In the **To** box, choose **French (France)**.

Figure 11-12
Using translation in the Research task pane
Research.xlsx
Funnel sheet

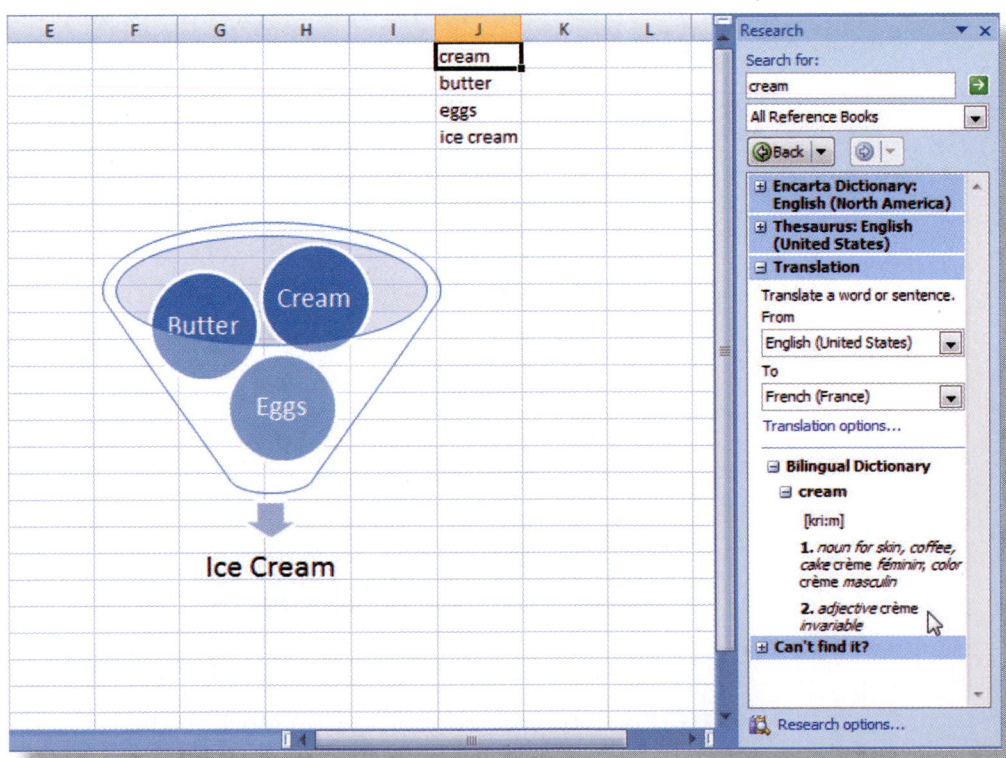

7. Click the Expand button ⊞ for **Bilingual dictionary** if it is not expanded. The translation for "cream" is "crème."

8. Select the shape and double-click **Cream** in the Text pane.

9. Key **La Creme**. You will add the accent on the "e" in the next exercise.

NOTE

Many languages include an article with a noun. In French, the articles are "le," "la," and "les." The translation tool does not include the article, although it does specify masculine or feminine.

10. Hold down ⟨Alt⟩ and click cell J2. The Translation group should be expanded, since you just used it. The French word is **beurre**.

11. Select the shape and double-click **Butter** in the Text pane. Key **Le Beurre**.

12. Hold down the ⟨Alt⟩ key and click cell J3.

13. Double-click **Eggs** in the Text pane and key **Les Oeufs**.

14. Hold down ⟨Alt⟩ and click cell J4. The dictionary translates both words.

15. In the Text pane, replace **Ice Cream** with **Creme Glace**.

16. Close the Research task pane.

Exercise 11-17 USE A SPECIAL SYMBOL

You should add the accent to the "e" in "Crème" so that the words are shown correctly in French. Accented characters are special symbols and can be easily inserted.

1. In the Text pane, click the first line. Then drag to select the first "e" in "Creme."

2. Click the **Insert** tab. In the **Text** group, click the Symbol button 🔣. The Symbol dialog box opens.

3. Click the **Font** arrow and key **c** to move to font names that begin with "C." Set the font to **Calibri**.

4. Scroll to find **è**, the accented lowercase "e." This is a *grave* accent.

TIP

When inserting a symbol for an accented character, use the same font as the rest of the text.

Figure 11-13
Inserting a symbol
Research.xlsx
Funnel sheet

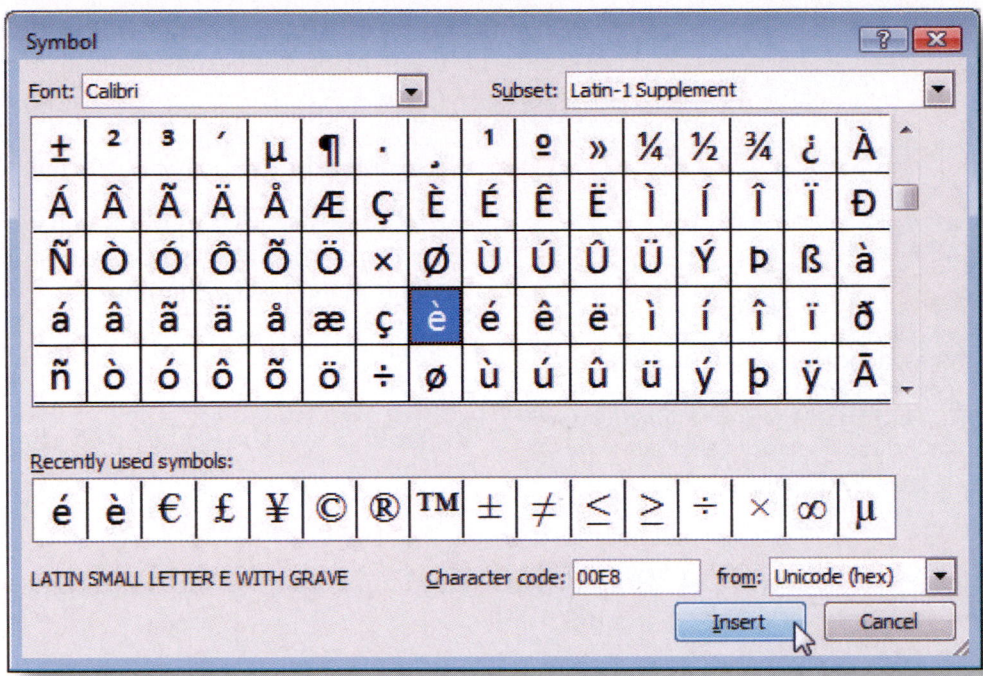

5. Click the character to select it and click **Insert**. Click **Close**. The accented è replaces the original character.

6. Make the same replacement in "Crème Glace."

7. In the Text pane, edit "Glace" to show the correct spelling "Glacée."

8. Close the Text pane. Delete the contents of cells J1:J4.

9. Drag the graphic so that its top-left handle starts in cell A1. Drag the bottom-right handle of the graphic frame to cell J25.

10. On the **SmartArt Tools Design** tab, choose **Polished** from the **SmartArt Styles**. Change the colors to one of the **Colorful** choices.

11. Click a worksheet cell.

Exercise 11-18   SET DOCUMENT PROPERTIES

Excel workbooks have properties. A *property* is a setting or attribute that is stored with the workbook when it is saved. Some properties can be edited, such as the author's name, a subject, or key words. Properties are shown in the Document Information Panel.

1. Click the Microsoft Office Button .

2. Hover over **Prepare** and choose **Properties**. The Document Information Panel opens at the top of the worksheet.

3. Triple-click in the **Author** box and key *[your first and last name]*.

4. Press Tab. Key **SmartArt Graphics** in the **Title** box.

5. Click in the **Comments** box and key the following:

   This workbook will be saved as Excel 97-2003 format for review by all shops.

Figure 11-14
Setting properties
Research.xlsx
Funnel sheet

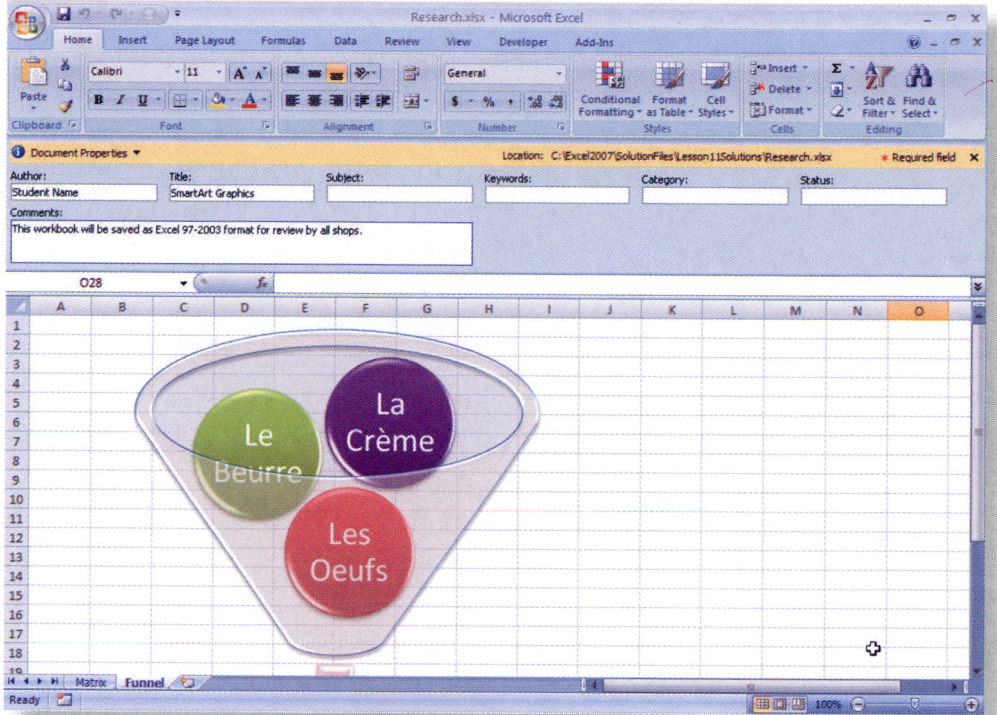

6. Close the Document Information Panel.

7. Save the workbook as *[your initials]*11-18.

8. Press F12. The Save As dialog box shows the current filename.

9. Click the **Save as type** arrow and choose **Excel 97-2003 Workbook**.

10. Edit the filename to *[your initials]*11-18a and click **Save**. The Compatibility Checker alerts you that the SmartArt graphics will not be editable in the earlier versions of Excel.

11. Click **Continue**. Close the workbook.

Using Online Help

Excel has many types of SmartArt graphics. You can use Help to learn about many of the layouts available for use in a workbook.

USE HELP TO LEARN ABOUT SMARTART GRAPHICS

1. In a new workbook, click the Microsoft Office Excel Help button.

2. Find and review topics about images and graphics.

3. Close the Help window when you are finished.

Lesson 11 Summary

- You can place images on a sheet or a chart. Images can be taken from a disk or the Clip Organizer.
- Pictures have properties that depend on how the image was originally created. You can edit some of these properties.
- You can use pictures in headers and footers. Some images, based on their size and color, can be used to mimic a watermark.
- Pictures have most of the same style elements as shapes.
- Cropping an image enables you to hide or mask part of the picture.
- SmartArt graphics include many common business diagrams including Cycle, Target, Radial, Venn, and Pyramid designs.
- SmartArt graphics include organization charts with various levels to illustrate relationships among workers.
- Most SmartArt graphics have a Text pane for easy text entry and editing.
- SmartArt graphics have their own styles and colors. Many can be easily changed into another layout, too.
- SmartArt graphics are not linked to worksheet data.
- You can use the Research task pane to find words that mean the same thing in the same or a different language.
- Document properties include information such as the author name, a title, the subject, key words, and general comments.

LESSON 11		Command Summary	
Feature	**Button**	**Task Path**	**Keyboard**
Clip art		Insert, Illustrations	
Crop picture		Picture Tools Format, Size	
Cycle diagram		Insert, Illustrations	
Document properties		Microsoft Office, Prepare, Properties	
Header/footer picture		Insert, Header & Footer, Header & Elements	
Organization chart		Insert, Illustrations	
Picture/image from file		Insert, Illustrations	
Research		Review, Proofing	Alt + [click]
Symbol, insert		Insert, Text	

Concepts Review

True/False Questions

Each of the following statements is either true or false. Indicate your choice by circling T or F.

T F   1. The font size in a SmartArt graphic adjusts to fit the shape.

T F   2. To crop a picture, you must first rotate it.

T F   3. A thesaurus translates words into another language.

T F   4. Picture Tools are contextual tools for editing a picture inserted from a disk.

T F   5. The text boxes in an organization chart are called *shapes*.

T F   6. Only a few of the SmartArt graphics include a Text pane.

T F   7. Accents for words translated into another language are automatically inserted in the label.

T F   8. In the Research task pane, you can find and use images from the Clip Organizer.

Short Answer Questions

Write the correct answer in the space provided.

1. Name three categories of SmartArt graphics in Excel.

_____

2. How can you display this character: **á**?

_____

3. What type of reference includes words that mean the same thing?

_____

4. What term describes the process of hiding part of a picture?

_____

5. Describe the pointer used to drag a graphic.

_____

6. How can you include your name and a general comment with a workbook?

_____

7. How do you enter text in a shape in a SmartArt graphic?

_____

8. How can you restyle a SmartArt graphic with different colors or shadows?

_____

Critical Thinking

Answer these questions on a separate page. There are no right or wrong answers. Support your answers with examples from your own experience, if possible.

1. The Research task pane allows you to add additional reference sources to those that come with Excel. What types of references might be helpful to business workers? What references might help students?

2. Explore each of the SmartArt categories. Then list a business or school concept that might be appropriately illustrated by each general category.

Skills Review

Exercise 11-19

Insert a picture. Size, color, and copy a picture. Flip and align pictures.

1. Open **KowSales** and save it as *[your initials]***11-19**.
2. Insert a picture by following these steps:
   a. Click cell A1.
   b. Click the **Insert** tab. Click the Picture button .
   c. Find and select the **KowOwowTrans** file. Click **Insert**.
   d. With the four-pointed arrow, click and drag the image slightly down and to the right so you can see all the handles.

3. Size, color, and copy a picture by following these steps:

   a. On the **Picture Tools Format** tab, click the Dialog Box Launcher for the **Size** group.

   b. In the **Scale** group, double-click the value in the **Height** box, key **50**, and press Tab. Click **Close**.

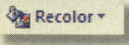

   c. In the **Picture Tools** group, click the Recolor button . Choose one of the **Light Variations**.

   d. Point at the picture and hold down Ctrl. Drag a copy of the picture to the right of the original.

   e. Hold down Shift and click the original image. Both images are selected. Point at either image, hold down Ctrl, and drag a copy of the pictures to the right of the labels in columns J:K.

   f. Select the first copy (at the left) and use a different **Light Variation** color. Select each of the other copies and choose a different color.

4. Flip and align pictures by following these steps:

   a. Click one of the images on the right. Hold down Shift and click the other picture on the right. Both pictures on the right should be selected.

   b. In the **Arrange** group, click the Rotate button . Choose **Flip Horizontal**.

   c. Hold down Shift and click the original image and then the first copy so that all four pictures are selected.

   d. In the **Arrange** group, click the Align button . Choose **Align Bottom**.

5. Click cell A12.

6. Click the Microsoft Office Button. Choose **Prepare** and **Inspect Document**. Remove all metadata and personal information.

7. Prepare and submit your work.

Exercise 11-20

Add a picture to a header/footer.

1. Open **KowSales** and save it as *[your initials]***11-20**.

2. Add a picture to a header by following these steps:

   a. Click the **Insert** tab. Click the Header & Footer button.

   b. Click in the right section. In the **Header and Footer Elements** group, click the Picture button.

   c. Navigate to the folder with **KowOwowTrans** and click to highlight the filename or thumbnail.

   d. Click **Insert**.

   e. In the **Header and Footer Elements** group, click the Format Picture button.

REVIEW

Background images do not print.

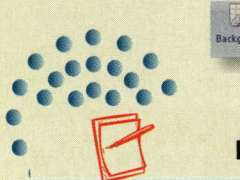

NOTE

You can use the same filename for the workbook and the Web page because they have different filename extensions.

f. Click the **Size** tab. In the **Scale** group, double-click the value in the **Height** box, key **50**, and click **OK**.

g. Key your name in the left section.

3. Click a cell in the worksheet. Press Ctrl+Home. Save the workbook.

4. Click the **Page Layout** tab. Click the Background button 📷. Navigate to the folder with **KKBack**. Insert the file.

5. Change the color of the labels in rows 1:2 to a color that complements the background.

6. Save the workbook as a Web page named *[your initials]***11-20**. Change the title for the Web browser to **K & K Sales**.

7. Prepare and submit your work.

Exercise 11-21

Create a hierarchy shape. Add text to an organization chart.

1. Create a new workbook named *[your initials]***11-21**. Rename **Sheet1** as **OrgChart**. Set landscape orientation.

2. Create a hierarchy shape by following these steps:

a. On the **Insert** tab, click the SmartArt button 📷.

b. Click **Hierarchy** and then click **Organization Chart**.

c. On the **SmartArt Tools Design** tab in the **SmartArt Styles** group, click the More button 📷. Find and choose **Inset**.

d. In the **SmartArt Styles** group, click the Change Colors button 📷. Choose **Colorful – Accent Colors**.

e. Click the assistant shape, the second icon vertically. Press Delete.

f. Click the border of the leftmost subordinate shape (bottom row).

g. On the **SmartArt Tools Design** tab in the **Create Graphic** group, click the arrow with the Add Shape button 📷. Choose **Add Shape Before**.

3. Add text to an organization chart by following these steps:

a. Click the first line in the Text pane.

b. Key **Heinrich Kraus** and press Shift+Enter. Key **President-Elect**.

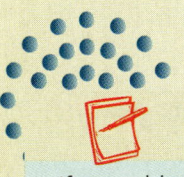

NOTE

If you add an unwanted shape, select it and press Delete.

c. Click the line below "President-Elect" in the Text pane. Key **Glenn Ladewig**.

d. Click the next line in the Text pane and key **Nassar Eassa**.

e. On the next line, key **Ted Artagnan**. On the last line, key **Maria Calcivechia**.

4. Hide the Text pane. Point at the border of the SmartArt shape to display the four-pointed arrow. Drag the shape so that its top-left selection handle is in cell A1. Drag the bottom-right selection handle to reach cell L25.

5. Click a worksheet cell. Insert WordArt using **Fill – Accent 2, Warm Matte Bevel** (fifth row) that displays **Owners Association**. Drag the WordArt shape so that is appears centered over the chart.

6. Center the worksheet horizontally.

7. Prepare and submit your work.

Exercise 11-22

Build a SmartArt diagram. Use the Research tool. Set document properties.

1. Create a new workbook named *[your initials]***11-22**. Rename **Sheet1** as **Venn**.

2. Build a SmartArt diagram by following these steps:

a. Click the **Insert** tab. Click the SmartArt button .

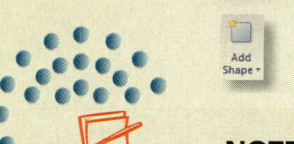

b. Open the **Relationship** pane. Find and click the **Basic Venn** icon. Click **OK**.

c. Click the arrow with the Add Shape button . Choose **Add Shape After**.

d. Click the first line in the Text pane and key **Finance**.

> **NOTE**
>
> For this diagram, it doesn't matter if you add the shape before or after the existing shapes.

e. On the second line in the Text pane, key **Marketing**.

f. On the third line, key **Owners**. On the last line, key **Human Resources**.

g. Click a cell within the diagram frame.

h. Close the Text pane. Drag the diagram so that the top-left corner starts in cell A5.

i. On the **SmartArt Tools Design** tab, click the Change Colors button . Choose **Dark 1 Outline**.

j. Key **Franchise Integration** in cell A1. Choose a font size and center the label across the diagram.

3. Center the sheet horizontally.

4. Select the diagram so that the frame is visible and no individual shape is selected. Press Ctrl+C. Click cell A24 and press Ctrl+V.

5. Use Research by following these steps:

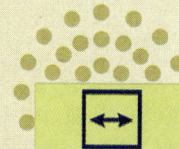

> **REVIEW**
>
> If you press Enter and add an extra shape, press Delete to remove it.

a. In cell J23, key **finance**. Key **marketing** in cell J24, **human resources** in cell J25, and **owners** in cell J26.

b. Hold down Alt and click cell J23. Verify that **All Reference Books** are used.

TIP

You can collapse references that you are not using.

c. Click the Expand button ☐ for **Thesaurus: English (US)**.

d. Place the mouse pointer on **investment** in the **money (n.)** category. Click the arrow and choose **Insert**.

e. Hold down [Alt] and click cell J24. Insert **promotion** from the **advertising (n.)** category.

f. Look up **human resources** and insert **workforce** in its place.

g. Look up **owners** but do not make a change. Close the Research task pane.

6. Edit a diagram by following these steps:

   a. Select the copied diagram.

   b. On the **SmartArt Tools Design** tab, click the Text Pane button 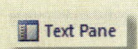. Drag the Text pane so that you can see the substitute words in column J and the diagram.

   c. Replace **Finance** in the Text pane with **Investment**. Replace **Marketing** with **Promotion**. Replace **Human Resources** with **Workforce**.

   d. Close the Text pane and delete the labels in column J.

7. Set document properties by following these steps:

   a. Click the Microsoft Office Button ☐.

   b. Choose **Prepare** and then choose **Properties**.

   c. Triple-click in the **Author** box and key *[your first and last name]*.

   d. Press [Tab]. Key **SmartArt Venn Diagram** in the **Title** box.

   e. Click in the **Comments** box and key the following:
      This worksheet illustrates two diagrams for the upcoming workshop.

   f. Close the Document Information Panel.

8. Prepare and submit your work.

Lesson Applications

Exercise 11-23

Build a SmartArt list diagram. Insert a picture.

1. Create a new workbook and save it as *[your initials]*11-23.

2. From the SmartArt **List** pane, create a **Vertical Picture Accent List** shape.

3. Key **Kowabunga** on the first line in the Text pane. Key **KowOwow** on the second line, and **Shakes and Malts** on the third line. Close the Text pane.

NOTE

Use the Format Shape dialog box to insert clip art.

4. Click the top circle shape to the left of the text. The Insert Picture dialog box opens. Navigate to the appropriate folder and insert **Kowabunga**. Insert **KowOwowTrans** in the second circle shape.

5. Right-click the third circle shape and choose **Format Shape**. On the **Fill** pane, choose **Picture or texture fill**. Click **ClipArt**. If you have a broadband connection, select **Include content from Office Online**. Search for an image about "ice cream" and/or "milk." Use a clip that seems appropriate. Click the image and click **OK**. Click the frame of the main shape to deselect any circles.

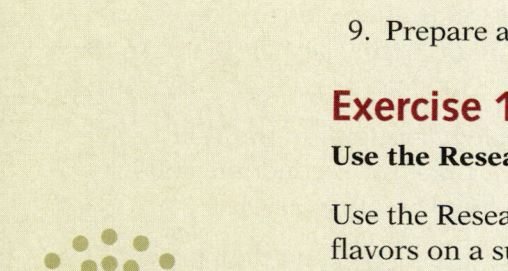

TIP

Use a corner handle to resize a shape horizontally and vertically at the same time.

6. On the **SmartArt Tools Design** tab, choose **Polished** and **Colorful Range – Accent Colors 2 to 3**.

7. Click a worksheet cell and insert a WordArt image using a color/style that will complement the SmartArt shape. Key **Klassy Kow Ice Cream**.

8. Position the WordArt so that it looks centered over the list shape. Size the WordArt for balance. Arrange both shapes so that they will appear centered on a portrait page.

9. Prepare and submit your work.

Exercise 11-24

Use the Research tool.

Use the Research task pane and other resources to change the names of the flavors on a supermarket order sheet from English to Spanish.

REVIEW

Hold down Alt and click the cell to open the Research task pane.

1. Open **SpanishOrderSheet** and save it as *[your initials]*11-24.

2. Look up **Vanilla** in cell A9 using the **Translation** tool with **Spanish (Spanish-International Sort)**. Key the Spanish spelling in cell A9.

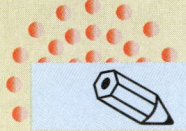

TIP

To insert a symbol, select the character in the formula bar or the cell and proceed as usual.

3. Repeat these steps to find a Spanish translation for each of the flavors. Use symbols if needed. Close the Research task pane.

4. Choose a different document theme for the order sheet. Then edit the document properties to show the name of the theme in the **Comments** area. Add your name as the **Author** and **Translated Sheet** as the **Title**.

5. Format the appropriate cells in row 3 with a bottom border that uses the second dotted style from the first column of line style choices in the Format Cells dialog box. Make row 3 **7.50 (10 pixels)** high.

6. Use a solid double-line bottom border for row 4 and make it the same height as row 3.

7. Create the same border arrangement for rows 25:26.

8. Prepare and submit your work.

Exercise 11-25

Create a hierarchy diagram.

The Hierarchy SmartArt pane includes charts that show relationships among people. Many of these graphics can be used to show relationships among events, activities, or ideas.

1. Create a new workbook and save it as *[your initials]*11-25.

2. Create a **Table Hierarchy** shape. There should be one top shape. Then add one shape before or after the two shapes on the second row, resulting in three shapes at the second level.

3. Key **Sales** in the top shape or the first line in the Text pane.

REVIEW

When you press [Enter] in the Text pane, a new shape at the same level is inserted.

4. In the leftmost shape on the second row, key **Campaigns**. In the middle shape, key **Locations**. In the rightmost shape, key **Products**.

5. Click the first line below **Locations** in the Text pane. Key **Geography**. Click the second line and key **Demographics**. Press [Enter] and key **Culture**.

6. Click after **Campaigns** in the Text pane. Press [Enter] and then press [Tab]. Key these three labels on the level below **Campaigns**.
   Timing
   Success Rate
   Cost

7. In three shapes below **Products**, key these labels:
   Appeal
   Cost Structure
   Portability

8. Choose a style and colors. Position the shape so that it starts at cell A1. Set landscape orientation and size the shape to fill the page.

9. Prepare and submit your work.

Exercise 11-26 ◆ Challenge Yourself

Link a picture of cells.

You can paste a "picture" of cells so that it acts like an image from a disk. A cell picture can be pasted or linked.

NOTE

A linked cell picture has fewer editable attributes than shapes. Use the Format Picture dialog box to add fill and border color.

1. Open **WeeklyData** and save it as *[your initials]***11-26**.

2. Insert a sheet and create a WordArt object that says **California Totals**. Position the WordArt so that it starts in cell A1. Name the sheet **Picture**.

3. Copy cells F4:F18 on the **WeeklySales** sheet. Click cell C10 on the **Picture** sheet. Click the arrow with the Paste button. Choose **As Picture** and then **Paste as Picture Link**. The linked cell picture is an object with selection handles.

4. Position the picture so that it is centered below the WordArt. Format the object to have a light fill color that complements your WordArt. Choose an appropriate line color, too.

5. Return to the **WeeklySales** sheet. Delete the weekly values (not totals) for two of the cities.

6. Prepare and submit your work.

On Your Own

In these exercises you work on your own, as you would in a real-life work environment. Use the skills you've learned to accomplish the task—and be creative.

Exercise 11-27

Open **SpanishOrderSheet** and use the Research tool to translate the flavors into another language for which the dictionary is installed on your computer. Save the workbook as *[your initials]***11-27**. Prepare and submit your work.

Exercise 11-28

Create a new workbook and save it as *[your initials]*11-28. Create a hierarchy shape that illustrates your ancestors and descendants (if appropriate). Format the shape according to your tastes. Prepare and submit your work.

Exercise 11-29

In a new workbook, create one each of the Matrix and Pyramid SmartArt shapes to illustrate a business or social concept or idea. Create the shape, add text, and style the diagram. Save your workbook as *[your initials]*11-29. Prepare and submit your work.

Unit 3 Applications

Unit Application 3-1

Create and format a combination chart.

Klassy Kow Ice Cream sells ice cream to supermarkets in cases that hold 6, 12, 18, or 24 half-gallon cartons. You have been asked to create a chart that plots the cost per case and the number of cartons per case.

NOTE

The markup is added to the cost to reach the selling price.

1. Open **ICCases** and save it as *[your initials]*u3-1 in a folder for Unit 3.

2. In cell C6, key a formula to determine the cost per case. Copy the formula and use Currency format.

3. In cell D6, key a formula to multiply the per-case cost by 1 plus the markup for the month. Copy the formula and use Currency format.

4. Use empty rows to create an attractive border arrangement for the worksheet. Insert/delete rows if necessary.

5. Use the labels and values in columns A, C, and D to create a clustered column chart on a separate sheet. As the chart title, key **Cost and Selling Price Comparison**. Choose a chart style.

6. Change the chart type for both currency values to a line chart with markers. Show the data labels for all three series.

7. Format the line and its markers and the column so that the chart is attractive and easy to interpret. Position the legend at the left.

8. Edit the document properties to show your name as the author.

9. Prepare and submit your work.

Unit Application 3-2

Insert WordArt. Insert a shape.

The Marketing Department tracks promotions and incentives to determine which are the best sales generators. You have been asked to create a worksheet that shows recent promotions and the resulting increase in sales.

TIP

Group the sheets and delete them at once.

1. Create a new workbook and save it as *[your initials]*u3-2. Delete **Sheet2** and **Sheet3**. Rename **Sheet1 Promotions**.

2. Key the information in Figure Unit3-1, starting in column B.

Figure Unit 3-1

	B	C
1	Promotions	Sales Increase
2	Guess gumballs	12%
3	Tip calculator	8%
4	10% Off	15%
5	Multiplication table	8%

> **NOTE**
>
> If you keyed the data starting in column A, move it to the right.

3. Make each row **52.50 (70 pixels)** tall.

4. Insert WordArt and key **Klassy Kow Ice Cream**. Rotate the shape 90° left and drag it to column A to fill the same space as the data rows.

5. Insert a rounded corner rectangle shape in columns D:F and key the following:

   These are company-wide averages. Individual shops experience various increases based on location, weather, and other factors.

6. Format the shape and the data with your own choices.

7. Prepare and submit your work.

Unit Application 3-3

Insert a SmartArt shape.

1. Create a new workbook and save it as *[your initials]*u3-3. Delete **Sheet2** and **Sheet3**. Rename **Sheet1 Radial**.

2. Insert a Radial Cycle shape. In the middle object, key **Increased Sales**.

3. Key additional text as follows:

Top shape	**Local promotion on radio and in newspapers.**
Left shape	**State-wide coupon campaign and free decal with purchase.**
Bottom shape	**Regional TV ads with free gift with purchase.**
Last shape	*[Key your own campaign idea for increasing sales.]*

4. Choose a style and colors. Position and size the shape to display well in landscape orientation.

5. Prepare and submit your work.

Unit Application 3-4 ◆ Using the Internet

Build a pie chart.

Search office supply and computer equipment Web sites to build a price list for six items in an office. You might include objects such as a desk, a chair, a bookcase, file cabinet(s), a computer, a monitor, or a printer. For each item, list the name and a price.

Build a pie chart that shows the proportion each item represents of the total cost for all six items. Use a main title for the chart that includes your name. You might need a legend, depending on your other design choices. Place the chart on a separate sheet. Save the workbook as *[your initials]*u3-4. Prepare and submit your work.

A Professional Approach

POWERPOINT 2007

Pat R. Graves

Amie Mayhall

There is more to learning a presentation graphics program like Microsoft Office PowerPoint 2007 than simply keying text on colored backgrounds and calling the result a presentation. You need to know how to use PowerPoint in a real-world situation. That's why all the lessons in this text relate to everyday business tasks. The text will show you how to create well-organized presentations that are designed effectively, too.

As you work through the lessons, imagine yourself working as an intern for Good 4 *U*, a fictional New York restaurant.

Good 4 *U* Restaurant

The Good 4 *U* restaurant has been in business for only a little more than three years, but it's been a success from the time it served its first veggie burger. The restaurant, which features healthy food and has as its theme the "everyday active life," seems to have found an award-winning recipe for success. (Figure CS-1 shows the interior of the largest dining room in the restaurant. It features plants and a wide expanse of windows looking out over Central Park South, a tree-lined avenue on the south side of New York's Central Park.)

Figure CS-1 Interior of Good 4 *U* restaurant and a sampling of the fresh food prepared daily

The food at Good 4 *U* is all low-fat. The menu features lots of vegetables (all organic, of course) as well as fish and chicken. The restaurant doesn't serve alcohol, instead offering fruit juices and sparkling water. Good 4 *U*'s theme of the "everyday active life" is reflected on the restaurant's walls with running, tennis, and bicycling memorabilia. This theme reflects the interests of the two co-owners: Julie Wolfe, who led the New York Flash to two Women's Professional Basketball Association championships in her 10 years with the team, and Gus Irvinelli, who is an avid tennis player and was selected for the U.S. amateur team. Even the chef, Michele Jenkins, leads an everyday active life—she rides her bicycle 10 miles a day in and around Central Park.

Two years ago, Roy Olafsen was a marketing manager for a large hotel chain. He was overweight and out of shape. In the same week that his doctor told him to eat better and exercise regularly, Roy received a job offer from Good 4 *U*. "It was too good to pass up," he said. "It was my chance to combine work and a healthy lifestyle." As you work through the text, you'll discover that Good 4 *U* is often involved in health-oriented as well as athletic events.

In your work as an intern at Good 4 *U* restaurant, you will meet many of the people who work at Good 4 *U* and will interact with the four key people shown in Figure CS-2. You will be doing most of your work for Roy Olafsen, the marketing manager.

All the presentations you will use and create in this course relate to the Good 4 *U* restaurant. As you work with the presentations in the text, note the following things:

- The types of presentations needed in a small business to carry on day-to-day business.
- The design of presentations. Real businesses must often focus on designing eye-catching, informative presentations for customers. The business's success often depends on developing attractive and compelling presentations that sell its services to customers.

Figure CS-2 Key employees

Julie Wolfe
Co-Owner

Gus Irvinelli
Co-Owner

Michele Jenkins
Head Chef

Roy Olafsen
Marketing Manager

As you use this text and become more experienced with Microsoft Office PowerPoint 2007, you will also gain experience in creating, editing, and designing the sort of presentations generated in a real-life business environment.

In your first meeting with Roy Olafsen, he gave you the following tips for designing presentations. These guidelines can be applied to any presentation.

Tips for Designing Presentations

- Prepare a distinctive title slide. Make sure the title identifies the presentation content.

- Maintain a consistent color scheme throughout the presentation for a sense of unity.

- Keep the background simple, and modify it to help create a unique theme for your presentation.

- Choose colors carefully so all text can be seen clearly. You must have a high contrast between background colors and text colors for easy reading.

- Write lists with parallel wording and be concise. Limit bulleted text to no more than seven words on a line and no more than seven lines on a slide.

- Avoid small text. Body text on slides, such as for bulleted lists, should be no smaller than 24 points. Text for annotations may be slightly smaller, but not less than 20 points. Establish a hierarchy for text sizes based on text importance and then use those sizes consistently.

- Think and design visually to express your message. Use graphics such as boxes, lines, circles, and other shapes to highlight text or to create SmartArt graphics that show process diagrams and relationships. Illustrate with pictures and clip art images.

- Select all images carefully to make your presentation content more understandable. They should not detract from the message. Avoid the temptation to "jazz up" a slide show with too much clip art.

- Keep charts simple. The most effective charts are pie charts with three or four slices and column charts with three or four columns. Label charts carefully for easy interpretation.

- Provide some form of handout so your audience can keep track of the presentation or make notes while you are talking.

- Include multimedia elements of animation, transitions, sound, and movies if these elements strengthen your message, engage your audience, aid understanding, or make your presentation more compelling.

- Your final slide should provide a recommendation or summary to help you conclude your presentation effectively.

unit 1

BASIC SKILLS

Lesson 1   Getting Started in PowerPoint   PP-6

Lesson 2   Developing Presentation Text   PP-36

Lesson 3   Revising Presentation Text   PP-76

Unit 1   APPLICATIONS   PP-110

Getting Started in PowerPoint

OBJECTIVES

After completing this lesson, you will be able to:

1. Explore PowerPoint.

2. View a presentation.

3. Add text using placeholders.

4. Name and save a presentation.

5. Prepare presentation supplements.

6. End your work session.

MCAS OBJECTIVES

In this lesson:
PP07 4.3.6
PP07 4.4.2
See Appendix

Estimated Time: 2 hours

PowerPoint is an easy-to-use presentation graphics program you can use to create professional-quality presentations. PowerPoint can be used in a variety of settings by people in many different career fields. For example, a day care worker may develop a presentation showing parents pictures of their children in all of the year's activities, or a minister may utilize PowerPoint to display notes on the sermon or song lyrics for the congregation. An instructor may use it for notes for a lecture to help students keep focused and their notes organized, or a hotelier may develop a presentation to help market the hotel at conferences and meetings. PowerPoint is also an effective tool for creating flyers and other printed products because of its versatile drawing and layout tools.

This lesson begins with an overview of many PowerPoint features and will help you become accustomed to the application window.

Exploring PowerPoint

If you are already familiar with other Microsoft Office 2007 programs, you'll feel right at home with PowerPoint. Although a number of new features appear in the PowerPoint window shown in Figure 1-1, it's easy to recognize similarities to Microsoft Word and Microsoft Excel.

TABLE 1-1 Main Parts of the PowerPoint Window

Part of Window	Purpose
Title bar	Contains the name of the presentation.
Quick Access toolbar	Located by default at the top of the PowerPoint window and provides quick access to commands that you use frequently.
Microsoft Office Button	Located in the upper left-hand corner and contains commands to open, save, print, and share your PowerPoint file with others.
Ribbon	Consists of task-oriented tabs with commands organized in groups.
Tabs	Task-oriented collections of commands. In addition to the standard tabs, there are other tabs which appear only when they are useful for the type of task you are currently performing.
Groups	Logical sets of related commands and options.
Command buttons	Buttons designed to perform a function or display a gallery of options.
Slide pane	The area where you create, edit, and display presentation slides.
Notes pane	The area where you can add presentation notes for the presenter.
Slides and Outline pane	The area that can display either an outline of the presentation's text or *thumbnails*—miniature pictures—of the presentation's slides. You choose either Outline or Slides by clicking the appropriate tab. (If this pane is not displayed, click the Normal view button.)
Scroll bars	Used with the pointer to move a slide or outline text right or left and up or down. You can also use the vertical scroll bar to move from slide to slide.
Status bar	Displays information about the presentation you are working on.
View buttons	Buttons used to switch between Normal view, Slide Sorter view, and Slide Show view.

Figure 1-1
Main features in
PowerPoint's Normal
view

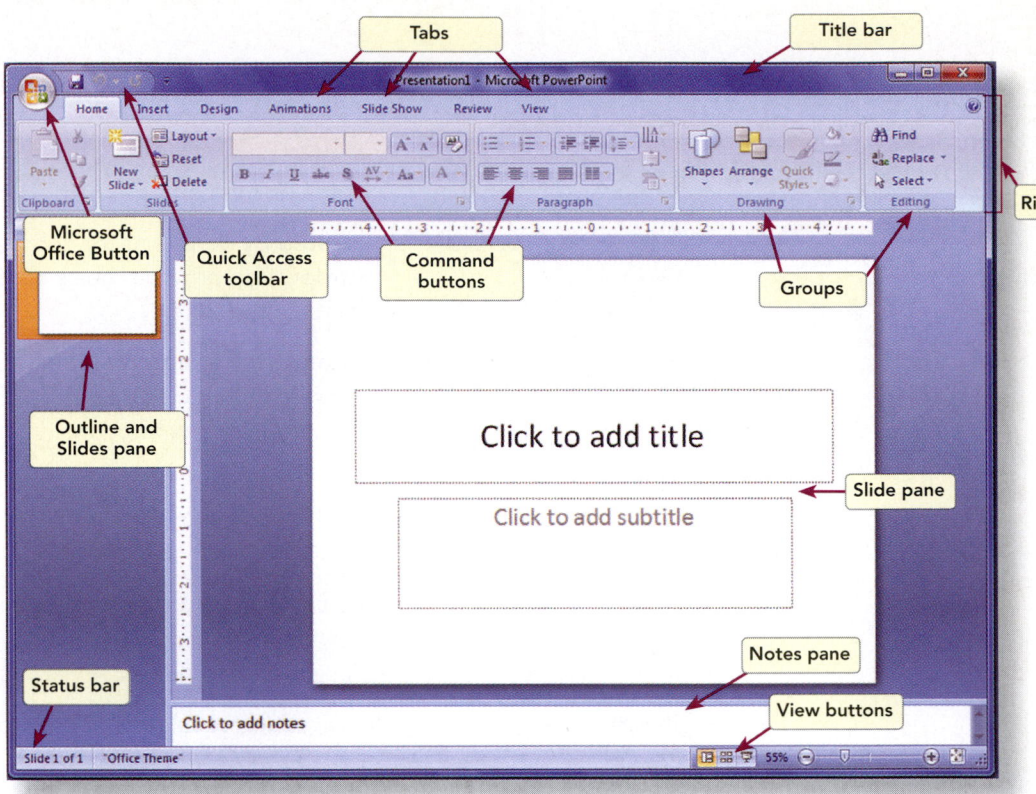

Exercise 1-1 IDENTIFY PARTS OF THE POWERPOINT WINDOW

The first step to becoming familiar with PowerPoint is to identify the parts of the window. The *Ribbon* contains seven task-oriented tabs: Home, Insert, Design, Animations, Slide Show, Review, and View. Commands are organized in logical groups with command buttons and other controls. ScreenTips will help you identify command buttons and other objects. A *ScreenTip* is the box displaying an object's name and sometimes a brief description that appears under a command button or other object when you point to it. Within the Ribbon groups are drop-down galleries that easily present formatting options, graphics choices, layouts, and more.

Figure 1-2
ScreenTip over the
Microsoft Office
Button

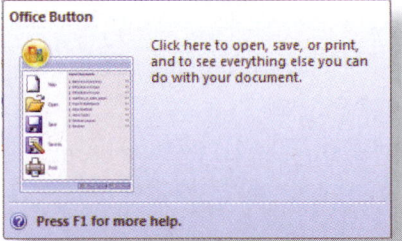

1. Using Figure 1-1 as a guide, move your pointer over items in the PowerPoint window to identify them by name using ScreenTips similar to Figure 1-2.

Exercise 1-2 USE THE QUICK ACCESS TOOLBAR

The *Quick Access toolbar* is a customizable toolbar containing a set of common commands that function independently of the tab that is currently displayed. This toolbar's default location is above the Ribbon. It can be moved under the Ribbon, but this location requires more space.

1. Click the drop-down arrow at the end of the Quick Access toolbar.

2. Choose **Show Below the Ribbon**.

3. Click the drop-down arrow again and choose **Show Above the Ribbon** to return to the default position.

Exercise 1-3 OPEN AN EXISTING PRESENTATION

When you first open PowerPoint, a new blank presentation automatically appears, ready for you to add text and graphics. However, in this exercise you open an existing PowerPoint presentation. The presentation was created for this lesson to give you an overview of many PowerPoint features.

1. Point to the Microsoft Office Button and click the left mouse button to open a menu.

2. Choose **Open**.

3. In the Open dialog box, navigate to the appropriate drive and folder for your student files according to your instructor's directions.

4. When you locate the student files, click the arrow next to the Views button  (see Figure 1-3) in the Open dialog box to display a menu of view options.

Figure 1-3
Folders listed in the Open dialog box

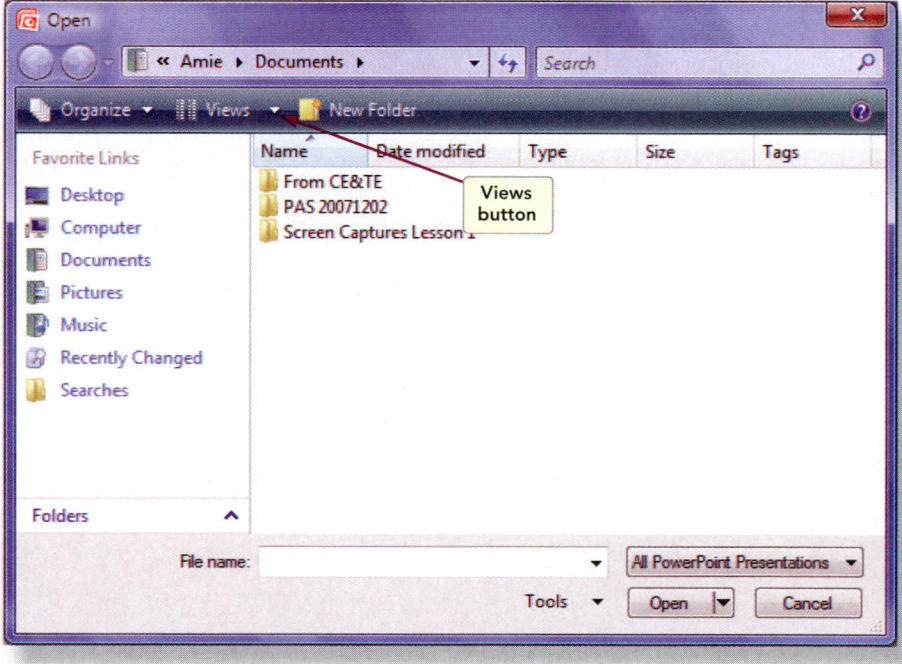

NOTE

Your instructor will advise you where to locate the files for this course. For more information about working with files, folders, and directories in Windows, refer to "File Management" at the Professional Approach Online Learning Center at **www.mhhe.com/pas07**.

5. Choose **Small Icons** to list all files by name.

6. Click the Views button  again and choose **Details** to see the type of file and the date when it was last modified.

7. Locate the file **ThreeYr1** (use the scroll bar if you need to) and click once to select the file.

8. Click **Open**. (You can also double-click the file's name to open it.) PowerPoint opens the file in Normal view.

NOTE

The presentations you create in this course relate to the case study at the front of this text about Good 4 U, a fictional restaurant.

Exercise 1-4   WORK WITH RIBBONS, TABS, GROUPS, AND COMMAND BUTTONS

PowerPoint organizes command buttons in a logical way. On the Ribbon, the tabs reflect tasks or activities you commonly perform and provide easy access to the commands. Within each tab, the commands are divided into related groups of buttons and other controls.

Live Preview is a feature that allows you to see exactly what your changes will look like before clicking or selecting an effect. Sometimes the available effects are presented in a *gallery* that displays thumbnails of different options you can choose.

1. Click the Insert tab on the Ribbon.

2. Identify each of the groups located on the Insert tab: Tables, Illustrations, Links, Text, and Media Clips.

3. These groups each contain command buttons that either provide options through dialog boxes or through galleries of options.

Exercise 1-5   USE MICROSOFT OFFICE POWERPOINT HELP

Microsoft Office provides a *Help* feature that is an excellent reference tool for reinforcing skills presented in a lesson and for finding more information on any PowerPoint feature. Each program in Microsoft Office has a separate Help window.

1. Click Microsoft Office PowerPoint Help button  located on the upper-right of the Ribbon or you can press F1. The Help window will appear on top of your open PowerPoint presentation.

NOTE

If you are connected to the Internet, Help will automatically open a browser and search your topic. If this happens, you will have to close the browser and the Help window.

2. Key **Ribbon** in the search box located on the help window, and then press ⌨Enter.

3. Scroll through the list of options that display and select **Use the Ribbon**.

4. Read and scroll through the entire Help window.

5. When you have finished, click the Close button in the upper-right corner of the Help window to close it and return to PowerPoint.

Viewing a Presentation

PowerPoint provides multiple views for working with your presentations. Using these various views, you can work in outline format, rearrange slides in *Slide Sorter view*, or work on an individual slide in the Slide pane of Normal view.

Exercise 1-6 USE NORMAL AND SLIDE SORTER VIEWS

The Normal view is the best for entering text directly on a slide and planning the design of your presentation. *Normal view* is the default view when you open PowerPoint. The *Slide Sorter view* presents a window of *slide thumbnails*, which are miniature versions of the slides. To rearrange slides, you can click on a thumbnail then hold down the left mouse button while you *drag* it to a new position. Slide Sorter view makes it easy to apply special slide-show effects.

1. From the View tab, in the Presentation Views group, choose the Slide Sorter button.

2. Click and drag slide 7 to place it before slide 6. You will be able to tell where your slide is when dragging by the vertical line that appears.

3. From the View tab, in the Presentation Views group, choose the Normal button to return to Normal view.

Exercise 1-7 USE THE SLIDES AND OUTLINE PANE

In Normal view, the *Slides and Outline pane* is at the left of the Slide pane. It provides some alternative ways to work with your presentation. The Outline tab shows only slide titles and listed text with *bullets*, small circular shapes, in front of each listing. The Outline tab allows you to enter just your text content as an outline without modifying the design or adding graphics to

Figure 1-4
Working with the Slides and Outline pane

Outline and Slides tabs

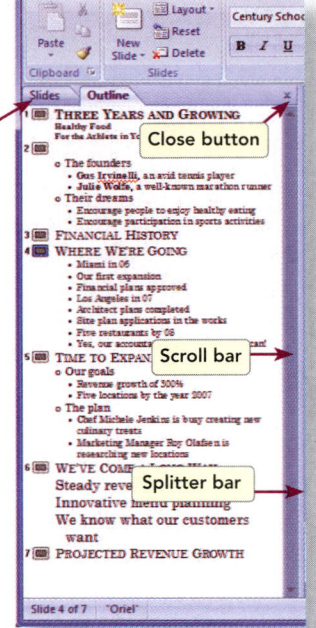

your slide. The Slides tab provides thumbnails similar to the slide sorter view.

1. Click the **Outline** tab at the top of the Slides and Outline pane. The Outline pane displays the presentation's text in an outline format.

2. Point to the right border of the Slides and Outline pane. When the splitter appears, drag the border about an inch to the right. This increases the size of the Slides and Outline pane.

3. Scroll in the outline text until you see the text for slide 4.

4. Working in the Outline tab, change each of the years (06, 07, and 08) to **2007, 2008**, and **2009**. The first line, for example, should read **Miami in 2007**. Notice that as you work, your changes are reflected in the Slide pane.

5. Click in front of Miami, then from the Home tab, in the Paragraph group, choose the Decrease List Level button to promote the item by moving it to the left. Apply this same treatment to Los Angeles in 2008 and Five Restaurants by 2009. This distinguishes the main items in the list from the more detailed items under them.

NOTE

When you have several bulleted lists, you can key them all in outline format if that's the way you like to work.

6. Click the Close button 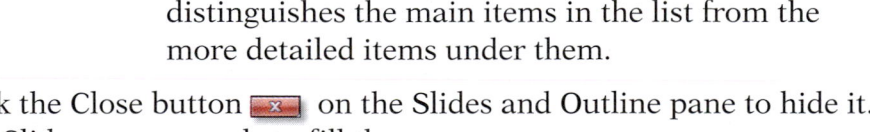 on the Slides and Outline pane to hide it. The Slide pane expands to fill the space.

7. From the View tab, in the Presentation Views group, choose the Normal view button . The Slides and Outline pane is displayed again.

8. Click the **Slides** tab at the top of the Slides and Outline pane. The Slides and Outline pane becomes smaller and the size of the Slide pane increases.

Exercise 1-8   MOVE FROM SLIDE TO SLIDE

PowerPoint provides several ways to move from slide to slide in a presentation:

• Use the pointer to drag the scroll box.

• Use the pointer to click the Previous slide ⬆ or Next slide ⬇ buttons.

• Use the ⎡PageUp⎤ and ⎡PageDown⎤ keys on the keyboard.

Figure 1-5
Moving from slide
to slide

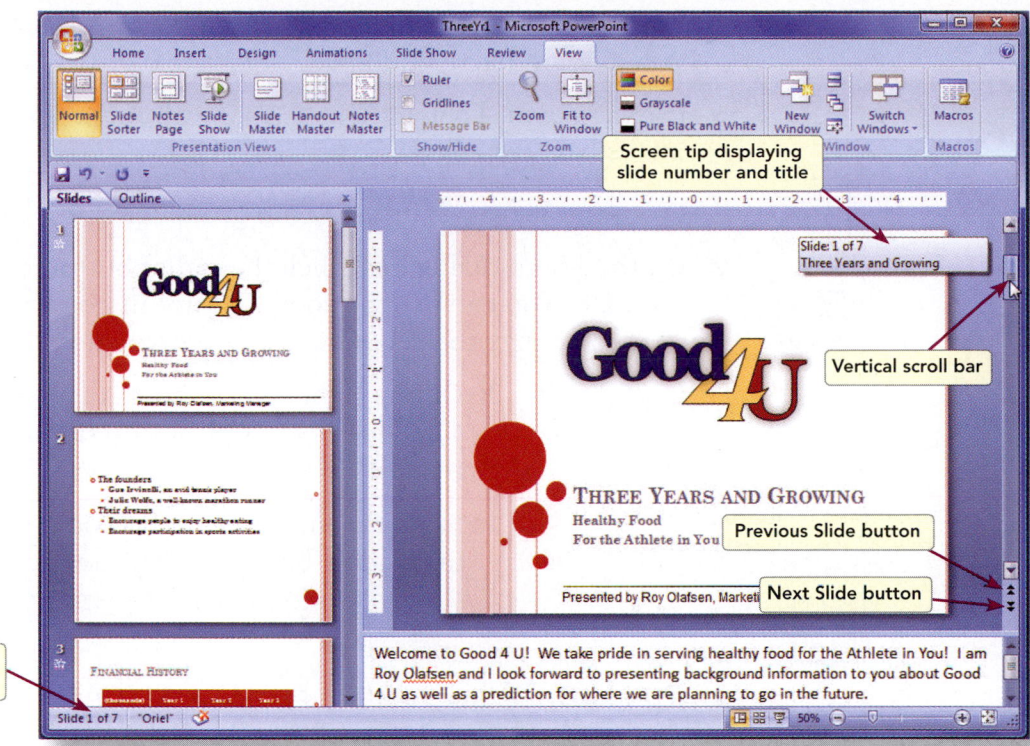

Slide number
indicator

1. Drag the vertical scroll box on the Slide pane to the bottom of the scroll bar. Notice the box that displays slide numbers and slide titles as you drag. When you release the mouse button at the bottom of the scroll bar, slide 7 appears in your window. Notice slide 7 has a highlighted border around it in the Slide pane. This identifies it as the current slide.

2. Drag the scroll box up to display slide 6. Notice that Slide 6 of 7 is indicated on the left side of the status bar.

 3. Click the Previous Slide button 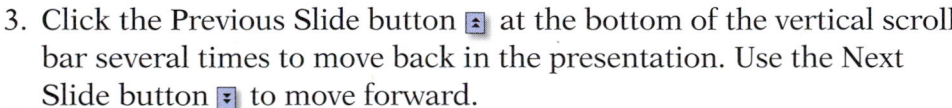 at the bottom of the vertical scroll bar several times to move back in the presentation. Use the Next Slide button 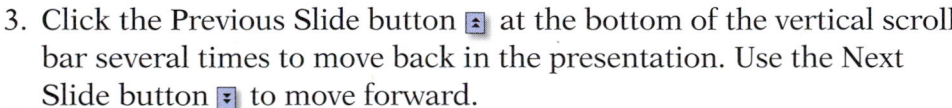 to move forward.

 4. As an alternative to clicking the Next Slide button 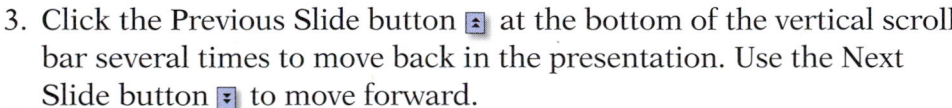 and the Previous Slide button 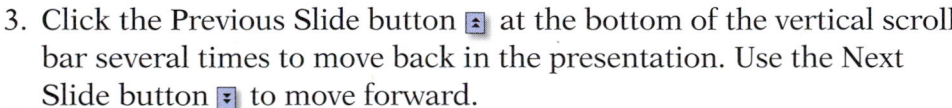, press ⌜PageDown⌟ and ⌜PageUp⌟ on your keyboard several times. Use this method to move to slide 2. Check the status bar for the slide number.

Exercise 1-9   USE THE ZOOM AND FIT TO WINDOW

PowerPoint provides two different ways to *zoom* and *fit to window*. Zoom is a great tool for magnifying your slide so you can see small details for precise alignment and corrections. The fit to window command will change from the current zoom settings to fit in the window that is open.

- From the View tab, in the Zoom group, choose the Zoom or Fit to Window command buttons.

- Use the Zoom slider and Fit to Window buttons on the right end of the status bar.

1. From the View tab, in the Zoom group, click the Zoom button  .

2. On the Zoom dialog box, click the radial button beside **200%** and click **OK**. You can use the zoom feature in normal or slide sorter view to change the percentage of what you are viewing.

3. On the right end of the status bar is a Zoom slider. Click the Zoom out button (a minus) until you reach **170%**.

> ✏️ **TIP**
>
> You can also click and drag the Zoom slider toward the minus to zoom out and toward the plus to zoom in.

4. From the View tab, in the Zoom group, choose the Fit to Window button . This reduces the size of your slide to be viewable in the window.

Exercise 1-10 RUN A SLIDE SHOW

A *slide show* displays slides sequentially in full-screen size. One way to start a slide show is to click the Slide Show command button. After you begin running a slide show, PowerPoint provides navigation tools to move from slide to slide. You may start a slide show from any slide by moving to the slide you wish to start on and clicking the Slide Show command button.

1. Move to slide 1 if it is not currently displayed. Click the Slide Show button located on the status bar to the left of the Zoom slider. The first slide in the presentation fills the screen.

> ✏️ **TIP**
>
> As an alternative to clicking the left mouse button, you can press the [Spacebar] to move forward. Also, you can press [N] which means "next" to move forward and [P] which means "previous" to move backward. You can also use the right and left arrow keys or [PageDown] and [PageUp] to move forward and backward.

2. Click the left mouse button to move to slide 2. The left mouse button is one of many ways to move forward in a slide presentation.

3. Press [N] on the keyboard to move to the next slide, slide 3.

Exercise 1-11 OBSERVE ANIMATION EFFECTS

Animation effects are the special visual or sound effects used as objects are displayed on the screen or removed from view. *Transition effects* are the effects seen in the process of changing between slides.

1. Press ⓝ again to move to slide 4, which is titled "Where We're Going."

2. Using the left mouse button, click anywhere to see a sample of a PowerPoint text animation. Click twice more to see the remaining text on this slide.

3. Press ⓝ again to move to slide 5. Notice the Box Out transition effect between slides 4 and 5.

4. Click the left mouse button two times to bring in the text from slide 5.

5. Press ⓝ to move to slide 6. Press ⓝ three more times to bring in the text for slide 6. Notice the Entrance and Emphasis effects placed on this text. If your sound is on, you should also hear sound effects with each text item.

6. Press ⓝ to move to slide 7 and ⓝ again to finish the presentation.

7. Press Esc or ⊟ (minus) to end the slide show.

Adding Text Using Placeholders

Adding and editing text in PowerPoint is very similar to editing text in a word processing program. You click an *I-beam* to position the *insertion point* where you want to key new text. An I-beam is a pointer in the shape of an uppercase "I." An insertion point is a vertical blinking bar indicating where the text you key will be placed. You can also drag the I-beam to select existing text. The keys Enter, Delete, and Backspace work the same way as in a word processing program.

It is important to understand that you *activate* a placeholder when you click the I-beam in it, making it ready to accept text.

Exercise 1-12   KEY PLACEHOLDER TEXT

Text on the slide is contained in text *placeholders*. Placeholders are used for *title text* (the text that usually appears at the top of a slide), *body text* (text in the body of a slide), and other objects, such as pictures. Placeholders help keep design layout and formatting consistent within a presentation.

Body text often contains *bullets* (small dots, squares, or other symbols) to indicate the beginning of each item in a list; therefore, this text is sometimes called bulleted text. Bullets can be decorative, also, for an attention-getting effect.

1. Move to slide 2, click in the Title Text Placeholder to activate the placeholder. Notice the box that surrounds the text. The border is made up of tiny dashed lines, and sizing handles indicates that the text box is activated and in edit mode, meaning you can edit and insert text.

NOTE

Notice that the pointer changes from an I-beam ⊤ inside the border to an arrow pointer ▸ outside the border. When the pointer rests on top of the border, it becomes a four-pointed arrow ✛, which can be used to move the text placeholder. When the pointer rests on top of a sizing handle, a two-pointed arrow appears.

2. Key the text **Where We Came From**.

3. Click anywhere on the line of text that begins "Gus Irvinelli."

4. Without clicking, move the pointer outside the border to the right and then back inside.

5. Drag the I-beam across the text "an avid" to select it as shown in Figure 1-6. (Click to the left of "an avid," hold down the left mouse button, drag the I-beam across the two words, and then release the mouse button.)

Figure 1-6
Selecting text to edit it

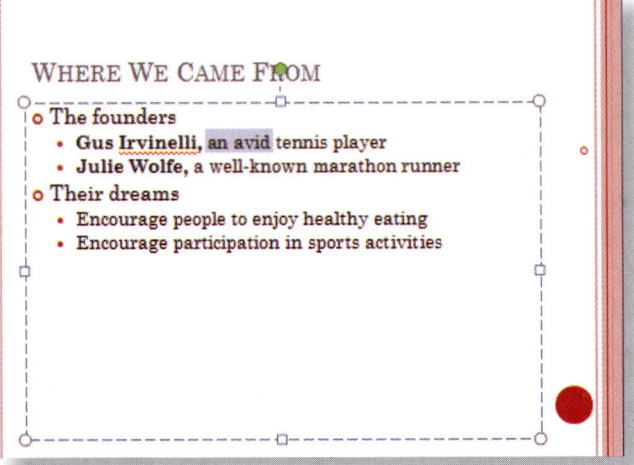

6. Key **a professional** to replace the selected text. (You don't need to delete selected text before keying new text.)

NOTE

Bulleted text lists the points being made in a slide presentation. This presentation uses open circle and solid dot bullets. Bullets can be changed to fit your presentation needs.

7. Click the I-beam to place the insertion point to the right of the words "healthy eating," near the bottom of the slide.

8. To insert a new line, press Enter. Notice that a new dimmed bullet appears at the beginning of the new line.

9. Key **Make their financial investment grow** on the new blank bullet line.

10. Click a blank part of the slide area to deactivate the text box. To make sure you are clicking a blank area, click when the pointer is a simple arrow, not an I-beam or a four-pointed arrow.

Exercise 1-13   **CHANGE AND RESET PLACEHOLDER LAYOUT**

Placeholders can be moved, resized, and rearranged on your slide. The layout feature of PowerPoint can be used to choose different layouts or reset the placeholder back to the original.

1. Still working on slide 2, click in the title placeholder to activate it.

2. Move your pointer to the outer border of the title placeholder.

3. When your pointer turns to a four-pointed arrow ⊕ (see Figure 1-7), click and drag the title placeholder to the bottom of the slide.

Figure 1-7
Selecting a placeholder

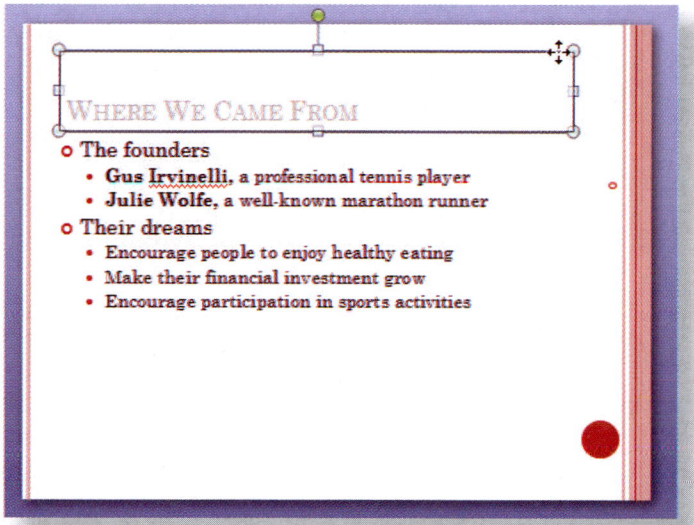

4. From the Home tab, in the Slides group, click the Layout command button 🗔, and choose the **Title and Content Layout** to reposition the placeholders to their original position.

Naming and Saving a Presentation

In PowerPoint, presentations are saved as files. When you create a new presentation or make changes to an existing one, you must save the presentation to make your changes permanent. Until your changes are saved, they can be lost if there's a power failure or a computer problem.

The first step in saving a document is to give it a *filename*. Filenames can be up to 255 characters long.

Throughout the exercises in this book, your document filenames will consist of two parts:

• The number of the exercise, such as **1-15**.

• **Your initials**, which might be your initials or an identifier your instructor asks you to use, such as **rst**.

When you're working with an existing file, choosing the **Save** command (or clicking the Save button on the Quick Access toolbar) replaces the file with the file on which you're working. After saving, the old version of the file no longer exists and the new version contains all your changes.

You can give an existing presentation a new name by using the **Save As** command. The original presentation remains unchanged and a second presentation with a new name is saved as well.

Exercise 1-14 CREATE A FOLDER FOR SAVING YOUR FILES

> **NOTE**
>
> Your instructor will advise you of the proper drive or folder to use when creating your lesson folders.

Before saving a file, you need to decide where you want to save it: in a folder on your fixed disk drive, on a jump drive, floppy disk or other removable medium, or on a network drive.

When you save a file, it's a good idea to create separate folders for specific categories to help keep your work organized. For example, you might want to create folders for different projects or different customers. In this course, you will follow these steps to create a new folder for each lesson's work before you begin the lesson.

1. Click the Microsoft Office Button , choose **Save As** then **PowerPoint Presentation**. The Save As dialog box appears.

> **NOTE**
>
> Even though you clicked Cancel to close the Save As dialog box, your new folder has been created. You could have saved your presentation before closing the Save As dialog box, but you will do that in the next exercise instead.

2. Using the list box at the top or links on the left, follow your instructor's directions to navigate to the location where you should create your folder. If you will be using a jump drive or other media, put it in your computer's drive now.

3. Click the Create New Folder button  on the Save As dialog box toolbar as shown in Figure 1-8.

Figure 1-8
Creating a new folder in the Save As dialog box

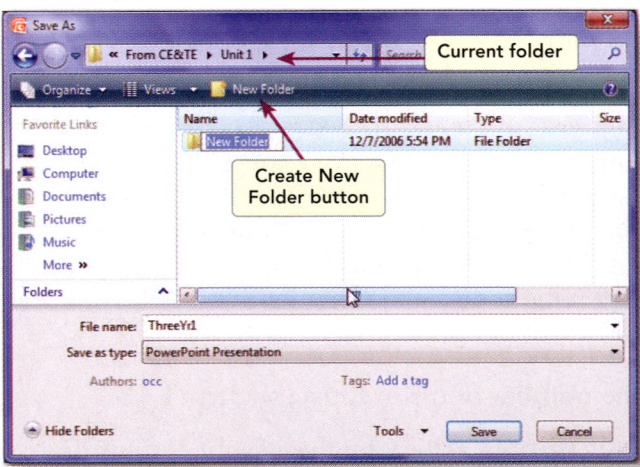

4. With the words New Folder selected, key **Lesson 1** and click off of the folder. A yellow folder icon with the name "Lesson 1" appears.

5. Click **Cancel** to close the Save As dialog box.

Exercise 1-15   NAME AND SAVE A PRESENTATION

To name files, you can use uppercase letters, lowercase letters, or a combination of both. Filenames can also include spaces. For example, you can use "Good 4 U Sales Report" as a filename.

1. Click the Microsoft Office Button 📀, choose **Save As** to reopen the Save As dialog box.

2. Navigate to the drive and folder where you created your new Lesson 1 folder.

3. Double-click the **Lesson 1** folder to open it.

4. In the **File name** text box, key **[1-15your initials]**.

5. Click **Save**. Your document is saved and named for future use. Notice that the title bar displays the new filename.

Preparing Presentation Supplements

Although the primary way of viewing a presentation is usually as a slide show, you can also print PowerPoint slides, just as you print Word documents or Excel worksheets. PowerPoint provides a variety of print options, including printing each slide on a separate page or printing several slides on the same page. You should utilize the PowerPoint Print Preview option when preparing to print.

Throughout this course, to conserve paper and speed up printing, you usually print a *handout* instead of full-size slides. A handout contains several scaled-down slide images on each page (one, two, three, four, six, or nine to a page) and is often given to an audience during a presentation.

Exercise 1-16   PREVIEW A PRESENTATION

The PowerPoint *Print Preview* feature lets you see what your printed pages will look like before you actually print them. You can view preview pages in black and white, grayscale, or color.

1. Click the Microsoft Office Button 📀.

2. Point to the arrow next to **Print**.

3. Click **Print Preview**. The Preview window opens, showing you how the printed slide will appear on paper. The Print Preview Ribbon (see Figure 1-9) is displayed at the top of the window.

Figure 1-9
Print Preview Ribbon

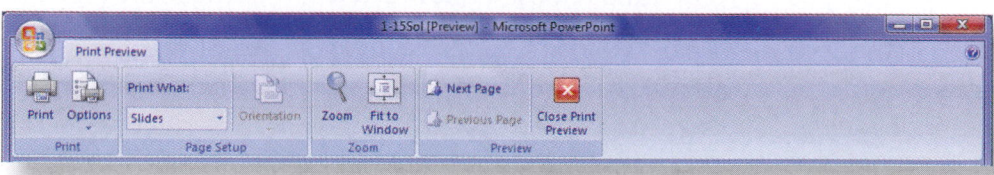

TABLE 1-2 Print Preview Ribbon Buttons

Toolbar Button	Name	Purpose
	Print	Open the Print dialog box.
	Options	Choose from a variety of options and preview them before printing.
	Print what	Choose between printing slides, handouts, notes pages, or an outline.
	Orientation	Switch the pages between portrait (vertical) and landscape (horizontal) layouts.
	Zoom	Change the magnification in the Preview window.
	Fit to window	Zoom the presentation so that the slide fills the window.
	Next page	Display the next page to be printed.
	Previous page	Display the previous page to be printed.
	Close Print Preview	Close the Print Preview window and return to Normal view.

4. From the Print Preview tab, in the Preview group, click the Next Page button. Page 2 of the printout is displayed.

5. Move your pointer to the middle of the slide. Notice that the pointer is in the shape of a magnifying glass.

6. Click the magnifying glass pointer in the center of the slide. The display is magnified.

7. Click again. The display returns to its regular size.

8. Click the Close the Print Preview window button.

Exercise 1-17   **PRINT A SLIDE, NOTES PAGE, OUTLINE, AND HANDOUT**

You can start the printing process in one of the following ways:

- Click the Microsoft Office Button, point to the arrow next to **Print**, and choose **Print Preview**. From the Print Preview Ribbon, in the Print group, click the Print button.

- Click the Microsoft Office Button, and choose **Print**.

- Press Ctrl+P.

- From the Quick Access toolbar, click the Quick Print button 🖨.

The first method opens the Print Preview window, which you learned in Exercise 1-16. The next two methods open the Print dialog box, where you can choose printing options. The last method, Quick Print 🖨, should be used with caution. You must first customize the Quick Access Toolbar to make the button available. This feature prints a presentation with the most recently used print options and does not open the print options dialog box. Usually this will result in printing your entire presentation with one slide on a page.

Printing an outline view is a nice feature if you want to print text only and avoid the slide thumbnails. Printing notes pages allows the speaker to record notes and print them along with an image of the slide. Printing several slides on a single page is a handy way to review your work and to create audience handouts. It's also a convenient way to print class assignments. You can create handouts in the Print Preview window or in the Print dialog box.

1. To print the first slide in your presentation, display slide 1, click the Microsoft Office Button 🔵, and then choose **Print**. The Print dialog box displays PowerPoint's default settings and indicates the designated printer as shown in Figure 1-10.

Figure 1-10
Print dialog box

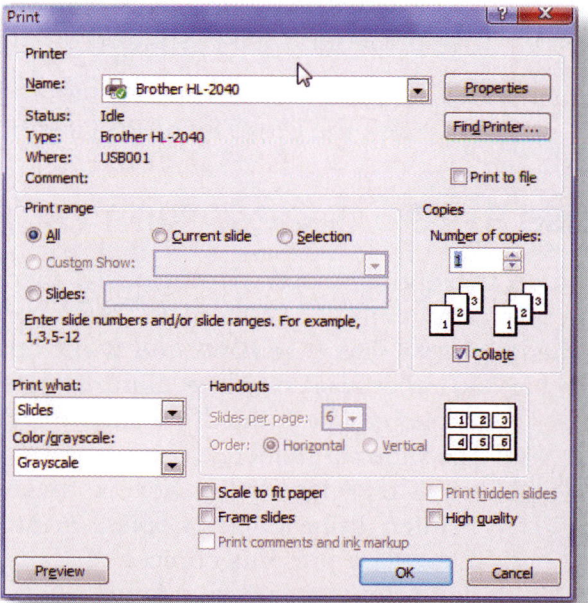

2. At the top of the Print dialog box, click the down arrow in the **Name** box. This is where you choose another printer, if one is available. Follow your instructor's directions to choose an appropriate printer from the list.

3. In the **Print range** option box, choose **Current Slide**.

NOTE

The information below the Name box applies to the selected printer. For example, "Status" indicates if the printer is idle or currently printing other documents.

> **TIP**
>
> You can create a presentation that uses overhead transparencies by printing your slides on transparency film. Before printing, insert transparency sheets directly into your printer (choosing the correct type of transparency for a laser or ink-jet printer).

> **TIP**
>
> If two slides are not displayed in the Print Preview screen, click the **Print** button, and under **Print range**, choose **All**. In the **Print what** drop-down list, choose **Handouts**. Then, under the **Handouts** heading, choose **2** from the drop-down list. Last of all, click **Preview** to return to **Print Preview**. This reverses the action where you chose Current Slide.

4. From the **Print what** drop-down list box, choose **Slides**.

5. Click **OK** to start printing.

6. Click the Microsoft Office Button 🔘, point to the arrow next to **Print**, and choose **Print Preview**. From the Print Preview tab, in the Page Setup group, click the arrow next to the **Print what** list box and then choose **Handouts (2 Slides per page)**. Two slides are displayed on the preview page. This is what would print if you chose to print at this point.

7. Still working in the Page Setup group, click the Orientation button 📄 and choose **Landscape**.

8. Open the **Print what** list box and then choose **Outline View** (this provides text only).

9. Open the **Print what** list box and then choose **Notes Pages** (this provides a snapshot of the slide as well as speaker notes).

10. Open the **Print what** list box again and choose **Handouts (9 Slides per page)**. Now the entire presentation is displayed on one page.

11. From the Print Preview tab, in the Preview group, click the Close Print Preview button ❌.

Exercise 1-18   CHOOSE PRINT OPTIONS

In addition to the options covered previously, there are two options for printing in black and white. The *Grayscale* option converts the presentation colors to shades of gray. The *Pure Black and White* option converts all colors to either black or white, eliminating shades of gray. Multiple copies can be printed, too, and the *Collate* option will print the slides in sequence.

The Print dialog box is divided into several areas: Printer, Print range, Copies, Print what, and Handouts. Each area presents choices that let you print exactly what you want in a variety of layouts.

> **NOTE**
>
> Because the Pure Black and White option simplifies your presentation graphics, it can sometimes speed up printing time.

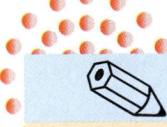

> **TIP**
>
> To print consecutive slides, you can use a hyphen. For example, key **2-4** to print slides 2 through 4. To print a combination of slides, you can key the range **1,3, 5-9, 12** to print slides 1, 3, 5 through 9, and 12.

1. Still working in **1-15your initials**, click the Microsoft Office Button 🔘 and choose **Print** to open the Print dialog box.

2. Under **Print range**, click **Slides** and key **1,2** in the text box to print only slides 1 and 2.

3. Under **Copies**, in the **Number of copies** box, key **2**. The **Collate** check box is selected by default to print the slide show from beginning to end two times.

4. From the **Print what** drop-down list box, choose **Notes Pages**.

5. If you have a black-and-white printer, choose **Grayscale** from the **Color/grayscale** list box. If you have a color printer, you can choose Color from the list box but the grayscale will conserve your colored ink/toner.

6. Click the **Scale to fit paper** check box to expand items to the full width of the page.

7. Click **OK.**

8. Open the Print dialog box again and set the following options:

   - For **Print range**, choose **All** to print all slides.

   - For **Number of copies**, key **1**.

   - In the **Print what** list box, choose **Handouts**.

   - Under **Handouts**, choose **3 Slides per page**.

   - From the **Color/grayscale** list box, choose **Pure Black and White**.

   - Click the **Frame slides** check box if it is not already checked.

9. Click **OK** to print the presentation handout and close the Print dialog box.

10. Click the Microsoft Office Button , and choose **Save As**.

> **NOTE**
>
> You are still on landscape orientation since you set that in a previous exercise.

11. In the **File name** text box, key **[1-18your initials]**.

12. Click **Save**. Your document is saved and named for future use. Notice that the title bar displays the new filename.

Ending Your Work Session

After you finish working on a presentation and save it, you can close it and open another file or you can exit the program.

To close a presentation and exit PowerPoint, you can:

- Click the Microsoft Office Button and choose **Close** or **Exit PowerPoint**.

- Use keyboard shortcuts. Ctrl+W closes a presentation and Alt+F4 exits PowerPoint.

- Use the Close button in the upper-right corner of the window.

Exercise 1-19   CLOSE A PRESENTATION AND EXIT POWERPOINT

1. Click the Microsoft Office Button .

2. Choose **Close** to exit the presentation.

3. Click the Close button in the upper-right corner of the window to exit PowerPoint.

Lesson 1 Summary

- Microsoft PowerPoint is a powerful graphics program used to create professional-quality presentations for a variety of settings.

- Identify items in the PowerPoint window by pointing to them and waiting for their ScreenTips to appear.

- PowerPoint command buttons are arranged in groups that can be accessed by clicking tabs on the Ribbon.

- The Quick Access toolbar contains a set of commands independent of the tab that is currently displayed. The toolbar includes commonly used commands such as save, undo, redo, and print.

- PowerPoint Help window is a great place to look for additional information on a topic or steps to completing a task.

- Key and edit text on a slide in the same way as you would in a word processing program.

- Use the Slide Show button to run a slide show. A slide show always starts with the slide that is currently selected.

- To print handouts that contain more than one slide on a page, use the Print dialog box or Print Preview window to select from the **Print what** options.

- Printing options provide a variety of ways to print your presentation: as slides, handouts, notes pages, and outline view.

LESSON 1		Command Summary	
Feature	**Button**	**Ribbon**	**Keyboard**
Open a presentation		Microsoft Office Button, Open	Ctrl + O
Display Slides and Outline pane		View tab, Presentation Views group, Normal	
Zoom		View tab, Zoom group, Zoom	
Help		Help button	F1
Normal view		View tab, Presentation Views group, Normal	
Slide Sorter view		View tab, Presentation Views group, Slide Sorter	
Next Slide			PageDown
Previous Slide			PageUp
Slide Show		View tab, Presentation Views group, Slide Show	F5
Save		Microsoft Office Button, Save; Quick Access toolbar, Save button	Ctrl + S
Save with a different name		Microsoft Office Button, Save As	
Next Slide (Slide Show view)		Right-click, Next	N , PageDown
Previous Slide (Slide Show view)		Right-click, Previous	P , PageUp , Backspace
End a slide show		Right-click, End Show	Esc or −
Layout		Home tab, Slides group, Layout	
Print Preview		Microsoft Office Button, Print arrow, Print Preview	
Print		Microsoft Office Button, Print; Quick Access toolbar, Quick Print button	Ctrl + P
Close a presentation		Microsoft Office Button, Close	Ctrl + W or Ctrl + F4
Exit PowerPoint	X Exit PowerPoint	Microsoft Office Button, Exit PowerPoint	Alt + F4

Concepts Review

True/False Questions

Each of the following statements is either true or false. Select your choice by indicating T or F.

T   F   1. When you start PowerPoint, it automatically displays a blank presentation.

T   F   2. Editing text in PowerPoint is similar to editing text in a word processing program.

T   F   3. ScreenTips identify command buttons by name only.

T   F   4. In the Slides and Outline pane, you can display either slide thumbnails or outline text, but not both at the same time.

T   F   5. You can edit text in Normal view or in the Outline tab.

T   F   6. You can display multiple slides as thumbnails in Slide Sorter view.

T   F   7. When viewing a slide show, pressing the plus sign moves to the next slide.

T   F   8. If you choose the Quick Print button 🖶 on the Quick Access toolbar, you can choose exactly which items to print.

Short Answer Questions

Write the correct answer in the space provided.

1. Where on the PowerPoint window are the View buttons located?

_____

2. What are the names of the three View buttons?

_____

3. If the Slides and Outline pane is not displayed, what button can you click to make it appear?

_____

4. What shape is the pointer when you move it over a text box?

_____

5. How would you save a copy of your presentation under a different filename?

_____

6. Name all the ways to use the keyboard for moving to the previous slide during a slide show.

_____

7. Which keys can you press to stop a slide show?

_____

8. What is the maximum number of slides you can print on a handout page?

_____

Critical Thinking

Answer these questions on a separate page. There are no right or wrong answers. Support your answers with examples from your own experience, if possible.

1. In this lesson you learned how to display slide thumbnails in the Slides and Outline pane and also in Slide Sorter view. Which way do you prefer to view thumbnails and why? What advantages and disadvantages do you think there are for each option?

2. You can produce slide shows, printouts, 35 mm slides, overhead transparencies, and other presentation media with PowerPoint. Why might you choose one medium over another? What factors would influence your decision?

Skills Review

Exercise 1-20

Open a file, identify parts of the PowerPoint window, key and edit text, and save as a new file.

1. Open a presentation by following these steps:
   a. Click the Microsoft Office Button 🔘.
   b. Choose Open.
   c. Choose the appropriate drive and folder, according to your instructor's directions.
   d. Double-click the file **Answers**.
2. Click anywhere on the text "Click to add subtitle" and key **your name**.
3. Select the two question marks in the text "Exercise 1-??" by dragging the I-beam across them. Key **20**.
4. To move to slide 2, click the Next Slide button 🔽 at the bottom of the vertical scroll bar.

5. Key the answers to the questions on slide 2 by following these steps:

   a. Click to position the insertion point after the word "Answer:" and press ⎡Spacebar⎤.

   b. Key the **answer**.

   c. Click after each of the words "Answer" and key the **answers to the next three questions**. Explore PowerPoint and remember to use your ScreenTips to help you answer the questions.

6. Save the presentation as **[1-20your initials]** in your Lesson 1 folder by following these steps:

   a. Click the Microsoft Office Button, choose **Save As** to open the Save As dialog box.

   b. Choose your Lesson 1 folder from the appropriate drive and folder, following your instructor's directions.

   c. Key the filename **[1-20your initials]** in the **File name** text box.

   d. Click **Save**.

Exercise 1-21

Edit text on a slide, save a presentation, run a slide show, preview and print a presentation, and end your work session.

1. Open the file **GoodFood**.

2. Notice on the status bar and by viewing the thumbnails in the Slides and Outline pane that this is a three-slide presentation (slide 1 of 3 now appears). Move to slide 3 by dragging the vertical scroll box.

3. Make corrections to the slide's text as shown in Figure 1-11.

Figure 1-11

```
Just Sweet Enough

     Carob Pecan Yogurt Cream Pie
                            s                      a
This light and fluffy desert has an all-natural grahm cracker crust,

great flavor, and very little sugar.

     Key Lime Soufflé
    intense                      chef
The striking lime flavor is Michelle's secret. Made from organic key

limes, sweetened with white grape juice, and thickened with organic egg

whites.
```

4. Move to slide 2, and notice that two items show the name of a dish and two items show the descriptions. The descriptions should be indented to distinguish them from the name of each dish; therefore, place your insertion point before each description and press Tab to indent those lines.

5. Run the presentation as a slide show by following these steps:

   a. Display slide 1. Click the Slide Show button on the status bar.

   b. After slide 1 appears, click the left mouse button to advance to the next slide.

   c. Click the left mouse button three more times to return to Normal view.

6. Save the presentation as **[1-21your initials]** in your Lesson 1 folder.

7. Print slides 1 and 3 only by following these steps:

   a. Click the Microsoft Office Button.

   b. Choose **Print** to open the Print dialog box.

   c. In the **Print range** area, click **Slides** and key **1,3** in the text box.

   d. From the **Print what** drop-down list, choose **Slides**. Choose **Grayscale**, and click **OK**.

8. Close the presentation by clicking the Close button in the upper-right corner of the PowerPoint window.

Exercise 1-22

Work with views, edit text, run a slide show, save a presentation, preview and print a presentation, and close a presentation.

1. Open the file **DressCd1**.

2. View the presentation's text in outline format by following these steps:

   a. If the Slides and Outline pane is not displayed, click the Normal view button.

   b. Click the Outline tab.

   c. Point to the Outline pane's right vertical border.

   d. When you see the splitter bar, drag it to the right to the center of the screen to see the text on these slides. Move the splitter bar back to its original position.

3. Click the Slide Sorter view button to view the presentation in Slide Sorter view.

4. Double-click slide 1 in Slide Sorter view to change back to Normal view.

5. Create a subtitle on slide 1 by following these steps:

   a. Click the text placeholder containing the text "Click to add subtitle."

   b. Key **your name**.

   c. Press Enter to start a new line; then key **today's date**.

6. Run a slide show and navigate within the show by following these steps:

    a. Click the Slide Show button 🖵 on the status bar.

    b. Advance through the slides by pressing PageDown several times.

7. Save the presentation as **[1-22your initials]**.

8. Preview the presentation before printing by following these steps:

    a. Click the Microsoft Office Button 📄, point to the arrow beside **Print**, and choose **Print Preview**.

    b. In the **Print what** drop-down list, choose **Handouts (4 slides per page)**.

    c. In the **Options** drop-down list box, point to **Color/Grayscale** and then choose **Grayscale**.

    d. In the **Options** drop-down list box, be sure there is a check beside **Frame Slides**. If it is not checked, click **Frame Slides**.

    e. Click the **Print** button 🖶.

    f. Click **OK**.

9. Click Close Print Preview 🗙 to close the Print Preview window and then close the presentation.

Exercise 1-23

Key text on a slide, save the file, and print.

1. Open the file **SpEvent1**.

2. Display slide 2.

3. Insert a new line of bulleted text by following these steps:

    a. Click the I-beam to the right of the word "team" at the end of the line "National In-Line Skate demo team."

    b. Press Enter to start a new line with an automatic bullet.

    c. Key **Autograph session with Marsha Miles**.

4. Edit the text you keyed by following these steps:

    a. Click the I-beam between the words "with" and "Marsha" to position the insertion point.

    b. Key **aerobic video star** and insert any necessary spaces.

5. Save the presentation as **[1-23your initials]** in your Lesson 1 folder.

6. Print the slides full size by following these steps:

    a. Click the Microsoft Office Button 📄.

    b. Choose **Print** to open the Print dialog box.

    c. In the **Print what** drop-down list box, choose **Slides**.

    d. In the **Color/Grayscale** drop-down list box, choose **Grayscale**.

    e. Click **Preview**.

    f. Click the Next Page button 🔽 to preview slide 2.

    g. Click the Print button 🖶 and then click **OK**.

    h. Click the Close Print Preview button 🗙 to close the Preview window.

7. Close the presentation by clicking the Close button 🗙.

Lesson Applications

Exercise 1-24

Edit text, change presentation views, save, print, and close a presentation.

1. Open the file **Party1**.

2. Using the Slide pane, make the changes to slides 2 and 3 as shown in Figure 1-12.

Figure 1-12

Entertainment

Slide 2

- Audition bands
    o Charlie's Dingbats
    o The Electrolytes
    o ~~Wired Rabbits~~ Pure Power
- Contact Marsha Miles
    o Is she willing to lead dance-style aerobics?
    o Is she available New Year's Eve?

Menu

Slide 3

- Michele needs suggestions by November 1
- Staff tasting party to be held December 25
- Menu printing deadline is December 10

3. Save the presentation as **[1-24your initials]**.

4. View each slide in the presentation as a slide show.

5. Preview the presentation as handouts, three slides per page, grayscale, framed, and then print it.

6. Close print preview and then close the presentation.

Exercise 1-25

Edit text, run a slide show, save, print, and close a presentation.

1. Open the file **JulyFun1**.

2. Move to slide 2. Working in the Slide pane, change "am" in the first and second bullets to **a.m.**, and change the date in the last bullet to **June 25**.

3. Click the Outline tab and drag the Outline pane's right border to make it wider.

4. Working on slide 3 in the outline area, change the age in the second bullet from "21" to **18**. Save the presentation as **[1-25your initials]**.

5. Click the Slides tab and display slide 1. Run a slide show of the presentation, clicking to display each new slide and text animation.

6. Preview and then print the presentation as handouts, six slides per page, grayscale, framed.

7. Close the presentation.

Exercise 1-26

Edit text, change presentation views, save, print, and close a presentation.

1. Open the file **DressCd2**.

2. On slide 1, key the word **Personnel** to the left of "Training" so the title reads "Personnel Training Session."

3. Locate the last line of text on slide 2 (which begins "Under no circumstances"). Position the insertion point at the end of that line and key **while on the job**.

4. Locate the last line of text on slide 3. Position the insertion point between "Good 4 U" and "test" and key **proficiency** (the phrase should read "Good 4 U proficiency test").

5. Click the Outline tab and make the Outline pane wide enough to work comfortably. Scroll down to display the outline text for slide 4.

6. Working on slide 4 in the Outline pane, delete the periods at the ends of the two sentences that begin "Guests."

7. Below the third bullet, change "Shirts are" to **T-shirts will be**.

8. Save the presentation as **[1-26your initials]**.

9. Preview and then print the presentation as handouts, four slides per page, grayscale, framed.

10. Close the presentation.

Exercise 1-27 ◆ Challenge Yourself

Edit text, print a slide and handouts, and close a presentation.

1. Open the file **RacePrep**.

2. Using whichever view you choose, edit slide 2 and slide 3 as shown in Figure 1-13.

Figure 1-13

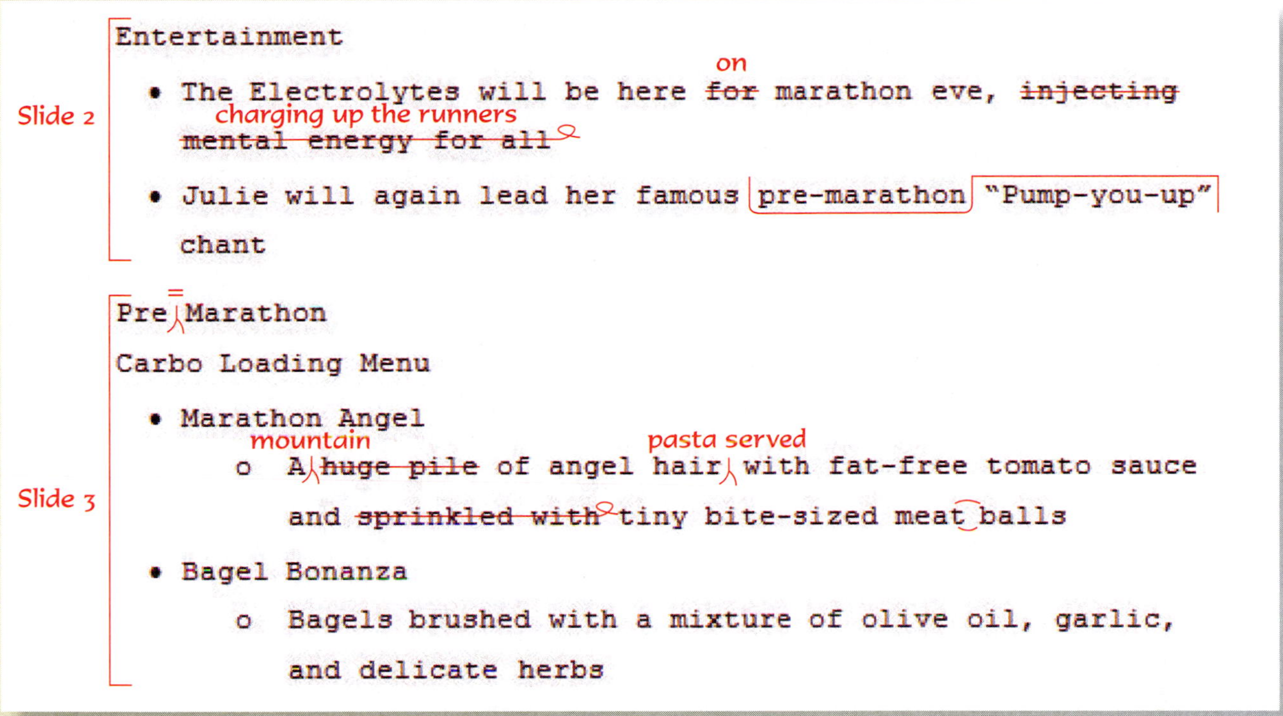

Entertainment

Slide 2
- The Electrolytes will be here ~~for~~ marathon eve, ~~injecting~~ (on) charging up the runners ~~mental energy for all~~

- Julie will again lead her famous pre-marathon "Pump-you-up" chant

Pre Marathon

Carbo Loading Menu

Slide 3
- Marathon Angel
  - A ~~huge pile~~ (mountain) of angel hair with fat-free tomato sauce (pasta served) and ~~sprinkled with~~ tiny bite-sized meat balls

- Bagel Bonanza
  - Bagels brushed with a mixture of olive oil, garlic, and delicate herbs

3. Save the presentation in your Lesson 1 folder as **[1-27your initials]**.

4. View the presentation in Slide Sorter view.

5. Run the presentation as a slide show, beginning with slide 1.

6. Preview and then print all slides in grayscale, framed.

7. Print the presentation as handouts, three slides per page, grayscale, framed.

8. Close print preview and then close the presentation.

On Your Own

In these exercises you work on your own, as you would in a real-life work environment. Use the skills you've learned to accomplish the task—and be creative.

Exercise 1-28

Open the file **SpEvent1**. Change slide 2 so that its title is **Summer Events**. Edit the slide's bullets by changing the events to be for June and July, describing activities relating to summer sports such as swimming, softball, sand volleyball, or others. Save the presentation as **[1-28your initials]**. Preview and then print the presentation as handouts, two slides per page.

Exercise 1-29

Open the file **GoodFood**. On slide 2, replace the text describing the pasta dishes with pasta creations from your imagination. On slide 3, replace the text describing the desserts with your own combination of sweet delights. Be sure the desserts you describe use healthy ingredients.

Save the presentation as **[1-29your initials]**. Preview and then print the presentation as handouts, three slides per page.

Exercise 1-30

Open the file **Fruitjuices**. On slide 2, promote each of the list levels that begin with the word variations. After the word variations under each type of juice, key your own creation of combinations of juices that could create new juice titles. Get creative with your juice combinations since the Good 4U restaurant described in the case study at the beginning of this text prides itself in serving healthy food and drinks. Save the presentation as **[1-30your initials]**. Preview and then print the presentation as handouts, landscape orientation, two slides per page.

Developing Presentation Text

OBJECTIVES

After completing this lesson, you will be able to:

1. Create a new blank presentation.
2. Use the font group commands.
3. Adjust text placeholders.
4. Work with bullets and numbering.
5. Work with text boxes.

Estimated Time: 1³/₄ hours

MCAS OBJECTIVES

In this lesson:
PP07 1.1.1
PP07 1.5
PP07 2.1.1
PP07 2.1.2
PP07 2.1.3
PP07 2.1.4
PP07 2.2.3
PP07 2.2.5
PP07 2.2.6
See Appendix

You can add interest to a PowerPoint presentation by varying the appearance of text—that includes changing the font, text style, bullet shape, or position of text. You can change text appearance before or after you key it. Always strive for readability and continuity within your presentation.

In this lesson you will learn how to change text attributes such as color, font, font style, and font size. You will also work with bullets and numbering for easy-to-read lists and use different ways of indenting your text. You will change the indent settings, set tab stops, adjust line spacing, and manipulate text in other ways. Several keystrokes you will use to quickly move around on slides or within your presentation are shown in Table 2-1.

Creating a New Blank Presentation

To create a new blank presentation, you can begin with either:

- A *design theme*, which adds uniform colors and design background to each slide in the presentation.

- A blank presentation (simple text on a plain background), to which you can later apply a design template.

You build each slide by choosing a slide layout and keying slide text.

Exercise 2-1   START A NEW BLANK PRESENTATION

One way to create a presentation is to start with a blank slide, focusing first on content, and then adding color and other design elements later.

NOTE

If PowerPoint is already open and a blank title slide is not displayed, click the Microsoft Office Button 🔘 and choose **New**. Choose Blank Presentation and click **Create**.

1. Start PowerPoint. A blank title slide appears, ready for your text input, as shown in Figure 2-1.

Figure 2-1
Title slide

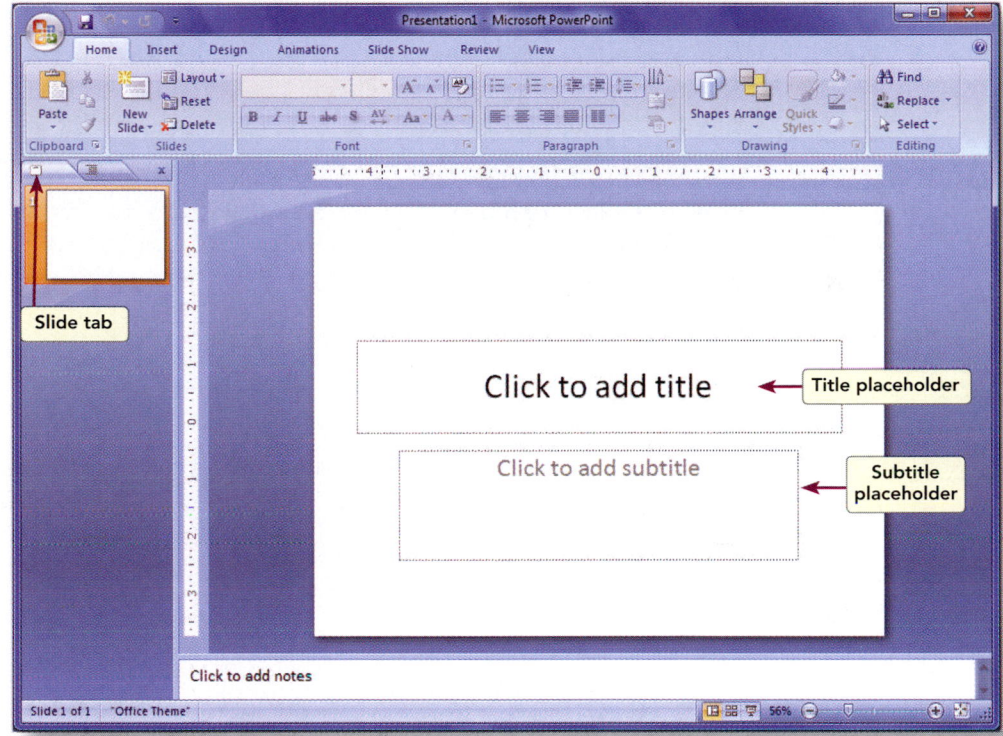

2. Click the title placeholder to activate it and key **For the Pleasure of Your Company**.

3. Click the subtitle placeholder and key **Plan Your Next Event with Good 4 U**.

NOTE

The documents you create in this course relate to the case study in the front of this text about Good 4 U, a fictional restaurant business.

4. Position the insertion point after the word "Event" in the subtitle; then press ⏹Shift⏹+⏹Enter⏹. The subtitle is now split into two lines. Delete the space before "with" on the second line of the subtitle.

5. Split the title text into two lines so that "Your Company" appears on the second line.

TABLE 2-1 Using the Keyboard to Navigate on a Slide and in a Presentation

Keystrokes	Result
Ctrl + Enter	Selects and activates the next text placeholder on a slide. If the last placeholder (subtitle or body text) is selected or activated, pressing Ctrl + Enter inserts a new slide after the current slide. Pressing Ctrl + Enter never selects other objects on a slide (including text boxes) that are not placeholders.
Esc	Deactivates the currently activated text placeholder or text box and selects the entire text box instead. If a text box is selected but not activated, pressing Esc deselects the text box.
Tab	If a text placeholder or text box is activated, inserts a tab character at the insertion point; if not activated, selects the next object on the slide. If the insertion point is between a bullet and the first text character on a line, pressing Tab demotes the bulleted text. Pressing Tab repeatedly when no objects are activated cycles through all the objects on a slide but never moves to another slide.
Shift + Tab	If a text box or text placeholder is not activated, selects the previous object on a slide. If the insertion point is between a bullet and the first text character on the line, promotes the bulleted text.
Esc, Tab	Moves to the next object on a slide, regardless of whether a text box is activated. It never inserts a new slide.
Shift + Enter	If a text box or text placeholder is activated, inserts a new line (but not a new paragraph) at the insertion point.
Enter	If a text box or text placeholder is activated, inserts a new paragraph, including a bullet if in a body text placeholder. If a text box or text placeholder is selected but not activated, selects all the text in the object.
Ctrl + M	Inserts a new slide after the current slide.

Exercise 2-2 ADD NEW SLIDES AND USE SLIDE LAYOUTS

To add a new slide after the current slide in a presentation, you can do one of the following:

*   From the Home tab, in the Slides group, click the New Slide button 📄 .

*   Press Ctrl + M.

*   When a placeholder is selected, press Ctrl + Enter one or more times until a new slide appears.

When a new slide first appears on your PowerPoint window, you don't need to activate a placeholder to start keying text. When no placeholder is selected, as long as your slide pane is active, the text you key automatically goes into the title text placeholder. Knowing this can speed up the process of developing a presentation.

1. From the Home tab, in the Slides group, click the top of the New Slide button 📄 . A new slide appears, containing a title text placeholder and a body text placeholder.

2. Key **Excellent Service**. The text appears automatically in the title placeholder.

Figure 2-2
Keying text on a slide

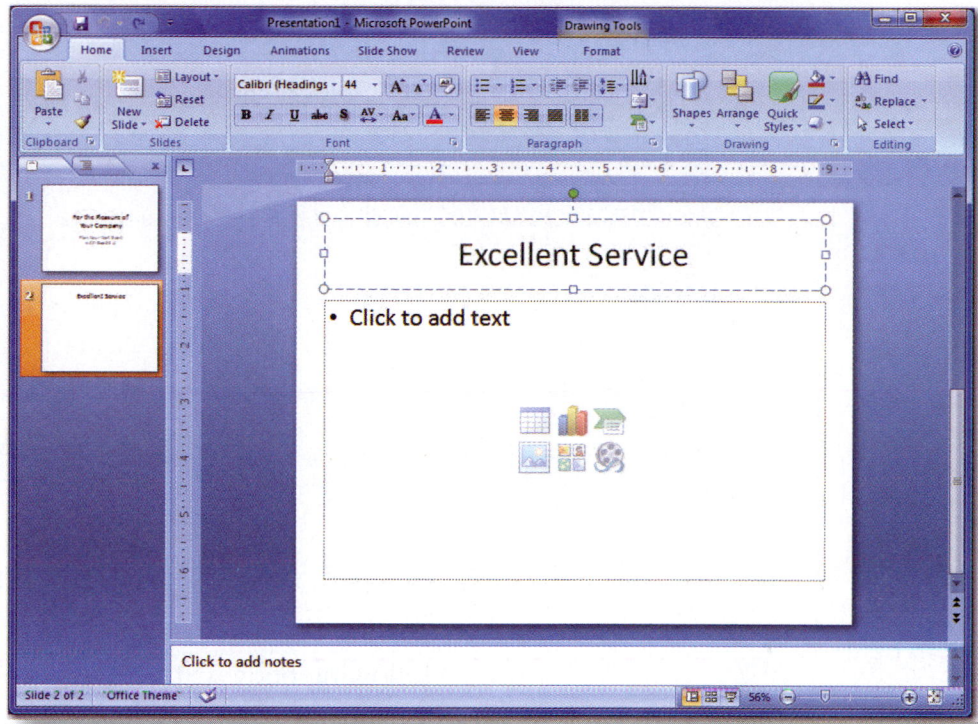

3. Press [Ctrl]+[Enter] or click the body text placeholder to activate it and key the following text, pressing [Enter] at the end of each bulleted line:

    *   **We put your employees and guests at ease**
    *   **We make your company look good**
    *   **We adhere to promised schedules**
    *   **We provide a professional and courteous staff**
    *   **We guarantee customer satisfaction**

4. Press [Ctrl]+[M] to create a new text slide.

5. Key **A Delightful Menu** as the title and then key the following body text:

    *   **High-quality, healthy food**
    *   **Variety to appeal to a broad range of tastes**

6. From the Home tab, in the Slides group, click the down arrow on the New Slide button 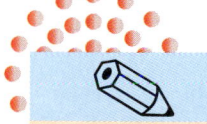 to see thumbnail *slide layouts* with their names, as shown in Figure 2-3. Layouts contain placeholders for slide content such as titles, bulleted lists, charts, and shapes that you will learn about in other lessons.

TIP

When you insert a new slide in a presentation, it uses the same layout as the previous slide (unless the previous slide was the title slide). You learn how to change slide layouts later in this lesson.

Figure 2-3
Inserting a new slide by using the slide layouts

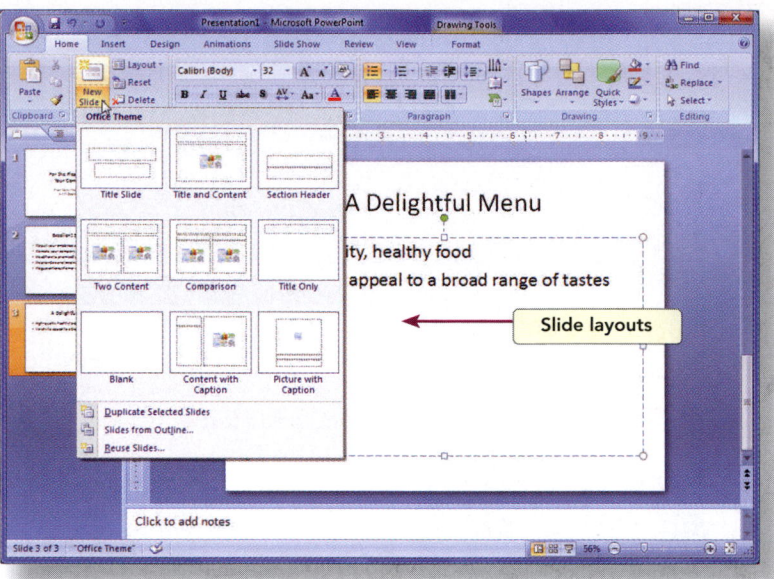

7. Click the **Title and Content** slide layout.

8. Key **High-Energy Fun** as the title and then key the following body text:

   • **Athletic decor**

   • **Sports promotions**

9. Notice that PowerPoint's AutoCorrect feature automatically adds the accent mark to the word "décor."

TIP

PowerPoint's *AutoCorrect* feature automatically corrects common spelling and other errors as you key text. It can be turned on or off, and you can customize it so it will find errors that you frequently make.

10. Press Ctrl+M to insert another slide; then key **A Healthy Atmosphere** as the title and key the following body text:

    • **Smoke-free**

    • **Alcohol optional**

    • **We sell none**

    • **We'll gladly serve your own**

11. Move to slide 4 ("High-Energy Fun") and from the Home tab, in the Slides group, click the down arrow on the New Slide button. Click the **Two Content** slide layout.

12. Key **Events That Are Good 4 U** as the title and then key the following bulleted text in the left body text placeholder:

    • **High-energy meetings**

    • **Productive lunches**

    • **Company celebrations**

    • **Celebrity promotions**

13. Key the following bulleted text in the right body text placeholder:

    • **Entertaining customers**

    • **Demonstrating products**

14. Notice how each slide is numbered in the Slides and Outline pane.

15. Create a new folder for Lesson 2 and save the presentation **[2-2your initials]** in your new Lesson 2 folder.

16. Close the presentation.

Using the Font Group Commands

One way to change the appearance of text in your presentation is by changing the font. A font is a set of characters with a specific design. You can change the *font face* (such as Times New Roman or Arial) and the *font size*. Fonts are measured in *points* (there are 72 points to an inch) indicating how tall a font is.

It is useful to understand that different fonts can take up different amounts of horizontal space, even though they are the same size. For example, a word formatted as 20-point Arial will be wider than a word formatted as 20-point Garamond, as shown in Figure 2-4.

Figure 2-4
Comparing fonts

20 point Arial:	**Formatting**
20 point Garamond:	Formatting

Another way to change the appearance of text is by applying text attributes. For example, you can apply a text style (such as bold or italic) and effect (such as underline or shadow). You use the Font group commands, shown in Figure 2-5 and described in Table 2-2, to change selected text.

Figure 2-5
The Font group on the Home tab

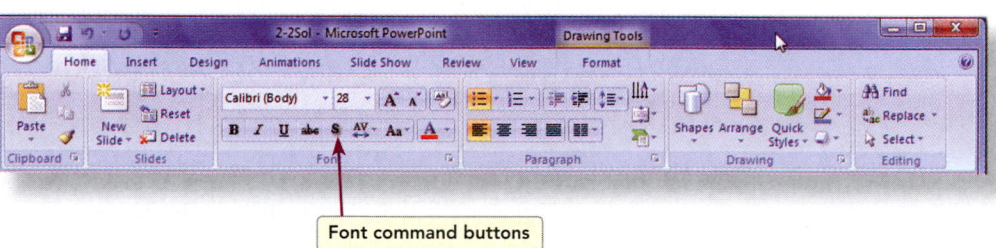

Font command buttons

TABLE 2-2 The Font Group Formatting Command Buttons

Button	Purpose
Century Gothic (Γ ▾) Font	Enables you to choose a font face for selected text or for text to be keyed at the insertion point.
36 ▾ Font Size	Enables you to choose a font size for selected text or for text to be keyed at the insertion point.
A▴ Increase Font Size	Increases the size of selected text by one font size.
A▾ Decrease Font Size	Decreases the size of selected text by one font size.
Aa Clear All Formatting	Removes all formatting from the selected text.
B Bold	Applies the bold attribute to text.
I Italic	Applies the italic attribute to text.
U Underline	Applies the underline attribute to text.
S Shadow	Applies a text shadow.
abc Strikethrough	Draws a line through selected text.
AV ▾ Character Spacing	Increases or decreases the space between characters.
Aa ▾ Change Case	Applies different capitalizations such as uppercase, lowercase, or sentence case.
A ▾ Font Color	Changes text color.

Exercise 2-3 CHANGE THE FONT FACE AND FONT SIZE

One convenient way to apply text formatting is to first key the text, focusing on content, and then select the text and apply formatting, such as by changing the size or font. Keep in mind that no more than two or three fonts should be used in a presentation. Also remember that the font size should be large enough for easy reading when the presentation is displayed on a large projection screen.

Another thing to be aware of is the type of font you choose. The font drop-down list displays all the fonts available for your computer. On the left side of each font is a symbol indicating the font type. *Truetype* fonts have the following symbol: ⊤. If you plan to show your presentation on a different computer or print it with a different printer, it is best to choose a Truetype font.

The Increase Font Size A▴ and Decrease Font Size A▾ buttons change the size of all the text in a selected placeholder by one font size increment as shown in the font size box on the formatting toolbar. If several sizes of text are used in the placeholder, each size is changed proportionately. For example, if a text placeholder contains both 24-point text and 20-point text, clicking the Increase Font Size button  will change to the point sizes 28 and 24 at the same time.

Many of the buttons used to format text are toggle buttons. A *toggle button* switches between on and off when you click it. The Shadow button ⓢ is an example of a toggle button: click it once to apply a shadow, once again to remove it. Other examples of toggle buttons are Bold ⓑ, Italic ⓘ, and Underline ⓤ.

Figure 2-6
Font drop-down list

1. Open the file **Health1**.

2. Examine the Font group and locate the command buttons listed in Table 2-2.

3. On slide 1, click the title placeholder to activate it and key **Heart**.

4. Select the word you just keyed.

5. In the Font group, click the down arrow next to the Font box. A drop-down list of available fonts appears, as shown in Figure 2-6.

6. From the drop-down list, choose **Arial Black**. As you can see, text formatting in PowerPoint is similar to text formatting in a word processing program.

Figure 2-7
Font size drop-down list

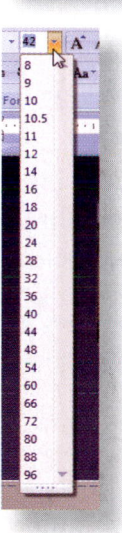

7. With "Heart" still selected, click the down arrow next to the Font Size box, as shown in Figure 2-7. Choose **66**. The text size increases to 66 points.

8. Click the Decrease Font Size button 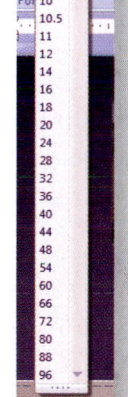. The font size decreases by one size increment. Notice the number "60" displayed in the Font Size box.

9. Click the Increase Font Size button ⒜ twice. The font size increases by two size increments, to 72 points (the equivalent of 1 inch tall).

NOTE

Theme colors are preselected groups of colors that provide variations suitable for many presentation needs. However, font colors or other graphic colors may need more emphasis than using the Theme colors will provide.

Exercise 2-4 APPLY BOLD, ITALIC, COLOR, AND SHADOW

Sometimes it's convenient to apply text formatting as you key. This is particularly true with bold, italic, and underline if you use the following keyboard shortcuts:

- Ctrl + B for bold

- Ctrl + I for italic

- Ctrl+U for underline
- Ctrl+S for shadow

TIP

A shadow can help to make the shapes of characters more distinctive. Be sure you always have a high contrast in color between your text colors and your background colors (light on dark or dark on light) for easy reading. Apply a shadow when it helps to make your text stand out from the background color and apply the same type of shadow in a similar way for unity of design in your presentation.

1. Position the insertion point to the right of "Heart" and press Spacebar. Click the Bold button **B** (or press Ctrl+B) and then the Italic button *I* (or press Ctrl+I) to turn on these attributes.

2. Key **Smart!** The word is formatted as bold italic as you key. Notice that this word is also 72-point Arial, like the previous word.

3. Double-click the word "Heart" to select it then press Ctrl+B to make it bold.

4. Select the word "Heart."

5. From the Home tab, in the Font group, locate the Font Color button . Click its down arrow to open the Font Color menu showing Theme colors and Standard colors, as shown in Figure 2-8.

6. Drag your pointer over the row of standard colors and you will see the live preview of that color before it is applied. Click the red box and the color is applied.

Figure 2-8
Font color menu

7. Click in the word "Smart" to deselect "Heart." "Heart" is now red.

8. Select both of the two words in your title placeholder. From the Home tab, in the Font group, click the Shadow button **S**. Now the text appears to "float" above the slide background with a soft shadow behind it.

Exercise 2-5 CHANGE THE CASE OF SELECTED TEXT

If you find that you keyed text in uppercase and want to change it, you don't have to re-key it. By using the Change Case button **Aa**, as shown in Figure 2-9, you can change any text to **Sentence case, lowercase, UPPERCASE, Capitalize Each Word**, or **tOGGLE cASE**. You can also cycle through uppercase, lowercase, and either title case or sentence case (depending on what is selected) by selecting text and pressing Shift+F3 one or more times.

Figure 2-9
Change Case dialog box

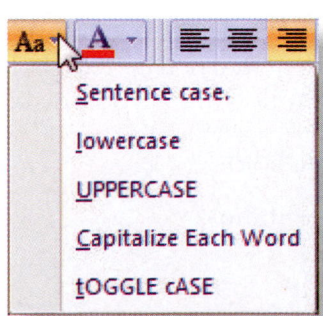

1. Move to slide 3.

2. Use the I-beam pointer to select the title "walk to good health," which has no letters capitalized.

3. From the Home tab, in the Font group, click the down arrow on the Change Case button . Choose **Capitalize Each Word**. This option causes each word to begin with a capital letter.

4. Select the word "To" in the title. Press [Shift]+[F3] two times to change it to lowercase.

5. Select the first item in the body text placeholder by clicking its bullet. This text was keyed with [Caps Lock] accidentally turned on.

6. From the Home tab, in the Font group, click the Change Case button and choose **tOGGLE cASE**. This option reverses the current case, changing uppercase letters to lowercase, and lowercase letters to uppercase.

7. Select the two bulleted items under "Walking" (beginning with "reduces" and "lowers") by dragging your I-beam across all the words.

8. From Home tab, in the Font group, click the Change Case button and choose **Sentence case**. Now only the first word in each item is capitalized.

Exercise 2-6   CHANGE LINE SPACING WITHIN PARAGRAPHS

You can control *line spacing* by adding more space between the lines in a paragraph or by adding more space between paragraphs. Increased line spacing can make your text layout easier to read and enhance the overall design of a slide.

To change spacing between lines within a paragraph, you can use the Line Spacing button to change the space between lines within a paragraph by increments of 0.5 lines.

Figure 2-10
Line spacing sizes

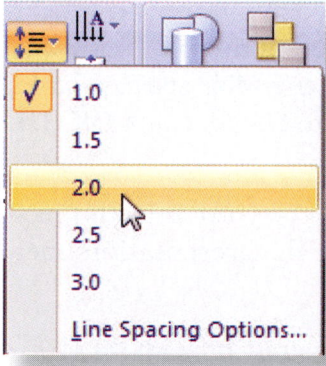

1. Move to slide 2. Click within the first bulleted item, which is considered a paragraph in the placeholder.

2. From the Home tab, in the Paragraph group, click the Line Spacing button and a drop-down list of sizes appear, as shown in Figure 2-10.

3. Click 2.0 and the line spacing of the first paragraph increases.

4. Usually you will want to change the line spacing for an entire text placeholder. Select the placeholder.

5. From the Home tab, in the Paragraph group, click the Line Spacing button , and change the line spacing to 1.5 lines.

Exercise 2-7 CHANGE LINE SPACING BETWEEN PARAGRAPHS

The default paragraph line spacing measurement is single. Using the Paragraph dialog box, you can add space by inserting points for before or after paragraphs to expand the space between them. In PowerPoint, each bulleted item in a list is treated as a paragraph.

1. Still working on slide 2, click within the second bulleted item (a paragraph) then in the Paragraph group, click the Dialog Box Launcher 🔲 to open the Paragraph dialog box, as shown in Figure 2-11.

Figure 2-11
Paragraph dialog box

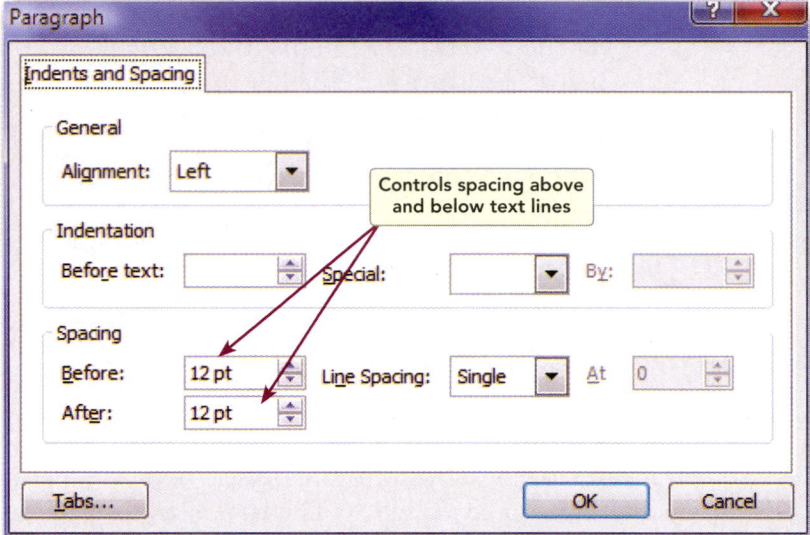

2. In the Spacing section, change the **Before** setting by clicking the spin-box up arrow twice to 18 points. Click **OK**.

3. To make all paragraph spacing uniform, select the entire text placeholder and open the Paragraph dialog box. Change the **Before** spacing to 12 points and the **After** spacing to 12 points. Change the Line spacing setting to **Single**. Click **OK**. The text is now evenly spaced in the placeholder.

4. Save the presentation as [**2-7your initials**] in your Lesson 2 folder but do not print it. Leave the presentation open for the next exercise.

Exercise 2-8 USE THE FONT DIALOG BOX TO MAKE MULTIPLE CHANGES

The Font dialog box is a convenient place to apply several font attributes all at one time. In addition to choosing a font, font style, and font size, this dialog box enables you to choose various effects, such as underline or shadow, and a font color.

1. Go to slide 1 and select the words "Diet and Exercise" in the subtitle. Notice that handles appear around the entire subtitle placeholder, but the colored area showing selection appears only around the text. This has happened because the placeholder is much bigger than the three words that are keyed in it.

2. Right-click the selected text to display the shortcut menu. Choose **Font** to open the Font dialog box, as shown in Figure 2-12.

3. Choose the following options in the Font dialog box:

   - From the **Latin text font** list box, choose **Arial**.
   - From the **Font style** list box, choose **Bold Italic**.
   - From the **Size** list box, key **48**.
   - For **Underline style**, choose **Wavy heavy line**.
   - For **Underline color**, choose **Dark red**.
   - Notice the additional options available in this dialog box.

TIP

Underlining is not the best way to emphasize text. Underlining can cut through the bottom of letters (the descenders) causing the text to be more difficult to read. And because underlining is used so much for hyperlinks on the Internet, underlining seems to have the connotation of a hyperlink. So emphasize your text in different ways, such as by using a larger font size, more dramatic color, or bold.

Figure 2-12
Font dialog box

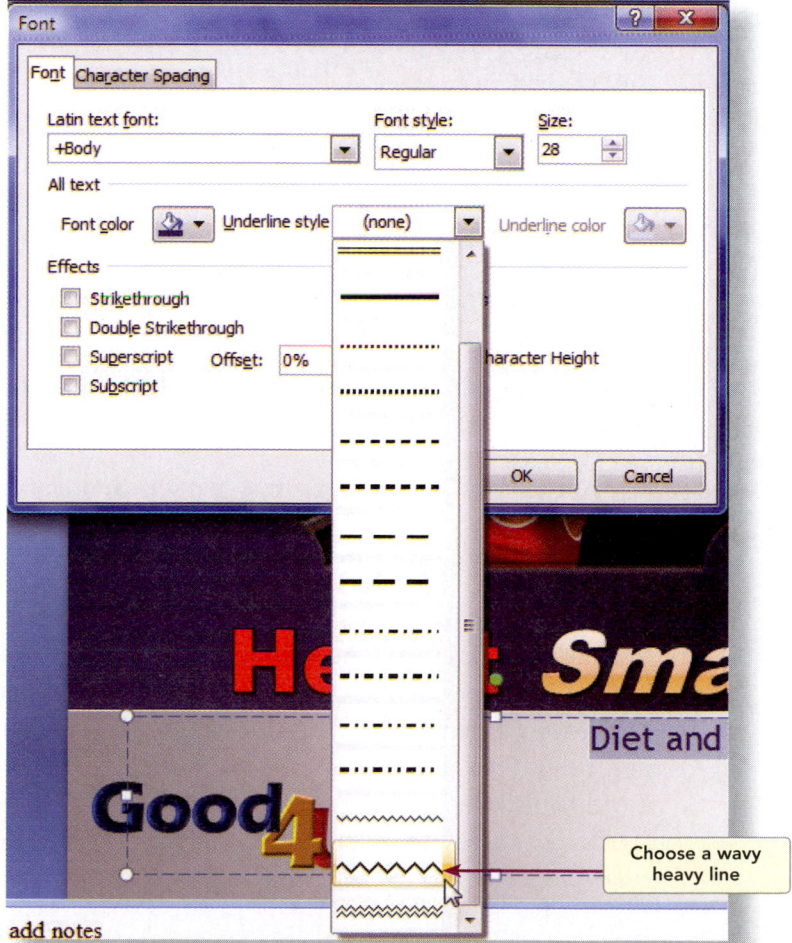

4. Click **OK** to close this dialog box.

5. Select the word "Heart" and then from the Home tab, in the Font group, click the Underline button ⟨u⟩ to turn on underlining. Click the Underline button again to turn off this attribute.

NOTE

You can change text attributes in the Outline tab in the same way as in the Slide tab.

6. With the word "Heart" still selected, change the size to 80 points.

7. Save the presentation as **[2-8your initials]** in your Lesson 2 folder.

8. Preview and then print the title slide only, grayscale, framed.

Adjusting Text Placeholders

You can change formatting features for an entire placeholder by first selecting the placeholder and then choosing the formatting. For example, you can change the text size, color, or font.

You can select placeholders several ways:

- Click the border of an active placeholder with the four-pointed arrow ⊕.

- Press ⟨Esc⟩ while a placeholder is active (when the insertion point is in the text).

- Press ⟨Tab⟩ to select the next placeholder on a slide (only when a text box or text placeholder is not active).

You can deselect placeholders several ways:

- Press ⟨Esc⟩ to deselect a placeholder or other object. (Press ⟨Esc⟩ twice if a text placeholder or text box is active.)

- Click an area of the slide where there is no object.

Exercise 2-9   SELECT A TEXT PLACEHOLDER

Selecting and applying formatting to an entire placeholder can save time in editing.

1. On slide 3, click anywhere in the title text to make the placeholder active. Notice that the placeholder is outlined with small dashes to create a border showing the size of the rectangle. Circles are positioned on the corners and squares are positioned at the midpoint of all four sides, as shown in Figure 2-13. When the placeholder looks like this, the insertion point is active (an I-beam) and you are ready to edit the text within the placeholder.

Figure 2-13
Selecting a text
placeholder

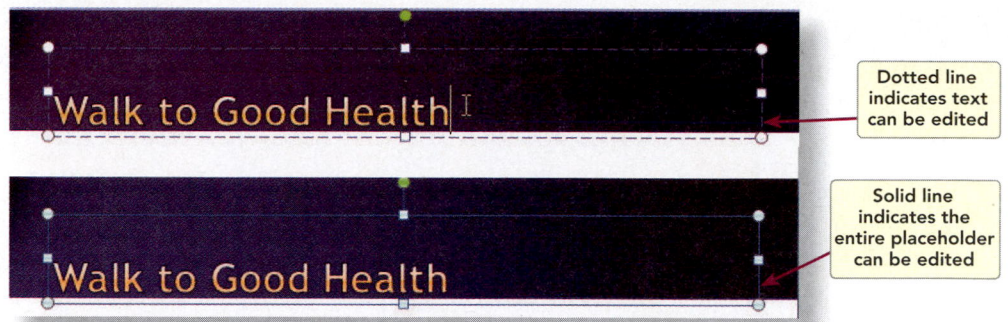

> Dotted line indicates text can be edited

> Solid line indicates the entire placeholder can be edited

2. Point to any place on the dotted line border but not on a circle or square. When you see the four-pointed arrow ⊕, click the border. Notice that the insertion point is no longer active and the border's appearance has changed slightly—it is now made up of a solid line instead of a dashed line. This indicates that the placeholder is selected. You can make changes to all of the text within it, the fill color of the placeholder, the size of the placeholder, or the position of the placeholder.

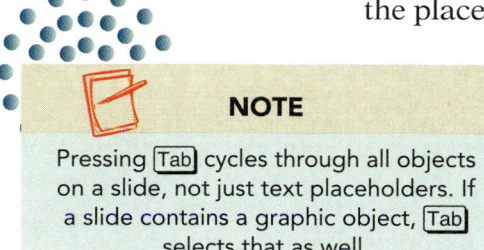

NOTE

Pressing [Tab] cycles through all objects on a slide, not just text placeholders. If a slide contains a graphic object, [Tab] selects that as well.

3. Press [Tab]. Now the body text placeholder is selected.

4. Press [Esc] to deselect the body text placeholder. Now nothing on the slide is selected.

5. Still working on slide 3, click inside the title placeholder text and then press [Esc]. This is another way to select an active placeholder.

6. Click the Increase Font Size button A five times. The font size increases to 60 points.

7. Click the Decrease Font Size button A two times until the font size is 48 points.

8. Press [Tab] to select the body text placeholder. Notice the 23+ in the Font Size box. This indicates that there is more than one font size in the placeholder, and the smallest size is 23 points.

9. Click any text in the first bullet. Notice that its font size is 26 points. Notice also that when you click text inside a placeholder, its border is no longer selected. (The dashed line returns to the border showing that you are editing the text.)

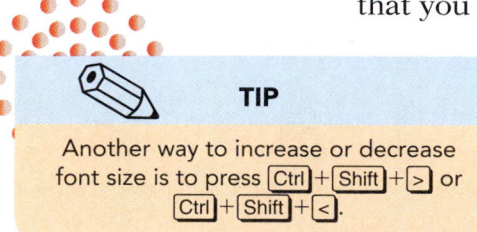

TIP

Another way to increase or decrease font size is to press [Ctrl]+[Shift]+[>] or [Ctrl]+[Shift]+[<].

10. Click the first sub-bullet text, which is 23 points.

11. Press [Esc] to reselect the entire placeholder.

12. Click the Increase Font Size button A twice so that 28+ appears in the Font Size box.

13. From the Home tab, in the Font group, click the down arrow on the Font Color button and choose Standard color dark blue (the color sample second from the right), making all the body text on this slide dark blue.

14. Still working in the Font group, click the Shadow button to test that effect. Now all the text has a shadow, but with the colors being used, the text looks blurred. Remove the Shadow by clicking the Shadow button again.

15. Leave the presentation open for the next exercise.

Exercise 2-10 CHANGE TEXT HORIZONTAL ALIGNMENT

Bulleted items, titles, and subtitles are all considered paragraphs in PowerPoint. Just as in a word processing program, when you press Enter, a new paragraph begins. You can align paragraphs with either the left or right placeholder borders, center them within the placeholder, or justify long paragraphs so that both margins are even. However, the last alignment option should be reserved for longer documents such as reports when you want a formal appearance. Fully justified text is not appropriate for presentation slides.

You can change text alignment for all the text in a placeholder or for just one line, depending on what is selected.

1. Move to slide 5 and select the body text placeholder.

2. Position the insertion point in the first line, "Earn Good 4 U discounts."

3. From the Home tab, in the **Paragraph** group, click the Align Right button . The text in the first line aligns on the right.

4. Click the Align Left button and the paragraph aligns on the left.

5. Select the placeholder border and click the Center button . Both lines are centered horizontally within the placeholder. Because the lines are centered, remove the bullets by clicking on the Bullet list button .

6. Make the text bold.

7. Leave the presentation open for the next exercise.

Exercise 2-11 RESIZE A PLACEHOLDER

At times you will want to change the way text is positioned on a slide. For example, you might want to make a text placeholder narrower or wider to control how text wraps to a new line, or you might want to move all the text up or down on a slide. You can change the size and position of text placeholders in several ways:

• Drag a *sizing handle* to change the size and shape of a text placeholder. Sizing handles are the four small circles on the corners and the squares on the border of a selected text placeholder or other object.

• Drag the placeholder border to move the text to a new position.

• Change placeholder size and position settings by using the Format Shape dialog box.

To change the size or shape of a placeholder, you must first select it, displaying the border as a solid line with sizing handles. It is important to make sure that you're dragging a sizing handle when you want to change a placeholder's size.

By dragging a corner sizing handle, you can change both the height and width of a placeholder at the same time.

1. Display slide 5 and select the body text placeholder. Notice the small white circles and squares on the border. These are the sizing handles, as shown in Figure 2-14.

2. Position the pointer over the bottom center sizing handle.

3. When the pointer changes to a two-pointed vertical arrow ⬍, hold down your left mouse button and drag the bottom border up until it is just below the second line of text.

4. As you drag, the border moves and the pointer turns into a crosshair ⊞. When you release the mouse, the border adjusts to the new position.

Figure 2-14
Resizing a
placeholder

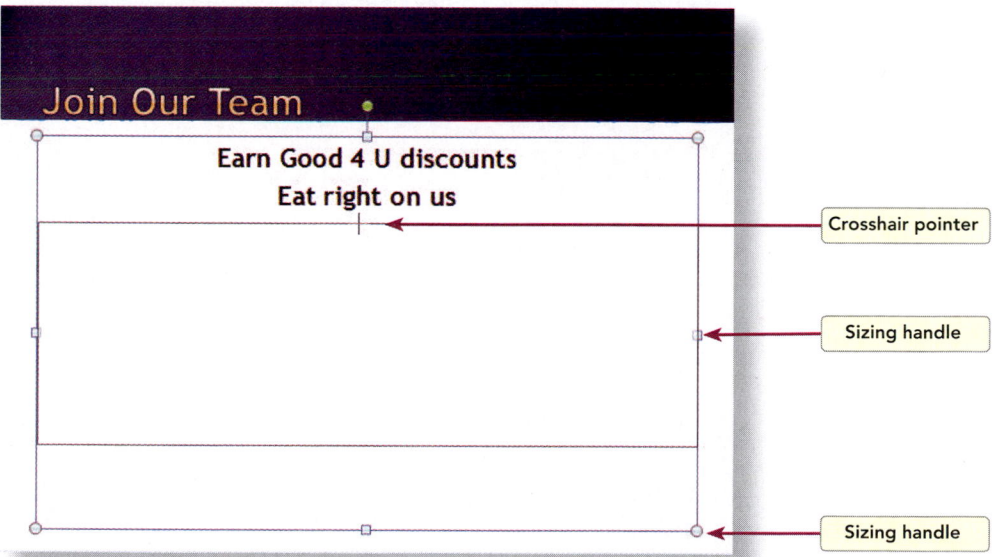

5. Position your pointer over the lower-left-corner sizing handle; then drag it toward the center of the text. Both the height and width of the placeholder change.

6. Click the Undo button once to restore the placeholder to its previous size.

7. Leave the presentation open for the next exercise.

Exercise 2-12   MOVE A PLACEHOLDER

As with changing the size of a placeholder, to change a placeholder's position you must first select it. Drag any part of the placeholder border except the sizing handles when you want to change its position.

> **TIP**
>
> To fine-tune the position of an object, hold down [Alt] while dragging or press the arrow keys to "nudge" an object. Press [Ctrl] + arrow keys to nudge an object in very small increments.

1. Select the body text placeholder on slide 5.

2. Position the pointer over the placeholder border anywhere except on a sizing handle. The pointer changes to the four-pointed arrow ⊕.

3. Drag the four-pointed arrow ⊕ down until the placeholder appears vertically centered on the white area of the slide, as shown in Figure 2-15.

Figure 2-15
Moving a placeholder

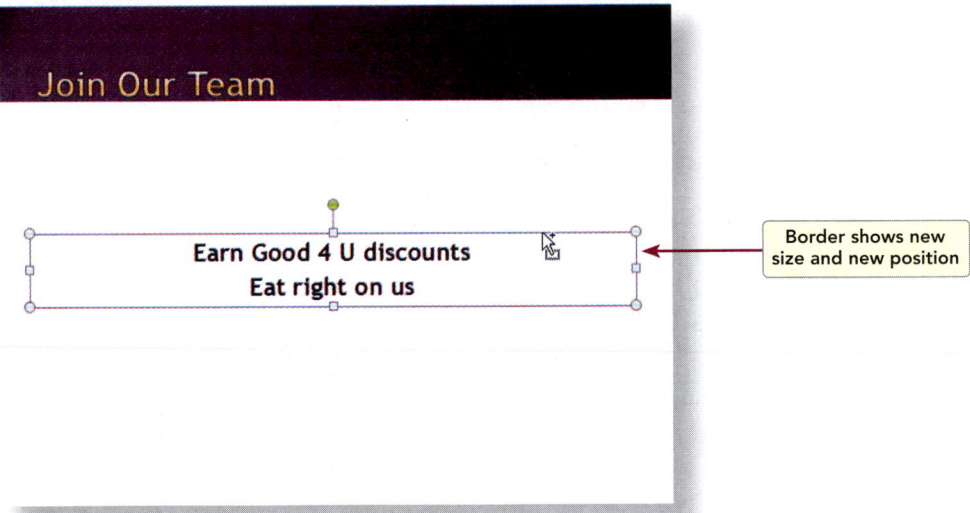

4. Deselect the placeholder. The text is now attractively placed on the slide.

5. Move to slide 1 and save the presentation as **[2-12your initials]** but do not print it.

6. Leave the presentation open for the next exercise.

Working with Bullets and Numbering

When you work with body text placeholders, each line automatically starts with a bullet. However, you can turn bullets off when the slide would look better without them. You can remove bullets, add new ones, change the shape and color of bullets, and create your own bullets from pictures. The Bullets and Numbering buttons are both found in the Paragraph group.

Exercise 2-13   REMOVE BULLETS

As you have learned in previous exercises, the Bullets button can turn bullets off and on. Depending on how your text is selected, you can affect a single bullet or all the bulleted lines in a body placeholder when you use the Bullets button. The Bullets button is another example of a toggle button.

1. Display slide 2. Click within the body text to activate the placeholder. Press [Esc] to select the entire placeholder.

2. From the Home tab, in the Paragraph group, click the Bullets button. This turns bullets off for the entire placeholder and moves the text to the left.

3. Click the Bullets button again to reapply the bullets.

4. Click within the first bulleted item, "Exercise regularly," and click the Bullets button to turn off the bullet.

5. Click the Bullets button again to reapply the bullet.

Exercise 2-14   PROMOTE AND DEMOTE BULLETED TEXT

As you create bulleted items, a new bullet is inserted when you press [Enter] to start a new line. When you want to expand on a slide's main points, you can insert indented bulleted text below a main point. This supplemental text is sometimes referred to as a sub-bullet or a level 2 bullet. PowerPoint body text placeholders can have up to five levels of indented text, but you will usually want to limit your slides to two levels.

To *demote* body text, you increase its indent level by moving it to the right. To *promote* body text, you decrease its indent level by moving it to the left. These changes can be made by moving the insertion point before the text and pressing [Tab] to demote (increase indent) or [Shift]+[Tab] to promote (decrease indent) or by using the Increase List Level or Decrease List Level buttons found on the Home tab, in the Paragraph group.

1. With slide 2 displayed, move your insertion point after "regularly" then press [Enter] to create a new bulleted line.

2. Press [Tab] to indent to the second-level bullet and key **Walk 30 minutes daily** then press [Enter].

3. Notice that the text is now indented automatically to the second-level bullet.

4. Key **Alternate aerobic and weight training** then press [Enter].

5. To return to the first-level bullet, press [Shift]+[Tab].

6. Key **Get sufficient rest**.

7. Leave the presentation open for the next exercise.

NOTE

If you press [Tab] when the insertion point is within the text placeholder, you insert a tab character instead of demoting text.

Exercise 2-15 CHANGE THE COLOR AND SHAPE OF A BULLET

The Bullets gallery provides just a few choices to change the shape of a bullet. The Bullets dialog box provides many more choices to change the bullet shape by choosing a character from another font. Fonts that contain potential bullet characters include Symbol, Wingdings, and Webdings. Another source of bullet characters is the Geometric Shapes subset available for most other fonts.

1. Working on slide 2, select the body text placeholder.

2. From the Home tab, in the Paragraph group, click the down arrow on the Bullets button ▤▾ to see the gallery options, as shown in Figure 2-16.

3. Click the checkmark bullet option.

Figure 2-16
Bullets and Numbering gallery

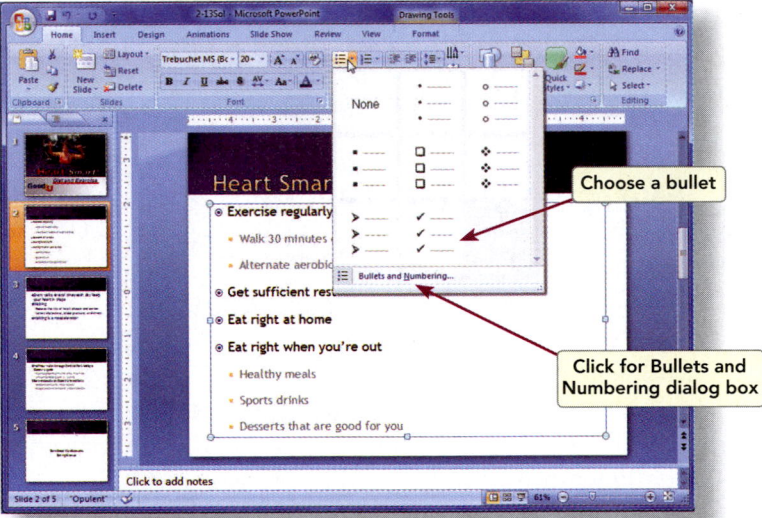

4. With the body text placeholder still selected, click the Bullets button again and then choose **Bullets and Numbering** at the bottom.

5. In the Bullets and Numbering dialog box, as shown in Figure 2-17, click the **Bulleted** tab.

Figure 2-17
Bullets and Numbering dialog box

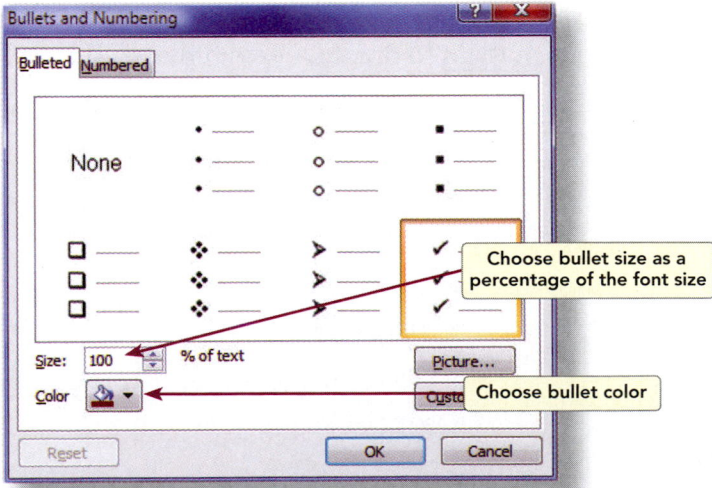

6. In the **Color** box, choose a Standard red.

7. In the **Size** box, click the down arrow several times until **80** is displayed. Click **OK**. All bullets on slide 2 are now red checks, sized at 80 percent of the font size.

8. Select the first line of bulleted text then press [Ctrl] while you use your I-beam pointer to select the text of the remaining three level-one bulleted text lines.

9. From the Home tab, in the Paragraph group, click the Bullets button down arrow then choose **Bullets and Numbering**.

10. Click **Customize** to open the Symbol dialog box, shown in Figure 2-18.

11. In the **Font** drop-down list (upper-left corner of the dialog box), scroll to the top and choose **Monotype Corsiva** if it is not displayed.

12. In the **Subset** drop-down list (upper-right corner), choose **Geometric Shapes** (near the bottom of the list). Several characters suitable for bullets appear in the dialog box grid.

Figure 2-18
Symbol dialog box

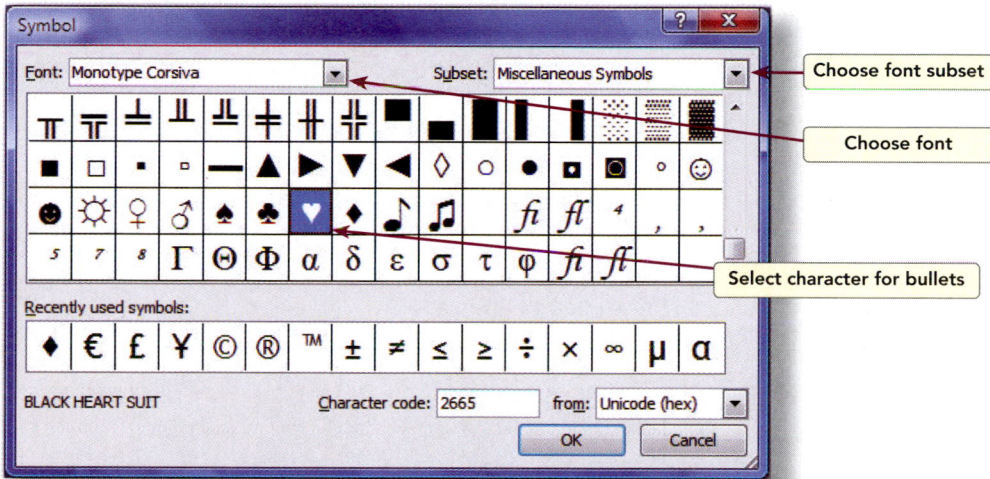

13. Click the heart bullet to select it; then click **OK**. The Symbol dialog box closes, and the Bullets and Numbering dialog box reappears.

14. Change the **Size** to **110%** and leave the **Color** on a Standard **red**. Click **OK**. The selected three bullets on the slide change to red hearts. While the percentage you use is related to the size of the font for that bulleted item, symbols vary in size. So you may need to try more than one adjustment before you accept a size that is pleasing to you.

15. Leave your presentation open for the next exercise.

Exercise 2-16   CREATE A BULLET FROM A PICTURE

A picture bullet can add a unique or creative accent to your presentation. A picture bullet is made from a graphic file and can be a company logo, a special picture, or any image you create with a graphics program or capture with a scanner or digital camera.

1. Display slide 3 and select the text of the first two bullets (but not the sub-bullets).

2. From the Home tab, in the Paragraph group, click the Bullets button down arrow then choose **Bullets and Numbering**.

3. Click the **Picture** to open the Picture Bullet dialog box. The Picture Bullet dialog box displays a variety of colorful bullets. You can choose from one of these bullets or you can import a picture file of your own.

4. Key the search text **walking**. Click the check box to include content from Office Online then click **Go**.

5. Look through the images to find a simple one that would represent a person walking for exercise, as shown in Figure 2-19.

6. Click the picture of a person walking to select it and then click **OK**. The bullets are replaced with picture bullets, but they are too small.

Figure 2-19
Inserting a picture bullet

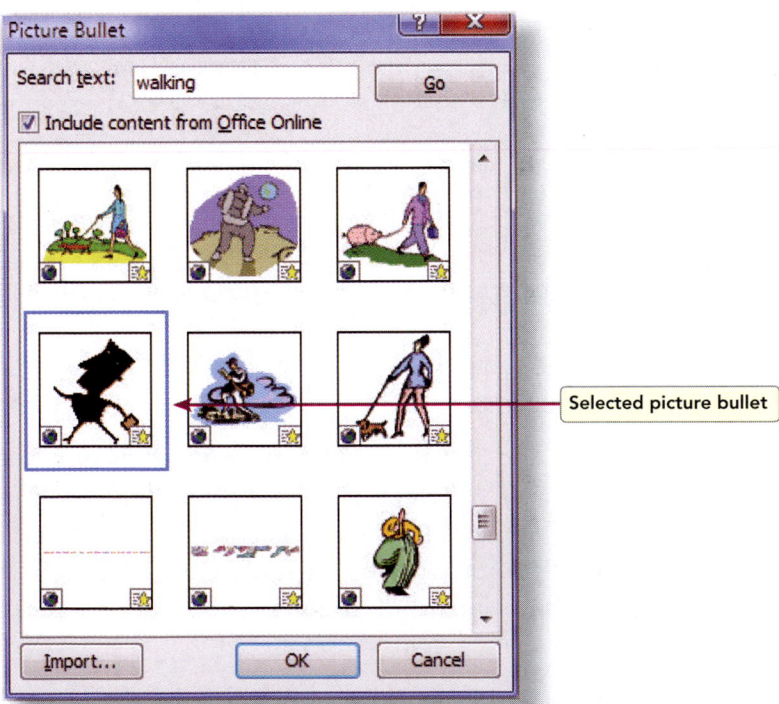

7. With the two bullet items still selected, reopen the Bullets and Numbering dialog box. In the **Size** box, change the size to **200**%. Click **OK**.

NOTE

If the AutoFit Options button ⊞ appears near the placeholder, click it and choose **AutoFit Text to Placeholder**.

8. Using the steps outlined above, change the bullet for the last bulleted item ("Walking is a mood elevator") to the picture of the walker and size it to match the other bullets.

9. Leave your presentation open for the next exercise.

Exercise 2-17   CREATE NUMBERED PARAGRAPHS

Instead of using bullet characters, you can number listed items. A numbered list is useful to indicate the order in which steps should be taken or to indicate the importance of the items in a list.

Using the **Numbered** tab in the Bullets and Numbering dialog box, you can apply a variety of numbering styles, including numbers, letters, and Roman numerals. You can also create a numbered list automatically while you key body text.

1. Display slide 5 and select the body text placeholder.

2. From the Home tab, in the Paragraph group, click the Align Text Left button ▤.

3. Select all the text in the placeholder and delete it.

4. With the placeholder activated, key **1.** and press ⎚Tab⎚. Key **Walk with us**.

5. Press ⎚Enter⎚. The second line is automatically numbered "2."

6. Key **Eat with us** and press ⎚Enter⎚.

7. Key **Do what's Good 4 U**. The slide now has three items, automatically numbered 1 through 3.

8. Your text may have resized to be smaller because earlier you made this placeholder just tall enough for two text lines. Press ⎚Esc⎚ to select the placeholder, then use the bottom sizing handle to drag down and increase the placeholder size to see all three items.

9. From the Home tab, in the Paragraph group, click the down arrow on the Numbers button ▤▾ to see several different numbering styles. Then click **Bullets and Numbering** to open the Bullets and Numbering dialog box and click the **Numbered** tab.

10. Click the first numbered option. In the **Color** box, choose **Red** and change the size to **100**% of text. Click **OK**.

TIP

You can control the numbering style that is applied automatically by keying your first item with the style you want, such as 1. or A.

11. Move to slide 1 and save the presentation as **[2-17your initials]** in your Lesson 2 folder.

12. Preview and then print the presentation as handouts, six slides per page, grayscale, framed. Leave the presentation open for the next exercise.

Exercise 2-18   **USE THE RULER TO ADJUST PARAGRAPH INDENTS**

A text placeholder will have one of three types of paragraph indents that affect all text in a placeholder. These paragraph indents are:

- *Normal indent*—where all the lines of the paragraph are indented the same amount from the left margin.

- *Hanging indent*—where the first line of the paragraph extends farther to the left than the rest of the paragraph.

- *First-line indent*—where only the first line of the paragraph is indented.

These paragraph indents are controlled by the Paragraph dialog box shown in Figure 2-20 that is accessed through the Paragraph Dialog Box Launcher.

Figure 2-20
Paragraph Indent
dialog box

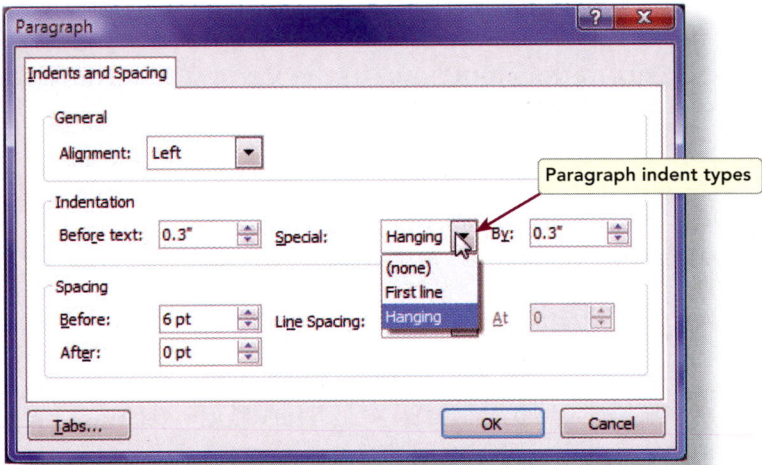

You can also set indents by using the ruler. If the ruler is displayed, you can see and manipulate *indent markers* when you activate a text object for editing. Indent markers are the two small triangles and the small rectangle that appear on the left side of the ruler.

At times you might want to change the distance between the bullets and text in a text placeholder. For example, when you use a large bullet (as you did in Exercise 2-16), the space that it requires may cause the text that follows it to word-wrap unevenly. You can easily adjust this spacing by dragging the indent markers. The following steps will guide you through this process.

NOTE

The Ruler is a toggle command. Choose it once to display the rulers; choose it again to hide them.

1. Display slide 3. Notice how the text does not align correctly and the square second-level bullets are not indented enough.

2. From the View tab, in the Show/Hide group, click to select the **Ruler**. The vertical and horizontal rulers appear, as shown in Figure 2-21.

Figure 2-21
Horizontal and
vertical rulers

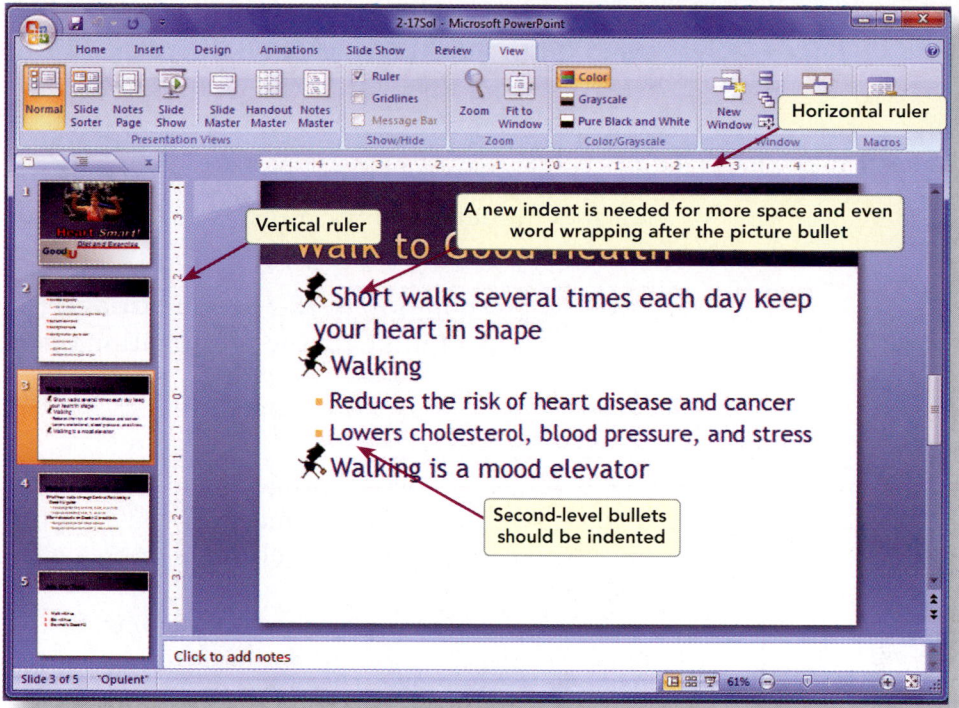

NOTE

You must have an insertion point somewhere inside a text box to change settings on the ruler. The appearance of the ruler reflects whether the entire placeholder is selected or the insertion point is active within the placeholder. If text is already in the placeholder, it must be selected for any ruler changes to apply to the text.

3. Click anywhere within the placeholder as if you were planning to edit some text. Notice the indent markers that appear on the horizontal ruler. Also notice that the white portion of the ruler indicates the width of the text placeholder.

4. Select all of the text in the placeholder.

5. Point to the first-line indent marker on the ruler (triangle at the top of the horizontal ruler, shown in Figure 2-22) and drag it to the right, to the 1-inch mark. The first line of each bulleted item beginning with the picture bullet is now indented the same way.

Figure 2-22
Indent markers

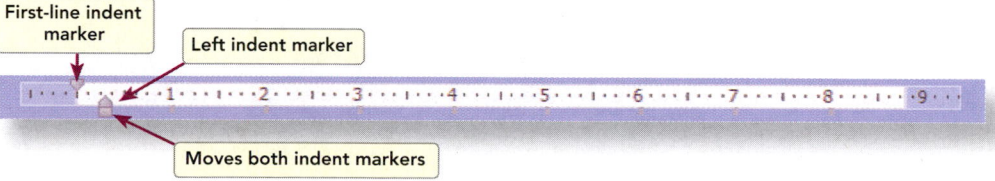

6. Drag the small rectangle (below the triangle on the bottom of the ruler) to the 1-inch mark on the ruler. Notice that both triangles move when you drag the rectangle.

7. Drag the left indent marker (triangle at the bottom of the ruler) to the right to the 2-inch mark on the ruler and the text will word-wrap with even alignment after the picture bullet.

8. Select the text in the lines beginning with square bullets. Drag the first-line indent marker to the 2.5-inch mark on the ruler. Drag the left indent marker to the 3-inch mark on the ruler. Now the text has much better alignment.

9. Save the presentation as **[2-18your initials]** in your Lesson 2 folder but do not print it. Leave the presentation open for the next exercise.

Working with Text Boxes

Until now, you have worked with text placeholders that automatically appear when you insert a new slide. Sometimes you'll want to use *text boxes* so you can put text outside the text placeholders or create free-form text boxes on a blank slide.

 You create text boxes by clicking the Text Box button  found on the Insert tab, in the Text group, and then dragging the pointer to define the width of the text box. You can also just click the pointer, and the text box adjusts its width to the size of your text. You can change the size and position of text boxes the same way you change text placeholders.

NOTE

You can also click and drag the text tool pointer to create a text box in a specific width. The text you key will wrap within the box if it does not fit on one text line. You can use the resizing handles to increase or decrease the text box width. You can practice making other text boxes on this slide and then click Undo as needed to return to just the first text box.

Exercise 2-19   CREATE A TEXT BOX

When you use the Text Box button to create a single line of text, you are free to place that text anywhere on a slide, change its color and font, and rotate it. This type of text is sometimes called floating text.

1. Display slide 5.

2. From the Insert tab, shown in Figure 2-23, in the Text group, click the Text Box button.

Figure 2-23
Insert tab

3. Place the pointer below the "G" in "Good 4 U" and click. A small text box containing an insertion point appears, as shown in Figure 2-24.

Figure 2-24
Creating floating text

1. **Walk with us**
2. **Eat with us**
3. **Do what's Good 4 U**

4. Key **Join Our Team Today!** Notice how the text box widens as you key text.

5. Leave the presentation open for the next exercise.

Exercise 2-20 CHANGE THE FONT AND FONT COLOR

You can select the text box and change the font and font color using the same methods as you did with text placeholders.

1. Click the text box border to select it. Change the text to 44-point, bold, shadowed.

Figure 2-25
Placement for floating text

2. With the text box selected, choose an attractive script font such as Monotype Corsiva or Script MT Bold.

3. Using the Font color button, change the text color to red.

4. Using the four-pointed arrow ⊕, move the floating text box to the bottom-right corner of the slide. See Figure 2-25 for placement.

Exercise 2-21 ROTATE AND CHANGE TEXT DIRECTION

You can *rotate* almost any PowerPoint object—including text boxes, place-holders, and clip art—by dragging the green rotation handle that appears at the top of a selected object. You can also control rotation of text boxes and placeholders by using the Format Shape dialog box.

To *constrain* the rotation of an object to 15-degree increments, hold down [Shift] while rotating.

When text is in a rotated position, it can be awkward to edit. Fortunately, when you select a rotated text box for editing, it conveniently returns to a horizontal position while you revise the text.

> **TIP**
>
> You can key a precise angle of rotation measurement on the 3-D Rotation tab of the Format Shape dialog box in the Z area.

1. On slide 5, click "Join Our Team Today!" and drag the text box up slightly so that you will have enough space to angle it on the slide.

2. Point to the green rotation handle at the top of the text box and drag it to the left. Notice the circling arrow pointer that appears while you drag.

3. Position the text box as shown in Figure 2-26.

Figure 2-26
Rotating a text box

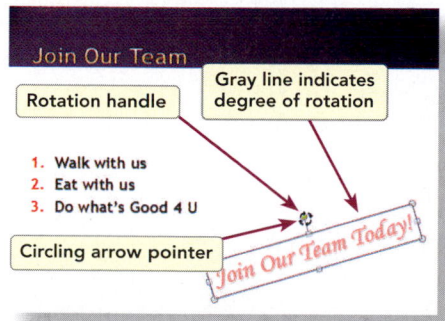

4. With the "Join Our Team Today!" text box selected, press Ctrl+C to copy.

5. Move to slide 4 and press Ctrl+V to paste.

6. Rotate the copied text box to make it straight again, then change the text to read **Offered Daily!** The text box should resize itself to fit this text.

7. With the text box selected, from the Home tab, in the Paragraph group, click Text Direction then choose **Rotate All Text 270°** to make the text read from the bottom up.

8. Reposition this rotated text on the right of the slide.

9. Save the presentation as **[2-21your initials]** in your Lesson 2 folder but do not print it. Leave the presentation open for the next exercise.

Exercise 2-22 WRAP TEXT AND CHANGE ALIGNMENT

When you drag the pointer to define the width of a text box, *word wrapping* is automatically turned on. As you key, your insertion point automatically jumps to a new line when it gets to the right side of the box. The height of the box automatically adjusts to accommodate additional text lines.

1. Move to slide 2, "Heart Smart Living."

2. From the Insert tab, in the Text group, click the Text Box button.

3. Position your pointer to the right of "Exercise regularly"; then drag to the right to create a rectangle that is about 2 inches wide (use the ruler as a guide).

4. In the text box, key **Be consistent wherever you are!**

5. Click the text box border to select it; then increase the font size to 28 points, bold, and red; and then right-align the text. Resize the text box if necessary to match Figure 2-27 and position the text box as shown.

Figure 2-27
Text wrapped in a text box

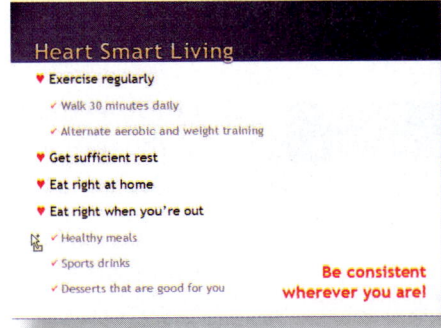

6. Save the presentation as **[2-22your initials]** in your Lesson 2 folder and print a handout page with six slides per page, grayscale, and framed.

Lesson 2 Summary

- Creating a presentation by starting with a blank presentation lets you concentrate on textual content. Anytime during the process, you can choose a design and color theme.

- Keyboard shortcuts are a big time-saver when creating a presentation. For example, Ctrl+Enter moves to the next text placeholder and Ctrl+M inserts a new slide.

- When you add a new slide, you can choose a slide layout. Slide layouts can be either text layouts or content layouts containing different arrangements of placeholders.

- After a slide is added, you can change the layout of the current slide or of a group of selected slide thumbnails.

- Before keying text in a placeholder, activate it by clicking inside it.

- Using the Outline pane is a quick way to enter slide titles and bulleted text.

- A font is a set of characters with a specific design, for example, Arial or Times New Roman.

- Font size (the height of a font) is measured in points, with 72 points to an inch. Fonts of the same size can vary in width, some taking up more horizontal space than others.

- Many formatting buttons are toggle buttons, meaning that the same button is clicked to turn an effect on and clicked again to turn it off.

- Change text attributes and effects such as bold, italic, and text color by first selecting the text and then clicking the appropriate buttons on the Home tab in the Font group. Or, apply formatting before you key text.

- The Font dialog box, accessible through the Font dialog box launcher, enables you to apply multiple formatting styles and effects all at one time.

- When a text placeholder is selected, formatting that you apply affects all the text in the placeholder.

- Text in placeholders can be aligned with the left or right side of the placeholder, centered, or justified.

- Body text placeholders are preformatted to have bulleted paragraphs. Bullets for selected paragraphs or placeholders are turned on or off by clicking the Bullets button.

- Use the Bullets and Numbering dialog box to change the shape, size, and color of bullets or numbers.

- Graphic files can be used as picture bullets.

- Paragraph indents can be adjusted in text placeholders and text boxes by dragging indent markers on the ruler when a text object is selected.

- To display the ruler for a text object, from the View tab, in the Show/Hide group, choose **Ruler**, and then activate the text object as if to edit the text.

- Bulleted text always uses a hanging indent. Changing the distance between the first-line indent marker (top triangle) and the left indent marker (bottom triangle) on the ruler controls the amount of space between a bullet and its text.

- Indent and tab settings apply only to the selected text object and all the text in the text box. To create more than one type of indent or tab setting, you must create a new text object.

- Line spacing and the amount of space between paragraphs are controlled using the Line Spacing button ![icon] and dialog box. Line and paragraph spacing can be applied to one or more paragraphs in a text object, or to the entire object.

- Text boxes enable you to place text anywhere on a slide. From the Insert tab, in the Text group, click the Text Box button ![icon], then click anywhere on a slide or draw a box and then start keying text.

- Text in a text box can be formatted by using standard text-formatting tools. Change the width of a text box to control how the text will word-wrap.

- When you select a text box on a slide, a green rotation handle appears slightly above the top-center sizing handle. Drag the rotation handle left or right to rotate the object.

LESSON 2		Command Summary	
Feature	**Button**	**Menu**	**Keyboard**
Create new presentation	![icon]	Microsoft Office Button, New	Ctrl + N
Insert new slide	![icon]	Home tab, Slides group, New Slide	Ctrl + M
Activate placeholder			Ctrl + Enter
Deactivate placeholder			Esc
Insert line break			Shift + Enter
Move to next placeholder			Ctrl + Enter
Decrease List Level	![icon]		Shift + Tab or Alt + Shift + ←
Increase List Level	![icon]		Tab
Decrease Font Size	![icon]	Home tab, Font group, Decrease Font Size	Ctrl + Shift + <
Increase Font Size	![icon]	Home tab, Font group, Increase Font Size	Ctrl + Shift + >
Bold	![icon]	Home tab, Font group, Bold	Ctrl + B
Italic	![icon]	Home tab, Font group, Italic	Ctrl + I
Underline	![icon]	Home tab, Font group, Underline	Ctrl + U

continues

LESSON 2		Command Summary *continued*	
Feature	Button	Menu	Keyboard
Shadow	S	Home tab, Font group, Shadow	
Font Color	A ▾	Home tab, Font group, Font Color	
Apply a font	Century Gothic (E ▾	Home tab, Font group, Font	Ctrl + Shift + F
Change font size	36 ▾	Home tab, Font group, Font Size	Ctrl + Shift + P
Change case	Aa ▾	Home tab, Font group, Change Case	Shift + F3
Align Text Left	▤	Home tab, Paragraph group, Align Text Left	Ctrl + L
Center	▤	Home tab, Paragraph group, Center	Ctrl + E
Align Text Right	▤	Home tab, Paragraph group, Align Text Right	Ctrl + R
Justify	▤	Home tab, Paragraph group, Justify	Ctrl + J
Turn bullets on or off	▤ ▾	Home tab, Paragraph group, Bullets	
Turn numbering on or off	▤ ▾	Home tab, Paragraph group, Numbering	
Change paragraph spacing	▤ ▾	Home tab, Paragraph group, Line Spacing	
Text Box	A▤	Insert Tab, Text group, Text Box	
Change text box options		Drawing Tools Format tab	

Concepts Review

True/False Questions

Each of the following statements is either true or false. Select your choice by indicating T or F.

T F   1. You can add text to a new presentation by using a blank presentation.

T F   2. You can add a new slide by pressing Ctrl+Y.

T F   3. You can display slide thumbnails and the Outline pane at the same time.

T F   4. You can use Ctrl+Enter both to activate the next slide placeholder and to insert a new slide.

T F   5. You can change selected text from uppercase to lowercase by using the Shift+F3 keyboard shortcut.

T F   6. Sentence case capitalizes the initial letter of all words in a paragraph.

T F   7. You can drag a sizing handle to reposition a placeholder.

T F   8. To move a text box, the pointer must remain on the border and not touch a sizing handle.

Short Answer Questions

Write the correct answer in the space provided.

1. Name two ways to insert a new slide.

_____

2. Which key do you press to insert another bullet at the same level?

_____

3. Which command buttons change font size?

_____

4. What must you do before you can change an attribute for existing text?

_____

5. How do you change the distance between bullets and text?

_____

6. What is the difference between line spacing and paragraph spacing?

_____

7. How do you create a text box that adjusts its width to the width of the text you key?

_____

8. How can you rotate a text box in 15-degree increments?

_____

Critical Thinking

Answer these questions on a separate page. There are no right or wrong answers. Support your answers with examples from your own experience, if possible.

1. Explain how font faces can affect a presentation. Can you use too many fonts in a presentation? Explain your answer.

2. Under what circumstances might you choose to use a text box instead of a text placeholder?

Skills Review

Exercise 2-23

Create a new presentation, add new slides, and insert a new slide with a different layout.

1. Start PowerPoint.

2. Complete the title slide by following these steps:
   a. Key **Healthy Eating** as the first line of the title (you don't have to click the text "Click to add title" to begin keying the title slide text).
   b. Press Enter to start a new title line.
   c. Key **for Young Athletes** to complete the title.
   d. Press Ctrl+Enter.
   e. Key the subtitle **A Good 4 U Seminar**.

3. Add a new slide with the **Title and Content** layout by following these steps:
   a. Press Ctrl+M.
   b. Key **Basic Food Groups** as the title.
   c. Key the following bulleted text:
      - **Fats, oils, and sweets**
      - **Dairy products**
      - **Meat, poultry, fish, eggs, beans, and nuts**
      - **Fruits and vegetables**
      - **Rice, bread, and pasta**

4. From the Home tab, in the Slides group, click the top of the **New Slide** button ▢ to insert a third slide.

5. Key **Elements of a Healthy Diet** as the title of the slide and the following bulleted text:

   - **Choose a variety of foods**
   - **Eat moderate amounts**
   - **Choose low-fat foods**
   - **Choose fresh, unprocessed foods**
   - **Avoid candy and junk foods**

6. Move to slide 1 and save the presentation as **[2-23your initials]** in your Lesson 2 folder.

7. Preview and then print the presentation as handouts, three slides per page, grayscale, framed. Close the presentation.

Exercise 2-24

Change font size, apply text attributes to selected text, and change the case of selected text.

1. Open the file **ComWalk**.

2. On slide 1, change font size and color and apply bold and shadow effects for the title by following these steps:

   a. Select the title text "Power Walking" by dragging the I-beam pointer across the text.

   b. From the Home tab, in the Font group, change the Font Size to **36** points.

   c. From the Home tab, in the Font group, click the Font Color button ▣ drop-down list and choose **red**.

   d. Still working in the Font group, click the Bold button ▣ and the Shadow button ▣.

3. On slide 3, increase the font size for the title by following these steps:

   a. Move to slide 3 and select the title text.

   b. From the Home tab, in the Font group, click the Increase Font Size button ▣ several times until 36 appears in the Font Size box.

4. On slide 5, use the Font dialog box to change the title text formatting by following these steps:

   a. Select the title text.

   b. From the Home tab, in the Font group, click the Font dialog box launcher ▣.

   c. Choose the font style **Bold** and change the font color to **red**.

   d. In the **Size** box, choose **36** points.

   e. Click **OK**.

5. Change the case of text on slide 5 by following these steps:

    a. Select the last bulleted item by clicking its bullet.

    b. From Home tab, in the Font group, click the Change Case button [Aa▾].

    c. Choose **tOGGLE cASE**.

6. Using step 4 above as a guide, change the title text formatting on slides 2, 3, 4, and 6 to match slide 5. On slide 6, if necessary, resize the placeholder slightly on the right side so that the title fits on one line.

7. Move to slide 1 and save the presentation as **[2-24your initials]** in your Lesson 2 folder.

8. Preview and then print the presentation as handouts, six slides per page, grayscale, framed. Close the presentation.

Exercise 2-25

Adjust indents using the ruler.

1. Open the file **EmpAward**.

2. Move to slide 2.

3. Create first-line indents by following these steps:

    a. Click within the text box to activate the ruler.

    b. Select the bulleted text.

    c. From the Home tab, in the Paragraph group, click the Bullet button [▤] to remove the bullets from the body text placeholder.

    d. If the ruler is not displayed, click the View tab, in the Show/Hide group, and choose **Ruler**.

    e. Drag the first-line indent marker (top triangle) to the right, to the 1-inch mark on the ruler.

    f. Drag the small rectangle to the left, to the zero point on the ruler.

4. Move to slide 3 and change the spacing before the bullets by following these steps:

    a. Select all of the text in the body text placeholder.

    b. Drag the left indent marker (bottom triangle) to the right one tick mark, to the 0.5-inch position on the ruler.

5. Move to slide 4 and select all the text. Increase the space between the bullets and text by one tick mark on the ruler. Resize the placeholder on the right so the text does not word-wrap. Move the oval shapes that emphasize the words "week" and "paid" up and slightly to the right.

6. Move to slide 6 and modify the line spacing by following these steps:

    a. Select both paragraphs (the quotation and hobbies).

    b. From the Home tab, in the Paragraph group, choose the Dialog Box Launcher and change the Before paragraph spacing to **0**. Now the text will fit better on the slide.

7. Save the presentation as **[2-25your initials]** in your Lesson 2 folder.

8. Print the presentation as handouts, six slides per page, grayscale, framed. Close the presentation.

Exercise 2-26

Change text box settings and page setup options.

1. Open the file **Upgrade1**.

2. On the title slide, make these changes:

   a. Title placeholder—Change to 66 points, shadow, and **Pink**, **Accent 2** color.

   b. Subtitle placeholder—Change to 40 points and left alignment. Resize the placeholder to fit the text and then position the placeholder on the lower right of the slide.

3. On slide 2, make the following changes to the body text placeholder:

   a. Remove the bullet and make the first line of the paragraph indent to the 1.5-inch mark on the ruler.

   b. Move the placeholder slightly to the right so the left paragraph edge aligns with the word "Why" in the slide title.

4. On slide 3, from the Insert tab, in the Text group, click the text box button ⊡ and create three text boxes under each of the pictures to identify the equipment categories. For all three text boxes, use the font Corbel, 24 points, bold, and the **Orange, Accent 1** color.

   Kitchen Equipment
   Tableware
   Computer Equipment

5. Center align the text in each text box and then center the text boxes below each of the three pictures as shown in Figure 2-28.

Figure 2-28
Text box alignment

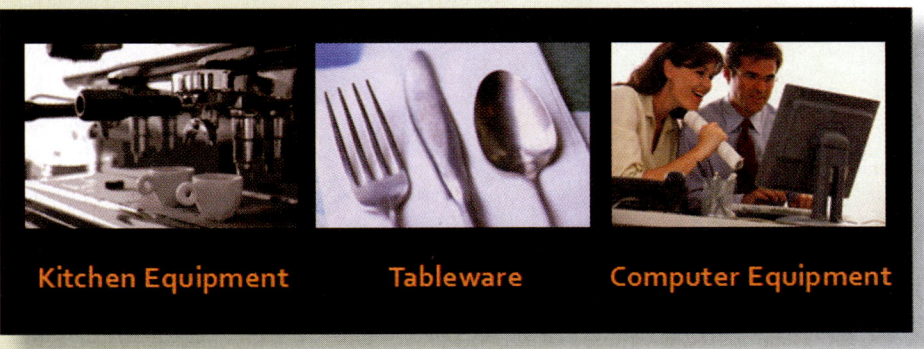

6. Move to slide 6, move the picture of the computer up and to the right, even with the rainbow colored line under the slide title.

7. Save the presentation as **[2-26your initials]** in your Lesson 2 folder.

8. Preview and then print the presentation as handouts, six slides per page, grayscale, landscape, framed. Close the presentation.

Lesson Applications

Exercise 2-27

Create a new blank presentation and add slides using different slide layouts.

1. Start a blank presentation.

2. Create a title slide with the text **First in Food Safety** as the title and **Good 4 U Employee Training** as the subtitle.

3. Using the text in Figure 2-29, create three slides. For slides 2 and 3, use the **Title and Content** layout. For slide 4, use the **Two Content** layout and key the first three bulleted items in the left placeholder and the last three bulleted items in the right placeholder.

Figure 2-29

Slide 2

Our Food Safety Programs
- Food handler training
- Management inspections
- Safety supervisors on-site
- Reports to USDA

Slide 3

Safe Food-Handling Practices
- Wear gloves, hair nets, and beard nets
- Wash hands before and after handling food
- Wear clean uniforms
- No smoking

Slide 4

Food Procurement
- Know your suppliers
- Prefer local growers
- Prefer organic food
- Insist on freshness
- Insist on cleanliness
- Test for pesticides

4. Check both body text placeholders for extra blank lines and remove them if necessary.

5. Move to slide 1 and save the presentation as **[2-27your initials]** in your Lesson 2 folder.

6. Preview and then print the presentation as handouts, four slides per page, grayscale, framed, landscape. Close the presentation.

Exercise 2-28

Work with indents, tabs, line spacing, and page setup options.

1. Open the file **Inventory**.

2. Move to slide 2, and apply the following formatting changes:

   - Change the first-level bullet to a large solid square from the Wingdings 2 font.

   - Use the ruler to increase the space between the bullet and text for even word-wrapping of the text.

   - Change the paragraph after spacing to 12 points.

3. On slide 3, make the following changes to the body text placeholder:

   - Change the bullets to a numbered list, formatting the numbering at 100% of text size.

   - Reduce the width of the text placeholder to approximately 7 inches, making the line endings more even.

   - Change the paragraph after spacing to 12 points.

4. On slide 4, select the three first-level bulleted items and make these changes:

   - Change the bullets to a numbered list, formatting the numbering at 100% of text size.

   - Change the indent on the second-level bullets so the bullet is indented 1.25 inches and the text is indented 1.5 inches.

   - Select the second-level bullet on item 1, item 2, and the second-level bullet on item 3 then change the paragraph after spacing to 12 points.

5. On slide 5, do the following:

   - Remove the bullets.

   - Press Tab after Miami and Tucson so the dates are aligned.

   - Change the line spacing to 2.

   - Adjust the size of the placeholder to fit the text.

   - Center the placeholder horizontally so you have even spacing on both sides of the text.

6. On slide 6, do the following:

   - Increase the size of the placeholder on the right so no lines word wrap.

   - Change the line spacing to 2.

7. Save the presentation as **[2-28your initials]** in your Lesson 2 folder.

8. Print as handouts, six slides per page, grayscale, landscape, framed. Close the presentation.

Exercise 2-29

Add slides, promote and demote text, insert a text box, and move bullets and slides.

1. Open the file **Marketing**.

2. On slide 1, increase the size of the title to 60 points and move the placeholder to the left slightly so the text aligns evenly with the picture on the left.

3. Select the subtitle placeholder then make the text right aligned and bold.

4. On slide 2, key the title **Our Products** and make it bold.

5. Still working on slide 2, move the picture to the left of the slide. Make a text box and key the following items. Press [Enter] after each item.

   - **Merchandise**
   - **Food services**
   - **Honeys and confections**
   - **T-shirts**
   - **Caps**

6. Select the text box and change the font size to 28 and the paragraph line spacing to 1.5.

7. Add bullets to the list and then customize them to choose Arrow Bullets in a blue color that works well with your design theme colors.

8. Resize the text box as needed so the lines do not word wrap.

9. Align the bulleted list beside the picture as shown in Figure 2-30.

Figure 2-30

10. Move to slide 1 and save the presentation as **[2-29your initials]** in your Lesson 2 folder.

11. Preview and then print the presentation as handouts, two slides per page, grayscale, landscape, framed. Close the presentation.

Exercise 2-30 ◆ Challenge Yourself

Work with indents, line spacing, and text box settings.

1. Open the file **Party2**.

2. On slide 2, remove all the bullets and hanging indents from both body text placeholders. Make the text in the left placeholder bold, resize the placeholder and move it under the slide title so it is aligned on the left.

3. Resize the "Directions" text placeholder and position it as shown in Figure 2-31 aligned on the left.

Figure 2-31
Slide 2

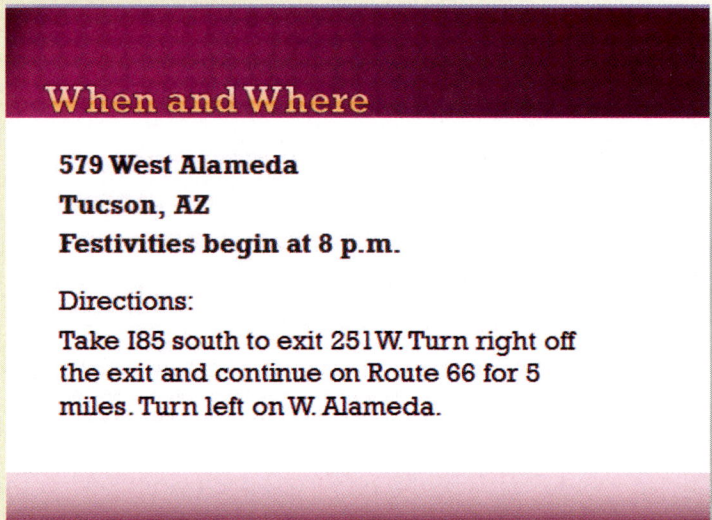

4. Move to slide 4 and create text boxes to key the text below. Center align all the text and use a black font. Use 20 points for the text and 24 points for the heading in each section. Add spacing of 12 points after the heading in each section. Refer to Figure 2-32.

Figure 2-32
Slide 5

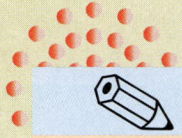

TIP

A quick way to create these boxes is to make the first one, adjust all formatting settings, then select the text box, and press Ctrl + D three times to duplicate that text box for the other shapes. Then reposition and edit each one.

5. Save the presentation as **[2-30your initials]** in your Lesson 2 folder.

6. Preview and then print the presentation as handouts, four slides per page, grayscale, landscape, scale to fit paper, framed. Close the presentation.

On Your Own

In these exercises you work on your own, as you would in a real-life work environment. Use the skills you've learned to accomplish the task—and be creative.

Exercise 2-31

Locate a recipe for a food dish that you enjoy. Organize the recipe steps to make it easy to teach someone to make it. Put the steps into an outline with at least four main points suitable for slide titles. Create the outline by using any method that is comfortable for you (index cards, Word, PowerPoint, etc.). From the outline, create a PowerPoint presentation with a title slide. Save the presentation as **[2-31your initials]**. Preview and then print the presentation as an outline and as handouts.

Exercise 2-32

Assume you are on a planning committee for a student organization or for your employer that has the responsibility to plan a holiday banquet. Create a slide show to guide discussion at your first meeting as your group starts planning this project. Identify all the tasks that must be accomplished before the event, and plan for the various courses of the meal, such as salad, main dish, side items, and dessert. Using the skills that you have learned up to this point, format the text attractively. Save the presentation as **[2-32your initials]**. Preview and then print the presentation as handouts.

Exercise 2-33

Imagine that you work at a car dealership where the computer system needs to be replaced. Research computer systems online, and create a presentation for your boss recommending what brand and options would be appropriate. Be sure to include a slide describing the costs and a slide with the benefits of choosing this system. Provide the URL addresses for the sites where you found the information. Create at least six slides using different slide layouts. Save the presentation as **[2-33your initials]**. Preview and then print the presentation as an outline and as handouts.

Lesson 3

Revising Presentation Text

OBJECTIVES

MCAS OBJECTIVES

In this lesson:
PP07 1.2.1
PP07 1.3
PP07 1.4.2
PP07 1.5
PP07 2.2.1
PP07 2.2.4
PP07 2.3.2
See Appendix

After completing this lesson, you will be able to:

1. Select, rearrange, and delete slides.

2. Use the clipboard.

3. Check spelling and word usage.

4. Insert headers and footers.

5. Apply a consistent background and color theme.

6. Add movement effects.

Estimated Time: 1½ hours

When using PowerPoint, it is important to review your presentation to ensure that it flows logically, is free of errors in spelling and grammar, and is consistent in its visual representation. Many PowerPoint tools will help with this important task.

Selecting, Rearranging, and Deleting Slides

Just as you frequently rearrange paragraphs or sentences in a word processing document, you will often need to rearrange or delete slides in a PowerPoint presentation. You can change the arrangement of slides by dragging them to a new position in the Slides tab, in the Outline tab, or in Slide Sorter view.

You can delete selected slide thumbnails by pressing Delete on your keyboard.

Exercise 3-1   SELECT MULTIPLE SLIDES

If you select multiple slides, you can move them to a new position all at one time. You can also delete several selected slides at one time. In addition, you can apply transitions, animations, and other effects to a group of selected slides.

There are two ways to select multiple slides:

Figure 3-1
Selecting contiguous slides

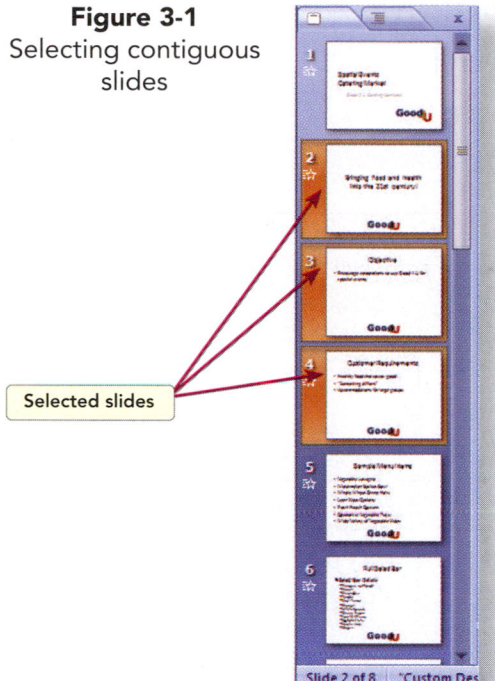

Selected slides

- To select *contiguous slides* (slides that follow one after another), click the first slide in the selection and then hold down Shift while you click the last slide in the selection.

- To select *noncontiguous slides* (slides that do not follow one after another), click the first slide and then hold down Ctrl while you click each slide you want to add to the selection, one at a time.

1. Open the file **SpEventCatering**.

2. In the Slides and Outline pane, click the Slides tab to display slide thumbnails if they are not already displayed.

3. Without clicking, point to each thumbnail one at a time and notice that a ScreenTip appears displaying the title of the slide.

4. Click the thumbnail for slide 2 ("Bringing Food and Health . . .") to select it.

5. Hold down Shift and click the slide 4 thumbnail ("Customer Requirements"). Release Shift.

   Slides 2, 3, and 4 are all selected, as indicated by the heavy borders around their thumbnails, as shown in Figure 3-1. This is a contiguous selection.

6. With Shift released, click slide 3. Now it is the only slide selected.

7. Hold down Ctrl and click slide 1. Slide 1 and slide 3 are both selected. This is a noncontiguous selection.

8. While holding down Ctrl, click slide 5. Now three noncontiguous slides are selected, as shown in Figure 3-2. You can add as many slides as you want to the selection if you hold down Ctrl while clicking a slide thumbnail.

Figure 3-2
Selecting noncontiguous slides

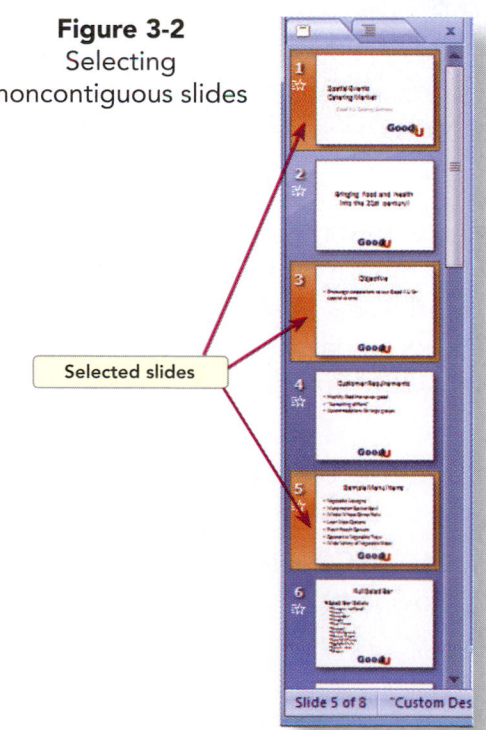

Selected slides

Exercise 3-2   REARRANGE SLIDE ORDER

The Slides tab is a convenient place to rearrange slides. You simply drag selected slide thumbnails to a new position. *Slide Sorter View* enables you to see more thumbnails at one time and is convenient if your presentation contains a large number of slides. You select slides in Slide Sorter view in the same way as in the Slides tab.

1. Click the Slide Sorter View button .

2. Click the slide 2 thumbnail to select it.

Figure 3-3
Moving a slide in the Slide Sorter View

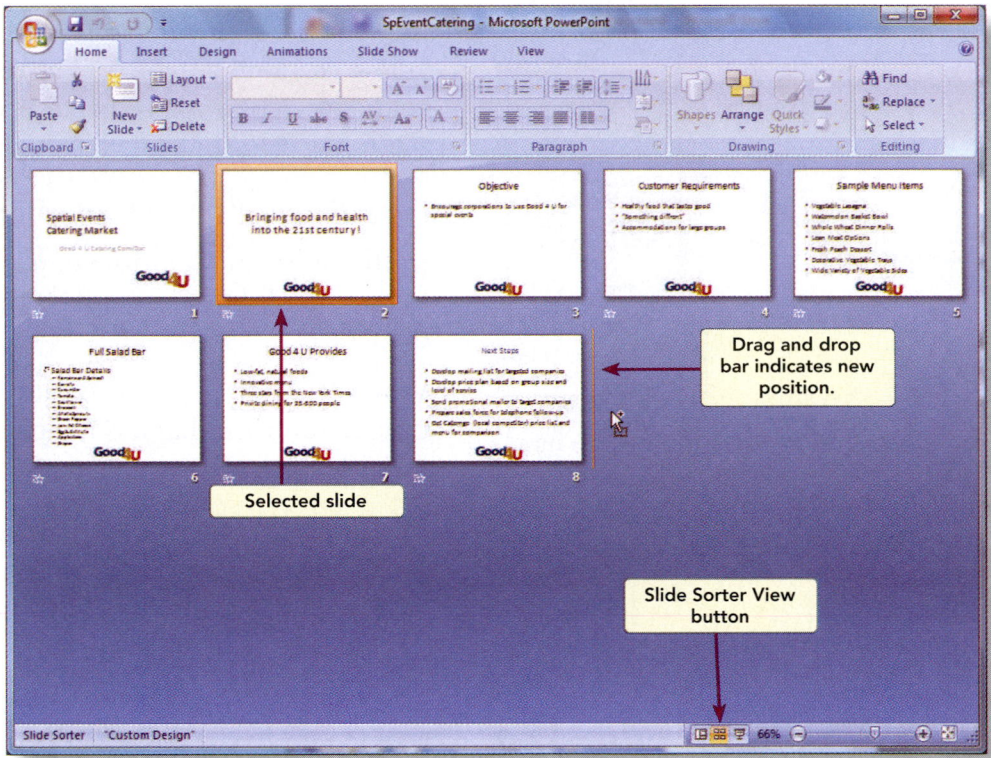

NOTE

While you are dragging, be sure not to release the left mouse button until it is pointing where you want the selection to go. Otherwise, you might either cancel the selection or drop the slides in the wrong place.

3. Position the pointer within the selected slide's border, press the left mouse button, and drag the pointer after the eighth slide, as shown in Figure 3-3. Notice the drag-and-drop bar (the vertical line) as you drag. The vertical line indicates where the slide will go.

4. Release the mouse button. Slide 2, titled "Bringing Food and Health . . . ," becomes slide 8.

5. Using Ctrl, make a noncontiguous selection of slides 3 ("Customer Requirements") and 6 ("Good 4 U Provides").

6. Point to either slide in the selection and drag the selection after the first slide. Both slides move to the new position.

7. Check to make sure your slides are in the following order. If not, rearrange your slides to agree.

   Slide 1: Special Events Catering Market (This slide has a spelling error that you will correct later.)

   Slide 2: Customer Requirements

   Slide 3: Good 4 U Provides

   Slide 4: Objective

   Slide 5: Sample Menu Items

   Slide 6: Full Salad Bar

   Slide 7: Next Steps

   Slide 8: Bringing Food and Health into the 21st Century!

8. Double-click slide 1 to display it in Normal view.

Exercise 3-3 DELETE SLIDES

When you want to delete slides, you first select them (in the Slides tab or in Slide Sorter view) the same way you select slides you want to move. You delete them by pressing Delete on your keyboard or clicking the Delete button on the Home tab, in the Slides group.

REVIEW

To advance through a slide show, click the left mouse button, press the Spacebar, press PageDown, or press N.

1. Working in Normal view, display the Slides tab if it is not already showing.

2. Click the slide 4 thumbnail to select it. The slide 4 title should be "Objective."

3. Press Delete on your keyboard. Slide 4 is deleted and the new slide 4 becomes selected.

4. Move to slide 1 and click the Slide Show button to start a slide show.

5. Advance through the slides (using any method), reading the text and observing the built-in animation effects.

6. Create a new folder for Lesson 3. Save the presentation as **[3-3your initials]** in the Lesson 3 folder. Do not print the presentation at this point, and do not close it.

Using the Clipboard

The *Cut*, *Copy*, and *Paste* commands are almost universally available in computer programs. When you cut selected text or a selected object, it is removed from the presentation and placed on the *Clipboard*, a temporary storage space. When you copy text or an object, it remains in its original place and a copy is placed on the Clipboard. When you paste a Clipboard item, a copy of the item is placed at the location of the insertion point and the item remains on the Clipboard to use again if needed.

Each item you cut or copy is stored on the Clipboard, which can hold up to 24 items at a time. Clipboard items can be viewed and managed by using the Clipboard task pane. When working with the Office Clipboard, it is important to understand that unlike the Cut command, Delete does not save items to the clipboard.

The following cut, copy, and paste keyboard shortcuts are big time-savers when you do extensive editing:

- Ctrl + C   Copy

- Ctrl + X   Cut

- Ctrl + V   Paste the most recent item stored on the clipboard.

Exercise 3-4   USE CUT, COPY, AND PASTE TO REARRANGE SLIDES

In the previous objective, you learned how to rearrange slides by dragging their thumbnails. This exercise presents another way to arrange slides by using the clipboard. From the Home tab, in the Clipboard group, you can open the Clipboard task pane by clicking the Dialog Box Launcher 🔲.

Figure 3-4
Using the Clipboard task pane

Number of items in the Clipboard

Slide that has been cut

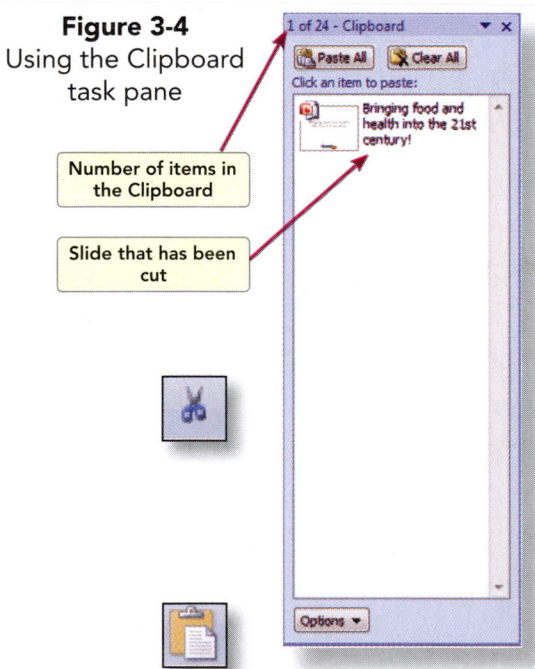

1. With the **[3-3your initials]** presentation open, from the Home tab, in the Clipboard group, click the Dialog Box Launcher 🔲 to display the Clipboard task pane, as shown in Figure 3-4.

2. On the Slides tab, click the thumbnail of slide 7 ("Bringing Food and Health into the 21st Century!").

3. From the Home tab, in the Clipboard group, click the Cut button ✂. This removes the slide and stores it on the clipboard.

4. Select the thumbnail for slide 1 ("Spatial Events Catering Market"). Later you will change the spelling of the first word.

5. From the Home tab, in the Clipboard group, click the Paste button 📋. The cut slide (on the clipboard) is inserted (or pasted) after slide 1. This accomplishes the same thing as if you moved the slide by dragging its thumbnail.

6. Select the slide 1 thumbnail ("Spatial Events Catering Market"). From the Home tab, in the Clipboard group, click the Copy button. Notice that two slides are stored on the Clipboard task pane.

7. Move to slide 7 ("Next Steps"). From the Home tab, in the Clipboard group, click the Paste button to paste ("Spatial Events Catering Market"). A copy of the slide is inserted at the end of the presentation to use for making a concluding comment.

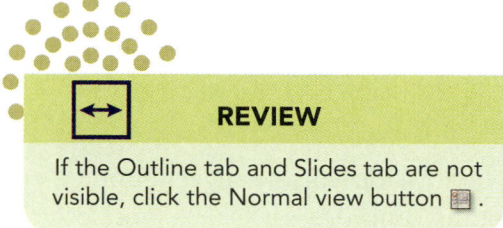

REVIEW

If the Outline tab and Slides tab are not visible, click the Normal view button.

8. Move to slide 8, the pasted slide.

9. Delete the subtitle text and key the following text in its place on four lines:

Catering Market Slogan:
Make Your Event Special
Call Good 4 U at
800-555-1234

10. Move to slide 1 and save the presentation as **[3-4your initials]**. Keep the presentation open for the next exercise.

Exercise 3-5   USE CUT, COPY, AND PASTE TO REARRANGE TEXT

Figure 3-5
Text and slides stored on the Office Clipboard

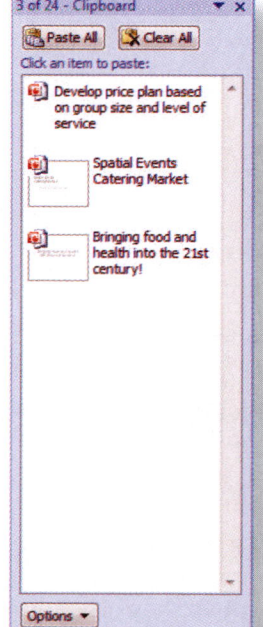

Just as you cut, copy, and paste slides, you can cut, copy, and paste text, and store it on the Office Clipboard. The Paste Options button appears near a pasted item if the item's *source* formatting is different from the formatting of similar elements in its *destination* presentation. A clipboard item's source is the presentation or other document from which it was cut or copied. Its destination is the presentation or other document in which it is pasted.

1. Display slide 7 ("Next Steps").

2. Activate the body text placeholder; then click the second bullet to select all its text.

3. Press Ctrl+X to cut the text from the slide. It appears on the Clipboard task pane. Notice the difference between text and slides on the Clipboard, as shown in Figure 3-5.

4. Click in front of the text in the first bulleted item.

5. Click the first item on the Clipboard task pane ("Develop price plan . . .") to insert that text as the first bulleted item.

6. Move to slide 6 ("Full Salad Bar").

7. Select the title text "Full Salad Bar," and press Ctrl+C to copy the text from the slide.

8. Move to slide 5, and click after the text "Wide Variety of Vegetable Sides," press Enter to create a new bullet, and press Ctrl+V. Notice that a Paste Options button 📋 appears each time you paste.

9. Click the Paste Options button 📋 that appears underneath the new bulleted item, and choose **Keep Source Formatting** from the drop-down list. Notice that the new bulleted item font size does not match that of the other bullets.

10. Click the Paste Options button 📋 again. This time choose **Use Destination Theme**, as shown in Figure 3-6. The bullet design changes to match the size of the other bulleted items.

NOTE

You can use paste options when you paste slides, text, or objects within the same presentations or between multiple presentations.

Figure 3-6
Viewing the Paste Options button

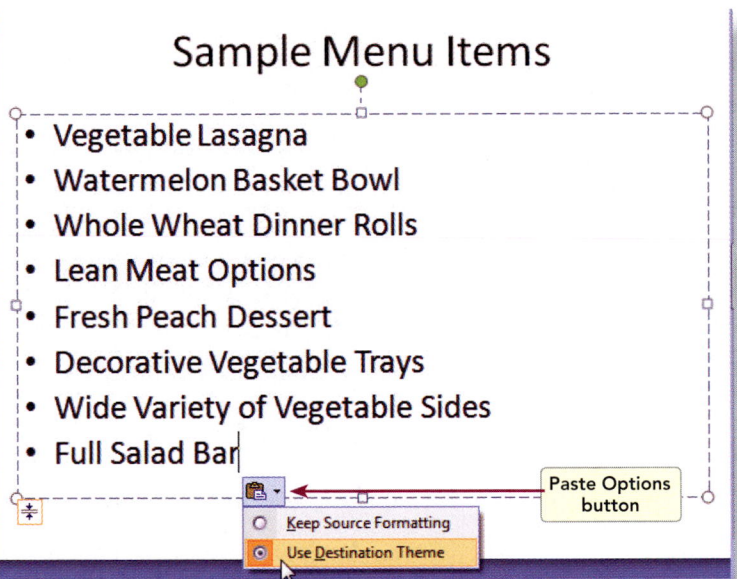

Exercise 3-6   CLEAR THE CLIPBOARD TASK PANE

The Clipboard task pane is a quick way to see a series of items that have been cut or copied to the Clipboard. The advantage of using the Clipboard to paste items is that you can have several items on the Clipboard and then choose

Options ▾

which ones you want to paste instead of having to paste immediately after copying or cutting. If you have copied a lot of items, however, you may want to clear the Clipboard task pane.

The Clipboard Options button Options ▾ allows you to control the settings of the Clipboard task pane.

1. If the Clipboard task pane is not open, from the Home tab, in the Clipboard group, click the Clipboard Dialog Box Launcher .

2. Click the Clipboard Options button Options ▾ at the bottom of the task pane, as shown in Figure 3-7.

Clear All

3. Choose **Show Office Clipboard Automatically** to enable the Clipboard to automatically pop up when you use the cut, copy, or paste commands.

Figure 3-7
Viewing the clipboard task pane options

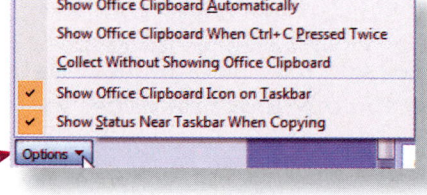

Clipboard Options button

4. At the top of the Clipboard task pane, click the Clear All button Options ▾ on to clear all of the contents held in the Clipboard.

5. Click Close on the Clipboard task pane.

Exercise 3-7   USE UNDO AND REDO

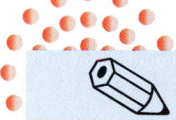

The *Undo* button on the Quick Access toolbar reverses the last action you took. You can undo a series of editing actions, including keying or deleting text, promoting or demoting items, or deleting slides. By using Undo more than once, you can undo multiple actions. The *Redo* button found beside the Undo button reapplies editing commands in the order you undid them.

> **TIP**
>
> By default, PowerPoint can undo the last 20 actions. You can increase or decrease this number by choosing the Microsoft Office Button, PowerPoint Options, Advanced tab, and changing the Maximum number of undos. Increasing the number uses up more RAM memory on your computer.

In PowerPoint, unlike Word, Undo and Redo are cleared when you save a presentation. In other words, you cannot undo or redo actions performed before saving a presentation. Therefore, in PowerPoint, don't save unless you are sure you won't want to undo an action.

1. Move to slide 7 ("Next Steps"). Click at the end of the second bulleted line and press Enter.

2. Click the Undo button . Notice the new bullet is removed and your insertion point is back at the end of the first line.

3. Click the Redo button . The bullet is back and ready to accept text beside it.

4. On the new bulleted line, type the text below:

Fully develop a menu choices plan

5. Press Ctrl+Z, the keyboard shortcut for Undo. Part of your text will go away.

6. Press Ctrl+Y, the keyboard shortcut for Redo. The text that was taken away in step 5 is now back on your screen.

7. In the Slides and Outline pane, click on slide 6, and press Delete on your keyboard. Notice the slide is deleted.

8. Press Ctrl+Z to undo this deletion and put the slide back into place.

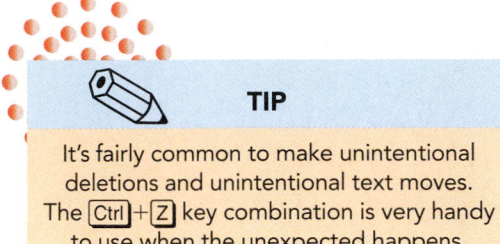

TIP

It's fairly common to make unintentional deletions and unintentional text moves. The Ctrl+Z key combination is very handy to use when the unexpected happens.

Exercise 3-8   USE FORMAT PAINTER

If you use Word or Excel, you may be familiar with the *Format Painter* tool. This tool makes it easy to copy the formatting, for example, the font size, color, and font face, from one object to another object on the same slide or within a presentation.

When you copy the format of an object, many default settings associated with that object are copied as well.

1. On slide 6, select the title "Full Salad Bar."

2. From the Home tab, in the Clipboard group, click the Format Painter button ✦. The Format Painter picks up the font formatting of this title.

3. Click within the word "cucumber" on the same slide. The text appears with the same formatting as the title. Click the Undo button ⤺.

4. Select the title "Full Salad Bar" once again and double-click the Format Painter button ✦. Double-clicking keeps the Format Painter active, so you can copy the formatting to more than one object.

5. Move to slide 7, and click on "Next" in the title. Notice when you just click a word, it changes only that single word.

6. Click "Steps" to format it the same way.

7. Click the Format Painter button ✦ again or press Esc to restore the standard pointer.

Checking Spelling and Word Usage

PowerPoint provides many tools to edit and revise text, and improve the overall appearance of a presentation:

- *Spelling Checker*, which corrects spelling by comparing words to an internal dictionary file.

- *Research*, which allows you to search through reference materials such as dictionaries, encyclopedias, and translation services to find the information you need.

- *Thesaurus*, which offers new words with similar meanings to the word you are looking up.

- *Find* and *Replace*, which allows you to find a certain word or phrase and replace it with a different word or phrase.

Exercise 3-9   CHECK SPELLING

The *Spelling Checker* in PowerPoint works much the same as it does in other Microsoft Office applications. It flags misspelled words with a red wavy underline as you key text. It can also check an entire presentation at once. The Spelling Checker is an excellent proofreading tool, but it should be used in combination with your own careful proofreading and editing.

1. In slide 1, a word in the subtitle has a red wavy underline indicating a spelling error. Right-click the word. Choose the correct spelling ("Committee") from the short-cut menu and click to accept it.

2. Notice the spelling of "Spatial" in the title. This is an example of a word that is correctly spelled but incorrectly used. The Spelling Checker can't help you with this kind of mistake. Change the spelling to **Special**. Do this on slide 8 also.

3. Move to slide 1 and run the Spelling Checker for the entire presentation. From the Review tab, in the Proofing Group, click the Spelling button 🔲 or press F7.

4. PowerPoint highlights "diffrent," the first word it doesn't find in its dictionary. It displays the word in the Spelling dialog box and suggests a corrected spelling, as shown in Figure 3-8.

Figure 3-8
Using the spelling checker

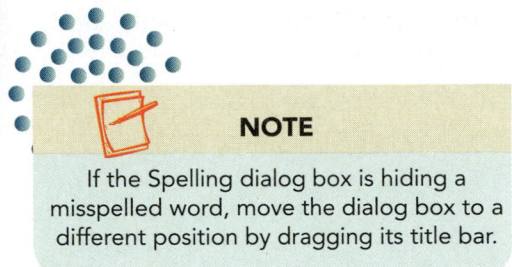

NOTE

If the Spelling dialog box is hiding a misspelled word, move the dialog box to a different position by dragging its title bar.

5. Click **Change** to apply the correct spelling of "different."

6. When the spelling checker locates "Privite," click **Change** on the correct spelling of "Private."

7. At the next spelling error "Caterngo," click **Ignore** because this is the correct spelling of the company name.

8. Click **OK** when the spelling check is complete.

Figure 3-9
Research task pane with definitions

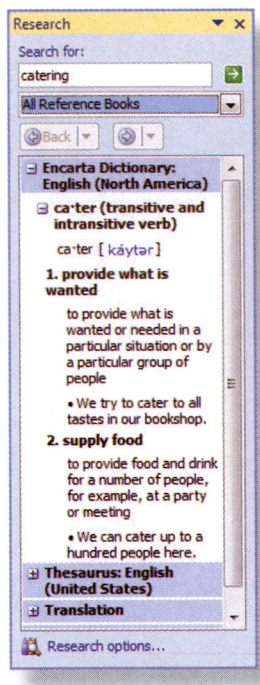

Exercise 3-10   USE RESEARCH

Research is a handy reference tool to look up many facets of a word. For example, when you research the word "catering," you find information about the definition of the word from the dictionary, synonyms in the thesaurus, and an area where you can translate this word into another language.

1. From the Review tab, in the Proofing group, click the Research button 📖.

2. On the Research task pane in the **Search for** box, type **catering** and press ⌷Enter⌷.

3. Look in the definition area and notice that the context for the word "catering" is definition number 2, as shown in Figure 3-9.

4. On the Thesaurus task pane, click the Close button ⌷x⌷.

Exercise 3-11   USE THE THESAURUS

The *Thesaurus* is used to find words with similar meanings. This tool is extremely helpful when the same word becomes repetitious and you would like to use a similar word, or if you are looking for a more appropriate word with a similar meaning.

1. On slide 6, put your insertion point on the word "Full." From the Review tab, in the Proofing group, click the Thesaurus button 📖. On the Research task pane, the word "full" is automatically placed in the **Search for** box, a search has already been performed, and the results displayed, as shown in Figure 3-10.

Figure 3-10
Search word highlighted and Thesaurus task pane

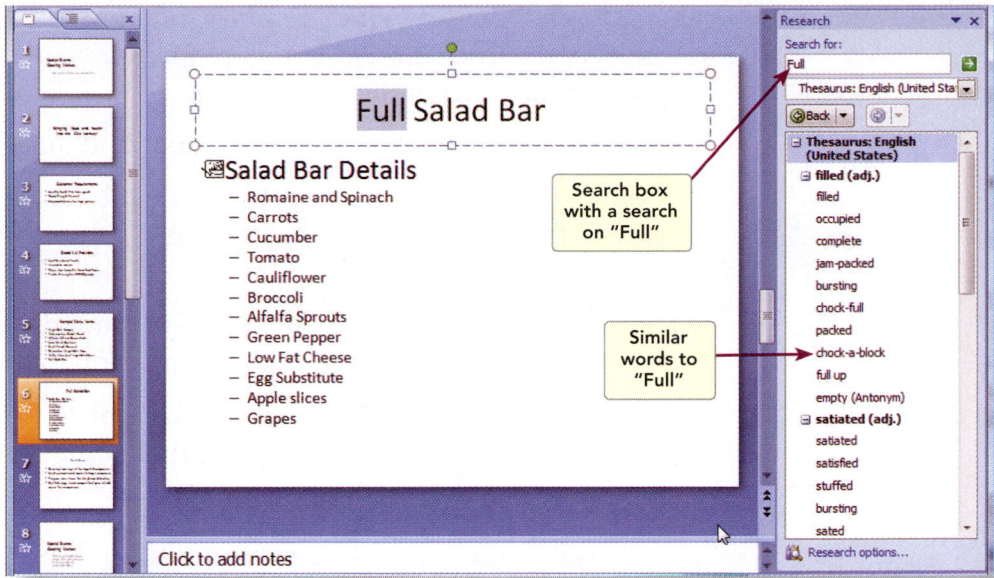

2. Scroll down until you find the word "extensive." Click the down arrow beside extensive, and choose **Insert**. Notice that the word "Full" is replaced by the word "Extensive," and the slide now reads "Extensive Salad Bar."

3. Click the Thesaurus task pane Close button ☒.

Exercise 3-12 USE FIND AND REPLACE

When you create presentations—especially long presentations—you often need to review or change text. In PowerPoint, you can do this quickly by using the Find and Replace commands.

The *Find* command locates specified text in a presentation. The *Replace* command finds the text and replaces it with a specified alternative.

1. Move to slide 1. From the Home tab, in the Editing group, click the Find button (or press Ctrl+F) to open the Find dialog box.

2. In the **Find what** text box, key **full**, as shown in Figure 3-11.

Figure 3-11
Find dialog box with text selected

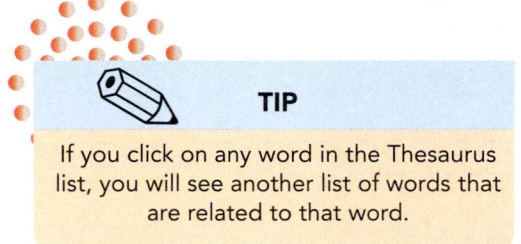

3. Click the Find Next button 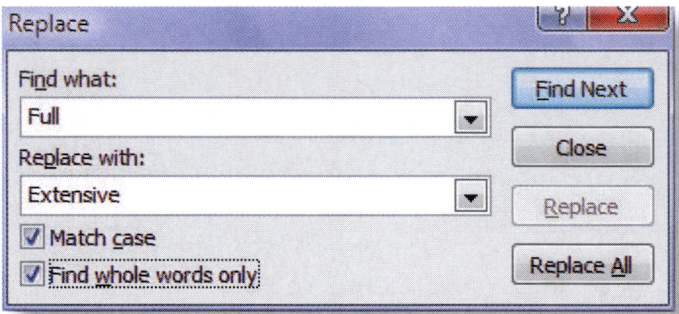 and PowerPoint locates and selects the text. This could be used if you were looking for a particular word in the presentation.

4. Click the Close button ⊠ to close the Find dialog box.

5. Move back to slide 1. From the Home tab, in the Editing group, click the Replace button `Replace` (or press Ctrl+H) to open the Replace dialog box.

6. In the **Find what** text box, key **Full** if it is not displayed already. In the **Replace with** text box, key **Extensive** as shown in Figure 3-12.

7. Check **Match case** and **Find whole words only**, to ensure that you find only the text "Full" and not words that contain these letters (such as "fuller" or "fullest").

Figure 3-12
Replace dialog box

8. Click the Find Next button and PowerPoint finds the first occurrence of "Full." Click the Replace button `Replace`. Click the Find Next button `Find Next` once again. A dialog box appears to tell you the search is completed. Click **OK**.

9. Click the Close button ⊠ to close the Replace dialog box.

10. Return to slide 1 and save the presentation as **[3-12your initials]** in your Lesson 3 folder. Leave the presentation open for the next exercise.

> **TIP**
>
> If you're certain about what you're looking for, you can use the Replace All button `Replace All` to replace all occurrences of text in one step.

Inserting Headers and Footers

You can add identifying information to your presentation, such as header or footer text, the date, or a slide or page number. See Table 3-1. A *header* is text that appears at the top of each notes page or handouts page. A *footer* is text that appears at the bottom of each slide, notes page, or handouts page. Header and footer text appears in special header and footer placeholders.

 As is true in Word and Excel, the Header and Footer button 🖹 is on the Insert tab in the Text group. In PowerPoint, this command opens the Header and Footer dialog box, which has two tabs: the Slide tab and the Notes and Handouts tab.

TABLE 3-1 Adding Identifying Information to Presentations

Information	Description
Date and Time	Current date and time—can be updated automatically or keyed
Header	Descriptive text printed at the top of the page on notes and handouts pages only
Page Number	Number placed in the lower-right corner of notes and handouts pages by default
Slide Number	Number placed on slides, usually in the lower-right corner
Footer	Descriptive text printed at the bottom of slides, notes pages, and handouts pages

Exercise 3-13   ADD SLIDE DATE, PAGE NUMBER, AND FOOTER

Using the Slide tab in the Header and Footer dialog box, you can add information to the footer of all slides in a presentation by clicking **Apply to All**, or you can add footer information to only the current slide by clicking **Apply**.

1. Working on the presentation **[3-12your initials]**, from the Insert tab, in the Text group, click the Header and Footer button 📄. Notice the two tabs in the Header and Footer dialog box, one for adding information to slides and one for adding information to notes and handouts, as shown in Figure 3-13. Click the Slide tab.

Figure 3-13
Header and Footer dialog box, Slide tab

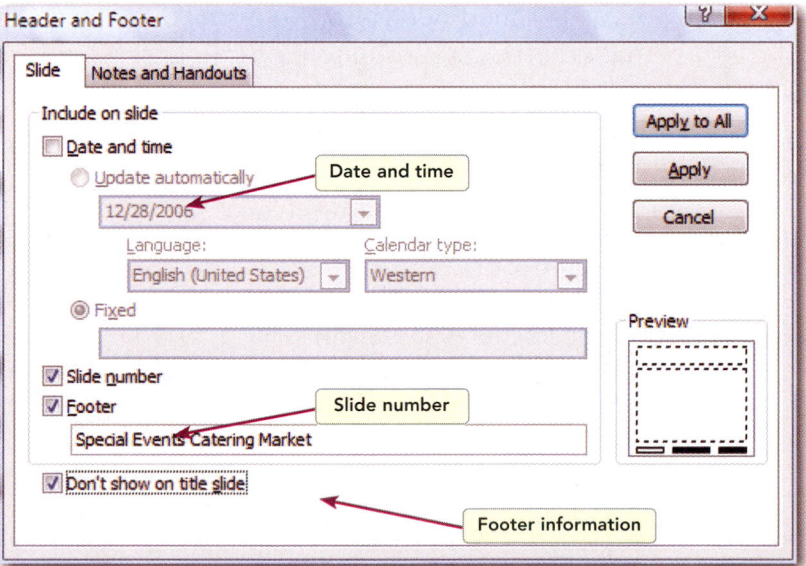

2. In the **Preview** box, notice the positions for the elements you can place on a slide. As you enable each element by selecting its check box, PowerPoint indicates where the element will print with a bold outline.

3. Click the **Slide number** check box to select it.

4. Click the check box labeled **Don't show on title slide**. When this box is checked, footer and page number information does not appear on the slides using the title slide layout.

5. Clear the **Date and Time** check box so there is no check.

6. Click the **Footer** check box and key **Special Events Catering Market**.

7. Click **Apply to All**. The presentation now has footer information including slide numbers at the bottom of each slide except the title slide.

8. Move to slide 1 and click the Slide Show button 🗐 on the Status bar to view the presentation. Notice the footer information and slide number at the bottom of the slide.

Exercise 3-14   ADD HANDOUT DATE, PAGE NUMBER, AND HEADER

Using the Notes and Handouts tab, you can insert both header and footer information on notes pages and handouts that are usually printed.

1. From the Insert tab, in the Text group, click the Header and Footer button 🖹. On the Header and Footer dialog box, click the Notes and Handouts tab as shown in Figure 3-14.

2. Under the **Date and time** option, click **Update automatically** to add today's date. Each time you print the presentation handout, it will include the current date. You can choose different date and time formats from the drop-down list.

Figure 3-14
Header and Footer dialog box, Notes and Handouts tab

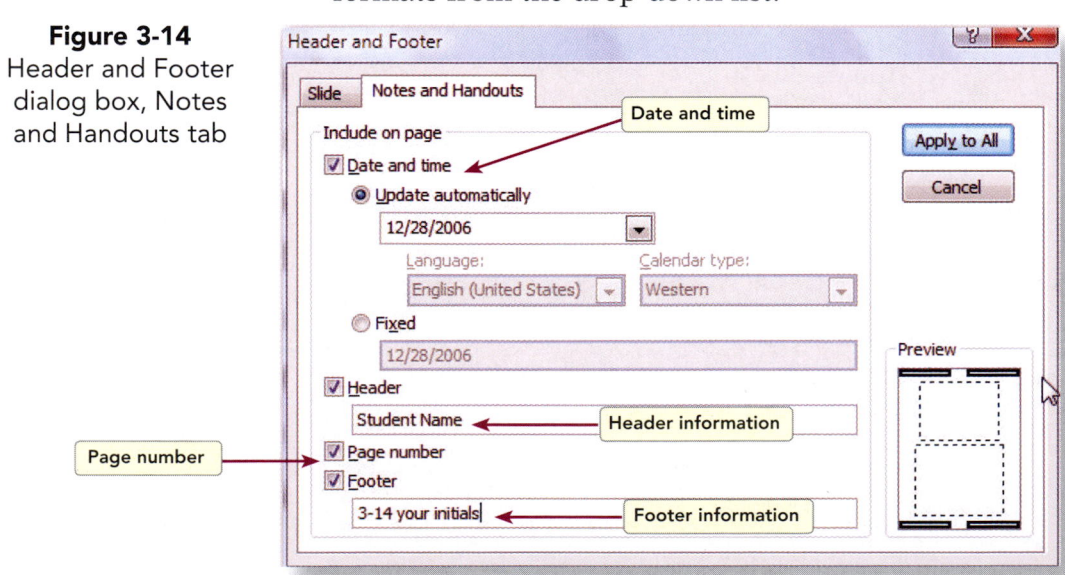

3. Make sure **Header** is checked and key **Your Name** in the header text box. The header is printed in the upper-left corner of a notes or handouts page.

4. Make sure the **Page number** option is checked. Page numbers are printed at the bottom right of the page.

5. Make sure the **Footer** check box is selected. Then key the filename **[3-14your initials]** in its text box.

6. Click **Apply to All** to add this information to all handouts pages you print (but not to individual slides).

7. Save the presentation as **[3-14your initials]** in your Lesson 3 folder.

Applying a Consistent Background and Color Theme

When you create a new blank presentation, the presentation contains no special formatting, colors, or graphics. Sometimes it's convenient to work without design elements so that you can focus all your attention on the presentation's text. Before the presentation is completed, however, you will usually want to apply a *design theme* to add visual interest. You can apply a design theme or change to a different one at any time while you are developing your presentation.

Exercise 3-15 **SELECT A DESIGN THEME**

The presentation that you have been working on in this lesson contains no theme. To select a design theme, from the Design tab, in the Themes group, click a design theme. The process to change a design theme is the same as to apply it for the first time.

1. From the Design tab, in the Themes group, click the More button 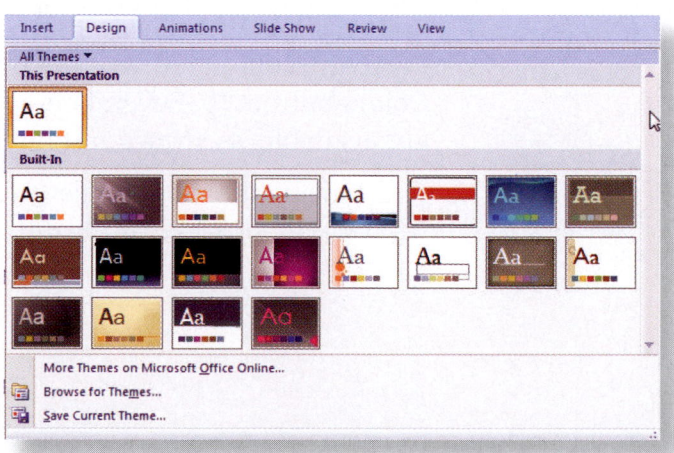 to display the theme choices shown as thumbnails.

Figure 3-15
Applying a design theme

2. Use the vertical scroll bar in the All Themes window to view the many design thumbnails. The window is divided by "This Presentation" and "Built-In." Links are available for "More Themes on Microsoft Office Online," "Browse for Themes," and "Save Current Theme," as shown in Figure 3-15.

3. Point to one of the design theme thumbnails. Notice the live preview working as you point to one of the design themes; PowerPoint automatically previews what that design theme will look like applied to your presentation. A ScreenTip also appears to indicate the name of the theme you are previewing or choosing.

4. Point to several design themes to sample what your presentation will look like with them applied.

5. Right-click any design theme thumbnail. Notice that you can apply the slide design to matching slides, all slides, or selected slides.

6. Click **Apply to All Slides**. The design theme that you selected is applied to all the slides in your presentation.

7. Locate the **Flow** design theme in the list of design theme thumbnails and click it. By clicking on the design theme, it automatically changes all slides in the presentation. (If **Flow** is not available on your computer, use a different theme.)

8. Notice that each thumbnail on the Slides tab shows the new theme design. Note also that the name of the template appears at the left on the status bar below the slide.

9. Move to slide 1 and view the presentation as a slide show; then return to slide 1 in Normal view.

Exercise 3-16   CHANGE THEME COLORS

You can apply different built-in colors to the current design theme by changing the *theme colors*. To display the built-in theme colors, from the Design tab, in the Themes group, click the Colors button.

NOTE

You can choose to apply to selected slides, matching slides, or all slides on each of the theme elements including designs, colors, fonts, and effects.

1. From the Design tab, in the Themes group, click the Colors button. Several choices for theme colors are available, as shown in Figure 3-16.

2. Point to any theme color set to see a live preview of what it will look like applied to your presentation.

Figure 3-16
Theme Colors drop-down list

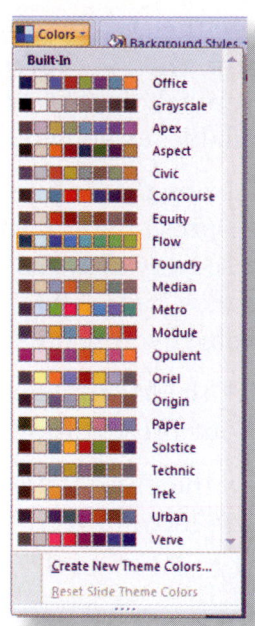

3. Click any theme color to apply it to your presentation.

4. Click the **Aspect** theme color to apply it to your presentation.

5. View the presentation as a slide show; then return to Normal view.

6. Move to slide 8.

7. From the **Design** tab, in the Themes group, click the Colors button.

8. Right-click on the **Office** theme color and choose **Apply to Selected Slides**. Notice that the color of only slide 8 changes to make this closing slide look a little different from the other slides.

Exercise 3-17   CHANGE THEME FONTS

You can apply different built-in fonts to the current design theme by changing the *theme font*. To display the built-in theme fonts, from the Design tab, in the Themes group, click the Fonts button.

Figure 3-17
Theme Font drop-down list

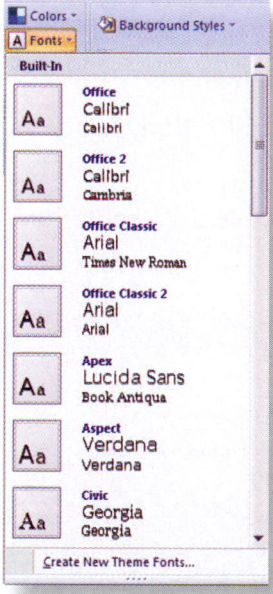

1. From the Design tab, in the Themes group, click the Fonts button . Several choices for theme fonts are available, as shown in Figure 3-17.

2. Point to any theme font to see a live preview of what it will look like applied to your presentation. A ScreenTip will pop up showing the name of the theme font.

3. Click any theme font to apply it to your presentation.

4. Click the **Oriel** Theme Font (Century Schoolbook) to apply it to your presentation.

5. View the presentation as a slide show; then return to Normal view.

Exercise 3-18   CHANGE THEME EFFECTS

You can apply different built-in effects to the current design theme by changing the *theme effects*. To display the built-in theme effects, from the Design tab, in the Themes group, click the Effects button.

Figure 3-18
Theme Effect drop-
down list

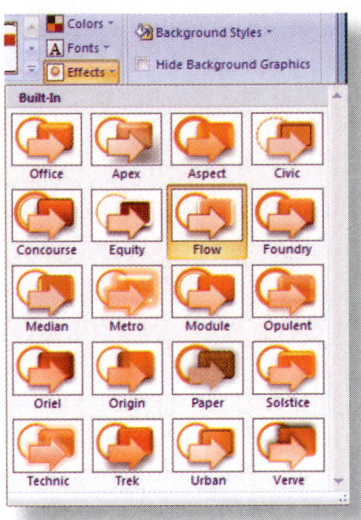

1. From the Design tab, in the Themes group, click the Effects button [⊙]. Several choices for theme effects are available, as shown in Figure 3-18.

2. Click any theme effects to apply it to your presentation. Right now you may not see any changes because these effects are most noticeable when applied to graphics you will use in later lessons.

3. Click the **Metro** theme effects to apply it to your presentation.

4. View the presentation as a slide show; then return to Normal view.

Exercise 3-19   CREATE NEW THEME FONTS

Although many built-in theme fonts are available, it is sometimes better to choose your own. You can accomplish this by creating new theme fonts.

1. From the Design tab, in the Themes group, click the Fonts button [A].

2. Click **Create New Theme Fonts** at the bottom of the Font Theme drop-down list.

3. Click the drop-down arrow under **Heading font**, and choose **Gloucester MT Extra Condensed**, as shown in Figure 3-19.

4. Click the drop-down arrow under **Body font**, and choose **Goudy Old Style**.

5. In the Name box, key **Special Event Presentation Font Theme**.

Figure 3-19
Create New Theme
Fonts dialog box

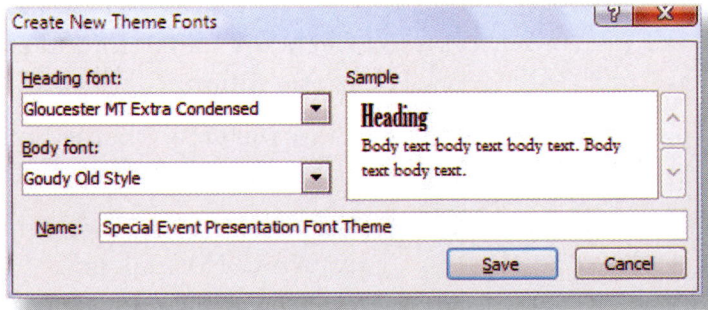

6. Click **Save**. Notice the change in the fonts of your presentation.

7. Save the presentation as **[3-19your initials]** in your Lesson 3 folder.

Adding Movement Effects

A *slide transition* is an effect that appears between two slides as they change during a slide show. You can choose to make one slide blend into the next in a checkerboard pattern, a fade pattern, or choose from many other effects. Transitions can have an effect like turning pages of a book. Movement can be applied to all slides in a presentation to control how they enter and exit the screen.

Exercise 3-20   APPLY SLIDE TRANSITIONS

Transitions can be applied to individual slides, to a group of slides, or to an entire slide show. To apply transitions, from the Animations tab, in Transition to This Slide group, click the More button ⬇ to display transition options. Click on the transition that you would like to apply.

1. Move to slide 1 and from the Animations tab, in the Transition to This Slide group, click the More button ⬇ to view all of the transition options shown as thumbnails.

Figure 3-20
Choosing the Box Out transition

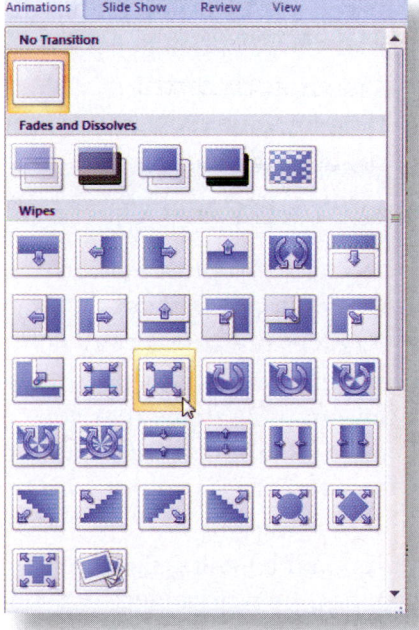

2. Point to several transitions and notice that the live preview shows you how this transition effect will look applied to your slide.

3. Choose **Box Out** from the list of transitions, as shown in Figure 3-20. This applies the transition to slide 1 only.

4. From the Animations tab, in the Transitions to This Slide group, click the Apply to All button ⬚. This applies the transition to all slides in the presentation.

5. View the presentation as a slide show, and notice the Box Out transition between slides.

Exercise 3-21   ADJUST SOUNDS AND SPEEDS

Transitions also have the option to include sounds during the transition, and you can adjust the speed at which the transition occurs.

1. Move to slide 1. From the Animations tab, in the Transitions to This Slide group, click the drop-down arrow in the Transition Speed list box.

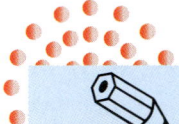

2. Choose **Medium** to slow the speed of the transition a little. This applies only to slide 1.

3. From the Animations tab, in the Transitions to This Slide group, click the Apply to All button . This applies the transition speed to all slides in the presentation.

4. Click the drop-down arrow in the Transition Sounds list box, and point to several sounds to listen to the possibilities for transition sounds.

5. Move to slide 1 and choose **Applause** from the Transition Sounds list box to apply the applause sound.

6. Still working in the Transitions to this Slide group, for **Advance slide** select **On mouse click** if it is not already checked.

7. View the presentation as a slide show to hear this sound as slide 1 appears.

8. Save the presentation as **[3-21your initials]** in your Lesson 3 folder.

9. Print the presentation as handouts, grayscale, framed, three slides per page.

TIP

Try not to apply transition effects randomly. You might choose one transition for most of your presentation and then select one or two other effects to better emphasize the slide content as it appears. Be careful about using sounds, too, because they may detract from your presentation unless specifically suited to your content.

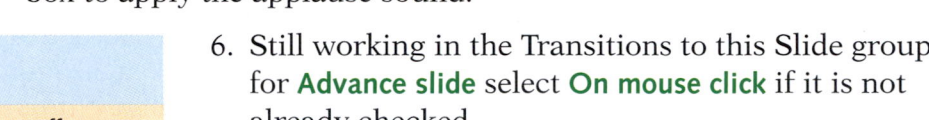

Lesson 3 Summary

- To change the order of slides in a presentation, use either the Slides and Outline pane or the Slide Sorter view. Select the slides you want to move; then drag them to a new location. You can also delete selected slides.

- The Clipboard can store up to 24 items that you cut or copy from a presentation. The items can be text, entire slides, or other objects. Insert a Clipboard item at the current location in your presentation by clicking the item.

- Text can be moved or copied by using the Cut, Copy, and Paste commands. Slides can also be rearranged by using these commands.

- The Paste Options button ⬚ enables you to choose between a pasted item's source formatting and its destination formatting. The source is the slide or placeholder from which the item was cut or copied, and the destination is the location where it will be pasted.

- PowerPoint enables you to undo—and if you change your mind—redo multiple editing actions. The default number of available undos is 20. When you save a presentation, the list of undos is cleared.

- The Format Painter button ⬚ enables you to copy formatting from one object to another. This is a great time-saver if you applied several effects to an object and want to duplicate the effects.

- Double-clicking the Format Painter button ✅ keeps it active, so that multiple objects can receive the copied format. Click the Format Painter button ✅ again to turn it off.
- Right-clicking a word flagged with a red wavy line provides a shortcut list of suggested spelling corrections. You can spell check an entire presentation at one time by using the Spelling dialog box.
- Use the Research task pane to research items in the dictionary, thesaurus, and translator all at once.
- Use the Thesaurus task pane to find words with similar meanings.
- The Find command and the Replace command search your entire presentation for specified text. The Replace feature enables you to automatically make changes to matching text it finds.
- Headers and Footers can appear at the top and bottom of notes and handouts pages. Footers can also appear at the bottom of slides. They are commonly used to provide page numbers, dates, and other identifying information common to an entire presentation.
- Design Themes are a great way to add color, design, fonts, and effects all at once.
- There are several built-in Theme Colors, Theme Fonts, and Theme Effects. You can access these from the Design tab, in the Theme group.
- Design themes, Theme Colors, Theme Fonts, and Theme Effects can be applied to individual slides, to a group of selected slides, or to an entire presentation.
- Slide transitions add visual interest to slide shows. They can be applied to individual slides, a group of slides, or an entire slide presentation.
- Transition sounds and speed can be adjusted to add interest in a presentation.

LESSON 3		Command Summary	
Feature	**Button**	**Ribbon**	**Keyboard**
Select contiguous slides			Shift + click left mouse button
Select noncontiguous slides			Ctrl + click left mouse button
Delete selected slides	🗙	Home, Slides group, Delete	Delete
Cut selected object or text	✂	Home, Clipboard group, Cut	Ctrl + X
Copy selected object or text	📋	Home, Clipboard group, Copy	Ctrl + C
Paste (insert) cut or copied object or text	📋	Home, Clipboard group, Paste	Ctrl + V

continues

LESSON 3		Command Summary *continued*	
Feature	**Button**	**Ribbon**	**Keyboard**
Paste options			
Display Clipboard task pane		Home, Clipboard group, Dialog Box Launcher	
Clear the Clipboard task pane	Clear All	Clipboard task pane, Clear All	
Copy formatting of an object		Home, Clipboard group, Format Painter	
Undo		Quick Access toolbar, Undo	Ctrl + Z
Redo		Quick Access toolbar, Redo	Ctrl + Y
Spelling checker	ABC	Review, Proofing group, Spelling	F7
Research definitions		Review, Proofing group, Research	
Thesaurus		Review, Proofing group, Thesaurus	
Find		Home, Editing group, Find	Ctrl + F
Replace	Replace	Home, Editing group, Replace	Ctrl + H
Header and footer		Insert, Text group, Header and Footer	
Apply Design Theme		Design, Themes group, Design Theme	
Choose Theme Colors		Design, Themes group, Colors	
Choose Theme Fonts	A	Design, Themes group, Fonts	
Choose Theme Effects		Design, Themes group, Effects	
Slide transition		Animation, Transition to This Slide group	

Concepts Review

True/False Questions

Each of the following statements is either true or false. Select your choice by indicating T or F.

T   F   1. The only way to change the order of slides is to drag them to a new position in Slide Sorter view.

T   F   2. The Clipboard can store up to 24 items that you cut or copy from a presentation.

T   F   3. The keyboard shortcut for undoing a task is Ctrl+Z.

T   F   4. You can use the Format Painter tool to copy formatting from one slide to another.

T   F   5. You can put headers on slides, but not on handouts.

T   F   6. You can activate the Spelling Checker by pressing F1.

T   F   7. The Find command is located on the Review tab.

T   F   8. Slide transitions appear when you move from one slide to the next while presenting a slide show.

Short Answer Questions

Write the correct answer in the space provided.

1. How do you select two noncontiguous slides at the same time?

2. How do you change the color theme of just one slide in a presentation?

3. Name two ways to copy a selection of text.

4. What is the default number of actions that you can undo using the Undo feature in PowerPoint?

5. How do you use the Thesaurus?

6. When you use the Header and Footer dialog box to add slide numbers to a presentation, where do the numbers usually appear on the slides?

_____

7. How would you apply a transition to all of the slides in a presentation?

_____

8. What feature can you use to copy the formatting of selected text to new text?

_____

Critical Thinking

Answer these questions on a separate page. There are no right or wrong answers. Support your answers with examples from your own experience, if possible.

1. PowerPoint enables the user to choose a different design theme, color, font, effect, transition, and animation for each slide. How can these effects be applied consistently and why is it important to portray consistency throughout the presentation?

2. You can use headers and footers to identify your slides, handouts, and notes pages. What information is most important to include? Why?

Skills Review

Exercise 3-22

Add text, rearrange slides, and delete slides.

1. Open the file **Resort**.
2. On slide 1, replace "Student Name" with **your name**.
3. On slide 2, change the title "Customer Requirements" to **Vacationer's Expectations**.
4. On slide 3, insert a new bullet line after the first bullet point and key **Our name associated with gourmet dining**.
5. On slide 4, insert the following text into the blank body text placeholder: Key **Miami Beach** and press [Enter]; key **Palm Springs** and press [Enter]; and key **Niagara Falls**.
6. Reverse the position of slides 2 and 3 by following these steps:

   a. Click the Slides tab on the Slides and Outline pane.

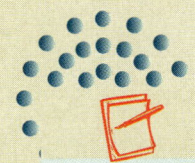

NOTE

If the Slides and Outline pane is not displayed, click the Normal view button to display it.

   b. Position your pointer on the right border of the Slides tab and drag the Splitter bar to the right to enlarge the slide thumbnails.

   c. Click the slide 3 thumbnail to select it.

   d. Drag slide 3 up until the drag-and-drop bar (the horizontal line) is between slides 1 and 2.

   e. Release your mouse button.

7. Reverse the position of slides 5 and 6.

8. Select slide 7 ("Key Benefits") and press [Delete] on your keyboard.

9. Move to slide 1 and save the presentation as **[3-22your initials]** in your Lesson 3 folder.

10. Preview and then print the presentation as handouts, nine slides per page, grayscale, framed.

11. Close the presentation.

Exercise 3-23

Rearrange slides, use cut and paste, and check spelling.

1. Open the file **EatGuide**.

2. Move to slide 3 ("Basic Food Groups") and cut the text "Use Sparingly" by using the following steps:

   a. Click the I-beam pointer before "Use" and drag to select "Sparingly."

   b. From the Home tab, in the Clipboard group, click the Cut button 🔹 .

3. Move to slide 7, and paste the copied text by following these steps:

   a. Click the I-beam pointer in the body text placeholder after "Sweets."

   b. Press [Enter] two times.

   c. From the Home tab, in the Clipboard group, click the Paste button 📋 .

4. Promote "Use Sparingly" so it is even with the word "Examples."

5. In the Slide pane, drag slide 10 below slide 3.

6. Check spelling in the presentation by following these steps:

   a. Move to slide 1.

   b. From the Review tab, in the Proofing group, click the Spelling button ✅ .

   c. Make corrections if needed, and click **OK** when the Spelling Checker has completed checking the document.

7. Move to slide 1 and save the presentation as **[3-23your initials]** in your Lesson 3 folder.

8. Preview and then print the presentation as handouts, four slides per page, landscape, grayscale, framed. Close the presentation.

Exercise 3-24

Apply a design theme, use the Undo command, and change the theme color.

1. Start a new presentation.
2. Apply a design theme by following these steps:
   a. From the Design tab, in the Themes group, click the More button 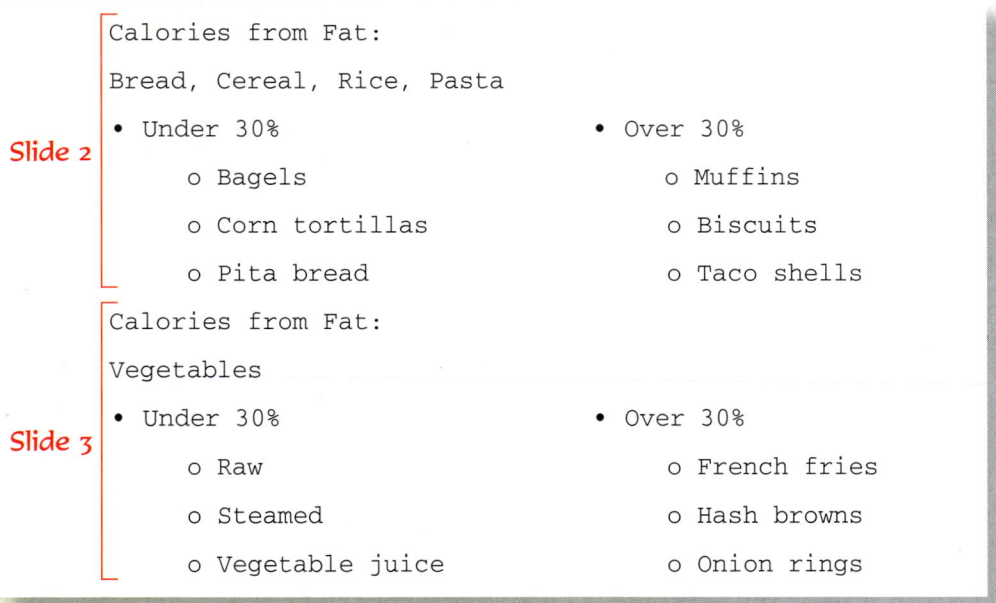 to show more design themes.
   b. Click on the **Verve** design theme to apply it to the presentation.
3. On the first slide, key **Smart Diet Options** for the presentation title. Key **Choosing Low-Fat Foods** for the subtitle.
4. Insert a new slide with the **Two Content** layout.
5. Key the title for slide 2 (on two lines) and bulleted text for slide 2 shown in Figure 3-21, demoting the bulleted text below "Under 30%" and "Over 30%" as shown.
6. Insert a new slide with the **Two Content** layout. Key the title for slide 3 (on two lines) and bulleted text for slide 3 shown in Figure 3-21, demoting the bulleted text below "Under 30%" and "Over 30%" as shown.

Figure 3-21
Content for slide 2 and 3

```
Calories from Fat:

Bread, Cereal, Rice, Pasta

• Under 30%                    • Over 30%
    o Bagels                       o Muffins
    o Corn tortillas               o Biscuits
    o Pita bread                   o Taco shells
```
Slide 2

```
Calories from Fat:

Vegetables

• Under 30%                    • Over 30%
    o Raw                          o French fries
    o Steamed                      o Hash browns
    o Vegetable juice              o Onion rings
```
Slide 3

7. View the presentation as a slide show starting on slide 1. Return to Normal view when you're finished.
8. Apply a different design theme by following these steps:
   a. From the Design tab, in the Themes group, click the More button 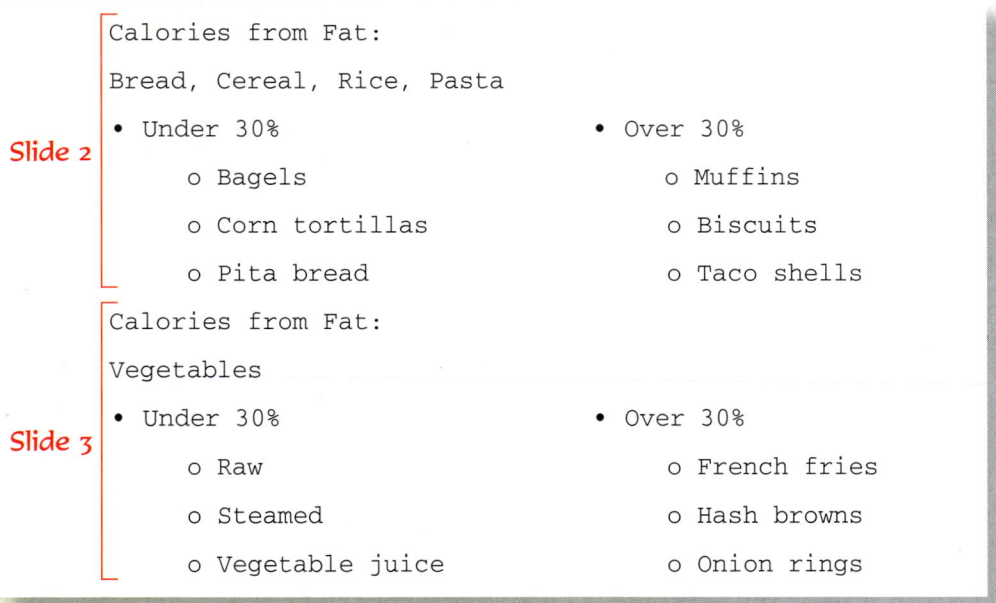 to view the design theme options.
   b. Click on the **Concourse** design theme to apply it to the presentation.
   c. Scroll through the presentation to view the applied design.
9. Change the presentation's theme colors by following these steps:
   a. From the Design tab, in the Themes group, click the Colors button to display the built-in theme colors.
   b. Click **Opulent** to apply to the color theme to your presentation.

10. Click the Undo button 🔁 to compare the new theme colors with the previous ones.

11. Click the Redo button 🔁 to reapply the color change.

12. Check spelling in the presentation.

13. Create a handout header and footer; include the date and your name as the header, and the page number and text **[3-24your initials]** as the footer by following these steps:

    a. From the Insert tab, in the Text group, click the Header and Footer button 🖼 .

    b. Click the Notes and Handouts tab.

    c. Check **Date and Time** and then select the **Update Automatically** option.

    d. Check the **Footer** box and key **[3-24your initials]** in the Footer text box.

    e. Make sure **Page number** is checked.

    f . Click **Apply to All**.

14. Move to slide 1 and save the presentation as **[3-24your initials]** in your Lesson 3 folder.

15. Preview and then print the presentation as handouts, three slides per page, grayscale, framed. Close the presentation.

Exercise 3-25

Add headers and footers to a presentation, change the theme color, and apply a slide transition.

1. Open the file **Takeout**.

2. On slide 1, replace "Student Name" with your name.

3. Add a transition effect by following these steps:

    a. From the Animations tab, in the Transition to This Slide group, click the More button 🔽.

    b. From the list of slide transitions, in the category of Fades and Dissolves, select **Dissolve**.

    c. Click the arrow to open the Transition Sound drop-down list and choose **Cash Register** for the sound.

    d. Click the arrow to open the Transition Speed drop-down list and choose **Medium** for the speed.

    e. From the Animations tab, in the Transition to This Slide group, click the Apply to All button 🖼.

4. Add a footer and slide numbers by following these steps:

    a. From the Insert tab, in the Text group, click the Header and Footer button 🖼 .

    b. Click the Slide tab.

    c. Check **Slide number**.

    d. Check **Footer** and key your name as a footer.

  e. Click **Don't show on title slide** so that the footer and slide number do not print on slide 1.

  f. Click **Apply to All**.

5. Scroll through the presentation to check the footer and slide numbers. Notice that with this theme the footer shows at the top of the slide.

6. Create a handout header and footer; include the date and your name as the header, and the page number and text **[3-25your initials]** as the footer.

7. Save the presentation as **[3-25your initials]** in your Lesson 3 folder.

8. View all slides as a slide show.

9. Print all the slides as handouts, six slides per page, grayscale, framed. Close the presentation.

Lesson Applications

Exercise 3-26

Rearrange slides, cut and paste text, and check spelling.

1. Open the file **SafeFd1**.

2. On slide 4, cut the bulleted items in column 2 and paste them at the bottom of column 1. Ignore the Paste Options button 📋 that appears because the text is formatted correctly.

3. Change the layout of slide 4 to the **Title and Content** layout.

4. Edit text in slide 4 and demote bullets as shown in Figure 3-22.

Figure 3-22
Completed slide

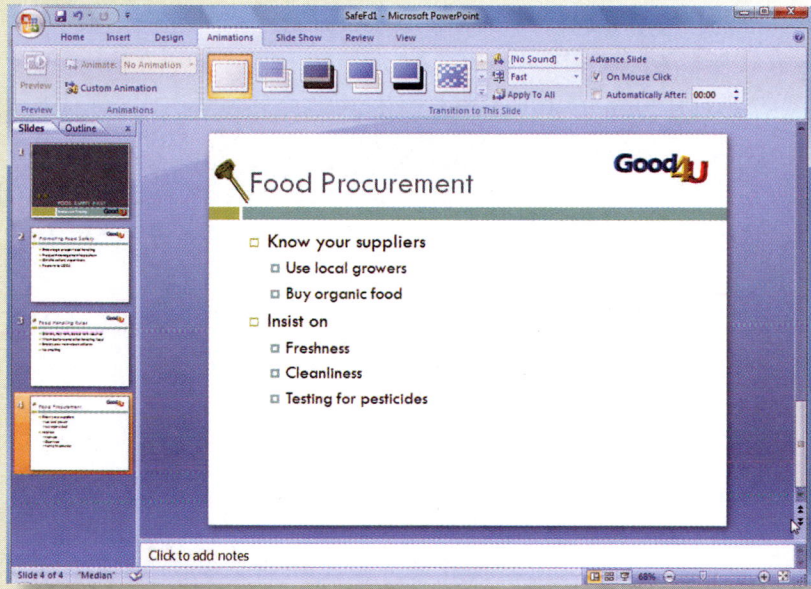

5. Add a new slide 5 using the **Title and Content** layout, containing the text shown in Figure 3-23.

Figure 3-23
Slide 5 Content

```
Inspections
• Training inspections
    o Scheduled
    o Cooperative
• Internal evaluation inspections
• USDA inspections
```

6. Check spelling in the presentation.

7. Move to slide 1 and save the presentation as **[3-26your initials]** in your Lesson 3 folder.

8. View the presentation as a slide show.

9. Preview and then print the presentation as handouts, four slides per page, grayscale, framed. Close the presentation.

Exercise 3-27

Delete and reorder slides, check spelling, find and replace text, and add a header and footer.

1. Open the file **Premium**.

2. On slide 1, change the subtitle text to the following:

   Item 1: Water bottle
   Item 2: Visor
   Item 3: Knee pads

3. Make a noncontiguous selection that includes the thumbnails for slides 2 ("Introduction"), 7 ("Real Life"), and 8 ("What This Means").

4. Delete the selected slides.

5. Click the Replace button [Replace] and replace each occurrence of the word "Topic" with the word "Item." Use the **Match case** and **Find whole words only** options so that you replace only "Topic" and not "Topics" or "topic."

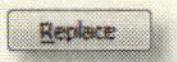

6. Edit slides 2 ("Topics of Discussion") through 6 ("Next Steps") so they contain only the text shown in Figure 3-24.

Figure 3-24
Content for slide 2 through 6

Slide 2
```
Topics of Discussion ——— Title
• Introduce new premium items to give away
at special events
• All premium items will contain the Good 4 U logo
```

Slide 3
```
Item 1: Water Bottle ——— Title
• Made of durable plastic
• Excellent for outdoor sports and indoor workouts
```

Slide 4
```
Item 3: Knee Pads ——— Title
• Made of durable vinyl/foam
• Essential protection for skaters
```

Slide 5
```
Item 2: Visor ——— Title
• Made of white cotton blend
• Adjustable, one size fits all
• Ideal for tennis, running, walking
```

Slide 6
```
Next Steps ——— Title
• Create designs
• Produce prototype items
• Analyze production costs
```

7. Reverse the order of slide 5 ("Item 3: Visor") and slide 4 ("Item 2: Knee Pads").

8. Check spelling in the presentation.

9. View the presentation as a slide show.

10. Add your name to the handout header and the filename **[3-27your initials]** to the handout footer, and set the date and time to update automatically.

11. Move to slide 1 and save the presentation as **[3-27your initials]** in your Lesson 3 folder.

12. Preview and then print the presentation as handouts, six slides per page, grayscale, framed.

Exercise 3-28

Check spelling, add a header and footer, apply a design theme, change the theme colors, and add transitions.

1. Create a new presentation, using the text shown in Figure 3-25.

Figure 3-25
Presentation content

2. Apply the design theme **Foundry**.

3. Apply the color theme **Median**.

4. Check spelling in the presentation.

5. Add the **Wedge** slide transition to all slides.

6. Add slide numbers to all slides.

7. Create a handout header and footer; include the date and your name as the header, and the page number and text **[3-28your initials]** as the footer.

8. Move to slide 1 and save the presentation as **[3-28your initials]** in your Lesson 3 folder.

9. Preview and then print slide 3 in full size in grayscale or in color if available.

10. Preview and then print the entire presentation as handouts, six slides per page, grayscale, framed. Close the presentation.

Exercise 3-29 ◆ Challenge Yourself

Rearrange and delete slides, cut and paste text, check spelling, add a handout header/footer, change a design theme, change a color theme, add transition effects.

1. Open the file **CookCon1**.

2. On slide 1, key the subtitle **Rules, Judging, and Prizes**.

3. Add a new slide using the **Title and Content** layout after the title slide, using the text shown in Figure 3-26.

Figure 3-26
Slide content

```
Contest Rules
• Submit an original written recipe and dish
    o Good 4 U Restaurant, Saturday, June 7
    o 10 a.m. to noon
• Judging is from noon to 2 p.m.
• Judges' decisions are final
• Anyone may enter except Good 4 U employees and their
  families
```

4. Change slide 5 ("Ingredients to Use") to a **Two Content** layout; then cut the body text from slide 3 and paste it in the second column of slide 5.

5. Change the title of slide 5 to **Recipe Ingredients**. Insert a new line at the top of the first column. Key **Use** on the new line and demote all the text below it. Insert **Avoid** at the top of the second column and demote all the text below it.

6. Delete slide 3 ("Ingredients to Avoid"); then rearrange the remaining slides where needed so that they appear in the following order:

   Slide 1: Recipe Contest   Slide 4: Awards

   Slide 2: Contest Rules   Slide 5: Judging Criteria

   Slide 3: Recipe Ingredients

7. Change the design theme to **Equity** and the color theme to **Apex**.

8. Check spelling in the presentation.

9. Review the presentation as a slide show.

10. Add the **Newsflash** transition with **Medium** speed to all slides in the presentation.

11. Create a handout header and footer; include the date updated automatically and your name as the header, and the page number and text **[3-29your initials]** as the footer.

12. Move to slide 1 and save the presentation as **[3-29your initials]** in your Lesson 3 folder.

13. Preview and then print the presentation as handouts, six slides per page, grayscale, framed. Close the presentation.

On Your Own

In these exercises you work on your own, as you would in a real-life work environment. Use the skills you've learned to accomplish the task—and be creative.

Exercise 3-30

Imagine that you are organizing a drawing for your local community college to raise money for an internship banquet and updated technology for the business department. Local businesses have donated interesting products, and business students will sell tickets for a drawing to determine who will receive the products. Decide how you might organize such an event and prepare a slide show to promote it. Rearrange slides and copy and paste text as necessary to get them in a logical order. Apply a design theme of your choice to the first and last slides in your presentation and apply a different but complementary design theme to the other slides. Add a handout footer with your name and the file name in it. Check spelling in the presentation. Save the presentation as **[3-30your initials]**. Preview and then print the presentation as handouts.

Exercise 3-31

Create a presentation describing briefly a personal hobby that you have, i.e., scrapbooking, building guitars, quilting, riding motorcycles. Create at least six slides using a design theme, theme color, theme effects, and slide transitions. Copy and paste as necessary to put the text in a logical sequence. Rearrange or delete slides as necessary to finalize your presentation. Check spelling in the presentation. Add page numbers to the slides. Save the presentation as **[3-31your initials]**. Preview and then print the presentation as handouts.

Exercise 3-32

Choose a children's story, for example, a Dr. Seuss classic, Berenstain Bears, or Frog and Toad's adventures. Create a presentation that includes a title slide with the subject title being the title of the book and the author's name for the subtitle. After the title slide, insert multiple slides describing the major points of the story. Rearrange slides and copy and paste text as necessary to get them in a logical order. Choose a design theme and theme color that conveys the mood of the book. Add transition effects. Add page numbers to the slide. Check the spelling in the presentation. Save the presentation as **[3-32your initials]**. Preview and then print the presentation as handouts.

Unit 1 Applications

Unit Application 1-1

Copy and delete slides, edit slide text, check spelling, add header and footer information to handouts and slides, modify bullet color, use the format painter, and choose print options.

1. Open the file **ThreeYr2**.

2. Use Slide Sorter view to move slide 2 ("Projected Revenue Growth") after slide 7.

3. Delete the newly numbered slide 2 ("Presenting Good 4 U").

4. Move slide 4 ("Financial History") after slide 5.

5. On slide 2, add the title **Who We Are** and delete the text "Their dreams" and the subtext below it.

6. Move to slide 3, which contains blank placeholders, and add the title **What We Want** and key these bulleted items:

   • **To encourage healthy eating**
   • **To promote participation in sports activities**
   • **To expand our market base**

7. Change the bullets on slide 3 to a new color that matches the theme color in the presentation.

8. Move to slide 8. Change the bullets on slide 8 to the square bullets used throughout the presentation using Format Painter.

9. Check spelling in the presentation (assume that all proper names are spelled correctly).

10. View the presentation as a slide show, starting on slide 1.

11. Create a header and footer for handouts that includes today's date as a fixed date, your name as the header, and the filename **[U1-1your initials]** as the footer.

12. Using the Header and Footer dialog box, add a slide number to all slides, including slide 1.

13. Move to the first slide and save the file as **[U1-1your initials]** in a new folder for Unit 1 Applications.

14. Preview and then print the presentation as handouts, four slides per page with landscape orientation, pure black and white, framed.

15. Close the presentation.

Unit Application 1-2

Rearrange slides, edit text, change bullet color, find and replace text, check spelling and style, add slide transitions, add slide numbers, and add handout headers and footers.

1. Open the file **NewFood1**.

2. Find the word "desert" and replace it with **dessert**.

3. On slide 5 ("Just Sweet Enough"), delete the sentence that begins "The striking lime flavor."

4. On slide 3 (the first "Pasta Delights" slide), change the title to **Salad Delights**.

5. Select all the bulleted text on slide 3 and delete it, leaving a blank body text placeholder. In the placeholder, key the text shown in Figure U1-1.

Figure U1-1

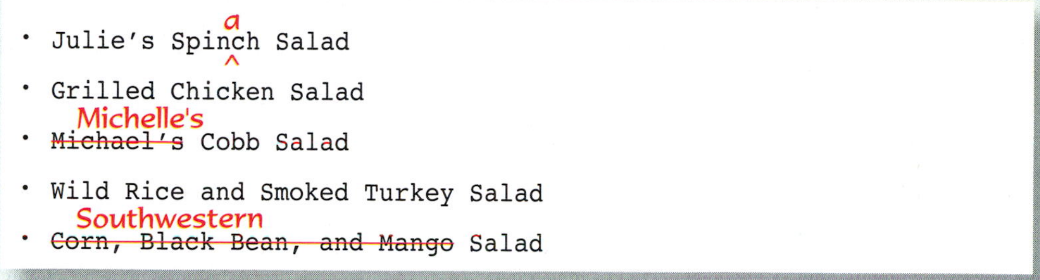

- Julie's Spinch Salad *(a inserted above "Spinch")*
- Grilled Chicken Salad
- ~~Michael's~~ **Michelle's** Cobb Salad
- Wild Rice and Smoked Turkey Salad
- **Southwestern** ~~Corn, Black Bean, and Mango~~ Salad

6. Change the color of the bullets in slide 3 to a new color that matches the current theme color.

7. Move slide 2 with the subtitle text "A New Dining Event" to the end of the presentation. (It will become slide 6.)

8. Move the new slide 5 ("Appetizer Specials") after slide 1 so that it becomes slide 2. Increase the size of the body text placeholder slightly so the size of the text will match the other body text placeholders.

9. Check spelling in the presentation.

10. Use the Thesaurus to replace the word "Event" on slide 6. Choose "experience" to replace it from the Thesaurus window. Use cut and paste and insert words as needed to get the text on slide 6 to read **A New Experience in Dining**.

11. Add the **Shape Diamond** slide transition to all slides.

12. Add a **Drum Roll** transition sound to only the first slide.

13. Add slide numbers to all slides except the title slide layouts. Add a handout header that contains your name, add a handout footer that contains the filename **[U1-2your initials]**, with the page number and current date.

14. Save the presentation as **[U1-2your initials]** in your Unit 1 Applications folder.

15. Preview and then print the entire presentation as handouts, six slides per page, grayscale, framed.

16. Print slide 2 of the presentation in full size, grayscale, framed.

17. Close the presentation.

Unit Application 1-3

Create slides, change theme colors, change slide layout, apply text formatting, change text alignment, replace text, and change bullets.

1. Open the presentation **PowerWalk**.

2. Change the theme color to **Metro**.

3. On slide 1, change the slide title font to Arial Black and take the title off ALL CAPS.

4. Make the subtitle stand out more:
   - Make "Good 4 U" bold.
   - Increase the font size of "4" by one font size increment.
   - Move the placeholder up slightly so all text fits in the green area.
   - Right-align the subtitle text.

5. Working in either the Slide tab or the Outline tab, create slides 2 through 4 using the text shown in Figure U1-2. Use the **Title and Content** layout.

Figure U1-2

```
          ┌ Objectives
Slide 2   │    • Encourage morning power walkers to breakfast at G4U
          └    • Make G4U a social center for power walkers
          ┌ Strategies
          │    • Guided walks
Slide 3   │    • Seminars
          │    • G4U merchandise
          └    • Advertising
          ┌ Cost/Benefits Analysis
          │    • Costs
          │       _ Walk guides' salaries
          │       _ Seminar leaders' salaries
          │       _ Merchandise costs
Slide 4   │       _ Advertising costs
          │    • Benefits
          │       _ Increase breakfasts served
          │       _ Increase repeat business
          │       _ Increase merchandise sales
          └       _ Increase general sales
```

6. On slide 1, copy the text Good 4 U. Use the Replace command to change all instances of "G4U" to Good 4 U.

7. On slide 2, change the title text font to Arial Black and increase the size by one increment.

8. Double-click the Format Painter then apply this new formatting to the title on slides 3 and 4.

9. On slide 4, make the following changes:

   - Change the slide layout to **Comparison**.
   - Move the "Benefits" bullet and all its second-level bullets into the right column by cutting and pasting the text.
   - Cut "Costs" and "Benefits" and put them into their respective comparison heading boxes.
   - Increase the size of "Costs" to 32 points and make it bold. Use the Format Painter to give "Benefits" the same treatment.
   - Change the color of bullets on this slide to **Pink, Accent 2**. and make them 80 percent of the text size.

10. Check spelling in the presentation.

11. View the presentation as a slide show.

12. Create a handout header and footer; include the date and your name as the header, and the page number and text **[U1-3your initials]** as the footer.

13. Move to slide 1 and save the presentation as **[U1-3your initials]** in your Unit 1 Applications folder.

14. Preview and then print the presentation as handouts, landscape orientation, four slides per page, grayscale, framed.

15. Close the presentation.

Unit Application 1-4 ◆ Using the Internet

Research a topic, create a presentation, use cut and paste, rearrange slides, apply a design theme, change theme color, change theme font, add slide and handout header/footer, check spelling, modify bullets, add a text box, and add transition effects.

Use the Internet to research a self-help topic. Choose something that interests you, such as weight loss, anti-aging, body toning, exercise, quit smoking, spirituality, personality improvement, etc. The following is a list of suggested information to gather:

- Background on the topic.
- Who might be interested in this topic.
- Main points to begin the process of self-help in this area.

- Any other information that you think would be useful for a presentation.

- Be sure to cite where you found the information.

Use the material you researched to prepare an informative presentation on your subject. Be sure to include at least five slides in the presentation. Choose any design theme, a new theme color, a new theme font, and new theme effects. Format the presentation attractively. Add a transition to all slides in the presentation.

Use cut and paste and rearrange slides as necessary to get presentation information into a logical sequence.

Change bullets in the presentation to a new shape and color. Add at least one text box within the presentation.

In the slide footer, include the text **Prepared by** followed by your name. Include the slide number on all slides but not the date. In the handout footer, include the text **[U1-4your initials]**. In the handout header, key **Presented to** and then identify to whom you would be giving this presentation (instructor or class). Include in the handout the date you would be delivering the presentation as a fixed date.

Check spelling in the presentation and save it with the filename **[U1-4your initials]** in your Unit 1 Applications folder. Practice delivering the presentation. Preview and then print the presentation handouts, choosing an appropriate number of slides per page, grayscale, framed. Close the presentation.

unit 2

PRESENTATION ILLUSTRATION

Lesson 4   Working with Graphics   PP-116

Lesson 5   Creating Tables   PP-166

Lesson 6   Creating Charts   PP-210

Lesson 7   Creating Diagrams with SmartArt
           Graphics   PP-248

UNIT 2   APPLICATIONS   PP-289

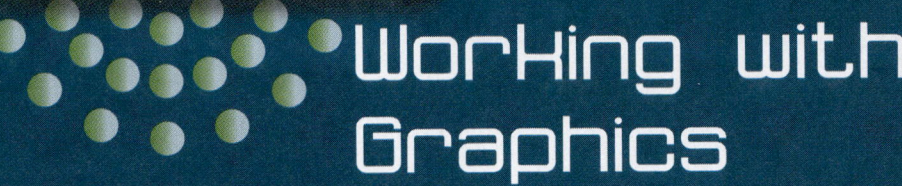

Working with Graphics

MCAS OBJECTIVES

In this lesson:
PP07 2.2.2
PP07 2.2.7
PP07 3.3.1
PP07 3.3.2
PP07 3.3.3
PP07 3.3.4
PP07 3.4.1
PP07 3.4.2
PP07 3.5.1
PP07 3.5.2
PP07 3.5.3
See Appendix

OBJECTIVES

After completing this lesson, you will be able to:

1. Work with shapes.

2. Insert clip art images.

3. Insert and enhance pictures.

4. Create WordArt.

5. Create a photo album.

Estimated Time: 2 hours

An effective presentation slide show consists of more than text alone. Although text may carry most of the information, you can use several types of objects to help communicate your message or draw attention to key points. For example, you can add shapes, free-floating text objects, clip art images, and photographs to help illustrate your presentation.

After you add an object to a slide, you can change its size, position, and appearance. In this lesson, you will concentrate on some basic drawing skills and begin to explore some of the many special effects made possible in PowerPoint 2007.

Working with Shapes

PowerPoint provides a variety of tools you can use to create original drawings. These tools are available in three tabs: Home, Insert, and Drawing Tools Format. In this lesson, you learn basic drawing skills. In later lessons, you learn how to enhance simple shapes and create more complex drawings.

When drawing shapes, the ruler can help you to judge size and positioning. When the ruler is displayed, it appears in two parts: the horizontal measurement is across the top of the slide and the vertical measurement is on the left. By default, the ruler measures in inches; the center of the slide (vertically and horizontally) appears as zero. A dotted line on each ruler indicates the horizontal and vertical position of your pointer.

TABLE 4-1 Tools for Basic Drawing

Button	Name	Purpose
	Select	Selects an object. This tool is automatically in effect when no other tool is in use.
	Picture	Inserts a bitmap or photo image from a file.
	Clip Art	Inserts a clip art object, which could be drawings, sounds, movies, or stock photography.
	Photo Album	Creates a presentation made of pictures with each one on a separate slide.
	Shapes	Opens the Shapes gallery, which contains predefined shapes you can draw.
	Line	Draws a straight line.
	Arrow	Draws an arrow.
	Rectangle	Draws a rectangle or square.
	Oval	Draws an oval or circle.
	Text Box	Inserts text anywhere on a slide.
	WordArt	Creates a Microsoft WordArt object on a slide.
	Shape Fill	Fills a shape with colors, patterns, or textures.
	Shape Outline	Changes the color of a shape's outline or the color of a line.
	Shape Effects	Adds a visual effect such as shadow, glow, or bevel.

Exercise 4-1   DRAW SHAPES—RECTANGLES, OVALS, AND LINES

In this exercise, you practice drawing several *shapes* on a blank slide. To draw a shape, click the appropriate drawing tool button (such as the Line ◺, Rectangle ▭, or Oval ◯); then drag the *Crosshair pointer* ⊞ on your slide until the shape is the size you want.

You can draw multiple shapes with the same drawing tool by using the *Lock Drawing Mode* option. This keeps the button activated, so you can draw as many of the same shapes as you want without the need to reclick the button. This feature is deactivated when you click another button.

If you don't like an object that you created, you can easily remove it from your slide. Simply select the object by clicking it, and then press Delete on your keyboard.

As you draw with different tools, the ones you have used appear at the top of the list in a **Recently Used Shapes** category of the Shapes gallery; however, each tool is also shown in a related group when you access the entire Shapes gallery.

1. Open the presentation file **Opening1**.

2. Insert a new slide after slide 2 and use the **Blank** layout. You will use this slide to practice drawing.

3. If the rulers are not showing, right-click on the blank slide and choose **Ruler** from the short-cut menu.

> **NOTE**
>
> Three of the slides in this presentation were created by using the Blank slide layout. The Blank slide layout contains no text placeholders. The text that appears on the slides is placed in text boxes as shown in Lesson 2.

4. While watching the horizontal ruler at the top of the slide, move your pointer back and forth, observing the dotted line on the ruler indicating the pointer's position. While moving your pointer up and down, observe the dotted line on the vertical ruler. From the Home tab, in the Drawing group, click the Shapes button then click the Rectangle button . The pointer changes to a crosshair pointer .

5. Notice that zero is placed at the midpoint of the slide on both the vertical ruler and the horizontal ruler. Move the crosshair pointer ⊞ to the 3-inch mark on the horizontal ruler to the left of the zero and to the 2-inch mark on the vertical ruler above the zero.

> **NOTE**
>
> The green handle just above the rectangle is a *rotation handle*. It can be used to rotate a shape in the same way it was used to rotate a text box in the previous lesson.

6. Click and hold the left mouse button. Drag diagonally down and to the right until you reach the 2-inch mark below the zero on the vertical ruler and the 3-inch mark to the right of the zero on the horizontal ruler. Release your mouse button. A blue rectangle with a white outline appears. See Figure 4-1 to compare the size and placement of the completed rectangle.

Figure 4-1
Drawing a shape on a slide

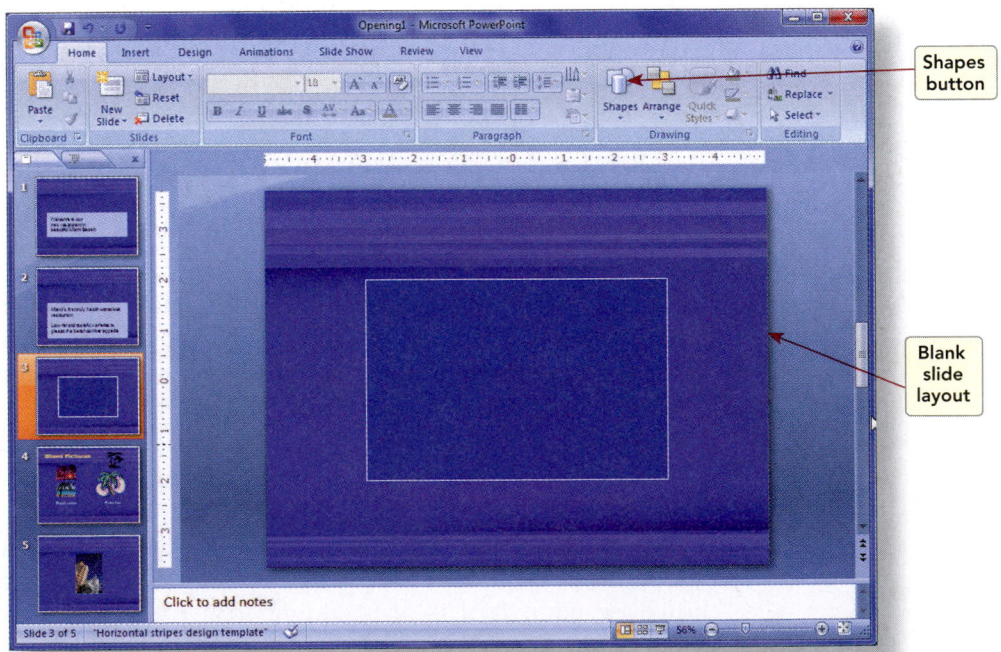

7. From the Home tab, in the Drawing group, click the Shapes button ▢ , and then choose the Oval button ▢ .

8. Draw a small oval (approximately one-inch wide) on the inside of the rectangle that you previously drew, using the same method that you used to draw the rectangle.

9. From the Home tab, in the Drawing group, click the Shapes button ▢ , and then right-click the Line button ◺ and choose **Lock Drawing Mode**. Drag your pointer diagonally to draw a line from the left corner of the rectangle to the outline of the oval.

10. Because the drawing mode is locked, notice that the pointer is still the crosshair pointer ⊞ showing that the Line button ◺ is still selected. Draw three more lines from each corner of the rectangle to the outline of the oval.

11. Your screen should look similar to the back of an envelope with a seal, as shown in Figure 4-2.

Figure 4-2
Drawing an oval
and lines

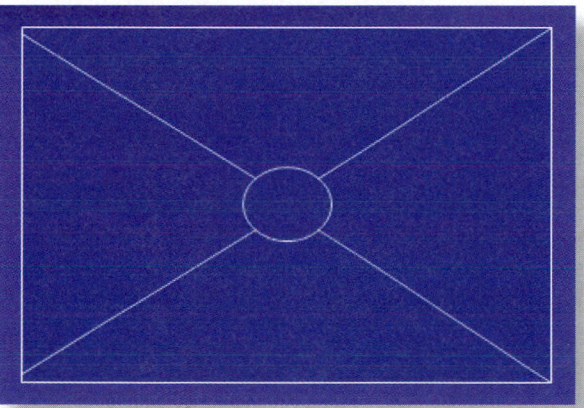

12. Click the Line button ◺ again to deactivate it.

13. Hold Shift down while you click to select all four lines and the oval then press Delete to remove them all at once. The slide should now contain one rectangle only.

Exercise 4-2   DRAW HORIZONTAL CONSTRAINED LINES

You use Shift to *constrain* a shape as you draw it on a slide. For lines, constraining enables you to make perfectly straight horizontal or vertical lines. If you try to angle a constrained line, lines are limited to angles in increments of 45 degrees.

When using Shift to constrain a shape, it's important to release your mouse button before releasing Shift. Otherwise, you might accidentally move the pointer when Shift is no longer in effect, resulting in a shape that is no longer constrained.

> **NOTE**
>
> Depending on the settings of your computer and the size of your screen, you may need to use a different percent so you can focus on the rectangle and not the entire slide.

> **REVIEW**
>
> To insert a footer on one slide only, move to the slide before opening the Header and Footer dialog box; then click **Apply** instead of **Apply to All**.

> **NOTE**
>
> The documents you create in this course relate to the case study about Good 4 U, a fictional restaurant business described at the beginning of this text.

Figure 4-3
Drawing horizontal lines

1. Still working on slide 3, from the View tab, in the Zoom group, click the Zoom button. On the Zoom dialog box, key **150** percent and click **OK**. Scroll as needed to display the rectangle. Zooming in on the area will make it easier to see what you're doing when you work on detailed objects.

2. From the Home tab, in the Drawing group, right-click the Line button then choose **Lock Drawing Mode**. You're going to draw several constrained lines without needing to reclick the Line button each time you draw.

3. Position the crosshair pointer ⊞ on the left side of the rectangle on the vertical ruler's zero marker, hold down [Shift], and drag straight across to the right side of the rectangle. (As you drag, notice that the line remains straight, even if you move the pointer up or down a little.)

4. Release the mouse button first, and then release [Shift].

5. With the Line button still activated, position the crosshair pointer ⊞ at the left end of the rectangle again about a half inch above where you drew the last line. Hold down [Shift] and drag to the right edge of the rectangle. Release the mouse button, and then release [Shift]. Continue this process until the rectangle is full of horizontal lines a half inch apart, as shown in Figure 4-3.

6. Press [Esc] to release the locked drawing mode.

7. From the View tab, in the Zoom group, click **Fit to Window** to display the entire slide.

8. Insert a footer only on slide 3 that contains Your Name, a comma, and the text **[4-2your initials]**. (Do not include the date.)

9. Create a new folder for Lesson 4. Save the presentation as **[4-2your initials]** in the new Lesson 4 folder. Print only slide 3, full size, grayscale, and framed. Keep the presentation open for the next exercise.

Exercise 4-3   ADD CONNECTOR LINES

Sometimes two or more shapes need to be connected with a line; therefore, PowerPoint provides a variety of *connector lines* for this purpose. These lines are either straight connectors, elbow connectors (with 90-degree angles between connected shapes), or curved connector lines. Some lines have arrowheads on one or both ends to show a relationship or movement between the shapes when creating a diagram.

1. Insert a new slide after slide 3 using the **Blank** layout.

2. On the new slide 4, from the Home tab, in the Drawing group, click the Shapes button ⬜ and then choose the Rounded Rectangle button ⬜. Notice that a ScreenTip will appear that labels each drawing tool button.

3. Position the crosshair pointer ⊞ on the left of your slide then click and drag to create a rectangle as shown in Figure 4-4.

4. Repeat this process to create a similar rectangle on the right of the slide.

5. Now select the Elbow Connector button ⌐. Point to the left rectangle and you will see a red square appear on all four sides of this rectangle. These are *connection sites* where the line and rectangle can be joined.

6. Click the red square at the bottom. This step connects the beginning portion of your line.

7. Now drag the line to the right until you connect to the red square on the left side of the second rectangle.

8. Notice that the connector line has two yellow diamond shapes. These are *adjustment handles* that enable you to change the horizontal or the vertical portions of the line. Adjust the line as shown in Figure 4-4.

Figure 4-4
Elbow connector lines

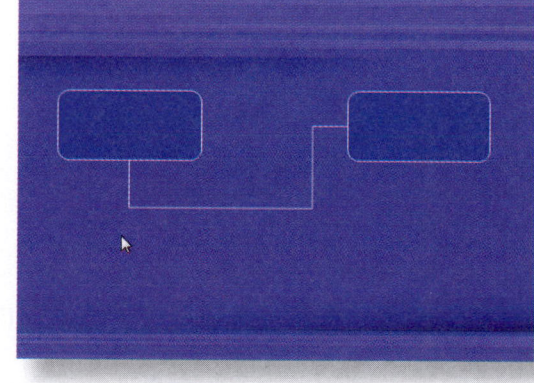

9. With the connector line still selected, press Delete to remove the connector line.

10. Now add a different connector line. Click the Curved Double-Arrow Connector button 🔁 and repeat the process of connecting the bottom of the left rectangle with the left side of the rectangle on the right.

Figure 4-5
Double-arrow connector lines

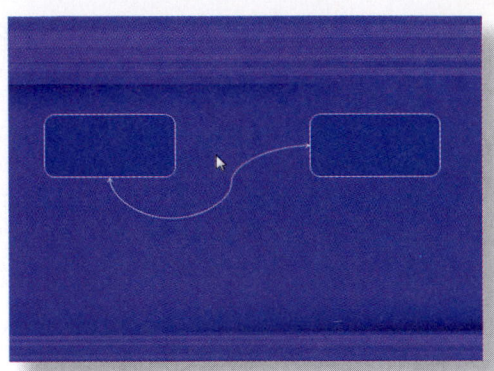

11. Notice how the adjustment handles affect the curve of the line as you move them horizontally or vertically. Adjust the line as shown in Figure 4-5.

Exercise 4-4   CREATE SQUARES AND CIRCLES

When you constrain other shapes, such as rectangles or ovals, they grow at an equal rate horizontally and vertically as you draw, creating symmetrical objects such as squares and circles.

> **NOTE**
>
> Your square might look more like a rectangle if your monitor's horizontal size and vertical size are not perfectly synchronized. Your square will print correctly, even if it is distorted on your screen.

1. Insert a new slide after slide 4 using the **Blank** layout.

2. On the new slide 5, from the Home tab, in the Drawing group, click the Shapes button 🔲 and then choose the Rectangle button 🔲.

3. Position the crosshair pointer ⊞. on the left of your slide.

4. Press and hold Shift then drag diagonally down and to the right, ending near the center of the slide. Release the mouse button first, and then release Shift. See Figure 4-6 for the approximate size and placement of the completed square.

Figure 4-6
Drawing a circle and a square

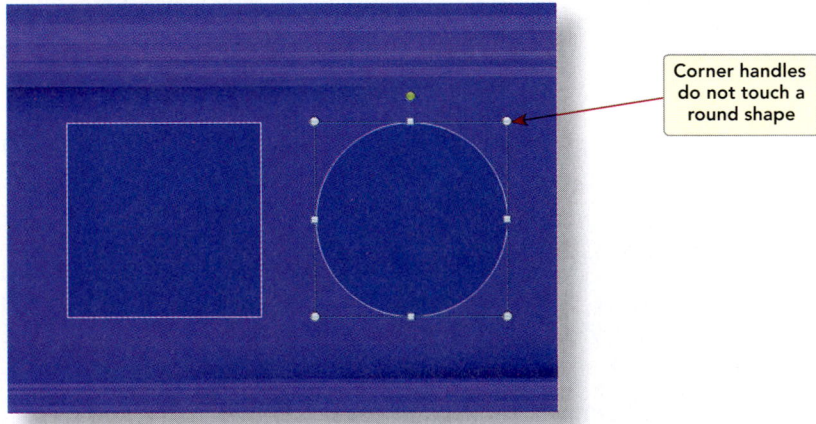

Corner handles do not touch a round shape

5. From the Home tab, in the Drawing group, click the Shapes button 🔲 and choose the Oval button 🔘.

6. Position your pointer to the right of the square.

7. While pressing ⎡Shift⎤, drag diagonally down and to the right to create a circle the same size as the square. Your screen should resemble Figure 4-6. Both the square and the circle in this example have a **Height** and **Width** measurement of 3.5 inches.

8. Notice that with a circular shape, the corner handles do not touch the shape.

9. Save the presentation as **[4-4your initials]** in your Lesson 4 folder, but do not print it. Leave it open for the next exercise.

Exercise 4-5   RESIZE AND MOVE SHAPES

A shape that you draw is resized in the same way that you resize a text placeholder: Select it, and then drag one of its sizing handles. Holding down ⎡Shift⎤ and/or ⎡Ctrl⎤ while dragging a sizing handle has the following effects on an object:

- ⎡Shift⎤ preserves a shape's *proportions,* meaning that its height grows or shrinks at the same rate as its width, preventing shapes from becoming too tall and skinny or too short and wide.

- ⎡Ctrl⎤ causes a shape to grow or shrink from the center of the shape, rather than from the edge that's being dragged.

- ⎡Ctrl⎤+⎡Shift⎤ together cause a shape to grow or shrink proportionately from its center.

You reposition a shape by dragging it with the four-pointed arrow 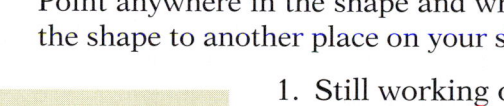. Point anywhere in the shape and when you see the four-pointed arrow, drag the shape to another place on your slide.

NOTE

These techniques also apply to resizing and moving clip art and photo images, too.

1. Still working on slide 5, select the circle by clicking anywhere inside it, and then point to its bottom center sizing handle. Your pointer changes to a two-pointed vertical arrow ⎡↕⎤.

2. Drag the handle down. As you drag, the pointer changes to a crosshair ⎡+⎤. The circle has changed into an oval and is now larger.

3. Drag the bottom-left corner handle diagonally up and to the left. The oval is now wider and flattened, taking on an entirely new shape.

4. Click the Undo button ⎡↺⎤ twice to restore the circle to its original size and shape.

5. Point to the circle's lower-left corner sizing handle. While holding down ⎡Shift⎤, drag diagonally out from the circle's center, making it larger. (Don't worry if the circle overlaps the rectangle.) The circle retains its original shape. Press ⎡Ctrl⎤+⎡Z⎤ to Undo this action and revert the circle to the original size.

6. While holding down both Ctrl and Shift, drag the lower-left corner sizing handle toward the center of the circle. The circle becomes smaller, shrinking evenly from all edges. With this technique, all expanding and contracting of the size occurs from the shape's center, as shown in Figure 4-7.

Figure 4-7
Resizing a shape from its center

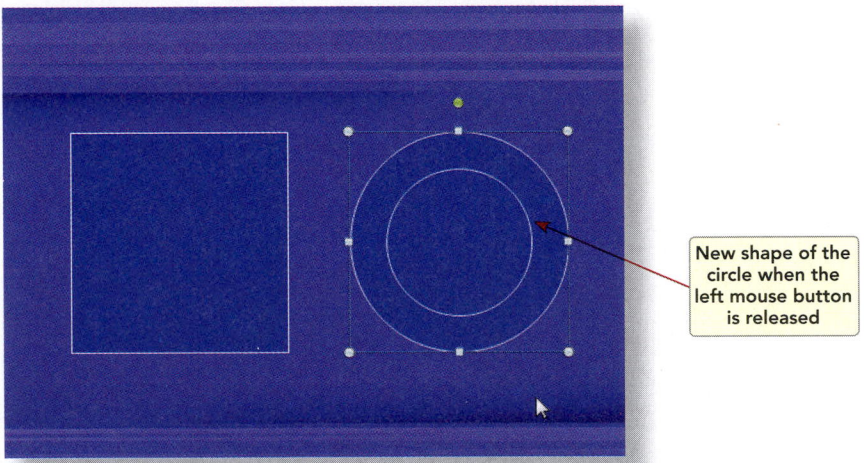

New shape of the circle when the left mouse button is released

7. Select the circle and press Delete to remove it.

8. Select the square shape and then from the the Drawing Tools Format tab, in the Size group, key **4.5** in both the **Height** and **Width** boxes.

9. Point in the square so you see the four-pointed arrow ⊕ then drag the square to the middle of the slide

10. To control precise sizing and positioning, click the **Dialog Box Launcher** in the Size group.

TIP

If you like working with the ruler measurements, you can precisely size and position objects without the need to open the Size and Position dialog box, but keep in mind that the rulers measure distances from the center of the slide. So, if you point to the two-inch mark at the right of the zero mark on the horizontal ruler, you need to do some math to figure out how far you are from either edge of the slide. The Position tab on the Size and Position dialog box lets you choose to measure either from the center of the slide or from its top left corner.

11. On the Size tab in the **Size and Position** dialog box, click the **Lock aspect ratio** option to keep the vertical and horizontal sizing in the same ratio as a shape (or other object) is resized. This can be very important when working with photographs.

12. Click the Position tab then change the **Horizontal** position of the square to be 2.75 inches from the top left corner and the **Vertical** position to be 1.75 inches down from the top left corner.

13. Click the Close button ⊠.

14. Save the presentation as **[4-5your initials]** in your Lesson 4 folder, but do not print it. Leave it open for the next exercise.

Exercise 4-6   USE ADJUSTMENT HANDLES TO MODIFY SHAPES

The rectangles, ovals, and lines that you have created are very simple shapes. Many additional shapes are available, as shown in Figure 4-8.

Shape tools are arranged in nine different categories, as shown in Figure 4-8. You resize all of these shapes in the same way, and many shapes include one or more adjustment handles which enable you to change the shape dimensions after it is drawn.

Figure 4-8
Additional shapes in the Shapes gallery

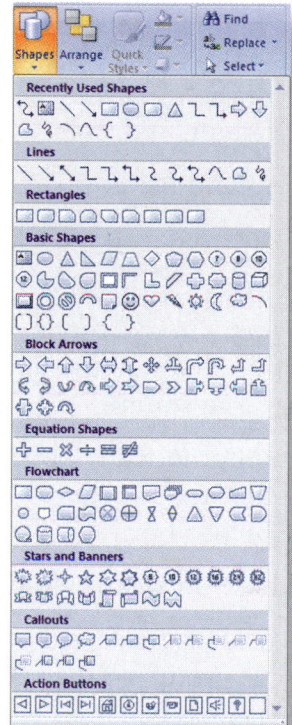

1. You no longer need slides 3 and 4 where you practiced making shapes. From the Slides and Outline pane, select each of these slide thumbnails and press Delete to remove them.

2. Now working on slide 3, from the Home tab, in the Drawing group, click the Shapes button 🔲 to display the Shapes gallery.

3. In the **Stars and Banners** category, point to the various shape buttons and read their ScreenTips to see what each one is called.

4. Right-click the 5-Point Star button ☆ and choose **Lock Drawing Mode**. Draw several stars in different sizes positioned randomly on the slide with some stars overlapping. Place stars on the rectangle and on the blank area of the slide.

5. Press Esc to exit the locked drawing mode.

6. Select one of the stars and drag its yellow diamond-shaped adjustment handle 🔶 toward the center to make the points more narrow, as shown in Figure 4-9.

7. Press Ctrl+Z several times until there is only a square left on the slide.

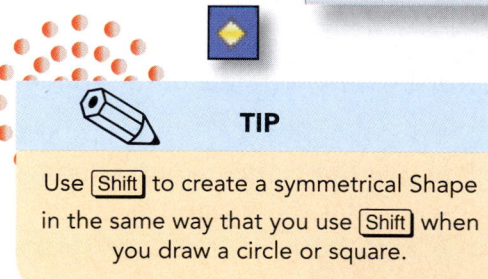

TIP

Use Shift to create a symmetrical Shape in the same way that you use Shift when you draw a circle or square.

Figure 4-9
Dragging an adjustment handle

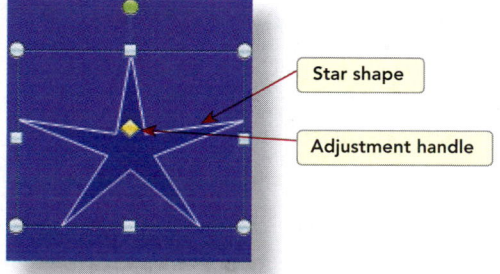

Star shape

Adjustment handle

8. From the Home tab, in the Drawing group, click the Shapes button 🔲 and in the **Basic Shapes** category, click the Sun button ☼. Draw a sun, about two inches in diameter, in the upper right corner of the slide.

9. Drag the adjustment handle ◆ toward the center of the Sun shape to make the center circle smaller and the points longer.

Exercise 4-7   **PLACE TEXT IN A SHAPE AND ROTATE**

You can easily transform a shape into an attention-getting background for text. Simply select the shape and key the text (or paste it from the clipboard). You can format and edit the text in the same way as in a text placeholder. The text in a shape is centered by default.

1. Select the Sun shape on slide 3 and press ⌈Delete⌋.

2. From the Home tab, in the Drawing group, click the Shapes button 🔲 to display the Shapes gallery.

3. In the **Stars and Banners** category, choose the 16-Point Star button ⚙ then click and drag to draw this shape in the upper right of the slide. It should slightly overlap the large square.

4. Key **Grand Opening**. The text automatically appears in the center of the star in the same color as the star's outline. Notice the dashed-line border similar to a text placeholder border.

5. Click the star's outline anywhere between two sizing handles to select it.

6. From the Home tab, in the Font group, change the size from 18 points to 28 points and apply bold. The text becomes too large for the star.

7. Drag the center sizing handle on the left side to make the star wide enough to contain the text without word wrapping. Part of the star shape will be over the square shape.

Figure 4-10
Inserting text in a shape

8. Drag the top-center sizing handle down to flatten the star, as shown in Figure 4-10.

9. Click on the green rotation handle and drag it slightly to the left to rotate the star.

10. Drag the star down until it overlaps the lower-right corner of the square, as shown in Figure 4-11.

Figure 4-11
Rotating a shape
with text

11. Compare slide 3 with Figure 4-11 and make any necessary adjustments.

12. Create a handout header and footer: Include the date and your name as the header, and the page number and text **[4-7your initials]** as the footer.

13. Move to slide 1 and save the presentation as **[4-7your initials]** in your Lesson 4 folder.

Inserting Clip Art Images

Included with Microsoft Office is a collection of ready-to-use images known as clip art, also called *clips*, that you can insert on PowerPoint slides. The *clip art* collection includes *vector drawings*—images made up of lines, curves, and shapes that are usually filled with solid colors. It also includes *bitmap pictures*—photographs made up of tiny colored dots that are made from scanned photographs or a digital camera. These photographs can be accessed from the Insert Clip Art task pane.

You can insert clip art and picture images into a PowerPoint presentation in two ways:

- Search for Clip Art. On the Insert tab, in the Illustrations group, click the Clip Art button 🖼 to display the Clip Art task pane where you can search for appropriate images from Microsoft's Clip Organizer collection. Also, if your slide uses a layout that includes a content placeholder, double-click the Clip Art button 🖼 to display the Clip Art task pane.

- Insert Picture from File. On the Insert tab, in the Illustrations group, click the Picture button 🖼 to insert picture files stored on a hard drive, removable drive, or network drive. This method is useful for inserting your own images that you have stored on your computer and that are not part of the Microsoft Clip Organizer collection.

Exercise 4-8   FIND CLIP ART THEN MODIFY A SEARCH

Each clip art image that Microsoft provides has *keywords* associated with it that describe the subject matter of the picture. You use keywords to find the art you need for your presentation.

Clip art images (and other media such as photographs, sound, and movie files) are organized into collections and media types. You can choose to search all collections and types or to select a particular type. If you know that you want a photograph only, be sure to select that type of media only to make the search more efficient.

If you search for a keyword and don't find any images, or you don't find one you like, you can modify your search and try again.

1. If you have Internet access, but are not connected, make a connection now (unless your instructor tells you otherwise).

2. Move to slide 2, and then from the Insert tab, in the Illustrations group, click the Clip Art button . The Clip Art task pane, as shown in Figure 4-12, is displayed on the right.

Figure 4-12
Clip Art task pane

3. In the Clip Art task pane, click the **Search in** list box arrow. Be sure that **Everywhere** is checked. All categories in the Microsoft Clip Organizer will be searched and, if you are connected to the Internet, Microsoft Office Online will be searched, too.

4. Close the list box by clicking anywhere on your screen.

5. Click the **Results should be** list box arrow. In this list box, you can choose to search all media types or limit your search to specific types. These options are helpful if you have a large number of media files stored on your computer, or you are searching on the Internet. Check only the Clip Art category and remove all other checks.

6. In the **Search for** text box at the top of the Clip Art task pane, key **food** and then click **Go**. The **Results** box shows thumbnails (miniature images) of clips that match the search word, as shown in Figure 4-13.

Figure 4-13
Search results

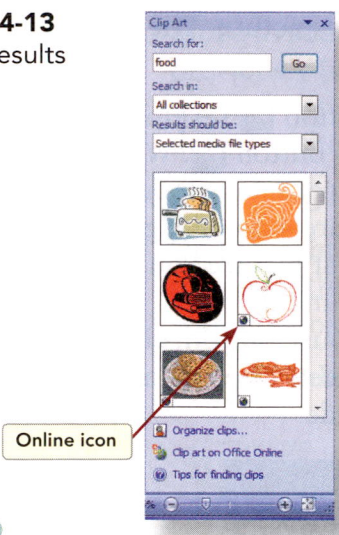

Online icon

7. Use the scroll bar to review some of the thumbnails.

8. In the **Search for** box, key **bananas** and then click **Go**. Thumbnails of pictures with bananas should appear in your **Results** box. If you do not find a picture you like, modify the search using a different keyword.

Exercise 4-9 PREVIEW AND INSERT CLIP ART IMAGES

You can preview images in a larger format, so you can see more detail before choosing one of them.

1. Without clicking, point to a clip art thumbnail in the task pane. As your pointer is over an image, a ScreenTip showing keywords, image dimensions, size, and file format appears. A gray bar with a downward pointing triangle appears on the right side of the thumbnail that changes to blue when you point to it.

2. Choose a picture you would like to insert.

3. Click the gray bar beside the picture you have chosen to display a menu of options. You can also display this menu by right-clicking a thumbnail.

4. Choose **Preview/Properties**. In addition to displaying an enlarged picture, this dialog box also shows you the filename and more detailed information about the image, as shown in Figure 4-14.

NOTE

Clips from the Microsoft Office Online collection have an online icon  in the lower left corner of the image thumbnail. When you do a search from all categories, some clips will have a musical note, indicating that they are sound files. Some clips will have an animation icon  displayed in the lower right corner, indicating that they are movies.

Figure 4-14
Preview/Properties dialog box

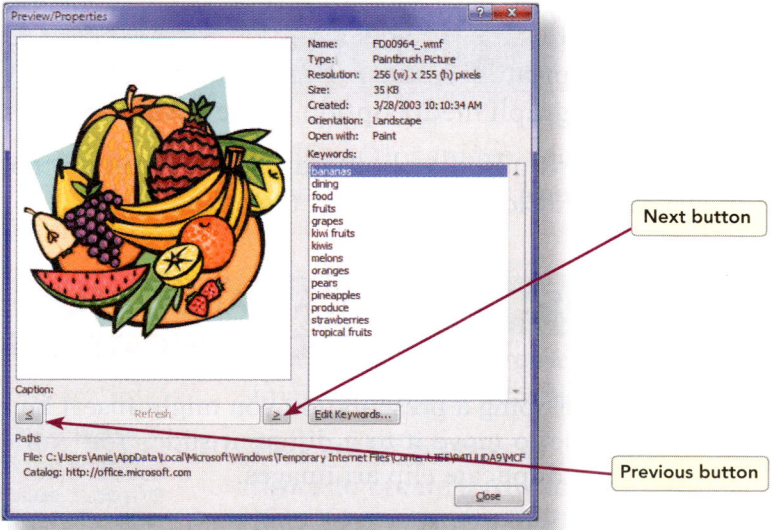

Next button

Previous button

4. With the Picture selected, click the Picture Tools Format tab. Change the Height to **5 inches** and the Width will automatically change to **3.7 inches**.

5. Move the picture to the left of the slide.

6. Keep your presentation open for the next exercise.

Exercise 4-17   ADJUST CONTRAST AND BRIGHTNESS

Sometimes a picture may be too dark to show needed details, or colors are washed out from too much sunshine when the picture was taken. PowerPoint's *Brightness* and *Contrast* adjustments can fix these problems. Adjusting the brightness changes the picture's overall lightness while adjusting contrast affects the difference between its lightest and darkest areas.

Figure 4-24
Brightness drop-down list

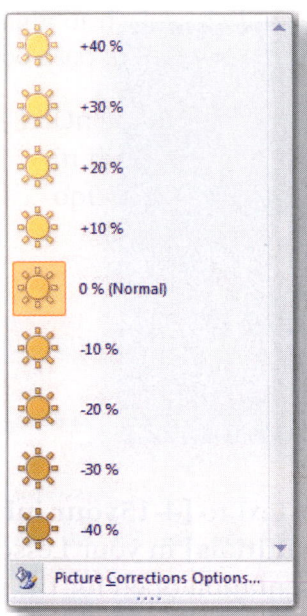

1. On slide 6, select the picture and press `Ctrl`+`D` to duplicate it. Position the second image on the right of the slide. Use it to make the color adjustments in this exercise so you can compare your changes to the original.

2. With the second picture selected, from the Picture Tools Format tab, in the Adjust group, click the Brightness button. A drop-down list appears showing adjustments in 10 percent increments, as shown in Figure 4-24, to increase or decrease the brightness of the picture.

3. Drag your pointer over the various amounts and study the effect on the picture. Click on **+10%** to increase the brightness.

Figure 4-25
Contrast drop-down list

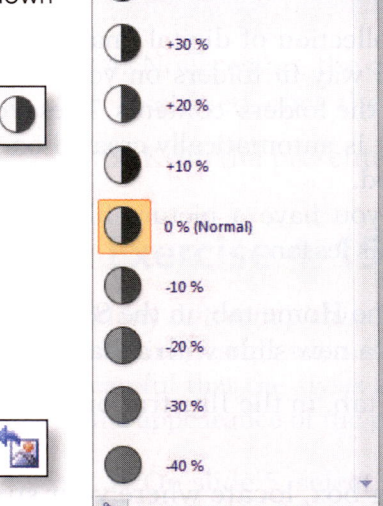

4. Click the Contrast button. Again, a drop-down list appears showing adjustments in 10 percent increments, as shown in Figure 4-25, to increase or decrease the lightness of the picture.

5. Drag your pointer over the various amounts and study the effect on the picture. Click on **+20%** to increase the contrast.

6. Now click the Reset Picture button to restore the picture's original colors and size. Change the height to 5 inches again.

7. Sometimes these 10 percent increments change a picture's colors too much, so you might need to adjust them more gradually to get good results. Click the Brightness button 🔅 then choose **Picture Correction Options** to open the Format Picture dialog box. Move this dialog box away from the picture so you can see the results of your changes as you make them.

8. Both the Brightness and Contrast can be adjusted by dragging the sliders to the left or right. You can also enter numbers in the spin boxes or click up or down to change in 1 percent increments.

9. This time change the Brightness to **14%** and the Contrast to **24%**. Click **Close**.

10. The picture appears a little clearer now when you compare the one changed on the right with the original version on the left, as shown in Figure 4-26.

Figure 4-26
Image-adjusted picture

11. Update the handout footer text to **[4-17your initials]**. Save the presentation as **[4-17your initials]** in your Lesson 4 folder, but do not print it. Leave the presentation open for the next exercise.

Exercise 4-18   CHANGE A PICTURE SHAPE

Any picture that is inserted on a slide can be made to fill a shape for an unusual and creative treatment.

1. On slide 6, from the Home tab, in the Slides group, click the New Slide button 🔲 to add a new slide with a **Blank** layout.

2. On slide 7, insert another picture from your Clip Art task pane. If the search from earlier in the lesson is not displayed, then search again for Miami photograph images.

3. Click the image that shows a beach and buildings. It has an unusual appearance because the image is angled.

4. With this image selected, from the Picture Tools Format tab, in the Picture Styles group, click the Picture Shape button. Try several of these shapes by clicking on the buttons in any of the categories. The image becomes the fill for that particular shape.

5. In the **Basic Shapes** category, select the **Heart** shape.

6. Continue to the next exercise.

Exercise 4-19   ADD A BORDER TO A PICTURE

The line that surrounds pictures is referred to as a Picture Border. This line can be shown in different colors and *line weights* (thicknesses) or in different styles (solid lines or dashes) to create a border around a picture just as you have used an outline on other shapes.

1. With the heart-shaped picture selected, from the Picture Tools Format tab, in the Picture Styles group, click the Picture Border button. As you drag your pointer over these colors, you can see how the color will look if selected.

Figure 4-27
Picture in a shape
with a border

2. From the colors that appear, in the **Standard Colors** group, click the **Red** color.

3. Click the Picture Border again and click **Weight**. Choose **3 pt** for a thicker red line, as shown in Figure 4-27.

4. Continue to the next exercise.

Exercise 4-20   APPLY PICTURE EFFECTS

Special effects can be applied to pictures as well as other shapes you create. To apply these effects to pictures, you will use the Picture Effects button on the Picture Tools Format tab. Many different customized settings are possible. Picture effects are available in seven categories:

- *Preset*—a collection of images with several different settings already applied.

- *Shadow*—displays a shadow behind the picture that can be adjusted in different ways to change direction, thickness, and blurring effect.

- *Reflection*—causes a portion of the image to be displayed below the image as though reflecting in a mirror or on water.

- *Glow*—adds a soft color around the picture edges that makes the picture stand out from the background.

- *Soft Edges*—changes a picture's normal hard edges to a soft, feathered appearance that gradually fades into the background color.

- *Bevel*—makes the picture looked dimensional with several different options available such as a raised button.

- *3-D Rotation*—enables the picture to be angled in different ways with perspective settings that change the illusion of depth.

1. On slide 7, select the heart-shaped picture. From the Picture Tools Format tab, in the Picture Styles group, click Picture Effects 🔲.

Figure 4-28
Picture Effects categories

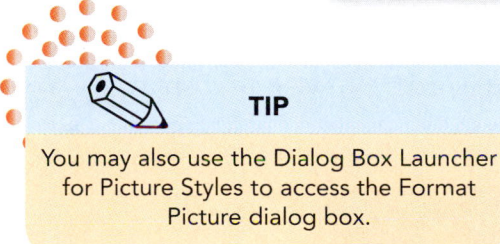

2. The drop-down list of effect categories appears, as shown in Figure 4-28. Each of these categories has several variations that you can see on your image as you drag your pointer over the effect thumbnail.

3. From the **Shadow** category, in the **Outer** subcategory, click the shadow named **Offset Diagonal Bottom Right** to apply a soft shadow.

4. Adjustments can be made to how the shadow appears. Click the Picture Effects button 🔲, click **Shadow** and then choose the **Shadow Options** at the bottom of this gallery.

5. From the dialog box that appears, key these numbers for each of the following settings:

  - Transparency   **20%**
  - Size   **100%**
  - Blur   **10 pt**
  - Angle   **40°**
  - Distance   **15 pt**

> **TIP**
>
> You may also use the Dialog Box Launcher for Picture Styles to access the Format Picture dialog box.

6. Click **Close** to accept these settings. Your heart shape should now look like Figure 4-29.

Figure 4-29
Format Picture shadow settings and shadow effects

7. Update the handout footer text to **[4-20your initials]**. Save the presentation as **[4-20your initials]** in your Lesson 4 folder, but do not print it. Leave the presentation open for the next exercise.

Creating WordArt

WordArt can create special effects for decorative text that are not possible with standard text-formatting tools. You can stretch or curve text and add special shading, 3-D effects, and much more.

Exercise 4-21   **CREATE AND MODIFY WORDART TEXT**

In this exercise, you create a WordArt object, and then modify it by changing its shape and size. Make sure you key and proofread WordArt objects carefully.

1. Display slide 3 with the building photograph.

Figure 4-30
WordArt Styles gallery

2. From the Insert tab, in the Text group, click the WordArt button [A]. The WordArt Styles gallery appears, as shown in Figure 4-30.

3. Point to the blue WordArt style that is called **Fill – Accent 2, Warm Matte Bevel** and click to select it. WordArt appears in the middle of your slide with sample text. At this point, you edit the text to replace the sample text, as shown in Figure 4-31, with the words you wish to display.

Figure 4-31
WordArt as it first appears

4. With the WordArt object selected key **Good For You** and delete any extra letters.

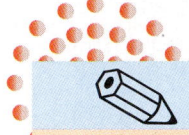

TIP

Many different styles are displayed in the WordArt gallery using the colors of your current theme. When applied, some of the styles may need color adjustments so the text is easily readable on the background color.

5. Click anywhere on the blank part of the slide to accept these changes and the bevel effect of this style becomes more evident.

6. To edit WordArt text, simply select the text and change it. In this case change the wording to **Good 4 U**.

7. Move the WordArt object to the upper left of the slide above the picture as shown in Figure 4-32.

Figure 4-32
WordArt showing positioning

8. Update the handout footer text to **[4-21your initials]**. Save the presentation as **[4-21your initials]** in your Lesson 4 folder, but do not print it. Leave the presentation open for the next exercise.

Exercise 4-22   APPLY WORDART EFFECTS

Figure 4-33
Text Effects

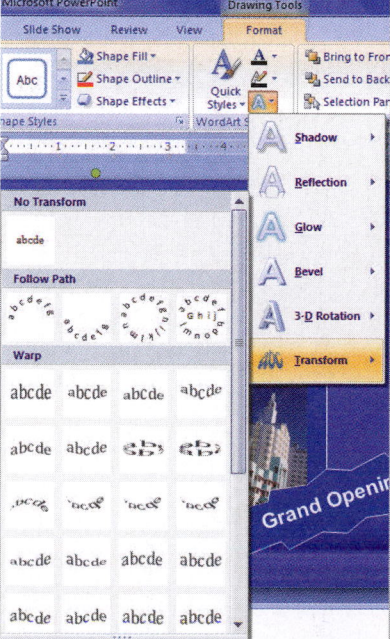

The same types of effects you have applied to pictures can be applied to WordArt. From the Drawing Tools Format tab, in the WordArt Styles group, the Text Effects are shown in Figure 4-33. In Exercise 4-20 you were introduced to these effects when applying them to a picture: Shadow, Reflection, Glow, Bevel, and 3-D Rotation. But the last category, *Transform*, is unique to WordArt because it enables you to change your text into different shapes.

1. Still working on slide 3, with the Good 4 U WordArt selected, click the Drawing Tools Format tab, in the WordArt Styles group, click the Text Effects button and choose **Transform**.

2. The default for WordArt text is No Transform because text will appear straight. When you drag your pointer over the various effects shown in this gallery, you will see that effect being applied to your text. The text sample on each of the buttons gives you an indication of the particular effect.

Figure 4-34
Using Transform to apply the Deflate Bottom Warp effect

3. From the Warp category, choose the effect **Deflate Bottom** that causes the text in the middle of the WordArt to become smaller.

4. Move the WordArt to the top of the picture so the letters G and U just slightly overlap with the blue rectangle as shown in Figure 4-34.

5. Keep your presentation open and continue to the next exercise.

Exercise 4-23 EDIT WORDART TEXT FILL AND TEXT OUTLINE COLORS

The *Text Fill* color of WordArt text can be changed as well as the *Text Outline* color and the weight of the outline. The outline goes around the edge of each letter. Making it thick emphasizes the outline; making it thin provides less emphasis but still makes the text look quite different than if no outline is applied.

1. Move to slide 7.

2. From the Insert tab, in the Text group, click the WordArt button ⓐ. For the style, click the white WordArt style that is called **Fill – White, Warm Matte Bevel** and click to select it.

3. Key **We Love Miami Beach!** then select the text. From the Home tab, in the Font group, change the font size to 44 points.

4. Move the WordArt object above the heart, centered horizontally on the slide.

5. With the WordArt selected, from the Drawing Tools Format tab, in the WordArt Styles group, click the Text Fill button ⓐ. From the Standard Colors, choose **Red**.

6. Now the WordArt color is almost too intense with such a bright red on the blue background. So apply a line color to tone down this effect.

7. With the WordArt selected, from the Drawing Tools Format tab, in the WordArt Styles group, click the Text Outline button 🖊.

8. Choose **More Outline Colors**, and then from the Colors dialog box, choose **Black**. Click **OK**.

9. Click the Text Outline button , click **Weight**, and choose **1 pt**.

10. Now change the shadow effect so it better matches the heart shape. From the Drawing Tools Format tab, in the WordArt Styles group, click the Dialog Box Launcher button .

11. From the Format Text Effects dialog box, choose **Shadow**. Change to these settings: Transparency **20%**, Size **100%**, Blur **4 pt**, Angle **45°**, distance, **2 pt**. Click **Close**.

12. From the Drawing Tools Format tab, in the WordArt Styles group, click the Text Effects button , click **Transform**, and from the Warp category, choose **Wave 2**.

13. Resize and adjust any necessary spacing so your slide resembles Figure 4-35.

Figure 4-35
Completed WordArt object

14. Update the handout footer to show **[4-23your initials]**.

15. Save the presentation as **[4-23your initials]** in your Lesson 4 folder and print it as handouts with nine slides per page. Close the presentation.

Creating a Photo Album

A presentation consisting of mostly pictures can be created quickly using PowerPoint's *Photo Album* feature. Picture files can be inserted from different locations on your computer and will be displayed with one picture on a slide. The pictures can be displayed at full screen size or framed in different shapes. Also, text can accompany each picture at the time you create the photo album, or text can be added to the individual slides. When complete, your saved photo album can be displayed just as any other presentation.

While this feature can be important for business situations, it could also be very helpful for creating a display for open house functions, or even wedding or birthday celebrations.

Exercise 4-24   CREATE ALBUM CONTENT BY INSERTING NEW PICTURES

In your Lesson 4 student data files you have a folder named **Salads** containing five pictures for this exercise. Copy the **Salads** folder to your storage location.

1. Open PowerPoint if necessary. Start a new blank presentation.

2. From the Insert tab, in the Illustrations group, click the top of the Photo Album button 🖼️. The Photo Album dialog box appears, as shown in Figure 4-36.

Figure 4-36
Photo Album dialog box

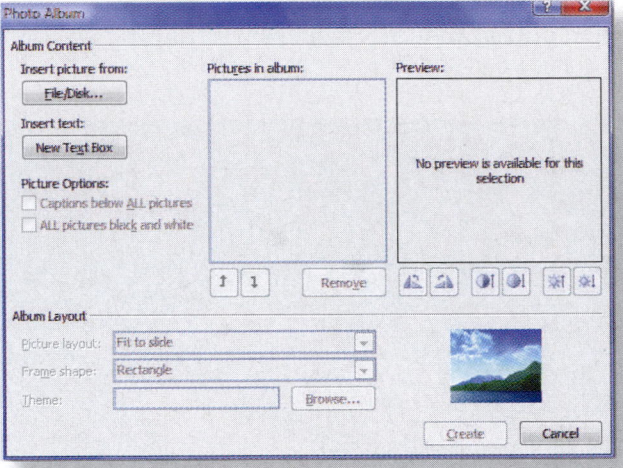

3. Click the File/Disk button  then choose the storage location where you have the **Salads** folder. Select the folder name then click **Open**.

4. Select all of the picture files and click **Insert**.

5. At the bottom of the dialog box, notice the **Album Layout** options. By default, the **Picture layout** is **Fit to slide**. This option will expand each picture to fill your computer's screen. Click **Create**.

6. Each picture appears on a separate slide and a title slide has been created.

7. Continue to the next exercise to edit the Photo Album settings.

Exercise 4-25   ADJUST PICTURE ORDER, BRIGHTNESS, AND CONTRAST

Using the Format Photo Album dialog box, pictures can easily be reordered by selecting the picture name and clicking the up or down arrows. Pictures can be rotated if their orientation needs to change and even the brightness and contrast can be adjusted. These changes can be made at the time you create the Photo Album or later by editing it.

1. From the Insert tab, in the Illustrations group, click the lower half of the Photo Album button 🖼 then click **Edit Photo Album**.

2. Highlight picture 5, **tuna**, that has a vertical orientation. Click the up arrow twice to position it in the middle of the other four pictures.

3. Highlight picture 2, **avocado**, click twice on the Increase Contrast button 🔲.

4. Highlight picture 1, **apples**, and click once on the Increase Brightness button 🔲 and click twice on the Increase Contrast button 🔲.

5. Click **Update** to accept these changes.

6. Continue to the next exercise.

Exercise 4-26   CONTROL ALBUM LAYOUT

Album Layout allows you to change the Picture layout from **Fit to slide** to different options with one to four pictures on a slide. You can choose to display titles for each slide or change to one of seven different Frame shapes for the pictures. Using Picture Options, you can choose to place captions below all pictures.

1. From the Insert tab, in the Illustrations group, click the lower half of the Photo Album button 🖼 then click **Edit Photo Album**.

2. For **Picture Layout**, change to **1 picture**.

3. Now **Picture Options** are available. Click **Captions below ALL pictures**.

4. For **Frame shape**, select several of the available options and notice how the effect is displayed in the thumbnail area on the right. Select **Simple Frame, White**.

Figure 4-37
Photo Album edited options

5. Now apply a background theme that will provide soft coloring on the background behind the pictures. For the Theme, click Browse [Browse...] and choose **Apex** then click **Select**. (You may have to navigate to your themes for Office 2007.)

6. Be sure the options on your Edit Photo Album dialog box match Figure 4-37. Click **Update**.

7. Now the pictures appear a little smaller on the slide and have a white frame with a subtle shadow effect, as shown in Figure 4-38. The **Apex** theme provides a soft background that is subtle and does not detract from the pictures.

Figure 4-38
Slide with framed picture

8. Notice that the file names for each picture now appear in text boxes below each picture. This text could now be changed to a more descriptive title for each salad.

9. On slide 1, key **New Salads** for the presentation title and key **Good 4 U** for the subtitle. Change the subtitle text size to 36 points and apply bold.

10. Add a header on the handout page with **[4-26your initials]** and nothing in the footer.

11. Save the presentation as **[4-26your initials]** in your Lesson 4 folder.

12. Print a handout copy with six slides on a page in portrait orientation. For print options, choose **Scale to Fit Paper** so each slide appears larger on the page.

13. Close your presentation.

Lesson 4 Summary

- In addition to text placeholders, PowerPoint provides a variety of objects that you can use to enhance the visual appearance of your slides. These include shapes, text boxes, clip art, and pictures.

- PowerPoint's drawing tools enable you to create a variety of shapes including squares, circles, rectangles, ovals, and straight lines drawn at any angle.

- To draw a shape, from the Insert tab, in the Illustrations group, click the Shapes button ⬚, choose a shape, and then drag diagonally on your slide to create the shape in the size you need.

- If you don't like a shape you drew, select it and press Delete to remove it from your slide, or press Ctrl +Z to undo the action.

- Press [Shift] while drawing a line or other shape to constrain it. Constraining a shape makes it perfectly symmetrical, for example, a circle or a square, or it can make a line perfectly straight.

- Press [Ctrl] while drawing a shape to make it grow in size from the center instead of from one edge.

- Change the size of a drawn object by dragging one of its sizing handles (small white circles on its border) with a two-pointed arrow [↕].

- To preserve an object's proportions when resizing it, hold down [Shift] while dragging a corner sizing handle.

- Move a drawn object by pointing to it and when the four-pointed arrow [✛] appears, drag the object to a new position.

- The Shapes gallery has many predefined shapes that are organized into several categories.

- When a shape is selected, text that you key appears inside the shape.

- Use the Clip Art task pane to search for clip art and photograph images. If you are connected to the Internet, the task pane's **Search** command will automatically search the Microsoft Office Online collection.

- To see the file properties of a clip art image or photograph, point to a clip art thumbnail in the Clip Art task pane, and then click the vertical bar that appears on the right side of the thumbnail (or right-click the thumbnail).

- Using the **Cut, Copy,** and **Paste** commands, you can easily move or copy clip art or other images from one slide to another or from one presentation to another.

- Using the **Duplicate** command is the quickest way to create a copy of an object on the same slide.

- Resize a clip art image by dragging one of its sizing handles. If you want to preserve proportions, drag a corner handle. If you want to distort the proportions, drag one of the side handles.

- From the Picture Tools Format tab, in the Adjust group, use tools to change a picture's brightness, contrast, and colors.

- Clip art images (vectors, bitmaps, or scanned images) can be cropped. Cropping is trimming away edges of a picture, much like using scissors to cut out a picture from a newspaper or magazine.

- WordArt enables you to create special effects with text that are not possible with standard text-formatting tools.

- WordArt is modified by using the WordArt Styles and Text Effects to change its appearance in many different ways. These options are available on the Drawing Tools Format tab when a WordArt object is selected.

- PowerPoint's Photo Album feature can be used to quickly create a presentation consisting mostly of pictures. One or more pictures can be placed on each slide with a choice of different framing techniques.

- Once a photo album is created, it can be modified by choosing the Edit Photo Album option to rearrange pictures, request captions and add a theme. A photo album is saved as any other presentation.

LESSON 4		Command Summary
Feature	**Button**	**Ribbon**
Rectangle		
Oval		
Line		
Constrained line	Shift +	
Square	Shift +	
Circle	Shift +	
Shapes		Home tab, Drawing group, Shapes or Insert tab, Illustrations group, Shapes
Search for Clip Art and Photographs		Clip Art task pane, Search
Insert Pictures		Insert tab, Illustrations group, Picture
Adjust Picture Brightness		Picture Tools Format tab, Adjust group, Contrast
Adjust Picture Contrast		Picture Tools Format tab, Adjust group, Brightness
Adjust Picture Color		Picture Tools Format tab, Adjust group, Recolor
Change Picture Shape		Picture Tools Format tab, Picture Styles group, Picture Shape
Apply Picture Border		Picture Tools Format tab, Picture Styles group, Picture Border
Picture Effects		Picture Tools Format tab, Picture Styles group, Picture Effects
Crop a Picture		Picture Tools Format tab, Size group, Crop
Insert WordArt		Insert tab, Text group, WordArt
Apply WordArt Styles		Drawing Tools Format tab, WordArt Styles group, Quick Styles
Change WordArt Color		Drawing Tools Format tab, WordArt Styles group, Text Fill
Change WordArt Outline		Drawing Tools Format tab, WordArt Styles group, Text Outline
Apply WordArt Text Effects		Drawing Tools Format tab, WordArt Styles group, Text Effects

Concepts Review

True/False Questions

Each of the following statements is either true or false. Select your choice by indicating T or F.

T F   1. You can type text only in an existing placeholder.

T F   2. Use [Shift] with ▢ to create a square.

T F   3. Every Shape includes an adjustment handle.

T F   4. A green handle on a PowerPoint object indicates that the object can be rotated.

T F   5. ☆ is found in the Basic category of the Shapes gallery.

T F   6. When you want to change the height of an object, but not the width, press [Shift] while dragging a corner sizing handle.

T F   7. To apply a frame or shadow effect to a picture, choose a Picture Style.

T F   8. WordArt enables you to create special effects with text.

Short Answer Questions

Write the correct answer in the space provided.

1. How do you draw a perfect circle?

2. What kind of handle is the yellow diamond?

3. How can you make a picture have a different shape?

4. What happens if you apply a bevel effect to a picture or shape?

5. Which task pane is used to search for a photograph?

6. What setting on the Format Picture dialog box will cause a shadow to appear from a particular direction?

7. How do you resize an object?

_____

8. How do you change the shape of a WordArt object?

_____

Critical Thinking

Answer these questions on a separate page. There are no right or wrong answers. Support your answers with examples from your own experience, if possible.

1. Consider the Shapes gallery and explain how three different shapes could help you to illustrate or draw attention to a concept you need to explain.

2. Describe how Picture Styles can enhance the appearance of a photograph.

Skills Review

Exercise 4-27

Create shapes, key text in a shape, and use the Format Shape dialog box.

1. Open the file **Seminar1**. Move to slide 3.
2. Use the drawing tools to create the shapes shown in Figure 4-39. First, create the wide rectangle that appears on top of the triangle by following these steps:

Figure 4-39
Drawing shapes

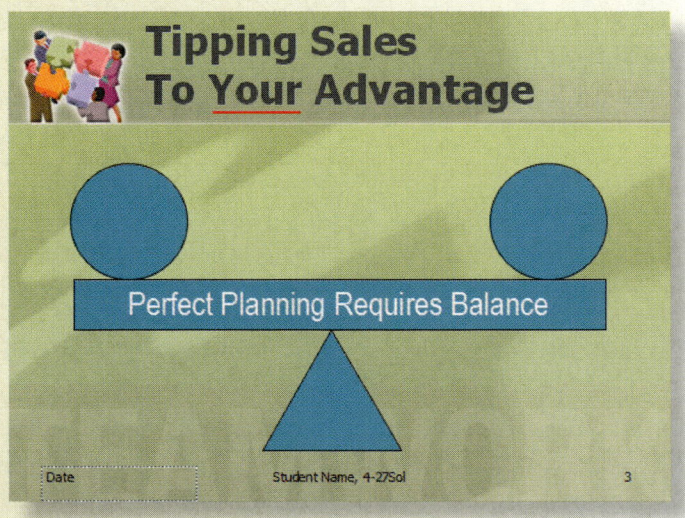

   a. From the Insert tab, in the Illustrations group, click the Shapes button 🔲 then the Rectangle button ▭.

   b. Position the crosshair pointer ⊞ on the left of the slide.

   c. Drag the pointer diagonally down and to the right, creating a wide rectangle, like the one shown in Figure 4-39. Release the mouse button. (Don't worry about the exact size or position. You size and place it in the next step.)

3. Precisely size and position the rectangle by following these steps:

   a. Select the rectangle, and from the Drawing Tools Format tab, in the Size group, click the Dialog Box Launcher.

   b. In the **Height** text box change the size to **0.75** inches and in the **Width** text box change the size to **8** inches.

   c. Click the **Position** tab. Key **1** inches in the **Horizontal** text box and **4** inches in the **Vertical** text box. Click **Close**.

4. Key text in the rectangle by following these steps:

   a. Select the rectangle.

   b. Key **Perfect Planning Requires Balance**.

   c. From the Home tab, change the font to Arial Narrow, the size of the text to 36 points, the text color to white, and alignment to center.

5. Create the triangle shown in Figure 4-39 by following these steps:

   a. From the Insert tab, in the Illustrations group, click the Shapes button 🔲, then from the **Basic Shapes** category, click the Isosceles Triangle button △.

   b. Position the pointer at the bottom center of the new rectangle.

   c. Drag diagonally down and to the right to create a triangle then center it under the rectangle.

6. Draw a circle by following these steps:

   a. From the Insert tab, in the Illustrations group, click the Shapes button 🔲, then from the **Basic Shapes** category, click the Oval button ⬭.

   b. Position the crosshair pointer ⊞ above the left end of the rectangle, hold down Shift, and drag diagonally to draw a circle approximately the same size as the one in Figure 4-39.

   c. Hold down Ctrl while using the arrow keys on your keyboard to fine-tune the circle's position.

7. Select the circle then press Ctrl + D to duplicate it. Drag the second circle to the other end of the rectangle, positioning it appropriately.

8. Create a horizontal line on slide 3 by following these steps:

   a. From the Insert tab, in the Illustrations group, click the Shapes button 🔲, then from the **Lines** category, click the Line button ◥.

   b. Position the pointer below the Y in the word *Your*.

   c. Hold down Shift and drag to the right to draw a straight line below the word. Release the mouse button first, and then release Shift.

d. From the Drawing Tools Format tab, in the Shape Styles group, click the Dialog Box Launcher to access the Format Shape dialog box. Change the Line Width to **3** points and then on the Line Color tab change the Line color to **Red, Accent 2**.

e. Adjust the position of the line, if necessary.

9. Check spelling in the presentation.

10. Create a footer for slide 3: Include the slide number, date, and your name, followed by a comma and the text **[4-27your initials]**.

11. Create a handout header and footer: Include the date and your name as the header, and the page number and text **[4-27your initials]** as the footer.

12. Move to slide 1 and save the presentation as **[4-27your initials]** in your Lesson 4 folder.

13. Print slide 3 in full size, framed. Preview and print the presentation as handouts, four slides per page, grayscale, landscape, framed. Close the presentation.

Exercise 4-28

Insert a picture from a file, crop a clip art image, search for and insert a clip art image, and place text on a shape.

1. Open the file **Seminar2**.

2. On slide 1, insert the picture file **Logo1** (from your student files) by following these steps:

   a. From the Insert tab, in the Illustrations group, click the Picture button ▨.

   b. Browse to find the student data files for Lesson 4, and click on **Logo1**.

   c. Click **Insert**.

3. Now remove the white color in the image by following these steps:

   a. From the Picture Tools Format tab, in the Adjust group, click the Recolor button ▨ and choose **Set Transparent Color**. Your pointer will change to a pen.

   b. Click on the white area to make it transparent.

4. Resize the logo to make it slightly smaller.

5. Position the logo at the bottom of the slide below the white graphic shape that is on the background.

6. Move to slide 2 and, in the content placeholder, click the Clip Art button ▨. The Clip Art task pane will appear.

   a. In the **Search for** box, key **refrigerator**. In the **Results should be** box, select Clip Art and then click **Go**.

   b. Look for an image that most closely resembles a commercial-grade refrigerator, and then insert it by clicking its thumbnail.

7. Resize the image proportionately from the center by following these steps:

   a. Select the image.

   b. Hold down Ctrl while dragging a corner handle.

c. When the image is the size you want, release ⌈Ctrl⌉ first, and then release the mouse button.

8. Crop clip art by following these steps:

   a. Move to slide 3. Select the image on the right side of the slide.

   b. From the Picture Tools Format tab, in the Size group, click the Crop button ⊞.

   c. Drag the top cropping handle down to just above the square containing the chef's hat.

   d. Drag each of the side cropping handles in, so that only the squares containing the chef's hat and the rolling pin remain.

   e. Click a blank area on the slide to deactivate the Crop button ⊞.

   f. Increase the size of the cropped image and position it beside the list with balanced spacing above and below the image.

9. On slides 4 and 6, search for and insert clip art images appropriate to the slide text content and the overall presentation design. Crop and/or resize the images if necessary.

10. On slide 2, at the bottom, insert a text box and key **Ask for our list of wholesale appliance dealers** and change the font to 24-point Arial Narrow, italic. Position the text box on the lower left.

11. Check spelling in the presentation.

12. Create a handout header and footer: Include the date and your name as the header, and the page number and text **[4-28your initials]** as the footer.

13. Move to slide 1 and save the presentation as **[4-28your initials]** in your Lesson 4 folder.

14. Preview, and then print the presentation as handouts, six slides per page, grayscale, framed. Close the presentation.

Exercise 4-29

Insert and size a picture from a file, adjust its contrast and brightness, and create WordArt.

1. Open the file **Seminar3**.

2. Replace the title on slide 1 with a WordArt text object by following these steps:

   a. Highlight the title text and turn off bold.

   b. From the Insert tab, in the Text group, click the WordArt button and choose the **Fill - Accent 2, Matte Bevel** (on the last row).

   c. Delete the original placeholder with the title.

   d. Reposition the WordArt where the title placeholder was located.

3. Change the shape of a WordArt object by following these steps:

   a. Select the WordArt object.

   b. From the Drawing Tools Format tab, in the WordArt Styles group, click the Text Effects button ⓐ▾ , then select **Transform**.

c. Select the **Chevron Up** shape and the text will increase in size when this effect is applied.

d. Hold down Ctrl and drag the bottom center sizing handle up slightly to decrease the height of the WordArt shape.

4. Add the Good 4 U logo to the title slide by following these steps:

a. Delete the subtitle placeholder.

b. From the Insert tab, in the Illustrations group, click the Picture button.

c. Navigate to the drive and directory where your Lesson 4 student data files are stored and select the file **Logo1**. Click **Insert**.

d. Drag the logo to the bottom of the subtitle placeholder in the center of the slide, as shown in Figure 4-40.

Figure 4-40
WordArt effect

5. Create a handout header and footer: Include the date and your name as the header, and the page number and text **[4-29your initials]** as the footer.

6. Save the presentation as **[4-29your initials]** in your Lesson 4 folder.

7. Preview, and then print the presentation as handouts, four slides per page, grayscale, landscape, framed. Close the presentation.

Exercise 4-30

Create shapes and rotate, add text, insert a picture from a file, and adjust image settings.

1. Open the file **Seminar4**. Replace the word *"Date"* on slide 1 with today's date.

2. Create a left arrow shape by following these steps:

a. Move to slide 3 and from the Insert tab, in the Illustrations group, click the Shapes button. In the **Block Arrows** category click **Left Arrow** (the second shape in the first row).

b. Position the crosshair pointer + at the top of the tallest bar in the fourth quarter of the chart, and then click and drag to create an arrow.

3. Rotate a shape by following these steps:

a. Select the arrow then drag the green rotation handle above the arrow to the left until the arrow points down at about a 45-degree angle.

b. Reposition the arrow, so it points to the top of the tallest bar, as shown in Figure 4-41.

4. Draw a text box in the space at the right of the chart. Change the font to 20-point Arial, bold, and left-align the text. Key **Los Angeles division sales expected to double in the 4th quarter**.

Figure 4-41
Adding a text box to clarify an important point

5. On slide 2, insert the **Restaurant1** picture from your student data files.

   a. Resize the picture to make it slightly smaller.

   b. From the Picture Tools Format tab, in the Adjust group, access the Picture Correction Options dialog box and adjust the **Contrast** and **Brightness** by **+5** percent.

   c. From the Picture Tools Format tab, in the Picture Styles group, apply the **Reflected Bevel, Black** picture style.

6. On slide 4, the picture that is already positioned on this slide is very dark.

   a. Adjust the contrast and brightness to improve the image.

   b. Apply the **Reflected Bevel, Black** picture style to match the other picture treatment.

7. Below the picture on slide 4, insert a text box with the words **Only the finest produce!**

   a. Format the text in a size, font, and color to match slide 3 (Arial, 20 point, bold).

   b. Position the text centered below the picture.

8. On slide 5, from the Insert tab, in the Illustrations group, click the Shapes button 🔲, then in the **Stars and Banners** category click the **5-Point Star**. Draw a star then position and size it so the star covers the gold rectangle on the right side of the horizontal line.

9. Place text in the star by following these steps:

   a. Select the star.

   b. Key **Star**, press ⟦Enter⟧, and key **Team**. Make the text Arial Black in 32 points.

   c. Adjust the size of the star, if necessary, to fit the text.

10. Check spelling in the presentation.

11. Create a handout header and footer: include the date and your name as the header, and the page number and text **[4-30your initials]** as the footer.

12. Move to slide 1 and save the presentation as **[4-30your initials]** in your Lesson 4 folder.

13. Preview, and then print the presentation as handouts, six slides per page, grayscale, framed. Close the presentation.

Lesson Applications

Exercise 4-31

Work with lines, text effects, shapes, and clip art.

1. Open the file **Market1**.

2. On slide 1, select the title text and apply the Text Effects of **Circle Bevel** and **Outer Offset Bottom Shadow**.

3. Draw a thin horizontal rectangle below the title text that extends under the title to the right edge of the slide.

4. Delete the subtitle placeholder. Draw a rectangle, approximately three inches wide. Position it attractively on the lower right side of the slide.

5. Use the Clip Art task pane to search for a photograph image by using the search word **meeting**. Choose a picture that has a horizontal orientation and is appropriate in style, content, and color for this slide.

6. Resize and crop the picture, if necessary, to make it fit on the solid-color area on the lower right of the slide using the rectangle as a border for the picture. Select an **Outer Offset Bottom Shadow** effect, as shown in Figure 4-42.

Figure 4-42
Drop shadow effect

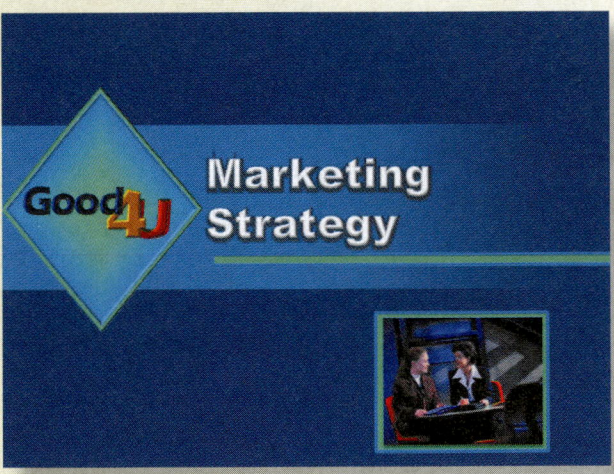

7. On slide 2, resize the body text placeholder to allow space on the right of the slide for a picture.

8. Find a similar picture to the one on slide 1 but in portrait orientation. Size and/or crop it as needed then add the same shadow effect. Position it on the right beside the bulleted list.

9. Check spelling in the presentation.

10. Create a handout header and footer: Include the date and your name as the header, and the page number and text **[4-31your initials]** as the footer.

11. Move to slide 1 and save the presentation as **[4-31your initials]** in your Lesson 4 folder.

12. Preview, and then print the presentation as handouts, six slides per page, grayscale, framed. Close the presentation.

Exercise 4-32

Insert pictures, apply effects, rotate, and insert WordArt.

1. Open the file **Orientation**.

2. On the title slide, select the clip art image, copy it, then delete it from this slide.

3. Move to slide 3 and add a slide with a blank layout to create slide 4. Paste the clip art image from slide 1 on slide 4.

4. On the title slide, increase the title text placeholder font size to 54 points. Increase the size of this placeholder so the text fits on two lines. Adjust the horizontal position so the left edge of the text aligns with the left edge of the horizontal blue shape.

5. On the title slide, in the subtitle placeholder, key **Your Name**, press Enter and key the **Current Date**.

6. Search for photograph images using the word "dining." Insert three photographs. You may need to crop them to reduce the image size to better feature one part of the picture. Adjust the size of these images for each to be 2.5 inches wide.

7. Add a Picture Style to all three of the photographs using **Drop Shadow Rectangle**.

8. Rotate these pictures and position them with even spacing on the left side of the slide as shown in Figure 4-43. (Your pictures may be different ones.)

Figure 4-43
Positioning of pictures

9. On slide 2, change the second bulleted item into two bulleted items and revise the wording:

   • **Company History**
   • **Company Vision**

10. Insert two new slides after slide 3; use the **Title and Content** slide layout. Key the text in Figure 4-44 on slides 4 and 5.

Figure 4-44
Text for slides

Slide 4
```
Who's Who
   • Julie Wolfe and Gus Irvinelli are the
     co-owners of the restaurant
   • Michele Jenkins is the head chef
   • Roy Olafsen is the marketing manager
```

Slide 5
```
Summary
   • Good 4 U is growing rapidly with our new franchising
     philosophy
   • Our healthy living message has worldwide appeal
   • We are relying on you, our new employees, to help us grow
```

11. If necessary, adjust the size of the text placeholders so the text fits within them without changing to a smaller size.

12. On slide 6, insert WordArt for the words **Welcome to Good 4 U** and make it fit on one line, left aligned. Adjust WordArt colors and effects to be appropriate for the presentation theme colors. Use the same Bookman Old Style font that is used in the slide titles.

13. Position the clip art image and the WordArt text for a pleasing arrangement.

14. Check spelling in the presentation.

15. Scroll through the presentation and check each slide to make sure the images and text are positioned appropriately.

16. Create a handout header and footer: Include the date and your name as the header, and the page number and text **[4-32your initials]** as the footer.

17. Move to slide 1 and save the presentation as **[4-32your initials]** in your Lesson 4 folder.

18. Preview, and then print the presentation as handouts, six slides per page, grayscale, framed. Close the presentation.

Exercise 4-33

Create shapes, insert and resize pictures, and insert WordArt.

1. Open the file **Investors**.

2. Using the Outline tab, insert the body text for each slide, as shown in Figure 4-45.

3. Click on the Slides tab and move to slide 1.

4. On slide 1, delete the title text and its placeholder. Create a WordArt title using the same text, **Attracting Investors**. Use the WordArt Quick Style **Gradient Fill - Accent 1** in the third row, fourth column.

5. With the WordArt selected, use the Text Effect of **Transform** to change its shape to **Deflate Bottom**.

6. Resize the WordArt to stretch across the slide with a height of 2.5 inches and a width of 9.0 inches. Move it up slightly from the center of the slide. Delete the subtitle placeholder.

7. On slide 2, on the shape on the right, key **Investors are our building blocks** with a font size of 36 points and bold. Resize the shape with a height of 3 inches and a width of 3 inches so the text word-wraps on three lines. Adjust the shape's position so it is even with the bulleted list on the left.

8. On slide 3, remove the bullets from the body text placeholder and center its text. Remove the indent for the second line of text. Adjust the size of the placeholder so the text fits on three lines and move it to the bottom of the slide to make room for a picture above it.

Figure 4-45
Text for slides

Slides	Outline

1. **Attracting Investors**
2. **Objectives**
   - Obtain investors to establish Good 4 U as a franchise
   - Revisit the current business plan
   - Hire a marketing consulting firm
3. **Our Specialties**
   - Organic fruit and vegetables
   - Fresh juices
   - Innovative cuisine
4. **What Investors Want**
   - High-profile location
   - Hotel or storefront
   - City with tourism, such as Miami or New York
   - "Curb Appeal"

9. Search for and insert a picture of fruit and a picture of vegetables. You can use the content placeholder or the Insert tab to access the Clip Art task pane so you can look for the images. Adjust the size and image settings of the pictures, if necessary. Apply a Picture Style of **Simple Frame, White**.

10. On slide 4, search for a picture of New York and insert it. Resize the picture so that it fits on top of the shape on the right of the slide. The picture should be approximately four inches wide. Apply the same Picture Style of **Simple Frame, White** and then resize the shape so it fits evenly behind the picture.

11. On slide 5 draw a **Right Arrow** shape and rotate it so it points up slightly. Duplicate this arrow by pressing Ctrl+D and position the second arrow above the first one. Repeat for two more arrows. The arrows should angle up across the slide, as shown in Figure 4-46.

Figure 4-46
Arrow positioning

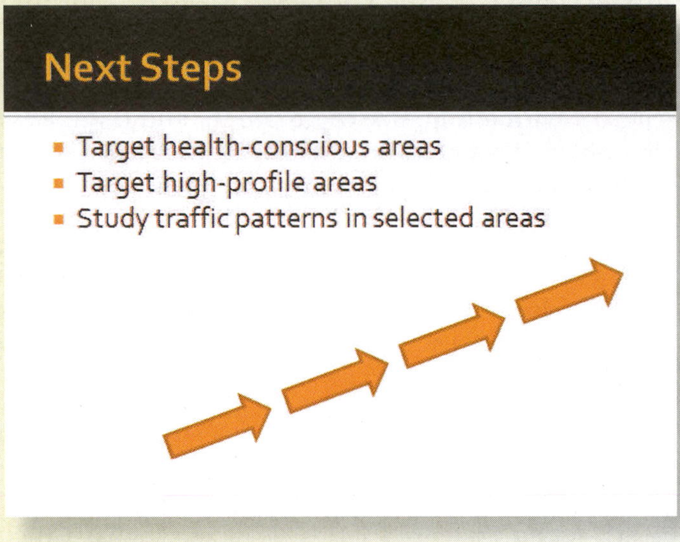

12. Review each slide, and make changes to the size and position of any objects that should be adjusted.

13. Check spelling in the presentation.

14. Create a handout header and footer: Include the date and your name as the header, and the page number and filename **[4-33your initials]** as the footer.

15. Move to slide 1 and save the presentation as **[4-33your initials]** in your Lesson 4 folder.

16. Preview, and then print the presentation as handouts, six slides per page, grayscale, framed. Close the presentation.

Exercise 4-34 ◆ Challenge Yourself

Create a photo album presentation, insert WordArt, and adjust Text Effects.

1. Start a new blank presentation.

2. From the Insert tab, in the Illustrations group, click **Photo Album**.

3. On the Photo Album dialog box, insert the five pictures from the **Cooking classes** folder.

4. Rearrange the picture order to put Chopping first followed by **Slicing**, **Sauce making**, **Pastry baking**, and **Bread baking**.

5. For the Album layout, choose the Picture Layout of **1 picture**.

6. For Frame shape, choose **Simple Frame, Black**.

7. For Theme, click **Browse** and then choose **Foundry**.

8. Click **Create**. Once the slides appear, choose the Design tab, Colors, and choose **Office** theme colors.

9. On slide 1, for the title text key **Cooking Classes** for the slide title. For the subtitle key **by Michele Jenkins, Head Chef** and make it bold.

10. Insert WordArt with the text **Back by Popular Demand** using the Quick Style of **Fill – Accent 2, Matte Bevel**. Change the font size to 40 points.

11. Rotate the WordArt and position it on the upper left of the slide.

12. Insert a text box below the subtitle to show the class dates:

    October 17 and 18, 9-10:30 a.m.

    November 7 and 8, 2-3:30 p.m.

    Registration required

13. Use right alignment for the text box so it matches the title and subtitle positioning.

14. On slide 2, insert a text box and, using the font size of 18 points, key **Efficient food handling methods**.

15. Center this text box under the picture.

16. Press Ctrl+C to copy the text box and paste it on slide 3. Edit the text to be **Fresh fruits and vegetables**.

17. Repeat this process for slides 4, 5, and 6, as shown in Figure 4-47, using this text:

    | Slide 4 | **Savory sauces** |
    | Slide 5 | **Pastry for a crowd** |
    | Slide 6 | **Breads like Grandma made** |

Figure 4-47

18. Create a handout header and footer. Include the date and your name as the header, and the page number and filename **[4-34your initials]** as the footer.

19. Save the presentation as **[4-34your initials]**. Preview, and then print the presentation as handouts.

On Your Own

In these exercises you work on your own, as you would in a real-life work environment. Use the skills you've learned to accomplish the task—and be creative.

Exercise 4-35

Imagine that you are about to open a new retail store or restaurant. Using the content and layout of the Miami Beach presentation from this lesson as a general guide, create a presentation with at least five slides announcing the opening of your business. Use clip art, text boxes, shapes, WordArt, and, if possible, scanned photos to illustrate your presentation. Include a transition effect. Save the presentation as **[4-35your initials]**. Preview, and then print the presentation as handouts.

Exercise 4-36

Create a presentation entitled "Gift Suggestions for [*choose occasion or person*]." Select five or more suitable items from mail-order catalogs and create a separate slide describing each item, including the price and why you selected it. If you have access to a scanner, scan each item's picture from the catalog and insert it on the appropriate slide. If a scanner is not available, insert a suitable clip art image on each slide. Use your own creativity and the tools learned in this and previous lessons to add interest to the slides. Save the presentation as **[4-36your initials]**. Preview, and then print the presentation as handouts.

Exercise 4-37

Prepare a photo album presentation as a gift for a family member or friend to commemorate a special occasion when you took several pictures. If you do not have a digital camera, then you can scan printed photos. Create an appropriate theme for your presentation based on the occasion by choosing a suitable background design theme and theme colors. Add clip art, text boxes, shapes, and WordArt to illustrate your presentation like a scrapbook. Save the presentation as **[4-37your initials]**. Preview, and then print the presentation as handouts.

Lesson 5

Creating tables

OBJECTIVES

After completing this lesson, you will be able to:

1. Create a table.

2. Draw a table.

3. Modify a table structure.

4. Align text and numbers.

5. Enhance the table.

6. Create a tabbed table.

MCAS OBJECTIVES

In this lesson:
PP07 2.1.6
PP07 3.7
PP07 3.7.1
PP07 3.7.2
PP07 3.7.3
PP07 3.7.4

See Appendix

Estimated Time: 2 hours

Tables display information organized in rows and columns. Once a table is created, you can modify its structure by adding columns or rows, plus you can merge and split cells to modify your table's design. Table content can be aligned in different ways for easy-to-read layouts. Color can be applied to highlight selected table cells or to add table borders. Working with tables in PowerPoint is similar to working with them in Word.

Creating a Table

A *table* consists of rows, columns, and cells. *Rows* consist of individual cells across the table horizontally. *Columns* consist of individual cells aligned vertically down the table. The *cell* is the intersection between the column and a row.

PowerPoint provides several convenient ways to create a table. With each method, you specify the number of columns and rows that you need.

- Insert a new slide, choose the **Title and Content** layout, and click the Insert Table button 🔲.

- From the Insert tab, in the Tables group, click the Table button 🔲 and choose **Insert Table**.

- From the Insert tab, in the Tables group, click the Table button 🔲, and drag the mouse to select the correct number of rows and columns.

- Draw a table using the Draw table pen tool. To access this tool, click the Insert tab then in the Tables group, choose the Table button 🔲 and then click **Draw Table**. Using the Pencil Pointer, click and drag to create the size of the table and then divide it into columns and rows.

- Create a tabbed table using tab settings.

When you insert a table into your presentation, your Ribbon will change to show the Table Tools Design and Layout tabs. These tabs contain many options for formatting and modifying the table you have created.

Exercise 5-1   INSERT A TABLE

When you use the Insert Table button 🔲, you may define a table's dimensions by dragging down and across a grid to determine the number of rows and columns.

1. Open the file **Briefing1**. Insert a new slide after slide 1 that uses the **Title Only** slide layout. Key the title **Employment Levels 2006**. Resize the placeholder so the title fits on one row.

2. From the Insert tab, in the Tables group, choose the Insert Table button 🔲. A grid appears for defining the size of the table by selecting squares that represent table cells.

3. Drag your pointer down three squares and across four squares to define a 4 by 3 Table (four columns by three rows), as shown in Figure 5-1, then click your left mouse button to accept the table size.

Figure 5-1
Defining a table

4. Point to the table's border and use the four-pointed arrow ✛ to move the table down and to the right about one-half inch.

5. Key the text shown in Figure 5-2. Use your pointer to click into the first cell of the table, and then press Tab to move from cell to cell. Entering text in a PowerPoint table is similar to entering text in a Word table.

6. Leave the presentation open for the next exercise.

Figure 5-2
Table with text

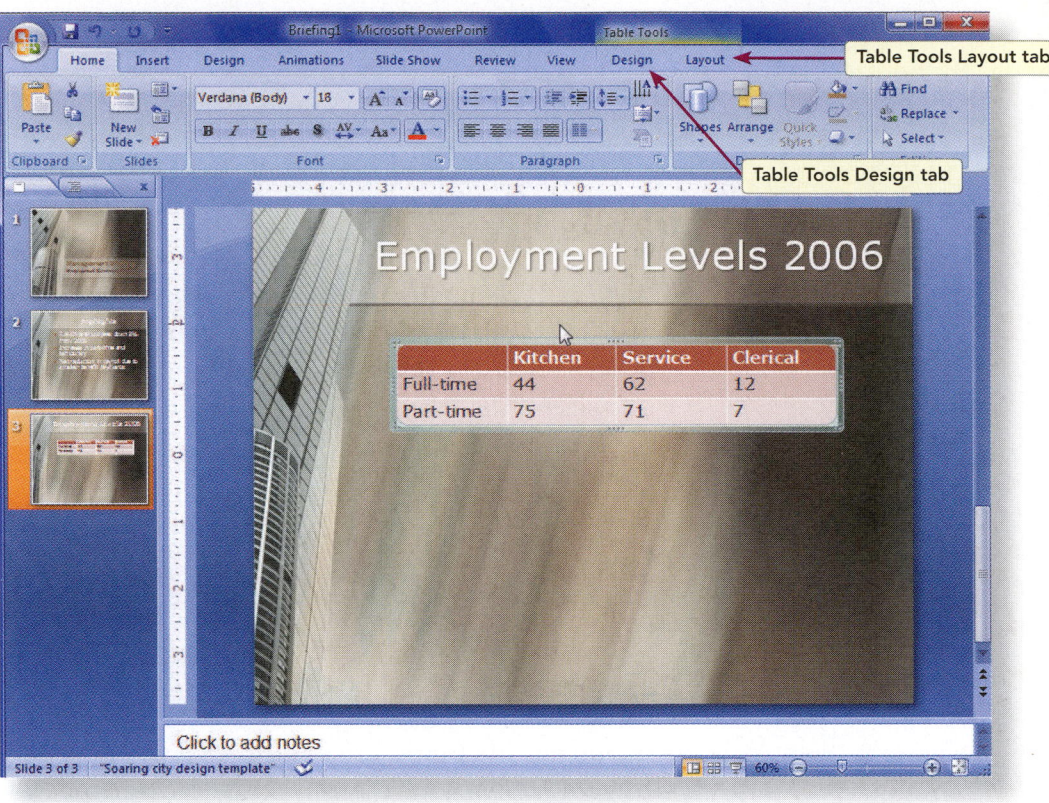

Exercise 5-2   NAVIGATE IN A TABLE

There are several ways to navigate in a table:

NOTE

When a cell is blank, pressing the left arrow key ← or the right arrow key → moves the insertion point left or right one cell. If text is in a cell, the left and right arrow keys move the insertion point one character to the left or right.

NOTE

If you reach the end of the table move to step three. If you accidentally press Tab at the end of the table, it will add a new row to the table. Use the Undo Button to reverse this action.

- Click the cell with the I-beam.

- Use the arrow keys ←, →, ↑, or ↓.

- Press Tab to move forward or Shift+Tab to move backward.

1. Click in the first table cell. Notice the insertion point in the cell you clicked.

2. Press Tab several times. The insertion point moves through cells from left to right. When you reach the end of a row, pressing Tab moves the insertion point to the beginning of the next row.

3. Press Shift+Tab several times. The insertion point moves through cells from right to left.

4. Press each arrow key several times and observe the movement of the insertion point.

5. Leave the presentation open for the next exercise.

Exercise 5-3   SELECT TABLE STYLES

A *Table Style* is a combination of formatting options, including color combinations, based on your theme colors. A table style is applied automatically to any table that you add through the Insert Table feature. Thumbnails of table styles are shown in the Table Styles gallery found on the Table Tools Design tab in the Table Styles group, as shown in Figure 5-3. When your pointer is over any thumbnail in the gallery, you will see a live preview of what your table will look like if you apply this style.

1. Right-click in any of the table cells and choose **Select Table** from the short-cut menu.

2. From the Table Tools Design tab, in the Table Styles group, choose the More button to open the Table Styles Gallery.

Figure 5-3
Table Tools Design
tab

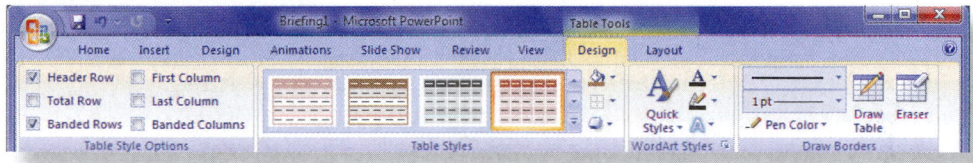

3. Place your pointer over several of the styles to see the ScreenTip with the name of the style and preview the effect on your table.

4. From the **Best Match for Document** category, choose **Themed Style 1, Accent 6** by clicking on the thumbnail. Notice how this table style blends well with the background.

5. Leave the presentation open for the next exercise.

Exercise 5-4   APPLY TABLE STYLE OPTIONS

Table Style Options can be used to apply a table style to specific parts of your table.

- To emphasize the first row of the table, select the **Header Row** check box.

- To emphasize the last row of the table, select the **Total Row** check box.

- To have alternating striped rows, select the **Banded Rows** check box.

- To emphasize the first column of the table, select the **First Column** check box.

- To emphasize the last column of the table, select the **Last Column** check box.

- To have alternating striped columns, select the **Banded Column** check box.

1. With the table selected, from the Table Tools Design tab, in the Table Style Options group, click the **First Column** check box. Notice that the text in the first column now appears bold.

TIP

If you were comparing the number of kitchen staff versus the number of clerical staff, this formatting style would make the document easier to read. However, if you were comparing the number of full-time versus the number of part-time employees, the Banded Rows would be a better choice.

2. Click the **Header Row** check box to uncheck the box. Notice that the deep brown disappears and the banded rows alternate starting with the first row.

3. Click the Undo button to reapply the Header Row formatting.

4. Click the **Banded Rows** check box to uncheck the box.

5. Click the **Banded Columns** check box to apply a check in the box.

6. Leave the presentation open for the next exercise.

Drawing a Table

The Draw Table feature in PowerPoint provides a different method of creating a table. From the Insert tab, in the Tables group, click the Table button, and choose **Draw Table**. Using this method allows you to control the exact size of the table using the pencil pointer to draw.

Exercise 5-5 USE PENCIL POINTER TO DRAW A TABLE

To draw a table, you first drag the *Pencil pointer* diagonally down and across to create a rectangle the approximate size of the table's outside border. Then you draw horizontal and vertical lines within the table to divide it into columns and rows.

1. Insert a new slide after slide 3 that uses the **Title Only** slide layout. Key the title **Employment Levels 2007**. Resize the placeholder to fit the text on one row.

2. From the Insert tab, in the Tables group, click the Table button, and then choose **Draw Table**.

3. Using the pencil pointer, drag from under the left edge of the title (down and to the right) to create a rectangle that fills the available space. See Figure 5-4 for size and placement. At this point, you have a one-cell table.

Figure 5-4
Using the Pencil pointer

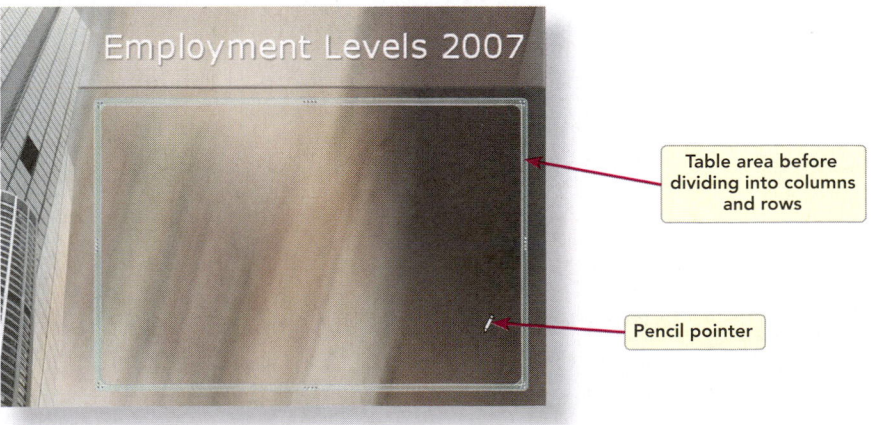

4. The Pencil pointer creates rows and columns when you draw borders within the table area. Be sure the pointer is inside the table before you start drawing so the lines you draw divide the table space. If the pointer touches the table border, a new table will be created. (If this happens, press Ctrl+Z to undo the action and try again.)

NOTE

For now, don't worry if your table cell sizes do not perfectly match Figure 5-5 or if your text wraps within the cell. You will learn how to adjust cell sizes later in the lesson.

5. With the table selected, from the Table Tools Design tab, click the Draw Table button and draw a line through the middle of the table area. Each time you draw a line, one cell is split into two cells. Because you are drawing horizontal lines now, the cells you are splitting create the table rows. Draw two more horizontal lines to create four rows in the table as shown in Figure 5-5.

6. Now, split the table with four vertical lines extending from the top of the table to create 5 columns.

7. From the Table Tools Design tab, in the Draw Borders group, click **Draw Table** to turn off the pencil pointer.

8. Key the table text shown in Figure 5-5. Leave the presentation open for the next exercise.

Figure 5-5
Drawing a table

Exercise 5-6 — CHANGE TABLE TEXT DIRECTION

Text direction changes can affect the appearance of a table and how it fits within a given space. If the title is the only long part about the column, changing the column title text direction allows you to fit more columns in a given area. Text direction in a table can be changed in two ways:

NOTE

Some of your titles may wrap onto the next line even in the middle of words. You will fix this in a later exercise.

- From the Table Tools Layout tab (see Figure 5-6), in the Alignment group, select the Text Direction button .

- From the Home tab, in the Paragraph group, select the Text Direction button.

Figure 5-6
Table Tools Layout
tab

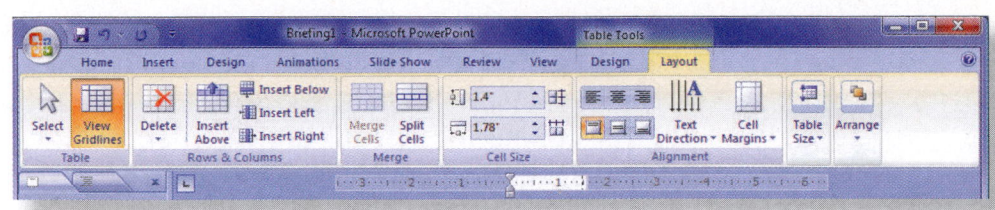

Figure 5-7
Text Direction drop-
down list

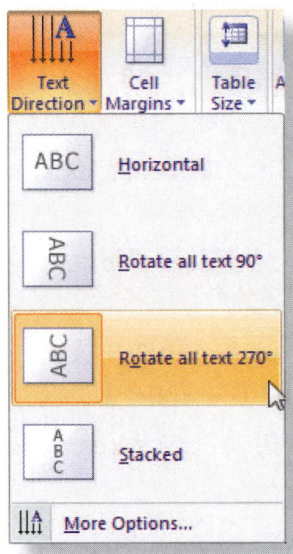

1. Click in the cell that reads **Mgmt**.

2. From the Table Tools Layout tab, in the Alignment group, click Text Direction button.

3. From the drop-down list, choose **Rotate all text 270°** as shown in Figure 5-7.

4. Notice how the text reads going up in the cell. Change the text direction in the same manner for **Kitchen**, **Service**, and **Clerical**.

Exercise 5-7   APPLY SHADING AND BORDERS

When you first draw a table, the table cells contain no shading, allowing the slide's background to show. You can apply a shading color or other shading alternatives, such as a gradient, or picture effect to one or more cells in your table. Applying shading to a table is similar to applying shading to other PowerPoint objects. All of the shading options are available from Table Tools Design tab, in the Table Styles group, from the Shading button drop-down list. Applying shading involves two-steps:

• First, select the cells to which you want to apply the shading effect.

• Second, click the Shading button and choose the shading you wish to apply.

Table borders are the lines forming the edges of cells, columns, rows, and the outline of the table. From the Table Tools Design tab, in the Table Styles group, the Borders button drop-down list enables you to apply borders to all the cells in a selection, to just an outside border, or to just the inside borders separating one cell from another. Applying table borders is a three-step process:

• First, select the cells to which you want to apply the border effect.

• Second, select the border style, border width, and border color you want.

• Third, click the Borders button and choose an option from the drop-down list.

1. On slide 4, with the table active, select all the cells in the top row by moving your pointer to the left of row 1 until you get a solid black arrow pointing at the row. Click to select the whole row.

2. From the Table Tools Design tab, in the Table Styles group, click the Shading button  and choose **Gray-25%, Accent 4, Darker 25%** from the Theme Colors area.

3. Change the font color for the selected row to **Gray-25%, Accent 4, Darker 90%**.

4. Select the first column in the table by pointing to the top of the first column until you get a solid black arrow pointing down at the column. Apply the same **Gray-25%, Accent 4, Darker 25%**, and change the font color to **Red, Accent 1, Darker 50%**.

5. Select all the cells that contain numbers by clicking in the first number cell and dragging your pointer down and to the right to the last number cell.

6. From the Table Tools Design tab, in the Table Styles group, click the Shading button  and apply a white color. With these cells still selected, change the font color to the **Red, Accent 1, Darker 50%** matching the first column.

7. Click outside the table to observe the effect. Now the table has an appearance that distinguishes it from the slide background. Compare your table to Figure 5-8.

REVIEW

The Font Color button 🅰 is on the Home tab, in the Font group. You can also right-click to access the floating font group to make font changes.

Figure 5-8
Shading applied to a table

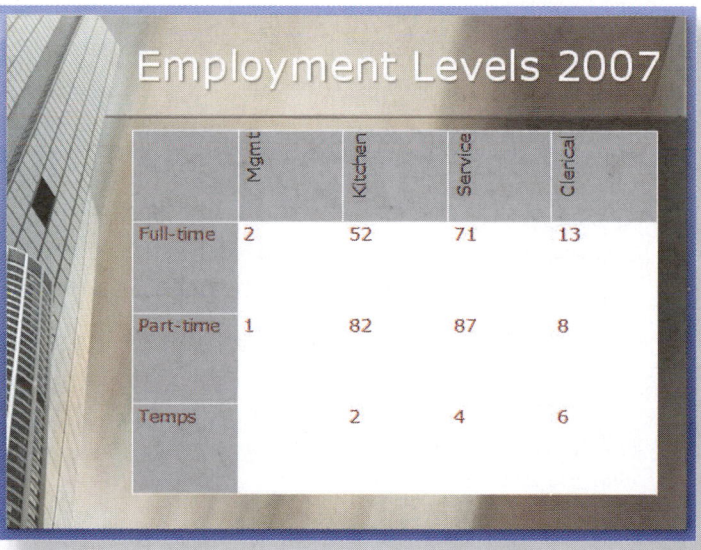

8. Select the whole table by right-clicking any cell within the table and choosing **Select Table** from the short-cut menu.

9. From the Table Tools Design tab, in the Draw Borders group, click the Pen Weight button 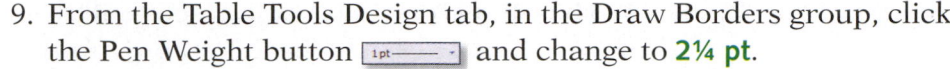 and change to **2¼ pt**.

10. Still working in the Draw Borders group, click the Pen Color button , and choose **Red, Accent 1**.

11. Click the Borders button in the Table Styles group, and choose **Top Border**. Repeat this step for the **Bottom Border** and the **Inside Horizontal Border**. Click outside the table to deselect the table and notice the difference in the table with some added borders.

Exercise 5-8 CHANGE BORDER AND SHADING COLORS

Table Border and Shading styles can be changed at any point while creating your presentations.

1. Select any cell in your table. From the Table Tools Design tab, in the Draw Borders group, click Pen Style and choose the second style down (a dashed line).

2. Click the Pen Weight button and choose **1½ pt**.

TIP

You can use the pencil tool to change the color and style of a border. Set the border options in the Draw Borders group. Then, instead of clicking the Borders button, use the pencil to click the borders you want to change.

3. Click the Pen Color button and choose **Gray-25%, Accent 4**.

4. Right-click in the table and choose **Select Table**.

5. Click the drop-down list arrow for the Borders button, and choose **Inside Borders**, as shown in Figure 5-9. The inside borders of the table are now dashed lines.

Figure 5-9
Borders button drop-down list

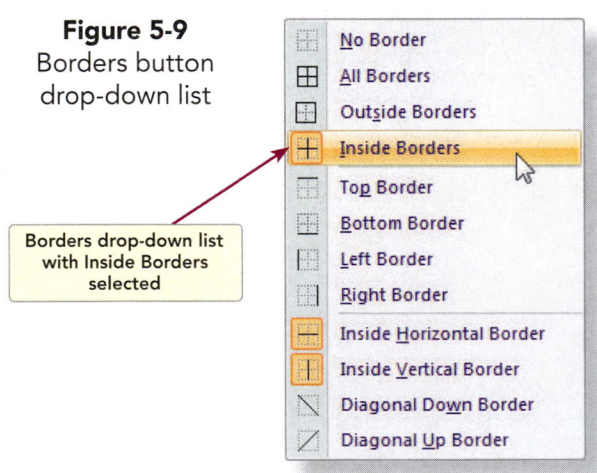

Borders drop-down list with Inside Borders selected

6. Still working on slide 4, select row 2 of the table. From the Table Tools Design tab, in the Table Styles group, click the Shading button and choose **White, Text 1** to change the Shading to white for row 2.

7. Select row 3 of the table. Still working in the Table Styles group, click the Shading button and choose **Gray-25%, Accent 4, Darker 25%** to change the shading to gray for row 3.

8. Select row 4 of the table. Click the Shading button and choose **White, Text 1** to change the Shading to white for row 4, as shown in Figure 5-10.

Figure 5-10
Completed table

Exercise 5-9 ERASE CELL BORDERS

The *Eraser* can be used to delete borders between cells.

1. Click in the last cell of the table on slide 4. Click Tab one time. Notice that PowerPoint automatically inserts another row below the last row in the table.

2. From the Table Tools Design tab, in the Draw Borders group, choose the Eraser.

3. Click each of the four borders that divide the last row of the table into five cells. Notice that as you click each border, it disappears. When all four are removed, the last row is turned into one cell.

4. Press Esc to turn off the Eraser. Click in the last row and key **Estimated Projection**. Your table may now extend past the bottom of the slide. This will be corrected later.

5. Create a new folder for Lesson 5 and save the presentation as **[5-9your initials]** in your new Lesson 5 folder.

6. Leave the presentation open for the next exercise.

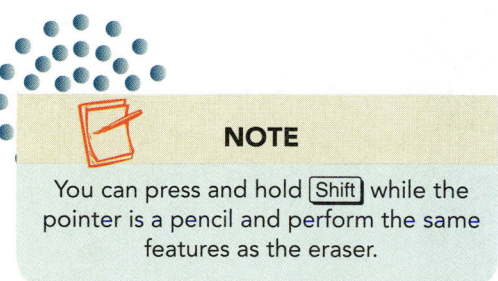

NOTE

You can press and hold Shift while the pointer is a pencil and perform the same features as the eraser.

Modifying Table Structure

When you create a table, you decide how many rows and columns the table should have. After entering some data, you might discover that you have too many columns or perhaps too few rows. Or, you might want one row or column to have more or fewer cells than the others. You can modify your table structure by inserting or deleting columns, merging a group of cells, or splitting an individual cell into two or more cells.

Exercise 5-10 INSERT AND DELETE ROWS AND COLUMNS

Columns and rows can be inserted using three methods:

- From the Table Tools Layout tab, in the Rows & Columns group, choose which option you would like to insert.

- Right-click a cell in the table and use commands on the short-cut menu.

- Insert a row at the bottom of the table by pressing Tab if you're in the last cell of the last table row. This is convenient if you run out of rows while you're entering data.

Columns can be inserted either to the right or the left of the column that contains the active cell. The column formatting of the active column is copied to the new column or the table style is applied. Rows can be inserted above or below the row that contains the active cell. The row formatting of the active row is copied or the table style is applied to the new row.

1. Move to slide 2, select the "Kitchen" column.

2. Right-click the selected column and click **Insert** and choose **Insert Columns to the Left** from the short-cut menu, as shown in Figure 5-11. A new column appears to the left of "Kitchen." It is the same size as the "Kitchen" column and has the formatting of the table style applied. The table is wider to accommodate the extra column.

Figure 5-11
Inserting a column through the short-cut menu

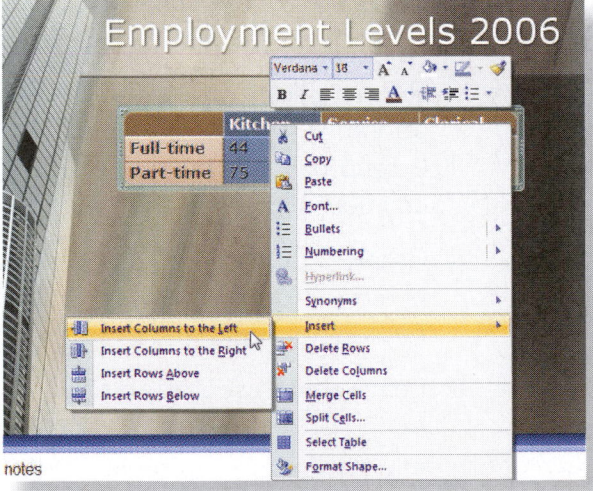

3. Click the blank cell in the upper-left corner of the table.

4. From the Table Tools Layout tab, in the Rows & Columns group, click the Insert Right button. A new column appears to the right of the selected cell, and it is the same size and formatted with the selected table style.

5. Click any cell in column B (the last column that was inserted).

6. From the Table Tools Layout tab, in the Rows & Columns group, click the Delete button 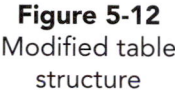 then choose **Delete Columns**. The new column is deleted, and the table is resized. Your table should now have one blank column located to the left of the "Kitchen" column and some of your titles may be wrapped to two lines. This will be fixed later.

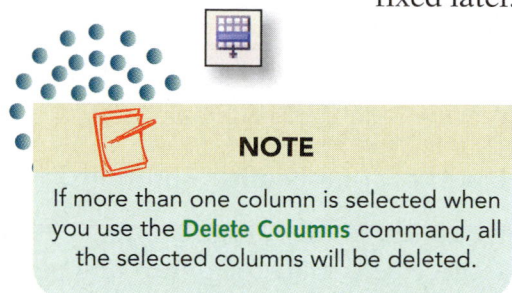

7. Still working on the Table Tools Layout tab, in the Rows & Columns group, select one cell in the second table row and click the Insert Below button 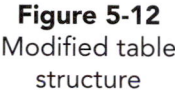.

8. Click the last cell in the last row, containing the number "7." Press ⟨Tab⟩. A new row is inserted at the bottom of the table.

9. Select cells in the blank row below the text "Full-time," right-click the selected cells, and choose **Delete Rows** from the short-cut menu.

10. Complete the table by keying the information shown in Figure 5-12 into the blank row and blank column.

Figure 5-12
Modified table structure

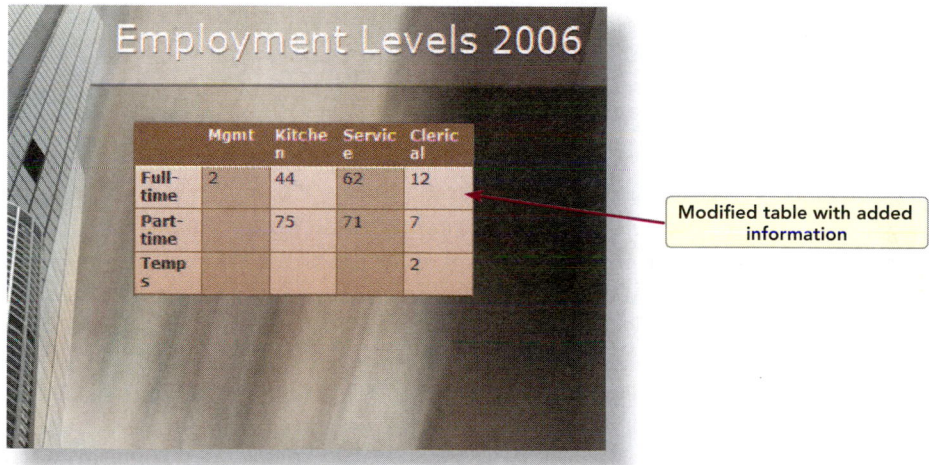

Modified table with added information

Employment Levels 2006

	Mgmt	Kitchen	Service	Clerical
Full-time	2	44	62	12
Part-time		75	71	7
Temps				2

Exercise 5-11   MERGE AND SPLIT CELLS

As you discovered when drawing the table, you can split cells by drawing a line through them with the pencil pointer ⟨✎⟩. You can also split a cell by using the *Split Cells* button ⟨⊞⟩ on the Table Tools Layout tab in the Merge group, or by right-clicking the cell and choosing **Split Cells** from the short-cut menu.

Cells can be merged together in several ways. As you learned in a previous exercise, the Eraser button ⟨⊞⟩ removes borders between two adjacent cells to create one cell. You can merge cells by selecting two or more cells, and then from the Table Tools Layout tab, in the Merge group, click the *Merge Cells* button 🔲 or by right-clicking the selected cells and choosing **Merge Cells** from the short-cut menu.

1. Move to slide 4. At the bottom of the table, click the cell containing the text "Estimated Projection."

2. From the Table Tools Layout tab, in the Merge group, click the Split Cells button 🔲. Change the number of columns to **1** and the number of rows to **2**. The selected cell becomes two cells.

3. Click **OK**.

4. In the new cell, key **Revised Figures**.

5. Select the first three cells in the second row that begins "Full-time."

6. Still working on the Table Tools Layout tab, in the Merge group, click the Merge Cells button 🔲. The three cells transform into one wide cell. The text and numbers from the merged cells all appear in one cell.

7. Click the Undo button 🔄 to return the merged cells to their previous state.

8. Leave the presentation open for the next exercise.

Exercise 5-12   APPLY A DIAGONAL BORDER

Borders can be placed diagonally within a cell. For example, if you are using a PowerPoint table to create a calendar, you might want to put two dates in the same square, separated by a diagonal line. Applying a diagonal border in this way does not create two separate cells, but is merely a line drawn within one cell. You can make it look like two cells by carefully placing text inside the cell.

1. Still working on slide 4, select the two rows at the bottom of the table, and then right-click and choose **Merge Cells** from the short-cut menu to combine the two cells into one. The text "Revised Figures" now appears on a separate line below "Estimated Projection" in one cell.

2. With the table active, move to the bottom of the table in the center at the sizing handle, and click and drag up to fit within the slide.

3. From the Table Tools Design tab, in the Draw Borders group, change the pen style to a **dashed line**, **1½-point**, **Gray-25%**, **Accent 4**, **Darker 50%** gray line. Your pointer has been changed to a pencil.

4. Position the pencil tool near, but not touching, the lower-left corner of the cell in the last row. Draw a diagonal line across the cell to the upper-right corner, as shown in Figure 5-13.

Figure 5-13
Using the pencil pointer to add a diagonal border

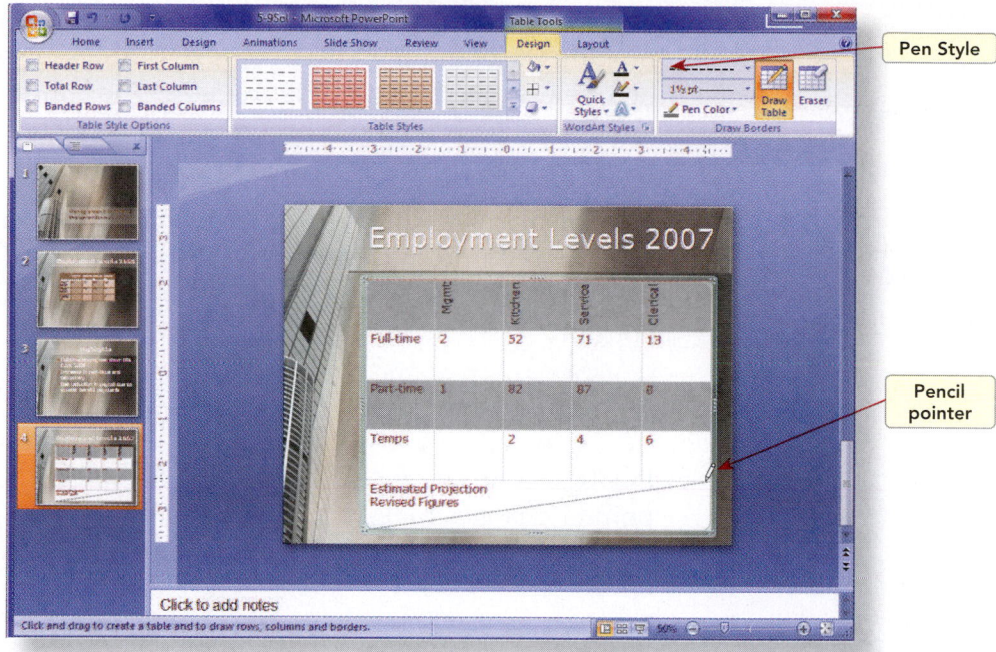

NOTE

Be careful where you start drawing. If you touch one of the cell borders with the pencil, the formatting of that border might change. If that happens, use Undo to restore it.

5. Press [Esc] to turn off the pencil pointer. Deselect the table to see the result. In a later exercise, you will apply text alignment to give this the appearance of a split cell.

Exercise 5-13 **DISTRIBUTE COLUMN WIDTH AND ROW HEIGHT**

If you decide to add rows or columns, or if you decide to make a column wider, the table may no longer fit on a slide. You can make a table smaller or larger by dragging its sizing handles, and you can change the height of rows and the width of columns individually by dragging cell borders. You can also choose the exact height and width of the cells by using the Cell Size group on the Table Tools Layout tab.

From the Table Tools Layout tab, in the Cell size group, use the *Distribute Columns* button to easily adjust several columns to be the same width. The *Distribute Rows* button works in a similar way.

1. Move to slide 2, move your pointer over the right border of the first column until the pointer changes to a two-pointed arrow ⊕.

2. Using this pointer, click and drag the column border to the right making the column wide enough so that the text "Part-time" appears on one line, as shown in Figure 5-14. The column width increases, and the adjacent column becomes smaller. Now the second column might be too narrow for the word "Kitchen."

3. Use the arrow pointer ⊞ to double-click the right border of the "Kitchen" column. Double-clicking a right border makes the column wide enough to accommodate the widest text line in the column.

4. Double-click the right border of each of the remaining columns to allow the widest text to be all on one line.

5. Position your pointer on the bottom border of the first row. When the pointer changes to ⊞ , click and drag the bottom border down, so that the row is approximately half again its original height.

Figure 5-14
Resizing column
width and row height

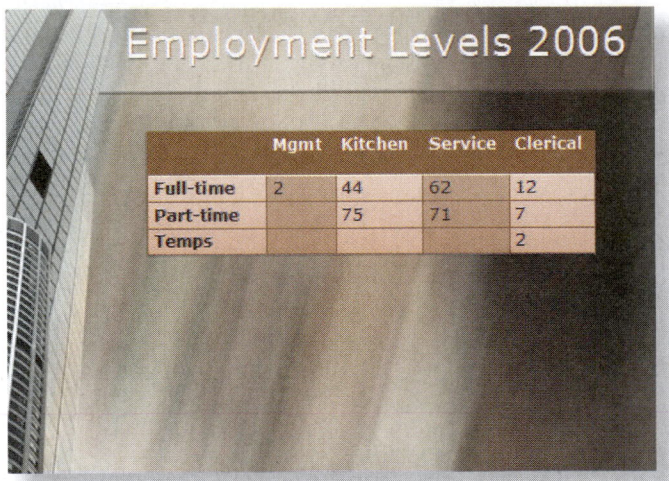

6. Move to slide 4. Select the "Mgmt," "Kitchen," "Service," and "Clerical" columns by dragging across the second, third, fourth, and fifth cells in any row (or drag the small, black, down-facing arrow ⊡ just above the top border of the four columns).

7. From the Table Tools Layout tab, in the Cell Size group, click the Distribute Columns button ⊞. The four selected columns are now all the same width.

8. Select the second through fourth cells in the first column.

9. Click the Distribute Rows button ⊞. Now the second through fourth rows are exactly the same height.

10. Select the last row of the table. From the Table Tools Layout tab, in the Cell Size group, change the height to **.7"** so the table fits better on the slide.

11. Create a handout header and footer: Include the date and your name as the header, and the page number and text **[5-13your initials]** as the footer.

12. Save the presentation as **[5-13your initials]** in your Lesson 5 folder.

Aligning Text and Numbers

Text and numbers in a table cell can be aligned vertically or horizontally. You can specify that text or numbers appear at the top, middle, or bottom of a cell, and be horizontally left-, center-, or right-aligned.

In addition, you can use *Cell Margin* settings to refine even further the position of text and numbers in a cell. A cell margin is the space between the text in a cell and its borders.

Exercise 5-14   ALIGN TEXT AND NUMBERS HORIZONTALLY

Text is aligned horizontally within cells in the same manner that you align text in other PowerPoint objects by using the alignment buttons on the Home tab, in the Paragraph group, or by right-clicking to access the floating font group.

1. On slide 2, select the cells in the first row that contain the text "Mgmt," "Kitchen," "Service," and "Clerical."

2. From the Home tab, in the Paragraph group, click the Center button ▤. The text is horizontally centered in each cell.

3. Select all the cells that contain numbers and right-click. From the floating font group that appears, click the right-align button ▤.

4. Move to slide 4. In the last row of the table, select the text "Revised Figures." From the Home tab, in the Paragraph group, click the right-align button ▤. This gives the appearance that the cell is actually split instead of just having a border in it.

Exercise 5-15   CHANGE THE VERTICAL POSITION OF TEXT IN A CELL

The appearance of a table is often improved by changing the vertical alignment of text or objects within cells.

1. On slide 4, select the cells in the first row that contain the text "Mgmt," "Kitchen," "Service," and "Clerical."

2. From the Table Tools Layout tab, in the alignment group, choose the Center Vertically button ▤. The text in the selected cells is now in the center of the cells.

3. Select all the cells in the second, third, and fourth rows.

4. Click the Align Bottom button ▤. The text moves to the bottom edge of the cells.

Exercise 5-16   USE MARGIN SETTINGS TO ADJUST THE POSITION OF TEXT IN A CELL

Sometimes, the horizontal and vertical alignment settings do not place text precisely where you want it to be in a cell. You might be tempted to use Spacebar to indent the text, but that usually doesn't work well.

You can precisely control where text is placed in a cell by using the cell's margin settings, combined with horizontal and vertical alignment, as shown in Figure 5-15. For example, you can right-align a column of numbers and also have them appear centered in the column.

1. Move to slide 2. Select all the cells that contain numbers (blank cells in the third and fourth rows, too).

Figure 5-15
Using the Cell Text Layout dialog box to control cell margins

2. From the Table Tools Layout tab, in the Alignment group, click Cell Margins . From the drop-down list, click **Custom Margins**.

3. Click the **Vertical alignment** list box arrow to see the other settings. Choose **Middle**.

4. Under Internal margin, change the **Right** setting to **0.5"** and then click **OK**. The numbers are still right-aligned, but some space is between the cell border and the numbers, as shown in Figure 5-16.

5. Select all the cells in the first column containing text and change the left margin to **0.2"**.

Figure 5-16
Table with improved alignment

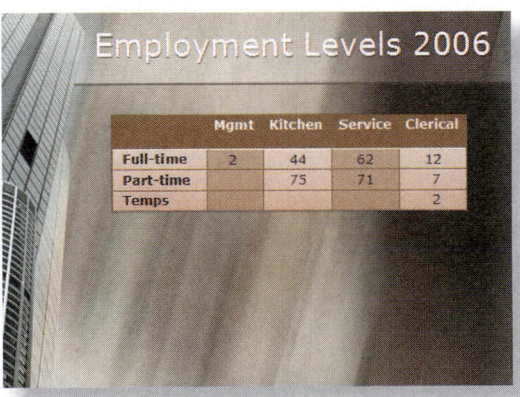

Exercise 5-17   RESIZE A TABLE

To resize the entire table, drag one of the sizing handles. When you drag, make sure the pointer is one of these shapes ⬍, ⬌, ⤢, and not the pointer used for changing column width ⊞ or row height ⊟.

If you hold down Shift while dragging a corner sizing handle, the table will resize proportionately. Whenever possible, depending on how large or small you make the table, the relative proportions of row heights and column widths are preserved.

1. Move to slide 4, and click anywhere inside the table. Notice the eight sizing handles around the border (one in each corner, and one in the middle of each side). They work just like sizing handles on other PowerPoint objects.

2. Using the diagonal two-pointed arrow ⤢, drag the lower-right corner up and to the left about ½ inch. The table becomes smaller, and the relative size of the rows and columns is preserved. Notice that your titles are wrapping onto two lines again.

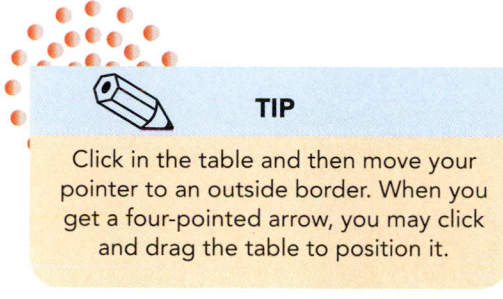

TIP

Click in the table and then move your pointer to an outside border. When you get a four-pointed arrow, you may click and drag the table to position it.

3. Select the entire table and change the font size to 24 points. Resize the first row and first column as necessary to get the titles all on one row, as shown in Figure 5-17.

4. Position the table attractively on the slide by using the same method that you use to move text boxes or other objects.

Figure 5-17
Resized table

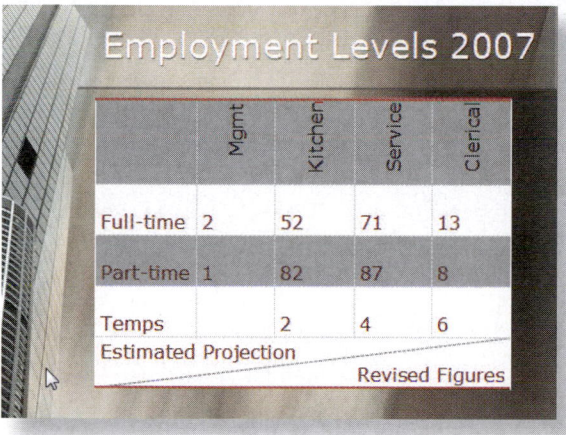

	Mgmt	Kitchen	Service	Clerical
Full-time	2	52	71	13
Part-time	1	82	87	8
Temps		2	4	6

Employment Levels 2007

Estimated Projection
Revised Figures

Enhancing the Table

You can enhance a table by adding one of the many three-dimensional effects available in PowerPoint 2007. Graphic images and shading effects also improve the appearance of tables.

Images can be added in open cells or across the full table; shading effects can be applied in the same manner.

Exercise 5-18   **APPLY AND MODIFY A CELL BEVEL EFFECT**

The *Cell Bevel* effect is a dimensional effect that can be applied to make cells look raised and rounded or pressed in, as shown in Figure 5-18. The Cell Bevel effect is found on the Table Tools Design tab, in the Table Styles group, under the Effects button .

1. On Slide 4, select the whole table. From the Table Tools Design tab, in the Table Styles group, click the Effects button. A drop-down list displays effects that can be applied to a table.

2. Choose **Cell Bevel** then choose **Riblet**. Notice the effect that is applied to the table.

3. With the table still selected, click the Effects button and choose **Cell Bevel** and **No Bevel**. This removes the bevel effect.

4. Click the Effects Button again, choose **Cell Bevel**, then choose **Relaxed Inset**.

Figure 5-18
Bevel effect applied to a table

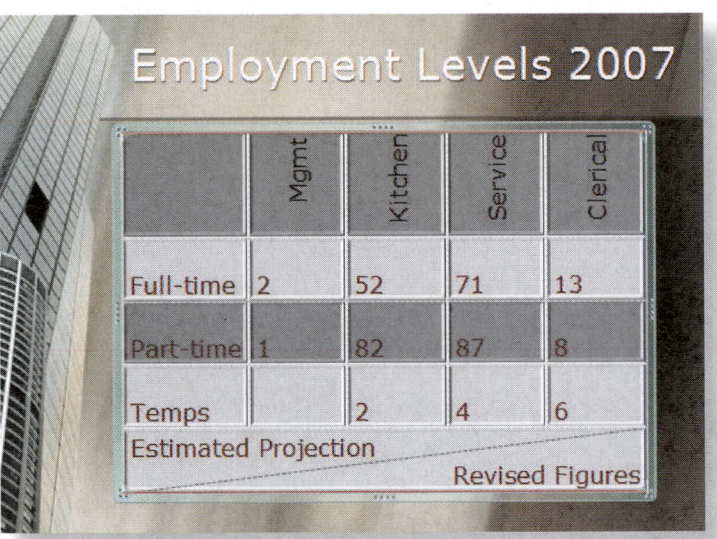

Exercise 5-19   **APPLY AND MODIFY A SHADOW EFFECT**

Another dimensional effect is the *Shadow* effect. You may modify where the shadow is cast, what color the shadow is, and many other aspects of the shadow. The shadow effect can be applied from the Table Tools Design tab in the Table Styles group, under the Effects Button.

1. Still working on slide 4, select the table. From the Table Tools Design tab, in the Table Styles group, click the Effects button. A drop-down list displays effects that can be applied to a table.

2. Choose **Shadow** and move your pointer over several of the options. Notice the effect that the shadow has on the table.

3. Without selecting a shadow, choose **Shadow Options** at the bottom of the drop-down list. The Format Shape dialog box appears and allows you to control every aspect of the shadow.

4. Under **Presets**, in the **Outer** group, choose **Offset Diagonal Bottom Right**.

5. Under **Color**, choose **Red, Accent 1, Darker 25%**.

6. Change the other settings as follows:

   - Transparency, **34%**

   - Size, **100%**

   - Blur, **4 pt.**

   - Angle, **180°**

   - Distance, **13 pt.**

7. Click **Close** on the dialog box to return to your presentation. Notice the effect that the shadow applies to your table, as shown in Figure 5-19.

Figure 5-19
Shadow effect applied to table

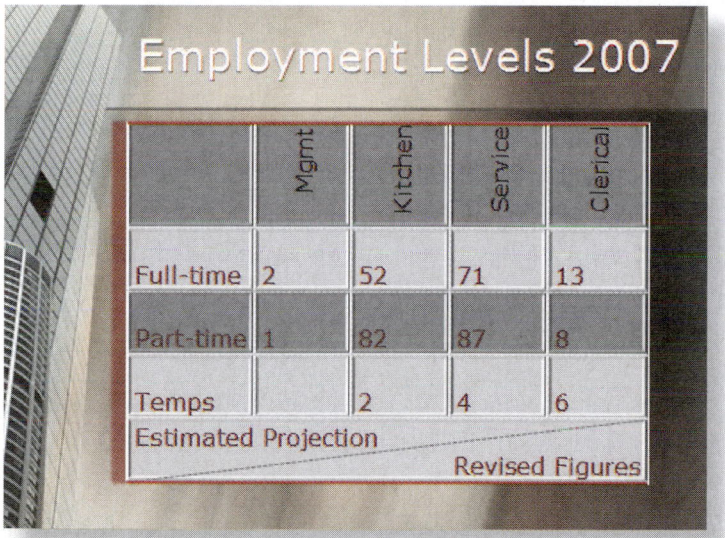

Exercise 5-20   APPLY AND MODIFY A REFLECTION EFFECT

The *Reflection* effect makes the table appear to be reflecting on a body of water or a mirror. Several preset reflection effects are available to be applied to a table. The Reflection effect is found on the Table Tools Design tab, in the Table Styles group, under the Effects button 🔲.

1. Move to slide 2, and select the table.

2. From the Table Tools Design tab, in the Table Styles group, click the Effects button 🔲. A drop-down list displays effects that can be applied to a table.

3. Choose **Reflection** and move your pointer over several of the options. Notice the effect that each reflection has on the table.

4. Choose the **Half Reflection, 8 pt Offset** option. The lower half of the table is reflected and the reflection is offset from the bottom of the table, as shown in Figure 5-20.

5. Leave the presentation open for the next exercise.

Figure 5-20
Reflection effect applied to a table

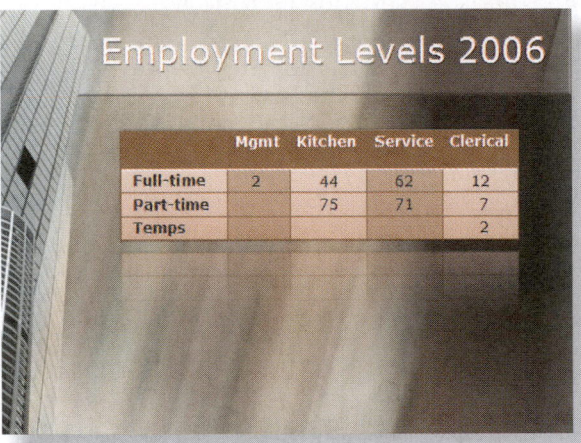

Exercise 5-21   INSERT A PICTURE AND APPLY GRADIENT SHADING

Pictures within a table can help viewers understand the context of the data in the table. Gradient shading on rows or columns can add interest or perhaps make text easier to read.

1. On slide 4, with the table active, click in the first cell of the table.

2. From the Table Tools Design tab, in the Table Styles group, click the Shading button ⬛▾ and choose **Picture**. A picture can be inserted in one cell, a selection of cells, or an entire table.

3. Locate your student files for Lesson 5, and double-click on **Employees** to insert the picture into the table.

4. Select the last four cells in the first row in the table. Still working on the Table Tools Design tab, in the Table Styles group, click the Shading button ⬛▾ and choose **Gradient**.

5. In the **Light Variation** category, choose the **Linear Down** pattern of gradient fill.

6. Select row three and apply the **Linear Down** pattern of gradient fill.

7. Select row five and apply the color **Gray-25%, Accent 4, Darker 25%** first, then repeat the process of applying a **Linear Down** pattern of gradient fill for row five.

8. Click outside the table to observe the effects. Compare your table to Figure 5-21.

Figure 5-21
Gradient shading effects applied to a table

9. Update the handout footer to include the text **[5-21your initials]**.

10. Save the presentation as **[5-21your initials]** in your Lesson 5 folder. Leave it open for the next exercise.

Creating a Tabbed Table

In this lesson, you have learned several ways to create tables using PowerPoint's table tools. You can also create tables through tab settings using the *Ruler*. Sometimes information can be effectively displayed with just a very simple table.

Exercise 5-22   SET AND EDIT TABS

In PowerPoint you set tabs on the Ruler the same way you set tabs in Word, and they are left-aligned by default. However, PowerPoint's default tabs are set at one-inch intervals. To set your own tabs, click the Tab Type button (in the upper-left corner of the Slide pane, where the two rulers meet) to choose the alignment style. Then click the ruler at the location where you want to set a tab.

1. Insert a new slide after slide 4 that uses the **Title Only** slide layout.

2. From the View tab, in the Show/Hide group, check the box beside the **Ruler** if the Ruler is not displayed already.

3. Key the title **Employment Change Summary**. The title will appear on two lines.

4. Draw a text box starting an inch to the left and below the word "Employment" and extending it to the right to a similar position (approximately seven inches wide).

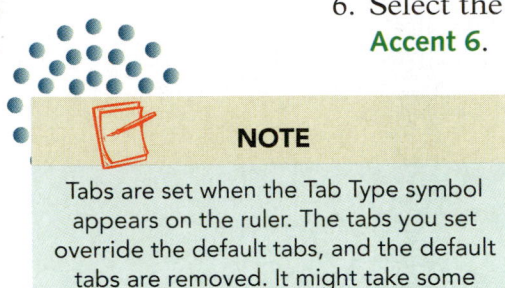

5. Key the following, pressing ⎣Tab⎦ where indicated: **Department** ⎣Tab⎦ **Status** ⎣Tab⎦ **2006** ⎣Tab⎦ **2007** ⎣Tab⎦ **% Change**.

6. Select the text box, apply bold, and change the font color to **Brown, Accent 6**.

7. Click anywhere within the text box to activate the text box ruler. If the ruler is still not showing, click the View tab and choose **ruler** in the show/hide group.

8. Click the Tab Type button 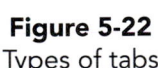 at the left end of the horizontal ruler. Each time you click the button, a different tab type icon appears, enabling you to cycle through the four tab type choices, as shown in Table 5-1 and Figure 5-22.

NOTE

Tabs are set when the Tab Type symbol appears on the ruler. The tabs you set override the default tabs, and the default tabs are removed. It might take some practice before you are comfortable with tab type selection and tab placement.

TABLE 5-1 Types of Tabs

Tab	Purpose
⌞	Left-aligns text at the tab setting
⌴	Centers text at the tab setting
⌟	Right-aligns text at the tab setting
⌴	Aligns decimal points at the tab setting

Figure 5-22
Types of tabs

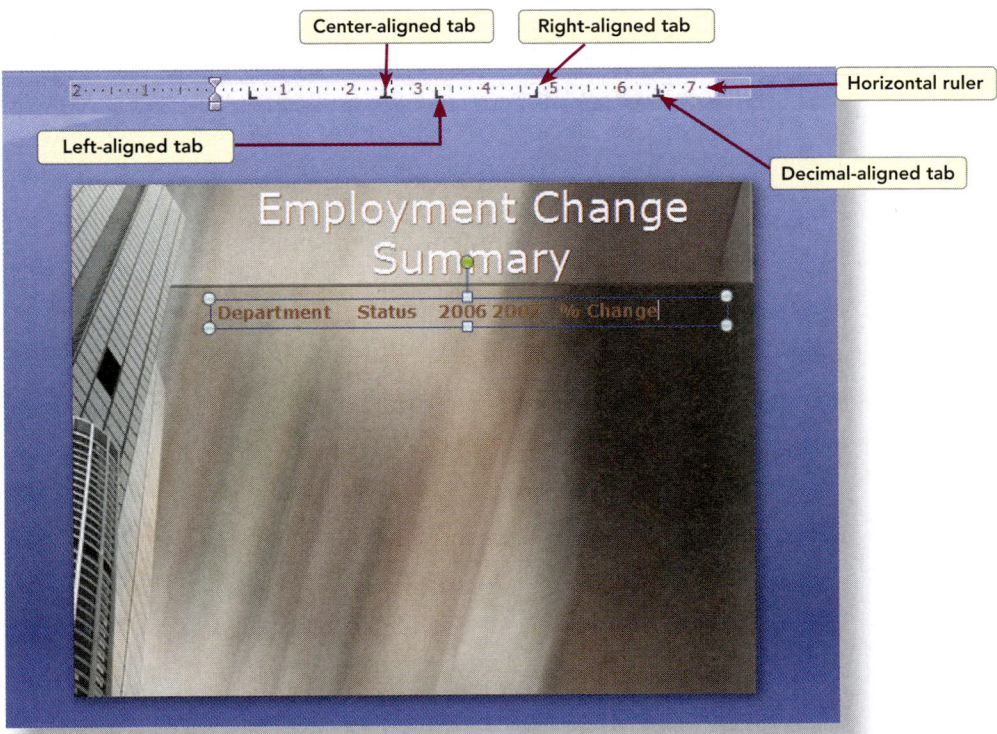

9. Click the Tab Type button 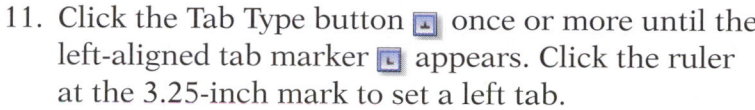 one or more times until the left-aligned tab button appears. Click the ruler at the .5-inch position to set a left tab.

10. Click the Tab Type button once until the center-aligned tab button appears. Click the ruler at the 2.5-inch position. The text "Status" moves so that it is centered under the tab marker.

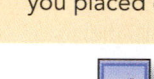

> **TIP**
>
> When setting tabs, you might want to increase the zoom setting for an enlarged view of the ruler. After tabs are set, tabbed text that you key will automatically align under the tab markers you placed on the ruler.

11. Click the Tab Type button once or more until the left-aligned tab marker appears. Click the ruler at the 3.25-inch mark to set a left tab.

12. Click the Tab Type button once or more until the right-aligned tab marker appears. Click the ruler at the 4.75-inch mark to set a right-aligned tab.

13. Click the Tab Type button once or more until the decimal-aligned tab marker appears. Click the ruler at the 6.5-inch mark to set a decimal-aligned tab.

14. Click on the first tab setting, a left-aligned tab marker, and click and drag it down and off the ruler. This removes the tab.

15. Leave the presentation open for the next exercise.

Exercise 5-23   CREATE A TABBED TABLE

A tabbed table is created by making a series of tabs within a text box. Since you have set the tabs, now you just need to enter text using the set tabs.

1. Working in the text box you created on slide 5, position the insertion point at the end of the text line and press Enter to start a new line of text.

2. Key the table text, shown in Figure 5-23, pressing Tab between columns and pressing Enter at the end of each line. The text box will increase in size as the text is keyed.

Figure 5-23
Creating a tabbed table

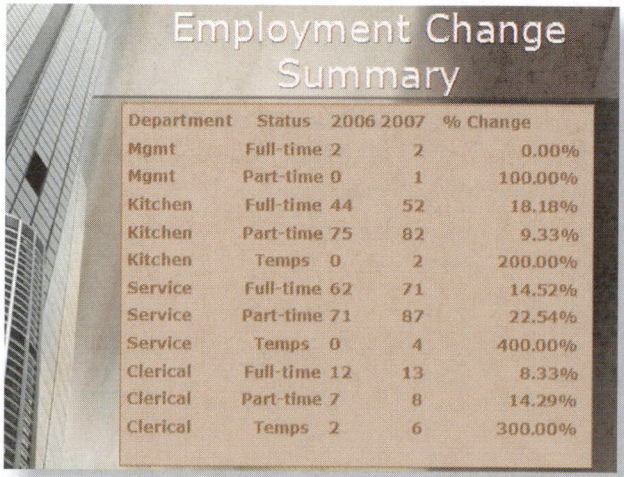

Department	Status	2006	2007	% Change
Mgmt	Full-time	2	2	0.00%
Mgmt	Part-time	0	1	100.00%
Kitchen	Full-time	44	52	18.18%
Kitchen	Part-time	75	82	9.33%
Kitchen	Temps	0	2	200.00%
Service	Full-time	62	71	14.52%
Service	Part-time	71	87	22.54%
Service	Temps	0	4	400.00%
Clerical	Full-time	12	13	8.33%
Clerical	Part-time	7	8	14.29%
Clerical	Temps	2	6	300.00%

3. Select the entire text box by clicking its border. From the Drawing Tools Format tab, in the Shape Styles group, click the Shape Fill button ⬚ and add shape fill of **Brown, Accent 6, Lighter 60%**.

4. From the Drawing Tools Format tab, in the Shape Styles group, click the Shape Outline button ⬚ and add a shape outline of **Brown, Accent 2**.

5. Select the text in the table, and from the Home tab, in the Paragraph group, change the line spacing to **1.5**.

6. Highlight the text in the text box. Drag the center-aligned tab marker from the 2.5-inch position on the ruler to 2.25 inches. The entire column moves to the left.

7. Drag the center-aligned marker down and off the ruler to remove it. The table realigns in an unattractive way that does not make sense.

8. Click the Undo button ⬚ once to restore the table's appearance.

9. Update the handout footer text to **[5-23your initials]** as the footer.

10. Save the presentation as **[5-23your initials]** in your Lesson 5 folder.

11. View the presentation as a slide show; then preview and print the presentation as handouts, six slides per page, grayscale, landscape, scale to fit paper, framed.

Lesson 5 Summary

- Tables offer a convenient way to quickly organize material on a slide. From the Insert tab, in the Table group, you can use the Insert table button ⬚ to insert a table. You can insert a table by choosing a content slide layout. You can "draw" a table directly on a slide by using the Draw Table button ⬚. Lastly, you can create a tabbed table through setting tabs.

- Before you can apply special formatting to table cells, you must first select those cells. You can select individual cells, groups of cells, or the entire table.

- Use the buttons on the Table Tools Design tab, in the Table Styles group, to apply fill effects and border effects to individual cells, a group of cells, or the entire table.

- Change the overall size of a table by dragging one of its sizing handles with a two-pointed arrow.

- Change the width of a column by dragging or double-clicking its border. Change the height of a row by dragging its border.

- Rows and columns can be easily inserted or deleted as you develop a table. Select at least one cell in the row or column where you want to insert or delete; then use buttons on the Table Tools Layout tab.

- While keying text in a table, a quick way to insert a new row at the bottom is to press Tab when you reach the last table cell.

- Occasionally, you might want one row or column to have more or fewer cells than the others. You can make this happen by merging a group of cells or splitting an individual cell into two cells.

- A diagonal line can be added to a cell to make it appear to be split into two cells. Careful placement of text within the cell completes this illusion.

- Applying and removing shading effects is similar to applying shading effects to other PowerPoint objects. Table and cell fills can be gradients, textures, or pictures.

- Before applying a border to cells or the entire table, choose the border style, border width, and border color from the Table Tools Design tab in the Draw Borders group. Then select cells and choose an option from the Borders button ▦ drop-down list or use the pencil pointer to apply it to the borders you want to change.

- Use the text alignment buttons on the Home tab in the Paragraph group to control the horizontal position of text in a cell.

- Use the Align Top ▤, Center Vertically ▤, and Align Bottom ▤ buttons on the Table Tools Layout tab in the Alignment group to control the vertical position of text within a cell.

- To fine-tune the horizontal or vertical position of text, change a cell's margin settings by using the Cell Margins button ▭ on the Table Tools Layout tab in the Alignment group.

- Add and modify 3-D effects by selecting the table and clicking the Effects button ▣ on the Table Tools Design tab.

- Click the Tab Type button ▣ on the left edge of the ruler to change the type of tab. The button cycles through four tab types: left-aligned, centered, right-aligned, and decimal.

- Create a tabbed table by using a text box and setting tabs to control how the information is indented. Remove tabs or move tabs as needed by clicking and dragging.

LESSON 5		Command Summary	
Feature	**Button**	**Ribbon**	**Keyboard**
Insert table	▦	Insert, Tables group, Table	
Navigate in a table			Tab; Shift+Tab; ↓; ↑; ←; →
Column, select		Table Tools Layout, Table group, Select, Select Column	

continues

LESSON 5		Command Summary *continued*	
Feature	**Button**	**Ribbon**	**Keyboard**
Row, select		Table Tools Layout, Table group, Select, Select Row	
Table, select		Table Tools Layout, Table group, Select, Select Table	
Apply Shading Effect to cells		Table Tools Design, Table Styles group, Shading	
Select Table Styles		Table Tools Design, Table Styles group, More	
Change Table Style		Table Tools Design, Table Style group, More	
Add Header Row		Table Tools Design, Table Style Options group	
Change Text Direction		Table Tools Layout, Alignment group, Text Direction	
Apply Border Effects		Table Tools Design, Draw Borders group	
Erase Cell Borders		Table Tools Design, Draw Table group, Eraser	
Align Table Text Vertically		Table Tools Layout, Alignment group	
Set Table Cell Margins		Table Tools Layout, Alignment group, Margins	
Distribute Columns Evenly		Table Tools Layout, Cell Size group, Distribute Columns	
Distribute Rows Evenly		Table Tools Layout, Cell Size group, Distribute Rows	
Insert Table Columns		Table Tools Layout, Rows & Columns group	
Insert Table Rows		Table Tools Layout, Rows & Columns group	
Delete Table Columns		Table Tools Layout, Rows & Columns group, Delete	
Draw a Table		Insert, Tables group, Table, Draw Table	
Merge Table Cells		Table Tools Layout, Merge group, Merge Cells	
Split a Table Cell		Table Tools Layout, Merge group, Split Cells	
Apply 3-D Effects		Table Tools Design, Table Styles group, Effects	

Concepts Review

True/False Questions

Each of the following statements is either true or false. Select your choice by indicating T or F.

T F   1. You can adjust the width of individual columns in a table, but row heights must all be the same.

T F   2. Effects can be used to give the table a 3-D look.

T F   3. You don't need to be exact when you define the size of a table because it's easy to insert rows and columns later.

T F   4. Borders are available in only one width.

T F   5. Text in a table cell can have its vertical position adjusted, independent of other cells.

T F   6. When you insert a new column, it is always inserted to the left of the currently selected column.

T F   7. Cell margins work the same way as text box margins.

T F   8. You can remove a tab marker by dragging it off the ruler.

Short Answer Questions

Write the correct answer in the space provided.

1. What do you call the intersection between a column and a row?

_____

2. Other than dragging down all the cells or using a button on the Ribbon, how can you select a column in a table?

_____

3. What tab contains the Center Vertically button?

_____

4. What method can be used to select the entire table?

_____

5. What three types of 3-D effects are available to apply to the table?

_____

6. What are the three methods to merge cells in a table?

_____

7. What is different about splitting a cell diagonally from splitting it horizontally or vertically?

_____

8. What's the quickest way to make a group of selected columns of varying widths all the same width?

_____

Critical Thinking

Answer these questions on a separate page. There are no right or wrong answers. Support your answers with examples from your own experience, if possible.

1. Why might you choose to put information in a table instead of in a bulleted placeholder?

2. Tables can be created in three ways: inserting, drawing, or tabbing. Why would you choose one method over another? What criteria would affect which method you use?

Skills Review

Exercise 5-24

Create a table, key text, apply table styles.

1. Open the file **CookOff** and move to slide 4, which contains the WordArt title "The Winning Fare."
2. Insert a new table by following these steps:
   a. From the Insert tab, in the Tables group, click the Table button .
   b. On the grid that appears, drag to define a (2 × 4) table two columns wide by four rows long.
3. Key text in the table by following these steps:
   a. Click the upper-left cell to select it, and then key: **Name**
   b. Press Tab to move to the next cell, and then key: **Recipe Description**

4. Key the text shown in Figure 5-24 for the remaining cells.

Figure 5-24
Table text

Amy Grand	Hot Tomato Salsa
Juanita McLeod	Raspberry Cream Pie
William Steinberg	Roasted Chicken and Vegetables

5. Apply a table style from the **Best Match for Document** category following these steps:
   a. Select the table by right-clicking within the table and choosing **Select Table** from the short-cut menu.
   b. From the Table Tools Design tab, in the Table Styles group, click the More button ▾.
   c. From the **Best Match for Document** category, choose **Themed Style 1, Accent 1**.
   d. Move the table down a little to position it better on the slide.
6. Create a slide footer for the current slide (slide 4 only) containing today's date and the text your name **[5-24your initials]**.
7. Move to slide 1 and save the presentation as **[5-24your initials]** in your Lesson 5 folder.
8. View the presentation as a slide show from slide 1.
9. Print slide 4 only. If you have a color printer, print it in color.

Exercise 5-25

Draw a table, apply border and shading options.

1. Open the file **Operate2**.
2. Insert a new slide after slide 3 that uses the **Title Only** layout. Key the title **Capital Equipment 2007**. From the View tab, in the Show/Hide group, click the checkbox beside **Ruler** if it is not checked already.
3. Draw a new table by following these steps:
   a. From the Insert tab, in the Tables group, click the Table button ▦ and choose **Draw Table**.
   b. Use the Pencil pointer to draw a table from under "Capital" to under "2007" and down about 3.5 inches on the ruler.
   c. Click and drag two vertical borders to create three columns.
   d. Click and drag four horizontal borders to create five rows.
   e. Press Esc to turn off the Pencil pointer.

4. For the table text, key the information shown in Figure 5-25.

Figure 5-25
Table text

	Column 1	Column 2	Column 3
Row 1		Leased	Bought
Row 2	Kitchen	9,450	24,350
Row 3	Dining	14,400	18,650
Row 4	Office	10,500	25,500
Row 5	Other	8,252	16,300

5. Apply Shading effects to table cells by following these steps:
   a. Move the pointer to the outside of the table beside row 1, when you get a right-facing arrow click to select all the cells in the first row.
   b. From the Table Tools Design tab, in the Table Styles group, click the list box arrow on the Shading button.
   c. Choose **Aqua, Text 2, Lighter 40%**.
   d. Click the list box arrow on the Shading button again and choose **Gradient**.
   e. In the **Variations** category, choose **From Center**.
   f. With the first row still selected, change the font color to a deep blue, **Indigo, Accent 6, Darker 50%**. Apply bold to the first row.

6. Make all the columns the same width and all the rows the same height by following these steps:
   a. Select the entire table by right-clicking within the table and choosing **Select Table**.
   b. From the Table Tools Layout tab, in the Cell Size group, click the Distribute Columns button.
   c. From the Table Tools Layout tab, in the Cell Size group, click the Distribute Rows button.
   d. With the table still selected, change the font size of the entire table to 24 points.

7. Remove all the table's borders by following these steps:
   a. Select the entire table.
   b. From the Table Tools Design tab, in the Table Styles group, click the arrow on the Borders button and choose **No Border**.

8. Select all cells with numbers and the column heading cells, and make them right aligned.

9. Create a handout header and footer: Include the date and your name as the header, and the page number and text **[5-25your initials]** as the footer.

10. Move to slide 1 and save the presentation as **[5-25your initials]** in your Lesson 5 folder.

11. View the presentation as a slide show; then preview and print the presentation as handouts, four slides per page, grayscale, landscape, framed. Close the presentation.

Exercise 5-26

Draw a table; insert and delete rows and columns; adjust column and row width; apply formatting for text, shading, and borders.

1. Open the file **Operate3**.
2. Display slide 5, titled "Reservation Requests."
3. Draw a table on slide 5 by following these steps:
   a. From the **Insert** tab, in the Tables group, click the Table button and choose **Draw Table**.
   b. Use the Pencil pointer to draw a table from under "Average" to under "Number" and down about 3.5 inches on the ruler.
   c. From the Table Tools Design tab, in the Draw Borders group, click the Pen Color button and choose **Light Blue, Accent 6, Darker 50%**.
   d. If your pointer is not a Pencil pointer, click the Draw Table button.
   e. Within the table, draw four vertical lines (to create five columns) and three horizontal lines (to create four rows). They don't need to be the same size.
   f. Press Esc to turn off the Pencil pointer.
4. For the table's text, key the data in Figure 5-26. It's okay if the text wraps within cells; you will fix the layout in the next few steps.

Figure 5-26
Table text

	Column 1	Column 2	Column 3	Column 4	Column 5
Row 1		Brunch	Lunch	Dinner	Late Night
Row 2	Weekday	3	35	75	3
Row 3	Weekends	21	12	100	15
Row 4	Memorial Day	7	5	12	4

5. Select the table and make it bold. Make all the numbers blue.
6. If the text "Weekday" or "Weekends" wraps to a second line, make the table a little wider by dragging either the right- or left-center sizing handle. Make sure the pointer appears as.
7. Insert a new row between "Weekends" and "Memorial Day" by following these steps:
   a. Right-click "Memorial Day."
   b. Choose **Insert** from the short-cut menu and choose **Insert Above**.
   c. If the table extends below the bottom of the slide, make the table smaller by dragging the bottom-center sizing handle up.

8. Insert a new column to the left of "Brunch" by following these steps:

   a. Click anywhere in the "Brunch" column.

   b. Click the Table Tools Layout tab, in the Rows & Columns group, choose **Insert Left**.

9. Delete a column and a row by following these steps:

   a. Select the entire "Late Night" column (which might extend beyond the right edge of the slide).

   b. Right-click the selection and choose **Delete Columns** from the short-cut menu.

   c. Select the "Memorial Day" row. Right-click the selection and choose **Delete Rows** from the short-cut menu.

10. In the second column, key **Breakfast** for the column heading. Key **5** for "Weekday" and **18** for "Weekends." Change the "Weekday" cell to **Weekdays**.

11. Key the following information in the new row:

    Holidays `Tab` **6** `Tab` **9** `Tab` **15** `Tab` **94**.

12. Move the table to a new position and change its size by following these steps:

    a. Right-click anywhere inside the table and choose **Select Table** from the short-cut menu.

    b. Move your pointer over the table's border until you see the four-pointed arrow ⊕. If necessary, drag the table so it is positioned on the white area of the slide so all numbers are easy to read.

    c. Make the table wider by dragging the right-center sizing handle to the right until all text and numbers are on one line. Before you drag, make sure the pointer appears as ↔.

13. Make all the columns the same width and all the rows the same height. Then adjust the first column size as needed to fit all on one line.

14. Align text horizontally by following these steps:

    a. Select the first row by clicking the first cell and dragging down to the last cell.

    b. From the Home tab, in the Paragraph group, click the Center button ▤ (or press `Ctrl`+`E`).

    c. Select all the cells that contain numbers by dragging diagonally across the cells.

    d. Click the Align Right button ▤ (or press `Ctrl`+`R`) to right-align the numbers.

15. Change cell margin settings by following these steps:

    a. Make sure all the cells that contain numbers are selected.

    b. From the Table Tools Layout tab, in the Alignment group, choose the Cell Margins button ▦ and choose **Custom Margins**.

    c. In the **Internal margin** section, key **0.5"** in the **Right** text box. Click **OK**.

16. Change the vertical alignment of text and numbers in their cells by following these steps:

    a. Select the entire table from Table Tools Layout tab, in the Table group, choose the Select button 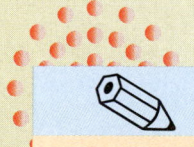 and **Select Table**.

    b. Still working on the Table Tools Layout tab, in the Alignment group, click the Center Vertically button.

17. Create a handout header and footer: Include the date and your name as the header, and the page number and text **[5-26your initials]** as the footer.

18. Move to slide 1 and save the presentation as **[5-26your initials]** in your Lesson 5 folder.

19. View the presentation as a slide show; then preview and print the presentation as handouts, six slides per page, grayscale, framed. Close the presentation.

Exercise 5-27

Insert a table, merge cells, work with tabbed tables.

1. Open the file **Tucson1**.

2. Insert a new slide after slide 2 and use the **Title and Content** layout. Key **Appetizers** as the title.

3. Set a decimal tab at the 4.5-inch on the ruler by following these steps:

    a. Click in the body text placeholder.

    b. Click the Tab Type marker until the Decimal Tab Marker appears.

    c. Click on the ruler at the 4.5-inch mark.

4. Key the following in the body text placeholder, pressing [Tab] before each price:

Wild Rice Soup	Tab	**5.25**
Dill Cucumber Salad	Tab	**4.50**
Four Bean Salad	Tab	**4.25**

5. Insert a new slide after slide 3 and use the **Title Only** layout. Key **Entrees** as the title.

6. Insert a table with three columns and seven rows.

7. Merge the cells in rows three, five, and seven using the following steps:

    a. Select the cells in row three.

    b. From the Table Tools Layout tab, in the Merge group, choose the Merge Cells button.

    c. Repeat the process for row five and row seven.

TIP

You can use right tabs instead of decimal tabs to align numbers if all the numbers in the list have the same number of decimal places.

8. Key the text as shown in Figure 5-27 into your table.

Figure 5-27
Table text

	Column 1	Column 2	Column 3
Row 1	**Entrée**	**Dinner**	**Lunch**
Row 2	Chicken Fajitas	9.50	6.25
Row 3	Chunky chicken, Monterey Jack cheese, tomatoes, and olives wrapped in a flour tortilla		
Row 4	Dijon Chicken Rolls	9.95	6.50
Row 5	Rolled boneless chicken breast filled with spicy bread crumbs and dressed with a Dijon sauce		
Row 6	Thai Stir Fry	10.25	7.50
Row 7	Tasty shrimp with fresh garden vegetables served over your choice of wild or white rice		

9. Move the table down and resize as necessary the table, columns, and rows.
10. Center the text vertically in the table.
11. Create a handout header and footer: Include the date and your name as the header, and the page number and text **[5-27your initials]** as the footer.
12. Save the presentation as **[5-27your initials]** in your Lesson 5 folder.
13. Preview and then print the presentation as handouts, four slides per page, grayscale, landscape, framed. Close the presentation.

Lesson Applications

Exercise 5-28

Create a presentation with a table slide, apply table styles, arrange and format text, and change column widths and table size.

1. Open the file **Print1**.

2. Insert three slides after slide 1. Use the **Title and Content** layout for all three slides.

3. On slide 4, select the Table button ▦ from the content placeholder and select the correct number of columns and rows before keying the information in. Select the entire table and change the font to red. On the table, each cell in the first row should contain two lines of text.

4. Key the text in Figure 5-28.

Figure 5-28
Presentation content

Slide 2

Print Advertising 2007
- Campaigns use a variety of print media
- Each medium targets a specific market segment
- Every campaign must meet specific sales objectives

Slide 3

Coupon Redemption
- Effective measure of return on investment
- Used for promotional purposes in a variety of print media

Slide 4

Coupons Redeemed 2006

	Column 1	Column 2	Column 3	Column 4
Row 1	Newspaper Magazine	Coupons Redeemed	Average Check	Cost of One Ad
Row 2	NY Times	414	$31.50	$6,800
Row 3	NY Magazine	476	$25.00	$2,850
Row 4	NY Runner	1,063	$23.50	$975
Row 5	NY Health	125	$16.25	$650

5. On slide 4, change the Table style to **Themed Style 2, Accent 4** in the **Best Match for Documents** category.

6. For the entire table, change all right and left cell margins to 0.2 inches. Using the pointer ⊞, double-click each column border so that each column self-adjusts to fit the widest text in the column.

7. Center the headings for the columns containing numbers.

8. Right-align all numbers.

9. Vertically center all text and numbers in the table.

10. Adjust the overall size and position of the table for attractive positioning on the slide, as shown in Figure 5-29.

Figure 5-29
Completed table slide

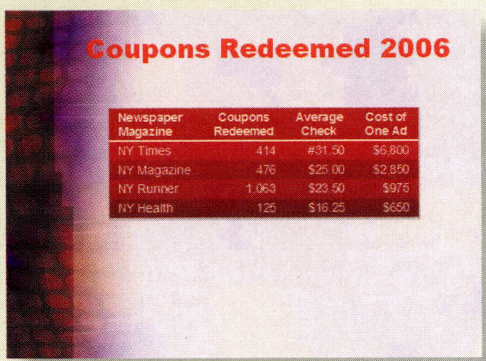

11. Create a slide footer for the current slide (slide 4) containing today's date and the text your name, **[5-28your initials]**.

12. Create a handout header and footer: Include the date and your name as the header, and the page number and text **[5-28your initials]** as the footer.

13. Save the presentation as **[5-28your initials]** in your Lesson 5 folder.

14. Print the current slide (slide 4) in full size.

15. View the presentation as a slide show; then preview and print the presentation as handouts, four slides per page, grayscale, landscape, framed. Close the presentation.

Exercise 5-29

Insert a table slide; insert rows; change row height, column width, alignment, and cell margins; and apply a 3-D effect.

1. Open the file **Ads2**.

2. On slide 1, change "Student Name" to Your Name.

3. Insert a table on a new slide after slide 1 and key the text shown in Figure 5-30.

Figure 5-30
Table text

Advertising Effectiveness

	Column 1	Column 2	Column 3
Row 1		New	Total
		Customers	Revenue
Row 2	Newspaper	28%	30%
Row 3	Radio	10%	5%
Row 4	Yellow Pages	6%	12%

4. Resize the title placeholder to fit on one line.

5. Apply the following formatting to the table's text:

- Center the text in the first row.

- Right-align all the numbers and apply a cell right margin, so that the numbers appear centered under their headings.

- Apply a 0.25-inch left margin to all the cells in the first column.
- If necessary, adjust the column width of the first row so that "Yellow Pages" is on one line.

6. Insert a row above "Yellow Pages" with the following text:

   Mailers   12%   18%

7. Make the table easy to read by adjusting the column widths, row heights, and vertical alignment of cells, as necessary. Resize and reposition the table appropriately on the slide.

8. Change the table style to **Themed style 1, Accent 1**.

9. Select all of the text in the table except the first row and change the font to **Gray-50%, Background 2, Darker 50%**.

10. Add a **Convex** cell bevel to the entire table.

11. Create a slide footer for the current slide (slide 2) containing today's date and your name and the text **[5-29your initials]**.

12. Create a handout header and footer: Include the date and your name as the header, and the page number and text **[5-29your initials]** as the footer.

13. Check spelling and change any words that need to be corrected.

14. Save the presentation as **[5-29your initials]** in your Lesson 5 folder.

15. Print slide 2 in full size.

16. View the presentation as a slide show; then preview and print the presentation as handouts, six slides per page, grayscale, landscape, framed. Close the presentation.

Exercise 5-30

Create a tabbed table.

1. Start a new blank presentation. Use the **Concourse** design theme with the **Equity** color theme.

2. On slide 1, key a two-line title with the text **Good 4 U** and **Softball Schedule**.

3. Key **Spring/Summer 2008** for the subtitle.

4. Find a softball clip art image and insert it on the title slide in the color bar at the bottom. Duplicate the softball several times, and resize the images to look as though they are getting smaller. See Figure 5-31 for an example.

Figure 5-31
Slide 1

5. Using the **Title Only** layout, create slide 2 as shown in Figure 5-32. Key the table and its heading all in one text box and format the table as follows:

   • Set appropriate tabs.

   • Add bold to the headings.

   • Change the font size to 20 points.

   • Position the table appropriately on the slide.

6. Add the same softball used in slide 1 to the bottom left corner of slide 2.

Figure 5-32
Slide 2

7. Using the **Title and Content** layout, create slide 3 as shown in Figure 5-33.

8. Copy and paste the softball from slide 2 onto slide 3 and insert a softball image recolored to match the theme colors on the right of the slide.

Figure 5-33
Slide 3

9. Check spelling in the presentation. The names of team members are spelled correctly; do not make any changes.

10. Create a handout header and footer: Include the date and your name as the header and the page number and filename **[5-30your initials]** as the footer.

11. Save the presentation as **[5-30your initials]** in your Lesson 5 folder.

12. Preview and then print the presentation as handouts, three slides per page, landscape, grayscale, scale to fit paper, framed. Close the presentation.

Exercise 5-31 ◆ Challenge Yourself

Edit and format a presentation including a table slide, add data, change alignment, change table colors, and merge cells.

1. Open the file **MktSum**.

2. Create a table on a new slide after slide 3 using the layout **Title Only** layout. Key the title **Marketing Expenses 2006**.

3. Draw a table using the Pencil pointer. Change the font of the first row to 28 points, brown, and bold. Center the first row vertically and horizontally within the cell. Use Figure 5-34 for as an example to create the table.

Figure 5-34
Table slide

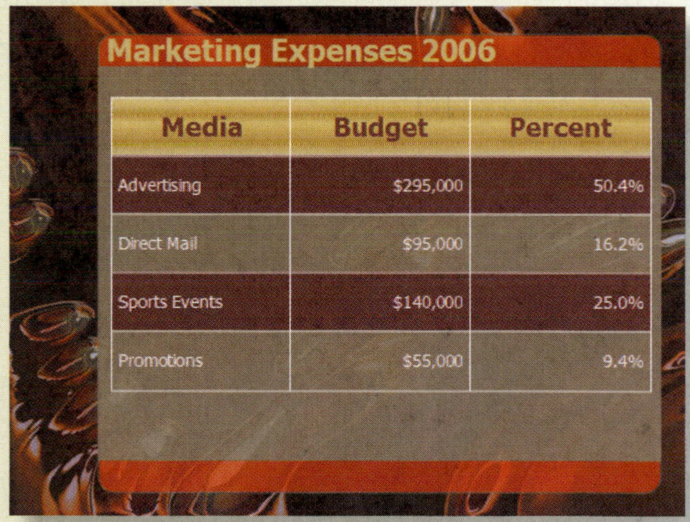

4. Use appropriate alignment techniques, fill colors, and border treatments. Use a preset gradient color for the heading row fill for a gold appearance. (This option is found under More Gradients.)

5. Distribute the columns and rows evenly.

6. Using the **Title and Content** layout, insert a new slide after slide 4 with the title **Estimated Budget 2007**. Use Figure 5-35 as an example to create the table. Choose an appropriate table style to coordinate with the theme.

7. Adjust the size of the columns, rows, and table as necessary to present an attractive table.

8. Select the table and choose the Reflection Effect of **Half Reflection, 4 pt offset**.

Figure 5-35
Table slide

9. Create a handout header and footer: Include the date and your name as the header, and the page number and text **[5-31your initials]** as the footer.

10. Check spelling in the presentation.

11. Save the presentation as **[5-31your initials]** in your Lesson 5 folder.

12. View the presentation as a slide show; then preview and print the presentation as handouts, six slides per page, grayscale, framed. Close the presentation.

On Your Own

In these exercises you work on your own, as you would in a real-life work environment. Use the skills you've learned to accomplish the task—and be creative.

Exercise 5-32

Use a recipe to create a series of slides describing a prepared dish. Create a title slide with the name and where the recipe came from, and, if possible, a picture of the finished dish. Add one or two slides describing in general terms what the dish contains and why it is good. Create a series of slides containing tables that present the ingredients and steps to create the recipe.

Design your own table structures to present the information in a way that you think is easy to understand using inserted tables with table styles, tables that you draw, and tabbed tables. Format your presentation attractively; picking up colors, fonts, and other style features that accent the recipe that you have chosen. Save your presentation as **[5-32your initials]**. Preview, and then print the presentation as handouts.

Exercise 5-33

Find a schedule of events from your local newspaper or other source, for example, a movie schedule, your class schedule, the TV listings, or a schedule of community or school events. Create a presentation containing a table that lists those events in a way you think is easy to understand. Create a second table listing the three events or classes you think are the most interesting in one column and a description of those events in a second column. The presentation should include a title slide, two table slides, and any other slides you think will enhance your presentation. Use your creativity to make the tables interesting and fun to view. Be sure to resize the table and cells as needed and add borders, shading, and effects to add interest. Save the presentation as **[5-33your initials]**. Preview, and then print the presentation as handouts.

Exercise 5-34

Create a single-slide presentation with a personal grocery or other shopping list in table format. (If you have a long list, use two or more slides.) Create columns based on the categories of items you need to purchase. For example, frozen meat, canned goods, refrigerated items, etc. List items that you need to buy in each section of a grocery store under the proper column heading. Format your table attractively and in keeping with your own personality (making sure it is easy to read). If you create a really thorough list, you can print copies and circle what you need to purchase each time you go to the store. Save the presentation as **[5-34your initials]**. Preview, and then print the presentation as a full-size slide(s).

Lesson 6

Creating Charts

OBJECTIVES

MCAS OBJECTIVES

In this lesson:
PP07 3.6
PP07 3.6.1
PP07 3.6.2
PP07 3.6.3
PP07 3.6.4
See Appendix

After completing this lesson, you will be able to:

1. Create a chart.

2. Format a column chart.

3. Use different chart types.

4. Work with pie charts.

5. Enhance chart elements.

Estimated Time: 1½ hours

Charts, sometimes called graphs, are diagrams that display numbers in pictorial format. Charts illustrate quantitative relationships and can help people understand the significance of numeric information more easily than when they view the same information in a table or in a list. Charts are well suited for making comparisons or examining the changes in data over time.

Creating a Chart

PowerPoint provides several ways to start a new chart. You can add a chart to an existing slide, or you can select a slide layout with a chart placeholder at the time you create a new slide. Here are two methods of inserting a chart:

- From the Insert tab, in the Illustrations group, click the Chart button.

- On a new slide with the Title and Content layout, click the Insert Chart icon in the center of the placeholder.

Microsoft Excel is opened using either method of creating charts. Microsoft Excel holds the chart data in a *worksheet* and this data is linked to Microsoft PowerPoint where the chart is displayed. If changes are made to the data in Microsoft Excel, the chart is automatically updated in Microsoft PowerPoint.

If Microsoft Excel is not installed on your computer when you start a new chart, Microsoft Graph will open with a sample *datasheet*. A datasheet provides rows and columns in which you key the numbers and labels used to create a chart. Advanced features of charting with Excel are not available with Microsoft Graph.

Exercise 6-1   CHOOSE A SLIDE LAYOUT FOR A CHART

Several slide layout choices are suitable for charts. For example, the **Title and Content** layout works well for one chart on a slide; the **Two Content** layout works well for a chart combined with text or an image.

1. Open the file **Finance1**.

2. Insert a new slide after slide 1 that uses the **Title and Content** slide layout, as shown in Figure 6-1. Key the slide title **Sales Forecast**. This layout contains a placeholder suitable for one chart. When you want to place more than one chart or other element on a slide, use one of the other Content layouts.

Figure 6-1
Choosing a slide layout for a chart

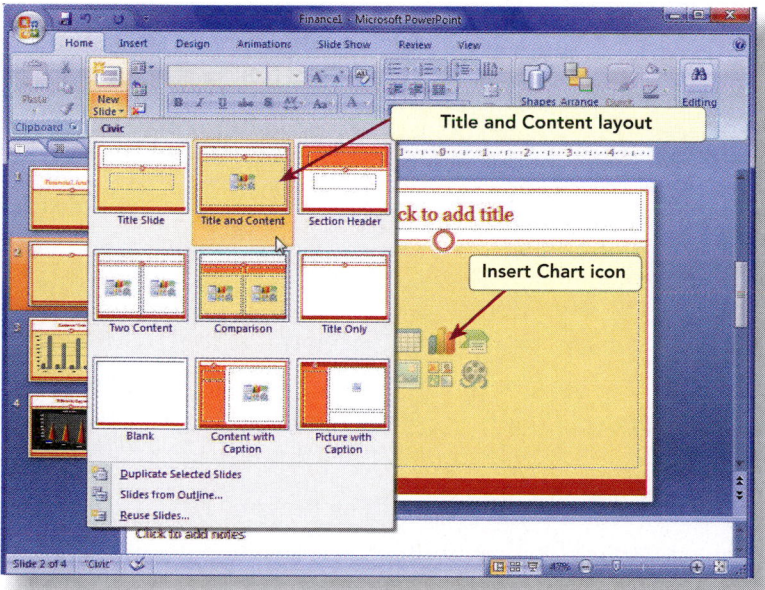

3. Click the Insert Chart icon ▦ in the center of the content placeholder.

4. Point to the options in the Insert Chart dialog box, and notice the different chart types displayed. Choose the **3-D Clustered Column Chart**, and click **OK**. Microsoft Excel opens displaying a worksheet with sample data, and a chart is inserted into PowerPoint. Chart-related tabs appear on the Ribbon.

Exercise 6-2   EDIT THE DATA SOURCE

Each worksheet contains rows and columns. Each number or label is in a separate *cell*—the rectangle formed by the intersection of a row and a column.

As you enter data, you can monitor the results on the sample chart. You key new infor mation by overwriting the sample data or by deleting the sample data and keying your own data.

Figure 6-2
Creating a chart

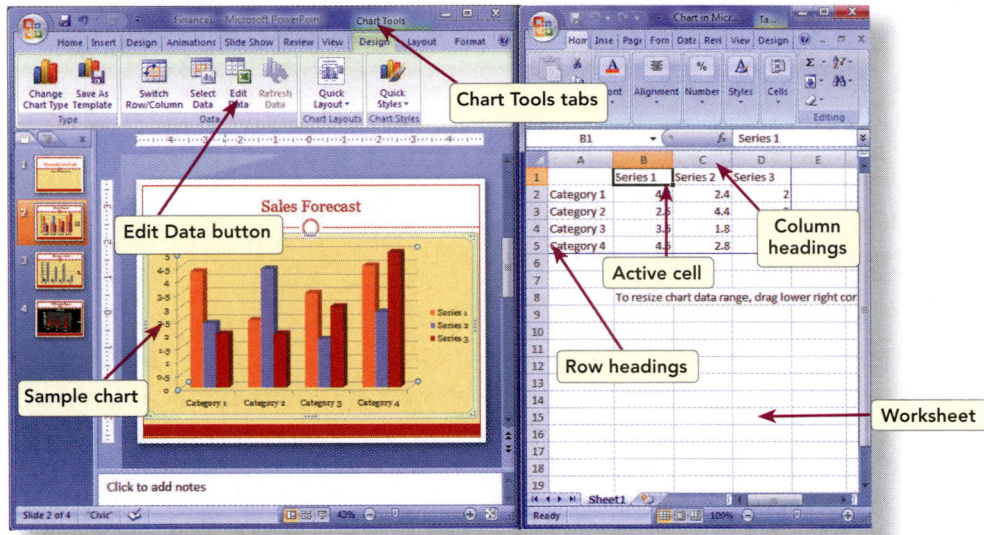

1. On the worksheet, click the words "Series 1." A heavy black border, which indicates that this is the active cell, surrounds the cell that contains "Series 1," as shown in Figure 6-2. Notice that when working on the worksheet, your pointer is a white cross ⊕, called a *cell pointer*.

2. Move around the worksheet by clicking on individual cells. Then try pressing Enter, Tab, Shift+Enter, Shift+Tab, and the arrow keys to explore other ways to navigate in a worksheet.

3. Click cell B2 (the cell in column B, row 2 that contains the value 4.3) then key **10** and press Enter. The chart data will automatically update in PowerPoint.

4. Click cell B2 with the value "10" which represents Category 1 of Series 1.

5. Press Delete to delete the contents of cell B2 and press Enter. Notice that the first column in the chart is no longer displayed.

6. Click and drag the pointer from cell B3 to cell B5 to select the rest of the numbers in the Series 1 column.

7. Press [Delete] and then for Series 1 no columns are displayed in the chart. Because the Series 1 column is still included on the worksheet, however, space still remains on the chart where the columns were removed and Series 1 shows in the legend.

8. Click the box in the upper-left corner of the worksheet where the row headings meet the column headings, as shown in Figure 6-3. The entire worksheet is selected.

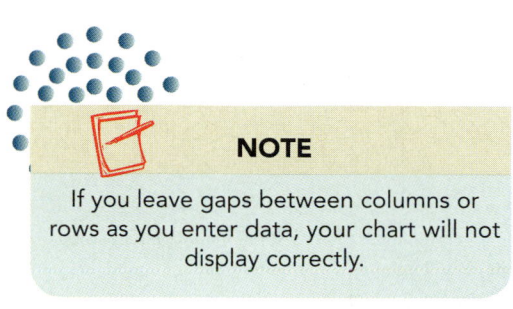

NOTE

If you leave gaps between columns or rows as you enter data, your chart will not display correctly.

Figure 6-3
Editing the worksheet

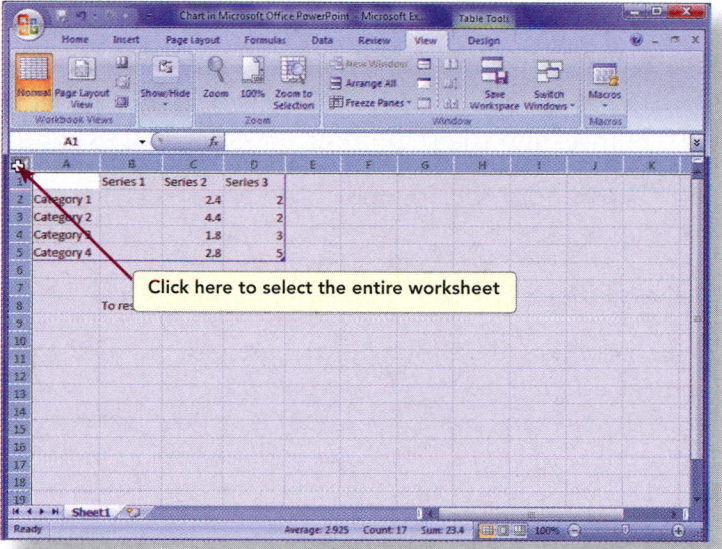

TIP

You do not need to be concerned about number formatting in the worksheet. If any of the labels or numbers do not fit in a cell, move to the right of the column heading for the cell until you get the two-pointed arrow and double-click. This will adjust the column to fit the longest line of text.

9. Press [Delete]. The worksheet is now blank and ready for you to key new data. Notice that the columns in the chart are removed.

10. Click the first cell in the upper-left corner. All the cells in the worksheet are deselected.

11. Close Microsoft Excel. The worksheet is not visible. The worksheet can be closed at any point and accessed when you wish.

12. From the Chart Tools Design tab, in the Data group, choose the Edit Data button ⊞ . This reopens the worksheet and you can now enter new data.

13. Key the numbers and labels shown in Figure 6-4. Be sure to put the labels in the top row and left-most column. Notice how the chart grows as you key data.

Figure 6-4
Worksheet with new data

	A	B	C	D	E
1		2008	2009	2010	
2	New York	920	1130	1450	
3	Miami	500	850	1210	
4	Los Angeles	350	760	990	
5					

Row heading

14. Notice on the chart in Microsoft PowerPoint, there is a blank area on the chart. In the sample chart, there were four categories. To fix this, row 5 must be deleted. Click on the row heading number for row 5. Right-click, and choose **Delete**. This will update the chart to remove the blank space where the fourth category columns were displayed before, and the remaining columns will expand to fill the chart area.

15. Leave both files open for the next exercise.

Exercise 6-3   SWITCH ROWS/COLUMN DATA

When you key data for a new chart, Microsoft Excel interprets each row of data as a *data series*. On a column chart, each data series is usually displayed in a distinct Theme color. For example, on the current chart, the 2008 worksheet column is one data series and is displayed in orange on the chart. The 2009 worksheet column is a second data series, displayed in blue on the chart, and the 2010 worksheet column is a third data series, displayed in dark red.

When creating your worksheet, you might not know whether it is best to arrange your data in rows or columns. Fortunately, you can enter the data and easily change the way it is displayed on the chart.

1. In PowerPoint, click on the slide 2 chart area to continue modifying this chart.

2. From the Chart Tools Design tab, choose the Switch Row/Column button ▣ . The chart columns are now grouped by year instead of by city. The years are displayed below each group of columns.

3. Click the Switch Row/Column button ▣ again to group the chart columns by city. Your chart should look like the one shown in Figure 6-5.

4. Create a slide footer for the current slide (slide 2 only) containing today's date and the text your name, **[6-3your initials]**.

5. Create a new folder for lesson 6. Save the presentation as **[6-3your initials]** in your folder for Lesson 6.

6. Print the current slide (slide 2) in full size. If you have a color printer, print it in color.

Figure 6-5
Chart with new data

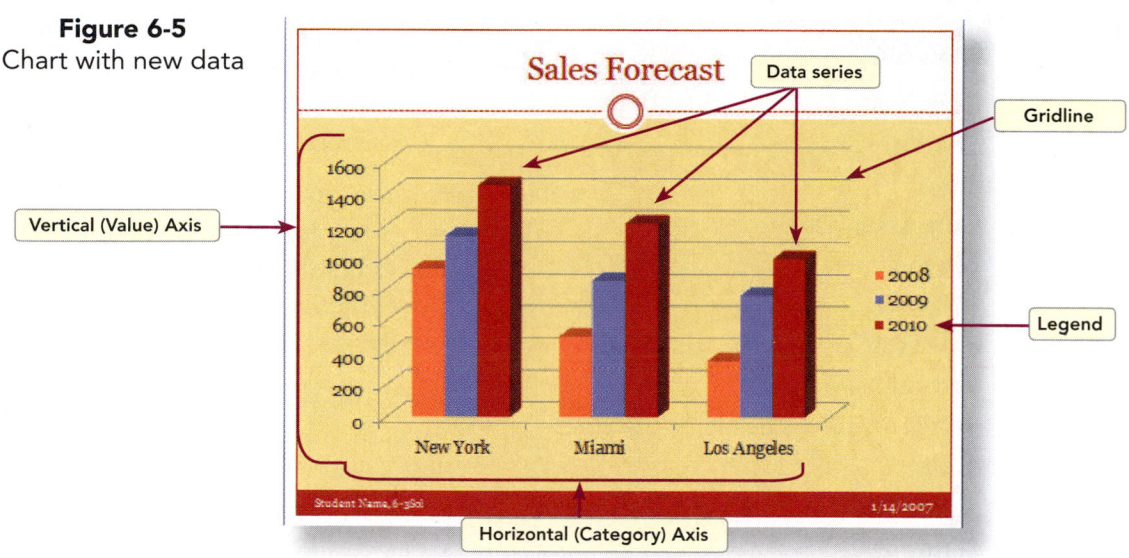

Formatting a Column Chart

You can apply a wide variety of format options to charts by changing the colors, gradients, fonts, and number formats of a chart. Some of these options are appropriate based on the particular chart type being used. In this lesson you have been working with a **3-D Clustered Column** chart.

You can alter the appearance of your chart's axes by changing text color, size, font, and number formatting. You can also change scale and tick mark settings. The *scale* indicates the values that are displayed on the value axis and the intervals between those values. *Tick marks* are small measurement marks, similar to those found on a ruler, that can show increments on the *Vertical (Value) Axis* (on the left for column charts) and the *Horizontal (Category) Axis* (on the bottom for column charts).

To make these changes, use the Format Axis dialog box, which you display in one of the following ways:

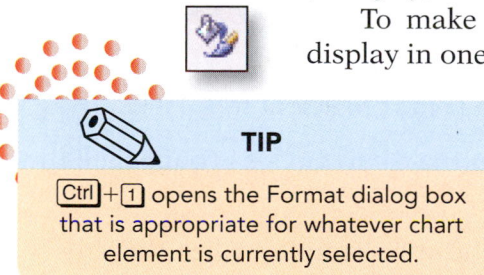

TIP

Ctrl + 1 opens the Format dialog box that is appropriate for whatever chart element is currently selected.

- Click on the Chart Tools Format tab, in the Current Selection group, choose the area you want to format and click the Format Selection button.

- Right-click an axis and choose Format Axis from the shortcut menu.

Exercise 6-4   EXPLORE PARTS OF A CHART

PowerPoint provides several tools to help you navigate around the chart and ScreenTips to help you select the part of the chart on which you want to work.

1. Click on the chart to select it.

Figure 6-6
Chart elements list

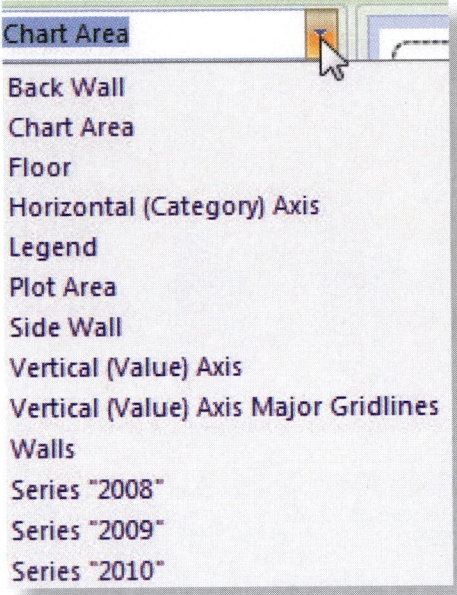

2. Move the pointer over the words "New York." The ScreenTip identifies this part of the chart as the Horizontal (Category) Axis.

3. Point to one of the horizontal gray lines (gridlines) within the chart. The ScreenTip identifies these lines as Vertical (Value) Axis Major Gridlines.

4. Move the pointer around other parts of the chart to find the Plot Area, Chart Area, and Legend Entries. Each of these areas can be formatted with fill colors, border colors, and font attributes.

5. From the Chart Tools Format tab, in the Current Selection group, the chart element that is currently selected is displayed. Click the **Chart Elements** list box arrow to see a list of the various chart elements as shown in Figure 6-6.

6. Choose **Floor** from the list to select the chart floor. Sometimes it's easier to select the chart's smaller elements this way.

7. Close the Excel worksheet, but keep the chart open for the next exercise.

Exercise 6-5   CHANGE CHART STYLES

Microsoft PowerPoint provides preset *Chart Styles* that can be applied to a chart to enhance its appearance.

1. On slide 2, click anywhere inside the chart to select it.

2. From the Chart Tools Design tab, in the Chart Styles group, click the More button.

3. Move your pointer over several of the style samples. Click the **Style 4** chart style, as shown in Figure 6-7.

Figure 6-7
Chart styles drop-down gallery

4. Notice the effect that applying a style has on the selected chart. The chart still coordinates with theme colors, but has three blue colors applied.

5. Leave the presentation open for the next exercise.

Exercise 6-6   FORMAT THE VERTICAL (VALUE) AND HORIZONTAL (CATEGORY) AXES

The Vertical (Value) Axis and the Horizontal (Category) Axis can be formatted through the Format Axis dialog box to change fonts, scales, units, and more options.

1. On slide 2, point to one of the numbers on the left side of the chart. When you see the Vertical (Value) Axis ScreenTip, right-click to open the shortcut menu.

2. Using the floating font group, change the font to **Arial**, **Bold**, **18 points**.

3. Right-click on the value axis again to reopen the shortcut menu and choose **Format Axis**. Click the **Number** option at the left of the dialog box, then in the **Category** box, choose **Currency**. Change the decimal places to **0** because all numbers in the worksheet are even numbers. Change the Symbol to **$ English (U.S.)**.

4. Click **Axis Options** at the left of the dialog box. In the **Maximum** box, choose **Fixed** and key **1500** to set the largest number on the value axis.

5. In the **Major unit** box, choose **Fixed** and key **500** to set wider intervals between the numbers on the value axis.

6. Click **Close**. The chart now shows fewer horizontal gridlines, and each value is formatted as currency with a dollar sign, as shown in Figure 6-8.

Figure 6-8
Formatting the
value axis

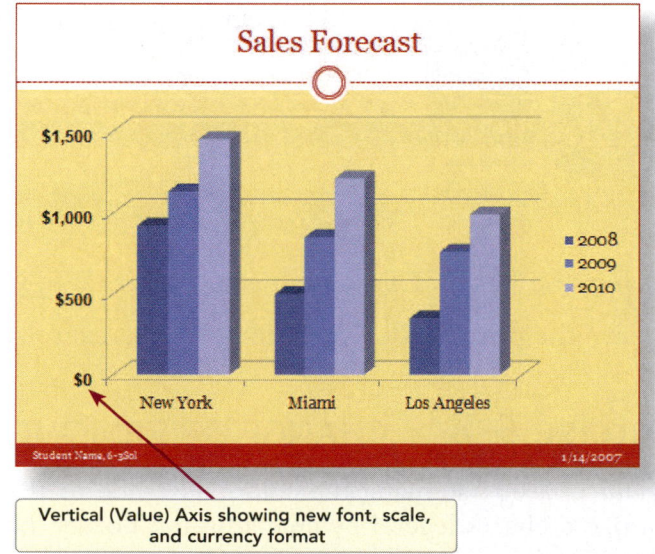

Vertical (Value) Axis showing new font, scale, and currency format

7. Right-click the text "New York" on the horizontal (category) axis.

8. Using the floating font group, change the font to **Arial**, **Bold**, **18 points**.

9. Leave the presentation open for the next exercise.

Exercise 6-7 — APPLY DIFFERENT CHART LAYOUTS

Chart Layouts control the position where different chart elements appear on the chart. PowerPoint provides many different preset layouts.

1. Move to slide 3 and click anywhere within the chart area.

2. From the Chart Tools Design tab, in the Chart Styles group, click **Style 2**.

3. From the Chart Tools Design tab, in the Chart Layouts group, click the Quick Layout button .

4. Select **Chart Layout 2**. Notice the new position of several chart elements. Also, the vertical (value) axis is gone and it has been replaced with data labels showing the values on the columns, as shown in Figure 6-9.

Figure 6-9
Choosing a chart layout

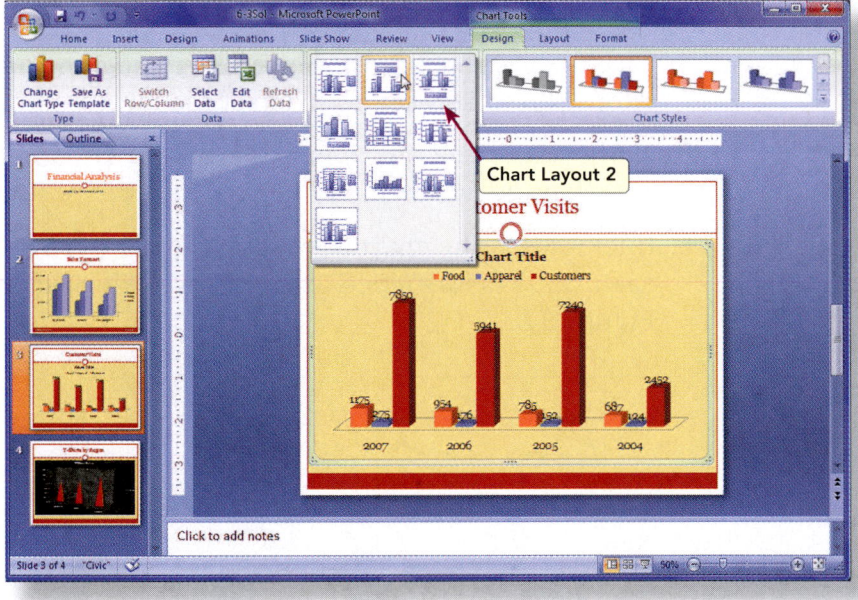

5. Select the "Chart Title" text box and press ⌈Delete⌋ to remove it.

6. Leave the presentation open for the next exercise.

Exercise 6-8 — CHANGE OR REMOVE THE LEGEND

A *Legend* is a box showing the colors assigned to the data series. You can customize a chart's legend by changing the border, background colors, and font attributes.

1. Move to slide 2, and right-click the legend box.

2. Using the Floating Font group, change the font to **Arial**, **Bold**, **18 points**.

3. Right-click the legend box again and choose **Format Legend** so you can make several changes at once. Click the **Fill** option at the left of the dialog box, choose **Solid Fill**, and select the gold accent color to change the legend background.

TIP

Choosing a fill color, even if it is the same as the background, can make it difficult to choose good grayscale settings for printing.

4. Click **Legend Options** at the left of the dialog box and under legend position, choose **Top**. Click **Close**. The legend appears above the chart with gold background color. Note that sizing handles surround the legend.

5. Using a right or left sizing handle, resize the legend box to make it wider so there is more space between the legend items and all three items are still visible.

6. Point to the center of the legend to select it. Drag the legend down so it fits below the top gridline and above the columns, as shown in Figure 6-10. Adjust the width of the legend if it overlaps any columns.

Figure 6-10
Legend repositioned

Exercise 6-9   APPLY OR REMOVE GRIDLINES

The chart style you used on slide 3 removed the chart gridlines. In situations where numbers are displayed within the chart, gridlines may not be needed. *Gridlines* are the thin lines that can be displayed for major and minor units on vertical or horizontal axes. They align with major and minor tick marks on the axes when those are displayed. Gridlines make quantities easier to understand.

1. Still working on slide 2, click anywhere within the chart area.

2. From the Chart Tools Layout tab, in the Axes group, choose the Gridlines button 🔲.

3. Choose **Primary Horizontal Gridlines** and **Minor Gridlines**. Notice that there are many horizontal gridlines now instead of only gridlines on the major units, as shown in Figure 6-11.

Figure 6-11
Gridlines options

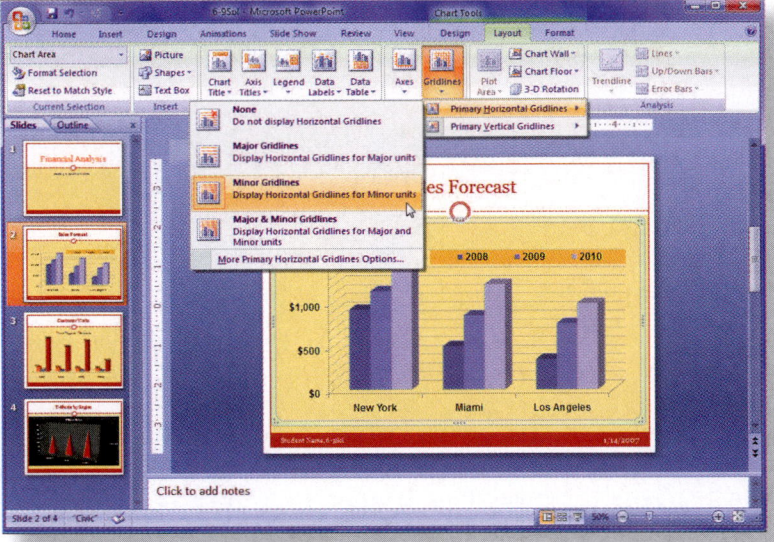

4. Update your slide footer for the current slide (slide 2 only) containing today's date and the text your name, **[6-9your initials]**.

5. Save the presentation as **[6-9your initials]** in your Lesson 6 folder.

Using Different Chart Types

In addition to the 3-D Clustered Column chart, PowerPoint offers a wide variety of chart types. Other types include bar, area, line, pie, and surface, in both two- and three-dimensional layouts. In addition, you can include more than one chart type on a single chart, such as a combination of lines and columns.

If you are working on a two-dimensional (2-D) chart, you can add a secondary axis, so that you can plot data against two different scales. For example, air temperature could be compared to wind speed, or number of customers could be compared to dollar sales. A secondary axis is also a good choice if you need to display numbers that vary greatly in magnitude. For example, sales generated by a small local brand could be compared with national sales trends.

Exercise 6-10   SWITCH TO OTHER CHART TYPES

Sometimes a different chart type can make data easier to understand. You can change chart types in the following ways:

- From the Chart Tools Design tab, in the Type group, click the Change Chart Type button to open the Change Chart Type dialog box.

- Right-click the chart area; then choose **Change Chart Type** from the shortcut menu.

1. Move to slide 3 and click the chart area to activate the chart. This chart compares dollar sales to number of customer visits. Because of the different types of data, the sales figures are not easy to understand.

2. Right-click the chart and choose **Change Chart Type** from the shortcut menu. On the Change Chart Type dialog box, chart types are organized by category, as shown in Figure 6-12.

Figure 6-12
Changing to a different chart type

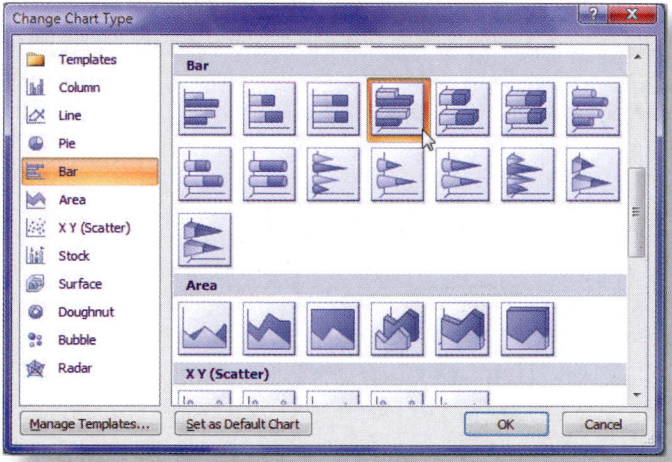

3. Click **Bar** at the left of the dialog box and choose the **Clustered Bar in 3-D** thumbnail and click **OK**. The chart's vertical columns change to horizontal bars.

4. Here is another way to change to a different chart type. From the Chart Tools Design tab, in the Type group, choose the Change Chart Type button. The Change Chart Type dialog box opens again.

5. Click **Column** at the left of the dialog box and several column chart thumbnails appear. Point to different thumbnails and notice the description that appears in the ScreenTip.

6. Select the **Clustered Column** type in the upper left of this category. Click **OK**. The chart changes to a two-dimensional column chart.

7. Leave the presentation open for the next exercise.

Exercise 6-11   ADD A SECONDARY CHART AXIS

The chart on slide 3 ("Customer Visits") contains dollar values for apparel and food sales, and also unit values for number of customer visits. Plotting customer visits on a secondary axis will improve the chart by making it easier to interpret.

If you are working with a 3-D chart, you must change it to a 2-D chart (as you did in the previous exercise), before you can add a secondary axis.

1. Select the chart on slide 3.

2. From the Chart Tools Design tab, in the Chart Layouts group, change the chart layout to **Layout 1** and delete the chart title text box.

3. Right-click one of the "Customers" columns and choose **Format Data Series** from the shortcut menu. Click **Series Options** at the left of the dialog box.

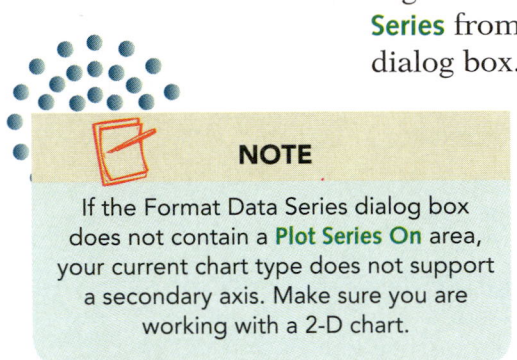

NOTE

If the Format Data Series dialog box does not contain a **Plot Series On** area, your current chart type does not support a secondary axis. Make sure you are working with a 2-D chart.

4. In the **Plot Series On** area of the dialog box, select **Secondary axis**. Click **Close**. Now the orange and blue columns have become taller, and a new scale has been added on the right, as shown in Figure 6-13. In the following exercises you will improve the appearance of this chart.

5. Leave the presentation open for the next exercise.

Figure 6-13
Adding a secondary axis

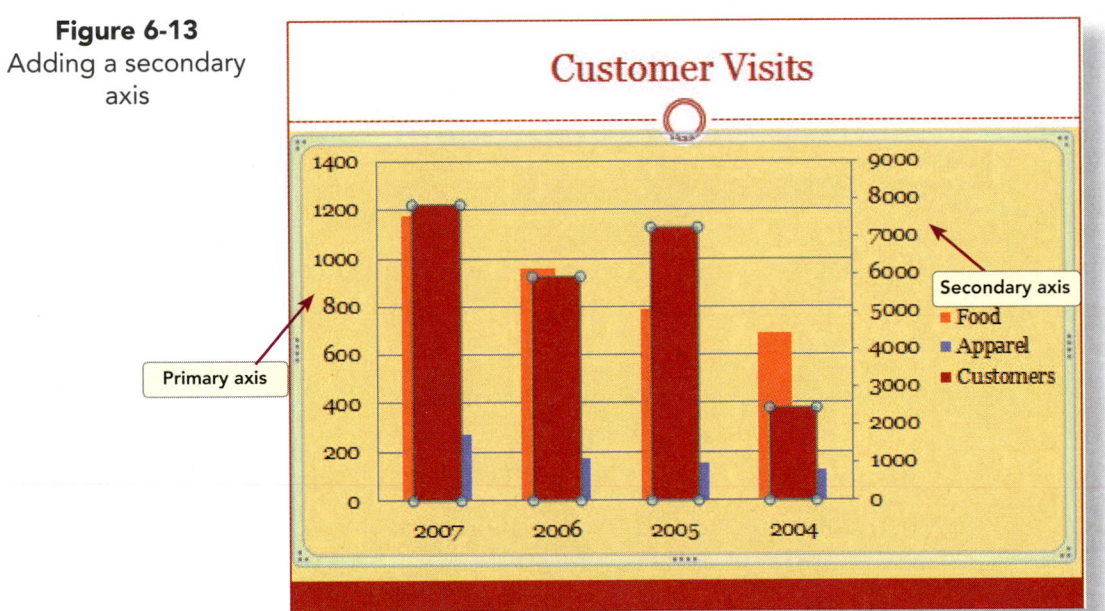

Exercise 6-12   COMBINE CHART TYPES

A good way to distinguish between different data types on a single chart is to assign different chart types. For example, with the current chart, the "Customers" data series can be shown as a line or an area, while the sales data can remain as columns, as shown in Figure 6-14.

1. Still working on slide 3 select the "Customers" data series if not already selected.

2. Right-click the data series and choose **Change Series Chart Type** from the shortcut menu. Click the **Area** category at the left of the dialog box and choose the **Area** chart type. Click **OK**.

Figure 6-14
Area and column
combination chart

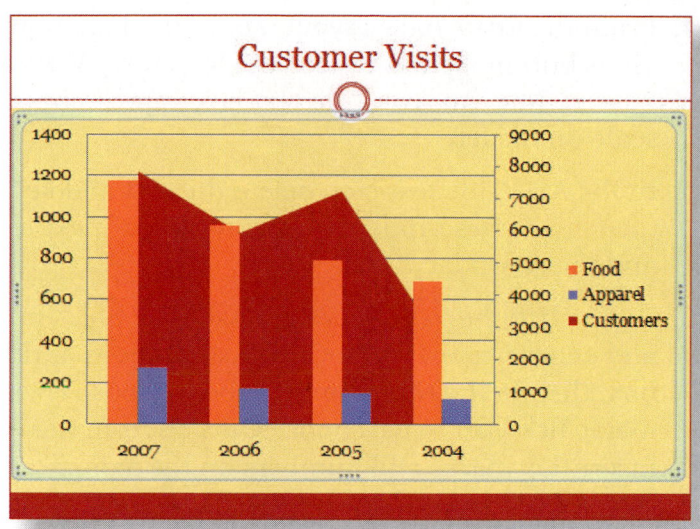

3. Click the "Customers" area to select it then right-click and choose **Change Series Chart Type** from the shortcut menu. Choose the **Line** category at the left of the dialog box and click the **Line** chart type. Click **OK**.

4. Right-click the red line representing "Customers" and choose **Format Data Series** from the shortcut menu.

5. Click **Line Style** option at the left of the dialog box, and change the **Width** to **3 points**.

6. Choose the **Line Color** option at the left of the dialog box, and change the **Color** to **Red Accent 3, Darker 50%**. Click **Close**.

7. Leave the presentation open for the next exercise.

Exercise 6-13   FORMAT A PRIMARY AND SECONDARY AXIS

Proper formatting and labeling on a chart is always important to ensure that viewers understand the information you want to convey. This is even more important when you have both a primary and secondary axis scale on the chart.

1. On slide 3, click the chart area to select it.

2. From the Chart Tools Layout tab, in the Labels group, click the Axis Titles button and choose the **Primary Vertical Axis Title** and **Rotated Title**.

3. In the Axis Title text box located on the primary vertical axis, delete the text and key **Sales (thousands)**. The size of the text box will adjust automatically. Figure 6-15 indicates the position of the text on the chart.

4. From the **Chart Tools Layout** tab, in the Labels group, click the Axis Titles button  and choose the **Secondary Vertical Axis Title** and **Rotated Title**. An Axis Title text box appears beside the secondary axis scale on the left.

5. In the Axis Title text box, delete the text and key **Customer Visits (hundreds)**. Descriptive titles now appear next to both the primary and the secondary axes.

6. Right-click the **Vertical (Value) Axis** (the Sales numbers on the left) and choose **Format Axis**. Click **Axis Options** at the left of the dialog box; then in the **Major unit** text box, choose **Fixed** and key **500**. Under **Major Tick Mark Type**, choose **Outside** from the list box. This will insert tick marks and numbers on the axis.

7. Click **Number** at the left of the dialog box. In the **Category** list box, choose **Currency**. Change the **Decimal places** to **0**. Under symbol, choose **$ English (U.S.)**. Click **Close**.

8. Right-click the **Secondary Vertical (Value) Axis** (the Customers numbers on the right) and choose **Format Axis**. Click **Axis Options** at the left of the dialog box, and change the value in the **Major unit** text box to **Fixed** and **1500** to reduce some of the number labels. Click **Close**.

9. Click outside the chart area to return to view your changes.

10. Click the Legend then right-click and choose **Format Legend**. For the Legend Position choose **Top**. Click **Close**. Now the chart appears more balanced with the scales evenly spaced on each side.

TIP

It is best to avoid using red and green in the same chart to distinguish between data on column and bar charts. Some individuals have difficulty distinguishing between those two colors.

Figure 6-15
Completed combination chart

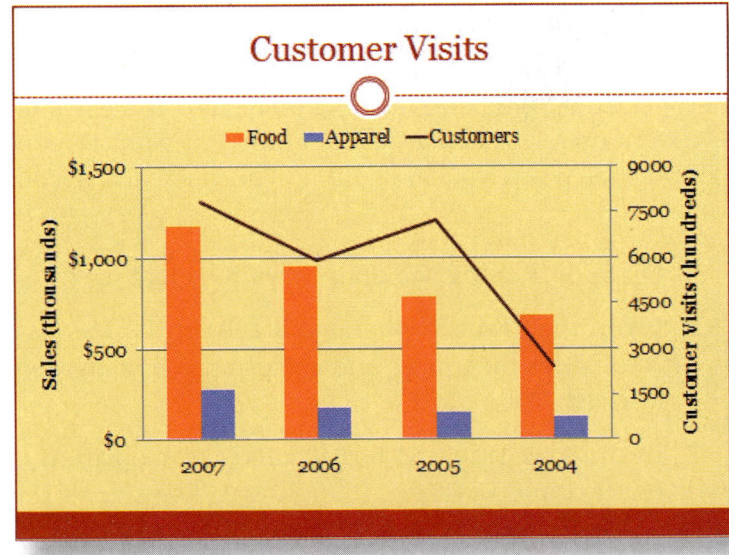

11. Create a slide footer for only slide 3 that includes the date and the text your name, **[6-13your initials]**. Save the presentation as **[6-13your initials]** in your Lesson 6 folder.

12. Print slide 3 only in full size. Leave the presentation open for the next exercise.

Working with Pie Charts

A *pie chart* is a simple, yet highly effective, presentation tool that shows individual values in relation to the sum of all the values—a pie chart makes it easy to judge "parts of a whole." Each value is displayed as a slice of the pie.

A pie chart can show only one data series. To show more than one data series, use more than one pie chart.

Exercise 6-14   CREATE A PIE CHART

In this exercise, you create a pie chart to display the breakdown of the restaurant's sales by category.

If your worksheet contains more than one series, a pie chart uses the first column of numbers. You can change to a different row or column by selecting the series you wish to use.

1. Insert a new slide after slide 3 that uses the **Title Only** layout. This layout provides a white background.

2. Key the title **2007 Sales Categories**.

3. From the Insert tab, in the Illustrations group, click the Chart button.

4. Click the **Pie** category at the left of the dialog box and choose the first chart type that appears in the pie chart category called **Pie**. Click **OK**. Microsoft Excel opens and displays a sample worksheet, and in PowerPoint you will see a sample pie chart reflecting that data.

5. On the worksheet, click the box in the upper-left corner to select all the sample data, and then delete it.

Figure 6-16
Worksheet for Pie chart

	A	B	C
1		2007 Sales	
2	Food	3339	
3	Beverage	2933	
4	Apparel	1529	
5	Other	906	

6. Key the data shown in Figure 6-16.

7. Close the Excel worksheet to view the chart and leave the presentation open for the next exercise.

Exercise 6-15   ADD PIE SLICE LABELS

You can add labels to the chart's data series and edit those labels individually.

1. Click one of the pie slices to select the Chart Series data.

2. From the Chart Tools Layout tab, in the Labels group, click the Data Labels button and click **More Data Label Options**.

3. Click **Label Options** at the left of the dialog box and make several changes under the **Label Contains** heading:

   a. Select both **Category name** and **Percentage**.

   b. Deselect **Value** and **Show Leader Lines**.

   c. Click **Close**.

4. Data labels now appear on the pie slices. With the addition of the data labels, the pie is now smaller; however, the legend is no longer needed since the slices are each labeled, as shown in Figure 6-17.

NOTE

Depending on the pie chart, sometimes parts of the data labels might be hidden by the edges of the chart placeholder. In this case, you need to resize the pie by using the plot area sizing handles.

5. Right-click the legend box and choose **Delete** from the shortcut menu. The pie chart becomes a little larger.

6. Click any data label. All the data labels are selected. Right-click on one of the labels, and use the floating font group to change the font to Arial, 16 points, bold, and italic. Click outside the pie to turn off this selection.

7. Click the data label "Other 10%" twice to select just that label. As with columns, click once to select all labels, and click again to select just one. You can now edit the selected label's text.

8. Click within the text to display an insertion point. Delete the word "Other" (but not "10%"), and key in its place **Take-out**.

9. Click anywhere within the chart to deselect the label that now appears separated from the pie.

10. Click on the "Take-Out 10%" label two times to select just that label. Right-click and choose **Format Data Label**. Under the Label Position heading, choose **Inside End**. Click **Close**. Now the label is positioned on the slice.

11. Because the slide title identifies what the pie contains, the pie chart title for 2007 sales can be removed. Select this text box and press Delete. The pie will expand to fill the available space.

Figure 6-17
Pie chart with data labels

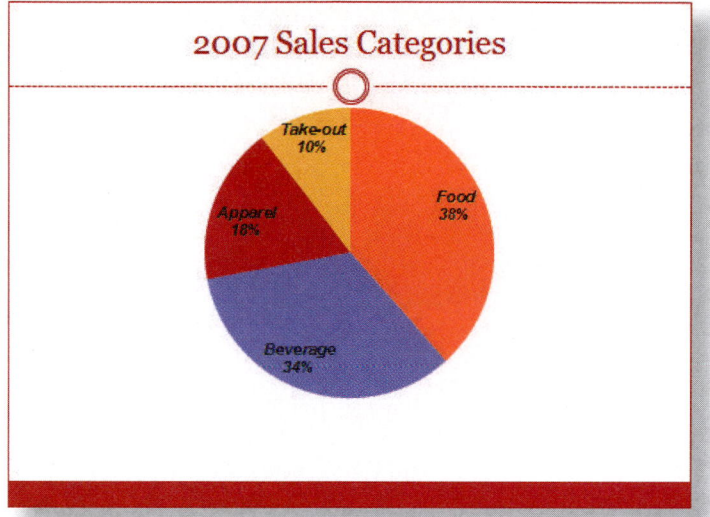

Exercise 6-16   APPLY 3-D ROTATION

You can enhance the appearance of your pie chart with additional effects, such as changing to a 3-D appearance and rotating the angle of the pie or *exploding* a slice (dragging it out from the center of the pie) for emphasis.

1. Click to select the chart. From the Chart Tools Design tab, in the Type group, click the Change Chart Type button , and select **Pie in 3-D**. The pie now has a perspective treatment. Click **OK**.

2. From the Chart Tools Layout tab, in the Background group, click the 3-D Rotation button . At the bottom of the Format Chart Area dialog box, click **Default Rotation** and the pie becomes more dimensional but almost flat.

3. In the **Perspective** box, key **0.1˚**.

4. Under the Rotation heading, change the **X degree** to **35˚** to move the "Take-out" slice to the right. Click **Close**.

5. Click the center of the pie once to select all the slices. Notice that each slice has selection handles where the slices join.

6. Click the "Take-out" slice so you have handles on that slice only (be careful not to select the label) and drag it slightly away from the center of the pie. This is called *exploding a slice*.

7. The labels for two slices move away from their respective slices. Select just the "Apparel 18%" label, right-click, choose **Format Data Label** and select the Label Position of **Inside End**. Click **Close**.

8. Select just the "Take-out 10%" label and drag it over to fit on top of the exploded slice, as shown in Figure 6-18.

Figure 6-18
Pie chart with
3-D rotation and
exploded slice

9. In Normal view, select the chart area and use the corner sizing handles to increase its size to make the pie chart larger to fill the slide.

10. Create a slide footer for slide 4 only that includes the date and the text your name, **[6-16your initials]**.

11. Save the presentation as **[6-16your initials]** in your Lesson 6 folder.

12. Print slide 4 only in full slide size. Leave the presentation open for the next exercise.

Enhancing Chart Elements

You can add many interesting effects to charts. In addition to changing colors, you can add shapes or pictures that help you make a particular point or highlight one aspect of the data. You can also annotate your charts with text to clarify or call attention to important concepts.

Exercise 6-17 ADDING SHAPES FOR EMPHASIS

Shapes can be combined with text or layered in some way to emphasize the point you need to make. For this exercise, you will combine an arrow and text.

1. Move to slide 5 ("T-Shirts by Region").

2. Because this chart reflects only one data series, the legend at the side is not needed. Select the legend and press Delete.

3. Because the slide title identifies the content of this chart, the chart title is redundant; therefore, select the chart title and press Delete.

4. From the Insert tab, in the Text group, click the Text Box button ; and click and drag above the Miami column to create a space to enter the text, change the font color to white, and key **L.A. may top Miami in 2008**.

5. Select the text inside the text box, right-click, and use the floating font group to change the text to 18-point Arial, bold, italic.

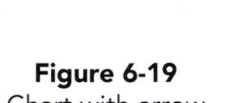

TIP

You may want to use Zoom to enlarge the slide so you can more easily use the arrow's rotation handle.

6. From the Insert tab, in the Illustrations group, click the Shapes button 🗔; then from the Block Arrow category, click the **Left Arrow** shape. Draw an arrow above the Los Angeles chart shape. Change the shape fill color to a gold that coordinates with the theme and remove the shape outline. Reposition and resize the arrow and text box as needed to appear as shown in Figure 6-19.

Figure 6-19
Chart with arrow and text box

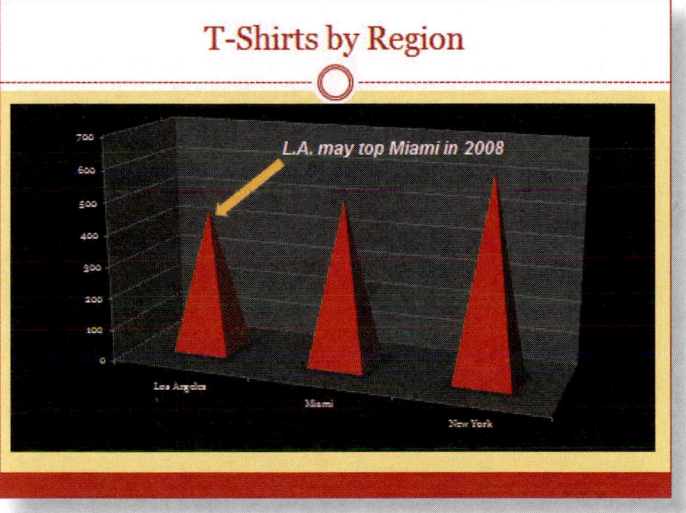

7. Create a slide footer for slide 5 that includes the date and the text your name, **[6-17your initials]**.

8. Save the presentation as **[6-17your initials]** in your Lesson 6 folder.

9. Print slide 5 in full size. If you have a color printer, print it in color. Leave the presentation open for the next exercise.

Exercise 6-18   CHANGE COLORS IN CHART AREAS

You can change the colors of individual chart areas, columns, or an entire data series. Shape fill effects, including textures and gradient fills, can be used the same way you use them for other PowerPoint shapes. You can also change the outline style of columns, bars, and other chart elements.

1. Move to slide 2 and click to select the chart. Point to one of the darkest blue columns, the 2008 series. Notice the ScreenTip that appears, identifying the data series.

2. Click any light blue column, the 2010 series. All the light blue columns are selected, as indicated by the box that is displayed around each selected column.

3. Click the light blue column for Los Angeles. Now the Los Angeles column is the only one selected. Clicking once selects all the columns in a series; clicking a second time (not double-clicking) changes the selection to just one column.

4. Click one of the darkest blue columns to select all of the 2008 series.

5. From the Chart Tools Format tab, in the Shape Styles group, click the Shape Fill button . Click a darker blue.

6. Click the darker blue column for Los Angeles, and then change to **Orange, Accent 1**. The Los Angeles column is now a different color from the other columns in its series. Click the Undo button 🔄 to return the column to the darker blue to match the other columns in the series.

> **TIP**
>
> You can change colors and fills on each part of the chart. Be sure to select the element that you would like to change before beginning to change colors or gradients, or add a picture.

7. Select the columns that contain the light blue fill color, the 2010 series. Click the Shape Fill button and choose **Ice Blue, Accent 5**. Click the Shape Fill button 🪣 again and choose **Gradient**. Under the Light Variations category, select **Linear Up** so the lightest color is at the top of the column.

Exercise 6-19   ADD A PICTURE FILL BEHIND CHART

A picture can help communicate the meaning of the chart by illustrating the data in some way. For instance, if you are discussing T-shirts as in this exercise, it is appropriate to have a shirt picture in the chart background.

1. Move to slide 5.

2. Change the font color of the text on both axes and in the text box to black to make it easier to read once a picture has been added.

3. With the chart active, from the Chart Tools Layout tab, in the Current Selection group, choose **Chart Area** from the Chart Elements drop-down list. Click the Format Selection button 🪣.

4. Choose **Fill** at the left of the dialog box; then choose **Picture or texture fill** and click **File** under the Insert from heading.

5. Navigate to your student files and click the file **t-shirt**. Click Insert. Click Close. The picture fills the background of your chart. You need to recolor other parts of the chart so the T-shirt is visible in the background, as shown in Figure 6-20.

6. Click the gray area behind the chart shapes, the Back and Side Walls. Right-click and choose **Format Walls**. Choose **No Fill** and click **Close**.

7. Right-click the Vertical (Value) Axis numbers and change the font to **Arial**, **18 points**, and **bold**.

8. Right-click the Horizontal (Category) Axis labels and change the font to **Arial**, **18 points**, and **bold**.

9. Adjust the position of the text box or arrow if necessary.

10. Update the slide footer for slide 5 to include the text **[6-19your initials]**.

Figure 6-20
Chart with picture background

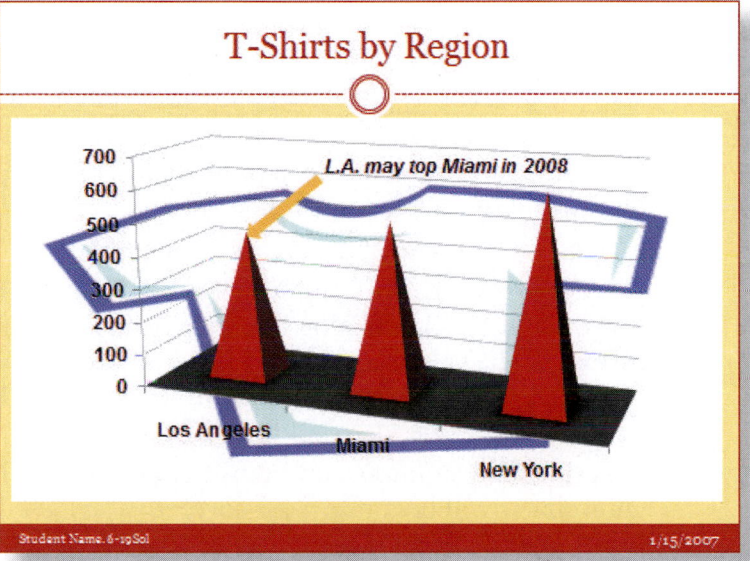

11. View the presentation as a slide show, starting with slide 1.

12. Create a handout header and footer: Include the date and your name as the header, and the page number and text **[6-19your initials]** as the footer.

13. Move to slide 1 and save the presentation as **[6-19your initials]** in your Lesson 6 folder.

14. Preview, and then print, the presentation as handouts, six slides per page, grayscale, landscape, scale to fit paper, and framed. Close the presentation.

Lesson 6 Summary

- Charts are diagrams that display numbers in pictorial format. Charts illustrate quantitative relationships and can help people understand the significance of numeric information more easily than viewing the same information as a list of numbers.

- When you start a new chart, a sample worksheet appears in Microsoft Excel. A worksheet is where you key the numbers and labels used to create a chart.

- The worksheet contains rows and columns. You key each number or label in a separate *cell*—the rectangle formed by the intersection of a row and a column.

- On the worksheet, key labels are in the first row and column.

- A data series is a group of data that relates to a common object or category. Often, more than one data series is displayed on a single chart.

- Use the Switch Row/Column button ⊞ to change how a data series is displayed on a chart.

- A wide variety of chart types are available including column, bar, area, line, pie, and surface with many different chart format options.

- Several Content Layouts are suitable for charts. Two Content Layouts also make it easy to combine a chart and body text on the same slide.

- Use the Chart Elements drop-down list to select specific parts of a chart or you can use ScreenTips to identify parts as you point to them.

- Special fill and border effects, including textures and gradient fills, can be used in charts the same way you use them for other PowerPoint objects.

- Use the Format Axis dialog box to modify the units, font, and number format of the value axis or secondary value axis. Modify the unit settings to specify the range of numbers displayed and increments between numbers.

- Axis titles are an important part of charts. Careful labeling ensures that your charts will be interpreted correctly.

- A legend is a box showing the colors assigned to each data series. Customize a chart's legend by changing the border, background colors, and font attributes.

- Use a secondary axis when you need to plot two dissimilar types of data on the same chart. A secondary axis is available only for a 2-D chart type.

- Proper formatting and labeling on a chart is important when your chart has both a primary and secondary axis.

- A good way to distinguish between different data types on a single chart is to assign different chart types. For example, use columns for one type of data and lines for the other type.

- A pie chart shows individual values in relation to the sum of all the values. Each value is displayed as a slice of the pie.

- A pie chart can show only one data series. To show more than one data series, use more than one pie chart.

- The plot area of a chart is the area containing the actual columns, bars, or pie slices. It can be formatted with or without a border and a fill effect.
- Exploding a pie slice (dragging it out from the center of the pie) emphasizes the slice.
- Use the Insert tab to add shapes and text boxes. Use text boxes wherever annotation is needed to clarify the chart's meaning.
- Charts can be enhanced by adding pictures, colors, and 3-D effects.

LESSON 6		Command Summary	
Feature	Button	Task Path	Keyboard
Insert a chart		Insert, Illustrations group, Chart	
Display worksheet		Chart Tools Design, Data group, Edit Data	
Insert axis titles		Chart Tools Layout, Labels group, Axis Titles	
Insert or remove a legend		Chart Tools Layout, Labels group, Legend	
Switch data series between columns and rows		Chart Tools Design, Data group, Switch Row/Column	
Format a chart object		Chart Tools Format, Current Selection group, Format Selection	Ctrl + 1
Change the chart type		Chart Tools Design, Type group, Change Chart Type	
Add a secondary axis		Chart Tools Format, Current Selection group, Format Selection (with Data series selected)	
Add data labels		Chart Tools Layout, Labels group, Data Labels	
Change chart style		Chart Tools Design, Chart Styles group, Chart Layout	
Apply different chart layouts		Chart Tools Design, Chart Layouts group, More	
Add/Remove gridlines		Chart Tools Layout, Axes group, Gridlines	

Concepts Review

True/False Questions

Each of the following statements is either true or false. Select your choice by indicating T or F.

T F   1. PowerPoint offers only one slide layout choice for slides with charts.

T F   2. The sample worksheet in Microsoft Excel is always blank when you create a new chart.

T F   3. You cannot see the chart while you are working on the worksheet.

T F   4. You can change the colors of columns in a chart to whatever you find appealing.

T F   5. The units shown on the value axis are set by PowerPoint and cannot be changed.

T F   6. Every chart must include a legend.

T F   7. You must use a two-dimensional chart if you want to include a secondary axis.

T F   8. Double-clicking a pie slice or column enables you to change its size.

Short Answer Questions

Write the correct answer in the space provided.

1. How can you delete all of the sample data in the worksheet at one time?

   _____

2. How do you change the grouping of the data series on a chart from columns to rows?

   _____

3. While working on a chart, how do you display the worksheet if it is not visible?

   _____

4. What type of number formatting do you apply to values to display dollar signs?

   _____

5. What group found on the Chart Tools Format tab can you use to select different parts of a chart?

   _____

6. Which button can you click to change the color of a selected pie slice?

_____

7. How can you change the font size for chart labels without opening a dialog box or using the Ribbon?

_____

8. On a 2-D column chart, how can you change one of the data series to be displayed as an area chart?

_____

Critical Thinking

Answer these questions on a separate page. There are no right or wrong answers. Support your answers with examples from your own experience, if possible.

1. How do you decide if a chart is needed in your presentation? Do you think a presentation can have too many charts? Explain your answer.

2. Imagine that you are trying to explain to someone how you spend your waking hours during a typical day. Can you think of a chart that would break down your activities into different categories and show how much time you spend on each during the day? Describe the chart's appearance and the values that you would include.

Skills Review

Exercise 6-20

Insert a column chart.

1. Open the file **FinSum1**.
2. Create a chart by following these steps:
   a. Insert a new slide after slide 2 that uses the **Title and Content** layout.
   b. Key **2007 Quarterly Earnings** for the title.
   c. Click the Insert Chart icon ▦ in the center of the content placeholder.
   d. Choose a **3-D Clustered Column** chart and click **OK**.
   e. In Microsoft Excel, click the upper-left box on the worksheet to select all the existing data and press Delete.
   f. Key the data shown in Figure 6-21.

◢	A	B	C	D	E	F
1		Q1	Q2	Q3	Q4	
2	New York	1888	2008	2116	1543	
3	Los Angeles	1743	1799	1844	1539	
4	Miami	1634	1439	1783	1469	
5						

3. Click in any cell of row 5 that was used in the sample worksheet. Right-click and then choose **Delete** from the shortcut menu. Choose **Entire Row**; then click **OK**. This step removes the unused row and the empty space on the chart.

4. Close Microsoft Excel.

5. Click the chart once in Normal view to select it; then use the chart's corner sizing handles to reduce the chart's height by approximately 0.5 inches and adjust the chart's position for even spacing on the slide.

6. Edit the chart by following these steps:

   a. Be sure the chart is selected; then from the Chart Tools Design tab, in the Data Group, click Edit Data 📊.

   b. Click cell E3 (Q4 for Los Angeles) to select it.

   c. Key **1849** to replace the value "1539." Press [Enter].

   d. Still working on the Chart Tools Design tab, in the Data group, click the Select Data button 📊. In the Select Data Source dialog box, click the **red arrow** at the end of the Chart Data Range box.

   e. Click in Cell A1 and drag the pointer through E4 (the end of the data).

   f. Click the **red arrow** again, and click **OK**.

   g. Still working on the Chart Tools Design tab, in the Data group, click the Switch Row/Column button 📊.

   h. Close Microsoft Excel.

7. Create a handout header and footer: Include the date and your name as the header, and the page number and text **[6-20your initials]** as the footer.

8. Move to slide 1 and save the presentation as **[6-20your initials]** in your Lesson 6 folder.

9. View the presentation as a slide show; then preview and print it as handouts, three slides per page, grayscale, framed. Close the presentation.

Exercise 6-21

Edit and format an existing chart, change chart style, format the legend.

1. Open the file **Finance2**.

2. Edit the chart on slide 4 by following these steps:

   a. Click the chart to activate it.

   b. From the Chart Tools Design tab, in the Data group, click the Edit Data button 📊 to open Microsoft Excel.

   c. On the worksheet, click cell B3 containing the value "−2%" and key **2** to overwrite the negative value with a positive value. Press [Enter].

   d. Close Microsoft Excel.

3. Change the style of the chart by following these steps:

   a. From the Chart Tools Design tab, in the Chart Styles group, choose the More button ▾.

   b. Choose **Style 25**.

4. Change the font for the Horizontal (Category) Axis labels by following these steps:

   a. Click the category axis label "2007" to select the category axis.

   b. Right-click on the axis and make the following changes from the floating font group: Choose the **Tahoma** font, a **20 point** font size, and the **Brown, Background 2** font color.

5. Format the Vertical (Value) Axis by following these steps:

   a. Right-click a number on the value axis and choose **Format Axis**.

   b. For **Major unit** choose **Fixed** and key **.05**. Click **Close**.

   c. Right-click on the axis and make the following changes from the floating font group: Choose the **Tahoma** font, a **20 point** font size, and the **Brown, Background 2** font color.

6. Format the legend by following these steps:

   a. Right-click the legend and choose **Format Legend** from the shortcut menu.

   b. Under the Legend Position heading, choose **Top Right** and click **Close**.

   c. Use the floating font group to change the legend font to **Tahoma** at a **16 point** font size.

7. Create a handout header and footer: Include the date and your name as the header, and the page number and text **[6-21your initials]** as the footer.

8. Move to slide 1 and save the presentation as **[6-21your initials]** in your Lesson 6 folder.

9. View the presentation as a slide show; then preview and print the presentation as handouts, four slides per page, grayscale, landscape, framed. Close the presentation.

Exercise 6-22

Add a chart, format chart axes, add a secondary axis, and combine chart types.

1. Open the file **Finance3**.

2. Add a slide after slide 3 with the **Title and Content Layout**.

3. Key the title **2007 Special Events Revenue**.

4. Click the Insert Chart button 📊 in the content placeholder. In the Column category, choose the **Clustered Column** chart. Delete the sample data and key the information in Figure 6-22. So that you can see all of the words entered into each cell of the worksheet in Microsoft Excel,

select the cells in the worksheet; then from the Home tab, in the Cells group, click **Format** then choose **AutoFit Column Width**.

Figure 6-22
Worksheet

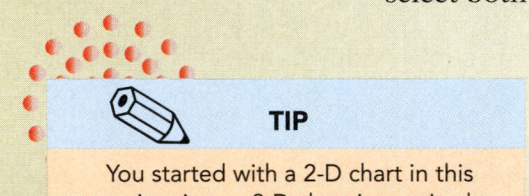

	A	B	C	D	E	F
1		1st Quarter	2nd Quarter	3rd Quarter	4th Quarter	
2	Special Events	71	141	118	149	
3	Total Revenue	800	1076	1149	1207	
4						

5. Once the data is keyed, click on the row 4 heading and drag down to select both rows 4 and 5. Right-click and choose **Delete**.

TIP

You started with a 2-D chart in this exercise since a 2-D chart is required to add a secondary axis.

6. In Microsoft PowerPoint, from the Chart Tools Design tab, in the Data group, click the Select Data button. In the Select Data Source dialog box, in the Chart data range box, change the D to an E and click **OK**.

7. From the Chart Tools Design tab, in the Data group, click the Switch Row/Column button.

8. Close Microsoft Excel.

9. Add a secondary axis to the chart by following these steps:

   a. Right-click one of the "Total Revenue" columns and choose **Format Data series** from the shortcut menu.

   b. In the **Plot Series On** area, click **Secondary axis**. Click **Close**.

10. Change the chart type for the "Total Revenue" columns by following these steps:

    a. Be sure the columns in this data series are still selected.

    b. From the Chart Tools Design tab, in the Type group, click Change Chart Type button.

    c. In the **Line** category, choose the **Line** chart.

    d. Click **OK**.

11. Change the formatting of the line for the data series by following these steps:

    a. Select the line (being careful not to select the gridlines) then right-click and choose **Format Data Series** from the shortcut menu.

    b. Click **Line Style** at the left of the dialog box and change the **Width** to **8 points**.

    c. Click **Marker Options** at the left of the dialog box and change the **Marker Type** to **Built-In** and the size to **15**.

    d. Click **Marker Fill** at the left of the dialog box and change to a **Solid Fill** then make the color **Tan, Text 2**. Click **Close**.

12. Format the secondary value axis by following these steps:

    a. Right-click one of the numbers on the right side of the chart (on the Secondary Vertical (Value) Axis) and choose **Format Axis**.

    b. Change the **Major unit** to **Fixed** and key **500**.

    c. Click **Number** at the left of the dialog box and choose **Currency**. For **Decimal places** key **0** and for **Symbol** choose **$ English (United States)**. Click **Close**.

d. Right-click the secondary axis again and use the floating font group to change the font to **Arial**.

13. Apply the following formatting to the Vertical (Value) Axis (on the left side of the chart) using the same process as for the secondary axis.

a. Right-click the Vertical (Value) Axis and choose **Format Axis**.

b. Change the **Maximum** to **Fixed** and **250** and the **Major unit** to **Fixed** and **50**.

c. Click **Number** at the left of the dialog box and choose **Currency**. For **Decimal places** key **0** and for **Symbol** choose **$ English (United States)**. Click **Close**.

d. Right-click the vertical axis again and use the floating font group to change the font to **Arial**.

14. Change the formatting of the Horizontal (Category) Axis. Right-click the category axis and change the font to **Arial** using the floating font group.

15. Add chart titles and a legend by following these steps:

a. Click to activate the chart.

b. From the Chart Tools Layout tab, in the Labels group, click the Axis Titles button 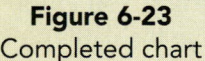.

c. Choose **Primary Vertical Axis Title** and **Rotated Title**.

d. Select the text that appears in the text box; delete it, and key **Special Events (thousands)**.

e. Still working on the Chart Tools Layout tab, in the Labels group, click the Axis Titles button.

f. Choose **Secondary Vertical Axis Title** and **Rotated Title**.

g. Select the text that appears in the text box; delete it, and key **Total Revenue (thousands)**.

16. Right-click the legend and choose **Format Legend** from the shortcut menu and change the legend position to **Top**. Click **Close**.

17. Reposition the chart, so it is centered horizontally on the slide, as shown in Figure 6-23.

Figure 6-23
Completed chart

18. Create a handout header and footer: Include the date and your name as the header, and the page number and text **[6-22your initials]** as the footer.

19. Move to slide 1 and save the presentation as **[6-22your initials]** in your Lesson 6 folder.

20. View the presentation as a slide show; then preview and print the presentation as handouts, four slides per page, grayscale, landscape, framed. Close the presentation.

Exercise 6-23

Create and format a pie chart; add shapes, text boxes, and color.

1. Open the file **Apparel2**.

2. Insert a new slide after slide 2 that uses the **Title and Content** layout. Key the title **Apparel Mix— 2007**.

3. Create a pie chart by following these steps:

   a. Click the Insert Chart button 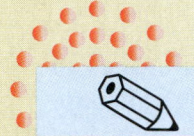 in the center of the content placeholder.

   b. Click the **Pie** category and choose the **Pie in 3-D** chart type. Click **OK**.

   c. On the worksheet, clear the sample information and key the information shown in Figure 6-24.

TIP

To use an em dash (the long straight line), key two hyphens with no space around them. Then space once after 2007 and the two hyphens will change to an em dash, a more contemporary punctuation mark. This adjustment is controlled with PowerPoint's AutoCorrect feature.

Figure 6-24
Worksheet

	A	B	C
1		Unit Sales	
2	T-Shirts	4208	
3	Bike Jerseys	1112	
4	Visors	528	
5	Knee Pads	663	
6	Elbow Pads	967	
7			

4. The sample data that you earlier deleted established a range of cells for the chart. However, not all of the current data is displayed in that range. Notice on the pie chart that no slice for Elbow Pads is included even though it is keyed on the worksheet.

5. From the Chart Tools Design tab, click **Select Data**. On the worksheet, notice that row 6 has not been included in the selection. Highlight all the cells for the data you entered (A1 through B6) then click **OK**. Now all of the items have a slice.

6. Close Microsoft Excel.

7. Format a pie slice by following these steps:

   a. Click the dark blue pie slice "T-shirts" once to select the entire pie.

   b. Click the dark blue slice again to select the individual slice.

   c. From the Chart Tools Format tab, in the Shape Styles group, click the Shape Fill button and choose **Light Blue** from the Standard Colors category. This sets the color apart from the other blues.

   d. Click these slices and change to the following standard colors: Bike Jerseys, light green; Visors, yellow; Knee Pads, red; and Elbow Pads, purple.

8. Right-click the pie's legend and choose **Delete** from the shortcut menu.

9. Add data labels by following these steps:

    a. Activate the chart.

    b. From the Chart Tools Layout tab, in the Labels group, click the Data Labels button 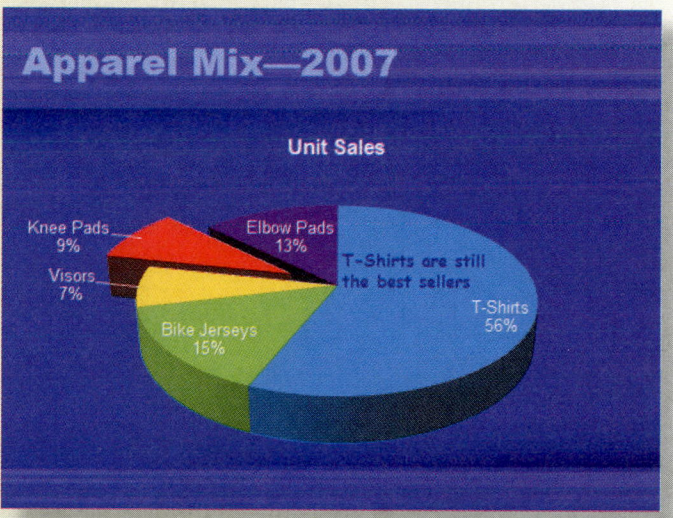 and choose **More Data Label Options**.

    c. In the Label Contains area, select the **Category name** and the **Percentage** check boxes and deselect the **Value** check box.

    d. In the Label Position area, choose **Best Fit**.

    e. Click **Close**.

10. Explode a pie slice by following these steps:

    a. Select the red "Knee Pads" slice by clicking it twice.

    b. Drag the slice slightly away from the center of the pie. The pie chart will become slightly smaller because of the additional space this requires. Therefore, increase the chart area slightly to compensate for this change.

    c. Center the chart area horizontally on the slide.

11. Insert a text box by following these steps:

    a. From the Insert tab, in the Text group, click the Text Box button.

    b. Click outside the chart area; draw the text box and key **T-Shirts are still the best sellers**.

    c. Move the text box on top of the large light blue T-shirt pie slice. Change the text box font to **18-point Comic Sans MS, bold, Dark Blue, Accent 1**. Resize the box so the text fits on two lines as shown in Figure 6-25.

Figure 6-25
Exploded slice and text box

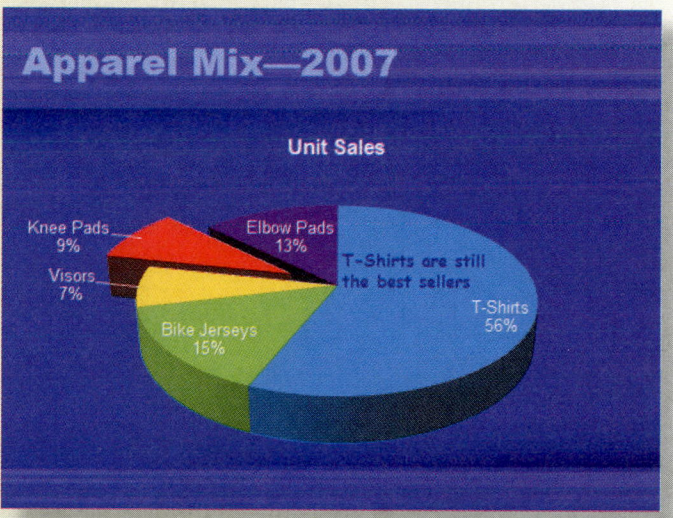

12. Create a handout header and footer: Include the date and your name as the header, and the page number and text **[6-23your initials]** as the footer.

13. Move to slide 1 and save the presentation as **[6-23your initials]** in your Lesson 6 folder.

14. View the presentation as a slide show; then preview and print the presentation as handouts, four slides per page, grayscale, framed. Close the presentation.

Lesson Applications

Exercise 6-24

Create a presentation containing a column chart and format the chart.

1. Start a new presentation using the **Median** design theme and the **Aspect** theme color.

2. Using the text in Figure 6-26, create a three-slide presentation; use the **Title Slide** layout for slide 1, and the **Title and Content** layout for slides 2 and 3. The first line of each is the title for the slide.

Figure 6-26

Slide 1 | Three Years of Phenomenal Sales

Slide 2 |
Highlights
- New York revenue still increasing
- Miami and Los Angeles meeting goals
- Revenues reach 120% of budget

Slide 3 | Sales by Region-2005 to 2007

3. Right-align the title on slide 1.

4. On slide 3, create a 3-D Clustered Column chart by using the data shown in Figure 6-27. Delete row 5.

Figure 6-27
Worksheet

	A	B	C	D	E
1		New York	Los Angeles	Miami	
2	2005	5650	4183	3843	
3	2006	8753	5892	6388	
4	2007	11332	9852	8487	
5					

5. Close Microsoft Excel.

6. Change the Vertical (Value) Axis options to have a **Maximum** of **12000** and a Major unit of **3000**. Change its Number formatting to **$ English (U.S.)** with no decimals.

7. Change to **Chart Style 3**.

8. For the value and category axes and legend, change the font to 16 points, not bold.

9. Move the legend to the bottom. Resize, if necessary.

10. Reposition the chart to keep spacing on both sides even. Resize if needed.

11. Create a handout header and footer: Include the date and your name as the header, and the page number and text **[6-24your initials]** as the footer.

12. Move to slide 1 and save the presentation as **[6-24your initials]** in your Lesson 6 folder.

13. View the presentation as a slide show; then preview and print it as handouts, three slides per page, grayscale, framed. Close the presentation.

Exercise 6-25

Create and format a pie chart.

1. Open the file **Expense2**.

2. Insert a new slide after slide 1 that uses the **Title and Content** layout. Key the title **Expense Breakdown**.

3. Create a 2-D pie chart on the new slide 2 by using the data from Figure 6-28.

Figure 6-28
Worksheet

	A	B
1		2007 Expenses
2	Food	2190
3	Payroll	1813
4	Depreciation	577
5	Lease	1737
6		

4. Add **Percentage** data labels only to the chart. Make them bold and change the font size to 32 points.

5. Increase the legend font to 20 points, bold.

6. Change the chart title size to 28 points, bold and move it to the top left of the chart area.

7. Change the chart to a **Pie in 3-D**.

8. Explode the "Food" slice of the pie slightly.

9. If any of the percentage labels move off the slices, then right-click, choose **Format Data Label**, and choose the Label Position **Inside End** or click and drag them onto the slices of the pie.

10. Create a handout header and footer: Include the date and your name as the header, and the page number and text **[6-25your initials]** as the footer.

11. Move to slide 1 and save the presentation as **[6-25your initials]** in your Lesson 6 folder.

12. View the presentation as a slide show; then preview and print it as handouts, six slides per page, grayscale, scaled for paper, framed. Close the presentation.

Exercise 6-26

Insert a chart; change the chart to a combination chart; format the chart text, data series, and legend; add a secondary axis; and add a shape.

1. Open the file **Earnings2** and apply the **Oriel** design theme using the **Concourse** theme color.

2. Resize and reposition the title on slide 1 so that it is right above the subtitle.

3. Insert a new slide between slides 2 and 3 that uses the **Title and Content** layout. Key the title **Gross Income**.

4. Create a clustered column chart on the new slide by using the data in Figure 6-29.

Figure 6-29

	A	B	C	D	E
1		2005	2006	2007	
2	San Francisco	1246	2033	5432	
3	Miami	2734	4630	6325	
4	Los Angeles	2871	4126	7235	
5	New York	3566	5135	7555	
6	Year Total	10417	15924	26547	
7					

5. Select all of the rows and columns in the worksheet so that all data is included in the chart.

6. Switch Row/Column.

7. Close Microsoft Excel.

8. Be sure you are using a 2-D column chart.

9. Plot the "Year Total" data series on a secondary axis. Change the chart type for the series to **Line Chart**. Format the line in a matching color and change the width to **10**.

10. Change the font for the Vertical (Value) Axis, Horizontal (Category) Axis, the Secondary Vertical (Value) Axis, and Legend to 16-point Arial (not bold).

11. For the Vertical (Value) Axis (on the left), change the units to minimum **0** and maximum to **8,000** displayed **Fixed** at major units of **2,000** and change the Number formatting to **Currency** with no decimal places.

12. Format the Secondary Vertical (Value) Axis (on the right) with the units to minimum **0** and maximum to **30,000** displayed **Fixed** at major units of **5,000** and change the Number formatting to **Currency** with no decimal places.

13. Move the legend to the bottom of the chart.

14. Expand the width and height of the chart area.

15. Expand the width of the legend so all parts of the legend fit on one line. Apply a light blue fill to the legend area to distinguish it from the slide background.

16. Apply a gradient fill to the columns in each data series. After the first data series has been changed, you will need to reset the fill color for each series selected and then apply the gradient coloring. Choose **Linear Up** in the Dark Variations category so the lightest color is on top.

17. Click outside the chart area to deselect the chart.

18. Now work in the area at the top of the chart to create these graphic elements and then move them into position when complete. You might want to use Zoom to increase the size of the slide so you can work better in detail.

    a. Create a text box centered above the chart. Key **Impressive!** in the text box. Change the font to 24-point Arial.

    b. Draw a small, **5-Point Star** with a yellow fill and red outline.

    c. Place the star on the top of the New York column for the year 2007.

    d. Place the text box above the columns near the star, as shown in Figure 6-30.

Figure 6-30
Completed chart

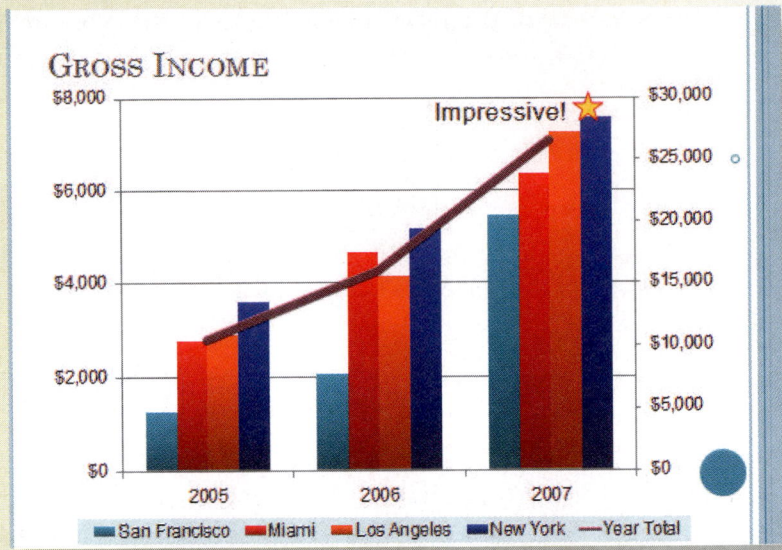

19. Create a handout header and footer: Include the date and your name as the header, and the page number and text **[6-26your initials]** as the footer.

20. Move to slide 1 and save the presentation as **[6-26your initials]**.

21. View the presentation as a slide show; then preview and print slide 3 in grayscale.

22. Close the presentation.

Exercise 6-27 ◆ Challenge Yourself

Insert a chart; change the chart style; apply gridlines; format the chart text, data series, and legend; add a picture fill to a chart; and add a shape.

1. Open the file **Suppliers**.

2. On slide 1, key **Your Name** as the subtitle.

3. Insert a new slide after slide 2 that uses the **Title and Content** layout. For the slide title, key **Produce Cost Comparison**.

4. Create a **3-D Clustered Column** chart on the new slide by using the data in Figure 6-31. On your worksheet in Microsoft Excel, select all of the cells for the chart, then from the Home tab, in the Cells group, click Format and choose **AutoFit Column Width** so all text is visible in the cells.

Figure 6-31
Worksheet

	A	B	C	D	E
1		Frankie's Food	Distributing by Dano	Patty's Produce	
2	Apples (20 lb)	10.99	11.84	9.85	
3	Lettuce (24 ct)	27.45	29.75	25.29	
4	Cucumbers (bushel)	19.8	20.25	19.45	
5	Tomatoes (case)	9.55	10.85	9.12	
6					
7					

5. Change the chart style to **Style 7**.

6. Change the **Floor** color to the orange that matches the slide design.

7. Select the legend and change to a **Top** position.

8. Deselect the chart. Draw a rectangle shape over "Patty's Produce" in the legend area then change the Fill color to **None** and the outline to **Orange**.

9. Add a text box on the right and key **Lowest Costs**. Change the Fill color to **Orange** and the text color to **Dark red** and font size to **18 points**.

10. Add an arrow from the text box pointing to "Patty's Produce." Change the Fill color and the Outline color to **Orange**, as shown in Figure 6-32.

Figure 6-32
Completed chart

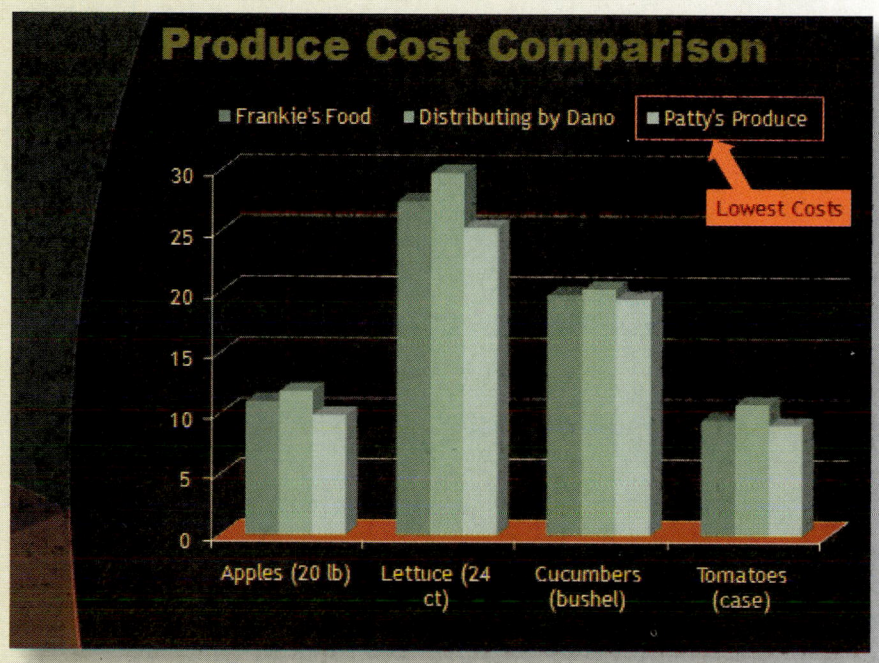

11. Insert a new slide after slide 3 using the **Title and Content** layout. For the slide title, key **Lead Time Comparison**.

12. Insert a **Line with Markers** chart and enter the data below in Figure 6-33 into the chart. Delete columns C and D and row 5.

13. Select the data from A1 through B4 so that the chart appears correctly.

Figure 6-33
Worksheet

	A	B
1		Days from Order to Delivery
2	Frankie's Food	7
3	Distributing by Dano	10
4	Patty's Produce	4
5		

14. Remove the legend. If the chart title did not automatically appear, title the chart **Days from Order to Delivery**.

15. Increase the width of the line to 8 points and make it **Dark red, Accent 2**. Change the Marker Options to **Built-in** and increase the marker size to 28 points and make it **Orange**.

16. Reposition the chart to fit evenly on the dark area of the slide.

17. Draw a green, **5-pointed star** and place it in front of the supplier's name with the lowest lead time.

18. Change the font color of the Value and Category Axes and the chart title to **Dark red, Accent 2**.

19. Insert the picture **Apple** from your data files into the background of the chart.

20. Change the gridline color to orange, as shown in Figure 6-34.

Figure 6-34
Completed chart

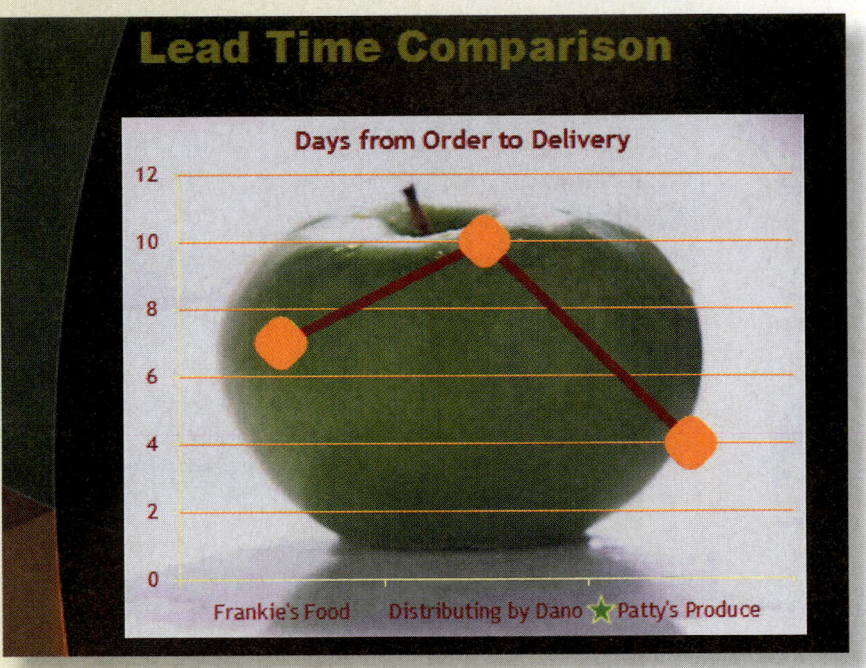

21. Create a handout header and footer: Include the date and your name as the header, and the page number and the text **[6-27your initials]** as the footer.

22. Move to slide 1 and save the presentation as **[6-27your initials]**.

23. View the presentation as a slide show; then preview and print it as handouts, four slides per page, grayscale, landscape, framed. Close the presentation.

On Your Own

In these exercises you work on your own, as you would in a real-life work environment. Use the skills you've learned to accomplish the task—and be creative.

Exercise 6-28

Obtain a list of stock quotes either online or from the *Wall Street Journal*. Create a chart listing at least five of your stock picks. Compare the prices of each stock visually through a chart. Create another chart showing the percentage change in stock value since closing the day before compared with the other stocks you have chosen. In addition, create a separate slide for each stock, giving details about the company. Format the presentation in a way that will hold a viewer's attention. Save your presentation as **[6-28your initials]**. Preview, and then print the presentation as handouts.

Exercise 6-29

Make a list of your activities during a typical weekday, including the actual time you spend on each activity. Group your activities into no more than eight categories. Make sure the times add up to 24 hours. Add a second set of times listing the amount of time you should be spending on each activity, and a third set of times listing the amount of time you would prefer to spend. (Don't be too serious about the times—make it fun.) Create a column or bar chart to represent these times, and then add three pie chart slides, one for each set of times (actual, should, prefer). Add a title slide and a conclusion slide. Use your creativity to make the charts interesting and fun to view including colors, pictures, shapes, and 3-D rotation. Save the presentation as **[6-29your initials]**. Preview, and then print the presentation as handouts.

Exercise 6-30

Research the information about your state of residence from the current census and other online resources. Prepare slides to explain the facts that you find using bulleted lists and charts. Find some statistics about diversity within your state, home ownership in your state compared to the national average, types of businesses, etc., and create at least two charts to display the statistics. Add a title slide and a conclusion slide. Format your presentation attractively, save it as **[6-30your initials]**, and then print handouts.

Creating Diagrams with SmartArt Graphics

OBJECTIVES

After completing this lesson, you will be able to:

1. Choose SmartArt graphics.
2. Enhance diagrams.
3. Prepare an organization chart.
4. Create other diagrams with SmartArt.
5. Change diagram types and orientation.

Estimated Time: 1½ hours

MCAS OBJECTIVES

In this lesson:
PP07 3.1.1
PP07 3.1.2
PP07 3.2.1
PP07 3.2.2
PP07 3.2.3
PP07 3.2.4
PP07 3.2.5
PP07 3.2.6
PP07 3.2.7
PP07 3.3.1
PP07 3.5.1
See Appendix

Using diagrams is a very important way to illustrate presentation content. *Diagrams* provide a visual representation of information that can help an audience understand a presenter's message. For example, diagrams can be used to show the steps of a process or the relationship between managers and subordinates. An audience can see the process or relationship because it is portrayed with graphic shapes and connecting lines or layered in some way to show these sequences and relationships. In this lesson you will create diagrams using SmartArt, a new feature of PowerPoint that contains a wide range of predesigned diagrams that can be customized in many different ways.

Choosing SmartArt Graphics

A *SmartArt graphic* is a diagram that can be inserted on your slide and then the parts of the diagram can be filled in with identifying text. Or if you have text in a bulleted list or in text shapes, the text items can be converted to a SmartArt diagram. You will use both of these techniques in this lesson.

 From the Insert tab, in the Illustration group, click the SmartArt button to see the Choose a SmartArt Graphic dialog box shown in Figure 7-1. You can display thumbnails of all possible diagrams, or you can click one of the seven categories to look at them by diagram type. On the right side of this

dialog box, the diagram is displayed in a larger size with a definition below to help you decide if this is the right type of illustration for your communication needs. The white lines that you see on the sample diagram represent where your text will appear when you label each part of the diagram.

Figure 7-1
Choose a SmartArt
Graphic dialog box

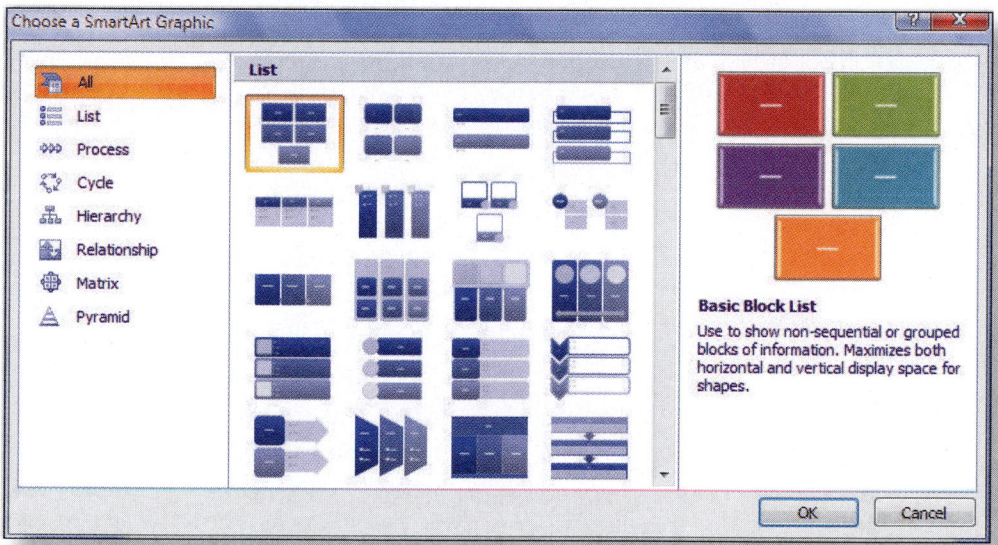

Exercise 7-1   USE DIAGRAMS FOR COMMUNICATION PURPOSES

Preparing a few bulleted lists is a simple way to create a series of slides for a presentation. However, a presentation including only bulleted lists is not very appealing to an audience from a visual standpoint and may not be the best way to communicate the meaning of your message an audience needs to understand.

NOTE

Search for SmartArt descriptions in PowerPoint's Help to find a comprehensive list of all SmartArt graphics organized by category. Each graphic is displayed with descriptions of the layout and tips for situations where each would be appropriate.

As you develop your presentation content, you should be considering your message from the viewpoint of the audience and not just thinking about what you need to say. To help your audience visualize these concepts and remember them, plan alternative ways to illustrate concepts, such as including pictures, charts, and shapes, to draw attention to key points. Also, you can choose from an extensive array of SmartArt graphics. These graphics are diagrams that are arranged in seven categories, as listed in Table 7-1.

TABLE 7-1 SmartArt Graphics Diagram Types

Diagram Type	Purpose
List	Provides an alternative to listing text in bulleted lists. List diagrams can show groupings, labeled parts, and even directional concepts through how the shapes are stacked. Several diagrams show main categories and then subtopics within those categories.

continues

TABLE 7-1 SmartArt Graphics Diagram Types   *continued*

Diagram Type	Purpose
Process	Shows a sequence of events or the progression of workflow such as in a flowchart. These diagrams show connected parts of a process or even converging processes using a funnel technique. Several diagrams with arrows can portray conflict or opposing viewpoints.
Cycle	Represents a continuous series of events such as an ongoing manufacturing or employee review process. A cycle can be arranged in a circular pattern or with slices or gears to reflect interconnected parts. A radial cycle begins with a central part and then other parts extend from the center.
Hierarchy	Illustrates reporting relationships or lines of authority between employees in a company such as in an organization chart. These connections are sometimes called parent-child relationships. Hierarchy diagrams can be arranged vertically or horizontally such as in a decision tree used to show the outgrowth of options after particular choices are made.
Relationship	Shows interconnected, hierarchical, proportional, or overlapping relationships. Some of these diagrams also appear in different categories.
Matrix	Allows placement of concepts along two axes or in related quadrants. Emphasis can be on the whole or on individual parts.
Pyramid	Shows interconnected or proportional relationships building from one direction such as a foundational concept on which other concepts are built.

Exercise 7-2   USE LISTS TO SHOW GROUPS OF INFORMATION

NOTE

If you added a fourth bulleted item, the shapes on the slide would become a little smaller so all shapes could be displayed.

In this exercise you will create a List diagram in two different ways:

- Start with a blank slide and key SmartArt content using a Text pane.
- Start with existing bulleted text and convert to SmartArt.

1. Open the file **Organize**.

2. Move to slide 1. From the Home tab, in the Slides group, click the New Slide button  to insert a new slide using the **Title and Content layout**. On the content placeholder, click the SmartArt button .

3. Click the **List** category. Click the **Vertical Box List** thumbnail then click **OK**.

4. From the SmartArt Tools Design tab, in the Create Graphic group, click the Text pane button . A text box will appear on the left, as shown in Figure 7-2, where you can key the text after each bullet for each of the shapes in this diagram.

Figure 7-2
Entering SmartArt text

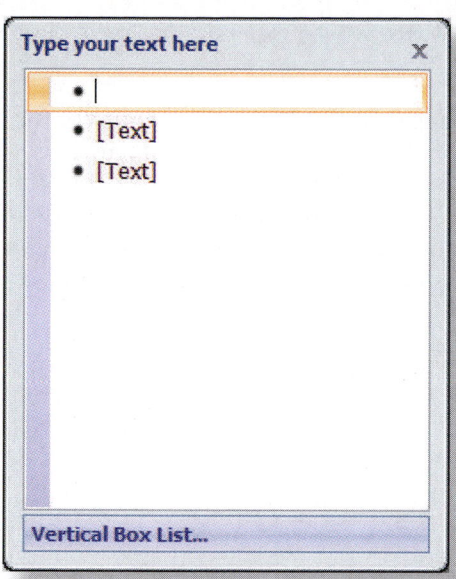

5. For the first item, key **New Procedure**.

6. Click after the second bullet and key **New Philosophy**; click after the third bullet and key **New Department**. Notice that the text you keyed as bulleted items now appears on the shapes.

7. Close the Text pane.

8. For the slide title, key **Organizational Changes** as shown in Figure 7-3. This type of list diagram will work best when you have limited information for first-level bulleted points and no subpoints in a list.

Figure 7-3
Vertical Box List diagram

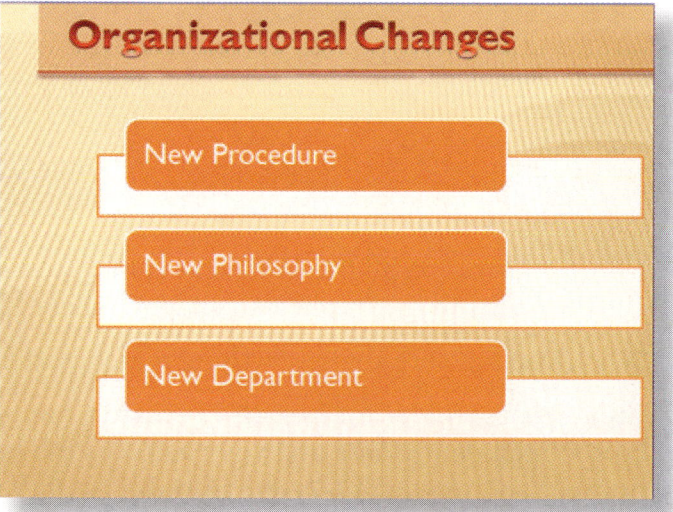

NOTE

If you already have bulleted text on a slide, then that text can be converted to a SmartArt diagram. In the following steps, you will show both the first-level and second-level text shown on slide 3.

9. In the Slides and Outline pane, click slide 3 and press Ctrl+D to duplicate the slide. Once your diagram is prepared on slide 3 and you have confirmed that all the text is appropriately displayed, you can delete slide 4 with the bulleted list. But for now, it is a good idea to leave one slide as originally prepared so it is available for comparison.

10. Now highlight all of the bulleted text on slide 3.

11. From the Home tab, in the Paragraph group, click the Convert to SmartArt Graphic button .

12. Click **More SmartArt Graphics** to access all categories and click the **List** category.

13. Click the **Horizontal Bullet List** thumbnail then click **OK**.

14. The first-level bulleted items appear in the top rectangles and the second-level bulleted items appear in the bottom rectangles with bullets. The color treatment of the first-level words is more dominant than what appears for the subpoints, as shown in Figure 7-4.

Figure 7-4
Horizontal Bullet List
diagram

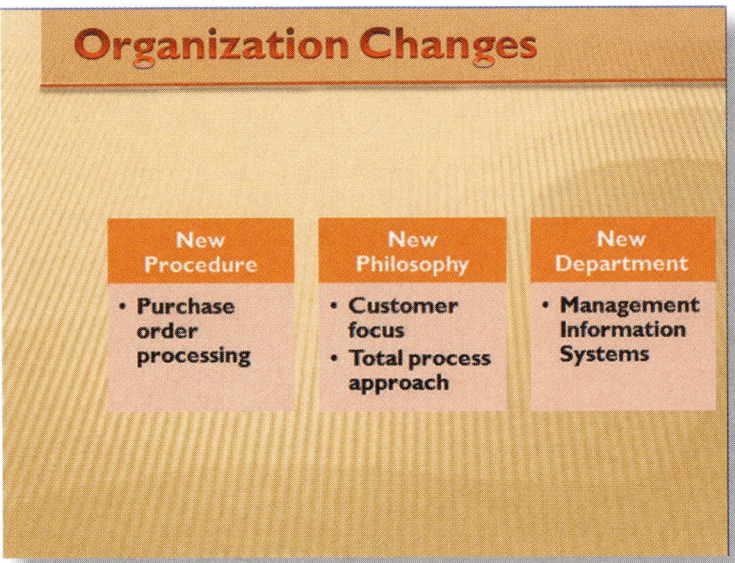

15. Now confirm that all the same text is included in the diagram on slide 3 that is in the duplicated slide 4 bulleted list.

16. When you are sure that everything matches, delete slide 4.

17. Create a new folder for Lesson 7. Create a handout header and footer. Include the date and your name as the header, and the page number and the text **[7-2your initials]** as the footer. Save the presentation as **[7-2your initials]** in your new Lesson 7 folder. Leave the presentation open for the next exercise.

Exercise 7-3   USE PROCESS DIAGRAMS TO SHOW SEQUENTIAL WORKFLOW STEPS

A *process diagram* reflects concepts or events that occur sequentially. Generally speaking, one part must be finished before the next part begins. Many variations for how these processes can be portrayed are available through SmartArt.

1. Move to slide 3. From the Home tab, in the Slides group, click the New Slide button 🖻.

2. On the slide 4 content area, click the SmartArt button 🖳 then choose the **Process** category.

3. Examine the different options in this category and then click the **Basic Process** thumbnail and click **OK**. A three-part diagram appears as shown in Figure 7-5. You can enter text directly in the placeholders on each diagram shape, or you can click the Text pane button ⋮ on the left to open enter text.

4. For this exercise, key directly in each of the shapes. As you key, the text will automatically word-wrap in the shape and become smaller to fit within that shape. Therefore, you need to be careful when using this method to keep the words you enter very concise.

5. Click in the first rectangle shape and key **Survey customer needs**.

6. Click in the second rectangle shape and key **Analyze survey results**.

7. Click in the third rectangle shape and key **Develop product plan**.

Figure 7-5
Basic Process
diagram

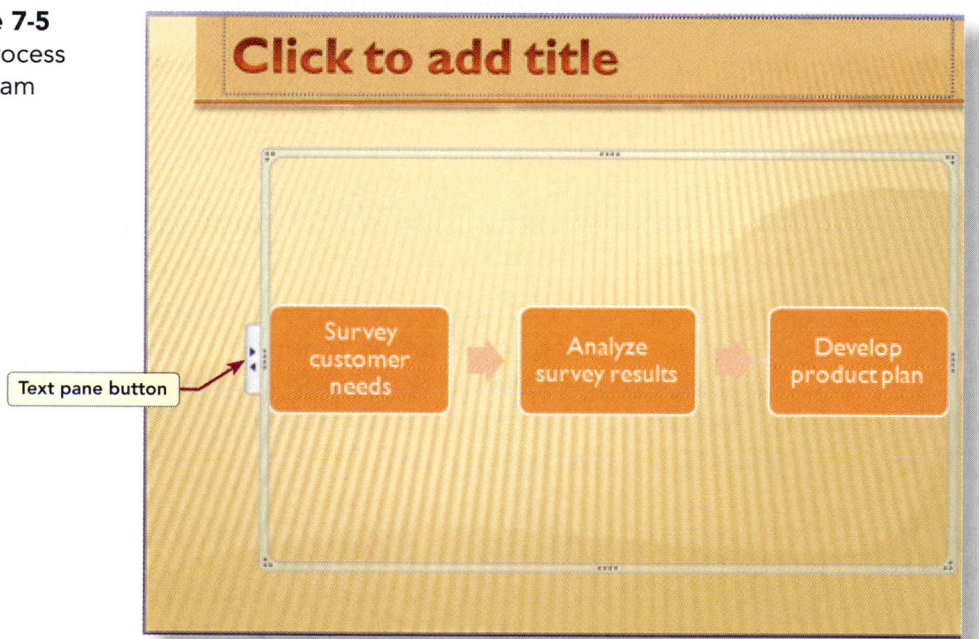

8. Because you need to include a fourth step in this process, you need to increase the size of the SmartArt area. Point to the top left corner of the SmartArt border and drag it close to the left edge of the slide.

9. Select the third shape in the diagram then click the Text pane button ⋮ to open the bulleted text dialog shape. Notice that this text is highlighted in the bulleted text dialog shape.

10. Click at the end of the word "plan" and press ⏎Enter then key **Introduce new products**. A fourth shape is added and text size automatically adjusted again.

11. Close the Text pane.

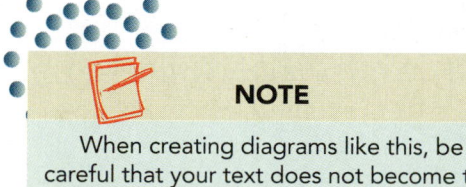

NOTE

When creating diagrams like this, be careful that your text does not become too small for easy reading. Later in this lesson you will make the text larger on this slide.

12. For the slide title, key the text **New Development Process**.

13. Update the handout footer text to **[7-3your initials]**. Save the presentation as **[7-3your initials]** in your Lesson 7 folder. Leave the presentation open for the next exercise.

Exercise 7-4   USE CYCLE DIAGRAMS TO SHOW A CONTINUING SEQUENCE

The *cycle diagram* is used to communicate a continuing sequence. In this exercise you will use the same information as you did in slide 4, but display it in a cycle. Instead of creating the diagram first, however, you will enter text using a bulleted list and then convert the list into a SmartArt graphic.

1. Insert a new slide after slide 4 and key the title **New Development Cycle**.

2. In the content placeholder key four bulleted items:

   Survey customer needs
   Analyze survey results
   Develop product plan
   Introduce new products

3. Select the listed text and right-click. From the pop-up menu, choose **Convert to SmartArt** then click the **Basic Cycle** thumbnail.

4. Select the four shapes. From the SmartArt Tools Format tab, in the Shape Styles group, click the Shape Fill button and choose (**Orange, Accent 1, darker 25%**) to apply a darker theme fill color. Select the four arrows and apply a darker theme color (**Orange, Accent 1, darker 50%**), as shown in Figure 7-6.

Figure 7-6
Completed Basic
Cycle diagram

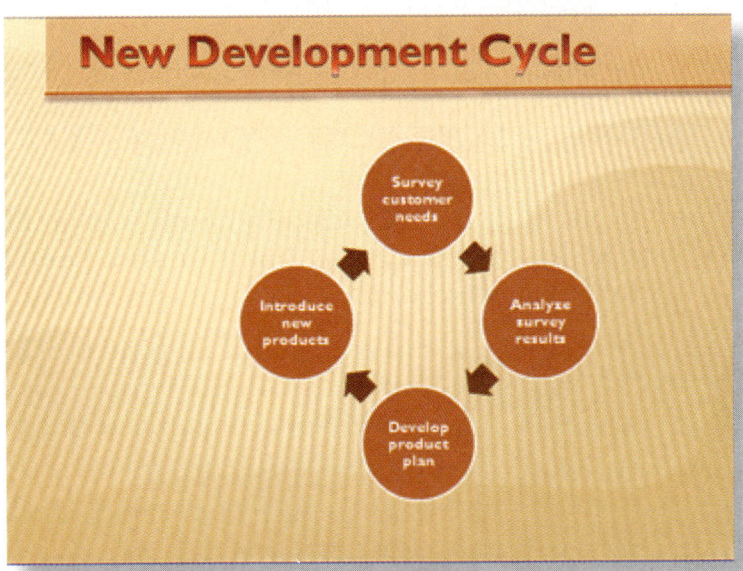

5. Update the handout footer text to **[7-4your initials]**.

6. Move to slide 1 and save the presentation as **[7-4your initials]** in your Lesson 7 folder.

7. Preview, and then print the entire presentation as handouts, six slides per page, grayscale, framed. Leave the presentation open for the next exercise.

Enhancing Diagrams

Once a SmartArt graphic is inserted on your slide, its appearance can be altered using the effects you have learned to apply to shapes. However, additional options exist for customizing these diagrams, and you will work with these design options in the next exercises.

Exercise 7-5   APPLY SHAPE QUICK STYLES

One of the quickest ways to change the appearance of shapes within a diagram is to apply *Quick Styles*. These styles include more than one preset adjustment.

1. On slide 2, select the three rectangle shapes that contain text content.

2. From the Home tab, in the Drawing group, click the Quick Styles button 🖌. A gallery of preset styles appears in an array of theme colors, as shown in Figure 7-7.

Figure 7-7
Shape Quick Styles

3. As you move your pointer horizontally, you will see different colors applied to the selected shapes. As you move your pointer vertically, you will see different effects such as outlines, beveling, and shadows.

4. To use a darker color and apply a shadow effect to the shapes, click on **Light 1 Outline, Color Fill - Accent 2**.

Exercise 7-6   ADJUST 3-D FORMAT AND ROTATION

In the previous exercises, the shapes have a *2-D* orientation—you see the shapes in dimensions of height (up/down measurement) and width (left/right measurement). Three-dimensional (*3-D*) settings add a perspective dimension to create the illusion of depth. For example, a square can look like a cube. Rotation settings enable you to tilt shapes on the screen.

1. Move to slide 4 and select the four rectangles.

2. From the Home tab, in the Drawing group, click the Shape Effects button ⊡ then choose **3-D Rotation**.

3. From the gallery of options, choose **Perspective Heroic Extreme Left**, as shown in Figure 7-8.

Figure 7-8
3-D Rotation effects

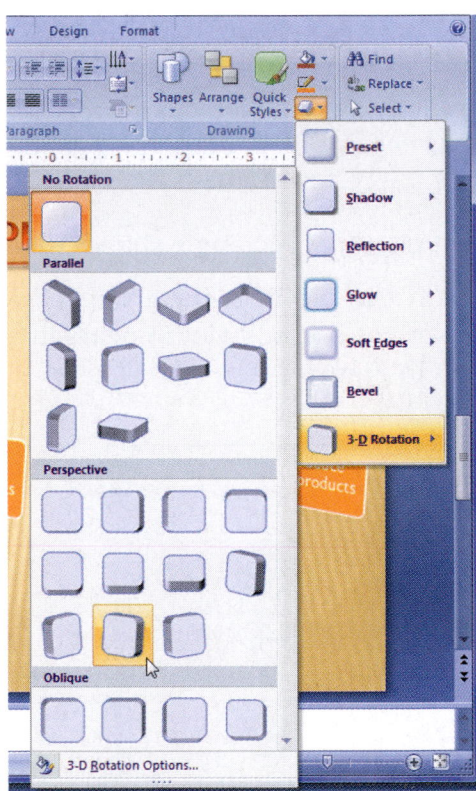

4. Now add two more shape effects to customize this diagram. With the rectangle shapes selected,

   a. click the Shape Effects button ⊡, choose **Bevel**, and then choose the **Circle** bevel.

   b. click the Shape Effects button ⊡, choose **Shadow**, and then from the Outer category choose **Offset Diagonal Top Right**.

   c. click anywhere on the slide to turn off the selection.

5. Select the three arrows and apply the same **Bevel** and **Shadow** effects that were applied to the shapes in step 4.

Exercise 7-7   ADJUST THE OVERALL SIZE AND LAYOUT OF THE DIAGRAM

Diagrams can be resized like any other PowerPoint object. However, you must always be sure the text is still readable if the size of shapes is reduced. You may need to use only a single word on small shapes if their size becomes small. In this exercise, you will experiment with a couple of sizing techniques.

1. Duplicate slide 4 then make the following changes on the slide 5 diagrams.

2. Notice that the four rectangles and connecting arrows extend across the complete slide so you don't have any extra horizontal room

unless the shapes become smaller. Resize the SmartArt area by dragging the right side about a half inch to the left. The text on the shapes becomes slightly smaller.

3. Resize the top and bottom of the SmartArt area so it is just large enough to contain the shapes.

4. Drag this diagram up to fit directly under the slide title.

5. With the diagram selected, press Ctrl + D to duplicate the diagram. Position the second diagram evenly below the first one. Duplicating is a quick way to make a second diagram because you can simply edit the text on each shape for new wording without having to reset the Shape Effects.

6. On the second diagram, expand its space then change the position of the shapes, as shown in Figure 7-9. Follow these steps:

   a. Resize the bottom border of the duplicated SmartArt area to increase the size of available space for positioning shapes.

   b. Select the first rectangle and drag it to the upper left. Notice that the arrow between this rectangle and the second one automatically repositions itself.

   c. Select the second rectangle and move it to the left.

   d. Select the third rectangle and move it to the left and down slightly. Be careful that you allow enough space for the arrow.

   e. Select the fourth rectangle and move it to the left and down slightly.

   f. Adjust rectangle positioning by nudging (using the arrow keys) so the arrows remain approximately the same size.

7. Now you are still portraying the four-step process because of the connecting arrows that show the direction. But with only one diagram in this arrangement, you would have enough room on the slide for a picture or some other graphic element to accompany the diagram.

Figure 7-9
A Process diagram
arranged two ways

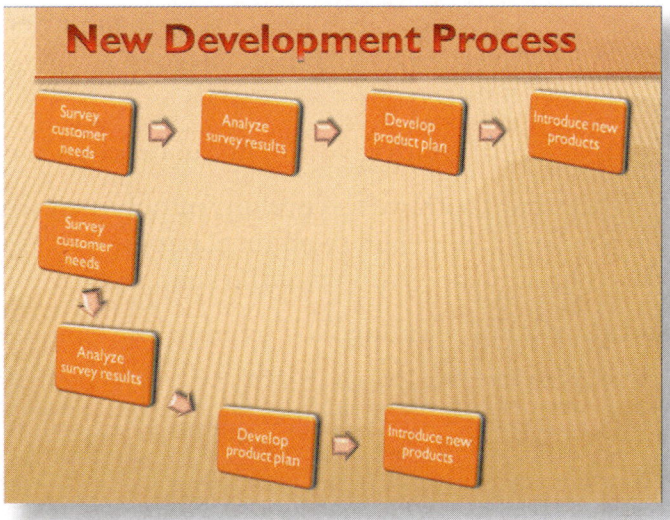

8. Update the handout footer text to **[7-7your initials]**.

9. Move to slide 1 and save the presentation as **[7-7your initials]** in your Lesson 7 folder. Leave the presentation open for the next exercise.

Exercise 7-8   ADD SHAPES

In Exercise 7-3, you added a shape so you already have some experience in modifying SmartArt. The different diagrams add shapes in different places, so the shape you have selected when you add another shape is important because the new shape is normally connected to the selected one in some way.

1. Move to slide 6 and create a new slide with the **Title and Content** layout. Key **Adding SmartArt Shapes** as the slide title. Click the SmartArt button 🖼 in the content placeholder.

2. From the List category, choose the **Stacked List** then click **OK**.

3. Now edit the text on each shape as follows:

    a. In the circle on the left, key **One**, then for the related text key **First item** and **Second item**.

    b. In the circle on the right, key **Two**, then for the related text key **First item** and **Second item**.

    c. Notice that the text will automatically resize and word-wrap for each shape.

4. Now under the left circle labeled "One," click the "First item" text to select that shape. From the SmartArt Tools Design tab, in the Create Graphic group, click the bottom part of the Add Shape button 🔲 then choose **Add Shape After**. A new shape appears below the first item and the diagram has been resized. Key **New item** in this shape.

5. Now select the left circle labeled "One." Click the bottom part of the Add Shape 🔲 then choose **Add Shape After**. This time a second circle with a related rectangle shape is added, as shown in Figure 7-10.

6. In the added circle, key **New**; in the related shape, key **New item**.

7. Notice that you have the options of before and after as well as above and below when you are adding shapes, so it is very important that you choose where you want the shape to go.

8. Also, you can rearrange the order of the shapes in a diagram. Select the circle labeled "New." From the SmartArt Tools Design tab, in the Create Graphic group, click the Right to Left button ⇄ and the diagram is displayed from right to left. Click the button again to display the diagram from left to right.

Figure 7-10
Adding SmartArt
shapes

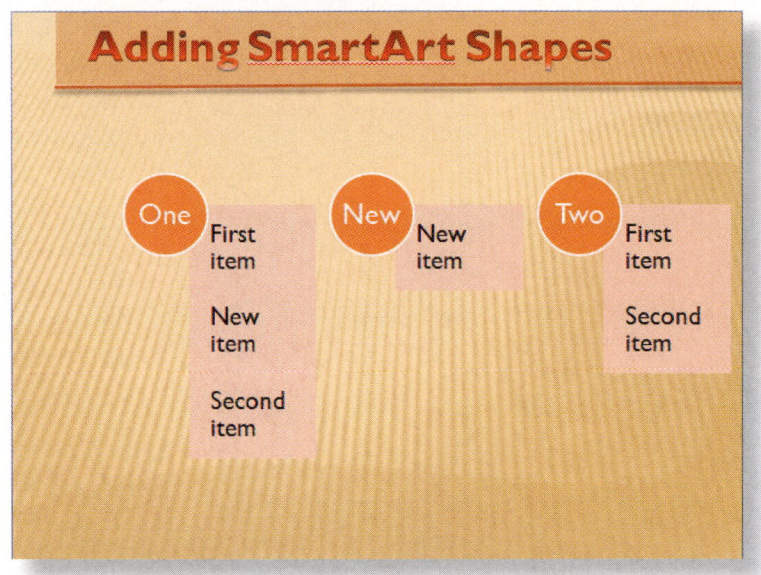

Exercise 7-9 **CHANGE COLORS AND
RESET THE GRAPHIC**

You have already used Quick Styles to change a diagram's appearance.
Many more options are available from the SmartArt Tools Design tab, in the
SmartArt Styles group, as shown in Figure 7-11.

1. On slide 7 select the SmartArt diagram. From the SmartArt Tools
   Design tab, in the SmartArt Styles group, click the More button ⬇ to
   see the complete gallery of SmartArt Styles arranged in two categories,
   Best Match for Document and 3-D. As you point to these thumbnails
   you will see that effect applied to your diagram.

Figure 7-11
SmartArt Styles

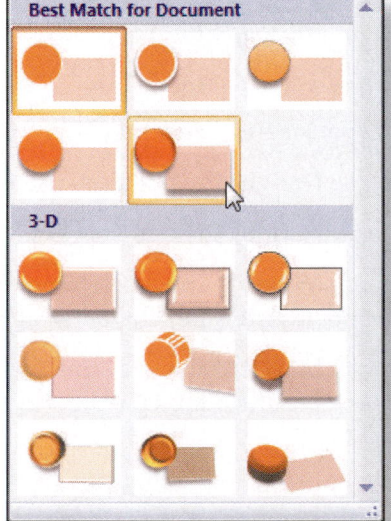

2. Click the **Intense Effect** thumbnail
   and this effect is automatically
   applied.

3. With your SmartArt diagram
   selected, from the SmartArt Tools
   Design tab, in the SmartArt Styles
   group, click the Change Colors
   button 🎨. Colors are arranged in
   eight categories: Primary Theme
   Colors, Colorful, and six Accent
   colors. The current color is selected,
   as shown in Figure 7-12.

Figure 7-12
Change colors for a
SmartArt diagram

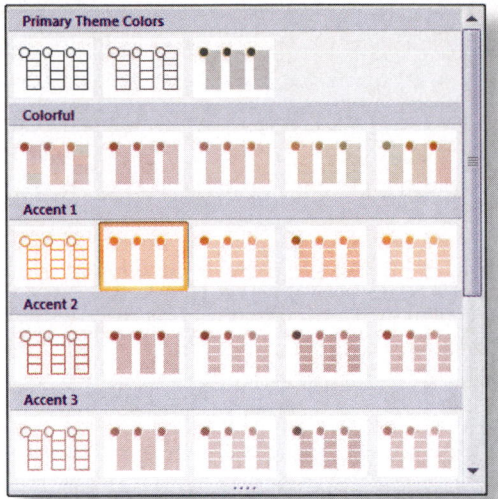

4. Point to different thumbnails in this gallery of colors and consider the changes on your slide. Notice that colors change as you go down the list between the various accent colors in the presentation's design theme. Then as you go across different line and shading treatments are used.

5. Select the **Gradient Loop – Accent 5** color.

6. If you are not pleased with your change, it is always easy to remove it. From the SmartArt Tools Design tab, in the Reset group, click the Reset Graphic button 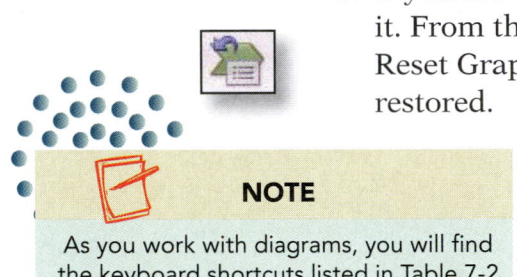 and the original style of your diagram is restored.

7. Update the handout footer text to **[7-9your initials]**.

8. Move to slide 1 and save the presentation as **[7-9your initials]** in your Lesson 7 folder. Leave the presentation open for the next exercise.

NOTE

As you work with diagrams, you will find the keyboard shortcuts listed in Table 7-2 helpful because they provide a quick way to move between shapes, select shapes, or select the text within the shapes.

TABLE 7-2 Using the Keyboard to Navigate in SmartArt Graphics

Key	Result
F2	Toggles the current shape between being selected and activated.
Esc	Deactivates a selected shape.
Enter	Activated shape: Inserts a new text line.
← or →	Selected shape: Nudges the position of the shape left or right.
↑ or ↓	Selected shape: Nudges the position of the shape up or down.
Tab	Selected shape: Moves to the next shape. Activated shape: Inserts a tab character at the insertion point.
Shift + Tab	Selected shape: Moves to the previous shape. Activated shape: Inserts a tab character at the insertion point.

Preparing an Organization Chart

Organization charts are most commonly used to show a hierarchy such as the lines of authority or reporting relationships in a business. You start an organization chart in the same way as other SmartArt graphics, but it is important to consider superior and subordinate relationships.

Exercise 7-10   CREATE AN ORGANIZATION CHART

When you start a new organization chart, you begin with a default arrangement of five rectangular shapes. Each shape is positioned on a *level* in the chart, which indicates its position in the hierarchy. The top shape indicates the highest level with a direct line down to the second level (such as the president of a company and the managers who report to the president). The shape that branches from the central line reflects a supporting position (such as an assistant to the president).

1. Insert a new slide after slide 7 that uses the **Title and Content** layout. Key the title **New Management Structure**.

2. In the content placeholder click the SmartArt button 🖼️ .

3. Choose the **Hierarchy** category then click the **Organization Chart** thumbnail and click **OK**. A chart with five shapes appears with text placeholders that show text in a large size. The text size will become smaller as you key text.

4. Move your pointer to the top shape in the chart and click inside the text placeholder. Notice the dashed outline that indicates the shape is activated.

5. Key **Julie Wolfe &** then press Enter and key **Gus Irvinelli** to position the names on two lines. You will later format this text to fit on one line.

6. Press Enter to start a new line and key **Co-owners**.

7. Press Esc to deactivate text editing. The shape now has a solid outline.

8. Press Tab to move to the first lower-level shape.

9. Key the following three items on three lines:

   Administration
   Michael Peters
   Administration Mgr

10. The text becomes smaller to fit in the shape. Press F2 to deactivate text editing.

11. Press Tab to move to the second shape on the lower level. Key the following items on three lines:

    Sales & Marketing
    Roy Olafsen
    Marketing Mgr

12. Press F2 then press Tab to move to the third shape and key the following items on three lines:

    Operations
    Michele Jenkins
    Head Chef

13. Press F2 then press Tab to move to the shape that branches from the central line and press Delete.

14. Click outside the SmartArt area to deactivate the organization chart, as shown in Figure 7-13.

Figure 7-13
Organization chart

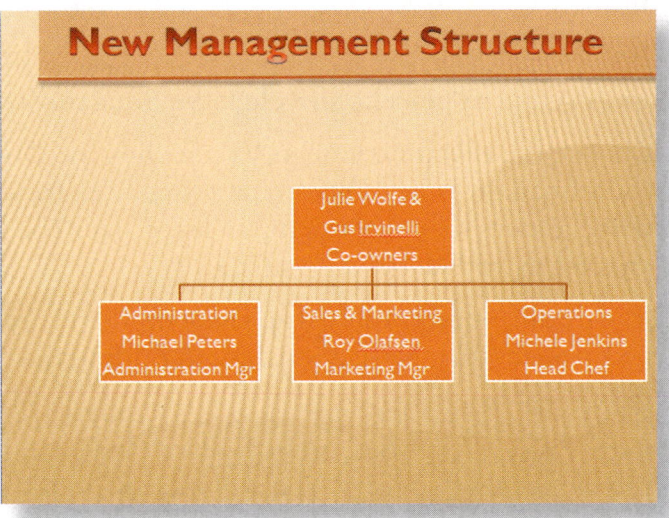

15. Update the handout footer text to **[7-10your initials]**.

16. Save the presentation as **[7-10your initials]** in your Lesson 7 folder. Leave the presentation open for the next exercise.

Exercise 7-11   INSERT SUBORDINATE SHAPES

The organization of many companies changes frequently. You might need to promote, demote, or move organization chart shapes as the reporting structure changes or becomes more complex.

To expand your organization chart as shown in Figure 7-14, you can insert additional shapes of the following types:

- *Subordinate shapes*—shapes that are connected to a superior shape (a shape on a higher level).

- *Coworker shapes*—shapes that are connected to the same superior shape as another shape.

- *Assistant shapes*—shapes that are usually placed below a superior shape and above subordinate shapes.

Figure 7-14
Structure of an
organization chart

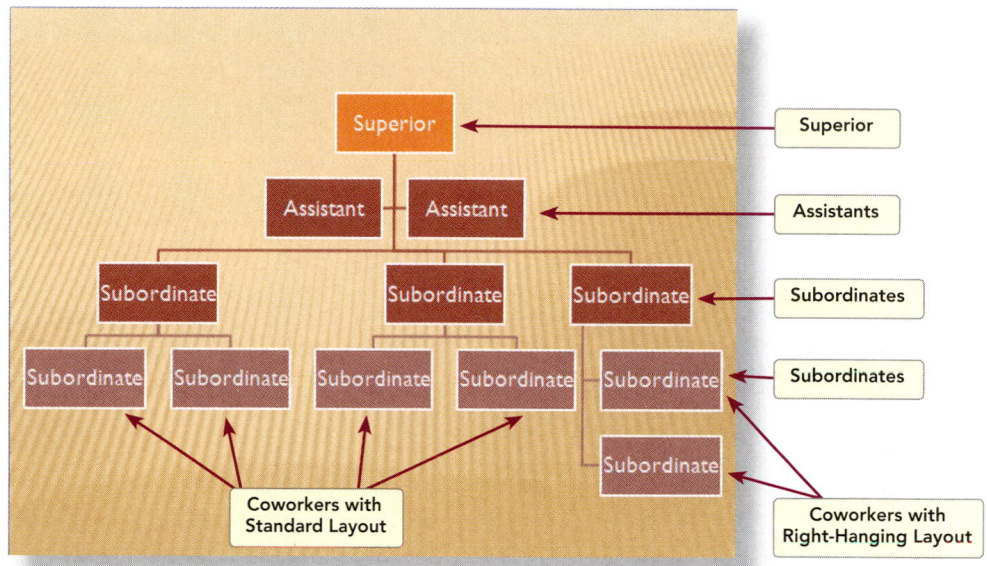

To add *subordinate shapes*, first select the shape that will be their superior; then from the SmartArtTools Design tab, in the Create Graphic group, click the Add Shape button .

1. Still working on slide 8, select the first shape on the second level, with the name "Michael Peters."

Figure 7-15
Adding organization
chart shapes

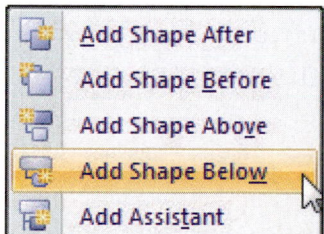

2. From the SmartArt Tools Design tab, in the Create Graphic group, click the lower half of the Add Shape button 🔲 then from the pop-up list select **Add Shape Below**. A shape appears below the selected shape with a connecting line and now the new shape is selected.

3. Click the lower half of the Add Shape button 🔲, then from the pop-up list select **Add Shape Before**, as shown in Figure 7-15. Now two shapes show a reporting relationship to Michael Peters. They are currently shown with a **Right-Hanging Layout**. All the shapes automatically become smaller, so the chart will fit on the slide.

4. Repeat this process to add one shape under Roy Olafsen and three shapes under Michele Jenkins. Once again the shapes are resized to fit, but the text is now too small to read. This will be corrected later.

NOTE

Both Add Shape After and Add Shape Before insert new shapes at different levels. Add Shape Above inserts a new shape in the level above, which would be a superior position. Add Shape Below inserts a new shape in the level below, which would be a subordinate position. Add Assistant inserts a new shape between levels.

Exercise 7-12 ADD ASSISTANT AND COWORKER SHAPES

Assistant shapes are used for positions that provide administrative assistance or other support. They are inserted below a selected shape, but above the next-lower level.

Coworker shapes are inserted at the same level as the selected shape and report to the same superior as the selected shape.

1. On slide 8, select the level 1 shape.

2. From the SmartArt Tools Design tab, in the Create Graphic group, click the Add Shape button 🖰 and choose **Add Assistant**. A new shape is inserted between levels 1 and 2.

3. Select the shape below Michael Peters to add another shape at the same level. From the SmartArt Tools Design tab, in the Create Graphic group, click the Add Shape button 🖰 and choose **Add Shape Before**. A new shape is inserted at the same level—this represents a coworker.

4. Repeat step 3 to add one shape under Roy Olafsen.

5. Now increase the slide size so you can more easily see the text. From the View tab, in the Zoom group, click the Zoom button 🔍 and choose **200%** then click **OK**.

6. On the enlarged slide, scroll to locate the assistant shape below the level 1 shape. Key **Troy Scott**, press Enter, then key **Assistant** so this text fits on two text lines.

7. In the three shapes under Michael Peters, key the following employee information on two text lines in each shape. After the text is entered, press F2 or Esc to deactivate the shape and then press Tab to move to the next shape.

MIS	Billing	HR
Chuck Warden	**Sarah Conners**	**Chris Davis**

8. After keying the text in Chris Davis's shape, press Esc to deactivate the text shape. Press Tab one time to move to Roy Olafsen's shape, and press Tab to move to the first shape under Roy Olafsen.

9. In the two shapes under Roy Olafsen, key the following employee information:

Events	Marketing
Ian Mahoney	**Evan Johnson**

10. In the first two shapes under Michele Jenkins, key the following and leave the last shape blank:

Kitchen	Purchasing
Eric Dennis	**Jessie Smith**

11. Notice that the organization chart again adjusted the text to a smaller size, as shown in Figure 7-16. From the View tab, in the Zoom group, click the Fit to Window button 🖰.

Figure 7-16
Organization chart
with text

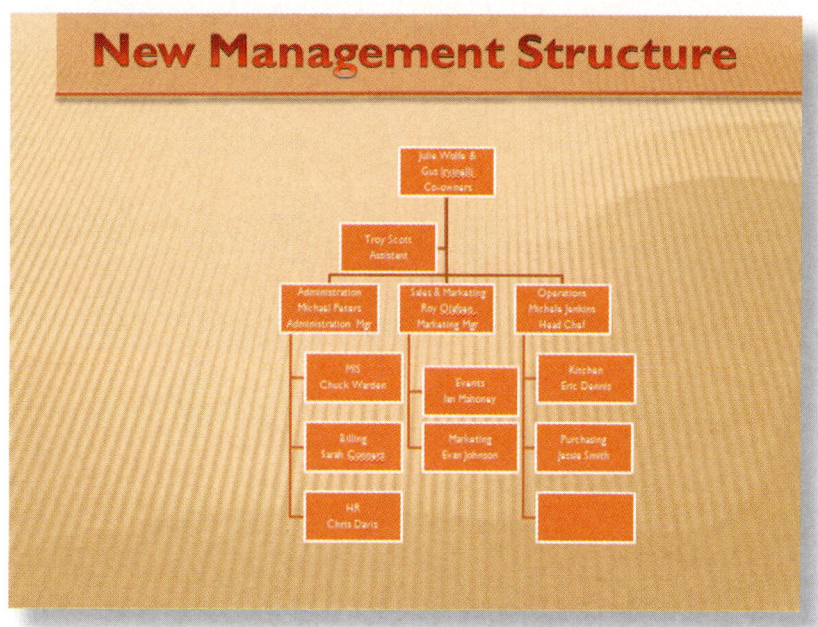

Exercise 7-13　CHANGE LAYOUT, DELETE, AND REARRANGE SHAPES

The layout of the organization chart can be changed to show subordinates in a *standard* format or a *hanging indent* format. A shape can be repositioned to a higher level by promoting (moving up) or repositioned to a lower level by demoting (moving down). An entire group of connected shapes can be moved right or left. If you have more shapes than necessary, you can delete them at any time.

1. On slide 8, select the shape for Michael Peters. From the SmartArt Tools Design tab, in the Create Graphic group, click the Layout button and choose **Standard**. The subordinate shapes below Michael Peters (co-workers) are now arranged side by side instead of in a vertical, hanging arrangement.

2. Select the blank subordinate shape below Michele Jenkins and press Delete .

3. Select the shape for Eric Dennis and click the Promote button . It moves up a level and the connected shape moves with it. Click the Undo button .

4. Click Roy Olafsen's shape and change the Layout to **Standard**. Repeat this process to change the Layout for Michele Jenkins's shape to **Standard**.

5. This arrangement communicates nicely the three levels of the organization as shown in Figure 7-17; however, the text is very small. The next steps will rearrange the layout so each shape can be a little larger.

Figure 7-17
Organization chart with standard layout

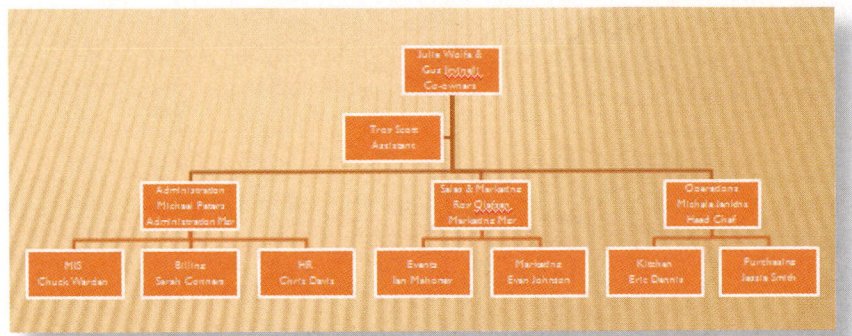

6. Select the shape for Michael Peters. From the SmartArt Tools Design tab, in the Create Graphic group, click the Layout button and choose **Right Hanging**. Repeat this process to apply the **Right Hanging** indent to the other two level 2 shapes.

7. Select the shape of Sarah Conners and click the Demote button. Now this shape is indented under Chuck Warden.

8. Select the shape for Michael Peters and click the Right to Left button and this entire branch of the chart is reordered to appear on the right, as shown in Figure 7-18.

Figure 7-18
Organization chart with hanging indent layout

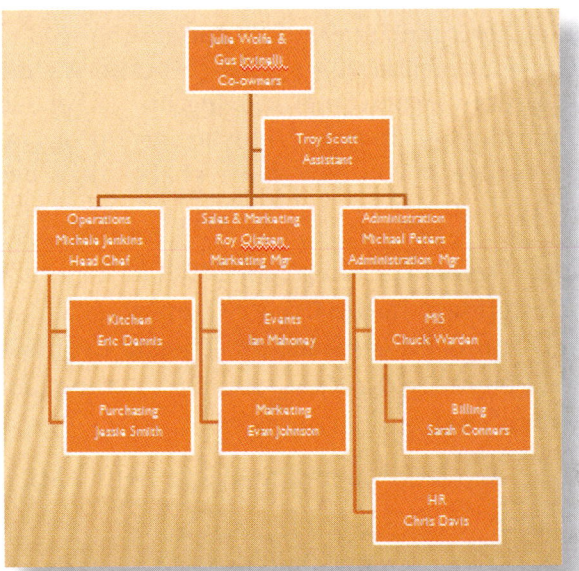

9. Update the handout footer text to **[7-13your initials]**.

10. Save the presentation as **[7-13your initials]** in your Lesson 7 folder. Leave the presentation open for the next exercise.

Exercise 7-14   CHANGE SHAPE SIZING AND STYLES

The entire SmartArt area can be made larger to accommodate charts with several levels. Selected shapes can be resized, and connected shapes repositioned so the text fits better. Text can be made larger, too.

1. On slide 8, resize the SmartArt area by dragging its border to expand it horizontally on both sides as well as vertically.

2. Select the level 1 shape and resize it horizontally to make it wider so both names fit on one line.

3. Select all three level 2 shapes and resize horizontally and vertically to allow a little more room in each shape.

4. Select all of the chart's shapes and increase the font size to 16 points in bold. Adjust the horizontal size of shapes if the text word-wraps.

5. Now spread apart the related shapes in the chart for easier reading. Select the Michael Peters shape and the related shapes below him. Press Ctrl and the right arrow about five times to move this branch to the right. The connecting lines automatically adjust.

6. Select the Michele Jenkins shape and the related shapes below her. Press Ctrl and the left arrow about five times to move this branch to the right.

7. With the SmartArt area selected, from the SmartArt Tools Design tab, in the SmartArt Styles group, click the Change Colors button and select the **Colorful – Accent Colors** thumbnail.

8. You can also change the color of individual shapes. Select the Assistant shape and then from the SmartArt Tools Format tab, in the Shape Styles group, choose a Shape Fill that will make the fill color a little lighter.

9. From the SmartArt Tools Design tab, in the SmartArt Styles group, examine the effect of different SmartArt Styles on the chart. Click the SmartArt Styles More button 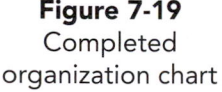 then choose the **Intense Effect**, as shown in Figure 7-19.

10. Update the handout footer text to **[7-14your initials]**. Save the presentation as **[7-14your initials]** in your Lesson 7 folder. Leave the presentation open for the next exercise.

Figure 7-19
Completed
organization chart

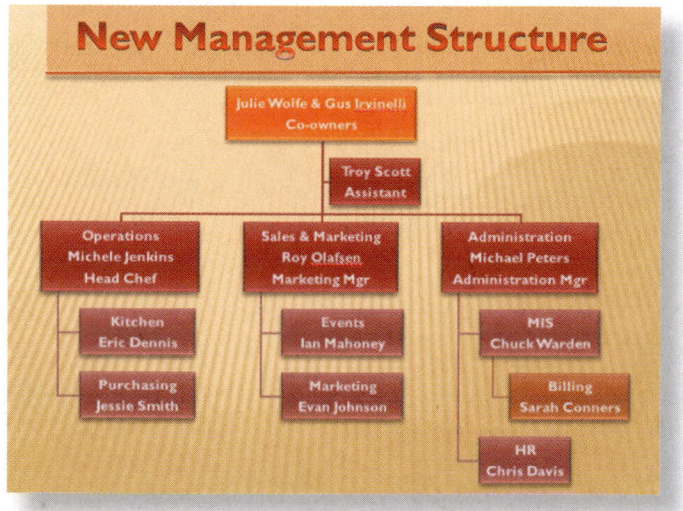

Creating Other Diagrams with SmartArt

The seven categories of PowerPoint SmartArt graphics offer many options to illustrate your thoughts in a visual way. This exercise will focus on three diagrams in the Relationship category.

Exercise 7-15   CREATE A RADIAL DIAGRAM

A *radial diagram* starts with a central circle (level 1) with four circles (level 2) connected to and surrounding the center circle. You can insert as many additional circles as you need to illustrate your message.

1. Insert a new slide after slide 8 that uses the **Title and Content** layout. Key the title **New Customer Philosophy**.

2. From the content placeholder click the SmartArt button 🖼.

3. Choose the **Relationship** category, then click the **Basic Radial** thumbnail and click **OK**. A chart appears with four circle shapes that radiate from the center circle with text placeholders.

4. Click the center circle, then from the SmartArt Tools Design tab, in the Create Graphic group, click the Add Shape button 🔲 and a new circle is added to the diagram. It becomes the selected circle.

5. Press Delete to remove this new shape.

6. With the center circle selected, key **Customer**.

7. Think about your positioning as though referring to the face of a round clock. Click the top outer circle (12 o'clock position) and key the information shown under "12 o'clock" in Figure 7-20. Press Enter after the individual words, so the information appears on three text lines.

8. Click the circle at the 3 o'clock position and key the corresponding text.

9. Working in a clockwise direction, key the remaining text shown in Figure 7-20 in the remaining outer circles.

NOTE

If PowerPoint automatically capitalizes the second and third word in each circle, change the letters to lowercase. Automatic capitalization is caused by the AutoCorrect in PowerPoint. You can turn off this feature, if you wish, by clicking the Microsoft Office button 🔘, click the PowerPoint Options button 🔲 PowerPoint Options, choose **Proofing**, click **AutoCorrection Options**, deselect **Capitalize first letter of sentences**, then click **OK**.

Figure 7-20
Radial diagram text

12 o'clock	3 o'clock	6 o'clock	9 o'clock
Satisfy	Provide	Provide	Resolve
customer	courteous	excellent	problems
needs	service	quality	promptly

10. From the SmartArt Tools Design tab, in the SmartArt Styles group, click the Change Colors button 🔲 and choose **Colored Fill – Accent 6**. Then click the SmartArt Styles More button 🔽 and look at the effect of different options as you point to them. Choose the **Cartoon** style.

11. Drag the borders of the SmartArt area to increase the size of the diagram.

12. Choose the center shape, then from the SmartArt Tools Format tab, in the Shape Styles group, choose a darker shade of the shape fill color to emphasize the center, as shown in Figure 7-21.

13. Update the handout footer text to **[7-15your initials]**. Save the presentation as **[7-15your initials]** in your Lesson 7 folder. Leave the presentation open for the next exercise.

Figure 7-21
Radial diagram

Exercise 7-16   CREATE A GEAR DIAGRAM

Gears have spokes that stick out and lock with other gears to make them turn. The turning of each gear is dependent on the other gears. Therefore, the *gear diagram* communicates interlocking ideas that are shown as shapes.

1. Insert a new slide after slide 9 that uses the **Title and Content** layout. Key the title **Interlocking Ideas**.

2. From the content placeholder click the SmartArt button 🖼️.

3. Choose the **Relationship** category, then click the **Gear** thumbnail and click **OK**. A chart with three shapes and directional arrows appears. Key the text as shown in Figure 7-22.

4. From the SmartArt Tools Design Tab, in the SmartArt Styles group, choose the SmartArt Styles More button ⬇ and choose the **3-D Inset style**.

5. Resize and reposition the SmartArt graphic attractively.

Figure 7-22
Completed Gear diagram

6. Update the handout footer text to **[7-16your initials]**. Save the presentation as **[7-16your initials]** in your Lesson 7 folder. Leave the presentation open for the next exercise.

Exercise 7-17   INSERT A CONTINUOUS PICTURE LIST

The *Continuous Picture List* contains round placeholders for pictures and a horizontal arrow to communicate that the items shown represent interconnected information.

1. Insert a new slide after slide 10 that uses the **Title and Content** layout. Key the title **New Desserts**.

2. From the content placeholder click the SmartArt button 🖼.

3. Choose the **Relationship** category, then click the **Continuous Picture List** thumbnail and click **OK**. A chart appears with three shapes that each contain a small circle with a picture placeholder.

4. Click the first picture placeholder to access the Insert Picture dialog shape. Navigate to where your student files are located, select the **cake** picture, and click **Insert**.

5. Repeat this process on the next two placeholders, inserting the **cookies** picture in the middle shape and the **strawberry** picture in the right shape.

6. Now key text below each of the pictures as shown in Figure 7-23 and the text will automatically resize:

   Fruit Cake Holiday Delight
   Oatmeal and Raisin Cookies
   Cream Cake and Strawberries

7. From the SmartArt Tools Design tab, in the SmartArt Styles group, click the More button ⬇ and select the **3-D, Polished** style.

8. Resize and reposition the SmartArt graphic attractively on the slide.

9. Update the handout footer text to **[7-17your initials]**. Save the presentation as **[7-17your initials]** in your Lesson 7 folder. Leave the presentation open for the next exercise.

Figure 7-23
Continuous Picture List

Changing Diagram Types and Orientation

Once a SmartArt diagram is created, the type of diagram can easily be changed by selecting a thumbnail from a different category. However, the levels of your information may not translate well into some layouts. The orientation of a diagram can be changed if an appropriate layout can be used. Shapes within the SmartArt area can also be repositioned by dragging them.

Exercise 7-18   CHANGE DIAGRAM TYPES

At any time during the development of your SmartArt diagram, you can apply a different SmartArt graphic to create a different diagram. Level 1 information and level 2 information will be reformatted to fit the new layout, so the layout you choose must have matching levels.

NOTE

Because this is a List diagram, you see those choices first. You could access all diagrams by clicking the More button ⬇.

1. Move to slide 3 and select it in the Slides and Outline pane. Press Ctrl+C to copy the slide, move to the end of your slide series, and press Ctrl+V to paste the slide after slide 11.

2. Now working on slide 12, select the SmartArt graphic, then from the SmartArt Tools Design tab,

in the Layouts group, click on several different Layout thumbnails to consider the different diagrams that are available. Notice how the level 1 and level 2 information is arranged and consider the emphasis that each level receives. The next three steps will point out specific diagrams to try and what you should notice in each one.

3. Click the **Table Hierarchy** thumbnail. This layout does not distinguish between the levels; level 1 information is placed above level 2, but no color or lines are used to show any connecting effect or relationship between the levels.

4. Click the **Grouped List** thumbnail. Now it is easy to see that certain items relate to other items because the shapes used for level 1 create a sort of container for the shapes used for level 2 information. It tends to emphasize level 2 text.

5. Click the **Vertical Arrow List**. This layout clearly distinguishes between the two levels and it works well for bulleted lists of information. The arrows on which level 2 information is displayed communicate that the level 2 information is an outgrowth of level 1.

6. The fill color on the arrows blends too much with the slide background to be easily visible, so change the colors and the style to make the arrows stand out more. From the SmartArt Tools Design tab, in the SmartArt Styles group, click Change Colors 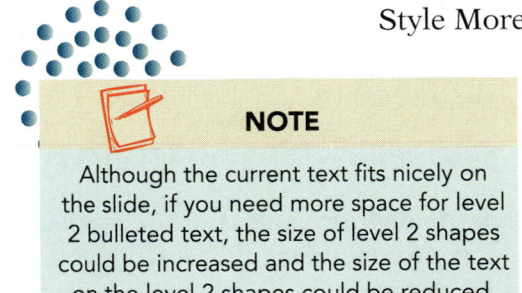 then choose **Colorful Range – Accent Colors 5 to 6**. Then click the SmartArt Style More button and choose the **3-D, Polished** style.

7. Select the three arrows, then from the SmartArt Tools Format tab, in the Shape Styles group, click the Shape Fill button and choose the **Orange, Accent 6, Lighter 40%** color. Now the arrows still blend with the theme design, but they are easier to see, as shown in Figure 7-24.

8. Leave your presentation open for the next exercise.

NOTE

Although the current text fits nicely on the slide, if you need more space for level 2 bulleted text, the size of level 2 shapes could be increased and the size of the text on the level 2 shapes could be reduced.

Figure 7-24
Diagram with changed layout

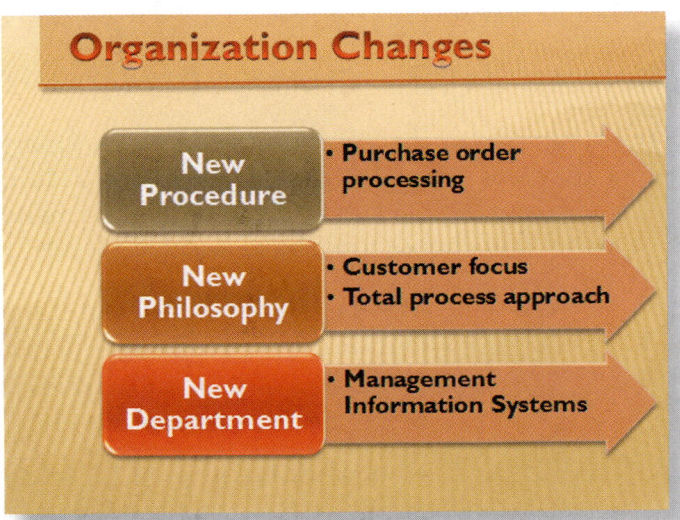

Exercise 7-19 CHANGE THE ORIENTATION OF DIAGRAMS

Because of the particular information a diagram must contain, the information may need to be displayed in a different orientation than the original SmartArt shape provides. For example, instead of a top to bottom orientation, it might need to be left to right.

1. From the Slides and Outline pane, select slide 8 and copy it. Move to the last slide in your presentation and paste the slide.

2. Now on slide 13, select the SmartArt diagram. From the SmartArt Tools Design tab, in the Layouts group, click the More button 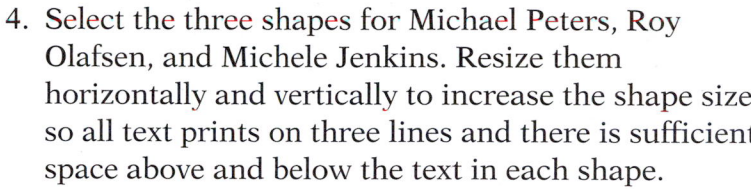 and choose the **Horizontal Hierarchy** layout. The shapes are now positioned horizontally as in a decision-tree diagram.

3. While the shapes are still connected, the sizes should be adjusted on some of them.

NOTE

Within the SmartArt area, shapes can be repositioned; therefore, a diagram such as the one on slide 7 could be redesigned manually to show the circles in a vertical arrangement and the shapes extending horizontally to the right.

4. Select the three shapes for Michael Peters, Roy Olafsen, and Michele Jenkins. Resize them horizontally and vertically to increase the shape size so all text prints on three lines and there is sufficient space above and below the text in each shape.

5. Select the MIS shape and all the ones below it and the Billing shape. Resize these shapes horizontally so each name fits on one text line, as shown in Figure 7-25.

6. Increase the vertical size of the Julie Wolfe & Gus Irvinelli shape.

Figure 7-25
Diagram with different orientation

7. Update the handout footer text to **[7-19your initials]**.

8. Save the presentation as **[7-19your initials]** in your Lesson 7 folder. Print the presentation as handouts in landscape orientation with nine slides on a page.

9. Close the presentation.

Lesson 7 Summary

- SmartArt graphics are used to represent information in a visual manner.
- SmartArt graphics are arranged into seven different categories that include a wide variety of diagrams such as organization charts, radial diagrams, list diagrams, and relationship diagrams.
- The SmartArt Tools Design tab has command buttons to insert shapes and modify the predefined diagram layouts. Shapes can be added and removed.
- List diagrams provide an alternative to listing information in a bulleted list because concise text can be placed on shapes that help to communicate categories and subtopics.
- Process diagrams show a sequence of events or the progression of workflow.
- Cycle diagrams communicate a continuous or ongoing process.
- Hierarchy diagrams are used to describe a hierarchical structure, showing who reports to whom, and who is responsible for what function or task.
- Pyramid diagrams show interconnected or proportional relationships.
- Relationship diagrams contain interconnected shapes that reflect relationships in some way.
- Matrix diagrams display two axes in related quadrants that emphasize the whole or the individual parts.
- An organization chart is a type of hierarchy chart in a tree structure, branching out to multiple divisions in each lower level.
- When a chart shape is promoted, it moves up a level. When a chart shape is demoted, it moves down a level.
- A SmartArt Text pane provides a quick way to enter the text that labels diagram shapes.
- List diagrams can show both level 1 and level 2 information, but text must be concise for easy reading.
- Text entered in SmartArt shapes automatically resizes to fit the shape; if shapes increase in size, the text they contain increases in size.
- An existing bulleted list can be converted to a SmartArt graphic.
- Quick Styles provide choices for color and effect changes such as outlines, beveling, and shadows that can be applied to any selected shape.
- SmartArt Styles consist of predefined effects that work well together for diagrams.
- An illusion of depth is created with 3-D style options.
- Shapes can be repositioned within the SmartArt area.
- The Change Colors option provides many possible variations of theme colors.

- If color changes made to a SmartArt graphic are unacceptable, the colors can be reset to their original colors.
- Several layouts in the List category have placeholders for pictures.

LESSON 7		Command Summary
Feature	Button	Ribbon
Create a graphical list or diagram on a slide.		Insert, Illustrations group, Insert SmartArt Graphic
Change text from a bulleted list to a diagram		Home, Paragraph group, Convert to SmartArt Graphics
Pick from choices for shape color and effects		Home, Drawing group, Quick Styles
Rearrange diagram direction or sequencing of shapes		SmartArt Tools Design, Create Graphic group, Right to Left
Open a gallery of thumbnails showing available options		Available on many Ribbons, More
Select from variations of theme colors		SmartArt Tools Design, SmartArt Styles group, Change Colors
Change back to original formatting		SmartArt Tools Design, Reset group, Reset Graphic
Create additional shapes within a diagram		SmartArt Tools Design, Create Graphic group, Add Shape
Change organization chart layout		SmartArt Tools Design, Create Graphic group, Layout
Increase the level of a selected bulleted item or shape		SmartArt Tools Design, Create Graphic group, Promote
Decrease the level of a selected bulleted item or shape		SmartArt Tools Design, Create Graphic group, Demote
Change the color of a selected shape		SmartArt Tools Format, Shape Styles group, Shape Fill

Concepts Review

True/False Questions

Each of the following statements is either true or false. Select your choice by indicating T or F.

T F   1. SmartArt contains a wide range of diagrams organized in seven different categories.

T F   2. All the shapes in a diagram must be the same color.

T F   3. An organization chart is an example of a hierarchy diagram.

T F   4. List diagrams can show both level 1 and level 2 information as long as the text is written concisely.

T F   5. If you add too many shapes to an organization chart, you can always delete the extra shapes.

T F   6. Quick Styles provide color and effect choices for selected shapes.

T F   7. SmartArt Styles can be applied to individual shapes in a diagram.

T F   8. The Change Colors option provides choices from Standard Colors.

Short Answer Questions

Write the correct answer in the space provided.

1. How do you create a SmartArt Graphic?

2. What feature enables you to quickly key text to create a SmartArt Graphic?

3. How can you convert an existing bulleted list to a diagram?

4. If you have created a Process diagram, how can you change it to a Cycle diagram?

5. Describe how to change the size of a SmartArt shape.

6. If you have six subordinates reporting to one superior, how do you change the six shapes so they are stacked vertically in two columns?

7. Which categories of SmartArt graphics provide picture placeholders?

8. What type of diagram is used to illustrate a continuous, ongoing relationship?

Critical Thinking

Answer these questions on a separate page. There are no right or wrong answers. Support your answers with examples from your own experience, if possible.

1. When developing your presentation content and making decisions about which SmartArt graphic to use, why is it important to consider your audience's viewpoint?

2. Organization charts are by nature rather detail-oriented. Based on what you learned about designing presentations, how can you ensure that an organization chart is easy to interpret?

Skills Review

Exercise 7-20

Create a list diagram.

1. Open the file **Retail**. Insert a new slide after slide 3 that uses the **Title and Content** layout. Key the title **New Retail Items**. If the text moves to the top of the title placeholder, then from the Home tab, in the Slides group, click the Reset button 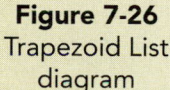 .

2. Insert a Trapezoid List SmartArt graphic by following these steps:
   a. Click the SmartArt button in the content placeholder.
   b. From the **List** category, choose the **Trapezoid List** and click **OK**. A SmartArt graphic will appear with three trapezoid shapes with title and list placeholders.
   c. From the SmartArt Tools Design tab, in the Create Graphic group, click the Text pane button to open the Text pane on the left as shown in Figure 7-26.

Figure 7-26
Trapezoid List diagram

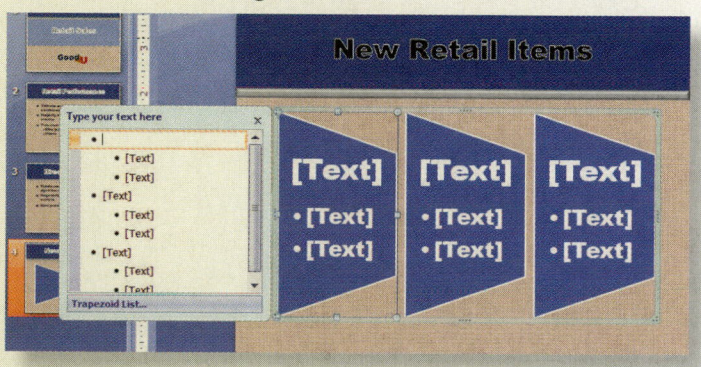

3. The first-level bullet will be the heading in each shape, and the second-level bullet will be the items listed in each shape. Two bulleted items first appear, but as you add a third and fourth item, the text will adjust its size to fit in the shape.

4. Working in the Text pane or directly on each shape, key the text to complete all three shapes as shown in Figure 7-27.

Figure 7-27
Completed
Trapezoid List
diagram

5. Close the Text pane.

6. Create a slide footer for slide 4 only including today's date and the text your name, **[7-20your initials]**.

7. Save the presentation as **[7-20your initials]** in your Lesson 7 folder. Print only slide 4 in full size. Close the presentation.

Exercise 7-21

Create a simple organization chart, change theme colors, and format shapes.

1. Open the file **Kitchen1**. Insert a new slide after slide 3 that uses the Title and Content layout. Key the title Operations.

2. Start an organization chart by following these steps:

   a. From the content placeholder, click the SmartArt button 🖼.

   b. In the Hierarchy category, click the Organization Chart thumbnail then click OK.

   c. In the top shape, key:

   Michele Jenkins
   Head Chef & Operations Mgr

    d. Press [Esc] to deactivate the shape. Click the assistant shape and press [Delete].

    e. In the first shape on the second level, key:

Eric Dennis
Asst Chef & Kitchen Mgr

    f. Press [Esc], press [Tab] to move to the next shape, and then key:

Claudia Pell
Maitre d' & Service Mgr

    g. Press [Esc], press [Tab] to move to the right shape, then press [Delete].

3. Insert subordinate shapes by following these steps:

    a. Select Eric Dennis's shape.

    b. From the SmartArt Tools Design tab, in the Create Graphic group, click the Add Shape button 🔲 then choose **Add Shape Below**.

    c. Now the second shape is selected. To add a second shape at the same level, click the Add Shape button 🔲 then choose **Add Shape After**.

    d. Key the following information in the two shapes:

First shape	**Second shape**
G. Robinson	**S. Stefano**
Sr. Cook	**Sr. Cook, Weekends**

    e. Select Claudia Pell's shape. Using the previous steps b and c, insert two shapes below Claudia Pell and key the following information:

First shape	**Second shape**
T. Domina	**T. Conway**
Banquets	**Facilities & Maint**

4. Change the layout:

    a. Click the shape for Eric Dennis. From the SmartArt Tools Design tab, in the Create Graphic group, click the Layout button 🔲 and choose **Standard** to make the shapes below Eric Dennis appear beside each other.

    b. Repeat this process for the Claudia Pell shape.

5. On all shapes, make the employee names (but not their titles) bold.

6. From the SmartArt Tools Design tab, in the SmartArt Styles group,

    a. click the Change Colors button 🔲 and select Primary Theme Colors of **Dark 2 Outline**.

    b. click the More button 🔽 and choose the **Intense Effect** style.

7. Move the SmartArt graphic up and slightly to the left so it is balanced better on the slide, as shown in Figure 7-28.

8. Create a slide footer for only slide 4 containing today's date and the text your name, **[7-21your initials]**.

Figure 7-28
Completed slide

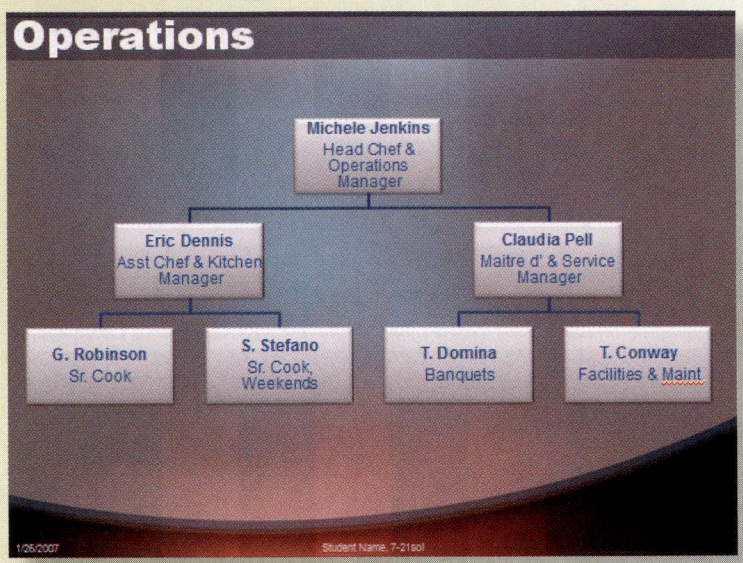

9. Move to slide 1 and save the presentation as **[7-21your initials]** in your Lesson 7 folder.

10. Print slide 4 in full size. Close the presentation.

Exercise 7-22

Create cycle and process diagrams.

1. Open the file **Health**.

2. Insert a new slide after slide 1 that uses the **Title and Content** layout. Key the title **Heart Smart Living**.

3. Create a cycle diagram by following these steps:

   a. Click the SmartArt button 🔲 in the content placeholder.

   b. In the **Cycle** category, click the **Block Cycle** thumbnail. Click **OK**.

   c. With one of the shapes selected, press Delete so you have four shapes in the diagram.

4. Insert text on the diagram by following these steps:

   a. In the top shape, key the text **Get enough** Enter **sleep**.

   b. Press Esc. Click the shape at the 3 o'clock position and key **Eat right when** Enter **you're out**.

   c. Move to the text shape at the 6 o'clock position and key **Eat right** Enter **at home**.

   d. In the text shape at the 9 o'clock position, key **Exercise** Enter **regularly**.

5. Format the four text shapes. Press Ctrl while you click each of the four shapes to select them. Make the following changes:

   a. Make the text bold.

   b. Increase the font size to 20 points then stretch the shapes horizontally so the text in each shape fits on two text lines.

   c. Right-click one of the shapes and from the shortcut menu choose **Change Shape**, then select an oval. Resize the oval shapes if necessary.

6. Insert a new slide after slide 4 that uses the **Title and Content** layout. Key the title **Do What's Good 4 U**.

7. Create a process diagram by following these steps:

   a. Click the SmartArt button 🖼 in the content placeholder.

   b. In the **Process** category, click the **Continuous Block Process** thumbnail. Click **OK**.

   c. With one of the shapes selected, from the SmartArt Tools Design tab, in the Create Graphic group, click the Add Shape button 🔲 and then choose **Add Shape After** so you have four shapes in the diagram.

8. In the first shape on the left, key **Join Our Team!!** Notice that in the small shapes of this diagram the text automatically word-wraps with one word on each line. Key the other text as follows:

   a. Second—**Eat With Us**

   b. Third—**Play With Us**

   c. Fourth—**Walk With Us**

9. Create a handout header and footer: Include the date and your name as the header, and the page number and text **[7-22your initials]** as the footer.

10. Move to slide 1 and save the presentation as **[7-22your initials]** in your Lesson 7 folder.

11. Preview, and then print the entire presentation as handouts, six slides per page, grayscale, landscape, framed. Close the presentation.

Exercise 7-23

Add, promote, demote, and rearrange shapes in an existing organizational chart.

1. Open the file **Kitchen2**. Move to slide 3 and click the organization chart to make it active.

2. Add three subordinate shapes to the G. Robinson level 2 shape, and key the information shown in Figure 7-29.

Figure 7-29
Content for organization chart

First shape	Second shape	Third shape
Pastry	Cooks	Banquets
G. Gordon	L. Tilson	T. Domina
J. Lemmer	S. Mason	J. Fulman

3. Adjust the format by following these steps:

   a. Select the level 3 Banquets shape and then from the SmartArt Tools Design tab, in the Create Graphic group, click the Promote button ⬦ to move it up to level 2.

   b. Select the level 2 Facilities shape then from the SmartArt Tools Design tab, in the Create Graphic group, click the Layout button ⬦ and choose **Left Hanging**.

   c. Using the sizing handles on the organization chart border, make the chart larger, as shown in Figure 7-30.

   d. Make the text on all shapes bold.

   e. Apply the **Moderate Effect** SmartArt Style.

   f. In all shapes, change the first text line to 14 points and the font color to **Gray-80%, Text 2, Darker 25%**.

Figure 7-30
Completed slide

4. Create a handout header and footer: Include the date and your name as the header, and the page number and text **[7-23your initials]** as the footer.

5. Move to slide 1 and save the presentation as **[7-23your initials]** in your Lesson 7 folder.

6. Print the organization chart slide in full size. Preview, and then print the entire presentation as handouts, three slides per page, grayscale, framed. Close the presentation.

Lesson Applications

Exercise 7-24

Create a process diagram and a list diagram and apply SmartArt styles.

1. Open the file **Market1**.

2. On slide 3, select the two bulleted items. From the Home tab, in the Paragraph group, click the Convert to SmartArt Graphic button 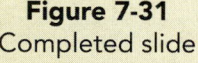. Choose **More SmartArt Graphics**.

3. Choose the **Process** category and consider which diagrams would best show these two different media categories. Click the **Arrow Ribbon** thumbnail and then click **OK**.

4. The two words are now positioned on a shape with arrows pointing in two directions.

5. Because this is such a simple shape and only two words are used, the SmartArt graphic is very large. Resize it to make the diagram smaller so it does not overpower the slide.

6. For slides 4 and 5, consider the type of diagrams that would be well suited for these lists that contain one item on level 1 and four or more items on level 2. Plan to use the same diagram on both slides.

7. On slide 4, select the bulleted list and from the Home tab, in the Paragraph group, click the Convert to SmartArt Graphic button 📄 and choose **More SmartArt Graphics**.

8. From the **List** category, choose the **Pyramid list** thumbnail and click **OK**. Now the text is positioned over a pyramid shape that can imply volume or levels of importance.

9. Repeat this process to convert the bulleted text on slide 5 to the same diagram. This time the height of the text shapes is smaller because six items are listed.

10. For slides 4 and 5, apply the SmartArt Style **Metallic Scene**, as shown in Figure 7-31.

Figure 7-31
Completed slide

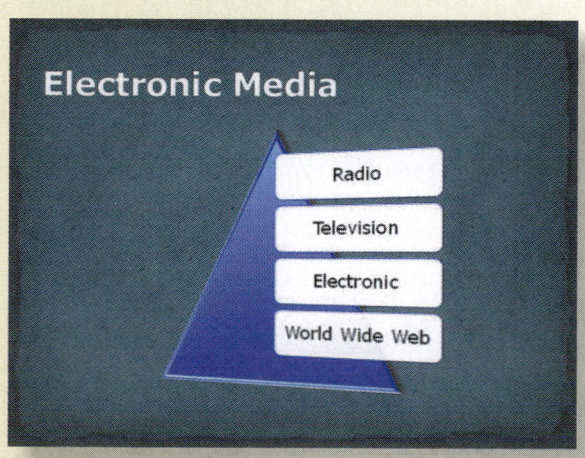

11. Create a handout header and footer: Include the date and your name as the header, and the page number and text **[7-24your initials]** as the footer.

12. Move to slide 1 and save the presentation as **[7-24your initials]** in your Lesson 7 folder.

13. Print the presentation as handouts with six slides on a page, scale to fit paper, and framed. Close the presentation.

Exercise 7-25

Create an organization chart and adjust layout.

1. Open the file **MISdept**.

2. Insert a new slide after slide 2 that uses the **Title and Content** layout. Key the title **MIS Department Organization**.

3. Create an organization chart using a horizontal hierarchy with the information shown in Figure 7-32.

Figure 7-32
Organization chart text

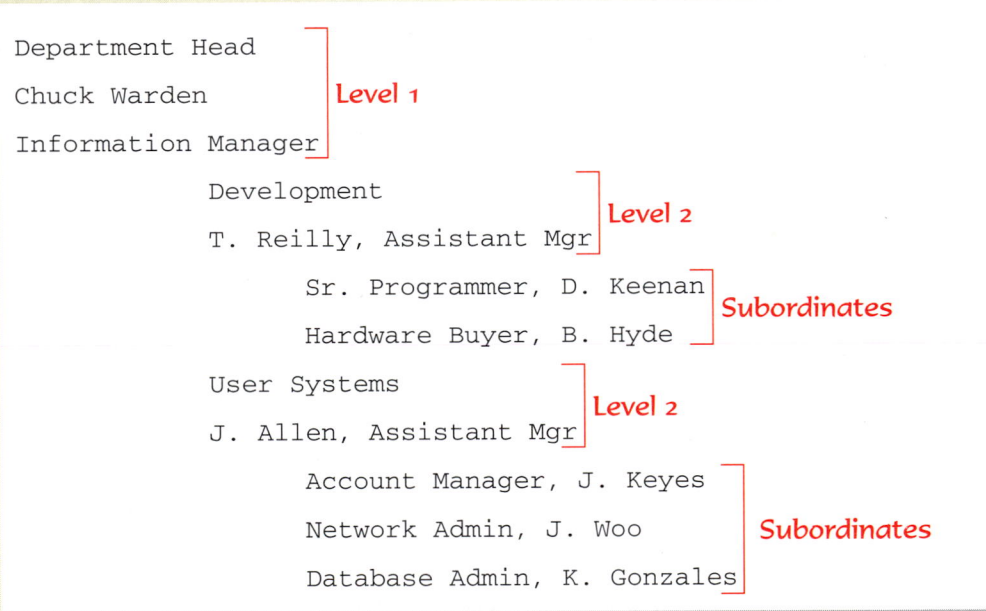

```
Department Head
Chuck Warden              Level 1
Information Manager

        Development
        T. Reilly, Assistant Mgr    Level 2
                Sr. Programmer, D. Keenan
                Hardware Buyer, B. Hyde     Subordinates
        User Systems
        J. Allen, Assistant Mgr     Level 2
                Account Manager, J. Keyes
                Network Admin, J. Woo       Subordinates
                Database Admin, K. Gonzales
```

4. Change the font of all diagram text to 14 points and apply bold.

5. Adjust the shape sizing to avoid word-wrapping of the job titles, but keep the size uniform at each level.

6. Change the colors to **Gradient Loop – Accent 2**.

7. Adjust the position of other shapes to spread them out in the SmartArt area as shown in Figure 7-33.

Figure 7-33
Completed
organization chart

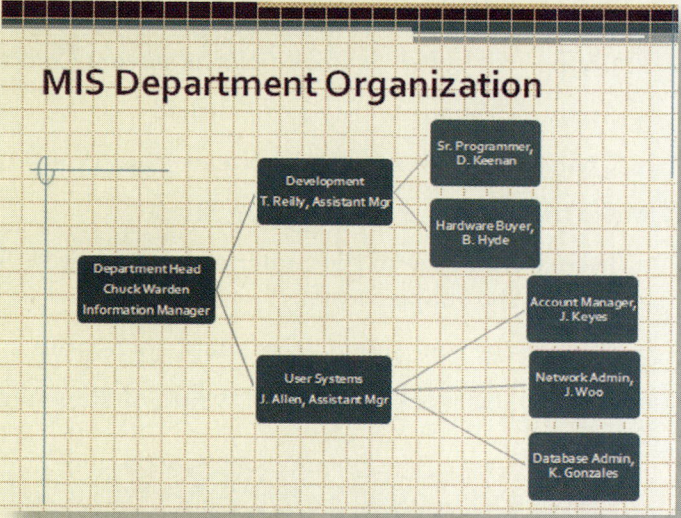

8. Create a slide footer for slide 3 containing today's date, and the text your name, **[7-25your initials]**.

9. Move to slide 1 and save the presentation as **[7-25your initials]** in your Lesson 7 folder.

10. Preview then print slide 3 in full size. Close the presentation.

Exercise 7-26

Create a radial diagram on a promotional flyer.

1. Open the file **NewYear**. Create a SmartArt graphic in the content placeholder for this single-page flyer.

2. From the **Cycle** category, choose the **Basic Radial** thumbnail.

3. Add five additional shapes (for a total of nine plus one in the center).

4. Increase the size of the SmartArt area to fill the available space.

5. Key the text **Great Food** in the center circle; then key the text in Figure 7-34 in the outer circles, starting with the 12 o'clock position moving in a clockwise direction.

Figure 7-34
Diagram text

```
Poached Salmon
Texan Tofu
Fresh Fruit
Pecan Pie
Peanut Soup
Veggies & Dip
Green Beans
Corn Relish
Spring Rolls
```

6. Make these design changes:

    a. Change the colors to click **Colorful-Accent Colors**.

    b. Apply the SmartArt Style of **Polished**.

    c. Change the font size for all circles to 16 points. Apply bold.

7. Make these changes to the center shape:

    a. Increase the size of the center shape and press ⌗Shift⌗ while you resize to keep the shape round.

    b. Change the font size for this shape to 24 points.

    c. Change the shape to a 16-point star, as shown in Figure 7-35.

Figure 7-35
Completed flyer

8. Save the presentation as **[7-26your initials]** in your Lesson 7 folder.

9. Preview, and then print the slide using color if possible. Close the presentation.

Exercise 7-27 ◆ Challenge Yourself

Convert bulleted lists to appropriate diagrams.

1. Open the file **Market3** and examine the slide content.

2. For slide 2, convert the bulleted text to an **Upward Arrow** SmartArt graphic from the **Process** category.

3. Increase the text size to 20 points and then resize the text boxes as necessary to avoid words being cut off in the middle. Change the colors to one of the colorful options and apply the **Moderate Effect** SmartArt Style.

4. For slides 4 and 5, convert both lists to the **Multidirectional Cycle** SmartArt graphic. Change the colors to one of the accent colors and apply a **Moderate Effect** SmartArt Style. Change the text color to black and font size to 28 points.

5. Reduce the vertical size of the SmartArt graphic on slides 4 and 5 so the diagrams are not quite so large and a little more space is allowed after the slide titles.

6. Create a handout header and footer: Include the date and your name as the header, and the page number and text **[7-27your initials]** as the footer.

7. Move to slide 1 and save the presentation as **[7-27your initials]** in your Lesson 7 folder.

8. Preview and then print the entire presentation as handouts, six slides per page, scale to fit paper, and framed. Close the presentation.

On Your Own

In these exercises you work on your own, as you would in a real-life work environment. Use the skills you've learned to accomplish the task—and be creative.

Exercise 7-28

Think of a familiar activity and create a process diagram indicating the steps in the process. For example, baking a cake, preparing for a camping trip, or paying a bill. Keep the process fairly simple—no more than 10 steps—and format it so that it is easy to understand and attractive to view. Add a title slide and one or two additional slides giving information about the process. Save the presentation as **[7-28your initials]**. Preview and then print the presentation as handouts.

Exercise 7-29

Create an organization chart of your family tree, starting with one set of great-grandparents and including all the descendants that come from that branch. If you don't want to create your own family tree, choose a famous person, a pedigreed pet, or an imaginary figure. Include a title slide for your presentation and one or two slides describing something of interest about one or more of the people (or pets) on your chart. Use your own creativity to format the presentation and the chart attractively. Save the presentation as **[7-29your initials]**. Preview and then print the presentation as handouts.

Exercise 7-30

Create a diagram to describe a relationship between several functions or departments at your school, work, or other organization. For example, a drama club might have a director, stagehands, costume designer, actors and actresses, musicians, and a playwright. Choose any of the SmartArt diagram types except the organization chart. Add a title slide and one or two other slides describing some aspect of the relationship. Save the presentation as **[7-30your initials]**. Preview and then print the diagram as a full-size slide.

Unit 2 Applications

Unit Application 2-1

Work with WordArt, work with images, group objects, and create a table.

1. Open the file **Runner1**.

2. On slide 1, key **Good 4 U** as the title and **Proud Sponsor of the Fall Festival Marathon** as the subtitle.

3. Find a clip art image of a runner and insert it into the slide. Position the clip art in the bottom right corner of the text area of the title slide.

4. Recolor the image to match one of the colors in the presentation.

5. Resize the image so it does not overlap the subtitle text.

6. Change the picture style to **Drop Shadow Rectangle**. Your completed slide 1 should look similar to Figure U2-1.

Figure U2-1
Completed title slide

7. Working in the Outline pane, key the text shown in Figure U2-2, inserting new slides where needed.

Figure U2-2
Presentation data

8. On slides 2 and 4, remove the bullets from the body text placeholders.

9. On slide 4, insert the **Fireworks** picture from your student data files and position it in the bottom right corner of the slide. Rotate the image so the rockets point toward the text and increase the size slightly, as shown in Figure U2-3.

Figure U2-3
Finished slide with
rotated picture

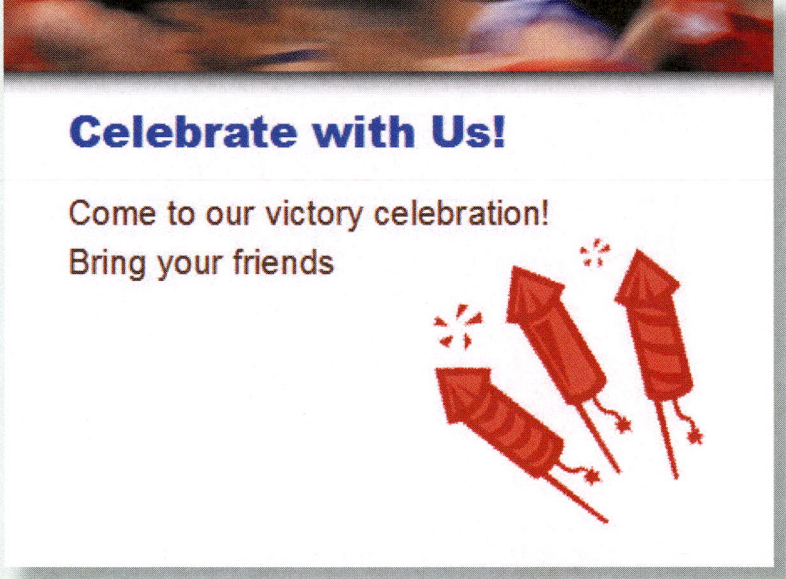

10. Insert a new slide after slide 4 that uses the **Blank layout**. Insert a clip art image of a race. Resize the picture proportionately so it almost fills the open space on the slide. If the picture is an odd size, crop it where necessary so it is the same size and shape as the slide. Adjust the picture's brightness settings to soften the colors so WordArt will be readable when placed above the image.

11. Create a WordArt text by using **Fill – Accent 2, Warm Matte Bevel**. Key the following text on three lines and center this text over the image:

    Award Ceremony
    6 p.m.
    Central Park

12. Increase the text size to 60 points and change the text color to **Dark Blue, Background 1**.

13. Check spelling in the presentation.

14. Create a handout header and footer: Include the date and your name as the header, and the page number and text **[U2-1your initials]** as the footer.

15. Create a Unit 2 Application folder. Move to slide 1 and save the presentation as **[U2-1your initials]** in your Unit 2 Applications folder.

16. Preview and then print the presentation as handouts, six slides per page, grayscale, framed. Close the presentation.

Unit Application 2-2

Add a table, insert a chart, create a SmartArt cycle diagram; add a shape and a text box to a chart.

1. Open the file **HeadCount**. Apply the **Verve** design theme and use the **Trek** theme color.

2. Insert a new slide after slide 3 that uses the **Title and Content** layout, and key the title **Current Breakdown**.

3. Create a table with five columns and four rows and key the data shown in Figure U2-4.

4. Merge two cells for "Kitchen" and two cells for "Service."

5. Adjust the column widths so that the text fits attractively, and align the text to match the figure. The overall table dimensions should be approximately 6.25 inches wide by 3 inches tall.

6. Change the Table Style to **Dark Style 1 – Accent 6**.

7. Vertically center all of the text in the table.

8. Position the table attractively on the slide.

Figure U2-4
Table data

	Kitchen		Service	
	F/T	P/T	F/T	P/T
Weekdays	13	8	19	9
Weekends	7	13	9	16

9. Insert a new slide after slide 4 that uses the **Title and Content** layout, and key the title **Past, Current, Projected**. Create a Clustered column chart by using the data shown in Figure U2-5.

Figure U2-5
Chart worksheet
data

	A	B	C
1		Full-time	Part-time
2	2006	41	30
3	2007	40	35
4	2008	48	46
5	2009	38	61

10. Apply a gradient fill to each series of columns. Move the legend to the bottom.

11. Draw a text box at the top of the chart; key the text **Projecting 61 P/T, 38 F/T!**. Change the text to 24 points and make it bold. Resize the text box so the text fits all on one line.

12. Draw an arrow from the text to the top of the 2009 columns.

13. Insert a new slide after slide 5. Use the **Title and Content** layout, and key the title **Plan for Increasing P/T Headcount**.

14. On the new slide 6, insert a Basic Cycle SmartArt Graphic showing the five steps in Figure U2-6 starting with the top shape in the 12 o'clock position and moving clockwise.

Figure U2-6
Data for Basic Cycle
SmartArt graphic

Step 1	Advertise P/T positions
Step 2	T. Scott to schedule interviews
Step 3	M. Peters to interview and hire employees
Step 4	J. Farla to train
Step 5	L. Klein to assign schedules

15. Apply the **3-D, Polished** Style and make the text bold. Resize the graphic to fill the open area of the slide.

16. Apply the **Wipes, Split Vertical Out** transition to all of the slides.

17. View the presentation as a slide show.

18. Create a slide footer for all slides, except the title slide, containing today's date, and the text your name, **[U2-2your initials]**.

19. Create a handout header and footer: Include the date and your name as the header, and the page number and the text **[U2-2your initials]** as the footer.

20. Move to slide 1 and save the presentation as **[U2-2your initials]** in your Unit 2 Applications folder.

21. Preview and then print the entire presentation as handouts, six slides per page, grayscale, landscape, framed. Close the presentation.

Unit Application 2-3

Create a presentation with an organizational chart and a diagram.

1. Start a new presentation that uses the **Solstice** design theme and the **Apex** theme color.

2. Insert two additional slides and key the text shown in Figure U2-7. Use the **Title Slide** layout for the first slide, the **Two Content** layout for the second slide, and the **Title and Content** layout for the third slide.

Figure U2-7
Presentation text

```
            Good 4 U Senior Management
Slide 1
                 Current and Future Organization

            Why Change What Works?
               •  Current structure designed for a single-restaurant
Slide 2           company
               •  Management must be positioned for a national, multi-
                  restaurant organization

            Future Structure
               •  Reorganization planned for 2008
               •  Designed to capitalize on the individual talents of
                  co-owners
Slide 3        •  Company will be split into two functional areas
               •  Chef and Administration Managers will report to Julie
                  Wolfe
               •  Marketing and Information Managers will report to Gus
                  Irvinelli
```

3. On slide 1, insert an appropriate clip art or picture showing managers, a business setting, etc. Recolor it to match the presentation theme color.

4. On slide 2, insert a Radial Cycle SmartArt graphic in the content placeholder.

5. Insert two more shapes on the Radial diagram, making a total of six shapes in the outer circle plus a center shape.

6. Make the diagram as large as possible without interfering with the other text on the slide.

7. Key **Good** Enter **4 U** in the center shape. For the other shapes, key the text shown in Figure U2-8, starting with "New York" in the 12 o'clock position and moving clockwise.

Figure U2-8
Data for Radial Cycle SmartArt graphic

New Enter York

Miami

Los Enter Angeles

San Enter Francisco

Tucson

More Enter soon

8. Change the SmartArt Style to **3-D, Metallic Scene** and change the colors to **Gradient Loop – Accent 3**. Resize the bulleted text placeholder to reduce its width. Resize the diagram to make it as large as possible without overlapping the bulleted text placeholder.

9. Insert a new slide after slide 2 that uses the **Title and Content** layout. Give it the title **Current Organization**.

10. On slide 3, create a Hierarchy Organization Chart SmartArt graphic for the Good 4 U restaurant by using Figure U2-9. Arrange the chart boxes in an attractive and functional way.

Figure U2-9
Data for organization chart SmartArt graphic

Julie Wolfe, Gus Irvinelli, Co-owners —— Level 1

   Michele Jenkins, Head Chef —— Level 2

      Claudia Pell, Maitre d' ⎤
                            Level 3
      Eric Dennis, Assistant Chef ⎦

   Roy Olafsen, Marketing Manager —— Level 2

      Jerry Wayne, Sales ⎤
                            Level 3
      Jane Kryler, Promotions ⎦

   Chuck Warden, Information Manager —— Level 2

      Tanya Reilly, Development ⎤
                            Level 3
      Jerry Allen, User Systems ⎦

   Michael Peters, Administration Manager —— Level 2

      Robert Lee, Purchasing ⎤
      Carol Lynne, Personnel   Level 3
      Sharon Ray, Payroll ⎦

11. Increase the size of the chart, making it as large as possible.

12. Choose the style **3-D, Metallic Scene**. Change the colors to **Colorful - Accent Colors**.

13. Insert a slide after slide 4 using the **Title and Content** layout. Give it the title **What We Expect**. Create a table showing the positive effects that the restructuring will have on the business. See Figure U2-10 for the table data.

Figure U2-10
Table data

Positive Effects of the Restructuring
Questions/Concerns to be handled in a more timely manner
Increase in responsiveness to customers
A more focused business ready to expand into new markets
Increase in adaptability of business if turnover takes place
Empowering employees will increase job satisfaction
Tap into the skills and expertise of owners

14. Resize the table and reposition the table attractively and apply **Themed Style 1 – Accent 6** to the table.

15. Review all slides, adjusting the size and position of elements where needed.

16. View the presentation as a slide show.

17. Create a slide footer for all slides containing today's date, and the text your name, **[U2-3your initials]**.

18. Create a handout header and footer: Include the date and your name as the header, and the page number and the text **[U2-3your initials]** as the footer.

19. Move to slide 1 and save the presentation as **[U2-3your initials]** in your Unit 2 Applications folder.

20. Preview and then print the entire presentation as handouts, six slides per page, grayscale, landscape, framed. Close the presentation.

Unit Application 2-4 ◆ Using the Internet

Write and design a presentation that uses graphics, numerical charts, tables, organization charts, and SmartArt graphics.

Use the Internet to research a topic of current interest that would lend itself to a presentation including graphics, numerical charts, tables, SmartArt graphics, and/or organization charts. You decide what your topic will be.

Here are a few topics to give you ideas, but you are not limited to these topics:

- The impact of increased security for air travel.

- Enrollment information at your local college or university.

- How global warming is affecting weather patterns.

- How the financial health of Hollywood is affected by the overall economy.

- The problems caused by overuse of antibiotics.

- The growth of computer use in the general population.

Illustrate the information you gathered by using a variety of graphics, charts, tables, and SmartArt graphics. Be sure to include at least five slides and format them in an attractive way. Prepare a slide listing the resources you used. When the presentation is complete check spelling.

In the slide footer, include the text **Prepared by** followed by your name. Include the slide number, but not the date, on all slides. In the handout footer, include the completed filename **[U2-4your initials]**. In the handout header, key **Presented to** and then identify to whom you would be giving this presentation. Include in the handout the date that you would be delivering the presentation.

Save the presentation as **[U2-4your initials]** in your Unit 2 Applications folder. Practice delivering the presentation. Preview and then print the presentation handouts with an appropriate number of slides per page, grayscale, framed. Close the presentation.

A Professional Approach

ACCESS 2007

Jon Juarez

John Carter

Database programs such as Microsoft Access are very powerful. There's more to learn about databases than just how to enter data or execute simple queries. You also need to know how to use Access in a real-world situation. Therefore, this book focuses on everyday business tasks. As you work through the lessons, imagine yourself working as an intern for Carolina Critters, Inc., a fictional company that manufactures stuffed animals, located in Charlotte, North Carolina.

Carolina Critters, Inc.

Carolina Critters, Inc., was formed in 1946 by Hector Fuentes upon his return from serving in the U.S. Navy in World War II. Hector's son Carlos took over the company in 1962 and ran it until 1997, when Carlos's daughter Lisa assumed the presidency.

Originally, Carolina Critters produced stuffed teddy bears, rabbits, squirrels, and other cuddly animals. The company has branched out over the years and now offers five product lines and 25 products, producing more than $25 million in annual sales. Today, the stuffed animals from Carolina Critters—ranging from traditional teddy bears and cats and dogs to dinosaurs and endangered species—sell in department stores and toy stores across the nation. The company also sells products via the Internet.

In your work as an intern at Carolina Critters, you interact primarily with the four key people shown in Figure CS-1. The databases you use relate to Carolina Critters. As you work, take the time to notice the following:

- The unusual method Carolina Critters has for manufacturing its stuffed animals.

- The types of database activities required in a small business to carry on its day-to-day activities.

Figure CS-1

Lisa Fuentes
President

James McCluskie
Vice President, Chief Financial Officer

Frances Falcigno
Sales and Marketing Manager

Jin Yan
Manufacturing Manager

Method of Manufacturing

Carolina Critters, Inc., uses an unusual method of manufacturing. It does not buy each individual component for a stuffed animal (e.g., material for the outer shell, plastic joints for arms and legs, felt pads for paws, specially made eyes, extruded plastic components for the nose or claws, clothes, stuffing). Instead, it has approached a small number of suppliers and contracted with them for kits that contain all the precut, preweighed, preformed materials required to manufacture a specific stuffed animal. For example, Robinson Mills, Inc., a supplier in Passaic, New Jersey, provides the kit for "Granny Bear."

unit 1

UNDERSTANDING ACCESS DATABASES

Lesson 1   Getting Started with a
            Database   AC-6

Lesson 2   Viewing and Modifying
            Records   AC-36

Lesson 3   Finding, Filtering, Sorting, and
            Summarizing Data   AC-70

Lesson 4   Creating New Databases and
            Tables   AC-98

UNIT 1   APPLICATIONS   AC-131

Getting Started with a Database

OBJECTIVES

After completing this lesson, you will be able to:

1. Identify basic database structure.

2. Work with a Microsoft Access database.

3. Identify components of Access.

4. Navigate Access recordsets.

5. Modify datasheet appearance.

6. Print and save a recordset.

7. Manage Access files.

MCAS OBJECTIVES

In this lesson:
AC07_3.2
AC07_5.6
AC07_5.5
AC07_6.1.2
AC07_6.1.3
AC07_6.2.2

Estimated Time: 1 1/2 hours

Databases are part of your daily life. Telephone directories are databases that you can use to find phone numbers for people or companies. Banks use databases to track account balances. Information about you is stored in many databases. Your school keeps track of where you live, when you enrolled, what courses you've taken, what grades you've received, and when you will graduate, as well as other important academic information.

A *database* is a logically organized collection of data. The most common type of database in use today follows the relational model. Other types of models include flat, hierarchical, network, and dimensional.

Identifying Basic Database Structure

Microsoft Access follows the relational model for its design. In a relational model database like Access, all data are stored in tables. A *table* is the major database object that stores all data in a subject-based list of rows and columns. A database table looks similar to a table displayed in a spreadsheet program or a word processor.

Tables are made up of records and fields. A *record* is a complete set of related data about one entity or activity. A record is displayed as a row in a table. Examples of records include a phone directory listing, a sales transaction, or a bank deposit. Records are composed of related fields. A *field* is the smallest storage element that contains an individual data element within a record. A field is displayed as a column in a table.

Figure 1-1
Data organization

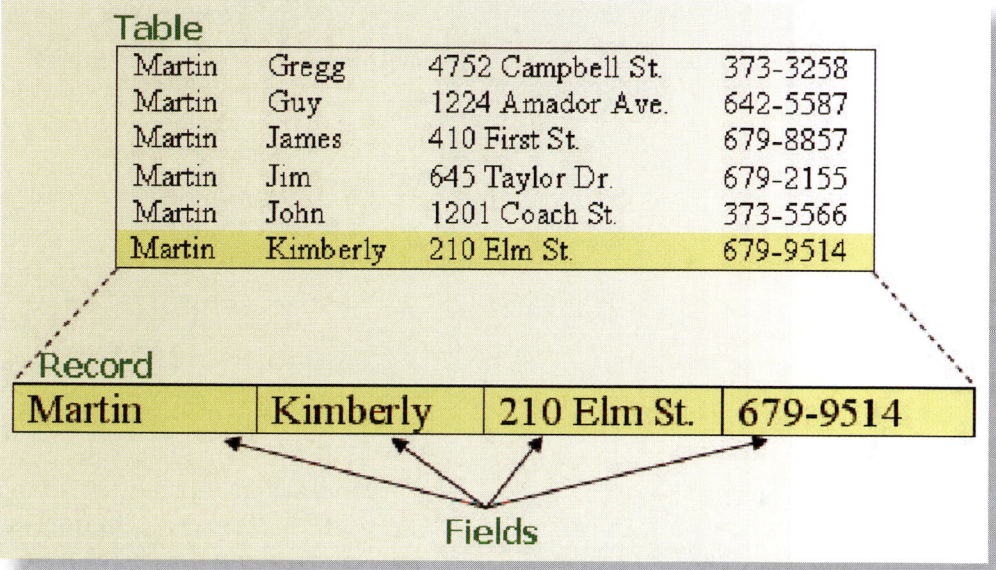

A group of related fields make up a record. A group of related records make up a table, and a group of related tables make up a relational model database.

Figure 1-2
Data hierarchy

Although all data are stored in tables, most often you use other objects to locate, organize, and modify recordsets. A *recordset* is a Microsoft object-oriented data structure consisting of grouped records. A recordset can be as small as a single field or as large as two or more combined tables.

Major objects in an Access database include the following:

- Tables store data about people, activities, items, and events. A table consists of records made up of fields. The information in a table appears in rows (records) and columns (fields), similar to an Excel worksheet.

- Queries organize data in the database. You can specify criteria or conditions to show records and fields from one or more tables. You can also create queries to perform actions.

- Forms display data. With a form you can view, add, and edit fields and records in a table.

- Reports are used to print data. When designing a report, you can sort records, calculate totals, and add graphics to make the report attractive and easy to read.

Figure 1-3
Major object orientation

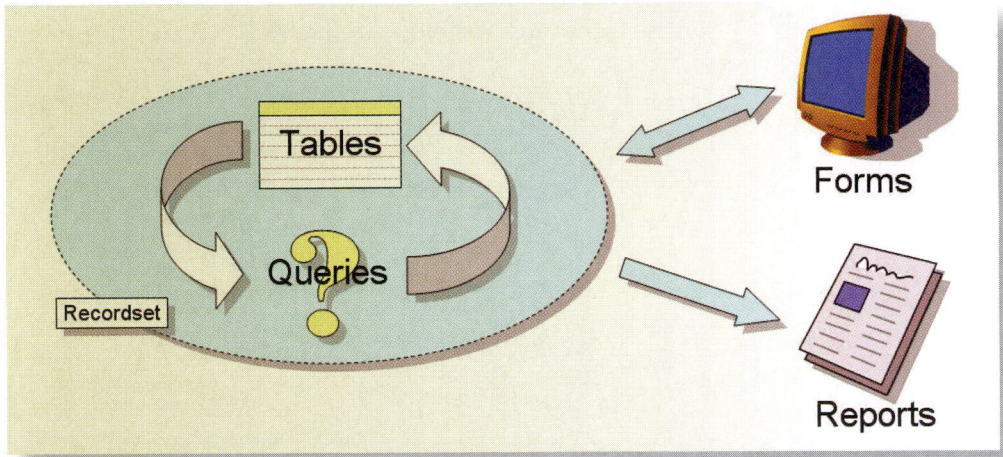

NOTE

In this course, the database with which you work involves a Case Study about Carolina Critters, a fictional company that manufactures stuffed animal kits (see the frontmatter of the book).

A recordset is most often displayed as either a form or a report. A form is a major database object used to display information in an attractive, easy-to-read screen format. Forms can be used to display, add, edit, or delete recordsets. A report is a major database object used to display information in a printable page format. Reports can only display recordsets.

Working with a Microsoft Access Database

Because of the complexity of a database, Access limits certain file operations. When a database is open, you cannot move or rename the file. Therefore, before you begin working with a database, you must place the file in a suitable location. The storage medium in which the file is located must provide enough space to allow the database to grow, and you must have rights to modify the file.

Exercise 1-1   MANAGE A DATABASE

At the beginning of each lesson, you will be required to copy the lesson files into a folder on your hard drive or another storage device such as a USB drive. Student files are located online or are available from your instructor. The files you need for a lesson can be found in its corresponding folder. For example, in the first lesson, you will need the folder **Lesson 01**, which contains the database

NOTE

Check with your instructor for the specific location of files used in this lesson.

CC01. If you need help copying files to your computer, ask your instructor or lab manager for assistance.

1. Locate the **Lesson 01** folder.

2. Double-click the folder **Lesson 01** to see its content.

3. Right-click the file **CC01** and from the shortcut menu, choose **Copy**.

4. Right-click an unused part of the folder and from the shortcut menu, choose **Paste**.

5. Right-click the new file and from the shortcut menu, choose **Rename**. Rename the file to *[your initials]*-**CC01**.

6. Right-click *[your initials]*-**CC01** and from the shortcut menu, choose **Properties**. Make certain that the Read-only attribute check box is not checked.

Figure 1-4
Properties dialog box

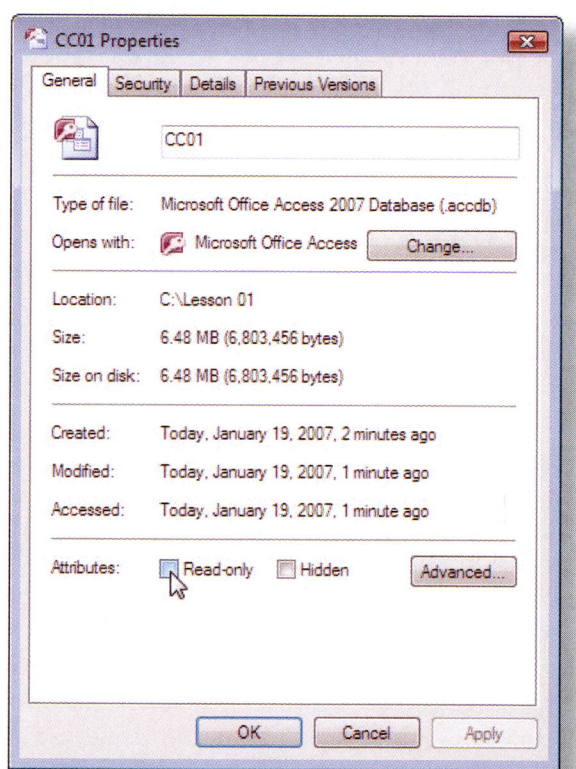

7. Click **OK** to close the dialog box. Close Windows Explorer.

NOTE

Windows provides many ways to start applications. If you have problems, ask your instructor for help.

Exercise 1-2   START A DATABASE

The first screen that appears after starting Access is Getting Started with Microsoft Office Access. From this screen, you can create a new database, open an existing database, or view featured content from Microsoft Office Online.

1. Click the Start button and choose **All Programs**.

2. Click on the Microsoft Office folder and choose Microsoft Office Access 2007. This will start Access.

Figure 1-5
Getting Started window

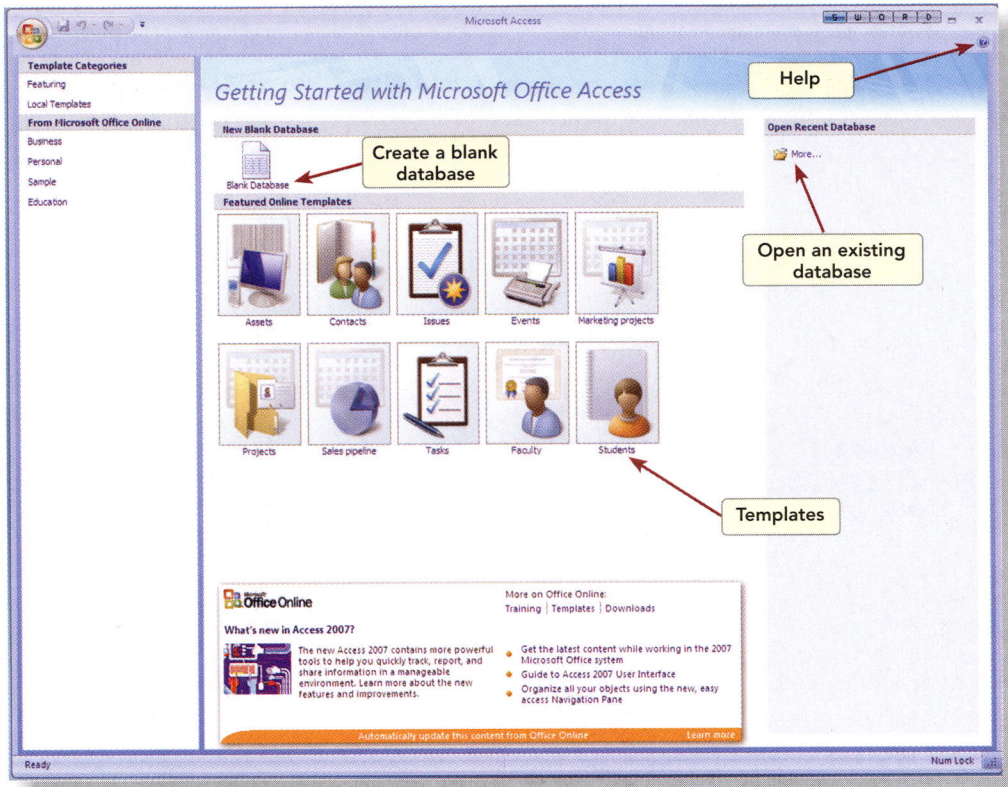

Exercise 1-3   OPEN A DATABASE

By double-clicking on the file icon of a database, you open it in the default mode. The default mode is set to Shared for most databases. Shared mode is a method of opening a database in which multiple users can read and write to the database at the same time. Access databases can be opened in several different modes, including Shared, Read-only, Exclusive use, and Exclusive Read-only.

Each time you open a database, a security alert displays on the Message Bar. The Message Bar alerts you that the database may contain malicious code. Because all Access databases contain program code, this message normally displays.

1. In the **Open Recent Database** section, click **More**.

2. Locate the folder **Lesson 01**. Select the file *[your initials]*-**CC01** and click **Open**.

3. In the Message Bar a **Security Warning** message states that certain content is disabled. Click **Options**. The **Microsoft Office Security Options** dialog box appears.

4. Click **Enable this content** and click **OK**.

Identifying Components of Access

You will use the Office Button to print and manage file operations. You will use command tabs and ribbons to complete a specific tasks. The commands in each ribbon are organized by command groups.

You will use the Navigation Pane to control major database objects. The Navigation Pane is the rectangular area on the left side of the database window that organizes major database objects. All major objects are accessed through the Navigation Pane.

Figure 1-6
Getting Started
window
CC01.accdb

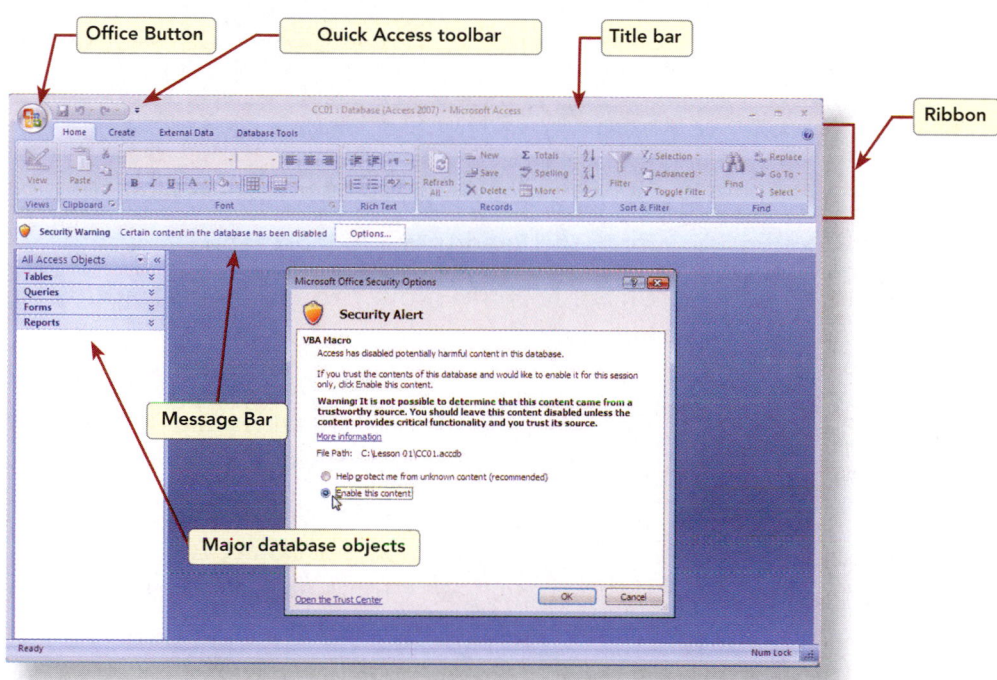

Exercise 1-4   MANIPULATE THE NAVIGATION PANE

The Navigation Pane displays the major database objects. Access allows you to organize these objects by categories and groups. You can open an object by double-clicking it or by right-clicking and selecting Open from the shortcut menu.

The Carolina Critters database organizes objects by the category **Object Type** and grouped by **All Tables**. Access allows you to change the layout of the Navigation Pane.

1. In the Navigation Pane, click the **Tables** group. This will expand the group and show all the tables in this database.

Figure 1-7
Navigation Pane
CC01.accdb

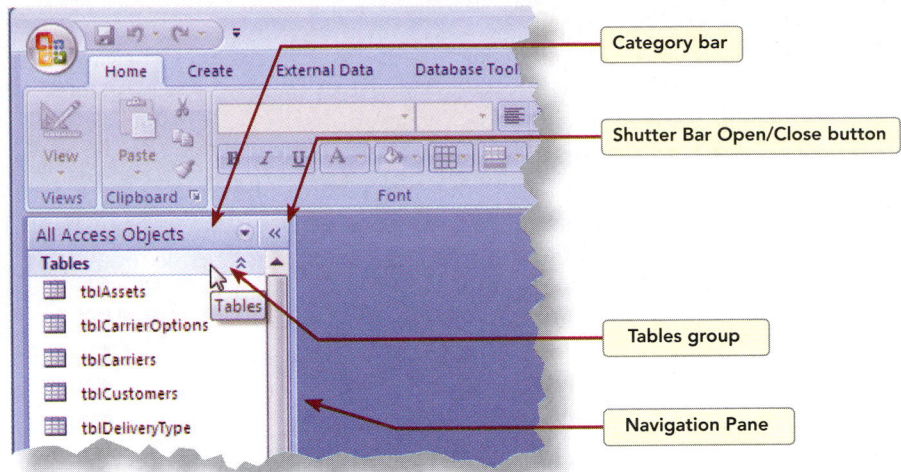

2. Click the **Tables** group again. This collapses the group.

3. Click the **Reports** group to expand the group.

4. Click the **Forms** group. You can have multiple groups expanded at any time.

Figure 1-8
Navigation Pane
options
CC01.accdd

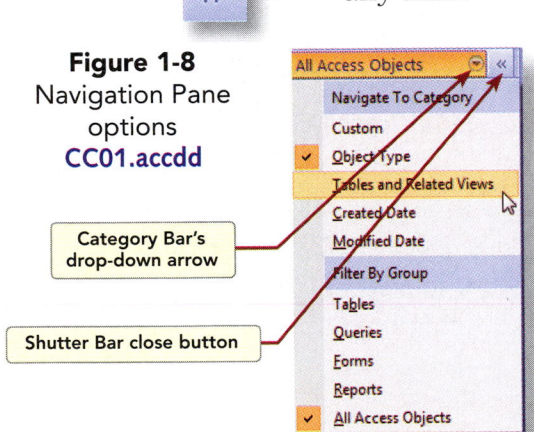

5. Click on the Category bar's drop-down arrow and select **Tables and Related Views**. Objects are now grouped by related major objects.

6. Click on the Category bar's drop-down arrow and select **Object Type** to return the Navigation Pane to its original layout.

7. Click the Shutter Bar button « to collapse the Navigation Pane. This allows you to see more data on the screen.

8. Click the Shutter Bar button » to expand the Navigation Pane.

Exercise 1-5   EXPLORE TABS, RIBBONS, AND GROUPS

Access uses tabs, ribbons, and groups, similar to other Microsoft Office applications. Some Access commands are the same as in Word and Excel. Other commands are unique to Access. Hovering over a command displays its ScreenTip. A *ScreenTip* is the name of or information regarding a specific object. This information can include images, shortcut keys, and descriptions.

When you click on a command tab, a unique set of command groups will appear in the ribbon. A *command group* is a collection of logically organized commands.

1. In the command tab **Home**, in the **Clipboard** group, you will find the Cut ✄ command. Hover your mouse pointer over this command to display its ScreenTip.

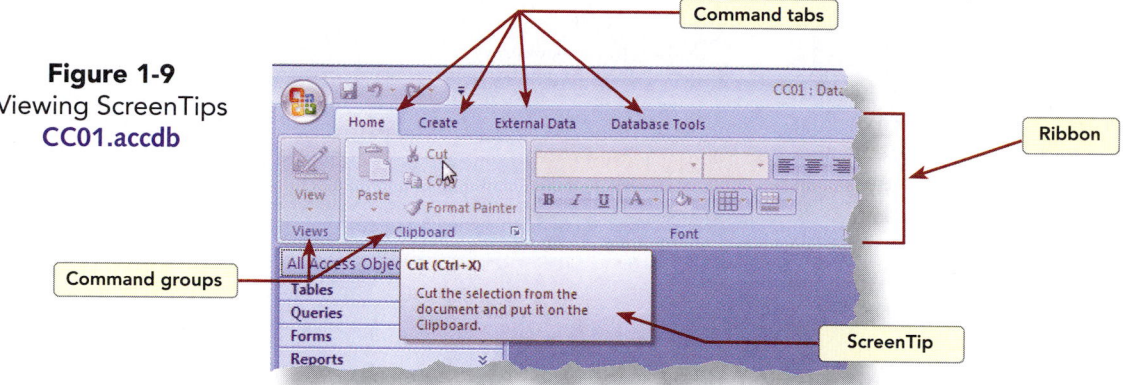

Figure 1-9
Viewing ScreenTips
CC01.accdb

2. In the command tab **Create**, in the **Forms** group, hover your mouse pointer over the Form ▦ command. Read the ScreenTip.

3. Click the **Home** command tab.

Exercise 1-6   OPEN AND CLOSE MAJOR OBJECTS

In this textbook, the names of the database objects use the Leszynski Naming Convention. The Leszynski Naming Convention is a method of naming objects that emphasizes the use of three-letter prefixes to identify the type of object. This convention does not use spaces or underscores and is widely used by software developers and programmers worldwide.

Table 1-1 Leszynski Naming Convention for Major Objects

Prefix	Object Type	Example
tbl	Table	**tblEmployees**
qry	Query	**qryKitSuppliers**
frm	Form	**frmStuffedAnimals**
rpt	Report	**rptQuarterlySales**

1. In the Navigation Pane, expand the **Tables** group.

2. Double-click the table **tblEmployees** to open it. The table that contains the employee's information is now open.

Figure 1-10
Open a table
CC01.accdb
tblEmployees

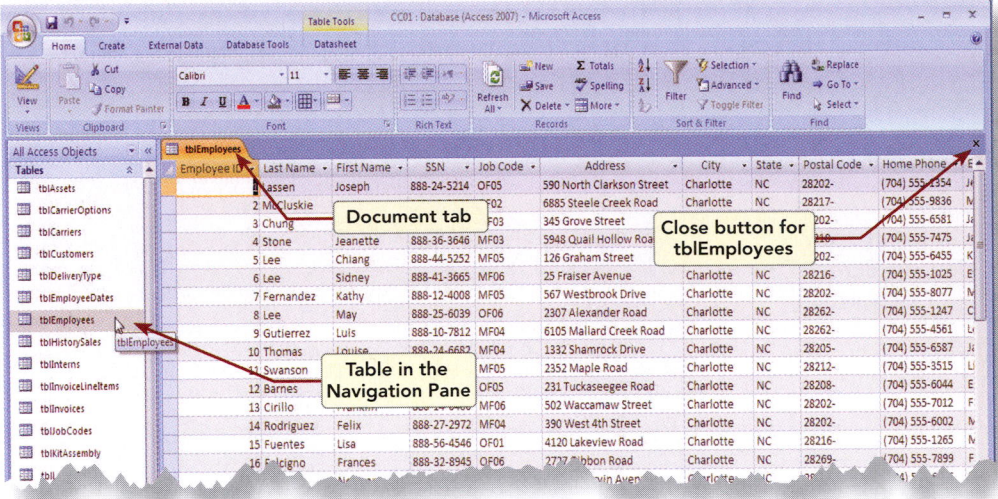

3. Click the Close button ⊠ to close the table **tblEmployees**.

4. In the Navigation Pane, collapse the **Tables** group.

5. Expand the **Queries** group, right-click the query **qryCustomerContact**, and select **Open** from the shortcut menu.

6. Right-click the document tab for **qryCustomerContact**, then select **Close** from the shortcut menu.

Exercise 1-7   EXPLORE DATASHEET AND DESIGN VIEWS

Each major database object has multiple views. The view that allows you to see a recordset is called the Datasheet View. A *Datasheet View* is a screen view used to display data in rows and columns, similar to a spreadsheet. Records are displayed as rows and fields are displayed as columns.

In addition to the Datasheet View, objects can be displayed in Design View. A *Design View* is a screen view used to modify the structure of a major object.

Switching between different views can be completed by

• Selecting, from the **Home** command tab in the **View** control group, the option arrow for the View command ⊠.

• Using the View Shortcut buttons (lower right corner of the screen.)

• Right-clicking the object and selecting the view.

1. In the **Queries** group of the Navigation Pane, double-click **qryProductPrice**. This will open the query in Datasheet View.

2. In the command group **Views**, click the option arrow for the View command ⊠ and select Design View. In this view, you can see the tables that are used to create this query.

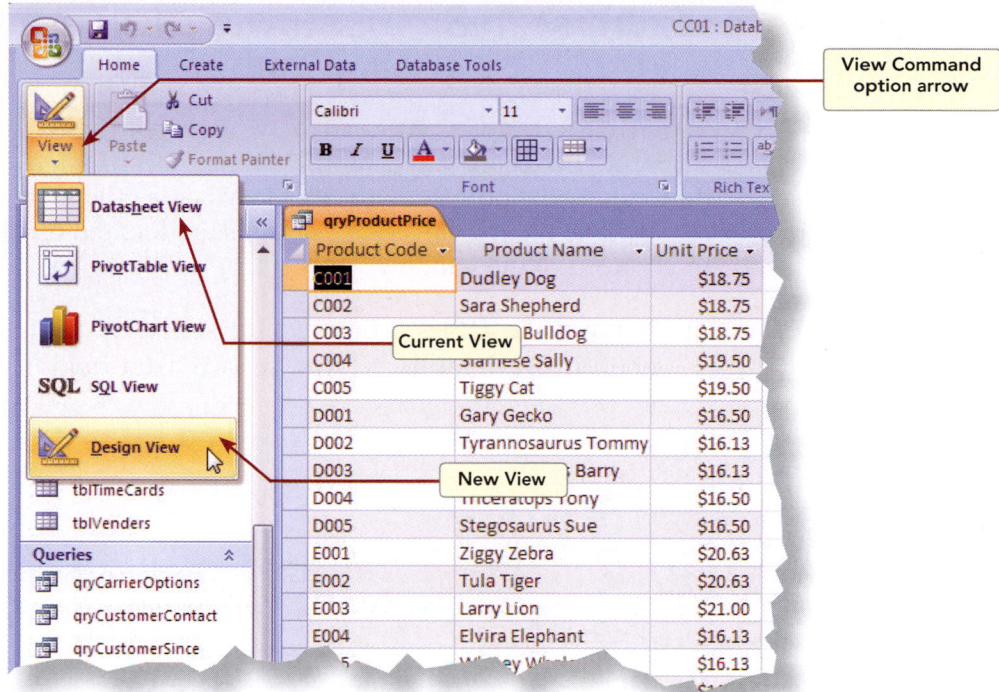

3. Right-click the document tab for the query, then select Datasheet View.

4. In the Navigation Pane, expand the **Tables** group.

5. Double-click **tblStuffedAnimals**. This opens the table in Datasheet View.

6. Right-click the document tab for the table, then select Design View. This is where you define the structure of the table.

7. Right-click the document tab for the table, then select **Close All**. This will close all open documents.

8. Collapse both the **Tables** and **Queries** groups.

Navigating Access Recordsets

Datasheet View has two modes: edit mode and navigation mode. *Edit Mode* is the mode in which changes to the content of a field can be made and the insertion point is visible. The insertion point looks like an I-beam. *Navigation Mode* is the mode in which an entire field is selected and the insertion point is not visible.

By using the scroll bars, navigation buttons, and keyboard shortcuts, you can navigate around large datasheets.

Exercise 1-8   USE NAVIGATION BUTTONS IN A TABLE

In navigation mode, you can move between fields by using the keyboard shortcuts or record navigation buttons. *Record navigation button* is an icon that moves the pointer within a recordset to the next, previous, first, or last record. The record navigation buttons are located on the navigation bar near the bottom of the window.

1. Expand the **Tables** group. Double-click the table **tblKitAssembly** to open it. By default, the first record, first field, is selected.

Figure 1-12
Navigation buttons
CC01.accdb
tblKitAssembly

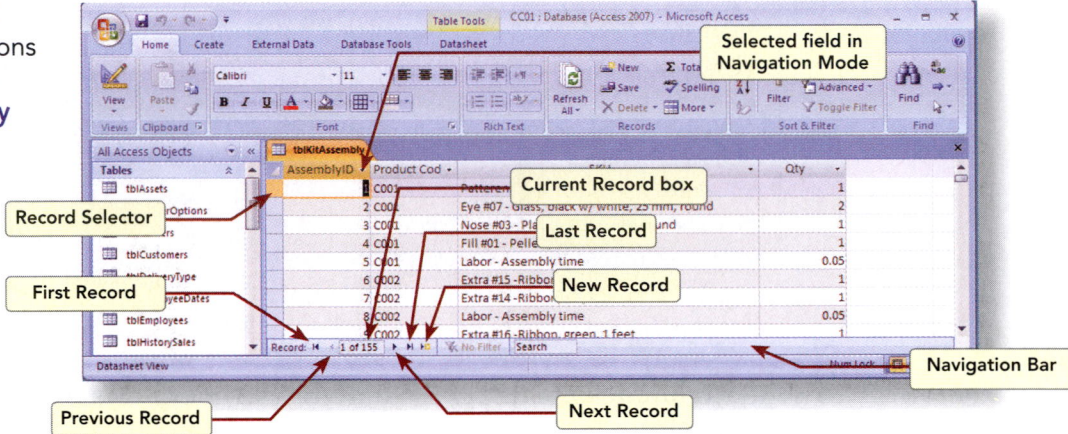

2. In the Navigation Bar, click the Next Record button once. The **AssemblyID** for the second record is highlighted.

3. Click the Previous Record button to return to the previous record.

4. Click the Last Record button to move to the last record in the table.

5. Click in the **Current Record** box. Delete the number in the box and key **75** and press Enter. The pointer moves to the seventy-fifth record.

6. Right-click the document tab for the table, then select **Close**. Collapse the **Tables** group.

Exercise 1-9   USE NAVIGATION SHORTCUT KEYS IN A QUERY

Just as in a table's Datasheet View, you can use both the navigation buttons and keyboard shortcuts to navigate through a recordset.

1. Expand the **Queries** group. Double-click the query **qrySales** to open it.

2. Press Ctrl+End to move to the last field in the last record.

3. Press Home to move to the first field in the current record.

4. Press Ctrl+Home to move to the first field in the first record.

5. Press End to move to the last field in the current record.

6. Press ↓ to move to the last field of the second record.

7. Right-click the document tab for the table, then select **Close**, and collapse the **Queries** group.

Table 1-2 Keyboard Shortcuts

Action	Shortcut
Move down one screen	PageDown
Move to the current field in the first record	Ctrl+↑
Move to the current field in the last record	Ctrl+↓
Move to the current field in the next record	↓
Move to the current field in the previous record	↑
Move to the first field in the current record	Home
Move to the first field in the first record	Ctrl+Home
Move to the last field in the current record	End
Move to the next field	Tab or →
Move to the previous field	Shift+Tab or ←
Move up one screen	PageUp
Place the pointer in the Specific Record Box	F5

Modifying Datasheet Appearance

In Access, a datasheet appears similar to a table displayed in Excel or Word. Just as in the other applications, in Access, you can hide, display, and resize columns and rows. You can also use formatting tools to change the appearance of text. Each format setting globally affects all text in every column and row.

Exercise 1-10   HIDE AND UNHIDE COLUMNS

When a table contains more fields than can be viewed on a single screen, you must scroll horizontally through the window. To reduce the number of fields shown at one time, you can hide columns within the datasheet.

1. Expand the **Tables** group. Double-click the table **tblHistorySales** to open it. There are nine fields in this table.

2. Click on the column header for the field **Employee** and drag through **ShipDate**. The four selected columns are highlighted.

Access 2007

Figure 1-13
Selecting multiple
columns
CC01.accdb
tblHistorySales

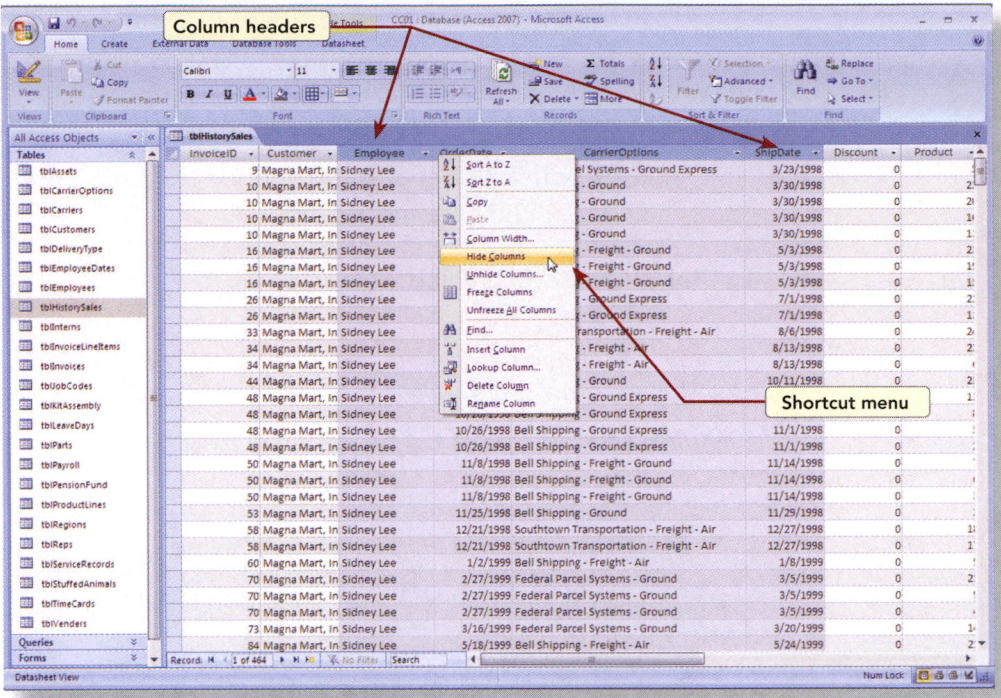

3. Right-click on the column header for the field **Employee** and select **Hide Columns**.

4. Right-click on the column header for the field **Customer** and select **Unhide Columns**.

5. Select the check box for **OrderDate** and **ShipDate**.

6. Click **Close**.

7. Right-click the document tab for the table, then select **Close**. A dialog box appears, prompting you to save the changes to the table. Click **Yes** to accept the changes.

NOTE

When you change the appearance or design of a major database object, Access prompts you to save the changes.

Exercise 1-11   CHANGE COLUMN WIDTHS AND ROW HEIGHTS

By default, all columns in a datasheet are the same width. You can change the width of each column to optimize your view of the data or the title for each field. You also can make columns narrower if too much blank space is included in a field.

You adjust row heights similarly to adjusting column widths. Although column widths can be set individually, row heights cannot. The row height is a global setting that applies to all rows in the entire datasheet.

1. Double-click the table **tblHistorySales** to open it.

2. Place the pointer on the vertical border between the column headers for **Customer** and **OrderDate**. Notice that the pointer changes to a vertical bar between a two-headed arrow. This is the resize pointer.

3. Drag the pointer to the right approximately one inch to allow enough space so the complete customer name is displayed for each record.

Figure 1-14
Resize a column
CC01.accdb
tblHistorySales

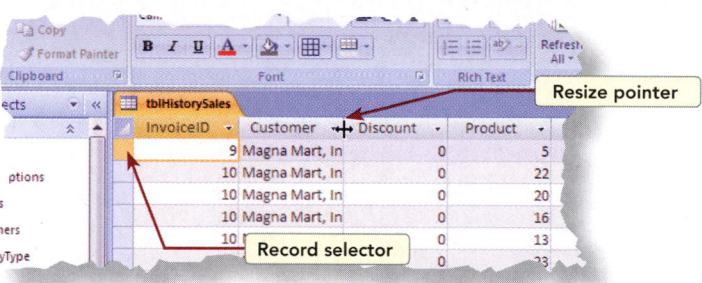

4. Right-click on the record selector for the first row.

5. Form the shortcut menu, select **Row Height**.

6. In the **Row Height** dialog box, key **25** and click **OK**. Notice that all rows are now taller.

7. Right-click on the record selector for any record and select **Row Height**.

8. Click the **Standard Height** check box and click **OK**.

Exercise 1-12   USE THE FONT COMMAND GROUP

You can increase the readability of data by applying specific format commands from the Font command group. Some commands, such as bold, underline, and italics, apply to the entire datasheet. Other commands, such as align left, center, and align right, can be applied to selected fields in the datasheet.

1. In the command group **Font**, hover your mouse pointer over the word **Calibri**. The ScreenTip states that this is the **Font** command.

2. Click the **Font**'s drop-down arrow and select **Microsoft Sans Serif**. The font has been applied to the entire datasheet.

3. The command to the right of **Font** is **Font Size**. Change the **Font Size** to **16**.

4. Place the resize pointer on the vertical border between the column headers for **OrderDate** and **ShipDate**.

5. Double-click to automatically adjust the column width of **OrderDate**.

6. Double-click the right side of the column header for **ShipDate** to automatically adjust its width.

7. Select the field **InvoiceID** by clicking its column header. Click the Center ≣ command. Only one field has been affected.

8. Press [Home] to deselect the column.

9. In the lower right corner of the command group, **Font** is a command called Alternate Fill/Back Color ▦▾. Click its drop-down arrow to show the available colors.

10. In the **Standard Theme Colors**, select **Brown 2** (row 3, last column) as the alternate color.

Figure 1-15
Changing datasheet
appearance
CC01.accdb
tblHistorySales

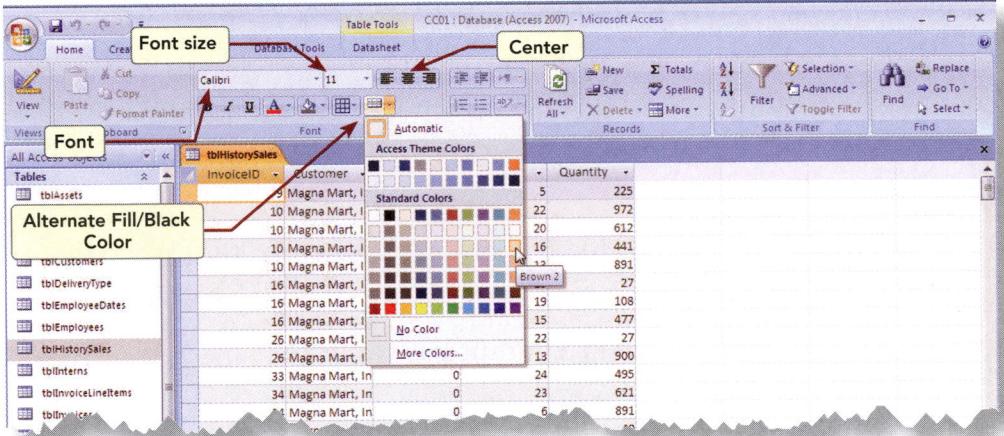

11. To the far right of the document tab for the table **tblHistorySales**, click the close button ×. Click **Yes** to save the changes.

12. Collapse the **Tables** group.

Printing and Saving a Recordset

You can print or save the Datasheet View of a table or query. The steps you take to print a datasheet are similar to the steps for printing in other Microsoft Office applications such as Word or Excel. You can also create an electronic XPS file of your printout. *XPS* is an XML Paper Specification (XPS) file format that preserves document formatting and enables file sharing of printable documents. The XPS format ensures that when the file is viewed online or is printed, it retains the original format.

Exercise 1-13   PRINT A QUERY

You can print a table or a query as it appears in Datasheet View. You can use any of these methods:

• Click the Office Button 🔘 and then choose **Print**.

• Press [Ctrl]+[P].

When you use the Office Button or the keyboard method, the Print dialog box displays to allow you to change print options.

1. Expand the **Queries** group. Double-click the table **qryProductPrice** to open it.

2. Press Ctrl + P to open the **Print** dialog box.

Figure 1-16
Print dialog box
CC01.accdb
qryProductPrice

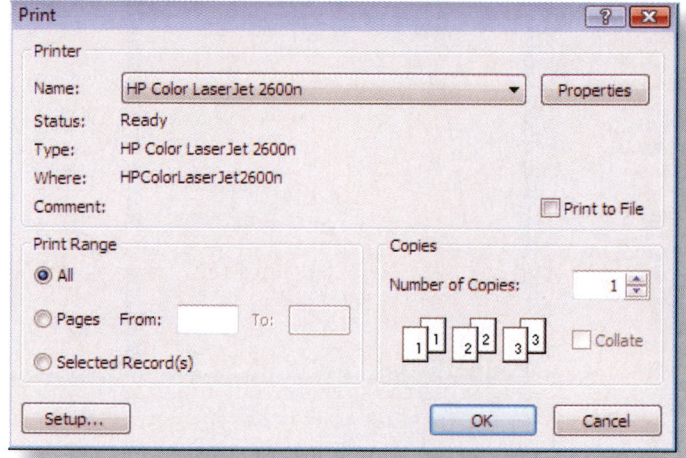

3. Based on your classroom procedure, you can either print the table or cancel the print process. To cancel, click **Cancel**. To print the datasheet, click **OK**. If you are uncertain, ask your instructor.

4. To the far right of the document tab for the query **qryProductPrice**, click the Close button ×.

5. Close the query and collapse the **Queries** group.

Exercise 1-14 PRINT A TABLE

Before printing a datasheet, you can use Print Preview to determine whether to change the page orientation from portrait (vertical layout) to landscape (horizontal layout). Landscape is often the better option when a datasheet contains numerous fields or wide columns.

1. Expand the **Tables** group. Double-click the table **tblInterns** to open it.

2. Click the Office Button 🌑. From the **Print** option, choose **Print Preview**.

3. Click the Last Page navigation button ▶| to display the last page.

4. From the **Print Preview** command tab, in the command group **Preview**, click the Two Pages command 🗐 to view both pages.

Access 2007

Figure 1-17
Print preview
CC01.accdb
tblInterns

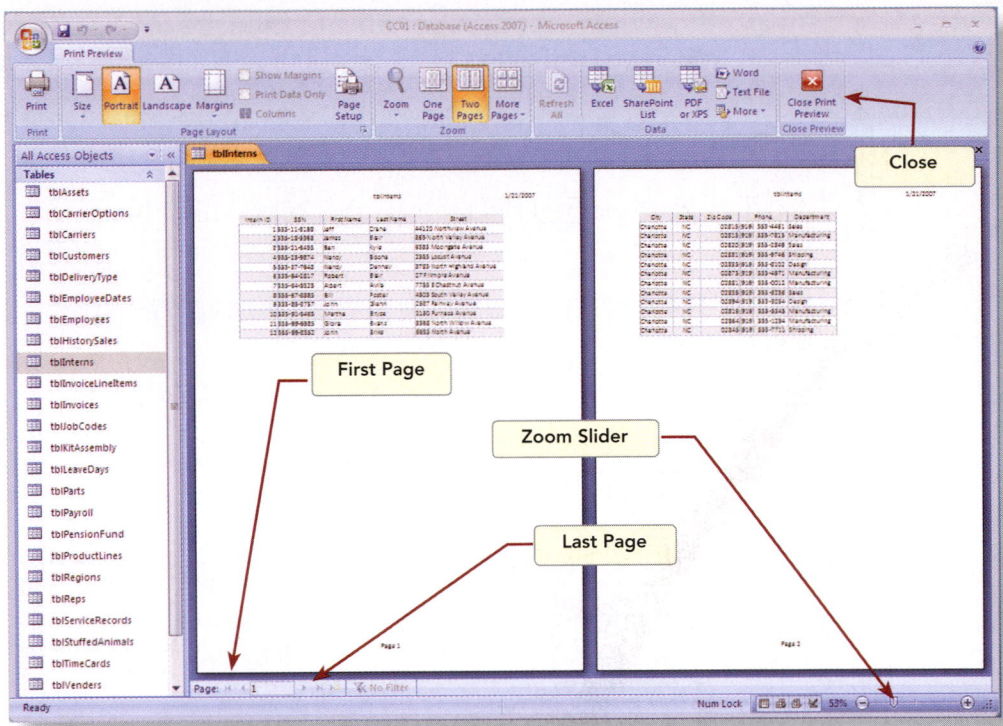

5. From the **Print Preview** command tab, in the command group **Page Layout**, click the Landscape command to reduce the total number of pages to print.

6. Based on your classroom procedure, you can either print the table or cancel the print process. To cancel, click **Cancel**. To print the datasheet, click **OK**. If you are uncertain, ask your instructor.

7. From the **Print Preview** command tab, in the **Command** group **Close Preview**, click the Close Print Preview command . This will return you to the table Datasheet View.

Exercise 1-15   PUBLISH A TABLE

In addition to printing a paper copy, you can create an electronic XPS file. The XPS format preserves document formatting and enables file sharing of printable documents. You can publish a document in high quality or reduced quality. Reduced quality is similar to draft quality printing. High quality produces a better printout but also increases the size of the file saved.

1. Double-click the table **tblKitAssembly** to open it.

2. Click the Office Button. Hover your mouse pointer over the More Options arrow of the **Save As** option and choose **PDF or XPS**.

Figure 1-18
Office Button
options
CC01.accdb
tblKitAssembly

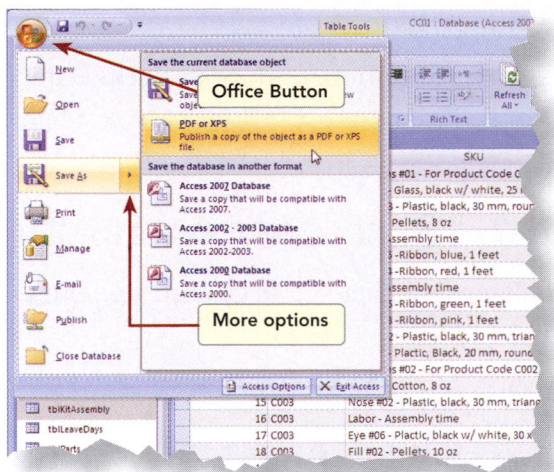

3. Change the location to the location where you will be storing your homework.

4. Click to the right of the file name and key in a hyphen and your initials.

5. Click the **Open file after publishing** check box.

6. Click **Publish** to create the XPS file. Your file has been opened in Internet Explorer.

7. Close Internet Explorer.

8. Right-click the **tblKitAssembly** tab and select **Close All**.

9. Collapse the **Tables** group.

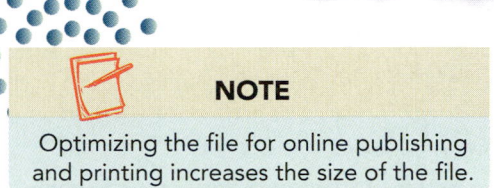

NOTE

Optimizing the file for online publishing and printing increases the size of the file.

Managing Access Files

Access, similar to many database applications, is designed to utilize space quickly, but not necessarily effectively. Normal database activities, such as adding, deleting, and moving data, can make the file unnecessarily large. After performing extensive work on a database, you should compact the data to save disk space.

The database expands and is usually not as efficiently organized on the disk as it could be. After compacting, you can back up the database to a new location, back it up with a new name, close it, or exit the program.

Exercise 1-16   USE COMPACT AND REPAIR

The Compact and Repair Database command reclaims unused space and improves database efficiency. After compacting an inefficient database, many activities will perform quicker.

1. Click the Office Button 🔵.

2. From the **Manage** option, choose **Compact and Repair Database**.

Exercise 1-17   BACK UP A DATABASE

By default, the backup file is saved to the same location as the original file. The default name is the original database name with the current date appended to the end. You can change both default values.

1. Click the Office Button 🔘.

2. From the **Manage** option, choose **Back Up Database**.

3. Click **Save**.

Exercise 1-18   CLOSE A DATABASE AND EXIT ACCESS

Now that you have compacted and backed up your database, you can close your database and Access.

1. Click the Office Button 🔘.

2. Click **Close Database**. This closes your database but not Access.

3. Click the Office Button 🔘.

4. Click **Exit Access**.

Lesson 1 Summary

- An Access database is relational, the most common type of database in use today.
- Major Access database objects include tables, queries, forms, and reports.
- A record is composed of related fields, a table is composed of related records, and a database is composed of related tables.
- A recordset is a Microsoft object-oriented data structure consisting of grouped records.
- A recordset is most often displayed as either a form or a report.
- An opened database cannot be moved or renamed.
- Shared mode is the default mode for most databases. This mode allows multiple users to use the database simultaneously.
- When opening a database, a security alert displays on the Message Bar alerting you that the database may contain malicious code.
- In the Navigation Pane, major objects are organized by categories and groups.
- The Leszynski Naming Convention is a method of naming objects that emphasizes the use of three-letter prefixes to identify the type of object.
- Datasheet View and Design View are two methods of displaying each major object.
- Edit mode allows contents of fields to be changed.
- Navigation mode allows movement between fields.
- The columns and rows of a datasheet can be hidden, displayed, or resized.

- Format changes to a datasheet affect all text in every column and row.
- In a datasheet, column widths can be changed individually; row heights must all be the same.
- In a datasheet, some format commands can be applied to individual fields; other commands apply to the entire datasheet.
- The Quick Print command sends a document directly to the default printer without allowing changes to the print options.
- Documents can be printed or published in portrait or landscape orientation.
- Publishing a document as an XPS file in either reduced quality or high quality preserves document formatting.
- Normal database activities such as adding, deleting, and moving data can unnecessarily increase the size of a database file.
- The Compact and Repair Database command reclaims unused space and improves database efficiency.

LESSON 1		Command Summary	
Feature	**Button**	**Task Path**	**Keyboard**
Close active object	✕		Ctrl + W or Ctrl + F4
Close database		Office Button, Close Database	
Column width		Shortcut menu, Column width	
Collapse Navigation Pane	«		
Compact database		Office Button, Manage, Compact, and Repair Database	
Database Properties		Shortcut menu, Properties	
Datasheet View		Views, View, Datasheet View	
Design View		Views, View, Design View	
Exit Access	✕	Office Button, Exit Access	Alt + F4
Expand Navigation Pane	«		
Font Face		Font, Font	
Font Size		Font, Font Size	
Go to record			F5
Hide Columns		Shortcut menu, Hide Columns	

continues

LESSON 1		Command Summary *continued*	
Feature	**Button**	**Task Path**	**Keyboard**
Jump to next screen or record			`Page Down`
Jump to pervious screen or record			`Page Up`
Move to beginning of field text			`Home`
Move to end of field text			`End`
Move to first record	 ⏮		`Ctrl` + `Home`
Move to last record	 ⏭		`Ctrl` + `End`
Move to next field			`Tab`
Move to next record	 ▶		
Move to previous field			`Shift` + `Tab`
Move to previous record	 ◀		
Open database			`Ctrl` + `O`
Page Layout		Office Button, Print, Print Preview, Page Layout	
Print Preview		Office Button, Print, Print Preview	
Print		Office Button, Print	`Ctrl` + `P`
Row Height		Shortcut menu, Row Height	
Save		Office Button, Save	`Ctrl` + `S`
Unhide Columns		Shortcut menu, Unhide Columns	

Concepts Review

True/False Questions

Each of the following statements is either true or false. Indicate your choice by circling T or F.

T F   1. A record is the smallest storage element within a database.

T F   2. Through a form, you can edit fields in a recordset.

T F   3. A row displayed in a datasheet may have a different height than the other rows.

T F   4. You can use the navigation buttons to move to a specific record.

T F   5. A recordset must include two or more fields.

T F   6. A security alert normally displays when opening an Access database.

T F   7. The Leszynski Naming Convention emphasizes the use of spaces and underscores to identify types of objects.

T F   8. When you hide a column in Datasheet View, you are deleting the record from the table or query.

Short Answer Questions

Write the correct answer in the space provided.

1. What is the Leszynski Naming Convention prefix for table names?

_____

2. In Datasheet View, which buttons do you use to move to different records?

_____

3. What is a collection of logically organized commands?

_____

4. What shortcut menu command displays a hidden column?

_____

5. Where is the Quick Print button located?

_____

6. Which navigation button would move the insertion point from Record #3 to Record #2?

_____

7. What format command allows alternating rows of a datasheet to display in different colors?

_____

8. Which database utility improves database efficiency and reduces storage requirements?

_____

Critical Thinking

Answer these questions on a separate page. There are no right or wrong answers. Support your answers with examples from your own experience, if possible.

1. Why would you need to open more than one table at a time? When might you need to hide one or more columns before printing a table?

2. How are navigation buttons different from scroll bars? When would you use scroll bars? When would you use navigation buttons?

Skills Review

Exercise 1-19

Manage a database and identify its components.

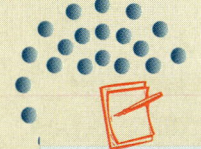

NOTE

If you have the file *[your initials]*-CC01 from the lesson, you can skip to Step 2.

1. Copy and rename a database by following these steps:
   a. Open the folder **Lesson 01**.
   b. Right-click the file **CC01**, and from the shortcut menu, choose **Copy**.
   c. Right-click an unused part of the folder. From the short-cut menu, choose **Paste**.
   d. Right-click the new file, and from the shortcut menu, choose **Rename**. Rename the file to *[your initials]*-**CC01**.
   e. Right-click *[your initials]*-**CC01,** and from the shortcut menu, choose **Properties**. Make certain that the Read-only attribute check box is not checked. Click **OK**.

2. Open a database by following these steps:
   a. Locate *[your initials]*-**CC01** and double-click it.
   b. In the Message Bar's **Security Warning**, click the **Options** button. The **Microsoft Office Security Options** dialog box appears.
   c. Click **Enable this content** and click **OK**.

3. Identify objects by following these steps:

   a. In the Navigation Pane, click the **Tables** group to expand the group.

   b. Create a Word document called *[your initials]*-Skills-01 and record the answer to the following question:

   How many tables are in the database?

   c. Record your answer in the new Word file and place "Ex 1-19 – Step 3b" next to your answer.

   d. In the Navigation Pane, click the **Tables** group to collapse the group.

   e. In the Navigation Pane, click the **Reports** group to expand the group.

   f. Answer the following question:

   How many reports are in the database?

   g. Record your answer in the same Word file as in step 3c and place "Ex 1-19 – Step 3f" next to your answer.

   h. In the Navigation Pane, click the **Reports** group to collapse the group.

   i. Add your name, class information, and today's date to the Word file.

4. Print/Save the Word file *[your initials]*-**Skills-01** by following these steps:

   a. Click the Office Button . From the **Print** option, choose Print Preview.

   b. Depending on your classroom procedures, either:

   • Click the Print command to print the datasheet, or

   • Click the XPS command to publish the datasheet.

Exercise 1-20

Navigate records. Resize rows and columns. Print/Save a table.

1. The database *[your initials]*-**CC01** is required to complete this exercise.

   a. Double-click the database *[your initials]*-**CC01**.

   b. In the Message Bar, press **Options**. In the dialog box, click **Enable this content** and click **OK**.

2. Navigate records in a table by following these steps:

   a. In the Navigation Pane, click the **Tables** group to expand the group.

   b. Double-click the table **tblAssets** to open it.

   c. In the Navigation Bar, click the Next Record button twice to move to the third record.

   d. Press Tab to move to the second field.

   e. Press Ctrl + Home to move to the first field in the first record.

3. Resize rows and columns in Datasheet View by following these steps:

   a. Place the pointer on the vertical border between the column headers for **Asset ID** and **Asset Name**.

b. With the two-headed arrow showing, drag the pointer to the left to remove the extra white space. Make sure that you can still see all of the data.

    c. Right-click on the record selector for the first row.

    d. In the **Row Height** dialog box, key **40** and click **OK**.

4. Print/Save the Datasheet View of a table by following these steps:

    a. Click the Office Button . From the **Print** option, choose Print Preview .

    b. Depending on your classroom procedures, either:

- Click the Print command to print the datasheet, or
- Click the XPS command to publish the datasheet.

5. Close an object by following these steps:

    a. Right-click the **tblAssets** tab. From the shortcut menu, select **Close**.

    b. In the Navigation Pane, collapse the **Tables** group.

Exercise 1-21

Change views of a table. Modify a table. Hide fields. Print/Save a table.

1. The database *[your initials]*-**CC01** is required to complete this exercise.

    a. Double-click the database *[your initials]*-**CC01**.

    b. In the Message Bar, press **Options**. In the dialog box, click **Enable this content** and click **OK**.

2. Change the view by following these steps:

    a. In the Navigation Pane, expand the **Tables** group.

    b. In the **Tables** group of the Navigation Pane, double-click **tblCustomers**.

    c. In the command group **Views**, click the option arrow for the View command and select Design View.

    d. Right-click the document tab for the table, then select Datasheet View .

3. Hide fields by following these steps:

    a. Click on the column header for the field **Billing Address** and drag through **Region**.

    b. Right-click on the column header of a selected column and select **Hide Columns**.

    c. Click on the column header for the field **After Hours** and drag through **Initial Order**.

    d. Right-click on the column header of a selected column and select **Hide Columns**.

4. Print/Save the Datasheet View of a table by following these steps:

   a. Click the Office Button . From the **Print** option, choose Print Preview .

   b. Depending on your classroom procedures, either:

      • Click the Print command 🖶 to print the datasheet, or

      • Click the XPS command 📄 to publish the datasheet.

5. Close an object by following these steps:

   a. Right-click the **tblCustomers** tab. From the shortcut menu, select **Close**.

   b. Click **No** when Access asks you if you want to save the changes.

   c. In the Navigation Pane, collapse the **Tables** group.

Exercise 1-22

Manage the datasheet of a query. Print/Save a query. Compact and close a database.

1. The database *[your initials]*-**CC01** is required to complete this exercise.

   a. Double-click the database *[your initials]*-**CC01**.

   b. In the Message Bar, press **Options**. In the dialog box, click **Enable this content** and click **OK**.

2. Change the view by following these steps:

   a. In the Navigation Pane, expand the **Queries** group.

   b. In the **Queries** group of the Navigation Pane, double-click **qryCarrierOptions**.

   c. Right-click the document tab for the query, then select Design View.

   d. In the command group **Views**, click the option arrow for the View command 📐 and select Datasheet View.

3. Change datasheet colors by following these steps:

   a. In the command group **Font**, click the down arrow for Alternate Fill/Back Color 🎨.

   b. In the **Standard Theme Colors**, select **Maroon 2** (row 3, column 6) as the alternate color.

4. Print/Save the Datasheet View of a query by following these steps:

   a. Click the Office Button 🔵. From the **Print** option, choose Print Preview 🔍.

   b. Depending on your classroom procedures, either:

      • Click the Print command 🖶 to print the datasheet, or

      • Click the XPS command 📄 to publish the datasheet.

5. Close an object by following these steps:

   a. Right-click the **qryCarrierOptions** tab. From the shortcut menu, select **Close**.

   b. Click **Yes** when Access asks you if you want to save the changes.

   c. In the Navigation Pane, collapse the **Queries** group.

6. Compact and close the database by following these steps:

   a. Click the Office Button .

   b. From the **Manage** option, choose **Compact and Repair Database**.

   c. Click the Office Button .

   d. Select **Close Database**.

   e. Click the Office Button .

   f. Select **Exit Access**.

Lesson Applications

Exercise 1-23

Open a database and explore major objects.

1. Open *[your initials]*-**CC01** and enable all content.

2. Open **qryKitCosts** in Datasheet View.

3. Change the **Font Size** to **14** and apply italic .

4. Size each column to fit its longest data and column title.

5. Save the changes to the query.

6. Print/Save the datasheet in portrait orientation.

7. Close all objects and collapse all groups in the Navigation Pane.

Exercise 1-24

Modify and Print/Save the Datasheet View of a query.

1. With database *[your initials]*-**CC01** open, open **qryCarrierOptions** in Datasheet View.

2. Apply the Alternate Fill/Back Color  of **Medium Gray 2** (row 3, column 3).

3. Change the **Font** to **Courier New** and the **Font Size** to **16**.

4. Size each column to fit its longest data and column title.

5. Print/Save the Datasheet View in Landscape orientation.

6. Close the query, save changes to the datasheet, and collapse the query group in the Navigation Pane.

Exercise 1-25

Modify and Print/Save the Datasheet View of a table.

1. With database *[your initials]*-**CC01** open, open **tblVenders** in Datasheet View.

2. Hide all columns except **Vender ID**, **Contact Name**, and **Phone Number**.

3. Size each column to fit its longest data and column title.

4. Resize the row height to approximately twice its current height.

5. Print/Save the table in **Portrait** orientation.

6. Close the query, save changes to the datasheet, and collapse the table group in the Navigation Pane.

Exercise 1-26 ◆ Challenge Yourself

Switch views. Change the row height, font, and orientation. Print/Save a table. Compact a database.

1. With database *[your initials]*-**CC01** open, expand the **Tables** group and **Query** group in the Navigation Pane.

2. Create a Word document called *[your initials]*-**Apps-01** and record the answers to the following questions.

3. Which query has the most records?

4. Which table has the fewest records?

5. What table is the source for the recordset used by **qryFullName**?

TIP

The Design View of a query displays source tables and queries.

6. Include your name, class information, and today's date on your answer sheet.

7. Print/Save the Word file.

8. Close all objects and collapse all groups in the Navigation Pane.

9. Close the database file and exit the application software.

On Your Own

In these exercises you work on your own, as you would in a real-life work environment. Use the skills you've learned to accomplish the task—and be creative.

Exercise 1-27

Assume that you are forming a new club or professional association. Begin analyzing your needs on paper. Determine the name of your organization. Write one or two paragraphs describing the mission or purpose of your group. After you have completed this exercise, continue to the next exercise.

NOTE

The "On Your Own" exercises in this text are all related. They form a single project. To complete the project, you must do all the "On Your Own" exercises in each lesson.

Exercise 1-28

Now think about the specific type of information your club or association will need to track its membership. Write a bulleted list of information you want to collect for each member (e.g., first name, email address). You should have no fewer than seven items. Continue to the next exercise.

Exercise 1-29

Using the list you created in Exercise 1-28, gather information about five potential members. On a single sheet of paper, record the data you collected. Submit your work for Exercises 1-27 through 1-29 to your instructor.

Viewing and Modifying Records

OBJECTIVES

After completing this lesson, you will be able to:

1. Modify recordsets in a table.

2. Modify recordsets through a query.

3. Use Office editing tools.

4. View and modify recordsets through a form.

5. Manage attachments.

6. Preview, print, and save data using a report.

MCAS OBJECTIVES

In this lesson:
AC07_3.1
AC07_3.2
AC07_3.4
AC07_5.5
AC07_5.6

Estimated Time: 1¹/₂ hours

In Lesson 1, you learned about the database environment including major objects such as tables, queries, forms, and reports. In this lesson, you learn to add, edit, delete, and print data. You learn how to use time-saving edit commands like duplicate, copy, and paste. You also learn how to store images in tables.

You will work directly with data in a table or as a recordset through a query, form, or report. A query creates a recordset based upon an entire table, a portion of a table, or a combination of one or more tables. Although you can look at an entire table in Datasheet View, more often it is easier to use a query and form.

Modifying Recordsets in a Table

Records are routinely added to a database. For example, when a new student enrolls in your school, a record is added to your school's database. If a new employee begins working at Carolina Critters, the company must add the person's information to the database. On other occasions, a record might be deleted if the information will no longer be used.

Exercise 2-1   OPEN A DATABASE

In addition to the database file, in this lesson you will use several text and image files. These files are located in the **Lesson 02** folder. Before opening the Access database, you must move and rename the file.

1. Locate the folder **Lesson 02**. Double-click the folder **Lesson 02** to see its contents.

2. Right-click the file **CC02** and, from the shortcut menu, choose **Rename**. On the keyboard, press Home to move to the beginning of the file name. Key your initials and then a hyphen. Press Enter to accept the new name.

3. Double-click *[your initials]*-**CC02** to open the database.

4. In the **Security Warning** message bar, click the **Option** button. The **Microsoft Office Security Options** dialog box appears.

5. Click **Enable this content** and click **OK**.

TIP

If a Read only message appears in the Message bar, you will need to close the database, deselect the Read-only property, and reopen the file.

Exercise 2-2   EDIT FIELDS IN A TABLE

You do not need to "save" when you make changes to a record. Access automatically saves your changes as soon as you move the insertion point to another record.

You can determine if a record has been saved by the shape of pointer in the Record Selector. Two shapes can appear in the Record Selector:

- A pencil icon appears while you are adding or editing text. This indicates the record changes have not been saved.

- An asterisk marks a new record.

1. In the Navigation Pane, expand the **Tables** group and double-click **tblCustomers** to open it in Datasheet View.

2. In the first record, click in the **Company Name** field. This places the insertion point in the field.

3. Press End to move the insertion point to end of the data in the field.

4. Press Ctrl + Backspace to delete "Inc."

NOTE

Notice the pencil icon in the record selector indicates that the record has been modified.

Access 2007

Figure 2-1
Modifying a record
CC02.accdb
tblCustomers

5. Key **LLC**.

6. In the **Contact Name** field of the first record, double-click on "Peterson" to select the word.

7. Key **Butler** to change the last name.

8. In the **Billing Address** field for **Customer ID** #7's record, click between the "7" and the "6."

9. Press ⟨Delete⟩ once and key **1**. You have changed "2876" to "2871."

10. Press ⟨Tab⟩ to move to the field **City**. Press the space bar to delete the data.

11. Press ⟨Esc⟩ to undo the deletion of the data.

12. Press ⟨↓⟩ to save the changes to the record. Notice that the pencil icon has disappeared from the record selector.

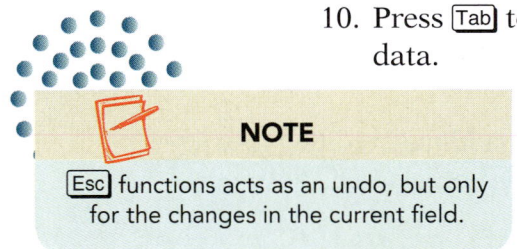

NOTE

⟨Esc⟩ functions acts as an undo, but only for the changes in the current field.

Exercise 2-3   ADD A RECORD IN A TABLE

When adding records in Datasheet View, you add the records to the end of the table. The last row of the table in which the new record will be added is marked by an asterisk in the Record Selector. You move to the new record row by any of the following steps:

- Right-click the selected record and, on the shortcut menu, select **New Record**.

- Click the New Record command ⊞.

- From the **Home** command tab, in the command group **Records**, select the New command ⊞ New.

- ⟨Ctrl⟩+⟨+⟩.

 New

1. From the command tab **Home**, in the command group **Records**, click the New command . This moves the insertion point to the empty record at the bottom of the table.

2. Key the customer information below to create a new record. Press Tab to move from one field to the next.

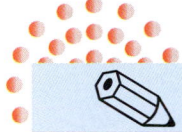
Customer ID:	21
Company Name:	Checker Toys
Contact Name:	Kathy Prince
Billing Address:	8854 Elm Street
City:	Knoxville
State:	TN
ZIP Code:	39725-6458
Region Name:	1
Phone Number:	(423)555-3456
Fax Number:	(423)555-3457
After Hours:	*Press* Tab
Tax Exempt:	*Press* Spacebar *to add a checkmark*
Initial Order:	8/5/07

3. Press ↑ to leave the new record, which will save the changes.

4. Press Ctrl+PageUp to return to the first field in the record.

Exercise 2-4   DELETE A RECORD IN A TABLE

There are times when you find that records are no longer needed and should be removed from a table. An example might be that you find a record that was entered into the wrong table.

To delete one or more records, you must first select the record(s) that you intend to delete. After selecting the record(s), you can use one of four methods:

- Select a record and press Delete.

- Right-click a selected record and, on the shortcut menu, select **Delete Record**.

- From the command tab **Home**, in the command group **Records**, select the Delete command × .

- Ctrl+-.

1. In the **Datasheet View** of the table **tblCustomers**, click on the Record Selector to select the record for "Crafts & More."

Figure 2-2
Selecting a record
for deletion
CC02.accdb
tblCustomers

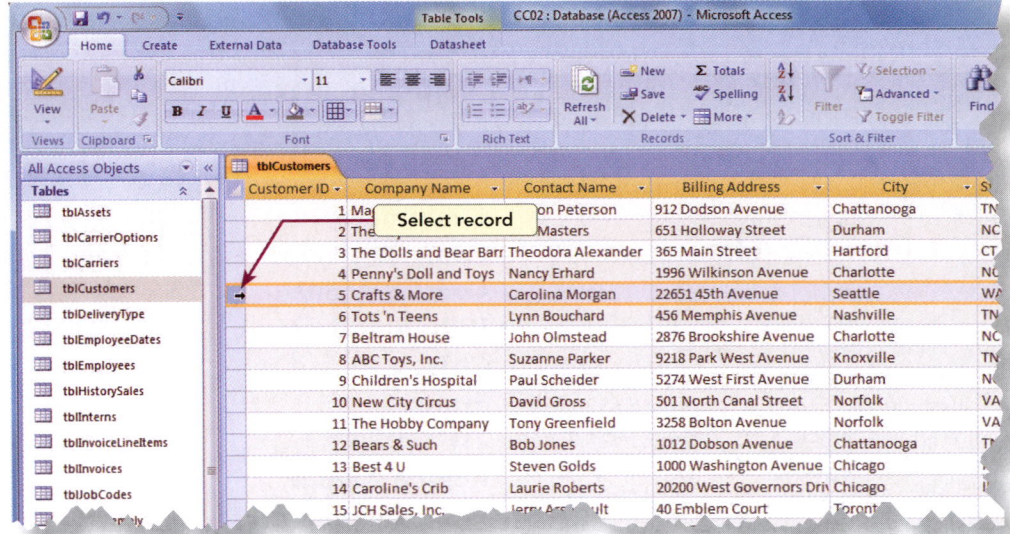

2. Press Delete. The record disappears, and a dialog box opens asking you to confirm the deletion.

Figure 2-3
Dialog box
confirming deletion
CC02.accdb
tblCustomers

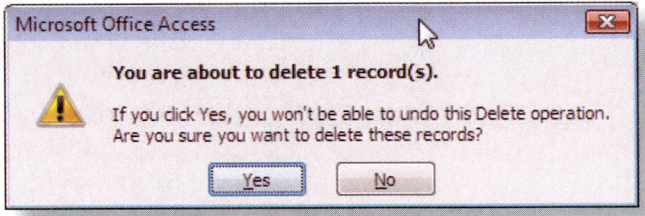

3. Click **Yes**. Access deletes the record.

4. Click anywhere in the **Company Name** field for "New City Circus" to make it the current record.

5. Press Ctrl + - and then click **Yes** to confirm the deletion.

6. In the Navigation Pane, collapse the **Tables** group.

Modifying Recordsets through a Query

When you use a query to make changes to data, you are making changes to the recordset. Although the records display in a query, the data are actually stored in a table. When you edit a record in a query, the data in the underlying table are changed automatically.

Although records can be added directly into a table, more often queries are used to enter data. An advantage to editing through a query over a table is that the recordset of a query does not have to display all the records or fields in the table. Using a query allows you to view only the relevant fields and records.

Exercise 2-5 EDIT FIELDS THROUGH A QUERY

When editing a record, you can insert text or use the **Overtype** mode to key over existing text. Use Insert to switch between **Insert** and **Overtype** mode.

1. In the **Queries** group of the Navigation Pane, double-click the **qryCustomersContact**. Notice that there are only 19 records.

2. In the record for **Customer ID** #11, in the field **Contact Name**, click to the right of the "n" in Greenfield.

3. Press Insert to switch to **Overtype** mode.

Figure 2-4
Overtype mode
CC02.accdb
qryCustomersContact

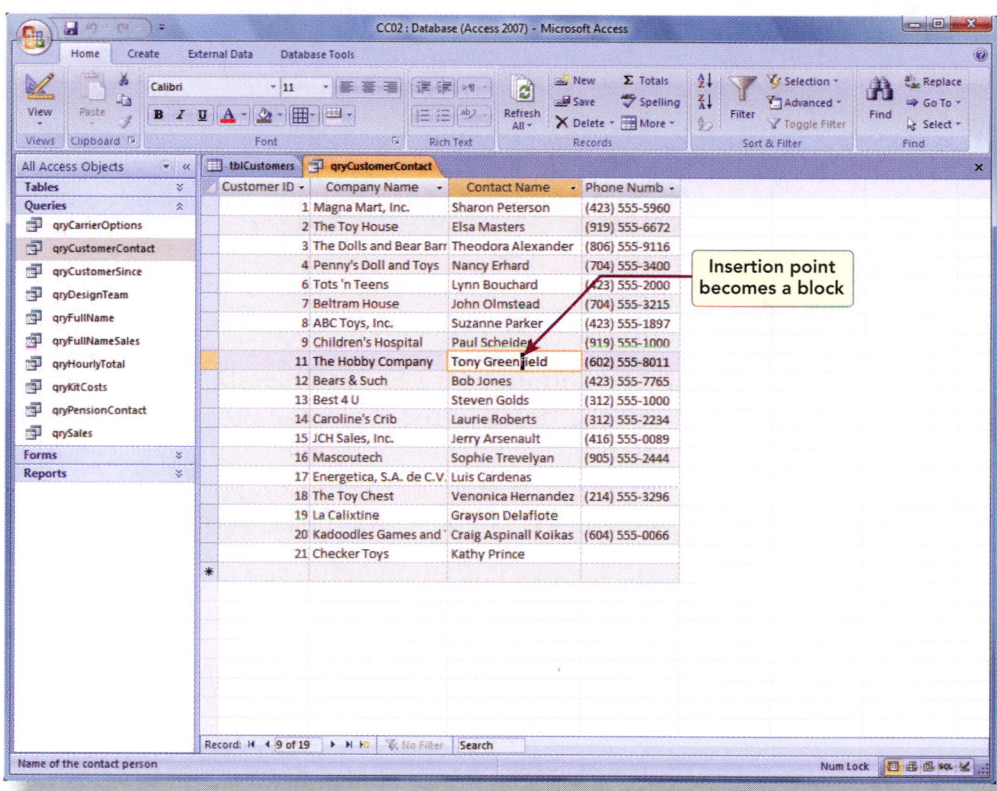

4. Key **stein**.

5. In the "Tots 'n Teens" record, in the **Contact Name** field, select "B" of "Bouchard."

6. Key **Leachman** over the old name.

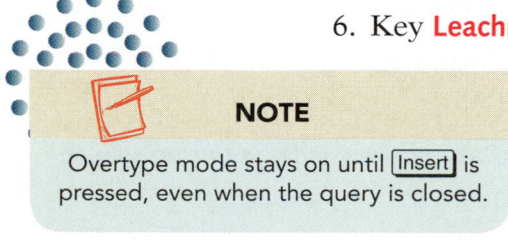

> **NOTE**
>
> Overtype mode stays on until Insert is pressed, even when the query is closed.

7. Press Insert to return to **Insert** mode.

8. Press Ctrl+S to save the record.

9. Click the **tblCustomers** tab to see the changes made through the query.

Exercise 2-6   ADD A RECORD THROUGH A QUERY

The additions made in the query's recordset are simultaneously made to the underlying table. The corresponding fields in a table are updated through a query even when the query recordset does not include all the fields in the source table.

1. Click on the **qryCustomersContact** tab and press Ctrl+⊞ to move to a new record.

2. Key the customer information below to create a new record. Press Tab to move from one field to the next.

NOTE

In this text, to help identify your work, you often are asked to key an identifier such as your name or initials.

Customer ID:	22
Company Name:	New City Circus
Contact Name:	*Key [your full name]*
Phone Number:	(602) 555-1800

3. Press Shift+Enter to save the record.

4. Click the **tblCustomers** tab and look for the New City Circus record.

5. From the command tab **Home**, in the command group **Records**, click the Refresh All command ⊞.

6. You should now see **Customer ID** "22." Because the query did not use all the fields in the table, the record is incomplete.

Exercise 2-7   DELETE A RECORD THROUGH A QUERY

Similarly to adding a record through a query, you can delete a record through a query.

1. Click the **qryCustomersContact** tab and click the record selector for New City Circus.

2. Right-click the selected record. From the short-cut menu, select **Delete Record.** Click **Yes** to confirm the deletion.

NOTE

When you deleted the record while in the query **qryCustomersContact**, Access automatically refreshed the query. By selecting **Refresh All**, you tell Access to refresh the data being displayed in all open objects.

3. Click the **tblCustomer** tab. Notice that the record for New City Circus has "#Deleted" in each cell.

4. From the command tab **Home**, in the command group **Records**, click the Refresh All command ⊞.

5. Right-click the **tblCustomer** tab. From the shortcut menu, select **Close All**.

6. In the Navigation Pane, collapse the **Queries** group.

Using Office Editing Tools

Similar to Word and Excel, Access uses AutoCorrect. *AutoCorrect* is an application feature that automatically corrects commonly misspelled words. The AutoCorrect Options button appears next to text being automatically corrected. Choices within the button allow you to customize the correction process. You can undo the correction, cancel future automatic corrections for this error, or turn off the AutoCorrect option completely.

The Office Clipboard is a feature available in Microsoft Word, Excel, PowerPoint, Access, and Outlook. You can use this clipboard to collect and paste multiple items. The contents of the Office Clipboard are deleted when you close Access. If you have multiple Office programs running, the contents of the Office Clipboard are deleted after you close the last Office program. You can copy items while using any program that provides copy and cut functionality, but you can only paste items into a Microsoft Office application.

Exercise 2-8 USE AUTOCORRECT

Text edit commands are used to make changes to the data within a record. AutoCorrect corrects commonly misspelled words as you key text. For example, if you type "teh," AutoCorrect will change it to "the." AutoCorrect also can fix many capitalization errors.

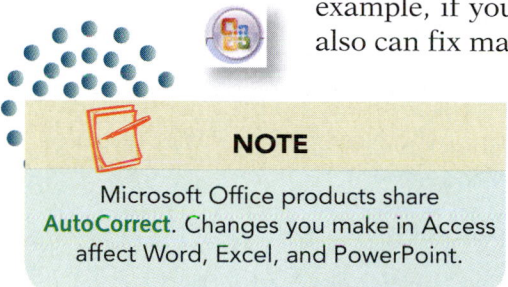

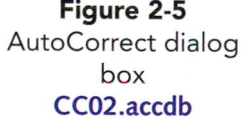

> **NOTE**
>
> Microsoft Office products share **AutoCorrect**. Changes you make in Access affect Word, Excel, and PowerPoint.

1. Click the Office Button and choose Access Options button.

2. In the left pane, click **Proofing**.

3. In the right pane, click the **AutoCorrect Options** button. This opens the AutoCorrect dialog box.

Figure 2-5
AutoCorrect dialog box
CC02.accdb

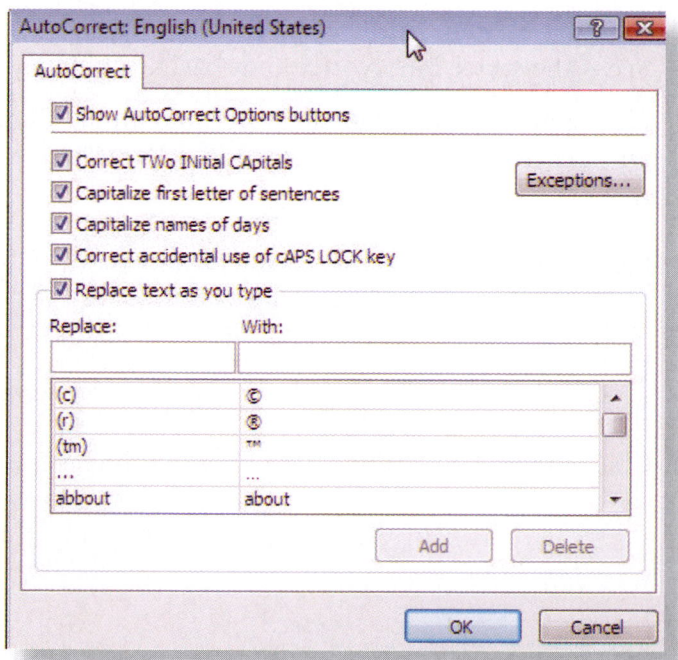

4. Make sure all check boxes are checked.

5. Scroll down the list of entries to see which words are in the **AutoCorrect** dictionary.

TABLE 2-1 AutoCorrect Options

Options	Description
Show AutoCorrect option buttons	Option button appears after a word was automatically corrected.
Correct TWo INitial CApitals	Corrects words keyed with two initial capital letters, such as "THis."
Capitalize first letter of sentences	Capitalizes the first letter in a sentence.
Capitalize names of days	Capitalizes days of the week and months.
Correct accidental use of cAPS LOCK key	Corrects words keyed with Caps Lock on but Shift key pressed, such as cAPS.
Replace text as you type	Makes corrections as you work.

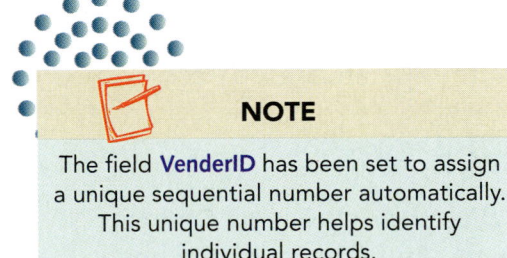

NOTE

The field **VenderID** has been set to assign a unique sequential number automatically. This unique number helps identify individual records.

6. Click **OK** to close the **AutoCorrect Options** dialog box.

7. Click **OK** to close the **Access Options** dialog box.

8. In the **Tables** group of the Navigation Pane, double-click the table **tblVenders**.

9. Press Ctrl + ＋ to add a new record.

10. Press Tab to move to the **Vender Name** field.

11. Key **ACN**.

12. Press the space bar. Notice that "ACN" changed to "CAN."

13. Place your pointer over the corrected word. Click the **AutoCorrect Options** icon when it appears and select **Change back to ACN**.

14. Key **Inc.** to complete the field.

15. Press Tab to move to the **Contact Name** field.

16. Key **TIm Herat**. Press Tab. Notice that AutoCorrect corrected the name to "Tim Heart."

17. Press ↑ to save changes to the record.

18. Click the Close command ✕ for the table.

Exercise 2-9   USE COPY, PASTE, AND THE OFFICE CLIPBOARD

You can copy a block of text from one part of a table to another. There are three ways to copy and paste text:

- From the ribbon, click the Copy command  and Paste command buttons.

- Press Ctrl + C (copy) and Ctrl + V (paste).

- Right-click and, from the shortcut menu, choose **Copy** and **Paste**.

TIP

Unlike the Office Clipboard, the Windows Clipboard only stores the last item copied. On both Clipboards, text can be pasted repeatedly. However, when you copy new information using the Windows Clipboard, the old information on the Windows Clipboard is replaced by the new information.

NOTE

F2 selects an entire content of a field.

NOTE

When you press Ctrl + ;, Access will enter the current system date, according to your computer.

When you copy the second text block, the Office Clipboard pane opens. You can use the Office Clipboard to paste multiple blocks of text. From that pane, you can select the item you want to paste.

You can duplicate the data from a field in the previous record to the same field in the current record by pressing Ctrl + ' (apostrophe). The Duplicate command copies one field at a time.

You can also paste an entire record from one location to another by using the Paste Append command.

1. In the Navigation Pane, double-click the query **qryCustomerSince**.

2. Find the record for "Energetica" and click in the field **Company Name**.

3. Press F2 to select the whole field.

4. Press Ctrl + ' to copy the content field from the previous record.

5. Double-click the word "Hospital" and key **Corner**.

6. Press Tab to move to the next field.

7. Press Ctrl + ; to replace the old date with today's date. Press Tab to save the changes.

8. From the command tab **Home**, in the lower-right corner of the command group **Clipboard**, click the dialog box launcher to open the **Clipboard** pane.

Figure 2-6
Clipboard group
CC02.accdb
qryCustomerSince

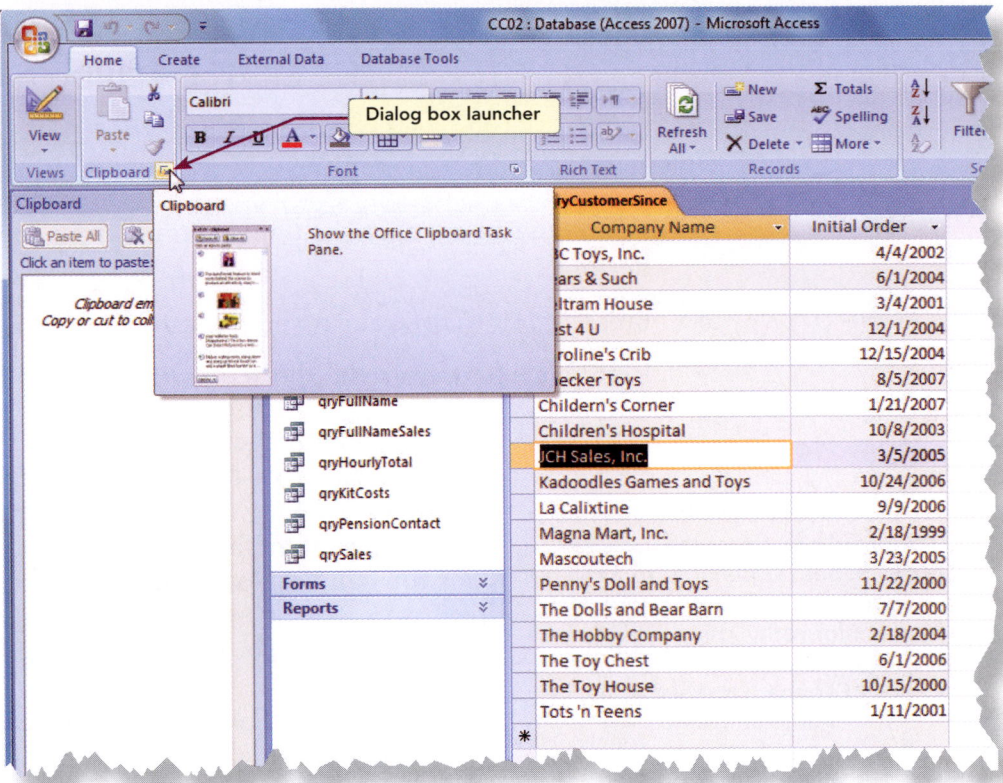

NOTE

The Office Clipboard holds up to 24 copied items.

TIP

In the Clipboard, the icon next to each copied item indicates the application from which the item was copied.

9. In the first record's **Company Name** field, click between the "s" and ",". Press Shift+End to select ", Inc."

10. Click Ctrl+C to copy. Notice that the selected text has been added to the **Clipboard**.

11. In the 16th record's (The Hobby Company) **Company Name** field, double-click the word "Company" to select it.

12. From the command tab **Home**, in the command group **Clipboard**, click the Copy command 📋. There are now two items in the **Clipboard**.

13. In the 13th record's (Mascoutech) **Company Name** field, click to the right of the data and press the spacebar to add a space.

14. Press Ctrl+V to paste the last text copied.

15. In the 17th record's (The Toy Chest) **Company Name** field, click to the right of the data.

16. From the Clipboard pane, click ", Inc." to paste the text.

17. In the 18th record's (The Toy House) **Company Name** field, click to the right of the data.

18. From the Clipboard pane, click ", Inc." to paste the text.

19. Click the **Clipboard** Close command ⊠.

20. Right-click the **qryCustomerSince** tab. From the short-cut menu, select **Close**.

21. In the Navigation Pane, collapse the **Queries** group.

Exercise 2-10   USE UNDO

In a previous exercise you used ⎡Esc⎤ to cancel changes in a field. You will now use the Undo command ⟲, which can affect fields, records, or even major objects.

Access remembers changes to the record and lets you undo most edits. If you accidentally delete text in a field, you can use the Undo command to reverse the action. One exception to this is if you delete a record, it can't be undone. There are two ways to undo an action:

- On the **Quick Access Toolbar**, click the Undo command ⟲.

- Press ⎡Ctrl⎤+⎡Z⎤.

1. In the Navigation Pane, double-click the table **tblRegions**.

2. In the field **Region Name**, double-click "Southeast."

3. Press ⎡Delete⎤ to delete the data.

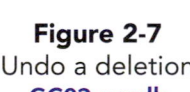

4. In the **Quick Access Toolbar**, click the Undo command ⟲.

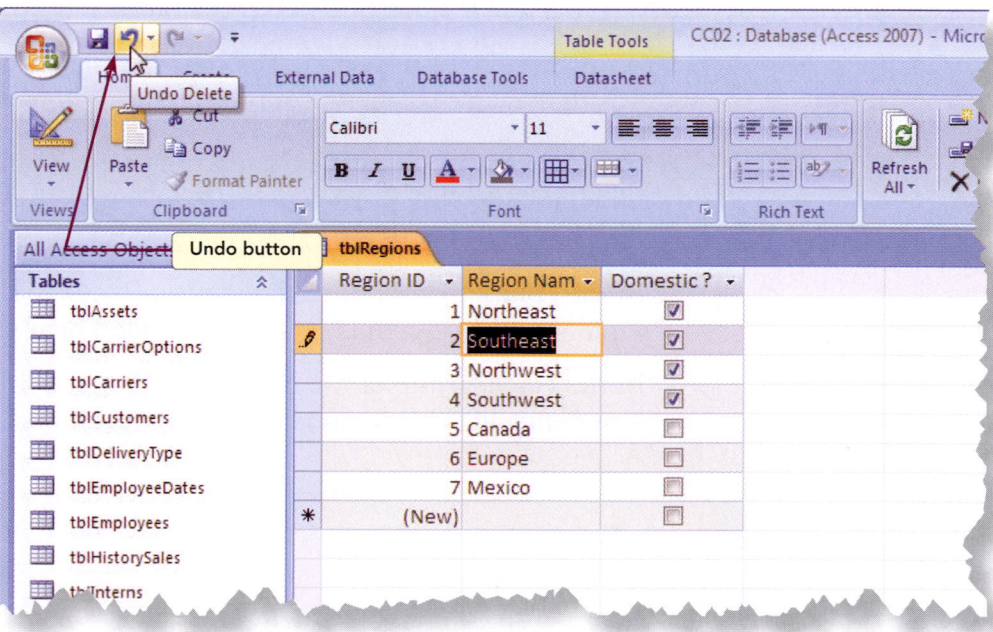

Figure 2-7
Undo a deletion
CC02.accdb
tblRegions

5. Click the Record Selector for Region ID "2" and press `Delete`.

6. Read the dialog box and then click **Yes** to confirm the deletion.

7. Press `Ctrl`+`Z` to attempt to undo the deletion. Nothing happens because once a record is deleted, it can't be undone.

8. Right-click the **tblRegions** tab. From the shortcut menu, select **Close**.

9. In the Navigation Pane, click the table **tblRegions** to select it. Do not open the table.

10. From the command tab **Home**, in the command group **Records**, click the Delete command `×`.

11. In the dialog box, click **Yes**. The table is deleted.

12. Press `Ctrl`+`Z` to undo the deletion.

13. In the Navigation Pane, collapse the **Tables** group.

Viewing and Modifying Recordsets through a Form

A form is a major Access object. A form is designed to be used on a computer screen. Through a form, you can enter, view, sort, edit, and print data. Most often when making changes to records, it is easier to use a form rather than a table. A form uses the same navigation buttons, scroll bars, and text editing features as a table.

Exercise 2-11   NAVIGATE THROUGH FORMS

A form is linked to a recordset. The fields displayed through a form are the same as in the table or query from which they originate.

1. In the **Forms** group of the Navigation Pane, double-click the form **frmInternList**. This form is using the Continuous Form view to display data.

2. In the **Forms** group of the Navigation Pane, double-click the form **frmInterns**. This form is using the Single Form view.

3. In the **Forms** group of the Navigation Pane, double-click the form **frmInternSplit**. This form is using the Split Form view.

Figure 2-8
Multiple open
documents
CC02.accdb
frmInternSplit

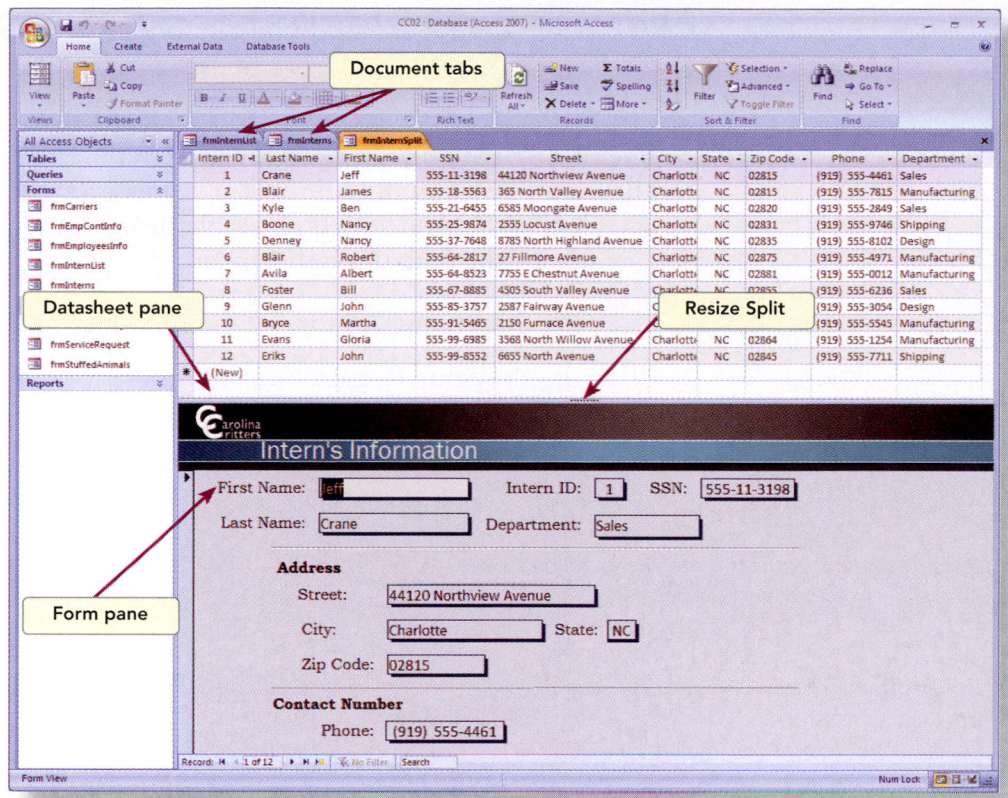

4. Click the document tab for the form **frmInternList**.

5. Press Tab to move the cursor to the second field (**SSN**) in the first record.

6. Press Ctrl+PageDown to move to the second record.

7. Press Ctrl+End to move to the last field in the last record.

8. Click the document tab for the form **frmInterns**.

9. Press Tab 5 times. Notice the selected field order is not always left to right or top down.

10. Press PageDown to move to the next record. Notice that the field Street is still selected.

11. In the Record Navigation tool, click the Last Record button ⏭. The record for John Eriks is now visible.

12. Click the document tab for the form **frmInternSplit**.

13. Press Tab to move through the first record. Notice that the fields in the form are not in the same order as in the datasheet.

14. Press PageDown to move to the next record. Notice that the information in the selected record and the form are the same.

Exercise 2-12   EDIT FIELDS THROUGH A FORM

You can edit data in a form with the same shortcuts you use in a table or a query. For example, [Backspace] deletes a single character and the keyboard combination [Ctrl]+[Delete] deletes everything to the right of the insertion point.

The data displayed in each field of a form are stored in a table. Just as you can change the data stored in a table through the table's Datasheet View, you can change the data through a form.

1. Click the document tab for the form **frmInternList**.

2. Click the Previous Record button ◂ until you get to the "Gloria Evens" (**Intern ID** 11) record.

3. In the **Street** field, click to the left of "Avenue" and press [Ctrl]+[Delete].

4. Key **Boulevard**. Notice the pencil icon in the record selector.

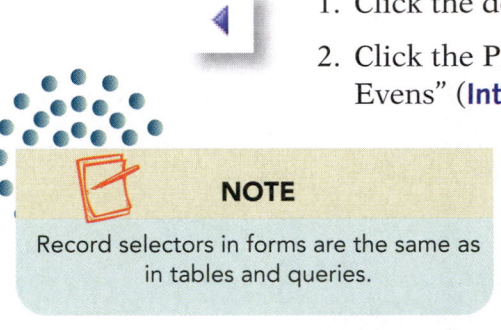

NOTE

Record selectors in forms are the same as in tables and queries.

Figure 2-9
Edit data in a form
CC02.accdb
frmInternList

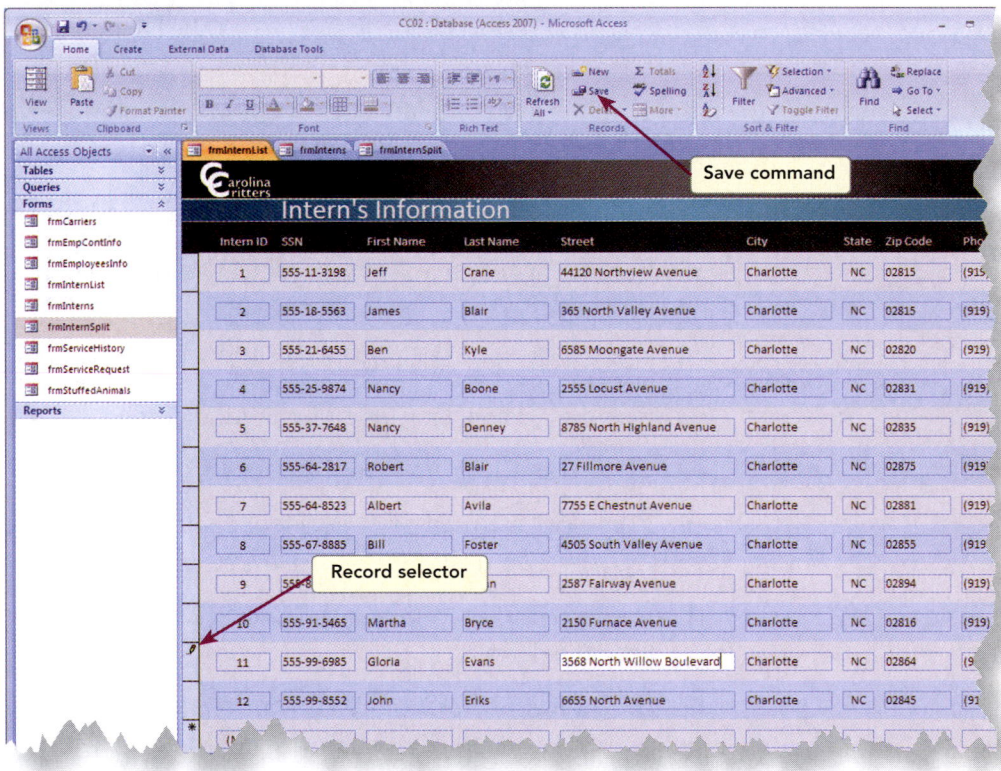

5. From the command tab **Home**, in the command group **Records**, click the Save command . Notice the pencil icon is no longer in the record selector.

6. Click the document tab for the form **frmInternSplit**.

7. In the datasheet at the top of the form, click anywhere in the record for "Nancy Boone" (**Intern ID** 4.)

8. Double-click the **City** field for the selected record to select all content.

9. Key **Garner** and press Enter. Notice that the data in the **City** field have changed in the lower part of the form.

10. Press ↓ to save the changes to the record.

11. Click in any field in the form (lower half.)

Exercise 2-13 ADD RECORDS THROUGH A FORM

A form can make it easier for you to add records. A well-designed form utilizes field placement to improve the efficiency of data entry.

1. From the command tab **Home**, in the command group **Records**, click the New command 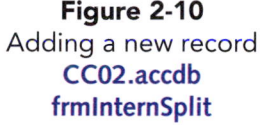. The record selector will display an asterisk until you key new data.

2. Key the following new record, pressing Tab between entries:

First Name:	*Key [your first name]*
Last Name:	*Key [your first name]*
SSN:	555-99-7845
Department:	Administration
Street:	825 Canal Street
City:	Cary
State:	NC
Zip Code:	27513
Phone:	(919) 555-1601

Figure 2-10
Adding a new record
CC02.accdb
frmInternSplit

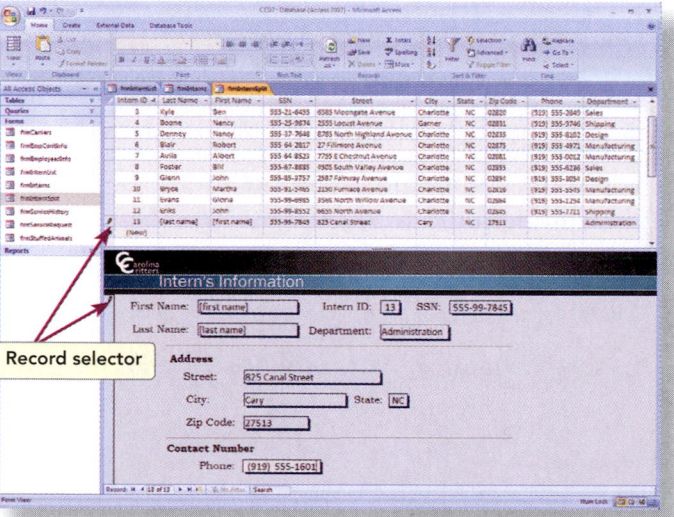

3. Press Ctrl + S.

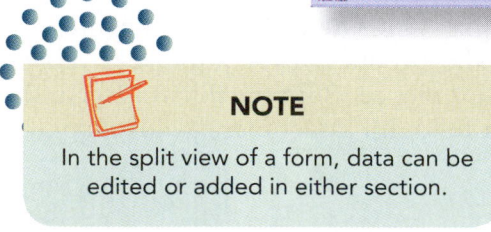

NOTE

In the split view of a form, data can be edited or added in either section.

Exercise 2-14 DELETE RECORDS THROUGH A FORM

You can delete the current record by using all the same methods you used when deleting a record in a table.

1. Click the document tab for the form **frmInternList**.

2. Click in any field for the intern "James Blair" (**Intern ID** 2.)

3. From the command tab **Home**, in the command group **Records**, click the Delete command ×⃒ option arrow and choose the Delete Record command ⍖.

Figure 2-11
Delete options
CC02.accdb
frmInternList

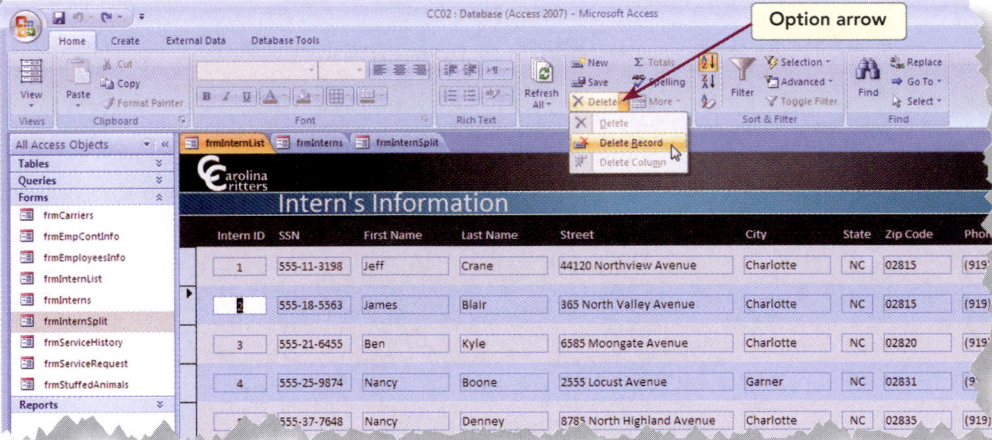

4. Click **Yes** to confirm the deletion.

5. Click the document tab for the form **frmInternSplit**. Notice that there is a row with "#Deleted" in each field.

6. From the command tab **Home**, in the command group **Records**, click the command Refresh All ⍟.

7. Right-click the **frmInternSplit** tab. From the shortcut menu, select **Close All**.

8. In the Navigation Pane, collapse the **Forms** group.

Managing Attachments

Some tables include an image with each record. The Stuffed Animals table includes a field with an illustration of the product. The Employees table includes a field with a photograph of the employee. Both the illustration and the photograph are images attached to a field. All attachment fields display as a paperclip in datasheet view.

In addition to images, you can attach certain types of data files such as documents, worksheets, or text files. The **Attachments** window allows you to add, remove, open, or save an attachment. Attached files cannot be larger than 256 megabytes or be non-data files such as programs, system files, or batch files.

Exercise 2-15 ATTACH AN IMAGE

When attaching an image, you must know the location of the file and in which record the file will be stored.

1. In the **Tables** group of the Navigation Pane, double-click the table **tblStuffedAnimals**.

2. Locate the record for "Larry Lion" (**Product ID** 13.)

3. Double-click the attachment field. The **Attachments** dialog box appears.

Figure 2-12
Adding an attachment
CC02.accdb
tblStuffedAnimals

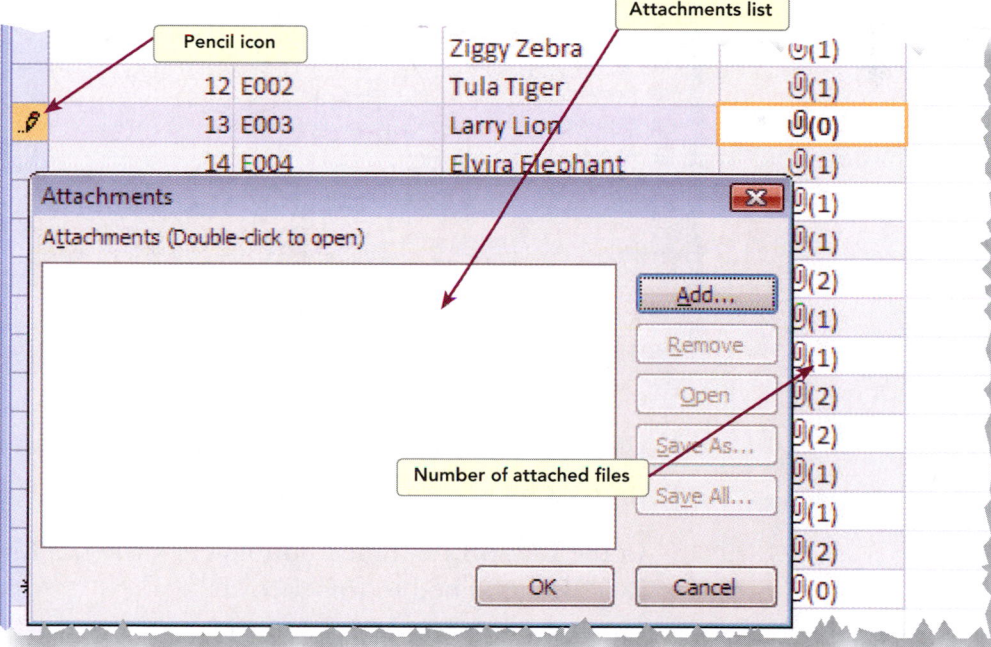

4. The names of attached files appear in the Attachments list. Click **Add**.

5. Locate the **Lesson 02** folder. Double-click the file **Lin003**.

6. Click **OK**.

7. Press Ctrl+S to save the changes in the record.

8. Close the table by right-clicking the table's document tab and choosing **Close**.

9. In the Navigation Pane, collapse the **Tables** group.

10. In the **Forms** group of the Navigation Pane, double-click the form **frmStuffedAnimals**.

11. Press ⌈PageDown⌉ until you get to the "Larry Lion" record.

12. Click the picture. A mini toolbar appears above the image.

Figure 2-13
Attachments in a
form
CC02.accdb
frmStuffedAnimals

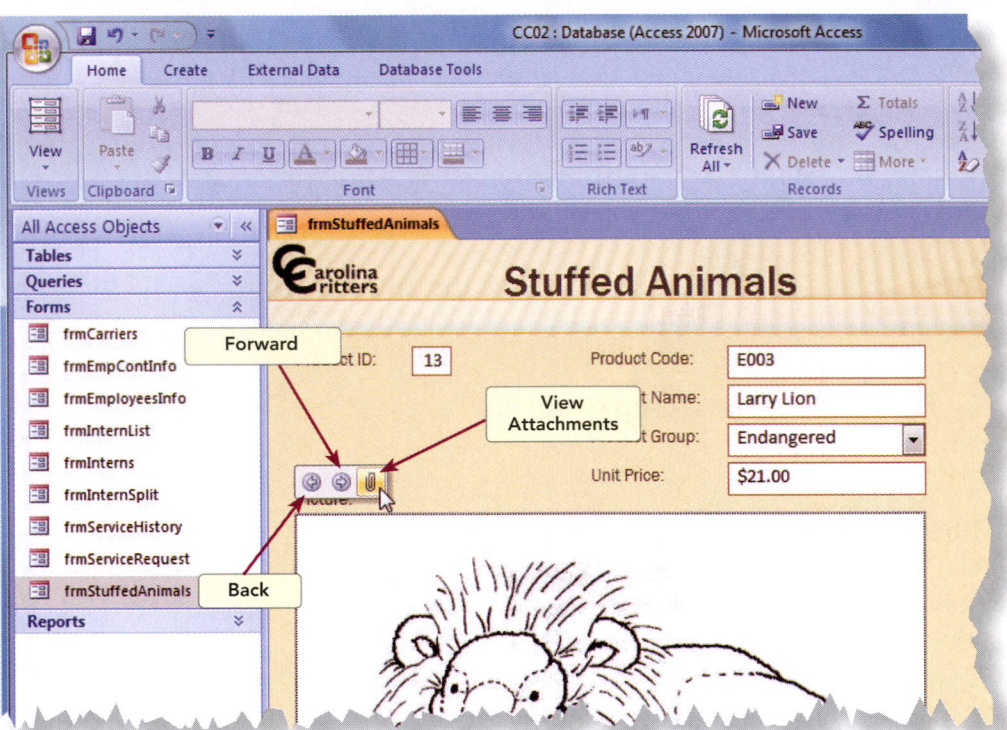

13. On the mini toolbar, click the **View Attachments** button.

14. In the **Attachments** dialog box, click **Add**.

15. In the **Lesson 02** folder, double-click the file **Lin003c**. You now have two files attached to this record.

16. Click **OK**.

17. Click the picture to open the mini toolbar.

18. On the mini toolbar, click the Forward button to see the second file.

Exercise 2-16   **EXTRACT AN IMAGE FROM THE DATABASE**

Extracting is different than removing an image. When you remove an image, you delete that image from the record. When you extract an image, you save a copy of the image as an external file without affecting the original image.

1. Press PageDown until the data for "Theodore Bear" (**Product ID** 22) is displayed in the form.

2. Double-click the image of the product. This opens the **Attachment** dialog box.

3. Click **Save As**.

4. In the **Save Attachment** dialog box, change the **File name** to **Theodore Bear.bmp**.

5. Check the file path in the location bar. Change if needed.

6. Click **Save** to save a copy of the image outside of the database.

7. Click **OK** to close the **Attachment** dialog box.

8. Close the form by right-clicking the form's document tab and choosing **Close**.

9. In the Navigation Pane, collapse the **Forms** group.

> **REVIEW**
>
> Closing a major object after modifying or adding a record will save the changes.

Previewing, Printing, and Saving Data Using a Report

Just as forms are designed to view data on a screen, reports are designed to view data on paper. A form is designed to fit on a standard computer screen, while a report is designed to fit on a sheet of paper.

Use the Microsoft Office Button or keyboard methods, to open the Print dialog box. From the Print dialog box, you can set a print range or change the page orientation.

Exercise 2-17   PREVIEW A REPORT

Print Preview shows you how the selected report prints on paper. *Print Preview* is a method for displaying on the screen how an object will appear if printed on paper.

1. In the **Reports** group of the Navigation Pane, double-click the report **rptInternsByDept**.

2. Right-click the report's document tab and choose **Print Preview**.

3. From the command tab **Print Preview**, in the command group **Page Layout**, click the command **Portrait** Ⓐ.

4. In the lower-right corner is the zoom control. Click the Plus button ⊕ twice to zoom to 120%.

> **TIP**
>
> To use the Print Preview ribbon for tables, queries, and forms, you must click the Office Button ⒮ and click the **Print** option arrow.

Access 2007

Figure 2-14
Print Preview
CC02.accdb
rptInternsByDept

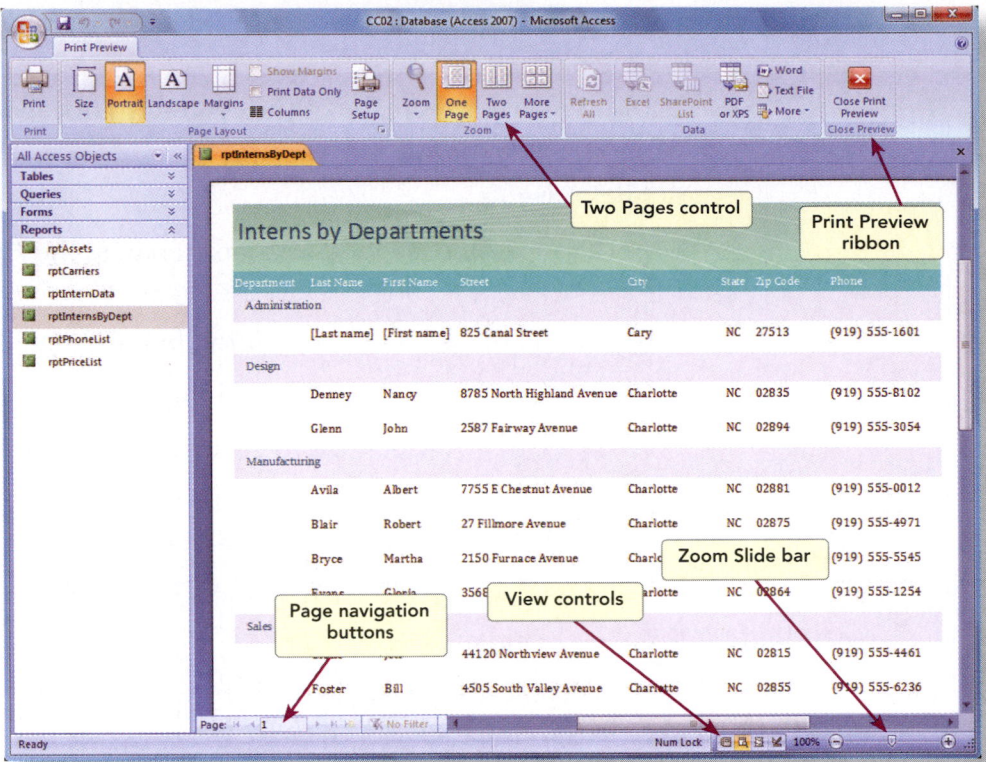

5. Click the Two Pages command ⬚. Notice that this report fits onto one page.

Exercise 2-18   PRINT A REPORT

Depending on the size of the report, you may need to change the page orientation or the margins. You can set the print orientation to landscape for a report similar to when printing a datasheet. You most often change the page orientation when records contain more fields than can print in portrait orientation.

1. In the **Reports** group of the Navigation Pane, double-click the report **rptInternData**.

2. At the right end of the status bar are the change view buttons. Click the **Print Preview** button 🔍.

3. Click the Two Pages button ⬚. Notice that this report has information on a second page.

4. From the command tab **Print Preview**, in the command group **Page Layout**, click the Margins command ⬚ option arrow and choose **Narrow**.

Figure 2-15
Changing margin
settings
CC02.accdb
rptInternData

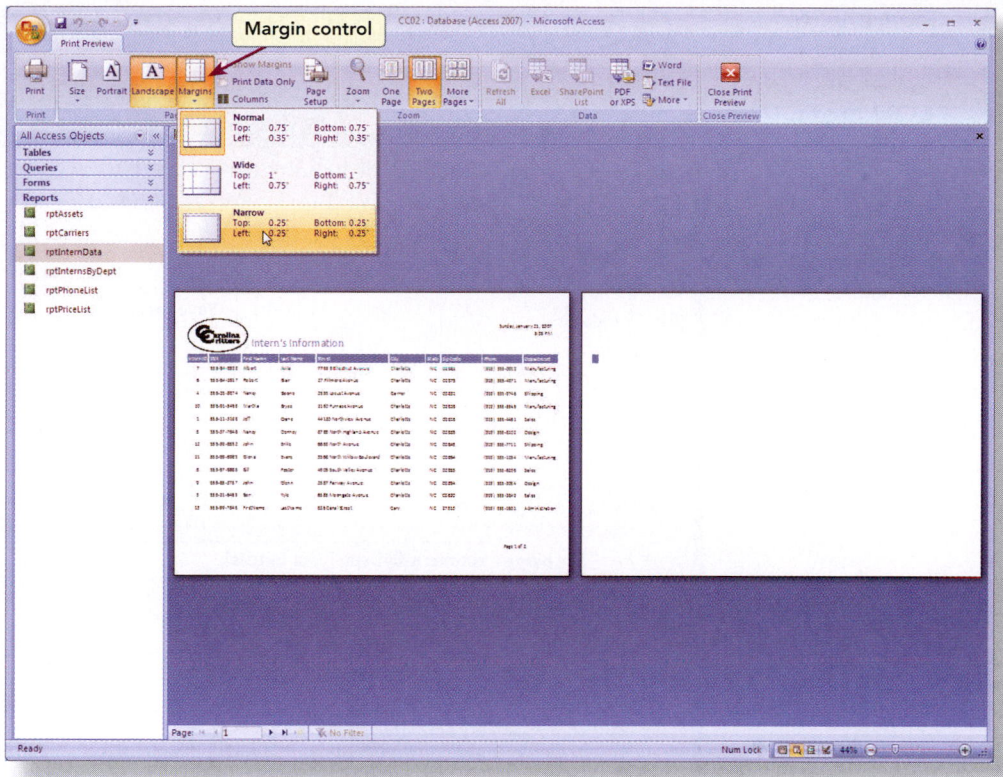

7. From the command tab **Print Preview**, in the command group **Print**, click the Print command 🖨. The **Print** dialog box opens.

8. Based upon your classroom procedure, you can either print the report or cancel the print process. To cancel, click **Cancel**. To print the report, click **OK**. If you are uncertain, ask your instructor.

Exercise 2-19   SAVE A REPORT TO A FILE

You can publish a report as an electronic XPS file just like when you publish a datasheet. A published report can be viewed or printed through Microsoft Internet Explorer.

1. From the command tab **Print Preview**, in the command group **Data**, click the PDF or XPS command 📄.

2. Change the location to the location where you will be storing your homework.

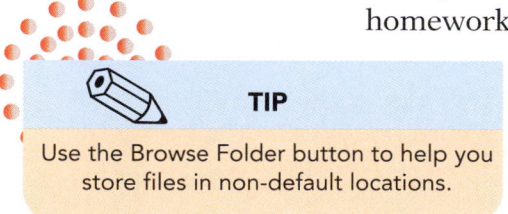

TIP

Use the Browse Folder button to help you store files in non-default locations.

3. Click to the right of the file name and key a hyphen and your initials.

4. Click the **Open file after publishing** check box.

Figure 2-16
Save a report
to a file
CC02.accdb
rptInternDat

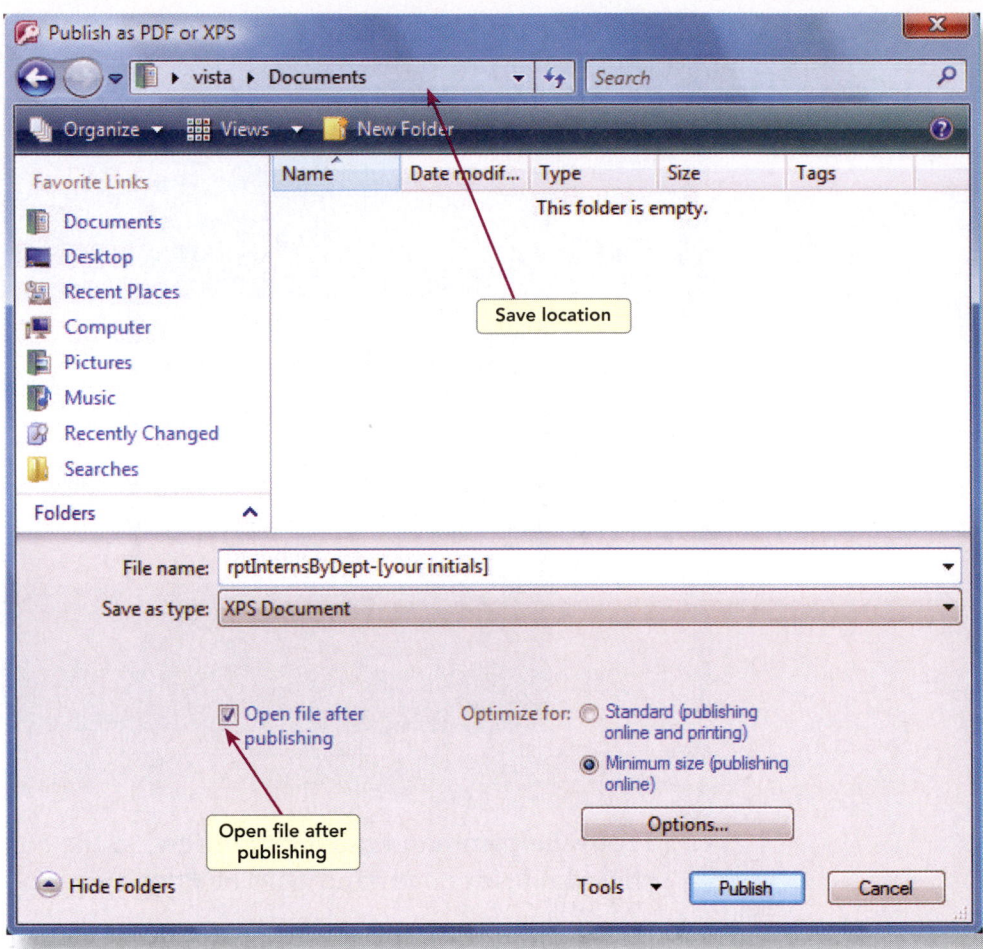

5. Click **Publish** to create the XPS file. Your file has been opened in Internet Explorer.

6. Close the Internet Explorer.

7. Right-click the **rptInternData** tab. From the shortcut menu, select **Close All**.

8. In the Navigation Pane, collapse the **Reports** group.

9. Click the **Office Button**.

10. Click **Exit Access**.

REVIEW

Optimizing the file for on-line publishing and printing increases the size of the file.

Lesson 2 Summary

- Access automatically saves changes to a record when you move the insertion point to another record.
- Records are stored in tables.
- Records can be added, edited, and deleted in a table, through a query, or through a form.
- You can delete records from a table by clicking on the Record Selector and pressing Delete.
- When editing a record, you can insert text or use the Overtype mode to key over existing text.
- AutoCorrect corrects commonly misspelled words.
- Press Ctrl+' to duplicate the contents in the field from the previous record.
- Press Ctrl+; to enter the current system date into a field.
- Press Ctrl+C to copy and Ctrl+V to paste text.
- Click the Undo button ⤺ to restore the previously deleted text.
- You can attach an image or document file to a record.
- Print Preview displays on the screen how an object will be printed.
- A published object can be viewed or printed at a later time.

LESSON 2		Command Summary	
Feature	**Button**	**Task Path**	**Keyboard**
Add record	New	Home, Records, New	Ctrl+[+]
Copy		Home, Clipboard, Copy	Ctrl+C
Delete record		Home, Records, Delete	Ctrl+[−]
Duplicate field			Ctrl+'
Insert current date			Ctrl+;
Paste		Home, Clipboard, Paste	Ctrl+V
Print			Ctrl+P
Save		Office Button, Print Preview, Data, XPS	
Refresh All		Home, Records, Refresh All	
Save record	Save	Home, Records, Save	Ctrl+Enter
Undo	⤺	Edit, Undo	Ctrl+Z

Concepts Review

True/False Questions

Each of the following statements is either true or false. Indicate your choice by circling T or F.

T F   1. The pencil icon appears in the Record Selector after data are saved.

T F   2. You can use the Undo button ↵ to restore up to 24 deleted records.

T F   3. When you enter or edit data through a form, you automatically update data in the underlying table.

T F   4. You can duplicate the data from a field in the previous record to the same field in the next record by pressing the keyboard shortcut Ctrl+D.

T F   5. Forms can be designed to show more than one record per screen.

T F   6. You can add records in a table, through a query, or through a form.

T F   7. Reports are designed to view data on paper.

T F   8. Only one image can be attached to each table.

Short Answer Questions

Write the correct answer in the space provided.

1. From which command group can you delete a record?

_____

2. In a table, where is a new record added?

_____

3. What is the keyboard shortcut to delete a record in a table or form?

_____

4. What Office feature automatically capitalizes days of the week?

_____

5. After copying text to the clipboard, what keyboard shortcut can be used to paste the text to a new location?

_____

6. In addition to the number of items held, how is the Office Clipboard different from the Windows Clipboard?

_____

7. What keystrokes are used to insert the current date into a field?

_____

8. Which command is carried out by pressing ⌈Ctrl⌉+⌈Z⌉?

_____

Critical Thinking

Answer these questions on a separate page. There are no right or wrong answers. Support your answers with examples from your own experience, if possible.

1. In addition to images, you can attach various types of files to a record. However, you cannot attach certain files such as those used by the operating system. Think about standardized file extensions and identify file extensions that cannot be used for an attachment.

2. When you delete a record from a table, it cannot be restored. Discuss different businesses in which you should never completely delete or remove records.

Skills Review

Exercise 2-20

Add and edit records in a table. Use Office Edit tools.

REVIEW

If you have the file *[your initials]*-CC02 from the lesson, you can skip to Step 2.

1. Copy and rename a database by following these steps:
   a. Open the folder **Lesson 02**.
   b. Right-click the file **CC02** and, from the shortcut menu, choose **Copy**.
   c. Right-click an unused part of the folder and, from the short-cut menu, choose **Paste**.
   d. Right-click the new file and, from the shortcut menu, choose **Rename**. Rename the file to *[your initials]*-**CC02**.
   e. Right-click *[your initials]*-**CC02** and, from the shortcut menu, choose **Properties**. Make certain that the **Read-only** attribute check box is not checked. Click **OK**.

2. Edit a record by following these steps:
   a. From the command tab **Home**, in the lower-right corner of the command group **Clipboard**, click the dialog box launcher to open the **Clipboard** pane.
   b. In the Navigation Pane, expand the **Tables** group and double-click **tblJobCodes**.

c. Locate the record for **Job Code** "MF06" and click in the **Job Title** field at the end of the word "Inspector."

d. Press [Delete] once to delete the "/".

e. Press [Shift]+[End] to select the word "packer."

f. Press [Ctrl]+[X] to cut the selected text.

3. Add a new record by following these steps:

a. Click the New Record navigation button .

b. Key **MF07** and press [Tab].

c. In the **Clipboard** pane, click "packer."

d. Press [Home] and [Delete]. Key **P**.

e. Press [End] and key *–[your last name]*.

4. Print/Save a datasheet by following these steps:

a. Click the **Office Button** . Hover your mouse pointer over the more options arrow for the **Print** option and click the Print Preview command .

b. Depending on your classroom procedures, either:

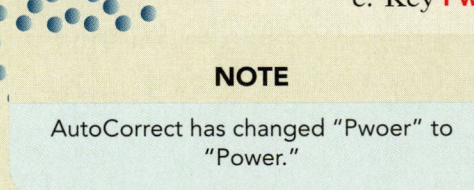

- Click the Print command to print the datasheet, or
- Click the XPS command to save the datasheet.

5. Close an object by following these steps:

a. Right-click the **tblJobCodes** tab. From the short-cut menu, select **Close**.

b. In the Navigation Pane, collapse the **Tables** group.

↔ **REVIEW**

Check with your instructor on how he or she wants your homework delivered.

Exercise 2-21

Edit data in a query. Add a record.

1. The database *[your initials]*-**CC02** is required to complete this exercise.

a. Double-click the database *[your initials]*-**CC02**.

b. In the Message bar, press **Options**. In the dialog box, click **Enable this content** and click **OK**.

2. Edit text by following these steps:

a. In the Navigation Pane, expand the **Queries** group and double-click **qryPensionContact**.

b. In the second record (Hopcorp Industries), double-click the last name (McLimans) in the **Contact Name** field.

c. Key **Pwoer**.

d. In the last record (Ajendro Economy), click in the **Phone Number** field.

e. Press [End] and [Backspace] twice to delete the last two digits in the phone number.

f. Key **23**.

NOTE

AutoCorrect has changed "Pwoer" to "Power."

3. Add a new record by following these steps:

   a. Right-click any record selector that is blank.

   b. From the shortcut menu, select **New Record**.

   c. Key the following to add another record:

Company Name:	Global Growth
Contact Name:	*Key [your full name]*
Phone Number:	(555) 214-7514

4. Print/Save a datasheet by following these steps:

   a. Click the Office Button. Hover your mouse pointer over the more options arrow for the **Print** option and click the Print Preview command.

   b. Depending on your classroom procedures, either:

     • Click the Print command to print the datasheet, or

     • Click the XPS command to publish the datasheet.

5. Close an object by following these steps:

   a. Right-click the **qryPensionContact** tab. From the shortcut menu, select **Close**.

   b. In the Navigation Pane, collapse the **Queries** group.

> **TIP**
>
> Data entry goes much faster if you press Tab between fields.

Exercise 2-22

Add and delete records through a form.

1. The database *[your initials]*-**CC02** is required to complete this exercise.

   a. Double-click the database *[your initials]*-**CC02**.

   b. In the message bar, press **Options**. In the dialog box, click **Enable this content** and click **OK**.

2. Add records by following these steps:

   a. In the Navigation Pane, expand the **Forms** group and double-click **frmServiceRequest**.

   b. Key the following to add two new records:

Asset ID:	CP303
Service Date:	*Press* Ctrl + ;
Employee ID:	8
Description:	Htis copier is placing a long black line down the center of every page.
Estimated Cost:	150
Asset ID:	LP201
Service Date:	*Press* Ctrl + ;
Employee ID:	30
Description:	Paper jams – *Key [your full name]*
Estimated Cost:	50

3. Delete a record by following these steps:

   a. In the Navigation Pane, expand the **Forms** group and double-click **frmServiceHistory**.

   b. Click on the Record Selector for the **Service ID** "002."

   c. From the command tab **Home**, in the command group **Records**, click the Delete command ✄.

   d. Click **Yes** to verify the deletion.

   e. In the Navigation Pane, collapse the **Forms** group.

4. Open a table in datasheet view by following these steps:

   a. In the Navigation Pane, expand the **Tables** group and double-click **tblServiceRecords**.

   b. Click and drag the bottom of the Record Selector for the first record and double the height of the row.

   c. Resize the field **Description** until all data can be seen.

5. Print/Save a datasheet by following these steps:

   a. Click the Office Button 🔲. Hover your mouse pointer over the more options arrow for the **Print** option and click the Print Preview command 🔍.

   b. From the command tab **Print Preview**, in the command group **Page Layout**, click the Landscape command 🄰.

   c. Depending on your classroom procedures, either:

   • Click the Print command 🖨 to print the datasheet, or

   • Click the XPS command 🗐 to publish the datasheet.

6. Close an object by following these steps:

   a. Right-click the **tblServiceRecords** tab. From the short-cut menu, select **Close All**. Save all changes.

   b. In the Navigation Pane, collapse the **Tables** group.

Exercise 2-23

Attach a file through a form. Preview and Print/Save a report.

1. The database *[your initials]*-**CC02** is required to complete this exercise.

   a. Double-click the database *[your initials]*-**CC02**.

   b. In the message bar, press **Options**. In the dialog box, click **Enable this content** and click **OK**.

2. Attach a file by following these steps:

   a. In the Navigation Pane, expand the **Forms** group and double-click **frmCarriers**.

   b. In the record for **Carrier ID** "C200," double-click the **Rates** field.

   c. In the **Attachment** dialog box, click **Add**.

    d. In the folder **Lesson 02**, double-click the file **FPS Rates.txt**.

    e. Click **OK**.

    f. In the Navigation Pane, collapse the **Forms** group.

3. Edit a record by following these steps:

    a. In the record for **Carrier ID** "C300," click the **Name** field and press End .

    b. Key *–[your last name]*.

4. Print/Save a report by following these steps:

    a. In the Navigation Pane, expand the **Reports** group and double-click **rptCarrier**.

    b. Click the Office Button . Hover your mouse pointer over the more options arrow for the **Print** option and click the Print Preview command .

    c. Depending on your classroom procedures, either:

      • Click the Print command to print the datasheet, or

      • Click the XPS command to publish the datasheet.

5. Close an object by following these steps:

    a. Right-click the **rptCarries** tab. From the short-cut menu, select **Close**.

    b. In the Navigation Pane, collapse the **Reports** group.

Lesson Applications

Exercise 2-24

Add records through a form.

1. Open *[your initials]*-**CC02** and enable all content.

2. In the form **frmEmpContInfo**, add the following new employees:

Employee ID:	40
Last Name:	Crowell
First Name:	Dennis
Address:	9404 Trinity Trace Lane
City:	Monroe
State:	NC
Postal Code:	28112
Home Phone:	(704) 555-6332
Employee ID:	41
Last Name:	Key *[your last name]*
First Name:	Key *[your first name]*
Address:	806 West Euclid St.
City:	Mooresville
State:	NC
Postal Code:	28115
Home Phone:	(704) 555-8254

3. Open the table **tblEmployees**. Hide all columns that were not used in **frmEmpContInfo**.

4. Resize each field so that all data can be seen.

5. Change the **Page Layout** to Landscape ⒶⒶ with **Wide Margins**.

6. Print/Save the datasheet.

7. Close the form and the table.

Exercise 2-25

Edit and delete records through a query.

1. Open *[your initials]*-**CC02** and enable all content.

2. Open **qryDesignTeam** in datasheet view.

3. Delete **Employee ID** "9" (Luis Gutierrez.)

4. Hide the fields **SSN**, **Job Code**, **Address**, **City**, and **State**.

5. Widen the field **Postal Code** to display the column heading.

6. Add the +4 postal code numbers in the field **Postal Code** for each record listed in Figure 2-17. (Not all the columns appear in the figure.)

Figure 2-17

Employee ID	Last Name	First Name	Postal Code
3	Chung	Sora	28202-**3024**
4	Stone	Jeanette	28210-**2202**
10	Thomas	Louise	28205-**1051**
14	Rodriguez	Felix	28202-**1114**
20	Floria	Maria	28214-**1133**
34	Voisine	Rebecca	28202-**1321**
37	White	Heidi	28211-**1044**
39	Boca-Larson	Janet	28210-**9712**

7. In the first record, change the fields **First Name** and **Last Name** to your name.

8. Change the **Page Layout** to Portrait . Resize fields so that all data can be seen on one page.

9. Print/Save the datasheet.

10. Close the table.

Exercise 2-26

Edit records in a table. Use Office Edit tools.

1. Open *[your initials]*-**CC02** and enable all content.

2. Open **tblLeaveDays** in datasheet view.

3. Use the Office Clipboard and navigation commands to find the records to be changed.

4. In the field **Leave Category**, change all occurrences of "Vacation" to **Annual**.

5. In the field **Leave Category,** change all occurrences of "Sick" to **Sick Leave**.

6. In the first record, replace the **Leave Category** data with your full name.

7. Print/Save the datasheet.

8. Close the table.

Exercise 2-27 ◆ Challenge Yourself

Attach an image in a table. Print/Save a report.

1. Open *[your initials]*-**CC02** and enable all content.

2. Open **tblAssets**.

3. Use the Internet to locate and save an image of a copier.

4. For the **Assets ID** "CP303," attach the image you found on the Internet.

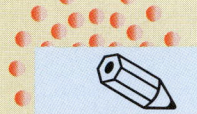

> **TIP**
>
> Try to find an image that is less than 100kb in size. This will keep your database from getting too large.

5. Change the name of the asset to your full name.

6. Print/Save the report **rptAssets**.

7. Close the table and exit the database.

On Your Own

In these exercises, you work on your own, as you would in a real-life work environment. Use the skills you've learned to accomplish the task—and be creative.

Exercise 2-28

Search the Web for companies that would sell products of interest to members of the club you formed in Lesson 1. If you are unable to locate any companies, search the Web for companies selling clothing that appeals to you. Write down at least five URLs (Web page addresses). Continue to the next exercise.

Exercise 2-29

On each of the five Web sites, determine what information the company asks a person when that person places an order or requests a catalog. On the same sheet of paper where you wrote down the five URLs, organize and write a bulleted list of customer information collected by the companies (for example: first name, e-mail). Continue to the next exercise.

Exercise 2-30

On a second sheet of paper, create a new field list by combining the list you created in Exercise 1-28 (in Lesson 1) with the list you created in Exercise 2-28. On a third sheet of paper, organize the items from your new list to sketch a form layout. Submit your work for Exercises 2-28 through 2-30 to your instructor.

Finding, Filtering, Sorting, and Summarizing Data

OBJECTIVES

After completing this lesson, you will be able to:

1. Find and replace data.

2. Use wildcards

3. Sort records.

4. Add and modify the totals row in datasheets.

5. Use filters.

6. Use the Database Documenter.

Estimated Time: 1¹/₂ hours

MCAS OBJECTIVES

In this lesson:
AC07 70-605 2.3.5
AC07 70-605 3.3
AC07 70-605 5.1.1
AC07 70-605 5.1.2
AC07 70-605 5.1.3
AC07 70-605 5.1.4
AC07 70-605 5.2.1
AC07 70-605 5.2.2
AC07 70-605 5.2.3
AC07 70-605 5.2.4
AC07 70-605 5.5
AC07 70-605 6.2.5

The main purpose of a database is to turn raw data into useful information. Often, databases are too complex to find specific information easily. To locate specific information, you can use Access tools to search, find, sort, and filter. By applying the proper combinations of tools, the cumbersome data becomes useful information.

Carolina Critters sells 24 different stuffed animal kits categorized into five different product lines. If you want to know which stuffed animal kits were most popular in Canada, you would total the quantities sold, sort the sales totals in descending order, and filter for only Canadian customers. You might often use a combination of tools to change data to information.

Finding and Replacing Data

Finding information can be time consuming if you have to scroll through several thousand records. Searches can be quicker when fields contain unique data. For example, if you know the social security number of a particular employee, you can find that person quickly because no two people share the same social security number. However, if you only know the person's last name, then the search can take quite a bit longer because your database may contain numerous employees who share the same last name.

Although most often, you will change single records, on occasion, you will find it necessary to update the same data listed in many records. Employees at Carolina Critters are classified by job titles. If the job title for a group of employees changes, then these changes need to be reflected throughout the entire table. To make the changes, you will need to find the original job titles and replace them with the updated job titles.

Exercise 3-1   USE THE SEARCH TOOL

Using the Search tool is a quick way to find data in a recordset. The Search tool begins its search at the first field of the first record and stops at the first match. If the recordset contains more than one match, only the first match is found. Because of this limitation, the Search tool is best used when searching for unique data, such as a social security number. The Search tool can be used on tables, queries, and forms.

1. Locate and open the **Lesson 03** folder.

2. Make a copy of **CC03** and rename it to *[your initials]*-**CC03**.

3. Open and enable content for *[your initials]*-**CC03**.

4. From the Navigation Pane, open the table **tblEmployees** in Datasheet View.

5. In the Navigation Bar, click in the **Search** tool.

> **NOTE**
>
> The Search tool is not case sensitive. Access treats uppercase and lowercase text the same.

Figure 3-1
Search tool
CC03.accdb
tblEmployees

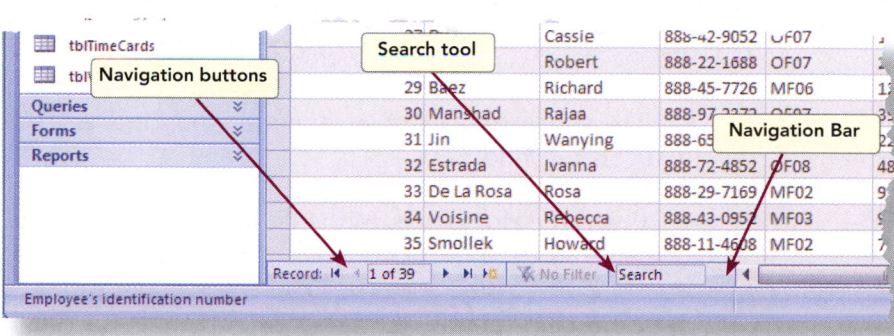

6. Key **r**. Starting from the upper left, the first "r" is selected.

7. Key **o**. Starting from the upper left, the first "ro" is selected.

8. Key **c**. The selection has moved to the 10th record.

9. Press Backspace three times to remove the content of the **Search** tool.

10. Key **raj**. The selection has moved to the **First Name** field of the 30th record.

> **NOTE**
>
> The content and application of the Search tool cannot be retained when you close an object.

11. Clear the content of the **Search** tool.

12. Key **888-5**. The selection has moved to the **SSN** field of the 15th record.

13. Close **tblEmployees**.

Exercise 3-2   USE THE FIND COMMAND

Similar to the **Search** tool, the **Find and Replace** dialog box finds matches in a recordset. However, there are two major differences. The **Find and Replace** command begins a search at the insertion point and includes options for fine-tuning how text is matched.

TABLE 3-1 Find and Replace Dialog Box Options

Option	Description
Look In	Sets the search for the current field or the entire table.
Match: Any Part of Field	Finds records with matching characters anywhere in the field.
Match: Whole Field	Finds records in which an entire field matches the value in the Find What text box.
Match: Start of Field	Finds records in which the beginning of a field matches the Find What entry.
Search: All	Searches forward to the end of the table and wraps back to the beginning.
Search: Up	Searches in the Up (backward) direction only.
Search: Down	Searches in the Down (forward) direction only.
Match Case	Finds exact uppercase and lowercase matches.
Search Fields As Formatted	Enables you to key data in its display format. To find a date that is stored as 1/25/01, you can key 25-Jan-01. This is the slowest search.

There are two ways of opening the **Find and Replace** dialog box with focus on the **Find** tab:

- From the **Home** tab, in the **Find** group, choose the Find command.

- Press Ctrl + F.

1. In the Navigation Pane, open the table **tblEmployees** in Datasheet View.

2. From the **Home** tab, in the **Find** group, choose the Find command.

3. In the **Find What** control, key **robert**.

Figure 3-2
Find option of the
Find and Replace
dialog box
CC03.accdb
tblEmployees

NOTE

To see the results of a search, you can drag the **Find and Replace** dialog box by its title bar to a location on the screen that doesn't conceal the results of the search.

4. Click **Find Next**. There is no "robert" found in the field **Employee ID**. Click the drop-down arrow for the control **Look In** and choose **tblEmployees**.

5. Click **Find Next**. The first occurrence of "robert" is located in the field **First Name**. To search in only one field, you must click in that field before starting the search.

6. Click anywhere in the datasheet and press [PageUp]. In the **Find and Replace** dialog box, click the drop-down arrow for the control **Match** and choose **Any Part of Field**.

7. Now the first occurrence of "robert" is located in the field **Emergency Contact**.

8. Click **Find Next** to find the next occurrence, until you reach the end of the table.

9. Read the message box and click **OK**.

10. Click **Cancel** to close the **Find and Replace** dialog box.

Exercise 3-3   USE THE REPLACE COMMAND

The **Replace** tab finds matches in the same way as the **Find** tab does. With Replace, you not only find the match, but you can also replace each matched value with a new value. You can replace either a single occurrence or every occurrence of the value.

When using the **Replace All** option, you must be careful that all occurrences in the recordset are values that you planned to replace. Sometimes, unanticipated errors can occur. For example, if you replace the word "form" with "report," then a field containing the word "information" will become "inreportation." You will not be able to use undo to correct these changes.

There are two ways of opening the **Find and Replace** dialog box with focus on the **Replace** tab:

- From the **Home** tab, in the **Find** group, choose the Replace command [icon].

- Press [Ctrl]+[H].

1. In the table **tblEmployees**, for the first record, click in the **Address** field.

2. Press [Ctrl]+[H] to open the **Find and Replace** dialog box.

3. In the **Find What** control, key **road**.

4. In the **Replace With** control, key **Street**.

5. Verify that the **Look In** control is set to **Address**.

6. Verify that the **Match** control is set to **Any Part of Field**.

7. Click **Find Next**. The first occurrence after the insertion point is selected.

8. Click **Replace** to replace the first occurrence of "road" with "Street" and to find the next occurrence of "road."

9. Click **Find Next** to skip this occurrence of "road" and move to the next.

10. Click **Replace**.

11. Change the content of the **Find What** control to **st.**.

12. Click **Find Next**. The abbreviation of "street" is selected.

13. Click **Replace All**.

14. Read the message box and click **Yes**.

15. Click **Cancel** to close the dialog box.

TIP

Make sure that you have keyed the period after "st."

Using Wildcards

Up to this point, you have used exact text when finding and replacing text. On occasion, you may not know the exact value you want to match. For example, you might need to find a particular stuffed animal. You may not know its exact name, but you know that the product name uses the word "dog." Not knowing the exact names, you would need to search using a wildcard. A *wildcard* is a character or group of characters used to represent one or more alphabetical or numerical characters.

Exercise 3-4   FIND DATA USING AN ASTERISK "*"

The asterisk (*) is a wild card that represents one or more characters. If you search for "Mar*" as a last name, you will match names such as "Mar," "Mart," "Martin," "Marigold," or "Marblestone." All fields matched will begin with "Mar," regardless of remaining characters in the field.

1. In the table **tblEmployees**, for the first record, click in the **Job Code** field.

2. Press Ctrl+F to open the **Find and Replace** dialog box.

3. In the **Find What** control, key **m***.

4. Click **Find Next**. "MF03" is selected.

5. Click **Find Next** twice. "MF05" is selected.

6. Click the drop-down arrow for the **Look In** control and choose **tblEmployees**.

7. Click **Find Next**. Notice that part of an address is now selected.

8. Click **Cancel** to close the dialog box.

Exercise 3-5   **FIND DATA USING A QUESTION MARK "?"**

The question mark (?) is a wildcard that represents a single character. If you search for "Mar?" as a first name, you will find names such as "Mari," "Mark," "Marv," or "Mary." All fields containing only four characters and starting with "Mar" will be matched. Fields containing more than four characters or not beginning with "Mar" will not be matched.

1. In the table **tblEmployees**, for the first record, click in the **Job Code** field.

2. From the **Home** tab, in the **Find** group, choose the Find command 🔍.

3. In the **Find What** control, key **OF??**.

4. In the **Look In** control, select **tblEmployees**.

5. In the **Match** control, select **Whole Field**.

6. Click **Find Next** to find the first occurrence of any field's content that is only four characters long that starts with "OF."

7. Click **Find Next** a few more times to see which different codes are found.

8. Click **Cancel**.

Sorting Records

In a table, records are displayed in the order in which they were entered. For example, whenever a new employee is hired, his or her name is added to the end of a table. Most often this order is not useful for all your needs.

You can change the sort order of the recordset depending on the information you need. When creating an employee phone list, you would sort the recordset by last and first name. When creating an organizational chart, you would sort by job title rather than by name.

Exercise 3-6   **SORT RECORDS IN DATASHEET VIEW**

You can sort data in three ways:

TIP

A small up or down arrow appears on the column header of a sorted column. This sort-order arrow appears to the right of the column header's drop-down arrow.

- From the **Home** tab, in the **Sort & Filter** group, choose Ascending ⬆ or Descending ⬇.

- On a column selector, click the option arrow and select the **Sort A to Z** or Sort **Z to A**.

- In a field, right-click and select the **Sort A to Z** or **Sort Z to A**.

1. In the table **tblEmployees**, in the **Job Code** field, click the option arrow on the column header, and choose **Sort A to Z**.

Figure 3-3
Apply Sort to a
column
CC03.accdb
tblEmployees

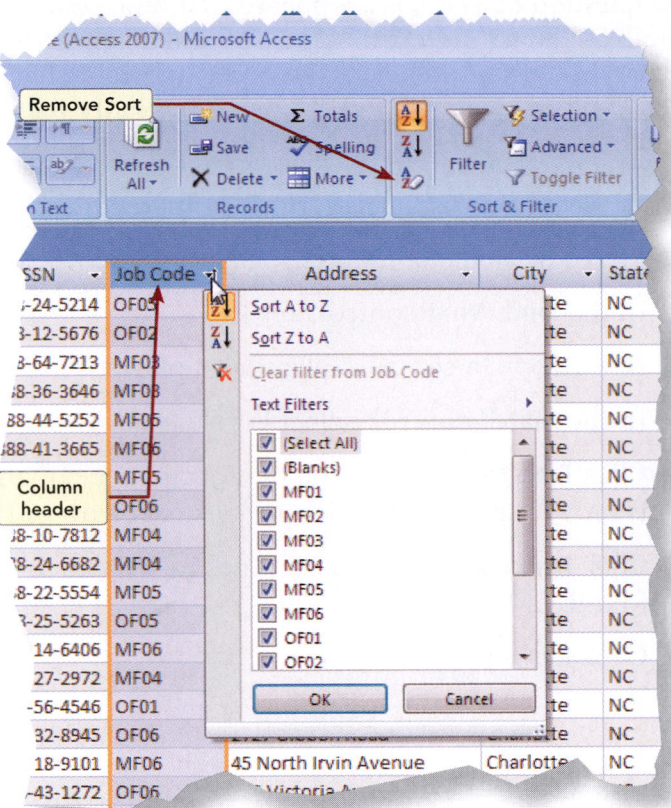

2. From the **Home** tab, in the **Sort & Filter** group, choose the Clear All Sorts command . Notice that the sort-order arrow no longer displays in the column header.

3. Select both the **Last Name** and the **First Name** fields.

4. Right-click the selected column headers and choose **Sort Z to A**. The table is now sorted by last name and then by first name.

5. In the Navigation Pane, open the query **qryEmployeePhone** in Datasheet View. This query gets its data from **tblEmployees**.

6. Click in the **Employee ID** field, click the option arrow on the column header, and choose **Sort Largest to Smallest**.

7. Click the document tab for **tblEmployees**. Notice that the sort order on the table is not affected when a sort order is applied to the query.

8. Right-click any document tab and choose **Close All**. Do not save any changes.

Exercise 3-7 SORT RECORDS IN A FORM

A form can be set to view a single record at one time or multiple records all at once. All forms can be sorted. When multiple records are displayed in a form, the sort order is observable. To see the results of a sort to a single record form, you will need to navigate through the recordset one screen at a time.

1. From the Navigation Pane, open the form **frmStuffedAnimals** in Form View.

2. Click in the **Product Code** field.

3. From the **Home** tab, in the **Sort & Filter** group, choose **Ascending** ↕. A different record now displays.

4. Press [PageDown] to move through all the records to see that the form is indeed sorted by **Product Code**.

5. Click in the **Product Name** field.

6. From the **Home** tab, in the **Sort & Filter** group, choose the Ascending command ↕.

7. Use the Record Navigation buttons to move through the records to see the change.

8. From the **Home** tab, in the **Sort & Filter** group, choose the Clear All Sorts command ↕.

9. Right-click the form's tab and select **Close All**. Do not save any changes.

Exercise 3-8 SORT RECORDS IN A REPORT

The recordset displayed in Layout View of a report can be sorted similarly to a recordset in Form View of a form. The Layout View of a report allows you to fine-tune the display of data, including sorting the fields and adjusting column widths.

1. From the Navigation Pane, open the report **rptEmployeePhone** in Form View. This report is sorted by Employee ID.

2. From the **Home** tab, in the **Views** group, click **View** and choose the **Layout View command** ▤.

NOTE

When in Layout or Design Views, contextual tabs are added to the ribbon.

3. Click the column heading **Last Name**. This selects the entire column of data.

4. Click the **Home** tab.

5. In the **Sort & Filter** group, choose the Ascending command ↕. (See Figure 3.4 on the next page.)

6. From the **Home** tab, in the **Views** group, click View, and choose the Report View command ▤.

Figure 3-4
Sort in a report
CC03.accdb
rptEmployeePhone

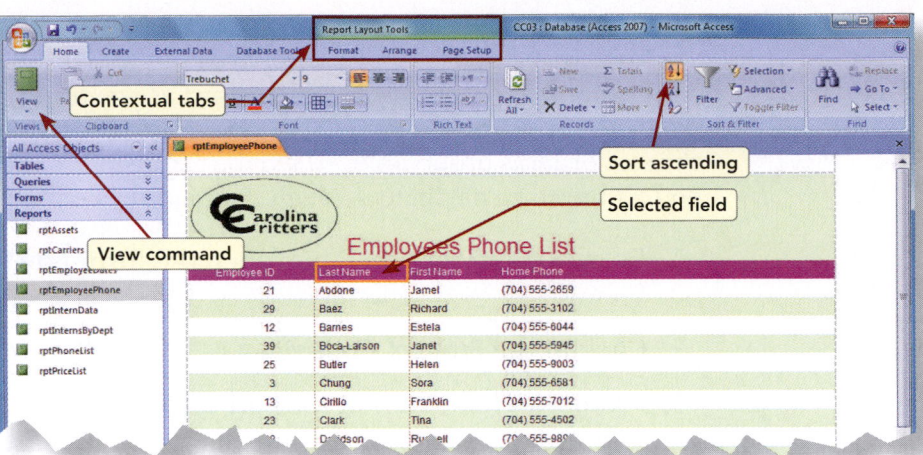

7. Right-click the report's tab and select **Close**.

8. Click **Yes** to save the changes.

Adding and Modifying the Totals Row in Datasheets

The **Totals** row is a feature that you can use to summarize data quickly. For example, if you need to know the amount of federal income tax paid by your employees this year, you would need to create a sum total for the federal income tax field in the payroll table.

Exercise 3-9   ADD A TOTALS ROW TO A QUERY

The Totals row uses an aggregate function to summarize a field. An *aggregate function* is a dynamic mathematical calculation that displays a single value for a specific field. Any change to a recordset automatically triggers recalculations of the aggregate functions located in the **Totals** row.

TABLE 3-2 Totals Row Aggregate Functions

Function	Description
Average	Calculates the average value for a column containing numeric, currency, or date/time data.
Count	Counts the number of items in a column.
Maximum	Returns the item with the highest value. For text data, the highest value is the last alphabetic value.
Minimum	Returns the item with the lowest value. For text data, the lowest value is the first alphabetic value.
Standard Deviation	Measures how widely values are dispersed from an average value.
Sum	Adds the items in a column containing numeric or currency data.
Variance	Measures the statistical variance of all values in the column containing numeric or currency data.

1. From the Navigation Pane, open the query **qryYrPay** in Datasheet View.

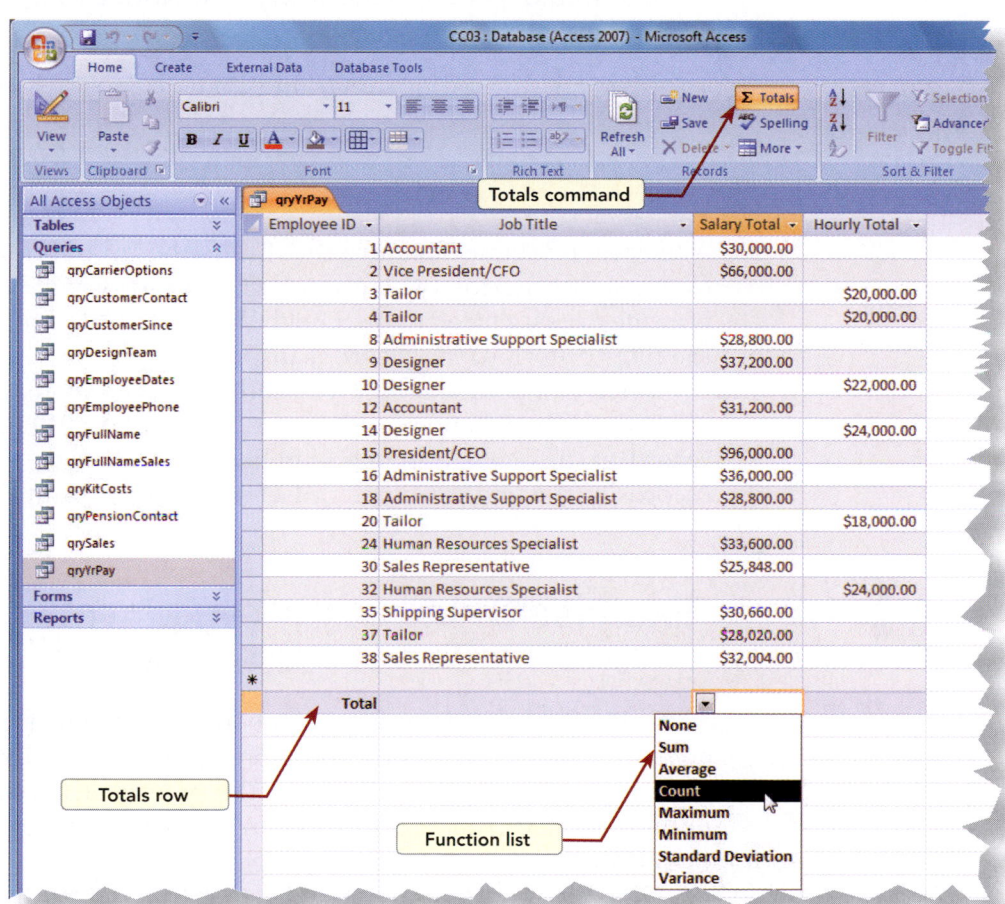

2. From the **Home** tab, in the **Records** group, choose the Totals command ∑. This adds a **Totals** row below the new record row.

3. In the **Totals** row, click in the **Salary Total** field. A drop-down arrow appears to the left of the field.

4. Click the drop-down arrow to display the list of available functions.

5. Choose **Count** from the list. There are 13 records that have **Salary Total** data.

Figure 3-5
Adding a Totals row
to a Datasheet
CC03.accdb
qryYrPay

Exercise 3-10   MODIFY A TOTALS ROW IN A QUERY

A Totals row is always present. Once you've created a Totals row in a datasheet, you can never truly delete it. You either modify it with a new function or hide it. Each time you display the Totals row, the functions that you last saved will appear.

1. In the query **qryYrPay**, click in the **Salary Total** field.

2. Click the drop-down arrow, and choose the function **Average**. The average of all data in the column displays.

3. In the **Totals** row, click in the **Hourly Total**.

4. Click the drop-down arrow and choose **Average**.

5. From the **Home** tab, in the **Records** group, choose the Totals command **Σ** to remove the **Totals** row.

6. Click the Close button **×** to close the query.

7. Click **Yes** to save the changes.

8. Reopen the query **qryYrPay**.

9. From the **Home** tab, in the **Records** group, choose the Totals command **Σ** to add the **Totals** row. Notice that the functions you added have been saved.

10. Click the Close button **×** and then click **Yes** to save the changes.

Using Filters

A *filter* is a database feature that limits the number of records displayed. A filter uses a criterion to determine which records will be displayed. A *criterion* is a rule or test placed upon a field. When the tested field in a record matches the filter criterion, the record is displayed.

Once you define a filter, you can toggle between apply or remove. When applied, a filter displays only matching records. When removed, the entire recordset displays. Whether applied or removed, the actual number of records in the underlying recordset remains constant.

Exercise 3-11   CREATE AND APPLY A FILTER BY SELECTION

Filter By Selection is a filter applied to a single field. The filter can be created to match the entire field or a portion of a field. The selection will be compared with field values in the recordset based upon a comparison option selected from a contextual menu. A contextual menu is a varying list of options based upon the item selected.

The filter options displayed depend upon the type of field and data selected. Options displayed for a date field differ from options displayed for a text field. Some options, such as "Begins With" or "Ends With," display only when the beginning portion or the ending portion of a text field is selected.

When filtering with more than one field, only records that match all filters will display. For example, if you need to list all employees who work as inspectors in the manufacturing department, you would create criteria for the department field and the job title field. Only records that match "Inspector" and "Manufacturing" will appear.

TABLE 3-3 Common Contextual Filter Options

Field Type	Filter Option
Date	Equals Does Not Equal On or Before On or After
Numeric	Equals Does Not Equal Less Than or Equal To Greater Than or Equal To Between
Text	Equals Does Not Equal Contains Does Not Contain Begins With Does Not Begin With Ends With Does Not End With

1. From the Navigation Pane, open the table **tblInvoices** in Datasheet View.

2. Click the Search tool and key **the t**. The Toy House customer is the first found.

3. Click in the highlighted field.

4. Press F2 to select the whole field.

5. From the **Home** tab, in the **Sort & Filter** group, click the Selection command .

6. From the menu, choose **Equals "The Toy House"**. There are 12 records for this customer.

Figure 3-6
Creating a filter by selection
CC03.accdb
tblInvoice

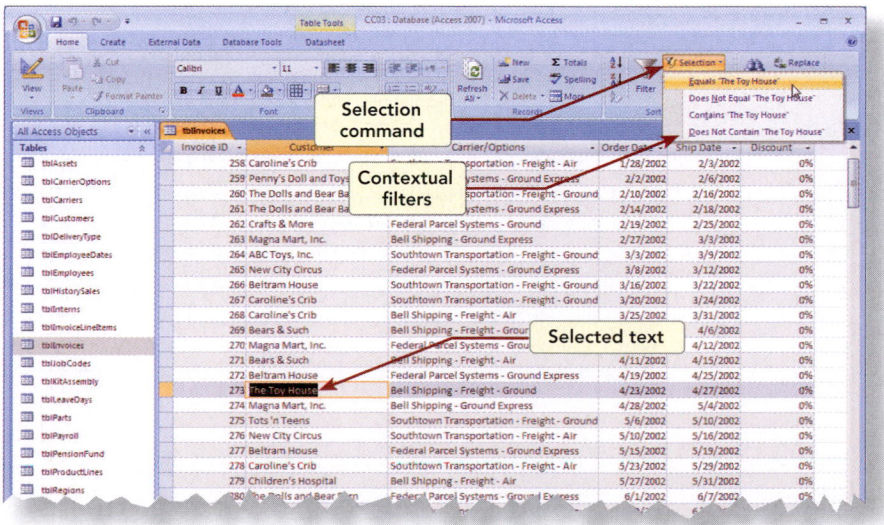

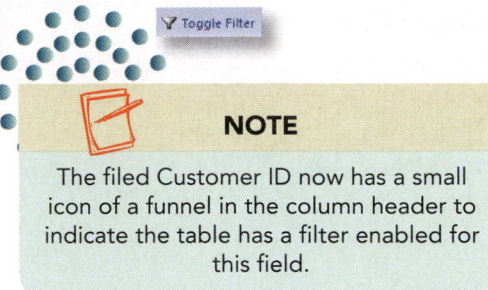

NOTE

The filed Customer ID now has a small icon of a funnel in the column header to indicate the table has a filter enabled for this field.

7. From the **Home** tab, in the **Sort & Filter** group, choose the Toggle Filter command. This disables the filter.

8. Press Ctrl + End to move to the last record in the table.

9. In the last record, select only the year (2007) in the **Order Date** field.

10. From the **Home** tab, in the **Sort & Filter** group, click the Selection command and choose **Ends With 2007**. There are 12 records for the year 2007.

11. From the **Home** tab, in the **Sort & Filter** group, click the Toggle Filter command to disable the filter.

12. Click in the **Carrier/Options** field of the first record. Make sure that no text is selected.

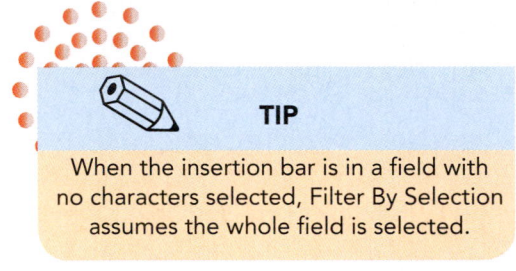

TIP

When the insertion bar is in a field with no characters selected, Filter By Selection assumes the whole field is selected.

13. From the **Home** tab, in the **Sort & Filter** group, click the Selection command and choose **Equals "Federal Parcel Systems – Groun…"**. Carolina Critter used this carrier 32 times.

14. Click the drop-down arrow next to the funnel icon in the column heading for the **Carrier/Options** field and choose **Clear filter from Carrier/Options**.

Figure 3-7
Clear a filter
CC03.accdb
tblInvoice

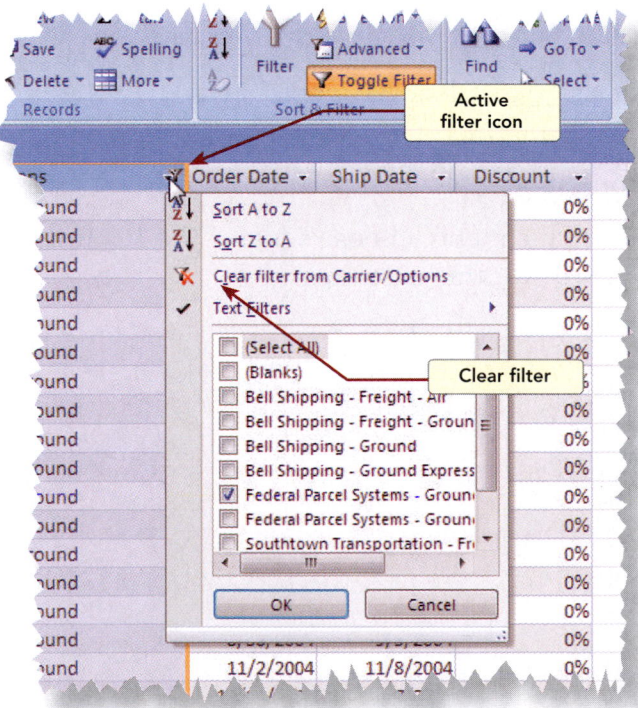

Exercise 3-12 FILTER FOR A SPECIFIC VALUE

When filtering for a specific value, you select one or more values from a pre-defined criteria list. Each item on a list can be "selected for" or "omitted from" the filter condition. When two or more criteria are selected, either criterion must match for the record to display. For example, if you select "NY" and "CA" for the state, then all records from New York and all records from California will display.

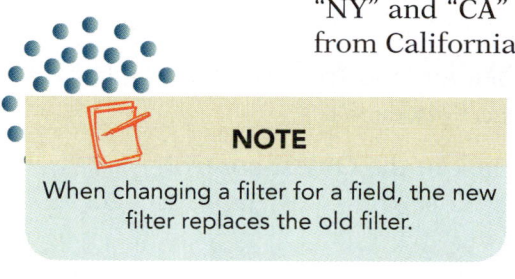

NOTE

When changing a filter for a field, the new filter replaces the old filter.

The criteria list is dynamically created on the basis of the unique values found in the field. The first two items in every criteria list will be "Select All" and "Blanks." "Select All" toggles between selecting and omitting all values. Selecting "Blanks" includes records where the criterion field is left empty.

1. With the table **tblInvoices** open, click in **Customer** for any record.

2. From the **Home** tab, in the **Sort & Filter** group, click the Filter command ▼.

3. In the menu, click the checkbox **(Select All)**. This removes all checkmarks.

4. Click the checkboxes for **Crafts & More** and **Carolina's Crib**.

5. Click **OK**. All records for both customers displays.

Figure 3-8
Filter Logic: Specific value
CC03.accdb

```
(Company Name = "Crafts & More") or (Company Name = "Carolina's Crib")
                              Condition
```

6. From the Navigation Pane, open the query **qryEmployeeDates** in Datasheet View.

7. Click in the **End Date** field for any record.

8. Click the drop-down arrow in the field's column header.

9. In the menu, uncheck the checkbox **(Select All)** and then check the checkbox for **(Blanks)**.

10. Click **OK** to apply the filter. Only records that do not have data in this field are shown.

11. Click the drop-down arrow in the **End Date** column header. From the menu, choose **Clear filter from End Date**.

Exercise 3-13 FILTER FOR A RANGE OF VALUES

Other contextual filter options, such as calendar filters, have even more options. If you filter on a date field, you can select to filter dates by days, weeks, months, quarters, or years. The options available will vary depending on the date selected and the current date. For example, if the date selected is within the current year, then "This Year" becomes an available filter option.

1. From the Navigation Pane, open the report **rptEmployeeDates**.

2. From the **Home** tab, in the **Views** group, click **View** and choose Layout View command .

3. Right-click the **Hire Date** column header, and from the menu, click **Data Filters**. From the menu, choose **Between…**

4. In the **Between Dates** dialog box, click in the **Oldest** control.

5. Key **1/1/2000** and press Tab.

Figure 3-9
Date Picker control
CC03.accdb
tblEmployeeDates

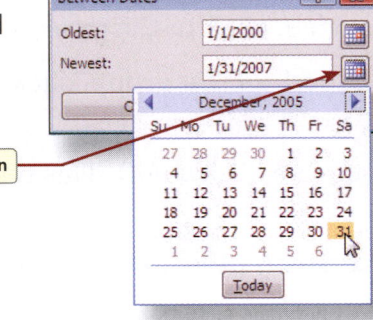

Date Picker button

6. Press the Date Picker button 📅 for the **Newest** control.

7. Use the left arrow to move through the calendar until you get to December, 2005. For the **Newest** control, click the 31st. This adds the date to the **Newest** control.

8. Click **OK**. Carolina Critters employees hired between 1/1/2000 and 12/31/2005 are shown.

Figure 3-10
Filter Logic: Range
of values
CC03.accdb

```
(Hire Date >= 1/1/2000)  and  (Hire Date <= 12/31/2005)
```

Condition

9. From the **Home** tab, in the **Sort & Filter** group, choose the Toggle Filter command.

10. Right-click the table's tab and choose **Close All**.

Exercise 3-14   CREATE AND APPLY A FILTER BY FORM

Filter By Form allows you to define a collection of criteria for one or more fields using a template. When using Filter By Form in a form, the template appears as a blank form. Alternatively, when using Filter By Form in a datasheet, the template appears as a blank datasheet.

Collections in Filter By Form are organized by tabs. The first tab is called "Look for" and is located in the lower-left hand corner of the template. In a tab, all conditions must be met for a record to be displayed. For example, in the "Look for" tab, if you defined the criterion "NY" for the state and the criterion "Albany" for city, then only records from "Albany, NY" will be included in the active recordset.

1. From the Navigation Pane, open the form **frmStuffedAnimals** in Form View.

2. From the **Home** tab, in the **Sort & Filter** group, click the Advanced command 🔲 and choose **Filter By Form**.

3. Click the drop-down arrow for the **Product Group** and choose **Endangered**.

Figure 3-11
Filter By Form
CC03.accdb
frmStuffedAnimals

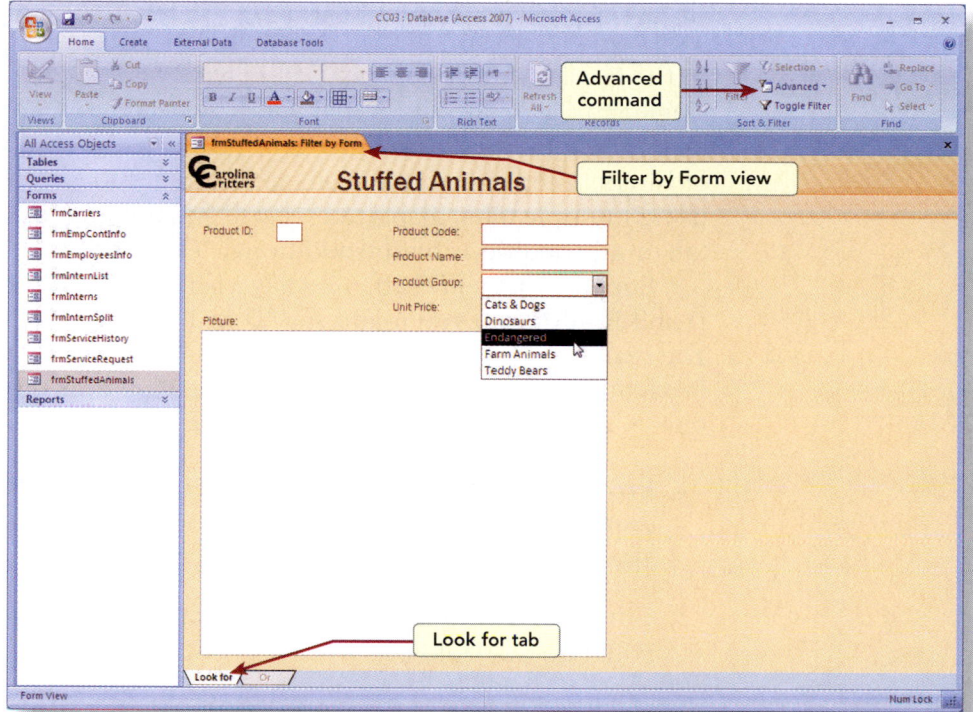

4. From the **Home** tab, in the **Sort & Filter** group, choose the Toggle Filter command 🔲. This returns you to the form and enables the filter. Five records match this filter.

5. Press Tab to move through the records.

6. From the **Home** tab, in the **Sort & Filter** group, click the Advanced command 🔲 and choose **Filter By Form**. The last setting for Product Group is still present.

7. Click in the **Unit Price** field, and key **>20** and press Enter.

8. From the **Home** tab, in the **Sort & Filter** group, choose the Toggle Filter command 🔲. Only three records display.

Access 2007

Figure 3-12
Filter Logic: Filter By Form
CC03.accdb

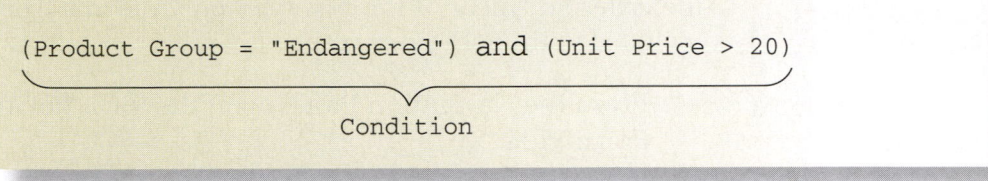

```
(Product Group = "Endangered") and (Unit Price > 20)
                          Condition
```

9. Press Tab to move through the records.

Exercise 3-15 USE FILTER BY FORM "OR" OPTION

In the previous exercise, you used Filter By Form to create a set of filters in a single tab. There are times that you may need to create a more complex filter using multiple tabs. The Filter By Form has the ability to add alternate sets of filters. Alternative collections of filters are located on the "Or" tab. When using multiple tabs, displayed records must match all conditions on the first tab or all conditions on the additional "Or" tabs.

Suppose that you need to display a list of stuffed animals in Product Groups D and E. Although you might say "D and E," this is actually an OR condition. You really want to display all the records that have "D" or "E" for a value in the Product Group field. Because both values are applied to the same field, you must place the first filter on the "Look for" tab and the second on the "Or" tab.

1. From the **Home** tab, in the **Sort & Filter** group, click the Advanced command 🔲 and choose **Filter By Form**. The filter is set to find "Endangered" animal kits that cost greater than $20.

2. Click the **Or** tab next to the **Look for** tab. This opens an alternative collection of fields.

3. Click the drop-down arrow for the **Product Group** and choose **Teddy Bears**.

4. Click in the **Unit Price** field, and key **>20**.

Figure 3-13
Filter Logic: Filter By Form with Or
CC03.accdb

```
((Product Group = "Endangered") and (Unit Price > 20)) or ((Product Group = "Teddy Bear") and (Unit Price > 20))
                    Condition 1                                              Condition 2
```

5. From the **Home** tab, in the **Sort & Filter** group, choose the Toggle Filter command ☑ Toggle Filter .

6. Press Tab to move through the records. There are seven records.

7. From the **Home** tab, in the **Sort & Filter** group, choose the Toggle Filter command ☑ Toggle Filter to disable the filter.

8. Click the Close button ✖ and then **Yes** to save the changes.

Using the Database Documenter

External documentation helps a database administrator manage changes to a database. An easy way to document a database is to create a report using the Database Documenter. The *Database Documenter* is an Access tool that lists the indexes, properties, relationships, parameters, and permissions of major database objects.

Assume you are the database manager for Carolina Critters and are asked to track healthcare expenses for the dependents of all employees. Before beginning the task, you would find it beneficial to see a list of all fields used in every table.

Exercise 3-16   GENERATE A REPORT FOR A TABLE

When documenting a single object, you most often include details for fields and indexes. By default, the Database Documenter does not include fields or indexes in its report. It is always a good idea to check which options are selected before printing a report.

1. From the **Database Tools** tab, in the **Analyze** group, choose the Database Documenter command .

2. In the **Documenter** dialog box, on the **Tables** tab, click the checkbox for **tblEmployees**.

Figure 3-14
Database
Documenter
CC03.accdb

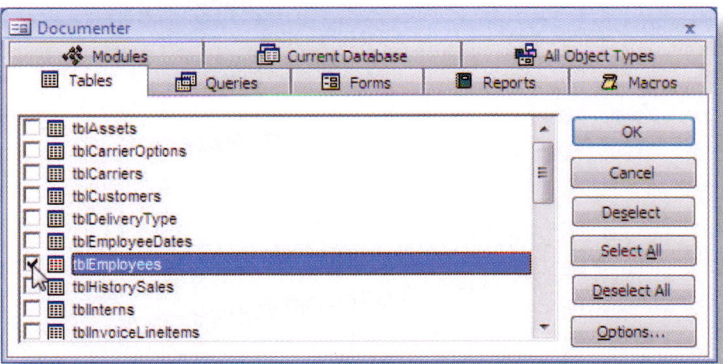

3. Click **Options** to open the **Print Table Definition** dialog box.

4. For the **Include for Table** section, check the **Properties**, **Relationships**, and **Permissions by User and Group**.

5. For the **Include for Fields** section, select **Names, Data Types, Sizes, and Properties**.

6. For the **Include for Indexes** section, select **Names, Fields, and Properties**.

7. Click **OK** to accept the changes and close the dialog box.

8. Click **OK** to view the report. This report contains more information than is needed.

9. Click the Close Print Preview command .

Exercise 3-17   PRINT/SAVE REPORTS FOR MULTIPLE OBJECTS

When documenting multiple objects, you may not wish to include the same level of the detail that you might for a single object report. For example, you may only need to see field names, data types, and sizes for all tables in your database.

1. From **Database Tools** tab, in the **Analyze** group, choose the Database Documenter command 📄.

2. In the **Documenter** dialog box, on the **Tables** tab, click **Select All**.

3. Click **Options** to open the **Print Table Definition** dialog box.

4. For the **Include for Table** section, only check **Properties**.

5. For the **Include for Fields** section, select **Names, Data Types, and Sizes**.

6. For the **Include for Indexes** section, select **Nothing**.

Figure 3-15
Print Table Definition
CC03.accdb

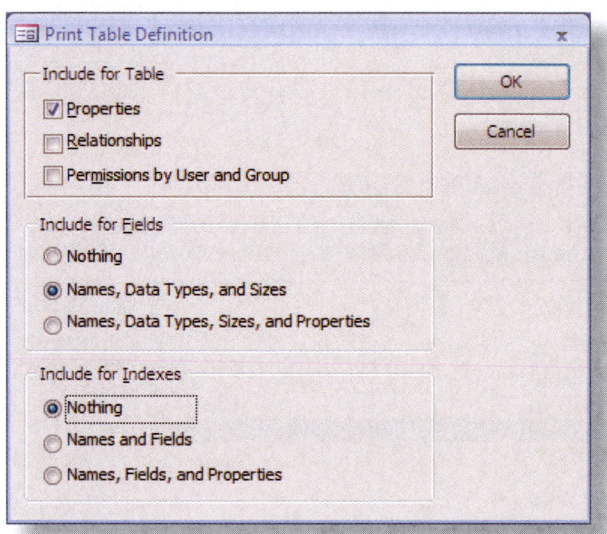

7. Click **OK** to accept the changes and close the dialog box.

8. Click **OK** to view the report. Notice that the information for each table now fits on one page.

 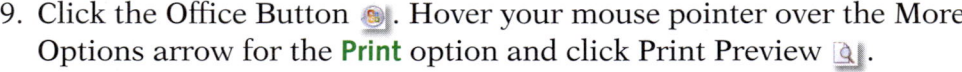 9. Click the Office Button 🔵. Hover your mouse pointer over the More Options arrow for the **Print** option and click Print Preview 🔍.

 10. Depending on your classroom procedures, click either the Print command 🖨 or the XPS command 📄.

 11. Click the Close button ✖ to close the database.

Lesson 3 Summary

- To locate specific information, you can use Access tools to search, find, sort, and filter.

- You can improve the search speeds by specifying unique data.

- The Search tool begins its search at the first field of the first record and stops at the first match.

- The **Find and Replace** command begins a search at the insertion point and includes options for fine-tuning how text is matched.

- A wildcard is a character or group of characters used to represent one or more alphabetical or numerical characters.

- The **Totals** row is a feature that you can use to calculate aggregate functions quickly.

- Each time you display the **Totals** row, the functions that you last saved will appear.

- A filter is a database feature that limits the number of records displayed.

- When applying a filter to a recordset, only records matching the criterion will display.

- The Filter By Selection options displayed depend upon the type of field and data selected.

- When filtering for a specific value, you select one or more values from a dynamically created list.

- The date filter options available vary depending on the date selected and the current date.

- Filter By Form allows you to define a collection of criteria for one or more fields using a template.

- The Filter By Form has the ability to add alternate sets of filters located on the "Or" tab.

- The Database Documenter is an Access tool that lists the indexes, properties, relationships, parameters, and permissions of major database objects.

LESSON 3		Command Summary	
Feature	**Button**	**Task Path**	**Keyboard**
Database Documenter		Database Tools, Analyze, Database Documenter	
Filter By Form		Home tab, Sort & Filter, Advanced, Filter By Form	
Filter Range of Values		Home, Sort & Filter, (data type) Filters	
Filter Selection		Home, Sort & Filter, Selection	

continues

LESSON 3		Command Summary *continued*	
Feature	**Button**	**Task Path**	**Keyboard**
Filter Specific Value		Home, Sort & Filter, Filter	
Find		Home tab, Find	Ctrl + F
Replace		Home tab, Find, Replace	Ctrl + H
Sort Ascending		Home, Sort & Filter, Ascending	
Sort Descending		Home, Sort & Filter, Descending	
Sort Remove		Home, Sort & Filter, Clear All Sorts	
Totals Rows		Home, Records, Totals	

Concepts Review

True/False Questions

Each of the following statements is either true or false. Indicate your choice by circling T or F.

T F   1. Templates can be used to create databases, tables, and queries.

T F   2. Press Ctrl+H to open the **Find and Replace** dialog box with a focus on the **Replace** tab.

T F   3. The asterisk (*) is a wildcard that represents one or more characters.

T F   4. The aggregate function average calculates values for columns containing text, numeric, currency, and date/time data.

T F   5. When applied, a filter displays only matching records.

T F   6. When the insertion bar is in a field with no characters selected, Filter By Selection assumes the whole field is selected.

T F   7. Only text fields can be created in Datasheet View.

T F   8. In Datasheet View, the column heading will display the Description property of a field.

Short Answer Questions

Write the correct answer in the space provided.

1. What shortcut keys open the **Find and Replace** dialog box with focus on the **Find** tab?

2. When using the Search tool, if a recordset contains more than one match, which match will be found?

3. What is a group of characters used to represent one or more alphabetical or numerical characters called?

4. In Filter By Form, what is the name of the first tab?

5. When using Filter By Form in a form, how will the template appear?

6. What action automatically triggers recalculations of the aggregate functions located in the **Totals** row?

7. What Find and Replace option finds records in which an entire field matches the value in the Find What text box?

_____

8. When creating a field in Datasheet View, what data type will be assigned to a street address?

_____

Critical Thinking

Answer these questions on a separate page. There are no right or wrong answers. Support your answers with examples from your own experience, if possible.

1. In addition to by month and by year, Access can filter data by quarters. Why do many businesses display financial information by calendar quarters?

2. Many businesses find it necessary to import tables into a database. Give an example of when a business might need to import data.

Skills Review

Exercise 3-18

Replace data in a table using a wildcard.

REVIEW

If you have the file *[your initials]*-**CC03** from the lesson, you can skip to Step 2.

1. Copy and rename a database by following these steps:
   a. Open the folder **Lesson 03**.
   b. Right-click the file **CC03** and from the shortcut menu, choose **Copy**.
   c. Right-click an unused part of the folder, and from the shortcut menu, choose **Paste**.
   d. Right-click the new file, and from the shortcut menu, choose **Rename**. Rename the file to *[your initials]*-**CC03**.
   e. Right-click *[your initials]*-**CC03**, and from the shortcut menu, choose **Properties**. Make certain that the Read-only attribute check box is not checked. Click **OK**.
2. Replace data by following these steps:
   a. In the Navigation Pane, open the table **tblPensionFund** in Datasheet View.
   b. Press Ctrl+H to open the **Find and Replace** dialog box.
   c. In the **Find What** control, key **st***.

d. In the **Replace With** control, key *[your initials]*.

e. Click the drop-down arrow for the **Look In** control and choose **tblPensionFund**.

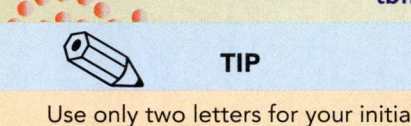

TIP

Use only two letters for your initials.

f. Click the drop-down arrow for the **Match** control and choose **Any Part of Field**.

g. Click the drop-down arrow for the **Search** control and choose **All**.

h. Click **Replace All** and click **Yes** in response to the message box.

i. Click **Cancel** to close the dialog box.

3. Print/Save a datasheet in landscape orientation by following these steps:

a. Click the Office Button 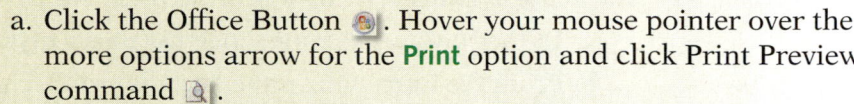. Hover your mouse pointer over the more options arrow for the **Print** option and click Print Preview command 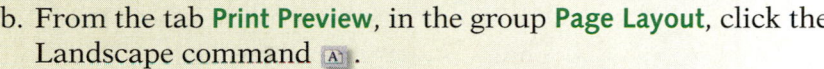.

b. From the tab **Print Preview**, in the group **Page Layout**, click the Landscape command.

c. Depending on your classroom procedures, click either the Print command or the XPS command.

4. Close an object by following these steps:

a. Right-click the **tblPensionFund** tab. From the shortcut menu, select **Close**.

Exercise 3-19

Sort records in a report.

1. The database *[your initials]*-**CC03** is required to complete this exercise.

a. Double-click the database *[your initials]*-**CC03**.

2. Sort data by following these steps:

a. In the Navigation Pane, open the report **rptInternData**.

b. From the tab **Home**, in the group **Views**, click the Layout command.

c. Right-click the column headers for **Intern ID** and choose **Sort Largest to Smallest**.

3. Print/Save a report in landscape orientation by following these steps:

a. Click the Office Button. Hover your mouse pointer over the more options arrow for the **Print** option and click Print Preview command.

b. From the tab **Print Preview**, in the group **Page Layout**, click the Landscape command.

c. Click the **Two Pages** command. Notice that this report contains information on a second page.

d. From the tab **Print Preview**, in the group **Page Layout**, click the Margins command option arrow and choose **Narrow**.

e. Depending on your classroom procedures, click either the Print command or the XPS command.

4. Close an object by following these steps:

    a. Right-click the **tblPensionFund** tab. From the shortcut menu, select **Close**.

    b. Click **Yes** to save the changes.

Exercise 3-20

Create a Totals Row in a query.

1. The database *[your initials]*-**CC03** is required to complete this exercise.

    a. Double-click the database *[your initials]*-**CC03**.

2. Create a Totals Row by following these steps:

    a. In the Navigation Pane, open the query **qryKitCosts** in Datasheet View.

    b. From the **Home** tab, in the **Records** group, choose Totals command .

    c. In the **Totals** row, click the drop-down arrow in the **Line Cost** field.

    d. Choose **Average** from the list.

3. Print/Save a report in landscape orientation by following these steps:

    a. Click the Office Button command . Hover your mouse pointer over the more options arrow for the **Print** option and click Print Preview command .

    b. Depending on your classroom procedures, click either the Print command or the XPS command .

4. Close an object by following these steps:

    a. Right-click the **qryKitCosts** tab. From the shortcut menu, select **Close**.

    b. Click **Yes** to save the changes.

Exercise 3-21

Filter a recordset. Create a Database Documenter report.

1. The database *[your initials]*-**CC03** is required to complete this exercise.

    a. Double-click the database *[your initials]*-**CC03**.

2. Create a Filter by following these steps:

    a. In the Navigation Pane, open the table **tblHistorySales** in Datasheet View.

    b. In the first record, in the **Ship Date** field, select only the year 1998.

    c. Right-click on 1998 and select **Ends With 1998**.

3. Close an object by following these steps:

    a. Right-click the **tblHistorySales** tab. From the shortcut menu, select **Close**.

    b. Click **Yes** to save the changes.

4. Create a Database Documenter report by following these steps:

a. From the **Database Tools** tab, in the **Analyze** group, choose Database Documenter command 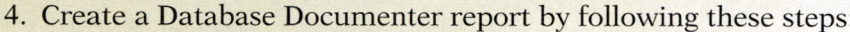.

b. In the **Database Documenter** dialog box, on the **Tables** tab, click the checkbox for **tblHistorySales**.

c. Click **Options** to open the **Print Table Definition** dialog box.

d. For the **Include for Table** section, only check **Properties**.

e. For the **Include for Fields** section, select **Nothing**.

f. For the **Include for Indexes** section, select **Nothing**.

g. Click **OK** to close the **Print Table Definition** dialog box.

h. Click **OK** to create the document report.

5. Print/Save a Database Documenter report by following these steps:

a. Depending on your classroom procedures, click either the Print command 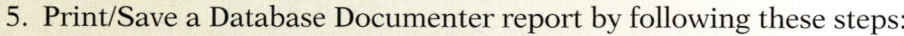 or the XPS command 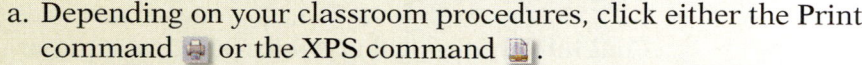.

Lesson Applications

Exercise 3-22

Replace data through a form.

1. Open *[your initials]*-**CC03** and enable all content.

2. Open the form **frmInternList** in Form View.

3. Replace all occurrences of **555** with **999**.

 4. Print/Save the form **frmInternList** in landscape orientation.

5. Close the form.

Exercise 3-23

Find information using wildcards. Create a Database Documenter Report.

1. Open *[your initials]*-**CC02** and enable all content.

2. Open the table **tblParts** in Datasheet View.

3. Locate all occurrences of **P*tic**.

4. Correct the misspelled words.

5. Filter the table to show only records that contain the word plastic.

 6. Print/Save the datasheet in landscape for **tblParts**.

Exercise 3-24

Filter for specific year and quarter. Sort a table. Print/Save a report.

1. Open *[your initials]*-**CC02** and enable all content.

2. Open the table **tblHistorySales**.

TIP

Use the date filter "between" 1/1/2001 and 3/31/2001.

3. Clear all filters and/or sorts.

4. Filter for records that were shipped during the first quarter of 2001.

5. Sort in descending order by **InvoiceID**.

 6. Print/Save a **Database Documenter** report for **tblHistorySales** that displays only the properties for the table.

Exercise 3-25 ◆ Challenge Yourself

Determine minimum, maximum, and average values.

1. Open the table **tblParts**.

TIP

You cannot complete this exercise in one step or view.

2. Create a Word document called *[your initials]*-**Apps-03**. and record the answers to the following questions.

3. Who are the eight Carolina Critters venders?

4. For each vender, list the minimum, maximum, and average value of the product cost field (PCost.)

5. Include your name, class information, and date.

 6. Print/Save the Word file *[your initials]*-**Apps-03**.

On Your Own

In these exercises, you work on your own, as you would in a real-life work environment. Use the skills you've learned to accomplish the task—and be creative.

Exercise 3-26

Review the Web sites you located in Exercises 2-28 and 2-29 of the companies that sell products that may be of interest to members of the organization you formed. Determine which companies allow products to be sorted or displayed by different conditions. On a sheet of paper, write down the fields that can be sorted or selected. Continue to the next exercise.

Exercise 3-27

For one of the Web sites, print three lists of products sorted or filtered by various methods. Write a brief description of the sort or filter being applied to each of the three printouts. Continue to the next exercise.

Exercise 3-28

Refer to the form you created in Exercise 2-30. Write down the fields that can be used to sort or filter the information displayed on the form. Sketch two new forms on the basis of your sorting and filtering parameters. Submit your work for Exercises 3-26 through 3-28 to your instructor.

Creating New Databases and tables

OBJECTIVES

After completing this lesson, you will be able to:

1. Create databases.

2. Create tables.

3. Add and delete fields in a table.

4. Control field appearance.

5. Control data integrity.

6. Manage external data.

Estimated Time: 2 hours

MCAS OBJECTIVES
AC07 70-605 1.1.1
AC07 70-605 1.1.2
AC07 70-605 1.1.3
AC07 70-605 2.1.1
AC07 70-605 2.1.2
AC07 70-605 2.2.1
AC07 70-605 2.2.2
AC07 70-605 2.2.3
AC07 70-605 2.3.1
AC07 70-605 2.3.3
AC07 70-605 2.3.4
AC07 70-605 2.4.1
AC07 70-605 2.4.1
AC07 70-605 2.4.2
AC07 70-605 2.4.4
AC07 70-605 3.4.3
AC07 70-605 3.5.1
AC07 70-605 5.4.1
AC07 70-605 5.4.2
AC07 70-605 6.2.3

Company databases maintain customer names, transaction histories, inventory levels, product pricing, and employee data. All of these data are vital pieces of information necessary to operate a company on a day-to-day basis.

The structure of a database is critical for a company's ability to convert data into useful information. A database must be both efficient and effective. It must be designed to improve data entry and protect the integrity of the data.

Creating Databases

Prior to creating a new database, you should analyze the needs of the people who will use it. You should plan for the type of data that will be stored, including how they will be entered and displayed.

There are two methods for creating a new database. One method uses templates to create a structured database containing major objects (e.g., tables, queries, forms, or reports). The second method creates a blank database without objects.

Exercise 4-1 CREATE A DATABASE USING A TEMPLATE

When creating a new database, you sometimes can find a database template on which to base your preliminary design. A *database template* is a ready-to-use database containing all the tables, queries, forms, and reports needed to perform a specific task.

For example, Access includes templates for tracking potential sales, organizing contact lists, and even maintaining grade sheets. Database templates can be useful even when you modify the pre-defined objects to better fit your needs.

> **NOTE**
> You will not need to keep a copy of this database. At the end of this exercise, you will delete the file. It is used only to demonstrate database templates.

1. Click the Start button  on the Windows task bar and point to **All Programs**.

2. Click **Office Access 2007** to start Access. (You might have to first point to a program group, such as Microsoft Office.)

3. Access opens into the **Getting Started with Microsoft Office Access** page.

4. Click in the **From Microsoft Office Online** section. Click **Business**.

Figure 4-1
Business Templates

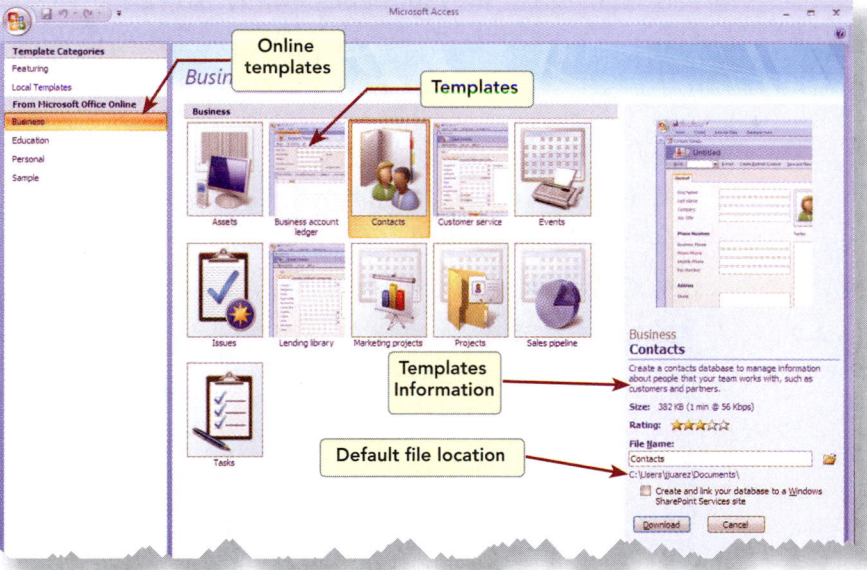

> **NOTE**
> Microsoft Templates do not follow the Leszynski Naming Conventions when naming a major object.

5. Click the **Contacts** template. The template's information appears on the right.

6. Click the **File Name** text box and change the file name to *[your initials]*-**Contact**.

7. Click **Download** to download and launch the template.

8. Click the Shutter Bar Open/Close button to expand the Navigation Pane. The Navigation Bar is organized by **Contacts Navigation**.

Access 2007

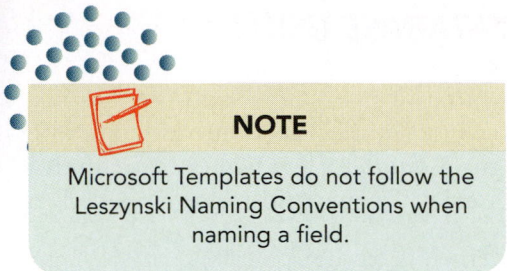

NOTE

Microsoft Templates do not follow the Leszynski Naming Conventions when naming a field.

9. Click the **Contacts Navigation** drop-down arrow and choose **Object Type**. This database has one table, one query, two forms, and two reports.

10. Right-click the document tab for the form **Contact List** and choose **Close**.

11. In the Navigation Pane, double-click the table **Contacts**.

12. From the **Home** tab, in the **Views** group, choose the View command . This is the Design View of the table.

13. Right-click the document tab for the table **Contacts** and choose **Close**.

Exercise 4-2   SET DATABASE PROPERTIES

Database properties do not change the functionality of the database. They only provide useful information to help identify the file. Some database properties, such as the title, author, and company, are defined when creating a new database. The information supplied comes from the operating system of the workstation on which the database is created.

1. Click the Office Button . Hover your mouse pointer over the **Manage** option and click Database Properties .

2. Click in the textbox for the **Title** property and key the name of your class.

3. Change the value for **Author** to *[your name]*.

4. In the property **Comments**, key **This database was created using the Microsoft Contacts template on** *[today's date]*.

5. Click **OK** to close the dialog box.

Figure 4-2
Changing properties

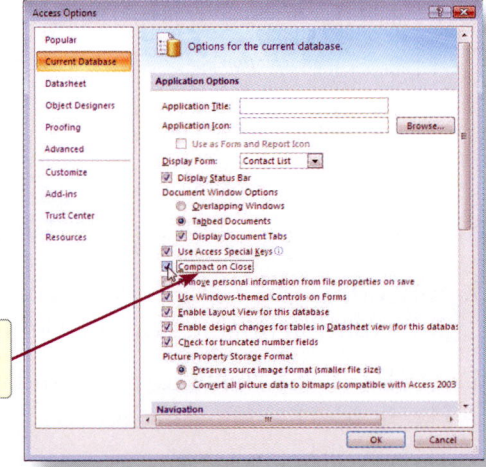

Compact on Close property

6. Click the Office Button and click the **Access Option** button.

7. On the left, click the **Current Database** category. Locate the **Compact on Close** property and click the check box to add a checkmark.

8. Click **OK** to close the **Access Option** dialog box.

9. Click **OK** to close and reopen the database.

10. Click the Office Button and click the Close Database button to close the database but not Access.

Exercise 4-3   CREATE A BLANK DATABASE

If you cannot find a database template to meet your needs, you must create a blank database from scratch. The process requires you to name the database and specify a location in which to save it. Once the database is created, you will be able to add other major objects, such as tables, queries, reports, and forms.

1. In the Getting Started with Microsoft Office Access page, click the Blank Database button.

Figure 4-3
Create a blank database

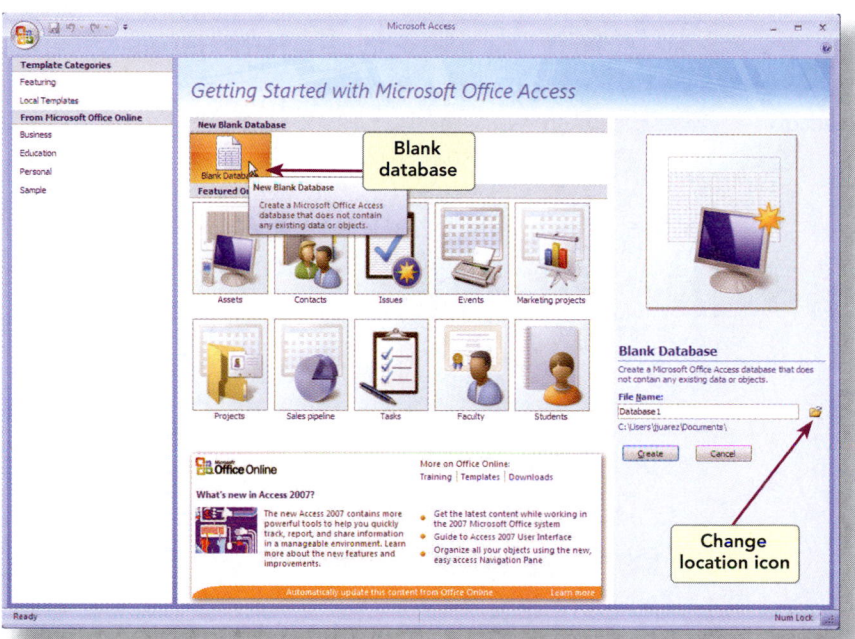

2. In the **File Name** textbox, key *[your initials]*-**Contacts2**.

3. Click **Create**. A new table opens in Datasheet View.

4. Click the Close button for the table. Notice that because the table does not contain fields, it is not listed in the Navigation Pane.

Creating Tables

In a well designed database, each table should store data for a unique purpose. For example, Carolina Critters has a table for employees. The data for employees are similar to the data for interns; however, each table has a unique purpose. When creating a new table, you should test your design by adding a few sample records. You may find that you will need to modify the design.

There are two methods for creating a new table. One method uses templates to populate a table with fields. The second method creates a blank table without fields.

Exercise 4-4   CREATE A TABLE USING A TEMPLATE

Table Templates are similar to database templates. Table Templates provide a quick and easy method to produce a table containing commonly used fields based upon a specific need. Tables created with a template provide the structure that you can modify later.

1. From the **Create** tab, in the **Tables** group, click the Table Templates command and choose **Contacts** from the list.

Figure 4-4
Table Wizard
dialog box
Contacts2.accdb

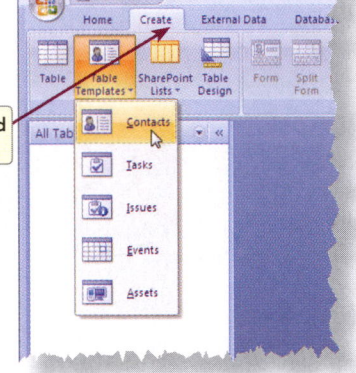

2. In the Quick Access toolbar, click the Save button.

3. In the **Save As** dialog box, key **Contacts** and click **OK**.

4. In the Navigation Pane, click the **All Tables** drop-down arrow and choose **Object Type**.

5. Click the Close button [×] for the table.

6. In the Navigation Pane, right-click the table **Contacts** and choose **Rename**.

7. Press [Home] and key **tbl**. Press [Enter] to accept that name change.

Exercise 4-5   CREATE A TABLE IN DESIGN VIEW

Design View offers you the greatest flexibility when defining field names, types, and properties. The type of field defined depends upon the data that will be stored. For example, prices will be stored as currency, names as text, and images as attachments. When data contains a mixed type of values, such as a street address that contains both numbers and text, you should use the Text data type.

TABLE 4-1 Access Data Types

Setting	Type of Data
Text	Alphanumeric characters. A text field can be a maximum of 255 characters long. Use Text as the data type for numbers that are not used in calculations, such as addresses or phone numbers.
Memo	Descriptive text such as sentences and paragraphs used for text greater than 255 characters in length or for text that uses rich text formatting.

continues

TABLE 4-1 Access Data Types   *continued*

Setting	Type of Data
Number	Numbers (integer or real). Data in a number field can be used in arithmetic calculations. Use Number as the data type when values will be used in calculations.
Date/Time	Formatted dates or times used in date and time calculations. Each value stored includes both a date component and a time component.
Currency	Money values used for storing monetary values (currency). Values can be used in arithmetic calculations and can display a currency symbol.
AutoNumber	A unique numeric value automatically created by Access when a record is added. Use AutoNumber as the data type for generating unique values that can be used as a primary key.
Yes/No	Boolean value displayed as check boxes. Use Yes/No as the data type for True/False fields that can hold one of two possible values.
Attachment	Pictures, images, binary files, or Office files. Preferred data type for storing digital images and any type of binary file.
Hyperlink	Navigation element for Internet sites, e-mail addresses, or file pathnames. Use Hyperlink Data as the data type for storing hyperlinks to provide single-click access to Web pages through a URL (Uniform Resource Locator) or files through a name in UNC (universal naming convention) format.

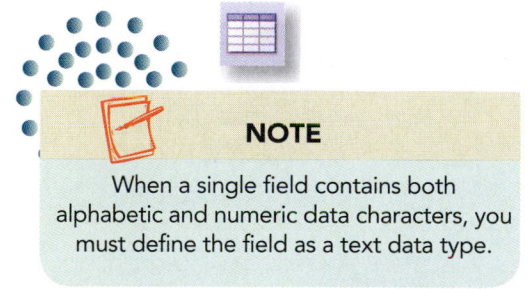

NOTE

When a single field contains both alphabetic and numeric data characters, you must define the field as a text data type.

1. From the **Create** tab, in the **Tables** group, choose Table. A new table is created and the ribbon now shows the contextual tab **Datasheet**.

2. In the **Views** group, choose Views to switch to Design View.

3. In the **Save As** dialog box, key **tblOrganization** and click **OK**. The table is now in Design View.

Figure 4-5
Design View of a table
Contacts2.accdb
tblOrganization

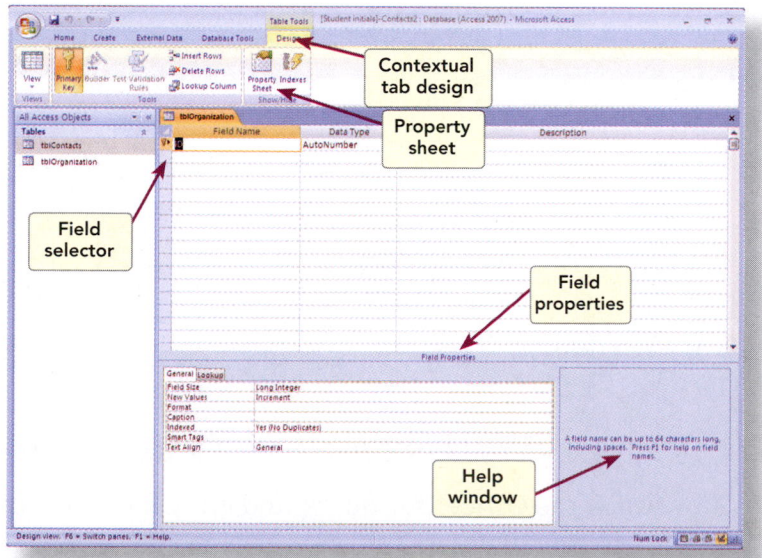

4. In the second row, click the **Field Name** column, and key **OrgNum**.

5. Press Tab to move to the **Data Type** column.

6. Click the drop-down arrow and choose **Number**.

7. Press Tab to move to the **Description** column. Key **Member identification number**.

8. Press Tab to move to the third row in the **Field Name** column. Key **OrgName**.

9. Press Tab to move to the **Data Type** column. The default data type is **Text**.

10. Press Tab and key **Organization name**.

11. Enter the following fields:

Field Name	Data Type	Description
Dues	**Currency**	**Organization dues**
Phone	**Text**	**Office phone number**
StartDate	**Date/Time**	**Member since**
Email address	**Hyperlink**	**Organization e-mail**
MemPhone	**Attachment**	**Members' phone lists**

12. Click the Close button ✕ for the table.

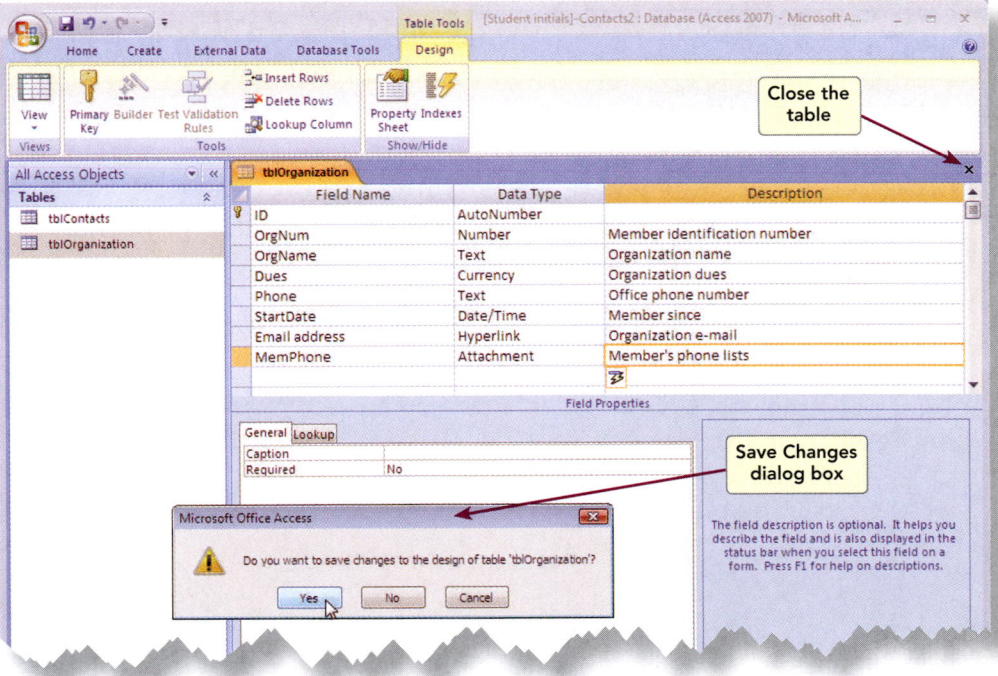

Figure 4-6
Structural changes to a table
Contacts2.accdb
tblOrganization

13. Click **Yes** to save the changes to the design of the table.

14. Click the Office Button 🔘 and click the Exit Access button 📁 to close the database and exit Access.

Exercise 4-6 COPY A TABLE STRUCTURE

When copying a table, you have three options. You can select to include only the structure, the structure and the data, or only the data. When copying only the structure, you create a table with only fields but no records. When copying only the data, you will add the records to a similarly structured table.

1. Locate and open the **Lesson 04** folder.

2. Make a copy of **CC04** and rename it to *[your initials]*-**CC04**.

3. Open and enable content for *[your initials]*-**CC04**.

4. In the Navigation Pane, double-click the table **tblEmployees**. This table has 39 records.

5. Click the Close button ⊠ for the table.

6. In the Navigation Pane, right-click the table **tblEmployees** and choose **Copy** from the menu.

7. From the **Home** tab, in the **Clipboard** group, click the Paste command 📋 .

8. In the **Paste Table As** dialog box, change the **Table Name** to **tblRetirees**.

9. In the **Paste Options** section, select **Structure Only**.

10. Click **OK**.

11. In the Navigation Pane, double-click the table **tblRetirees**. This table has no records. Only the structure of the employees table was copied.

Exercise 4-7 MODIFY TABLE PROPERTIES

Table properties do not change the functionality of the table. They only provide useful information to help identify the object. Most properties, such as owner or date/time modified, are automatically updated based upon the workstation settings.

1. In the Navigation Pane, right-click the table **tblRetirees**, and choose **Table Properties**.

Figure 4-7
Table properties
CC04.accdb
tblRetirees

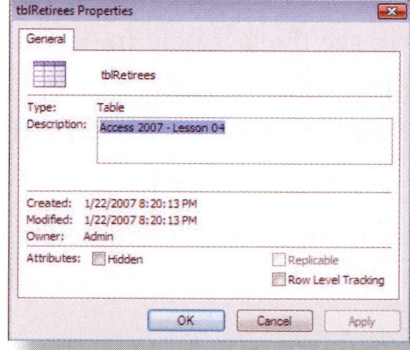

2. In the Description textbox, key **This table stores the information of all Carolina Critters retirees.**

3. Click **OK**.

4. In the Navigation Pane, double-click the table **tblRetirees**.

5. From the **Home** tab, in the **Views** group, choose the View command 🖉 .

6. From the **Design** tab, in the **Show/Hide** group, click the Property Sheet command. The Property Sheet appears. Notice that the **Description** property contains the text from step 2.

7. From the **Design** tab, in the **Show/Hide** group, click the Property Sheet command to close the Property Sheet.

8. Right-click the document tab for **tblRetirees** and choose **Close**.

Adding and Deleting Fields in a Table

When your company's needs for information change, so should your database. Making periodic adjustments to the table structures, such as adding or deleting fields, occasionally may be necessary.

Before adding any field to a table, you first should make certain that it does not duplicate an existing field's data. Adding a new field in one table to store data already in another table creates inefficient data design and can lead to data entry errors.

Deleting a field can be much more dangerous than adding one. Before deleting a field from a table, make certain that the data in the field will never be needed in the future. Many database administrators would rather move data to an archive table rather than delete historical information.

Exercise 4-8   ADD AND DELETE FIELDS IN DATASHEET VIEW

You also can insert and delete fields in Datasheet View. When inserting a text field in a datasheet, the default width of the field is 255 spaces. Each field will be named Field*n*, where *n* is a sequential number starting with one (1). Although the task of deleting a field from datasheet may appear similar to hiding the field, deleting a field is a permanent action that cannot be undone.

1. In the Navigation Pane, double-click the table **tblCustomers**.

2. From the **Home** tab, in the **Records** group, click the More command and choose **Unhide Columns** from the menu.

3. In the **Unhide Columns** dialog box, click the check box for **Add New Field**. Click **Close**.

4. Scroll horizontally to see the last field in the table.

5. In the **Add New Field**, for the first record, key **3.2%** and press Tab. The field is now called **Field1** and a new **Add New Field** column was added.

6. Click on the column header for **Field1**.

7. From the **Datasheet** tab, in the **Fields and Columns** group, choose Rename.

8. Key **Discount** as the new field name.

9. Scroll horizontally to see the first field in the table.

10. Click on the column header for the **After Hours**.

11. From the **Datasheet** tab, in the **Fields and Columns** group, choose Delete ⚓. Click **Yes** to confirm the deletion.

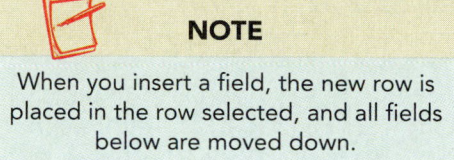

Exercise 4-9   ADD AND DELETE FIELDS IN DESIGN VIEW

Adding fields through Design View is more flexible than through Datasheet View. In addition to text, numeric, and date fields, you can define and size all field types.

> **NOTE**
>
> When you insert a field, the new row is placed in the row selected, and all fields below are moved down.

1. From the **Datasheet** tab, in the **Views** group, choose View ⬜ to switch to Design View.

2. Click on the field selector for **CompanyName**.

3. From the **Design** tab, in the **Tools** group, choose the Insert Row command ⬚.

Figure 4-8
Inserting a row
CC04.accdb
tblCustomers

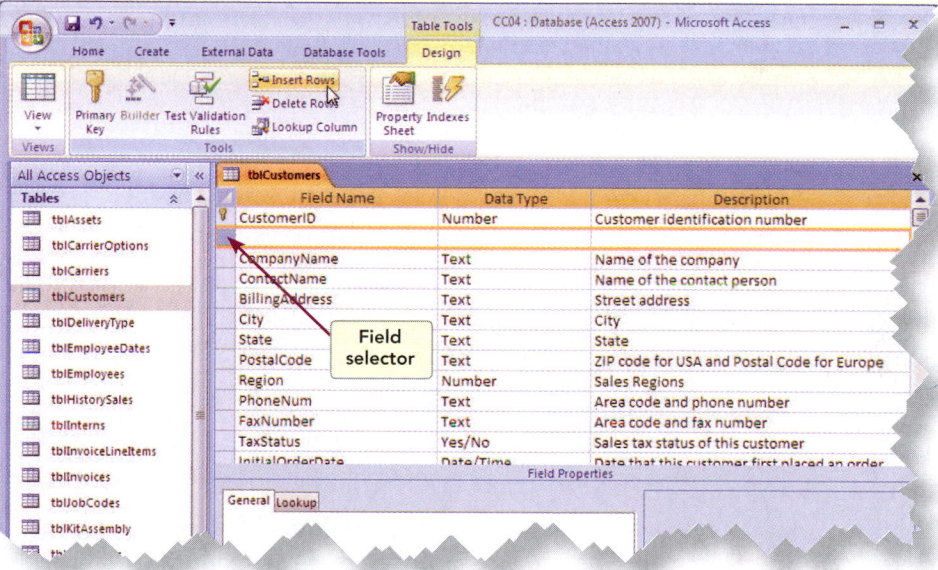

4. Click in the Field Name for the blank row and key **ID**.

5. Press ⌨Tab, click the drop-down arrow, and choose AutoNumber.

6. Click in the **Description** area for **CustomerID** and press ⌨F2 to select the whole description. Press ⌨Ctrl+⌨C to copy.

7. Click in the **Description** area for **ID** and press ⌨Ctrl+⌨V to paste.

8. From the **Design** tab, in the **Views** group, choose View ⬛ to switch to Datasheet View.

9. Click **Yes** to save the changes to the table's structure. The **ID** field has generated an incremental number starting at 1.

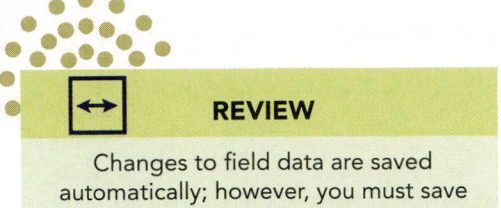

REVIEW

Changes to field data are saved automatically; however, you must save design changes to the table.

10. From the **Home** tab, in the **Views** group, choose View to switch to Design View.

11. Make certain the first field is selected.

12. From the **Design** tab, in the **Tools** group, choose Delete Rows . Click **Yes** to confirm the deletion.

13. Click in the **Field Name ID** and key **CutomerID**.

14. From the Quick Access Toolbar, click Save .

Controlling Field Appearance

NOTE

Spaces should not be used in field names. Spaces create additional requirements when using fields in advanced objects such as Macros and Modules.

Certain field properties control how a field appears to database users. A change to one of these properties only affects the field's appearance without changing the underlying structure or size of the field.

Changing a field's appearance may be for functional reasons, not merely cosmetic. For example, when most records use the same area code, you may change the default value for the phone number. This simple change may improve the speed, accuracy, and consistency of data entry.

TABLE 4-2 Text Field Properties

Property	Purpose
Field Size	Controls the size of a text field and can be up to 255 characters.
Format	Defines the appearance of data. Custom formatting changes the appearance of the data without changing the underlying record.
Input Mask	Displays a pattern for entering the data. Examples are the use of parentheses around an area code or hyphens in a social security number.
Caption	Sets a label or title for the caption. The caption replaces the field name as the column title in a datasheet and as the control label in forms and reports.
Default Value	Specifies the value that automatically appears in a field when creating a new record. The value can be accepted or changed.
Validation Rule	Condition specifying criteria for entering data into an individual field. A Validation Rule of ">100" requires values to be larger than 100.
Validation Text	Error message that appears when a value prohibited by the validation rule is entered. For the Validation Rule ">100," the Validation Text might be "You must enter a value greater than 100."
Required	Requires entry of a value in the field when set to "Yes."

Exercise 4-10 CHANGE FIELD PROPERTY CAPTION

When no caption is defined, the name of the field displays as its column heading on a datasheet or as its control label in a form or report. When a field caption is defined, the caption will be used instead.

1. In the Design View of **tblCustomers**, double-click the field **CustomerID** to select the **Field Name.** Press Ctrl + C.

2. In the **Field Properties** section, click in the **Caption** property.

3. Press Ctrl + V. Add a space between "Customer" and "ID."

Figure 4-9
Change the Caption
Property
CC04.accdb
tblCustomers

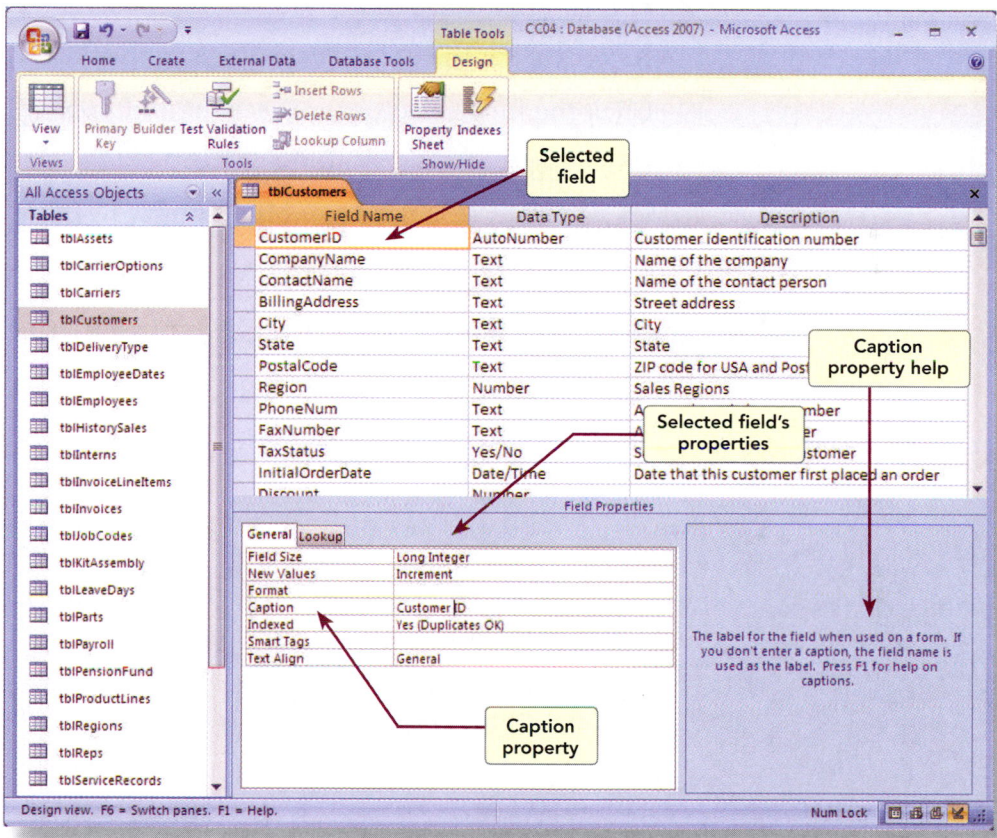

4. Double-click the **Field Name PhoneNum** and press Ctrl + C.

5. Press F6 to move to the **Field Properties** section.

6. Press Tab three times to move to the **Caption** property.

7. Press Ctrl + V. Add a space between "Phone" and "Num."

8. Press End and key **ber**.

9. In the Quick Access toolbar, click the Save button. Each column now has a more readable heading.

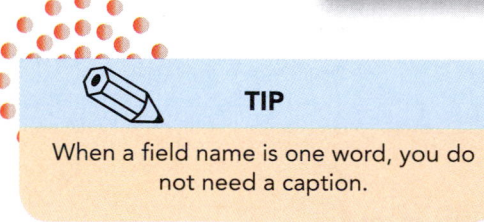

TIP

When a field name is one word, you do not need a caption.

Exercise 4-11   CHANGE FIELD PROPERTY DEFAULT VALUE

Setting a default value is useful when a significant number of records contain the same field value. For example, if the majority of your employees live in the same state, you might choose to set a default value for the state field. All new records will display the default value, and previously entered records will not be changed. Whenever a record contains a different value for the field, the user can key a new value to replace the default value.

1. Click the field selector for **TaxStatus** and press F6.

2. Press Tab until you reach the **Default Value** property.

3. Key **no** to set the default to no tax exemption.

4. Click the field selector for **Discount** and press F6.

5. Press Tab until you reach the **Default Value** property.

6. Key **0** (zero) to set the default to a 0% discount.

Exercise 4-12   CHANGE FIELD PROPERTY FORMAT

You can improve data entry by specifying formats. For example, you can set the format for a date to display the name of the month, set the format for currency to show dollar signs, or set the format for text to display as uppercase letters. For some data types, you can select from predefined formats. For others, you must enter a custom format.

1. In the Design View of **tblCustomers**, click the field selector for **InitialOrderDate** and press F6.

2. In the **Format** property, click the drop-down arrow, and choose **Medium Date**.

Figure 4-10
Setting the Format property
CC04.accdb
tblCustomers

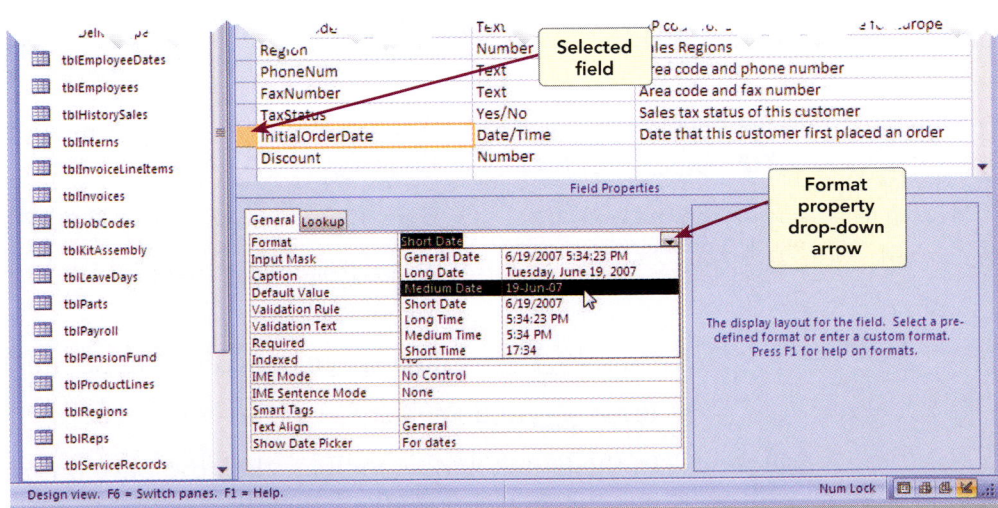

3. Press Ctrl + S to save the changes to the table.

4. From the **Design** tab, in the **Views** group, choose View to switch to Datasheet View. Scroll to see the **Initial Order** field. The appearance of the dates has changed.

5. From the **Home** tab, in the **Views** group, choose View to switch to Design View.

6. Click the field selector for **State** and press F6.

7. In the **Format** property, key **>**.

8. Press Ctrl + S to save the changes to the table.

9. From the **Design** tab, in the **Views** group, choose View to switch to Datasheet View.

10. In the **State** field for **Customer ID** "20", key **bc**. Press Tab. The data displays as upper case characters.

11. From the **Home** tab, in the **Views** group, choose View to switch to Design View.

> **TIP**
>
> A complete list of Text format symbols are located in the Appendix.

Exercise 4-13   CHANGE FIELD PROPERTY INPUT MASK

An input mask is used to format the display of data and control the format in which values can be entered. Input masks can be used for text or numeric data types. You can use the Input Mask Wizard for common formats such as telephone numbers and social security numbers.

TABLE 4-3 Input Masks

Character	Description
0	Digit (0 through 9, entry required; plus [+] and minus [−] signs not allowed).
9	Digit or space (entry not required; plus and minus signs not allowed).
#	Digit or space (entry not required; blank positions converted to spaces, plus and minus signs allowed).
L	Letter (A through Z, entry required).
?	Letter (A through Z, entry optional).

> **NOTE**
>
> A complete list of Input Mask symbols is located in the Appendix.

1. In the Design View of **tblCustomers**, click the field selector for **PhoneNum**, and press F6.

2. Click the **Input Mask** property row.

3. From the **Design** tab, in the **Tools** group, choose Builder.

Access 2007

Figure 4-11
Input Mask Wizard
dialog box
CC04.accdb
tblCustomers

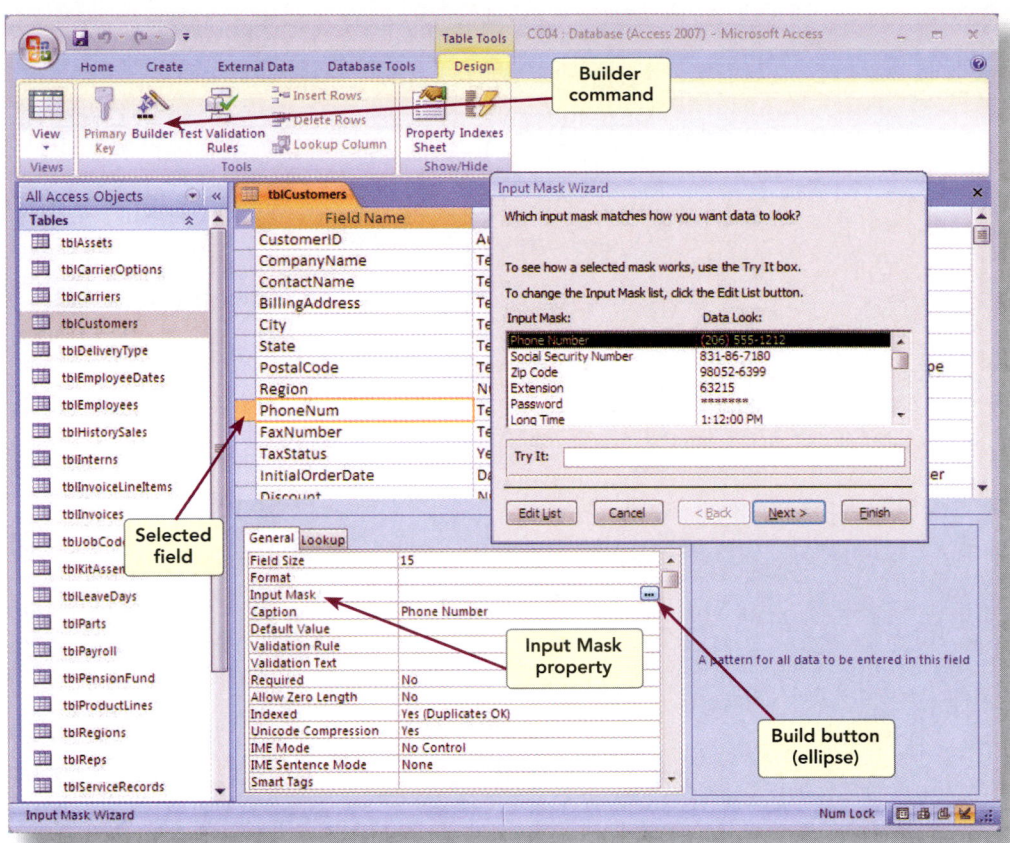

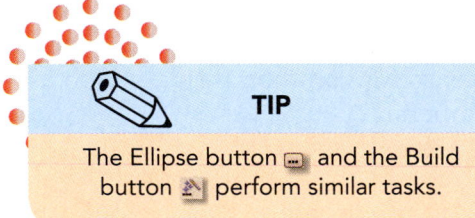

TIP

The Ellipse button and the Build button perform similar tasks.

4. The Input Mask Wizard lists several common masks and shows how the data are displayed. Select the **Phone Number** mask.

5. Click **Next**. The wizard asks if you want to change the **Input Mask**. Click in the **Try It** entry box.

6. Press [Home]. Key your phone number.

7. Click **Next**. The wizard asks how you want to store the data. Select **With the symbols in the mask, like this:**

8. Click **Next**. Read the final message and click **Finish**.

9. From the **Design** tab, in the **Views** group, choose View to switch to Datasheet View. Click **Yes**.

10. Locate the **Customer ID** 17. Scroll to the **Phone Number** field and enter your phone number.

11. From the **Home** tab, in the **Views** group, choose View to switch to Design View.

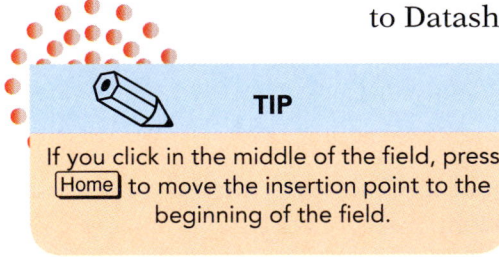

TIP

If you click in the middle of the field, press [Home] to move the insertion point to the beginning of the field.

Exercise 4-14   CHANGE FIELD PROPERTY DATE PICKER

Depending on the workstation's language settings, the date picker displays either to the right or left side of a Date/Time field. Clicking the date picker launches a calendar control from which you can select a date. If the field is empty, the Date Picker will default to the current date.

1. In the Design View of **tblCustomers**, click the field selector for **InitialOrder** and press F6.

2. Move to the **Show Date Picker** property, and click the drop-down arrow, and choose **For dates**.

3. From the **Design** tab, in the **Views** group, choose View ⊞ to switch to Datasheet View. Click **Yes** to save the changes.

4. Click in the first record's **IntialOrder** and click the Date Picker button 📅.

Figure 4-12
Date Picker
CC04.accdb
tblCustomers

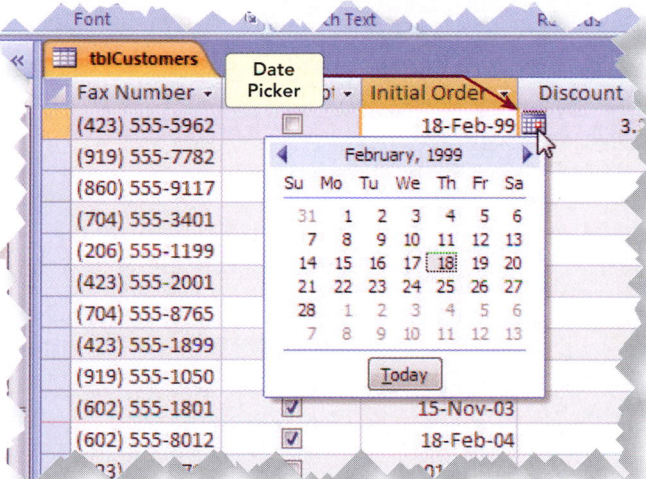

5. Press Esc to exit the field without saving any changes.

6. From the **Home** tab, in the **Views** group, choose View 🖉 to switch to Design View.

Controlling Data Integrity

Certain field properties restrict values stored in a field. A change to one of these properties can affect both the structure and the size of the field. Because these changes might alter your data, it's best to make them before adding data to a table. If a table already contains data and you are uncertain if your data will be affected, back up your database before making changes to the field properties.

Exercise 4-15   SET THE PRIMARY KEY

Most tables contain a primary key. A *primary key* is a field or set of fields in a table that provides a unique identifier for every record. Each record must store a unique value in a primary key field. Most often primary keys are numeric data types; however, other data types can be used.

1. In the Design View of **tblCustomers**, click the field selector for **CustomerID**.

2. From the **Design** tab, in the **Tools** group, choose the Primary Key command 🔑.

Figure 4-13
Set a Primary Key
CC04.accdb
tblCustomers

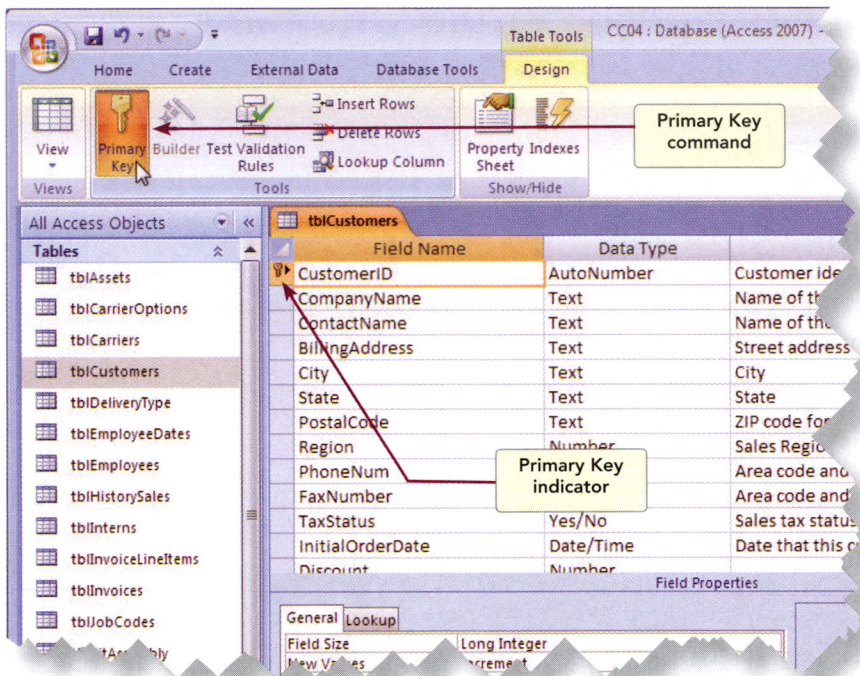

Exercise 4-16   SET THE FIELD PROPERTY FIELD SIZE

Changing the field size alters the space available to store data. The numeric value defined in the **Field Size** property is the maximum number of characters allowed for the storage of data. Changing the field size in Design View is different than changing the column width in Datasheet View.

1. In the Design View of **tblCustomers**, click the field selector for **CompanyName** and press F6.

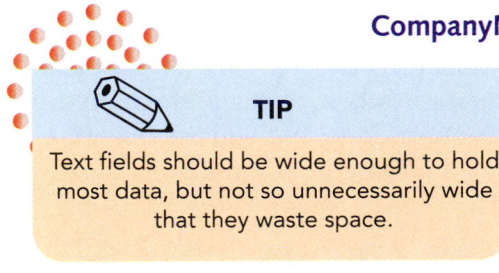

TIP

Text fields should be wide enough to hold most data, but not so unnecessarily wide that they waste space.

2. In the **Field Size** property, change 255 to **30**.

3. Read the message dialog box. Click **Yes**. If any record has stored more than 30 characters in the **CompanyName** field, characters beyond the first 30 characters would be deleted.

4. Select the **Discount** field selector and press F6.

5. For the **Field Size** property, click the drop-down arrow and choose **Single**. Changing from **Double** to **Single** reduces the field size from 8 bytes to 4 bytes.

6. Press Ctrl+S to save the changes to the table.

7. Click **Yes** to the message dialog box.

Exercise 4-17   SET THE FIELD PROPERTY VALIDATION TEXT AND RULES

A *Validation Rule* is a condition specifying criteria for entering data into an individual field. You define a validation rule to control what values can be entered into a field. You also can enter an optional validation text to match your rule. *Validation text* is an error message that appears when a value prohibited by the validation rule is entered.

For example, you could define the validation expression ">=100" for a quantity field to prevent a user from entering values less than 100. For the corresponding validation expression, you could enter "You must enter a number equal to or greater than 100."

When you set a validation rule for a field that contains data, Access will ask if you want to apply the new rule to the existing data. If you answer yes, Access evaluates the rule against the existing data in the table. If any record violates the validation rule, you will be notified that the data must be corrected before the rule can be applied.

The Test Validation Rule button checks the current data in the field to see if it matches the Rule. If not, Access prompts you to resolve the conflict.

1. In the Design View of **tblCustomers**, click the field selector for **Discount** and press F6.

2. Tab to the **Validation Rule** property and key **<=.05**. This rule will restrict users to enter a discount equal to or less than 5%.

3. Press Enter to move to the **Validation Text** property.

4. Key **The maximum discount is 5%. Please try again.**

5. Save the changes to the table. A data integrity dialog box appears, asking if you want to test the existing data with the new rules. Click **Yes**.

6. Switch to Datasheet View. Scroll horizontally to see the **Discount** field.

7. In the second record's **Discount** field, key **6** and press Enter.

Figure 4-14
Validation Text
dialog box
CC04.accdb
tblCustomers

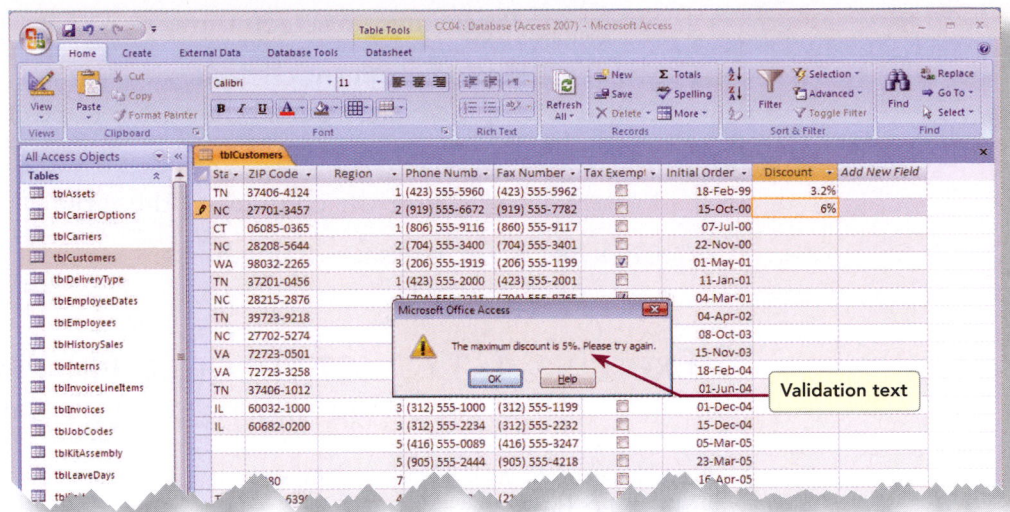

8. Click **OK** to close the dialog box. Delete the 6 and key **5**.

9. Press ⬇. The new data meets the **Validation Rule**.

10. Close the table.

Managing External Data

Whenever possible, a goal of yours should be to avoid requiring users to re-enter data already stored in an electronic format. Rather than re-keying the data, users should transfer the electronic data by importing it into the database. Importing data prevents errors that may occur when re-keying data.

Each time you import data, you create a copy of the original data. The original data remains in the source application while you work with a copy of the data in your database.

Exercise 4-18   **EXPORT A TABLE TO ACCESS**

You can export an Access table directly to another Microsoft application such as Word or Excel. Access tables can also be exported directly to non-Microsoft applications such as dBASE and Paradox. For applications not supported by Access, you can export a table using a file format such as text, XML, or HTML. When exporting a table, you can save the steps used in the export operation. Saving the steps can greatly decrease the time it takes to export the same table next time.

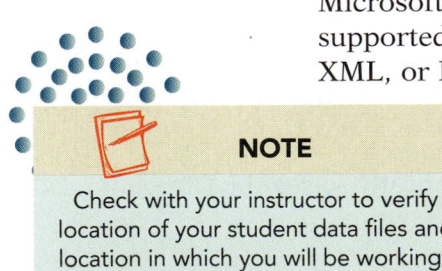

NOTE

Check with your instructor to verify the location of your student data files and the location in which you will be working. The folder "Documents" is often the default folder when you're creating or storing files.

1. Select the table **tblInterns** in the Navigation Pane.

2. From the **External Data** tab, in the **Export** group, click the More command ⬛More and choose **Access Database** from the menu.

Figure 4-15
Export a table
CC04.accdb

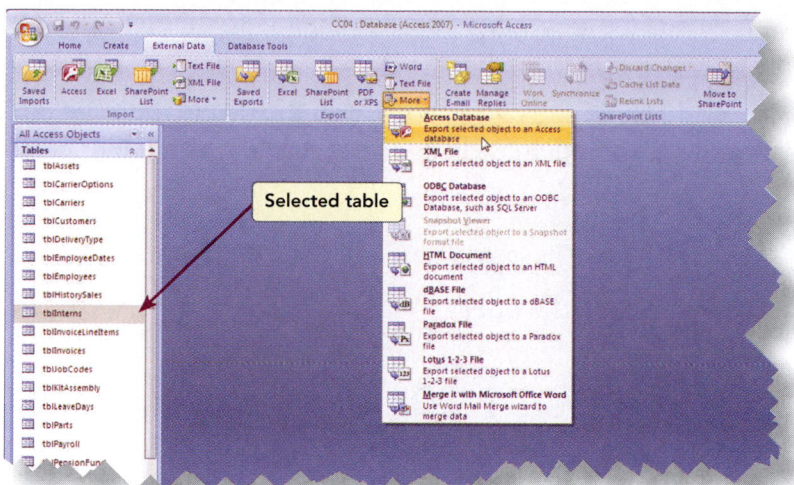

3. In the **Export – Access Database** dialog box, click **Browse**.

4. In the **File Save** dialog box, locate *[your initials]-***Contacts2,** that you created earlier in this lesson. Click **Save**.

5. Click **OK** to close the **Export – Access Database** dialog box.

NOTE

You may want to open the database *[your initials]-***Contacts2** to verify that the table has been exported.

Figure 4-16
Export dialog box
CC04.accdb

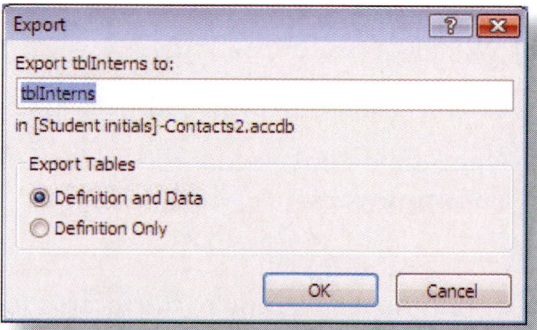

6. Click **OK** to export the table **tblInterns**.

7. Click **Close**.

Exercise 4-19   EXPORT DATA TO WORD

You can export a table, query, form, or report to Microsoft Word using the Access Export Wizard. A copy of the object's data will be stored as a Rich Text Format (RTF) file. For tables, queries, and forms, the visible fields and records appear as a table in the Word document. Hidden or filtered columns and records are not exported.

1. In the Navigation Pane, select the query **qryEmployeeDates**.

2. From the **External Data** tab, in the **Export** group, click the Word command 📄.

3. In the **Export – RTF File** dialog box, delete the "qry" from the file name.

4. Click the check box **Open the destination file after the export operation is complete.** Click **OK**.

5. View the table in Word, then exit Word.

6. Click **Close** without saving the export steps.

7. Close the query.

Exercise 4-20   IMPORT DATA FROM EXCEL

For most non-Access applications, a wizard steps you through the import process. When importing from an Excel workbook, you may select all columns and rows from a worksheet or just a range of cells. The ease of importing data greatly depends upon how the information is stored in the source workbook. Blank columns and rows in the worksheet add unnecessary fields and records to the imported data.

1. In the Navigation Pane, double-click the table **tblEmployees**. Notice that there are 39 employees in this table.

2. Close the table.

3. From the **External Data** tab, in the **Import** group, click the Excel command 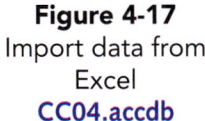.

4. In the **Get External Data – Excel Spreadsheet** dialog box, click **Browse**.

5. In the **File Open** dialog box, locate the folder **Lesson 04** and select the Excel file **Employees**.

6. Click **Open**.

7. Select the option **Append a copy of the records to the table:**, click the drop-down arrow, and choose **tblEmployees**.

Figure 4-17
Import data from
Excel
CC04.accdb

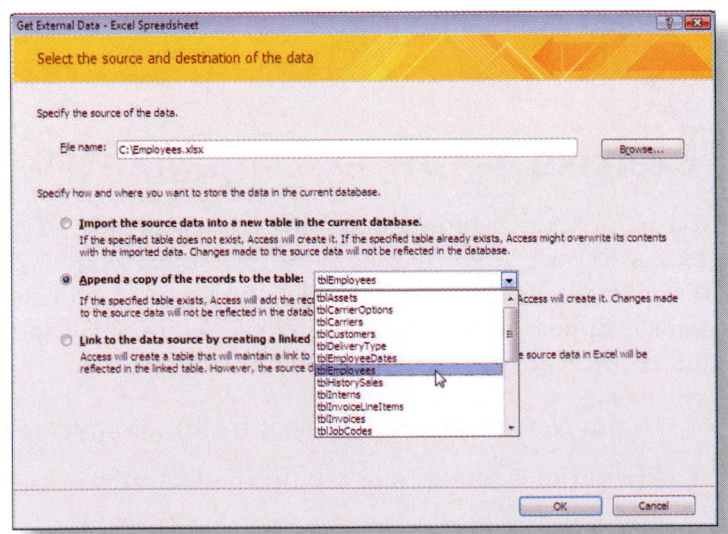

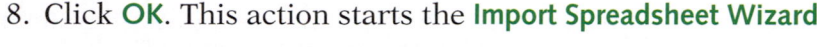
8. Click **OK**. This action starts the **Import Spreadsheet Wizard**.

9. In the first step in the **Import Spreadsheet Wizard**, you see the data from the Excel file. Click **Next**.

TIP

If you have any problems with any of the steps in a Wizard, just click **Cancel** and start over.

10. Click **Next**.

11. Click **Finish** and click **Close**.

12. Open **tblEmployees** in Datasheet View. There are now 42 records. Close the table.

13. Click the Office Button 🔘. Click the **Manage** and choose the Compact and Repair Database command 🔧.

14. Click the Office Button 🔘 and click **Exit Access** to close the database.

Lesson 4 Summary

- The two methods for creating a new database are using a template and creating a blank database.

- A database template is a ready-to-use database containing all the tables, queries, forms, and reports needed to perform a specific task.

- A new database created as a blank database does not contain objects or data.

- Some database properties come from the operating system of the workstation on which the database is created.

- Because database files can be quite large, you should not create a database on a diskette.

- The two methods for creating a new table are using a template and creating a blank table.

- Table Templates provide a quick and easy method to produce a table containing commonly used fields, based upon a specific need.

- When a single field contains both alphabetic and numeric data characters, you must define the field as text data type.

- When copying a table, you can select to include only the structure, the structure and data, or only the data.

- Before adding any field to a table, you first should make certain that it does not duplicate an existing field's data.

- When tables are created using Datasheet View, Access evaluates the data entered and determines the data type for each field.

- A caption is a field property that displays as a column heading in Datasheet View or as a control label in a form or report.

- Spaces should not be used in field names. Spaces create additional requirements when using fields in advanced objects such as macros and modules.

- An input mask is used to format the display of data and control the format in which values can be entered.
- Depending on the workstation's language settings, the date picker displays either to the right or left side of a Date/Time field.
- A primary key is a field or set of fields in a table that provides a unique identifier for every record.
- Changing the field size in Design View is different than changing the column width in Datasheet View.
- The data contained in a primary key field must be unique.
- A Validation Rule is a condition specifying criteria for entering data into an individual field.
- Validation text is an error message that appears when a value prohibited by the validation rule is entered.
- Importing data prevents errors that may occur when re-keying data.
- Data can be exported to another Microsoft application such as Word or Excel or non-Microsoft applications such as dBASE or Paradox.
- Data imported from another Access database, a non-Access database, or a non-database application can be added to an existing table or used to create a new table.
- The Manage Data Tasks dialog box displays and manages import and export operations previously saved.

LESSON 4		Command Summary	
Feature	**Button**	**Task Path**	**Keyboard**
Data, Export		External Data, Export	
Data, Import		External Data, Import	
Database, Create		Microsoft Office Button, New	
Database, Create, Blank		New Blank Database	
Database, Properties		Microsoft Office Button, Manage	
Field, Properties		Home, Views, Design View	
Field, Properties, Toggle			F6
Primary Key		Design, Tools, Primary Key	
Table, Create		Create, Tables	
Table, Properties		Right-click Object, Properties	
Table, Template		Create, Tables, Table Templates	

Concepts Review

True/False Questions

Each of the following statements is either true or false. Indicate your choice by circling T or F.

T F   1. After you create a table using a template, you can rename fields and change the data type of fields in Design View.

T F   2. When you create a table in Datasheet View, all fields are Text data types.

T F   3. The Table Template can create a new database.

T F   4. The primary key field in a table must contain unique data.

T F   5. Fields can be deleted only through Design View.

T F   6. When applying a validation rule to a field that contains data, Access asks if you want to apply the new rule to the existing data.

T F   7. In Datasheet View, the Description property of a field displays as the column header.

T F   8. When exporting a table to Microsoft Word using the Access Export Wizard, a copy of the object's data will be stored as a Rich Text Format (RTF) file.

Short Answer Questions

Write the correct answer in the space provided.

1. When must you create a blank database from scratch?

_____

2. When using the Leszynski Naming Conventions, what would you rename a table called Food Costs?

_____

3. Name the four ways to add a table to a database.

_____

4. What kind of data type does a Table Template use for a street address?

_____

5. What field data type can store more than 255 characters?

_____

6. In what view can you change the data type or description of a field?

_____

7. In Design View, which function key toggles the insertion point between the lower and upper panes?

_____

8. What kind of field must store unique or different data for each record?

_____

Critical Thinking

Answer these questions on a separate page. There are no right or wrong answers. Support your answers with examples from your own experience, if possible.

1. Access Table Templates uses field names such as StateOrProvince and PostalCode instead of State or ZIP Code. Why do you think Access does this? Give an example when using the default field names might not be appropriate.

2. Many businesses find it necessary to import tables into Access. Give an example when a business might need to import data.

Skills Review

Exercise 4-21

Create a blank database. Create a table using a template. Delete fields in Datasheet View and Design View. Rename fields.

1. Create a new database by following these steps:
   a. With Access running and no database open, in the **Getting Started with Microsoft Office Access** page, click the Blank Database button 📄.
   b. In the **File Name** textbox, key *[your initials]*-**Issues**.
   c. Verify the file location.
   d. Click **Create**.

2. Create a table, using a template, by following these steps:
   a. From the **Create** tab, in the **Tables** group, click Table Templates 📇 and choose **Issues** from the list.
   b. Press Ctrl + S.
   c. In the **Save As** dialog box, key **tblIssues** and click **OK**.

3. Delete fields in Datasheet View, by following these steps:

   a. Click on the column header for the **Description**.

   b. From the **Datasheet** tab, in the **Fields and Columns** group, choose Delete ▼.

   c. Click on the column header for the **Category**.

   d. From the **Datasheet** tab, in the **Fields and Columns** group, choose Delete ▼.

4. Delete and rename fields in Design View, by following these steps:

   a. From the **Datasheet** tab, in the **Views** group, choose View ✎ to switch to Design View.

   b. Click on the field selector for **Attachments**.

   c. Press Delete.

   d. Double-click on the field selector for **Title**.

   e. Key **Fullname**.

   f. Press Ctrl+S.

5. Change to Datasheet View and save the table. Add the following record:

   a. Enter the following data:

ID:	*Press* Tab
FullName:	*Key [your full name]*
Opened Date:	7/22/07
Status:	Resolved
Priority:	(1) High
Due Date:	8/1/08
Comments:	*Press* Tab

6. Print/Save the datasheet in landscape orientation by following these steps:

   a. Click the Office Button ⬤. Hover your mouse pointer over the more options arrow for the Print option and click Print Preview ◻.

   b. From the tab **Print Preview**, in the group **Page Layout**, click the Landscape command Ⓐ.

   c. Depending on your classroom procedures, click either the Print command ⬤ or the XPS command ◻.

Exercise 4-22

Edit field properties. Add records. Print/Save table definitions.

1. The database *[your initials]*-**CC04** is required to complete this exercise.

   a. Double-click the database *[your initials]*-**CC04**.

   b. Click the message bar and enable its content.

2. Change the field captions by following these steps:
   a. Open **tblInvoices**. Switch to Design View.
   b. In the top pane, click in the **CarrierOptions** field.
   c. Click in the **Caption** row in the bottom pane.
   d. Key **Carrier Options**.
   e. In the top pane, click in the **OrderDate** row.
   f. Click in the **Caption** row in the bottom pane.
   g. Key **Order Date** as the Caption.
   h. In the top pane, click in the **ShipDate** row.
   i. Click in the **Caption** row in the bottom pane.
   j. Key **Ship Date** as the **Caption**.
   k. Press Ctrl+S.

3. Change an input mast by following these steps:

   a. In the top pane, click in the **ShipDate** row and press F6.
   b. Click the **Input Mask** property row.
   c. From the **Design** tab, in the **Tools** group, choose the Builder button.
   d. Select the **Medium Date** mask. Click **Finish**.
   e. In the top pane, click in the **OrderDate** row and press F6.
   f. Click the **Input Mask** property row.
   g. From the **Design** tab, in the **Tools** group, choose the Builder button.
   h. Click **Yes** to save the changes to the design of the table.
   i. Select the **Medium Date** mask. Click **Finish**.

4. Change an input mask by following these steps:
   a. In the top pane, click in the **ShipDate** row and press F6.
   b. Move to the **Show Date Picker** property, click the drop-down arrow, and choose **For dates**.

   c. From the **Design** tab, in the **Views** group, choose View to switch to Datasheet View. Click **Yes** to save the changes.
   d. Close the table.

5. Print/Save a Database Documenter Report by following these steps:

   a. From the **Database Tools** tab, in the **Analyze** group, choose the Database Documenter command.
   b. In the **Documenter** dialog box, on the **Tables** tab, click the check box for **tblInvoices**.
   c. Click **Options**.
   d. For the **Include for Table** section, select **Properties**.
   e. For the **Include for Fields** section, select **Names, Data Types, Sizes, and Properties**.
   f. For the **Include for Indexes** section, select **Nothing**.
   g. Click **OK** to accept the changes and close the dialog box.
   h. Click **OK** to view the report.
   i. Depending on your classroom procedures, click either the Print command or the XPS command.

Exercise 4-23

Insert fields. Edit field properties. Add, delete, and edit fields. Add records.

1. The database *[your initials]*-**CC04** is required to complete this exercise.
   a. Double-click the database *[your initials]*-**CC04**.
   b. Click the message bar and enable its content.
2. Add fields by following these steps:
   a. Open **tblStuffedAnimals**. Switch to Design View.
   b. In the top pane, click in the **Picture** row.

   c. From the **Design** tab, in the **Tools** command group, select Insert Row .
   d. For the **Field Name**, key **MinimumOrder**.
   e. For the **Data Type**, select **Number**.
   f. Press F6 and change the **Field Size** to **Integer**.
   g. Tab to the **Validation Rule** property and key **>=100**. Click **Yes**.
   h. Tab to the **Validation Text** property and key **Minimum order must be equal to or greater than 100**.
   i. Close the table and save the changes.
3. Print/Save a Database Documenter Report by following these steps:
   a. From the **Database Tools** tab, in the **Analyze** group, choose Database Documenter .
   b. In the **Documenter** dialog box, on the **Tables** tab, click the check box for **tblStuffedAnimals**.
   c. Click **Options**.
   d. For the **Include for Table** section, select **Properties**.
   e. For the **Include for Fields** section, select **Names, Data Types, Sizes, and Properties**.
   f. For the **Include for Indexes** section, select **Nothing**.
   g. Click **OK** to accept the changes and close the dialog box.
   h. Click **OK** to view the report.
   i. Depending on your classroom procedures, click either the Print command 🖨 or the XPS command 📄.

Exercise 4-24

Import Excel data

1. The database *[your initials]*-**CC04** is required to complete this exercise.
   a. Double-click the database *[your initials]*-**CC04**.
   b. Click the message bar and enable its content.

2. Import Excel data by following these steps:

   a. From the **External Data** tab, in the **Import** group, choose Excel 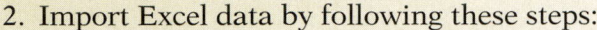.

   b. In the **Get External Data** dialog box, click **Browse**.

   c. Locate the **Lesson 04** folder and select **MoreSales**. Click **Open** and then **OK**.

   d. Click **Show Named Ranges** in the dialog box. Select **NewSales**.

   e. Click **Next**. Set the check box to select the **First Row Contains Column Headings**.

   f. Click **Next**. Click **Next**.

   g. Verify that **No primary key** is selected. Click **Next**.

   h. Verify that the **Import to Table** entry box shows **tblSales**. Click **Finish**.

   i. Do not save the import steps.

   j. Open **tblSales** in Datasheet View to see the new records. Close the table.

3. Print/Save a Database Report by following these steps:

   a. From the **Database Tools** tab, in the **Analyze** group, choose Database Documenter.

   b. In the **Documenter** dialog box, on the **Tables** tab, click the check box for **tblSales**.

   c. Click **Options**.

   d. For the **Include for Table** section, select **Properties**.

   e. For the **Include for Fields** section, select **Names, Data Types, and Sizes**.

   f. For the **Include for Indexes** section, select **Nothing**.

   g. Click **OK** to accept the changes and close the dialog box.

   h. Click **OK** to view the report.

   i. Depending on your classroom procedures, click either the Print command or the XPS command.

   j. Compact and close the database.

Lesson Applications

Exercise 4-25

Create a new database. Import data. Rename field.

1. Create a blank database named *[your initials]*-Venders.

2. Import **tblVenders** from *[your initials]*-**CC04**.

3. Rename the table **tblCCVenders**.

4. Add a hyperlink field named **WebSite** as the last field of the table.

5. Use the Database Documenter to Print/Save **tblCCVenders**. Set the Options to include the **Properties** for the table and **Names, Data Types, and Sizes** for the fields.

6. Compact and close the database.

Exercise 4-26

Delete a field in Datasheet View. Change field properties. Print table definition.

1. Open the *[your initials]*-**CC04** database.

2. Using the **Events** table template, create a table named **tblSalesEvent**.

3. Open the table in Design View. As the second field in the table, add a text field named **SalesRep** with a Field Size of **35**.

4. Change the field name **Start Time** to **StartDate**.

5. Change the field name **End Time** to **EndDate**.

6. Change the **Caption** for **SalesRep** to **Sales Representative**.

7. Change the **Caption** for **StartDate** to **Start Date**.

8. Change the **Caption** for **EndDate** to **End Date**.

9. Disable the **Date Picker** for the **StartDate** and **EndDate** fields.

10. Change the **Format** to **Short Date** for the **StartDate** and **EndDate** fields.

11. Use the Database Documenter to Print/Save **tblSalesEvents**. Set the **Options** to include the **Properties** for the table and **Names, Data Types, and Sizes** for the fields.

12. Delete the **Description** field.

13. Add the following record:

ID:	*Press* Tab
Sales Representative:	*Key [your name]*
Title:	*Key [class name]*
Start Date:	**1/1/07**
End Date:	*Key [today's date]*
Location:	*Key [name of your school]*
Attachments:	*Press* Tab

 14. Print/Save the datasheet for this table in landscape orientation.

Exercise 4-27

Create a table in Datasheet View. Set a primary key.

1. Open the *[your initials]*-**CC04** database, and create a new blank table.

2. In Datasheet View, add the following record:

ID:	*Press* Tab
Column 2:	**464-23-4824**
Column 3:	**Supplies**
Column 4:	**10/15/07**
Column 5:	**$14.85**
Column 6:	**Cleaning Supplies**
Column 7:	**Trash Bags, Soap, and Paper Towels**

TIP

To add a new field in Datasheet View, you must click in the Add New Field column.

3. Save the table as **tblEmpExp-***[your initials]*.

4. Delete the **ID** field and set **Field1** as the primary key.

5. Rename the field names to the following:

Field1:	**EmployeeID**
Field2:	**ExpenseType**
Field3:	**DatePurchased**
Field4:	**AmountSpent**
Field5:	**Purpose**
Field6:	**Description**

6. Enter the following record:

EmployeeID	**234-45-7890**
ExpenseType	**Supplies**
DatePurchased	**10/22/07**
AmountSpent	**25.34**
PurposeOfExpense	**Office Supplies**
Description	*Key [your full name]*

7. Resize columns so that all data are visible.

 8. Print/Save the table in landscape orientation.

9. Save and close the table.

10. Compact and close the database.

Exercise 4-28 ◆ Challenge Yourself

Create a blank database. Create a table from Design View, edit field properties, and enter records.

1. Create a blank database and name it *[your initials]*-**Applications**.

2. Create a new table named **tblPayments-***[your initials]*, and add the following fields:

Field Name	Data Type	Field Size
PaymentID	Autonumber	
CustomerID	Number	Integer
OrderID	Number	Long Integer
PaymentAmount	Currency	
PaymentDate	Date/Time	
Description	Text	40

3. Delete the Field **ID**.

4. Set **PaymentID** as the primary key.

5. Use the Database Documenter to Print/Save **tblPayments**. Set the **Options** to include the **Properties** for the table and **Names, Data Types, and Sizes** for the fields.

6. Enter the following record:

PaymentID	*Press* Tab
CustomerID	1
OrderID	20101
PaymentAmount	500
PaymentDate	11/14/07
Description	*Key [your first name]*
PaymentID	*Press* Tab
CustomerID	2
OrderID	20102
PaymentAmount	750
PaymentDate	1/26/08
Description	*Key [your last name]*
PaymentID	*Press* Tab
CustomerID	5
OrderID	20103
PaymentAmount	1000
PaymentDate	2/7/08
Description	*Key [your school's name]*

7. Size the columns to the widest text or title.

8. Print/Save the table's Datasheet View in landscape orientation.

9. Compact and close the database.

On Your Own

In these exercises, you work on your own, as you would in a real-life work environment. Use the skills you've learned to accomplish the task—and be creative.

Exercise 4-29

Using a Database Template, create a database to store the member information you collected and organized for the On Your Own exercises of Lessons 1 through 3. Enter the member information. Print the table. On the first sheet of your printout, write the name of the template you selected. Continue to Exercise 4-30.

Exercise 4-30

Review the structure of the main table in the database you created in Exercise 4-29. On a blank sheet of paper, list the fields, data types, and field sizes from the table that are most appropriate for your organization's needs. Add any additional fields that would improve the usability of the table. Without using a database template, create a blank database. Create a table to store the data. Enter the member information. Print the properties for the table. Continue to Exercise 4-31.

Exercise 4-31

Search the Templates section of the Microsoft Office home page. Locate a template that will enhance the database you created in the previous exercise. Using the template you located on the Internet, create a new database. Enter appropriate data for at least five records. Print the table. Submit to your instructor the printouts from Exercises 4-29 through 4-31 along with your field list from 4-30. Make sure your name, the date, and your class information is written on the printouts. Keep a copy of the three databases you created in Exercises 4-29 through 4-31. They may be used in subsequent lessons.

Unit 1 Applications

Unit Application 1-1

Edit and sort records in a table. Change font size and column width in Datasheet View. Print/Save a table. Use a filter. Add and delete records through a query. Print/Save a query.

1. From the **Unit 01** folder, copy the file **CCU1** and rename it *[your name]*-**CCU1**.

2. Open *[your initials]*-**CCU1** and enable its content.

3. Open **tblEmployees**. Change the font size of the Datasheet to **12**.

4. Size all columns wide enough to show the longest text or column heading for each field.

5. Hide all columns that are not shown in Table U1-1.

6. Make the changes shown in Table U1-1.

TABLE U1-1 Editing tblEmployees

Employees ID	Last Name	First Name	Job Code	Address	Emergency Contact
6	Lee	Sidney	**MF05**	25 **Frenger** Avenue	Etta Abrams
7	Fernandez	**Cassie**	**OF05**	567 Westbrook Drive	Maria Sanchez
8	Lee	May	OF06	**237** Alexander Road	Charles Finley
9	Gutierrez	Luis	**OF05**	6105 Mallard Creek Road	*[your full name]*

7. Sort the table in ascending order by **Last Name**.

8. Print/Save the table datasheet in portrait orientation. Make sure that all data fit on one page.

9. Unhide all the columns. Close **tblEmployees** and save the changes.

10. Open **qryDesignTeam**.

11. Filter the datasheet to only show **Job Codes** MF03 and MF04.

12. Find and delete Heidi White's record.

13. Add the following new record:

    Employee ID: **40**
    Last Name: *Key [your last name]*
    First Name: *Key [your first name]*
    SSN: **888-72-4852**
    Job Code: **MF04**
    Address: **152 Grandin Road**
    City: **Charlotte**
    State: **NC**
    Postal Code: **28208-4679**

 14. Select and Print/Save the datasheet in landscape orientation. Make sure that all fields are visible and fit on one page.

15. Save and close **qryDesignTeam**.

16. Compact and close the database.

Unit Application 1-2

Find and replace text. Copy and paste text in a table. Copy and paste a picture in a table. Delete and insert a picture in a form. Use filters and wildcards.

1. Open *[your initials]*-**CCU1** and enable its content.

2. Open **tblStuffedAnimals** in Datasheet View.

3. Find all product names that contain "Bear" and replace with "Teddy."

4. Add the following new record, leaving fields blank as shown.

    Product ID: *Press* Tab
    Product Code: **T006**
    Animal Name: **Tea Time Teddy**
    Illustration: *Attach* **TeaTeddy.jpg**

5. Open **frmStuffedAnimalsList**.

6. For **Product Code** T006, change the **Product Name** to *[your first name]'s* **Teddy**.

7. For **Product Code** T006, change the **Product Group** to "Teddy Bears."

NOTE

The image file can be found in the **Unit 01** folder.

8. Close **frmStuffedAnimalsList**.

9. Open **rptStuffedAnimalsList**.

10. Sort records by **Unit Price** in **Smallest to Largest** order.

11. Filter the report to show only the **Product Group** Teddy Bears.

12. Print/Save the report in **Portrait** orientation. Make sure all data fits one page.

13. Close the report.

14. Compact and close the database.

Unit Application 1-3

Add a table using the table template. Print/Save a table and its definition.

1. Create a new table using the **Table Template** tasks. Name the table **tbl***[your last name]*. Display the table in Design View.

2. For the **% Complete** field, change the **Field Size** to **Single**, the number of decimal places to **2**, the **Format** to **Percent**, and the **Caption** to **Completion Rate**.

3. Between the **% Complete** and **Start Date** fields, add a text field named **AssignedTo** with a **Caption** of **Assigned To**.

4. For each field with a **Data Type** of **Text**, change the **Field Size** to **40**.

5. Delete the **Attachments** and **Description** fields.

6. Save the changes to the table, change to Datasheet View, and key the following records:

ID	*Press* Tab
Title	New Year, New Toys
Priority	(1) High
Status	In Progress
Completion Rate	.8
Assigned to	Jeffrey Harrison
Start Date	12/01/07
Due Date	01/05/08

ID	*Press* Tab
Title	Easter Critters
Priority	(2) Normal
Status	In Progress
Completion Rate	.2
Assigned to	Janet Boca-Larson
Start Date	03/01/08
Due Date	04/04/08

ID	*Press* Tab
Title	Memorial Day Special
Priority	(3) Low
Status	Not Started
Completion Rate	.05
Assigned to	To be announced
Start Date	05/01/08
Due Date	05/31/08

7. Size rows and columns to print all data on one page in **Landscape** orientation. Print/Save the datasheet.

8. Print/Save a Database Documenter report for **tbl***[your name]*, showing only the table **Properties**, and **Names, Data Types, and Sizes** for all fields.

Unit Application 1-4 ◆ Using the Internet

Add data to a table. Modify a table. Print/Save recordsets.

1. Using the Internet search engine of your choice, locate a company that sells children's toys. Find the company (vender) name, address, city, state, postal code, and phone number.

2. Open *[your initials]*-**CCU1** and enable its content. Open **tblCustomers** in Datasheet View.

3. Key the company information. Use your full name for **CEO**.

4. After the **PostalCode** field, add a hyperlink field named **URL**. Enter the Web address for the company you located.

5. Hide all fields that were not used for the new customer.

6. Size all columns appropriately. Print/Save the table in landscape orientation on a single page. Change the font size if needed.

7. Close all objects.

8. Compact, back up, and close your database.

unit 2

DESIGNING AND MANAGING DATABASE OBJECTS

Lesson 5   Managing Data Integrity   AC-136

Lesson 6   Designing Queries   AC-170

Lesson 7   Adding and Modifying
            Forms   AC-210

Lesson 8   Adding and Modifying
            Reports   AC-248

UNIT 2   APPLICATIONS   AC-282

Managing Data Integrity

OBJECTIVES

After completing this lesson, you will be able to:

1. Create relationships between tables.
2. Work with referential integrity.
3. Work with subdatasheets.
4. Use the Lookup Wizard.
5. Use Analyzing tools.
6. Track object dependency.

MCAS OBJECTIVES

In this lesson:
AC07 70-605 1.2.1
AC07 70-605 1.2.3
AC07 70-605 1.2.2
AC07 70-605 2.4.3
AC07 70-605 2.3.2
AC07 70-605 6.2.4

Estimated Time: 1¹/₂ hours

Relationships are critical for properly designed databases. A *relationship* is a link or connection between two tables sharing a common field. Relationships change a flat database, containing isolated data, into a relational database, containing linked data. For tables to relate to each other, they must share common data.

Relationships must be planned; they do not just happen. Understanding them—and how to set them—takes time and practice. As you work more extensively with databases, you will learn more about creating and maintaining relationships.

Creating Relationships Between Tables

Relationships between tables can be graphically viewed in the Relationships window. Tables display as field lists. Related fields from each table are connected by a join line. Each end of the join line connects to the related fields in linked tables.

The related field between the two tables must be of the same data type and the same size. The related fields do not need to use the same name.

However, you will find it much easier to create and recognize relationships when the common fields use the same field name in both tables.

When you select a primary key in both related tables, you create a One-To-One relationship. A One-To-One relationship occurs when the common field is a primary key in the first table and a primary key filed in the second. This means one record in the first table can relate to only one record in the second table.

When you select a primary key in only one table, you create a One-To-Many relationship. A One-To-Many relationship occurs when the common field is a primary key in the first table and not a primary key field in the second. This means one record in the first table can relate to one or more records in the second table.

When you do not select a primary key in either table, you create an Indeterminate relationship. An Indeterminate relationship occurs when Access does not have enough information to determine the relationship between the two tables. The common fields in the first and the second table are not primary key fields.

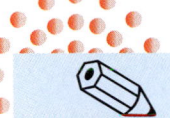

> **TIP**
>
> To resize a list box, you can use the left, right, and bottom borders. Clicking and dragging the top area (title bar) will move the list box

> **TIP**
>
> Make certain that you open the shortcut menu for the join line. The menu enables you to edit the relationship or delete the join line. If you accidentally open the shortcut menu for the Relationships window or for a field list, the menu displayed will not offer the option to edit relationships or to delete the join line.

> **NOTE**
>
> You will learn more about the types of relationships later in this lesson.

Exercise 5-1   LOOK AT AN EXISTING RELATIONSHIP

The Relationships window shows existing relationships in the current database. One or more relationships can be displayed at a time. When more than two tables are displayed, it is advantageous to arrange the tables to allow optimum viewing of all join lines.

1. Locate and open the **Lesson 05** folder.

2. Make a copy of **CC05** and rename it to *[your initials]*-**CC05**.

3. Open and enable content for *[your initials]*-**CC05**.

4. From the **Database Tools** tab, in the **Show/Hide** group, click Relationships command ⬚. This opens the Relationship window.

5. From the **Database Tools** tab, in the **Show/Hide** group, click the Relationships command ⬚. Any table that has a relationship with another table will open. The line connecting two tables represents the relationship between the tables.

6. Click and drag the bottom and right edges of the **tblEmployees** field list until all field names are visible.

7. Resize and move each field list to appear as shown in Figure 5-1.

Figure 5-1
Relationships
window with field
lists rearranged
CC05.accdb
Relationships
window

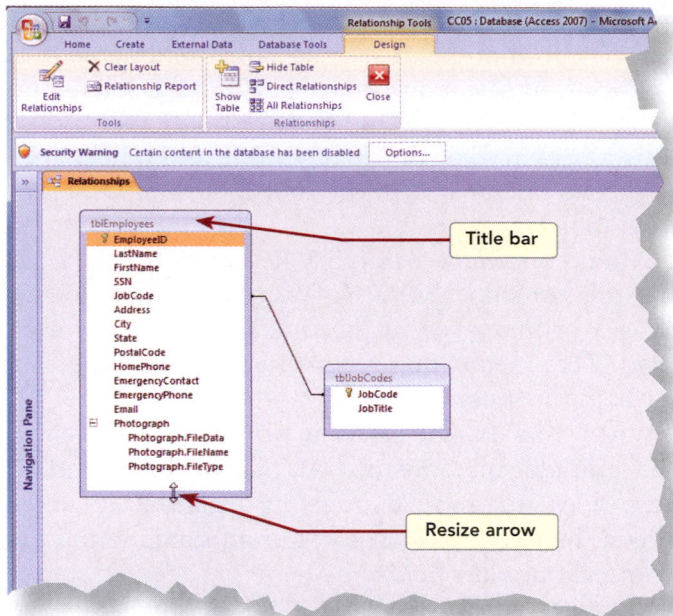

8. Right-click the sloping part of the join line between **tblEmployees** and **tblJobCodes** to open the shortcut menu for the join line.

Figure 5-2
Shortcut menu
CC05.accdb
Relationships
window

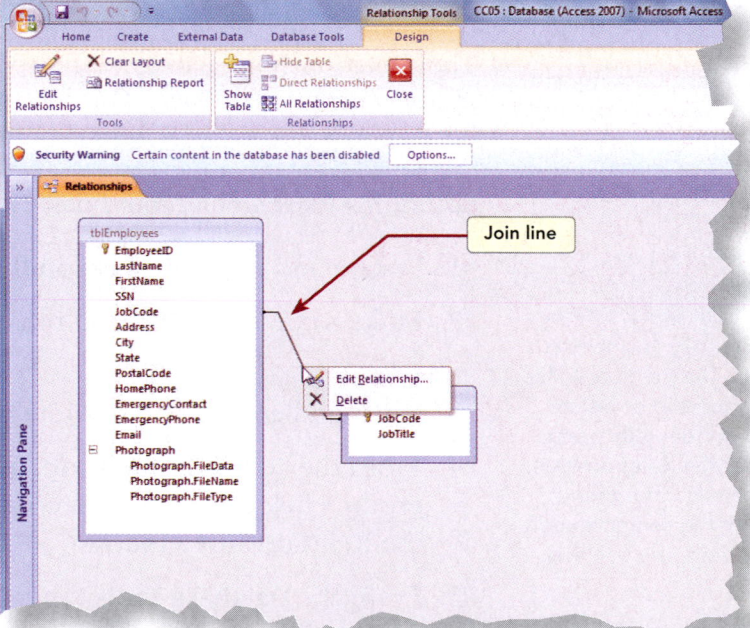

Figure 5-3
Edit Relationships
dialog box
CC05.accdb
Relationships
window

9. Choose **Edit Relationships**.

10. Click **Cancel** to close the dialog box.

Exercise 5-2   CREATE A RELATIONSHIP IN THE RELATIONSHIPS WINDOW

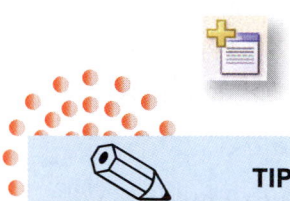

You can create different types of relationships depending on whether you choose a primary key as a common field. When a common field is a primary key in one table, it becomes a foreign key in the other table. A *foreign key* is a field that links to a primary key field in the related table.

1. From the **Design** tab, in the **Relationships** group, click the Show Table command. The **Show Table** dialog box lists the tables and queries that are in the database.

2. In the **Tables** tab, click **tblJobCodes**. Click **Add** to add its field list to the window.

3. Double-click **tblPayroll** and **tblTimcards**.

Figure 5-4
Show Table dialog box
CC05.accdb Relationships window

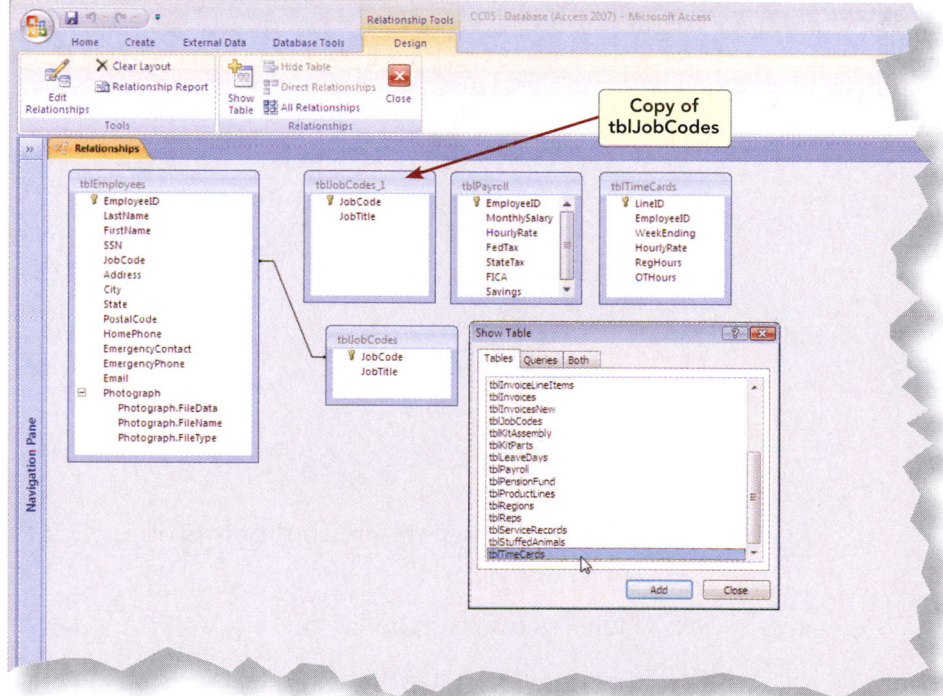

4. In the **Show Table** dialog box, click **Close**.

5. The table **tblJobCodes** has been entered twice. Click on the field list **tblEmployees_1** and press Delete to remove the copy.

6. In the **tblEmployees** field list, click the **EmpoyeeID** field. The field name has a key symbol because it is the primary key in this table.

7. Click and drag the **EmployeeID** field from the **tblEmployees** field list to the **EmployeeID** field in the **tblTimeCards** field list.

8. The **Edit Relationships** dialog box opens. The Relationship Type is One-To-Many because the EmployeeID (the primary key) appears only once in the table **tblEmployees** but can appear many times in the table **tblTimeCards**.

9. Click **Create**. A join line links the common field names.

10. Click and drag the **EmployeeID** field from the **tblEmployees** field list to the **EmployeeID** field in the **tblPayroll** field list.

11. The **Edit Relationships** dialog box opens. The Relationship Type is One-To-One because the EmployeeID (the primary key) appears only once in the table **tblEmployees** and only once in the table **tblPayroll**.

12. Click **Create**. A join line links the common field names.

13. Resize and move each field list to appear as shown in Figure 5-5.

Figure 5-5
Show Table
dialog box
CC05.accdb
Relationships
window

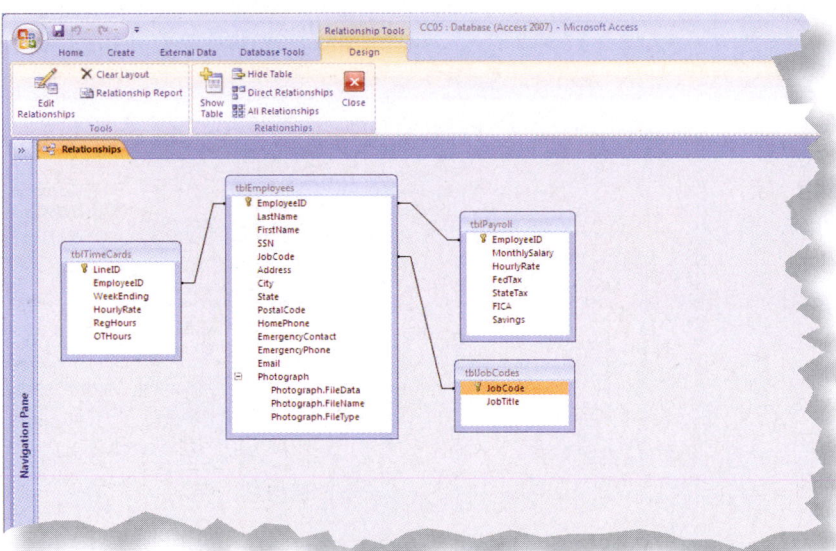

14. From the **Design** tab, in the **Tools** group, click the Clear Layout command .

15. Click **Yes** to clear the layout.

16. From the **Design** tab, in the **Relationships** group, click the All Relationships command ▦.

17. From the **Design** tab, in the **Tools** group, click the Clear Layout command ✕. Click **Yes** to clear the layout.

18. From the Navigation Pane, click and drag the tables **tblAssets** and **tblServiceRecords** into the Relationships window. Collapse the Navigation Pane.

NOTE

The Clear Layout button ✕ clears the way tables are arranged but does not delete the relationships between them.

19. Resize and move each field list so all fields are visible.

20. Click and drag the **AssetID** field from the **tblAssets** field list to the **AssetID** field in the **tblServiceRecords** field list. The Relationship Type is One-To-Many.

21. Click **Create**. From the Quick Access toolbar, click the Save button 📄.

22. From the **Design** tab, in the **Relationships** group, click the Close command ❌.

Exercise 5-3　PRINT/SAVE RELATIONSHIPS

Printing a Relationship Report helps a database administrator document and manage database integrity. A *Relationship Report* is a graphical report showing related tables. Each Relationship Report you create can be saved.

1. From the **Database Tools** tab, in the **Show/Hide** group, click the Relationships command 🔲.

2. From the **Design** tab, in the **Tools** group, click the Relationship Report command 🔲.

3. From the **Print Preview** tab, in the **Page Layout** group, click **Margins** and choose the Wide command 🔲 from the menu.

4. From the Quick Access toolbar, click the Save button 📄.

5. In the **Save As** dialog box, key **rptRelAssetsService** and press **OK**. This saved report can opened or printed at any time.

Figure 5-6
Save a Relationship
report
CC05.accdb
rptRelAsstesService

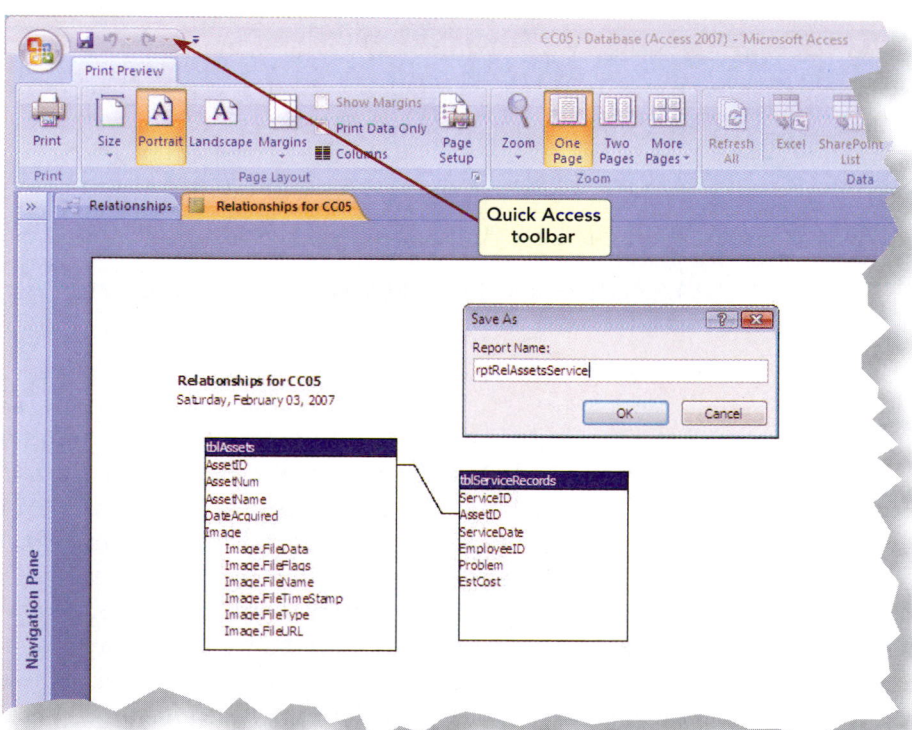

6. Click the Relationships tab to return to the Relationships window.

7. From the **Design** tab, in the **Relationships** group, click the All Relationships command 🔳.

8. Resize and move each field list to appear as shown in Figure 5-7.

Figure 5-7
Organize the
Relationships
window
**CC05.accdb
Relationships
window**

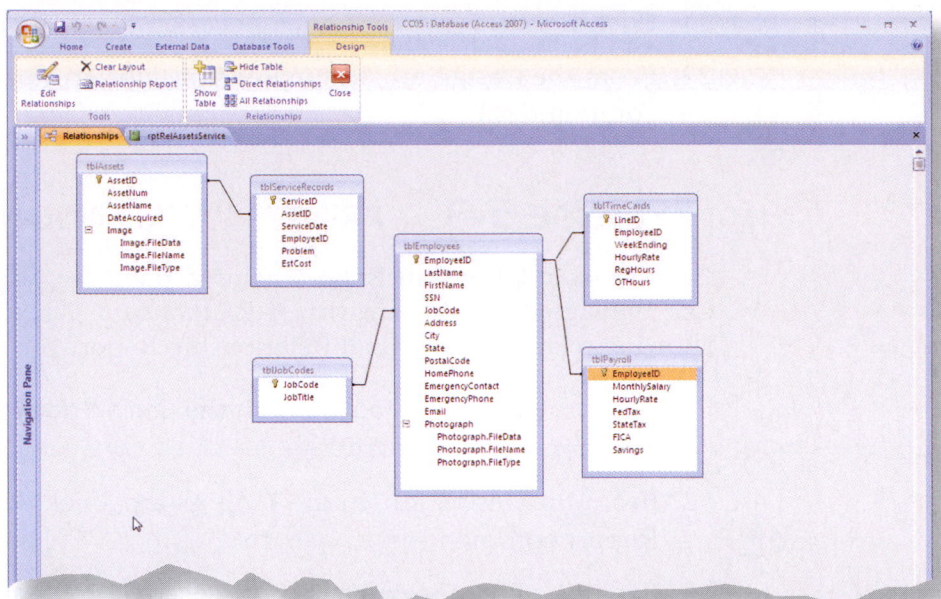

TIP

Avoid crossing join lines to improve the
readability of the relationships.

9. From the **Design** tab, in the **Tools** group, click the
   Relationship Report command .

10. From the **Print Preview** tab, in the **Page Layout** group,
    click **Margins** and choose the Wide command
    from the menu.

11. From the **Print Preview** tab, in the **Page Layout** group, click the
    Landscape command.

12. From the Quick Access toolbar, click the Save button.

13. In the **Save As** dialog box, key **rptRelAll** and press **OK**.

14. Right-click the **rptRelAll** document tab, and select **Close All**.

Working with Referential Integrity

The use of referential integrity helps reduce human error through accidental
deletions or other common errors. *Referential integrity* is a set of database
rules for checking, validating, and keeping track of data entry changes in
related tables. Enforcing referential integrity in two or more tables ensures
that field values are consistent throughout the entire database.

   For example, if you enforce referential integrity between the invoices
table and the customers table, then you can prevent someone from creating
an invoice without a corresponding customer. The enforced integrity also
prevents someone from deleting a customer that has active invoices.

Exercise 5-4   **ENFORCE REFERENTIAL INTEGRITY**

You can enforce referential integrity between tables in a One-To-Many
relationship. When referential integrity is enforced, the join line between
the tables displays a 1 for the "one" side of the relationship and an infinity

symbol (∞) for the "many" side. Referential integrity cannot be set for indeterminate relationships.

You can set referential integrity when the following conditions are met:

- The linking field from the main table is a primary key.

- The linked fields have the same data type.

- Both tables belong to the same Microsoft Access database.

1. Open **tblEmployees**. In the first record (EmployeeID # 1), change the **Job Code** to **OF55**.

2. Open **tblJobCodes**. Notice that there is no **Job Code** "OF55." Referential integrity would prevent this type of error from being made. Close both tables.

3. From the **Database Tools** tab, in the **Show/Hide** group, click the Relationships command ⊞.

4. Right-click the sloping part of the join line between **tblJobCodes** and **tblEmployees**. Select **Edit Relationships**. The Relationship Type is **One-To-Many**.

5. Click the check box to select **Enforce Referential Integrity** and click **OK**.

Figure 5-8
Enforcing referential integrity
CC05.accdb Relationships window

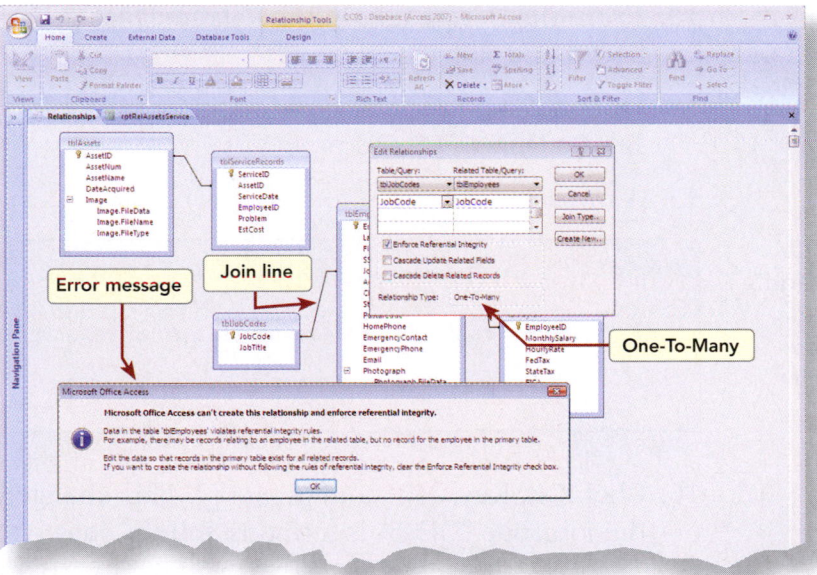

6. Read the error message and click **OK**.

7. Click **Cancel** to close the **Edit Relationships** dialog box without saving the changes.

8. Open **tblEmployees**. In the first record (EmployeeID # 1), change the **Job Code** back to **OF05**.

9. Close **tblEmployees**.

10. Click the **Relationships** tab to return to the Relationships window.

11. Right-click the sloping part of the join line between **tblJobCodes** and **tblEmployees**. Select **Edit Relationships**.

12. Click the check box to select **Enforce Referential Integrity** and click **OK**. This time, the changes were accepted, and the symbols "1" and "∞" have been added to the join line.

Figure 5-9
One-To-Many relationship
CC05.accdb
Relationships window

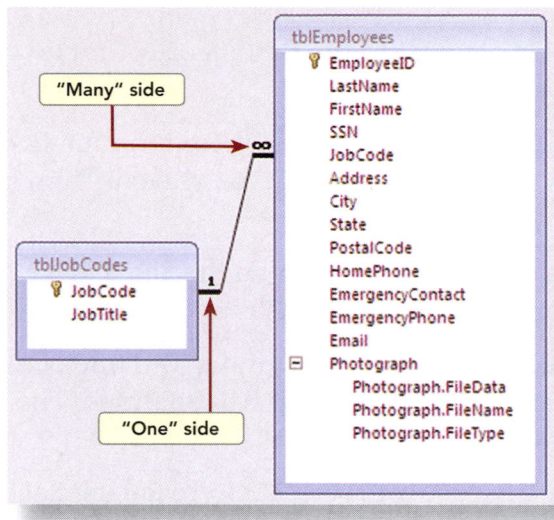

13. From the **Design** tab, in the **Relationships** group, click the Close command ![x].

14. Open **tblEmployees**. In the first record (EmployeeID # 1), change the **Job Code** to **OF55** and press ⬇.

15. A message box alerts you to a problem.

Figure 5-10
Referential Integrity finds an error
CC05.accdb
Relationships window

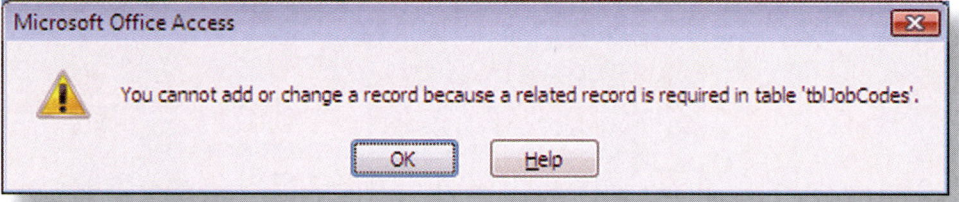

16. Click **OK**. Key **OF06** and press ⬇. This change was allowed because the job code "OF06" is found in **tblJobCodes**.

17. Close the table.

Exercise 5-5   REMOVE REFERENTIAL INTEGRITY

Referential integrity is a property of a relationship. When you remove referential integrity from a relationship, you merely remove the validation rules while preserving the original relationship between the tables.

1. From the **Database Tools** tab, in the **Show/Hide** group, click the Relationships command ![icon].

2. Right-click the sloping part of the join line between **tblEmployees** and **tblJobCodes**.

3. Choose **Edit Relationships** from the shortcut menu.

4. In the **Edit Relationships** dialog box, remove the checkmark from **Enforce Referential Integrity**. Click **OK**.

5. From the **Design** tab, in the **Relationships** group, click the Close command ❌. Save changes to the layout.

Working with Subdatasheets

A table on the "one" side of a One-To-Many relationship, by default, has a subdatasheet. A *subdatasheet* is a datasheet linked within another datasheet. A subdatasheet contains data related to the first datasheet. The common field linking the two datasheets is the primary key field in the main datasheet and the foreign key field in the linked datasheet.

Exercise 5-6   INSERT A SUBDATASHEET

You can insert a subdatasheet into a main datasheet even when a relationship does not exist between the two objects. When a relationship does not exist, Access automatically creates one. You can insert a subdatasheet into the Datasheet Views of tables and queries.

1. Open **tblJobCodes** in Design View.

2. From the **Design** tab, in the **Show/Hide** group, click the Property Sheet command 📄.

3. In the Property Sheet, the **Subdatasheet Name** property is set to **[None]**. Click on this property. Click the drop-down arrow and choose **Table.tblEmployees**.

4. Switch to Datasheet View and save the changes to the table.

5. Notice that the record selector now has an Expand icon ⊞ symbol. Click the Expand icon ⊞ for the Job Code "MF04."

Figure 5-11
Expanding a subdatasheet
CC05.accdb
tblJobCodes

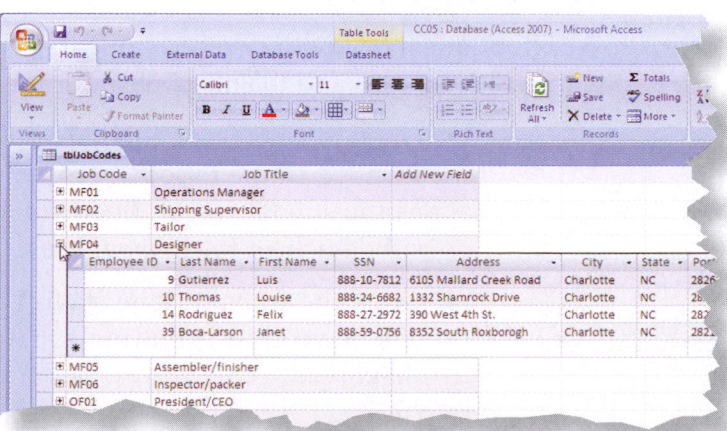

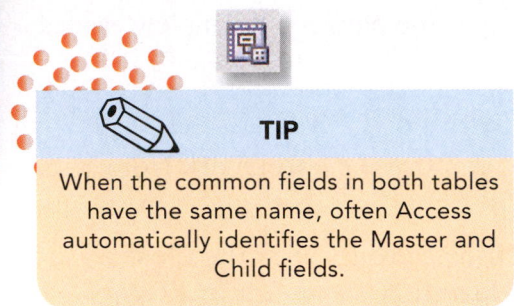

6. Click in the subdatasheet's first record.

7. From the **Home** tab, in the **Records** group, click **More**, and choose **Subdatasheet**, then the Subdatasheet command 📋 from the menu.

8. In the **Insert Subdatasheet** dialog box, choose **tblPayroll**.

Figure 5-12
Inserting a subdatasheet
CC05.accdb
tblJobCodes

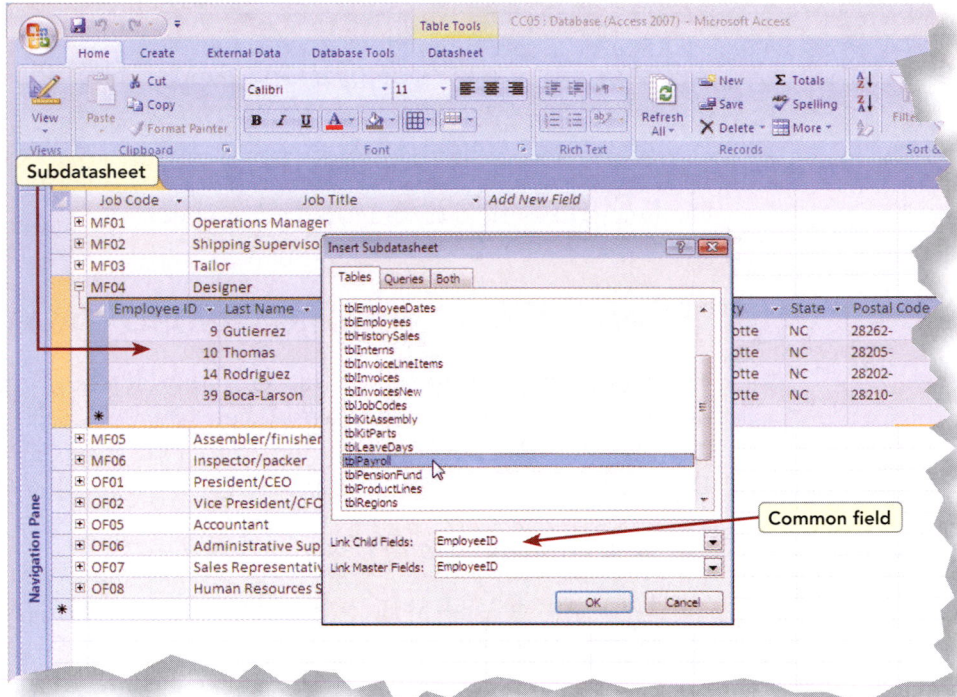

9. Click **OK**. Now the subdatasheet has its own subdatasheet.

10. Expand Employee #10 to see payroll information for that employee.

11. Click the Collapse icon button  to collapse the subdatasheet.

12. Close **tblJobCodes**. A **Save** dialog box appears, asking if you want to save both **tblJobCodes** and **tblEmployees**. Click **Yes**.

13. Open **tblEmployee**. This table now has the Expand icon ⊞. In the **tblJobCodes**, you added **tblEmployees** as the subdatasheet. Then you added **tblPayroll** as a subdatasheet for **tblEmpoyees**.

14. Click the Expand icon ⊞ for the first record. The payroll information for that employee is displayed.

Exercise 5-7   REMOVE A SUBDATASHEET

Not all subdatasheets need to be displayed in the main datasheet. If most database users do not need to use the subdatasheet, you should remove it from the main datasheet. Although a subdatasheet does not display in a main datasheet, the relationship between the two tables remains. You can remove a subdatasheet in Datasheet View.

1. While in the Datasheet View of **tblEmployees**, collapse the subdatasheet.

2. From the **Home** tab, in the **Records** group, click **More**, and choose **Subdatasheet**, then **Remove** from the menu.

3. Close **tblEmployees** and save the changes.

4. Open **tblJobCodes** and expand the subdatasheet for the first record. Notice that there is no longer a subdatasheet for the employee.

5. Close **tblJobcodes**. You were not asked to save because there were no changes to the table **tblJobCodes**.

Using the Lookup Wizard

Using lookup fields often improves data entry. A *lookup field* is a field property that displays input choices from another table and allows these choices to be selected from a list. Lookup fields are used often when specialized codes appear within databases.

Codes use less space than lengthy text describing the record. Some codes are readily understandable, such as two-letter abbreviations for state names. Other codes are less obvious and need a lookup field to become useful.

Exercise 5-8   CREATE A LOOKUP FIELD

In addition to reducing the amount of data stored in a table, a lookup field can improve the efficiency and consistency of data entry. The best fields to convert to a lookup value are those that contain a finite number of values. Lookup fields use list boxes to display a list of possible values. The Lookup Wizard guides you through a step-by-step process for creating the lookup field.

1. Open **tblInterns** in Datasheet View.

2. Click the column header for the field **Department**.

3. From the **Datasheet** tab, in the **Fields & Columns** group, click the Lookup Column command .

4. The Lookup Wizard dialog box appears. Verify that **I want the lookup column to look up the values in a table or query** is selected. Click **Next**.

5. From the list of tables, choose **Table: tblDepartments** and click **Next**.

Access 2007

6. Click the Add All button to move both fields from the Available Fields to the Selected Fields area.

7. Click **Next**. Click the first drop-down arrow and choose Department.

8. Click **Next**. Double-click the right edge of the column header to resize the column to fit the widest data.

9. Remove the checkmark from the **Hide key column** control. The **Department ID** field is displayed.

Figure 5-13
Showing the key column
CC05.accdb
tblInterns

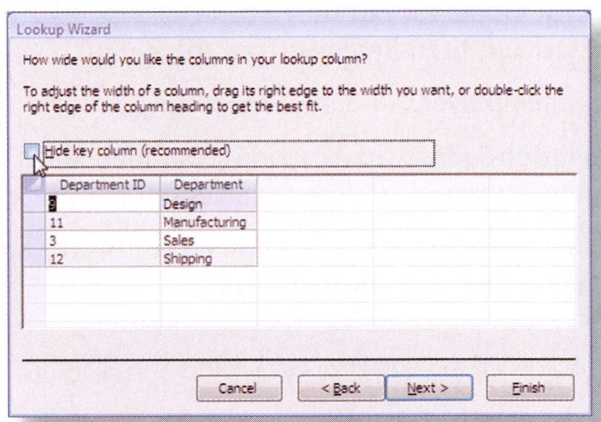

10. Click to add the checkmark to the **Hide key column** control.

11. Click **Next**. Key **Dept** as the label for the column. Click **Finish**.

Exercise 5-9   ADD DATA WITH A LOOKUP FIELD

Adding data to a field through a lookup field reduces the number of keystrokes necessary to enter a value. In this example, values in the lookup fields are listed alphabetically in ascending order.

1. Click in the first record's **Dept** field and key **s**. The combo box will display Sales. Press Enter to select Sales.

2. Click in the second record's **Dept** field. Click the drop-down arrow of the combo box to display the list of departments and choose **Manufacturing**.

Figure 5-14
Choose the value from the lookup column.
CC05.accdb
tblInterns

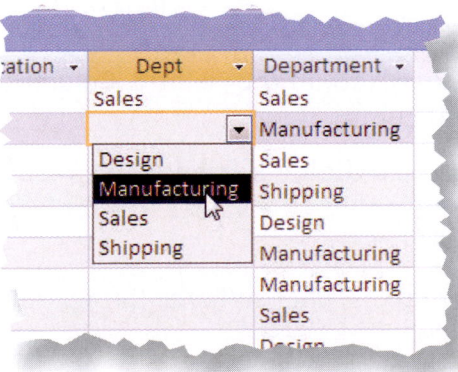

3. Press ↓ and key **s**. Press ↓ to move to the next record.

4. Key **sh**. Because there are two departments that start with the letter "S," you must key a second letter.

5. Finish adding the departments to the **Dept** field.

6. Now that the data in the **Dept** field matches the **Department** field, we can delete the old data. Click the column header for the **Department** field to select the column.

7. From the **Datasheet** tab, in the **Fields & Columns** group, click the Delete command. Click **Yes** in response to the warning message.

Exercise 5-10   MODIFY A LOOKUP FIELD

The list of values displayed in a lookup field can be limited or editable. A limited list does not allow the user to enter new values. An editable list does allow for new values to be entered.

1. Click in the first record's **Education** field and key **AA**.

2. Press Tab. An error message states that "AA" is not on the list.

3. Click **OK**. The lookup list expands to show the valid options. Press Esc twice.

4. Switch to Design View.

5. Click the field **Edu**.

6. Press F6 to move the field properties. Click the **Lookup** tab.

7. Notice that the **Limit To List** property is set to **Yes**. Read the description in the Help window.

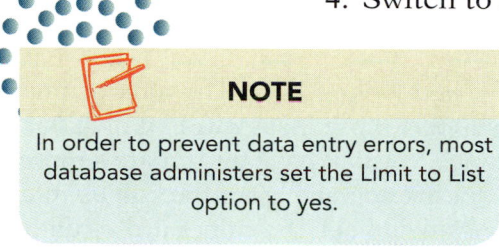

NOTE

In order to prevent data entry errors, most database administers set the Limit to List option to yes.

Figure 5-15
Limit To List property
CC05.accdb
tblInterns

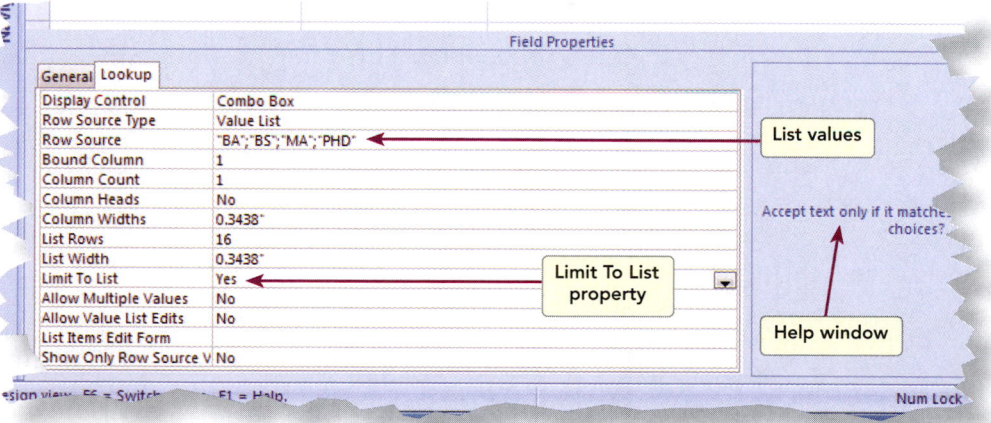

NOTE

If a lookup field has more than one column, the **Allow Value List Edits** property is ignored.

8. Click in the **Allow Value List Edits** property. Read the description in the Help window.

9. Change the **Allow Value List Edits** property to change the value from "No" to **Yes**.

10. Save the table and switch to Datasheet View.

11. Click in the first record's **Education** field and click the drop-down arrow. A small icon appears below the expanded list.

12. Click the Edit List icon . The **Edit List Items** dialog box opens.

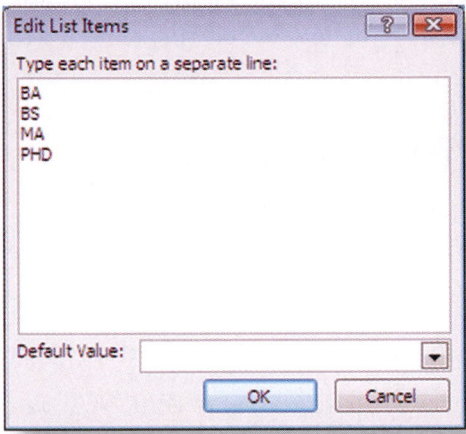

13. Press ⎡PageUp⎤ and key **AA**. Press ⎡Enter⎤.

14. Click **OK**.

15. Click in the first record's **Education** field and click the drop-down arrow. The list now has an Associates of Arts degree.

16. Key **A** and press ⎡Tab⎤.

17. Close **tblInterns** and save the changes.

Exercise 5-11   CREATE A MULTI-VALUED LOOKUP FIELD

A lookup field can be set to be a multi-valued lookup field. The idea behind multi-valued fields is to make it easy to support those instances in which you want to select and store more than one choice, without having to create a more advanced database design. Access 2007 doesn't actually store the values in a single field. Even though what you see is a single field, the values are actually stored independently and managed in hidden, system tables. The same wizard used to create lookup fields is used to create multi-valued lookup fields.

1. Open **tblRegions**. This table contains seven different sales regions.

2. Open **tblReps**. One sales representative can be assigned to many regions.

3. Switch to Design View.

4. Notice the field **Regions** has a **Data Type** of **Text**. Switch back to Datasheet View.

5. Select the **Regions** column.

6. From the **Datasheet** tab, in the **Fields & Columns** group, click the Lookup Column command ⊞.

7. In the **Lookup Wizard** dialog box, click **Next**.

8. From the list of tables, select **Table: tblRegions** and click **Next**.

9. In the **Available Fields** area, double-click **RegionID** and **RegionName** to move them to the **Selected Fields** area.

10. Click **Next**. Click the drop-down arrow and choose **RegionName**. Click **Next**.

11. Resize the **Region Name** column so all data can be seen. Click **Next**.

12. Name the field **Reg**.

13. Click to add the checkmark to the **Allow Multiple Values** control.

14. Click **Finish**.

Exercise 5-12   ADD DATA WITH A MULTI-VALUED LOOKUP FIELD

Each value stored in a multi-valued lookup field is linked to the source table or list. Values can be added or deleted from the field by using the check boxes next to each choice.

1. For the first record, click the drop-down arrow for the field **Reg**. Notice that this combo box has checkboxes next to each value.

2. Click the checkboxes for **Northeast** and **Northwest**.

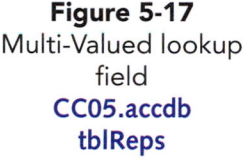
Figure 5-17
Multi-Valued lookup field
CC05.accdb
tblReps

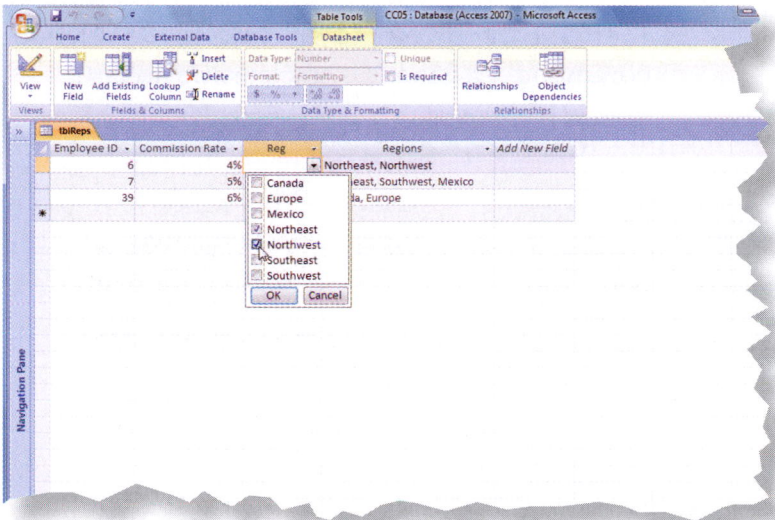

3. Close **OK**. Resize the column so you can see all the data.

4. Press ⬇ to move to the next record.

5. Click the drop-down arrow and add checkmarks to **Southeast**, **Southwest**, and **Mexico**. Click **OK**.

6. Press ⬇. Click the drop-down arrow and add checkmarks to **Canada** and **Europe**. Click **OK**.

7. Select the **Regions** column.

8. From the **Datasheet** tab, in the **Fields & Columns** group, click the Delete command ▥.

9. Click in the **Reg** field, on any record.

10. From the **Datasheet** tab, in the **Fields & Columns** group, click the Rename command ▧ and key **Regions**.

11. Switch to Design View.

12. Click in the **Regions** field. Notice the **Data Type** is **Number**. Only **RegionID** is being stored in this field.

13. Press F6. Click the **Lookup** tab. The **Allow Multiple Values** property is set to **Yes**.

14. Close both tables and save changes.

Exercise 5-13   VIEW RELATIONSHIPS CREATED BY LOOKUP FIELDS

When you create a lookup field, Access creates a relationship between the main table and the linked table. The relationship uses the lookup field as the common field. This relationship can be displayed in the Relationships window.

1. From the **Database Tools** tab, in the **Show/Hide** group, click the Relationships command.

2. From the **Design** tab, in the **Tools** group, click the Clear Layout command ✕. Click **Yes** to clear the layout.

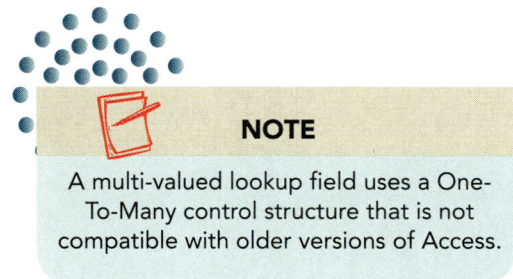

NOTE

A multi-valued lookup field uses a One-To-Many control structure that is not compatible with older versions of Access.

3. From the Navigation Pane, drag **tblInterns**, **tblDepartments**, **tblReps**, and **tblRegions** to the Relationships window. A join line appears between **tblReps** and **tblRegions**. Creating the lookup field produced this relationship.

4. Arrange the field lists so you can clearly see all fields and relationships.

Figure 5-18
Relationships created by lookup fields
CC05.accdb
Relationships window

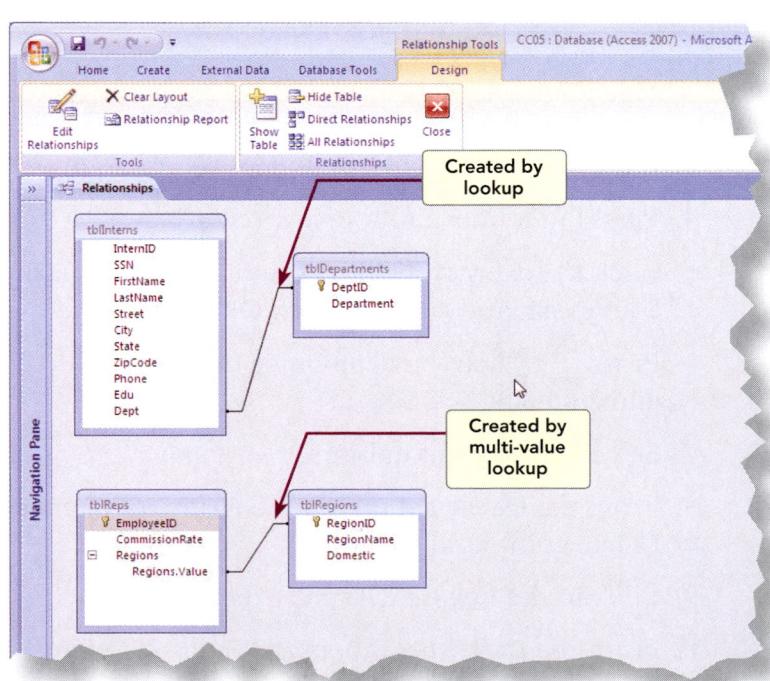

5. Double-click the join line between **tblInterns** and **tblDepartments** to open the Edit Relationships dialog box. This is a One-To-Many relationship. The main table is **tblDepartments**; it has the primary key. Click **OK**.

6. Double-click the join line between **tblReps** and **tblRegions** to open the Edit Relationships dialog box. This is a One-To-Many relationship. The main table is **tblRegions**; it has the primary key. Click **OK**.

7. Close the Relationships window. A message box asks if you want to save the changes to the layout. Click **Yes**.

Using Analyzing Tools

The Table Analyzer Wizard analyzes a database and recommends changes for normalization. *Normalization* is the process of restructuring a relational database for the purposes of organizing data efficiently, eliminating field redundancy, and improving data consistency.

The wizard analyzes table structures and field values. When the wizard identifies duplicated data or improper table structures, you are given the option to allow the wizard to automatically make changes to your database or for you to manually make changes.

Exercise 5-14   ANALYZE A TABLE

The Table Analyzer Wizard evaluates the contents of tables in your database. When a significant number of records contain repeating field values, the Analyzer will recommend that you split the table into two new tables. The structure and contents of the original table will be preserved.

1. Open **tblKitParts** in Datasheet View. You can see that there is redundancy in the Vender information.

2. Close the table.

3. From the **Database Tools** tab, in the **Analyze** group, click the Analyze Table command .

4. In the **Table Analyzer Wizard** dialog box, read the description of the problems that this wizard will try to analyze.

5. Click **Next**. Read the description of how the wizard will try to solve.

6. Click **Next**. From the list of tables, select **tblKitParts**.

7. Click **Next**. The default is to let the wizard decide what fields go in what tables.

8. Click **Next**.

9. Double-click the "Table1" field list header. Rename this table **tblParts**. This table will contain the part number (SKU), description of the part, and its cost.

10. Double-click the "Table2" field list header. Rename this table **tblVender**. This table will contain the unique data for the vender.

Figure 5-19
Table Analyzer
Wizard
CC05.accdb
Table Analyzer
Wizard

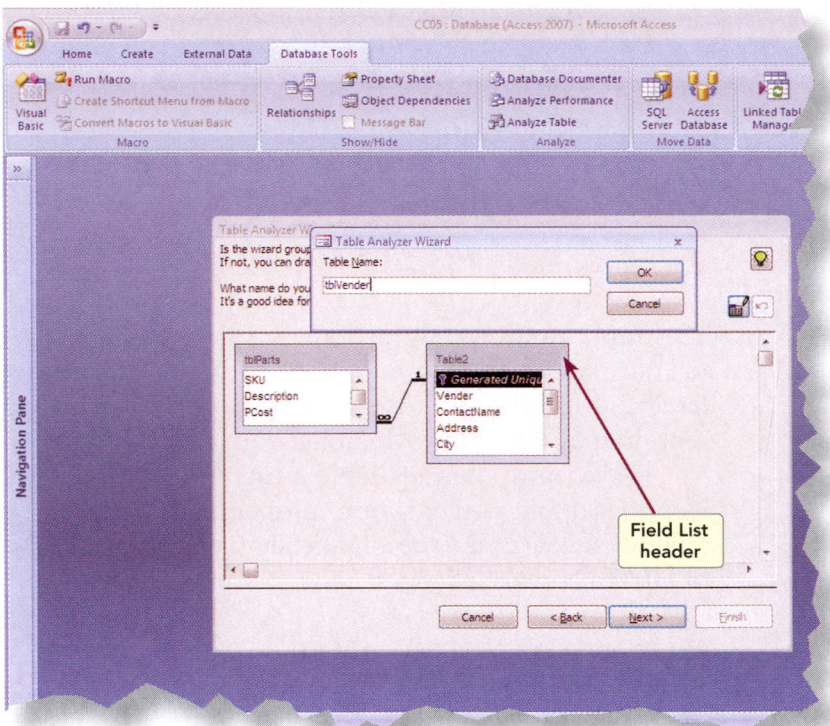

11. Click **Next**. In the field list **tblParts**, click **SKU** and click the Set Unique Identifier button 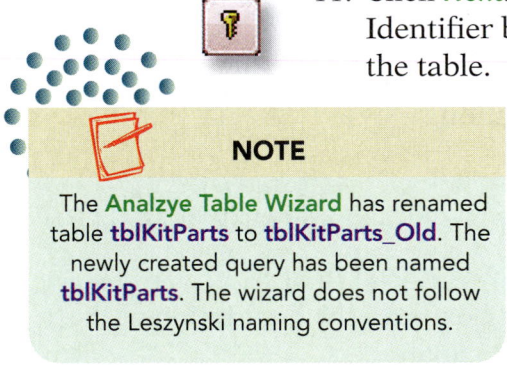. This action makes this field the Primary Key for the table.

> **NOTE**
>
> The **Analzye Table Wizard** has renamed table **tblKitParts** to **tblKitParts_Old**. The newly created query has been named **tblKitParts**. The wizard does not follow the Leszynski naming conventions.

12. Click **Next**.

13. If a dialog box appears identifying possible typographical errors, you will need to choose a value from the **Correction** list. For each record listed, in the **Correction** field, select **(Leave as is)**. Click **Next**.

14. In the last step, select **Yes, create the query option**.

15. Click **Finish**. If the Access Help appears, close the window.

16. The query opens in Datasheet View. Switch to Design View.

17. Notice that this query uses the two newly created tables. Resize the field lists so that all field names are visible.

18. Save and close the query.

19. In the Navigation Pane, right-click the query **tblKitParts** and choose **Rename**. Key **qryKitParts** and press Enter.

Exercise 5-15   ANALYZE PERFORMANCE

In addition to identifying redundant data, the Analyzer can identify data that can be converted to more efficient data types. Often the recommendations involve converting text data types to numeric values.

1. From the **Database Tools** tab, in the **Analyze** group, click the Analyze Performance command ![icon].

2. In the **Performance Analyzer** dialog box, on the **Tables** tab, click the check boxes for **tblEmployees** and **tblHistorySales.** Click **OK**.

3. In the **Analysis Results** section, you will see that the two tables that we selected have four **Ideas** and one **Recommendation**.

4. The table **tblHistorySales** is not indexed because the table does not contain a Primary Key field. Click the **Recommendation** for **tblHistorySales**.

5. Click **Optimize**. The red exclamation point has turned into a yellow checkmark.

6. The ideas that are listed refer to the fact that information stored as a number takes up less space than **Text** fields. Click on the first **Idea** in the section. Read the **Analysis Notes**.

7. This database needs these fields to stay **Text**. Click **Close**.

Tracking Object Dependency

Access provides a database tool to display information regarding dependencies among major objects. *Object dependency* is a condition of an object requiring the existence of another object. For example, the customers form depends upon the customers table.

Understanding dependencies helps you maintain database integrity. Before deleting an object, you first should track the dependencies for that object. For example, you might find a form is based upon a query rather than a table. Before deleting the query, you will need to decide if the form is necessary to the functionality of the database.

Exercise 5-16   VIEW OBJECT DEPENDENCY

An Object Dependency list can be generated for tables, queries, forms, and reports. The Object Dependency list displays:

• Objects that depend on the selected object, and.

• The object on which the selected object depends.

1. In the Navigation Pane, select **qryEmployeeDates**.

2. From the **Database Tools** tab, in the **Show/Hide** group, click the Object Dependencies command ![icon].

3. If a message dialog box appear, you will need to allow the wizard to analyze the database. The Object Dependencies Pane appears on the right side of the window.

Figure 5-20
Object
Dependencies Task
Pane
CC05.accdb
**Object Dependencies
Task Pane**

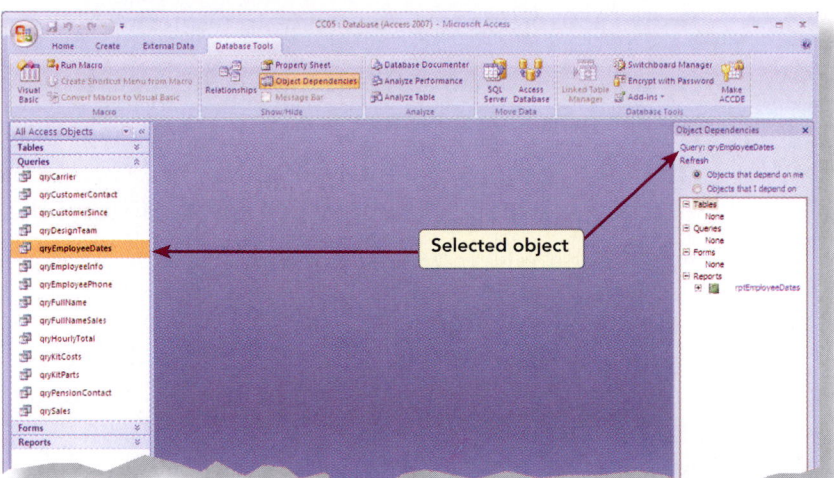

Figure 5-20
Object Dependencies Task Pane
CC05.accdb
Object Dependencies Task Pane

4. The first view is **Objects that depend on me** and it shows that the form **rptEmployeeDates** depends on the query **qryEmployeeDates**.

5. Click **rptEmployeeDates** in the pane. The report opens in Design View.

6. From the **Design** tab, in the **Tools** group, click the Property Sheet command . Click the **Data** tab. Notice that the **Record Source** property is set to **qryEmployeeDates**.

7. Close the Property Sheet and the report.

8. In the Object Dependencies Pane, click **Objects that I depend on**. This shows that the query **qryEmployeeDates** depends on the tables **tblEmployeeDates** and **tblEmployees**.

9. Click **tblEmployeeDates** to open the table in Design View.

10. Close the table.

Exercise 5-17   VIEW A MISSING DEPENDENCY

If a database object is not functioning properly, you should look at its dependency list. For example, if a form does not display data, the record source upon which it depends might be missing. Viewing "Objects that I depend on" identifies the source recordset for an object.

1. In the Navigation Pane, select **qryEmployeeInfo**.

2. In the Object Dependencies Pane, click **Refresh**. Notice that this object needs the table **tblEmployees**.

3. Click **Objects that depend on me**. Notice that this query is needed by the report **rptEmployeeInfo**.

4. In the Navigation Pane, right-click **qryEmployeeInfo** and choose **Delete** from the menu. Click **Yes** to confirm the deletion.

5. In the Navigation Pane, select, but do not open, **rptEmployeeInfo**.

6. In the Object Dependencies Pane, click **Objects that I depend on**. Click **Refresh**. You can see that **qryEmployeeInfo** is now missing. For the report to work, a new query would need to be created.

7. Close the Object Dependencies Pane.

8. Compact and repair the database, and then close it.

REVIEW

Remember to back up your database!

Lesson 5 Summary

- Relationships between tables change a flat database containing isolated data, into a relational database containing linked data.

- Graphical relationships between tables can be viewed in the Relationships window.

- Related fields must be of the same data type and size, but not have the same name.

- A One-To-One relationship occurs when the common field is a primary key in the first table and a primary key field in the second.

- A One-To-Many relationship occurs when the common field is a primary key in the first table and not a primary key field in the second.

- An Indeterminate relationship occurs when Access does not have enough information to determine the relationship between the two tables.

- One or more relationships can be displayed in the Relationships window.

- When a common field is a primary key in the first table, it becomes a foreign key in the second table.

- A Relationship report is a graphical report showing related tables.

- Referential integrity is a set of database rules for checking, validating, and keeping track of data entry changes in related tables.

- A subdatasheet is a datasheet linked within another datasheet containing related data.

- A lookup field is a field property that displays input choices from another table and allows these choices to be selected from a list.

- A multi-valued lookup field is a lookup field that can store more than one value per record.

- The Table Analyzer Wizard displays options for improving the table structures of your database based upon the field types and the values stored.

- Object dependency is a condition of an object requiring the existence of another object.

LESSON 5		Command Summary	
Feature	**Button**	**Task Path**	**Keyboard**
Collapse Subdatasheet			
Expand Subdatasheet			
Layout, Clear		Design, Tools, Clear Layout	
Lookup field, Create		Datasheet, Fields & Columns, Lookup Column	
Lookup field, Limit To List		Design View, Lookup, Limit To List	
Lookup field, Multi-valued, Create		Design View, Lookup, Allow Multiple Values	
Object Dependency		Database Tools, Show/Hide, Dependencies	
Primary Key, Set			
Referential Integrity, Enforce		Database Tools, Show/Hide, Relationships, Edit Relationships, Enforce Referential Integrity	
Relationship Report, Create		Design, Tools, Relationship Report	
Relationships, Report		Database Tools, Show/Hide, Relationships	
Relationships, Show All		Database Tools, Relationships, All Relationships	
Relationships, Table, Hide		Database Tool, Show/Hide, Relationships, Hide Table	
Relationships, Table, Show		Database Tool, Show/Hide, Relationships, Show Table	
Relationships, View		Database Tool, Show/Hide, Relationships	
Subdatasheet, Insert		Design, Show/Hide, Property Sheet	
Subdatasheet, Remove		Home, Records, More, Subdatasheet, Remove	
Table, Analyze Table		Database Tools, Analyze, Analyze Table	
Table, Analyze Performance		Database Tools, Analyze, Analyze Performance	

Concepts Review

True/False Questions

Each of the following statements is either true or false. Indicate your choice by circling T or F.

T F   1. A lookup field lets you select a value from a list instead of keying the value.

T F   2. When you clear the Relationships window, you also delete the relationships.

T F   3. The set of database rules for relationships is known as validating norms.

T F   4. A subdatasheet is a datasheet linked within another datasheet containing related data.

T F   5. Values in a lookup field are always listed in ascending order.

T F   6. Deleting the join line between two field lists in the Relationships window deletes the corresponding tables.

T F   7. The Relationships window can display more than one relationship at a time.

T F   8. Normalization is the process of restructuring a relational database for the purposes of organizing data efficiently, eliminating field redundancy, and improving data consistency.

Short Answer Questions

Write the correct answer in the space provided.

1. What graphic represents the relationship between two tables in the Relationships window?

_____

2. How do you delete a relationship in the Relationships window?

_____

3. When the common field is a primary key in one table, what does it become in the other table?

_____

4. In a One-To-Many relationship with referential integrity, how can you identify the table on the "many" side of the relationship?

_____

5. Referential integrity cannot be set for what type of relationship?

_____

6. What type of lookup field can store more than one value per record?

_____

7. What analyzing tool provides recommendations for restructuring a relational database for the purposes of organizing data efficiently, eliminating field redundancy, and improving data consistency?

_____

8. What is an association placed upon an object requiring the existence of another object known as?

_____

Critical Thinking

Answer these questions on a separate page. There are no right or wrong answers. Support your answers with examples from your own experience, if possible.

1. The One-To-Many relationship is the most commonly used relationship in business databases. Why do you think this is true?

2. Multi-valued lookup fields can be very useful for most types of data; however, some fields should not have more than one value. When shouldn't a field contain more than one value?

Skills Review

Exercise 5-18

Create a relationship in the Relationships window. Print a Relationship report.

1. Open a database by following these steps:
   a. Locate and open the **Lesson 05** folder.
   b. Make a copy of **CC05** and rename it to *[your initials]*-**CC05**.
   c. Open and enable content for *[your initials]*-**CC05**.
2. Create a relationship by following these steps:

   a. From the **Database Tools** tab, in the **Show/Hide** group, click the Relationships command ⬚.

   b. From the **Design** tab, in the **Tools** group, click the Clear Layout command ✕. Click **Yes** to save the changes.

c. From the **Design** tab, in the **Relationships** group, click the Show Table command .

   d. From the **Show Table** dialog box, double-click **tblStuffedAnimals** and **tblInvoiceLineItems**.

   e. Click **Close**.

   f. Resize the field lists so you can see every field.

   g. From the **tblStuffedAnimals** field list, click and drag the **ProductID** field to the **ProductID** field in the **tblInvoiceLineItems** field list.

   h. In the **Edit Relationships** dialog box, click **Create**.

3. Print/Save the Relationship report by following these steps:

   a. From the **Design** tab, in the **Tools** group, click the Relationship Report command .

   b. From the **Print Preview** tab, in the **Page Layout** group, click **Margins** and choose the Wide command from the menu.

   c. Save the report as **05-18-03d** and click the Close button .

   d. Print/Save the report **05-18-03d**.

   e. Close the report

   f. Close the Relationships window.

Exercise 5-19

Insert a subdatasheet. Modify a relationship to include Referential Integrity.

1. Insert a subdatasheet by following these steps:

   a. Open and enable content for *[your initials]*-**CC05**.

   b. Open **tblStuffedAnimals** in Datasheet View.

   c. From the **Home** tab, in the **Records** group, click **More**. Choose **Subdatasheet**, then **Subdatasheet** from the menu.

   d. From the list, select **tblKitAssembly** with the **Child** and **Master** fields **ProductID**.

   e. Click **OK**. Click **Yes** to create a new relationship.

   f. Close the table and save the changes.

2. Set Enforce Referential Integrity by following these steps:

   a. From the **Database Tools** tab, in the **Show/Hide** group, click the Relationships command .

   b. From the **Design** tab, in the **Tools** group, click the Clear Layout command .

   c. Click **Yes** to confirm the change.

   d. From the Navigation Pane, click and drag the tables **tblStuffedAnimals** and **tblKitAssembly** into the Relationships window.

   e. Resize the field lists so you can see all field names.

f. Right-click the sloping part of the join line between **tblStuffedAnimals** and **tblKitAssembly**. Choose **Edit Relationships**.

g. Click the check box to select **Enforce Referential Integrity** and click **OK**.

h. From the Quick Access Toolbar, click the Save button .

i. Close the Relationships window.

3. Print/Save the Database Documenter by following these steps:

a. From the **Database Tools** tab, in the **Analyze** group, click the Database Documenter command .

b. From the **Documenter** dialog box, click the **tblStuffedAnimals** check box.

c. Click **Options**.

d. Only include **Properties** and **Relationships** for tables and nothing else. Click **OK**.

e. Click **OK** to go to Print Preview.

f. From the **Print Preview** tab, in the **Page Layout** group, click **Margins** and choose the Wide command  from the menu.

g. Print/Save the report.

h. Close Print Preview.

Exercise 5-20

Create and use a lookup field. Print a Relationship report. Identify Object Dependency.

1. Delete a relationship by following these steps:

a. Open and enable content for *[your initials]*-**CC05**.

b. From the **Database Tools** tab, in the **Show/Hide** group, click the Relationships command .

c. From the **Design** tab, in the **Relationships** group, click the Show Table command .

d. From the **Show Table** dialog box, double-click **tblAssets** and **tblServiceRecords**. Click **Close**.

e. If there is no join line between **tblAssets** and **tblServiceRecords**, skip to step 1h.

f. Right-click the join line between the two tables and choose **Delete**.

g. Click **Yes** to verify the deletion of the relationship.

h. From the **Design** tab, in the **Relationships** group, click the Close command .

i. Click **No** to discard the layout changes.

j. Open **tblServiceRecords** in Datasheet View and select the field **Asset**.

k. Press Delete. Click **Yes** twice to verify the field deletion.

2. Create a lookup field by following these steps:

   a. Select the field **Service Date**.

   b. From the **Datasheet** tab, in the **Fields & Columns** group, click the Lookup Column command .

   c. In the **Lookup Wizard** dialog box, click **Next**.

   d. From the list of tables, select **Table: tblAssets** and click **Next**.

   e. In the **Available Fields** area, double-click **AssetID**, **AssetNum**, and **AssetName**.

   f. Click **Next**. Click the drop-down arrow and choose **AssetName**.

   g. Click **Next**. Resize the **Asset ID** and **Asset Name** columns so all data can be seen.

   h. Click **Next**. Name the field **Asset Name**.

   i. Click **Finish**.

3. Add data using a lookup field by following these steps:

   a. For the **Asset Name** field in the first record, click the drop-down arrow and choose **DC307**.

   b. Press [↓]. Click the drop-down arrow and choose **CD701**.

   c. Press [↓]. Click the drop-down arrow and choose **CP303**.

   d. Press [↓]. Click the drop-down arrow and choose **LP201**.

   e. Close the table.

4. Print/Save a datasheet by following these steps:

   a. Click the Office Button . From the **Print** option, choose Print Preview .

   b. From the **Print Preview** tab, in the **Page Layout** group, click the Landscape command .

   c. From the **Print Preview** tab, in the **Page Layout** group, click **Margins** and choose the Wide command from the menu.

   d. Print/Save the table.

   e. Close Print Preview and the table.

5. Print/Save a relationship by following these steps:

   a. From the **Database Tools** tab, in the **Show/Hide** group, click the Relationships command .

   b. From the **Design** tab, in the **Tools** group, click the Clear Layout command .

   c. From the Navigation Pane, click and drag the tables **tblServiceRecords** and **tblAssets** into the Relationships window.

   d. Resize the field lists so you can see all field names.

   e. From the **Design** tab, in the **Tools** group, click the Relationship Report command 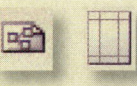.

   f. From the **Print Preview** tab, in the **Page Layout** group, click **Margins** and choose the Wide command 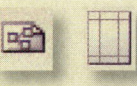 from the menu.

   g. Save the report as **05-20-05e** and click the Close button .

   h. Print/Save the report **05-20-05e**.

   i. Close the report and the Relationships window.

6. Identify Object Dependency by following these steps:

a. Select **tblServiceRecords**.

b. From the **Database Tools** tab, in the **Show/Hide** group, click the Object Dependencies command .

c. Create a Word document called *[your initials]*-**Skills-05-20** and record the answers to the following questions:

d. Select **Objects that depend on me**. What objects depend on **tblServiceRecords**?

e. Select **Objects that I depend on**. On what objects does **tblServiceRecords** depend?

f. Include your name, class information, and today's date on your answer sheet.

g. Close the Object Dependency Pane.

7. Print/Save the Word file *[your initials]*-**Skills-05-20**.

Exercise 5-21

Create and use a lookup field. Print/Save a relationship. Analyze performance of a table.

1. Create a lookup field by following these steps:

a. Open and enable content for *[your initials]*-**CC05**.

b. Open **tblStuffedAnimals** in Datasheet View and select the field **Product Group**.

c. From the **Datasheet** tab, in the **Fields & Columns** group, click the Lookup Column command [icon].

d. In the **Lookup Wizard** dialog box, click **Next**.

e. From the list of tables, select **Table: tblProductLines** and click **Next**.

f. In the **Available Fields** area, double-click **ProductGroup** and **ProductLine**.

g. Click **Next**. Click the drop-down arrow and choose **ProductLine**. Click **Next**.

h. Resize the **Name of Product Group** column so all data can be seen. Click **Next**.

i. Name the field **Product**.

j. Click **Finish**.

2. Add data using a lookup field by following these steps:

a. For the **Product** field in the first record, click the drop-down arrow and choose **Cats & Dogs**.

b. Press ⬇. Key **c**.

c. Do step 2b for every record that has the **Product Group** "C."

d. Press ⬇. Key **d**.

    e. Do step 2d for every record that has the **Product Group** "D."

    f. Press ⬇. Key **e**.

    g. Do step 2f for every record that has the **Product Group** "E."

    h. Press ⬇. Key **f**.

    i. Do step 2h for every record that has the **Product Group** "F."

    j. Press ⬇. Key **t**.

    k. Do step 2j for every record that has the **Product Group** "T."

3. Delete a column in Datasheet View by following these steps:

    a. Click the column header for **Product Group** to select the column.

    b. From the **Datasheet** tab, in the **Fields & Columns** group, click the Delete command ✖. Click **Yes** in response to the warning messages.

4. Rename a column in Datasheet View by following these steps:

    a. Select the column header for the field **Product** field.

    b. From the **Datasheet** tab, in the **Fields & Columns** group, click the Rename command ⬚ and key **Product Group**.

5. Print/Save a Datasheet View by following these steps:

    a. Click the Office Button ⬚. From the **Print** option, choose Print Preview ⬚.

    b. From the **Print Preview** tab, in the **Page Layout** group, click **Margins** and choose the Wide command ⬚ from the menu.

    c. Print/Save the table.

    d. Close Print Preview and the table. Save the changes.

6. Analyze a table by following these steps:

    a. From the **Database Tools** tab, in the **Analyze** group, click the Analyze Performance command ⬚.

    b. Click the **All Object Types** tab and click **Select All.** Click **OK**.

    c. Create a Word document called *[your initials]*-**Skills-05-21** and record the answers to the following questions:

    d. What are the Performance Analyzer's suggestions for the table **tblStuffedAnimals**?

    e. Include your name, class information, and today's date on your answer sheet.

    f. Print/Save the Word file *[your initials]*-**Skills-05-21**.

    g. Click the suggestion for **tblStuffedAnimals** and click **Optimize**.

    h. Close the Performance Analyzer window.

    i. Compact and close the database.

Lesson Applications

Exercise 5-22

Create a relationship between tables. Set referential integrity. Print/Save a relationship.

1. Open *[your initials]*-**CC05**.

2. Open the Relationships window and clear the layout.

3. Add **tblInvoices** and **tblCarriers** to the window. Size the field lists and identify the common field.

4. Create a One-To-Many relationship with referential integrity between the tables. Save and close the layout.

5. Print/Save the Relationship report for these two tables.

6. Save the report as **05-22-05**. Close the report.

7. Save and close the Relationships window.

Exercise 5-23

Insert a subdatasheet. Print a Database Documenter report.

1. Open *[your initials]*-**CC05**.

2. Open **tblCustomers** in Design View.

3. Set the Subdatasheet **Name** property to **tblInvoices.**

4. Print/Save a Database Documenter report for **tblCustomers**. For **Include for Table**, select **Properties** and **Relationships**. For **Include for Fields**, select **Nothing**. For **Include for Indexes**, select **Nothing**.

Exercise 5-24

Create a multi-value lookup field. Set referential integrity. Determine object dependencies. Print a Database Documenter report.

1. Open *[your initials]*-**CC05**.

2. Open **tblCarriers** in Datasheet View.

3. Create a multi-value lookup field called **Delivery Type** that links to **tblDeliveryType**.

4. In **tblCarriers**, complete the following records.

Southtown Transportation	Freight – Air
	Freight – Ground
Federal Parcel Systems	Ground
	Ground Express
Bell Shipping	Ground
	Ground Express
	Freight – Air
	Freight – Ground

5. Set Referential Integrity for the relationship between **tblCarriers** and **tblDeliveryType**.

6. Print/Save a Database Documenter report for **tblCarriers**. For **Include for Table**, select **Properties** and **Relationships**. For **Include for Fields**, select **Names, Data Types, Sizes, and Properties**. For **Include for Indexes**, select **Nothing**.

7. Create a Word document called *[your initials]*-**Apps-05** and record the answers to the following questions:

8. What tables, queries, forms, and reports depend on **tblCarriers**?

9. On what tables, queries, forms, and reports does **tblCarriers** depend?

10. Include your name, class information, and date.

11. Print/Save the Word file *[your initials]*-**Apps-05**.

Exercise 5-25 ◆ Challenge Yourself

Analyze a table. Create a table. Create a relationship. Print/Save a datasheet. Print/Save a Relationship report.

1. Open *[your initials]*-**CC05**.

2. Using the Table Analyzer Wizard, select **tblCustomers**.

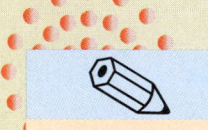

TIP

Do not let the wizard decide the fields and tables.

3. Create a new table named **tblStates** by dragging the **State** field out of **Table1**.

4. In **tblStates**, add records to include all 50 states and Washington DC.

5. Rename **Table1** to **tblCust**.

6. In **tblCust**, rename the Lookup field to **State**.

7. In Design View, move the **State** field between **City** and **PostalCode**.

8. Verify that **tblCust** has a lookup field listing all 51 options.

9. Print/Save the datasheet for **tblStates** on one page. Make certain that the records are sorted by State in ascending order.

10. Print/Save the Relationship report displaying only **tblCust** and **tblStates**.

11. Save the report as **05-25-10**.

12. Close the report and the Relationships window.

13. Compact, repair, and close the database.

On Your Own

In these exercises, you work on your own, as you would in a real-life work environment. Use the skills you've learned to accomplish the task—and be creative.

Exercise 5-26

Review the designs for the three databases you created in Exercises 4-29 through 4-31. Select one of the three databases to continue developing. Identify two additional tables you might need to make your database designs more useful. The relationships between the main table and the two additional tables should be One-To-Many. On a blank sheet of paper, list the field names, data types, field sizes, and attributes for the two new tables. Identify the common fields among the three tables. Continue to Exercise 5-27.

Exercise 5-27

Create the two tables you designed in Exercise 5-26. Add appropriate field properties to each table to make your design more useful. Create One-To-Many relationships with referential integrity between the tables. Test the referential integrity of the tables. Add at least five records to each empty table. Print the datasheet and a Database Documenter report for each table. Continue to Exercise 5-28.

Exercise 5-28

Search the Internet for images or graphics you might wish to use in your database. Design and create a new table to store the images. Create an appropriate relationship between this new table and the main table. Insert the images into the new table. Print a Relationship report displaying all four tables. Submit to your instructor the printouts from Exercises 5-27 through 5-28, along with your field list from 5-26. Keep a copy of the database you modified in this exercise. You will use it for the "On Your Own" exercises in subsequent lessons.

Lesson 6

Designing Queries

OBJECTIVES

After completing this lesson, you will be able to:

1. Create and modify select queries.

2. Add criteria and operators to a query.

3. Apply logical operators.

4. Modify query properties.

5. Add calculations to a query.

6. Create queries with Wizards.

7. Apply PivotChart / PivotTable Views.

Estimated Time: 1½ hours

MCAS OBJECTIVES

In this lesson:
AC07 70-605 2.5.6
AC07 70-605 4.1.1
AC07 70-605 4.1.2
AC07 70-605 4.1.4
AC07 70-605 4.2.1
AC07 70-605 4.2.2
AC07 70-605 4.2.4
AC07 70-605 4.2.5
AC07 70-605 4.2.6

In most relational databases, queries locate, add, modify, and delete records. The effectiveness and efficiency of a query depends upon its ability to access information quickly. When you design a query, you must select necessary fields, specify appropriate criteria, and sort recordsets.

Because queries make data more manageable, they often become the record source for reports and forms. For example, a report based on an employee table with 10,000 employees would show all 10,000 records. A report based on a query would show a subset of the table's records. This subset could specify information such as who is eligible for retirement, who is scheduled for evaluation, or who is on vacation this week.

As with any computer application, executing a query demands processing resources. Large databases and complicated queries take more processing time than small databases and simple queries. A skilled database administrator will be knowledgeable with the numerous types of queries available in a Microsoft Access database.

REVIEW

A query is similar to a filter in some respects. However, only a single filter can be saved per table, but multiple queries can be associated to a single table.

Creating and Modifying Select Queries

The most common type of query is a select query. A select query locates data from one or more tables and displays the results as a datasheet. In addition to grouping records, a select query can calculate sums, averages, and other types of totals.

You can use a wizard to design queries, but usually you can build a query quickly in Design View. The Query Design window has an upper and lower pane. The upper pane is the field list pane in which you choose the data source from one or more field lists. The lower pane is the design grid in which you specify criteria. The lower pane is also known as the QBE (Query by Example) grid.

Exercise 6-1   VIEW A SELECT QUERY AND ITS REPORT

Many reports and forms use a select query to limit the number of records and fields displayed. For example, rather than display all employees listed in the employee table, you can use a select query to display only names and phone numbers. When you view the results, the dynaset shows only the specified fields you specify in the design grid. A *dynaset* is a dynamic recordset that automatically reflects changes to its underlying data source.

1. Locate and open the **Lesson 06** folder.

2. Make a copy of **CC06** and rename it to *[your initials]*-**CC06**.

3. Open and enable content for *[your initials]*-**CC06**.

4. Open **qryEmployeePhone** in Design View. This query uses four fields from the table **tblEmployees**.

Figure 6-1
Query Design window
CC06
qryEmployeePhone

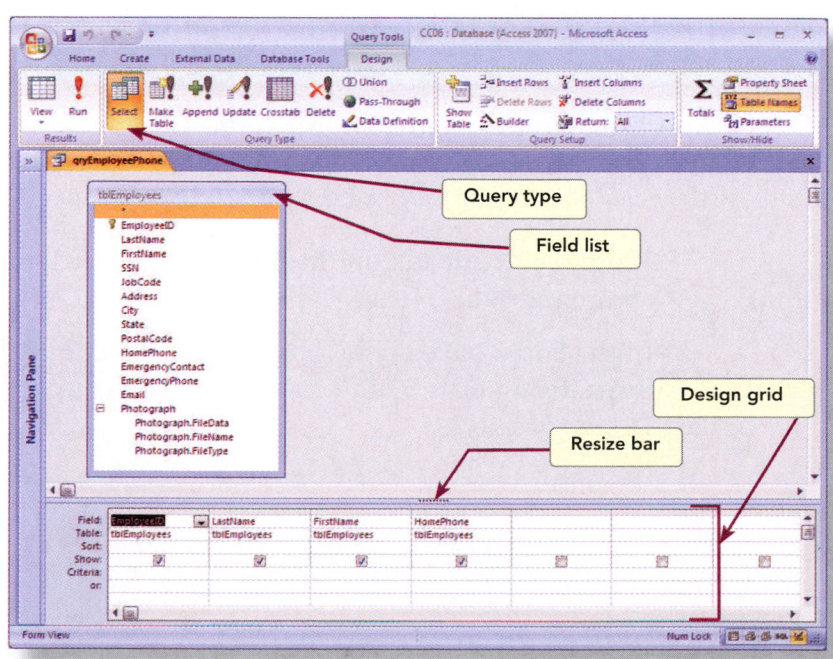

5. Open **rptEmployeePhone** in Design View.

6. From the **Design** tab, in the **Tools** group, click the Property Sheet command .

7. In the Property Sheet, click the **Data** tab. The **Record Source** property shows that this report is based on **qryEmployeePhone**.

Figure 6-2
Report's Property
Sheet
CC06
rptEmployeePhone

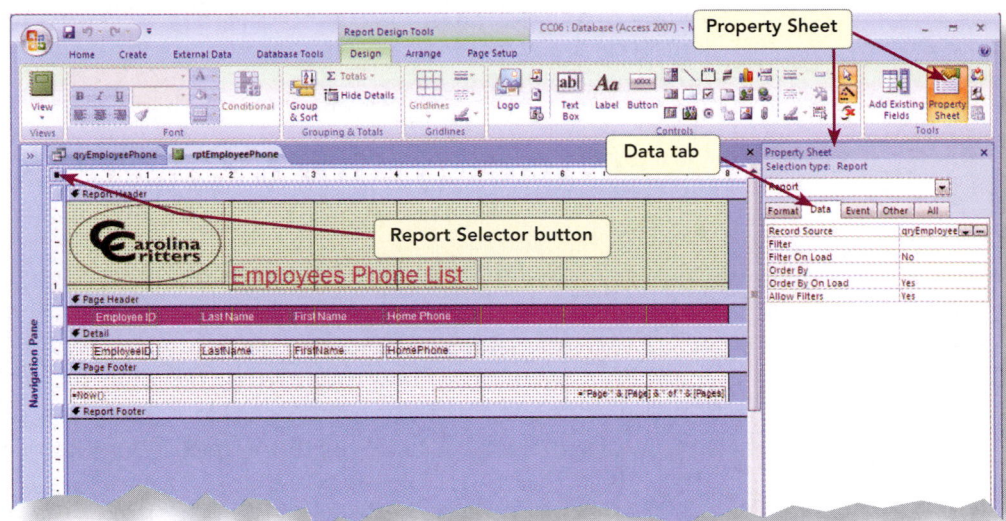

8. Right-click the document tab for **rptEmployeePhone** and choose **Close All**.

Exercise 6-2   CREATE A SELECT QUERY BASED ON A SINGLE TABLE

You define criteria and field lists in the Design View of a query. You display the resulting recordset through the datasheet of the query. When you view the results, only the fields and records that you specified will display.

1. From the **Create** tab, in the **Other** group, click the Query Design command .

2. In the **Show Table** dialog box, double-click **tblStuffedAnimals**. The **tblStuffedAnimals** Field List appears in the upper pane of the Query Design window.

Figure 6-3
Show Table
dialog box
CC06
qryAnimalPrices

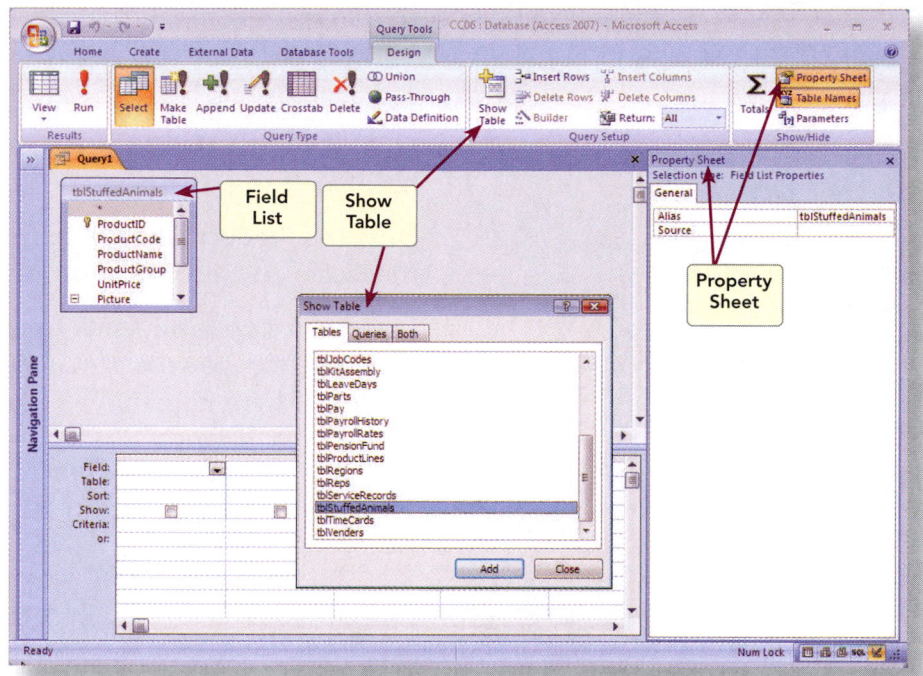

REVIEW

If you accidentally open two copies of the same Field List, right-click the second list and select **Remove Table**. You can also click the title bar of the Field List window and press [Delete] to remove the second copy.

3. Click **Close** in the **Show Table** dialog box.

4. Resize the Field List so all fields can be seen.

5. If the Property Sheet is not open, click the Property Sheet command [].

6. Click the **tblStuffedAnimals** Field List. The Property Sheet is now showing the properties of the table.

7. Click the blank area to the right of the Field List. The Property Sheet now shows the properties of the query.

8. From the Quick Access toolbar, click the Save button [].

9. In the **Save As** dialog box, key **qryAnimalPrices** and click **OK**.

Exercise 6-3   ADD FIELDS TO A QUERY

You can add fields to the design grid of a query by any of the three following ways:

* Double-click the field name in the Field List.

* Drag the field from the Field List to a **Field** row in the design grid.

* Click the **Field** row in the design grid and select a field name from the drop-down list.

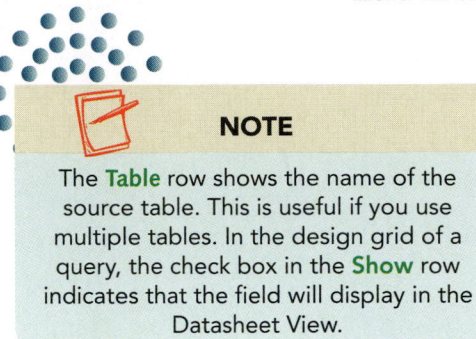

Access 2007

1. From the Field List, double-click **ProductName**. It appears as the first field in the **Field** row.

2. The Property Sheet now shows the properties of the field. Click the Property Sheet button to hide the Property Sheet.

3. Drag the **ProductGroup** field from the Field List to the **Field** row, second column.

4. In the third column, click the **Field** row, and then click its drop-down arrow. Choose **UnitPrice** from the list of field names.

NOTE

The **Table** row shows the name of the source table. This is useful if you use multiple tables. In the design grid of a query, the check box in the **Show** row indicates that the field will display in the Datasheet View.

Figure 6-4
Adding fields to the design grid
CC06
qryAnimalPrices

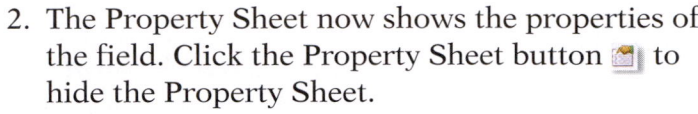
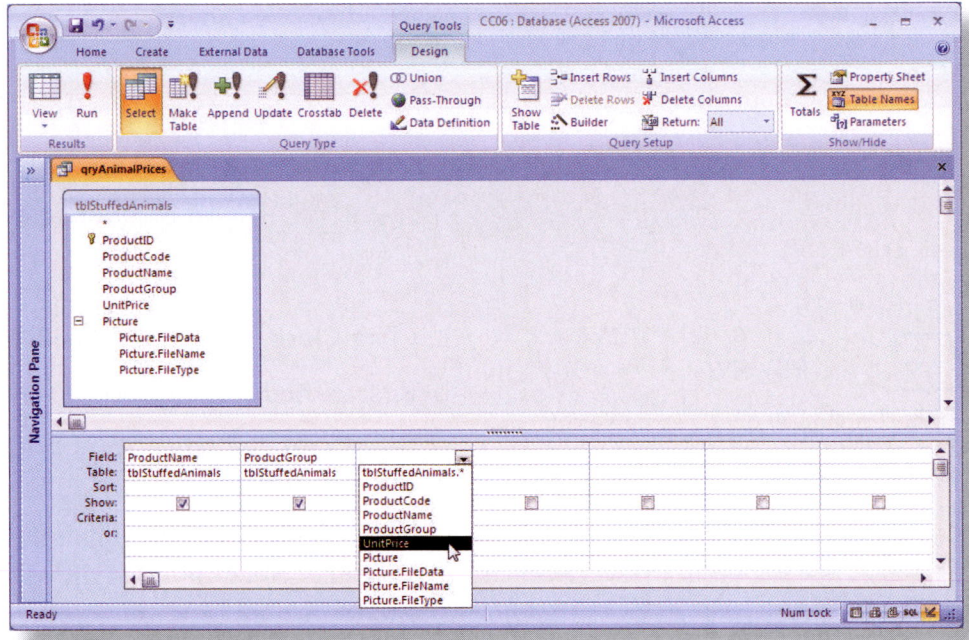

5. Save and close the query.

Exercise 6-4 CREATE A SELECT QUERY BASED ON TWO TABLES

A query is based upon one or more field lists. Each field list is a recordset created by a table or query. When you use two or more field lists, you must link the field lists through a common field.

1. From the **Create** tab, in the **Other** group, click the Query Design command.

2. In the **Show Table** dialog box, double-click **tblStuffedAnimals** and **tblProductLines**.

3. Double-click **tblProductLines** again to add a second copy. Click **Close**.

NOTE

When using more than one table in a query, they must always show a join line.

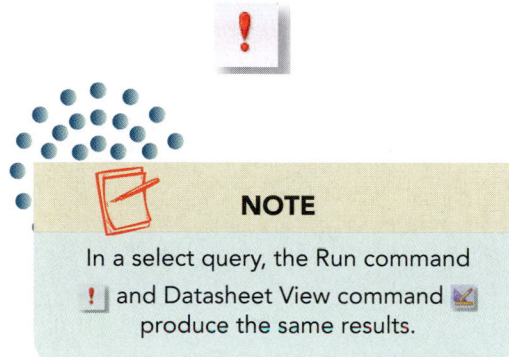

NOTE

In a select query, the Run command ❗ and Datasheet View command ▣ produce the same results.

4. The second copy of **tblProductLines** ends with "_1."

5. Resize and move the Field Lists so all fields can be seen.

6. From the **tblSuffedAnimals** Field List, double-click **ProductID** and **ProductName**.

7. From the **tblProductLines** Field List, double-click **ProductLine**.

8. From the **Design** tab, in the **Results** group, click the Run command ❗.

9. This query results in a dynaset of 120 records. Notice the many copies of the **Product Name**. Switch to Design View.

10. Right-click the **tblProductLines_1** Field List and choose **Remove Table**.

11. From the **Design** tab, in the **Results** group, click the Run command ❗.

12. The dynaset now contains only 24 records. The extra records come from having two unrelated tables in the query. Switch to Design View.

13. Save the query as **qryAnimalList**.

14. Close the query.

Adding Criteria and Operators to a Query

Adding criteria to a query is similar to adding criteria to a filter. One major difference is that more than one condition can be placed on multiple fields. When the query is executed, each condition placed as a criterion must be evaluated against field values for each record in the dynaset. The combination of conditions and operators is evaluated as a single criterion statement.

An *operator* is a word or symbol that indicates a specific arithmetic or logical relationship between the elements of an expression. Operators are used to create conditions. Operators can include arithmetic operators, such as the plus sign (+); comparison operators, such as the equals sign (=); or, logical operators, such as the word "And"; concatenation operators, such as "&" and "+"; and special operators such as "Like," "Between," or "In."

In addition to operators, a condition can also include one or more functions. A *function* is a procedure used in an expression. Most functions include multiple arguments. An *argument* is a reference in a function assigned as a single variable. Some functions such as "Date" do not require arguments. Other functions, such as "DateDiff," contain both required arguments and optional arguments.

TABLE 6-1 Types of Operators

Type	Definition	Examples
Arithmetic operator	A word or symbol that calculates a value from two or more numbers.	+, −, *, /, \, ^
Comparison operator	A symbol or combination of symbols that specifies a comparison between two values. A comparison operator is also referred to as a relational operator.	=, <>, <, <=, >, >=
Logical operator	A symbol, word, group of symbols, or group of words used to construct an expression with multiple conditions.	And, Or, Eqv, Not, Xor
Concatenation operator	A symbol, word, group of symbols, or group of words used to combine two text values into a single text value.	&, +
Special operators		Like, Between, In

Exercise 6-5   USE A SINGLE CRITERION

Text, numbers, or expressions can be used for criterion placed on a single field. Criterion using text values include leading and closing quotation marks. Criterion using date values include leading and closing pound signs (#). Numbers and expressions do not require leading or closing symbols.

1. Open **qryAnimalPrices** in Design View.

2. Click the **Criteria** row for **ProductGroup**. Key **c**.

Figure 6-5
Entering criteria
CC06
qryAnimalPrices

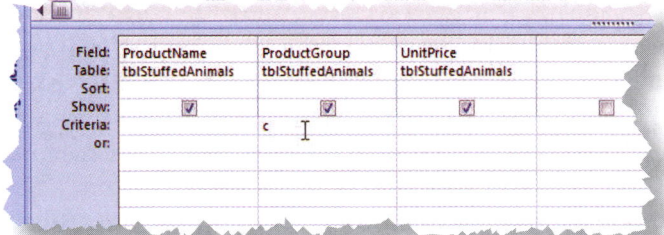

TIP

Text criterion is not case-sensitive.

3. From the **Design** tab, in the **Results** group, click the View command . Only those products in **Product Group** "C" (Cats & Dogs) are shown.

TIP

After you run a query, Access places leading and closing quotation marks around the text used as the criterion.

NOTE

This query has reduced the dynaset from 24 records to 5 records.

4. Switch to Design View.

5. Click in the **Criteria** row for **ProductGroup** and press [F2] to select the criterion. Then press [Delete].

6. In the **Criteria** row for **ProductGroup**, key **t**.

7. From the **Design** tab, in the **Results** group, click the View command [image]. Only those products in **Product Group** "T" (Teddy Bears) are shown.

8. Switch to Design View.

9. Click in the **Criteria** row for **ProductGroup** and press [F2]. Press [Delete] to remove the criteria.

10. Save and close the query.

Exercise 6-6   USE COMPARISON OPERATORS

Queries often use comparison operators to evaluate data. Comparison operators allow you to evaluate numbers, text, and dates. For example, the expression >10/17/07 would display all records with a date after October 17, 2007. The expression >=10/17/07 would display all records with a date on or after October 17, 2007.

When comparing text, fields are evaluated alphabetically. The expression <Smith would display all records that appear in a dictionary before the word "smith."

TABLE 6-2 Comparison Operators

Operator	Meaning
=	Equal
<>	Not equal
<	Less than
<=	Less than or equal to
>	Greater than
>=	Greater than or equal to

1. Open **qrySalesByOrderDate** in Datasheet View and notice that the dynaset is sorted by **OrderDate**.

2. Switch to Design View. Click in the **Criteria** row for **OrderDate**.

3. Key **>=8/23/05** and press [↓]. Access adds "#" around the date criteria.

4. Switch to Datasheet View. Records for which the **ShipDate** is on or after August 23, 2005, are displayed.

5. Switch to Design View. Click in the **Criteria** row for **OrderDate**. From the **Design** tab, in the **Query Setup** group, click the Delete Rows command .

6. Click in the **Criteria** row for **ShipDate**. Key **<=10/15/03** and display the dynaset. Records for which the **ShipDate** is on or before September 15, 2003, are displayed.

7. Delete the criteria.

Exercise 6-7   USE WILDCARDS IN CRITERIA

In much the same way, you might use wildcards in the Find command; you can use wildcards in a query. When using a wildcard in the Criteria row of a query, the Like operator compares the criterion condition to each record. When the keyword "Like" is not included in the criterion, Access automatically adds it.

1. For the **qrySalesByOrderDate**, in the **Criteria** row for **CompanyName**, key **the***.

Figure 6-6
Using the * wildcard
CC06
qrySalesByOrderDate

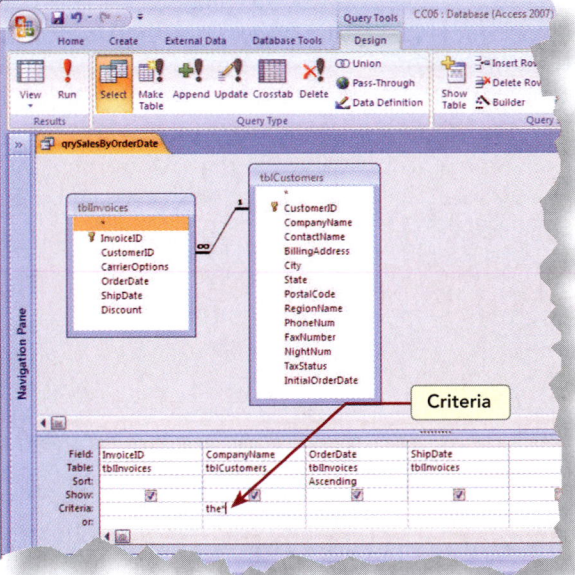

2. From the **Design** tab, in the **Results** group, click the Run command ![Run]. Records for which the companies name starts with "the" are displayed.

3. Switch to Design View. Access inserts the keyword "Like" and formats the text with quotes.

4. Press F2 and Delete.

5. In the **Criteria** row for **CompanyName**, key ***inc***.

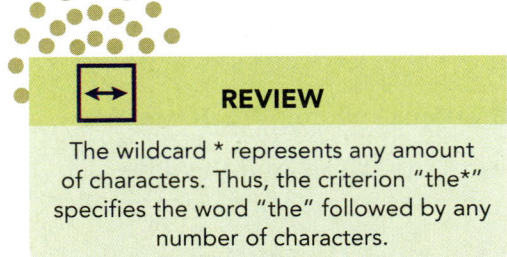

REVIEW

The wildcard * represents any amount of characters. Thus, the criterion "the*" specifies the word "the" followed by any number of characters.

6. Switch to view the dynaset. Records for which the companies name contains "inc" are displayed.

7. Switch to Design View. Delete the criteria.

8. In the **CompanyName Criteria** row, key ***b??r***. This means that only companies that begin with the letter "b" and has the fourth letter of "r" will display.

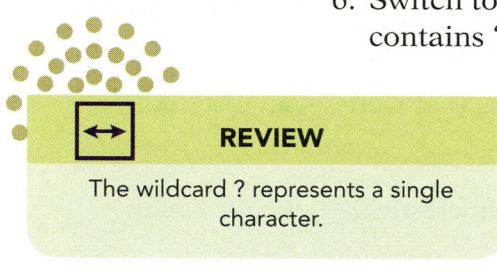

Figure 6-7
Using the * and ?
wildcards
CC06
qrySalesByOrderDate

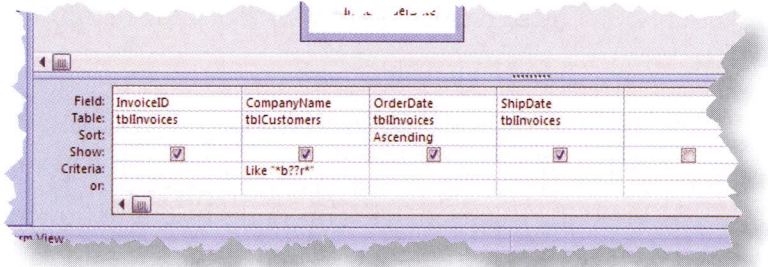

9. View the dynaset. Thirty-eight records are displayed.

10. Return to Design View and delete the criteria.

Exercise 6-8 USE KEYWORDS IN CRITERIA

Only the keywords "Like" and "Is" are automatically added to a criterion. All other keywords must be specified. Criterion expressions can be viewed in the Zoom box. You can open the Zoom box by pressing Shift + F2.

TABLE 6-3 Criteria Keywords

Keyword	Returns records in which the field . . .
Is Null	has no data, is "blank," or is "empty."
Between	value is between two numbers.
Like	value equals a defined text.
Not	value does not match the defined value.

1. With **qrySalesByOrderDate** in Design View, in the **tblInvoices** Field List, double-click the field **Discount** to add it to the Design Grid.

2. In the **Criteria** row for **Discount**, key **null** and press ⬇. Access has added the keyword "Is" to the criteria.

3. View the dynaset. There are 310 sales that were not given a discount.

4. Return to Design View.

5. Edit the **Discount** criteria to show **is not null**.

6. View the dynaset. There are 24 sales that were given discounts.

7. Return to Design View and delete the criteria.

8. Right-click in the **Criteria** row for **OrderDate** and choose **Zoom**.

9. In the **Zoom** dialog box, key **is between 1/1/05 and 12/31/05** and click **OK**.

10. View the dynaset. There were 65 sales in 2005.

11. Switch to Design View.

12. In the **Show** row, click to remove the checkmark for **OrderDate** and **ShipDate**.

13. View the dynaset. The two dates are not showing.

14. Return to Design View and delete the criteria.

15. Close the query and do not save the changes.

Applying Logical Operators

An AND criterion or an OR criterion compares two conditions in a single criterion statement. You use an AND criterion when two conditions must occur simultaneously for the statement to be true. You use an OR criterion when either condition must occur for the statement to be true.

The design grid of a query allows for AND and OR statements without using AND or OR as keywords. When you create an AND criterion, you enter all conditions on the same Criteria row of the design grid. When you create an OR criteria, you enter the conditions on different Criteria rows of the design grid.

Exercise 6-9   USE THE "AND" CRITERION

An AND condition can be created for a single field or multiple fields. When an AND condition is placed on a single field, the keyword AND must be placed between the two conditions. When an AND condition is placed on multiple fields, the keyword is not entered. When more than one field contains a condition on the same Criteria row, then an AND condition is automatically created by Access.

1. From the **Create** tab, in the **Other** group, click the Query Design command 🗗.

2. From the **Show Table** dialog box, double-click **tblCustomers** and click **Close**.

3. Resize the Field List so all field names can be seen.

4. Add the following fields to the query design grid; **CompanyName**, **BillingAddress**, **City**, **State**, **PostalCode**.

5. In the **CompanyName** column, click the drop-down arrow in the **Sort** row and choose **Ascending**.

6. Switch to Datasheet View to see the results. Resize the columns so all data are visible.

7. Right-click the document tab for the query and choose **Save**. Key **qryCustomerAddress** and click **OK**.

8. Switch to Design View.

9. In the **City** column, key **charlotte** in the **Criteria** row.

10. Switch to Datasheet View to see how many customers are in Charlotte. Return to Design View.

11. In the **BillingAddress** column, key ***brook*** in the same **Criteria** row.

Figure 6-8
AND criteria on the same row in the design grid
CC06
qryCustomerAddress

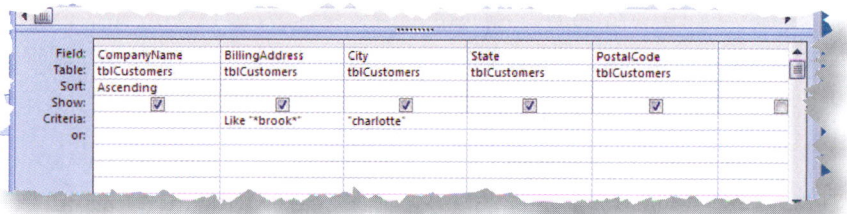

12. Switch to Datasheet View. Only records that matched both criteria are shown.

13. Switch to Design View. Click in the **Criteria** row for the **City** field. From the **Design** tab, in the **Query Setup** group, click the Delete Rows command ⊒×.

14. Click in the **Criteria** row for the **State** field. Key **tn and nc**.

15. Switch to Datasheet View. No records match the criteria because no customer's state can be both TN and NC.

Exercise 6-10   USE THE "OR" CRITERION

An OR condition also can be created for a single field or multiple fields. When an OR condition is placed on a single field, the keyword OR must be placed between the two conditions. When an OR condition is placed on multiple fields, the keyword is not entered. When multiple conditions are placed on multiple **Criteria** rows, then an OR condition is automatically created by Access.

Access 2007

1. Switch to Design View. Point to the right of the word "Criteria" in the **Criteria** row to display a black, right-pointing arrow. Click to select the **Criteria** row and press Delete.

Figure 6-9
Selecting a Criteria row
CC06
qryCustomerAddress

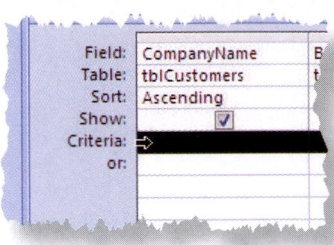

2. Click in the **Criteria** row for the **State** field and, key **tn**. View the dynaset to see the four matching records. Return to Design View.

3. Key **nc** in the row below "tn" to enter a second condition. The first **or** row is directly below the **Criteria** row.

Figure 6-10
OR criteria on separate rows in the design grid
CC06
qryCustomerAddress

Field:	CompanyName	BillingAddress	City	State	PostalCode
Table:	tblCustomers	tblCustomers	tblCustomers	tblCustomers	tblCustomers
Sort:	Ascending				
Show:	✓	✓	✓	✓	✓
Criteria:				"tn"	
or:				"nc"	

4. View the dynaset. Each record meets one of the OR conditions. Return to Design View.

5. Save and close the query.

6. Open **qryCustomerAddress** in Design View. Notice that Access has combined the two criteria to one row using the OR keyword.

7. Delete the criteria. Save and close the query.

Modifying Query Properties

Queries display specific data and sorted data. By setting specific properties for a query, you can display top values and sub datasheets. For example, if you need to list the five least expensive stuffed animals, you would sort the stuffed animals table by price in ascending order and apply the Top Value property. If you want to find the customers who generate the most revenue for your company, you would also use the Top Value property in a query.

Exercise 6-11   **FIND THE TOP AND BOTTOM VALUES**

When using the Top Values property, Access displays records based upon the defined sort order. If a query is sorted by a numeric value, then the top values will be based upon the sorted numeric field. If a query is sorted by a text field, then the top values will be based upon the sorted text field.

The Top Values property displays either a static number of records (such as the top five) or a percentage of all records in the dynaset (such as the top 5%). Depending on the sort order, Top Values can display either the highest (top) or lowest (bottom) values. For example, when you sort a numeric field in ascending order, the "top" of the list will be the lowest numbers. When you sort a numeric field in descending order, the "top" values are the largest numbers.

1. Open **qrySalesByAnimal** in Datasheet View. The dynaset shows sales by customer and product sold.

2. Switch to Design View. Click in the **Sort** row for the **InvoiceID** field. Click the drop-down arrow and choose **(not sorted)**.

3. Click in the **Sort** row for the **Qty** field. Click the drop-down arrow and choose **Descending**.

4. Switch to Datasheet View. The largest quantities of items sold per invoice are located at the top of the list.

5. Switch to Design View.

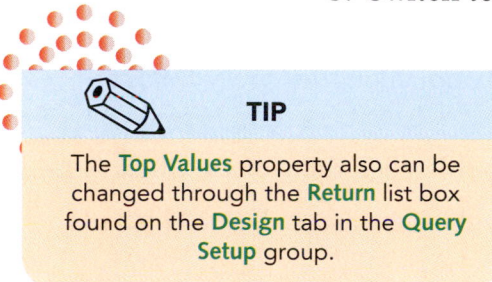

TIP

The **Top Values** property also can be changed through the **Return** list box found on the **Design** tab in the **Query Setup** group.

6. From the **Design** tab, in the **Show/Hide** group, click the Property Sheet command. Click anywhere above the **tblInvoiceLineItems** Field List. This changes the **Property Sheet** to display the **Query Properties**.

7. Click the **Top Values** property and the drop-down arrow. Choose **5**.

Figure 6-11
Top Values property
CC06
qrySalesByAnimal

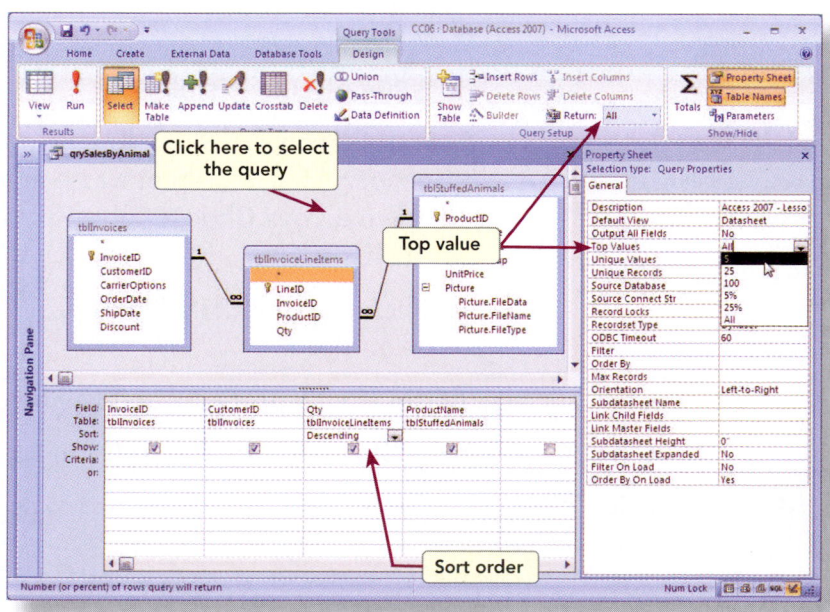

8. Switch to Datasheet View. Since the field **Qty** field is sorted in descending order, the five largest quantities are shown.

9. Switch to Design View. From the **Design** tab, in the **Query Setup** group, click the Return list box (Top Value) and choose **5%**.

> **NOTE**
>
> Remember to reset the **Top Values** property to "All." If you forget to reset the property and later prepare a report based on the query, you will print an incomplete dynaset.

10. Switch to Datasheet View. The top 5% quantities of sales results in 33 records being displayed.

11. Switch to Design View and reset the **Return** list box to **All**.

12. Close and save the query.

Exercise 6-12   CREATE A QUERY WITH A SUBDATASHEET

Just as a table can display a related table as a subdatasheet, a query can also contain a subdatasheet. A subdatasheet is created by defining a Subdatasheet Name as a query property.

1. From the **Create** tab, in the **Other** group, click the Query Design command .

2. From the **Show Table** dialog box, double-click **tblInvoices**. Click **Close**.

3. In the **tblInvoices** Field List, double-click the asterisk (*). This tells Access to use all the fields.

4. Switch to Datasheet View. All six fields have been included.

5. Save the query as **qryInvoices**.

6. Switch to Design View. Open the Property Sheet if it is not already visible.

> **NOTE**
>
> If the Property Sheet shows "Field Properties," click again in the top pane. You may also need to resize the Property Sheet to see all values.

7. In the Property Sheet for the query, click the property **Subdatasheet Name** and click the drop-down arrow. Choose **Table.tblInvoiceLineItems** from the list.

8. Click the **Link Child Fields** property and key **InvoiceID**.

9. Click the **Link Master Fields** property and key **InvoiceID**.

10. Close the Property Sheet and switch to Datasheet View.

11. Click the Expand button for any record to see which products were ordered.

12. Collapse the subdatasheet.

13. Close the query and save the changes.

Adding Calculations to a Query

The queries you have created so far have been select queries. Select queries display the dynaset as individual records similar to the datasheet of a table. A query can also display calculations. To display a calculation in a query, you must use an aggregate function. An aggregate function is a sum, average, maximum, minimum, or count for a group of records.

A query can also have a calculated field. A *calculated field* is a field that uses an expression or formula as its data source. You can add calculated fields to queries, forms, and reports.

Exercise 6-13 USE A FORMULA IN A CALCULATED FIELD

A calculated field does not store data in dynaset. The value of a calculated field is generated each time you run a query. Only the definition and properties of the calculated field are stored in the query object.

Since a calculated field is not part of the source dynaset, each calculated field must have a unique name. When a field does not have a name, Access assigns an alias name. The alias name for a calculated field displays as text followed by a colon. The alias displays in front of the calculation.

Calculated fields can be entered directly into the design grid or can be entered using the Expression Builder. The *Expression Builder* is an interface used to create a function, calculation, or expression.

TABLE 6-4 Parts of the Expression Builder

Part	Purpose
Expression box	White area at the top of the window that shows the formula as you build it. (Also called the preview area.)
Operator buttons	Set of buttons with common arithmetic and logical symbols below the Expression box.
Left panel	List of folders with objects available for use.
Middle panel	Contents of the folder selected in the left panel.
Right panel	Details or properties of the object selected in the middle panel.
Paste button	Command to paste a selected object, function, or expression into the expression box.

NOTE

If the Field List does not appear in the middle pane, close the Expression Builder, save the query, and re-open the Expression Builder.

1. Open **qryInvoiceLineItemCost** in Design View.

2. Click the empty **Field** row in the sixth column.

3. From the **Design** tab, in the **Query Setup** group, click the Builder command ⌐.

Figure 6-12
Building an expression for the query
CC06
qryInvoiceLineItemCost

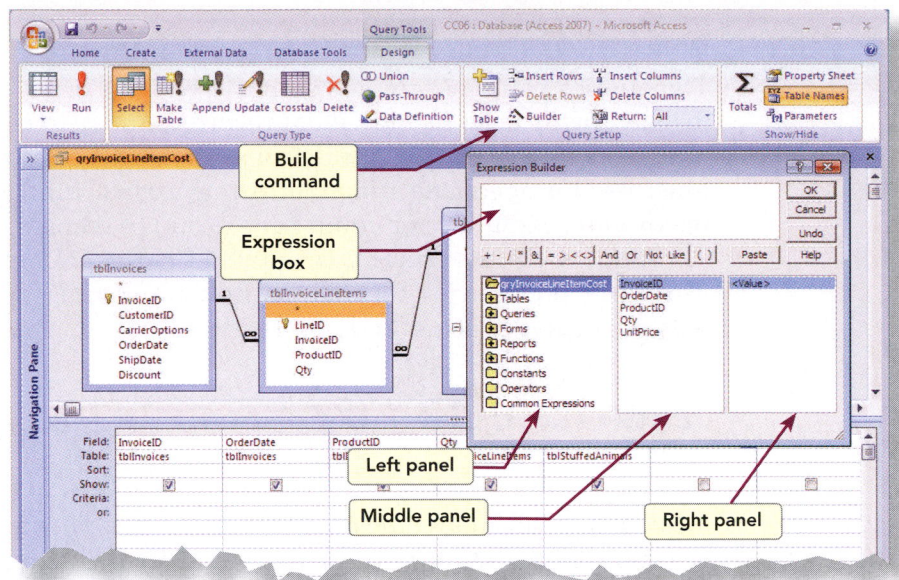

4. The current query is at the top of the left panel. In the middle panel, click the field **Qty**.

5. In the right panel, double-click **[Value]**. This action pastes the value of the **Qty** field to the expression box.

6. Press ⬚ to add the multiply symbol to the expression box.

7. In the middle panel, double-click the field **UnitPrice**.

Figure 6-13
Building a formula
CC06
qryInvoiceLineItemCost

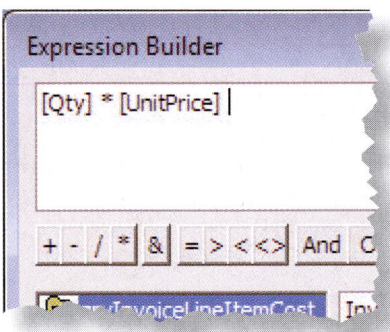

8. Click **OK** to close the **Expression Builder**.

9. Switch to Datasheet View. Notice that the last column shows the cost of each line item, or the unit price multiplied by the quantity.

10. Access has given the calculated field the alias of "Expr1." Switch to Design View.

11. Replace "Expr1" with **ItemCost**. Be certain to leave the colon after the field name.

12. From the **Design** tab, in the **Show/Hide** group, click the Property Sheet command 🗗. In the **Caption** property, key **Item Cost**.

13. In the **Format** property, click the drop-down arrow and choose **Currency**. In the **Decimal Places** property, key **2**.

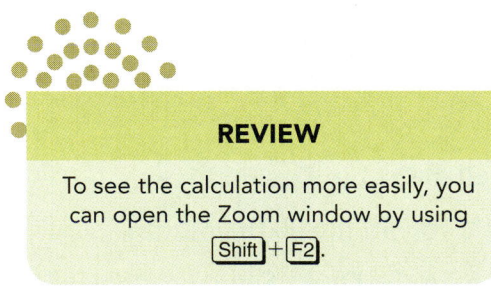

REVIEW

To see the calculation more easily, you can open the Zoom window by using

Shift + F2.

14. Close the Property Sheet.

15. Switch to Datasheet View.

16. Save and close the query.

Exercise 6-14   USE A FUNCTION IN A
CALCULATED FIELD

Calculated fields can be entered directly into the design grid or can be entered
using the Expression Builder.

TIP

You can key expressions directly in the
Field row without using the Expression
Builder.

NOTE

Functions use leading and ending
placeholders, << and >>. These
placeholders identify the argument(s)
used in the function.

1. Open **qrySalesByOrderDate** in Design View.

2. Click the empty **Field** row in the fifth column.

3. From the **Design** tab, in the **Query Setup** group, click
   the Builder command.

4. In the left panel, double-click **Functions** and click
   Built-In Functions.

5. In the middle panel, click **Date/Time**.

6. In the right panel, double-click **DateDiff**. This
   function has five parameters or values. We need to
   fill three of them.

7. In the expression box, click on **<<interval>>** and
   key **"d"**.

8. In the expression box, click on **<<date1>>**. In the left panel, click
   qrySalesByOrderDate. In the middle panel, double-click **OrderDate**.

9. In the expression box, click on **<<date2>>**. In the middle panel,
   double-click **ShipDate**.

10. Press [Delete] until you have deleted the remaining commas and
    placeholders. Do not delete the right parenthesis.

Figure 6-14
Building a function
**CC06
qrySalesByOrderDate**

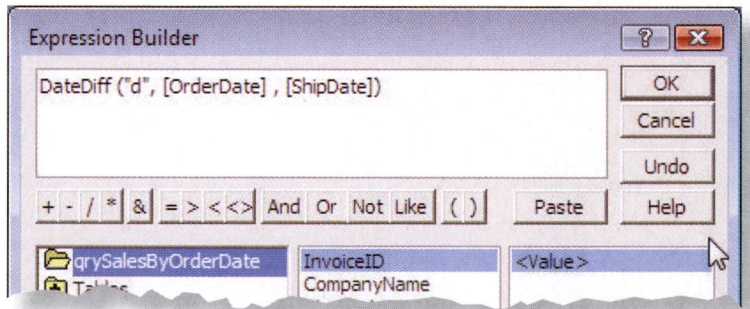

Access 2007

11. Click **OK**. Press ⬇. Access has added the alias "Expr1."

12. Replace the alias with **Turnover**.

13. From the **Design** tab, in the **Show/Hide** group, click the Property Sheet command 🖼. In the field **Turnover** Property Sheet, click in the **Format** property and key **#" Days"**.

14. Switch to Datasheet View. The difference between the order and shipping date is now listed in days.

15. Close and save the query.

Creating Queries with Wizards

Relationships and referential integrity prevent data duplication or unmatched relationships. However, when using data from other sources, such as an online Web site, the table you create might not follow your relationship rules. Access provides two query wizards to assist verifying the accuracy of your data. The Find Unmatched Records Query Wizard and the Find Duplicate Records Query Wizard create these special queries. Wizards can also be used to create a Crosstab query.

Exercise 6-15   USE THE SIMPLE QUERY WIZARD

When creating a query using a wizard, you must select the record source and the associated fields. The record source can be one or more related tables or queries.

1. From the **Create** tab, in the **Other** group, click the Query Wizard command 📇.

Figure 6-15
New Query Wizard
collection
CC06

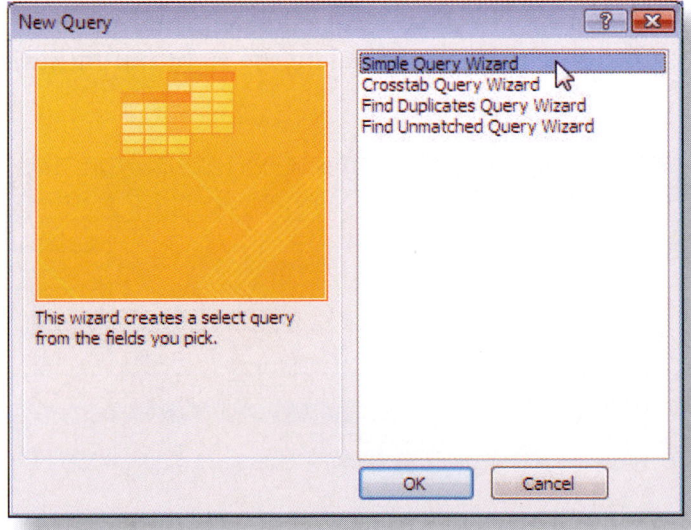

2. In the **New Query** dialog box, double-click **Simple Query Wizard**.

3. From the **Tables/Queries** list box, choose **Table: tblStuffedAnimals**.

4. In the **Available Fields** list, double-click **ProductName**.

5. From the **Tables/Queries** list box, choose **Table: tblKitAssembly**.

6. In the **Available Fields** list, double-click **Qty**.

7. From the **Tables/Queries** list box, choose **Table: tblParts**.

8. In the **Available Fields** list, double-click **Description** and **PCost**.

9. Click **Next**. The default type of select query is **Detail**. Click **Next**.

10. Delete the suggested title and key **qryProductParts**.

11. Click **Finish**. This dynaset lists the parts, quantity, and cost to make each kit.

12. Switch to Design View. Resize and move each Field List.

Figure 6-16
Query created by the
Simple Query Wizard
**CC06
qryProductParts**

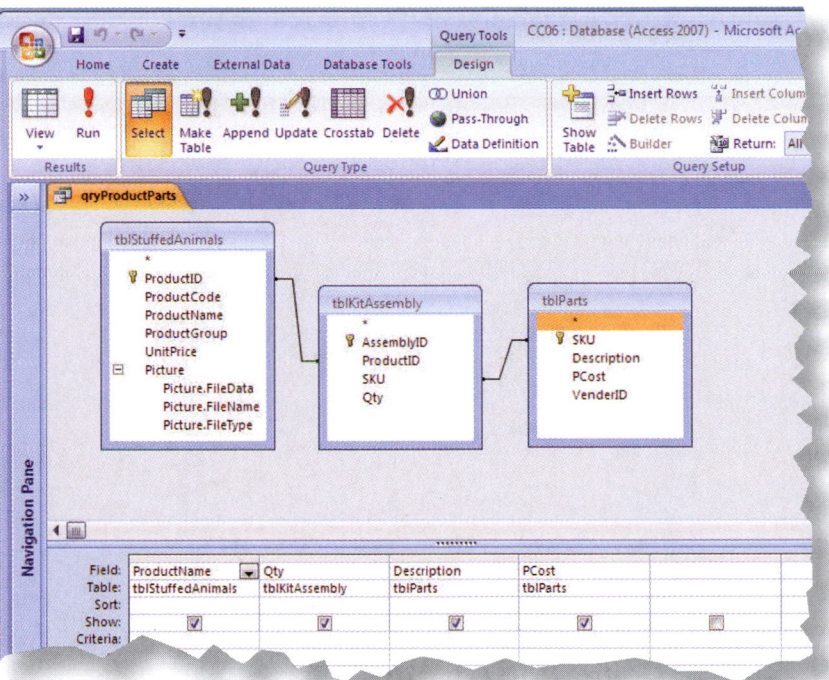

13. Close and save the query.

Access 2007

Exercise 6-16   USE THE CROSSTAB QUERY WIZARD

A crosstab query displays information similar to a spreadsheet. The Total row calculates the sum, average, count, or other totals. The Crosstab row defines the fields used for the data, column headings, and row headings. Data are grouped by two fields, one listed on the left and the other listed across the top.

1. From the **Create** tab, in the **Other** group, click the Query Wizard command 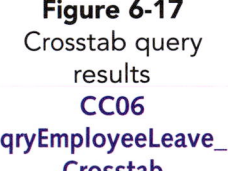.

2. In the **New Query** dialog box, double-click **Crosstab Query Wizard**.

3. In the **View** control, click **Queries**. From the list, select **Query: qryEmployeeLeave**. Click **Next**.

4. From the **Available Fields**, double-click **LastName** and **FirstName**. Click **Next**.

5. With **LeaveCategory** selected as the column heading, click **Next**.

6. With **LeaveDate** selected as the data to be shown, and **Count** as the **Function**, deselect the checkbox **Yes, include row sums**. Click **Next**.

7. Accept the suggested title and click **Finish**.

NOTE

Crosstab queries require that you have data suitable for summarizing. Many tables do not have fields appropriate to display as crosstabs.

Figure 6-17
Crosstab query results
**CC06
qryEmployeeLeave_
Crosstab**

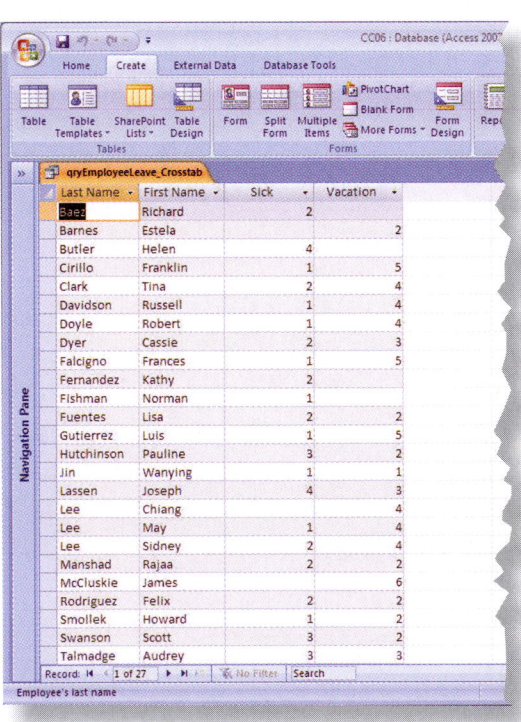

8. Switch to Design View. Two new rows were added to the design grid by the wizard: **Total** and **Crosstab**.

9. Close and save the query.

Exercise 6-17 USE THE FIND DUPLICATES QUERY WIZARD

The Find Duplicates Query Wizard analyzes a table for duplicate data. If duplicates are identified, you then decide what action to take, including deleting or editing the records. Because the Carolina Critters database has been normalized, you must first add a duplicate entry error to test the Find Duplicates Query that you will create.

1. Open **tblCustomers**. Copy the contents of the **Company Name** field for Customer "9."

2. Locate the record for the customer named "Magna Mart, Inc." Paste over "Magna Mart, Inc." Both records now have the same company name (a deliberate error). Close the table.

3. From the **Create** tab, in the **Other** group, click the Query Wizard command 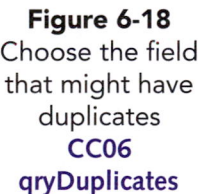.

4. In the **New Query** dialog box, double-click **Find Duplicates Query Wizard**.

5. From the list of table, select **Table: tblCustomers**. Click **Next**.

6. From the **Available fields** list, double-click **CompanyName**. Click **Next**.

Figure 6-18
Choose the field that might have duplicates
CC06
qryDuplicates

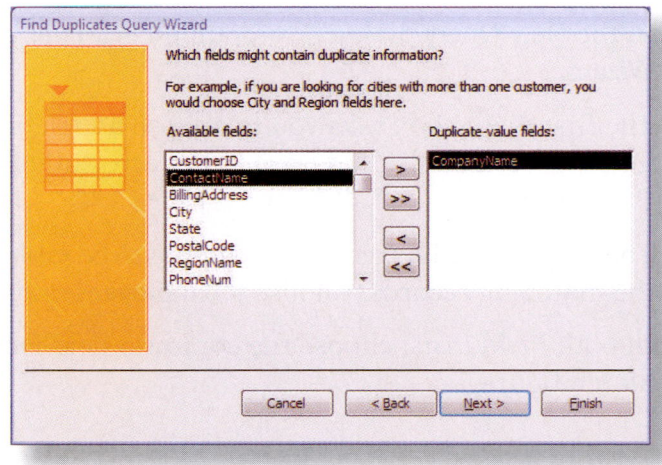

7. Click the Add All button to show all fields in the resulting dynaset. Click **Next**.

8. Delete the suggested title, and key **qryDuplicates**, and click **Finish**. The query shows the duplicate records. You could delete one now if that were the appropriate thing to do; however, do not delete anything.

9. For the **Customer ID** # 9, in the **Company Name** field, key **Magna Mart, Inc.**

10. From the **Home** tab, in the **Records** group, click the Refresh All command . The query runs again, but this time, there are no duplicates.

11. Close the query.

Exercise 6-18   USE THE FIND UNMATCHED QUERY WIZARD

The Find Unmatched Query Wizard finds unmatched, or orphaned, records. Since your database does not have any unrelated data, you must first add a deliberate error (an unmatched record) to test the Find Unmatched Records Query that you will create.

1. Open **tblReps** and add a new record for **Employee ID 999**. There is, of course, no employee with that ID. It is a deliberate error. Close the table.

2. From the **Create** tab, in the **Other** group, click the Query Wizard command 🔍.

3. In the **New Query** dialog box, double-click **Find Unmatched Query Wizard**.

4. The first dialog box asks you to choose a table that might have unmatched records. You created the error in **tblReps**, so choose it. Click **Next**.

5. The next dialog box asks you to choose the table that should have the matching records. Choose **tblEmployees** and click **Next**.

6. In both Field Lists, choose the common field **EmployeeID**. Click the Match button .

Figure 6-19
Match the common
field
CC06
qryNoEmp

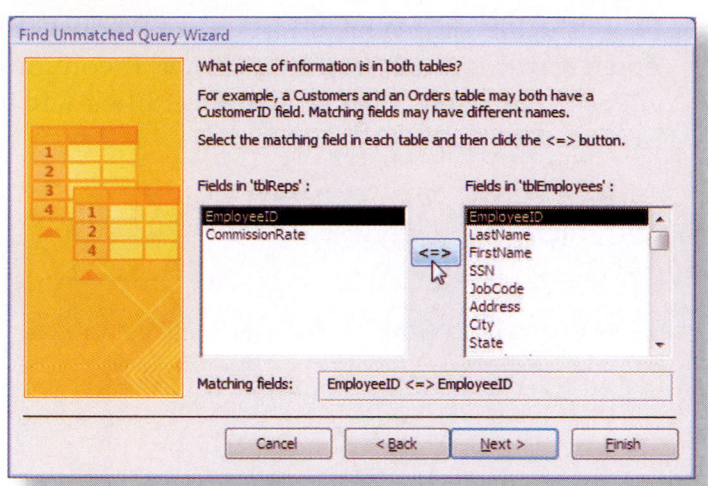

Figure 6-19
Match the common
field
CC06
qryNoEmp

7. Click **Next**. Click the Add All button to show all three fields in the query results. Click **Next**.

8. Delete the suggested title, and key **qryNoEmp**, and click **Finish**. The unmatched record you created is listed. The query shows you the problem record. Delete the record for **Employee ID** "999".

9. Close the query.

Applying PivotChart / PivotTable Views

PivotTables and PivotCharts are methods of viewing complex information in summarized formats. PivotTables and PivotCharts can automatically sort, count, and total data in a summarized format. You can change the summary's structure by dragging and dropping fields using a graphical interface.

You use a PivotTables and PivotCharts to analyze related totals or to compare related information from a large data set. In a PivotTable or PivotChart, each column or field in your source data becomes a PivotTable field that summarizes multiple rows of information. When you rearrange the fields in a PivotTable, the changes reflect as changes to columns in the related PivotChart. You can print PivotTables and PivotCharts similar to other objects.

Exercise 6-19   USE PIVOTTABLE VIEW

A *PivotTable* is an interactive table that combines and compares data in a summarized view. You create a PivotTable by using a graphical interface to drag and drop fields into appropriate column, row, and data locations.

1. Open **qryProductParts** in Design View.

2. From the **Design** tab, in the **Results** group, click the down arrow and choose PivotTable View.

3. From the PivotTable Field List, select **ProductName**. Click the drop-down arrow in the lower right corner. It contains a list of all drop zones in the chart. Choose **Row Area**. Click **Add to**.

Figure 6-20
Adding a field to a
PivotTable
CC06
qryProductParts

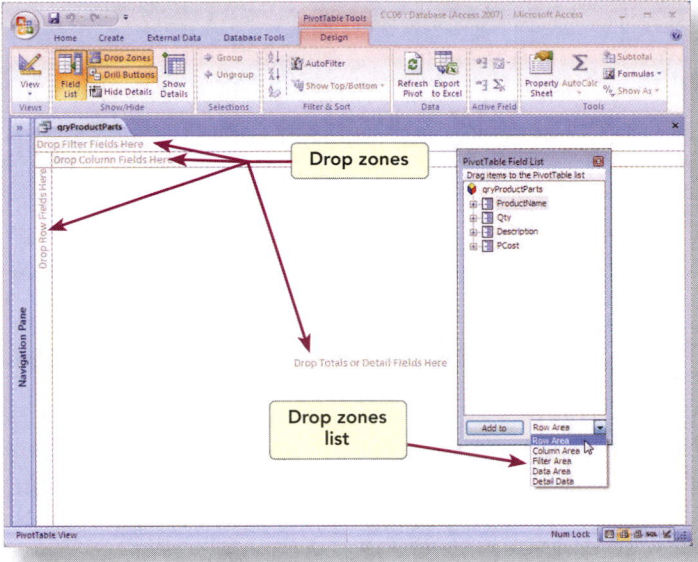

4. Drag the **Description** field from the **PivotTable** Field List into the **Drop Totals or Detail Fields Here** zone of the PivotTable.

5. From the **Design** tab, in the **Show/Hide** group, click the Field List command .

6. In the **Row Area** drop zone, click the **ProductName** button's drop-down arrow. Remove the checkmark for **All**. Add a checkmark to "Dudley Dog" and click **OK**.

7. Click the **ProductName** button's drop-down arrow. Add the checkmark for **All** and click **OK**.

8. Close and save the query.

Exercise 6-20   USE PIVOTCHART VIEW

A PivotChart View displays the same information as a crosstab query, including counts and sums of numeric fields. A *PivotChart View* is an interactive graphical representation of data displayed in a PivotTable.

A PivotChart displays field values which can be switched or pivoted to display different views of the same data. You set different levels of detail by dragging fields and items or by showing and hiding items in the field drop-down lists.

1. From the **Create** tab, in the **Other** group, click the Query Design command .

2. Double-click **tblStuffedAnimals** to add it to the grid and then close the **Show Table** dialog box.

3. Size the Field List.

4. Double-click **UnitPrice**, **ProductGroup**, and **ProductID** to add them to the design grid.

5. Save the query as **qryProductGroupsD&F**.

6. From the **Design** tab, in the **Results** group, click the down arrow and choose PivotChart View 📊.

7. Select **UnitPrice** from the Chart Field List. Click the drop-down arrow in the lower right corner. It contains a list of all drop zones in the chart. Choose **Data Area**.

8. Click **Add to**. An aggregate Sum function is automatically created.

NOTE

The Chart Field List displays a field name in a bold font whenever the field is used in the chart.

9. Drag the **ProductID** from the Chart Field List into the **Drop Category Fields Here** zone of the PivotChart. The Product IDs are listed at the bottom of the chart.

10. Drag the **ProductGroup** from the **Chart Field List** into the **Drop Series Fields Here** section of the PivotChart. Each Product Group has a different color.

11. From the **Design** tab, in the **Show/Hide** group, click the Field List command 📋 to remove the Field List.

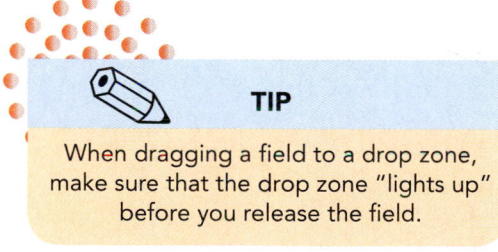

TIP

When dragging a field to a drop zone, make sure that the drop zone "lights up" before you release the field.

12. Drag the **ProductGroup** field button on top of the **ProductID** field button and slightly to the left. Both fields are now being used for the X-axis of the chart.

Figure 6-21
Two field x-axis
CC06
qryProductGroupsD&F

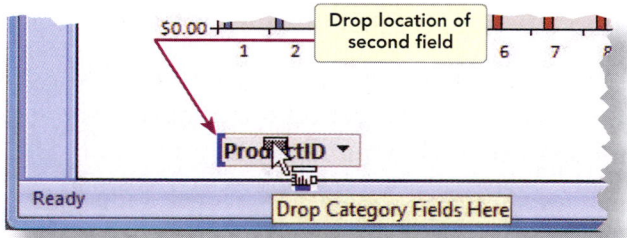

13. Click the drop-down arrow for **ProductGroup**. Deselect C, E, and T.

Access 2007

Figure 6-22
Product Groups D
and F
CC06
qryProductGroupsD&F

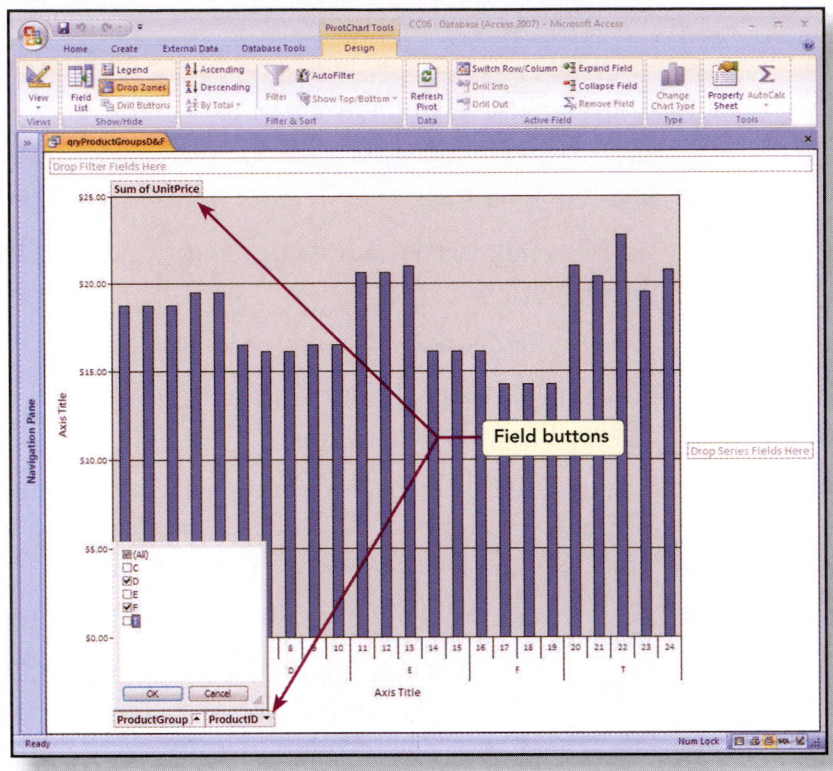

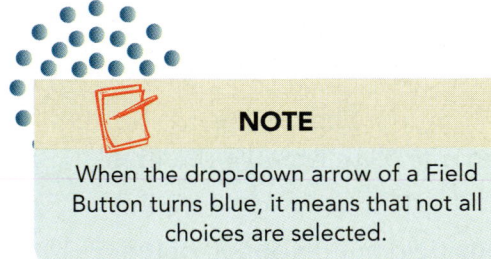

NOTE

When the drop-down arrow of a Field Button turns blue, it means that not all choices are selected.

14. Click **OK**. Only the Product IDs for product groups D and F are now visible.

15. Right-click the **Axis Title** at the bottom of the chart. Choose **Properties**. Click the **Format** tab. Key **Product ID / Product Group** as the new **Caption**.

16. Click the **Axis Title** to the left of the chart. Clicking on a new object automatically switches the Property Sheet to that new object. Key **List Price** as the new **Caption**. Close the Properties Sheet.

17. From the **Design** tab, in the **Show/Hide** group, click the Drop Zones command to remove the unused drop zones.

18. Switch to Datasheet View. Notice that making changes to the query's PivotChart has no effect on the dynaset. The PivotChart View is just another way of viewing the data.

19. Save and close the query.

20. Compact and close the database.

Lesson 6 Summary

- Only a single filter can be saved per table, but multiple queries can be associated to a single table.

- A select query, the most common type of query, locates data from one or more tables and displays the results as a datasheet.

- The Query Design window has an upper and lower pane. The upper pane is the Field List pane in which you choose the data source from one or more Field Lists. The lower pane is the design grid in which you specify criteria.

- A dynaset is dynamic recordset that automatically reflects changes to its underlying data source.

- In the design grid of a query, the check box in the **Show** row indicates that the field will display in the Datasheet View.

- When two or more tables are used in a query, the tables must be linked through a common field.

- In a query, more than one condition can be placed on multiple fields.

- An operator is a word or symbol that indicates a specific arithmetic or logical relationship between the elements of an expression.

- Operators can include arithmetic operators, comparison operators, logical operators, concatenation operators, and special operators.

- A function is a procedure used in an expression.

- An argument is a reference in a function assigned as a single variable.

- Criterion using text values include leading and closing quotation marks. Criterion using date values include leading and closing pound signs (#). Numbers and expressions do not require leading or closing symbols.

- When using a wildcard in the **Criteria** row of a query, the "Like" operator compares the criterion condition to each record.

- Only the keyword "Like" is automatically added to a criterion. All other keywords must be specified.

- Criterion expressions can be viewed in the Zoom box. You can open the Zoom box by pressing Shift + F2.

- An AND criterion exists when two conditions must occur simultaneously for the statement to be true.

- An OR criterion exists when one of two conditions must occur for the statement to be true.

- When using the Top Values property, Access displays records based upon the defined sort order.

- The Top Values property displays either a static number of records (such as the top five) or a percentage of all records in the dynaset (such as the top 5%).

- A calculated field is a field that uses an expression or formula as its data source.

- When a field does not have a name, Access assigns an alias name. The alias name for a calculated field displays as text followed by a colon.

- Calculated fields can be entered directly into the design grid or can be entered using the Expression Builder. The Expression Builder is an interface used to create a function, calculation, or expression.

- A crosstab query displays information similar to a spreadsheet. Crosstab queries require that you have data suitable for summarizing. Many tables do not have fields appropriate to display as a crosstab.

- The Find Duplicates Query Wizard analyzes a table for duplicate data.

- The Find Unmatched Query Wizard finds unmatched, or orphaned, records.

- A PivotTable is an interactive table that combines and compares data in a summarized view.

- A PivotChart is an interactive graphical representation of data displayed in a PivotTable.

LESSON 6		Command Summary	
Feature	Button	Menu	Keyboard
	<=>	Match	
		Home, Records, Refresh All	
	>>	Add All	
		Create, Other, Query Wizard	
		Design, Query Setup, Builder	
		Create, Other, Query Design	
Rows, Delete		Design, Query Setup, Delete Rows	
Query, View		Design, Results, View	
Query, Run	!	Design, Results, Run	
Query Design, View		Create, Other, Query Design	
Query, Properties, View		Design, Show/Hide, Properties Sheet	

Concepts Review

True/False Questions

Each of the following statements is either true or false. Indicate your choice by circling T or F.

T F   1. You cannot add records in a dynaset.

T F   2. You can build criteria by using logical and relational operators.

T F   3. You cannot use a query as the source of records for another query.

T F   4. You can add a field to a query in Design View by double-clicking the field name in the Field List window.

T F   5. Count and Sum are types of aggregate functions.

T F   6. Before using the Top Values property, you must sort a dynaset by its primary key.

T F   7. In the design grid, OR criteria are entered in the same row.

T F   8. The criteria "is not null" finds records with a blank or empty field.

Short Answer Questions

Write the correct answer in the space provided.

1. What is the grid name of the lower pane of a query in which you sort data and enter criteria?

_____

2. In what view do you see the dynaset of a query?

_____

3. What property displays the highest or lowest values?

_____

4. What type of criteria do you use when you want two conditions to be true at the same time?

_____

5. In the Design View of a query, what row displays "Group By" or "Count"?

_____

6. In Access, what keyword(s) means is "blank" or is "empty"?

_____

7. When you key a wildcard in a query, what operator does Access use to compare your criteria with each record?

_____

8. What symbol represents "not equal?"

_____

Critical Thinking

Answer these questions on a separate page. There are no right or wrong answers. Support your answers with examples from your own experience, if possible.

1. When an expression has two or more math operators, the Expression Builder follows the mathematical order of operations rules. List these rules, as well as all symbols used with each of them, and give examples of their use.

2. AND and OR criteria are common to databases, programming, and spreadsheets. You can build a logic table to help you visualize what happens with two criteria in these situations. Complete this table (on a separate sheet of paper) to show if the result is True or False (a match or no match).

Figure 6-23
Logic table

AND			OR		
First Criterion	Second Criterion	Answer ? (T/F)	First Criterion	Second Criterion	Answer ? (T/F)
T	AND T	=	T	OR T	=
T	AND F	=	T	OR F	=
F	AND T	=	F	OR T	=
F	AND F	=	F	OR F	=

Skills Review

Exercise 6-21

Create a select query. Add and remove fields to a query. Add a calculation. Sort a query. Print/Save a query's dynaset and Documenter report.

1. Open a database by following these steps:
   a. Locate and open the **Lesson 06** folder.
   b. Make a copy of CC06 and rename it to *[your initials]*-**CC06**.
   c. Open and enable content for *[your initials]*-**CC06**.

2. Create the query by following these steps:

a. From the **Create** tab, in the **Other** group, click the Query Design command 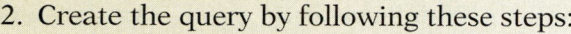.

b. In the **Show Table** dialog box, double-click **tblEmployees** and click **Close**.

c. Resize the Field List so all fields can be seen.

d. From the **tblEmployees** Field List, double-click **EmployeeID**, **LastName** and **FirstName**.

e. From the Quick Access toolbar, click Save . Name the query **06-21-**_[your initials]_.

3. Add a calculation to a query by following these steps:

a. In the design grid, click in the forth column.

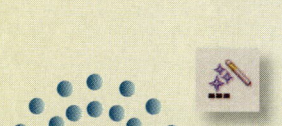

b. From the **Design** tab, in the **Query Setup** group, click the Builder command .

c. In the middle panel, double-click **LastName**.

d. In the expression box, after "[LastName]" key **&", "&** (ampersand, double quote, comma, space, double quote, amperstand.)

> **NOTE**
>
> Make sure that you add a space after the comma in the quotes.

e. In the middle panel, double-click **FirstName**.

f. Click **OK**.

g. Replace "Expr1" with **FullName**. Be certain to leave the colon after the field name.

4. Sort and delete fields by following these steps:

a. In the **Sort** row for **FullName**, click the drop-down arrow and choose **Ascending**.

b. In the design grid, select both the **LastName** and the **FirstName** fields. Press Delete to remove the fields from the design grid.

c. From the Quick Access toolbar, click Save 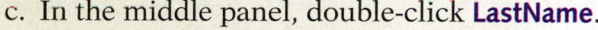.

d. From the **Design** tab, in the **Results** group, click the View command to switch to Datasheet View.

e. Size columns appropriately.

5. Print/Save a query's dynaset and Documenter report by following these steps:

a. Click the Office Button . From the **Print** option, choose Print Preview .

b. Print/Save the query.

c. Close **Print Preview** and the query.

d. From the **Database Tools** tab, in the **Analyze** group, click the Database Documenter command .

e. From the **Documenter** dialog box, click the query **06-21-**_[your initials]_ checkbox and click **Options**.

f. Only include **Properties** and **SQL** for the query and nothing else. Click **OK**.

g. Click **OK** to go to **Print Preview**.

h. From the **Print Preview** tab, in the **Page Layout** group, click **Margins** and choose the Wide command ⊞ from the menu.

i. Print/Save the report.

j. Close **Print Preview**.

Exercise 6-22

Create a query with a wizard. Add criteria to a query. Sort and hide a field. Print/Save a dynaset.

1. Use the Simple Query Wizard by following these steps:

   a. Open and enable content for *[your initials]*-**CC06.**

   b. From the **Create** tab, in the **Other** group, click the Query Wizard command ⊞ .

   c. In the **New Query** dialog box, double-click **Simple Query Wizard**.

   d. From the **Tables/Queries** list box, choose **Table: tblEmployees**.

   e. In the **Available Fields** list, double-click **LastName**, **FirstName**, and **JobCode**.

   f. From the **Tables/Queries** list box, choose **Table: tblJobCodes**.

   g. In the **Available Fields** list, double-click **JobTitle**.

   h. From the **Tables/Queries** list box, choose **Table: tblPay**.

   i. In the **Available Fields** list, double-click **EmpPay** and **PayClass**.

   j. Click **Next**. The default type of select query is **Detail**. Click **Next**.

   k. Delete the suggested title and key **06-22-***[your initials]*. Click **Finish**.

2. Add criteria to fields by following these steps:

   a. Switch to Design View. Resize and move each Field List.

   b. In the **Criteria** row for **JobCode**, key **mf03**, press ⬇, and key **mf04**.

   c. In the **Criteria** row for **PayClass**, key **2**, and press ⬇, and key **2**. Pay class 2 represents hourly employees.

3. Sort and hide a field by following these steps:

   a. In the **Sort** row for **JobTitle**, click the drop-down arrow and choose **Ascending**.

   b. In the **Show** row for **PayClass**, remove the checkmark. This field is only needed for criteria, so there is no need to include it in the final dynaset.

   c. Switch to Datasheet View. Resize each field appropriately.

4. Print/Save a query's dynaset by following these steps:

   a. Click the Office Button ⊞. From the **Print** option, choose Print Preview ⊞ .

   b. Print/Save the query.

   c. Close **Print Preview** and the query.

Exercise 6-23

Create a query in Design View. Add a criterion to a query. Sort and show the top 5% of records. Print/Save a dynaset and Database Documenter report.

1. Create a query in Design View by following these steps:

   a. Open and enable content for *[your initials]*-**CC06**.

   b. From the **Create** tab, in the **Other** group, click the Query Design command .

   c. In the **Show Table** dialog box, double-click **tblInvoices**, **tblInvoiceLineItems**, and **tblStuffedAnimals**. Click **Close**.

   d. Resize the Field List so all fields can be seen.

   e. From the **tblInvoices** Field List, double-click **InvoiceID**, **ShipDate**, and **CustomerID**.

   f. From the **tblStuffedAnimals** Field List, double-click **ProductName**.

   g. From the **tblInvoiceLineItems** Field List, double-click **Qty**.

   h. From the Quick Access toolbar, click Save . Name the query **06-23-***[your initials]*.

2. Add a criterion to a field by following these steps:

   a. In the **Criteria** row for **ShipDate**, key **between 10/1/2006 and 1/1/2007**.

3. Sort and show the top 5% of records by following these steps:

   a. In the **Sort** row for **Qty**, click the drop-down arrow and choose **Descending**.

   b. From the **Design** tab, in the **Query Setup** group, click the Return list box (Top Value) and choose **5%**.

   c. Switch to Datasheet View. Resize columns appropriately.

4. Print/Save a query's dynaset and Documenter report by following these steps:

   a. Click the Office Button . From the **Print** option, choose Print Preview .

   b. Print/Save the query.

   c. Close **Print Preview** and the query.

   d. From the **Database Tools** tab, in the **Analyze** group, click the Database Documenter command .

   e. From the **Documenter** dialog box, click the **06-23-***[your initials]* check box and click **Options**.

   f. Only include **Properties** and **SQL** for the query and nothing else. Click **OK**.

   g. Click **OK** to go to **Print Preview**.

h. From the **Print Preview** tab, in the **Page Layout** group, click **Margins** and choose the Wide command from the menu.

i. Print/Save the report.

j. Close **Print Preview**.

Exercise 6-24

Create a query in Design View. Add a criterion to a field. Modify a query PivotChart view. Print a PivotChart and Database Documenter report.

1. Create a query in Design View by following these steps:

   a. Open and enable content for *[your initials]*-**CC06**.

   b. From the **Create** tab, in the **Other** group, click the Query Design command 🗗.

   c. In the **Show Table** dialog box, double-click **tblEmployees** and **tblLeaveDays**. Click **Close**.

   d. Resize the Field List so all fields can be seen.

   e. From the **tblEmployees** Field List, double-click **JobCode**.

   f. From the **tblLeaveDays** Field List, double-click **LeaveDate** and **LeaveCategory**.

   g. From the Quick Access toolbar, click Save 🖫. Name the query **06-24-***[your initials]*.

2. Add a criterion by following these steps:

   a. In the **Criteria** row for **JobCode**, key **m***.

3. Modify a PivotChart view by following these steps:

   a. Switch to PivotChart View. From the Chart Field List, click the Expand button ⊞ for **LeaveDate By Month**. Drag the **Months** into the **Drop Category Fields Here** zone (bottom of the chart) of the PivotChart.

   b. From the Chart Field List, drag the **LeaveCategory** into the **Drop Series Fields Here** zone (right of the chart) of the PivotChart.

   c. From the Chart Field List, drag the **LeaveCategory** into the **Drop Data Fields Here** zone (middle of the chart) of the PivotChart. The default function for this data type is Count.

   d. Close the Chart Field List. From the **Design** tab, in the **Tools** group, click the Property Sheet command 🖺.

   e. On the PivotChart, click the Value Axis (left of the chart). In the **Properties** dialog box, click the **Format** tab. Change the **Caption** property to **Number of days**.

   f. On the PivotChart, click the Category Axis (bottom of the chart). In the **Properties** dialog box, change the **Caption** property to **Year to date**. Close the **Properties** dialog box.

   g. From the **Design** tab, in the **Show/Hide** group, click the Drop Zone command 🗗 to remove the zone markers.

h. From the **Design** tab, in the **Show/Hide** group, click the Legend command to add the Legend to the PivotChart.

i. Save the query.

4. Print/Save a query's dynaset and Database Documenter report by following these steps:

a. Click the Office button . From the **Print** option, choose Print Preview .

b. From the **Print Preview** tab, in the **Page Layout** group, click the Landscape command 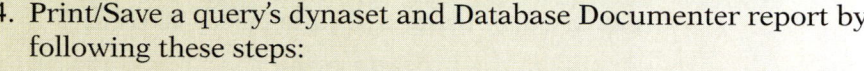 from the menu.

c. Print/Save the query's PivotChart View.

d. Close **Print Preview** and the query.

e. From the **Database Tools** tab, in the **Analyze** group, click the Database Documenter command .

f. From the **Documenter** dialog box, click the **06-24-[your initials]** check box and click **Options**.

g. Only include **Properties** and **SQL** for the query and nothing else. Click **OK**.

h. Click **OK** to go to **Print Preview**.

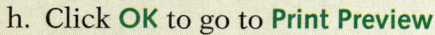

i. From the **Print Preview** tab, in the **Page Layout** group, click **Margins** and choose the Wide command from the menu.

j. Print/Save the report.

k. Close **Print Preview**.

Lesson Applications

Exercise 6-25

Create a query using a Simple Query Wizard.

1. Open *[your initials]*-CC06.

2. Launch the Simple Query Wizard.

3. From **tblEmployee**, use the fields **LastName** and **FirstName**. From **tblRegions**, add **RegionName**.

4. Save the query as **06-25-***[your initials]*.

5. Sort the dynaset in ascending order by **LastName**.

 6. Print/Save the Datasheet View of the query.

Exercise 6-26

Create query in Design View.

1. Using *[your initials]*-**CC06**, create a new query in Design View.

2. From **tblEmployees**, add the fields **LastName** and **FirstName**.

3. From **tblEmployeeDates**, add the field **HireDate** and remove the **Show** checkmark.

4. Create a calculated field using the function **DateDiff("yyyy",[HireDate], now())**. Set the format to **0" years"** and the alias to **Tenure**.

5. For the field **Tenure**, sort in descending order.

6. From **tblEmployeeDates**, add the field **EndDate**.

7. For the field **EndDate**, set the criterion to **Is Null** and remove the **Show** checkmark.

8. Set **Top Value** to **5**.

9. Name the query **06-26-***[your initials]*.

 10. Print/Save the Datasheet View of the query.

11. Print/Save a Database Documenter report displaying only the **Properties** and **SQL** options for the query.

Exercise 6-27

Create a query in Design View.

1. Using *[your initials]***-CC06**, create a new query in Design View.

2. Include **tblCustomers**, **tblInvoices**, **tblInvoiceLineItems**, and **tblStuffedAnimals**.

3. From **tblCustomers**, add **CompanyName**.

4. From **tblInvoiceLineItems,** add the field **Qty** field and remove the **Show** checkmark.

5. From **tblStuffedAnimals**, add the field **UnitPrice** and remove the **Show** checkmark.

6. Create a calculated field by multiplying the field **Qty** and by the field **UnitPrice**. Set the format to currency with two decimal places and the alias to **Revenue**.

7. In PivotChart View, perform the following actions:

   - Add **CompanyName** to the X-axis.

   - Add **Revenue** to the **Data** are with a default function of **SUM**.

   - Rename the X-axis to **Customers-***[your full name]*.

   - Rename the Y-axis to **Total Sales**.

   - Remove the drop zones.

8. Save the query as **06-27-***[your initials]*.

 9. Print/Save PivotChart View in Landscape layout.

 10. Print/Save a Database Documenter report displaying only the **Properties** and **SQL** options for the query.

Exercise 6-28 ◆ Challenge Yourself

Create a query in Design View.

1. Using *[your initials]***-CC06**, create a new query in Design View.

2. Include **tblEmployees**, **tblPayrollHistory**, **tblPayrollRates**, and **tblPay**.

3. From **tblEmployees**, add **LastName**, **FirstName**, and **JobCode**.

4. From **tblPayHistory**, add **PayNum** and **OvHr**.

5. From **tblPayrollRates**, add **OverTime**.

6. From **tblPay**, add **EmpPay**.

7. Create a calculated field using the expression **OvHr** multiplied by **EmpPay** multiplied by **OverTime**. Set the format to currency with two decimal places and the alias to **Over Time Cost**.

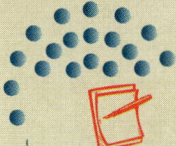

NOTE

Only eight records will appear in the dynaset when the criteria are properly applied.

8. Using a single **Criteria** row, perform the following:

   - For the field **JobCode**, set the criterion to **m***.
   - For the field **PayNum**, set the criterion to **>=23**.
   - For the field **OvHr**, set the criterion to **Is Not Null**.

9. Name the query **06-28-**_[your initials]_.

10. Print/Save the Datasheet View of the query in Landscape orientation.

11. Print/Save a Database Documenter report displaying only the **Properties** and **SQL** options for the query.

On Your Own

In these exercises, you work on your own, as you would in a real-life work environment. Use the skills you've learned to accomplish the task—and be creative.

Exercise 6-29

Review the design of the database that you modified in Exercise 5-28. On a sheet of paper, list information that a user of your database might need. Design three queries that might provide the information needed. Use a variety of query types. Write your name and Exercise 6-29. Before proceeding to the next exercise, have your instructor approve your database design and intentions. Continue to the next exercise.

Exercise 6-30

Create the queries you designed in Exercise 6-29. Enter at least five additional records into each table of the database. Print the tables. Review the design of the database. On a sheet of paper, design a dynaset that incorporates data from two or more tables. Identify the type of query needed to create the dynaset. On the same sheet of paper, list all fields to be used in the query. For each field, include the name of the table from which the field originates. Identify the key fields and any foreign fields. Write down the criteria that would be required for the query. Name the query appropriately. Write your name and "Exercise 6-30" on each sketch. Continue to the next exercise.

Exercise 6-31

Based on the designs that you created in Exercises 6-29 and 6-30, create the queries. Print the definitions for each query. Print a copy of the dynaset for each query. Submit to your instructor your designs and the printouts that you created for Exercises 6-29 through 6-31. Keep a copy of the database you modified in this exercise. You will use it for the On Your Own exercises in subsequent lessons.

Adding and Modifying Forms

OBJECTIVES

After completing this lesson, you will be able to:

1. Generate forms quickly.
2. Modify controls in layout view.
3. Work with form sections.
4. Modify controls in Design View.
5. Add calculated controls to a form.
6. Print/Save forms.

Estimated Time: 2 hours

MCAS OBJECTIVES

In this lesson:
AC07 70-605 2.5.2
AC07 70-605 2.5.3
AC07 70-605 2.5.4
AC07 70-605 2.5.7
AC07 70-605 2.5.8
AC07 70-605 2.7.1
AC07 70-605 2.7.2
AC07 70-605 2.7.3
AC07 70-605 2.7.4
AC07 70-605 2.7.5
AC07 70-605 2.7.7
AC07 70-605 5.5
AC07 70-605 5.6

Although you can enter, edit, and delete data directly in the datasheet of a query or table, database operators usually use forms to perform these activities. When you use the datasheet view of a table or a query, the dynaset can display only in columns and rows. When each record of the dynaset contains numerous fields, the entire record cannot be seen at once.

The limitations of a datasheet emphasize the need for forms. A form can be designed to view an entire record on a single screen. Other advantages of forms include the following:

- You can arrange data in an attractive format that may include special fonts, colors, shading, and images.

- You can design a form to match a paper source document.

- You can include calculations, functions, and totals in the form.

- You can display data from more than one table.

Generating Forms Quickly

The quickest way to create a form is to use the Form Wizard or to use a form tool. When using the Form Wizard, select the source dynaset(s), fields, layout, and style. The fields may come from multiple tables or queries, as long as a relationship exists between the recordsets.

When using either of the first three Form tools, all fields from the source dynaset are automatically placed on the form. You can use the new form immediately, or you can modify the form in Layout View or Design View. Database designers often use either the Form Wizard or a Form tool to create a beginning form that they can later modify and enhance.

Exercise 7-1   CREATE A FORM WITH A WIZARD

The Form Wizard lets you select fields, a layout, and a style. The layout determines whether the records are arranged in columns, rows, or a hybrid of columns and rows. The style automatically determines colors, backgrounds, and fonts used for the form.

> **NOTE**
>
> A form is created from a recordset and does not have to include all the fields from the query or table.

1. Locate and open the **Lesson 07** folder.

2. Make a copy of **CC07** and rename it *[your initials]*-**CC07**.

3. Open and enable content for *[your initials]*-**CC07**.

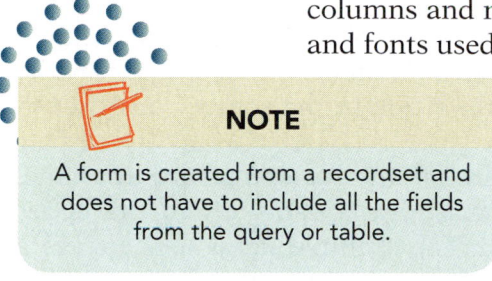

4. From the **Create** tab, in the **Forms** group, click **More Forms** and choose the Form Wizard command .

Figure 7-1
Form Wizard
CC07

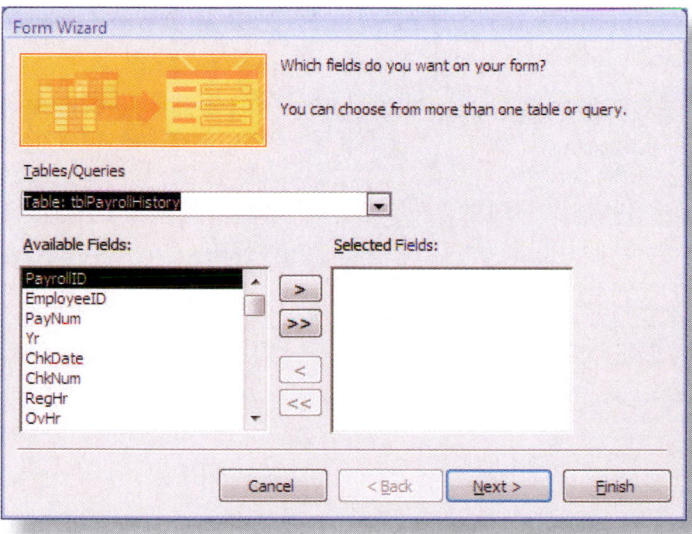

5. In the **Tables/Queries** drop-down box, choose **Table: tblPayrollHistory**.

6. The dialog box asks which fields to use in the form. Click the Add All button to choose all fields.

7. Click **PayrollID** in the **Selected Field** list. Click the Remove One button to move it back to the list on the left.

8. Click **Next**. The dialog box asks you to choose a layout. Click each layout to see a preview. Select **Tabular**.

Access 2007

9. Click **Next**. The next dialog box lists several styles. Click each style to see a preview. Select **Apex**.

10. Click **Next**. The dialog box asks for a title for the form. This title is used as both a title and the name of the form. Key **frmPayrollHistory**.

11. Select **Open the form to view or enter information** and then click **Finish**.

12. Close the form.

Exercise 7-2   GENERATE A FORM WITH ONE CLICK

When using the Forms tool, you can create a Simple Form, Split, or Multiple Items Form by selecting the appropriate command button located in the **Forms** group. Each command uses all the fields in the source recordset to create a pre-determined form.

The Simple Form tool creates a form for entering one record at a time. The Split Form tool creates a form that shows a datasheet in the upper section and a form in the lower section. The Multiple Items tool creates a form that shows multiple items in a datasheet, with one record per row.

1. In the Navigation Pane, select **tblPayrollHistory**.

2. From the **Create** tab, in the **Forms** group, click the Form command. The new form is now in Layout View and shows only one record.

Figure 7-2
New form in
Layout View
CC07
frmPayrollHistoryOne

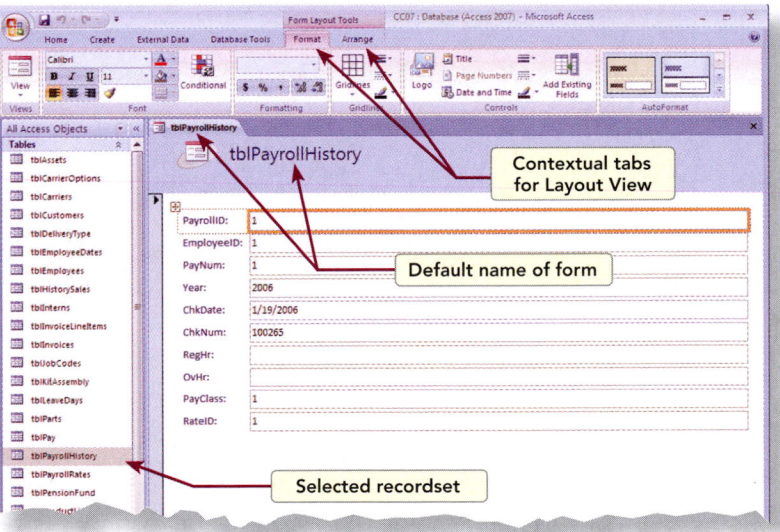

3. Right-click the new form's document tab and choose **Save**. The default name is the name of the recordset used to create the form.

4. In the **Save As** dialog box, key **frmPayHistoryOne** and click **OK**.

5. In the Navigation Pane, select **tblPayrollHistory** again.

6. From the **Create** tab, in the **Forms** group, click the Split Form command 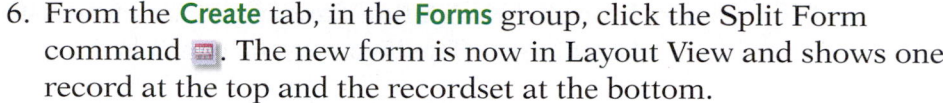. The new form is now in Layout View and shows one record at the top and the recordset at the bottom.

7. From the Quick Access toolbar, click the Save button to save the new form.

8. In the **Save As** dialog box, key **frmPayHistorySplit** and click **OK**.

9. In the Navigation Pane, select **tblPayrollHistory** again.

10. From the **Create** tab, in the **Forms** group, click the Multiple Items command . The new form is now in Layout View and shows all records.

11. Press Ctrl+S to save the new form.

12. In the **Save As** dialog box, key **frmPayHistoryList** and click **OK**.

13. In the Navigation Pane, select **tblPayrollHistory** again.

14. From the **Create** tab, in the **Forms** group, click **More Forms** and choose the Datasheet command . The new form is now in Datasheet View and shows all records.

15. Press Ctrl+S to save the new form.

16. In the **Save As** dialog box, key **frmPayHistoryData** and click **OK**.

17. Right-click any document tab and choose **Close All**.

Modifying Controls in Layout View

A *control* is a database object that displays data, performs actions, and lets you view and work with information that enhances the user interface, such as labels and images. Controls can be bound, unbound, or calculated.

A *bound control* is a control whose source of data is a field in a table or query. You use bound controls to display values from the dynaset. The values can be text, dates, numbers, Yes/No values, pictures, or graphs. An *unbound control* is a control without a source of data. You use unbound controls to display lines, rectangles, or pictures. A *calculated control* is a control whose source of data is an expression, rather than a field.

Exercise 7-3   MODIFY A CONTROL LAYOUT

A control layout assists you to horizontally and vertically align the controls within a form. A control layout is similar to a table in which each cell is a control. In addition to creating a control layout, you can switch a control layout between tabular and stacked, split one control layout into two, and change the padding or margins of the controls.

Control padding is the space between the gridline of the form and the control. A *control margin* is the specified location of information inside a control.

1. From the Navigation Pane, right-click **frmCustomers** and choose **Layout View**. The layout of the controls is known as Stacked.

Figure 7-3
Form in Layout View
CC07
frmCustomers

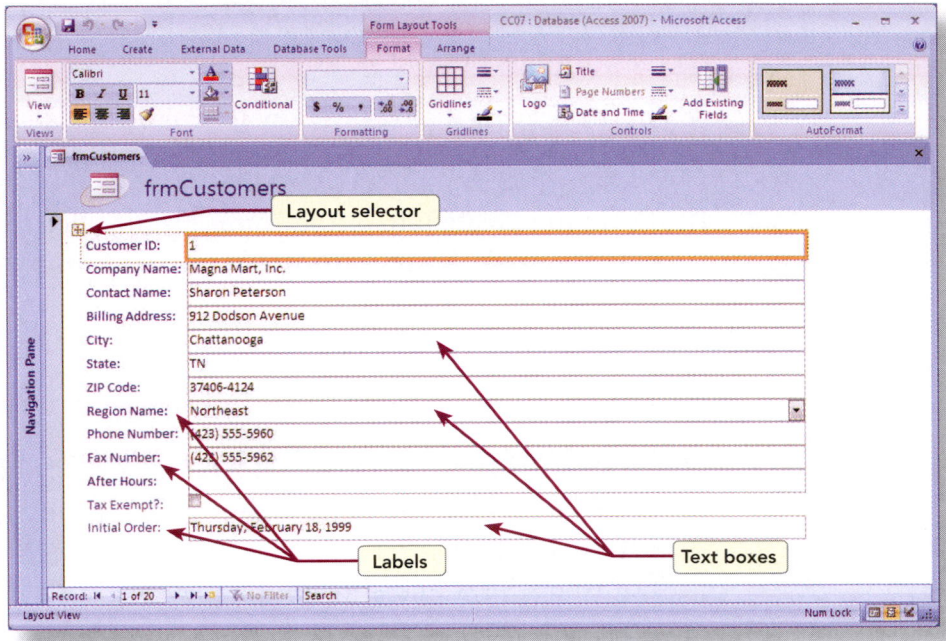

2. Click the Layout Selector command . This selects the entire control layout.

3. From the **Arrange** tab, in the **Control Layout** group, click **Control Padding** and choose the Narrow command . Space has been added between all controls.

4. From the **Arrange** tab, in the **Control Layout** group, click **Control Margins** and choose the Medium command . Space has been added between the content of the controls and the outside edge of the controls.

Exercise 7-4   RESIZE AND MOVE CONTROL LAYOUTS

Layout View is an efficient means to resize and move controls within a form. While viewing the source data on the form, you can rearrange the controls and adjust their sizes to improve the form's appearance and functionality.

1. Click the first text box (contains 1). An orange box indicates the selected control.

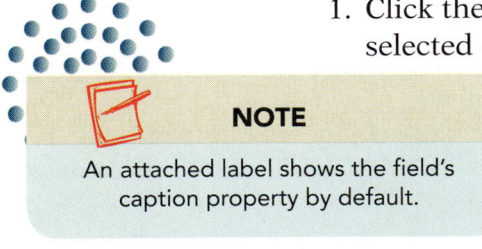

NOTE

An attached label shows the field's caption property by default.

2. Place your mouse pointer on the right edge of the select text box. When you see the resize pointer, drag it to the left to make the controls smaller, but make sure you still can see all the data.

Figure 7-4
Resize a text box in
Form Layout View
CC07
frmCustomers

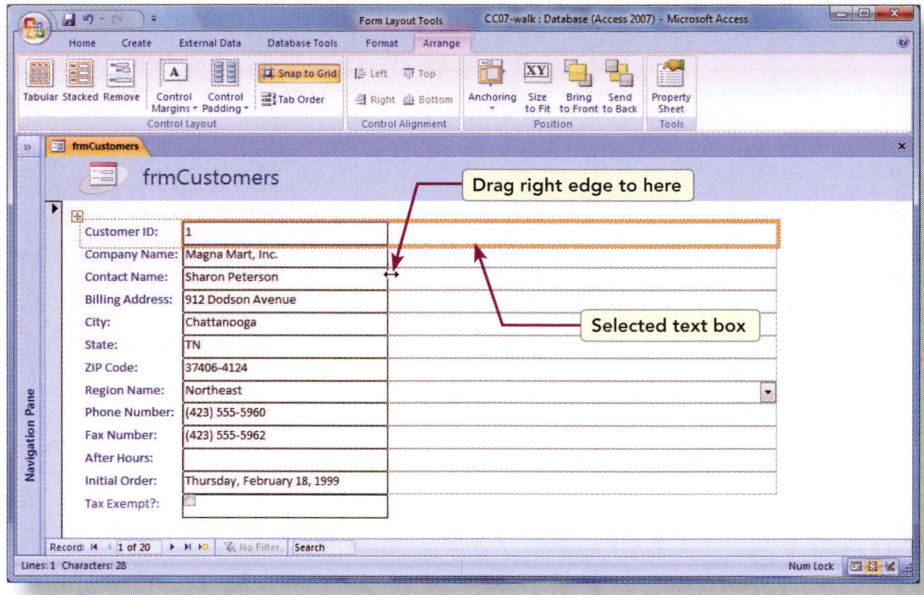

3. Click the **Billing Address** text box.

4. While pressing Shift, click the text boxes for **City**, **State**, and **Zip Code**. This action selects the four controls.

5. From the **Arrange** tab, in the **Control Layout** group, click the Stacked command. The four controls have created their own control layout.

6. Drag the new control layout so that it is located to the right of the other control layout and the top margins are aligned.

FIGURE 7-5
Moving a control
layout
CC07
frmCustomers

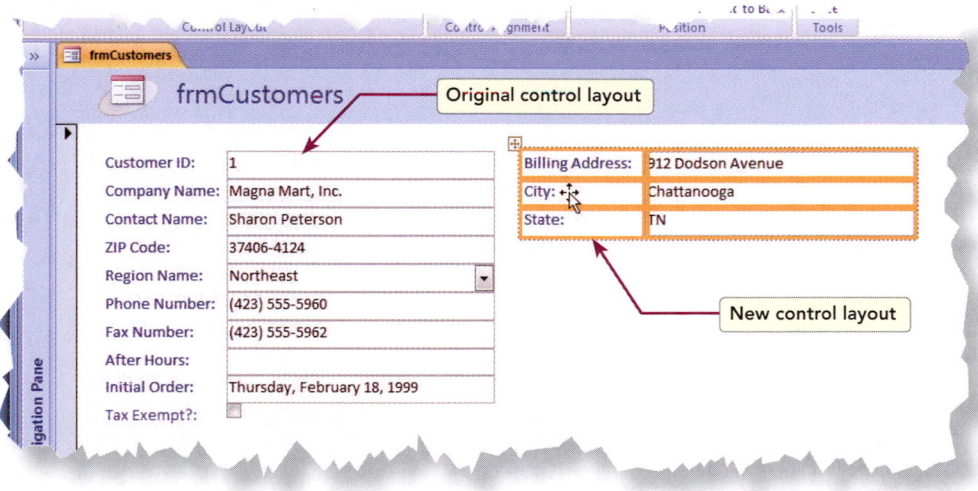

7. Click the **Phone Number** text box.

8. Press Shift and click the text box for **Fax Number**.

9. From the **Arrange** tab, in the **Control Layout** group, click the Stacked command.

10. Align the newest control layout under the **Zip Code** control. Leave about ¼ inch of space between the two control layouts.

11. Click the **After Hours** text box.

12. While pressing Shift, click the **Initial Order** text box and **Tax Exempt?** check box.

13. From the **Arrange** tab, in the **Control Layout** group, click the Stacked command 📇.

14. Drag the newest control layout down about ¼ inch below **Region Name**.

15. Save the form.

Exercise 7-5   ALIGN CONTROL LAYOUTS

When aligning selected controls, you change where the controls appear on the form. Selecting an alignment of "left" moves all controls so that the left edge of each control is aligned with the left edge of the control farthest to the left. Selecting "top" moves all controls so that the top edge of each control aligns with the top edge of the highest control. Aligning a control is different than aligning the text within a control. Aligning the text within a control does not change the placement of the control on the form, only the contents of the control.

Table 7-1 Alignment Options

Choose	To Do This
Left	Vertically align the left edges of the controls with the control that is the farthest to the left.
Right	Vertically align the right edges of the controls with the control that is the farthest to the right.
Top	Horizontally align the top edges of the controls with the control that is the highest.
Bottom	Horizontally align the bottom edges of the controls with the control that is the lowest.
To Grid	Align the uppermost corner of the selected control with the design grid.

1. Click the **Customer ID** text box. Click the layout selector for that control layout.

2. While pressing Shift, click the **Billing Address** text box. Now the layout selector is visible for the second control layout. While pressing Shift, click the layout selector for the second control layout. Both control layouts should now be selected.

Figure 7-6
Aligning two control
layouts
CC07
frmCustomers

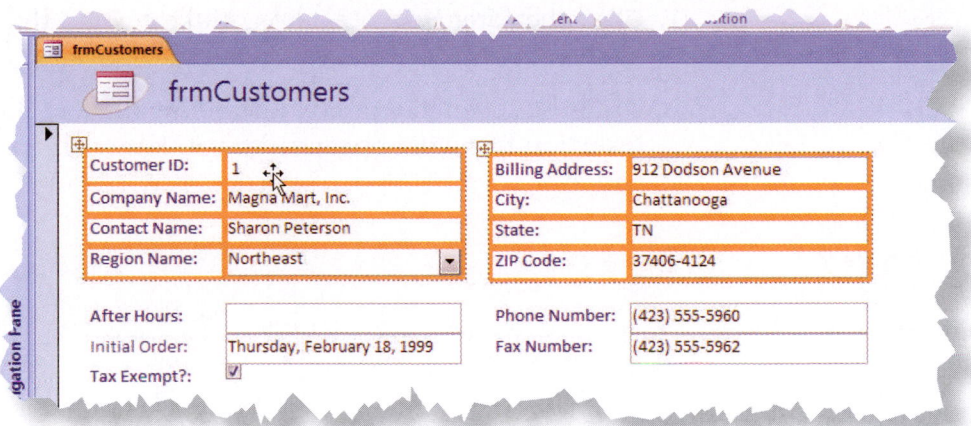

3. From the **Arrange** tab, in the **Control Alignment** group, click the Top command .

4. While pressing Shift, click the **Billing Address** layout selector. This action removes that control layout from the selection.

5. While pressing Shift, click the **After Hours** text box. Now that the layout selector is visible for the second control layout, click it. Both control layouts should now be selected.

6. From the **Arrange** tab, in the **Control Alignment** group, click the Left command .

7. Click the **Billing Address** text box. Click the layout selector for this control layout.

8. While pressing Shift, click the **Phone Number** text box. Now that the layout selector is visible for the second control layout, click it. Both control layouts should now be selected.

9. From the **Arrange** tab, in the **Control Alignment** group, click the Left command.

10. Save the form.

Exercise 7-6 REMOVE AND ADD CONTROLS TO A CONTROL LAYOUT

A single form can have multiple control layouts. For example, you might use a tabular layout to create a row of data for each record, and then one or more stacked layouts underneath that contain more data from the same record.

In tabular control layouts, controls are arranged in rows and columns like a spreadsheet, with labels across the top. Tabular control layouts always span two sections of a form; whichever section the controls are in, the labels are in the section above it.

In stacked layouts, controls are arranged vertically, like you might see on a paper form, with a label to the left of each control. Stacked layouts are always contained within a single form section.

1. Click the **After Hours** text box. Make certain that you do not click the control layout selector.

2. Drag the selected text box just below the **Fax Number** control. An insertion bar will appear to let you know where the control will be added.

Figure 7-7
Move a control to another control layout
CC07
frmCustomers

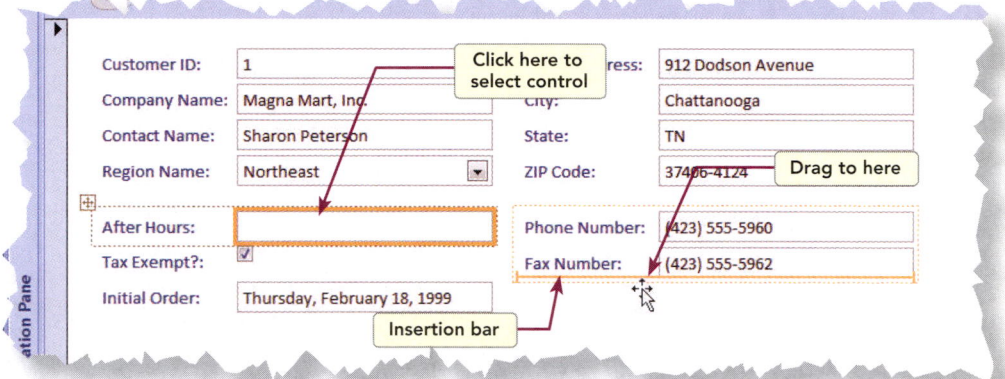

3. Select the layout selectors for the two bottom control layouts and align them Top .

4. Click the **After Hours** text box and press [Delete]. The field has been removed from the form.

5. From the **Format** tab, in the **Controls** group, click the Add Existing Fields command 📑.

6. You can resize the Field List by dragging its left edge.

7. From the Field List, click **NightNum**. Drag **NightNum** just below the **Fax Number** control.

Figure 7-8
Use the Field List to add a field
CC07
frmCustomers

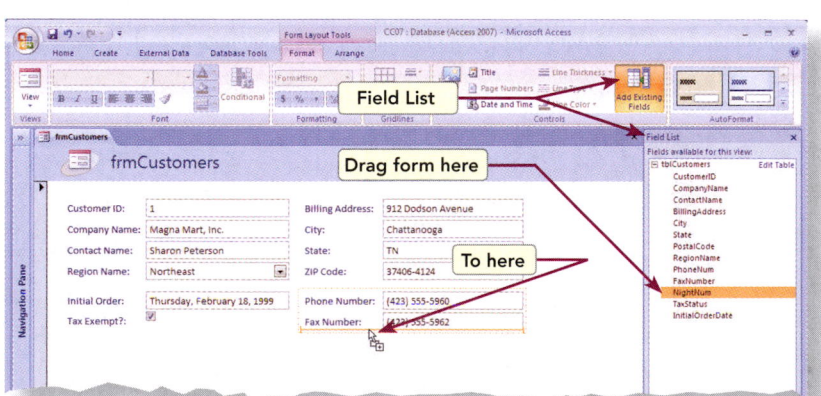

8. From the **Format** tab, in the **Controls** group, click the Add Existing Fields command 📑 to close the Field List.

9. From the **Format** tab, in the **Controls** group, click the Date and Time command .

Figure 7-9
Adding a Date and
Time control
CC07
frmCustomers

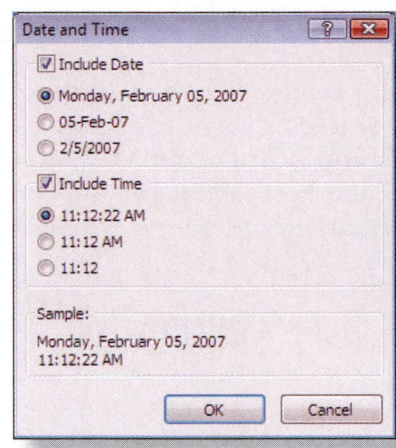

10. Click **OK**.

11. Click the **Billing Address** text box. While pressing Shift, click the Date and Time text boxes that you just added to the form.

12. From the **Arrange** tab, in the **Control Alignment** group, click the Left command .

13. Save the form.

Exercise 7-7   SET TAB ORDER

Tab order is a form setting that determines the movement of the insertion point through a form. The tab order determines where the insertion point goes when you press Tab in Form View. The usual order is left-to-right, top-to-bottom. When you move controls in Design View, the tab order might be changed and might not be what you expect.

1. From the **Format** tab, in the **Views** group, click the **View** command to switch to Form View.

2. Press Tab to determine how the insertion point moves through the form.

3. Switch to Layout View.

4. From the **Arrange** tab, in the **Control Layout** group, click the Tab Order command.

5. Click **Auto Order**. Click and drag the field selectors for **PhoneNum** through **NightNum**. Drag the three fields above **InitialsOrderDate**.

Figure 7-10
Tab Order
dialog box
CC07
frmCustomers

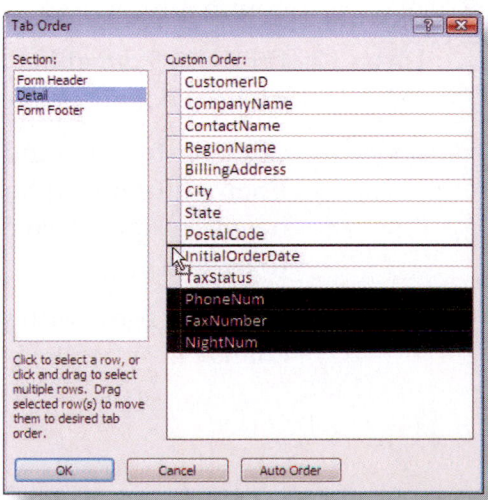

6. Click **OK**.

7. Switch to Form View.

8. Press Tab to move from text box to text box. Labels are not included in the Tab Order.

9. Save the form and switch to Layout View.

Exercise 7-8   FORMAT A FORM IN LAYOUT VIEW

You can easily refine the placement and size of controls through Layout View. Layout View allows you to modify the properties of controls by viewing the source data in each control. In Layout View, you can navigate through the dynaset to determine the best layout for the controls. In Layout View, you can apply an AutoFormat. *AutoFormat* is a tool that applies a predefined format to a form or report.

1. From the **Format** tab, in the **Controls** group, click the Title command.

2. Key **Customer Information**. Press [Enter].

3. From the **Arrange** tab, in the **Position** group, click the Size to Fit command [XY]. This tool only works on labels.

4. From the **Format** tab, in the **Font** group, click the Font Color command and choose **Automatic**.

5. Click in the blank area below all the controls.

6. From the **Format** tab, in the **Font** group, click the Fill/Back Color command.

7. From the **Access Theme Colors** section, choose **Access Theme 3** (third column, second row).

Figure 7-11
Pick a color
CC07
frmCustomers

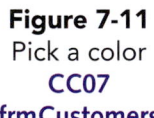

8. Click to the right of the **Date** control.

9. From the **Format** tab, in the **Font** group, click the Fill/Back Color command.

10. From the **Access Theme Colors** section, choose **Dark Header Background** (seventh column, first row).

11. Save the form. It's a good idea to always save before using the AutoFormat command.

12. From the **Formatting** tab, in the **AutoFormat** group, click the More arrow.

13. Click on **Trek** (second column, fifth row). Each AutoFormat has different sized header graphics, so controls usually need to be moved.

14. Close the form without saving the changes.

Working with Form Sections

A basic form contains controls only in a single section. Advanced forms use multiple sections. Some sections display on every screen or on every printed page. Other sections display only at specific times. The five form sections are as follows:

- **Detail** section is part of a form or report that displays data once for every row in the record source. This section makes up the main body of the form or report.

- **Form Header** section is a section of a form that displays once at the beginning of a form. This section often is used to display objects that would appear on a cover page, such as a logo, title, or date.

- **Form Footer** section is a section of a form that appears once at the end of a form. This section often is used to display summary information such as totals.

- **Page Header** section is a section of a form that displays at the top of each printed page. This section often is used to display title information or page numbers to be repeated on each page.

- **Page Footer** section is a section of a form that displays at the bottom of each printed page. This section often is used to display title information or page numbers to be repeated on each page.

The **Page Header** and **Page Footer** sections can only be seen in Print Preview or when the form is printed. The sections that initially appear in a form depend on the type of form originally created.

Exercise 7-9   OPEN AND SIZE FORM SECTIONS

When you scroll through a form, the **Form Header** always displays at the top of the screen. The **Form Footer** always appears at the bottom of the screen.

1. From the Navigation Pane, right-click **frmCustomers** and choose **Design View**. This form has two sections opened, **Form Header** and **Detail**.

2. Place the mouse pointer on the top of the **Form Footer** section bars. When the pointer changes to a two-headed arrow, click and drag up to the 3-inch mark on the vertical ruler.

3. Place the mouse pointer on the bottom of the **Form Footer** section bars. When the pointer changes to a two-headed arrow, click and drag down 1/2 inch.

Figure 7-12
Form Design View
CC07
frmCustomers

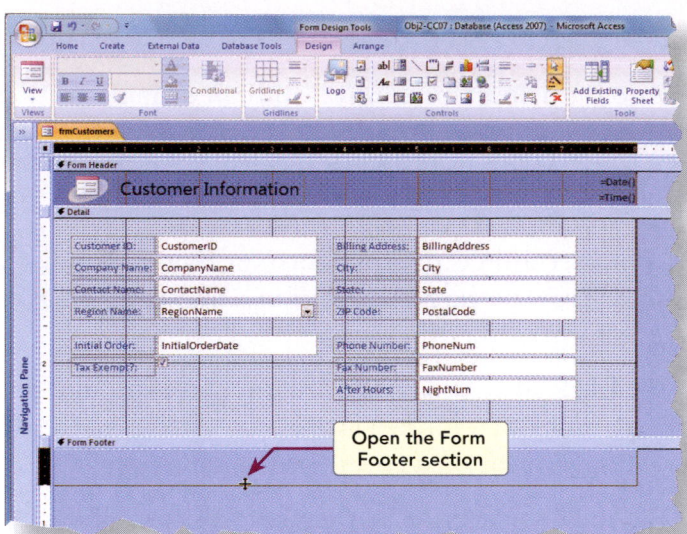

TIP

Each square of the design grid is 1 inch by 1 inch.

4. Drag the top border of the **Detail** section down to make the **Form Header** section about 1 inch tall.

5. From the **Arrange** tab, in the **Show/Hide** group, click the Page Header/Footer command 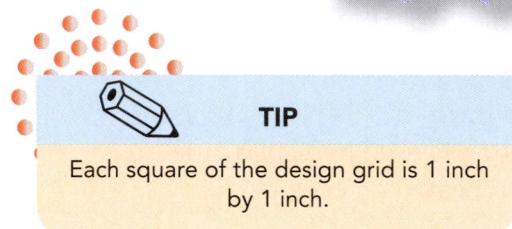.

6. Drag the top border of the **Detail** section down to make the **Page Header** section about ½ inch tall.

7. Drag the top border of the **Form Footer** section down to make the **Page Footer** section about ½ inch tall.

Figure 7-13
All Form sections expanded
CC07
frmCustomers

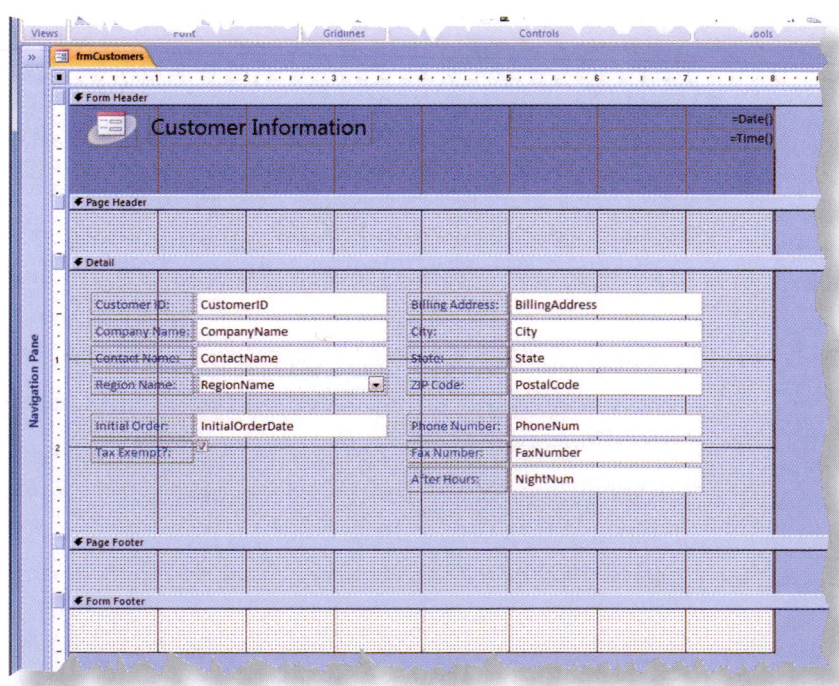

8. Save the form.

Exercise 7-10   ADD LABELS AND VIEW FORM SECTIONS

The Label tool in the Control command group is used to enter text or titles in a form. The text displayed in a label is independent of the recordset and does not change from record to record.

When you select a label or any other object, selection handles appear around the object. Selection handles are eight small black rectangles around an active object. The top left selection handle is known as the moving handle and is used to move the object without resizing it. The other seven handles are known as sizing handles. Sizing handles are any selection handles on a control except the top left one and are used to adjust the height and width of the object.

1. From the **Design** tab, in the **Controls** group, click the Label command. The pointer changes to a crosshair cursor with the letter A.

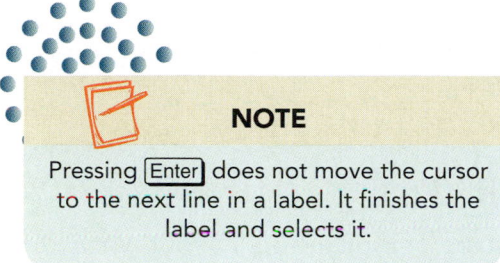

NOTE

Pressing Enter does not move the cursor to the next line in a label. It finishes the label and selects it.

2. Place the pointer in the **Form Header** section at the 4-inch mark, below the other controls. Click and drag down and to the right to draw a box about 2 inches wide and 5 dots tall. When you release the mouse button, you will see the box and a text insertion point.

3. Key **Form Header** and press Enter. The label box is selected and displays the eight selection handles around its edges.

Figure 7-14
Adding a label to the
Form Header
CC07
frmCustomers

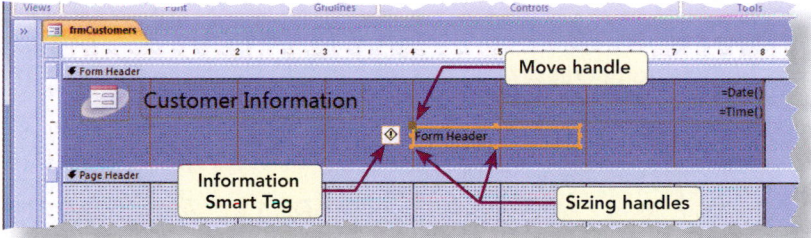

4. Click the Smart Tag. This label is not associated with another control. This is our intention. Choose **Ignore Error**.

5. Double-click any of the sizing handles. The label adjusts its size to fit the text.

6. In the **Page Header** section, add a label that is the same size as the one in the **Form Header** section. Key **Page Header** in the label.

7. In the **Page Footer** section, add a label that is the same size as the one in the **Form Header** section. Key **Page Footer** in the label.

8. In the **Form Footer** section, add a label that is the same size as the one in the **Form Header** section. Key **Form Footer** in the label.

9. Switch to Form View. You can see both the **Form Header** and **Form Footer**.

10. Press <kbd>PageDown</kbd> to move to the next record. There is no change in the **Form Header** or **Form Footer**.

11. Press <kbd>Ctrl</kbd>+<kbd>End</kbd> to move to the last record. There is no sign of the **Page Header** or **Page Footer**.

12. Click the Office button . Point at the **Print** option and click Print Preview 🔍. Click near the top of the preview to zoom in. You can see the **Form Header** and **Page Header** at the top of the first page.

13. Scroll down to see the **Page Footer**.

14. Click the Last Record button ▶|. After the last record, you can see the **Form Footer** appear.

15. From the **Print Preview** tab, in the **Zoom** group, click the More Pages command 🗇.

16. From the **Print Preview** tab, in the **Close Preview** group, click the Close Print Preview command ❎.

17. Close the form and save the changes.

Modifying Controls in Design View

> **NOTE**
>
> A form inherits the field properties of the table. Changes to the form's properties do not affect the table's properties.

Certain actions cannot be completed in Layout View. To perform these tasks, you will need to switch to Design View. Design View provides a more detailed view of the form's structure. In Design View, you can view the **Header**, **Detail**, and **Footer** sections. Unlike Layout View, when the form is in Design View, the form does not display the underlying data while making design changes.

Exercise 7-11   **FORMAT A FORM IN DESIGN VIEW**

When using Design View to modify the format of a form, you can begin by selecting a predefined format using AutoFormat.

1. From the Navigation Pane, right-click **frmAnimals** and choose **Design View**.

2. Click the **ProductID** text box.

3. From the **Arrange** tab, in the **AutoFormat** group, click the AutoFormat command 🖳 to expand the AutoFormat options.

4. Choose **Civic** (fifth column, first row). Because only the text box was selected, only it was formatted.

5. Click the Form selector.

Figure 7-15
The Form selector
CC07
frmAnimals

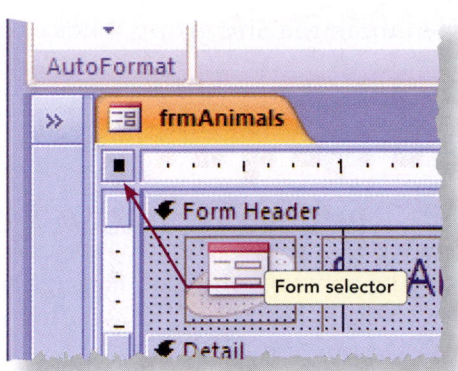

6. Choose **Civic** (fifth column, first row). The whole form is now formatted.

7. Right-click the form's document tab and choose **Form View**. To see how data look in the form, you must switch to either Layout or Form Views.

8. Switch to Design View.

9. Place your mouse pointer over the top edge of the **ProductID** text box. When a small, black, down arrow appears, click. All controls below the arrow are now selected.

Figure 7-16
All text boxes
selected
CC07
frmAnimals

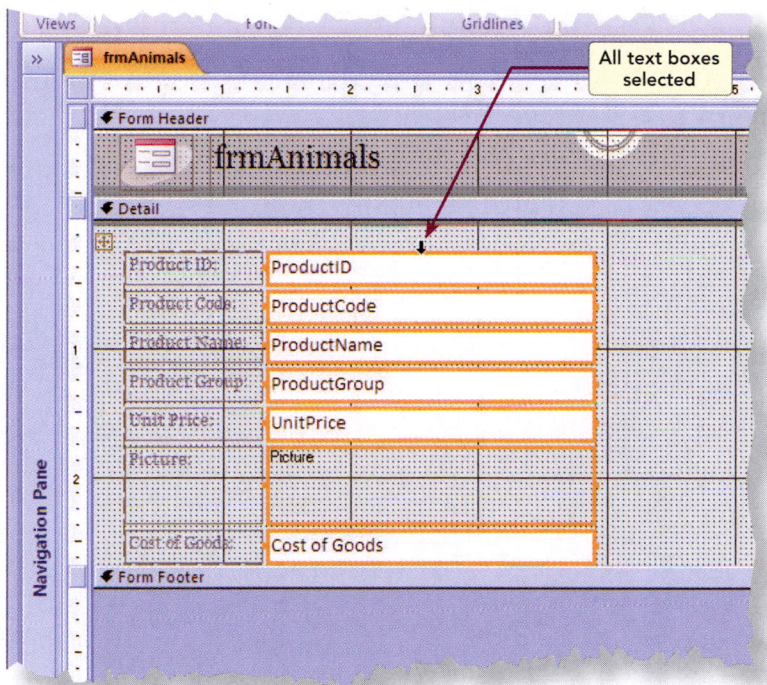

10. While pressing Shift, click the **Picture** control to remove it from the selection.

11. From the **Design** tab, in the **Controls** group, click the drop-down arrow for the Special Effect command ▭ and choose **Special Effects: Shadowed**.

12. From the **Design** tab, in the **Controls** group, click the drop-down arrow for the Line Type command ▤▾ and choose **Solid** (second option on the list.)

13. Click to the right of the selected controls to deselect them. You can now see your changes.

14. From the **Design** tab, in the **Controls** group, click the Title command ▣ and key **Product Information**.

15. From the **Arrange** tab, in the **Size** group, click the Size to Fit command .

16. Save the form.

Exercise 7-12 RESIZE AND MOVE CONTROLS

When resizing and moving controls, you can use the gridline marks in Design View. You can use the vertical and horizontal rulers to position the edges of each control.

1. Right-click the **ProductGroup** text box and choose **Delete**.

2. Click the **Picture** control. From the **Arrange** tab, in the **Control Layout** group, click the Remove command .

3. Click the **Picture** control label and press Delete.

4. Drag the Picture control to the right of the **ProductID** control.

5. Place your pointer to the middle bottom of the Picture control. When you see the resize arrow, drag down the bottom to 2.5 inches on the vertical ruler.

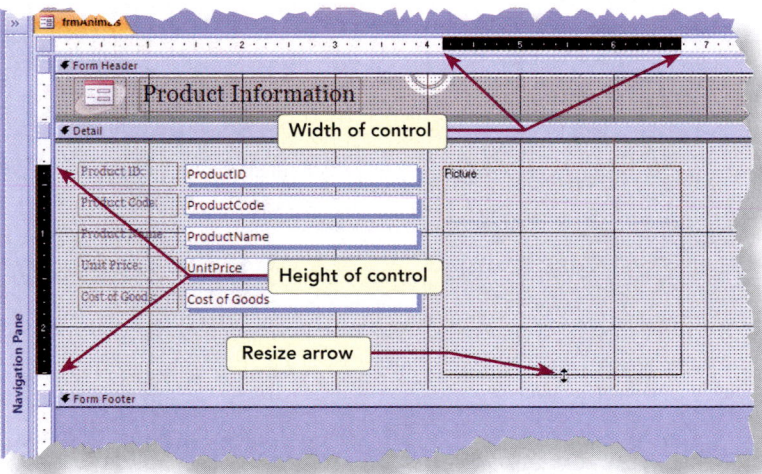

REVIEW

If you make an error deleting, sizing, or moving a control, click the Undo button and try again.

Figure 7-17
Moving a control
CC07
frmAnimals

6. Place your pointer in the vertical ruler to the left of the **ProductID** control. When you see a small, black, right arrow, click and drag until you are below the **Cost of Goods** control. This action selected all controls in the **Detail** section of the form.

7. From the **Arrange** tab, in the **Control Alignment** group, click the Top command to align the top of the control layout and the **Picture** control.

8. Click to the right of the **Picture** control to deselect the controls.

9. Place your pointer in the middle of the **Picture** control. With the move pointer, click and drag down ⅛th inch (one tick on the ruler).

10. Click the **UnitPrice** control. While pressing [Shift], click **Cost of Goods**.

11. From the **Arrange** tab, in the **Control Layout** group, click the Stacked command .

12. Drag the new control layout down until its bottom is at 2.5 inches on the vertical ruler.

13. Place your pointer over the top of the **ProductID** text box. When you see the small down arrow, click.

14. From the **Design** tab, in the **Font** group, click the Align Text Right command ▤.

15. Drag the right edge of the form to 7.5 inches on the horizontal ruler.

16. Deselect the controls.

17. Save the form.

Exercise 7-13   MODIFY PROPERTY SETTINGS

Every control has property settings. The property settings allow you to modify a control more precisely. For example, through the property settings, you can modify how an image will appear. The various Picture Size Mode settings for an image include the following:

• Clip Mode sizes an image to its original size.

• Stretch Mode sizes an image to fit the control without regard to the proportions of the original image.

• Zoom Mode sizes an image to fit the control while maintaining the proportions of the original image.

1. Double-click the **Picture** control to open the Property Sheet for this control.

2. On the **Format** tab, click the **Picture Size Mode**. Click the drop-down arrow and choose **Clip**. This mode shows the image at normal size.

3. Switch to Form View. The image does not fit the control.

4. Switch to Design View. Change the **Picture Size Mode** to **Zoom**.

5. Switch to Form View. This time the image fits the control.

6. Switch to Design View.

7. In the Property Sheet for the **Picture** control, click the **Picture Alignment** property.

8. Click the drop-down arrow and choose **Center**.

9. In the **Width** property, key **3**.

10. In the **Height** property, key **3**.

11. In the **Border Style** property, choose **Solid**.

12. In the **Border Width** property, choose **2 pt**.

13. In the **Back Style** property, choose **Normal**.

14. Switch to Form View.

Figure 7-18
Form View
CC07
frmAnimals

15. Switch to Design View. Close the Property Sheet.

16. Save the form.

Exercise 7-14   ADD A LABEL

Adding a label to a form helps identify the entire form or aspects of the form. For example, you might add a label to identify the department for which the form was created or a date on which the form was last modified. A label is not associated with data stored in the record source. A label is only associated to the major object to which it is attached.

1. Drag the bottom of the **Form Footer** section down ½ inch.

2. From the **Design** tab, in the **Controls** group, click the Label command Aa.

3. Place the pointer in the **Form Footer** section at the left edge. Click and key **Prepared by:** *[your full name]*.

4. Save the form.

Adding Calculated Controls to a Form

A calculated control in a form allows you to display the results of a calculation based upon one or more values. You create a calculated control by adding an expression to the Source Control property of a control. An expression can be any combination of mathematical operators, logical operators, constants, and functions.

Exercise 7-15 ADD UNBOUND TEXT BOXES

Although any control that has a Control Source property can be used as a calculated control, an unbound text box is the easiest control to change to a calculated control. An unbound text box inherits the format of the control layout to which it is added.

1. From the **Design** tab, in the **Controls** group, click the Text Box command . The pointer changes to a crosshair cursor with the letters "ab."

2. Click below the **Cost of Goods** control. This adds an unbound text with a label.

3. Drag the **Unbound** text box up until you see the insertion bar below the **Cost of Goods** control. The new text box inherits the format of the control layout.

4. Add a second text box to the form in the same manner as above.

5. Add the new text box to the same control layout as you did the last text box.

6. Select the **UnitPrice** text box, and drag its right edge to the 3-inch mark on the horizontal ruler.

Figure 7-19
New unbound text
boxes added
CC07
frmAnimals

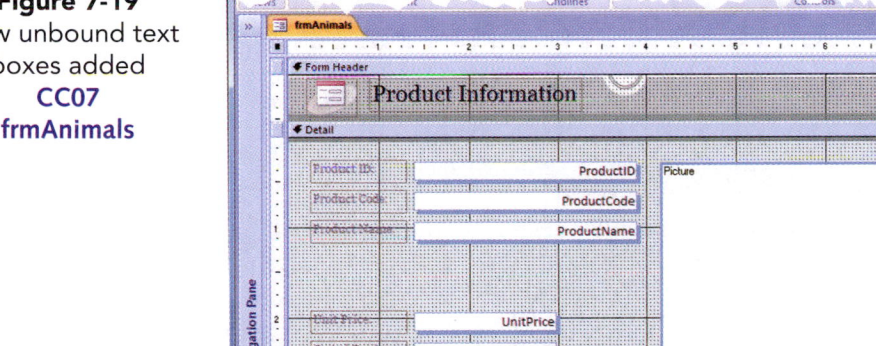

7. Save the form.

Exercise 7-16 ADD A CALCULATED CONTROL

You can use a calculated control to display the solution to a calculation. The calculation can be an expression or a function. For example, if you have a form displaying the number of items sold and the unit price for each item, you can add a calculated control to multiply the two fields and display a total price.

Access 2007

1. Double-click the first unbound text box to display its Property Sheet. Click the **Data** tab.

2. Click the **Control Source** property; read the status bar. Click the Build button to open the **Expression Builder** dialog box.

3. In the left panel, your **frmAnimals** form is shown as the current object at the top of the list.

4. In the middle panel, click **<Field List>**. The right panel shows the fields in the form.

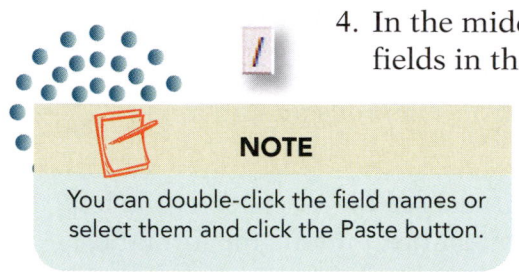

> **NOTE**
>
> You can double-click the field names or select them and click the Paste button.

5. In the right panel, double-click **UnitPrice**. It is pasted into the preview area with square brackets.

6. Click the Division button in the operator row.

7. In the right panel, double-click **Cost of Goods**.

Figure 7-20
Expression Builder
with an expression
CC07
frmAnimals

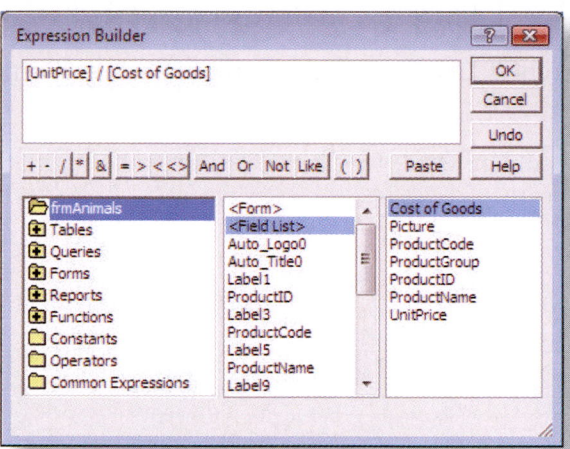

8. Click **OK** to close the **Expression Builder**. The equation appears in the unbound text box.

> **TIP**
>
> You must click the OK button to accept the changes in the Expression Builder.

9. Click the **Format** tab in the Property Sheet. Click the **Format** row and its drop-down arrow. Choose **Percent**.

10. Click the **Decimal Places** property and choose **2**.

11. Click the label of the text box you just modified. In the Property Sheet, click the **Caption** property and key **Points:**. Press ↓ to see the changes.

12. Click the second unbound text box. In its Property Sheet, click the **Data** tab.

13. Click the **Control Source** property and click the Build button.

14. In the **Expression Builder** dialog box, in the middle panel, click **<Field List>**.

15. In the right panel, double-click **UnitPrice**. Press ⊟.

16. In the right panel, double-click **Cost of Goods**. Click **OK**.

17. On the **Format** tab, click the **Format** property and choose **Currency**.

18. Click the label of the text box you just modified. In the Property Sheet, click the **Caption** property and key **Profit Margin:**.

19. Close the Property Sheet.

20. Switch to Form View. Press PageDown to view a few records.

Figure 7-21
Completed form
CC07
frmAnimals

21. Close and save the form.

Printing/Saving Forms

Although forms are designed to view data on a screen, on occasion you may need to print a form. If you choose to print the entire form, all records will display. Each record may display on a single page, on multiple pages, or on a portion of a page, depending on the size of the form and the size of the paper on which you print.

When printing a form, the **Page Header** and **Page Footer** sections will appear on each printed page. If a form is wider than the paper width, a single page of the form may print on two or more pages of paper. You can change the width of the form and the margins of the page to optimize the print quality of a form.

Exercise 7-17   PRINT SPECIFIC PAGES

As with other Office applications such as Word, you can print a specific page or range of pages. When printing a specific range of pages, you must enter a single page number, or a page range including the first page through the last page.

1. From the Navigation Pane, double-click **frmEmployeesInfo**.

2. Click the Office button ⊙. Point at the **Print** option and click Print Preview ⊙.

3. From the **Print Preview** tab, in the **Zoom** group, click the More Pages command  and choose **Four Pages**. Notice that each record is too wide to fit one page.

4. From the **Print Layout** group, click the Landscape command.

5. From the **Print Layout** group, click the **Margins** command, and choose the Normal command.

6. From the **Print Preview** tab, in the **Print** group, click the Print command. The report now fits on three pages.

7. In the **Print** dialog box, in the **Print Range** section, choose **Pages**.

8. In the **From** control, key **1**. The **To** control is now active.

Figure 7-22
Print dialog box
CC07
frmEmployeesInfo

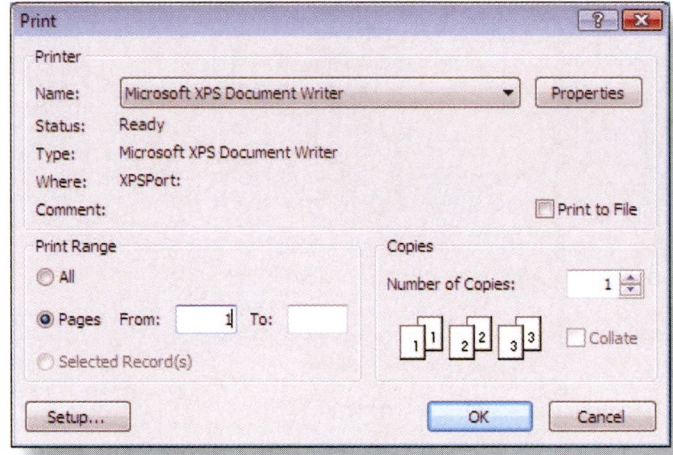

9. Click the **To** control and key **1**.

10. Based on your classroom procedure, you can either print the form or cancel the print process. To cancel, click **Cancel**. To print the form, click **OK**. If you are uncertain, ask your instructor.

11. From the **Print Preview** tab, in the **Close Preview** group, click the Close Print Preview command.

Exercise 7-18   PRINT ONE RECORD

When printing a single record, you must first select the record through the form. You cannot choose to print a single record through the Options in the Print or Print Preview commands.

1. In the Form View of **frmAnimals**, press PageDown until you reach the record for Barney Bulldog.

2. Click the record selector. The record selector is very tall in this form because the form is set to show only one record at one time.

3. Click the Office button. Point at the **Print** option and click Print.

4. In the **Print** dialog box, in the **Print Range** section, choose **Selected Record(s)**.

5. Based on your classroom procedure, you can either print the form or cancel the print process. To cancel, click **Cancel**. To print the form, click **OK**. If you are uncertain, ask your instructor.

Exercise 7-19 **PRINT MULTIPLE RECORDS**

Similar to printing a single record, you can print a contiguous range of records. The order in which the multiple records will print depends on how the dynaset is sorted.

1. Open **frmEmployeesInfo** in Form View.

2. Click the record selectors for **EmployeeID** "3."

3. Drag down to **EmployeeID** "23." These are all the employees whose last names start with "C".

Figure 7-23
Print dialog box
CC07
frmEmployeesInfo

39	Boca-Larson	Janet	8352 South Roxb
25	Butler	Helen	89 Grandin Road
3	Chung	Sora	345 Grove Street
13	Cirillo	Franklin	502 Waccamaw
23	Clark	Tina	789 West Trade S
18	Davidson	Russell	345 Victoria Aver
33	De La Rosa	Rosa	9355 Saturn Lane

4. Click the Office Button. Point at the **Print** option and click Print.

5. In the **Print** dialog box, in the **Print Range** section, choose **Selected Record(s)**.

6. Based on your classroom procedure, you can either print the form or cancel the print process. To cancel, click **Cancel**. To print the form, click **OK**. If you are uncertain, ask your instructor.

Exercise 7-20 **SAVE A RECORD**

Just as with other major objects, a form can be saved as a PDF or XPS file. To save a single record or range of records through a form, the record or records first must be selected.

1. Click the document tab for the form **frmAnimals**.

2. Press PageDown until you reach the Barney Bulldog record.

3. Click the record selector on the left side of the form.

4. Click the Office button. Point at the **Save As** option and click PDF or **XPS**.

5. In the **Publish as PDF or XPS** dialog box, click **Options**.

6. In the **Options** dialog box, in the **Range** section, click **Selected records** and click **OK**.

7. Change the location to where you will be storing your work.

8. Select either **PDF** or **XPS** as the file type.

9. Click **Publish**.

10. Close both forms.

11. Compact and close the database.

Lesson 7 Summary

- A form can be designed to view an entire record on a single screen.

- A form can include calculations, functions, and totals.

- The quickest way to create a form is to use the Query Wizard or a tool in the Forms group.

- The Form Wizard lets you select fields, a layout, and a style.

- When using the Forms tool, you can create a Simple Form, Split Form, or Multiple Items Form by selecting the appropriate command button located in the Forms group.

- A control is a database object that displays data, performs actions, or controls user interface information, such as labels and images. Controls can be bound, unbound, or calculated.

- A control layout assists you to horizontally and vertically align the controls within a form. A single form can have multiple control layouts.

- In Layout View of a form, you can rearrange and adjust the size of controls to improve the form's appearance and functionality.

- In Layout View, you can navigate through the dynaset to determine the best layout for the controls.

- Aligning a control is different than aligning the text within a control. Aligning the text within a control does not move the placement of the control on the form, but only the contents of the control.

- The five sections of a form include the **Detail**, **Form Header**, **Form Footer**, **Page Header**, and **Page Footer** sections.

- The **Page Header** and **Page Footer** sections can only be seen in Print Preview or when the form is printed.

- When you select a label or any other object, selection handles appear around the object.

- When resizing and moving controls, you can use the gridline marks, vertical ruler, and horizontal ruler to position the edges of each control.

- The property settings of a control allow you to modify a control more precisely.

- A **Picture Size Mode** can be set to **Clip Mode**, **Stretch Mode** or **Zoom Mode**.

- A label control is only associated with the major object to which it is attached.

- An unbound text box is the easiest control to change to a calculated control.

- A calculated control can contain an expression or a function.

- When printing a form, the **Page Header** and **Page Footer** sections will print on each vertical page.

- When printing a specific range of pages, you must enter a single page number, a list of page numbers separated by commas, or a page range including the first page through the last page.

- To print a single record, first you must select the record through the form. You cannot select to print a single record or range of records through the Options in the Print or Print Preview commands.

- The order in which multiple records will print depends on how the dynaset is sorted.

LESSON 7		Command Summary	
Feature	**Button**	**Path**	**Keyboard**
Controls, Add Existing Fields		Formatting, Controls, Add Existing Fields	
Controls, Align Text Right		Design, Font, Align Text Right	
Controls, Date and Time		Formatting, Controls, Date and Time	
Controls, Left		Arrange, Control Layout, Left	
Controls, Lines		Design, Controls, Line Type	
Controls, Margins		Arrange, Control Layout, Control Margins	
Controls, Padding		Arrange, Control Layout, Control Padding	
Controls, Remove		Arrange, Control Layout, Remove	
Controls, Right		Arrange, Control Layout, Right	
Controls, Special Effects		Design, Controls, Special Effects	
Controls, Stacked		Arrange, Control Layout, Stacked	
Controls, Tab Order		Arrange, Control Layout, Tab Order	

continues

LESSON 7		Command Summary *continued*	
Feature	**Button**	**Path**	**Keyboard**
Controls, Text Box, Add	abl	Design, Controls, Text Box	
Controls, Top		Arrange, Control Layout, Top	
Fields, Choose All	>>	Add All	Ctrl + A
Fields, Fill/Back Color		Formatting, Font, Fill/Back Color	
Fields, Font Color	A	Formatting, Font, Font Color	
Fields, Remove One	<	Remove One	
Fields, Size to Fit	XY	Arrange, Position, Size to Fit	
Form, AutoFormat		Formatting, AutoFormat	
Form, Control Layout Selector		Layout Selector	
Form, Create, Datasheet Form		Create, Forms, More Forms, Datasheet Form	
Form, Create, Multiple Form		Create, Forms, Multiple Form	
Form, Create, Simple Form		Create, Forms, Form	
Form, Create, Split Form		Create, Forms, Split Form	
Form, Page Header/ Footer View		Arrange, Show/Hide, Page Header/Footer	
Form, Title		Formatting, Controls, Title	
Form, Wizard		Create, Forms, More Forms, Form Wizard	
Forms, AutoFormat		Arrange, AutoFormat, AutoFormat	
Label, Add	Aa	Design, Controls, Label	
Print Preview, More Pages		Print Preview, Zoom, More Pages	
View, Form View		Formatting, Views, View	

Concepts Review

True/False Questions

Each of the following statements is either true or false. Indicate your choice by circling T or F.

T F   1. As you move controls on a form, the tab order adjusts so controls are always in left-to-right and top-to-bottom order.

T F   2. Every form contains a main section and a subsection.

T F   3. A Multiple Items Form shows multiple items in a datasheet, displaying one record per row.

T F   4. Control padding is the specified location of information inside a control.

T F   5. Aligning a control is the same as aligning the text within a control.

T F   6. The Page Header section of a form displays at the top of each printed page.

T F   7. The top left selection handle is known as the moving handle and is used to move the object without resizing it.

T F   8. A label is associated with the data stored in the record source.

Short Answer Questions

Write the correct answer in the space provided.

1. What section on a form displays data for each record?

   _____

2. What type of information might be displayed in the Form Header section?

   _____

3. Which command do you use when adding a calculated control to a form?

   _____

4. What opens when you click the Build button ⬛ in a query?

   _____

5. What is the name of the Picture Size Mode setting that sizes an image to its original size?

   _____

6. What determines where the insertion pointer moves when you press Tab in a form?

   _____

7. What command changes the text color in a label or a text box?

_____

8. When you select a label, what appears around the object?

_____

Critical Thinking

Answer these questions on a separate page. There are no right or wrong answers. Support your answers with examples from your own experience, if possible.

1. You can add, edit, delete, and search records through a datasheet of a table or query. When would it be more appropriate to use a form rather than a datasheet? When would it be more appropriate to use a datasheet?

2. In this lesson, you were introduced to some ideas about designing forms. What design principles should be followed when creating forms? How would the design differ from printed reports? Would the form design be different based on the database user's skill level and the confidentiality of the data?

Skills Review

Exercise 7-21

Create a multiple record form. Use AutoFormat and resize text boxes in Layout View.

1. Open a database by following these steps:
    a. Locate and open the **Lesson 07** folder.
    b. Make a copy of **CC07** and rename it *[your initials]*-**CC07**.
    c. Open and enable content for *[your initials]*-**CC07**.

2. Create a multiple record form by following these steps:
    a. In the Navigation Pane, right-click the query **qryAssets**, and choose **Copy**.
    b. In the Navigation Pane, right-click and choose **Paste**.
    c. In the **Paste As** dialog box, key **07-21-***[your initials]*.
    d. Select the query **07-21-***[your initials]*.
    e. From the **Create** tab, in the **Forms** group, click the Multiple Items command .
    f. From the Quick Access toolbar, click the Save button to save the new form by its default name.

3. Format a form in Layout View by following these steps:

   a. From the **Format** tab, in the **AutoFormat** group, click the More arrow.

   b. Click on **Equity** (fourth column, second row.)

   c. Click the column label **Date Acquired**.

   d. Drag the label's right edge to the right until each date, in each record, fits on one line.

   e. Click in the **Asset Name** field for the first record.

   f. Drag the text box's bottom edge up until you have reduced the row height in half.

   g. Press Ctrl+S to save the changes to the form.

4. Print/Save a form by following these steps:

   a. Click the Office button. From the **Print** option, choose Print Preview.

   b. Print/Save the form.

   c. Close **Print Preview** and the form.

Exercise 7-22

Create a single record form. Modify a form in Design View. Print/Save a form.

1. Create a single record form by following these steps:

   a. Open and enable content for *[your initials]*-**CC07**.

   b. In the Navigation Pane, select **qrySalesReps**.

   c. From the **Create** tab, in the **Forms** group, click the Form command.

   d. Press Ctrl+S. In the **Save As** dialog box, key **07-22-***[your initials]*.

2. Modify the Title label by following these steps:

   a. From the **Format** tab, in the **Views** group, click the View command down arrow and choose **Design**.

   b. From the **Design** tab, in the **Controls** group, click the Title command.

   c. Key **Sales Representatives Information** and press Enter.

   d. From the **Arrange** tab, in the **Size** group, click the To Fit command.

3. Resize controls in Design View by following these steps:

   a. Click the **EmployeeID** text box. Drag the right edge to the 4-inch mark on the horizontal ruler.

   b. Drag the top of the **Detail** bar up to the 1/2-inch mark on the vertical ruler.

   c. Drag the right edge of the form to the 5-inch mark on the horizontal ruler.

   d. Drag the bottom edge of the **Form Footer** bar down to the 1/2-inch mark on the vertical ruler.

TIP

Each section has its own vertical ruler that starts at 0 inches.

4. Add a label by following these steps:

   a. From the **Design** tab, in the **Controls** group, click the Label command .

   b. Click in the **Form Footer** section.

   c. Key **Prepared by:** *[your full name]*.

   d. Press Enter.

   e. Drag the new label to the left part on the section.

   f. From the Quick Access toolbar, click the Save button  to save the new form.

5. Print/Save a form by following these steps:

   a. Switch to Form View.

   b. Click the Office button . Point at the **Print** option and click Print Preview .

   c. Print/Save the form.

   d. Close **Print Preview** and the form.

Exercise 7-23

Create a simple form. Add and modify control in a form. Print/Save a single record in a form.

1. Create a single record form by following these steps:

   a. Open and enable content for *[your initials]*-**CC07**.

   b. In the Navigation Pane, select **qryVenders**.

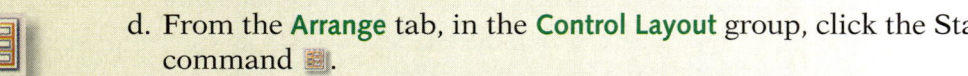

   c. From the **Create** tab, in the **Forms** group, click the Form command .

   d. Press Ctrl+S. In the **Save As** dialog box, key **07-23-***[your initials]*.

2. Modify controls by following these steps:

   a. Press PageDown until you reach the record for **Vender ID** number "1." This is the longest vender name.

   b. Drag the right edge of the **Vender ID** text box to reduce its width to just fit the contents of all fields.

   c. Click the **Phone Number** control. While pressing Shift, click **Fax Number**.

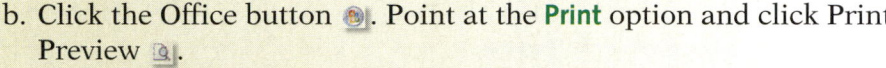

   d. From the **Arrange** tab, in the **Control Layout** group, click the Stacked command .

   e. Click the **City** control. While pressing Shift, click the **State** and **Zip Code** controls.

   f. From the **Arrange** tab, in the **Control Layout** group, click the Remove command .

g. Click the label for the **City** control (on the left). Press Delete.

h. Click the label for the **State** control and press Delete.

i. Click the label for the **Zip Code** control and press Delete.

j. Drag the **State** text box to the right of the **City** text box.

k. Drag the right edge of the **State** text box so its width is about 1/4 inch. Make sure that all data can be seen.

l. Drag the **Zip Code** text box to the right of the **State** text box.

m. Drag the right edge of the **Zip Code** text box to reduce its width to just fit the content of the field.

 n. Click the Layout Selector ⊞ for the **Phone Number** field and drag the control layout up under the **City** text box.

3. Add a label to a form by following these steps:

 a. From the **Format** tab, in the **Views** group, click the View command down arrow and choose Design View 📐.

b. Drag the bottom edge of the **Form Footer** bar down to the 1/2-inch mark on the vertical ruler.

 c. From the **Design** tab, in the **Controls** group, click the Label command Aa.

d. Click in the **Form Footer** section.

e. Key **Prepared by:** *[your full name]* and press Enter.

f. Drag the new label to the left part on the section.

4. Modify the Title label by following these steps:

 a. From the **Design** tab, in the **Controls** group, click the Title command 🔲.

b. Key **Vender Contact Information** and press Enter.

 c. From the **Arrange** tab, in the **Size** group, click the To Fit command XY.

d. Drag the right edge of the form to the 5-inch mark on the horizontal ruler.

 e. From the Quick Access toolbar, click the Save button 💾.

f. Switch to Form View.

g. Press PageDown until you reach **Vender ID** number "4" and click the record selector.

5. Print/Save a single record by following these steps:

 a. Click the Office button 🔘.

b. Click the **Save As** command and choose the PDF or XPS command 📄.

c. Change the location to where you will be storing your work.

d. Select either **PDF** or **XPS** as the file type.

e. Click **Options** and click **Selected Record(s)**. Click **OK**.

f. Click **Publish**.

g. Right-click the form's document tab and choose **Close**.

 h. According to your classroom procedure, print or submit PDF or XPS file.

Exercise 7-24

Create a form using a wizard. Add and modify controls. Add a calculated control. Print/Save a single page of a form.

1. Create a form using a wizard by following these steps:

   a. Open and enable content for *[your initials]*-**CC07**.

   b. From the **Create** tab, in the **Forms** group, click **More Forms** and choose the Form Wizard command 🔲.

   c. In the **Tables/Queries** drop-down box, choose **Table: tblEmployees**.

   d. In the **Available Fields** section, double-click **LastName** and **FirstName**.

   e. In the **Tables/Queries** drop-down box, choose **Table: tblEmployeeDates**.

   f. In the **Available Fields** section, double-click **HireDate**. Click **Next**.

   g. Select **Columnar**. Click **Next**.

   h. Select **Flow**. Click **Next**.

   i. Key **07-24-**_[your initials]_. Click **Finish**.

2. Modify controls in a form by following these steps:

   a. Switch to Layout View.

   b. Click the label for the **Last Name** control.

   c. Drag the label's right edge to the left so that there is about 1/2 inch of space after the label text.

   d. Click the **Hire Date** control.

   e. From the **Arrange** tab, in the **Control Layout** group, click the Stacked command 🔳.

   f. Drag the **Hire Date** control to the right of the **Last Name** control.

   g. While pressing ⟨Shift⟩, click the **Last Name** control.

   h. From the **Arrange** tab, in the **Control Alignment** group, click the Top command 🔲.

   i. Switch to Design View.

3. Add a calculation to a form by following these steps:

   a. From the **Design** tab, in the **Controls** group, click the Text Box command 🔲.

   b. Click below the **HireDate** text box.

   c. Drag the new unbound control up to the **HireDate** control until you see the insertion bar under the **HireDate** control.

   d. Double-click the unbound control. In the Property Sheet, click the **Data** tab.

   e. Click in the **Control Source** property and click the Build button 🔲.

   f. In the **Expression Builder** dialog box, in the left panel, double-click **Functions**. Click **Built-In Functions**.

   g. In the middle panel, click **Date/Time**. In the right panel, double-click **DateAdd**.

    h. In the expression box, click **<<interval>>** and key **"yyyy"**.

    i. In the expression box, click **<<number>>** and key **20**.

    j. In the expression box, click **<<date>>**.

    k. In the left panel, click **07-24-[Your Initials]**. In the middle panel, click **<Field List>**.

    l. In the right panel, double-click **HireDate**.

    m. Click **OK**.

    n. In the Property Sheet, click the **Format** tab. In the **Format** property, click the drop-down arrow and choose **Medium Date**.

    o. Click the label of the new control.

    p. In the **Caption** property, key **20-year Date**.

4. Add a label to a form by following these steps:

    a. Drag the bottom edge of the **Form Footer** bar down to the ½-inch mark on the vertical ruler.

    b. From the **Design** tab, in the **Controls** group, click the Label command .

    c. Click in the **Form Footer** section.

    d. Key **Prepared by:** *[your full name]* and press Enter.

    e. Drag the new label to the left part on the section.

    f. From the Quick Access toolbar, click the Save button to save the new form.

    g. Switch to Form View.

5. Print/Save a single record by following these steps:

    a. Click the Office Button.

    b. Click the **Save As** command and choose the PDF or XPS command.

    c. Change the location to where you will be storing your work.

    d. Select either **PDF** or **XPS** as the file type.

    e. Click **Options** and click **Page(s)**. Change **From:** to **3** and **To:** to **3**. Click **OK**.

    f. Click **Publish**.

    g. Right-click the form's document tab and choose **Close**.

    h. According to your classroom procedure, print or submit PDF or XPS file.

Lesson Applications

Exercise 7-25

Create a form by using the wizard. Change form width. Modify form sections. Add a label. Print/Save a record through a form.

1. Open and enable *[your initials]*-CC07.

2. Using the **Form Wizard**, create a **columnar** form using all fields in **tblEmployeeDates**.

3. Apply the **Trek** style to the form.

4. Save the form as **07-25-***[your initials]*.

5. Make the form 5 inches wide.

6. Using the **Font Size** of **20**, edit the title label to **Employee Dates**.

7. Add a label on the left edge of the **Page Footer**. Key **Prepared by:** *[your full name]*.

8. Close the **Page Header** (height of 0 inches).

9. Print/Save the only the record for **Employee ID** number "20."

10. Close the form.

Exercise 7-26

Generate a simple form. Modify controls. Add a label. Print/Save a group of records through a form.

1. Using *[your initials]*-CC07, create a **Multiple Items** form based on **qrySickDays**.

2. Apply the AutoFormat **Office** and rename the form **07-26-***[your initials]*.

3. Open the **Form Header** and edit the title label to **Employee Sick Days**. Make it **20**-point **Arial bold italic**. Size the control to fit the text.

4. Reduce the width of each column but making sure all data are visible.

5. Resize the form to 5 inches wide.

6. Add a label on the left edge of the **Form Footer**. Key **Prepared by:** *[your full name]*.

7. Align the **Form Header** and **Form Footer** labels to the left.

8. Save the form. Print/Save only the records for "Helen Butler." Make sure all data fit on one page.

9. Close the form.

Exercise 7-27

Create a form with the Form Wizard. Modify form controls. Add a form header with a label. Print/Save using a form.

1. Create a new form for **tblEmployees** by using the **Form Wizard**. Use these fields:

   EmployeeID
   LastName
   FirstName
   EmergencyContact
   EmergencyPhone

2. Use a **Columnar** layout and the **Flow** style. Name the form **07-27-**[your initials].

3. Change the form width to 6 inches.

4. Make all controls **18**-point **Times New Roman**. Size them to fit.

5. Widen the labels so all text can be seen.

6. Edit the title label and key **Emergency Information**. Make the label **24**-point **Times New Roman bold italic**. Show the label on a single line.

7. Add a label to the lower right section of the **Form Footer** and key **Prepared by:** [your full name].

8. Save the form.

 9. Find and Print/Save only the record for "Scott Swanson." Close the form.

Exercise 7-28 ◆ Challenge Yourself

Create a simple form. Modify controls. Add a calculated control. Print/ Save a single page of a form.

1. Create a simple form based on **qryHrWages**.

2. Apply the AutoFormat **None**.

3. Make all controls **14**-point **Arial**. Size them to fit.

4. Resize the labels so that all text can be seen.

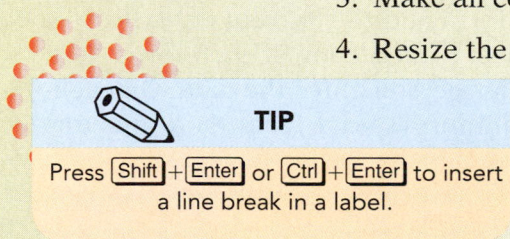

TIP

Press Shift + Enter or Ctrl + Enter to insert a line break in a label.

5. Resize the text boxes to about 2.5 inches wide.

6. Edit the title label to **Carolina Critters** on the first line. Key **Hourly Employee Wages** on the second line. Key **Confidential –** [your last name] on the third line.

7. Format the title label as **18**-point **Arial bold italic**. Size the title label and the form header as needed, and keep the label as a three-line title.

8. Change the form width to 6 inches.

9. Add an unbound text box to the bottom of the control layout. Edit its label to **Monthly Pay**.

10. Edit the **EmpPay** control's label to **Hourly Rate**.

11. Set the property **Control Source** for the unbound text box to **[EmpPay]*40*4**.

NOTE

The calculation "40*4" represents 40 hours per week and 4 weeks per month.

12. Set the format for the **Monthly Pay** text box to **Currency** with two decimal places.

13. Save the form as **07-28-[your initials]**.

14. Print/Save the first page of form. Close the form.

15. Compact and close your database. Exit Access.

On Your Own

In these exercises, you work on your own, as you would in a real-life work environment. Use the skills you've learned to accomplish the task—and be creative.

Exercise 7-29

Using the Form Wizard, create a form for the main table of the database you modified in Exercise 6-31. Include all fields from the table in your form. On the form printout, sketch changes that will improve each form. Using the Form Wizard, create forms for each additional table in your database. Print a copy of each form. On each form printout, sketch changes that will improve each form. On each form, write your name and "Exercise 7-29." Continue to Exercise 7-30.

Exercise 7-30

Modify your forms to incorporate the improvements you sketched. In the Form Footer of each form, include your name and Exercise 7-30. In the Form Header, include the name of the form and the current date. Print the data contained in each of your tables. Print a copy of each form. Test your redesigned forms by having another person enter the data. On each form printout, sketch changes that will improve your form. Continue to Exercise 7-31.

Exercise 7-31

Modify your forms appropriately. Analyze your database design. Determine if any additional forms might be required for queries or recordsets. Create any additional forms you might need. On each form, include your name and Exercise 7-31 in the Form Footer. Print a copy of each form. Submit the copies of the forms you printed in Exercises 7-29 through 7-31 to your instructor. Keep a copy of the database you modified in this exercise. You will use it for the On Your Own exercises in subsequent lessons.

Lesson 8

Adding and Modifying Reports

OBJECTIVES

After completing this lesson, you will be able to:

1. Generate reports quickly.
2. Modify controls in Layout View.
3. Work with report sections.
4. Work with controls in a report.
5. Use Format Painter and Conditional Formatting.
6. Create a multicolumn report and labels.

Estimated Time: 2 hour

MCAS OBJECTIVES

In this lesson:
AC07 70-605 2.6.1
AC07 70-605 2.6.2
AC07 70-605 2.6.4
AC07 70-605 2.6.5
AC07 70-605 2.6.6
AC07 70-605 2.6.7
AC07 70-605 2.7.1
AC07 70-605 2.7.4
AC07 70-605 2.7.5
AC07 70-605 2.7.6
AC07 70-605 2.7.7

A well-designed report can present information more effectively than other major objects. In a report you can:

- Display data in an attractive format that may include variations in fonts, colors, shading, and borders.
- Display sorted, grouped, or summarized information.
- Display images, graphics, charts, and logos.
- Display fields from more than one table.
- Display titles and headings.

In this lesson, you will learn how to create and modify reports. You will work with the Report Wizard, Design View, and Layout View. With reports, your design concerns are different than those with forms because when working with reports, you must account for margins, page breaks, and page orientation.

Generating Reports Quickly

Access provides a Wizards and tools to create reports using standardized styles. Depending on the Report tool you select, the report may have header and footer sections in addition to the section containing the record source detail.

Stacked style reports are commonly used when the width of data is too wide to display properly in tabular layout.

Exercise 8-1 CREATE A REPORT WITH A WIZARD

The Report Wizard allows you to select a record source and the fields to include in the report. When selecting multiple tables or queries as the record source, the objects must have a valid relationship already created. You can group and sort the fields in a report.

1. Locate and open the **Lesson 08** folder.

2. Make a copy of **CC08** and rename it *[your initials]*-**CC08**.

3. Open and enable content for *[your initials]*-**CC08**.

4. From the **Create** tab, in the **Reports** group, click the Report Wizard command 📷.

5. In the **Tables/Queries** drop-down box, choose **Query: qryStuffedAnimals**.

6. The dialog box asks which fields to use on the form. Double-click the following fields to add them to the **Selected Fields** section:

   ProductID
   ProductCode
   ProductName
   UnitPrice
   Picture

Figure 8-1
Report Wizard
dialog box
CC08.accdb

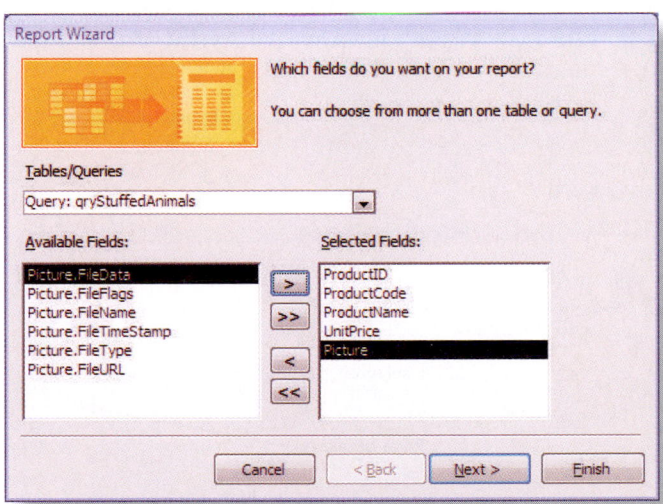

7. Click **Next**. This part of the Wizard asks you to add groups. This skill will be covered later in this lesson. Click **Next**.

8. Click the first combo box drop-down arrow and select **ProductName**. The report will be sorted by this field. Click **Next**.

9. In the **Layout** section, select **Columnar** and in the **Orientation** section, select **Portrait**. Click **Next**.

10. Click each of the different styles to view a small preview. Select **Paper**.

11. Click **Next**. Modify the title to **rptStuffedAnimals**.

12. You can choose to preview the report or modify the design. Select **Preview the report** and click **Finish**.

13. The report opens in Print Preview.

14. From the **Print Preview** tab, in the **Zoom** group, click the More Pages command and choose **Twelve Pages**.

15. From the **Print Preview** tab, in the **Close Preview** group, click the Close Print Preview command.

16. Close the report.

Exercise 8-2 GENERATE A REPORT WITH ONE CLICK

The Report tool is the quickest method to create a basic report based on a selected table or query. The report displays all fields from the source table or query. You can create a basic report and later modify it using Design or Layout View. The last style used on the workstation will be the default style used by the Report tool.

1. In the Navigation Pane, select **qryStuffedAnimals**.

2. From the **Create** tab, in the **Reports** group, click the Report command. The new report is now in Layout View showing multiple records.

Figure 8-2
Report in Layout View
CC08.accdb
rptStuffedAnimalsList

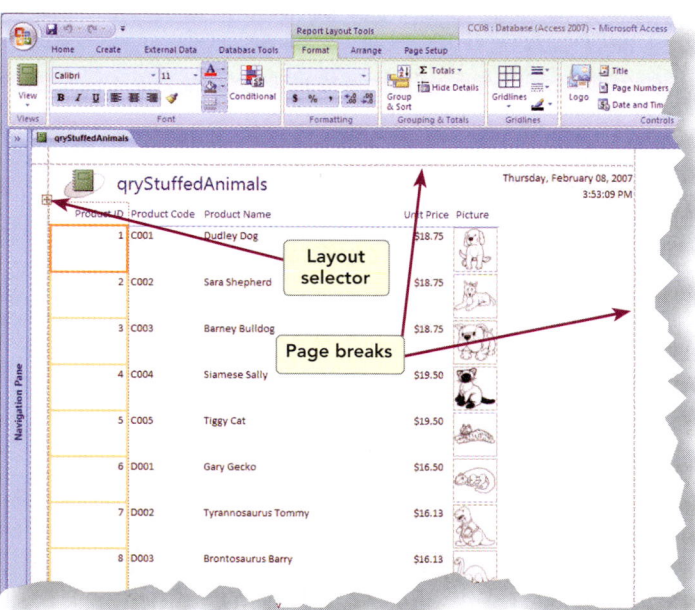

3. From the Quick Access toolbar, click the Save button 🖫 to save the new report.

4. In the **Save As** dialog box, key **rptStuffedAnimalsList** and click **OK**.

5. From the **Format** tab, in the **Views** group, click the Report View command 🔲.

6. Scroll down the report. Notice that there is only one page.

7. Right-click the report's document tab and choose **Print Preview**.

8. From the **Print Preview** tab, in the **Zoom** group, click the Two Page command 🔲. Only one page will display in Report or Layout View.

9. From the **Print Preview** tab, in the **Close Preview** group, click the Close Print Preview command 🔲.

10. Switch to Report View.

Modifying Controls in Layout View

Layout View for a report is very similar to Layout View for a form. You use Layout View to resize controls, adjust column widths, move columns, and change labels while viewing the actual data in the report. You also can insert or remove controls and set the properties for the report or a control.

Exercise 8-3 FORMAT A REPORT IN LAYOUT VIEW

Any report, including a basic report, can be modified in Layout View. You may find it easier to start by applying an AutoFormat to the report and then modifying the design.

1. Switch to Layout View for **rptStuffedAnimalsList**.

2. From the **Format** tab, in the **AutoFormat** group, click the More arrow 🔲 and choose **Origin** (4th column, 4th row).

3. Click the first record's **Product Code**.

4. From the **Format** tab, in the **Font** group, click the Center command 🔲.

5. Click the first record's **Picture**.

6. Drag the right edge to the right about ¼ inch.

7. Click the column heading **Picture**.

8. From the **Format** tab, in the **Font** group, click the Center command 🔲.

Figure 8-3
Formatting a report
in Layout View
CC08.accdb
rptStuffedAnimalsList

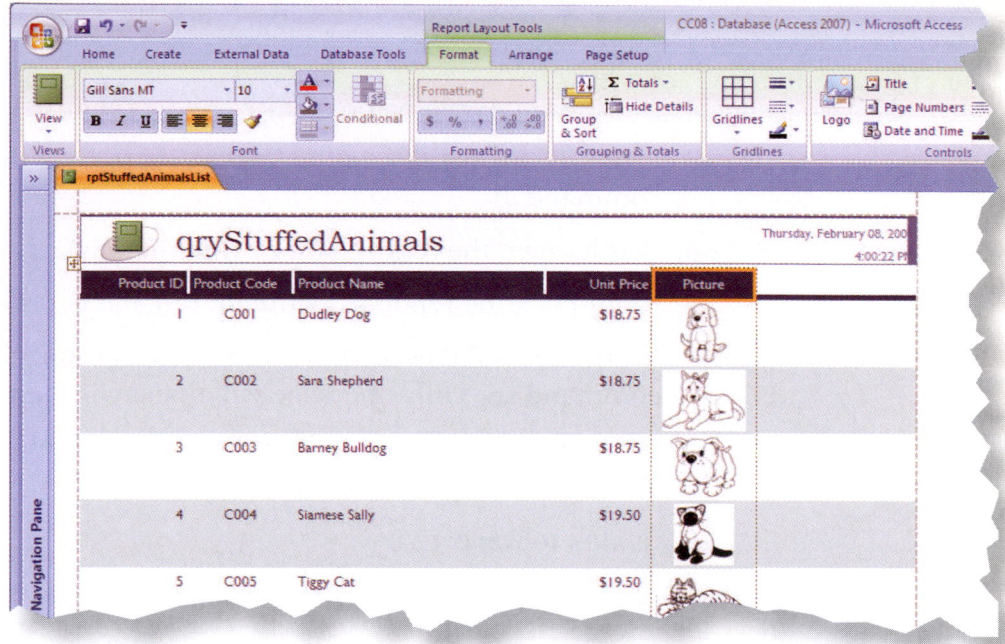

9. From the Quick Access toolbar, click the Save button 💾.

Exercise 8-4   ADD AND REARRANGE CONTROLS IN A REPORT

When you add fields in Layout View, a Field List pane displays. The top part of pane displays fields available in the current record source. The middle part of the pane displays fields available in related tables. The bottom part of the pane displays fields available in other tables.

1. Click the column heading **Product ID**.

2. Press ⏹Delete⏹. The other fields in the control layout have moved to the left.

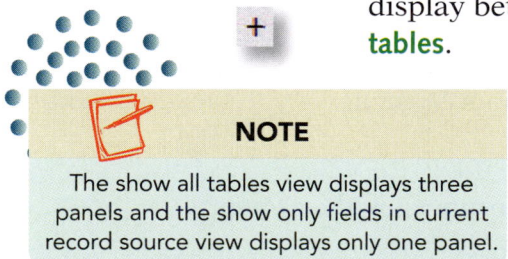

3. From the **Format** tab, in the **Controls** group, click the Add Existing Fields command ▦. The Field List pane appears.

4. Click the toggle button at the bottom of the Field List to switch the display between **Show only fields in current record source** to **Show all tables**.

> **NOTE**
>
> The show all tables view displays three panels and the show only fields in current record source view displays only one panel.

5. From the Field List, in the **Fields available in related tables:** panel, click the Expand button ⊞ for **tblProductLines**.

6. From **tblProductLines**, drag the field **ProductLine** to the left of **Product Code** in the report.

Figure 8-4
Adding a field to a
report in Layout View
CC08.accdb
rptStuffedAnimalsList

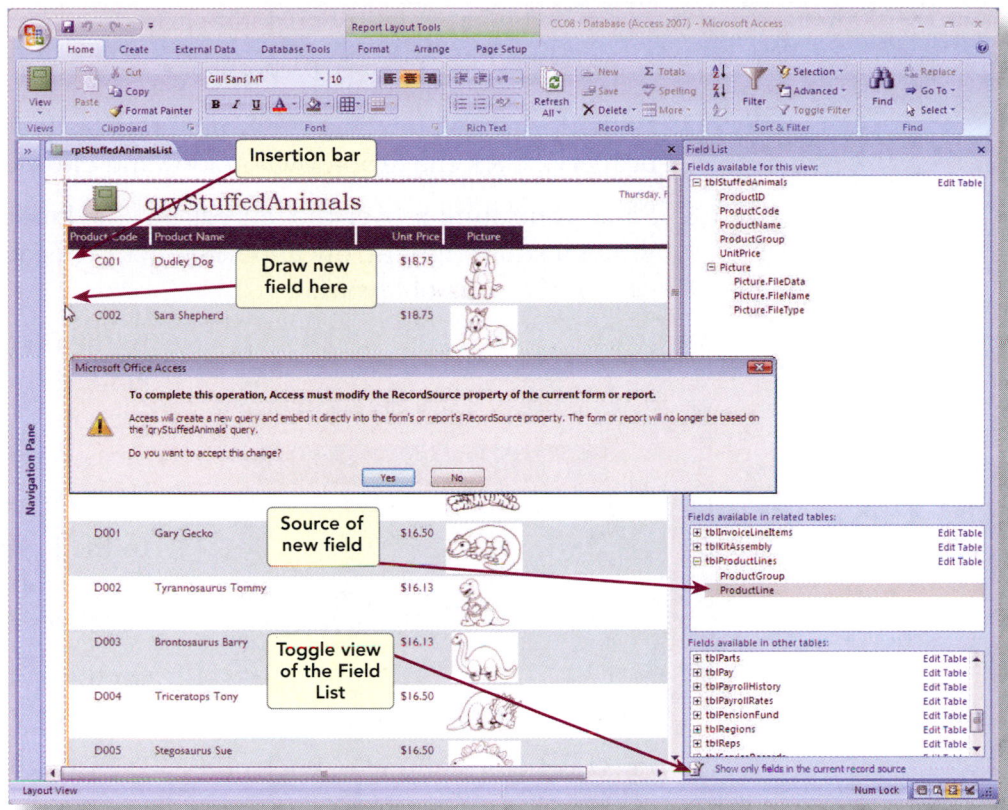

7. The warning dialog box states that the recordset must be modified to include the table and field just added. Click **Yes**.

8. From the **Format** tab, in the **Controls** group, click the Add Existing Fields command to remove the **Field List**.

9. Press Ctrl + S to save the report.

Exercise 8-5   FORMAT A REPORT USING THE PROPERTY SHEET

You can modify the properties of a control through its property sheet. For each property, you can change the paddings and margins. A padding is the space between the gridline of the report and the control. A margin is the specified location of information inside the control.

1. From the **Arrange** tab, in the **Tools** group, click the Property Sheet command .

2. Click the column header **Name of Product Group**.

3. In the Property Sheet, click the **Format** tab. Click in the **Caption** property.

4. Delete "Name of" from the field's **Caption**. Press ↓.

5. Change the field's **Width** property to **1.2**.

6. In the **Text Align** property, click the drop-down arrow and choose **Center**.

7. In the first record, click the **Product Group** text box.

8. In the Property Sheet, on the **Format** tab, click in the **Hide Duplicates** property, click the drop-down arrow, and choose **Yes**.

9. Place your pointer over the left edge of the **Product Group** text box. When a small right arrow appears, click. This action selects the data part of the control layout.

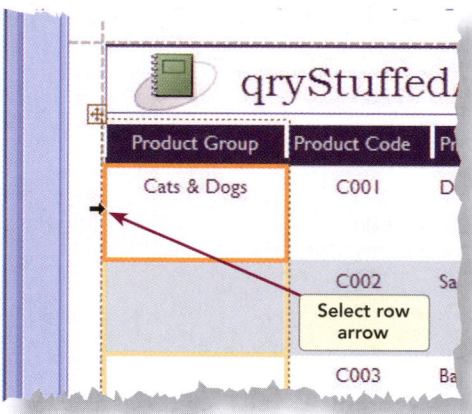

Figure 8-5
Select a row in Layout View
CC08.accdb
rptStuffedAnimalsList

10. In the first record, click the **Product Group** text box. While pressing Shift, click the text boxes for **Product Code**, **Product Name**, and **Unit Price**.

11. In the Property Sheet, on the **Format** tab, click in the **Top Padding** property and key **.15**.

12. On the **Format** tab, click in the **Top Margin** property and key **.15**.

13. Press ↓. The content of each control selected has moved down.

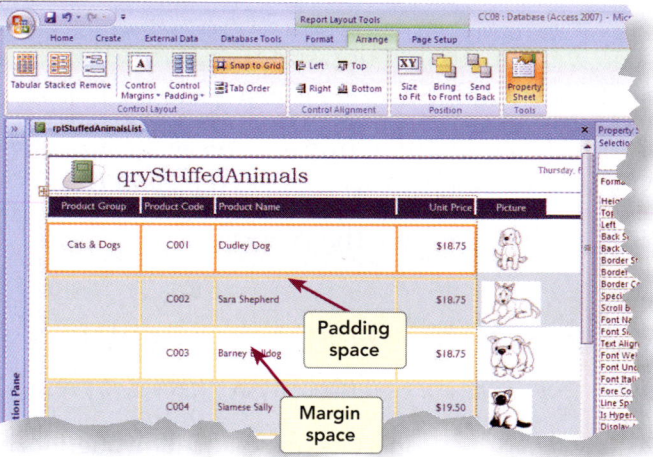

Figure 8-6
Setting the margin and padding properties
CC08.accdb
rptStuffedAnimalsList

14. From the Quick Access toolbar, click the Save button 💾.

15. Close the report.

Working with Report Sections

Reports can have numerous sections. The Detail section displays data from the record source. The **Report Header** or **Report Footer** section prints once at the beginning or end of the report (first or last page). Headers and footers can contain main titles, summary calculations, design lines, or even images. The **Page Header** and **Page Footer** sections print at the top and bottom of every page and are often used for page numbers and the date.

Reports may also have one or more Group Header/Footer sections. A Group Header/Footer prints either before or after a defined group.

TABLE 8-1 Sections of a Report

Name of Section	Purpose
Detail Section	Prints data once for every row in the record source.
Report Header	Prints once at the top (first page) of the report.
Report Footer	Prints once at the bottom (last page) of the report.
Page Header	Prints once at the top of every printed page.
Page Footer	Prints once at the bottom of every printed page.
Group Header	Prints once at the start of each group.
Group Footer	Prints once at the end of each group.

Exercise 8-6 CREATE A GROUPED REPORT USING A WIZARD

The Report Wizard is the quickest method for creating a grouped report.

1. From the **Create** tab, in the **Reports** group, click the Report Wizard command 🔍.

2. In the **Tables/Queries** drop-down box, choose **Query: qrySalesSummary**.

3. Click the Add All button >>.

4. Click **Next**. Click **RegionName** and click the Add One button >. This action will group the report by **RegionName**.

Figure 8-7
Grouping a report in the Report Wizard
CC08.accdb

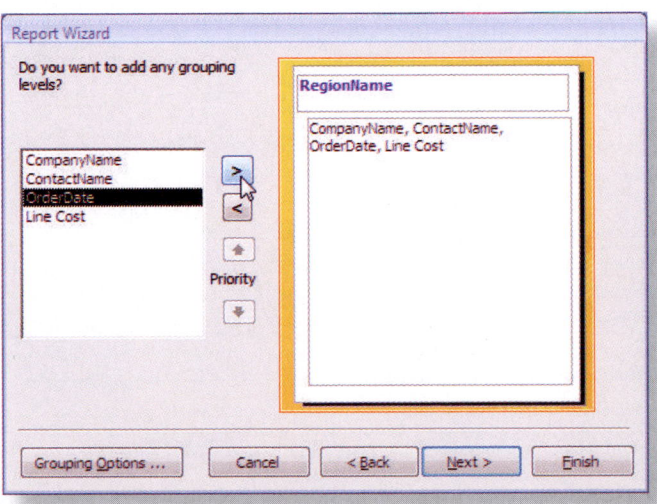

5. Click **Next**. Click the first combo box drop-down arrow and select **CompanyName**. The report will be sorted by this field.

6. Click **Summary Options**. You can pick what type of aggregate functions to add to the report.

7. Click the check boxes for **Sum** and **Calculate percent of total for sums**. Click **OK**.

8. Click **Next**.

9. Your options in the **Layout** section are different because you have added a group to the report. In the **Layout** section, select **Stepped** and in the **Orientation** section, select **Portrait**. Click **Next**.

10. Select **Oriel** as the style. Click **Next**.

11. Modify the title to **rptSalesSummaryByRegion**.

12. Select **Preview the report** and click **Finish**.

13. Scroll through the report. Notice the functions at the bottom of each **Region Name** grouping.

14. Close **Print Preview**.

15. The report opens in Design View. Notice that there are two new sections in the report: **RegionName Header** and **RegionName Footer**.

Exercise 8-7   ADD A GROUP SECTION IN DESIGN VIEW

A group organizes or categorizes a recordset by a particular field. Grouping allows you to separate records by displaying introductory and summary data. When using more than one group in a report, each subsequent group must be nested in the original group. You can group a report by up to 10 different fields.

1. From the **Design** tab, in the **Grouping & Totals** group, click the Group & Sort command. This action opens the **Group, Sort, and Total** pane.

Figure 8-8
Group, Sort, and Total pane
CC08.accdb
rptSalesSummary-ByRegion

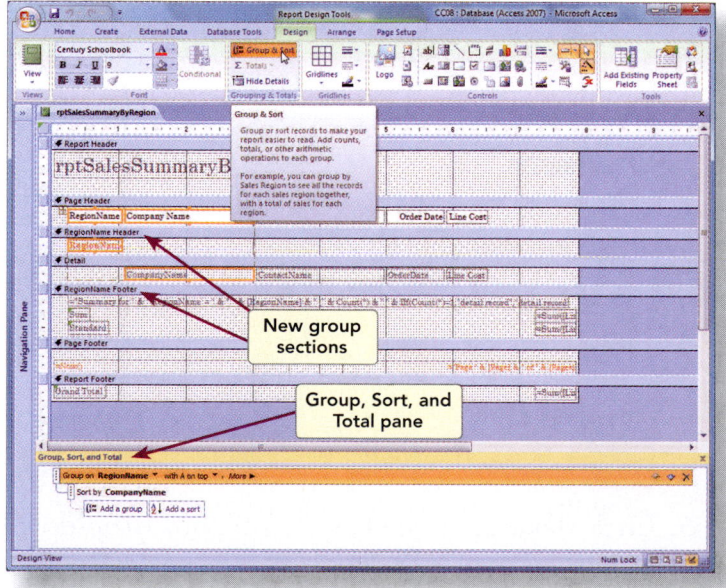

2. In the **Group, Sort, and Total** pane, click the **Sort by** level. Click the **CompanyName** drop-down arrow and choose **RegionName**.

3. Click the **Add a group** button and choose **CompanyName**. A new **CompanyName Header** section has been added above the **Detail** section but is empty.

Figure 8-9
Adding a new group
to the report
CC08.accdb
rptSalesSummary-
ByRegion

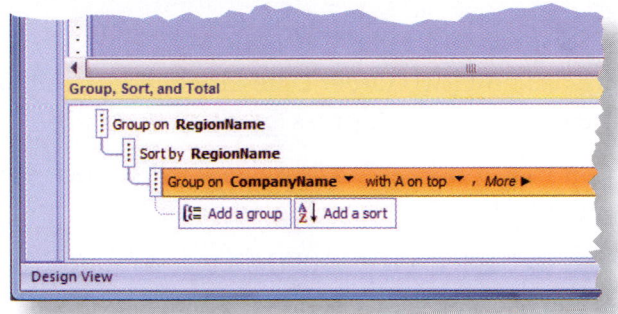

4. In the **Detail** section, click **CompanyName**. Make sure that you select only the text box.

5. While pressing [Shift], click **ContactName** text box.

6. Right-click the selected text boxes. From the menu choose **Layout**, then **Move Up a Section**. This action moves the text boxes into the **CompanyName Header** section.

7. Switch to Report View. The first three fields no longer repeat for each record.

8. Press [Ctrl]+[S] to save the report.

Exercise 8-8   ADD A GROUP SECTION
                    IN LAYOUT VIEW

You usually use a group header to display identifying labels. Group footers often display summary data such as totals or counts.

1. Switch to Layout View.

2. From the **Group, Sort, and Total** pane, click the **Add a group** button and choose **OrderDate**.

3. From the **Group, Sort, and Total** pane, in the **Group on OrderDate** level, click the **from oldest to newest** drop-down arrow and choose **from newest to oldest**.

4. From the **Group, Sort, and Total** pane, in the **Group on OrderDate** level, click the **by quarter** drop-down arrow and choose **by year**.

Figure 8-10
Group options
for dates
CC08.accdb
rptSalesSummary-
ByRegion

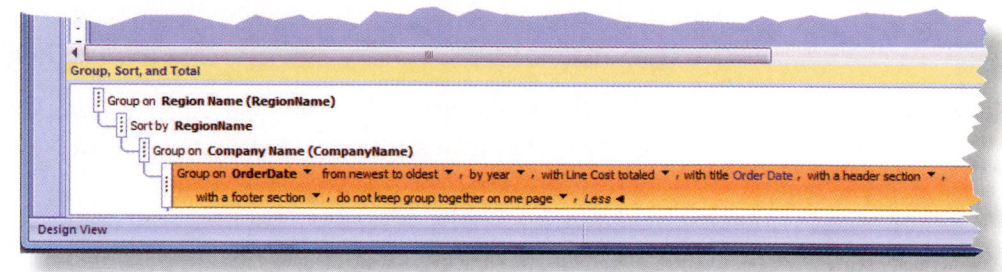

5. There are now two **Order Date** labels. Click the **Order Date** label next to the **Line Cost** label, press ⌨Delete.

6. Switch to Report View and review the report. The remaining **Order Date** control is now showing an error.

7. Switch to Design View and then return to Report View. The error is now gone.

8. Press ⌨Ctrl+⌨S to save the report.

Exercise 8-9   MODIFY GROUP OPTIONS

The default page break for a report occurs when the text reaches the bottom margin. If you do not want to split a group between pages, you can choose to keep the records together.

1. Switch to Layout View.

2. From the **Group, Sort, and Total** pane, in the **Group on OrderDate** level, click **More**.

3. Click the **with no totals** drop-down arrow. Click the **Total On** drop-down arrow and choose **Line Cost**.

Figure 8-11
Add an aggregate
function to a group
CC08.accdb
rptSalesSummary-
ByRegion

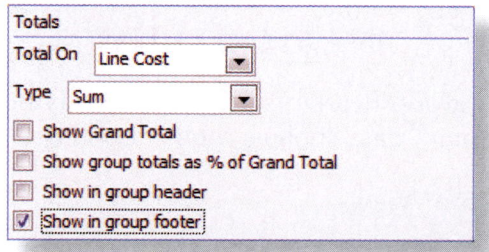

4. Click the check box **Show in group footer**.

5. From the **Group, Sort, and Total** pane, in the **Group on RegionName** level, click **More**.

6. In the **with title RegionName** option, click **RegionName**.

7. In the **Zoom** dialog box, add a space between **Region** and **Name**. Click **OK**.

8. From the **Group, Sort, and Total** pane, in the **Group on RegionName** level, click the **do not keep group together on one page** drop-down arrow and choose **keep header and first record together on one page**.

Figure 8-12
Page break options
CC08.accdb
rptSalesSummary-
ByRegion

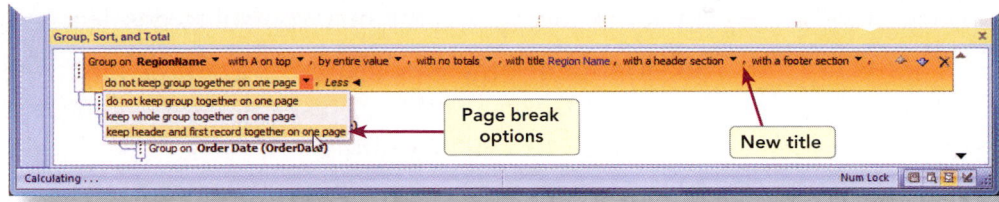

9. Right-click the **rptSalesSummaryByRegion** document tab and choose **Print Preview**. Scroll through the report.

10. Switch to Design View.

11. Press Ctrl+S to save the report.

Exercise 8-10 ADD A COMMON EXPRESSION CONTROL

When you place a summary expression, such as Count(*), in a group footer, the expression only will apply to the group. For example, assume that you create a report with a list of addresses grouped first by state and then by city. Placing the count function in the state group footer will count all records by state. Placing the count function in the city group footer will count all records by city.

1. From the **Design** tab, in the **Grouping & Totals** group, click the Group & Sort command to close the pane.

2. From the **Design** tab, in the **Controls** group, click the Text Box command. In the **Detail** section, click on the 7-inch mark on the horizontal ruler.

3. Drag the new text box to the left until you see the vertical insertion bar on the right side of the **Line Cost** text box. This adds the new control to the Control Layout.

Figure 8-13
Add a new text box
CC08.accdb
rptSalesSummary-
ByRegion

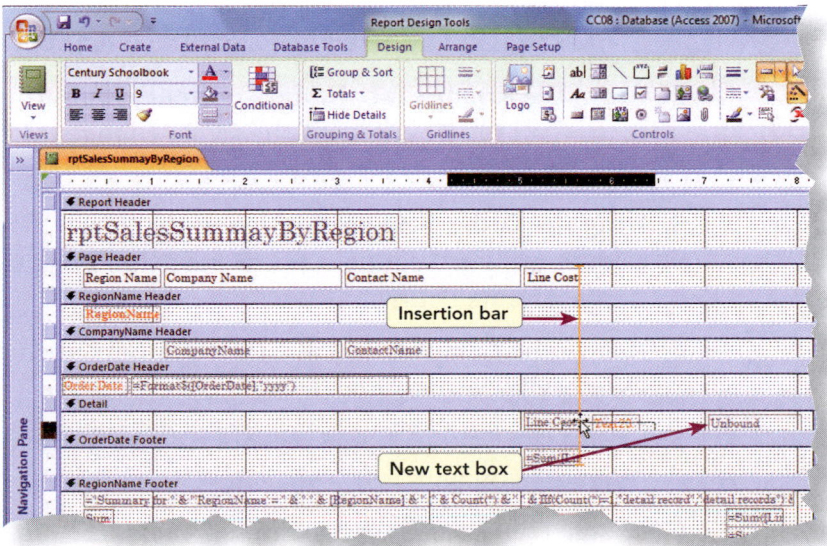

4. Click away from the new control to deselect it.

5. Right-click the new text box. From the menu, choose **Layout**, then **Move Down a Section**. This action moves the text boxes into the **OrderDate Footer** section.

6. From the **Design** tab, in the **Tools** group, click the Property Sheet command .

> **NOTE**
>
> The asterisk can be used in the Count function when you need to count just records and not the content of a field.

7. In the Property Sheet, on the **Data** tab, click in the **Control Source** property and key **=count(*)**.

8. Click the new text box's label.

9. In the Property Sheet, on the **Format** tab, click in the **Caption** property and key **Number of Orders**.

10. Close the Property Sheet.

11. Switch to Report View. There is now a Count function at the end of each **Order Date** section.

12. Press Ctrl+S to save the report.

Working with Controls in a Report

A report can contain bound controls, unbound controls, and calculated controls just like a form. In a report, you can move, resize, align, and format controls the same way you did in a form.

Exercise 8-11   MOVE AND RESIZE CONTROLS

Depending on the amount of changes you will need to make to a report, you may find that it will be easier for you to delete a control and then reinsert it rather than move it.

1. Switch to Layout View and select the **Order Date** control layout.

2. From the **Arrange** tab, in the **Control Layout** group, click the Tabular command . This moves the **Order Date** text box to another section than its label.

3. Drag the **Order Date** control layout to the right and up to **Contact Name** until you see the vertical insertion bar on the right side of the **Contact Name** control.

4. Resize the **Company Name** control to best fit the company "Kadoodles Games and Toys."

5. Resize the **Contact Name** control to best fit the contact "Craig Aspinall Koikas."

6. Resize the **Order Date** control to best fit the label **Order Date**.

7. Resize the **Line Cost** control to best fit the largest number on the column.

8. Resize the **Number of Orders** to fit the label.

9. Switch to Design View.

10. In the **RegionName Footer** section, there is a very long text box with an expression. Drag its right edge to the 7-inch mark.

11. Place your pointer in the horizontal ruler at the 7½-inch mark. When you see a black down arrow, click. This selects four text boxes in the lower right corner of the report.

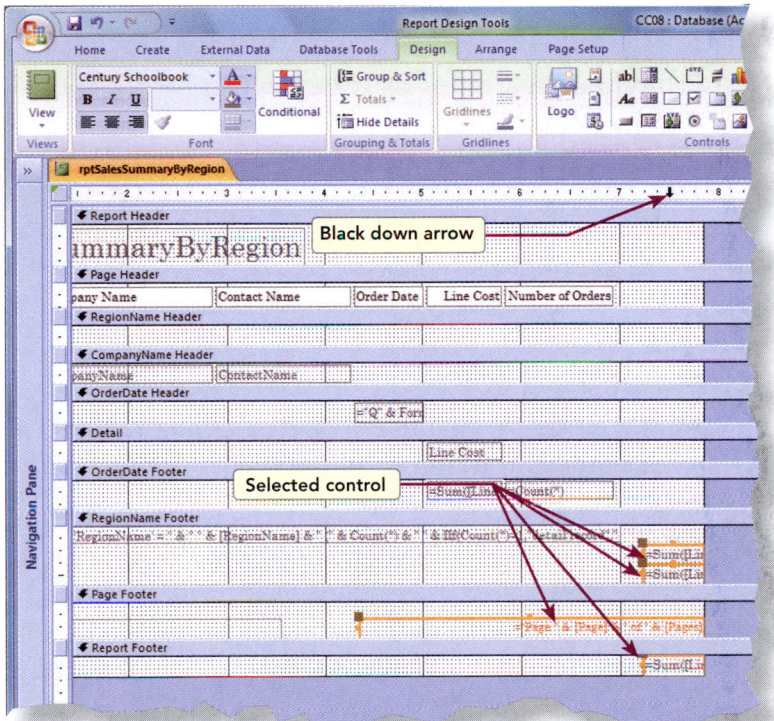

12. Drag the selected controls to the left until their right edges are at the 7-inch mark. Resize the report to the 7¼-inch mark.

13. Press Ctrl+S to save the report.

Exercise 8-12   ALIGN CONTROLS

When grouping fields in a report, the title of the field by default appears in the group header. When you move a control, such as a title, from one section to another, you will need to align the controls.

1. Switch to Layout View.

2. Click the first year under the **Order Date** label.

3. From the **Format** tab, in the **Font** group, click the Center command ▤ .

4. Click the **Line Cost** label.

5. From the **Format** tab, in the **Font** group, click the Center command 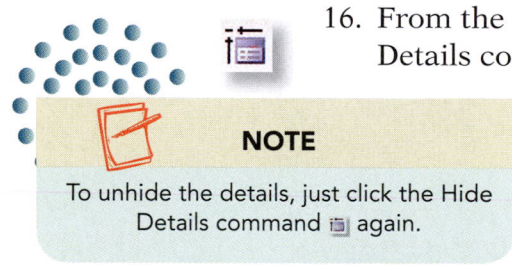.

6. Click the number under the **Number of Orders** label.

7. From the **Arrange** tab, in the **Tools** group, click the Property Sheet command.

8. In the Property Sheet, on the **Format** tab, click the **Right Margin** property and key **.5**. Close the Property Sheet.

9. Switch to Design View.

10. In the **RegionName Footer** section, there are three text boxes. Select the two small ones that start with "=Sum([Line…"

11. While pressing ⟨Shift⟩, click the text box in the lower right corner of the **Report Footer** section.

12. Drag the left edge of the text boxes to the 6-inch mark.

13. Move the three text boxes to the left so that they are under the **Line Cost** column.

14. In the **Report Header** section, edit the label to Sales Summary by Regions.

15. Switch to Layout View.

16. From the **Format** tab, in the **Grouping & Totals** group, click the Hide Details command.

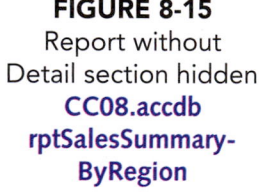

> **NOTE**
>
> To unhide the details, just click the Hide Details command again.

17. Right-click the first number under **Number of Orders**. From the menu, choose **Layout**, then **Move Up a Section**.

18. Switch to Print Preview.

FIGURE 8-15
Report without
Detail section hidden
CC08.accdb
rptSalesSummary-
ByRegion

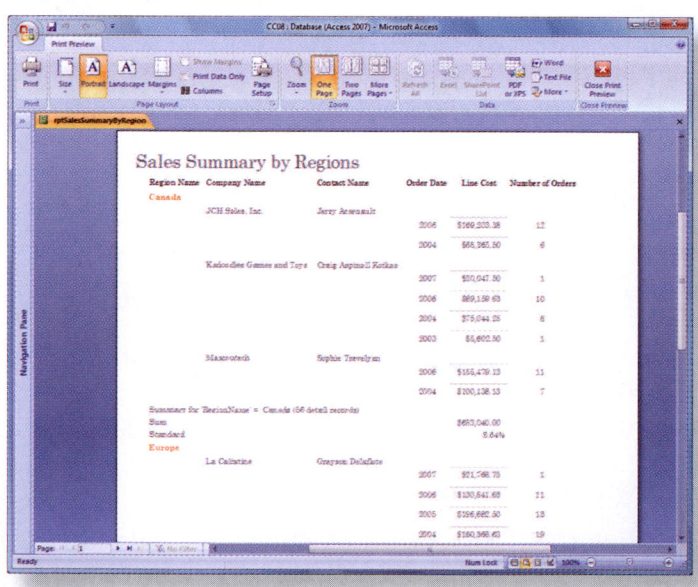

19. Press ⟨Ctrl⟩+⟨S⟩ to save the report.

Exercise 8-13   ADD LINES TO A REPORT

To make a report more visually appealing and distinguish information in each group, you can insert a horizontal line. Lines are added most often to the header sections of a report.

1. Switch to Design View.

2. Drag the top part of the **RegionName Header** section down ½ inch.

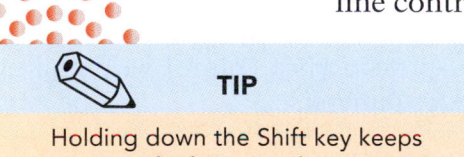

3. From the **Design** tab, in the **Controls** group, click the Line command ↘.

4. Click under the left edge of the **Region Name** label and drag to the 7¼ -inch mark on the horizontal ruler.

5. From the **Design** tab, in the **Tools** group, click the Property Sheet command 📑.

6. On the **Format** tab, click the **Height** property. If you dragged the line control across the page in a straight line, this number would be **0**. If needed, change this property to **0**.

7. Change the **Border Style** property to **Solid**.

8. Click the **Border Width** property, click the drop-down arrow, and choose **4 pt**.

9. Move the line control just below the labels.

10. Drag the top of the **RegionName Header** sections up to just below the line control.

TIP

Holding down the Shift key keeps the line straight.

11. Drag the top part of the **Page Footer** section down ½ inch.

12. From the **Design** tab, in the **Controls** group, click the Line command ↘.

13. While pressing Shift, click under the left edge of the **Standard** label and drag to the 6-inch mark on the horizontal ruler.

14. In the Property Sheet, on the **Format** tab, set the following properties:

Height	**0**
Border Style	**Dots**
Border Width	**2 pt**

15. Move the line control so that there are two rows of dots below the **Standard** control.

16. Resize the **Page Footer** section so that there are two rows of dots below the line control.

17. Switch to Print Preview.

Figure 8-16
Report with lines
added
CC08.accdb
rptSalesSummary-
ByRegion

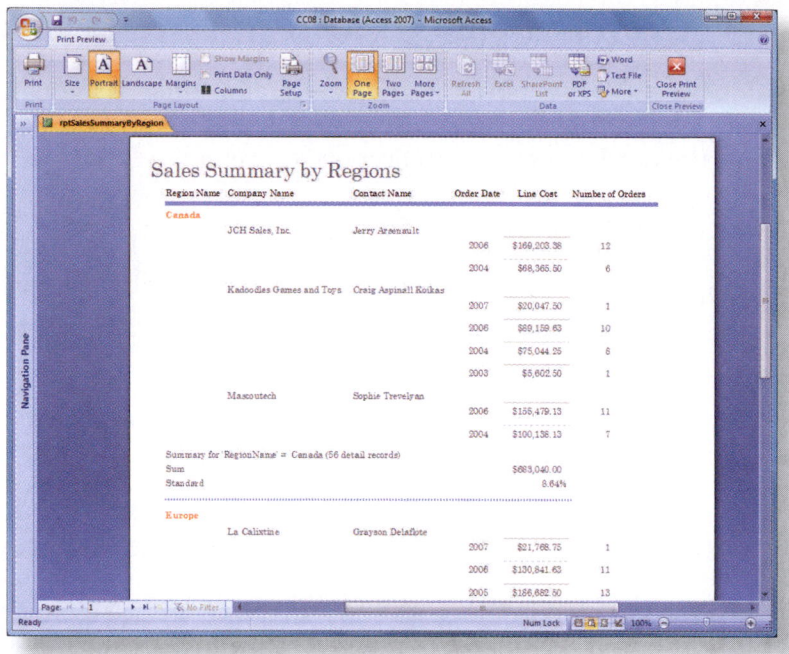

18. Press Ctrl + S to save the report.

19. Close Print Preview and switch to Design View.

Exercise 8-14   EDIT COMMON EXPRESSION CONTROLS

The Page Footer has two text boxes that use common expressions to display the date and page number. A common expression is a control with built-in commands to display dates, times, and page numbers.

1. In the **Page Footer** section, click the **=Now()** control. The Property Sheet shows that this is a text box.

2. In the Property Sheet, click the **Data** tab. The **Control Source** for this control is an Access common expression that displays the current date.

Figure 8-17
The =Now() Property
Sheet
CC08.accdb
rptSalesSummary-
ByRegion

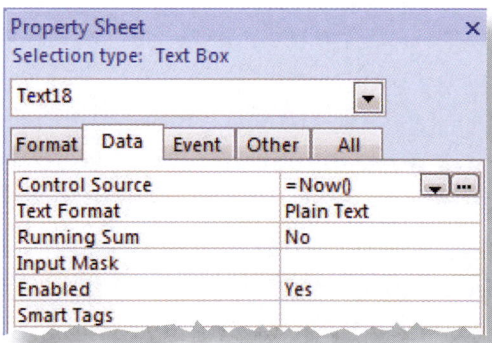

3. Click the **Format** tab. Click the **Format** property drop-down arrow and choose **Medium Date**.

4. In the **Page Footer** section, click the page number control.

5. In the Property Sheet, on the **Data** tab, click the **Control Source** property. Click the Build button ▣. The **Expression Builder** shows the Access code for this control.

6. Close the **Expression Builder** and click the **Format** tab. Change the **Width** property to **1.5**.

7. Close the Property Sheet.

8. Drag the page number control to the 7-inch mark.

9. Switch to Print Preview and review the report.

10. Press Ctrl+S to save the report.

Working with Format Painter and Conditional Formatting

Access has a **Format Painter** like Word and Excel. The *Format Painter* is a tool that copies the font, size, color, and alignment from one control to another. It saves you from having to set the individual properties for each control. To use the **Format Painter**, first select the control that has the desired formatting, click the **Format Painter** button, and then click the control to be changed.

You can also apply conditional formatting. Conditional formatting is formatting that displays in certain conditions, such as a style, color, or other setting. For example, you can set conditional formatting to show values over $15,000 in a different color, bolded, and underlined.

Exercise 8-15   USE THE FORMAT PAINTER

The calculated control should have the same format as the other controls in the **Detail** section. Use the **Format Painter** to match the control characteristics.

1. Switch to Layout View. Select the text box under the label **Region Name** that contains "Canada."

2. From the **Format** tab, in the **Font** group, change the **Font** to **Calibri**.

3. In the **Font** group, change the **Font Size** to **10**.

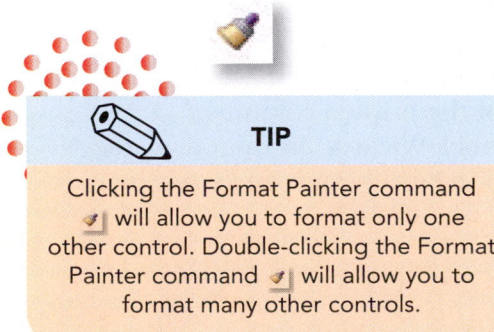

TIP

Clicking the Format Painter command ▨ will allow you to format only one other control. Double-clicking the Format Painter command ▨ will allow you to format many other controls.

4. From the **Format** tab, in the **Font** group, double-click the Format Painter command ▨. The pointer changes to an arrow with a paintbrush.

5. Click the first company under the **Company Name** label. The formats are copied.

6. Click the first contact under the **Contact Name** label. Press Esc to cancel the **Format Painter**.

7. Press Ctrl+S to save the report.

Exercise 8-16 USE CONDITIONAL FORMATTING

Many database designers use conditional formatting to call attention to records that are outside a specified parameter. Often managers use reports to track sales, production, and inventory levels. Conditional formatting helps quickly identify actions that may need to be taken. You can define up to three conditions.

1. Click the first number under the **Line Cost** label.

2. From the **Format** tab, in the **Font** group, click the Conditional command.

3. Press Tab to move to the second combo box. Click the drop-down arrow and choose **greater than or equal to**.

4. Press Tab and key **100000 (a one and 5 zeros.)**

5. In the bottom set of commands, click the Bold button **B** and the Font Color button **A** and choose the 7th row, 1st column.

Figure 8-18
Conditional
Formatting
dialog box
**CC08.accdb
rptSalesSummary-
ByRegion**

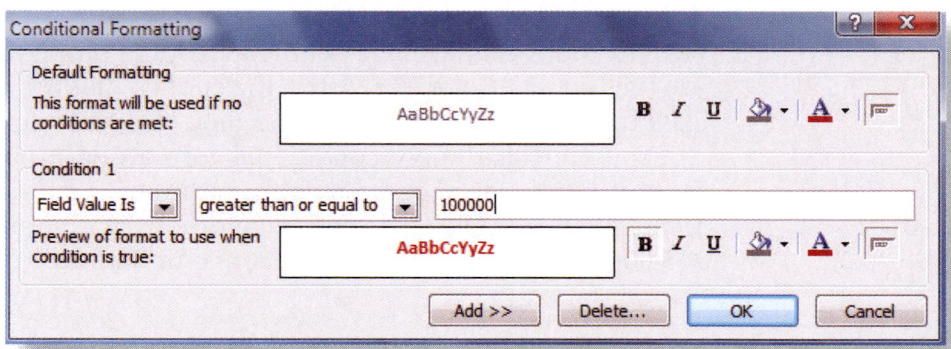

6. Click **OK**.

7. Values over $100,000 are now a different color.

8. Save and close the report.

Creating a Multicolumn Report and Labels

In addition to columnar and tabular reports, you can format a report to show the data in more than one column. You can use the Report Wizard or Design View to lay out the fields in a single column. Then use the **Page Setup** command to set the number and width of the printed columns.

You can also create labels using the Label Wizard, an option in the **New Report** dialog box. The Wizard lists common label brands and sizes, including mailing labels, package labels, CD labels, and more.

Exercise 8-17   CREATE A MULTICOLUMN REPORT

When creating a multicolumn report, you must define the number of columns, the number of rows, row spacing, column spacing, column width, and column height.

1. In the Navigation Pane, select **qryStuffedAnimals**.

2. From the **Create** tab, in the **Reports** group, click the Report command .

3. From the Quick Access toolbar, click the Save button. Key **rptMuliCol**.

4. Resize the **Product Code** control to just fit its label.

5. Resize the **Product ID** control to just fit its label.

6. Resize the **Product Name** controls to just fit the data.

7. Resize the **Unit Price** control to just fit its label.

8. Switch to Design View. In the **Detail** section, the **Picture** control's right edge, needs to be at 5 inches or less on the horizontal ruler.

NOTE

You can only see multiple columns in Print Preview.

Figure 8-19
Setting up a multicolumn report
CC08.accdb
rptSalesSummary-ByRegion

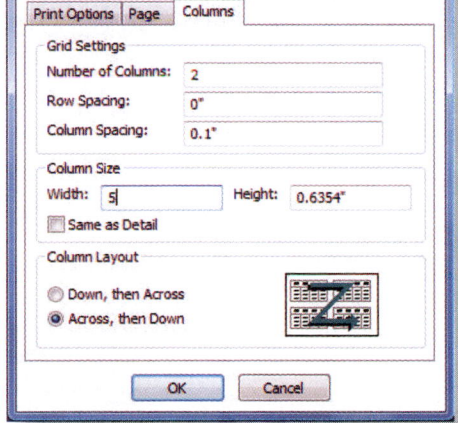

9. From the **Page Setup** tab, in the **Page Layout** group, click the Landscape command.

10. From the **Page Setup** tab, in the **Page Layout** group, click the Columns command.

11. Set the **Number of Columns** to **2** and the **Column Spacing** to **.1**.

12. Set the **Column Size Width** to **5**.

13. Click **OK**. Switch to Print Preview and view both pages.

14. Close and save the report.

Exercise 8-18   CREATE PACKAGE LABELS

The Label Wizard assists you in creating package labels. After you select a label type and size, the Label Wizard asks which fields to place on the label, which font to use, and how to sort the labels.

1. In the Navigation Pane, select **tblStuffedAnimals**.

2. From the **Create** tab, in the **Reports** group, click the Labels command.

3. In the **Label Wizard** dialog box, in the **Filter by manufacturer** section, choose **Avery**.

4. In the **Unit of Measure** section, choose **English**. In the **Label Type** section, choose **Sheet Feed**.

5. In the top list box, choose the **Product number** "8164." Click **Next**.

6. Set the **Font name** to **Times New Roman**, the **Font size** to **14**, the **Font weight** to **Normal**, and the **Text color** to black. Click **Next**.

7. Key **Product ID:** and press the spacebar twice.

8. In the **Available fields** section, double-click **ProductID** to place it in the **Prototype label** section.

9. Press ⌷Enter⌷ twice to leave a blank line in the **Prototype label** section.

10. Key **Product Name:** and press the spacebar twice. Double-click **ProductName**. Press ⌷Enter⌷ twice.

11. Key **Product Group:** and press the spacebar twice. Double-click **ProductGroup**.

Figure 8-20
Prototype for large labels
CC08.accdb
rptAnimalLabels

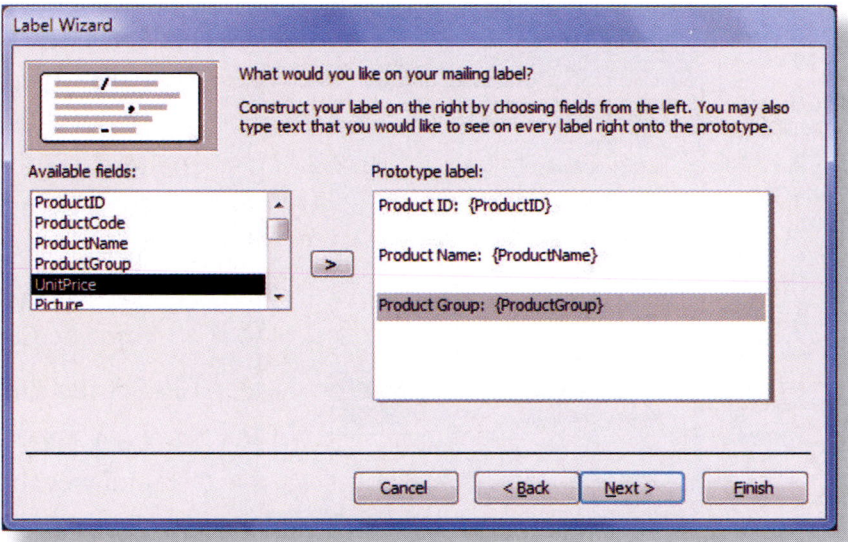

12. Click Next. In the **next** dialog box, double-click **ProductID** to add it to the **Sort by** section. Click **Next**.

13. Edit the report name to **rptAnimalLabels**. Select the option **Modify the label design**. Click **Finish**.

14. Switch to Design View.

Figure 8-21
Design View for large labels
CC08.accdb
rptAnimalLabels

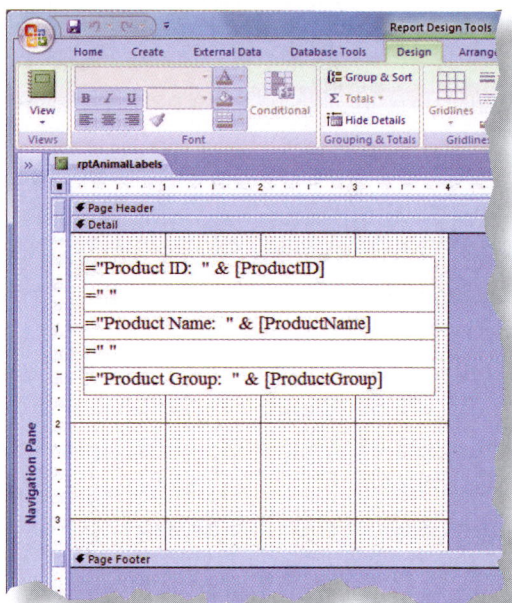

15. From the **Page Setup** tab, in the **Page Layout** group, click the Columns command ▦. Notice the **Number of Columns** is set to 2. Click **OK**.

16. Right-click the **rptAnimalLabel** document's tab and choose **Print Preview**.

17. If a warning message appears just click **OK**.

18. View all three pages.

19. Close Print Preview. Close and save the report.

20. Compact and repair the database and then close it.

Lesson 8 Summary

- A well-designed report can present information more effectively than other major objects can.

- Columnar style reports are most commonly used when the length of the data is too wide to display properly in tabular format.

- Depending on the report tool selected, the created report may have header and footer sections in addition to the detail section

- A Report tool is the quickest method to create a basic report.

- Before printing a report, it is good practice to view the report in Print Preview. In Print Preview, you can change the zoom size.

- When adding fields through Layout View, you will see a Field List pane.

- Padding specifies space between gridlines and controls. Margins specify the location of information in a control

- Reports can have numerous sections, including headers and footers.

- A group organizes or categorizes a recordset by a particular field. Groups can be nested up to 10 deep.

- The properties of controls can be modified.

- Simple reports can be created using the Report Wizard. A basic report can be created using the Report tool.

- Horizontal lines in a report can be created, moved, or resized, just like any other object.

- In a tabular report, each record displays on a separate line.

- Section properties can be viewed and modified in the property sheet.

- Group sections can organize and summarize information on the basis of categories.
- When adding or moving fields in a report, care should be given to aligning other controls in the header or footer to match the detail section.
- Controls should be sized and aligned to make the report easy to read.
- The date and page number are common controls created by the Report Wizard.
- The property sheet for each object in a report lists all the characteristics or attributes of that object.
- Calculated controls display the results of a numeric expression based on one or more fields in a record.
- Conditional formatting applies the property only when certain conditions are met.
- Records in a multicolumn report or label display in two or more columns.
- The Label Wizard can create non-standard labels.

LESSON 8		Command Summary	
Feature	**Button**	**Path**	**Keyboard**
Reports, Wizard		Create, Reports, Report Wizard	
Reports, Preview, Multiple Pages		Print Preview, Zoom, More Pages	
Reports, Create, Basic		Create, Reports, Report	
Reports, View, Report View		Formatting, Views, Report View	
Reports, Add Fields		Formatting, Controls, Add Existing Fields	
Control, Property Sheet		Arrange, Tools, Property Sheet	
Reports, Group and Sort		Design, Grouping & Totals, Group & Sort	
Reports, Grouping & Totals		Design, Grouping & Totals	
Line, Add		Design, Controls, Line	
Reports, Label		Create, Reports, Labels	

Concepts Review

True/False Questions

Each of the following statements is either true or false. Indicate your choice by circling T or F.

T F 1. The Field List pane appears in Design View.

T F 2. Use the Text Box button to add a calculated control to a report.

T F 3. Conditional formatting depends on criteria that you enter in the dialog box.

T F 4. Padding is the space between each section of a report.

T F 5. A Report Header prints at the top of every page.

T F 6. You cannot change the name of a control.

T F 7. An asterisk can be used in an aggregate function such as a count.

T F 8. Conditional formatting can be used to call attention to specific data in a report.

Short Answer Questions

Write the correct answer in the space provided.

1. What section of a report displays the data from each record?

2. When adding a field to a report in Layout View, what displays to allow you to select fields?

3. What is the quickest way to create a grouped report?

4. What is the name of the dialog box you use to select fields, common expressions, or arithmetic operators?

5. What does the expression =Now() do?

6. What tool should you use to add a calculated control to a report?

7. Which line property changes the width of the line?

8. What button on the toolbar copies the font and colors from one control to another?

Critical Thinking

Answer these questions on a separate page. There are no right or wrong answers. Support your answers with examples from your own experience, if possible.

1. You used the Line tool in this lesson to add a design element to a report. What other tools might add good design ideas for a printed report?

2. In this lesson, you learned how to change the size, position, and color of labels and text boxes using the property sheet. What are the advantages of using the property sheet instead of the mouse and toolbars?

Skills Review

Exercise 8-19

Create a label report. Modify the controls.

1. Open a database by following these steps:
    a. Locate and open the **Lesson 08** folder.
    b. Make a copy of **CC08** and rename it *[your initials]*-**CC08**.
    c. Open and enable content for *[your initials]*-**CC08**.

2. Create a label report by following these steps:
    a. In the Navigation Pane, select the table **qryCustomerContact**.
    b. From the **Create** tab, in the **Reports** group, click the Labels command .
    c. In the **Label Wizard** dialog box, in the **Filter by manufacturer** section, choose **Avery**.
    d. In the **Unit of Measure** section, choose **English**, and in the **Label Type** section, choose **Sheet Feed**.
    e. In the top list box, choose the **Product number** "5385." Click **Next**.
    f. Set the **Font name** to **Times New Roman**, the **Font size** to **16**, the **Font weight** to **Bold**, and the **Text color** to black. Click **Next**.
    g. In the **Available fields** section, double-click **CompanyName**.
    h. Press Enter twice.
    i. In the **Available fields** section, double-click **ContactName**.
    j. Press Enter.
    k. In the **Available fields** section, double-click **PhoneNum**.
    l. Click **Next**.
    m. In the **Available fields** section, double-click **CompanyName** and click **Next**.

n. Name the report **08-19-***[your initials]*.

o. Click **Finish**. In the warning dialog box, click **OK**.

p. Close the Print Preview to switch to Design View.

3. Modify controls by following these steps:

a. Click the **CompanyName** text box.

b. From the **Design** tab, in the **Font** group, click the Center command .

c. From the **Design** tab, in the **Font** group, click the **Font** command's drop-down arrow and choose **Arial Black**.

d. From the **Arrange** tab, in the **Size** group, click the To Fit command .

e. Move the **CompanyName** text box up until its bottom edge meets the top edge of the blank text box.

f. From the Quick Access toolbar, click the Save button .

g. Print/Save the first page of the report.

h. Right-click the form's document tab and choose **Close**.

Exercise 8-20

Create and modify a report. Modify sections and controls.

1. Create a report by following these steps:

a. Open and enable content for *[your initials]***-CC08**.

b. In the Navigation Pane, select **qryEmployeeDates**.

c. From the **Create** tab, in the **Reports** group, click the Report command .

d. From the Quick Access toolbar, click the Save button . Key **08-20-***[your initials]*.

2. Modify the control layout by following these steps:

a. With **08-20-***[your initials]* open, select the **Hire Date** control and press Delete.

b. Select the **EndDate** control and press Delete.

c. Select the **SSN** control label and click the Layout Selector command .

d. From the **Arrange** tab, in the **Control Layout** group, click the Stacked command.

e. Click the **Date of Birth** control.

f. From the **Arrange** tab, in the **Control Layout** group, click the Stacked command.

g. Drag the **Date of Birth** control to the open area to the right.

h. While pressing Shift, click the **SSN** control.

i. From the **Arrange** tab, in the **Control Alignment** group, click the Top command .

3. Modify a report section by following these steps:

   a. Switch to Design View.

   b. Drag the top of the **Page Footer** section until the **Detail** section is 1 inch tall.

   c. Select the control in the **Report Footer** section and press ⌷Delete⌷.

   d. Drag the bottom of the **Report Footer** section up until no more white area is visible. You have closed the section.

   e. In the **Report Header** section, select both the **Date** and the **Time** control. Drag the right edge to the 7-inch mark on the horizontal ruler.

   f. In the **Detail** section, if needed, drag the right edge of the **BirthDate** control to the 7-inch mark on the horizontal ruler.

   g. Resize the report to 7 inches wide.

4. Edit report labels by following these steps:

   a. In the **Report Header** section, edit the label to read **Employees Ages**. Switch to Design View.

   b. From the **Design** tab, in the **Controls** group, click the Label command ⒜.

   c. Click in the far left of the **Page Footer** section and key **Prepared by:** *[your full name]*.

5. Add a line control to a report by following these steps:

   a. From the **Design** tab, in the **Controls** group, click the Line command ⟍. Click in the lower left corner of the **Detail** section and drag it to the 7-inch mark on the horizontal ruler.

   b. From the **Design** tab, in the **Tools** group, click the Property Sheet command ⌸.

   c. On the **Format** tab, click the **Height** property and, if necessary, change this property to **0**.

   d. Close the Property Sheet.

6. Add a new control to a report by following these steps:

   a. Switch to Design View.

   b. From the **Design** tab, in the **Controls** group, click the Text Box command ⒜.

   c. Click under the **Date of Birth** control.

   d. Add the new unbound control by dragging the new control up to the **Date of Birth** control until you see the insertion bar below the **Date of Birth** control.

   e. Edit the new control's label to **Age**.

7. Add an expression to a control by following these steps:

   a. Double-click the new control's text box. In the Property Sheet, on the **Data** tab, click in the **Control Source** property. Click the Ellipses button ⌸.

   b. In the **Expression Builder**, in the left panel, double-click the folder **Functions** and then click **Built-In Functions**.

   c. In the middle panel, click **Date/Time**. From the right panel, double-click **DateDiff**.

d. In the expression box, click **<<Interval>>** and key **"yyyy"**.

e. In the expression box, click **<<date1>>**.

f. In the left panel, click **08-20-[your initials]**. In the middle panel, click **<Field List>**, and in the right panel, double-click **BirthDate**.

g. In the expression box, click **<<date2>>** and key **now()**.

h. In the expression box, click **<<firstweekday>>** and press Delete.

i. In the expression box, click **<<firstweek>>** and press Delete.

j. Delete the last two commas. Click **OK**.

 k. Print/Save the last page of the report.

l. Close and save the report.

Exercise 8-21

Create a report using the Report Wizard. Add and modify sections and controls.

1. Create a report with the Report Wizard by following these steps:

   a. Open and enable content for **[your initials]-CC08**.

   b. In the Navigation Pane, select **qryEmployeeDates**.

    c. From the **Create** tab, in the **Reports** group, click the Report Wizard command 🔍.

   d. Add the following field names to the **Selected Fields**:

   SSN
   EmployeeID
   HireDate

    e. Click **Next**. Click the Remove One button ◄ to remove the **EmployeeID** grouping. Click **Next**.

   f. Click the drop-down arrow for the first sort level. Choose **HireDate** and click **Next**.

   g. For the **Layout**, choose **Tabular**. For the **Orientation**, choose **Portrait**. Click **Next**.

   h. For the style, choose **Apex**. Click **Next**.

   i. Key **08-21-[your initials]** as the title of the report.

   j. Select the option to preview the report. Click **Finish**.

   k. Close Print Preview.

NOTE

The **Hire Date** field is leftmost in the report because it is the sort field.

2. Add a group to a report by following these steps:

    a. From the **Design** tab, in the **Grouping & Totals** group, click the Group & Sort command 📋.

   b. In the **Group, Sort, and Total** pane, click the **Add a group** button and choose **HireDate**. The section **HireDate Header** has been added.

   c. Right-click the text box **HireDate**. From the menu, choose **Layout** and click **Move up a Section**.

d. In the **Group, Sort, and Total** pane, click the **Group on HireDate** level, and click **More**.

e. In the **by quarter** option, click the drop-down arrow and choose **year**.

f. At the far right of the level, click the Promote button 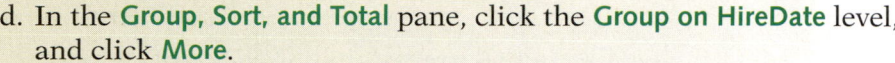 to move the Grouping above the Sort level.

g. In the **HireDate Header** section, click the **HireDate** text box.

h. From the **Design** tab, in the **Tools** group, click the Property Sheet command ◻.

i. On the **Format** tab, click the **Format** property and key **yyyy**.

j. Click the **Hire Date** label. In the Property Sheet, click the **Caption** property and key **Year**.

3. Add a field to a report by following these steps:

a. From the **Design** tab, in the **Tools** group, click the Add Existing Fields command ◻.

b. In the **Field List**, drag **HireDate** to the left side of the **SSN** text box in the **Detail** section.

4. Format the controls by following these steps:

a. Click the **Year** label.

b. From the **Design** tab, in the **Font** group, click the Center command ▤.

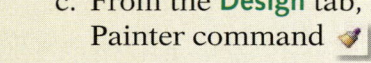

c. From the **Design** tab, in the **Font** group, double-click the Format Painter command ◢.

d. Click each of the labels in the **Page Header** section. Press ⎋Esc to turn off the **Format Painter**.

e. Click the **HireDate** text box in the **HireDate Header** section.

f. From the **Design** tab, in the **Font** group, click the Center command ▤.

g. From the **Design** tab, in the **Font** group, double-click the Format Painter command ◢.

h. Click the **SSN** and **EmployeeID** text boxes. Press ⎋Esc to turn off the **Format Painter**.

i. Save the report and preview it.

j. Print/Save the first page of the report. Close the report.

Exercise 8-22

Create a report using the Report Wizard. Add and modify sections and controls.

1. Create a report with the Report Wizard by following these steps:

a. Open and enable content for *[your initials]*-**CC08**.

b. From the **Create** tab, in the **Reports** group, click the Report Wizard command ◻.

   c. For each table, add the following field names to the **Selected Fields:**

tblProductLine	**ProductLine**
tblStuffedAnimals	**ProductName**
	UnitPrice
tblKitAssemblyLines	**SKU**
	QTY

   d. Click **Next**. View the data **by tblProductLines**. Click **Next**.

   e. Double-click **ProductName** to add a group. Click **Next**.

   f. Click the drop-down arrow for the first sort level. Choose **SKU** and click **Next**.

   g. For the **Layout**, choose **Stepped**. For the **Orientation**, choose **Portrait**. Click **Next**.

   h. For the style, choose **Solstice**. Click **Next**.

   i. Key **08-22-*[your initials]*** as the title for the report.

   j. Select the option to **Preview the report**. Click **Finish**.

   k. Close Print Preview.

2. Modify controls by following these steps:

   a. Click anywhere in the **Report Header** to deselect the other controls.

   b. In the **ProductID Header**, right-click the **UnitPrice** text box. From the menu, choose **Layout** and then **Move Up a Section**.

   c. From the **Design** tab, in the **Grouping & Totals** group, click the Group & Sort command .

   d. In the **Group, Sort, and Total** pane, click **Group on ProductID**. On the far right of this level, click the Delete button to delete the grouping.

   e. Switch to Layout View.

   f. From the **Page Setup** tab, in the **Page Layout** group, select the **Margins** arrow and select the Normal command .

   g. Rename the **Name of Product Group** label to **Product Group**.

   h. Resize the **Product Group** column to just fit its label.

   i. Resize the **Unit Price** column to just fit its label.

   j. Resize the **Qty** column to just fit its label.

   k. Resize the **SKU** column to just fit all data.

   l. Save and switch to Design View.

3. Set group options and print/save by following these steps:

   a. In the **Group, Sort, and Total** pane, click **Group on ProductGroup** and click **More**.

   b. Click the drop-down arrow for **do not keep together on one page** and choose **keep whole group together on one page**.

   c. Save the report and preview it.

    d. Print/Save the first page of the report. Close the report.

Lesson Applications

Exercise 8-23

Create a simple report. Add groups to a report. Apply Conditional Formatting

1. Open and enable content for *[your initials]*-**CC08**.

2. Create a simple report based on the **qryLastOrder**.

3. Save the report as **08-23-***[your initials]*.

4. Resize the columns so that all data can be seen.

5. Add a grouping for **RegionName** sorted in descending order.

6. Modify the title label to **Customers Last Order Report**.

7. Delete the **Time** control in the **Report Header** section and replace it with a label with the caption **Prepared by:** *[your full name]*.

8. Use the **Format Painter** to copy the format from the new label in the **Report Header** section to the **Date** control.

9. Add **Conditional Formatting** for the **Last Order Date** text box in the **Detail** section. If the date is in the year 2006, use the format **Bold** with a purple **Font Color**.

10. Delete the page control in the **Page Footer** section and close the section.

11. Make sure that all data and text can be seen.

 12. Print/Save the report. Close the report.

Exercise 8-24

Create a multicolumn report. Size controls. Add a label.

1. Open and enable content for *[your initials]*-**CC08**, create a simple report for **qryEmployeePhone**.

2. Delete the **Employee ID** control.

3. Resize the three controls in the **Detail** section so that the right edge of the **HomePhone** control is at the 3½-inch mark.

4. Save the report as **08-24-***[your initials]*.

5. Apply the AutoFormat **Civic** to the report.

6. Select the three labels in the **Page Header** section and make a copy. Place the copied labels to the right of the originals, starting at the 4-inch mark.

7. Change the report to use **2** columns that are **3.5** inches wide, with a column spacing of **.45**. The columns should run down and then across. The report must fit one page.

8. Select the three controls in the **Detail** section. Change their **Top Margin** property to **.1** and their **Height** property to **.30**.

9. Delete the page number control. Add a label with the caption **Prepared by:** *[your full name]*.

10. Edit the label in the **Report Header** section to **Employee Phone List**.

11. Use the **Group & Sort** command to add a sort by **Last Name** and then by **First Name**. Close the **LastName Header** and **FirstName Header** sections (height = 0).

 12. Print/Save the report. Close the report.

Exercise 8-25

Create a group report based on a query. Modify controls and sections.

1. Open and enable content for *[your initials]*-**CC08**.

2. Use the Report Wizard to create a report for **qryAnimalsByVender**.

3. Use all fields. Group by **ProductName** and **VenderName**. Use the summary options to add the **Sum** function for **LCost**. Use a stepped layout and portrait orientation. Use the **Urban** style. Name the report **08-25-***[your initials]*.

4. Change the title label to **Kit Costs by Vender**.

5. Resize each column so all data can be seen.

6. Delete the "Summary" controls in the **VenderName Footer** and **ProductName Footer** sections.

7. Delete the controls in the **Report Footer** section.

8. Move the text box in the **VenderName Footer** to the right of the text box in the **VenderName Header** section.

9. Delete the label in the **VenderName Footer** section and close this section.

10. Move the text box in the **ProductName Footer** to the left to place it under the **LCost** controls in the other sections.

11. In the **ProductName Footer** move the "Sum" label to the left until it is next to its text box.

12. Draw a straight line (2 pt) above the "Sum" label and text box.

13. Format the labels in the **Page Header** section to font size **14**. Change **LCost** to **Cost** add spaces where needed in the other labels.

14. Use the **Hide Details** command.

15. Add a label to right side of the **Report Header** with the caption **Prepared by:** *[your full name]*.

 16. Print/Save the first page of the report. Save and close report.

Exercise 8-26 ◆ Challenge Yourself

Create a report using the Report Wizard. Add and modify controls. Sort and group records in a report. Add a calculated control for a group. Add a line.

1. Open and enable content for *[your initials]*-**CC08**.

2. Create a report using the Report Wizard.

3. From **tblJobCodes**, select **JobTitle**. From **tblEmployees**, select **LastName** and **FirstName**. From **tblLeaveDays**, select **LeaveCategory** and **LeaveDate**.

4. You want to view the data by **tblJobCode**.

5. Add a group level for **LastName** and **LeaveCategory**. Choose the style **Access 2007**.

6. Save the report as **08-26-***[your initials]*.

7. Resize each control so all data can be seen. Double the height of the **Job Title** text box to better fit the data.

TIP

To move a Sort or Group up the list just click the Promote button.

8. Move the **FirstName** text box up to the **LastName Header** group.

9. Change the **EmployeeID** group's option to show the footer section and hide the header section.

10. Add a sort by **JobTitle**. Move **Sort by JobTitle** above **Group on JobCode**.

11. Add a text box to the **LeaveCategory Header** section. Drag the new text box until it has joined the control layout on the right side of the **LeaveCategory** control.

12. Set the unbound text box's **Control Source** property to **=Count(*)** and set its label **Caption** property to **Occurrences**. Resize the control to fit the label.

13. Center the content of this text box.

REVIEW

The default **Border Style** property for a new line is transparent. You will need to change this property to see the line.

14. In the **EmployeeID Footer** section, add a straight horizontal line starting at 1.5 inches and ending at 5 inches. Move the line to the top of the section. Resize the section to leave just enough room for the line.

15. Edit the title label to **Employee Leave Breakdown**.

16. Add spaces where needed in the **Page Header** labels.

17. Add a label in the far right of the **Report Header** section and key **Prepared by:** *[your full name]*.

 18. Print/Save the first page of the report. Save and close the report.

19. Compact the database and close it.

On Your Own

In these exercises you work on your own, as you would in a real-life work environment. Use the skills you've learned to accomplish the task—and be creative.

Exercise 8-27

Review the design of the database that you modified in Exercise 7-31. On a sheet of paper, sketch three reports that will enhance the usability of this database. On each sketched report, describe who would use the report, the reason that the information in the report is valuable, and the frequency with which the report will be printed. Name each report and give it a title that best describes the purpose for the report. Write your name and Exercise 8-27 on each sketch. Continue to Exercise 8-28.

Exercise 8-28

On the basis of the sketches you created in Exercise 8-27, create three reports. Select the style and layout most appropriate for each report. Arrange the controls as necessary. In the Page Footer, include your name and Exercise 8-28. In the Report Header, include the title of the report. Print a copy of each report. Continue to Exercise 8-29.

Exercise 8-29

Create a group for your report. Depending on your design, you may need to add a field to a table and enter appropriate data. Select the name, title, style, and layout most appropriate for the report. Arrange the controls as necessary. In the Page Footer, include your name and Exercise 8-29. Test your report in Print Preview. You may need to sort the records for the grouping to work appropriately. Print the report. Submit the copies of the sketches and reports that you printed in Exercises 8-27 through 8-29 to your instructor. Keep a copy of the database you modified in this exercise. You will use it for the On Your Own exercises in subsequent lessons.

Unit 2 Applications

Unit Application 2-1

Insert a subdatasheet. Modify a relationship. Create a validation rule, validation text, and form. Print/Save a datasheet, form, table, and relationship.

1. From the **Unit 02** folder, copy the file **CCU2** and rename it *[your initials]*-**CCU2**.

2. Insert **tblKitSuppliers** as a subdatasheet into the datasheet of **tblCampaigns** using **SupplierID** as the linking field.

3. Modify the One-to-Many relationship between **tblCampaigns** and **tblKitSuppliers**. Set the relationship to allow only suppliers found in **tblKitSuppliers** to be entered in **tblCampaigns**.

4. For **tblCampaigns**, create a **Validation Rule** for both date fields that will allow only start dates after December 31, 2006. Use the validation text **Enter a date after December 31, 2006**.

 5. Print/Save a Database Documenter Report for **tblCampaigns**. For **Include for Table**, select **Properties** and **Relationships**. For **Include for Fields**, select **Name, Data Types, and Sizes**. For **Include for Indexes**, select **Nothing**.

6. Using the Form Wizard, create a form that displays all the fields from **tblCampaigns**. Use a columnar layout with the **Oriel** style. Name the form **U2-01-***[your initials]*.

7. Using the newly created form, enter the following record:

Campaign:	**Sept 07**
Name:	**Back To School Critters**
Start Date:	**8/1/06** *(see Note below)*

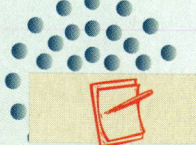

NOTE

This date violates the newly created validation rule.

8. Continue entering the record:

Start Date:	**8/1/07**
End Date:	**9/4/07**
Notes:	**We will have a new line of animals for this campaign. They will include Eddie Einstein Elephant and Alexander Graham Bear. Others will be developed by** *[your full name]*.
Supplier:	**CC-01** *(see Note below)*

NOTE

You won't be able to enter the supplier number. It violates the established referential integrity.

9. Change the **Supplier** to **CC-03**.

10. Print/Save only the record you just entered using the form **U2-01-***[your initials]*.

Unit Application 2-2

Modify a form. Create and modify a grouped report. Modify controls in forms and reports.

1. Using *[your initials]*-**CCU2**, edit **frmAnnualCampaign** by adding a label in the **Form Footer** section with the caption **Prepared by:** *[your full name]*.

2. In the **Form Header** section, add a title label with the caption **Carolina Critters Sales Campaigns**. Format the label as 14-point Arial bold with white text. Size the label to show the text on one line.

3. Resize the field labels to approximately 1-inch wide.

4. Move the **Supplier ID** controls above the **Name** controls.

5. View the form and save it.

6. Change the labels in the **Detail** section to the special effect **Etched**. Save the form.

7. Print/Save the record for **Campaign** "May 07" using **frmAnnualCampaign**. Close the form.

8. Using the Report Wizard, create a report for all the fields in **tblCampaigns**. When the wizard asks for a group, remove the **Supplier** group. Sort by **StartDate Ascending**. Make it a **tabular** report in **Landscape** orientation with an **Urban** style. Name the report **U2-02-***[your initials]*.

9. Delete the Campaign# text box and its label.

10. Change the **Name** label by adding the caption **Campaign Name**.

11. Move the **Start Date** control between **Campaign Name** and **End Date**.

12. Add a group for **SupplierID** and move it above the sort in the **Group, Sort, and Total** pane.

13. Edit the title label to **Sales Campaigns**. In the **Page Header** section, bold all the labels. Resize the labels to display all text.

14. In the far right of the **Report Header** section, add a label with the caption **Prepared by:** *[your full name]*.

15. Save, preview, print/save, and close the report.

Unit Application 2-3

Create a multicolumn report with conditional formatting.

1. Using *[your initials]*-**CCU2**, create a **Columnar** report for **qryInvoiceLineItemCost** using all the fields.

2. View the data by **tblInvoiceLineItems**. Group by **InvoiceID**. Sort by **Unit Price** in ascending order.

3. Apply an **Outline** layout in **Portrait** orientation. Apply the **Median** style.

4. Name the report **U2-03-***[your initials]*.

5. Resize the controls in the **Detail** section to fit in the left 3½ inches of the report.

6. Set up the page to show two columns. Decide how much space to leave between rows and columns and how wide to make the columns.

7. Set the **UnitPrice** field to appear in bold italics if the amount is greater than $17.

8. Change the title label in the **Report Header** to display **Invoice Line Items Report**.

9. In the far right of the **Report Header** section, add a label with the caption **Prepared by:** *[your full name]*. Format the new label the same as the title label but change the **Font Size** to **12** pt.

10. Change the **Product ID** label to **Product Name**.

 11. Print/Save the first page of the report. Save and close it.

Unit Application 2-4 ◆ Using the Internet

Carolina Critters is planning to photograph all aspects of its manufacturing process. You will need to research digital cameras for the company's president. Begin this task by searching the Internet for office supply venders that sell digital cameras priced between $200 and $700. Create a new table and form to enter the name of the camera manufacturer, the name/model of the camera, the store that sells the camera, and the price of the camera and an image of the camera. Using the form, enter data for at least four manufacturers and twelve cameras. Add your full name to the **Form Header**. Name the table **U2-04-T** and the form **U2-04-F**.

Design a report that displays the manufacturers, name/model of the cameras, stores, and prices. Group the data by manufacturer and sort by price in ascending order. On the **Page Footer** of the report, add your full name as a label. Name the report **U2-04-R**. Create and print/save the report.

 Print/Save the first record in the form. Print/Save the entire report on one page.

appendixes

Appendix A   Proofreaders' Marks

Appendix B   Standard Forms for Business Documents

Appendix C   Quick Reference Guide

APPENDIX A

Proofreaders' Marks

Proofreaders' Mark		Draft	Final Copy
⁋	Start a new paragraph.	ridiculous! If that is so	ridiculous!
			If that is so
⌒	Delete space.	to gether	together
#	Insert space.	Itmay be	It may not be
⟲	Move as shown.	it is (not) true	it is true
⁀	Transpose.	beleivable	believable
		is it so	it is so
◯	Spell out.	2 years ago	two years ago
		16 Elm St.	16 Elm Street
∧	Insert a word.	How much it?	How much is it?
℘ OR ―	Delete a word.	it may not be true	it may be true
∧ OR �	Insert a letter.	temperture	temperature
ℐ OR ∋	Delete a letter and close up.	committment to buny	commitment to buy
℘ OR ―	Change a word.	and if you won't	but if you can't
(Stet)	Stet (don't delete).	I was very glad	I was very glad
/	Make letter lowercase.	Federal Government	federal government
≡	Capitalize.	Janet L. greyston	Janet L. Greyston
∨	Raise above the line.	in her new book*	in her new book*
∧	Drop below the line.	H2SO4	H₂SO₄
⊙	Insert a period.	Mr Henry Grenada	Mr. Henry Grenada
⋏	Insert a comma.	a large old house	a large, old house
⌄	Insert an apostrophe.	my childrens car	my children's car
⌄⌄	Insert quotation marks.	he wants a loan	he wants a "loan"
= OR ⌃	Insert a hyphen.	a first-rate job	a first-rate job
		ask the coowner	ask the co-owner
¦M	Insert an em dash.	Here it is cash!	Here it is—cash!
¦N	Insert an en dash.	Pages 1–5	Pages 1–5
―	Insert underscore.	an issue of Time	an issue of Time
(ital)	Set in italic.	The New York Times	*The New York Times*

Proofreaders' Mark		Draft	Final Copy
(bf) ⌇⌇	Set in boldface.	(bf) the Enter key	the **Enter** key
(rom)	Set in roman.	(rom) the *most* likely	the most likely
( )	Insert parentheses.	left today (May 3)	left today (May 3)
⌐	Move to the right.	$38,367,000 ⌐	$38,367,000
⌐	Move to the left.	⌐ Anyone can win!	Anyone can win!
(ss) [	Single-space.	(ss) [I have heard / he is leaving	I have heard / he is leaving
(ds) [	Double-space.	(ds) [When will you / have a decision?	When will you / have a decision?
(+ 1 line)	Insert 1 line space.	Percent of Change / (+ 1 line) 16.25	Percent of Change / 16.25
(− 1 line)	Delete (remove) 1 line space.	Northeastern / (− 1 line) regional sales	Northeastern / regional sales

Standard Forms for Business Documents

Reference manuals, such as *The Gregg Reference Manual*, provide a variety of letter and memorandum styles, as well as styles for reports and other documents. Many businesses also have their own styles for documents. This appendix includes two basic styles—a business letter and a memorandum. It also shows the most common format for a continuation page (used for either letters or memos).

TABLE B-1 Parts of a Letter

Part of Letter	Location/Description
Heading	
Letterhead or return address	Often appears on preprinted stationery; can also be created in Word. Includes the company name, address, and other contact information.
Date line	Two inches from the top of the page on letterhead stationery or on the third line below a Word letterhead. Use date format shown in Figure B-1.
Opening	
Inside address	Starts on the fourth line below the date; consists of name and address (and possibly company name and job title) of person to whom you are writing.
Salutation	On the second line below the inside address; typically includes a courtesy title (Mr., Mrs., Ms., Miss) and ends with a colon.
Body	
Message	Content of the letter, single-spaced with one blank line between paragraphs.
Closing	
Complimentary closing	On the second line below the last line of the body of the letter. Common closings are "Sincerely" or "Sincerely yours" followed by a comma.
Writer's identification	On the fourth line below the closing, to leave space for a signature; includes the writer's name and job title (and sometimes the department).
Reference initials	On the second line below the writer's name and title; consists of the typist's initials in small letters.
Enclosure notation	On a new line below the reference initials if letter has an enclosure. Specify the number of enclosures. Can also use "Attachment" if enclosure is attached.
Optional features	Filename notation—indicates document name for reference purposes; delivery notation—method of delivery (other than regular mail); copy notation—people who will receive copies of the letter (usually begins with "c:" or "cc:")

Figure B-1
Business letter style

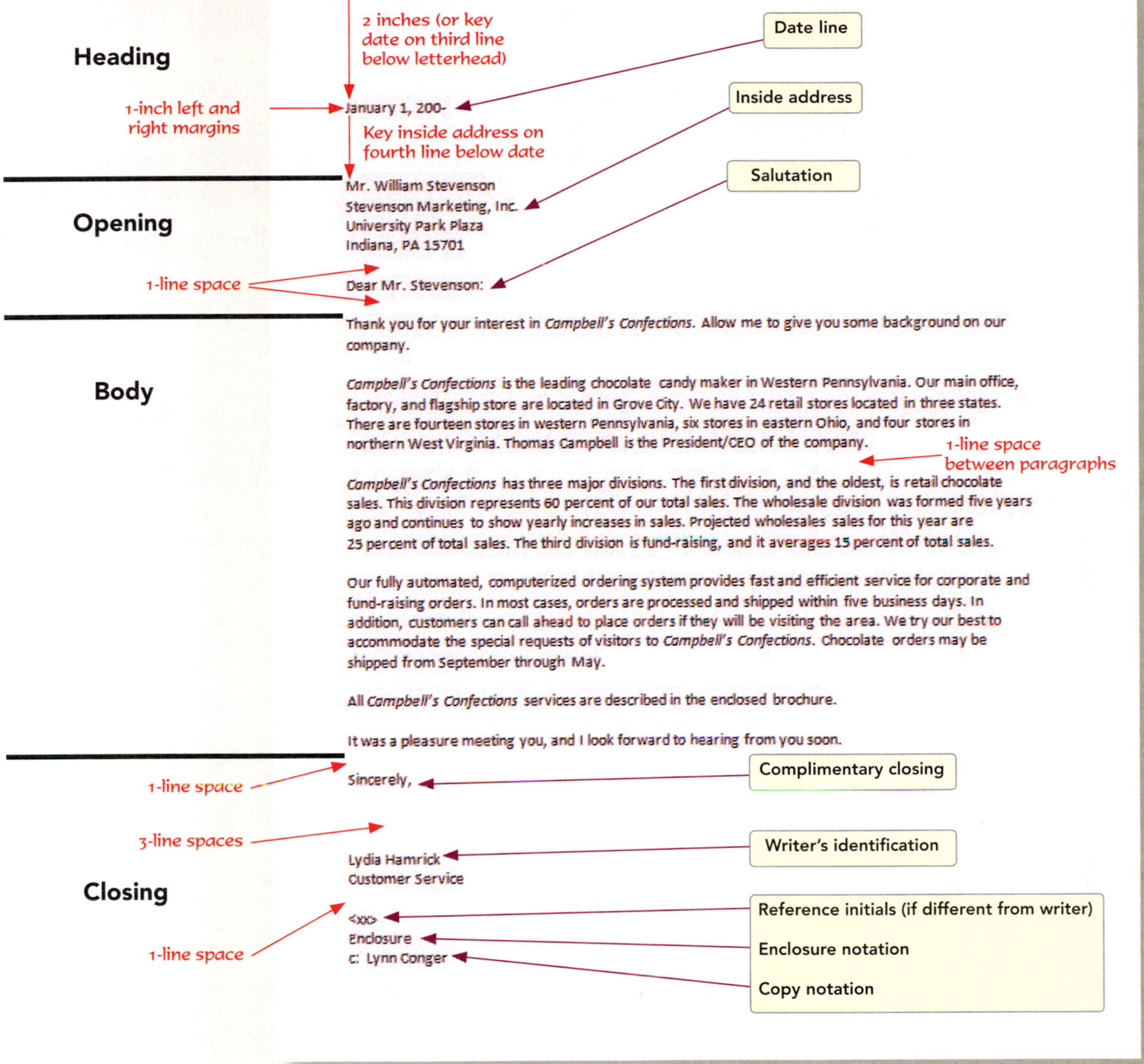

Heading

2 inches (or key date on third line below letterhead)

1-inch left and right margins

January 1, 200-

Date line

Inside address

Salutation

Key inside address on fourth line below date

Opening

Mr. William Stevenson
Stevenson Marketing, Inc.
University Park Plaza
Indiana, PA 15701

1-line space

Dear Mr. Stevenson:

Body

Thank you for your interest in *Campbell's Confections*. Allow me to give you some background on our company.

Campbell's Confections is the leading chocolate candy maker in Western Pennsylvania. Our main office, factory, and flagship store are located in Grove City. We have 24 retail stores located in three states. There are fourteen stores in western Pennsylvania, six stores in eastern Ohio, and four stores in northern West Virginia. Thomas Campbell is the President/CEO of the company.

1-line space between paragraphs

Campbell's Confections has three major divisions. The first division, and the oldest, is retail chocolate sales. This division represents 60 percent of our total sales. The wholesale division was formed five years ago and continues to show yearly increases in sales. Projected wholesales sales for this year are 25 percent of total sales. The third division is fund-raising, and it averages 15 percent of total sales.

Our fully automated, computerized ordering system provides fast and efficient service for corporate and fund-raising orders. In most cases, orders are processed and shipped within five business days. In addition, customers can call ahead to place orders if they will be visiting the area. We try our best to accommodate the special requests of visitors to *Campbell's Confections*. Chocolate orders may be shipped from September through May.

All *Campbell's Confections* services are described in the enclosed brochure.

It was a pleasure meeting you, and I look forward to hearing from you soon.

1-line space

Sincerely,

Complimentary closing

3-line spaces

Writer's identification

Closing

Lydia Hamrick
Customer Service

1-line space

<xx>
Enclosure
c: Lynn Conger

Reference initials (if different from writer)

Enclosure notation

Copy notation

Figure B-2
Continuation page header for two-page (or longer) letter or memo

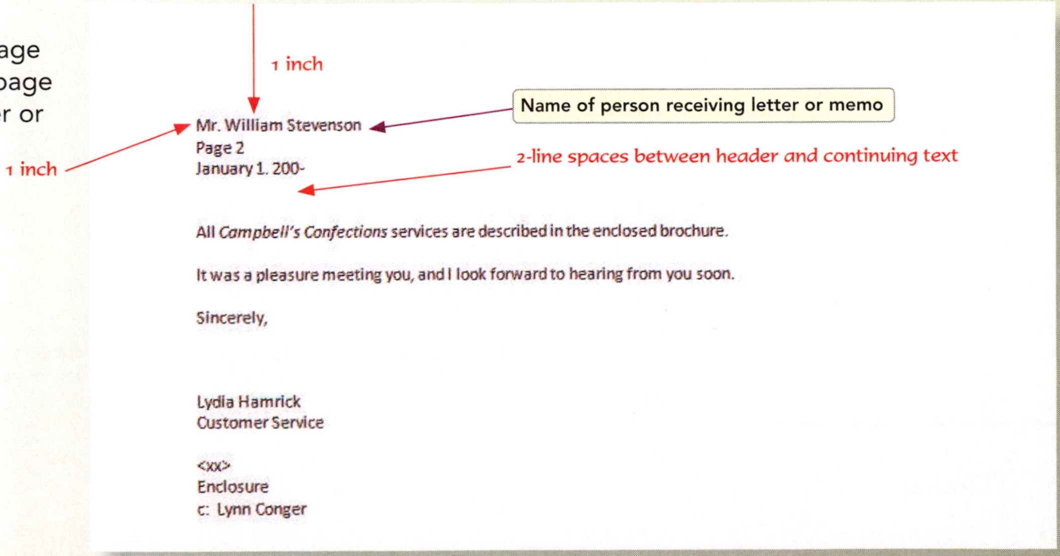

1 inch

1 inch

Mr. William Stevenson
Page 2
January 1, 200-

Name of person receiving letter or memo

2-line spaces between header and continuing text

All *Campbell's Confections* services are described in the enclosed brochure.

It was a pleasure meeting you, and I look forward to hearing from you soon.

Sincerely,

Lydia Hamrick
Customer Service

<xx>
Enclosure
c: Lynn Conger

TABLE B-2 Parts of a Memo

Part of Memo	Location/Description
Heading	Starts 2 inches from top of page using plain paper or letterhead stationery or on third line below memo letterhead. Consists of guide words ("MEMO TO," "FROM," "DATE," and "SUBJECT") in capital letters followed by a colon. Entries after guide words align at a 1-inch left tab setting. Use the date format shown in Figure B-3.
Body	Starts on the third line below the memo heading; contains the message, single-spaced with one blank line between paragraphs.
Closing	On the second line below the last paragraph; includes reference initials (the typist's initials in small letters). Might also include an enclosure notation, a file name notation, and a copy notation or distribution list.

Figure B-3
Memorandum style

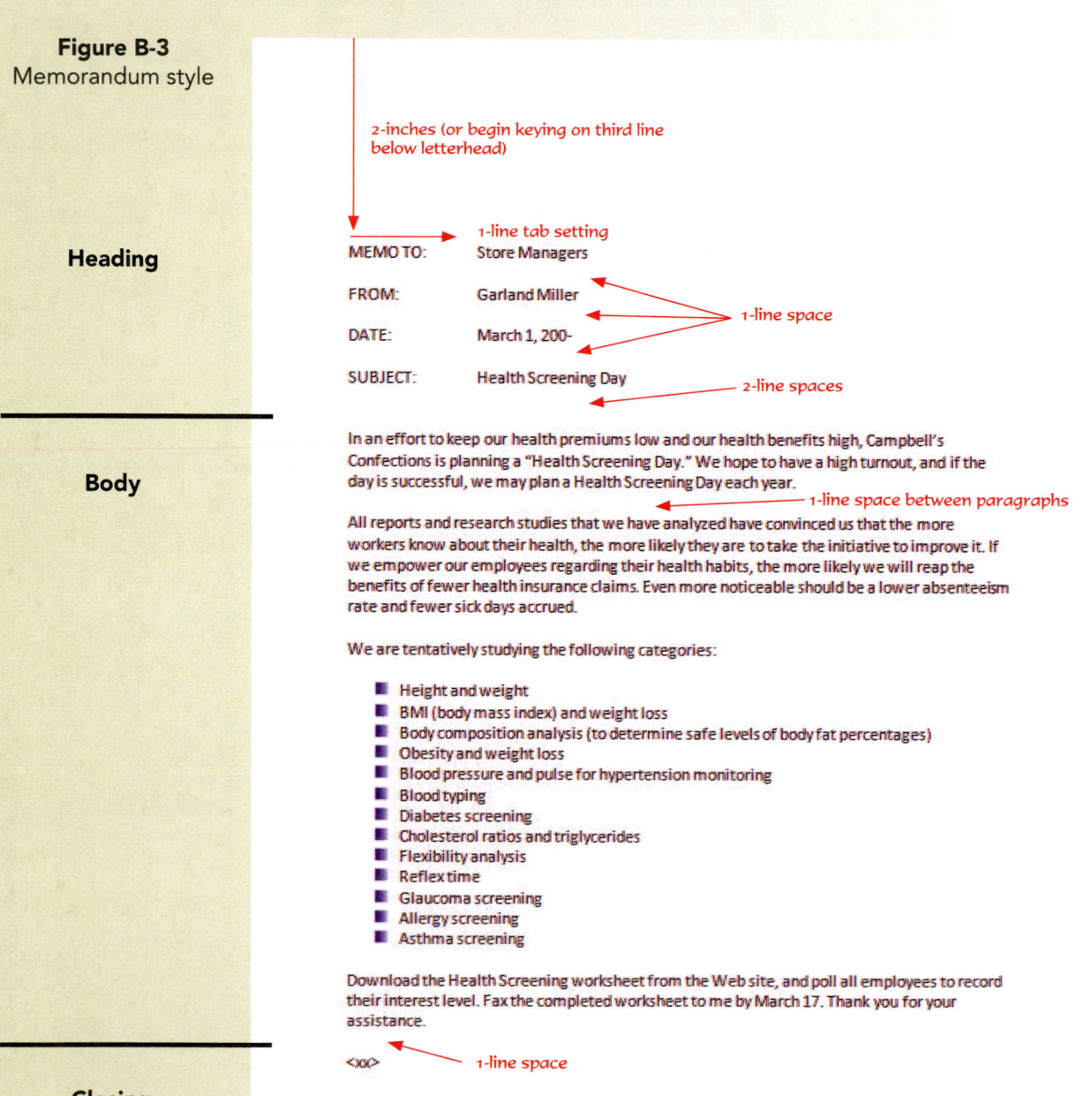

Quick Reference Guide

TABLE C-1 Prefixes for Major Objects—Leszynski Naming Conventions

Prefix	Object Type	Example
tbl	Table	tblEmployees
qry	Query	qryKitSuppliers
frm	Form	frmStuffedAnimals
rpt	Report	rptInventoryValue
mcr	Macro	mcrPreviewReport
bas	Module	basMyProgram

TABLE C-2 Prefixes for Control Objects—Leszynski Naming Conventions

Prefix	Object Type	Example
bof	Bound Object Frame	bofPhotos
cbo	Combo box	cboPaymentMethod
chk	Check box	chkCollate
cmd	Command button	cmdPrint
img	Image	imgEmployee
lbl	Label	lblEmployeeID
lin	Lines	linTitle
lst	List box	lstDepartments
opb	Option button	opbOrientation
opg	Option group	opgOrientation
pgb	Page break	pgbNewPage
rct	Rectangles	rctBox
sbf	Sub Forms	sbfLineItems
sbr	Sub Reports	sbrSales
tgb	Toggle	tgbCollated
txt	Text box	txtEmployeeID
uof	Unbound Object Frame	uofLogo

TABLE C-3 Variable Names—Microsoft Standards

Prefix	Object Type	Example
bln	Boolean	blnContinue
cur	Currency	curSalary
dat	Date	datHire
dbl	Double	dblCompanySales
err	Error	errReport
int	Integer	intItemNumber
lng	Long	lngPopulation
rst	Recordset	rstEmployees
sng	Single	sngRoomSize
str	String	strName

TABLE C-4 Custom Formats—Numbers and Currency

Symbol	Description
.(period)	Decimal separator
,(comma)	Thousand separator
"(double quotation)	Surrounds any text that you want users to see
0	Digit placeholder. Display a digit or 0
#	Digit placeholder. Display a digit or nothing
$	Display the literal character "$"
!	Forces left alignment
%	Percentage. The value is multiplied by 100 and a percent sign is appended
E- or e+	Scientific notation with a minus sign next to negative exponents and nothing next to positive exponents.
E+ or e+	Scientific notation with a minus sign next to negative exponents and a plus sign next to positive exponents.

TABLE C-5 Custom Formats—Date and Time

Symbol	Description
:	Time separator
/	Date separator
c	Same as the General Date predefined format
d	Day of the month in one or two digits (1 to 31)
dd	Day of the month in two digits (01 to 31)
ddd	First three letters of the weekday (Sun to Sat)
dddd	Full name of the weekday (Sunday to Saturday)
ddddd	Same as the Short Date predefined format
dddddd	Same as the Long Date predefined format
w	Day of the week (1 to 7)
ww	Week of the year (1 to 53)
m	Month of the year in one or two digits (1 to 12)
mm	Month of the year in two digits (01 to 12)
mmm	First three letters of the month (Jan to Dec)
mmmm	Full name of the month (January to December)
q	Date displayed as quarter of the year (1 to 4)
y	Number of the day of the year (1 to 366)
yy	Last two digits of the year (01 to 99)
yyyy	Full year (0100 to 9999)
h	Hours in one or two digits (0 to 23)
hh	Hours in two digits (00 to 23)
n	Minutes in one or two digits (0 to 59)
nn	Minutes in two digits (00 to 59)
s	Seconds in one or two digits (0 to 59)
ss	Seconds in two digits (00 to 59)
tttt	Same as the Long Time predefined format
AM/PM	Twelve-hour clock with the uppercase letters "AM" or "PM"
am/pm	Twelve-hour clock with the lowercase letters "am" or "pm"
A/P	Twelve-hour clock with the uppercase letters "A" or "P"
a/p	Twelve-hour clock with the lowercase letters "a" or "p"
[ ]	Stops resetting of seconds, minutes, hours, or days

TABLE C-6 Custom Formats—Text and Memo

Symbol	Description
@	Text character (either a character or a space) is required
&	Text character is not required
<	Force all characters to lowercase
>	Force all characters to uppercase

TABLE C-7 Custom Input Masks

Symbol	Description
0	Digit (0 to 9, entry required)
9	Digit or space (entry optional)
#	Digit or space (entry optional; spaces are displayed as blanks while in Edit mode, but blanks are removed when data are saved)
L	Letter (A to Z, entry required)
?	Letter (A to Z, entry optional)
A	Letter or digit (A to Z, entry required)
a	Letter or digit (A to Z, entry optional)
&	Any character or a space (entry required)
C	Any character or a space (entry optional)
<	Causes all characters to be converted to lowercase
>	Causes all characters to be converted to uppercase
!	Causes the input mask to display from right to left, rather than from left to right
\	Causes the character that follows to be displayed as the literal character
"abc"	Displays exactly what is between the quotation marks
.,:; - /	Placeholders (decimal, thousand, date and time separators)
Password	Any character typed in the control is stored as the character but is displayed as an asterisk (*)

TABLE C-8 Number Field Size Settings

Setting Precision	Stores Number From	Decimal	Storage Size
Byte 0 to 255	(None)		1 byte
Integer	–32,768 to +32,767	(None)	2 bytes
Long Integer	–2,147,483,648 to		
	+2,147,483,647	(None)	4 bytes
Single	-3.40×10^{38} to		
	$+3.40 \times 10^{38}$	7	4 bytes
Double	-1.79×10^{308} to		
	$+1.79 \times 10^{308}$	15	8 bytes
Decimal	-10^{28} to $+10^{28}$	28	12 bytes

TABLE C-9 Access 2007 Database Specifications

Attribute	Maximum
Access database (.accdb) file size	2 gigabytes
Number of objects in a database	32,768
Number of modules (including forms and reports modules)	1,000
Number of characters in an object name	64
Number of concurrent users	255

glossary

Glossary A	Word
Glossary B	Excel
Glossary C	PowerPoint
Glossary D	Access

Glossary A   Word

Active window   Window in which you are currently working that shows the title bar and taskbar button highlighted. (7)

Antonym   Word that is opposite in meaning to another word. (4)

Attribute   Setting, such as boldface or italics, that affects the appearance of text. (12)

AutoComplete   Automatic Word feature that suggests the completed word when you key the first four or more letters of a day, month, or date. (4)

AutoCorrect   Automatic Word feature that corrects commonly misspelled words as you key text. (4)

AutoFormat   Word feature that automatically changes formatting as you key text or numbers. (3)

AutoRecover   Word feature that automatically saves open documents in the background. The backup version of the document can be recovered in case the original is lost or damaged in a power failure or because of a system problem. (2)

AutoText   Word feature you can use to insert text automatically. (4)

Background pagination   Automatic process of updating page breaks and page numbers that occurs while you are creating or editing a document. (11)

Bar tabs   Used to make tabbed columns look more like a table with gridlines. A bar tab inserts a vertical line at a fixed position, creating a border between columns. (6)

Border   Line, box, or pattern placed around text, a graphic, or a page. (5)

Building Blocks   AutoText entries, cover pages, headers, footers, page numbers, tables, text boxes, and watermarks that are stored in galleries to be inserted in documents. (4) (11)

Bulleted list   List of items, each preceded by a bullet (•). Each item is a paragraph with a hanging indent. (5)

Character style   Formatting applied to selected text within a paragraph; includes font, font size, and font style. (12)

Click and type   Insert text or graphics in any blank area of a document. Position the insertion point anywhere in a document, click, and then type. Word automatically inserts paragraph marks before that point and also inserts tabs, depending on the location of the insertion point. (5)

Clipboard   Temporary storage area in the computer's memory used to hold text or other information that is cut or copied. (7)

Color set   Feature for applying color. It includes four colors for text and background, six accent colors, and two colors reserved for hyperlinks. (12)

Contiguous text   Any group of characters, words, sentences, or paragraphs that follow one another. (2)

Cut and paste   Method for moving text or other information by removing it from a document, storing it on the Clipboard, and then placing it in a new location. (7)

Document theme   Feature that includes colors, fonts, and effects which affect the overall appearance of a document. (12)

Drag and drop   Method for moving or copying text or other objects short distances by dragging them. (7)

Drop cap   Large letter that appears below the text baseline, usually applied to the first letter in the word of a paragraph. (3)

Em dash   Dash twice as wide as an en dash and used in sentences where you would normally insert two hyphens. (5)

En dash   Dash slightly wider than a hyphen. (5)

Facing pages   Document with a two-page spread. Right-hand pages are odd-numbered pages, and left-handed pages are even-numbered pages. (9)

Field   Hidden code that tells Word to insert specific information, such as a date or page number. In a data source table, each item of information contained in a record. (4) (9)

Filename   Unique name given to a document saved in Word. (1)

Find   Command used to locate text and formatting in a document. (8)

First-line indent   Indent for the first line of a paragraph. (5)

First-line indent marker   Top triangle on the left side of the ruler. Drag the indent marker to indent or extend the first line of a paragraph. (5)

Font   The design applied to an entire set of characters, including all letters of the alphabet, numerals, punctuation marks, and symbols. (3)

Footer   Text that appears in the bottom margin of a page throughout a section or document. (11)

Formatting mark   Symbol for a tab, paragraph, space, or another special character that appears on the screen, but not in the printed document. (2)

Gallery   List of design options for modifying elements of a page. (11)

Gutter margins   Extra space added to the inside or top margins to allow for binding. (9)

Hanging indent   Indentation of the second and subsequent lines of a paragraph. (5)

Hanging indent marker   Bottom triangle on the left side of the ruler. Drag the marker to indent the second and subsequent lines in a paragraph. (5)

Hard page break   Page break inserted manually. Does not move, regardless of changes in the document. (10)

Header   Text that appears in the top margin of a page throughout a section or document. (11)

I-beam   Shape of the mouse pointer when it is positioned in the text area. (1)

Indent   Increase the distance between the sides of a paragraph and the two side margins (left and right). (5)

Indent marker   On Word's horizontal ruler, small box or triangle that you drag to control a paragraph's indents. (5)

Insert mode   Mode of text entry that inserts text without overwriting existing text. (1)

Insertion point   Vertical blinking bar on the Word screen that indicates where an action will begin. (1)

Key Tips   Letters that appear over commands after you press the Alt key. Press the letter of the command you want to activate. The Key Tips may also be called *badges*. To turn off the Key Tips, press Alt again. (1)

Landscape   Page orientation setting in which the page is wider than it is tall. (9)

Leader characters   Patterns of dots or dashes that lead the reader's eye from one tabbed column to the next. (6)

Left and right indent   Indent left and right sides of paragraph (often used for quotes beyond three lines). (5)

Left indent   Indent paragraph from left margin. (5)

Left indent marker   Small rectangle on the left side of the ruler. Drag the marker to indent all lines in a paragraph simultaneously. (5)

Line break character   Character that starts a new line within the same paragraph. Insert by pressing Shift + Enter. (2)

Line space   Amount of vertical space between lines of text in a paragraph. (5)

Linked style   Paragraph formatting applied to selected text. (12)

List style   Formatting instructions applied to a list, such as numbering or bullet characters, alignment, and fonts. (12)

Margins   Spaces at the top, bottom, left, and right of the document between the edges of text and the edges of the paper. (9)

Microsoft Office Button   Button that displays the File menu which lists the commands to create, open, save, and print a document. (1)

Mirror margins   Inside and outside margins on facing pages that mirror one another. (9)

Multilevel list   Numbering sequence used primarily for legal and technical documents. (5)

Negative indent   Extends a paragraph into the left or right margin areas. (5)

Nonbreaking space   Space between words, defined by a special character, that prevents Word from separating two words. Insert by pressing Ctrl + Shift + Spacebar. (2)

Noncontiguous text   Text items (characters, words, sentences, or paragraphs) that do not follow one another, but each appears in a different part of a document. (2)

Nonprinting character   Symbol for a tab, paragraph, space, or another special character that appears on the screen, but not in the printed document. (2)

Normal style   Default paragraph style with the formatting specifications 11-point Calibri, English language, left-aligned, 1.15 line spacing, 10 points spacing after, and widow/orphan control. (12)

Numbered list   List of items preceded by sequential numbers or letters. Each item is a paragraph with a hanging indent. (5)

Ordinal number   Number indicating an order or position, for example, 1st, 2nd, or 3rd. (3)

Organizer   Feature that lets you copy styles from one document or template to another or copy macros from one template to another. (13)

Orientation   Setting to format a document with a tall, vertical format or a wide, horizontal format. (9)

Orphan   First line of a paragraph that remains at the bottom of a page. (10)

Overtype mode   Mode of text entry that lets you key over existing text. (1)

Pagination   Process of determining how and when text flows from the bottom of one page to the top of the next page in a document. (10)

Pane   Section of a window that is formed when the window is split. A split window contains two panes. (7)

Paragraph   Unique block of text or data that is always followed by a paragraph mark. (5)

Paragraph alignment   Determines how the edges of a paragraph appear. (5)

Paragraph mark   On-screen symbol (¶) that marks the end of a paragraph and stores all formatting for the paragraph. (1) (5)

Paragraph space   Amount of space (measured in points) before and after a paragraph; replaces pressing Enter to add space between paragraphs. (5)

Paragraph style   Formatting instructions applied to a paragraph; includes alignment, line and paragraph spacing, indents, tab settings, borders and shading, and character formatting. (12)

Placeholder text   In a template (or a new document based on a template), text containing the correct formatting, which you replace with your own information. (13)

Point   Measure of type size; 72 points equals 1 inch. (3)

Portrait   Page orientation setting in which the page is taller than it is wide. (9)

Positive indent   Indentation between the left and right margins. (5)

Proofreaders' marks   Handwritten corrections to text, often using specialized symbols. (1) (Appendix A)

Property   Any information, such as the filename, date created, or file size, that describes a document. (2)

Quick Access Toolbar   Toolbar containing frequently used commands and which is easily customized. (1)

Quick styles   Various formatting options for text and objects that display as thumbnails in a gallery.

Replace   Command used to replace text and formatting automatically with specified alternatives. (8)

Ribbon   Seven default tabs, each tab containing a group of related commands. (1)

Right indent   Indent paragraph from right margin. (5)

Right indent marker   Triangle on the right side of the ruler; drag the marker to indent the right side of a paragraph. (5)

Ruler   Part of the Word window that shows placement of indents, margins, and tabs. (1)

Sans serif   Font characteristic in which the font has no decorative lines, or serifs, projecting from its characters, such as Arial. (3)

ScreenTip   Brief explanation or identification or an on-screen item such as a Ribbon command. (1)

Scroll bar   Bar used with the mouse to move right or left and up or down within a document to view text not currently visible on screen. (1)

Section   Portion of a document that has its own formatting. (9)

Section breaks   Double-dotted lines that appear on screen to indicate the beginning and end of a section. (9)

Selection   Area of a document that appears as a highlighted block of text. Selections can be formatted, moved, copied, deleted, or printed. (2)

Serif   Font characteristic in which the font has decorative lines projecting from its characters, such as Times New Roman. (3)

Shading   Applying shades of gray, a pattern, or color to the background of a paragraph. (5)

Shortcut menu   Menu that opens and shows a list of commands relevant to a particular item that you right-click. (3)

SmartQuotes   Quotation marks that curl in one direction (") to open a quote and curl in the opposite direction (") to close a quote. (5)

Soft page break   Page break automatically inserted by Word and continually adjusted to reflect changes in the document. (10)

Special characters   Characters such as the trademark symbol ™ or those used in foreign languages. (5)

Split bar   Horizontal line that divides a document into panes. (7)

Split box   Small gray rectangle located just above the vertical scroll bar. You can drag it down to split a document into two panes. (7)

Status bar   Bar located at the bottom of the Word window that displays information about the task you are performing, shows the position of the insertion point, and shows the current mode of operation. (1)

Style   Set of formatting instructions that you apply to text. (12)

Style set   List of style names and their formatting specifications. (12)

Symbol   Special character, such as the copyright symbol ©. (5)

Synonym   Word that is similar in meaning to another word. (4)

Tab   Paragraph-formatting feature used to align text. (6)

Tab character   Symbol on the horizontal ruler that indicates a custom tab setting. (6)

Tab characters   Nonprinting characters used to indent text. (2)

Tab marker   Symbol on the horizontal ruler that indicates a custom tab setting. (6)

Tab stop   Position of a tab setting. (6)

Table style   Formatting instructions applied to a table, such as borders, shading, alignment, and fonts. (12)

Task pane   Pane to the right of the text area that provides access to a variety of functions. (4) (7) (12)

Template   File that contains formatting information, styles, and text for a particular type of document. (13)

Theme   Set of formatting instructions for the entire document. (12)

Thesaurus   Tool you can use to look up synonyms for a selected word. (4)

Title bar   Bar that displays the name of the current document at the top of the Word window. (1)

Widow   Last line of a paragraph that remains at the top of a page. (10)

Wildcard   Symbol that stands for missing or unknown text. (8)

Wingding   Font that includes special characters, such as arrows. (5)

3-D format   Style that applies a three-dimensional look to a shape. (10)

Absolute reference   A cell address that does not change when copied in a formula. (5)

Active cell   The cell that is ready for data outlined with a thick border. (1)

Adjustment handle   Yellow diamond handle on a shape used to change the appearance and design of the shape. (10)

Annuity   A series of equal payments made at regular intervals for a set period of time. (7)

Argument   Values or cell ranges between parentheses in a function; they are what a function needs to complete its calculation. (6)

Arithmetic mean   An average of values calculated by adding the values and then dividing the total by the number of values. (6)

Arithmetic operators   Math symbols for calculations (+, −, /, and *). (2)

Assistant shape   Shape that represents a helper. (11)

AutoCalculate   Feature that displays sums, averages, counts, maximums, or minimums in the status bar for selected cells. (2)

AutoComplete   Feature that displays a suggested label after the first character is keyed in a cell in the column. (4)

AutoCorrect   Excel feature that corrects common spelling errors as you type. (3)

AutoFill   Feature that copies or extends data from a cell or range to adjacent cells.

AutoFit   Sizes a column to fit its longest entry or sizes a row to the font. (2)

Axis   Horizontal or vertical line that encloses chart data. (9)

Axis title   Optional label for the axis. (9)

Background   An image that displays on screen for the worksheet. (5)

Bevel   3-D effect for shapes that resembles the edge of a tabletop. (10)

Border   Outline above, below, or around a cell or range of cells. (4)

Bounding box   Imaginary rectangular box or outline for shapes. (10)

Callout   Descriptive text enclosed in a shape with a pointer or arrow connector. (10)

Cell   Intersection of a column and row in a worksheet with an address or reference, such as cell B5. (1)

Cell address   Column letter and row number that identifies a location in the worksheet. (1)

Cell alignment   Feature that describes and sets how the contents of a cell are positioned within the cell. (4)

Cell reference   The cell address or location in the worksheet. (1)

Character space   Average width of a character in a font. (2)

Character string   Sequence of letters, numbers, or other symbols. (3)

Chart   Visual display of worksheet data. (9)

Chart area   Background of a chart. (9)

Chart object   Chart that appears on the same sheet as the worksheet data. (9)

Chart title   Optional title or name for the chart. (9)

Color scale   Solid cell fill of varying shades based on values within a range. (4)

Column   Vertical group of cells in a worksheet identified by alphabetic letter. (1)

Combination chart   Chart with series that used different chart types. (9)

Comment   A pop-up cell attachment with descriptive or explanatory text. (10)

Cost   The original price of an item or asset. (7)

Crop   Remove parts of an image from view. (11)

CSV   Filename extension for comma-separated values format, a simple text file. (8)

Data bar   Bar-shaped fill in a cell based on values within a range. (4)

Data label   Optional title for each value in a chart. (9)

Data marker   Object that displays individual values, such as a bar or column. (9)

Data point   One value from the data series. (9)

Data series   Collection of related values in the worksheet. (9)

Depreciation   Decline in the financial value of a business asset. (7)

Diagram   Object that illustrates an idea or concept. (11)

Document Inspector   Feature that lists metadata and other personal information in a workbook file so that such data can be removed. (10)

Document theme   Built-in set of fonts, colors, and effects used in a workbook. (2)

Drag-and-drop pointer   Four-pointed arrow that appears when the pointer rests on the edge of a cell. It is used to copy or cut a cell or range by dragging. (4)

Draw layer   Invisible, transparent working surface, separate from and on top of the worksheet, that holds drawing objects and images. (10)

Electronic spreadsheet software   Computer software that produces reports with calculations, list management, or charts. (1)

Embedded chart   Chart object; a chart that appears on the same sheet as the data. (9)

Exploded pie chart   Pie chart in which one or more slice(s) is detached from the rest of the pie. (9)

Exponentiation   Math operation that raises a number to a power. (2)

Extension   Four characters preceded by a period, added to a filename. (2)

Filename   Document name or identifier. (2)

Fill   Background pattern or color for a cell or range of cells. (4)

Fill handle   Small rectangle at the lower-right corner of a cell or range used for extending a series or copying data. (3)

Financial function   Formula that performs a common business calculation involving money. (7)

Folder   Storage location for work files on a disk. (1)

Footer   Data that print at the bottom of each page in a worksheet. (3)

Formula   Equation that performs a calculation on values in a worksheet. (2)

Formula AutoComplete   Feature that displays a list of functions and range names that match the spelling of what is keyed. (6)

Function   Built-in mathematical formula for common mathematical, statistical, financial, or other calculation. (2) (6)

Function Arguments   Dialog box that displays help and entry areas for completing a function. (6)

FV   Financial function argument that specifies the value of the cash at the end of the time period. (7)

GIF file   Graphics Interchange Format, a format for images used on a Web site. (11)

Gradient   Blend of colors used to fill charts and other objects. (9)

Gridline   Horizontal or vertical line in the chart plot area to mark values. (9)

Header   Data that print at the top of each page in a worksheet. (3)

Header row   First row in a table with descriptive labels for each column. (3)

HMTL   Hypertext Markup Language, a widely used format for Web pages. (5)

Home   Cell A1

Horizontal (category) axis   What is shown in a chart, created from row or column headings. (9)

Hyperlink   A clickable text or object that, when clicked, displays another file, another program, or an Internet site/address. (8)

Icon set   Set of three, four, or five icons displayed in a cell based on values within a range. (4)

Integer   A whole number or a number with no decimal or fractional parts. (8)

Interval   Number of steps between values or labels in a series. (3)

KeyTip   Keyboard shortcut that appears on screen when Alt is pressed.

Label   An entry in a cell that begins with a letter. (2)

Landscape   Print orientation that prints a horizontal page that is wider than it is tall. (5)

Leading zero   A zero shown as the first digit in a value. (4)

Legend   Chart object that explains the colors, textures, or symbols used in the chart. (9)

Life   Number of periods over which an asset is depreciated. (7)

Line break   Location in a label where text is split to a second line, made by pressing Alt + Enter. (5)

Live Preview   Feature that displays design changes before they are applied. (2)

Logical function   Formula that determines whether or not something is true. (7)

Mail-enabled   The ability to e-mail a file without closing the application. (8)

Math hierarchy   Mathematical rules that determine which part of a formula is calculated first. (5)

Metadata   Information that is included and saved with a document, such as the computer name, the user named, revision dates, etc. (10)

Microsoft Office button   Button next to the Quick Access toolbar that opens the File menu. (1)

Mixed reference   A cell address that adjusts either the row or the column when the formula is copied. (5)

Name Box   Text box in the formula bar that shows the current cell address. (1)

Nested function   A function inside another function. The second or third functions are used as arguments in the first function. (8)

Nper   Financial function argument that specifies the total number of payments or time periods. (7)

Numeric keypad   Set of number and symbol keys at the right of the keyboard. (4)

Object   Separate, clickable element or part of a worksheet. (3)

Office Clipboard   Temporary memory area that can hold up to 24 copied elements across Office products. (4)

Order of operation/precedence   Mathematical rules that determine which part of a formula is calculated first. (5)

Organization chart   Object that illustrates hierarchical relationships, usually among company workers. (11)

Page break   Code shown as a solid or dashed line to signal where the printer will start a new page. (7)

Page orientation   Print setting that determines landscape or portrait layout. (5)

Period   The time for which depreciation is calculated. (7)

Pick From Drop-Down List   Feature that displays a list of all labels already in a column. (4)

Pixel   A single screen dot. (2)

Plot area   Rectangular bounding area for the category and value axes. (9)

Point   1/72 of an inch, used to measure fonts. (2)

Portrait   Print orientation that prints a page that is taller than it is wide. (5)

Property   Setting or attribute that is stored with the workbook. (11)

PV   Financial function argument that specifies the current cash value of the money transaction. (7)

Quick Access toolbar   Customizable toolbar with buttons for frequently used commands. (1)

Range   A group of cells that forms a rectangle. (2)

Range address   Upper-left and lower-right cell addresses separated by a colon. (2)

Rate   Financial function argument that specifies the interest rate for the time period. (7)

Relative reference   A cell address that adjusts to the row or column where a copied formula is located. (5)

Replacement string   Sequence of characters that is exchanged for existing data in the Replace command. (3).

Ribbon   A set of command tabs with buttons, galleries, and controls. (1)

Rotation handle   Green oval handle (circle) on a shape used to rotate the shape using the mouse. (10)

Rounding   To make a value larger or smaller depending on a specified digit to the left or right of the decimal point. (8)

Row   Horizontal group of cells identified by a number in a worksheet. (1)

Salvage   The value of an asset after it has been depreciated. (7)

Scale   Size an image by a percentage so that it is proportional. (11)

Secondary axis   Separate set of values for a data series. (9)

Selection handles   Small black rectangles, circles, or dots that surround and indicate a selected or active object. (9)

Selection handles   Eight circles or rectangles surrounding the bounding box of shape. (10)

Selection pointer   White cross-shaped pointer used to select cells. Solid black arrow to select rows/columns. (2)

Serial number   Number system assigned to dates, counting from January 1, 1900, as 1.

Series   List of labels, numbers, dates, or times that follows a pattern. (3)

Shading   Background color or pattern for a cell or range of cells. (4)

Shape   Common, recognized figure, form, or outline. (10)

SmartArt   Graphic shapes that include lists, processes, hierarchies, cycles, matrices, and pyramids. (11)

Stop   A color in a gradient that refers to its position on the gradient's color scale. (9)

Style   Set of formatting specifications for labels and/or values. (7)

Subordinate shape   Shape that represents an employee. (11)

Subroutine macro   Command sequence that can be run from a workbook or from within another macro. (21)

Super ScreenTip   A box on screen with the name and purpose of a button when you hover over a button or control. (1)

Synonym   A word that means the same thing. (11)

Syntax   Structure or necessary parts and the order of those parts for a function. It is an equal sign (=), the function name, and the arguments in parentheses. (6)

Table   Data arrangement in rows with a single header row. A list of information with a row of headers followed by rows of data. (3)

Template   Model or sample workbook that can include labels, values, formulas, themes, styles, alignment settings, and borders. It is saved with an .xltx extension. (5)

Text box   Drawing object with no connector lines for displaying text. (10)

Text pane   Dialog box attached to a SmartArt shape used for entering text in an outline style. (11)

Texture   Grainy or non-smooth appearance used to fill charts and other objects. (9)

Thesaurus   Reference book that lists words with the same meaning. (11)

Tick mark   Line or marker on an axis to display values. (9)

Type   Financial function argument that specifies whether the payment/deposit is made at the beginning or end of the period. (7)

Value   An entry in a cell that begins with a number or an arithmetic symbol. (2)

Vertical (value) axis   Horizontal or vertical range of values from the worksheet.

Visualization   Format elements that display bars, colors, or icons with values for quick comparison. (4)

Volatile   Function characteristic that causes it to depend on the system in which the workbook is opened. (6)

Watermark   Text or image that appears behind printed data, similar to a background image. (11)

Whole number   Value without a fraction or decimal. (5)

Wildcard   Character that represents one or more letters or numbers. (3)

Windows Clipboard   Temporary memory area that holds cut or copied data. (4)

WordArt   Application that inserts shaped and colored text as an object. (10)

Workbook   Excel file that holds worksheets with data. A workbook has an .xlsx filename extension. (1)

Worksheet   Individual page or sheet in a workbook, shown by a tab at the bottom of the screen. (1)

XLS   Filename extension for files saved in previous Excel versions. (8)

XPS   XML Paper Specification file format for saving formatted files. (1)

Zoom size   Setting that controls how much of the worksheet appears at once on the screen. (1)

3-D rotation Effect that enables the picture to be displayed in a variety of dimensional treatments. (4)

Activate To select a placeholder by clicking it. An activated text placeholder can accept text that you key or it can be moved or resized. (1)

Adjustment handle Yellow diamond-shaped handle found on many shapes that is used to change a prominent feature of a shape. For example, you can change the size of an arrowhead relative to the body of the arrow, or you can change the tilt of a triangle. (4)

Album layout Used to change the layout of slides created with the Photo Album feature. (4)

Animation effects Special visual or sound effects used when objects are displayed on the screen or removed from view. (1)

Assistant shape Shape in an organization chart that is usually placed below a superior shape and above subordinate shapes. Usually, an assistant shape has no subordinates. (7)

AutoCorrect Feature that automatically corrects common spelling errors and typos as you key text. It can be turned on or off, and you can customize so it will find errors that you frequently make. (2)

Autofit options Contains options for fitting text into placeholders. (2)

Axis Line that borders one side of the chart plot area. A vertical (value) axis displays a range of numbers, and a horizontal (category) axis displays category names. (6)

Bar chart A chart that compares one data element with another data element using horizontal bars. (6)

Bevel Effect that makes a picture look dimensional with several different options available. (4)

Bitmap pictures Made up of tiny colored dots. The more you enlarge a bitmap, the more blurred it becomes. You can crop bitmaps and easily change the contrast and brightness. Other changes can be made only by using a paint-type graphics program. Examples of bitmaps are pictures created in a paint program, photographs and other images that come from a scanner, and images that come from a digital camera. (4)

Blank presentation One way to start a new presentation with no design elements displayed. (2)

Body text Text in the body of a slide or other document. On a PowerPoint slide, body text is usually placed in a body text placeholder and can be displayed as bulleted text. (1)

Brightness Adjusts the overall lightness of the colors in a picture. (4)

Bullet A small dot, square, or other symbol placed at the left of each item in a list or series of paragraphs. Bullets are often used in presentations and outlines. (1)

Case text Capitalization treatment: uppercase (all capital letters), lowercase (all small letters), sentence case (first letter only capitalized), title case (first letter of all words capitalized). (2)

Cell bevel effect A dimensional effect that can be applied to cells to give the appearance of a raised, rounded, or pressed in look. (5)

Cell margin Space between the text in a cell and its borders. (5)

Cell pointer Pointer in the shape of a white cross used to select cells in a Microsoft Excel worksheet or Microsoft Graph datasheet. (6)

Cell Rectangle formed by the intersection of a row and a column in a table or a worksheet. (5, 6)

Chart Diagram that displays numbers in pictorial format, such as slices of a pie shape, or rows of columns of varying height. Charts are sometimes called graphs. (6)

Chart layouts Control the position in which different chart elements appear on the chart. (6)

Chart styles Preset styles that can be applied to a chart to enhance the appearance through colors matching the document theme colors. (6)

Clip art Ready-to-use graphic images that you can insert in a presentation. (4)

Clipboard Temporary storage place for cut and copied items. Holds up to 24 items at a time. (3)

Clipboard options Allows the control of settings on the Clipboard task pane. (3)

Collate To print all the pages of a document before starting to print the first page of the next copy. When pages are not collated, all the copies of page 1 are printed first, then all the copies of page 2, etc. (1)

Column chart A chart that compares one data element with another data element using vertical bars. (6)

Columns Individual cells aligned vertically down the table or worksheet. (5)

Command buttons Buttons designed to perform a function or display a gallery of options. (1)

Connection sites Red squares that appear on a shape, clip art, or text box object when the connector tool is active or when a connector is selected. Connection sites indicate places where a connector can be attached to an object. (4)

Connector line Straight, curved, or angled line with special endpoints that can lock onto connection sites on a shape or other PowerPoint object. (4)

Constrain Used to draw objects in precise increments or proportions. For example, a line will be straight or angled in precise amounts, a rectangle will be square, and an oval will be round. When resizing an object, the correct size ratio is maintained. (2, 4)

Contiguous slides   Slides that follow one after another. For example, slides numbered 2, 3, and 4 are contiguous. See "Noncontiguous slides." (3)

Continuous picture list   Diagram that contains placeholders for pictures and a horizontal arrow to communicate that the items shown represent interconnected information. (7)

Contrast   Adjusts the intensity of the colors in a picture by adjusting the difference between the lightest and darkest areas. (4)

Copy   To copy a selected object or text from a presentation and store it on the clipboard without removing the selection from its original place. (3)

Coworker shape   Shape in an organization chart that is connected to the same superior shape as another shape. (7)

Crop   To trim the vertical or horizontal edges of a picture. (4)

Cropping handles   Short black markers on the sides and corners of a picture selected for cropping. When you drag one of these handles with the cropping tool, an edge of the picture is cut away (trimmed). (4)

Crosshair pointer   The shape of your pointer when drawing objects. (4)

Cut   To remove a selected object or text from a presentation and store it on the clipboard. (3)

Cycle diagram   Diagram used to illustrate a process that is continuous. (7)

Data series   Group of data that relates to a common object or category such as product, geographic area, or year. A single chart may display more than one data series. (6)

Datasheet   Table that is part of Microsoft Graph and in which you enter numbers and labels that are used to create a chart if you do not have Microsoft Excel installed on your computer. When you start a new chart, the datasheet appears automatically, containing sample data that you can delete or overwrite. (6)

Demote   To move selected text to the next-lower outline or heading level by increasing the indent level. (2)

Design template   Available online and used to add a uniform color theme and design background to each slide in a presentation. (2)

Design theme   Predesigned background graphics, theme colors, theme fonts, theme effects, and other formatting options that can be applied to presentations for a consistent presentation appearance. These can be customized for a particular topic or unique design. (3)

Destination   When working with clipboard objects, the presentation or other document in which the objects are pasted. (3)

Diagram   A visual representation of information. (7)

Distribute Columns   Adjusts columns to be the same width. (5)

Distribute Rows   Adjusts rows to be the same height. (5)

Drag   Selecting an object then holding down the left mouse button while moving the pointer to position the object in a different location. (1)

Duplicate   To make a second copy of a selected object on the same slide. (4)

Eraser   Used to delete table cell borders. (5)

Explode   To move a pie slice away from other slices in a pie chart to add emphasis. (6)

Filename   Unique name given to a PowerPoint presentation file, a Word document file, or files created by other applications. (1)

Find   Locates specified text in a presentation. (3)

First-line indent   Indent where the first line of the paragraph is indented farther to the right than the other lines in the paragraph. (2)

Fit to Window   Changes from the current zoom settings so the slide will fit in the window that is open. (1)

Font   A set of characters A–Z, in uppercase and lowercase, and related symbols in a specific design. (2)

Font face   Names of a set of characters with a specific design such as Times New Roman or Arial. (2)

Font size   Describes the size of a font and is measured in points. (2)

Footer   Text that appears at the bottom of each slide, notes page, or handouts page. (3)

Format Painter   Used to copy formatting from one object to another. (3)

Four-pointed arrow   Used to move placeholders and other objects without resizing them. Can also select text in a bulleted list by clicking the bullet. (2)

Gallery   A collection of thumbnails displaying different effect options you can choose. (1)

Gear diagram   Diagram that illustrates interlocking ideas. (7)

Glow   Effect that adds a soft color around the object edges that makes the object stand out from the background. (4)

Graph   See "Chart." (6)

Grayscale   Displays slides in shades of gray for printing on a black-and-white printer. (1)

Grid   A set of intersecting lines used to align objects that you can show or hide. (4)

Gridlines   The background lines on a chart that aid interpretation of data quantities. (6)

Group   To combine selected objects so that they behave as one object. (4)

Groups   Command buttons are broken into logical groups by type of task. (1)

Guides   Horizontal and vertical lines used to align objects. Guides do not display in Slide Show view or when printed. (4)

Handout   Printout that contains one, two, three, four, six, or nine PowerPoint slides on a page. (1)

Hanging indent   Indent where the first line extends farther to the left than the rest of the paragraph. Also can be used to describe a format of displaying an organization chart where each shape is displayed hanging under their superior and coworker shapes. (2, 7)

Header   Text that appears at the top of each slide, notes page, or handouts page. (3)

Help   A reference tool for getting assistance with PowerPoint. (1)

Hierarchy diagram   Diagram that illustrates reporting relationships or lines of authority between employees in a company. (7)

I-beam   Pointer that has the shape of an uppercase "I." The I-beam pointer is used to select text or mark the location where you can insert text. (1)

Indent markers   Two small triangles and one small rectangle that appear on the ruler to control the indents. (2)

Insertion point   Vertical flashing bar indicating the position where text that you key will be inserted. Clicking an I-beam pointer is one way to place an insertion point. (1)

Keyword   Word or words that describe the subject matter of your clip art search. (4)

Landscape   A horizontal orientation for slides or printed pages; the opposite of Portrait. (1)

Legend   Box showing the colors and formatting assigned to the data series or categories in a chart. (6)

Level   In organization charts, the position in the hierarchy of the organization being diagrammed. (7)

Line spacing   The spacing between lines of text within and between paragraphs. (2)

Line weight   Thickness of a line measured in points. (4)

List diagram   Diagram that provides an alternative to listing text in bulleted lists. (7)

Live Preview   A feature that allows you to see exactly what your changes will look like before selecting an effect. (1)

Lock drawing mode   Locks the drawing mode of the shape that is selected to avoid having to activate the shape to draw several of the same shapes. (4)

Matrix diagram   Diagram that allows placement of concepts along two axes or in related quadrants. (7)

Merge cells   To combine two or more table cells into one larger cell. (5)

Microsoft Office Button   Button that provides access to opening, saving, printing, and sharing your PowerPoint file with others. (1)

Noncontiguous slides   Slides that do not follow one after another. For example, slides numbered 1, 4, 5, and 7 are noncontiguous. See "Contiguous slides." (3)

Normal indent   Indent where all lines are indented the same amount from the left margin. (2)

Normal view   This view provides one place for viewing the different parts of your presentation and displays the Slides and Outline pane, Slide pane, and Notes pane. (1)

Notes pane   Area where you can add presentation notes for either the presenter or the audience. The Notes pane is located below the Slide pane. (1)

Nudge   To move an object in very small increments by using the arrow keys. (2, 4)

Organization chart   Diagram used to show the relationships and reporting structure of the people in an organization in a hierarchical format. (7)

Paste   To insert an item stored on the clipboard at the current location. (3)

Paste options   A button appears near a pasted item when the source formatting is different from the formatting of the destination presentation. (3)

Pencil pointer   Used to draw and recolor table borders and cells. (5)

Photo album   Creates a presentation consisting mostly of pictures that can be formatted to create electronic scrapbooks or photo albums. (4)

Picture border   The line that surrounds pictures. (4)

Picture effects   Many customizable special effects are available to apply to pictures such as shadows, glow, bevel effects, and soft edges. (4)

Picture shape   Used to change the shape of a picture to any of the shapes in the Shapes gallery. (4)

Picture style   A selection of preset treatments that can be applied to pictures to enhance the appearance of pictures. (4)

Pie chart   A chart that shows the proportions of individual components compared to the whole. (6)

Placeholder   Box that can contain title text, body text, pictures, or other objects. Most slide layouts contain placeholders. A placeholder's formatting, size, and position is set on a master slide and can be customized. (1)

Plot area   The area of a chart that displays the shapes such as bars or pie slices that represent the data. (6)

Points   The measurement unit of font size; one inch has 72 points. (2)

Portrait   A vertical orientation for slides or printed pages where the slide or page is taller than it is wide; the opposite of landscape. (1)

Print preview   Feature that enables you to see what your printed pages will look like before you actually print them. You can view preview pages in black and white, grayscale, or color. (1)

Process diagram   Reflects concepts or events that occur sequentially. (7)

Promote   To move selected text to the next-higher outline or heading level by decreasing the indent. (2)

Proofreaders' marks   Special notation used to mark up a printed draft with changes to be made before final printing. Some proofreaders' marks might be confusing if you are unfamiliar with them. For example, a handwritten "=" indicates that a hyphen is to be inserted. (1)

Proportions   Relationship between the height and width of an object. When an object is resized, its porportions will be preserved if both the height and width of the object change at the same rate or percentage. An object that is out of proportion is either too tall and skinny, or too short and wide. (4)

Pure Black and White Print option that converts all colors to either black or white, eliminating shades of gray. (1)

Pyramid diagram Diagram that illustrates relationships based on a foundation. (7)

Quick Access toolbar Toolbar that is located at the top of the PowerPoint window by default and provides access to commands that are used frequently. (1)

Quick Styles A gallery of preset effects used to change the appearance of shapes. (7)

Radial diagram Diagram that illustrates relationships focused on or directed from a central element. (7)

Recolor Used to change to different color modes or change to light and dark variations of the presentation's theme colors. (4)

Redo Reverses a previous action such as an editing change up to 20 actions if the save feature has not been used. (3)

Reflection An effect that gives the illusion that the object is reflecting off water by displaying a lighter transparent copy of the object. (4)

Regroup Recombine objects that were at one time part of the same group. (4)

Relationship diagram Diagram that shows interconnected, hierarchical, proportional, or overlapping relationships. Some of these diagrams also appear in other categories. (7)

Replace Locates specified text in a presentation and replaces it with different text that you specify. (3)

Research Searches reference materials such as dictionaries, encyclopedias, and translation services to find information you need. (3)

Reset picture Used to return a picture to its original state after its colors have been changed. (4)

Ribbon Consists of task-oriented tabs that each contain commands organized in logical groups. (1)

Rotate To change the positioning of an object determined in degree increments or freely turn it using the rotation handle. (2)

Rotation handle Green handle that appears above a selected object. You change the rotation of an object by dragging the rotation handle. (4)

Rows Individual cells arranged across the table or worksheet horizontally. (5)

Scale Specifies the range of values on a chart's value axis and the interval between values. (6)

ScreenTip Box that identifies the name of an on-screen object when you point to the object. (1)

Scroll bars Used in several areas of the application window to move what you see right or left, and up or down. You can also use the vertical scroll bar to move from slide to slide. (1)

Selection rectangle The shape that you draw by dragging the pointer to select objects on a slide. All objects contained inside the shape are selected. (4)

Shadow An effect that gives the illusion that there is light shining on an object producing a shadow. (4)

Shape One of a group of predefined shapes that are easy to draw. Available shapes include rectangles, circles, arrows, flowchart symbols, stars, banners, callouts, lines, and connectors. (4)

Sizing handles Small circles and squares around placeholders used to resize them. (2)

Slide layouts Contain placeholders for slide content such as titles, bulleted lists, charts, and shapes. (2)

Slide pane Area where you create, edit, and display presentation slides. (1)

Slide show The view that displays slides sequentially in full-screen size. Slides can advance manually or automatically with slide timings using a variety of transition effects. Slide shows can display movies and animated elements. (1)

Slide Sorter view Displays several thumbnails of slides making it easy to reorder, add, delete, or duplicate slides and set transition effects. (1, 3)

Slide thumbnail Miniature version of a graphic image. In PowerPoint, a miniature version of a slide is often referred to as a "thumbnail." (1)

Slide transition Visual effect that you can apply to enhance the way the screen changes during a slide show as you move from one slide to another. For example, the current slide could fade to a black screen before the next slide appears. (3)

Slides and Outline pane Area that can display either an outline of the presentation's text or thumbnails of the presentation's slides. You choose either Outline or Slides by clicking the appropriate tab. (1)

SmartArt graphic Categorized in seven major types of diagrams that produce a professional-looking visual representation of information. (7)

Snap to grid Feature that causes objects to align on the grid that may or may not be visible when working on a slide. (4)

Soft edges Effect that changes a picture's normal hard edges to a soft, feathered appearance that gradually fades into the background color. (4)

Source formatting The formatting of text and other elements that appear in the document from which the objects were cut or copied. (3)

Source When working with clipboard objects, the presentation or other document from which the objects were cut or copied. (3)

Spell checker Feature that corrects spelling by comparing words to an internal dictionary file. (3)

Split cells To divide a table cell into two smaller cells. (5)

Standard A format of displaying an organization chart where each shape is displayed in a hierarchy format. (7)

Status bar   Displays information about the presentation you're working on. It is located at the bottom of the PowerPoint window. (1)

Stock photography   Microsoft's online collection of photo images that can be searched by keyword. (4)

Subordinate shape   Shape in an organization chart that is connected to a superior shape reflecting a higher level. (7)

Table   Organized arrangement of information in rows and columns. (5)

Table borders   The lines forming the edges of cells, columns, rows, and the outside border of the table. (5)

Table style   Combination of formatting options, including color combinations based on theme colors. (5)

Tabs   Designed to be task oriented and contain groups of commands. Also, tabs can be used to align and indent text on a slide. Tab stops appear on the horizontal ruler. (1, 5)

Task pane   Area that appears at appropriate times on the right side of the PowerPoint window, displaying a list of commands that are relevant to certain tasks on which you are currently working. (3)

Text box   A free-form text object used to add text to slides. (2)

Text fill   Fill of WordArt and other text that can be a solid color, gradient fill, or other fill. (4)

Text outline   Outline of WordArt and other text that can be modified in color and thickness. (4)

Theme colors   Preset groups of colors for text, background, accent, and hyperlink colors. (2)

Theme effects   Selection of built-in effects that are applied to a presentation. (3)

Theme fonts   Selection of fonts that can be applied to a presentation. (3)

Tick marks   Small measurement marks, similar to the marks on a ruler, that cross a chart value or category axis. (6)

Title text   Text that usually appears at the top of a PowerPoint slide. Title text is usually placed in a title text placeholder. (1)

Toggle button   Switches between on and off when clicked. (2)

Transform   Effect that changes your text into different shapes. (4)

Transition effects   Visual or sound effects used when changing between slides. (1)

Transition, Slide   See "Slide transition." (3)

TrueType font   Font faces that are available universally on computers. (2)

Undo   Reverses the last action such as an editing change. PowerPoint can undo up to 20 actions if the Save feature has not been used. (3)

Ungroup   To separate a group of objects. When an object is ungrouped, each of its parts behaves as an individual object. (4)

Vector drawing   Picture made up of an arrangement of line segments and shapes that can be scaled to any size or aspect ratio without blurring. Vector drawings can be modified in PowerPoint by recoloring and by adding, removing, and rearranging individual elements. A shape is an example of a simple vector drawing. (4)

View buttons   Three buttons located on the lower-right corner of the PowerPoint window. You use these buttons to switch between Normal view (the default), Slide Sorter view, and Slide Show view. (1)

Word wrap   Text wraps to the next line when you reach the end of a placeholder or text box. (2)

WordArt   Text objects you create with special shading, shapes, and 3-D effects. (4)

Worksheet   Area in Microsoft Excel in which you enter numbers and labels that are used to create a chart. When you create a new chart, the worksheet in Microsoft Excel appears automatically, containing sample data that you can delete or overwrite. (6)

XML Paper Specification (XPS)   Preserves document formatting for viewing online or printing as originally designed. (14)

Zoom   Used in several areas of the application window to change the size at which you view that area. (1)

aggregate function   Dynamic mathematical calculation that displays a single value for a specific field. (2)

argument   A reference in a function assigned as a single variable. (6)

arithmetic operator   A word or symbol that calculates a value from two or more numbers. (6)

AutoCorrect   An application feature that automatically corrects commonly misspelled words. (2)

bound control   A control whose source of data is a field in a table or query. (7)

calculated control   A control whose source of data is an expression, rather than a field. (7)

calculated field   A field that uses an expression or formula as its data source. (6)

command group   A collection of logically organized commands. (1)

comparison operator   A symbol or combination of symbols that specifies a comparison between two values. (6)

concatenation operator   A symbol, word, group of symbols, or group of words used to combine two text values into a single text value. (6)

control   A database object that displays data, performs actions, and lets you view and work with information that enhances the user interface, such as labels and images. (7)

control margin   The specified location of information inside a control. (7)

control padding   The space between the gridline of the form and the control. (7)

criterion   A rule or test placed upon a field. (2)

database   A logically organized collection of data. (1)

Database Documenter   An Access tool used to display the indexes, properties, relationships, parameters, and permissions of major database objects. (3)

database template   A ready-to-use database containing all the tables, queries, forms, and reports needed to perform a specific task. (4)

Datasheet View   A screen view used to display data in rows and columns, similar to a spreadsheet. (1)

Design View   A screen view used to modify the structure of a major object. (1)

dynaset   A dynamic recordset that automatically reflects changes to its underlying data source. (6)

Edit Mode   The mode in which changes to the content of a field can be made and the insertion point is visible. (1)

Expression Builder   An interface used to create a function, calculation, or expression. (6)

field   The smallest storage element that contains an individual data element within a record. (1)

filter   A database feature that limits the number of records displayed. (3)

foreign key   A field that links to a primary key field in the related table. (5)

function   A procedure used in an expression. (6)

Join Line   A symbol representing a connection between related fields from two tables. (5)

logical operator   A symbol, word, group of symbols, or group of words used to construct an expression with multiple conditions. (6)

lookup field   A field property that displays input choices from another table and allows these choices to be selected from a list. (5)

Navigation Mode   The mode in which an entire field is selected and the insertion point is not visible. (1)

normalization   The process of restructuring a relational database for the purposes of organizing data efficiently, eliminating field redundancy, and improving data consistency. (5)

object dependency   A condition in which an object requires the existence of another object. (5)

operator   A word or symbol that indicates a specific arithmetic or logical relationship between the elements of an expression. (6)

PivotChart   An interactive graphical representation of data displayed in a PivotTable. (6)

PivotTable   An interactive table that combines and compares data in a summarized view (6)

primary key   A field or set of fields in a table that provides a unique identifier for every record. (3)

Print Preview   A method for displaying on the screen how an object will appear if printed on paper. (2)

record   A complete set of related data about one entity or activity. (1)

record navigation button   An icon that moves the pointer within a recordset to the next, previous, first, or last record. (1)

referential integrity   A set of database rules for checking, validating, and keeping track of data entry changes in related tables. (5)

Relationship Report   A link or connection between two tables sharing a common field. (5)

Relationship Report   A graphical report showing related tables. Each Relationship Report you create can be saved. (5)

ScreenTip   The name of or information regarding a specific object. (1)

special operator   A symbol, word, group of symbols, or group of words used to express a relationship between two values. (6)

subdatasheet   A datasheet linked within another datasheet. (5)

table   A major database object that stores all data in a subject-based list of rows and columns. (1)

unbound control   A control without a source of data. (7)

Validation Rule   A condition specifying criteria for entering data into an individual field. (4)

Validation Text   An error message that appears when a value prohibited by the validation rule is entered. (4)

wildcard   A character or group of characters used to represent one or more alphabetical or numerical characters. (3)

XPS   An XML Paper Specification (XPS) file format that preserves document formatting and enables file sharing of printable documents. (1)

Word Index

A

Access Keys, WD-10, WD-12
Add to Contacts, WD-103
Add to Dictionary option, WD-111
Adding
    contacts, WD-103
    to dictionary, WD-111
    footers, WD-324–WD-325
    headers, WD-324–WD-325
    page headers, WD-320–WD-323
    page numbers, WD-314–WD-318
    section footers, WD-324–WD-325
    section headers, WD-324–WD-325
Address(es)
    envelope format for, WD-274
    format for, WD-274
Address bar button, WD-37
Alignment
    bottom, WD-300
    centered, WD-169, WD-300
    justified, WD-300
    paragraph, WD-132–WD-135
    of sections, WD-299–WD-300
    of tabs, WD-169, WD-172
    top, WD-300
    vertical, WD-299–WD-300
All Caps, WD-76, WD-80
All Fonts, WD-68
Alphabetical sorting, WD-180
Alternate footers, WD-330–WD-332
Alternate headers, WD-330–WD-332
Antonyms, WD-113
Apply to (borders), WD-145
Arrow keys, WD-40
Ascending sort, WD-180
At Least option, WD-137
AutoComplete, WD-96–WD-98
AutoCorrect, WD-96–WD-101
    for borders formatting, WD-149
    control options for,
      WD-99–WD-100
    defined, WD-96
    description of, WD-111
    entries for, WD-98–WD-99
    exceptions in, WD-100–WD-101
    for lowercase initials, WD-101
    options for, WD-99–WD-100
    for shortcut keying, WD-98
    for spelling, WD-98–WD-99
    for symbols, WD-71, WD-157
AutoFormat, WD-83–WD-84
    for bulleted lists, WD-153–WD-154
    for character formatting,
      WD-83–WD-84
    of fractions, WD-83
    for hyperlinks, WD-83
    for lists, WD-153–WD-154
    for numbered lists,
      WD-153–WD-154
    of ordinals, WD-83
Automatic formatting
    with background repagination,
      WD-314–WD-315
    of borders, WD-149
    of bulleted lists, WD-153–WD-154
    of fractions, WD-84
    of hard page break,
      WD-292–WD-293
    of numbered lists,
      WD-153–WD-154
    of numbers, WD-84
    of ordinal numbers, WD-83
    of soft page break, WD-291
    of spacing, WD-203
    of symbols, WD-157
Automatic insertion
    of paragraph marks, WD-134
    of smart quotes, WD-157
    of tabs, WD-134
Automatic page breaks, WD-290
Automatic text keying, WD-96–WD-111
    with AutoComplete, WD-96–WD-98
    with AutoCorrect, WD-96–WD-101
    with AutoText, WD-103–WD-106
    date and time, WD-107–WD-108
    for grammar, WD-108–WD-109
    with smart tags, WD-101–WD-103
    for spelling, WD-108–WD-109
    wrapping, WD-13–WD-15
Automatic updates, WD-108
AutoRecover, WD-50–WD-51
AutoText, WD-103–WD-106
    creating entries for,
      WD-103–WD-105
    deleting entries for, WD-106
    editing entries for, WD-106
    inserting entries, WD-105–WD-106
    for months, WD-107
    on new page, WD-104
    in separate paragraph, WD-104
    for tables, WD-103
Available print area, WD-316

B

Back button, WD-37
Background repagination,
    WD-314–WD-315
Bar tabs, WD-169, WD-179–WD-180
Bars, split, WD-204
Basic character formatting,
    WD-69–WD-72
    applying, WD-70–WD-72
    with keyboard shortcuts, WD-71
    with mini toolbar, WD-72
    removing, WD-71–WD-72
    with ribbon, WD-70–WD-71
Blank and recent (templates), WD-381
Blue wavy lines, WD-108
Bold (format), WD-69
Bold and italic (format), WD-69
Borders, WD-143–WD-147
    application areas for, WD-145
    AutoCorrect for, WD-149
    automatic application of, WD-149
    defined, WD-143
    indents and, WD-145
    manual application of, WD-149
    for page decoration,
      WD-143–WD-14
    for paragraphs, WD-143–WD-145,
      WD-149
    ScreenTips for, WD-143
    selections for, WD-145
    for text, WD-145–WD-147
Borders and Shading dialog box,
    WD-143
Borders button, WD-143
Bottom alignment, vertical, WD-300
Bound documents, WD-265

Break(s), WD-290–WD-297
    automatic, WD-290
    column, WD-235
    continuous section, WD-297
    on even pages, WD-297
    hard page, WD-290,
      WD-292–WD-294
    line, WD-38, WD-39, WD-235,
      WD-294–WD-297
    manual line, WD-235
    on next page, WD-297
    for odd pages, WD-297
    page, WD-261, WD-290–WD-296
    paragraph, WD-294–WD-297
    in Print Layout view, WD-261
    section. *See under* Section breaks
    Show and Hide button for, WD-295
    soft, WD-290–WD-291, WD-293
Break dialog box, WD-297
Building Blocks Organizer, WD-105
Built-in styles, WD-351, WD-352, WD-354
Bullet(s), WD-150
    changing graphic of, WD-152,
      WD-153
    defining new, WD-153
    picture, WD-153
    selection by, WD-152
Bulleted lists, WD-150–WD-154
    AutoFormat for, WD-153–WD-154
    automatic creation of,
      WD-153–WD-154
    changing, WD-152–WD-153
    closing, WD-153
    continuing format for, WD-153
    creating, WD-150–WD-154
    defined, WD-150
    selecting, WD-152
Business documents, WD-328
By box (character spacing), WD-78

C

Calibri (font), WD-67
Cambria (font), WD-67, WD-274
Capitalization
    in cells, WD-98
    correcting improper use of, WD-98
    of days, WD-98
    of sentences, WD-98
    small, WD-76
    of weekdays, WD-98
Caps Lock, WD-16, WD-98
Case (text)
    changing, WD-80–WD-81
    correcting, WD-98
    matching, WD-226–WD-227
Cells, capitalization in, WD-98
Center alignment
    of tabs, WD-169
    vertical, WD-300
Change All option, WD-111
Change option, WD-111
Character(s)
    leader, WD-173
    for line breaks, WD-38, WD-39
    selecting, WD-45
    special, WD-155, WD-157,
      WD-233–WD-235
    symbols, WD-155–WD-156
    tab, WD-38, WD-39

Character (font) effects
   with Font dialog box,
      WD-74–WD-77
   highlighting, WD-81–WD-82
   keyboard shortcuts for, WD-77
Character formatting, WD-66–WD-84
   applying, WD-70–WD-72
   AutoFormat features for,
      WD-83–WD-84
   basic, WD-69–WD-72
   case changing, WD-80–WD-81
   copying, WD-79, WD-80
   drop caps, WD-82–WD-83
   Find and Replace for,
      WD-235–WD-236
   font basics for, WD-66–WD-69
   Font dialog box for, WD-72–WD-79
   with Format Painter button,
      WD-79, WD-80
   highlighting text, WD-81–WD-82
   with keyboard shortcuts, WD-71
   with mini toolbar, WD-72
   purpose of, WD-66
   removing, WD-71–WD-72
   with Repeat command, WD-79
   with ribbon, WD-70–WD-71
Character spacing
   changing, WD-77–WD-78
   with Font dialog box,
      WD-77–WD-78
Character Spacing tab (Font dialog
   box), WD-77
Character styles, WD-345,
   WD-350–WD-351
Clear Formatting button,
   WD-148
Clearing
   formatting, WD-148
   tabs, WD-173–WD-174
Click and Type, WD-134–WD-135
Clip Art button, WD-322
Clipboard, WD-194–WD-195. See also
   Office Clipboard
Close button, WD-21
Close command, WD-21
Close Print Preview button, WD-268
Close quotes, WD-157
Closing
   bulleted lists, WD-153
   documents, WD-20, WD-21
   File menu, WD-9
   Folders list, WD-20
   keyboard shortcuts for, WD-21
   numbered lists, WD-153
Colons (punctuation), WD-76
Color(s)
   fill, WD-148
   fonts and, WD-148
   readability and, WD-148
   shading, WD-148
   themes, WD-361
   for underlining, WD-75
Column, tabbed, WD-176–WD-181
Column breaks, WD-235
Combining
   keyboard shortcuts, WD-16
   paragraphs, WD-17
Commands, WD-12. See also specific
      types, e.g. Repeat command
   Font group, WD-70
   formats for, WD-10
   identifying, WD-12
   locations of, WD-9
   of Office Button, WD-10
   Ribbon, WD-10–WD-12
   unavailable, WD-11
   Word, WD-12

Compatibility, checking, WD-36
Compatibility Mode, WD-36
Completion, automatic. See
   AutoComplete
Contacts, adding, WD-103
Contiguous text, WD-47
Continuation page headers,
   WD-328–WD-330
Continuous section breaks, WD-297
Copy and Paste, WD-201–WD-202.
   See also Paste
   between multiple documents,
      WD-210
   using, WD-201–WD-202
Copying, WD-194–WD-196,
   WD-201–WD-204
   character formatting, WD-79,
      WD-80
   with Clipboard,
      WD-194–WD-196
   with copy and paste. See Copy
      and Paste
   with drag-and-drop,
      WD-202–WD-204
   between multiple documents,
      WD-209–WD-210
   paragraph formats,
      WD-149–WD-150
   styles to templates,
      WD-387–WD-388
Correction, automatic. See AutoCorrect
Correspondence. See Letters
Cover page, page numbers on,
   WD-318–WD-319
Create new document, WD-21
Create New Theme Colors dialog box,
   WD-362
Custom dictionary, WD-111
Custom tabs, WD-169
Cut-and-paste
   keyboard shortcuts for,
      WD-199
   methods for, WD-196
   moving text with,
      WD-196–WD-200, WD-210
   Office Clipboard for,
      WD-199–WD-200
   shortcut menu for,
      WD-197–WD-199
   Smart Cut-and-Paste feature,
      WD-203
   spacing and, WD-196, WD-203
   Standard toolbar for, WD-197

D

Dashes, as leader characters, WD-173
Date
   fields for, WD-107
   in letters and memos, WD-329
Date and time
   automatic insertion of,
      WD-107–WD-108
   fields for, WD-108
   in letters, WD-108
Date and Time (command), WD-107
Date and Time button, WD-322,
   WD-329
Days, capitalization of, WD-98
Decimal-aligned tabs, WD-169
Default styles, WD-351
Default templates, WD-377
Default themes, WD-359
Define New Bullet, WD-153
Deleted pages, Go To, WD-303
Deleting
   accidental, WD-49

AutoText entries, WD-106
   basic character formatting,
      WD-71–WD-72
   character formatting,
      WD-71–WD-72
   hard page breaks, WD-293
   page breaks, WD-293
   page numbers, WD-319
   pages, WD-303
   paragraph formats,
      WD-148–WD-150
   redo after, WD-43
   with Replace, WD-232–WD-233
   section breaks, WD-298
   selections, WD-49
   soft page breaks, WD-293
   spacing after, WD-203
   styles, WD-354
   text, WD-16
   Undo, WD-43
Descending sort, WD-180
Desktop publishing. See specific topics,
   e.g. Page formatting
Dictionary
   adding to, WD-111
   custom, WD-111
   for spell-check, WD-111
Different first page button, WD-322
Different Odd and Even Pages button,
   WD-322
Disk drive letter, WD-37
Document(s)
   AutoRecover of, WD-50–WD-51
   bound, WD-265
   business, WD-138
   closing, WD-20
   editing, WD-269–WD-270
   existing, WD-34–WD-38, WD-383
   grammar-check for,
      WD-109–WD-111
   margins, WD-258–WD-260
   moving within, WD-40–WD-43
   multiple, WD-204–WD-209
   multiple-page, WD-267–WD-268
   naming, WD-18–WD-19
   opening existing, WD-34–WD-38
   Print Preview for, WD-267–WD-270
   printing, WD-20
   properties, WD-51–WD-53
   recent, WD-20
   revised, WD-50–WD-51
   saving, WD-18–WD-19,
      WD-50–WD-51
   selecting, WD-45
   show text of, WD-322
   size of, WD-257, WD-270
   spell-check of, WD-109–WD-111
   standard, WD-257, WD-270
   switching between, WD-208
   as templates, WD-383
   templates attached to,
      WD-383–WD-386
   text of, WD-322
   themes, WD-359–WD-363
   types of, WD-19
Document footers, WD-323–WD-324
Document headers. See Page headers
Document Information Panel,
   WD-53
Document themes. See Theme(s)
.docx, WD-19
.dotm file, WD-377
Dotted lines
   as leader characters, WD-173
   purple, WD-101
.dotx file, WD-377
Double strikethrough, WD-76

Double-spaced paragraphs, WD-135
Draft view, WD-261
    page breaks in, WD-261, WD-262
    style area in, WD-358
Drag-and-drop
    alternatives to, WD-204
    for copying text, WD-202–WD-204
    over distance, WD-200, WD-204
    moving text with, WD-200–WD-201,
        WD-210–WD-211
    between multiple documents,
        WD-210–WD-211
Drop caps, WD-82–WD-83
Duplicating text, WD-44–WD-45

E

Editing, WD-269–WD-270
    AutoText entries, WD-106
    document properties,
        WD-51–WD-53
    insertion point and, WD-41
    keyboard shortcuts for, WD-15
    multiple documents,
        WD-206–WD-211
    in panes, WD-206
    in paragraphs, WD-17
    in Print Preview, WD-269–WD-270
    properties, WD-51–WD-53
    redo, WD-43–WD-44
    Repeat command for,
        WD-44–WD-45
    text. See Text editing
    Undo, WD-43–WD-44
Editing group, WD-225
Em dash, WD-157, WD-235
Emboss (font effect), WD-76
En dash, WD-157, WD-235
Engrave (font effect), WD-76
Envelopes
    address format for, WD-274
    default font for, WD-274
    font for, WD-274
    formatting for, WD-271–WD-275
    options for, WD-273–WD-275
    page formatting for, WD-271–WD-275
    printing, WD-271–WD-273
    test prints for, WD-273
Errors
    in document in entirety,
        WD-109–WD-111
    flagging, WD-108
    grammar-check for, WD-109–WD-111
    individual. See Individual errors
    spell-check of, WD-109–WD-111
Even page(s)
    alternate headers and footers for,
        WD-330–WD-332
    different, WD-322
    section breaks on, WD-297
Even page section break, WD-297
Exactly option (line spacing), WD-137
Exceptions, AutoCorrect,
    WD-100–WD-101
Existing documents, WD-34–WD-38
    opening, WD-34–WD-38
    as templates, WD-383
Exiting Microsoft Word, WD-21

F

Facing pages, WD-265–WD-266
Feed, manual. See Manual feed
Field(s), WD-107
    for date and time, WD-108
    for dates, WD-107

defined, WD-107
Find for, WD-235
on-screen update of, WD-108
printing, WD-107, WD-108
for time, WD-107
File(s). See also Document(s)
    .dotm, WD-377
    .dotx, WD-377
    inserting, into current document,
        WD-210
    naming, WD-18
    noncontiguous, WD-207
    opening, WD-36, WD-207
    reopening, WD-294
    types, WD-19
    view type of, WD-386
File extensions, WD-19, WD-377
File menu
    closing, WD-9
    keyboard shortcut for, WD-35
Filenames, WD-18, WD-50
Fill colors, WD-148
Find (command), WD-224–WD-231
    defined, WD-224
    for fields, WD-235
    with Find whole words only
        option, WD-228
    for footnotes, WD-235
    for formatted text, WD-230
    for graphics, WD-235
    with Match case option,
        WD-226–WD-227
    Next Find/Go To button, WD-229
    Previous Find/Go To button,
        WD-229
    scrolling vs., WD-224
    for section breaks, WD-235
    with Use wildcards options,
        WD-228–WD-229
    using, WD-224
Find all word forms, WD-233
Find and Replace. See also Replace
    for character formatting,
        WD-235–WD-236
    for column breaks, WD-235
    for em dash, WD-235
    for formatting,
        WD-235–WD-238
    of formatting guidelines, WD-239
    for line breaks, WD-235
    for manual line breaks, WD-235
    for paragraph formatting,
        WD-236–WD-238
    for paragraph marks, WD-235
    for special characters,
        WD-233–WD-235
Find Next (Replace), WD-231–WD-232
Find whole words only, WD-228
First page, different, WD-322
First-line indent markers,
    WD-141
Folders, WD-37–WD-38
Folders list, WD-20
Font(s), WD-66–WD-69
    availability of, WD-73
    basics of, WD-66–WD-69
    Calibri, WD-67
    Cambria, WD-67, WD-274
    changing, WD-67–WD-69
    choosing, WD-73–WD-74
    colors and, WD-148
    default, WD-274
    defined, WD-66
    for envelopes, WD-274
    Font dialog box and, WD-73–WD-74
    formatting, WD-66–WD-69
    Home tab for, WD-67, WD-70

measurement of, WD-67
Monotype Corsiva, WD-67
recently used, WD-68
Ribbon control over,
    WD-67–WD-69
sans serif fonts, WD-67
serif fonts, WD-67
shading and, WD-148
sizes of. See Font sizes
with special characters,
    WD-155
styles, WD-73–WD-74
Symbol font, WD-155
in themes, WD-66–WD-67,
    WD-68
types of, WD-67
Wingdings font, WD-155, WD-156
Font dialog box, WD-72–WD-79
    active, WD-74
    character effects with,
        WD-74–WD-77
    character spacing with,
        WD-77–WD-78
    with Font box active, WD-74
    font choice in, WD-73–WD-74
    font effects with, WD-74–WD-77
    for formatting, WD-72–WD-79
    opening, WD-72, WD-74
    with Size box active, WD-74
    styles, choosing with,
        WD-73–WD-74
    underline options in,
        WD-74–WD-77
    using, WD-72–WD-79
Font effects. See Character effects
Font group commands, WD-70
Font sizes
    bold appearance of, WD-69
    changing, WD-67–WD-69
    keyboard shortcuts for
        changing, WD-69
    Ribbon control over,
        WD-67–WD-69
Footer(s), WD-314
    alternate, WD-330–WD-332
    breaking link for, WD-326
    default position of,
        WD-329
    defined, WD-314
    in document, WD-323–WD-324
    for even pages, WD-330–WD-332
    linking, WD-326–WD-327
    position of, WD-329
    printer affecting, WD-316
    section, WD-324–WD-327
    selecting text in, WD-326
    tools for, WD-322
    unlinking, WD-326–WD-327,
        WD-332
    viewing, WD-316
Footer button, WD-322
Footer from Bottom button, WD-322
Footnote(s), WD-235
Foreign language characters, WD-155
Format indicators
    blue wavy lines, WD-108
    for grammar-check, WD-108
    green wavy lines, WD-108, WD-109
    purple dotted lines, WD-101
    red wavy lines, WD-108
    for spell-check, WD-108
Format Painter button, WD-79, WD-80
    character formatting with, WD-79,
        WD-80
    for paragraph formatting,
        WD-149
    for tabs, WD-172

Formatting, WD-230
  with AutoFormat. *See* AutoFormat
  automatic, WD-84
  basic character formatting,
      WD-69–WD-72
  character, WD-66–WD-84
  clearing, WD-148
  commands, WD-10
Find and Replace for,
      WD-235–WD-239
Find command for, WD-230
  of fractions, WD-84
  lack of, WD-225
  of numbers, WD-84
  page numbers, WD-317–WD-318
  paragraph, WD-132–WD-155
  revealing, WD-75
  sections, WD-298–WD-301
  of templates, WD-386–WD-387
Formatting characters. *See* Character
      formatting; Formatting marks
Formatting marks
  displaying, WD-67
  entering, WD-39–WD-40
Forward button, WD-37
Fractions, WD-83, WD-84

G
Gallery
  defined, WD-315
  Quick Style Gallery, WD-344,
      WD-354
Gallery heading (Building Blocks
      Organizer), WD-105
Go To, WD-301–WD-303
  for deleting pages, WD-303
  Next, WD-229
  Next Find, WD-229
  page, WD-302
  percentages, WD-303
  Previous Find, WD-229
  relative destination,
      WD-302–WD-303
  scrolling vs., WD-301
  section, WD-302
Go to Footer button, WD-322
Go to Header button, WD-322
Grammar-check, WD-108–WD-111
  automatic tools for,
      WD-108–WD-109
  of document in entirety,
      WD-109–WD-111
  indicators for, WD-108, WD-109
  for individual errors, WD-109
  options for, WD-49
  without spell-check, WD-110
  Undo for, WD-49
  weaknesses of, WD-109
Graphics
  AutoText for, WD-103
  Find for, WD-235
Green wavy lines, WD-108, WD-109
Gregg Reference Manual, The, WD-176,
      WD-379
Grouping, WD-70
Gutter margins
  defined, WD-265
  facing pages with,
      WD-265–WD-266

H
Hanging indent(s), WD-141, WD-150,
      WD-151
Hanging indent marker, WD-141

Hard page breaks, WD-290
  automatic adjustment of,
      WD-292–WD-293
  deleting, WD-293
Header(s), WD-314, WD-320–WD-323
  alternate, WD-330–WD-332
  breaking link for, WD-326
  of business letter, WD-328
  continuation, WD-328–WD-330
  default position of, WD-329
  defined, WD-314
  in document, WD-320–WD-323,
      WD-328–WD-330
  for even pages, WD-330–WD-332
  for letters, WD-328–WD-330
  linking, WD-326–WD-327
  of memo, WD-328
  position of, WD-329
  section, WD-324–WD-327
  selecting text in, WD-326
  tools for, WD-322
  unlinking, WD-326–WD-327,
      WD-332
Header button, WD-322
Header from Top button, WD-322
Header styles, WD-352
Help, online, WD-21–WD-22
Hidden (font effect), WD-76
Hide button, WD-38
Highlight button, WD-81
Highlighting
  for emphasis, WD-81, WD-82
  printing issues with, WD-82
  shading and, WD-82
  for sharing, WD-82
  text, WD-81–WD-82
Home tab, for fonts, WD-67, WD-70
Horizontal lines, WD-147
Horizontal scroll bar, WD-42
Hyperlinks, AutoFormat for, WD-83
Hyphenation
  dashes and, WD-157
  Find and Replace for, WD-235
  nonbreaking, WD-235
  nonbreaking Find and Replace for,
      WD-235

I
I-beam
  defined, WD-13
  movement within document,
      WD-40
Ignore All option, WD-111
Ignore Once option, WD-111
"In current document" styles, WD-351
"In use" styles, WD-351
Indent(s), WD-139–WD-142
  borders and, WD-145
  defined, WD-139
  hanging, WD-141, WD-150,
      WD-151
  indent buttons for,
      WD-140–WD-141
  keyboard shortcuts for, WD-141
  as lists, WD-150–WD-155
  in multilevel lists, WD-154
  negative, WD-140
  Paragraph dialog box for,
      WD-140–WD-141
  positive, WD-140
  ruler for, WD-141–WD-142
  setting, WD-139–WD-142
  shading and, WD-145
Indent button, WD-140–WD-141
Indent markers, WD-141
  first-line, WD-141

hanging, WD-141
right, WD-141
ScreenTips for, WD-141
Indicators, for format. *See* Format
      indicators
Individual errors, WD-109
Initials, WD-101
Insert Alignment Tab button, WD-322
Insert mode, WD-16
Insert Page Number button, WD-322
Insert tab, WD-210
Inserting
  AutoText entries, WD-105–WD-106
  files, WD-210
  special characters, WD-157
  symbols, WD-155–WD-156
  text, WD-16–WD-17
Inserting text, WD-16–WD-17
  alignment of, WD-134–WD-135
  Click and Type for,
      WD-134–WD-135
  with paragraph alignment,
      WD-134–WD-135
Insertion, automatic. *See* Automatic
      insertion
Insertion point
  canceling, WD-228
  defined, WD-12
  keyboard control over,
      WD-40–WD-41
  keyboard shortcuts for, WD-41
  at last location of edit, WD-41
  movement of, WD-40–WD-41
  paragraph formatting and, WD-134
  scrolling and, WD-40
  after Search, WD-227
Internet Address. *See* Hyperlinks
Italics, WD-69

J
Justified alignment, vertical, WD-300

K
Keep lines together, WD-294
Keep with next, WD-294
Key Tips, WD-10, WD-11
Keyboard
  clearing tabs with,
      WD-173–WD-174
  insertion point control with,
      WD-40–WD-41
  for moving within document,
      WD-40
  selection adjustment with,
      WD-48–WD-49
  tabs options with,
      WD-173–WD-174
Keyboard shortcuts
  basic character formatting with,
      WD-71
  for closing documents, WD-21
  combinations, WD-16
  for cut-and-paste, WD-199
  for File menu, WD-35
  for font size, WD-69
  for indents, WD-141
  for insertion point, WD-41
  for line spacing, WD-135
  for paragraph spacing, WD-139
  for selecting, WD-49
  for styles, WD-359
  for symbols, WD-71
  for text editing, WD-15
  for underline options, WD-77

Keying text, WD-12–WD-15
   with AutoComplete, WD-96–WD-98
   with AutoCorrect, WD-96–WD-101
   automatic. *See* AutoText
   automatically, WD-96–WD-111
   with AutoText, WD-103–WD-106
   date and time, WD-107–WD-108
   insertion point when, WD-13
   with smart tags, WD-101–WD-103
   spelling correction when,
      WD-13–WD-15
   tools for, WD-96–WD-114

L

Labels
   formatting for, WD-271,
      WD-275–WD-277
   printing, WD-271,
      WD-275–WD-277
Landscape orientation, WD-270
Leader characters, WD-173
Leader tabs, WD-169, WD-173
Left indent markers, WD-141
Left-alignment, WD-168, WD-169
Letters (correspondence)
   continuation page headers for,
      WD-328–WD-330
   date and time fields in, WD-108
   date in, WD-329
   headers for, WD-328
   manual feed, WD-275
Line breaks, WD-294–WD-297
   controlling, WD-294–WD-297
   Find and Replace for, WD-235
   manual, WD-235
   in paragraphs, WD-294–WD-297
   Show and Hide button for, WD-295
Line spacing, WD-135–WD-138
   changing, WD-135–WD-138
   defined, WD-135
   keyboard shortcuts for, WD-135
   paragraph dialog box for, WD-136
Line Spacing button, WD-135
Line-break characters, WD-38, WD-39
Lines. *See* Format indicators;
    specific types
Link to Previous button, WD-322,
   WD-326
Linked styles, WD-345, WD-350
Linking
   footers, WD-326–WD-327
   headers, WD-326–WD-327
   section footers, WD-326–WD-327
   section headers, WD-326–WD-327
   to Web. *See* Hyperlinks
Links, hypertext. *See* Hyperlinks
List style, WD-345
Lists, WD-150–WD-155
   AutoFormat for, WD-153–WD-154
   bulleted, WD-150–WD-154
   hanging indents and, WD-150,
      WD-151
   indents as, WD-150–WD-155
   indents in, WD-154
   multilevel, WD-154–WD-155
   multilevel styles for, WD-155
   numbered, WD-152–WD-154
   selecting, WD-152
   styles for, WD-155
Lowercase initials, WD-101

M

Magnifier button, WD-268
Manual feed, WD-272, WD-273, WD-275

Manual line breaks, WD-235
Manuals, for style, WD-83
Margins, WD-256–WD-267
   default, WD-256
   defined, WD-256
   for document, WD-258–WD-260
   with facing pages,
      WD-265–WD-266
   formatting, WD-256–WD-267
   gutter, WD-265–WD-266
   measurement of, WD-269
   mirror, WD-265
   movement in dialog box of,
      WD-260
   for page, WD-258–WD-261
   in Page Setup dialog box,
      WD-257–WD-262
   in Print Layout view, WD-269
   in Print Preview, WD-257, WD-269
   rulers and, WD-269
   rulers for changing,
      WD-262–WD-265
   for section, WD-262
   text in. *See* Footer(s); Header(s)
   viewing, WD-259
Margins button, WD-258, WD-268
Mark(s)
   formatting, WD-39–WD-40, WD-67
   for paragraphs. *See* Paragraph
      marks
Markers. *See also* Format indicators
   indent, WD-141
   tab, WD-169
Match case option, WD-226–WD-227
Memos
   date in, WD-329
   headers for, WD-328
Microsoft Office button. *See* Office
     Button
Microsoft Office Suite, WD-103
Microsoft Outlook, WD-103
Microsoft Word
   commands in, WD-12
   defined, WD-6
   exiting, WD-21
   identification of parts of,
      WD-9–WD-12
   online help for, WD-21–WD-22
   parts of, WD-9–WD-12
   previous versions of, WD-36
   screen of, WD-9–WD-12
   starting, WD-6–WD-8
Mini toolbar
   basic character formatting with,
      WD-71, WD-72
   for selections, WD-46
Mirror margins, WD-265
Monotype Corsiva (font), WD-67
Months, AutoText for, WD-107
Mouse (device)
   navigating with, WD-43
   scroll bars vs., WD-43
   selection adjustment with,
      WD-48–WD-49
   selections with, WD-46–WD-47
   slider of, WD-12
   for styles options, WD-352
   with wheel, WD-43
   zooming with, WD-12
Movement
   within document, WD-40–WD-43,
      WD-292
   between documents,
      WD-206–WD-207
   with I-beam, WD-40
   of insertion point, WD-40–WD-41

   with keyboard, WD-40–WD-41
   margin dialog box, WD-260
   with mouse, WD-43
   with panes, WD-206–WD-207
   scrolling, WD-41–WD-43
Moving text, WD-194–WD-201
   with Clipboard, WD-194–WD-196
   with cut-and-paste,
      WD-196–WD-200, WD-210
   with drag-and-drop, WD-200–WD-201,
      WD-210–WD-211
   between multiple documents,
      WD-209–WD-211
Multilevel List button,
     WD-154
Multilevel lists, WD-154–WD-155
   indents in, WD-154
   styles for, WD-155
Multiple documents, WD-204–WD-209
   copying text between,
      WD-209–WD-210
   drag-and-drop between,
      WD-210–WD-211
   editing text between,
      WD-206–WD-211
   moving text between,
      WD-209–WD-211
   opening, WD-207–WD-209
   panes for, WD-206–WD-207
   pasting text between, WD-210
   splitting, WD-204–WD-206
   windows for, WD-206–WD-211
Multiple option (line spacing),
     WD-137
Multiple selections, WD-46
Multiple-page documents,
     WD-267–WD-268
My Templates, WD-381

N

Name heading (Building Blocks
     Organizer), WD-105
Names and naming. *See also*
     Renaming
   documents, WD-18–WD-19
   filenames, WD-18, WD-50
   files, WD-18
   folders, WD-38
   styles, WD-349
Negative indents, WD-140
New Folder button, WD-37
New Style dialog box, WD-349
Newsletters, WD-320
Next button, WD-41
Next Find/Go To button, WD-229
Next Page button, WD-268
Next page section break, WD-297
Next Section button, WD-322
No Formatting button, WD-225
Nonbreaking hyphenation, Find and
     Replace for, WD-235
Nonbreaking space, WD-38, WD-39
Noncontiguous files, WD-207
Noncontiguous text
   character formatting for, WD-70
   selections of, WD-47–WD-48
Normal (format), WD-69
Normal style, WD-344, WD-354,
     WD-355
Normal template, WD-377
Note(s). *See* Footnote(s)
Number(s)
   automatic formatting of, WD-84
   ordinal, WD-84
   page. *See* Page numbers
   sequential, WD-150, WD-152

Numbered lists, WD-152–WD-154
  AutoFormat for, WD-153–WD-154
  automatic creation of,
    WD-153–WD-154
  changing, WD-152–WD-153
  closing, WD-153
  continuing format for, WD-153
  creating, WD-152–WD-154
  defined, WD-150
  selecting, WD-152
Numbering. *See* Page numbers
Numerals. *See* Number(s)
Numerical sorting, WD-180

O

Odd page(s)
  alternate headers and footers for,
    WD-330–WD-332
  different, WD-322
  section break, WD-297
Odd page section break, WD-297
Office Button (Microsoft),
    WD-8–WD-10
Office Clipboard, WD-194–WD-196
  Clipboard vs., WD-195
  copying text with,
    WD-194–WD-196
  for cut-and-paste, WD-199–WD-200
  defined, WD-195
  full, WD-202
  moving text with, WD-194–WD-196
  for pasting text, WD-202
  Replace for, WD-235
  storage of, WD-195, WD-202
  task pane of, WD-195–WD-196
Office Clipboard task pane,
    WD-195–WD-196
Office Suite (Microsoft), WD-103
One Page button, WD-268
100% button, WD-268
Online help, WD-21–WD-22
Open dialog box, WD-20, WD-36
Opening
  documents, WD-34–WD-38,
    WD-207–WD-209
  existing documents, WD-34–WD-38
  files, WD-36, WD-207
  Folders list, WD-20
  Font dialog box, WD-72, WD-74
  multiple documents,
    WD-207–WD-209
  noncontiguous files, WD-207
  Office Clipboard task pane,
    WD-196
  reopening and, WD-294
  templates, WD-386
Options (Print Preview), WD-268
Options (spell- and grammar-check),
    WD-111
Ordinal numbers, WD-83, WD-84
Organize button, WD-37
Organizer, WD-387–WD-388
  for Building Blocks. *See* Building
    Blocks Organizer
  for templates, WD-387–WD-388
Orientation
  landscape, WD-270
  page, WD-270–WD-271
  portrait, WD-270
Orientation button, WD-268
Orphans, widows and, WD-294
Outline (font effect), WD-76, WD-225
Outlook (Microsoft), WD-103
Overtype mode, WD-16, WD-17

P

Page(s)
  facing, WD-265–WD-266
  Go To, WD-302
  with gutter margins,
    WD-265–WD-266
  next, WD-268
  orientation of, WD-270–WD-271
  previous, WD-268
  shrink, WD-268
  size of, WD-268,
    WD-270–WD-271
Page break(s), WD-290–WD-296
  automatic, WD-290
  controlling, WD-294–WD-297
  in Draft view, WD-261, WD-262
  hard, WD-290, WD-292–WD-294
  in paragraphs, WD-294–WD-297
  in Print Layout view, WD-261
  Show and Hide button for, WD-295
  soft, WD-290–WD-291
Page break before, WD-294
Page formatting
  borders for, WD-143–WD-147
  for envelopes, WD-271–WD-275
  horizontal lines for, WD-147
  for labels, WD-271, WD-275–WD-277
  margins, WD-256–WD-267
  orientation, WD-270–WD-271
  Print Preview, WD-267–WD-270
  for printing, WD-277–WD-278
  size, WD-270–WD-271
Page headers
  adding, WD-320–WD-323
  continuation, WD-328–WD-330
  for letters, WD-328–WD-330
Page Layout
  pagination in, WD-300–WD-301
  sections in, WD-300–WD-301
Page length, WD-290
Page margins, WD-258–WD-261
Page numbers, WD-314–WD-319. *See
    also* Pagination
  adding, WD-314–WD-318
  changing, WD-319
  continuation of, WD-326
  on cover page, WD-318–WD-319
  on first page, WD-317
  format of, WD-317–WD-318
  location of, WD-314
  numerals for, WD-317
  position of, WD-317–WD-318
  previewing, WD-315–WD-316
  removing, WD-319
  roman numerals for, WD-317
  sections affecting, WD-326
  starting, WD-318–WD-319,
    WD-327–WD-328
  viewing, WD-316
Page Setup dialog box,
    WD-257–WD-262
Page Setup Dialog Box
    Launcher, WD-258
Pagination, WD-290
  in background, WD-314–WD-315
  in Page Layout, WD-300–WD-301
  in Print Preview, WD-300–WD-301
  repagination, WD-314–WD-315
  in sections, WD-300–WD-301
Panes
  defined, WD-204
  editing in, WD-206
  movement with, WD-206–WD-207
  moving between, WD-206–WD-207

  for multiple documents,
    WD-206–WD-207
  Office Clipboard task pane,
    WD-195–WD-196
  research task pane,
    WD-112–WD-114
  Reveal Formatting task pane,
    WD-75
  splitting documents into,
    WD-204–WD-206
  Styles task pane, WD-345, WD-348,
    WD-351, WD-354, WD-359
  task pane, WD-75,
    WD-112–WD-114,
    WD-195–WD-196, WD-345,
    WD-348, WD-351, WD-354,
    WD-359
Paragraph(s)
  aligning, WD-132–WD-135
  borders for, WD-143–WD-145,
    WD-149
  breaks in, WD-294–WD-297
  combining, WD-17
  copying formats for,
    WD-149–WD-150
  defined, WD-132
  editing, WD-17
  Find and Replace for,
    WD-236–WD-238
  Format Painter button for, WD-149
  formatting, WD-132–WD-155
  indenting, WD-139–WD-142
  insertion point and, WD-134
  line breaks in, WD-294–WD-297
  line spacing, WD-135–WD-138
  with lists, WD-150–WD-155
  measurement of, WD-138
  page breaks in, WD-294–WD-297
  removing formats for,
    WD-148–WD-150
  repeating formats for,
    WD-149–WD-150
  selecting, WD-45, WD-149, WD-348
  selections for, WD-134
  shading for, WD-143, WD-145,
    WD-148–WD-149
  single-spaced, WD-135
  sorting text in, WD-180
  spacing, WD-135, WD-138–WD-139
  splitting, WD-17
  styles. *See* Paragraph styles
  text editing in, WD-17
Paragraph alignment, WD-132–WD-135
  changing, WD-133–WD-134
  text insertion with,
    WD-134–WD-135
Paragraph dialog box
  for indents, WD-140–WD-141
  for line spacing, WD-136
Paragraph marks, WD-13, WD-39,
    WD-132
  automatic insertion of, WD-134
  defined, WD-13
  Find and Replace for, WD-235
  tabs and, WD-168
Paragraph spacing, WD-138–WD-139
  keyboard shortcuts for, WD-139
  single-spaced, WD-135
Paragraph styles,
    WD-345, WD-348–WD-350,
    WD-355–WD-356
Paste. *See also* Copy and paste
  formatting of, WD-198
  between multiple documents,
    WD-210

Office Clipboard for, WD-202
    spacing after, WD-203
    text, WD-202, WD-210
Paste All button, WD-200
Paste button, WD-197
Paste Options button, WD-197
Percentages, Go To, WD-303
Periods (punctuation), WD-76
Picture button
    for bullets, WD-153
    for headers and footers, WD-322
Placeholder text
    locating, WD-379
    selecting, WD-379
    in templates, WD-377
Plain Text (TXT) format, WD-19
Points (measurement) for fonts, WD-67
    for paragraph space, WD-138
Portrait orientation, WD-270
Positive indents, WD-140
Previewing
    page numbers, WD-315–WD-316
    show, WD-348
Previous button, WD-41
Previous Find/Go To button, WD-229
Previous Page button, WD-268
Previous Section button, WD-322
Print(s). See Printing
Print, test, WD-273
Print area, WD-316
Print button, WD-268
Print dialog box, WD-20
Print Layout view, WD-7, WD-262
    for margin adjustments, WD-262
    margins in, WD-269
    page breaks in, WD-261
Print Preview, WD-267–WD-270
    editing documents in,
        WD-269–WD-270
    margins in, WD-257, WD-269
    for multiple-page documents,
        WD-267–WD-268
    for page formatting,
        WD-267–WD-270
    pagination in, WD-300–WD-301
    sections in, WD-300–WD-301
    style area in, WD-358
    toolbar, WD-268
Printing
    documents, WD-20
    envelopes, WD-271–WD-273
    for envelopes, WD-273
    features for, WD-256
    fields and, WD-107, WD-108
    footers, WD-316
    highlighting text, WD-82
    labels, WD-271, WD-275–WD-277
    manual feed, WD-272, WD-273,
        WD-275
    options for, WD-277–WD-278
    page formatting and,
        WD-277–WD-278
    Quick Print, WD-20, WD-277
    shared, WD-20
    styles, WD-357–WD-359
Proofing Errors icon, WD-14, WD-108
Properties, document, WD-51–WD-53
    defined, WD-51
    editing, WD-51–WD-53
    reviewing, WD-51–WD-53
    search by, WD-51
Properties dialog box, WD-52
Publishing, desktop. See specific
    topics, e.g. Page formatting
Punctuation, underlining, WD-76
Purple dotted lines, WD-101

Q
Quick Access Toolbar, WD-9
    Key Tips, WD-11
    purpose of, WD-8
    role of, WD-9
Quick Parts button, WD-322
Quick Print, WD-20, WD-277
Quick Style Gallery, WD-344,
    WD-354
Quotations (punctuation)
    close, WD-157
    smart, WD-157

R
Readability
    colors affecting, WD-148
    shading affecting, WD-148
    tab and, WD-172
Rearranging multiple document
    windows, WD-209
Recent Documents, WD-20
Recently Used Fonts, WD-68
Recommended (styles), WD-351
Recovering documents, automatic,
    WD-50–WD-51. See also
    AutoRecover
Red wavy lines, WD-108
Redo, WD-43–WD-44
Reference numbers. See Page numbers
Removing. See Deleting
Renaming
    folders, WD-38
    styles, WD-352–WD-353
Reopening files, WD-294
Repagination, background,
    WD-314–WD-315
Repeat command, WD-79
    character formatting with, WD-79
    duplicating text with,
        WD-44–WD-45
    for text editing, WD-44–WD-45
    use of, WD-79
Repeating
    character formatting, WD-79
    paragraph formats,
        WD-149–WD-150
Replace, WD-224, WD-231. See also
    Find and Replace
    defined, WD-224
    deleting with, WD-232–WD-233
    with Find Next, WD-231–WD-232
    methods for, WD-231
    for Office Clipboard, WD-235
    with Replace All, WD-232
    Replace All vs., WD-232
Replace All, WD-232
Replacing. See Replace
    automatic, WD-98
    command for (), WD-231
    styles, WD-353–WD-354
Reports, WD-320
Research options, WD-114
Research task pane, WD-112–WD-114
Research tools, WD-113–WD-114
Resizing, WD-209. See also Size
    and sizing
Reveal Formatting task pane, WD-75
Review tab, WD-113
Revised documents, WD-50–WD-51
Ribbon
    access keys for, WD-12
    appearance of, WD-225
    basic character formatting with,
        WD-70–WD-71

font options in, WD-67–WD-69
font size options in, WD-67–WD-69
font sizes, changing with,
    WD-67–WD-69
fonts, changing with, WD-67–WD-69
minimizing, WD-11
purpose of, WD-8
on tabs, WD-10
View tab of, WD-12
Ribbon commands, WD-10–WD-12
    accessing, WD-10
    identifying, WD-10–WD-12
    unavailable, WD-11
Rich Text Format (RTF), WD-19
Right indent marker, WD-141
Right-aligned tabs, WD-169
Roman numerals, as page numbers,
    WD-317
RTF (Rich Text Format), WD-19
Rulers
    indents and, WD-141–WD-142
    margins and, WD-262–WD-265,
        WD-269
    purpose of, WD-8
    show, WD-268
    tabs and, WD-171–WD-175
    view, WD-205
Run Compatibility Checker, WD-36

S
Sans serif fonts, WD-67
Save. See Saving
Save As command, WD-18, WD-50
Save As dialog box, WD-36
Save command, WD-18
Saving, WD-18
    AutoRecover and, WD-50–WD-51
    command locations for, WD-9
    with different filename, WD-50
    documents, WD-18–WD-19,
        WD-50–WD-51
    naming files before, WD-18
    with new filename, WD-50
    revised documents,
        WD-50–WD-51
    styles, WD-347
Scale option, WD-77
Screen (Word), WD-8–WD-12
ScreenTips, WD-9
    for AutoComplete, WD-96
    borders and, WD-143
    for indent markers, WD-141
    for translations, WD-96
Scroll bars
    horizontal, WD-42
    mouse wheel vs., WD-43
    for moving within document,
        WD-40
    position of, WD-40
    purpose of, WD-8
    vertical, WD-40
Scrolling
    within document, WD-41–WD-43
    Find vs., WD-224
    Go To vs., WD-301
    insertion point and,
        WD-40
Search. See also Find
    dialog box after, WD-227
    by document properties, WD-51
    insertion point after,
        WD-227
    by properties, WD-51
    purpose of, WD-37

Section(s)
 alignment of, WD-299–WD-300
 defined, WD-260, WD-290
 formatting, WD-298–WD-301
 Go To, WD-302
 margins for, WD-262
 next, WD-322
 in Page Layout view,
  WD-300–WD-301
 page numbers in, WD-326
 pagination in, WD-300–WD-301
 previous, WD-322
 in Print Preview, WD-300–WD-301
 vertical alignment of,
  WD-299–WD-300
Section breaks, WD-260, WD-297
 Break dialog box for, WD-297
 continuous, WD-297
 defined, WD-297
 deleting, WD-298
 even page, WD-297
 Find for, WD-235
 next page, WD-297
 for odd and even pages, WD-297
 odd page, WD-297
Section footers, WD-324–WD-327
 adding, WD-324–WD-325
 linking, WD-326–WD-327
 unlinking, WD-326–WD-327
Section headers, WD-324–WD-327
 adding, WD-324–WD-325
 linking and unlinking,
  WD-326–WD-327
Select Browse Object menu, WD-42
Selected text. See Selections
Selecting
 bulleted lists, WD-152
 defined, WD-45
 in footers, WD-326
 in headers, WD-326
 keyboard shortcuts for, WD-49
 lists, WD-152
 numbered lists, WD-152
 paragraphs, WD-149, WD-348
 placeholder text, WD-379
 sentences, WD-45
 styles and, WD-345, WD-352
 tabbed columns, WD-178
 text, WD-45, WD-326
 vertically, WD-178
 word, WD-45
Selections, WD-45–WD-49
 adjusting, WD-48–WD-49
 for borders, WD-145
 by bullet, WD-152
 defined, WD-45
 deleting, WD-49
 keyboard control over,
  WD-48–WD-49
 mini toolbar for, WD-46
 with mouse, WD-46–WD-47
 mouse control over,
  WD-48–WD-49
 multiple, WD-46
 of noncontiguous text,
  WD-47–WD-48
 for paragraph formatting, WD-134
 replacing, WD-49
 by sequential numbers, WD-152
 with "smart-select," WD-46
 tab and, WD-170, WD-178
Sentences
 capitalization of, WD-98
 selecting, WD-45
 spacing after, WD-15

Sequential numbers
 lists with, WD-150
 selection by, WD-152
Serif fonts, WD-67
Shading
 button for, WD-148
 colors for, WD-148
 defined, WD-143
 dialog box for, WD-143
 fill colors for, WD-148
 fonts and, WD-148
 highlighting text and, WD-82
 indents and, WD-145
 for paragraphs, WD-143, WD-145,
  WD-148–WD-149
 readability and, WD-148
Shadow (font effect), WD-76
Shared printer, WD-20
Sharing, highlighting text for, WD-82
Shortcut(s). See Keyboard shortcuts
Shortcut menus, WD-72,
  WD-197–WD-199
Show Document Text button, WD-322
Show Preview (check box), WD-348
Show Ruler button, WD-268
Show White Space button, WD-265
Show/Hide button, WD-38
Shrink One Page button, WD-268
Single-spaced paragraphs, WD-135
Size and sizing. See also Resizing
 documents, WD-257, WD-270
 font. See Font sizes
 page, WD-268, WD-270–WD-271
Size box, active, WD-74
Size button, WD-268
Slider (mouse), WD-12
Small Caps, WD-76
Smart Cut-and-Paste feature, WD-203
Smart quotes, WD-157
Smart tags, WD-40, WD-101–WD-103
 defined, WD-97
 indicators for, WD-101
"Smart-select," WD-46
Soft page breaks, WD-290–WD-291
 automatic adjustment of, WD-291
 defined, WD-290
 deleting, WD-293
Solid lines, as leader characters,
  WD-173
Sorting
 alphabetical, WD-180
 ascending, WD-180
 defined, WD-180
 descending, WD-180
 numerical, WD-180
 in paragraphs, WD-180
 styles, WD-351
 in tabbed columns, WD-180
Space (area). See also Spacing
 line, WD-135
 white, WD-235
Space (formatting character), WD-39
 Find for, WD-235
 nonbreaking, WD-38, WD-39
Spacing. See also Space (area)
 automatic adjustment of, WD-203
 for business documents, WD-138
 character, WD-77–WD-78
 with cut-and-paste, WD-196
 after cutting, WD-203
 after deleting, WD-203
 line, WD-135–WD-138
 paragraph, WD-138–WD-139
 after pasting, WD-203
 after sentences, WD-15

Spacing option, WD-77
Special characters, WD-155, WD-157
 Find and Replace for,
  WD-233–WD-235
 fonts with, WD-155
 for foreign languages, WD-155
 inserting, WD-157
Spell-check, WD-108–WD-111
 AutoCorrect for, WD-98–WD-99
 automatic, WD-13–WD-15,
  WD-108–WD-109
 custom dictionary for, WD-111
 of document in entirety,
  WD-109–WD-111
 without grammar-check, WD-110
 indicators for, WD-108
 for individual errors, WD-109
 options for, WD-49
 suggested word from, WD-15
 Undo for, WD-49
 weaknesses of, WD-109
Split bars, WD-204
Splitting
 multiple documents,
  WD-204–WD-206
 into panes, WD-204–WD-206
 paragraphs, WD-17
Standard toolbar, WD-197
Starting, WD-6–WD-8. See also
 Opening
Starting page numbers,
  WD-318–WD-319,
  WD-327–WD-328
Statistics tab, WD-52
Status bar, WD-8
Strikethrough, WD-76
Style(s), WD-344–WD-359
 applying, WD-344–WD-347
 area for, WD-358
 based on, option, WD-357
 built-in, WD-351, WD-352, WD-354
 changing set for, WD-359
 character, WD-345, WD-350–WD-351
 copied, WD-387
 creating new, WD-347–WD-351
 default, WD-351
 defined, WD-344
 deleting, WD-354
 displaying, WD-357–WD-359
 for following paragraph,
  WD-355–WD-356
 font, WD-73–WD-74
 formatting with, WD-355
 header, WD-352
 "In current document," WD-351
 "In use," WD-351
 keyboard shortcuts for, WD-359
 linked, WD-345, WD-350
 list, WD-345
 modifying, WD-352–WD-353,
  WD-385
 mouse use for, WD-352
 for multilevel lists, WD-155
 naming, WD-349
 new, WD-349
 Normal, WD-344, WD-354, WD-355
 options for, WD-355–WD-359
 paragraph, WD-345,
  WD-348–WD-350
 printing, WD-357–WD-359
 recommended, WD-351
 renaming, WD-352–WD-353
 replacing, WD-353–WD-354
 saving, WD-347
 selecting and, WD-345, WD-352

sorting, WD-351
table, WD-345
to templates, WD-387–WD-388
types of, WD-345
Undo for, WD-353
Style area, WD-358
Style manuals, WD-83
Style sets, WD-359
available, WD-346
defined, WD-344
defining, WD-345
Styles based on, WD-357
Styles for following paragraph,
    WD-355–WD-356
Styles gallery, WD-344, WD-354
Styles task pane, WD-345, WD-348,
    WD-351, WD-354, WD-359
Subscript, WD-76
Suggested words, WD-15
Summary tab, WD-53
Superscript, WD-76
Superscript ordinals, WD-83
Symbol(s), WD-155–WD-156
AutoCorrect for, WD-71, WD-157
automatic creation of, WD-157
inserting, WD-155–WD-156
keyboard shortcuts for, WD-71
recently used, WD-156
Symbol font, WD-155
Synonyms, WD-113

T

Tab(s), WD-38, WD-39,
    WD-168–WD-175
adjusting settings for,
    WD-174–WD-175
alignment of, WD-172
automatic insertion of, WD-134
bar, WD-169, WD-179–WD-180
centered, WD-169
clearing, WD-173–WD-174
copying settings for, WD-172
custom, WD-169
decimal-aligned, WD-169
default, WD-168, WD-169, WD-321
defined, WD-168, WD-171
in dialog box, WD-232
Find and Replace for, WD-235
Format Painter button for, WD-172
keyboard options for,
    WD-173–WD-174
leader, WD-169, WD-173
left-aligned, WD-168, WD-169
paragraph marks and, WD-168
readability and, WD-172
Ribbon on, WD-10
right-aligned, WD-169
ruler options for, WD-171–WD-175
selections and, WD-170, WD-178
setting, WD-168–WD-173
Show and Hide button for, WD-171
types of, WD-169
Tab Alignment button, WD-172
Tab markers, WD-169
Tab stops, WD-168
Tabbed columns, WD-176–WD-181
bar tabs in, WD-179–WD-180
creating, WD-176–WD-180
selecting, WD-178
setting, WD-176–WD-177
sorting, WD-180
Table(s)
AutoText for, WD-103
sorting text in, WD-181

Table style, WD-345
Tabs dialog box
clearing tabs with,
    WD-173–WD-174
setting tabs with, WD-170–WD-171
Task panes, WD-195–WD-196
Office Clipboard, WD-195–WD-196
research, WD-112–WD-114
Reveal Formatting, WD-75
Styles, WD-345, WD-348, WD-351,
    WD-354, WD-359
Templates, WD-376–WD-388
attaching, to documents,
    WD-383–WD-386
benefits of, WD-376–WD-377
blank, WD-381
changes, effects of, WD-386
copying styles to, WD-387–WD-388
creating new, WD-380–WD-383
default, WD-377
defined, WD-376
documents as, WD-383
existing document as, WD-383
features of, WD-376–WD-377
file extension for, WD-377
formatting, WD-386–WD-387
modifying, WD-386–WD-387
My Templates, WD-381
for new document,
    WD-377–WD-380
Normal, WD-377
opening, WD-386
Organizer for, WD-387–WD-388
placeholder text in, WD-377
recent, WD-381
replacing, WD-386
styles and, WD-387–WD-388
using, WD-376–WD-380
Testing, printer, WD-273
Text
automatic. *See* Automatic text
    keying; AutoText
borders for, WD-145–WD-147
contiguous, WD-47
copying, WD-194–WD-196,
    WD-201–WD-204
editing. *See* Text editing
finding, WD-224–WD-231
formatting, WD-230
highlighting, WD-81–WD-82
keying. *See* Keying text
noncontiguous, WD-47–WD-48,
    WD-70
placeholder, WD-377
selecting, WD-45
selections of. *See* Selections
wrapping, WD-13–WD-15
Text areas, WD-8
Text editing, WD-15–WD-18
deleting text, WD-16
formatting characters for,
    WD-38–WD-40
inserting text, WD-16–WD-17
keyboard shortcuts for, WD-15
between multiple documents,
    WD-206–WD-211
in paragraphs, WD-17
redo command for, WD-43–WD-44
repeat command for,
    WD-44–WD-45
selecting text, WD-45–WD-49
Undo command for,
    WD-43–WD-44
Text flow, WD-290
Text wrapping, WD-13–WD-15

Theme(s), WD-344, WD-359–WD-363
applying, WD-359–WD-360
colors for, WD-362
create new, WD-362
customizing, WD-361–WD-363
default, WD-359
defined, WD-66, WD-344
fonts in, WD-66–WD-67
Theme Colors button, WD-361
Theme Fonts, WD-68
Thesaurus, WD-112–WD-113
Time fields, WD-107. *See also* Date
    and time
Title bar, WD-8
Toggles, underlining, WD-77
Toolbars
mini, WD-46, WD-71, WD-72
Print Preview, WD-268
Quick Access Toolbar, WD-9
Standard, WD-197
Top alignment, WD-300
Translation(s). ScreenTip for, WD-96
Translation Tool Tip button, WD-114
Triple-click, WD-46
Turn Off Translation ScreenTip,
    WD-96
Two Pages button, WD-268
TXT (Plain Text) format, WD-19
Type, Click and, WD-134–WD-135
Typefaces. *See* Font(s)

U

Unavailable commands, WD-11
Underlining, WD-69
colons, WD-76
color selection for, WD-75
Font dialog box options for,
    WD-74–WD-77
keyboard shortcuts for, WD-77
periods, WD-76
punctuation, WD-76
toggle for, WD-77
Undo
for accidental deletion, WD-49
deleting, WD-43
drop-down list for, WD-44
for grammar-check, WD-49
for spell-check, WD-49
for styles, WD-353
for text editing, WD-43–WD-44
Uniform Resource Locators. *See*
    Hyperlinks
Unlinking
footers, WD-326–WD-327, WD-332
headers, WD-326–WD-327, WD-332
section footers, WD-326–WD-327
section headers, WD-326–WD-327
Update Automatically option, WD-108
URLs. *See* Hyperlinks
U.S. Postal Service, WD-274
Use wildcards options,
    WD-228–WD-229

V

Vertical alignment, WD-299–WD-300
Vertical scroll bars, WD-40
Vertical selection, WD-178
View Ruler button, WD-205
View tab (Ribbon), WD-12
Viewing
file type, WD-386
footers, WD-316
margins, WD-259

Viewing—*Cont.*
    page numbers, WD-316
    rulers, WD-205
    styles, WD-357–WD-359
Views button, WD-37

W
Wavy lines. *See specific types, e.g.*
        Green wavy lines
Web address. *See Hyperlinks*
Web sites, picture bullets in, WD-153
Weekdays, capitalizing, WD-98
Wheel (mouse), WD-43
White space
    Find for, WD-235
    show and hide, WD-265

Widows, orphans and, WD-294
Wildcards (Find), WD-228–WD-229
Wingdings font, WD-155, WD-156
Word. *See* Microsoft Word
Word(s)
    Find, WD-228
    selecting, WD-45
    suggested, WD-15
    whole, WD-228
Word Help link, WD-21
Word Ribbon. *See* Ribbon
Wrapping, text, WD-13–WD-15
Writing tools, WD-96–WD-114
    AutoComplete, WD-96–WD-98
    AutoCorrect, WD-96–WD-101
    AutoText, WD-103–WD-106
    for date and time, WD-107–WD-108

for grammar, WD-108–WD-111
for research,
        WD-113–WD-114
research task pane,
        WD-112–WD-114
smart tags, WD-101–WD-103
for spelling, WD-108–WD-111
thesaurus, WD-112–WD-113

Z
Zoom button, WD-268
Zooming
    with mouse, WD-12
    for placeholder text,
        WD-379
    slider for, WD-12

Excel Index

Symbols

\# symbols
  in a cell, EX-218, EX-281
  column filled with, EX-159
\$ (dollar signs)
  in an absolute reference, EX-177
  adding to cell references, EX-179
  in a mixed reference, EX-177
% (percent sign) in a formula, EX-171
+ (addition) operator, EX-60
+ (plus sign), EX-168
+ sign, expanding a list, EX-394
− (minus sign), EX-168
− sign, collapsing a list, EX-394
− (subtraction) operator, EX-60
* (asterisk) in multiplication
    formulas, EX-15
* (multiplication) operator, EX-60
* wildcard, EX-87
/ (division) operator, EX-60
/ (forward slash) in division formulas,
    EX-171
^ (exponentiation) operator, EX-60
< (less than) operator, EX-239
<= (less than or equal to) operator,
    EX-239
<> (not equal to) operator, EX-239
= (equal to) operator, EX-239
= sign, identifying formulas, EX-60
> (greater than) operator, EX-239
>= (greater than or equal to)
    operator, EX-239
~ (tilde), EX-87, EX-185
? wildcard, EX-87

A

absolute references, EX-177, EX-179
accented characters, EX-397–EX-398
Accounting format, EX-74
Accounting Number Format button,
    EX-55, EX-74
Across Worksheets option, EX-220
active cell, EX-7, EX-11, EX-12
Add Shape button, EX-389
Add to Dictionary spelling
    option, EX-85
addition formulas, EX-168–EX-170,
    EX-193
adjustment handles, EX-347,
    EX-361–EX-362
Adobe PDF file, EX-28
ages, determining, EX-281–EX-282
Align button, EX-360, EX-374, EX-403
Align Text Right button,
    EX-135, EX-353
Alignment group, EX-135, EX-235
Alignment tab
  in the Format Cells dialog box,
    EX-136, EX-139
  in the Text control group, EX-224
Alt key, displaying KeyTips, EX-9
Alt + Enter, EX-137, EX-177, EX-235
AND function, EX-242–EX-243
annuity, EX-255
area charts, EX-317
Argument ScreenTip, EX-204
arguments of functions,
    EX-202–EX-203
arithmetic mean, EX-209

arithmetic operators, EX-60, EX-174
arithmetic symbols, EX-53
Arrange group, EX-360
arrow keys, EX-10, EX-41
arrows, block styles, EX-354
aspect ratio, EX-382
assistant shape in an organization
    chart, EX-389
asterisk (*) in multiplication formulas,
    EX-171
"auto" functions, EX-63
AutoCalculate
  checking results with, EX-65–EX-66
  results in the status bar, EX-175
AutoComplete, EX-120,
    EX-121–EX-122. *See also*
    Formula AutoComplete
AutoCorrect, EX-80–EX-81
  setting options for, EX-82–EX-83
AutoCorrect list, EX-85
AutoFill command, EX-93, EX-103
AutoFill Options button, EX-94,
    EX-96, EX-170, EX-171
AutoFitting, EX-51, EX-52
AutoShape, EX-378
AutoSum, EX-76
AutoSum button, EX-76, EX-203
  clicking, EX-129
  in the Editing group, EX-95
  in the Function Library group, EX-64
AVERAGE function,
    EX-65, EX-209–EX-210
AVERAGEIF function, EX-210
Axes button, EX-315
axis, EX-308. *See also* horizontal axis;
    vertical axis
axis title, EX-309

B

background, EX-186–EX-187, EX-383
Background button, EX-186, EX-196
background color, EX-316
Bar button in the Charts group, EX-321
bar charts, EX-317, EX-321–EX-322
basic shapes, inserting, EX-374
Basic Shapes group, EX-354–EX-357
bevels, gallery of, EX-351
block-style arrows, EX-354
blue dashed lines, page breaks as,
    EX-249–EX-250
bold, applying, EX-48
Bold button, EX-9
  clicking, EX-10, EX-228
  for the Font group, EX-8
  in the Mini toolbar, EX-354
Border tab, EX-141–EX-142, EX-182
borders, EX-139
  adding for printing, EX-182
  applying, EX-139–EX-142
  changing, EX-280–EX-281
  designing special, EX-157–EX-158
  removing, EX-280
Bottom Align button, EX-137
Bottom Border option, EX-140
Bottom cell alignment option, EX-134
Bottom Double Border option, EX-141
bounding box, EX-311, EX-312,
    EX-347
Breaks button, EX-250, EX-254
bubble charts, EX-317, EX-343

built-in formulas, EX-60–EX-61
business diagrams, EX-391

C

callouts, EX-347–EX-351, EX-373
Cancel button in the formula
    bar, EX-41
category axis. *See* horizontal axis
cell(s), EX-11
  aligning, EX-134–EX-139
  changing vertical alignment
    for, EX-137
  combining a selected range,
    EX-138
  with comments, EX-363
  copying, cutting, and pasting
    contents of, EX-123–EX-128
  counting empty in a range, EX-212
  deleting, EX-120
  inserting, EX-119
  moving to specific, EX-11–EX-13
  orientation of, EX-138–EX-139
  selecting all, EX-50
  selecting a range of, EX-47–EX-50
  spell-checking, EX-85
  text display spilling into adjacent,
    EX-42
cell A1, EX-11, EX-13, EX-24
cell addresses, EX-11, EX-89
cell alignment, EX-134
cell contents
  clearing, EX-22
  copying and pasting,
    EX-124–EX-126
  cutting and pasting,
    EX-123–EX-124
  editing, EX-20–EX-22
  replacing, EX-19–EX-20
cell entries, EX-40–EX-41
cell formats, copying, EX-46
cell picture, pasting or linking,
    EX-409
cell ranges. *See* ranges
cell references, EX-11
  as arguments, EX-203
  types of, EX-177
cell styles, EX-246
  applying, EX-98–EX-99
  clearing and reapplying, EX-247
  creating, EX-247–EX-248
  described, EX-96
  editing, EX-248
  using, EX-246–EX-247
Cell Styles button, EX-98, EX-109,
    EX-246, EX-247, EX-268
Cell Styles gallery, EX-98–EX-99,
    EX-246
cell values, EX-208
Center across selection cell alignment
    option, EX-134
Center Across Selection command,
    EX-135–EX-136
Center button
  in the Alignment group, EX-135,
    EX-137
  in the Home tab, EX-240, EX-374
Center cell alignment option, EX-134
centering pages for printing, EX-253
Change Chart Type box, EX-332
Change Chart Type dialog box, EX-328

Change Colors button, EX-388, EX-404
character space, EX-51
character string, locating, EX-86
chart(s), EX-306
    building with two series, EX-332–EX-333
    creating, EX-317–EX-322, EX-331–EX-332
    as graphic objects, EX-307
    moving, EX-321
    placing on sheets, EX-332
    printing, EX-308
    viewing, EX-307–EX-308
chart area, EX-308, EX-316
chart data, editing, EX-323–EX-327
Chart data range entry box, EX-326
chart elements, EX-308–EX-316
Chart Elements box, EX-315
chart layout, changing, EX-310
chart objects, EX-319–EX-320
chart sheets, creating and editing, EX-318–EX-319
Chart Styles gallery, EX-311
Chart tab, EX-18
chart title, EX-309, EX-311–EX-312
Chart Title button, EX-321
Chart Tools, EX-307
    Design tab, EX-318, EX-320
    Format tab, EX-307, EX-315, EX-320
    Layout tab, EX-315
chart types, EX-317
Choose a SmartArt Graphic dialog box, EX-388
Clear All button, EX-127, EX-128
Clear button in the Editing group, EX-22, EX-247, EX-268
clicking the mouse, EX-8
clip art, inserting, EX-383–EX-384
Clipboard task pane, EX-128
Close button, EX-29
Close Window button, EX-16
closing workbooks, EX-16
Clustered Column 2-D chart, EX-332
Collapse Formula Bar button, EX-180
Color box for a border line, EX-141, EX-142
color palette, EX-143
color scales, EX-146, EX-179–EX-180
colors, changing, EX-280–EX-281
column(s)
    AutoFitting a range of, EX-196
    freezing, EX-133
    hiding and unhiding, EX-131–EX-132
    inserting and deleting, EX-131
    resizing, EX-52
    selecting multiple with the mouse, EX-48
    working with, EX-128–EX-134
    in a worksheet, EX-11
column charts, EX-317
column headings, EX-7, EX-101–EX-102
column width, EX-51–EX-52
Column Width dialog box, EX-52
combination chart, EX-331–EX-334, EX-341
Comma Style button, EX-144, EX-145, EX-242
comma style with no decimal places, EX-247
command tabs, EX-7
    in the Ribbon, EX-6, EX-7, EX-8

comments, EX-88, EX-363
    closing and hiding, EX-365
    editing, EX-364
    inserting, EX-365, EX-375
    printing, EX-365
    using, EX-363–EX-367
Comments arrow, EX-365
comparison operators. See relational operators
Compatibility Checker dialog box, EX-290
conditional format, blank cells as, EX-112
conditional formatting, EX-146–EX-147, EX-179–EX-180, EX-214–EX-215
    based on common numerical rankings, EX-287
Conditional Formatting button, EX-287
    Icon Sets option, EX-230
    Manage Rules option, EX-148
Conditional Formatting Rules Manager dialog box, EX-147–EX-148, EX-180, EX-215
Conditional Formatting tasks, EX-146
constants, EX-203
Contextual Picture Tools, EX-381
Copy button, EX-171, EX-357
    in the Clipboard group, EX-123
    copying formulas, EX-62
Cost argument in a depreciation function, EX-260
COUNT function, EX-212–EX-213
Count option in AutoCalculate, EX-214
COUNTA function, EX-213–EX-214
COUNTBLANK function, EX-212
COUNTIF function, EX-229, EX-234
cropping images, EX-384–EX-385
CSV (comma-separated values) format, EX-290
CSV files, EX-290
Ctrl key, copying an object, EX-374
Ctrl + A, EX-49, EX-50
Ctrl + C, EX-123
Ctrl + End, EX-10, EX-34
Ctrl + Enter, EX-41, EX-170
Ctrl + G, EX-10, EX-12, EX-13
Ctrl + Home, EX-10, EX-12, EX-13
Ctrl + P, EX-25, EX-99, EX-308
Ctrl + PageDown, EX-10, EX-11
Ctrl + PageUP, EX-10, EX-11
Ctrl + V, EX-123, EX-125
Ctrl + X, EX-123
Currency format, EX-73
Current Date button, EX-101, EX-110
custom date formats, EX-221–EX-222
custom time format, EX-223–EX-224
Cut and Paste commands, EX-123
Cut button, EX-123
cycle diagrams, EX-391–EX-392

D
data
    copying with the Fill handle, EX-95
    replacing, EX-89–EX-90
data bars, EX-146–EX-148
data entry. See keying
data labels, EX-315, EX-316
data marker, EX-309
data point, EX-309
    adding to a data series, EX-323–EX-325
    deleting, EX-327

data series, EX-309
    adding and renaming, EX-325–EX-326
    changing the chart type for, EX-332
    deleting, EX-327
    using images, gradients, and textures for, EX-327–EX-331
data table(s), adding to charts, EX-322
data visualization, EX-146
date(s)
    determining, EX-281–EX-282
    displaying current, EX-101
    entering, EX-53–EX-58
    formats of, EX-53–EX-54
    keying, EX-219–EX-220
date and time arithmetic, EX-281–EX-284
date and time functions, EX-218–EX-225
date formats
    applying from the dialog box, EX-55–EX-56
    built-in, EX-219
    creating custom, EX-221–EX-222
DB (Declining Balance) function, EX-260–EX-262
DDB (double-declining balance) function, EX-271
decimal positions, increasing, EX-173
decimals, EX-276
Decrease Decimal button, EX-144, EX-242
Decrease Font Size button, EX-136, EX-253
Delete Cells button, EX-117, EX-118, EX-131
Delete dialog box, EX-120, EX-131
Delete Sheet option, EX-118
deleting
    cells, EX-120
    columns, EX-131
    rows, EX-131
depreciation, EX-259–EX-260
depreciation functions, EX-259–EX-263
Design tab for charts, EX-307
Details pane, EX-16, EX-17
diagrams, EX-391
Dialog Box Launcher
    in the Clipboard group, EX-127
    for the Font group, EX-8, EX-9
    in the Page Setup group, EX-100
dialog box, moving, EX-86
Direction choices for gradients, EX-330
Distributed cell alignment option, EX-134
division formulas, EX-171, EX-173, EX-193–EX-194
Document Information Panel, EX-366, EX-398–EX-399
Document Inspector, EX-365–EX-367
document properties, EX-398–EX-399
Document Theme gallery, EX-44
document themes
    changing, EX-42–EX-47
    defined, EX-42
dollar signs ($)
    in an absolute reference, EX-177
    adding to cell references, EX-179
    in a mixed reference, EX-177
doughnut charts, EX-317
drag-and-drop method, EX-126–EX-127, EX-171
draw layer, EX-346
Drawing Tools Format tab, EX-356, EX-357–EX-363, EX-374

E

Edit Comment button, EX-375
Edit Data Source dialog box, EX-325
Edit Formatting Rule dialog box,
    EX-148, EX-180,
    EX-215–EX-216, EX-288
Edit mode
    keyboard shortcuts in, EX-20
    selecting words, EX-21
    starting, EX-20, EX-22, EX-86,
        EX-179
Edit Shape button, EX-360
editing
    cell styles, EX-248
    worksheets, EX-17–EX-24
edits, undoing multiple, EX-23
electronic spreadsheet software, EX-6
elements. *See* chart elements
embedded charts. *See* chart objects
empty cells, EX-211, EX-212
Enable background error checking,
    EX-83
Enter button in the formula bar,
    EX-20, EX-41, EX-169
Enter key
    completing a Copy or Paste
        command, EX-63
    completing an entry, EX-41
Enter mode, EX-19, EX-41
entries. *See* cell entries
equal to (=) operator, EX-239
error(s)
    correcting spelling, EX-80–EX-81
    correcting with replace,
        EX-90–EX-91
Error Checking dialog box, EX-84
Error Checking Options button,
    EX-83, EX-90, EX-91, EX-129,
    EX-170
Error checking rules, EX-168
error indicator, EX-83
Error message box, EX-169–EX-170
error triangles, EX-170, EX-171. *See
    also* green triangles
Esc key, EX-9
Excel
    exiting, EX-29
    interface of, EX-8–EX-10
    screen, parts of, EX-7
    starting, EX-6, EX-8
Excel icon on the desktop, EX-8
Excel Options dialog box, AutoCorrect
    tab, EX-82
exclamation point within a diamond,
    EX-83
exiting Excel, EX-29
Expand Formula Bar button, EX-244
exploded pie chart, EX-342–EX-343
exponentiation operator (^), EX-60
Extend Selection mode, EX-50, EX-99,
    EX-137, EX-247
extensions, EX-59
Eye button, EX-307–EX-308, EX-357

F

F2, EX-86, EX-179
F5, EX-10, EX-18
File menu. *See* Microsoft Office
    Button
File Name button, EX-110
filenames, EX-35, EX-58–EX-59
files
    managing, EX-24–EX-25
    names, EX-58–EX-59
    printing, EX-25–EX-29

fill, EX-139
    adding for printing, EX-182
    methods for applying, EX-143
Fill Across Worksheets command,
    EX-220–EX-221
Fill button, EX-220
Fill cell alignment option, EX-134
Fill Color button, EX-143
Fill handle
    copying a formula with,
        EX-95–EX-96
    copying data with, EX-95
    defined, EX-93
Fill tab, EX-143, EX-144
Financial button, EX-255
financial functions, EX-238, EX-255
Find & Select button, EX-12, EX-87
Find and Replace dialog box,
    EX-87–EX-88, EX-89, EX-90,
    EX-92
Find command, EX-86–EX-87
floating currency symbol, EX-73,
    EX-195
folded corner shape, EX-360–EX-361
folders
    creating new, EX-24
    defined, EX-24
Font Color button, EX-56, EX-99,
    EX-353
font color, changing, EX-56–EX-57
Font group, EX-8, EX-9
font size, EX-45
font style, changing, EX-45
Font tab in the Format Cells dialog
    box, EX-9, EX-56, EX-57,
    EX-247
footer font, EX-253–EX-254
footers, EX-99
    adding to all sheets in a group,
        EX-224–EX-225
    changing margins, EX-200
    creating, EX-100
    inserting images in,
        EX-385–EX-386
    preparing, EX-99–EX-103
    sizing images in, EX-386
Format as Table button, EX-96,
    EX-109
Format As Table dialog box, EX-97
Format button, EX-51, EX-284
Format Cells dialog box
    Alignment tab, EX-136, EX-139
    applying borders, EX-141–EX-142
    applying date formats,
        EX-55–EX-56
    Border tab, EX-182,
        EX-280–EX-281
    building number formats, EX-144
    date formatting codes and samples
        in, EX-221
    Fill tab, EX-143, EX-144
    Font tab, EX-9, EX-56, EX-57,
        EX-247
    Number tab, EX-145,
        EX-221–EX-222,
        EX-223–EX-224, EX-248
    opening, EX-137
format codes, EX-225
Format Data Series dialog box, EX-328
Format Painter, EX-46–EX-47, EX-143
Format Picture button, EX-386,
    EX-387, EX-403
Format Picture dialog box, EX-386
Format Selection button, on the Chart
    Tools Format tab, EX-316,
    EX-327, EX-328, EX-331

Format Shape dialog box,
    EX-350–EX-351, EX-407
Format tab for charts, EX-307
Format Text button, EX-283
formats. *See also* number formats
    for dates, EX-219
    finding and replacing, EX-91–EX-92
    locating, EX-86
    resetting Find and Replace, EX-93
Formatting Only option, EX-125
formula(s), EX-17, EX-59
    building absolute references,
        EX-194–EX-195
    changing, EX-19
    copying, EX-62–EX-63,
        EX-95–EX-96, EX-178
    copying with the Fill handle,
        EX-95–EX-96
    creating with absolute references,
        EX-179
    displaying, EX-185–EX-186
    editing, EX-172
    entering basic, EX-59–EX-67
    listing built-in, EX-60–EX-61
    multiplication and addition in,
        EX-175–EX-176
    order of precedence,
        EX-174–EX-177
    replacing functions in, EX-90
    viewing, EX-19
Formula Auditing group, EX-84
Formula AutoComplete, EX-60–EX-61,
    EX-203–EX-204, EX-211,
    EX-241. *See also* AutoComplete
    displaying, EX-256
    highlighting a function name in,
        EX-204
formula bar, EX-7
    cell contents and, EX-17
    editing a formula in, EX-172
    sizing, EX-178
formula view, EX-232
Formulas command tab, EX-84
Formulas tab, EX-64
forward slash (/) in division
    formulas, EX-171
Freeze Panes button, EX-132, EX-133
Freeze Top Row option, EX-132
Full Screen view, EX-9
function(s)
    creating nested, EX-284–EX-288
    defined, EX-63, EX-65, EX-202
    replacing in a formula, EX-90
Function Arguments dialog box,
    EX-205–EX-206
    moving, EX-239
    opening, EX-210
    showing syntax, EX-258
Function Library group, EX-64,
    EX-207
funnel graphic, EX-396
future value, EX-256
FV (future value) argument,
    EX-255, EX-270
FV (future value) function,
    EX-258–EX-259

G

General style, EX-54–EX-55
GIF (Graphics Interchange Format)
    file, EX-381
Go To dialog box, EX-10, EX-12,
    EX-18
Go to Footer button, EX-101, EX-110,
    EX-253, EX-385

gradients, EX-329
    inserting in charts, EX-327
    using for a data series,
        EX-329–EX-330
grave accent, EX-397–EX-398
greater than (>) operator, EX-239
greater than or equal to (>=)
    operator, EX-239
green triangles, indicating errors,
        EX-22, EX-83, EX-170, EX-171
gridlines, EX-309
    on a chart, EX-322
    printing, EX-101–EX-102
grouping worksheets, EX-216–EX-218,
        EX-283–EX-284

H

header(s), EX-99
    adding to all sheets in a group,
        EX-224–EX-225
    preparing, EX-99–EX-103
Header & Footer button, on the Insert
        tab, EX-100, EX-110, EX-253,
        EX-385, EX-403
Header & Footer Tools Design tab,
        EX-253
Header and Footer Elements group,
        EX-101
Header button, EX-100, EX-308
Header dialog box, EX-224, EX-225
header row for table columns, EX-96
header/footer, adding a picture to,
        EX-403–EX-404
Hide & Unhide option, EX-284
hiding
    columns, EX-131–EX-132
    rows, EX-131–EX-132
hierarchy shape, EX-404
Hierarchy SmartArt pane, EX-408
high-low-close charts. *See* stock charts
Home, EX-10, EX-11
Home tab, EX-8, EX-9, EX-10, EX-116
horizontal alignment
    changing, EX-135
    options for cells, EX-134
horizontal (category) axis, EX-309,
        EX-315
horizontal scroll box, EX-14
hours, converting time to, EX-283
hovering, EX-11
.htm extension, EX-187
HTML file, EX-187
hyperlinks, EX-288
    creating, EX-288–EX-289
    editing or deleting, EX-289
    inserting, EX-297
    theme colors, EX-56
Hypertext Markup Language, EX-187

I

icon sets
    defined, EX-146
    using, EX-214–EX-216
IF function
    calculating a value,
        EX-241–EX-242
    creating a nested, EX-286–EX-287
    displaying text, EX-239–EX-240
    using, EX-238–EX-242
Ignore All spelling option, EX-85,
        EX-86
Ignore Once spelling option, EX-85,
        EX-86

images. *See also* pictures
    cropping, sizing, and styling,
        EX-384–EX-385
    for data series, EX-327–EX-328
    formatting and copying, EX-383
    inserting, EX-327, EX-380–EX-385,
        EX-385–EX-386
    scaling, EX-382
    sizing in footers, EX-386
Increase Decimal button, EX-173,
        EX-210
Increase Font Size button, EX-135,
        EX-136
indents, EX-137
Insert Cells button, EX-117
Insert Comment option, EX-365
Insert Copied Cells option, EX-125
Insert Cut Cells option, EX-124
Insert Date button, EX-224, EX-225
Insert dialog box
    General tab, EX-117–EX-118
    opening, EX-119, EX-129
Insert Function button, EX-205,
        EX-210
    in the formula bar, EX-212, EX-285
Insert Function dialog box, EX-64,
        EX-205, EX-211
Insert Hyperlink dialog box,
        EX-288–EX-289
Insert Page Break option, EX-251
Insert Picture dialog box, EX-381,
        EX-385
Insert Picture from File button,
        EX-381
Insert Sheet Name button, EX-224,
        EX-225, EX-283
Insert Worksheet tab, EX-116
inserting
    columns, EX-131
    rows, EX-129–EX-130
Inspect Document option, EX-366,
        EX-375
INT function, EX-276–EX-278
integer, EX-276
interval, setting, EX-93
Invalid Name Error, EX-90, EX-91
italic, applying, EX-48
Italic button, EX-45, EX-353

J

Justify cell alignment option, EX-134

K

keyboard shortcuts
    in Edit mode, EX-20
    selecting ranges with,
        EX-49–EX-50
keying
    dates, EX-219–EX-220
    times, EX-222–EX-223
KeyTips, EX-9

L

labels
    aligning, EX-40
    autofitting columns to, EX-52
    centering multiple rows of,
        EX-135–EX-136
    entering in a column, EX-120
    entering in worksheets,
        EX-40–EX-42
    formatting numbers as, EX-53
    repeating column A on each page,
        EX-252

landscape orientation, EX-183
Layout tab for charts, EX-307
layouts
    changing for charts, EX-320
    for SmartArt graphics, EX-393
leading zero, EX-144
Left (Indent) cell alignment option,
        EX-134
left mouse button, EX-8
left scroll arrow, EX-14
legend, EX-309, EX-310
less than (<) operator, EX-239
less than or equal to (<=) operator,
        EX-239
Life argument in a depreciation
        function, EX-260
line break, EX-177–EX-178
Line button, EX-339
line charts, EX-317, EX-331
Line Style pane, EX-377
Lines group in the Shapes gallery,
        EX-354
linked cell picture, EX-409
list diagram, EX-407
Live Preview, EX-43, EX-45
Logical button, EX-239, EX-268
logical functions, EX-238
logical tests, EX-241, EX-242

M

magnifying glass icon, EX-27
mail-enabled program, EX-291
Manage Rules option, EX-148
manual page breaks, EX-254
margin markers, dragging, EX-102,
        EX-184
Margins button, EX-185, EX-196
Margins tab, EX-184
markers for all margins, EX-251
marquee, moving, EX-46, EX-62
Math & Trig button, EX-208, EX-228
Math and Trig functions,
        EX-202–EX-209
math hierarchy, EX-174
MAX function, EX-65,
        EX-210–EX-211
Merge and Center button, EX-287
Merge and Center command, EX-138
metadata, EX-365
Microsoft Excel. *See* Excel
Microsoft Office Button, EX-6, EX-7,
        EX-8
    Close, EX-16
    Excel Options, EX-82
    Exit Excel, EX-29
    Open, EX-16
    Print, QuickPrint, EX-25, EX-26
    Save As, EX-24, EX-28
Microsoft Office Excel Help button,
        EX-30
Middle Align button, EX-137, EX-287,
        EX-374
MIN function, EX-210–EX-211
Mini toolbar
    for font editing, EX-21
    Increase Font Size button, EX-135,
        EX-136
    ScreenTips and, EX-135
    for text editing, EX-35
minus sign (−), EX-168
mixed references, EX-177, EX-181
month series, EX-93–EX-94
monthly payments for a loan,
        EX-255–EX-258
More button in the Table Styles group,
        EX-97

Most Recently Used list for functions, EX-229
mouse
　pointing to cells, EX-62
　selecting ranges, EX-47–EX-49
Move Chart button, EX-332
Move Chart dialog box, EX-321
moving marquee, EX-46, EX-62
multiplication formulas, EX-171, EX-193–EX-194

N

Name Box, EX-7, EX-11–EX-12
　clicking in, EX-13
　resizing, EX-355
#NAME? error, EX-90
named ranges. *See* range names
navigating in workbooks, EX-10–EX-16
navigation commands, EX-10
Navigation Pane, EX-16, EX-17
negative formula results, EX-256
negative numbers, EX-198, EX-259
nested functions, EX-203, EX-284–EX-288
New Folder button, EX-24, EX-59
New Workbook dialog box, EX-167–EX-168
noncontiguous ranges on a chart, EX-332
None button for borders, EX-280
Normal button, EX-9, EX-26, EX-110, EX-186
Normal cell style, EX-246
not equal to (<>) operator, EX-239
NOT function, EX-245
NOW() function, EX-223
Nper argument in financial functions, EX-255
nudging shapes, EX-360
Number format, EX-248
number formats, applying, EX-54–EX-55
Number group, EX-55, EX-173
Number of Pages button, EX-101, EX-253
number series, EX-94
Number tab in the Format Cells dialog box, EX-55, EX-56, EX-145, EX-221–EX-222, EX-223–EX-224, EX-248
numbers
　aligning in a cell, EX-36
　formatting, EX-53, EX-144–EX-145
　removing the decimal part of, EX-207
　storing the nondecimal part of, EX-276
numeric keypad, EX-119
Numerical Count option in AutoCalculate, EX-214

O

objects
　aligning, EX-360
　copying and moving, EX-357–EX-358
　defined, EX-87, EX-307, EX-346
Office Clipboard, EX-127
Office document theme, EX-51, EX-113
online help, EX-29–EX-30, EX-66–EX-67
Open dialog box, EX-17

OR function, EX-244–EX-245
order of calculation of arithmetic operations, EX-60
order of operation. *See* order of precedence
order of precedence, EX-174–EX-177, EX-194
organization chart, EX-387
　adding a shape to, EX-389
　adding text to, EX-390–EX-391, EX-404–EX-405
　creating and styling, EX-387–EX-388
Organize button, EX-16, EX-17
Orientation box, EX-138, EX-139
Outline button for borders, EX-280
Outline option on the Borders tab, EX-141, EX-142

P

page(s), centering for printing, EX-253
Page Break Preview button, EX-249, EX-250, EX-254, EX-269
page breaks, EX-248
　previewing and changing, EX-249–EX-250
　removing, EX-254
　removing and inserting, EX-250–EX-251
Page Layout tab, EX-183–EX-189
page layout view, EX-102–EX-103
Page Layout View button, EX-9
　in the status bar, EX-26, EX-100, EX-142, EX-183
　in the Workbook View group, EX-100
page margins, changing, EX-102, EX-183–EX-184
Page Number button, EX-101, EX-253
page orientation, EX-183
Page Orientation button, EX-196
Page Setup button, EX-100
Page Setup dialog box
　adding headers or footers, EX-224–EX-225
　applying settings to grouped sheets, EX-234
　Header/Footer tab, EX-224
　Margins tab, EX-184, EX-225
　Print Preview in, EX-225
　Sheet tab, EX-252
Page Setup group, EX-183, EX-184
parentheses
　changing the order of operations, EX-174
　showing negative numbers, EX-198
Paste button, EX-62, EX-123, EX-171, EX-357
Paste Options button, EX-62, EX-63, EX-124
Paste Special commands, EX-47
patterns, using as fill, EX-143–EX-144
PDF file, EX-28
percent sign (%) in a formula, EX-171
percent style, EX-173
Period argument in a depreciation function, EX-260
Pick From Drop-Down List, EX-120, EX-122
Picture button, EX-385, EX-387, EX-403
Picture Effects button, EX-383
Picture Tools Format tab, EX-382
pictures. *See also* images
　adding to a header/footer, EX-385–EX-387

　checking properties and scales, EX-382
　cropping, sizing, and styling, EX-384–EX-385
　flipping and aligning, EX-403
　formatting and copying, EX-383
　inserting, EX-327–EX-328, EX-380–EX-385
Pie button, EX-319
pie charts, EX-317, EX-319, EX-325
pixels, EX-51
"Please excuse my dear Aunt Sally", EX-175
plot area, EX-309, EX-316
plus sign (+), EX-168
PMT function, EX-255–EX-258
pointing, entering formulas by, EX-62
points, EX-51
Popular pane, EX-117
portrait orientation, EX-183
present value, EX-256
preset color blends, EX-329
preset color variations, EX-385
preset gradients, EX-341
preset styles, EX-385
Preview button, EX-28
Print button, EX-25, EX-99, EX-365
Print dialog box, EX-26, EX-27–EX-28, EX-99
print page numbers, EX-253–EX-254
Print Preview, EX-26, EX-99
Print Titles button, EX-252, EX-269
Print what group, EX-308
printer icon on the taskbar, EX-27
printing
　centering pages for, EX-253
　Excel files, EX-25–EX-29
properties, EX-398
PV (present value) argument, EX-255, EX-270

Q

Quick Access toolbar, EX-6, EX-7, EX-8
　Quick Print button, EX-25, EX-26
　Redo button, EX-23, EX-24
　Save button, EX-59
　Undo button, EX-22
Quick Print button, EX-25, EX-26
quotation marks in functions, EX-239, EX-268

R

radar charts, EX-317
radials, EX-391
range addresses, EX-47
range names, as arguments, EX-203
range of cells, spell-checking, EX-85
ranges
　defined, EX-47
　noncontiguous on a chart, EX-332
　selecting, EX-47–EX-50
Rate argument in financial functions, EX-255
read-only file, EX-25
Ready mode, EX-19, EX-20
Recolor button, EX-385, EX-403
red, negative numbers in, EX-259
Redo button, EX-23, EX-24
Redo command, EX-22, EX-23–EX-24
references, EX-177
relational operators, EX-239
relative references, EX-177, EX-178
Remove Page Break option, EX-254
renaming worksheets, EX-57–EX-58

Repeat command, EX-273
Repeated Word error, EX-86
Replace command, EX-87
Replace Format dialog box, EX-92
replacement string, EX-87
replacing
    data, EX-89–EX-90
    functions in formulas, EX-90
Research button, EX-394
Research Library, EX-393
Research task pane, EX-393–EX-397
Research tool, EX-407–EX-408
resizing
    columns, EX-52
    the Name Box, EX-355
    rows, EX-53
Review command tab, EX-364
Ribbon, EX-6, EX-7, EX-8
    applying number formats from,
        EX-54–EX-55
    collapsing/expanding, EX-10
Right (Indent) cell alignment option,
    EX-134
right mouse button, EX-8
right scroll arrow, EX-14
Rotate button, EX-363, EX-403
rotation, EX-362
rotation handle, EX-347, EX-362
ROUND function
    in nested functions, EX-284
    nesting SUM in, EX-285–EX-286
    using, EX-278–EX-281
rounded values, comparing,
    EX-279–EX-280
rounding a number, EX-278
row(s)
    deleting, EX-131
    hiding and unhiding,
        EX-131–EX-132
    inserting, EX-129–EX-130
    resizing, EX-53
    selecting multiple with the mouse,
        EX-48
    working with, EX-128–EX-134
row and column headings,
    EX-101–EX-102
row headings, EX-7
    row height, modifying,
        EX-51–EX-53, EX-109
Row Height dialog box, EX-53

S

Salvage argument in a depreciation
    function, EX-260
sans serif font, EX-43
Save As command, EX-59
Save As dialog box, EX-24, EX-25
    opening, EX-28, EX-29
    Web Page saving, EX-188
Save button on the Quick Access
    toolbar, EX-59
Save command, EX-59
saving workbooks, EX-58–EX-59
Scale to Fit group, EX-184, EX-185
scaling
    changing, EX-183–EX-184
    images, EX-382
scatter charts, EX-317, EX-342
screen resolution, EX-63
ScreenTip
    for chart elements, EX-311
    for a function, EX-211
    for a hyperlink, EX-289
scroll bars, EX-7, EX-14

scrolling through worksheets,
    EX-13–EX-14
secondary axis, EX-331,
    EX-333–EX-334
Select All button, EX-48, EX-228
Select Data button, EX-331
Select Data Source dialog box,
    EX-323, EX-324
Selection and Visibility pane,
    EX-337–EX-338
    using, EX-356–EX-357
selection handles, EX-347
    for chart elements, EX-311
    for a chart object, EX-319–EX-320
    for a graphic frame, EX-391
    for shapes, EX-358
Selection Pane button, EX-307,
    EX-337, EX-356
selection pointer, EX-47
selections, printing, EX-99
separators between empty rows and
    columns, EX-144
serial number system for dates,
    EX-218–EX-219
series. *See also* data series
    creating a number, EX-94–EX-95
    creating month and week,
        EX-93–EX-94
    defined, EX-93
serif font, EX-43
shading, EX-143. *See also* fill
Shadow gallery, EX-374
shape(s), EX-346
    adding, EX-354–EX-355
    adding and formatting, EX-377
    adding to organization charts,
        EX-389
    aligning and nudging, EX-360
    changing, EX-360–EX-361
    effects, EX-314
    features of, EX-347
    formatting multiple, EX-357
    inserting, EX-346–EX-369
    nudging selected, EX-353
    rotating, EX-362–EX-363
    sizing, EX-358–EX-359
    styles, EX-313–EX-314
Shape Effects button, EX-314,
    EX-373, EX-374
Shape Fill button, EX-314, EX-318,
    EX-327, EX-374
Shape Height box, EX-359
Shape Outline button, EX-357,
    EX-374
Shape Styles group, EX-318,
    EX-353–EX-354
Shape Width box, EX-359
Shapes button, EX-348, EX-354,
    EX-355
Shapes gallery, EX-354
Shapes Styles group, EX-313
Sheet Background dialog box,
    EX-186–EX-187
Sheet Options group, EX-185
sheet protection, removing, EX-348
sheets. *See* worksheets
Shift + F11, EX-116, EX-117
Shift + Tab, EX-10, EX-41
Shift key
    drawing an elliptical object,
        EX-374
    sizing a shape, EX-358
Show All Comments button, EX-364,
    EX-375
Show Margins in Print Preview,
    EX-251

Show/Hide Comment button, EX-365
Size and Properties dialog box,
    EX-359, EX-382
Size button, EX-388
Size group, EX-358, EX-359
sizing button, EX-355
sizing handle for a table, EX-99
sizing shapes, EX-358–EX-359
Smart Art button, EX-404
SmartArt, EX-387–
SmartArt button, EX-
SmartArt button, EX-388
SmartArt diagram, EX-405–EX-406
SmartArt graphics
    changing layouts for, EX-393
    reviewing topics about using,
        EX-334
SmartArt Tools, EX-388
solid fill, EX-143
special symbols, EX-397–EX-398
spelling
    checking, EX-84–EX-86
    correcting errors, EX-80–EX-81
Spelling button, EX-85, EX-107
Spelling dialog box, EX-84, EX-85
Split button, EX-133, EX-134
spreadsheet software, EX-6
stacking order for shapes, EX-356
Start button on the Windows
    taskbar, EX-8
starting Excel, EX-6, EX-8
statistical functions, EX-209–EX-214
status bar, EX-7
stock charts, EX-317, EX-344
Style box for a border line, EX-141,
    EX-142
styles. *See also* cell styles
    changing for charts,
        EX-320–EX-321
    predefined for charts, EX-311
Styles group, EX-96, EX-146
subordinate shape in an organization
    chart, EX-389
subtraction formulas, EX-168
    building, EX-193
    creating and copying,
        EX-170–EX-171
Sum button, EX-65
SUM function
    nesting, EX-285
    using, EX-203–EX-204
SUMIF function, EX-208–EX-209,
    EX-229
Super ScreenTips, EX-8
surface charts, EX-317
Symbol dialog box, EX-397–EX-398
synonyms, EX-394–EX-396
syntax of functions,
    EX-202, EX-203

T

Tab key, EX-10, EX-41
tab scrolling buttons, EX-7
table(s), EX-96
    changing the style of,
        EX-97–EX-98
    creating, EX-96–EX-97
    printing, EX-99
table styles, EX-97–EX-98
Table Styles gallery, EX-96–EX-98
Table Tools Design command tab,
    EX-97
templates, EX-166
    creating workbooks,
        EX-166–EX-168

text
  adding to shapes in an
    organization chart,
    EX-390–EX-391
  aligning in a cell, EX-36
  displaying with IF,
    EX-239–EX-240
  keying into a callout,
    EX-348–EX-349
  moving in the Text pane,
    EX-392–EX-393
  rotating in cells, EX-138–EX-139
Text Box button, EX-352,
    EX-353, EX-373
text boxes, EX-352–EX-354, EX-373
text display, spilling into adjacent
    cells, EX-42
Text Fill button, EX-376
Text Outline button, EX-376
Text pane
  moving text in, EX-392–EX-393
  toggling on/off, EX-388
  working in, EX-390
Text preview area, EX-141, EX-142
textures, EX-327, EX-330–EX-331
Theme Colors dialog box, EX-58
theme fonts, EX-43
themes. *See* document themes
Themes button, in the Page Layout
    Tab, EX-108
Themes group, EX-44
thesaurus, EX-393, EX-394–EX-396
tick mark, EX-309
tilde (~), EX-87, EX-185
time(s)
  converting to hours, EX-283
  keying and formatting,
    EX-222–EX-223
time functions, EX-218–EX-225
time passed, calculating, EX-282–EX-283
title bar, EX-7
TODAY() function, EX-218–EX-219,
    EX-223
Top 10 Items dialog box, EX-287
Top Align button, EX-137
Top cell alignment option, EX-134
top shape in an organization chart,
    EX-389
Top/Bottom Rules command,
    EX-287
translation, EX-396–EX-397
TRUNC function, EX-207
TRUNC Function Arguments dialog
    box, EX-207–EX-208
Type argument in financial functions,
    EX-255

U

Undo button
  clicking, EX-23, EX-178, EX-240
  on the Quick Access toolbar,
    EX-22, EX-120

Undo command, EX-22
Unfreeze Panes option, EX-133
Ungroup Sheets option, EX-284
ungrouping worksheets, EX-217
Unhide dialog box, EX-284
Unhide Rows option, EX-132
unhiding
  columns, EX-132
  rows, EX-132
unmerging cells, EX-138
Unprotect Sheet button, EX-348,
    EX-372
user templates. *See* templates

V

value(s)
  defined, EX-53
  entering, EX-53–EX-58
value (vertical) axis. *See* vertical axis
value series, EX-94
Venn diagram, EX-405–EX-406
vertical (value) axis, EX-309,
    EX-313
vertical alignment options for cells,
    EX-134, EX-137
vertical scroll box, EX-14
View switcher, EX-7
View tab, EX-9, EX-15
Views button, EX-16, EX-17
visualizations, EX-146
volatile function, EX-218

W

watermarks, EX-387
Web pages, saving workbooks as,
    EX-187–EX-189
week series, EX-94
white arrow pointer, EX-11
white cross pointer, EX-46
whole number, EX-171
wildcards, EX-87, EX-89
windows, freezing and splitting,
    EX-132–EX-134
Windows Clipboard, EX-123, EX-127
WordArt button, EX-376
WordArt Gallery, EX-367
WordArt images, EX-367–EX-369,
    EX-376
WordArt styles, EX-368
words, translating, EX-396–EX-397
workbook(s), EX-10
  closing, EX-16
  creating, EX-40–EX-67
  navigating, EX-10–EX-16
  navigation commands in, EX-10
  opening, EX-16–EX-17
  printing, EX-27–EX-28
  saving, EX-58–EX-59,
    EX-187–EX-189

starting new, EX-33
  using templates to create,
    EX-166–EX-168
Workbook Views group, EX-9
worksheet tabs, EX-7, EX-118,
    EX-218
worksheets, EX-10
  adding callouts to,
    EX-347–EX-349
  adding hyperlinks to, EX-288
  changing the default number of,
    EX-117
  copying, EX-185–EX-186,
    EX-217
  copying data from one to another,
    EX-220
  deleting, EX-117
  editing, EX-17–EX-24
  entering labels in, EX-41–EX-42
  grouping, EX-216–EX-218,
    EX-230–EX-231,
    EX-283–EX-284
  hiding and unhiding, EX-284
  inserting, EX-116–EX-117
  managing, EX-217–EX-218
  moving, EX-217–EX-218
  moving and deleting, EX-118
  moving between, EX-11
  previewing and printing,
    EX-26–EX-27
  printing portions of, EX-99
  renaming, EX-57–EX-58
  scaling the printing of,
    EX-183–EX-184
  scrolling through, EX-13–EX-14
  selecting all cells in, EX-48
  spell-checking, EX-84–EX-86
  viewing, EX-18–EX-19
Wrap Text setting, EX-137

X

x-axis, EX-313, EX-315
XLS format, EX-290
.xlsx extension, EX-25, EX-59
.xltx extension, EX-167
XPS (XML Paper Specification) file,
    EX-28–EX-29

Y

y-axis, EX-313

Z

Zoom button, EX-15
Zoom controls, EX-7
Zoom dialog box, EX-15
Zoom In button, EX-15, EX-44,
    EX-132
Zoom Out button, EX-15,
    EX-26

PowerPoint Index

A

Adjustment handles
    connector lines, PP-121
    shapes, PP-125–PP-126
Albums. *See* Photo Albums
Alignment. *See also* Tab settings
    paragraphs, PP-50
    text in tables, PP-181
Animation. *See* Movies
Arrowheads, on connector lines,
    PP-121–PP-122
Assistant shapes, PP-263, PP-264
Audio. *See* Music; Sound effects
AutoCorrect
    capitalization, PP-268
    options, PP-268
    spelling errors, PP-40
Axes. *See* Chart axes

B

Basic Process diagrams, PP-253
Bevel effect
    pictures, PP-141
    tables, PP-184
Bitmap pictures, PP-127. *See also* Clip
    art; Pictures
Black and White
    pictures, PP-136
    printing, PP-22
Body text, PP-15
Bold text, PP-43–PP-44
Borders. *See also* Lines
    erasing, PP-175
    picture, PP-140
    styles, PP-174
    table, PP-172–PP-174, PP-175
Boxes. *See* Shapes; Text boxes
Brightness, of pictures,
    PP-138–PP-139, PP-147
Bring to front command, PP-132
Bulleted lists
    converting to diagrams,
        PP-251–PP-252
    distance between bullets and text,
        PP-58–PP-60
    indents, PP-58–PP-60
    levels, PP-53
    promoting and demoting items,
        PP-53
Bullets
    colors, PP-54–PP-55
    pictures, PP-56–PP-57
    removing, PP-53
    shapes, PP-54, PP-55
    use of, PP-15
    working with, PP-52
Bullets and Numbering dialog box,
    PP-54–PP-55, PP-57
Bullets and Numbering gallery, PP-54

C

Capitalization, PP-44–PP-45, PP-268
Case, text, PP-44–PP-45
Cell pointer, PP-210
Cells, table. *See also* Tables
    aligning text, PP-181
    borders, PP-172–PP-174, PP-175
    definition, PP-166

diagonal lines in, PP-178–PP-179
    erasing borders, PP-175
    keying text, PP-167
    margins, PP-181, PP-182
    merging, PP-177–PP-178
    pictures, PP-186–PP-187
    shading, PP-172–PP-173
    splitting, PP-177–PP-178
Cells, worksheet, PP-210
Change Case dialog box, PP-44–PP-45
Chart axes
    formatting, PP-215–PP-216,
        PP-221–PP-222
    Horizontal (Category), PP-213,
        PP-214, PP-215–PP-216
    primary, PP-221–PP-222
    scale, PP-213
    secondary
        adding, PP-219–PP-220
        formatting, PP-221–PP-222
        uses, PP-218
    tick marks, PP-213
    Vertical (Value), PP-213, PP-214,
        PP-215–PP-216
Chart Layouts, PP-216
Chart Styles, applying, PP-214–PP-215
Charts
    adding shapes, PP-226–PP-227
    colors, PP-222, PP-227–PP-228
    creating, PP-208–PP-209, PP-223
    data labels, PP-224
    data sources
        datasheets, PP-209, PP-210
        editing, PP-210–PP-212
        worksheets, PP-208–PP-209
    elements, PP-213–PP-214
    enhancing, PP-226–PP-229
    fonts, PP-215
    formatting, PP-213, PP-215–PP-216
    gridlines, PP-214, PP-217–PP-218
    layouts, PP-216
    legends, PP-214, PP-216–PP-217
    navigating, PP-213–PP-214
    outline styles, PP-227–PP-228
    parts, PP-213–PP-214
    pictures in background,
        PP-228–PP-229
    pie, PP-223–PP-226
    slide layouts, PP-209
    styles, PP-214–PP-215
    switching row and column
        data, PP-212
    types, PP-209, PP-218
        changing, PP-218–PP-219
        combining, PP-220–PP-221
    uses, PP-208
Choose a SmartArt Graphic dialog
    box, PP-248–PP-249
Circles, drawing, PP-122–PP-123
Clip art. *See also* Pictures
    animated. *See* Movies
    copying and pasting, PP-131
    deleting, PP-131
    duplicating, PP-131
    files, PP-127
    finding, PP-127, PP-128–PP-129
    grouping, PP-132–PP-133
    inserting, PP-127, PP-129–PP-130
    moving, PP-123
    positioning, PP-130
    previewing, PP-129–PP-130

rearranging, PP-130–PP-131
    regrouping, PP-132
    resizing, PP-123, PP-130
    rotating, PP-131
    selecting, PP-130–PP-131
    ungrouping, PP-132
Clip Art task pane, PP-128
Clipboard
    automatic display, PP-83
    clearing, PP-82–PP-83
    cutting and pasting, PP-80
    using, PP-80
Clipboard Options button, PP-83
Clipboard task pane, PP-80,
    PP-82–PP-83
Clips. *See* Clip art; Movies; Sound effects
Color schemes. *See* Design themes
Colors. *See also* Grayscale option;
    Theme colors
    of bullets, PP-54–PP-55
    in charts, PP-222, PP-227–PP-228
    in pictures, PP-136
    of shapes in diagrams, PP-267
    of SmartArt graphics,
        PP-259–PP-260, PP-267
    standard, PP-44
    in tables, PP-173, PP-174
    text, PP-44, PP-47
    text boxes, PP-61
    of WordArt, PP-144–PP-145
Column charts, PP-212, PP-213
Columns, in tables
    definition, PP-166
    deleting, PP-177
    inserting, PP-176–PP-177
    widths, PP-179–PP-181
Columns, in worksheets, PP-210
Command buttons, PP-7, PP-10
Connection sites, shapes, PP-121
Connector lines
    adjustment handles, PP-121
    arrowheads, PP-121–PP-122
    curved, PP-121–PP-122
    drawing, PP-121–PP-122
    elbow, PP-121
    straight, PP-121
Constrained shapes
    lines, PP-119–PP-120
    ovals, PP-122–PP-123
    rectangles, PP-122–PP-123
Contiguous slides, selecting, PP-77
Continuous picture lists,
    PP-270–PP-271
Contrast, of pictures, PP-138–PP-139,
    PP-147
Copying. *See also* Duplicating
    clip art, PP-131
    to Clipboard, PP-80
    formatting, PP-82, PP-84
    keyboard shortcut, PP-80
    text, PP-81–PP-82
Coworker shapes, PP-263, PP-264
Creating
    charts, PP-208–PP-209, PP-223
    cycle diagrams, PP-254–PP-255
    folders, PP-18–PP-19
    list diagrams, PP-250–PP-252
    numbered lists, PP-57
    organization charts, PP-261–PP-262
    pie charts, PP-223
    presentations, PP-36–PP-37

process diagrams, PP-252–PP-254
slides, PP-36, PP-38
SmartArt graphics, PP-250–PP-252
tables
    drawing, PP-170–PP-171
    Insert Table button, PP-167
    methods, PP-166–PP-167
    tabbed table, PP-187–PP-190
text boxes, PP-60
theme fonts, PP-94
WordArt, PP-142–PP-143
Cropping handles, PP-135
Cropping pictures, PP-135–PP-136
Cropping tool, PP-135
Crosshair pointer, PP-117
Cutting
    to Clipboard, PP-80
    keyboard shortcut, PP-80
    text, PP-81–PP-82
Cycle diagrams. *See also* SmartArt
    graphics
    creating, PP-254–PP-255
    description, PP-250

D

Data series, switching row and column
    data, PP-212
Dates, in headers and footers,
    PP-89, PP-90
Deleting
    bullets, PP-53
    clip art, PP-131
    columns in tables, PP-177
    rows in tables, PP-177
    shapes, PP-117
    shapes in organization charts, PP-265
    slides, PP-76, PP-79
    tab settings, PP-189
Delivery methods, overhead
    transparencies, PP-22. *See also*
    Slide shows
Design templates. *See* Templates
Design themes. *See also* Theme colors
    applying, PP-91–PP-92
    effects, PP-93–PP-94
    fonts, PP-93, PP-94
    selecting, PP-91–PP-92
    using, PP-91
Destination formatting, PP-81, PP-82
Diagrams. *See* SmartArt graphics
Digital photographs. *See* Pictures
Distributing column width and row
    height, PP-179–PP-181
Documents. *See* Files; Presentations
Draw table pen tool, PP-167
Drawing. *See also* Lines
    circles, PP-122–PP-123
    connector lines, PP-121–PP-122
    Lock Drawing Mode, PP-117, PP-119
    ovals, PP-119
    rectangles, PP-118
    shapes, PP-116, PP-117–PP-119
    squares, PP-122–PP-123
    tables, PP-170–PP-171
    tools, PP-116, PP-117
    vector drawings, PP-127
Duplicating. *See also* Copying
    clip art, PP-131
    SmartArt graphics, PP-257

E

Editing
    chart data sources, PP-210–PP-212
    Photo Albums, PP-146–PP-148
    WordArt text, PP-143

Effects. *See also* Sound effects;
    Transitions
    animation, PP-14–PP-15
    bevel, PP-141, PP-184
    in Design themes, PP-93–PP-94
    galleries, PP-10
    glow, PP-140
    Live Preview, PP-10
    in pictures, PP-140–PP-141
    in pie charts, PP-225
    previewing, PP-10
    reflections
        pictures, PP-140
        in tables, PP-185–PP-186
    shading, PP-186–PP-187
    shadows
        pictures, PP-140
        in tables, PP-184–PP-185
        text, PP-44
    soft edges, PP-140
    tables, PP-183, PP-184–PP-187
    text, PP-41, PP-44
    theme, PP-93–PP-94
    3-D rotation
        diagram shapes, PP-256
        pictures, PP-141
        pie charts, PP-225–PP-226
    transition, PP-14–PP-15,
        PP-95–PP-96
    WordArt, PP-143–PP-144
Eraser tool, PP-175
Excel. *See* Worksheets

F

Files. *See also* Presentations
    locations, PP-10
    names, PP-17, PP-19
    pictures, PP-137–PP-138
    saving, PP-18–PP-19
Fill colors, WordArt, PP-144–PP-145.
    See also Colors
Find dialog box, PP-87–PP-88
Finding
    and replacing, PP-85, PP-88
    text, PP-87–PP-88
First-line indent, PP-58
Fit to window command, PP-13–PP-14
Floating text, PP-60
Folders, creating, PP-18–PP-19
Font dialog box, PP-46–PP-47
Font faces, PP-41, PP-42–PP-43
Font group commands, PP-41–PP-42
Fonts
    changing, PP-41, PP-42–PP-43, PP-47
    colors, PP-44, PP-47
    sizes, PP-41, PP-42–PP-43, PP-47, PP-49
    in text boxes, PP-61
    theme, PP-93, PP-94
    TrueType, PP-42
Footers
    dates in, PP-89, PP-90
    definition, PP-88
    of handouts, PP-89, PP-90–PP-91
    of notes pages, PP-89
    page numbers in, PP-89
    slide, PP-88, PP-89–PP-90
    slide numbers in, PP-89, PP-90
Format Axis dialog box, PP-215
Format Painter, PP-84
Format Photo Album dialog box,
    PP-146–PP-147
Format Picture dialog box, PP-139
Format Shape dialog box
    placeholder size and position, PP-51
    3-D Rotation tab, PP-61

Formatting
    charts, PP-213, PP-215–PP-216
    copying, PP-82, PP-84
    line spacing, PP-45–PP-46
    source and destination, PP-81, PP-82
    tables, PP-169
    text, PP-41
        alignment, PP-50
        bold, PP-43–PP-44
        case, PP-44–PP-45
        colors, PP-44, PP-47
        italic, PP-43–PP-44
        shadow, PP-44
        underlined, PP-43–PP-44, PP-47
    text placeholders, PP-48–PP-49

G

Galleries
    Bullets and Numbering, PP-54
    effects, PP-10
    Recolor, PP-136
    Shapes, PP-117, PP-125
    WordArt Styles, PP-142, PP-143
Gear diagrams, PP-269–PP-270
Glow effect, PP-140
Graphics. *See* Clip art; Pictures;
    Shapes; SmartArt graphics;
    WordArt
Graphs. *See* Charts
Grayscale option
    for pictures, PP-136
    printing, PP-22–PP-23
Gridlines, in charts, PP-214,
    PP-217–PP-218
Grouping clip art, PP-132–PP-133
Groups, command, PP-7, PP-8, PP-10

H

Handouts
    headers and footers, PP-89,
        PP-90–PP-91
    printing, PP-19, PP-21, PP-22
Hanging indent, PP-58
Header and Footer dialog box
    Notes and Handouts tab, PP-88,
        PP-89, PP-90–PP-91
    Slide tab, PP-88, PP-89–PP-90
Headers
    dates in, PP-89, PP-90
    definition, PP-88
    on handouts, PP-89, PP-90–PP-91
    on notes pages, PP-89
    page numbers in, PP-89
    slide, PP-88, PP-89–PP-90
    slide numbers in, PP-89, PP-90
Help feature, PP-10–PP-11
Hierarchy diagrams, PP-250. *See also*
    Organization charts; SmartArt
    graphics
Horizontal (Category) Axis
    formatting, PP-215–PP-216
    location, PP-214
    tick marks, PP-213
Horizontal Bullet List diagrams, PP-252

I

I-beam pointer, PP-15, PP-16
Illustrations. *See* Clip art; Drawing;
    Pictures; SmartArt graphics
Images. *See* Clip art; Pictures
Indents
    setting on ruler, PP-58–PP-60
    in text placeholders, PP-58–PP-60

Insert Chart dialog box, PP-209
Insert Clip Art task pane, PP-127
Insert Picture dialog box, PP-137–PP-138
Inserting. *See also* Keying text; Pasting
    clip art, PP-127, PP-129–PP-130
    columns and rows in tables,
        PP-176–PP-177
    photos in Photo Albums, PP-146
    pictures, PP-134–PP-135,
        PP-137–PP-138
    slides, PP-38–PP-41
    SmartArt graphics, PP-248–PP-249
    tables, PP-167
    text in shapes, PP-126–PP-127
Insertion point, text placeholders, PP-15
Italic text, PP-43–PP-44

K
Keyboard shortcuts
    copying, cutting, and pasting, PP-80
    moving objects, PP-131
    navigating SmartArt
        graphics, PP-260
Keying text
    in list diagrams, PP-250–PP-251
    in organization charts,
        PP-261–PP-262
    in process diagrams, PP-253
    in slides, PP-38
    in SmartArt graphics,
        PP-250–PP-251
    in tables, PP-167
    in text placeholders, PP-15–PP-16

L
Legends, chart, PP-214,
        PP-216–PP-217
Line spacing
    between paragraphs, PP-46
    within paragraphs, PP-45
Lines. *See also* Borders
    connector, PP-121–PP-122
    constrained (straight),
        PP-119–PP-120
    diagonal, in cells, PP-178–PP-179
    drawing, PP-119
    in tables, PP-170–PP-171
    weights, PP-140
List diagrams. *See also* SmartArt
        graphics
    creating, PP-250–PP-252
    description, PP-249
    keying text, PP-250–PP-251
Lists. *See* Bulleted lists; Numbered lists
Live Preview, PP-10
Lock aspect ratio option, PP-124
Lock Drawing Mode option, PP-117,
        PP-119

M
Margins, in tables, PP-181,
        PP-182
Masters. *See* Templates
Matrix diagrams, PP-250. *See also*
        SmartArt graphics
Microsoft Clip Organizer, PP-127,
        PP-128, PP-133
Microsoft Graph datasheets,
        PP-209, PP-210
Microsoft Office Online Collection,
        PP-129, PP-133
Mouse. *See* Pointers
Movies, finding, PP-129

Moving clip art, PP-123
    objects, PP-131
    pictures, PP-123
    shapes in organization charts,
        PP-265
    text placeholders, PP-17, PP-52
    WordArt, PP-143
Music. *See* Sound effects

N
Names, presentation, PP-17,
        PP-18, PP-19
Navigating
    charts, PP-213–PP-214
    presentations, PP-38
    slides, PP-38
    SmartArt graphics, PP-260
    tables, PP-167, PP-168
    worksheets, PP-210
Noncontiguous slides, selecting, PP-77
Normal indent, PP-58
Normal view, PP-11
Notes pages
    headers and footers, PP-89
    printing, PP-21, PP-22
Notes pane, PP-7
Numbered lists
    creating, PP-57
    styles, PP-57
    working with, PP-52

O
Objects. *See also* Pictures; Shapes;
        WordArt
    moving, PP-131
    outlines. *See* Lines
Open dialog box, PP-9
Opening
    PowerPoint, PP-9
    presentations, PP-9–PP-10
Organization charts
    creating, PP-261–PP-262
    formats, PP-265
    keying text, PP-261–PP-262
    shapes
        adding, PP-262–PP-264
        deleting, PP-265
        demoting, PP-266
        moving, PP-265
        promoting, PP-265
        rearranging, PP-265–PP-266
        types, PP-262–PP-263
    structure, PP-263
    uses, PP-261
Orientation, SmartArt graphics,
        PP-273. *See also* Rotating
Outlines
    printing, PP-21, PP-22
    promoting and demoting
        items, PP-12
    viewing, PP-11–PP-12
Output formats. *See* Delivery methods
Ovals
    constrained, PP-122–PP-123
    drawing, PP-119
Overhead transparencies, PP-22

P
Page numbers, in headers and footers,
        PP-89
Paragraph dialog box, PP-46, PP-58
Paragraphs. *See also* Text
    alignment, PP-50
    indents, PP-58–PP-60

line spacing between, PP-46
line spacing within, PP-45
Paste Options button, PP-81, PP-82
Pasting
    from Clipboard, PP-80
    keyboard shortcut, PP-80
    text, PP-81–PP-82
Pencil pointer, PP-170–PP-171
Photo Album dialog box, PP-146
Photo Albums
    background themes,
        PP-147–PP-148
    captions, PP-147
    editing, PP-146–PP-148
    frame shapes, PP-147
    inserting photos, PP-146
    layouts, PP-146, PP-147
    rearranging photos, PP-146–PP-147
    rotating photos, PP-146
    uses, PP-145
Photographs. *See* Pictures
Picture Bullet dialog box, PP-56
Picture tools, PP-133–PP-134
Picture tools format tab, PP-133
Pictures. *See also* Clip art; Photo
        Albums
    borders, PP-140
    brightness, PP-138–PP-139, PP-147
    as bullets, PP-56–PP-57
    changing colors, PP-136
    as chart backgrounds,
        PP-228–PP-229
    continuous picture lists,
        PP-270–PP-271
    contrast, PP-138–PP-139, PP-147
    cropping, PP-135–PP-136
    effects, PP-140–PP-141
    enhancing, PP-133–PP-134,
        PP-138–PP-139
    finding, PP-133, PP-134
    inserting, PP-134–PP-135,
        PP-137–PP-138
    moving, PP-123
    resizing, PP-123
    shapes, PP-139–PP-140
    styles, PP-136–PP-137
    in tables, PP-186–PP-187
Pie charts
    creating, PP-223
    effects, PP-225
    exploding slice, PP-225
    labels, PP-224
    rotating, PP-225–PP-226
Placeholders. *See* Text placeholders
Plot Area, PP-214
Pointers
    cell, PP-210
    crosshair, PP-117
    I-beam, PP-15, PP-16
    pencil, PP-170–PP-171
    shapes, PP-16
Points, PP-41
PowerPoint
    exiting, PP-23–PP-24
    exploring, PP-6–PP-8
    Help, PP-10–PP-11
    opening, PP-9
    window, PP-6–PP-8
Presentations. *See also* Delivery
        methods; Slide shows
    blank, PP-36–PP-37
    closing, PP-23–PP-24
    creating, PP-36–PP-37
    file locations, PP-10
    moving from slide to slide,
        PP-12–PP-13

names, PP-17, PP-18, PP-19
navigating, PP-38
opening, PP-9–PP-10
printing, PP-19, PP-20–PP-21
renaming, PP-18
saving, PP-17–PP-19
views
    Normal, PP-11
    Slide Sorter, PP-11, PP-78
    Slides and Outline pane,
       PP-11–PP-12
Previewing
  clip art, PP-129–PP-130
  effects, PP-10
  printing, PP-19–PP-20
Preview/Properties dialog box,
    PP-129–PP-130
Primary axis, PP-221–PP-222
Print dialog box, PP-21, PP-22
Print Preview, PP-19–PP-20
Print Preview Ribbon, PP-20
Printing
  black-and-white option, PP-22
  grayscale option, PP-22–PP-23
  handouts, PP-19, PP-21, PP-22
  methods, PP-20–PP-21
  notes pages, PP-21, PP-22
  options, PP-19, PP-22–PP-23
  outlines, PP-21, PP-22
  presentations, PP-19, PP-20–PP-21
  previewing, PP-19–PP-20
  slides, PP-21–PP-22
  on transparencies, PP-22
Process diagrams. *See also* SmartArt
    graphics
  creating, PP-252–PP-254
  description, PP-250
  keying text, PP-253
Proofreading, PP-85. *See also* Spelling
Pure Black and White option, PP-22
Pyramid diagrams, PP-250. *See also*
    SmartArt graphics

Q

Quick Access toolbar, PP-7,
    PP-8–PP-9, PP-21
Quick Print, PP-21
Quick Styles, PP-255

R

Radial diagrams, PP-268–PP-269
Recolor gallery, PP-136
Rectangles
  constrained, PP-122–PP-123
  drawing, PP-118
Redoing actions, PP-83
Reference tools, PP-85, PP-86
Reflection effect
  pictures, PP-140
  in tables, PP-185–PP-186
Regrouping clip art, PP-132
Relationship diagrams. *See also*
    SmartArt graphics
  continuous picture lists,
    PP-270–PP-271
  description, PP-250
  gear diagrams, PP-269–PP-270
  radial diagrams, PP-268–PP-269
Renaming presentations, PP-18
Replace dialog box, PP-88
Research, PP-85, PP-86
Reset Graphic button, PP-260
Resizing
  clip art, PP-123, PP-130
  Lock aspect ratio option, PP-124

pictures, PP-123
shapes, PP-123–PP-124,
    PP-125–PP-126
SmartArt graphics, PP-256–PP-258,
    PP-266–PP-267
tables, PP-179, PP-183
text placeholders, PP-17, PP-50–PP-52
Ribbon, PP-7, PP-8, PP-10
Rotating. *See also* 3-D rotation effect
  clip art, PP-131
  photos in Photo Albums, PP-146
  pie charts, PP-225–PP-226
  shapes, PP-126–PP-127, PP-256
  text boxes, PP-61–PP-62
Rotation handles
  on shapes, PP-118
  on text boxes, PP-61
Rows, in tables
  definition, PP-166
  deleting, PP-177
  heights, PP-179–PP-181
  inserting, PP-176–PP-177
Rows, in worksheets, PP-210
Ruler
  horizontal, PP-116, PP-118
  indent markers, PP-58, PP-59
  tabs, PP-187
  using to size and position objects,
    PP-116, PP-118, PP-124
  vertical, PP-116, PP-118

S

Save As dialog box, PP-18–PP-19
Saving
  files, PP-18–PP-19
  presentations, PP-17–PP-19
Scale, PP-213
ScreenTips, PP-8
Scroll bars, PP-7
Searching. *See* Finding
Secondary axis
  adding, PP-219–PP-220
  formatting, PP-221–PP-222
  uses, PP-218
Selecting
  clip art, PP-130–PP-131
  contiguous slides, PP-77
  design themes, PP-91–PP-92
  noncontiguous slides, PP-77
  slides, PP-77
  text placeholders, PP-48
Sepia option, PP-136
Shadow button, PP-43
Shadow effect
  pictures, PP-140
  in tables, PP-184–PP-185
  text, PP-44
Shape fill effects, in charts,
    PP-227–PP-228
Shapes. *See also* Lines; Organization
    charts
  adjustment handles,
    PP-125–PP-126
  in charts, PP-226–PP-227
  circles, PP-122–PP-123
  connection sites, PP-121
  constrained, PP-122–PP-123
  deleting, PP-117
  in diagrams
    adding, PP-258
    colors, PP-267
    Quick Styles, PP-255
    rearranging, PP-257, PP-267
    rotating, PP-256
  drawing, PP-116, PP-117–PP-119

inserting text, PP-126–PP-127
moving, PP-123
outlines. *See* Lines
ovals, PP-119, PP-122–PP-123
of pictures, PP-139–PP-140
proportions, PP-123
recently used, PP-117
rectangles, PP-118, PP-122–PP-123
resizing, PP-123–PP-124,
    PP-125–PP-126
rotating, PP-126–PP-127
rotation handles, PP-118
sizing handles, PP-123
squares, PP-122–PP-123
Shapes gallery, PP-117, PP-125
Size and Position dialog box, PP-124
Sizing handles. *See also* Resizing
  shapes, PP-123
  tables, PP-183
  text placeholders, PP-51
Slide layouts, choosing, PP-39–PP-40
Slide Masters. *See* Templates
Slide numbers, in headers and footers,
    PP-89, PP-90
Slide shows. *See also* Delivery
    methods; Presentations
  running, PP-14
  starting, PP-14
  transitions. *See* Transitions
Slide Sorter view, PP-11, PP-78
Slide transitions. *See* Transitions
Slides
  creating, PP-36, PP-38
  deleting, PP-76, PP-79
  headers and footers, PP-88,
    PP-89–PP-90
  inserting, PP-38–PP-41
  keying text, PP-38
  moving between, PP-12–PP-13
  navigating, PP-38
  printing, PP-21–PP-22
  rearranging, PP-78–PP-79,
    PP-80–PP-81
  selecting multiple, PP-77
  thumbnails, PP-11
  transitions. *See* Transitions
Slides and Outline pane, PP-7,
    PP-11–PP-12
Slides tab, PP-77, PP-78
SmartArt graphics. *See also*
    Organization charts
  adding shapes, PP-258
  choosing, PP-248–PP-249
  colors, PP-259–PP-260, PP-267
  continuous picture lists,
    PP-270–PP-271
  converting bulleted lists to,
    PP-251–PP-252
  creating, PP-250–PP-252
  cycle diagrams, PP-254–PP-255
  diagram types
    categories, PP-249–PP-250
    changing, PP-271–PP-272
  duplicating, PP-257
  enhancing, PP-255
  fonts, PP-267
  gear diagrams, PP-269–PP-270
  inserting, PP-248–PP-249
  keyboard shortcuts, PP-260
  keying text, PP-250–PP-251
  list diagrams, PP-250–PP-252
  navigating, PP-260
  orientation, PP-273
  process diagrams, PP-252–PP-254
  radial diagrams, PP-268–PP-269
  rearranging shapes, PP-257, PP-267

SmartArt graphics—*Cont.*
 resizing, PP-256–PP-258,
  PP-266–PP-267
 rotation, PP-256
 shape quick styles, PP-255
SmartArt Styles, PP-259, PP-267
Soft edges effect, PP-140
Sound effects. *See also* Music
 finding, PP-129
 transitions, PP-95, PP-96
Source formatting, PP-81, PP-82
Special effects. *See* Effects
Spelling
 AutoCorrect, PP-40
 checking, PP-84–PP-86
Squares, drawing, PP-122–PP-123
Status bar, PP-7
Stock photography, PP-133. *See also*
  Clip art
Subordinate shapes, PP-262–PP-263
Superior shapes, PP-263
Symbol dialog box, PP-55

T

Tab key, PP-49, PP-53
Tab settings
 default, PP-187
 deleting, PP-189
 in text placeholders, PP-53
 types, PP-187, PP-188–PP-189
 using ruler, PP-187, PP-189
Tabbed tables, PP-187–PP-190
Table Style Options, PP-169–PP-170
Table Styles, applying, PP-169–PP-170
Tables
 aligning text, PP-181
 borders, PP-172–PP-174
 cells, PP-166
 changing colors, PP-173, PP-174
 columns, PP-166
 creating
  drawing, PP-170–PP-171
  Insert Table button, PP-167
  methods, PP-166–PP-167
  tabbed table, PP-187–PP-190
 effects, PP-183
  cell bevel, PP-184
  pictures, PP-186–PP-187
  reflection, PP-185–PP-186
  shading, PP-186–PP-187
  shadow, PP-184–PP-185
 erasing borders, PP-175
 formatting, PP-169
 inserting, PP-167
 keying text, PP-167
 modifying structure, PP-175
  deleting columns and rows,
   PP-177
  distributing column width and
   row height, PP-179–PP-181
  inserting columns and rows,
   PP-176–PP-177
  merging cells, PP-177–PP-178

 splitting cells, PP-177–PP-178
 navigating in, PP-167, PP-168
 resizing, PP-179, PP-183
 rows, PP-166
 shading, PP-172–PP-173
 sizes, PP-167, PP-179
 sizing handles, PP-183
 styles, PP-169–PP-170
 tabbed, PP-187–PP-190
 text direction, PP-171–PP-172
Tabs, on ribbon, PP-7, PP-10
Templates, PP-36
Text. *See also* Fonts; Lists; WordArt
 cutting and pasting, PP-81–PP-82
 effects, PP-41, PP-44
 finding, PP-87–PP-88
 formatting, PP-41
  alignment, PP-50
  bold, PP-43–PP-44
  case, PP-44–PP-45
  colors, PP-44, PP-47
  entire placeholders, PP-48–PP-49
  italic, PP-43–PP-44
  shadow, PP-44
  underlined, PP-43–PP-44, PP-47
 inserting in shapes, PP-126–PP-127
 keying. *See* Keying text
Text boxes
 colors, PP-61
 creating, PP-60
 fonts, PP-61
 rotating, PP-61–PP-62
 tables in, PP-189–PP-190
 word wrapping, PP-62
Text Effects, WordArt, PP-143
Text fill colors, WordArt,
  PP-144–PP-145
Text outline, WordArt, PP-144–PP-145
Text placeholders
 activating, PP-15
 deselecting, PP-48
 formatting, PP-48–PP-49
 indents, PP-58–PP-60
 insertion point, PP-15
 keying text, PP-15–PP-16
 moving, PP-17, PP-52
 resizing, PP-17, PP-50–PP-52
 selecting, PP-48
 sizing handles, PP-51
Text styles, PP-41
Text tool pointer, PP-60
Theme colors
 changing, PP-92–PP-93
 definition, PP-43
 text, PP-44
Theme effects, PP-93–PP-94
Theme fonts, PP-93, PP-94
Themes. *See* Design themes
Thesaurus, PP-85, PP-86–PP-87
3-D rotation effect
 diagram shapes, PP-256
 pictures, PP-141
 pie charts, PP-225–PP-226
Thumbnails, PP-11

Tick marks, PP-213
Title bar, PP-7
Title text, PP-15
Toggle buttons, PP-43
Toolbars, Quick Access,
  PP-7, PP-8–PP-9, PP-21
Transform effect, WordArt,
  PP-143–PP-144
Transitions
 applying, PP-95
 definition, PP-95
 effects, PP-95–PP-96
 sounds, PP-95, PP-96
 speed, PP-95–PP-96
 viewing, PP-14–PP-15
Transparencies, PP-22
TrueType fonts, PP-42

U

Underlined text, PP-43–PP-44, PP-47
Undoing actions, PP-83–PP-84
Ungrouping clip art, PP-132

V

Vector drawings, PP-127. *See also* Clip art
Vertical (Value) Axis
 formatting, PP-215–PP-216
 location, PP-214
 tick marks, PP-213
Vertical Box List diagrams,
  PP-250–PP-251
Video clips. *See* Movies
View buttons, PP-7
Views
 Normal, PP-11
 Slide Sorter, PP-11, PP-78
 Slides and Outline pane,
   PP-11–PP-12

W

Washout option, PP-136
Word wrapping, PP-62
WordArt
 creating objects, PP-142–PP-143
 editing text, PP-143
 effects, PP-143–PP-144
 fill colors, PP-144–PP-145
 moving, PP-143
 outlines, PP-144–PP-145
WordArt Styles gallery, PP-142, PP-143
Worksheets
 chart data
  changing, PP-208–PP-209
  creating charts, PP-208
  entering, PP-210–PP-212
 navigating, PP-210

Z

Zooming, PP-13–PP-14

Access Index

*. *See* Asterisk "*" wildcard
=. *See* =Now() control
?. *See* Question mark "?" wildcard

A

Access. *See* Microsoft Access
Access Export Wizard, AC-117
Adding
    forms, AC-210–AC-247
    group sections, AC-256–AC-257
    labels, AC-223–AC-224, AC-228
    report sections, AC-257–AC-258
    reports, AC-248–AC-281
    totals rows, AC-78–AC-80, AC-94
    unbound text boxes, AC-229
    view form sections, AC-223–AC-224
Adding controls
    calculated, AC-229–AC-231,
        AC-242–AC-243
    common expression,
        AC-259–AC-260
    to a control layout, AC-217–AC-219
Adding data
    with a Lookup field,
        AC-148–AC-149
    with a multi-valued lookup field,
        AC-151–AC-152
Adding fields
    in Datasheet View, AC-106–AC-107,
        AC-122–AC-123, AC-127–AC-128
    in Design View, AC-107–AC-108,
        AC-122–AC-123
    to a query, AC-173–AC-174
    in a table, AC-106–AC-108, AC-125
Adding lines, to a report,
    AC-263–AC-264
Adding records,
    AC-123–AC-124, AC-129
    in a table, AC-38–AC-39
    through a form,
        AC-51, AC-63–AC-64, AC-66
    through a query, AC-42, AC-62–AC-63
Aggregate functions, AC-79
    adding to a group, AC-258
    defining, AC-185
Aligning
    control layouts, AC-216–AC-217
    controls, AC-261–AC-262
Alignment options, AC-216
All Form sections, AC-222
Analyze Table Wizard. *See* Table
    Analyzer Wizard
Analyzing tools, AC-153–AC-155
    for performance, AC-155,
        AC-164–AC-165
    for a table, AC-153–AC-154,
        AC-167–AC-168
AND criteria, AC-180–AC-181
Applications, AC-33–AC-34,
    AC-66–AC-68, AC-96–AC-97,
    AC-127–AC-129,
    AC-131–AC-134,
    AC-166–AC-168,
    AC-206–AC-208,
    AC-244–AC-246, AC-278–AC-284
Applying
    Filter By Form, AC-84–AC-86
    Filter By Selection, AC-80–AC-82

Arguments, AC-175
Arrows, AC-75
Asterisk "*" wildcard, finding data
    using, AC-74
Attached labels, AC-214
Attachments
    attaching a file through a form,
        AC-64–AC-65
    attaching an image, AC-53–AC-54,
        AC-68
    extracting an image from the
        database, AC-54–AC-55
    in a form, AC-54
    managing, AC-52–AC-55
Attachments window, AC-53
AutoCorrect, AC-43–AC-44
AutoFormat, AC-238–AC-239, AC-251
    defining, AC-220

B

Backing up databases, AC-23–AC-24
Blank databases, AC-101,
    AC-122–AC-123, AC-129
Bottom values, finding,
    AC-182–AC-184, AC-203–AC-204
Bound controls, AC-213
Browse Folder button, AC-57
Build button, AC-112
Business templates, AC-99

C

Calculated controls, AC-229, AC-265
    adding, AC-229–AC-231,
        AC-242–AC-243
    adding to a form, AC-228–AC-231
    adding unbound text boxes, AC-229
    defining, AC-213
Calculated fields, AC-185
Calculations, adding to a query,
    AC-185–AC-188
Calendar control, AC-84
Caption Property, changing, AC-109
Changing
    views of tables, AC-30–AC-31
    widths and row heights of
        columns, AC-18–AC-19,
        AC-29–AC-30, AC-34
Changing field properties
    caption, AC-109
    date picker, AC-113
    default value, AC-110
    format, AC-110–AC-111,
        AC-122–AC-123, AC-127
    input mask, AC-111–AC-112
Chart Field List, AC-195
Check box fields, AC-39
Child fields, AC-146
Clear Layout button, AC-140
Clip Mode, AC-227
Clipboard group, AC-46
Closing
    databases, AC-24, AC-31–AC-32
    major objects, AC-13–AC-14, AC-33
Collapse All command, AC-146
Columnar style reports, AC-249
Columns
    hiding and unhiding, AC-17–AC-18
    resizing, AC-19
Command groups, AC-12

Command summaries, AC-25–AC-26,
    AC-59, AC-89–AC-90, AC-120,
    AC-158, AC-198,
    AC-235–AC-236, AC-270
Common expression controls
    adding, AC-259–AC-260
    editing, AC-264–AC-265
Compact and Repair, AC-23,
    AC-31–AC-32, AC-34
Comparison operators,
    AC-177–AC-178
Components of Access, AC-11–AC-15,
    AC-28–AC-29
    exploring Datasheet and Design
        Views, AC-14–AC-15,
        AC-33–AC-34
    exploring tabs, ribbons, and
        groups, AC-12–AC-13
    manipulating the Navigation Pane,
        AC-11–AC-12
    opening and closing major objects,
        AC-13–AC-14, AC-33
Conditional formatting, AC-266
Contextual filter options, AC-81
Contextual tabs, AC-77
Control layouts
    aligning, AC-216–AC-217
    modifying, AC-213–AC-214
    resizing and moving,
        AC-238–AC-239
Control margins, AC-213
Control padding, AC-213
Control Source property, AC-229
Controlling
    appearance of fields,
        AC-108–AC-113, AC-125, AC-127
    data integrity, AC-113–AC-116
Controls. *See also* Adding controls
    aligning, AC-261–AC-262
    defining, AC-213
    resizing and moving,
        AC-226–AC-227, AC-260–AC-261
Controls in a report, AC-260–AC-265
    adding and rearranging,
        AC-252–AC-253
    adding lines to a report,
        AC-263–AC-264
    aligning, AC-261–AC-262
    editing common expression
        controls, AC-264–AC-265
    resizing and moving,
        AC-260–AC-261
Controls in Design View
    adding a label, AC-228
    formatting a form in Design View,
        AC-224–AC-226
    modifying, AC-224–AC-228
    modifying property settings,
        AC-227–AC-228
    resizing and moving,
        AC-226–AC-227
Controls in Layout View
    adding and rearranging in a report,
        AC-252–AC-253
    aligning control layouts,
        AC-216–AC-217
    formatting a form in, AC-220
    formatting a report in,
        AC-251–AC-252
    formatting a report using the
        Property Sheet, AC-253–AC-254

Controls in Layout View—*Cont.*
  modifying, AC-213–AC-220,
    AC-251–AC-254, AC-272–AC-276
  removing and adding, AC-217–AC-219
  resizing and moving,
    AC-238–AC-239
  setting tab order, AC-219
Copying, AC-45–AC-47
  table structure, AC-105
Count function, AC-260
Criteria and operators
  adding to a query, AC-175–AC-180,
    AC-202–AC-205
  AND criteria, AC-180–AC-181
  OR criteria, AC-181–AC-182
  using a single criterion,
    AC-176–AC-177
  using comparison operators,
    AC-177–AC-178
  using keywords in criteria,
    AC-179–AC-180
  using wildcards in criteria,
    AC-178–AC-179
Criteria row, AC-182
Crosstab Query Wizard, AC-188,
  AC-190–AC-191

D

Data. *See also* Adding data
  applications, AC-96–AC-97
  command summary, AC-89–AC-90
  and the Database Documenter,
    AC-87–AC-88
  exporting to Word, AC-117–AC-118
  and the Find command,
    AC-72–AC-73
  finding and replacing, AC-70–AC-74
  finding using a question mark "?",
    AC-75
  finding using an asterisk "*", AC-74
  importing from Excel,
    AC-118–AC-119, AC-125–AC-126
  "On Your Own" exercise, AC-97
  and the Replace command,
    AC-73–AC-74
  and the Search tool, AC-71
  sorting records, AC-75–AC-78,
    AC-96
  summary, AC-89
  using filters with, AC-80–AC-86,
    AC-94–AC-95
  using wildcards with, AC-74–AC-75
Data in a table, replacing,
  AC-92–AC-93, AC-96
Data integrity
  and analyzing tools, AC-153–AC-155
  applications, AC-166–AC-168
  command summary, AC-158
  controlling, AC-113–AC-116
  creating relationships between
    tables, AC-136–AC-142,
    AC-167–AC-168
  and the Lookup Wizard,
    AC-147–AC-153
  managing, AC-136–AC-169
  "On Your Own" exercise,
    AC-168–AC-169
  printing a Database Documenter
    Report, AC-166–AC-167
  printing and saving a Relationship
    Report, AC-167–AC-168
  setting the field property field size,
    AC-114–AC-115
  setting the field property validation
    text and rules, AC-115–AC-116

setting the primary key, AC-114,
    AC-128
  and subdatasheets, AC-145–AC-147
  summary, AC-157
  tracking Object Dependency,
    AC-155–AC-157
Data organization, AC-7
Data types, AC-102–AC-103
Data using a report, AC-55–AC-58,
    AC-64–AC-65
  previewing, AC-55–AC-56
  printing, AC-56–AC-57, AC-68
  saving to a file, AC-57–AC-58,
    AC-68
Data with a Lookup field, adding,
    AC-148–AC-149
Data with a multi-valued lookup field,
    adding, AC-151–AC-152
Database designers, AC-211
Database Documenter, AC-87–AC-88
Database Documenter Report
  generating for a table, AC-87,
    AC-94–AC-96
  for multiple objects, AC-88
  printing, AC-96, AC-166–AC-167
  saving, AC-96
Database objects
  adding and modifying forms,
    AC-210–AC-247
  adding and modifying reports,
    AC-248–AC-281
  applications, AC-282–AC-284
  designing and managing,
    AC-135–AC-284
  designing queries, AC-170–AC-209
  managing data integrity,
    AC-136–AC-169
  using the Internet, AC-284
Database templates, AC-99
Databases, AC-8–AC-10,
    AC-98–AC-101, AC-127. *See also*
    New databases and tables
  applications, AC-33–AC-34,
    AC-131–AC-134
  backing up, AC-23–AC-24
  changing properties, AC-100
  closing, AC-24, AC-31–AC-32
  command summary, AC-25–AC-26
  creating blank, AC-101,
    AC-122–AC-123, AC-129
  creating new, AC-98–AC-130
  creating using a template,
    AC-99–AC-100
  defining, AC-6
  finding, filtering, sorting, and
    summarizing data in,
    AC-70–AC-97
  getting started with, AC-6–AC-35
  identifying basic structure,
    AC-6–AC-8
  identifying components of Access,
    AC-11–AC-15, AC-28–AC-29
  and the Internet, AC-134
  managing, AC-8–AC-9,
    AC-28–AC-29
  managing Access files,
    AC-23–AC-24
  modifying appearance,
    AC-17–AC-20
  navigating Access recordsets,
    AC-15–AC-17, AC-29–AC-30
  "On Your Own" exercise,
    AC-34–AC-35
  opening, AC-10, AC-33, AC-37
  printing and saving a recordset,
    AC-20–AC-23

printing and saving a table,
    AC-30–AC-31
  setting properties, AC-100–AC-101
  starting, AC-9–AC-10
  summary, AC-24–AC-25
  understanding, AC-5–AC-134
  viewing and modifying records,
    AC-36–AC-69
Datasheet View, AC-14–AC-15,
    AC-33–AC-34
Datasheets
  adding and modifying the Totals
    row in, AC-78–AC-80
  changing column widths and row
    heights, AC-18–AC-19,
    AC-29–AC-30, AC-34
  changing views of a table,
    AC-30–AC-31
  hiding and unhiding columns,
    AC-17–AC-18
  hiding fields, AC-30–AC-31
  modifying a table, AC-30–AC-31
  modifying appearance of,
    AC-17–AC-20
  switching views, AC-34
  using the Font command group,
    AC-19–AC-20
Date picker, changing, AC-113
Default values, changing, AC-110
Delete options, AC-52
Deleting fields
  in Datasheet View, AC-106–AC-107,
    AC-122–AC-123, AC-127–AC-128
  in Design View, AC-107–AC-108,
    AC-122–AC-123
  in a table, AC-106–AC-108, AC-125
Deleting records
  from a table, AC-39–AC-40
  through a form, AC-52,
    AC-63–AC-64
  through a query, AC-42,
    AC-66–AC-67
Deletions, undoing, AC-47
Dependency. *See* Missing dependency;
    Object Dependency
Design grids, adding fields to,
    AC-174
Design View, AC-14–AC-15,
    AC-33–AC-34
  modifying controls in, AC-224
    AC-228
Designing database objects,
    AC-135–AC-284
Designing queries, AC-170–AC-209
Detail section, AC-221
Dialog boxes, confirming deletion,
    AC-40
Drop-down arrow, AC-196
Drop zones, AC-195
Dynasets, defining, AC-171

E

Edit Mode, AC-15
Edit Relationships dialog box,
    AC-138
Editing
  common expression controls,
    AC-264–AC-265
  data in a form, AC-50
  field properties, AC-123–AC-124,
    AC-129
  fields in a table, AC-37–AC-38
  lookup field lists, AC-150
Ellipses button, AC-112
Existing relationships, AC-137–AC-138
Exiting Access, AC-24

Expand All command, AC-146
Exporting data, to Word, AC-117–AC-118
Exporting tables, to Access, AC-116–AC-117
Expression Builder, AC-230
  defining, AC-187
  parts of, AC-185, AC-187
External data
  exporting a table to Access, AC-116–AC-117
  exporting to Word, AC-117–AC-118
  importing from Excel, AC-118–AC-119, AC-125–AC-126
  managing, AC-116–AC-119, AC-127
Extracting images, from the database, AC-54–AC-55

F

Field lists, AC-185
Field properties
  changing caption, AC-109
  changing date picker, AC-113
  changing default value, AC-110
  changing format, AC-110–AC-111, AC-122–AC-123, AC-127
  changing input mask, AC-111–AC-112
  editing, AC-123–AC-124, AC-129
  editing through a form, AC-50–AC-51
  editing through a query, AC-41, AC-62–AC-63, AC-66–AC-67
  setting field size, AC-114–AC-115
  setting validation text and rules, AC-115–AC-116
Fields. *See also* Adding fields
  adding and deleting in Datasheet View, AC-106–AC-107, AC-122–AC-123, AC-127–AC-128
  adding and deleting in Design View, AC-107–AC-108, AC-122–AC-123
  adding to a query, AC-173–AC-174
  child, AC-146
  controlling appearance, AC-108–AC-113, AC-125, AC-127
  defining, AC-7
  hiding, AC-30–AC-31
  master, AC-146
  printing and saving table definitions, AC-123–AC-124, AC-127–AC-128
Fields in a table
  adding and deleting in Datasheet View, AC-106–AC-107, AC-122–AC-123, AC-127–AC-128
  adding and deleting in Design View, AC-107–AC-108, AC-122–AC-123
  editing, AC-37–AC-38
Files
  attaching through a form, AC-64–AC-65
  backing up a database, AC-23–AC-24
  closing a database, AC-24, AC-31–AC-32
  exiting, AC-24
  managing, AC-23–AC-24
  optimizing, AC-23
  using Compact and Repair, AC-23, AC-31–AC-32, AC-34
Filter By Form
  creating and applying, AC-84–AC-86
  and the "Or" option, AC-86

Filter By Selection, creating and applying, AC-80–AC-82
Filters, AC-80–AC-86, AC-94–AC-95
  for data, AC-70–AC-97
  defining, AC-80
  logic of, AC-83–AC-86
  for a range of values, AC-83–AC-84, AC-97
  replacing data in a table, AC-96
  for a specific value, AC-83, AC-96
Find and Replace dialog box, AC-72–AC-73
Find command, AC-72–AC-73
Find Duplicate Records Query Wizard, AC-191–AC-192
Find Unmatched Query Wizard, AC-192–AC-193
Finding
  information, AC-96
  top and bottom values, AC-182–AC-184, AC-203–AC-204
Finding data, AC-70–AC-97
  using asterisk "*" wildcard, AC-74
  using question mark "?" wildcard, AC-75
Font command group, AC-19–AC-20
Foreign keys, AC-139
Form Footer section, AC-221
Form Header section, AC-221
Form Layout View, AC-214
Form sections, AC-221–AC-224
  adding labels and view form sections, AC-223–AC-224
  Detail section, AC-221
  opening and sizing, AC-221–AC-222
  Page Footer section, AC-221
  Page Header section, AC-221
Form Wizard, AC-210
Format Painter, AC-265
Formatting
  changing, AC-110–AC-111, AC-122–AC-123, AC-127
  setting properties, AC-110
Formatting forms
  in Design View, AC-224–AC-226
  in Layout View, AC-220
Formatting reports
  in Layout View, AC-251–AC-252
  using the Property Sheet, AC-253–AC-254
Forms
  adding and modifying, AC-210–AC-247
  adding calculated controls to a form, AC-228–AC-231
  applications, AC-244–AC-246
  command summary, AC-235–AC-236
  creating multiple record forms, AC-238–AC-239
  creating single record, AC-239–AC-240
  creating with a wizard, AC-211–AC-212, AC-242–AC-243
  defining, AC-7
  formatting in Design View, AC-224–AC-226
  formatting in Layout View, AC-220
  generating quickly, AC-210–AC-213
  generating with one click, AC-212–AC-213
  modifying controls in Design View, AC-224–AC-228
  modifying controls in Layout View, AC-213–AC-220
  navigating through, AC-48–AC-49

"On Your Own" exercise, AC-246–AC-247
  printing and saving, AC-231–AC-234, AC-239–AC-241
  printing multiple records, AC-233
  printing one record, AC-232–AC-233
  printing specific pages, AC-231–AC-232, AC-242–AC-243
  saving a record, AC-233–AC-234
  summary, AC-234–AC-235
  using AutoFormat, AC-238–AC-239
Formulas, in calculated fields, AC-185–AC-187
Functions
  building, AC-188
  in a calculated field, AC-187–AC-188
  defining, AC-175

G

Generating forms
  with one click, AC-212–AC-213
  quickly, AC-210–AC-213
Generating reports
  with one click, AC-250–AC-251
  quickly, AC-248–AC-251
  for a table, AC-87, AC-94–AC-96
Getting Started window, AC-11
Gridline marks, AC-226
Group Header/Footer sections, AC-255
Group options, modifying, AC-258–AC-259
Group sections
  adding in Design View, AC-256–AC-257
  adding in Layout View, AC-257–AC-258
Grouped reports, creating using a wizard, AC-255–AC-256
Groups, AC-12–AC-13

I

Identifying
  basic database structure, AC-6–AC-8
  components of Access, AC-11–AC-15, AC-28–AC-29
  Object Dependency, AC-162–AC-164, AC-166–AC-168
Images
  attaching, AC-53–AC-54, AC-68
  extracting from the database, AC-54–AC-55
Imports, data from Excel, AC-118–AC-119, AC-125–AC-126
Indeterminate relationships, AC-137
Information, finding, AC-96
Input mask, changing, AC-111–AC-112
Input Mask symbols, AC-111
Input Mask Wizard, AC-111–AC-112
Inserting, subdatasheets, AC-145–AC-146, AC-161–AC-162, AC-166
Insertion point, AC-15
The Internet, AC-134, AC-284
Internet Explorer, AC-57

J

Join lines, AC-137–AC-138

K

Key column, AC-148
Keyboard shortcuts, AC-15
Keys, primary, AC-114, AC-128
Keywords, using in criteria,
    AC-179–AC-180

L

Label tool, AC-223
Label Wizard, AC-266–AC-267
Labels
    adding, AC-223–AC-224, AC-228
    attached, AC-214
Landscape layout, AC-21
Layout View, modifying controls in,
    AC-213–AC-220,
    AC-251–AC-254, AC-272–AC-276
Leszynski Naming Convention, AC-13,
    AC-99–AC-100, AC-250
Limit To List property, AC-149
Lines, adding to a report,
    AC-263–AC-264
List boxes, resizing, AC-137
Logical operators
    applying, AC-180–AC-182
    using AND criteria, AC-180–AC-181
    using OR criteria, AC-181–AC-182
"Look for" tab, AC-84
Lookup fields, AC-147–AC-148,
    AC-162, AC-164
    creating, AC-147–AC-148, AC-162,
    AC-164
    defining, AC-147
    editing lists of, AC-150
    modifying, AC-149–AC-150
    multi-valued, AC-150–AC-151,
    AC-166–AC-168
    viewing relationships created by,
    AC-152–AC-153
Lookup Wizard, AC-147–AC-153
    adding data with a lookup field,
    AC-148–AC-149
    adding data with a multi-valued
    lookup field, AC-151–AC-152

M

Major objects, opening and closing,
    AC-13–AC-14, AC-33
Managing
    attachments, AC-52–AC-55
    data integrity, AC-136–AC-169
    database objects, AC-135–AC-284
    databases, AC-8–AC-9, AC-28–AC-29
    external data, AC-116–AC-119,
    AC-127
    files, AC-23–AC-24
Manipulating, Navigation Pane,
    AC-11–AC-12
Margins, AC-253
    changing settings, AC-57
Master fields, AC-146
Microsoft Access
    components of, AC-11–AC-15,
    AC-28–AC-29
    Datasheet and Design Views in,
    AC-14–AC-15, AC-33–AC-34
    exiting, AC-24
    Navigation Pane in, AC-11–AC-12
    opening and closing major objects,
    AC-13–AC-14, AC-33
    previous versions of, AC-152
    tabs, ribbons, and groups,
    AC-12–AC-13

Microsoft Internet Explorer, AC-57
Missing dependency, viewing,
    AC-156–AC-157
Modifying
    control layouts, AC-213–AC-214
    controls in Design View,
    AC-224–AC-228
    controls in Layout View, AC-
    213–AC-220, AC-251–AC-254,
    AC-272–AC-276
    forms, AC-210–AC-247
    group options, AC-258–AC-259
    lookup fields, AC-149–AC-150
    property settings, AC-227–AC-228
    records, AC-36–AC-69
    recordsets, AC-48–AC-52
    reports, AC-248–AC-281
    select queries, AC-171–AC-175,
    AC-200–AC-205
    tables, AC-30–AC-31
    totals rows in datasheets,
    AC-78–AC-80
Modifying properties
    of queries, AC-182–AC-184,
    AC-200–AC-202, AC-204–AC-205
    of tables, AC-105–AC-106,
    AC-123–AC-124
Moving
    control layouts, AC-238–AC-239
    controls, AC-226–AC-227,
    AC-260–AC-261
Multi-valued lookup fields,
    AC-150–AC-151, AC-166–AC-168
Multicolumn report and labels,
    AC-266–AC-269
    creating package labels,
    AC-267–AC-269
    for a query, AC-267
Multiple columns, selecting, AC-18
Multiple Items Forms, AC-212
Multiple open documents, AC-49
Multiple record forms, AC-238–AC-239
Multiple records, printing, AC-233

N

Navigation buttons, AC-15–AC-16
    in a table, AC-16
Navigation Mode, AC-15
Navigation Pane, manipulating,
    AC-11–AC-12
Navigation shortcut keys, in a query,
    AC-16–AC-17
Navigation techniques
    for recordsets, AC-15–AC-17,
    AC-29–AC-30
    through forms, AC-48–AC-49
New databases and tables,
    AC-98–AC-130
    adding and deleting fields in a
    table, AC-106–AC-108, AC-125
    adding records, AC-123–AC-124,
    AC-129
    applications, AC-127–AC-129
    command summary, AC-120
    controlling data integrity,
    AC-113–AC-116
    controlling field appearance,
    AC-108–AC-113, AC-125, AC-127
    creating databases, AC-98–AC-101,
    AC-127
    creating tables, AC-101–AC-106
    managing external data,
    AC-116–AC-119, AC-127
    "On Your Own" exercise, AC-130
    summary, AC-119–AC-120

New Query Wizard collection, AC-189
New records, adding, AC-51
New Report dialog box, AC-266
Normalization, AC-153
=Now() control, AC-264

O

Object Dependencies Task
    Pane, AC-156
Object Dependency
    defining, AC-155
    identifying, AC-162–AC-164,
    AC-166–AC-168
    tracking, AC-155–AC-157
    viewing, AC-155–AC-156
    viewing missing dependency,
    AC-156–AC-157
Object-oriented data structures, AC-7
Office Buttons, AC-11
    options, AC-11
Office Clipboard, AC-43, AC-45–AC-47
Office Edit tools, AC-43–AC-48,
    AC-61–AC-62, AC-67
    using AutoCorrect, AC-43–AC-44
    using Copy, Paste, and the Office
    Clipboard, AC-45–AC-47
    using Undo, AC-47–AC-48
"On Your Own" exercises,
    AC-34–AC-35, AC-68–AC-69,
    AC-97, AC-130, AC-168–AC-169,
    AC-208–AC-209,
    AC-246–AC-247, AC-281
One record, printing, AC-232–AC-233
One-To-Many relationships, AC-137,
    AC-142, AC-144
One-To-One relationships, AC-137
Opening
    databases, AC-10, AC-33, AC-37
    form sections, AC-221–AC-222
    major objects, AC-13–AC-14, AC-33
Operators. *See also* Logical operators
    comparison, AC-177
    defining, AC-175
    types of, AC-176
OR criteria, AC-181–AC-182
Overtype mode, AC-41

P

Package labels, AC-267–AC-269
Padding, AC-253
Page break options, AC-259
Page Footer section, AC-221, AC-231,
    AC-254, AC-264
Page Header section, AC-221, AC-231,
    AC-254
Page orientation, AC-21
Paste, AC-45–AC-47
Performance, analyzing, AC-155,
    AC-164–AC-165
Picture Size Mode settings, AC-227
PivotChart view, AC-194–AC-196,
    AC-204–AC-205
    applying, AC-193–AC-196
PivotTable view, AC-194
    applying, AC-193–AC-196
Placeholders, AC-187
Pointers, resizing, AC-19
Portrait layout, AC-21
Previewing
    data using a report, AC-55–AC-58,
    AC-64–AC-65
    reports, AC-55–AC-56
Primary keys, setting, AC-114, AC-128
Print dialog box, AC-21, AC-55

Print Preview, AC-22, AC-55–AC-56
Print Preview ribbon, AC-55
Print Table Definition, AC-88
Printing
    data using a report, AC-55–AC-58,
        AC-64–AC-65
    specific pages, AC-231–AC-232,
        AC-242–AC-243
Printing forms, AC-231–AC-234,
    AC-239–AC-241
Printing queries, AC-20–AC-21,
    AC-31–AC-33
Printing records
    multiple, AC-233
    single, AC-232–AC-233
Printing recordsets, AC-20–AC-23
Printing reports, AC-56–AC-57, AC-68,
    AC-96
    Database Documenter Report,
        AC-166–AC-167
    for multiple objects, AC-88
    Relationship Reports,
        AC-141–AC-142, AC-160–AC-162,
        AC-164–AC-168
Printing tables, AC-21–AC-22,
    AC-29–AC-31, AC-33–AC-34
    table definitions, AC-123–AC-124,
        AC-127–AC-128
Property settings, modifying,
    AC-227–AC-228
Property Sheets, AC-184
Publishing tables, AC-22–AC-23

Q
QBE (Query by Example) grid, AC-171
Queries
    adding calculations to,
        AC-185–AC-188
    adding criteria and operators to,
        AC-175–AC-180, AC-202–AC-205
    applications, AC-206–AC-208
    applying logical operators,
        AC-180–AC-182
    applying PivotChart and PivotTable
        views, AC-193–AC-196
    command summary, AC-198
    creating and modifying select
        queries, AC-171–AC-175,
        AC-200–AC-205
    creating with a subdatasheet,
        AC-184
    creating with wizards,
        AC-188–AC-193, AC-202
    and the Crosstab Query Wizard,
        AC-190–AC-191
    defining, AC-7, AC-170
    designing, AC-170–AC-209
    and the Find Duplicates Query
        Wizard, AC-191–AC-192
    and the Find Unmatched Query
        Wizard, AC-192–AC-193
    "On Your Own" exercise,
        AC-208–AC-209
    printing and saving, AC-20–AC-21,
        AC-31–AC-33
    and the Simple Query Wizard,
        AC-189–AC-190
    summary, AC-197–AC-198
Query Design window, AC-171
Query properties
    finding the top and bottom values,
        AC-182–AC-184, AC-203–AC-204
    modifying, AC-182–AC-184,
        AC-200–AC-202, AC-204–AC-205
Query Setup group, AC-183–AC-184

Query Wizard, AC-210
Question mark "?" wildcard, finding
    data using, AC-75

R
Ranges of values, filtering for,
    AC-83–AC-84, AC-97
Read-Only messages, AC-37
Record navigation button,
    AC-15–AC-16
Record selector, AC-37–AC-38, AC-51
Records. *See also* Adding records;
        New records
    adding, AC-123–AC-124,
        AC-129
    adding in a table, AC-38–AC-39
    adding through a form, AC-51,
        AC-63–AC-64, AC-66
    adding through a query, AC-42,
        AC-62–AC-63
    applications, AC-66–AC-68
    command summary, AC-59
    in Datasheet View, AC-75–AC-76
    defining, AC-7
    deleting from a table, AC-39–AC-40
    deleting through a form, AC-52,
        AC-63–AC-64
    deleting through a query, AC-42,
        AC-66–AC-67
    in a form, AC-77
    managing attachments,
        AC-52–AC-55
    modifying, AC-38
    "On Your Own" exercise,
        AC-68–AC-69
    previewing, printing, and saving
        data using a report, AC-55–
        AC-58, AC-64–AC-65
    in a report, AC-77–AC-78,
        AC-93–AC-94
    saving, AC-233–AC-234
    selecting for deletion, AC-40
    sorting, AC-75–AC-78,
        AC-96
    summary, AC-59
    unmatched, AC-192
    using Office Edit tools,
        AC-43–AC-48, AC-61–AC-62,
        AC-67
    viewing and modifying,
        AC-36–AC-69
Recordsets
    defining, AC-8
    editing fields in a table, AC-37–AC-38
    editing fields through a form,
        AC-50–AC-51
    editing fields through a query,
        AC-41, AC-62–AC-63, AC-66–AC-67
    modifying in a table, AC-36–AC-40,
        AC-61–AC-62, AC-67
    modifying through a query,
        AC-40–AC-42
    navigating, AC-15–AC-17,
        AC-29–AC-30
    navigating through forms,
        AC-48–AC-49
    opening a database, AC-37
    printing a table, AC-21–AC-22,
        AC-29–AC-30, AC-33–AC-34
    printing and saving, AC-20–AC-23
    printing and saving a query,
        AC-20–AC-21, AC-31–AC-33
    publishing a table, AC-22–AC-23
    using navigation buttons in a table,
        AC-16

using navigation shortcut keys in a
    query, AC-16–AC-17
viewing and modifying through a
    form, AC-48–AC-52
Referential Integrity, AC-142–AC-145
    defining, AC-142
    enforcing, AC-142–AC-144
    finding an error, AC-144
    modifying a relationship to
        include, AC-161–AC-162
    removing, AC-144–AC-145
Relational databases, AC-7
Relationship Reports, printing and
    saving, AC-141–AC-142,
    AC-160–AC-162, AC-164–AC-168
Relationships
    created by lookup fields,
        AC-152–AC-153
    defining, AC-136
    indeterminate, AC-137
    One-To-Many, AC-137, AC-142,
        AC-144
    One-To-One, AC-137
Relationships between tables,
    AC-136–AC-142, AC-167–AC-168
    creating in the Relationships
        window, AC-139–AC-141,
        AC-160–AC-161, AC-166
    looking at existing, AC-137–AC-138
Relationships window, AC-136
    organizing, AC-142
Remove Table, AC-173
Removing
    controls, AC-217–AC-219
    subdatasheets, AC-147
Replace All option, AC-73
Replace command, AC-73–AC-74
Replacing data, AC-70–AC-74
    in a table, AC-92–AC-93, AC-96
Report Footers, AC-254
Report Headers, AC-254
Report sections, AC-254–AC-260
    adding a group section in Design
        View, AC-256–AC-257
    adding a group section in Layout
        View, AC-257–AC-258
    creating a grouped report using a
        wizard, AC-255–AC-256
    modifying group options,
        AC-258–AC-259
Report tools, AC-248
Report Wizard, AC-249, AC-266
Reports
    adding and modifying,
        AC-248–AC-281
    applications, AC-278–AC-281
    command summary, AC-270
    controls in, AC-260–AC-265
    creating multicolumn,
        AC-266–AC-269
    creating using a wizard,
        AC-249–AC-250,
        AC-275–AC-277
    defining, AC-8
    with Format Painter and
        conditional formatting,
        AC-265–AC-266
    formatting in Layout View,
        AC-251–AC-252
    formatting using the Property
        Sheet, AC-253–AC-254
    generating for a table, AC-87,
        AC-94–AC-96
    generating quickly, AC-248–AC-251
    generating with one click,
        AC-250–AC-251

Reports—*Cont.*
modifying controls in Layout View,
AC-251–AC-254, AC-272–AC-276
"On Your Own" exercise, AC-281
previewing, AC-55–AC-56
printing, AC-56–AC-57, AC-68, C-96
saving, AC-57–AC-58, AC-68, AC-96
summary, AC-269–AC-270
Reports for multiple objects, printing
and saving, AC-88
Resizing
columns, AC-19
control layouts, AC-238–AC-239
controls, AC-226–AC-227,
AC-260–AC-261
list boxes, AC-137
pointers, AC-19
Return list box, AC-183
Ribbons, AC-12–AC-13
Rich Text Format (rtf) files, AC-117
Rows, inserting, AC-107

S
Saving
data using a report, AC-55–AC-58,
AC-64–AC-65
forms, AC-231–AC-234,
AC-239–AC-241
queries, AC-20–AC-21, AC-31–AC-33
records, AC-233–AC-234
recordsets, AC-20–AC-23
Saving reports, AC-96
to a file, AC-57–AC-58, AC-68
for multiple objects, AC-88
Relationship Reports, AC-141–AC-142,
AC-160–AC-162, AC-164–AC-168
Saving tables, AC-30–AC-31
table definitions, AC-123–AC-124,
AC-127–AC-128
ScreenTips, AC-12
Scroll bars, AC-15
Search tools, AC-71
Searches, AC-70
Select queries
adding fields to, AC-173–AC-174
based on a single table,
AC-172–AC-173
based on two tables, AC-174–AC-175
creating and modifying,
AC-171–AC-175, AC-200–AC-205
and their reports, AC-171–AC-172
Setting
database properties, AC-100–AC-101
field size, AC-114–AC-115
primary keys, AC-114, AC-128
Referential Integrity, AC-166–AC-168
tab order, AC-219
validation text and rules,
AC-115–AC-116
Shift key, AC-263
Shortcut menu, AC-138
Show Table dialog box,
AC-139–AC-140, AC-173
Simple Forms, AC-212
Single criteria, AC-176–AC-177
Single record forms, AC-239–AC-240
Sizing form sections, AC-221–AC-222.
See also Resizing
Sort-order arrow, AC-75
Sorting data, AC-70–AC-97
Sorting records, AC-75–AC-78, AC-96
in Datasheet View, AC-75–AC-76
in a form, AC-77
in a report, AC-77–AC-78,
AC-93–AC-94

Specific pages, printing,
AC-231–AC-232, AC-242–AC-243
Specific values, filtering for, AC-83,
AC-96
Split Forms, AC-212
Stacked layouts, AC-217–AC-218
Starting databases, AC-9–AC-10
Stretch Mode, AC-227
Student files, AC-8
Subdatasheets, AC-145–AC-147
defining, AC-145
inserting, AC-145–AC-146,
AC-161–AC-162, AC-166
removing, AC-147
Summarizing data, AC-70–AC-97
Summary expressions, AC-259

T
Tab order, setting, AC-219
Tab Order dialog box, AC-219
Table Analyzer Wizard,
AC-153–AC-154
Table definitions, printing and saving,
AC-123–AC-124, AC-127–AC-128
Table row, AC-174
Table structure, copying, AC-105
Table Wizard dialog box, AC-102
Tables, AC-101–AC-106. *See also* New
databases and tables
analyzing, AC-153–AC-154,
AC-167–AC-168
changing views of, AC-30–AC-31
copying a table structure, AC-105
creating in Datasheet View, AC-128
creating in Design View,
AC-102–AC-104, AC-129
creating using a template, AC-102,
AC-122–AC-123
defining, AC-6–AC-7
exporting to Access,
AC-116–AC-117
modifying, AC-30–AC-31
modifying properties of,
AC-105–AC-106, AC-123–AC-124
printing, AC-21–AC-22,
AC-29–AC-30, AC-33–AC-34
printing and saving, AC-30–AC-31
publishing, AC-22–AC-23
Tabs, AC-12–AC-13
Tabular control layouts, AC-217
Test Validation Rules button, AC-115
Text field properties, AC-108
Text format symbols, AC-111
Toolbox, AC-223
Tools
for analysis, AC-153–AC-155
Office Edit, AC-43–AC-48,
AC-61–AC-62, AC-67
for searches, AC-71
Top and bottom values, finding,
AC-182–AC-184, AC-203–AC-204
Totals rows in datasheets
adding and modifying,
AC-78–AC-80
adding to a query, AC-78–AC-79,
AC-94
modifying in a query,
AC-79–AC-80
Tracking, Object Dependency,
AC-155–AC-157

U
Unbound controls, AC-213
Unbound text boxes, adding, AC-229

Undo, AC-47–AC-48
Unmatched records, AC-192

V
Validation text and rules, setting,
AC-115–AC-116
Values
filtering for ranges of,
AC-83–AC-84, AC-97
filtering for specific,
AC-83, AC-96
View form sections, adding,
AC-223–AC-224
Viewing
missing dependency,
AC-156–AC-157
Object Dependency,
AC-155–AC-156
records, AC-36–AC-69
recordsets, through a form,
AC-48–AC-52
relationships created by lookup
fields, AC-152–AC-153
select queries and their reports,
AC-171–AC-172
Views. *See also* Datasheet View; Design
View; Layout View; PivotChart
view; PivotTable view
switching, AC-15, AC-34

W
The Web. *See* The Internet
Wildcards, AC-74–AC-75, AC-178
finding data using a question
mark "?", AC-75
finding data using an asterisk "*",
AC-74
finding information, AC-96
replacing data in a table,
AC-92–AC-93
using in criteria, AC-178–AC-179
Windows Clipboard, AC-45
Windows Explorer, AC-8
Wizards
Access Export Wizard, AC-117
Crosstab Query Wizard, AC-188,
AC-190–AC-191
Find Duplicate Records Query
Wizard, AC-188, AC-191–AC-192
Find Unmatched Query Wizard,
AC-188, AC-192–AC-193
Form Wizard, AC-210
Input Mask Wizard, AC-111
Label Wizard, AC-266–AC-267
Lookup Wizard, AC-147–AC-153
New Query Wizard collection,
AC-189
Query Wizard, AC-210
Report Wizard, AC-249, AC-266
Simple Query Wizard,
AC-189–AC-190
Table Analyzer Wizard,
AC-153–AC-154

X
XML Paper Specification (XPS)
files, AC-20
XPS format, AC-21–AC-22, AC-57

Z
Zoom Mode, AC-227
Zoom window, AC-179, AC-186